MW00565559

WITHDRAWN

ENCYCLOPEDIA OF

Social
Psychology

REF
Hm
1007
E53
2007
v.2

Library & Media Ctr.
Carroll Community College
1601 Washington Rd.
Westminster, MD 21157

ENCYCLOPEDIA OF
Social
*P*sychology

2

Roy F. Baumeister
Florida State University

Kathleen D. Vohs
University of Minnesota

EDITORS

A SAGE Reference Publication

SAGE Publications
Los Angeles • London • New Delhi • Singapore

Copyright © 2007 by SAGE Publications, Inc.

All rights reserved. No part of this book may be reproduced or utilized in any form or by any means, electronic or mechanical, including photocopying, recording, or by any information storage and retrieval system, without permission in writing from the publisher.

For information:

 SAGE Publications, Inc.
2455 Teller Road
Thousand Oaks, California 91320
E-mail: order@sagepub.com

SAGE Publications Ltd.
1 Oliver's Yard
55 City Road
London EC1Y 1SP
United Kingdom

SAGE Publications India Pvt. Ltd.
B 1/I 1 Mohan Cooperative Industrial Area
Mathura Road, New Delhi 110 044
India

SAGE Publications Asia-Pacific Pte. Ltd.
33 Pekin Street #02-01
Far East Square
Singapore 048763

Printed in the United States of America.

Library of Congress Cataloging-in-Publication Data

Encyclopedia of social psychology/editors, Roy F. Baumeister, Kathleen D. Vohs.
  p. cm.
Includes bibliographical references and index.
ISBN 978-1-4129-1670-7 (cloth)
  1. Social psychology—Encyclopedias. I. Baumeister, Roy F. II. Vohs, Kathleen D.

HM1007.E53 2007
302.03—dc22   2007014603

This book is printed on acid-free paper.

07 08 09 10 11 10 9 8 7 6 5 4 3 2 1

Publisher:	Rolf A. Janke
Acquisitions Editor:	Michael Carmichael
Developmental Editors:	Carole Maurer, Paul Reis
Reference Systems Manager:	Leticia Gutierrez
Project Editor:	Tracy Alpern
Copy Editors:	Colleen B. Brennan, Robin Gold
Typesetter:	C&M Digitals (P) Ltd.
Indexer:	Julie Sherman Grayson
Cover Designer:	Candice Harman
Marketing Manager:	Carmel Withers

Contents

List of Entries

Reader's Guide

This Reader's Guide performs two functions within the encyclopedia. One, the headings alone describe, at a broad level, the kinds of topics covered in the field of social psychology. Looking at the overarching categories, one can see that social psychology studies cognition (thought) and action, helpful and hurtful behaviors, emotions and decisions, culture and evolution, the self and social relationships, as well as health and problematic behaviors. That's quite a range of topics! The second purpose of the Reader's Guide is related to the first in that it helps readers who are already interested in a topic find new topics that may be of interest. In this way, the Reader's Guide provides links among topics. Either way it is used, we hope that you find yourself reading entries from all of the general categories, given the wealth of interesting and important information to learn here.

Action Control

Action Identification Theory
Adaptive Unconscious
Apparent Mental Causation
Approach-Avoidance Conflict
Authenticity
Auto-Motive Model
Autonomy
Behavioral Contagion
Choking Under Pressure
Control
Controlled Processes
Decision Making
Delay of Gratification
Drive Theory
Ego Depletion
Excitation-Transfer Theory
Extrinsic Motivation
Feedback Loop
Free Will, Study of
Goals
Grim Necessities
Guilty Pleasures
Habits
Helplessness, Learned
Home-Field Advantage and Disadvantage

Hormones and Behavior
Implementation Intentions
Intrinsic Motivation
Ironic Processes
Learned Helplessness
Learning Theory
Locus of Control
Mental Control
Meta-Awareness
Mindfulness and Mindlessness
Modeling of Behavior
Nonconscious Processes
Overjustification Effect
Procrastination
Reasoned Action Theory
Regulatory Focus Theory
Risk Taking
Rubicon Model of Action Phases
Scripts
Self-Awareness
Self-Control Measures
Self-Defeating Behavior
Self-Determination Theory
Self-Discrepancy Theory
Self-Efficacy
Self-Handicapping
Self-Regulation

Intergroup Emotions
Intergroup Relations
Jigsaw Classroom
Leadership
Minimal Group Paradigm
Minority Social Influence
Optimal Distinctiveness Theory
Organizational Behavior
Other–Total Ratio
Outgroup Homogeneity
Polarization Processes
Power
Procedural Justice
Realistic Group Conflict Theory
Ringelmann Effect
Risky Shift
Robbers Cave Experiment
Roles and Role Theory
Rumor Transmission
Scapegoat Theory
Self-Categorization Theory
Self-Stereotyping
Sex Roles
Social Compensation
Social Dominance Orientation
Social Identity Theory
Social Impact Theory
Social Justice Orientation
Social Loafing
Social Power
Socioeconomic Status
Subtyping
System Justification
Territoriality
Token Effects

Health

Binge Eating
Biopsychosocial Model
Buffering Effect
Bulimia
Coping
Depression
Hardiness
Health Psychology
Sexual Desire

Social Neuroscience
Social Psychophysiology
Stress and Coping
Tend-and-Befriend Response
Testosterone

History

Bennington College Study
Bobo Doll Studies
History of Social Psychology
Logical Positivism
Reductionism
Robbers Cave Experiment
Stanford Prison Experiment
Thematic Apperception Test

Influence

Compliance
Conformity
Debiasing
Door-in-the-Face Technique
Fear Appeals
Foot-in-the-Door Technique
Forced Compliance
Forewarning
Heuristic-Systematic
    Model of Persuasion
Influence
Informational Influence
Ingratiation
Ingratiator's Dilemma
Inoculation Theory
Mere Exposure Effect
Milgram's Obedience to Authority Studies
Minority Social Influence
Normative Influence
Norms, Prescriptive and Descriptive
Persuasion
Reactance
Reciprocity Norm
Reference Group
Resisting Persuasion
Scarcity Principle
Self-Fulfilling Prophecy
Sleeper Effect

Spreading of Alternatives
Sunk Cost
Visceral Influences

Methods

Autobiographical Narratives
Behavioral Economics
Bennington College Study
Big Five Personality Traits
Bobo Doll Studies
Bogus Pipeline
Content Analysis
Control Condition
Critical Social Psychology
Cross-Lagged Panel Correlation
Deception (Methodological Technique)
Demand Characteristics
Discursive Psychology
Dynamical Systems Theory
Ecological Validity
Ethnocentrism
Experimental Condition
Experimental Realism
Experimentation
Experimenter Effects
Falsification
Forced Compliance Technique
Identity Status
Implicit Association Test
Individual Differences
LISREL
Logical Positivism
Lost Letter Technique
Meta-Analysis
Mundane Realism
Nonexperimental Designs
Operationalization
Order Effects
Path Analysis
Placebo Effect
Quasi-Experimental Designs
Reductionism
Research Methods
Self-Reports
Semantic Differential
Social Desirability Bias

Social Relations Model
Sociometric Status
Structural Equation Modeling
Thematic Apperception Test
Twin Studies

Personality

Achievement Motivation
Agreeableness
Androgyny
Attachment Styles
Authoritarian Personality
Babyfaceness
Big Five Personality Traits
Central Traits Versus
    Peripheral Traits
Control Motivation
Curiosity
Defensive Pessimism
Depression
Expertise
Extraversion
Gender Differences
Genetic Influences on Social Behavior
Hardiness
Hostile Masculinity Syndrome
Identity Status
Implicit Personality Theory
Individual Differences
Introversion
Locus of Control
Masculinity/Femininity
Metatraits
Narcissism
Narcissistic Entitlement
Need for Affiliation
Need for Closure
Need for Cognition
Need for Power
Neuroticism
Personalities and Behavior Patterns,
    Type A and Type B
Personality and Social Behavior
Power Motive
Rejection Sensitivity
Self-Complexity

Social Cognition

Social Projection
Spontaneous Trait Inferences
Spreading of Alternatives
Subliminal Perception
Subtyping
Symbolic Interactionism
Theory of Mind
Thin Slices of Behavior
Three-Dimensional Model of Attribution
Transactive Memory
Value Pluralism Model

Subdisciplines

Applied Social Psychology
Consumer Behavior
Critical Social Psychology
Discursive Psychology

Environmental Psychology
Ethology
Evolutionary Psychology
Eyewitness Testimony, Accuracy of
Forensic Psychology
Health Psychology
History of Social Psychology
Organizational Behavior
Peace Psychology
Personality and Social Behavior
Political Psychology
Positive Psychology
Religion and Spirituality
Social Cognitive Neuroscience
Social Neuroscience
Social Psychophysiology
Sociobiology
Sociological Social Psychology

J

JEALOUSY

Definition

Jealousy is an unpleasant emotion that arises when one perceives that some important aspect of one's relationship with another, or the relationship itself, is being threatened by someone else (a rival). For example, a person is likely to experience jealousy if his or her romantic partner appears to be emotionally or sexually interested in someone else. The term *jealousy* also applies to feelings that arise in other types of interpersonal relationships, such as when children exhibit distress over parents showering attention on a new sibling or when a person feels upset over being excluded by friends who are socializing together. Thus, jealousy requires the involvement of three individuals (the self, the partner, and the rival), which is sometimes referred to as a *love triangle*.

The proposed function of jealousy is to motivate behaviors that will reestablish the relationship between the self and the partner and break up the threatening liaison between the partner and rival. Because close personal relationships provide individuals with many physical and psychological benefits, it is important to have psychological predispositions toward maintaining them. In evolutionary terms, it is likely that people who established and protected their relationships typically produced more offspring. Thus, the psychological traits that helped maintain relationships would have been selected for and passed down to us through our genes. One possibility is that jealousy may have originally evolved as a response to competition of siblings who are rivals for a parent's time, attention, resources, and so forth, and was later usurped for the purpose of keeping friendships and romantic relationships together.

Background

Although few would doubt that jealousy involves negative feelings, there is no unanimous consensus on the exact nature of the distress. The feelings we call jealousy may be a blend of other more basic feelings, particularly of anger, fear, and sadness. One possibility is an individual may experience all of these emotions simultaneously during a jealous episode. Another possibility is, rather than experiencing several different emotions at once, a person experiences a series of different emotions over the course of a single jealousy episode. Which emotion is experienced would depend on what one focused or ruminated on. For example, thinking about the loss of the relationship might elicit sadness, while thinking about the partner's betrayal might elicit anger. A final possibility is that jealousy is its own distinct emotional state that elicits feelings and behaviors that are different from other emotions such as fear and anger.

Importance and Consequences of Jealousy

Jealousy can have powerful personal and social consequences. While it sometimes can lead to positive outcomes by redirecting a loved one's attention to the self and reestablishing bonds, it also can have serious negative costs. For example, jealousy is frequently implicated as a factor in spousal abuse and often ranks as the third or fourth most common motive in nonaccidental homicides across cultures.

The first signs of jealousy appear to occur early in life. Some research suggests that a parent merely directing attention to another child is, in and of itself, sufficient to elicit jealousy in infants as young as 6 months. These infants displayed more negative emotion when their mothers interacted with a life-like baby doll, relative to when their mothers behaved the same way toward a nonsocial toy (e.g., a book). This suggests that complex cognitions are not needed to elicit at least some primitive form of jealousy in infants. However, with development, social and cognitive factors become increasingly important. Even by preschool age, the specifics of a social triangle influence whether jealousy arises. For example, 4-year-olds demonstrated more jealousy when their mothers interacted with a similar-aged peer than when she interacted with an infant, whereas younger infants' jealousy was not affected by the rival's age. Thus, one of the changes that occurs with development is that a person's appraisal or assessment of the exact nature and meaning of the loved one and rival's interactions become increasingly important in whether jealousy is experienced.

Research on the social-cognitive aspects of jealousy has emphasized two factors that make a loved one's involvement with another particularly threatening: (1) when it challenges some aspect of a person's self-concept, self-regard, or other self-representations, and (2) when it decreases the quality of the primary relationship. In other words, people ask themselves questions about the meaning of their loved one's relationship to the rival: "What does this say about me? Am I unlovable, unattractive, boring, et cetera?" and "Will this rival relationship impact the important things I get from my relationship with my partner such as attention, affection, and support?" The answers to these questions will affect the intensity of jealousy over potential rival relationships.

Individual Differences

Many have wondered whether men or women are more jealous. While studies occasionally find men to be more jealous, others find women to be more jealous. Overall, there seems to be no major consistent differences in men's and women's jealousy. It was once believed that in men jealousy was a stronger motive for murder than in women. However, careful analyses of murder motives, taking into account men's overall greater propensity for violence, show that a woman who commits murder is as likely to be motivated by jealousy as a man who commits murder.

One theory that has received a great deal of recent attention predicts that gender differences should exist in jealousy over a romantic partner's infidelity: Men should feel more jealous over sexual betrayal and women over emotional betrayal. This view claims that in our evolutionary past, different threats impacted the number of children that any given man or woman could have. (The basic tenet of modern evolutionary theory is that we inherited our psychological and/or physical traits from the ancestral people who reproduced the most.) Since fertilization occurs internally within women, men can never know with 100% certainty that an offspring is indeed their own. Thus, ancestral man faced the threat of spending resources (food, time) on children that might not be his own. This would decrease the number of biological children that he had and increase those of someone else, which would help pass the other man's genes on instead of his own. Hence, the theory suggests, men who were particularly vigilant to sexual infidelity could prevent this from happening. Thus, modern men should be particularly jealous of sexual infidelity. Women, however, cannot be tricked into bringing up someone else's offspring, so they should not be particularly jealous of sexual infidelity per se. Instead, ancestral woman had to be concerned that her mate might give his resources to other women and their children, which would decrease the chances of the woman's own children surviving and reproducing. Thus, present-day women should be particularly jealous over emotional infidelity. Inherent in this is the assumption that a man's emotional involvement is a proxy for his spending resources on another. This hypothesis drew apparent support from early work that found when people were forced to predict whether a partner's sexual or emotional infidelity would be more upsetting, more men than women picked sexual infidelity. However, recent research with other measures and with people who have actually experienced a loved one's infidelity have not found consistent gender differences in jealousy over sexual and emotional infidelity.

Why might evolution have failed to produce gender differences? One possibility is that a more general jealousy reaction may have benefited both genders.

Infidelity rarely occurs abruptly; now, and presumably in the ancestral past, those people who would stray engage in flirting behaviors (e.g., increased eye contact and smiling) well before they have sex. These same behaviors can signal the beginnings of emotional interest, sexual interest, or both. Thus, there may be no need for men and women to have evolved jealous reactions tuned to different events. Instead, both sexes might best prevent either form of infidelity by being alert to the common early warning signs of either. This hypothesis is consistent with the emerging evidence that men and women show similar reactions to sexual and emotional infidelity.

Gender differences, however, are found in one type of jealousy, namely, clinical cases of *pathological jealousy* (also called *morbid jealousy*). Patients suffering form this disorder show a usually delusional conviction that their romantic partner is cheating on them. Before making this diagnosis, clinicians must think that the patient has weak and implausible evidence of betrayal or has an exaggerated reaction. Patients with pathological jealousy experience intense negative feelings and strong urges to check up on and spy on their partner and sometimes behave aggressively. Men make up approximately 64% and women 36% of pathological jealousy cases. Recent research suggests that, in some cases, pathological jealousy is a form of obsessive-compulsive disorder, which sometimes can be successfully treated with the antidepressant medication, fluoxetine.

Christine R. Harris

See also Attachment Theory; Emotion; Need to Belong

Further Readings

Harris, C. R. (2004). The evolution of jealousy. *American Scientist, 92,* 62–71.

Salovey, P. (Ed.). (1991). *The psychology of jealousy and envy.* New York: Guilford Press.

JIGSAW CLASSROOM

Social psychologist Elliot Aronson introduced the jigsaw classroom in 1971, while a professor at the University of Texas at Austin. It was first used as a teaching/learning strategy to help defuse a potentially explosive situation in Austin—its racially segregated schools were slowly desegregating. The primary purpose of the technique was to help teachers eliminate desegregated social patterns that emerged in racially diverse classrooms; likewise, it was applied by teachers for defusing violence in desegregated schools, as well as easing social problems among diverse students.

It is frequently used in elementary and secondary classrooms and, although less a fixture in college classrooms, it is nonetheless applicable. The name *jigsaw* is derived from its method of having each student become an informational puzzle piece; that is, students assemble in small groups in which each member becomes an expert at his or her subject or learning task. Each individual shares his or her information with the other members and then presents it to the entire class. Aronson believed the learning environment in traditional classrooms was full of competition, which created an atmosphere of turmoil and hostility. He believed that traditional classrooms often have the tendency to favor the "good" or more advanced students, ignoring those that are less advanced with different learning styles or needs.

The concept's original purpose was to reduce racial conflict and promote minority students' learning motivation and learning outcome. Another rationale for the jigsaw method underscored the idea that each individual learner was unique, and his or her role as a team member emphasized his or her contribution to the team through the learning process. Specifically, the method utilized cooperative learning, similar to a jigsaw puzzle, with each piece presenting each student's part in helping other students understand the entire project. Each student is essential because each is responsible for a segment of the project that the teacher assigns to that particular group. In other words, students of jigsaw classrooms have to cooperate and work with each other. Otherwise, their assignments cannot be completed. This cooperation is thought to be a valuable tool in preventing tragic events, such as the Columbine shootings in 1999. Jigsaw classrooms allow students to appreciate each team member's contribution and presence. As a result, hostility and anger diminish when students work together cooperatively.

In jigsaw classrooms, teachers can follow 10 steps to implement the jigsaw techniques:

1. Teachers divide the entire class into small groups, with each group consisting of five to six students; the exact number of team members and teams

depends on both the number of students in that class and the complexity level of the project. Most important, each team should be as diverse as possible, highlighting differences like gender, ethnicity, cultural background, and ability.

2. Teachers assign a student as the discussion leader for each session on a rotating basis. The team leader's duty is to call on other team members in a fair manner to make sure that each member participates evenly.

3. Teachers divide that particular school day's learning task into several segments, making sure they match the number of students.

4. Teachers assign each student on every team the responsibility for one segment.

5. Teachers allow each student enough time to read over his or her segment in order to become familiar with it.

6. Each student on each jigsaw team is responsible for a specific segment. The group gets together as "expert groups," discussing and exchanging their research results. After that, they rehearse the presentation they will make to their individual jigsaw team.

7. Teachers request students to return to their jigsaw team.

8. Students present their segment findings to their team, while other teams' members are encouraged to ask questions for clarification.

9. Teachers visit each jigsaw team, observing the process and helping team members successfully complete the learning task. In addition, if any team member attempts to dominate or disrupt the team, the teacher should implement an appropriate intervention. However, it is recommended that the team leader handle the entire learning task, instead of involving the teacher. The teacher can train team members how to intervene when faced with difficult members.

10. This step centers on assessment. Teachers should administer a quiz based on the group's particular learning task, which helps students understand cooperative learning.

Jigsaw classrooms have several advantages compared to traditional teaching methods. From a teacher's perspective, (a) it is easy to implement within the classroom, (b) it can be easily combined with other teaching strategies, (c) there is no time limitation or requirement when using the strategy, and (d) it increases both retention and achievement of minority students. For students, benefits include that it (a) is an efficacious method of learning; (b) disperses personality conflicts and/or tension in diverse classroom, while creating a more amicable learning environment; (c) encourages students' listening to their peers; (d) succeeds in fostering friendships while creating mutual respect among students, regardless of their individual differences; (e) promotes students' learning motivation and engagement in their tasks more actively; (f) builds up less advanced learners' self-confidence; (g) promotes team building skills; and (h) improves students' research ability, such as gathering information, organizing their resources, and so on.

A teacher might experience several difficulties when implementing a jigsaw classroom strategy. First, teachers have to ensure that students have ample research resources to complete their project. Second, teachers need to spend more time helping less advanced students so they do not produce inferior work within their respective jigsaw group. Third, when dominant students try to control the group, teachers need to be able to effectively deal with the situation. Fourth, teachers need to encourage bright students to develop the mind-set that helping their team members is an excellent method to prevent boredom.

Cary Stacy Smith
Li-Ching Hung

See also Group Performance and Productivity; Prejudice; Stereotypes and Stereotyping

Further Readings

Aronson, E. (2000). *The jigsaw classroom*. Retrieved December 10, 2006, from http://www.jigsaw.org

Aronson, E., & Patnoe, S. (1997). *Jigsaw classroom*. New York: Longman.

JUSTICE MOTIVE

Definition

The justice motive is the idea that people have a basic motive for justice; that is, people have a need to believe that people get what they deserve. Research on the justice motive emphasizes the importance of justice to people as a goal unto itself. Its origins lie in a basic understanding people develop early in life about the kind of world they must be able to assume if they are to get what they deserve. Evidence for people's need for justice has been derived from research that examines people's reactions to injustice. There is also reason to believe that sometimes when people are concerned about justice, it is the result of another need or concern they have, and in this case, justice motivation derives from other motives.

Justice and Psychology

A useful place to start a discussion of justice motivation is the concept of justice itself. Psychology researchers approach the topic of justice differently than lawyers and legal philosophers do, and often differently from how it appears in people's everyday lives, where justice is commonly associated with the law, police, and the courts.

For psychologists, justice is about the thoughts and feelings people have about the relation between the value of people and their outcomes. Psychological research on justice builds on the observation that people are good at evaluating other people, on one hand, and evaluating their experiences (e.g., winning a lottery, finding love, becoming ill) and resources (e.g., wealth and material possessions) on the other. Psychologists refer to experiences and resources combined as a person's outcomes.

People can rapidly decide whether someone they meet for the first time is a good or bad person; indeed, it is one of the first things people want to know. Of course, each person also has an evaluative sense of him- or herself as a good or not-so-good person, referred to in psychology as *self-esteem*. People are also good at evaluating outcomes. Getting sick for most people is bad, and getting an increase in salary is good.

When considering justice, the question is how does a person's evaluations of people (including themselves) line up with his or her evaluations of their outcomes? When a good person (like you good reader) experiences a good outcome, such as a good-sized salary increase, others view the situation as just, because there is correspondence in their evaluation of the person and the person's outcome: good with good. However, when the same good person experiences a bad outcome, such as being laid off from his or her job, others will be inclined to view the situation

as unjust, because the evaluations are inconsistent: good with bad. People are similarly sensitive to the outcomes of bad people. When a bad person such as a criminal has good outcomes such as a life of comfort, people view the situation as unjust, but when the same bad person has a bad experience, say, losing all his or her money, the situation is just.

There are of course many intriguing variations and complexities in how people think and feel about justice, including the relative nature of justice judgments; what one person considers just and fair is often different from what others see as just. As you might imagine, this relativity has all sorts of interesting implications, but this entry will set these aspects of justice aside and turn to its primary focus: motivation for justice.

Justice Motivation

Why do people care about justice? Psychologists interested in answering this question often approach it in terms of motivation. When a person demonstrates a need or desire to reach a goal, others say he or she is motivated. In motivational terms, people care about justice because of a need they have to experience justice in their own lives and in their social world. Where does the need for justice come from? Interestingly, psychological research has suggested a number of possible origins that fall into two categories depending on the goal involved.

Some scholars argue that justice is an ultimate goal people can have, an end unto itself. In this case, the need for justice is understood to be a distinct motive that cannot be reduced to other motives, such as self-interest. This is important because it raises the possibility that people may sometimes be motivated to achieve justice at the expense of self-interest. The ultimate goal approach to justice motivation is the one that argues that it is psychologically meaningful to talk about a distinct justice motive.

The second approach to justice motivation assumes that when people demonstrate a need for justice, they do so as a means to arriving at another goal. In other words, justice is an instrumental rather than ultimate goal. This would be the case, for instance, if people believe that complying with justice rules will help maximize their outcomes: "If everybody plays by the rules, we'll all get what we want." The instrumental goal perspective on justice motivation means that when people appear to have a need for justice, that need is derivative of another need or concern. The list of needs people have that can give rise to a secondary concern with justice continues to grow, with self-interest arguably at the top of the list. A number of psychological justice theories assume that self-interest is a central goal that people are trying to achieve; the theories differ on whether self-interest motivation is pursued for self-gains in the short term or the long term. The short-term view is that people will behave justly when it is in their self-interest to do so and unjustly when it is not. The longer-term view points out that self-interest needs must be met in the context of ongoing relations with others, which gives rise to a social exchange view of justice and self-interest. If people enter into relations with others motivated to gain resources over time, it is in their self-interest to commit to social exchange (justice) rules that govern how resources will be distributed and what processes will be used to make decisions.

Other, less-resource-oriented theories suggest that people's need for justice arises from other concerns, such as a desire to be regarded positively by others, the need for control, concerns associated with uncertainty, and a basic concern with morality. Examination of these various perspectives is beyond the scope of this entry, but their number and diversity highlights the complexity of justice motivation. Thus, when someone expresses a concern about justice, it is useful to remember that his or her concern may reflect a basic need for justice or derive from another concern, such as increasing the chances of getting what he or she wants or getting respectful treatment from others in order to feel valued.

The Justice Motive

The idea that people have a basic motive for justice has been characterized as the need to believe that people get what they deserve. Because people in this context refer to both oneself and others, the need essentially means that people need to believe in a just world where they not only experience justice in their lives but where it is also important that others experience justice as well.

People's concern about justice in the world helps explain why people can be upset by injustices that happen to other people they do not know and who may live far away and in very different circumstances than their own. Not surprisingly, given this description, the most extensive theoretical account of the justice motive comes from the just-world theory, a theory developed and researched for many years by the social psychologist Melvin Lerner.

Origins

According to Melvin Lerner, the justice motive originates in the realization people develop in childhood that to have the things they want in life, they have to engage in activities in the present that they assume will result in payoffs in the future. In other words, people come to understand delay of gratification. Many of the rewards they value most, such as a rewarding career, require them to work toward a future goal. Put in justice terms, people assume that as good people working toward a future reward, the reward will in fact be forthcoming when the future point arrives, because by that point, they deserve it.

The assumption this reasoning is based on is the foundation for the justice motive. For people to believe they will get the rewards they deserve in the future, they must also believe they live in a world where people do in fact get what they deserve. Indeed, to sustain people's efforts to achieve their goals in the future, they must believe in such a world because if they cannot assume people get what they deserve, what is the point of working toward future goals? Lerner argues accordingly that when people reach the point in their childhood (around age 4) when they come to understand delay of gratification, they make a personal contract with the world. This contract says that for them to be able to believe in that they will get what they deserve, they must at the same time believe that the world is a just place. This is also what makes the fates of other people important. One's sense of the world as a just place is based not only on one's own experience, but also on the experiences of others and if others experience injustice, that is threatening to one's need to believe in a just world.

Evidence

The most compelling evidence for the justice motive comes from research examining people's reactions to injustice. The reasoning is as follows: If people have a need for justice, they should be motivated in the face of injustice to respond in ways that are consistent with achieving justice. A common research strategy is to expose people to scenarios involving the suffering of an innocent victim. This can be done by having research participants read a story or watch a video where they learn about something bad happening to a good person through no fault of that person. Such experiences create temporary distress, as a result of the injustice associated with the victim's suffering, in much the same way one feels a sense of unfairness and upset when one learns about the suffering of innocents in the news. Evidence of other people's unjust suffering is upsetting because it threatens one's belief in a just world.

If people are motivated to achieve the goal of justice in their lives, they should respond in such situations in ways that are consistent with achieving that goal. The research suggests this is in fact the case, but there are some intriguingly different ways people do this, some with undesirable consequences. The most straightforward thing people can do is engage in justice-restoring behavior. For instance, they might try to compensate an innocent victim or find justice in punishing the person responsible for the injustice. Such behavioral reactions can be very effective in helping people maintain their just-world beliefs, and it is likely many altruistic deeds one observes in life are based in a desire for justice.

However, people are not always able to address injustice through their own actions, for any number of reasons: The size of the injustice is too large or too far away, they do not have the means to address the injustice, or they may assume their efforts will be ineffective. Does this mean they abandon their need to believe in a just world when they cannot fix injustice themselves? The answer from psychological research is "no." In lieu of action, people make psychological adjustments in how they think about events that allow them to sustain the belief. One of the intriguing but troubling ways people do this is to blame the victim. Through selective consideration of the facts, people can convince themselves that a victim or victims are somehow responsible for their suffering and hence deserve their fate. If one can convince oneself that others deserve their suffering, then one removes any threat to one's ability to believe that the world is a just place. Unfortunately, victim blaming is a common phenomenon. Justice motive research helps researchers understand why this is so, given the importance of people's need to believe in a just world. There are other psychological adjustments people can make in the service of the justice motive, but the important point is that there

is extensive evidence that people are motivated to address injustice either behaviorally or psychologically, and the reliability with which they do so provides compelling evidence of the justice motive.

John H. Ellard

See also Blaming the Victim; Just-World Hypothesis; Social Exchange Theory

Further Readings

Hafer, C. L., & Bègue, L. (2005). Experimental research on just-world theory: Problems, developments, and future challenges. *Psychological Bulletin, 131,* 128–167.

Lerner, M. J. (1980). *The belief in a just world: A fundamental delusion.* New York: Plenum.

JUST-WORLD HYPOTHESIS

Definition

The just-world hypothesis is the belief that, in general, the social environment is fair, such that people get what they deserve. The concept was developed in part to help explain observations that to preserve a belief that the world is a just place, people will sometimes devalue a victim. A just world is defined as a world in which people *do* get what they deserve. The just-world hypothesis is important because it suggests that people may treat certain victims badly, oddly enough, out of a desire to sustain their belief in justice. It also suggests that people may go to great lengths to maintain a sense that the world is just, giving evidence that the human motivation for justice is very strong.

Background and History

The seminal experiment illustrating this phenomenon was conducted by Melvin Lerner and Carolyn Simmons in the 1960s. In this experiment, people watched on a television monitor a woman who appeared to be receiving painful electric shocks from a researcher. In actuality, the footage was prerecorded and the events were only simulated by actors. As the woman did nothing to deserve the shocks she was receiving, she can be seen as suffering unjustly. People who watched this unjust suffering described the victim's character quite negatively if they could not compensate her (or at least were not sure they could compensate her) and if they thought that they would continue to see her suffer. People described the victim's character most negatively when they also believed that she was behaving altruistically; that is, she chose to suffer for their sake. The findings were explained by suggesting that people have a strong need to believe that the world is a just place in which individuals get what they deserve. Victims who continue to suffer through no fault of their own (and especially very good people, like the altruistic woman in the early experiment) threaten this belief in a just world. As a way of dealing with that threat and maintaining a belief in a just world, people may try to restore justice by helping or compensating victims. When it is not possible to help or compensate victims, people may reinterpret the situation by, for example, claiming that a particular victim is a bad or otherwise unworthy person. By devaluing or derogating the victim in this way, his or her fate seems more deserved and people's sense of justice is maintained.

There was much controversy about how to interpret the results of the original experiment. For example, some researchers suggested that people devalued the victim to reduce their own feelings of guilt at letting her continue to suffer. However, further experiments showed that people sometimes devalue a victim of injustice even when they could not have played any role in the victim's situation. This and other proposed alternatives were, for the most part, dealt with through further study and argumentation, leading to a general acceptance of the notion that people will sometimes devalue a victim of injustice because they need to believe in a just world.

More Recent Research

Since the early period of experimentation in the 1960s and 1970s, social psychologists have continued to conduct research on the just-world hypothesis. There have been two main traditions in this later research. First, researchers have continued to conduct experiments to study how people respond when they see, read about, or are otherwise exposed to victims who presumably threaten the need to believe in a just world. This research has tended to focus on victims of HIV/AIDS, rape, and cancer. Although some researchers have claimed that a number of these experiments have flaws that make it difficult to interpret the results, there is agreement that several of the investigations generally support the just-world hypothesis.

Another tradition in the later research on the just-world hypothesis has involved using a questionnaire to measure the extent to which people actually believe that the world is a just place. Researchers then test whether people who believe more strongly in a just world, according to the questionnaire, hold certain attitudes. These studies have shown, for example, that the more people claim that they believe the world is just, the more negative attitudes they have toward the poor, groups of people who are discriminated against in society, and other people who might be seen as victims of injustice. These findings are consistent with the just-world hypothesis.

Implications

The just-world hypothesis has several important implications for reactions to victims of injustice. For example, the research suggests that if people feel they cannot help or compensate victims of injustice who continue to suffer, they may react defensively. They may reason that the victims deserved their fate either because of the kind of people they are or because of the way they behaved. If people respond in this way, they may be less likely to react in a more positive manner, like working toward minimizing injustice or offering emotional support.

It is important to note that the just-world hypothesis is actually part of a broader theory called *justice motive theory* or *just-world theory*. The theory includes propositions about how and why a belief in a just world develops in children, the different forms that a belief in a just world might take, the many strategies (aside from blaming and derogating victims of injustice) that people use to maintain a belief in a just world, and the various ways in which justice is defined for different kinds of social relationships.

Carolyn L. Hafer

See also Blaming the Victim; Discrimination; Justice Motive

Further Readings

Hafer, C. L., & Bègue, L. (2005). Experimental research on just-world theory: Problems, developments, and future challenges. *Psychological Bulletin, 131,* 128–167.

Lerner, M. J. (1980). *The belief in a just world: A fundamental delusion.* New York: Plenum.

Lerner, M. J., & Miller, D. T. (1978). Just-world research and the attribution process: Looking back and ahead. *Psychological Bulletin, 85,* 1030–1051.

KELLEY'S COVARIATION MODEL

Definition

Harold Kelley's covariation principle is a central model within attribution theory, an area of social psychology that is concerned with the scientific analysis of the psychology of everyday people. Attribution theory was originally introduced by Fritz Heider in 1958 and assumes that we all want to understand and explain events. For instance, we ask why we succeeded at a task or why our friend liked a movie. The answers to such "why questions" (e.g., "I am smart" or "The movie was good") are called causal attributions. Kelley's model explains how laypersons arrive at such attributions; hence, it is a scientific theory about naive theories.

Analysis

For both scientists and laypersons, explanations consist of *effects* to be explained (e.g., success at a task or liking a movie) and *causes* that are used as explanations (e.g., high ability or the quality of the movie). Kelley's model applies to all types of psychological effects that laypersons explain, ranging from achievement outcomes to emotional states, and it can be applied to self-perception (e.g., "Why did I fail?") as well as to other perception ("Why did you fail?").

Kelley distinguishes attributions to causes that reside within the person, the entity, and the circumstances. *Person* attributions (e.g., "She is a movie fanatic" or "She is smart") rely on stable factors residing within the person to explain, for example, that person's enjoyment of a movie or his or her success. *Entity* attributions imply tracing back the effect to stable properties of the object the person interacts with (e.g., we explain the enjoyment with the quality of the movie, or success with task ease). Finally, *circumstance* attributions are made when explaining an effect with transient and unstable causes (e.g., when enjoyment is traced back to a happy mood or success is attributed to luck).

But how do we come to explain a specific effect with one of such causes?

Kelley postulates that laypersons use methods akin to those used by scientists, most importantly, experiments. In such experiments, independent and dependent variables are differentiated. For instance, a researcher investigating the influence of color on mood will manipulate color as the independent variable (e.g., putting half of the participants in a blue room and the other half in a red room). Subsequently, she assesses, as the dependent variable, participants' mood in both rooms. In such experiments, the independent variables are often conceived of as causes or determinants of the dependent variables (e.g., color might be conceived of as a determinant of mood), and the dependent variables are the effects.

From this point of view, events to be explained by lay scientists (e.g., success or liking a movie) are the dependent variable, and the possible causes of the event are independent variables. For instance, when I succeed at a task and I ask myself, "Why did I succeed?" success is the dependent variable (i.e., the effect) and the possible causes—the task (entity), my ability (person), or luck (circumstances)—are independent variables.

Whether an effect is attributed to the person, the entity, or the circumstances depends on which of the causes (independent variables) the effect (dependent variable) covaries with. Covariation refers to the co-occurrence of the effect and a cause. To decide whether the *entity* is the cause, one has to assess whether the effect covaries (co-occurs) with the entity—more specifically, whether there is variation of the effect across objects (entities). Covariation with the entity is given when the effect is present if the entity is present and when the effect is absent when the entity is absent. For instance, when a person succeeds at Task 1 but fails at Tasks 2, 3 and 4, the effect (i.e., success) is present when Task 1 (i.e., the entity) is present, and it is absent when Task 1 is absent (i.e., when Tasks 2, 3, and 4 are present). In this example, the effect covaries with the task (entity): The manipulation of this independent variable results in an effect of the dependent variable; that is, the task "makes a difference." If, however, the individual succeeds at all tasks in addition to Task 1, the effect (success) does not vary with tasks (there is no covariation between the effect and the entity), or the manipulation of the independent variable (task) does not result in a change of the dependent variable (outcome).

Kelley labels information about the covariation between entities and effects *distinctiveness*. Distinctiveness is considered high when the effect covaries with the entity (e.g., the person succeeds only at Task 1). Low distinctiveness indicates a lack of covariation between the entity and the effect (i.e., the individual succeeds at all tasks; the task "does not make a difference").

Information about the covariation of an effect with persons is called *consensus*. If the effect covaries with the person (only Person 1 succeeds at Task 1, and Persons 2, 3, and 4 fail), there is low consensus (the manipulation of the independent variable "person" results in a change of the dependent variable). If covariation with this independent variable (i.e., the person) is lacking, there is high consensus (i.e., everybody succeeds at Task 1). Finally, high *consistency* reflects that an effect is always present whenever a certain cause (i.e., the person or the entity) is present. By contrast, low consistency is indicative of the fact that an effect is sometimes present when the cause is absent and sometimes absent when the cause is present.

Kelley suggests that there are three combinations of consistency, consensus, and distinctiveness information which give rise to unambiguous person, entity,

and circumstance attributions. We make person attributions when the effect covaries with the person and not with the remaining two causes (entity and circumstances). This data pattern characterizes, for instance, a situation in which a person succeeds at a task at which nobody else succeeds (low consensus), if he or she also succeeds at this task at different points of time (high consistency) and performs other tasks just as well (low distinctiveness). In this situation, we should attribute success to the person (e.g., his or her ability).

Attributions to the entity should be made when the effect covaries with the entity (the person succeeds only at this but not at other tasks; high distinctiveness) and not with the person (everybody succeeds at this task; high consensus) or the point of time (the person always succeeds at this task; high consistency). This pattern is again characterized by the fact that the effect (e.g., success) covaries with one cause (i.e., the entity) but not with the remaining two causes (i.e., the person or points in time).

Finally, attributions to the circumstances should be made when there is low consensus, high distinctiveness, and low consistency—for example, when a person who usually fails at Task 1 succeeds at it at a specific point of time (low consistency), other persons fail at Task 1 (low consensus), and the individual fails most other tasks (high distinctiveness). This covariation pattern differs from the cases that lead to person and entity attributions, as the effect covaries with all of the three possible causes and not (as was the case for the ideal patterns for person and entity attributions) with only one cause.

Kelley's prediction that people make unambiguous attributions to the person, entity, and circumstances in these three patterns of information is empirically well established. The model has sparked numerous theoretical developments and empirical investigations in the field of attribution and causal induction and continues to be influential into the present. It has been used as a normative model to assess errors and biases, and it served as a conceptual tool for the analyses of a wide range of social psychological phenomena ranging from attribution in close interpersonal relations to attributions of changes in one's heart rate. Current refinements and extensions of Kelley's model focus on whether it specifies all attributionally relevant information and on the cognitive processes involved in making attributions.

Friedrich Försterling

See also Attributions; Attribution Theory; Fundamental
Attribution Error; Person Perception

Further Readings

Försterling, F. (2001). *Attribution: An introduction to theory,
research and applications.* East Sussex, UK: Psychology
Press.

Kelley, H. H. (1973). The processes of causal attribution.
American Psychologist, 28, 107–128.

KIN SELECTION

Definition

Otherwise known as inclusive fitness theory, kin
selection refers to the theory that people have evolved
to favor others who are genetically related to them.
The logic of the theory is that a gene can propagate
itself through two routes. The first is by increasing the
likelihood that the body in which it resides (the *self*)
will survive and reproduce (e.g., by leading to the
selection of nutritious foods and fertile mates). The
second is by increasing the reproduction of close relatives (kin) who also possess copies of the same gene
(e.g., by leading the self to help kin in ways that
increase the chances that they will reproduce and the
gene will be passed on). Some of your kin are more
closely related to you than others and therefore are
more likely to carry your genes. Thus, because you
share 50% of your genes with your siblings, but only
12.5% with your cousins, you should be much more
likely to help siblings than cousins. According to the
theory of inclusive fitness, parental care for offspring
is a special case of kin selection, as it is yet another
case of people (or animals) providing care for closely
related kin who carry shared genetic material.

History and Modern Usage

The theory of kin selection is widely regarded as the
most important theoretical development in evolutionary thinking since Charles Darwin, as it proposes a
mechanism that explains why individuals would
altruistically help others (i.e., why they would provide
resources to someone else at a cost to themselves).
The idea of altruism seems counterintuitive from a
Darwinian perspective, as any behavior that increases
the likelihood that another individual will survive or
reproduce at a cost to one's own survival or reproduction should be selected against. But if this altruistic
behavior enhances the survival or reproduction of a
related individual to a greater degree than it diminishes one's own chances, then, according to the theory, such behavior would be selected for. To give
a concrete example, I may be willing to endanger
myself by alerting my siblings when there is a predator afoot, even if my own shouting makes the predator
more likely to see me. Although this behavior puts me
at risk, it has the potential to result in greater replication of the genes that I carry than if I kept quiet and
one or more of my siblings were killed.

William von Hippel
Martie G. Haselton

See also Altruism; Evolutionary Psychology; Reciprocal
Altruism

Further Readings

Buss, D. M. (2004). *Evolutionary psychology: The new
science of the mind* (2nd ed.). Boston: Allyn & Bacon.

Daly, M., Salmon, C., & Wilson, M. (1997). Kinship: The
conceptual hole in psychological studies of social
cognition and close relationships. In J. Simpson &
D. T. Kenrick (Eds.), *Evolutionary social psychology*
(pp. 265–296). Mahwah, NJ: Erlbaum.

L

LAW OF SMALL NUMBERS

Definition

The law of small numbers refers to the incorrect belief held by experts and laypeople alike that small samples ought to resemble the population from which they are drawn. Although this is true of large samples, it isn't for small ones. So the "law" of small numbers isn't really a law at all, but a fallacy. And as such, it is a law you should feel free to break.

Analysis

To provide an example, suppose you have an urn containing marbles—half of them red and half of them blue (statisticians love urns . . . especially ones with marbles in them). Suppose further that without looking, you draw 100 of them. What are the odds that about half of them will be blue? Although it is unlikely that *exactly* half will be blue (i.e., you probably won't draw exactly 50 blue marbles), the odds are good that it will be close with a sample of 100. With 1,000, the odds are even better—and they keep getting better until your sample reaches infinity (a fact known as the law of *large* numbers).

But suppose instead you draw a smaller sample, say, only two marbles. There, the odds of half of them being blue is much lower . . . only 50%, to be exact. And with a sample of only one, the odds drop to zero. So whereas large samples tend to resemble the population from which they are drawn, smaller samples do not.

The problem is that for most of us, this fact is counterintuitive. People tend to expect small samples to behave just like large ones, a fallacy that leads to all sorts of errors in everyday judgment and decision making.

For instance, when people are asked to mentally generate a sequence of "random" coin tosses, their sequences tend to be anything but. That is, people expect there to be many more alternations than would be expected by chance. In other words, they expect not only the entire sequence to contain approximately 50% heads, but each *portion* of the sequence to contain approximately 50% heads as well.

The same is true in the world of sports. When people observe a basketball player make several baskets in a row, they assume it must because he or she is "hot." They forget that because the sample size is small, such coincidences are not only unsurprising, they are inevitable. In fact, when a group of scientists examined the shooting pattern of professional players, they found something remarkable—there is no such thing as the "hot hand" in basketball. That is, players are no more likely to make a shot after making the previous shot (or shots) than after missing the previous shot (or shots). Despite this fact, people continue to believe in the hot hand, one of several by-products of the mistaken belief in the law of small numbers.

Jeremy Burrus
Justin Kruger

See also Decision Making; Gambler's Fallacy; Hot Hand Effect; Research Methods

Further Readings

Gilovich, T. (1991). *How we know what isn't so: The fallibility of human reason in everyday life.* New York: Free Press.

Tversky, A., & Kahneman, D. (1971). Belief in the law of small numbers. *Psychological Bulletin, 76,* 105–110.

LAY EPISTEMICS

The concept of lay epistemics concerns the process through which individuals (lay persons and scientists alike) attain their subjective knowledge. A theory of lay epistemics has been outlined in two volumes by Arie W. Kruglanski published 15 years apart, and the relevant empirical research has been presented in numerous theoretical and research articles in the scientific literature in personality and social psychology. The theory of lay epistemics describes the cognitive and motivational factors that determine the formation and alteration of human knowledge on all topics. Knowledge is defined in terms of propositions (or bodies of propositions) in which individuals have a given degree of confidence. This conception requires that the contents of knowledge be considered by the individual, implying a phase of hypothesis generation, and that they be assessed as to their validity (their warrant of confidence), implying a phase of hypothesis testing.

According to the lay epistemic theory, hypotheses are tested via relevant evidence. Relevance, in turn, is determined by preexisting inference rules that in an individual's mind tie the evidence to the conclusion in an if-then fashion. This theory assumes that all inferences or judgments are rule based, including such automatic and unconscious judgments as involved in people's perceptions of objects in their environment, the (erroneous) inferences they may draw from momentary mood states to their general levels of life-satisfaction and so on. By assuming the inevitability of rules in the mediation of judgments, the lay epistemic theory affords a unimodel that integrates numerous dual process models proposed in different domains of social cognition.

In principle, the individual may continue generating further and further rule-like hypotheses linking the same category of evidence to different conclusions. For instance, one might link one's good mood at a given moment to one's general level of happiness and success, but also consider the alternative possibility that the good mood was caused by a drink one had just imbibed, by the fact that one's country won a soccer match, and so on. Given such a plethora of alternative possibilities, the individual may feel confused and uncertain. To attain certainty, therefore, one's generation of alternative possibilities must come to a halt. The theory of lay epistemics identifies two categories of conditions affecting the cessation (or conversely, the initiation) of hypothesis generation: long-term capability and epistemic motivation. Long-term capability relates to the availability of constructs in memory pertinent to a given issue or question, and short-term capability relates to their momentary accessibility. Epistemic motivations are conceptualized as the cognitive state the knower wants to attain. Two issues are critical here:

1. Whether the knower desires to achieve or desires to avoid the state of cognitive closure, defined as a firm judgment on a topic and contrasted with confusion and ambiguity

2. Whether such desired or undesired judgment has specific (appealing or unappealing) contents (e.g., a desirable content might be that one is healthy, and an undesirable one that one is not) or is nonspecific—its desired or undesired nature stemming from its constituting a judgment (closure) or an absence of judgment (a lack of closure)

This analysis yields a typology of four motivational orientations, referred to as needs for the following:

1. Specific closure

2. Avoidance of specific closure

3. Nonspecific closure

4. Avoidance of nonspecific closure

Each motivational orientation is assumed to depend on the perceived benefits of attaining or costs of failing to attain the correspondent epistemic state (e.g., 1 through 4 in the previous list). Such costs and benefits can differ across situations (e.g., under time pressure, uncertainty may be more unpleasant than in the absence of pressure) as well as be based on stable individual characteristics. For instance, some individuals more than others may desire nonspecific closure (e.g., be intolerant of uncertainty or ambiguity), some individuals more than others may desire to avoid a specific closure (e.g., being labeled as a failure), and so forth. The epistemic motivations have been shown to exert important influence on individual judgment and decision-making processes (by initiating or halting such processes), and on such interindividual phenomena as persuasion, communication, empathy, and bargaining. The need for nonspecific closure in particular has been shown to lead to a behavioral syndrome referred to as *group-centrism* that includes pressures toward opinion uniformity, endorsement of autocratic leadership, ingroup favoritism and outgroup derogation, the rejection of opinion deviates, and an intolerance of diversity.

Contributions of the Lay Epistemic Theory

The lay epistemic theory has contributed to the understanding of social psychological phenomena in two distinct ways:

1. By generating novel testable predictions explored in empirical research

2. By affording a conceptual integration of numerous, heretofore separate, topics in social cognition

Such predictions concerned individuals' cognitive and social interaction styles, their political preferences, and their reactions to events around them (e.g., to organizational change taking place in their work place). The predictions also concerned the conditions under which the information given would affect the individuals' judgments and those under which it would not, despite its obviousness to external observers. These issues have considerable real-world relevance relating as they do to (1) circumstances in which individuals fail to "see it coming" in military, political, or technological realms fostering immense debacles (e.g., the Pearl Harbor surprise attack, or the breakdowns of the *Challenger* and *Columbia* space shuttles), (2) conditions affording or forestalling intercultural communication, and so on.

Its broad, content free nature allowed the lay epistemic theory to integrate numerous specific domains of social psychological inquiry including the synthesis of attribution with cognitive consistency theories and an integration of the plethora of dual process models under a common set of principles.

Arie W. Kruglanski

See also Cognitive Consistency; Dual Process Theories; Motivated Cognition

Further Readings

Chaiken, S., & Trope, Y. (1999). *Dual process theories in social psychology.* New York: Guilford Press.

Kruglanski, A. W. (1989). *Lay epistemics and human knowledge: Cognitive and motivational bases.* New York: Plenum.

Kruglanski, A. W. (2004). *The psychology of closed mindedness.* New York: Psychology Press.

Kruglanski, A. W., Erb, H. P., Pierro, A., Mannetti, L., & Chun. W. Y. (2006). On parametric continuities in the world of binary either ors. *Psychological Inquiry, 17*(3), 153–163.

Kruglanski, A. W., Pierro, A., Mannetti, L., & DeGrada, E. (2006). Groups as epistemic providers: Need for closure and the unfolding of group centrism. *Psychological Review, 113*(1), 84–100.

Kruglanski, A. W., & Thompson, E. P. (1999). The illusory second mode, or the cue *is* the message. *Psychological Inquiry, 10*(2), 182–193.

Kruglanski, A. W., & Thompson, E. P. (1999). Persuasion by a single route: A view from the unimodel. *Psychological Inquiry, 10*(2), 83–110.

Kruglanski, A. W., & Webster, D. M. (1996). Motivated closing of the mind: "seizing" and "freezing." *Psychological Review, 103*(2), 263–283.

LEADERSHIP

People are obsessed with leaders. People gossip about the boss; airport bookshops bulge with leadership books; current affairs analyzes the actions of leaders; and much of organizational science is about leadership. This is not surprising. Leaders have enormous influence over their followers—leaders make decisions for their followers and shape the course of their lives and even the type of people they are, and so followers are focused on how effective their leaders are; how they are elected, appointed, and deposed; and whether they lead for good or for evil.

Definition

Leadership is a process whereby an individual, or clique, is able to influence others to internalize a collective vision and mobilize them toward attaining that vision. Effective leadership transforms people's goals and ambitions, even their identities, and replaces self-oriented behavior with group-oriented behavior. The exercise of power over people to force them, through rewards and punishments, to comply with commands and bend to one's will is not leadership.

Personality Attributes of Great Leaders

Although leadership is a group process (leaders require followers), leadership research has a long history of focusing on attributes of leaders alone that make them effective—great leaders. The 19th-century belief that leaders are born rather than made is no longer in vogue—research has failed to find "great leader" genes. However, the idea that some people have personalities, however acquired, that predispose them to lead effectively in all situations, whereas others do not, has attracted enormous research attention. A definitive review published in 2002 concluded that three of the Big Five personality dimensions are associated with effective leadership: Extraversion, Openness to Experience, and Conscientiousness. Overall, however, personality does not allow people to differentiate between effective and ineffective leaders very reliably.

What Do Effective Leaders Do?

Maybe some leadership behaviors are more effective. One reliable distinction that has emerged is between a leadership style that pays more attention to the group task and getting things done (task-oriented leadership) and one that pays attention to relationships among group members (socioemotional leadership). Most groups require both types of leadership and people who are capable of being both task-focused and socio-emotionally focused tend to be the most effective.

Interactionist Perspectives

However, different situations and different group activities call for different emphases on the task or on relationships—in which case, the relative effectiveness of task-oriented and relationship-oriented leaders may be contingent on properties of the leadership situation. This idea is reflected in Fred Fiedler's contingency theory of leadership, very popular in the 1970s; one strength of this theory was that Fielder had a novel way to measure both leadership styles (the least-preferred coworker scale) and classify how well structured situations were. Generally, relationship-oriented leadership was most effective unless the group task was very poorly structured or very well structured.

Another interactionist perspective is normative decision theory. Leaders can choose to make decisions autocratically (subordinate input is not sought), consultatively (subordinate input is sought, but the leader retains authority to make the final decision), or as a genuine group decision (leader and subordinates are equal partners in shared decision making). The relative efficacy of these strategies is contingent on the quality of leader-subordinate relationships and on task clarity and structure. Autocratic leadership is fast and effective if leader-subordinate relationships are good and the task is well structured. When the task is less clear, consultative leadership is best, and when leader-subordinate relations are poor, group decision making is best.

A third interactionist theory is path-goal theory, which assumes that a leader's main function is to motivate followers by clarifying the paths that will help them attain their goals. Leaders do this by directing task-related activities (structuring) or by addressing followers' personal and emotional needs (consideration). Structuring is most effective when followers are unclear about their goals and how to reach them, and consideration is most effective when the task is boring or uncomfortable.

Transactional Leadership

Another way to look at leadership is as a transaction between leaders and followers—the leader does something benefiting followers, and followers in turn allow the leader to lead. Eric Hollander coined the term *idiosyncrasy credit* to describe a transaction in which leaders who initially conform to group norms and therefore serve the group well are subsequently rewarded by the group by being allowed to be idiosyncratic and innovative—key features of effective leadership.

One key transactional leadership theory is leader-member exchange (LMX) theory. Because leaders have to relate to many subordinates, they differentiate among them and develop different LMX relationships with different subordinates—the quality of these relationships range from those based on mutual trust, respect, and obligation (high-quality LMX relationships), to those mechanically based on the formal employment contract between leader and subordinate (low-quality relationships). Effective leadership rests on the development of high-quality LMX relationships with as many subordinates as possible—these relationships motivate followers and bind them to the group.

Transformational Leadership and Charisma

Leaders typically are innovative and able to mobilize followers to buy and implement their new vision for the group—they are transformational. Transformational leadership is characterized by (a) careful attention to followers' needs, abilities, and aspirations, (b) challenging followers' basic thinking, assumptions, and practices, and (c) exercise of charisma and inspiration. Charisma is central for transformational leadership (there is much talk about charismatic or visionary leaders and leadership), which has engaged a debate among scholars (a) about whether this is a return to older personality perspectives on leadership, and (b) about how one can distinguish between charisma in the service of evil (Slobodan Milošević) and charisma in the service of good (Nelson Mandela).

Stereotypes of Leadership

According to leader categorization theory, people have stereotypical expectations (schemas) about the attributes an effective leader should have in general, or in specific leadership situations. Once a person categorizes someone as a leader, the person automatically engages the relevant leadership schema—the better the match is between the leader's actual characteristics and the leadership schema, the more favorable are the person's evaluations of the leader and his or her leadership.

Stereotypical expectations might affect leadership in two other ways. According to status characteristics theory, in a task-oriented group, a person's evaluations of effective leadership rest on whether he or she believes the leader has the attributes to perform the group task, called *specific status characteristics,* and whether the leader is a member of a high-status group in society and therefore possesses attributes that are valued in society, called *diffuse status characteristics.*

Role congruity theory focuses on gender and leadership. The argument is that stereotypes of women typically do not match well with schemas of effective leadership, and thus in many leadership situations, women find it difficult to be endorsed as effective leaders. There is an incongruity between the attributes of the leadership role and the stereotypical attributes of women.

Social Identity and Leadership

According to the social identity theory of leadership, a key function of leadership is to forge, transform, and consolidate one's identity as a group member—one's social identity. The implication of this is that if membership in a group is important to a person, particularly to his or her sense of self, the person is more likely to be influenced by a leader who matches his or her understanding of what the group stands for (a leader who is *prototypical* of the group) than by one who does not. Effective leadership in such groups rests significantly on being perceived by one's followers as being prototypical, even to the extent that general attributes of good leadership decline in importance. One reason why leaders who are prototypical members of subjectively important groups can be effective is that followers believe that because their identity and that of the group are closely matched, the leaders treat members fairly and must be acting in the best interest of the group, so they are therefore trusted and allowed to be innovative.

Michael A. Hogg

See also Attributions; Schemas; Social Identity Theory

Further Readings

Goethals, G. R., Sorenson, G. J., & Burns, J. M. (Eds.). (2004). *Encyclopedia of leadership.* Thousand Oaks, CA: Sage.

Hogg, M. A. (2007). Social psychology of leadership. In A. W. Kruglanski & E. T. Higgins (Eds.), *Social psychology: A handbook of basic principles* (2nd ed.). New York: Guilford Press.

Yukl, G. (2002). *Leadership in organizations* (5th ed.). Upper Saddle River, NJ: Prentice Hall.

LEARNED HELPLESSNESS

What happens when people encounter obstacles in solving problems and are unable to avoid negative outcomes (e.g., academic failure, interpersonal rejection)? Will they persevere in trying to control the course of events and invest more efforts in improving their performance or give up and withdraw from the frustrating situation? What are the consequences of this painful experience for a person's emotional state and psychological functioning? Dealing with these questions, hundreds of experimental studies, conducted during the 1970s and 1980s, have exposed people to inescapable failures in a wide variety of tasks and have found that participants apparently give up trying, passively succumb to the failure, and show performance deficits in a subsequent task. These responses, which reflect the emotional and behavioral interference produced by the inability to control undesirable life events, have been labeled "learned helplessness."

Research

The first study of learned helplessness was conducted with dogs by Martin E. P. Seligman and Steven F. Maier in 1967. In this study, dogs were randomly divided into three groups. One group (the neutral group) received no electric shock. A second group (the escape group) received 64 electric shocks, which dogs could escape by pressing a panel located on either side of their heads. In the third group (the helplessness group), each dog received the same number and duration of shocks to those received by a dog in the escape group. However, whereas dogs in the escape group ended the shock by their own responses, dogs in the helplessness group could not control shock termination (which came only when the dog from the escape group delivered the required response).

Twenty-four hours later, all the dogs performed a new learning task (jump over a barrier to avoid electric shocks). Dogs in the helplessness group showed worse performance in the new task than dogs in both the escape and neutral groups. Specifically, dogs in the helplessness group seemed to accept the shock without any resistance and were unlikely to cross the barrier to escape from it. In addition, they were slow to learn to avoid the shock even when they discovered the contingency between barrier jumping and shock termination. Although they jumped over the barrier occasionally and in so doing stopped the shocks, they rarely jumped again on the next trial. Importantly, although dogs in the escape group were also exposed to aversive shocks, they showed no performance deficits in the new task. On this basis, Seligman and Maier concluded that lack of control rather than the mere exposure to aversive events produced the performance deficits observed in the helplessness group.

In 1975, Donald Hiroto and Seligman extended the study of learned helplessness to humans. In their experiment, undergraduates performed a series of concept formation tasks. In each trial of these tasks, two different geometrical patterns, each composed of five attributes (e.g., shape, color), appeared on each side of a card. Participants were asked to try to figure out which of five attributes (e.g., a star-shape figure) the experimenter had arbitrarily designated as the target attribute. In each of the trials, participants indicated whether the target attribute appeared on the right or left side of the card, and the experimenter told them whether their choice was correct or not. After the 10th card, participants indicated what they thought the target attribute was and were told whether they succeeded or not to learn the concept.

During these tasks, participants were randomly divided into three groups. In the neutral group, participants performed no task and simply waited for the second part of the experiment. In the solvable group, participants received veridical feedback on each trial and at the end of the task. On this basis, participants could learn the target attribute and control the experimenter's feedback by their own responses. Participants in the third group, the unsolvable group, were exposed to uncontrollable feedback. For them, the experimenter did not select any attribute, instead providing a predetermined, random schedule of "correct" and "incorrect" responses during the trials. After the 10th trial, participants in this group were uniformly told that they failed to learn the target attribute.

Following the concept formation task, all the participants performed a new task in which they were asked to learn how to escape from an aversive noise. Findings revealed that participants in the unsolvable group were less likely to learn to escape from the noise than were participants in the solvable and neutral groups. According to Hiroto and Seligman, the exposure to unsolvable problems might have led people to develop expectancies that they have no available response or strategy for controlling outcomes and altering negative course of events. This expectation can be generalized to the subsequent task, thereby reducing motivation to undertake the new activity ("Why invest efforts in trying to solve a problem if I have no suitable response for solving it?") and interfering with task performance.

Depression and Learned Helplessness

These initial findings were replicated in hundreds of subsequent studies and extended to a wide variety of tasks. The theoretical and empirical interest in the performance effects of unsolvable problems dramatically increased when Seligman claimed in 1975 that learned helplessness is a precursor of depression. That is, exposure to uncontrollable adverse circumstances and the resulting expectancy of lack of control can result in depression. According to Seligman, both people exposed to uncontrollable events and those suffering from depression show lowered response initiation, lack of assertiveness and aggression, loss of appetite, feelings of sadness and hopelessness, and extreme passivity. Moreover, several researchers have found similar performance deficits among nondepressed people exposed to unsolvable problems and depressed people exposed to solvable or no problems.

Originally, Seligman argued that the expectation of lack of control is the main psychological mechanism that explains performance deficits and depression following exposure to uncontrollable events. However, with the progress of research and theory, Lyn Abramson, Seligman, and John Teasdale claimed in 1978 that the attributions a person makes about the causes of the failure to control negative events can also explain why and when expectancies of lack of control result in generalized performance deficits and depression. If a person decides that failure is due to stable and global factors that can persist in the future and recur in other situations (e.g., intelligence), the expectancy of control tends to be generalized to new and different tasks and to result in global performance deficits. By contrast, if failure is explained by unstable and specific factors (e.g., tiredness), neither the expectation of uncontrollability nor performance deficits tend to be recorded in new situations. Moreover, if a person believes that failure is due to internal causes that reflect on his or her abilities and personality, expectancy of lack of control can result in depression (e.g., "I'm a failure"). In contrast, attribution of the failure to external causes (a difficult task, others' bad intentions) can result in anger and aggression rather than depression.

Beyond expectancies of control and causal attributions, subsequent studies have revealed the importance of other psychological mechanisms that can explain the emergence of performance deficits and depression following exposure to uncontrollable events. For example, the perceived importance of the failure for one's goals and aspirations can moderate these effects, with higher personal relevance of the failure amplifying performance deficits and depression. The direction of attention toward one's feelings, thoughts, and inner states (*self-focus*) also amplifies the performance and emotional deficits produced by uncontrollable events. In addition, exposure to unsolvable problems elicits anxiety, worries, and doubts about one's personal value, which divert attention away from task-relevant activities and can impair task performance. Moreover, people may withdraw effort from the new task as a means to protect their personal value from further damage. Although this self-defeating decision results in performance deficits, people have a good excuse for the failure—poor performance was caused by lack of effort rather than lack of ability.

Implications

In the 30 years since the work of Seligman and his colleagues, learned helplessness has become a thriving area of research and has been applied to understanding problems in school achievement; post-traumatic stress symptoms; the detrimental effects of the death of a beloved, chronic illnesses, and aging; and maladaptive reactions of battered women who decide to remain close to their abusive partners. In all these cases, the painful recognition that one has no control over the course and outcome of personal and interpersonal events can result in passivity, resignation, hopelessness, and loss of vigor to effectively cope with ongoing demands for adjustment and to restore one's emotional well-being.

Mario Mikulincer

See also Depression; Locus of Control; Self-Defeating Behavior

Further Readings

Abramson, L. Y., Seligman, M. E. P., & Teasdale, J. D. (1978). Learned helplessness in humans: Critique and reformulation. *Journal of Abnormal Psychology, 87,* 49–74.

Mikulincer, M. (1989). Cognitive interference and learned helplessness: The effects of off-task cognitions on performance following unsolvable problems. *Journal of Personality and Social Psychology, 57,* 129–135.

Mikulincer, M. (1994). *Human learned helplessness: A coping perspective.* New York: Plenum.

Peterson, C., & Seligman, M. E. P. (1984). Causal explanations as a risk factor for depression: Theory and evidence. *Psychological Review, 91,* 347–374.

Seligman, M. E. P. (1975). *Helplessness: On depression, development and death.* San Francisco: Freeman.

LEARNING THEORY

Definition

The meaning of this term seems simple: Learning theory is the theory about how learning is achieved. Unfortunately, things are not that simple. A fundamental problem is that the term *learning theory* seems to suggest that there is a single, true theory of learning. Although one cannot exclude the possibility that such a theory might be developed, at present, nothing even comes close to the overarching learning theory. It is unlikely that such a theory will ever be formulated, if only because there are so many different types of learning. The next paragraphs will discuss two general types of learning: non-associative and associative learning. Afterward, this entry will focus on theories about associative learning because people often have these theories in mind when they use the term *learning theory.*

Context and Importance

Different types of learning can be characterized on the basis of a number of criteria. One of those criteria is whether the change in behavior is caused by the mere repeated presentation of a single stimulus or event or because one stimulus or event is paired with another stimulus or event. These types of learning are called non-associative and associative learning, respectively. Non-associative learning is a fundamental type of learning that can be seen even in very simple organisms. But the mere fact of being exposed to a stimulus or event also has an important impact on human behavior. For instance, when you enter a room for the first time, you might pay attention to the ticking of the clock that is present in the room. But it is likely that you will no longer notice the ticking of the clock after a while. So one possible effect of repeated presentation of a stimulus or event is that one habituates to it: One's initial reaction to the stimulus or event decreases in intensity because of the repeated presentation. But stimulus presentations can have a whole range of other effects. For instance, the first time that you hear a new song on the radio, you often don't like it as much as after you have heard it a few times. This shows that repeated stimulus presentation can change one's liking for the presented stimulus.

Associative learning can be defined as changes in behavior that are due to the repeated pairing of different stimuli or events. The term *conditioning* is basically a synonym for associative learning. There are two basic types of conditioning. First, Pavlovian or classical conditioning refers to a change in the reaction to a stimulus that is caused by this stimulus being paired with another stimulus. For instance, a dog might initially not react to the sound of a bell, but might start to salivate upon hearing the bell (i.e., change in behavior) when the ringing of the bell is paired repeatedly with the delivery of food (i.e., pairing two stimuli). Second, operant or instrumental conditioning refers to changes in behavior that are the result of a behavior being paired with a certain stimulus. For instance, rats will press a lever more frequently (i.e., change in behavior) if that behavior is followed by the delivery of food (i.e., pairing of the behavior and a stimulus). The main difference between the two forms of conditioning is that the animal or person does not have any control over the events in Pavlovian conditioning (e.g., the bell and food are paired no matter what the dog does) but does have an impact on the events in operant conditioning (e.g., the food is presented only if the rat presses the lever).

For most of the 20th century, behaviorist theories dominated research on conditioning. These theories postulated that conditioning occurs in an automatic, unconscious way and does not involve any cognitive processes. This long-standing dominance of behaviorist theories has led to a tendency to use the term *learning theory* to refer to these theories. But use of the term *learning theory* is problematic. First, the behaviorist theories focused mainly on associative forms of learning and not on other forms. Hence, none of these theories provides a theory of all forms of learning. Second, behaviorist theories cannot account for a wide variety of findings in research on conditioning.

Since the end of the 1960s, it is clear that cognitive processes do play an important role in conditioning. For instance, ample evidence indicates that conditioning in humans depends heavily on whether the person is aware of the link between the associated events (e.g., the fact that the bell always precedes food). In fact, there is little evidence for automatic, unconscious conditioning in humans.

Implications

Some have concluded, on the basis of these results, that conditioning does not occur in humans and that learning theory does not apply to humans. But conditioning does occur in humans because the behavior of people changes as the result of pairing two stimuli or a behavior and a stimulus. For instance, people do stop at railway crossings because they have learned that the flickering of the lights will be followed by the arrival of a train. Likewise, they will often start to dislike a certain food when eating that food was followed by nausea. It remains useful to see these associatively induced changes in behavior as forms of conditioning because this provides a framework for studying and understanding these behaviors. Which processes (i.e., automatic or controlled) are involved in conditioning is an important question. Probably several types of processes can play a role under certain conditions. But this question needs to be answered by research rather than by claiming that conditioning is only conditioning if it is the result of certain (i.e., automatic and unconscious) processes. Because of these potential dangers, it seems best to avoid using the term *learning theory* unless one specifies which specific theory one has in mind.

Jan De Houwer

See also Attention; Controlled Processes; Mere Exposure Effect

Further Readings

Domjan, M. (2005). *The essentials of conditioning and learning* (3rd ed.). Belmont, CA: Wadsworth/Thomson Learning.

Schwartz, B., Wasserman, E. A., & Robbins, S. J. (2002). *Psychology of learning and behavior* (5th ed.). New York: W. W. Norton.

LISREL

Definition

LISREL (LInear Structural RELations modeling) was one of the first statistical computer packages used for structural equation modeling. Created by Karl Jöreskog and Dag Sörbom, it remains one of the most popular programs for such analyses, although numerous other programs exist, including EQS, Proc Calis within SAS, and Amos. As with all structural modeling programs, LISREL provides an extremely powerful and flexible way to analyze complex data.

LISREL essentially assesses the extent to which theorized relations between variables are consistent with observed relations between those variables. The researcher begins by theorizing how a set of variables should be related to each other. For example, he or she might theorize that many measured variables (e.g., a verbal test, math test, reaction time test) all relate to a single underlying construct of generalized intelligence (IQ). This is an example of a "latent variable model." IQ is not measured directly; rather, its existence is inferred because a variety of measured or "observed" variables (the various tests) are themselves highly related to each other. If the researcher collects the data and the measured tests are not all highly related to each other, a model that assumes a single latent variable may not "fit" the observed data. LISREL provides the researcher with specific, quantitative estimates of the extent to which the theorized model fits the observed data.

Popular uses of LISREL include tests for the presence of a single latent variable, multiple latent variables, and even latent variables that are nested hierarchically. A model that tests only for the presence of latent variables is often referred to as a "confirmatory factor model." Other common uses of LISREL include tests of models in which the researcher theorizes a chain of direct and indirect influences among variables. The variables included in such a "path" model can be either observed or latent variables or a mixture of the two. They may all be measured at a single point in time or involve multiple time-points. Indeed, structural modeling programs like LISREL are often used to analyze longitudinal data.

When analyzing data using LISREL, the researcher is provided a variety of statistics that are useful in determining how well or poorly the model fits the observed data. These include statistics for individually theorized associations among variables as well as statistics that assess the model as a whole. In addition, the researcher is provided statistics that pinpoint sources of ill fit. Armed with these statistics, the researcher is often tempted to modify the originally theorized model in an attempt to provide a better fitting model. Although such modifications will improve fit, they run the risk of capitalizing on chance fluctuations in the data and should be replicated in a separate sample before they are trusted.

LISREL and other structural equation modeling programs provide powerful tools for testing complex models of psychological phenomena. At the same time, they require a fair amount of mathematical ability and statistical sophistication to use properly.

Jay Hull

See also Structural Equation Modeling

Further Readings

Byrne, B. (1998). *Structural equation modeling with LISREL, PRELIS, and SIMPLIS: Basic concepts, applications, and programming.* Mahwah, NJ: Erlbaum.

Byrne, B. (2006). *Structural equation modeling with EQS: Basic concepts, applications, and programming.* Mahwah, NJ: Erlbaum.

du Toit, M., & du Toit, S. (2001). *Interactive LISREL: User's Guide.* Lincolnwood, IL: Scientific Software.

Kline, R. B. (2004). *Principles and practice of structural equation modeling* (2nd ed.). New York: Guilford Press.

LOCUS OF CONTROL

Who determines one's fate? Is it the person or outside forces beyond the person's control? This question lies at the root of the concept of locus of control. People who believe they are in control of their destinies have an internal locus of control (internals). Those who believe that luck and powerful others determine their fate have an external locus of control (externals).

Measurements

Locus of control is usually measured by questionnaires, just as personality traits are; however, locus of control is more an attitude than a trait—it measures how one thinks the world works. Some researchers have called locus of control a *generalized expectancy*—in other words, a person's usual expectation about how things work.

One of the first locus of control measures was Julian Rotter's Internal-External Locus of Control Scale, first published in 1966 and used in thousands of articles. Rotter's measure consists of 23 forced-choice pairs; the respondent must choose one of the two statements, one internally oriented and the other externally oriented. For example, one of the pairs is "People's misfortunes result from the mistakes they make" (internal) versus "Many of the unhappy things in people's lives are partly due to bad luck" (external). Most items are general, though a few deal with specific circumstances such as school ("In the case of the well-prepared student there is rarely if ever such a thing as an unfair test") or world affairs ("By taking an active part in political and social affairs, the people can control world events"). These are both internal items.

The most popular measure of locus of control in children is the Children's Nowicki-Strickland Internal-External Control Scale. Other scales measure more specialized aspects of control; there has been an especially large amount of research on health locus of control. Several scales (of both general and health locus of control) are multidimensional, as many researchers agree that external control should be divided into control by fate or chance and control by powerful others.

Research

Research has consistently shown that externality is related to negative outcomes. Externals report lower subjective well-being, are more likely to be depressed, display more anxiety, and cope poorly with stress. Externals have weakened self-control and a lessened ability to delay gratification (meaning that they have a difficult time choosing long-term gains over short-term pleasures, something necessary for many life situations, particularly college!)

Externals also consistently achieve less in school, as shown in two meta-analyses and numerous individual studies. A widely publicized report by James Coleman and his colleagues concluded that internal locus of control was a better predictor of school achievement in minority children than any other variable. Children with an internal locus of control see more reason to study and try hard because they believe it will make a difference; externals believe that it won't matter, compromising their performance.

Several studies have also linked externality to increased juvenile delinquency. Externality may also lead to a victim mentality, in which people blame others for their problems. Some authors have argued that the victim mentality encourages self-loathing and the expectation of low functioning and achievement.

Externality on health locus of control also leads to negative outcomes such as decreased success in stopping smoking or losing weight. People who are external in locus of control are also less likely to make and keep dentist and doctor appointments; they are also less likely to use birth control consistently. People who truly believe that fate controls everything are less likely to take control of their health.

Differences

Locus of control differs along many dimensions. Men tend to be more internal than women, Whites more internal than minorities, middle-class people more internal than lower-class people, and older people more internal than younger people. These four results suggest that people with more power are more internal.

Locus of control also differs by generation: More recent generations are more external and thus more likely to believe that outside forces determine their fates. This generational shift is so large that the average college student in the 2000s would score at the 80th percentile on the original 1960 distribution (where, of course, the average 1960s college student would score at the 50th percentile). This increase in externality may be at the root of some current trends, such as blaming others for problems. For example, civil lawsuits are more common, and there is anecdotal evidence that students (and their parents) are now more likely to argue with teachers and professors. Externality may also help explain the high rates of anxiety and depression observed in recent years. Many young people are also disinclined to get involved in political action or even vote; voter participation has steadily declined over this period, especially for voters ages 18 to 24.

There are also cultural differences in locus of control. Members of more interdependent and traditional cultures often have a more external locus of control. Stricter adherence to social and religious rules may encourage externality. There has been debate about whether externality may be adaptive in some cases. Many researchers believe that externality is a negative characteristic because it is correlated with poor outcomes. However, other researchers have pointed out that in reality, control is sometimes an illusion and there are some things that people must accept as being out of their control.

Jean M. Twenge

See also Achievement Motivation; Blaming the Victim; Control; Illusion of Control; Power; Self-Defeating Behavior

Further Readings

Rotter, J. B. (1966). Generalized expectancies for internal versus external control of reinforcement [Whole issue]. *Psychological Monographs, 80*(1), 1–28.

Rotter, J. B. (1971). External control and internal control. *Psychology Today, 5,* 37–59.

Twenge, J. M., Zhang, L., & Im, C. (2004). It's beyond my control: A cross-temporal meta-analysis of increasing externality in locus of control, 1960–2002. *Personality and Social Psychology Review, 8,* 308, 319.

LOGICAL POSITIVISM

Definition

Logical positivism, also called logical empiricism, was an early 20th-century philosophical movement that held that a statement was meaningful only if it could be verified or confirmed through experience. Logical positivism relied exclusively on observable events for knowledge about the world, and therefore considered non-observable events to be basically meaningless. In other words, the only truth is what science can prove.

History, Problems, and Modern Significance

A. E. Blumberg and Herbert Feigl coined the term *logical positivism* in 1931 to describe the philosophical principles of the Vienna Circle, a group of European scholars. Logical positivists rejected philosophical inquiries on the grounds that there was no possible way of verifying them in experience. For example, the statement "abortion is wrong" reflects a person's disapproval of abortion, or attempts to convince others to also disapprove of abortion. In either case, the statement itself does not convey any direct information about the existence or nature of abortion, and is therefore (according to logical positivism) meaningless (e.g., what you think about abortion does not really matter because it is just your opinion). Logical positivists consequently proposed science to be the source for all knowledge about the world because science is grounded in concrete experience and publicly observable events (unlike, for instance, observations gained from introspection). If propositions were inextricably tied to science, logical positivists argued, they could not be too far from the truth.

Logical positivism collapsed in the 1940s, largely because of the sharpness of its inevitably created yes-or-no dichotomies: Either a statement is verifiable or it is not, either a statement is scientific or unscientific. Ironically, this created severe problems because such statements themselves cannot be conclusively verified. Moreover, basing all conclusions on directly observable data creates problems as well. For example, a person with a headache might complain of pain, lie down, or take aspirin. However, someone faking a headache might objectively exhibit the same overt symptoms. A pure reliance on the observable data would presumably lead to the errant conclusion that both people have headaches, when only one actually does.

Problems notwithstanding, logical positivism has nonetheless left its mark on psychology. The behaviorists in particular quite enthusiastically adopted the premise that scientists should study behavior rather than thought. Most importantly, logical positivism helped endow psychology with the enduring sentiment that one can transform complex propositions about cognitive phenomena into scientifically testable hypotheses about overt behavior and do so in a way that other researchers—and ideally the general public—can clearly understand the results.

Scott J. Moeller
Brad J. Bushman

See also Experimentation; Lay Epistemics

Further Readings

Passmore, J. (1967). Logical positivism. In P. Edwards (Ed.), *The encyclopedia of philosophy* (Vol. 5, pp. 52–57). New York: Macmillan.

LONELINESS

Definition

Loneliness is defined as the distressing experience that occurs when one's social relationships are perceived to be less in quantity, and especially in quality, than desired. Being alone and experiencing loneliness are not the same thing. People can be alone without feeling lonely and can feel lonely even when with other people. Loneliness is associated with depressive symptoms, poor social support, neuroticism, and introversion, but loneliness is not synonymous with these psychological characteristics. Loneliness is typically thought of as a stable trait, with individual differences in the set-point for feelings of loneliness about which people fluctuate depending on the specific circumstances in which they find themselves. Loneliness changes very little during adulthood until 75 to 80 years of age when it increases somewhat. Loneliness puts people at risk for mental and physical disease and may contribute to a shortened life span.

History and Theory

Although loneliness has always been part of human existence, it has a relatively short psychological history. John Bowlby's attachment theory emphasized the importance of a good attachment bond between the infant and caregiver, and this theory was a forerunner to theories of loneliness. From this perspective, loneliness is the result of insecure attachment patterns that lead children to behave in ways that result in being rejected by their peers. Rejection experiences hinder the development of social skills and increase distrust of other people, thereby fostering ongoing loneliness.

Attachment theory formed a foundation for an influential psychological theory of loneliness developed by Robert S. Weiss. Weiss identified six functions or needs of social relationships that, if in short supply, contribute to feelings of loneliness. These needs are attachment, social integration, nurturance, reassurance of worth, sense of reliable alliance, and guidance in stressful situations. Weiss went on to distinguish loneliness from social isolation (e.g., a lack of social integration) and loneliness from emotional isolation (e.g., the absence of a reliable attachment figure). As would be predicted by attachment theory, Weiss maintained that friendships complement but do not substitute for a close, intimate relationship with a partner in staving off loneliness. Widows who remarry have been found to escape from loneliness, but those who merely have other friends still feel somewhat lonely about not having a husband.

Another theoretical perspective holds that loneliness is characterized by personality traits that are associated with, and possibly contribute to, harmful interpersonal behavioral patterns. For instance, loneliness is correlated with social anxiety, social inhibition (shyness), sadness, hostility, distrust, and low self-esteem, characteristics that hamper one's ability to interact in skillful and rewarding ways. Indeed, lonely individuals have been shown to have difficulty forming and maintaining meaningful relationships. They are also less likely to self-disclose to peers, and this helps to explain why they report a lack of intimacy with close friends.

The cognitive approach to loneliness is based on the fact that loneliness is characterized by distinct differences in perceptions and attributions. Lonely individuals tend to look at their world through dark-tinted glasses: They are more negative than are nonlonely individuals about the people, events, and circumstances in their world, and they tend to blame themselves for not being able to achieve satisfactory social relationships. The "perceived discrepancy" definition of loneliness provided previously represents the cognitive perspective. In addition, the cognitive approach largely takes account of the attachment and behavioral perspectives by explaining how (a) failure to meet the need for attachment, social integration, nurturance, and other social needs, results in perceived relationship discrepancies that are experienced as loneliness, and (b) loneliness is perpetuated by way of a self-fulfilling prophecy in which poor social skills result in unsatisfactory personal relationships that, in turn, result in negative self-attributions that lead to further social isolation and relationship dissatisfaction.

Theories of the self have contributed to theories of loneliness by demonstrating the importance of individual, relational, and collective selves. These self-identities correspond to aspects of the experience of loneliness or conversely, the experience of connectedness. For example, at the individual level, if a person's self-concept expands to include an intimate other (e.g., a marital partner), the person is less likely to experience a sense of isolation than if his or her self-concept fails to include his or her partner. Similarly, a network of close friends and relatives protects against relational loneliness, and group affiliations and memberships protect against collective loneliness.

All these theories of loneliness fit under the umbrella of an evolutionary account of loneliness. According to the evolutionary model, hunter-gatherers who, in times of famine, chose not to return to share their food with mother and child (i.e., did not place a high priority on maintaining social or family bonds) may have survived themselves, but the same genes that allowed them to ignore their family also made it less likely their genes would survive past the child's generation. In contrast, hunter-gatherers inclined to share food with their family may have lowered their own chances of survival but increased the survival odds of their offspring, thereby propagating their genes. Of course, a hunter-gatherer who survives a famine may then live to have another family another day, suggesting that no single strategy is necessarily best. Such an evolutionary scenario suggests that humans might inherit differing tendencies to experience loneliness. Adoption and twin studies among children and adults have confirmed that loneliness has a sizable heritable component.

Correlates and Consequences

Practically and ethically, loneliness cannot be easily manipulated in an experimental setting. This has posed a challenge to researchers attempting to distinguish between the causes and consequences of loneliness. One creative approach to this obstacle was a paradigm that employed hypnotic suggestion. Using this strategy, highly hypnotizable individuals were asked to relive a time when they felt lonely, and after return from this hypnotic state, to relive a time when they felt highly socially connected. While in these states of social disconnection and connection, participants completed a set of psychosocial measures. The results showed that the states and dispositions that differentiate lonely and nonlonely individuals in everyday life also varied with manipulated feelings of loneliness. That is, when participants were induced to feel lonely, compared with nonlonely, they scored higher, not only on a measure of loneliness, but also in shyness, negative mood, anger, anxiety, and fear of negative evaluation, and lower on measures of social skills, optimism, positive mood, social support, and self-esteem. Conversely, when individuals were induced to feel that their intimate, relational, and collective social needs were being met, they became characterized by states and dispositions that were generally more positive and engaged. This experimental study suggests that loneliness has features of a central trait—central in the sense that loneliness influences how individuals construe themselves and others, as well as how others view and act toward these individuals.

One example of differential construals is that lonely individuals form more negative social impressions and interpret the behavior of others in a more negative light than do nonlonely individuals. Negative social expectations tend to elicit behaviors from others that match these expectations. This reinforces the lonely individual's expectations and increases the likelihood that the individual will behave in ways that push away the very people who could satisfy his or her social needs. This has been demonstrated in experimental studies in which perceived social threats (e.g., competition, betrayal) cause lonely individuals to respond more quickly and intensely with distrust, hostility, and intolerance.

The negative, self-protective lens through which lonely individuals view their social world also influences how they interpret and cope with stressful circumstances. Lonely individuals are more likely to disengage or withdraw from stressors, whereas nonlonely individuals are more likely to actively cope (e.g., problem solve) and seek tangible and emotional support from others. Passively coping or withdrawing from stressful circumstances is reasonable in certain instances, but when applied generally to everyday hassles, it can lead to an accumulation of stress that becomes increasingly taxing and oppressive. Increased stress may be at least partially responsible for the risk of mental and physical disease in lonely individuals. For instance, loneliness has been associated with elevated levels of stress hormones, poorer immune functioning, and health-jeopardizing changes in cardiovascular functioning.

Individual Differences

Individual differences in loneliness are typically measured using paper-and-pencil questionnaires developed for this purpose. The most frequently used instrument is the UCLA Loneliness Scale, first developed at the University of California at Los Angeles by Daniel Russell and his colleagues. Responses to the 20 items on this scale provide an overall measure of loneliness along a continuum from low to high levels of loneliness. Other loneliness scales have been designed to measure different dimensions of loneliness (e.g., social and emotional loneliness). Some individuals are reluctant or ashamed to report they are lonely, so most loneliness scales avoid using the terms *lonely* and *loneliness*.

Louise Hawkley

See also Attachment Theory; Need to Belong; Rejection; Self

Further Readings

Cacioppo, J. T., Hawkley, L. C., & Berntson, G. G. (2003). The anatomy of loneliness. *Current Directions in Psychological Science, 12,* 71–74.

Ernst, J. M., & Cacioppo, J. T. (1999). Lonely hearts: Psychological perspective on loneliness. *Applied and Preventive Psychology, 8,* 1–22.

LOOKING-GLASS SELF

Definition

The looking-glass self is the process by which people evaluate themselves based on how others see them. According to this theory, people first imagine how they appear to others. Second, they imagine how others judge them based on that appearance. Third, people have an emotional reaction to that imagined judgment, such as pride or embarrassment. This self-evaluation influences the person's sense of self-worth or self-esteem. In short, the looking-glass self theory suggests that we come to know ourselves by reflecting on how others see us.

History and Modern Usage

The looking-glass self was first proposed by Charles Horton Cooley. According to Cooley, self-perceptions are based on reflected appraisals of how others see us (i.e., our impression of others' impressions of us), which are in turn based on how others actually see us.

The looking-glass self theory is controversial for two reasons. First, this view supposes that people have a good idea of how significant others see them. Psychological research reveals that people's beliefs about how others see them are not very accurate. Indeed, our reflected appraisals of how we think others see us are much more closely related to how we see ourselves than to how others see us. Some researchers have argued that this evidence implies that the looking-glass self theory is actually backward—it could be that people simply assume others see them the same way they see themselves.

The second reason why the looking-glass self theory is controversial is that other theories of self-perception provide alternative explanations for how people form their self-views. For example, self-perception theory claims that self-views are based on direct observations of one's own behavior, rather than on how we imagine others see us. Nevertheless, our impressions of what others think of us are extremely important to us. People go to great lengths to obtain feedback about how others see them, such as posting their photographs on a Web site where others will rate their attractiveness. Some researchers have even proposed that the main purpose of self-esteem is to serve as an internal "sociometer"—a gauge of our relative popularity or worth among our peers.

Some evidence indicates that people's reflected appraisals of how others see them influence their self-views and their behavior, particularly in close relationships. Research on romantic relationships suggests that our reflected appraisals of how our partners see us may be particularly important in this context. This is especially true for people who have doubts about how their partner feels about them. People with negative impressions of how their partner sees them tend to cause strain and dissatisfaction in their relationships.

Simine Vazire

See also Person Perception; Self; Self-Concept; Self-Perception Theory; Symbolic Interactionism

Further Readings

O'Connor, B. P., & Dyce, J. (1993). Appraisals of musical ability in bar bands: Identifying the weak link in the looking-glass self chain. *Basic and Applied Social Psychology, 14,* 69–86.

Shrauger, J. S., & Schoeneman, T. J. (1979). Symbolic interactionist view of the self-concept: Through the looking-glass darkly. *Psychological Bulletin, 86,* 549–573.

Loss Aversion

Definition

Loss aversion refers to people's tendency to prefer avoiding losses to acquiring gains of equal magnitude. In other words, the value people place on avoiding a certain loss is higher than the value of acquiring a gain of equal size. Consider, for instance, the subjective value of avoiding a loss of $10 compared with gaining $10. Usually, people say that the former has a higher value to them than the latter. Such a preference seems striking, given that, objectively, $10 is $10, regardless whether it is lost or gained. Nevertheless, the aversion toward incurring losses is a strong and reliable effect, and the value of avoiding a loss is usually twice as high as the value of acquiring an equivalent gain.

Theoretical Explanation

Loss aversion can be explained by the way people view the value of consequences. Specifically, the value of a certain consequence is not seen in terms of its absolute magnitude but in terms of changes compared with a reference point. This reference point is variable and can be, for example, the status quo. Starting from this reference point, every increase in a good is seen as a gain, and the value of this gain rises with its size. Importantly, this rise does not follow a linear trend but grows more slowly with ever-increasing size. Contrarily, starting from the reference point, every decrease is seen as a loss. Now, the value is negative and decreases with the size of the loss. This decrease also slows down with ever-decreasing size, however, not as fast as on the gain side. Therefore, a gain does not increase subjective value at the same rate as a loss of the same size decreases subjective value. Given that individuals are assumed to maximize subjective value, they should express a preference for avoiding the loss. Hence, as suggested in the beginning, people usually prefer avoiding a loss of $10 compared with ensuring a gain of equal size. In general, this may be because bad events have a greater power over people than good events.

Background and History

Daniel Kahneman and Amos Tversky were first to fully recognize the importance of the loss aversion phenomenon for a better understanding of human decision making. They made loss aversion a central part of their prospect theory, which explains human decision making in situations when outcomes are uncertain. Of importance, the idea of different values for equivalent gains and losses strongly contradicted the assumptions held so far in classic theories of decision making; namely, that gains and losses of the same size should have the same value for people. However, as abundant empirical evidence in favor of the loss aversion phenomenon demonstrated, the grief of losing is stronger than the pleasure of gaining.

In subsequent research on the phenomenon of loss aversion, the effect was demonstrated in many domains, including, for example, economic, medical, and social decision making. In addition, it was shown that loss aversion is not limited to decisions under uncertainty but also occurs in situations in which the outcomes of alternatives are certain.

Implications

A prominent implication of loss aversion in decisions with uncertain outcomes is a shift from risk-averse to risk-seeking behavior depending on whether a situation is framed as a gain or as a loss. Given that reference points are not fixed but depend on the specific situation, two alternatives that are equivalent from the standpoint of rational decision making (receiving $10 versus not losing $10) can result in different choices if one of the decisions is seen in the context of gains and the other in the context of losses. Consider the so-called Asian Disease Problem with which Kahneman and Tversky confronted participants in an experiment. In this problem, participants were told about a hypothetical outbreak of an unusual Asian disease threatening to kill 600 people in the United States. Participants had to choose between two alternatives to counteract this disease. One alternative was risky, saving all 600 people with a probability of one-third but otherwise all 600 people would be killed. In the other alternative, 200 people were saved and 400 were killed. If this problem was presented in a gain frame by mentioning how many lives in each alternative could be *saved*, most participants avoided risk and opted for the certain option. But if the problem was presented in a loss frame by mentioning how many people could *die* in each alternative, participants opted for the risky alternative. This puzzling result can be explained by loss aversion. The higher value of avoiding losses compared with gains makes the one-third probability of nobody getting killed much more attractive in the loss frame than it is in the gain frame (framed as saving 600 lives). Consistent with the assumptions of the prospect theory, people seem to avoid risk in gain frames while seeking risk in loss frames.

Other implications of loss aversion occur for decisions with certain outcomes. One of these implications is the status quo bias. This is the tendency to remain at the status quo because the disadvantages of changing something loom larger than the advantages of doing so. The mere ownership effect (also called endowment effect) is a related phenomenon also explained by the differences in the value of losses and gains. Here, the mere possession of an object makes it more valuable to a person relative to objects the person does not own and to the value the person would have assigned to the object before possessing it. This is because giving the object away means a loss to the person, and following the loss aversion phenomenon, losses weigh more heavily than gains. The compensation for giving up a good, therefore, is usually higher than the price the person would pay for it to possess it (which would mean to gain it). Both the status quo bias and the endowment effect have strong implications for economic and social situations.

Patrick A. Müller
Rainer Greifeneder

See also Bad Is Stronger Than Good; Mere Ownership Effect; Prospect Theory

Further Readings

Baumeister, R. F., Bratslavsky, E., Finkenauer, C., & Vohs, K. D. (2001). Bad is stronger than good. *Review of General Psychology, 5,* 323–370.

Kahneman, D., & Tversky, A. (1979). Prospect theory: An analysis of decision under risk. *Econometrica, 47,* 263–291.

Tversky, A., & Kahneman, D. (1991). Loss aversion in riskless choice: A reference dependent model. *Quarterly Journal of Economics, 106,* 1039–1061.

LOST LETTER TECHNIQUE

Definition

The lost letter technique is used to measure people's attitudes by dropping stamped letters addressed to various organizations in public areas and then recording how many of the letters are returned via the mail. It is assumed that people will be more likely to return a letter if it is addressed to an organization that they support than if it is addressed to an organization they do not support. For example, a Democrat who finds a lost letter should be more likely to mail it when it is addressed to a Democratic candidate's headquarters than to a Republican candidate's headquarters.

History and Modern Usage

In one of the first studies to use the lost letter technique, Stanley Milgram and his colleagues dropped stamped letters in a variety of public locations. The letters were addressed to one of four recipients: "Medical Research Associates," "Friends of the Communist Party," "Friends of the Nazi Party," or a private individual. People were less likely to return the letters if they were addressed to the Communist Party (25% returned) or the Nazi Party (25% returned) than if they were addressed to the Medical group (72% returned) or the private individual (71% returned). These results suggest that people were less likely to mail letters to organizations they did not support.

To verify that the response rates reflected people's attitudes, Milgram conducted additional studies. In one study, the researchers were able to correctly predict U.S. presidential election results in different election wards using the lost letter technique. Letters addressed to the Committee to (a) Elect (Barry) Goldwater, (b) Defeat Goldwater, (c) Elect (Lyndon) Johnson, and (d) Defeat Johnson were dropped in various election wards. Election wards that supported Johnson in the election were more likely to return the pro-Johnson and anti-Goldwater letters than the pro-Goldwater/anti-Johnson letters. The opposite results were found in wards that ended up supporting Goldwater in the election.

Later researchers have used the lost letter technique to study helping behavior. By varying the characteristics of the letters, researchers can identify the factors that increase the chances that people will help by mailing the letter. Some of these studies have used post cards and e-mails instead of sealed letters. This modification has allowed researchers to determine the impact of the type of message on helping behavior.

The lost letter technique allows researchers to determine people's attitudes or the factors that influence helping behavior without directly asking them (known as an unobtrusive measure). Because participants are unaware that they are participating in a study, they will not alter their behavior to "look good" for the experimenter.

Pamela L. Bacon

See also Altruism; Attitudes; Helping Behavior; Research Methods

Further Readings

Milgram, S., Mann, L., & Harter, S. (1965). The lost-letter technique: A tool of social research. *Public Opinion Quarterly, 29,* 437–438.

Vaes, J., Paladino, M. P., & Leyens, J. P. (2002). The lost e-mail: Prosocial reactions induced by uniquely human emotions. *British Journal of Social Psychology, 41,* 521–534.

LOVE

Definition

Love is often thought of as an intense and positive emotion that can be experienced for a variety of close others, including a romantic partner or spouse, close friends, children, parents, and other relatives. For more than three decades, social psychologists and other social scientists have been studying love. The type of love that has been most frequently measured and studied is the love experienced for a romantic partner. However, when social scientists began measuring love, they realized that there were many different types or subtypes, even in regard to a romantic partner.

Types

An initial distinction was made between *liking* and *love.* One of the first psychologists to study love, Zick Rubin, discovered that people could distinguish between attitude statements that measured liking (items that referred to respect, positive evaluation, and perceptions of similarity) and attitude statements that measured love (items that referred to dependency, caring, and exclusiveness). His liking and love scales have been used in several research studies that have generated a number of interesting findings including (1) liking and loving are only modestly associated; (2) those who have higher scores on the love scale spend more time eye-gazing with their partner; and (3) higher scores on love are predictive of staying together over time.

Social psychologists next distinguished between various types of love. The first distinction was between *passionate love* and *companionate love.* Passionate love is intense, exciting, and has the potential for both ecstasy (when things are going well) and despair (when things are not going well). Companionate love, however, is less intense and is referred to as affection that develops between two people whose lives are intertwined. Research suggests that in most dating and newly married relationships, both types of love exist. Passionate love tends to develop first, although it is also likely to dissipate first over time. Companionate love may take longer to develop but is likely to remain stable and not erode with the passage of time. Passionate love, as the more intense type of love, may sometimes increase because of misattribution of arousal. A person can become aroused because of an extraneous source such as consumption of caffeine or a frightful experience and then mistakenly attribute the arousal to passionate love for another, especially if the other is physically attractive. Although passionate love declines over years of marriage, research has revealed that if couples engage in exciting and novel activities together, the passion can be rekindled.

In a more recent typology, six types or styles of loving have been identified. These are *eros* (intense, passionate love), *ludus* (game-playing love), *storge* (friendship love), *pragma* (practical love), *mania* (obsessive, dependent love) and *agape* (selfless love). These love styles may be considered to be attitudes or orientations toward a particular person (e.g., a romantic partner) but also may be considered to be stable orientations toward relationships. For example, some people may be thought of as erotic lovers, likely to experience this particular style of love regardless of the partner. However, people's lovestyle experiences also may change as a function of the partner's style of loving and how he or she behaves toward the other partner. The two types of love that are experienced to the greatest degree, especially among young adults, are eros and storge. In fact, most romantic relationships may have a combination of these two types of love. People experience a low level of ludus, which is good because this type of love does not lead to healthy and long-lasting relationships. Consistent gender differences have been found in the experience of love styles. Ludus is experienced to a greater degree by men than by women, and storge and pragma are experienced to a greater degree by women.

Love also has been described as a triangle, having three primary components: *intimacy, passion,* and *commitment* (pictorially presented as a triangle). Each component (triangle side) can range from low to high so that a number of different triangle shapes and sizes are possible. Intimacy refers to warmth, understanding, caring, support, and connection. Passion is characterized by physical attraction and arousal. Commitment refers to the decision to stay in the relationship and maintain it. The triangular model of love yields eight different love types ranging from nonlove (no intimacy, no passion, and no commitment) to consummate love (high on all three components). Romantic love, often experienced in young college romances, includes intimacy and passion but rarely includes long-term commitment. An empty-shell marriage has commitment, but may no longer have passion or intimacy.

Researchers have identified many other types of loving, including unrequited love (in which one loves another but isn't loved back), limerence (an intense dependent type of love), lust, and friendship love. Although most social scientific research has focused on love for one specific person, typically a romantic partner, love can also be experienced for pets, God, strangers, and all of humanity. Compassionate love, for example, is the type of love that focuses on selfless caring for others, especially those who are in need or distressed. It's similar to empathy but more enduring. Some nonprofit organizations, such as the Fetzer Institute located in Kalamazoo, Michigan, have recently become interested in promoting scientific study on compassionate love. The hope is that the more that can be learned about this type of love, including love as expressed for all of humanity, the more likely researchers can identify ways to increase it.

Attitudes About Love

Social scientists also have been interested in examining people's attitudes about love. How important do people believe love is for entering and maintaining marriage (i.e., do love and marriage go together?) Do people believe that love is necessary to have premarital sex? What are people's romantic attitudes about love? For example, do they believe in love at first sight and that love conquers all? These beliefs are important to study for many reasons, including that the attitudes and beliefs people have will affect their behaviors. Survey studies indicate that most young adults believe that one should not enter marriage without love. The disappearance of love from marriage over time is thought to be a sufficient reason for a divorce by most people. Although some young adults indicate that they believe that sex is okay in a casual relationship and even in a "hook-up," most young adults and especially women and female adolescents believe that love and affection are necessary for premarital sexual activity. Finally, young adults have many romantic beliefs about love, including that if you love someone, other obstacles can be overcome and a love partner and relationship can be perfect. These beliefs have sometimes been referred to as *positive illusions* and have been found to be good for relationships because they contribute to people engaging in actions that lead to positive events in the relationship.

Falling in Love

Many people can remember the first time they had an upsurge of affection for another and may have labeled this turning point in the relationship "falling in love." Researchers have identified the factors that lead to initial attraction as well as falling in love. People report that they fall in love because of desirable characteristics of the other (e.g., kindness, physical attractiveness) and because the other expresses attraction toward them, such as through eye contact. Falling in love can lead to an increased feeling of self-worth, at least in the initial stage and especially if it's reciprocated.

Determinants of Love

Researchers also have tried to identify the factors that make love grow over time or at least not decrease. The most common way of studying determinants of love is to survey individuals about their relationship and have them complete a scale to measure how much they love their partners, and then also have them complete measures on several factors that are predicted to be associated with love. A design that follows the relationships over time is more useful than data at only one point in time for determining causal directions. Research has indicated that feelings of love are associated with factors such as self-disclosure, equity (fair exchange of resources), frequent and satisfying sex, and positive beliefs about the relationship. Research done by Diane Felmlee and Susan Sprecher also indicates that love increases when parents and friends support the relationship. Each of these factors that have been identified as determinants of love, however, also can be consequences of love. That is, when people feel more love, their self-disclosure, sex, fair exchange, and attempts to seek support from family and friends for the relationship may increase.

Implications

Love is important to relationships, to individuals, and to society. Relationships that are loving are more likely to be satisfying and last over time. Individuals who experience love and support by others and also feel love for others are more likely to have high levels of mental and physical health. Society also benefits from people forming loving connections with each other. Love leads to reproduction (and replacement of members in a society), familial relationships for the raising of children to adulthood, and humanitarian efforts toward others. Social psychological investigation has helped significantly to expand the knowledge regarding the multidimensional nature of this important concept of love, as well as the attitudes associated with it. The scientific community and society has much to gain from the continued investigation of this pivotal and central human emotion.

Susan Sprecher
Diane Felmlee

See also Companionate Love; Emotion; Intimacy; Positive Illusions; Romantic Love; Triangular Theory of Love

Further Readings

Felmlee, D., & Sprecher, S. (2006). Love. In J. E. Stets & J. H. Turner (Eds.), *Handbook of sociology of emotions* (pp. 389–409). New York: Springer.

Hatfield, E., & Sprecher, S. (1986). Measuring passionate love in intimate relationships. *Journal of Adolescence, 9,* 383–410.

Hendrick, S. S., & Hendrick, C. (1992). *Romantic love.* Newbury Park, CA: Sage.

Sprecher, S., & Toro-Morn, M. (2002). A study of men and women from different sides of earth to determine if men are from Mars and women are from Venus in their beliefs about love and romantic relationships. *Sex Roles, 46,* 131–147.

LOWBALLING

Definition

Lowballing is a strategy to increase compliance. In lowballing, the person making a request gets another person (i.e., the target of compliance) to make a commitment to a particular course of action. After making that commitment, the requester reveals hidden costs associated with the requested course of action. The target of compliance is then more likely to follow through with the request (i.e., to comply) than if the hidden costs had been revealed at the time of the initial request.

Examples

Car salespeople have been observed using the lowball strategy to increase the likelihood that the customer will purchase a car. In this situation, the salesperson negotiates with the customer to arrive at a sales price that the customer feels is a good deal. After the customer commits to that price (e.g., via oral agreement, signing paperwork, putting money down), the salesperson takes the agreement to the manager for approval. Upon returning, the salesperson indicates that the manager will only approve a purchase price of $500 more than the previously agreed-upon price. Because the customer initially made a commitment to purchase the car, he or she is likely to follow through on the purchase, even though it is no longer that good of a deal. In this scenario, the initial price was a lowball offer, which the salesperson never intended to honor.

Lowballing also occurs in nonsales situations. For example, a professor asks students to help move boxes of books from the office building to the library. After the students agree, the professor reveals that the students must arrive on campus at 7:30 A.M. to help. Because the students have already agreed to help the professor, they are more likely to follow through than if they had initially been asked to help early in the morning.

The Importance of Commitment

The lowballing effect depends on the target of compliance making a public commitment to the initial request. For several reasons, it is difficult for the target of compliance to back out of the commitment. First, the target of the lowball feels a commitment to the person who made the request (e.g., the customer "made a deal" with the salesperson). Second, the target feels a commitment to the course of action involved (e.g., the customer made a commitment to buy a car). And finally, once the target has made the commitment, he or she becomes excited about the prospect of the course of action involved (e.g., while the salesperson "discusses the offer with the manager," the customer envisions driving home in the new car). Given these forms of commitment, the customer is likely to follow through with the behavior, even though it is more costly than the original commitment (e.g., the customer buys the car even though the actual purchase price is higher than the initial agreement).

Research suggests that the lowballing technique is robust, in that it remains effective even when the targets of compliance are aware of the strategy and its effectiveness.

Kathryn A. Morris

See also Compliance; Foot-in-the-Door Technique; Influence

Further Readings

Burger, J. M., & Cornelius, T. (2003). Raising the price of agreement: Public commitment and the lowball compliance procedure. *Journal of Applied Social Psychology, 33,* 923–934.

M

MARITAL SATISFACTION

Definition

Marital satisfaction is a mental state that reflects the perceived benefits and costs of marriage to a particular person. The more costs a marriage partner inflicts on a person, the less satisfied one generally is with the marriage and with the marriage partner. Similarly, the greater the perceived benefits are, the more satisfied one is with the marriage and with the marriage partner.

Components and Mechanisms

Cognition

In perceiving whether a spouse's behavior is costly or beneficial, cognitions, or thoughts about the behavior, are important. If one's spouse performs a negative (costly) behavior, this may be attributed either to characteristics of the spouse (for example, he or she is lazy), or instead to circumstances surrounding the spouse's behavior (for example, it was an especially taxing day at work, and he or she doesn't feel like making dinner). In the case of marital satisfaction, attributing costly behavior to characteristics of one's spouse, rather than to circumstances surrounding his or her behavior, is associated with decreased marital satisfaction, as well as marital deterioration. These maladaptive attributions occur more often with negative behaviors in marital problem-solving discussions, and these attributions do not appear to be a result of either partner being depressed, having a neurotic personality, or tending toward physical aggression. The way

people interpret behavior appears to be related to how satisfied they are with their marriage.

Intimately related to an individual's thoughts about behaviors are the individual's feelings about behaviors, or affect. Research on affect and marital satisfaction is not conclusive yet; some studies have shown that negative affect is related to decreased marital satisfaction, whereas others have shown it has no effect or even increases it. Future research needs to clarify more specifically how negative affect is related to marital satisfaction.

Physiology

There is a well-established relationship between being married and maintaining physical well-being. This, in the most immediate sense, is established by the physiological functioning of the two married individuals. Recent research has indicated that married couples who are more satisfied with their relationship also exhibit greater synchrony among their physiological systems compared with those married couples who are less satisfied. That is, maritally satisfied couples are more likely to maintain synchrony among each partner's electrodermal (or electrical resistance of the skin) and heart rate systems, which may be a mechanism by which married couples maintain greater physical well-being than unmarried individuals.

Interaction Patterns

Patterns of interaction between spouses can affect how satisfied they are with their marriage. The pattern most often related to marital dissatisfaction is one of demand/withdrawal. In this pattern, one partner (often the wife) criticizes or nags the other about change, while the other partner (usually the husband) evades the confrontation and discussion. It operates such that initial criticism leads to disengagement, which leads to further confrontation and even further disengagement. This pattern has clear implications for marital satisfaction, with both parties developing dissatisfaction.

Social Support

Another component of satisfaction within a marriage is the degree of social support for each of the partners and for the relationship. Support processes are reliably associated with good marital functioning, as well as with healthful outcomes within families. A marriage partner who provides good social support for his or her spouse contributes to the spouse's marital satisfaction.

Violence

Physical violence also is closely linked with marital satisfaction. Individuals involved in physically abusive relationships are more likely to be dissatisfied with their marriage than are individuals not involved in abusive relationships. Escalation to physical violence can result from many factors, one of which is alcohol use. And somewhat surprisingly, some form of physical aggression is present in 57% of newlywed marriages, indicating that the relationship between violence and marital satisfaction may not be as straightforward as is often presumed.

Contextual Factors

Many factors enter into assessments of marital satisfaction: a spouse's personality, his or her performance of mate-guarding behaviors, his or her likelihood of infidelity, the desirability of each partner, the presence of children, and others. If one partner perceives that the other is inflicting costs (or being troublesome) in these domains, he or she may move to address them through discussions with the partner, or by seeking a new or additional partner who may better suit the person.

Spousal Personality Characteristics

How satisfied a person is with his or her marriage seems to be related to, in part, the personality characteristics of his or her spouse. Personality is often gauged by five dimensions, including Extraversion (surgency, dominance, extraversion vs. submissiveness, introversion), Agreeableness (warm, trusting vs. cold, suspicious), Conscientiousness (reliable, well organized vs. undependable, disorganized), Neuroticism (emotional stability, secure, even-tempered vs. nervous, temperamental) and Openness to Experience (intellect, perceptive, curious vs. imperceptive). Marital dissatisfaction is most often related to a spouse's emotional instability, but dissatisfaction is also related to having a partner who is low in Conscientiousness, low in Agreeableness, and low in Openness/intellect. People married to those with these personality characteristics often complain that their spouses are neglectful, dependent, possessive, condescending, jealous, unfaithful, unreliable, emotionally constricted, self-centered, sexualizing of others, and abusive of alcohol. Thus, the personality characteristics of each spouse contribute greatly to the relationship, culminating in satisfying marriage or its ending in divorce.

Spousal Mate Guarding

Even after finding a suitable partner and forming a lasting relationship, challenges associated with maintaining that relationship ensue. Men and women often attempt to prevent another person from encroaching on their marriage by performing mate-guarding behaviors. Some of these behaviors can actually inflict costs on the spouse and, consequently, are related to lessened marital satisfaction. These mate-guarding behaviors include monopolizing the partner's time (for example, she spent all of her free time with him so he could not meet other women), threatening or punishing infidelity (for example, he hit her when he caught her flirting with someone else), and being emotionally manipulative (for example, she threatened to harm herself if he ever left). Marriages in which one or both partners frequently perform these costly guarding behaviors are more often dissatisfied marriages.

Spousal Susceptibility to Infidelity

Being unfaithful can unmistakably cause problems in marriages. Discovered infidelities raise issues of honesty, trust between the partners, commitment, and, ultimately, love. Because a spouse's infidelity has the potential to inflict these emotional costs, marital satisfaction appears to be negatively related to the likelihood that a spouse will be unfaithful. That is, the more likely one's partner is to be unfaithful, the less satisfied one is with his or her marriage and marriage partner.

Mate Value

Mate value can be thought of as the desirability of a partner, a composite of a variety of characteristics including physical attractiveness, intelligence, and personality. Marriages in which there is a discrepancy between the partners in mate value are marriages in which both partners are more likely to be unfaithful, signaling marital dissatisfaction. When a husband, for example, is perceived as having a higher mate value than his wife, he, as well as she (perhaps for retaliatory reasons), is more likely to be unfaithful to their marriage. The lower marital satisfaction associated with this contextual marital difficulty, of differing mate values between the partners, appears as an indicator to the higher mate value individual that he or she might seek a better-matched partner elsewhere.

Children

The introduction of a child drastically changes the marital context. Marital satisfaction is influenced by, and has influences on, children. The presence of children in a marriage has the paradoxical effect of increasing the stability of the marriage (when the children are young, at least), while decreasing marital satisfaction. That is, parenthood makes a marriage less happy but more likely to last. In addition, marital strife, an indicator of dissatisfaction, has been shown to factor into the well-functioning differences between children who come from divorced homes and children who do not.

Additional Factors

In addition, family background factors, such as the relationship satisfaction of one's parents' marriage, are related to marital satisfaction in an individual's current marriage. Perhaps surprisingly, parental marital satisfaction seems to be more closely related to one's own present marital satisfaction than is one's parents' divorce.

Adult attachment styles also are related to marital satisfaction, in that securely attached adults are more often satisfied in their marriage than are those individuals who are avoidant or anxiously ambivalently attached. Some circumstances, like traumatic events (for example, hurricanes, or testicular cancer), appear to actually strengthen marital satisfaction. Stressors in economic or work-related realms often contribute to decreased marital satisfaction, however. For example, displaying negative affect in marital relationships has been shown to be more frequent among blue-collar, rather than white-collar, employees.

Marital satisfaction, in addition to verbal aggression and conflict frequency, appears also to be related to the performance of joint religious activities (like praying together) and to perceptions of the sacredness of their relationship. And although not a direct measure of marital satisfaction, but replete with implications, the presence of available alternative partners in one's environment is related to a greater likelihood of divorce.

Marital Satisfaction Over Time

One component of marital satisfaction is an understanding of the factors that influence it presently, a sort of snapshot of it, but it's also important to understand how these factors play a role in its development over time.

Marital satisfaction was once believed to follow a U-shaped trajectory over time, such that couples began their marriages satisfied, this satisfaction somewhat waned over the years, but resurfaced to newlywed levels after many years together. This was found to be the case in studies with cross-sectional data, where marital satisfaction was assessed once, drawn from participants with a variety of ages, but is now actually better understood by following the marital satisfaction trajectory of particular couples over the years. It now seems that, on average, marital satisfaction drops markedly over the first 10 years, and continues to gradually decrease over the subsequent decades. There are individual differences in the path that marital satisfaction follows over time, however, as not all marital satisfaction decreases in a linear way (a slow, steady decrease), but may include more dramatic decreases at times, or may even increase. One study found a minority of couples in their sample reported increasing levels of marital satisfaction over time.

To date, the many contextual variables mentioned earlier, like the presence of children, mate value discrepancies, and likelihood of infidelity, in conjunction with particular personality characteristics of the marriage partners, most notably neuroticism and emotional stability, have been identified as contributors to the general decrease in marital satisfaction over time.

Measuring Marital Satisfaction

Assessing marital satisfaction in research is often done through self-report surveys, in which participants respond to a variety of questions assessing their satisfaction with different facets of their marriage. The concept of marital satisfaction is not necessarily gauged by assessing a lack of dissatisfaction in the relationship; factors that lead to marital distress are not necessarily the inverse of factors that promote satisfying relationships. Factors that promote healthy relationships and are present in satisfying, long-term marriages are important to consider, as well. Thus, thorough measures of marital satisfaction assess qualities that contribute negatively, as well as uniquely positively, to the marriage.

Emily A. Stone
Todd K. Shackelford

See also Big Five Personality Traits; Close Relationships; Happiness; Love; Positive Illusions

Further Readings

Bradbury, T. N., Fincham, F. D., & Beach, S. R. H. (2000). Research on the nature and determinants of marital satisfaction: A decade in review. *Journal of Marriage and the Family, 62,* 964–980.

Buss, D. M. (2003). *The evolution of desire* (Rev. ed.). New York: Basic Books.

Buss, D. M., & Shackelford, T. K. (1997). Susceptibility to infidelity in the first year of marriage. *Journal of Research in Personality, 31,* 193–221.

Karney, B. R., & Bradbury, T. N. (1997). Neuroticism, marital interaction, and the trajectory of marital satisfaction. *Journal of Personality and Social Psychology, 72,* 1075–1092.

Shackelford, T. K., & Buss, D. M. (2000). Marital satisfaction and spousal cost-infliction. *Personality and Individual Differences, 28,* 917–928.

MARKET PRICING

See RELATIONAL MODELS THEORY

MASCULINITY/FEMININITY

Definition

The terms *masculinity* and *femininity* refer to traits or characteristics typically associated with being male or female, respectively. Traditionally, masculinity and femininity have been conceptualized as opposite ends of a single dimension, with masculinity at one extreme and femininity at the other. By this definition, high masculinity implies the absence of femininity, and vice versa. In other words, people can be classified as either masculine or feminine. Contemporary definitions propose that masculinity and femininity are separate dimensions, allowing for the possibility that individuals may simultaneously possess both masculine and feminine attributes.

The Single-Factor Approach

The Attitude Interest Analysis Survey (AIAS) was the first attempt to measure masculinity versus femininity. To develop the test, hundreds of scale items—including measures of attitudes, emotions, personality traits, and occupational preferences—were given to American junior high and high school students in the 1930s. Only items that elicited different responses from girls and boys were included in the final version of the measure. Items that the typical girl endorsed—such as ignorance, desire for a small income, and a fondness for washing dishes—received femininity points. Items that the typical boy endorsed—such as intelligence, desire for a large income, and dislike of tall women—received masculinity points. Because these items clearly reflect gender stereotypes and role expectations prevalent at the time the scale was developed, responses to these items may simply reflect the desire to be a "normal" man or woman. It is not surprising then that the AIAS was less reliable than other standard measures of personality and was not related to other criteria of masculinity and femininity (e.g., teachers' ratings of students' masculinity and femininity). Because of these methodological issues and a lack of theoretical basis, the AIAS is no longer used today.

Multifactorial Approaches

Contemporary scales of masculinity/femininity have abandoned the single-factor approach in favor of multifactorial models. In the 1970s, the Bem Sex Role Inventory (BSRI) introduced the concept of androgyny by allowing for combinations of two independent dimensions of masculinity and femininity. Importantly, the items on the BSRI were not developed using differences in the responses typical of males and females, as was the AIAS. Instead, the BSRI was developed by asking male and female respondents to indicate how desirable it was for an American man or woman to possess various traits. The final version of the scale is composed of 20 femininity items, 20 masculinity items, and 20 neutral items. Respondents indicate how much each adjective is self-descriptive. Based on these responses, people may be classified as feminine (high femininity, low masculinity), masculine (low femininity, high masculinity), androgynous (high femininity, high masculinity), or undifferentiated (low femininity, low masculinity).

The Personal Attributes Questionnaire (PAQ), another measure of masculinity/femininity developed in the 1970s, also assumes that dimensions of masculinity and femininity are independent dimensions. Scale items for this measure were developed in ways similar to the development of the BSRI. The scale consists of 16 socially desirable items designed to measure instrumental traits (e.g., competitive), often associated with males, and expressive traits (e.g., gentle), often associated with females. Although the BSRI and PAQ are similar in content, they differ in their theoretical implications.

Currently, the BSRI is used within the framework of gender schema theory as a measure of men and women's degree of sex-typing. Sex-typed individuals (i.e., men classified as masculine or women classified as feminine) are said to be gender-schematic—or to use gender as a way to organize information in their world. Strong gender schemas develop through strong identification with gender roles, in turn leading to attitudes and behaviors consistent with gender role expectations. Thus, masculinity and femininity scores on the BSRI reflect a tendency to conceptualize the world in terms of male and female.

In contrast, the creators of the PAQ have rejected the notion that there is one underlying factor of masculinity and one factor of femininity. Instead, multiple gender-related phenomena, such as physical attributes, occupational preferences, and personality traits, contribute to multiple factors that contribute to gender identity—or one's own sense of maleness and femaleness. From this perspective then, PAQ and BSRI scores do not represent the global concepts of masculinity/femininity or gender schemas. Rather, they are simply measures of instrumental and expressive traits, one of many factors contributing to gender identity. Thus, scores should only be related to gender-related behaviors to the extent they are influenced by instrumentality and expressiveness.

Correlates of Masculinity/Femininity

In support of gender schema theory, initial studies demonstrated that BSRI scores predicted gender-related behaviors such as nurturance, agency, and expressiveness. For example, in one study, students who were categorized as feminine or androgynous displayed more nurturing behaviors while interacting with a baby compared with masculine or undifferentiated students. However, the creators of the PAQ argue that BSRI scores are only predictive of instrumental and expressive behaviors. Empirical evidence supports this claim. Some studies have found little or no relationship between the BSRI and typical measures of gender attitudes and behaviors. Failure to predict related gender constructs may be indicative of psychometric flaws or problems with the underlying theory.

Measuring masculinity/femininity in a theoretically meaningful way continues to be problematic. Currently, the multifactor gender identity perspective of masculinity and femininity has received stronger empirical support than other models. Despite theoretical criticisms, both the BSRI and PAQ remain frequently used measures in gender research.

Ann E. Hoover
Stephanie A. Goodwin

See also Gender Differences; Stereotypes and Stereotyping

Further Readings

Bem, S. L. (1974). The measurement of psychological androgyny. *Journal of Consulting and Clinical Psychology, 42,* 155–162.

Lippa, R. A. (2005). *Gender, nature, and nurture.* Mahwah, NJ: Erlbaum.

Spence, J. T., & Helmreich, R. L. (1980). Masculine instrumentality and feminine expressiveness: Their relationship with sex role attitudes and behaviors. *Psychology of Women Quarterly, 5,* 147–163.

MATCHING HYPOTHESIS

Definition

The matching hypothesis refers to the proposition that people are attracted to and form relationships with individuals who resemble them on a variety of attributes, including demographic characteristics (e.g., age, ethnicity, and education level), personality traits, attitudes and values, and even physical attributes (e.g., attractiveness).

Background and Importance

Theorists interested in relationship development believe that similarity plays a key role in the process by which people select their friends and romantic partners. During the initial phase of relationship formation, when two people have not yet become good friends or committed partners, they assess the extent to which they resemble one another in demographic background, values and interests, personality, and other characteristics. The perception of similarity promotes feelings of mutual rapport and positive sentiment between the two, as well as the expectation that further interaction will be rewarding. These feelings, in turn, increase the likelihood that their relationship will continue to develop.

Evidence

There is ample evidence in support of the matching hypothesis in the realm of interpersonal attraction and friendship formation. Not only do people overwhelmingly prefer to interact with similar others, but a person's friends and associates are more likely to resemble that person on virtually every dimension examined, both positive and negative.

The evidence is mixed in the realm of romantic attraction and mate selection. There is definitely a tendency for men and women to marry spouses who resemble them. Researchers have found extensive similarity between marital partners on characteristics such as age, race, ethnicity, education level, socioeconomic status, religion, and physical attractiveness as well as on a host of personality traits and cognitive abilities. This well-documented tendency for similar individuals to marry is commonly referred to as *homogamy* or *assortment*.

The fact that people tend to end up with romantic partners who resemble them, however, does not necessarily mean that they prefer similar over dissimilar mates. There is evidence, particularly with respect to the characteristic of physical attractiveness, that both men and women actually prefer the most attractive partner possible. However, although people might ideally want a partner with highly desirable features, they might not possess enough desirable attributes themselves to be able to attract that individual. Because people seek the best possible mate but are constrained by their own assets, the process of romantic partner selection thus inevitably results in the pairing of individuals with similar characteristics.

Nonetheless, sufficient evidence supports the matching hypothesis to negate the old adage that "opposites attract." They typically do not.

Pamela C. Regan

See also Attraction; Close Relationships; Equity Theory; Social Exchange Theory

Further Readings

Berscheid, E., & Reis, H. T. (1998). Attraction and close relationships. In D. T. Gilbert, S. T. Fiske, & G. Lindzey (Eds.), *The handbook of social psychology* (4th ed., pp. 193–281). New York: McGraw-Hill.

Kalick, S. M., & Hamilton, T. E. (1996). The matching hypothesis re-examined. *Journal of Personality and Social Psychology, 51,* 673–682.

Murstein, B. I. (1980). Mate selection in the 1970s. *Journal of Marriage and the Family, 42,* 777–792.

MEANING MAINTENANCE MODEL

Definition

People expect that certain experiences will be associated with one another. For example, if a person goes out to dinner, he or she expects the waiter to bring what he or she ordered. If a person sees a crow, he or she expects it to be black. People expect that good people will be rewarded in life, bad people will be punished, and that their friends will be kind to them. Sometimes, however, these expectations are violated by unusual experiences. Sometimes the waiter brings the wrong breakfast, and sometimes friends are cruel. Sometimes tragedies befall nice people, villains prosper, or an albino crow lands on a neighbor's roof.

The meaning maintenance model (MMM) proposes that whenever these *expected associations* are violated by unexpected experiences, it goes against people's shared desire to maintain meaning, or to feel that their experiences generally make sense. Often, when people's expectations are violated, they can revise them ("A white crow? Hmm . . . I guess that some crows can be white as well as black"), or they can reinterpret the experience so that it no longer appears to violate their expectations ("A white crow? I guess I didn't see it right. It must have been a dove").

Alternatively, violated expectations can prompt people to seek out or remind themselves of other experiences that still do make sense to them ("Weird. A white crow? Hmm . . . maybe I'll watch that movie again . . . the one I've seen a dozen times before"). MMM proposes that when people's expected associations are violated, they often reaffirm other expected associations that haven't been violated, even if the expected associations being reaffirmed don't have much to do with the expected associations that were violated to begin with. MMM calls this process *fluid compensation* and proposes that expected associations are substitutable with one another when they attempt to restore a feeling that their experiences generally make sense.

What Is Meaning?

Meaning comprises the expected associations that connect people's experiences to one another—*any* experience, and *any* way that experiences can be connected. Meaning is what connects people's experiences of the people, places, objects, and ideas all around them (e.g., hammers to nails, cold to snow, fathers to sons, or dawn to the rising sun). Meaning is what connects experiences of one's own self (e.g., one's thoughts, behaviors, desires, attributes, abilities, roles, and past incarnations), and meaning is what connects one to the outside world (e.g., purpose, value, belonging). Despite the many ways that people can connect their experiences, meaning always manifests as expected associations that allow them to feel that these experiences make sense.

Why Do People Maintain Meaning?

The idea that people have a general desire to maintain expected associations was suggested by many Western existentialists in the mid-19th and 20th centuries, including Søren Kierkegaard, Martin Heidegger, and Albert Camus. These philosophers imagined that all humanity shared a common desire to see their experiences as connected to one another in ways that generally made sense. Science, religion, and philosophy were imagined to be different ways of connecting one's experiences of the outside world, connecting elements of one's own self, and ultimately, connecting oneself to the world around him or her. These connections were called *meaning,* and when people experience something, anything, that isn't connected to their existing expected associations, it was said to be *meaningless;* such experiences could only be considered meaningful once people have found a way of connecting them to their existing expected associations. According to the existentialists, feelings of meaninglessness could be evoked by any experience that violated one's expected associations, be it a simple error in judgment, an unexpected observation, a surreal image, feeling alienated from lifelong friends, or thoughts of one's own mortality, as death was thought to represent one's final disconnection from the world around him or her.

When experimental psychologists began to talk about meaning in the early 20th century, they used a novel term that was introduced by the English psychologist Fredric Bartlett. Bartlett called these expected associations *schemas.* Where the existentialists once spoke of meaning, psychologists focused their attention on different kinds of schemas, scripts, worldviews, and paradigms, eventually using many different terms to express the same essential concept: expected associations that connect people's experiences to one another in ways that make sense.

Psychologists have now spent the better part of a century exploring the specific functions served by different kinds of expected associations. For example, some unconscious paradigms focus people's attention, which in turn enables them to memorize and recall their experiences. Other scripts provide people a basis for predicting different events in their environment, and allow them to influence their outcomes. Social schemas help people understand their place in society and how they are expected to behave. Many worldviews help people cope with tragedy and trauma by connecting these events to beliefs about a higher purpose and cultural values. Although many theories explore the many functions of meaning, MMM is unique in proposing a general desire to maintain meaning beyond whatever functions it may serve.

How Do People Maintain Meaning?

Different kinds of psychologists have different theories that try to explain how people maintain expected associations. For example, developmental psychologists speak of Jean Piaget's theory of equilibrium, and many social psychologists are influenced by Leon Festinger's cognitive dissonance theory. Like MMM, these theories propose that people strive to connect their experiences to one another through a series of expected associations, while acknowledging that, from time to time, people are exposed to experiences that violate these expectations.

To date, these and other meaning maintenance accounts propose that people deal with violated expectations in one of two ways: revision or reinterpretation. When people have an experience that doesn't make sense, they will either revise their expectations to include the unusual experience (e.g., "A white crow? Some crows *are* white"; "Death as the end of life? Death is a *part* of living"), or they may reinterpret the unusual experience such that it no longer appears to violate their expectations (e.g., "I did that boring job for no reward? I must have done it because the job was actually fun and interesting"; "Tragedy befalling virtuous people? It wasn't a tragedy because it made them stronger"). In addition to revision and reinterpretation, MMM proposes a third way that people deal with violations of expected associations; in the face of meaninglessness, people often reaffirm other, generally unrelated expected associations to restore a general feeling that their experiences make sense.

MMM proposes that people maintain expected associations to satisfy their desire to feel that their experiences make sense, beyond any specific function that expected associations may serve. When unusual experiences violate expected associations, this violation compromises the specific function served by those expected associations and challenges people's general desire to have experiences make sense. When people try to restore a general sense of meaningfulness, expected associations become substitutable for one another; reaffirming one set of expected associations (e.g., social affiliation) may be as good as reaffirming another set of expected associations (e.g., self-concept) when expected associations are violated that serve an entirely different function (e.g., visual schema). The meaning framework being reaffirmed may have no bearing whatsoever on the meaning framework that was originally violated, so it can be said that expected associations are substitutable with one another in this fluid compensation process.

There is much evidence in the social psychological literature for substitutable fluid compensation. For example, researchers have shown that if people experience unexpected inconsistencies in their lives, they may reaffirm their adherence to social values that have nothing whatsoever to do with those inconsistencies. Similarly, if people have their self-concept violated by unexpected failure feedback, they may respond by

reaffirming their connection to an established social group that has no bearing on the aspect of self that was violated. Making people uncertain about their visual perceptions may prompt them to more vigorously reaffirm unrelated social values, as does making people feel that they are connected to a group of people that they normally see as being quite different from themselves.

Another example of substitutable compensatory reaffirmation involves reminding people about their eventual death, which in turn prompts them to reaffirm other expected associations more vigorously. This reaffirmation can manifest itself as many different behaviors—seeking greater affiliation with others, showing increasing dislike of people who criticize their current affiliations, or even as seeking patterned associations within seemingly random strings of letters. Although many separate theories attempt to explain these individual behavioral phenomena, MMM proposes that all of these studies (and many, many more) demonstrate the same general psychological impulse: One meaning framework is threatened, and another, unrelated meaning framework undergoes compensatory reaffirmation.

Travis Proulx

See also Cognitive Dissonance Theory; Terror Management Theory

Further Readings

Heine, S., Proulx, T., & Vohs, K. (2006). The Meaning Maintenance Model: On the coherence of social motivation. *Personality and Social Psychological Review, 10,* 88–111.

Media Violence and Aggression

Definition

Violent media includes all forms of mass communication that depict the threat to use force, the act of using force, or the consequences of the use of force against animate beings (including cartoon characters or other species as well as humans). There are many forms of media, including TV programs, movies, video games, comic books, and music. More than five decades of scientific data lead to the irrefutable conclusion that exposure to violent media increases aggression. About 300 studies involving more than 50,000 subjects have been conducted on this topic.

Violent Media Effects

Exposure to violent media can have several undesirable effects. One effect is that people who consume a lot of violent media become less sympathetic to victims of violence. In one study, people who played violent video games assigned less harsh penalties to criminals than did those who played nonviolent games. People also perceive victims as injured less and display less empathy toward them after exposure to violent media. One reason why people may become more tolerant of violence and less sympathetic toward victims is because they become desensitized to it over time. Research has shown that after consuming violent media, people have lower heart rate and blood pressure in response to real depictions of violence.

In addition to desensitizing people to the effects of violence, violent media also increase aggressive thoughts. One result is that people who consume a lot of violent media are more likely to attend to hostile information and expect others to behave in a hostile manner. They may also interpret ambiguous situations in the worst possible light, assuming that the behavior of others reflects hostility rather than other, more positive traits such as assertiveness. Some researchers have also found that violent media also increase aggressive feelings. Most importantly, exposure to violent media also makes people act more aggressively toward others.

Violent Video Games

Although most studies have focused on violent television and movies, the same general pattern of effects appears to be present after exposure to different forms of media, including violent music, violent comic books, and violent video games. The effects of violent video games on people's attitudes toward victims of violence are of particular concern. Feeling empathy requires taking the perspective of the victim, whereas violent video games encourage players to take the perspective of the perpetrator. Violent video games should also have a larger effect on aggressive behavior than violent TV programs and films. Watching a violent TV program or film is a passive activity, whereas playing a violent video game is active. Research has shown

that people learn better when they are actively involved. Viewers of violent shows may or may not identify with violent characters, whereas players of violent video games are forced to identify with violent characters. Any rewards that come from watching violent shows are indirect. The rewards that come from playing violent video games are direct. The player gets points or advances to the next level of the game by killing others. The player also sees impressive visual effects and hears verbal praise (e.g., "Nice shot!" "Impressive!") after behaving aggressively.

Different Types of Violent Media Studies

Experimental studies have shown that exposure to media violence causes people to become more tolerant of aggressive behavior and to behave more aggressively toward others immediately after exposure. Although laboratory experiments involving noise blasts and electric shocks have been criticized for their somewhat artificial nature, field experiments have produced similar results. For example, in one field experiment, delinquent boys who were shown violent films every night for five nights were more likely than were those shown nonviolent films to get into fights with other boys. Similar effects have been observed with nondelinquent children who saw a single episode of a violent children's television program.

Another criticism about experimental studies is that they do not measure actual criminal violence. Although acting aggressively is not always a desirable trait, it is not the same as breaking the law or committing serious acts of violence. But stories of copycat violence tend to make the public most concerned about the effects of violent media. Eric Harris and Dylan Klebold, the students who killed 13 people and wounded 23 in the Columbine massacre, were both avid players of violent video games. Before the massacre, both of them played a specially modified version of the video game Doom. In a videotape released after the massacre, Harris refers to his gun as "Arlene," which is the name of the protagonist's love interest in the Doom novels. This connection suggests that consuming violent media and aggression are related, but does violent media actually cause criminal violence?

It would be difficult, if not impossible, to conduct a safe and ethical laboratory study on the effect of violent media on violent behavior. However, it is probably not so much the immediate effect of media violence on violent crime that is of concern but, rather, the aggregated long-term effects. Children are exposed to about 10,000 violent crimes in the media per year, and each of these has a cumulative effect on their thoughts, feelings, and actions. Longitudinal studies have shown that exposure to violent media is related to serious violent and antisocial behavior. For example, the amount of violent media consumed as a child is related to how many fights a person will get into in high school. Similarly, men who watched violent media during childhood were nearly twice as likely to have assaulted their spouse 15 years later. In another longitudinal study, consumption of violent media at age 14 predicted violent crimes committed at age 22.

What Types of Media Are Most Harmful?

All violent media do not have the same effect, and all people are not affected the same way by violent media. For example, how violence is depicted is important. Both realistic violence and violence that goes unpunished increase the likelihood of aggression. Also, pairing violence with sex seems to have a particularly strong effect on men's aggressive attitudes and behavior toward women.

Who Is Most Affected by Violent Media?

Who watches violent media is also important. A number of personality traits seem to place some viewers at greater risk than others. One key variable is the trait of aggressiveness. People who are characteristically aggressive seem to be more affected by violent media than are people who are not characteristically aggressive. However, the relationship between trait aggression and violent media is complex, and these findings only represent trait differences at a single point in time. Exposure to media violence also causes trait aggressiveness, which in turn increases the likelihood of aggressive behavior. This suggests that the short-term effects of violent media observed in experimental research may become increasingly pronounced within individuals as they are repeatedly exposed to violence, leading to a downward spiral into greater levels of aggression.

Importantly, longitudinal studies have also addressed the causal direction of this downward spiral. It could be argued that people who behave aggressively are more likely to watch violent television. Researchers have found that although exposure to aggressive media as a child is related to acts of aggression later in life, aggression as a child is unrelated to exposure to violent media as a young adult, effectively ruling out the possibility that a predisposition to watch violent media is causing this effect.

Gender norms or sex differences may also play a role. Some studies have found that boys are more influenced by media violence than girls are, but these effects are inconsistent. Other researchers find little difference between boys and girls. Longitudinal studies may provide some explanation for this inconsistency. Gender differences in aggression have decreased over time, possibly because more aggressive female models have appeared on TV and because it has become more socially acceptable for females to behave aggressively.

When someone is exposed to violent media is also important. Although all age groups are equally susceptible to the short-term effects of violent media on aggression, exposure to violent television at a young age is a particularly strong predictor of violent behavior in later life. It is not yet clear whether this finding is simply a result of additional years of exposure to violent media or a result of exposure to violence during a critical period of children's social development.

Implications

Although many individual differences moderate the impact of violent media on aggressive and even violent behavior, on the whole, consumption of violent media increases aggressive and antisocial behavior. The effect of violent media on aggression is not trivial, either. Although the typical effect size for exposure to violent media is small by conventional standards and is thus dismissed by some critics, this small effect translates into significant consequences for society as a whole, which may be a better standard by which to measure the magnitude of the effect. A recent review found that the effect of exposure to violent media is stronger than the effect of secondhand smoke on lung cancer, the effect of asbestos on cancer, and the effect of lead poisoning on mental functioning. Although media violence is not the only factor that increases aggression and violence, it is an important factor.

Brad J. Bushman
Jesse J. Chandler

See also Aggression; Empathy; Gender Differences; Individual Differences; Intimate Partner Violence

Further Readings

Anderson, C. A., Berkowitz, L., Donnerstein, E., Huesmann, R. L., Johnson, J. D., Linz, D., et al. (2003). The influence of media violence on youth. *Psychological Science in the Public Interest, 4,* 81–110.

Anderson, C. A., & Bushman, B. J. (2002). Media violence and societal violence. *Science, 295,* 2377–2378.

Bushman, B. J., & Anderson, C. A. (2001). Media violence and the American public: Scientific facts versus media misinformation. *American Psychologist, 56,* 477–489.

Bushman, B. J., & Anderson, C. A. (2002). Violent video games and hostile expectations: A test of the general aggression model. *Personality and Social Psychology Bulletin, 28,* 1679–1686.

Huesmann, L. R., Moise-Titus, J., Podolski, C. L., & Eron, L. D. (2003). Longitudinal relations between children's exposure to TV violence and their aggressive and violent behavior in young adulthood: 1977–1992. *Developmental Psychology, 39,* 201–221.

MEMORY

Definition

Most contemporary researchers discuss three elements to the concept of memory: (1) Memory is the place or storage area where social and nonsocial information is held; (2) memory is also the specifics or content of an experience or event, also referred to as the *memory trace*; and (3) *memory* is the term used to describe the mental process through which people learn, store, or remember this information. In addition, when discussing memory and memory processes, researchers often refer to the related concept of a *mental representation*. A mental representation is an encoded construction that people can access, store, retrieve, and use in a variety of ways. For example, each person has a mental representation of his or her mother. The collections of feelings, beliefs, and knowledge you have about your mother constitute your mental representation of her.

Background and History

Memory is a topic that has enjoyed the attention of academics and thinkers for literally thousands of years. Almost 2,500 years ago, Plato argued that memory was a wax tablet whereupon one's everyday experiences left their impressions. An important consequence of this characterization, one that was accepted as truth for some time, is that once a memory is encoded it is set and unchangeable. Although a memory can be forgotten for some time, it could eventually be completely and accurately retrieved. Conversely, Aristotle argued that memories were associations among different stimuli and experiences. This idea was further developed by the likes of John Locke and David Hume in the 1600s and 1700s. An associative network allows for a greater fluidity of memory and implies that memories and mental representations may change or be forgotten over time. This latter view is more consistent with current psychological thought.

One of the most comprehensive early approaches to human memory was published by Hermann Ebbinghaus in his 1885 book on the subject. Ebbinghaus's work focused on the learning of new information (typically nonsense words), and he developed curves to describe how people learned and subsequently forgot new information. Many of his results have laid the foundations for current thought on learning and memory for new information. Some time later, Sir Frederic Bartlett began focusing on how existing knowledge influenced learning and memory. He proposed that memory was actually a constructive process and that people, in trying to recollect, often reconstructed memories from the fragments that were available. Since these early findings, understanding memory processes has been a focus in a number or areas of psychology including perception, behaviorism, verbal learning, and neuroscience. Consistent with this broad focus in the psychological literature, memory and memory effects have been a core subject of study in social psychology.

Development of Models of Memory

Within the concept of memory, researchers have made a distinction between *explicit* (often referred to as *declarative*) and *implicit* (often referred to as *nondeclarative*) memory. Explicit memory can be defined as the conscious or intentional act of trying to remember something (such as your mother's birthday), whereas implicit memory can be thought of as the way in which people's memories and prior experiences (i.e., mental representations) affect the way they think about and process information in their social worlds. An example of this would be how people's attitudes about a topic (their beliefs or opinions stored in memory) affect how they process incoming information about that topic. For example, your attitude toward your mother influences your definition of what represents a good versus a bad mother. Importantly, with implicit memories, people are not necessarily aware that their memories have an influence on them. Explicit memory can be further divided into *episodic* memory (memory for specific events) and *semantic* memory (memory for the meaning of things, such as words).

In the 1950s, researchers began to carefully delineate different models of memory. Two types of memory models that have substantially affected the field of social psychology are the related concepts of *associative networks* and *schemas*. The associative network model posits that memories are simply the collected associations between different nodes of concepts, sensations, and perceptions. These nodes are linked by being repeatedly associated with each other. Every time the memory is accessed or activated, the associative link between the nodes is strengthened. The more often this happens, the easier the association (i.e., the memory) is to activate. Associative network models fundamentally propose a bottom-up processing strategy whereby larger meanings are constructed from the associations among linked concepts.

Conversely, schemas can be defined as more comprehensive representations in memory that provide a framework for interpreting new information. As such, schemas suggest a top-down processing strategy. New information is incorporated into existing schemas, and this information is understood in relation to it. Whereas the associative network approach suggests that people incorporate new information by creating novel associations, schema theory suggests people understand new information by relating it to their existing knowledge and expectations. Far from being contradictory, these processes work in a complementary fashion, depending on the requirements of the situation.

Memory in the Context of Social Psychology

Although research into memory has been conducted primarily by cognitive psychologists, it is a core research area within social psychology as well. Imagine that you could not remember the people you met from day to day. Each time you saw your roommate, friends, or family members, you would need to get to know them all over again. Clearly, memory is essential to our social interactions.

Consequently, a substantial amount of research in social psychology has explored how associative networks and schemas play a role in everyday social experience. A significant amount of research suggests that people go into situations with certain expectations. These expectations are based on their previous experiences and beliefs (i.e., their mental representation about an event, person, or situation). For example, researchers have demonstrated that people have a general tendency to recall and recognize attitude-consistent information better than they recall attitude-inconsistent information. Although the strength of the overall effect has been debated, people prefer information that is consistent with their attitudes. Given certain circumstances, however, memory biases can be eliminated or even reversed. For example, some evidence suggests that under certain conditions, people will actively try to counterargue attitude-inconsistent information they encounter, and this may result in better recall for the attitude-inconsistent information.

Similar findings have been reported in the impression formation literature. That is, when people meet a person for the first time, their expectations about the person (e.g., stereotypes about specific groups and their members) or the situation (e.g., a script or set of beliefs about how an event, such as a romantic encounter, should unfold) can influence how they perceive and judge that person. If they expect someone to be nice, they will remember him or her as being pleasant and friendly. Interestingly, if their expectations are particularly strong when they encounter schema-incongruent information, that inconsistent information may be remembered better (i.e., they may begin to create a new associative network or information). Thus, as with the attitude literature, people tend to demonstrate a confirmatory bias, but if their expectations are strong, the inconsistent information may be particularly salient and thus may be remembered better. Although there has been debate in the literature about how and when these effects occur, mental representations and memory affect how people interact with their social worlds.

Applications of Memory Research

The social psychological aspects of memory research have been applied to real-world settings in several areas. For example, police and the courts have had a necessary interest in human memory. Much of what happens in the court system relies on people's memories and how their mental representations influence information processing. Issues such as interviewing witnesses, eyewitness identification, and jury decision making have all received a great deal of attention in the social psychological literature. Within the area of eyewitness memory, one popular area of research has been the exploration of false memories. A significant amount of empirical research indicates that false memories are relatively easy to create and that these memories can be held with as much confidence and clarity as true memories. This further reinforces the concept of memory as malleable over time and retrieval as a reconstructive process.

Outside of the social psychological literature, memory research has been applied to, and conducted in, several areas such as clinical psychology (e.g., exploring long- and short-term amnesia; the role of memory in schizophrenia, dementia, and depression), developmental psychology (e.g., exploring how memory skills and processes develop in childhood and progress through adolescence, adulthood, and old age), and of course, cognitive psychology (e.g., exploring basic processes in attention, perception, and memory modeling). Thus, memory and memory research have been and will continue to be major focuses within social psychology and the broader psychological literature.

Steven M. Smith

See also Eyewitness Testimony, Accuracy of; Metacognition; Primacy Effect, Memory

Further Readings

Schacter, D. L. (1996). *Searching for memory: The brain, the mind and the past.* New York: Basic Books.

Smith, E. R. (1998). Mental representation and memory. In D. T. Gilbert, S. T. Fiske, & G. Lindzey (Eds.), *The handbook of social psychology* (Vol. 1, pp. 391–445). Boston: McGraw-Hill.

MENTAL ACCOUNTING

Definition

Mental accounting is a theory that describes how people think about money. This theory suggests that people track and coordinate their financial activities by partitioning money into mental accounts, which are used to make spending decisions. Examples of mental accounts might include an "entertainment account" or an "education account," each representing money specifically budgeted for that endeavor.

Mental accounting represents a shift from traditional economic theory, which suggests that people think about their assets as a single account representing their total state of wealth. According to economic theory, spending decisions are based on a purchase's utility relative to all other potential purchases. Mental accounting instead suggests that spending decisions are based on utility relative only to other purchases in the relevant account.

Background

The concept of mental accounting first emerged with studies about spending behavior related to sunk costs (money spent on a future event that cannot be refunded). Mental accounting research has since expanded to include more in-depth analyses of spending behavior as well as how mental accounts are opened and closed and how income is apportioned to accounts.

Evidence

The following examples illustrate the findings of mental accounting research.

Sunk Costs

One early mental accounting study examined whether people would attend a basketball game in the middle of a blizzard. Those who purchased a ticket in advance choose to go see the game, despite not wanting to drive in bad weather. In contrast, people planning to purchase a ticket at the game decide to stay home to avoid driving in poor conditions. This difference can be attributed to the observation that for advance ticket holders, the mental account for "basketball game viewing" remains open until the game is attended. If the game is not attended, the account may remain open indefinitely, which can be a source of mental discomfort.

Assignment of Activities to Accounts

Research investigating assignment of activities to mental accounts presents scenarios like the following:

Scenario 1: Imagine that you spent $20 on a ticket to go see a concert. When you get to the concert, you pull out your wallet and realize that you have lost the ticket you'd bought. If you want to see the concert, you need to buy another $20 ticket. Would you buy the ticket?

Scenario 2: Imagine you go to the concert without a ticket, planning to buy one there. When you pull out your wallet, you realize that you have lost a $20 bill. Tickets to the show cost $20. Would you buy the ticket?

People are less likely to buy a ticket after losing a ticket (Scenario 1) than after losing $20 (Scenario 2). This is inconsistent with traditional economic theory because the scenarios are economically equivalent; in both versions, the choice to skip the concert means having $20 less and the choice to see the concert means having $40 less in overall wealth.

Mental accounting better explains the results of this ticket-buying study. In the first scenario, both $20 expenditures are charged to the "entertainment" account, which makes it seem like $40 is being spent on the concert ticket. In the second scenario, the lost $20 is charged to the "general fund" account and only the $20 spent on the ticket is charged to the "entertainment" account, which makes it seem like the ticket cost only $20.

Transaction Utility

Research on transaction utility (the perception and experience of outcomes) reveals that altering the purchase context causes people to be willing to pay different prices for the same product. In one study, participants were asked how much money they would spend on a bottle of beer. Half the participants were told they could buy the beer from a nearby resort, and half the participants were told they could buy the beer from a nearby grocery store. People report they are willing to pay $2.65 for a bottle of beer purchased from an expensive resort but only $1.50 for the same bottle of beer when purchased from a grocery store. Economic theory predicts that willingness to pay should not be influenced by factors like the product's source. Mental accounting research reveals that this is not actually the case and that people perceive and experience outcomes differently depending on the context; the same beer is charged to different mental accounts based on the particular circumstances of the purchase.

Mental Accounting in Real Life

Mental accounting has been studied using hypothetical scenarios like those described earlier and in the field within diverse populations. One field study investigated mental accounting in taxi drivers, finding that drivers tend to work longer on days when they are making less money and quit earlier on days when they are making lots of money. This study revealed that taxi drivers have a mental account for income that fills each day. Once the account has been filled, the workday can be considered over. Economic theory predicts that drivers would work longer on high-earning days and quit earlier on slow days in the interest of making the most money possible per hour worked, but this is exactly the opposite of what most drivers do. Drivers seem unwilling to close the income account each day until they receive a fixed amount of money.

Another study found that people treat windfalls (unexpected income) differently than earnings from a paycheck. These two sources of income correspond to different mental accounts, and as such, people tend to spend the money differently. Regular earnings are used for predictable expenses and bonuses are used for special luxury purchases. Economic theory, however, predicts that people would treat all income the same regardless of source. As this is not the case, mental accounting provides a better description of how people think about money.

Importance and Implications

Mental accounting helps illustrate that economic theory cannot always account for people's behavior. It demonstrates that money is not always treated as representing an overall state of wealth and that psychological factors are important to consider in predicting everyday behavior when it comes to earning or spending money.

Joanne Kane
Ethan Pew

See also Behavioral Economics; Gain–Loss Framing; Prospect Theory; Sunk Cost

Further Readings

Thaler, R. H. (1999). Mental accounting matters. *Journal of Behavioral Decision Making, 12,* 183–206.

MENTAL CONTROL

Definition

Mental control refers to the ways in which people control their thoughts and emotions to remain in agreement with their goals. People engage in mental control when they suppress a thought, concentrate on a feeling or sensation, restrain an emotional response, or strive to maintain a mood. Mental control proves difficult for most people, and the study of mental control has implications for the treatment of a wide range of psychological disorders.

History and Background

The scientific study of mental control is relatively new to psychology. Before 1987, the term *mental control* did not appear in any searches of the psychological literature. The tendency for people to exert control over their thoughts and emotions has been observed culturally for more than a century, however. Perhaps the most famous instance of mental control came from the Russian writer Leo Tolstoy, who described a time in which he instructed his younger brother to sit in a corner and not to think of a white bear. Once challenged to suppress thoughts of a white bear, the younger Tolstoy stood in the corner, confused, and frustrated at having to suppress unwanted thoughts of a white bear. The earliest notion of mental control in the psychological literature came from the writings of Sigmund Freud on the study of repression, which he described as the tendency for people to discard certain thoughts out of consciousness unintentionally. Repression occurs outside of conscious awareness, based on motives of which the person is unaware, and results in the elimination of both a particular memory and the memory that represents the event of repression. Although the Freudian view of repression held a dominant place in psychology throughout the early 20th century, research investigating this view has yielded little supportive evidence. In the 1980s, researchers began to consider the impact of conscious efforts to suppress unwanted thoughts. The tendency for people to exert mental control over unwanted thoughts has been widely documented in both normal individuals and those with a wide variety of mental disorders, such as depression, obsessions and compulsions, and post-traumatic stress. These researchers sought to examine the results of attempted suppression on subsequent cognition, emotion, and behavioral tasks.

Suppression Cycle

Early mental control researchers sought to determine the process by which people exert mental control. Daniel Wegner and colleagues have shown that when people exert mental control, they often do so in a cyclical manner. People asked to suppress the thought of a white bear, for example, begin suppression with a self-distraction phase in which they plan to distract themselves (e.g., "I'll think of something else"). The second phase involves choosing a distracter (e.g., "I'll think about a book"), which results in the intrusive return of the unwanted thought (e.g., "The white bear is there again"). When the unwanted thought has returned, the cycle repeats with a return to the plan to self-distract (e.g., "Now I'll think of something else").

This suppression cycle comprises two main cognitive processes—controlled distracter search and automatic target search. Controlled distracter search involves a conscious search for thoughts that are not the unwanted thought, which is carried out with the goal of replacing the unwanted thought. Automatic target search entails searching for any sign of the unwanted thought, and this process detects whether the controlled distracter search is successful at replacing the unwanted thought. Research has shown that the availability of potential distracters in the environment influences the distracters that people use while exerting mental control. People also rely on their current mental states to serve as distracters during suppression. For example, people suffering from depression have been shown to choose depressing distracters during suppression. Another study showed that people who were induced into a positive or negative mood selected distracters that were related to their mood. These findings suggest that mental control is a process that involves the initial suppression of the unwanted thought or emotion and the search for materials in the environment that are related or unrelated to the suppressed thought or emotion.

Consequences

Although much research has investigated the process by which people exert mental control in their everyday lives, other research has examined what the aftereffects of exerting mental control may be. Wegner and colleagues have shown consistently that exerting mental control over some particular event or object causes people to show a greater level of obsession or preoccupation with the suppressed object than do people who had never suppressed a thought or emotion regarding the particular event or object. This rebounding effect was first observed in a study by Wegner and colleagues. Some participants in this study were instructed to suppress the thought of a white bear, whereas other participants completed a similar task but were not asked to suppress the thought of a white bear. After participants had completed this initial task (in which they either suppressed the thought of a white bear or not), participants were asked to think of a white bear and to ring a bell every time a white bear came to mind. Participants who had suppressed the thought of a white bear during the initial task rang the bell more than did participants who had not suppressed the thought of a white bear during the initial task. Thus, the initial act of suppressing the thought of a white bear led to increased activation of the concept of a white bear in the mind of these participants.

Another consequence of exerting mental control is impaired self-control. Roy Baumeister and colleagues have demonstrated that participants who suppressed a thought on an initial task showed impaired performance on a subsequent self-control task compared with participants who had not previously suppressed a thought. These findings suggest that mental control is an effortful process that can cause impairments in a person's ability to engage in self-control successfully.

C. Nathan DeWall

See also Ego Depletion; Ironic Processes; Motivated Cognition; Self-Control Measures; Self-Regulation

Further Readings

Baumeister, R. F., Bratslavsky, E., Muraven, M., & Tice, D. M. (1998). Ego depletion: Is the active self a limited resource? *Journal of Personality and Social Psychology, 74,* 1252–1265.

Wegner, D. M., Schneider, D. J., Carter, S., III, & White, L. (1987). Paradoxical effects of thought suppression. *Journal of Personality and Social Psychology, 53,* 5–13.

MERE EXPOSURE EFFECT

Definition

The mere exposure effect describes the phenomenon that simply encountering a stimulus repeatedly somehow makes one like it more. Perhaps the stimulus is a painting on the wall, a melody on a radio, or a face of a person you pass by every day—somehow all these stimuli tend to "grow on you." The mere exposure effect is technically defined as an enhancement of attitude toward a novel stimulus as a result of repeated encounters with that stimulus. Interestingly, the mere exposure effect does not require any kind of reward for perceiving the stimulus. All that is required is that the stimulus is merely shown, however briefly or incidentally, to the individual. So, for example, briefly glimpsing a picture or passively listening to a melody is enough for the picture and melody to become preferred over pictures and melodies that one has not seen or heard before. In short, contrary to the adage that familiarity breeds contempt, the mere exposure effect suggests just the opposite: Becoming familiar with a novel stimulus engenders liking for the stimulus.

Background

The mere exposure effect was first systematically examined by Robert Zajonc, who reported his findings in the influential 1968 article "Attitudinal Effects of Mere Exposure." He presented two kinds of evidence in support of the mere exposure effect. The first kind of evidence was correlational and established a relationship between the frequency of occurrence of certain stimuli and their evaluative meaning. For example, Zajonc reported that words with positive rather than negative meanings have a higher frequency of usage in literature, magazines, and other publications. Thus, the word *pretty* is used more frequently than *ugly* (1,195 vs. 178), *on* is more frequent than *off* (30,224 vs. 3,644), and *first* is more frequent than *last* (5,154 vs. 3,517). Similar findings have also been obtained with numbers, letters, and other apparently neutral stimuli. However, this evidence is correlational, so it is impossible to say if stimulus frequency is the cause of positive meaning or if positive meaning causes the stimulus to be used more frequently. To alleviate concerns associated with the correlational evidence, Zajonc also presented experimental evidence. For example, he performed an experiment and showed that nonsensical words as well as yearbook pictures of faces are rated more favorably after they have been merely exposed to participants. Since then, researchers have experimentally documented the mere exposure effect using a wide variety of stimuli, including simple and complex line drawings and paintings, simple and complex tonal sequences and musical pieces, geometric figures, foods, odors, and photographs of people. Interestingly, the participants in those experiments included college students, amnesic patients, rats, and even newborn chicks, suggesting that the mere exposure effect reflects a fairly fundamental aspect of psychological functioning.

Conditions Affecting Strength

During this research, scientists have discovered several conditions that modify the strength of the mere exposure effect. Thus, the mere exposure effect is stronger when exposure durations are brief. In fact, the mere exposure effect is sometimes stronger with subliminal rather than supraliminal presentations. The mere exposure effect is also stronger when the repetition scheme is heterogeneous (i.e., with the exposures of a stimulus being interspersed with the presentations of other stimuli) rather than homogeneous (i.e., with all the exposures being of the same stimulus). Furthermore, the magnitude of the mere exposure effect reaches a peak after 10 to 20 stimulus exposures and thereafter levels off. Finally, stronger mere exposure effects are elicited by more complex stimuli and when the experimental situation is set up such that boredom is minimized. In fact, boredom and saturation can sometimes reverse the generally positive effect of mere exposure— a phenomenon certainly experienced by the reader when a massively repeated advertising jingle becomes simply annoying. Some reversals of the mere exposure effect have also been reported with stimuli that are initially negative, though it is unclear whether the increased negativity is due to exposure per se or rather to the unpleasantness that comes from repeated induction of negative affect.

Implications

Some studies on the mere exposure effect suggest that the phenomenon has wide-ranging personal and social implications. It may influence who people become attracted to; what products, art, and entertainment

they enjoy; and even their everyday moods. Regarding interpersonal attraction, one study found that subjects shown a photograph of the same person each week for four weeks exhibited greater liking for that person than when compared with subjects shown a photograph of a different person each week. In another study, preschoolers who watched *Sesame Street* episodes that involved children of Japanese, Canadian, and North American Indian heritage were more likely to indicate that they would like to play with such children than were preschoolers who had not seen these episodes.

In the domain of advertising, researchers have shown that unobtrusive exposure to cigarette brands enhances participants' brand preference and their purchase intentions. Even people's aesthetic inclinations are shaped by mere exposure. For example, adult preferences for impressionistic paintings were found to increase as the frequency of occurrence of the images of the paintings in library books increased. In another study, subjects were incidentally exposed to various pieces of orchestral music at varying frequencies. Again, as the number of exposures to a piece of orchestral music increased, then so did the subjects' liking ratings for the music.

Apparently, mere repeated exposure may even boost mood states of individuals. In one experiment, subjects were subliminally exposed to either 25 different Chinese ideographs (single exposure condition) or to 5 Chinese ideographs that were repeated in random sequence (repeated exposure condition). Assessment of subjects' overall mood states indicated that those subjects in the repeated exposure condition exhibited a more positive mood than did those subjects in the single exposure condition.

Theoretical Interpretations

There are many theoretical interpretations of exactly how mere repeated exposure enhances our liking for the stimulus. One class of explanations seeks the answer in simple biological processes common to many organisms, including mammals and birds. Thus, it has been proposed that organisms respond to a novel stimulus with an initial sense of uncertainty, which feels negative. Repeated exposure can reduce such uncertainty, and thus engender more positive feelings. A related proposal suggests that organisms approach novel stimuli expecting possible negative consequences and that the absence of such consequences during repeated exposure is experienced as positive.

Finally, those biologically inspired proposals emphasize that mere familiarity with a stimulus can serve as a probabilistic cue that a stimulus is relatively safe (after all, the individual survived to see it again).

A competing class of explanations seeks the answer in more perceptual and cognitive processes and treats the mere exposure effect as a kind of implicit memory phenomenon. One proposal suggests that repeated exposure gradually strengthens a stimulus memory trace and thus enhances the ease of its later identification. This ease of perception can elicit positive affect because it allows people to better deal with the stimulus in a current situation. The positive affect created by the ease of perception may, of course, generalize to the nature of the stimulus, or participants' own mood, explaining a relatively wide scope of mere exposure effects. Importantly, for this process to occur, participants should not know why the stimulus is easy to process. Otherwise, they are unlikely to attribute the sense of positivity from the ease of perceiving the stimulus to an actual preference for the stimulus. This idea explains why mere exposure effects are stronger when stimuli are presented subliminally and when stimuli are not recognized from the exposure phase. Furthermore, the ease of perception idea explains why the mere exposure effect is more easily obtained for more complex stimuli because their memory traces are more likely to benefit from progressive strengthening by repetition. Finally, the perceptual account of the mere exposure effect fits well with many other studies suggesting that other ways of enhancing the ease of stimulus perception of a single stimulus (e.g., via stimulus contrast, duration, clarify, or priming) tend to enhance participants' liking for those stimuli in ways comparable to repetition.

The debate, however, over the exact mechanism by which repeated mere exposure exerts its effects is far from resolved and will no doubt be a hot topic in the psychological literature for some time to come.

Troy Chenier
Piotr Winkielman

See also Attitudes; Attraction; Priming; Memory

Further Readings

Bornstein, R. F. (1989). Exposure and affect: Overview and meta-analysis of research 1968–1987. *Psychological Bulletin, 106,* 265–289.

Bornstein, R. F., & D'Agostino, P. R. (1994). The attribution and discounting of perceptual fluency: Preliminary tests of a perceptual fluency/attributional model of the mere exposure effect. *Social Cognition, 12,* 103–128.

Lee, A. Y. (2001). The mere exposure effect: An uncertainty reduction explanation revisited. *Personality and Social Psychology Bulletin, 27,* 1255–1266.

Winkielman, P., Schwarz, N., Fazendeiro, T., & Reber, R. (2003). The hedonic marking of processing fluency: Implications for evaluative judgment. In J. Musch & K. C. Klauer (Eds.), *The psychology of evaluation: Affective processes in cognition and emotion* (pp. 189–217). Mahwah, NJ: Erlbaum.

Zajonc, R. B. (1968). Attitudinal effects of mere exposure. *Journal of Personality and Social Psychology, 9,* 1–27.

MERE OWNERSHIP EFFECT

Definition

The mere ownership effect refers to an individual's tendency to evaluate an object more favorably merely because he or she owns it. The endowment effect is a related phenomenon that concerns the finding that sellers require more money to sell an object than buyers are willing to pay for it. Taken together, these phenomena indicate that ownership is a psychologically meaningful variable that can influence the way that one thinks about and evaluates objects in the external world.

Context and Importance

The mere ownership effect has been hypothesized to occur because people are motivated to see themselves in a positive light. Thus, the mere ownership effect illustrates the importance of the self in mediating how people interpret the world.

Self-concept refers to the beliefs a person holds about the self. Self-esteem refers to how much a person likes or dislikes the self. Because people are motivated to maintain high self-esteem, people strive to see themselves in a positive light. This tendency toward self-enhancement can take many forms. For example, people tend to underestimate the likelihood of experiencing a negative event such as an illness or accident. Similarly, individuals overestimate their abilities on skills such as driving a car or behaving in a morally correct way. People also focus selectively on positive, rather than negative, beliefs about themselves.

People show indirect self-enhancement by positively evaluating targets associated with the self. For example, people evaluate their own groups more positively than others' groups. The basis for association can include significant dimensions such as race or irrelevant dimensions such as a shared birth date.

Explaining Ownership Effects

The mere ownership effect is a form of indirect self-enhancement similar to the bias people show regarding their own, rather than others', groups. The concept of ownership creates a psychological association between the owner and the object. To the extent that an owner sees the owned object in a favorable light, he or she can then indirectly come to see the self in a more favorable light, as well.

The endowment effect is thought to operate for a different reason than self-enhancement. The endowment effect works because of the different way that people think about gains and losses. People tend to be more distressed by losses than they are made happy by gains. For example, people would probably be more irate by a $10-a-week pay cut than they would be made happy by a $10-a-week raise. In other words, the absolute value of their change in emotional state would be larger for a loss than a gain.

According to the gain–loss explanation for the endowment effect, selling a possession is perceived as a loss. In contrast, buying is seen as a gain. The seller's reluctance to accept a loss causes him or her to ask for a little extra compensation that potential buyers are unwilling to provide.

Both the mere ownership effect and the endowment effect reflect an important conflict that has occurred between psychology and economics. If people behaved in the purely rational fashion that economics assumes, then the endowment effect and the mere ownership effect would not occur. From the perspective of economics, the object is the same regardless of who owns it. The idea that owners think about the object differently than nonowners do indicates that a full understanding of economics will have to acknowledge psychological principles.

Evidence

Evidence for the mere ownership effect has been demonstrated using laboratory-based experiments. In the ownership condition, an individual is provided with ownership of an object, typically justified as a gift for participating. Participants are later asked to rate the owned object as well as other, nonowned objects. In the nonownership condition, participants rate the objects in the absence of ownership. Generally, the same object is rated as more attractive when it is owned rather than not owned.

In research on the endowment effect, a miniature economy is created in which half the participants are each provided ownership of an object and the other half are not. Potential sellers are asked to indicate the lowest price they would accept to sell the object, whereas potential buyers are asked to indicate the highest price they would pay to buy the object. Typically, the average seller's price is higher than the average buyer's price.

One possible limitation of these kinds of experiments is that giving someone a gift may encourage the recipient to evaluate it in a positive manner to show appreciation rather than because he or she actually sees the item in a more positive light. To address this problem, researchers have asked people to evaluate objects that they already own. They found that people listed a greater number of positive traits associated with their own cars rather than others' cars.

Implications

The self is a complex concept that consists of many parts, including achievements, ancestors, descendants, and education. The self also consists of what one owns. The mere ownership effect illustrates there is a relationship between one's possessions and how one sees oneself.

Given the existence of the mere ownership effect and the endowment effect, at first glance, a person might wonder how it could be that anything ever sells. In the course of a typical negotiation, people may come to realize that they need to reduce their aspirations for transactions to occur. In addition, ownership effects do not operate for all possessions or even for the same possession at different points in time.

James K. Beggan

See also Gain–Loss Framing; Self; Self-Concept; Self-Enhancement; Self-Esteem

Further Readings

Beggan, J. K. (1992). On the social nature of nonsocial perception: The mere ownership effect. *Journal of Personality and Social Psychology, 62,* 229–237.

Csikszentmihalyi, M., & Rochberg-Halton, E. (1981). *The meaning of things: Domestic symbols and the self.* Cambridge, UK: Cambridge University Press.

Kahneman, D., Knetsch, J. L., & Thaler, R. H. (1990). Experimental tests of the endowment effect and the Coase theorem. *Journal of Political Economy, 98,* 1325–1348.

META-ANALYSIS

Meta-analysis uses statistical techniques to summarize results from different empirical studies on a given topic to learn more about that topic. In other words, meta-analyses bring together the results of many different studies, although the number of studies may be as small as two in some specialized contexts. Because these quantitative reviews are analyses of analyses, they are literally meta-analyses. The practice is also known as *research synthesis,* a term that more completely encompasses the steps involved in conducting such a review. Meta-analysis might be thought of as an empirical history of research on a particular topic, in that it tracks effects that have accumulated across time and attempts to show how different methods that researchers use may make their effects change in size or in direction.

Rationale and Procedures

As in any scientific field, social psychology makes progress by judging the evidence that has accumulated. Consequently, literature reviews of studies can be extremely influential, particularly when meta-analysis is used to review them. In the past three decades, the scholarly community has embraced the position that reviewing is itself a scientific method with identifiable steps that should be followed to be most accurate and valid.

At the outset, an analyst carefully defines the variables at the center of the phenomenon and considers the history of the research problem and of typical studies in the literature. Usually, the research problem will be defined as a relation between two variables, such as the influence of an independent variable on a dependent variable. For example, a review might consider the extent to which women use a more relationship-oriented leadership style compared with men. Typically, the analyst will also consider what circumstances may change the relation in question. For example, an analyst might predict that women will lead in a style that is more relationship-oriented than men and that this tendency will be especially present when studies examine leadership roles that are communal in nature (e.g., nurse supervisor, elementary principal).

Analysts must next take great care to decide which studies belong in the meta-analysis, the next step in the process, because any conclusions the meta-analysis might reach are limited by the methods of the studies in the sample. As a rule, meta-analyses profit by focusing on the studies that use stronger methods, although which particular methods are "stronger" might vary from area to area. Whereas laboratory-based research (e.g., social perception, persuasion) tends to value internal validity more than external validity, field-based research (e.g., leadership style, political attitudes) tends to reverse these values.

Ideally, a meta-analysis will locate every study ever conducted on a subject. Yet, for some topics, the task can be quite daunting because of sheer numbers of studies available. As merely one example, in their 1978 meta-analysis, Robert Rosenthal and Donald B. Rubin reported on 345 studies of the experimenter expectancy effect. It is important to locate as many studies as possible that might be suitable for inclusion using as many techniques as possible (e.g., computer and Internet searches, e-mails to active researchers, consulting reference lists, manual searching of related journals). If there are too many studies to include all, the analyst might randomly sample from the studies or, more commonly, narrow the focus to a meaningful subliterature.

Once the sample of studies is in hand, each study is coded for relevant dimensions that might have affected the study outcomes. To permit reliability statistics, two or more coders must do this coding. In some cases, an analyst might ask experts to judge methods used in the studies on particular dimensions (e.g., the extent to which a measure of leadership style is relationship-oriented). In other cases, an analyst might ask people with no training for their views about aspects of the reviewed studies (e.g., the extent to which leadership roles were communal).

To be included in a meta-analysis, a study must offer some minimal quantitative information that addresses the relation between the variables (e.g., means and standard deviations for the compared groups, F tests, t tests). Standing alone, these statistical tests would reveal little about the phenomenon.

When the tests appear in a single standardized metric, the effect size, the situation typically clarifies dramatically. The most common effect sizes are d (the standardized mean difference between two groups) and r (the correlation coefficient gauging the association between two variables). Each effect size receives a positive or negative sign to indicate the direction of the effect. As an example, a 1990 meta-analysis that Blair T. Johnson and Alice H. Eagly conducted to examine gender differences in leadership style defined effect sizes in such a way that positive signs were stereotypic (e.g., women more relationship-oriented) and negative signs were counterstereotypic (e.g., men more relationship-oriented). Typically, d is used for comparisons of two groups or groupings (e.g., gender differences in leadership style) and r for continuous variables (e.g., self-esteem and attractiveness).

Then, the reviewer analyzes the effect sizes, first examining the mean effect size to evaluate its magnitude, direction, and significance. More advanced analyses examine whether differing study methods change, or moderate, the magnitude of the effect sizes. In all of these analyses, sophisticated statistics help show whether the studies' effect sizes consistently agree with the general tendencies. Still other techniques help reveal which particular studies' findings differed most widely from the others, or examine the plausibility of a publication bias in the literature. Inspection for publication bias can be especially important when skepticism exists about whether the phenomenon under investigation is genuine. In such cases, published studies might be more likely to find a pattern than would unpublished studies. For example, many doubt the existence of so-called Phi effects, which refers to "mind reading." Any review of studies testing for the existence of Phi would have to be sensitive to the possibility that journals may tend to accept confirmations of the phenomenon more than disconfirmations of it.

Various strategies are available to detect the presence of publication bias. As an example, Rosenthal and Rubin's fail-safe N provides a method to estimate the number of studies averaging nonsignificant that would change a mean effect size to being nonsignificant. If the number is large, then it is intuitively implausible that publication bias is an issue. Other, more sophisticated techniques permit reviewers to infer what effect size values non-included studies might take and how the inclusion of such values might affect the mean effect size. The detection of publication bias is especially important when the goal of the meta-analytic review is to examine the statistical significance or the simple magnitude of a phenomenon. Publication bias is a far less pressing concern when the goal of the review is instead to examine how study dimensions explain when the studies' effect sizes are larger or smaller or when they reverse in their signs. Indeed, the mere presence of wide variation in the magnitude of effect sizes often suggests a lack of publication bias.

Interpretation and presentation of the meta-analytic findings is the final step of the process. One consideration is the magnitude the mean effect sizes in the review. In 1969, Jacob Cohen informally analyzed the magnitude of effects commonly yielded by psychological research and offered guidelines for judging effect size magnitude. Table 1 shows these standards for d, r, and r^2; the latter statistic indicates the extent to which one variable explains variation in the other. To illustrate, a small effect size ($d = 0.20$) is the difference in height between 15- and 16-year-old girls, a medium effect ($d = 0.50$) is difference in intelligence scores between clerical and semiskilled workers, and a large effect ($d = 0.80$) is the difference in intelligence scores between college professors and college freshmen. It is important to recognize that quantitative magnitude is only one way to interpret effect size. Even very small mean effect sizes can be of great import for practical or applied contexts. In a close race for political office, for example, even a mass media campaign with a small effect size could reverse the outcome.

Ideally, meta-analyses advance knowledge about a phenomenon not only by showing the size of the typical effect but also by showing when the studies get larger or smaller effects, or by showing when effects

Table 1 Guidelines for Magnitude of d and r

	Effect Size Metric		
Size	d	r	r^2
Small	0.20	.100	.010
Medium	0.50	.243	.059
Large	0.80	.371	.138

Source: Adapted from Cohen (1969).

Note: r appears in its point-biserial form.

reverse in direction. At their best, meta-analyses test theories about the phenomenon. For example, Johnson and Eagly's meta-analysis of gender differences in leadership style showed, consistent with their social-role theory hypothesis, that women had more relationship-oriented styles than men did, especially when the leadership role was communal in nature.

Meta-analyses provide an empirical history of past research and suggest promising directions for future research. As a consequence of a carefully conducted meta-analysis, primary-level studies can be designed with the complete literature in mind and therefore have a better chance of contributing new knowledge. In this way, science can advance the most efficiently to produce new knowledge.

Blair T. Johnson

See also Research Methods

Further Readings

Cohen, J. (1969). *Statistical power analysis for the behavioral sciences.* New York: Academic Press.

Cooper, H. M., & Hedges, L. V. (Eds.). (1994). *The handbook of research synthesis.* New York: Russell Sage.

Johnson, B. T., & Eagly, A. H. (2000). Quantitative synthesis of social psychological research. In H. T. Reis & C. M. Judd (Eds.), *Handbook of research methods in social and personality psychology* (pp. 496–528). London: Cambridge University Press.

Lipsey, M. W., & Wilson, D. B. (2001). *Practical meta-analysis.* Thousand Oaks, CA: Sage.

META-AWARENESS

To have an experience is not necessarily to know that one is having it. Situations such as suddenly realizing that one has not been listening to one's spouse (despite nodding attentively) or catching oneself shouting, "I'm not angry," illustrate that people sometimes fail to notice what is going on in their own heads. The intuition that there is a difference between having an experience and recognizing it permeates everyday language, as illustrated by the popular expression "getting in touch with your feelings" and the famous lyrical refrain "if you're happy and you know it, clap your hands." A variety of psychological terms have been used to characterize how people vary in their awareness of their thoughts and feelings, including *metacognitive awareness, private self-awareness, reflective awareness, introspective awareness, higher-order consciousness, second-order consciousness, autonoetic consciousness,* and *mindfulness.* Nevertheless, typically when researchers consider the awareness associated with psychological phenomena, the question boils down to whether a particular phenomenon is conscious. Attitudes are implicit or explicit, thoughts are conscious or unconscious, behaviors are automatic or controlled. Routinely, discussions fail to acknowledge the possibility that a thought, feeling, or action could be experienced without being explicitly noticed.

In this entry, the term *meta-awareness* is used to refer to the explicit noticing of the content of experience. Importantly, meta-awareness need not be assumed to be a distinct state of consciousness; rather, it may merely entail a particular topic for the focus of attention, that is, "What am I thinking or feeling." Because this is just one of many possible directions in which attention can be focused, it follows that meta-awareness is intermittent. The answer to this question represents a description of one's state, rather than the state itself, so it offers individuals the opportunity to step out of the situation, which may be critical for effective self-regulation. However, it also raises the possibility that in the redescription process, individuals might get it wrong.

Two types of dissociations follow from the claim that meta-awareness involves the intermittent re-representation of the contents of consciousness. Temporal dissociations occur when one temporarily fails to attend to the contents of consciousness. Once the focus of conscious turns onto itself, translation dissociations may occur if the re-representation process misrepresents the original experience.

Temporal Dissociations

Temporal dissociations between experience and meta-awareness are indicated in cases in which the induction of meta-awareness causes one to assess aspects of experience that had previously eluded explicit appraisal. A variety of psychological phenomena can be thought of in this manner.

Mind-Wandering During Reading

Everyone has had the experience while reading of suddenly noticing that although his or her eyes have continued to move across the page, one's mind has been entirely elsewhere. The occurrence of mind-wandering during attentionally demanding tasks such as reading is particularly informative because it is incompatible with successfully carrying out such tasks and thus suggests that individuals have lost meta-awareness of what they are currently thinking about. Additional evidence that mind-wandering during reading is associated with an absence of meta-awareness comes from studies in which individuals report every time they notice their minds wandering during reading, while also being probed periodically and asked to indicate whether they were mind-wandering at that particular moment. Such studies find that participants are often caught mind-wandering by the probes before they notice it themselves. These findings demonstrate that individuals frequently lack meta-awareness of the fact that they are mind-wandering, even when they are in a study in which they are specifically instructed to be vigilant for such lapses.

Automaticity

Automatic behaviors are often assumed to be nonconscious. However, there is a peculiarity to this designation because it is difficult to imagine that individuals lack any experience corresponding to the automatic behaviors. Consider a person driving automatically while engaging in some secondary task (e.g., talking on the cell phone). Although such driving is compromised, one still experiences the road at some level. Similarly, when people engage in habitual consumptive behaviors, for example, smoking or eating, they presumably experience what they are consuming, yet may fail to take explicit stock of what they are doing. This may explain why people often unwittingly relapse in habits they are trying to quit. In short, it seems that rather than being unconscious, many automatic activities may be experienced but lacking in meta-awareness.

Moods

At any given time, people's experience is being colored by the particular mood that they are in. They may be happy because it is sunny out, or grumpy because they've had a bad day at work. However, because people often fail to notice their moods, moods can have undue influence on people's judgments and behaviors. When in an unnoticed bad mood, people may be more likely to snap at their partners, and when in an unnoticed good mood, they may be more likely to believe that their lives are going particularly well.

Translation Dissociations

If meta-awareness requires re-representing the contents of consciousness, then it follows that some information may become lost or distorted in the translation. Examples of translation dissociations include the following.

Verbal Reflection

Some experiences are inherently difficult to put into words: the appearance of a face, the taste of a wine, the intuitions leading to insights. If individuals attempt to translate these inherently nonverbal experiences into words, then the resulting re-representations may fail to do justice to the original experience. Consistent with this view, studies have demonstrated that when people attempt to describe their nonverbal experiences, performance disruptions can ensue. Importantly, verbal reflection does not hamper performance when individuals describe experiences that are more readily translated into words.

Motivation

In some situations, individuals may be explicitly motivated to misrepresent their experiences to themselves. For example, individuals who are homophobic would clearly not want to recognize that they were actually aroused by viewing graphic depictions of homosexual acts. Nevertheless, when homophobes were shown explicit movies of individuals engaging in homosexual acts, their degree of sexual arousal was significantly greater than that of controls. In this case, individuals may experience the arousal but, because of their strong motivation to ignore it, fail to become meta-aware of that experience. A similar account may help explain why individuals labeled as "repressors" can show substantial physiological (galvanic skin response) markers of experiencing stress when shown stressful videos but report experiencing no stress. Because they are highly motivated to deny their stress, they simply do not allow themselves to acknowledge it.

Faulty Theories

If individuals have a particularly strong theory about what they should be experiencing in a particular situation, this may color their appraisal of their actual experience. A compelling recent example of this comes from people's reports of their experience of catching a ball. Most people believe that as they watch a ball, their eyes first rise and then go down following the trajectory of the ball. Indeed, this is the case when one watches someone else catch a ball. However, when people catch a ball themselves, they actually maintain the ball at precisely the same visual angle. Nevertheless, when people who just caught a ball are asked what they experienced, they report their theory of what they think should have happened rather than what they actually experienced.

Future Applications

Because researchers have tended to overlook the fact that people can fluctuate in their meta-awareness of experience, there are many unanswered questions about this intriguing aspect of consciousness. The following are just two examples.

Implicit Attitudes

In recent years, considerable attention has been given to implicit attitudes with the assumption that such attitudes are unconscious. The Implicit Association Test, for example, has been applied in countless contexts to reveal attitudes that are assumed to be below the threshold of awareness. However, it is possible that implicit attitude measures may, at least sometimes, reveal attitudes that people experience but are unwilling or unable to acknowledge to themselves. For example, implicit racists may indeed experience some aversion when seeing members of another race, but may simply fail to acknowledge this aversion to themselves.

Individual Differences

Although there are a variety of personality measures that assess the degree to which individuals focus on their internal states, relatively little research has examined whether there are reliable differences in people's ability to accurately gauge their internal states. In recent years, there have been major advances in psychophysiological and behavioral measurements of emotion, thereby making it increasingly possible to assess emotional state without having to rely on self-report measures. This raises the fascinating question of whether some people are more accurate in identifying changes in their emotional responses than others. It seems quite plausible that individuals who show greater coherence between self-reported changes in

affective states and other measures might be particularly effective in affective self-regulation because they are more "in touch" with their feelings.

Jonathan W. Schooler
Jonathan Smallwood

See also Consciousness; Implicit Attitudes; Individual Differences; Mindfulness and Mindlessness; Mind-Wandering; Self-Awareness

Further Readings

Schooler, J. W. (2001). Discovering memories in the light of meta-awareness. *The Journal of Aggression, Maltreatment and Trauma, 4,* 105–136.

Schooler, J. W. (2002). Re-representing consciousness: Dissociations between consciousness and meta-consciousness. *Trends in Cognitive Science, 6,* 339–344.

Schooler, J., & Schreiber, C. A. (2004). Experience, meta-consciousness, and the paradox of introspection. *Journal of Consciousness Studies, 11*(7–8), 17–39.

Schooler, J. W., & Schreiber, C. (2005). To know or not to know: Consciousness, meta-consciousness, and motivation. In J. P. Forgas, K. R. Williams, & W. von Hippel (Eds.), *Social motivation: Conscious and non-conscious processes* (pp. 351–372). New York: Cambridge University Press.

METACOGNITION

Definition

Metacognition means "thinking about cognition," and given that cognition generally refers to the processes of thinking, metacognition means "thinking about thinking." Metacognitive strategies are what people use to manage and understand their own thinking processes. Metacognition refers to *knowledge* about cognitive processes ("I'm bad at names"), *monitoring* of cognitive processes ("I'll remember that equation"), and *control* of cognitive processes ("Using flash cards works for me" or "I'll need to spend at least 2 hours studying this").

Background

People are often in situations in which they are required to evaluate the contents of their memory. When people are approached on a busy street and are asked for directions, how do they know if they know the directions or not? When studying a list of items to be remembered, how do people know how much time they should spend studying each item for memorization? Furthermore, how do people know that they know the name of a movie they once saw, even though they cannot produce the name of the movie? These phenomena fall under the category of metacognition. Metacognition is a broad category of self-knowledge monitoring. Metamemory is a category of metacognition that refers to the act of knowing about what you remember.

Metacognition is generally implicated in the knowledge, monitoring, and controlling of retrieval and inference processes involved in the memory system. Knowledge refers to the evaluation of conscious experience. Monitoring refers to how one evaluates what one already knows (or does not know). Processes involved in metacognitive monitoring include ease of learning judgments, judgments of learning, feeling of knowing judgments, and confidence in retrieved answers. Metacognitive control includes learning strategies such as allocation of study time, termination of study, selection of memory search strategies, and decisions to terminate the search.

Metacognition involves the monitoring and control of what is called the meta-level and the object-level, with information flowing between each level. The meta-level is the conscious awareness of what is or is not in memory, whereas the object-level is the actual item in memory. The meta-level essentially creates a model of the object-level, giving people the sense of awareness of that object's existence in memory. Based on this meta-level model, people can quickly evaluate what they know or think they know so they can decide whether they should spend the effort trying to recall the information. An example of how the meta-level works might be the person being asked directions by a traveler. Before attempting to recall the directions, the person will determine if he or she even knows the directions before he or she begins to try to recall the specific directions. Once the meta-level evaluates the memory state of the object-level and determines that the directions are known, a search for specific details would follow.

Given that metacognition involves the memory system, it will be helpful to briefly review the processes of human memory. Memory proper can be divided into three separate processes: (1) acquisition, (2) retention, and (3) retrieval. Acquisition is how people get information in memory. Acquiring information could be reading a text passage, watching a movie, or talking to someone. The second stage, retention, refers to the maintenance of knowledge so that it is not forgotten or overwritten. The third and final stage is retrieval of the stored information. Retrieval, for example, might be the recall of the information (e.g., giving the traveler the directions) or the recognition of the information (e.g., marking the correct answer on a multiple choice test). Depending on which aspect of the memory stage is involved, different monitoring and control processes are involved.

The Metacognitive System

The metacognitive system consists of two types of monitoring: (1) prospective, occurring before and during acquisition of information, and (2) retrospective, occurring after acquisition of information. Ease of learning and judgments of learning are examples of prospective monitoring.

Ease of learning involves the selection of appropriate strategies to learn the new information and which aspect of the information would be easiest to learn. For example, if the traveler decides that the directions are too difficult to remember, he or she might attempt to write them down, or he or she may ask for directions based on geographical locations rather than street-by-street directions. One way researchers study ease of learning is by having students participating in a memorization study indicate which items on a list would be easier to learn (ease of learning judgments). Participants would then be allowed a specific amount of time to learn the list during acquisition. Following a period when the information is retained in memory, a recall or recognition test would follow. The researcher then compares the ease of learning judgments with the memory performance to determine how well the judgments predicted performance. The findings indicate that ease of learning judgments can be accurate in predicting learning.

Judgments of learning occur during and after the acquisition stage of memory. Participants in a study examining judgments of learning may be asked to study a list of items and then asked to indicate which items they had learned the best. Or participants may be asked to provide judgments of learning after a retention period, just before the memory test is administered. Similar to the ease of learning judgments, judgments of learning are compared with a later memory test to determine how accurate the participants were in their judgments. Research has found that judgments of learning become more accurate after practice trials. It is not known if judgments of learning are based on ease of learning or if they are based on previous recall trials.

Feeling of knowing can be either prospective or retrospective. Feeling of knowing is typically measured as an indication of how well a participant thinks he or she will be able to recognize the correct answer to a question in a subsequent multiple-choice task. Feeling of knowing studies typically use a recall-judgment-recognition task whereby participants are asked general information questions (sometimes trivia questions). If the participant is unable to recall the answer, he or she is then asked to provide a judgment evaluating the likelihood that he or she will be able to recognize the answer when seen in a multiple choice type test. When compared with recognition performance, feelings of knowing judgments are generally greater than chance, but far from perfect predictors of recognition. However, research on feeling of knowing has helped establish that people are able to provide accurate self-reports of their metacognitive states.

Confidence judgments are retrospective because they are taken after the retrieval of an item from memory. For example, after an eyewitness to a crime identifies someone from a lineup, he or she is often asked to provide an evaluation of his or her confidence in the identification either on a scale (e.g., from 1–10) or in terms of a percentage ("I'm 100% sure"). Confidence judgments are varyingly related to the accuracy of recall, depending on the type of information that is being recalled (verbal, spatial, pictorial), how much time the person had to study the information, or the context within which the judgment is being taken, among other factors. In some instances, such as in the eyewitness identification example, the relationship between confidence and accuracy is low, and thus confidence is not necessarily predictive of correct identification performance.

Metacognitive monitoring is studied by having participants provide judgments of their metacognitive state (e.g., "I know that," "I remember that," "I don't know," "I'm not sure"). A more naturally occurring metacognitive state is when a person has difficulty retrieving an item from memory yet has a sense that retrieval is imminent. This is commonly referred to as a tip-of-the-tongue state. In a tip-of-the-tongue state, a person is often able to partially recall bits and pieces of information related to the sought-after item. Researchers have often used partial recall created

while in a tip-of-the-tongue state as a "window" into the memory process because they can examine the types of partial information being recalled in relation to the properties of the memory item actually sought. It is believed that tip-of-the-tongue states are more than a memory curiosity and that they serve as a mechanism to evaluate one's memory state and direct metacognitive control.

Ease of learning, judgments of learning, feeling of knowing, and confidence are ways metacognitive monitoring is examined. These processes are interrelated with metacognitive control. As with monitoring, metacognitive control is different for the different stages of memory. Control during the acquisition of memory can involve the selecting of the different types of processes to use. For example, if the item to be remembered is thought to be easy, very little processing may be allocated to the item. However, if an item is thought to be difficult, more elaborate rehearsal may be allocated. Control over the allocation of the amount of time given to study each item also occurs at the acquisition phase. For example, when studying for an exam, a student may decide to spend more time on a particular item that he or she feels will be eventually learned and little to no time on an item that is thought to be too difficult to learn and thus resulting in a waste of time. This control process is related to ease of learning. Finally, the decision to terminate study is a control process occurring at the acquisition phase. This decision is usually related to judgments of learning.

Metacognitive control over search strategies occurs during the retrieval of memory. These include the selection of search strategies and the termination of search. How elaborate a search does a person conduct for an item in memory? When approached and asked for directions in an unfamiliar part of town, it is not reasonable to exert too much time and energy attempting recall. However, if approached while in a familiar area, more effort may be allocated to a search. This process is related to the feeling of knowing. Tip-of-the-tongue states also influence retrieval strategies. When in a tip-of-the-tongue state, a person may spend so much time and cognitive resources to recall the information he or she becomes preoccupied and at times immobilized.

Otto H. MacLin

See also Controlled Processes; Learning Theory; Memory; Self-Awareness

Further Readings

Leonesio, J., & Nelson, T. (1990). Do different metamemory judgments tap the same underlying aspects of memory? *Journal of Experimental Psychology: Learning, Memory, and Cognition, 16*(3), 464–470.

Metcalfe, J., & Shimamura, A. (1994). *Metacognition: Knowing about knowing.* Cambridge: MIT Press.

Nelson, T. (1992). *Metacognition: Core readings.* Boston: Allyn & Bacon.

Perfect, T., & Schwartz, B. L. (2002). *Applied metacognition.* New York: Cambridge University Press.

Schwartz, B. L. (2001). *Tip-of-the-tongue states: Phenomenology, mechanism, and lexical retrieval.* Mahwah, NJ: Erlbaum.

METATRAITS

Definition

The term *metatraits* refers to differences in the extent to which people possess a given trait. Consider the trait of friendliness. People may differ not only in how friendly they are, but also in how much friendliness is relevant to their personality and guides their behavior. Friendliness may be a central aspect of Jane's personality and influence how she acts in many situations (e.g., with friends, romantic partners, coworkers, family members). However, friendliness may not be very relevant to Sue's personality, and therefore will not predict how friendly she acts around different people. The existence of metatraits means that when people measure a person's standing on a given trait (e.g., Agreeableness), they need to know not only where the person stands on the trait (e.g., how agreeable he or she is), but also how relevant the trait is to his or her personality (e.g., is agreeableness a relevant trait for the individual?).

When someone asks you to describe your personality, you will likely give a description that includes at least some personality traits. When describing other people, people also frequently describe the personality traits they possess. One person you know may be shy, responsible, and determined, whereas another person you know may be open to new experiences, extraverted, and lazy. Most psychologists agree that people's personality can be defined, at least in part, based on their standing on personality traits.

Although psychologists agree that an individual's personality consists of where he or she stands on particular traits, they disagree about whether different traits are more important and relevant to some individuals than others. Researchers who adopt a *nomothetic* approach to personality argue that an individual's personality can be understood by finding out where he or she falls on a relatively small number of traits, and that one does not need to understand how these traits differ in their importance or relevance to the individual. Researchers who adopt an *idiographic* approach to personality argue that some traits are more relevant to some individuals than to others, and that failing to consider differences in how relevant traits are to individuals leads to important information being lost about the individual's personality. The concept of metatraits comes from the idiographic approach to personality.

Measurement

Although it is relatively straightforward to measure a person's standing on a personality trait (e.g., to measure Extraversion, one might ask individuals to rate how outgoing they are, how much they like to be around others), it has proven more difficult to measure how relevant that trait is to the individual. One approach researchers have taken is to see how variable people's responses are to items measuring the same personality trait. Imagine you are completing a 10-item scale assessing your ability to empathize with others. If you respond very differently to items that are all supposedly measuring empathy, then an argument could be made that where you stand on empathy is not as relevant to your personality as to someone who responds in a consistent manner to all the items. Although this approach is reasonable, one problem with the method is that factors other than the relevance of the trait may produce variability in item responses (e.g., poor intelligence, laziness).

Therefore, researchers have recommended additional measures to assess metatraits. Some researchers have measured metatraits by seeing how stable people's responses to a personality trait scale are over three administrations (separated by at least a week). The more stable an individual's scores on the personality trait, the more relevant that trait is to the individual. Other researchers have recommended measuring trait relevance by measuring how fast someone responds to items measuring a trait (the faster the individual responds, the more relevant the trait), or by counting how many times a trait is mentioned when a person describes his or her life story (the more times a trait is mentioned when talking about yourself, the more relevant the trait to your personality).

Evidence of Importance

Understanding metatraits is important because the relevance of a given trait to an individual's personality is expected to determine whether the trait influences the individual's experience and behavior. Early research supported the hypothesis that personality traits would better predict behavior when the trait was more relevant to the individual. However, other researchers failed to replicate this relationship. More recently, researchers have found that the relationship between a person's self-ratings of personality and other people's ratings of the person's personality is stronger for those traits most relevant to his or her personality. This suggests that other people are more accurate at rating a person on traits more relevant to his or her personality. Recent research has shown that personality is a better predictor of objective job performance when the traits being assessed are more relevant to the individual's personality.

Future Research

An exciting area for future research on metatraits is whether some personality traits are more relevant to people in general than others. For example, researchers have argued five primary traits underlay our personality: Extraversion, Openness to Experience, Agreeableness, Conscientiousness, and Neuroticism. These traits may be more relevant to people in general than are traits such as empathy, self-consciousness, and body image. The differences among traits in their relevance to individuals emphasize the importance of developing measures to assess how relevant a given trait is to the population of interest. To take an extreme example, imagine a culture in which personal ambition is de-emphasized and individuals are expected to do what they are told by authorities. In such a culture, the trait of achievement striving would not be relevant to the population, and therefore if members of this culture were to complete a measure of achievement striving, their scores on the measure would be largely meaningless. Understanding the relevance of a trait to different samples will help researchers select participants for whom scores on the trait are most meaningful.

Thomas W. Britt

See also Big Five Personality Traits; Individual Differences; Personality and Social Behavior; Personality Judgments, Accuracy of; Traits

Further Readings

Baumeister, R. F., & Tice, D. M. (1988). Metatraits. *Journal of Personality, 56,* 571–598.

Bem, D. J., & Allen, A. (1974). On predicting some of the people some of the time: The search for cross-situational consistencies in behavior. *Psychological Review, 81,* 506–520.

Britt, T. W., & Shepperd, J. A. (1999). Trait relevance and trait assessment. *Personality and Social Psychology Review, 3,* 108–122.

Dwight, S. A., Wolf, P. P., & Golden, J. H. (2002). Metatraits: Enhancing criterion-related validity through the assessment of traitedness. *Journal of Applied Social Psychology, 32,* 2202–2212.

Paunonen, S. V. (1988). Trait relevance and the differential predictability of behavior. *Journal of Personality, 56,* 599–619.

MILGRAM'S OBEDIENCE TO AUTHORITY STUDIES

Nations and cultures differ among themselves in countless ways, ranging from something as superficial as how people dress, to more serious matters, such as unwritten rules of appropriate social conduct. But one of the universals of social behavior that transcends specific groups is the presence of hierarchical forms of social organization. That is, all civilized societies seem to have people in positions of authority who are recognized as having the power or the right to issue commands that others feel obligated to follow. Most of the time, these authority–follower relationships serve useful functions. For example, children need to listen to parents to teach them right from wrong, that it is dangerous to cross the street when the light turns red, and countless other things. But there is also a potentially darker side to commands from authorities: their ability to lead their followers to act in ways that violate the followers' sense of right or wrong.

The most dramatic and powerful demonstration of this dark side of obedience was provided by a classic series of experiments on obedience to authority conducted by Stanley Milgram as a beginning assistant professor at Yale University in 1961–1962. The work was stimulated by his attempt to shed some light on the Holocaust—the systematic murder of six million Jewish men, women, and children during World War II by the Germans, aided by their allies. For Milgram, obedience seemed a likely explanation to pursue because it was generally known that Germany society placed a high value on unquestioning obedience to authorities. In fact, initially his plan was to repeat his experiment in Germany, after completing his research with American subjects. This plan was scrapped after completing his research at Yale because he found such a high degree of obedience among his American subjects that he saw no need to go to Germany.

Yale was Milgram's first academic position after receiving his Ph.D. in social psychology from Harvard University. Although he was very creative and, later in his career, he conducted many other inventive studies, none surpassed his very first experiments, the obedience studies, in their importance and fame.

Obedience Experiments

The subjects in the obedience experiments were normal adults who had responded to an ad in the *New Haven Register,* recruiting volunteers for a study of memory. When a subject arrived in Milgram's lab, he was met by the experimenter, who explained that his job was to try to teach another subject—the learner—to memorize a list of adjective–noun pairs. During the testing phase, each time the learner made a mistake, the subject-teacher was to punish the learner with an electric shock by pressing one of a row of 30 switches on a very realistic looking "shock generator." Above each switch was a voltage label, beginning with 15 volts and ending with 450 volts. The experimenter told the teacher-subject that the rule was that on each subsequent error he had to give the next, more intense shock. So, on the first mistake, he would press the first switch, which supposedly delivered 15 volts; then the next time the learner erred, the teacher would press the next switch, corresponding to 30 volts, and so on. And he was to continue with the procedure until the learner memorized all the word-pairs.

The learner, seated in an adjacent room, was to receive the shocks via electrodes attached to his wrist. In actuality, the shock box was a fake, well-crafted prop that did not really deliver shocks, and the learner was in cahoots with the experimenter, deliberately making mistakes on specific trials and responding

with a scripted set of increasingly agonizing and pitiful protests. For example, at 120 volts, he yelled, "Ugh! This really hurts," and by 195 volts he was howling, "Let me out of here! My heart's bothering me! . . ." Whenever the subject hesitated, the experimenter commanded him to continue with such prepared prompts as "The experiment requires that you continue." Despite the learner's apparent suffering and the fact that the experimenter—though he projected an aura of technical proficiency—had no punitive means to enforce his commands, more than 60% of the subjects were fully obedient, continuing to "shock" the victim to the 450-volt maximum.

Importance

Did we need Milgram to teach us that people tend to obey authorities? Of course not. What he *did* show that was eye-opening was just how powerful this tendency is—powerful enough to override moral principles. When acting autonomously, people don't generally hurt or harm an innocent individual who did nothing to merit harsh treatment. Yet, when commanded by an authority, most subjects readily did just that.

What is the psychological mechanism that enables an authority's commands to transform a normally humane individual into a pitiless tormentor? According to Milgram, when a person accepts the legitimacy of an authority—that the authority has the right to dictate one's behavior—that acceptance is accompanied by two changes in the person's mental set. First, the person relinquishes responsibility for his or her actions to the authority, and in so doing yields to the authority's judgments about the morality of what the person is requested to do. Second, the person accepts the authority's definition of the situation. So, if the authority sees someone as deserving of punishment, the person will also adopt that viewpoint.

Almost as important to know about the obedience experiments as what they tell us is what they *don't* tell us. It would be a mistake to conclude from Milgram's results that beneath the veneer of civility that people usually exhibit in their social relations they are actually ruthless and vicious, and their pent-up meanness is held in check by the rules and laws of society. That is, Milgram's laboratory merely created the opportunity for his subjects to give expression to their normally repressed sadistic tendencies. In other words, according to this view, Milgram's experiments don't enlighten people about the unexpected power of authorities, but merely expose the force of people's destructive natures that are normally bottled up.

Milgram carried out more than 20 different versions of his obedience experiment, in addition to the one described. One of them clearly demolishes this contrary view. In this experiment, the beginning is very similar to Milgram's other conditions. The teacher-subject "punishes" the learner for each mistake with increasingly intense shocks, while the learner, sitting on the other side of the wall, complains more and more vehemently. This continues to 150 volts, when something unusual happens. The experimenter tells the teacher that they will have to stop because the learner's complaints are unusually strong, and he is concerned about the learner's well-being. Suddenly, a protesting voice is heard from the adjacent room. The learner *insists* that the experiment continue. His friend who had been a previous participant in the experiment told him that he went all the way, and to stop now would be a blot on his own manliness. If bottled-up destructive urges were the underlying cause of the subjects' behavior, they couldn't have asked for a better excuse to vent them. And yet, not *one single* subject continued beyond this point. The experimental authority's command was to stop, and everybody obeyed his commands.

The revelatory power of the obedience experiments goes beyond the vivid demonstration of people's extreme readiness to obey authorities, even destructive ones. Milgram's experiments also serve as powerful sources of support for one of the main lessons of social psychology: To paraphrase Milgram himself, often it is not the kind of person you are but, rather, the kind of situation you find yourself in that will determine how you act.

Among Milgram's series of experiments, a subset of four, the four-part proximity series, speaks directly to this point. In these experiments, Milgram varied the physical and emotional distance between the subject-teacher and the learner. At one end, in the condition of greatest distance, the Remote condition, the teacher and learner are separated by a wall, and there is only minimal complaint from the learner: He bangs on the wall twice during the whole shock sequence. In the second condition—the Voice-Feedback condition—the two are brought closer, at least emotionally. They are still in separate rooms, but now vocal protests are introduced into the procedure. With increasing voltages, the learner's complaints get more urgent and shrill. In the third condition—the Proximity (close

and near) condition—distance is further reduced by seating the learner next to the teacher. Now the teacher not only hears the learner's screams, but also sees him writhing in pain. In the fourth and final condition, the teacher-learner distance is reduced to zero. In this variation, rather than being hooked up to electrodes, the learner gets punished by having to actively place his hand on a shock plate. At 150 volts, he refuses to continue doing that and so the experimenter instructs the teacher to force his hand onto the electrified plate. The results: The amount of obedience gradually declined as teacher–learner distance was reduced. Although in the first condition, the Remote condition, 65% were fully obedient, only 30% continued giving the whole range of shocks in the last one, the Touch-Proximity condition.

Implications

An important long-range consequence of Milgram's research is the regulations that are now in place in the United States and many other countries to safeguard the well-being of the human research subject. The ethical controversy stirred up by the obedience experiments, in which many subjects underwent an unanticipated and highly stressful experience—together with a handful of other ethically questionable experiments—led the U.S. government to enact regulations governing human research in the mid-1970s. The centerpiece of these regulations is the requirement that any institution conducting research with human subjects have an institutional review board (IRB) that screens each research proposal to ensure that participants will not be harmed. Ironically, the IRBs themselves have become a focus of controversy, especially among social psychologists. Most would agree that, in principle, they play an important role. However, many researchers believe that sometimes IRBs are overzealous in carrying out their duties and disapprove experiments that are essentially benign and harmless, thereby stifling research that could potentially result in valuable advances in our knowledge.

Milgram's productive career was a relatively short one. He died of heart failure on December 20, 1984, at age 51. But the legacy of his obedience experiments lives on, serving as continuing reminders of people's extreme willingness to obey authorities. And, having been enlightened about this, people can try to be more vigilant in guarding themselves against unwelcome commands. When ordered to do something that is immoral or just plain wrong, stop and ask yourself, "Is this something I would do on my own initiative?"

Thomas Blass

See also Aggression; Compliance; Deception (Methodological Technique); Influence; Relational Models Theory

Further Readings

Blass, T. (Ed.). (2000). *Obedience to authority: Current perspectives on the Milgram paradigm.* Mahwah, NJ: Erlbaum.

Blass, T. (2004). *The man who shocked the world: The life and legacy of Stanley Milgram.* New York: Basic Books.

Milgram, S. (1963). Behavioral study of obedience. *Journal of Abnormal and Social Psychology, 67,* 371–378.

Milgram, S. (1974). *Obedience to authority: An experimental view.* New York: Harper & Row. (A 30th anniversary edition, with an added preface by Jerome Bruner, was published in 2004 by HarperCollins.)

MIMICRY

Mimicry refers to the unconscious and unintentional imitation of other people's accents, speech patterns, postures, gestures, mannerisms, moods, and emotions. Examples of mimicry include picking up regional accents or expressions when on vacation, or shaking one's leg upon observing another person's leg shaking.

Background

In the 1970s and 1980s, research on mimicry focused on exploring the relationship between behavioral mimicry (i.e., shared motor movements) and rapport between interaction partners. The two were found to be positively correlated. For example, counselors who mimic the postures of their clients are perceived by their clients to be more empathetic, warm, genuine, with more expertise; mothers and babies who share motor movements have more rapport; and classrooms characterized by high teacher–student rapport have more shared movements.

By the 1990s, researchers agreed that mimicry is related to empathy, rapport, and liking. However, because the thrust of the early research was on demonstrating an association between behavioral mimicry

and rapport, rather than on demonstrating experimentally that mimicry does occur and the conditions under which it occurs, several questions remained to be explored. One question concerned the ubiquity of mimicry. Does mimicry occur above chance levels in a social interaction? Another question concerned how the effects are produced. Does mimicry lead to rapport or does rapport lead to mimicry? Moreover, early research paid little attention to the fact that most mimicry occurs without conscious intention or awareness. If people's behaviors passively and unintentionally change to match those of others in their social environments, then what are the minimal conditions needed to produce these chameleon effects? Do people mimic strangers or just friends? Do people need to have an active goal to get along with and be liked by the interaction partner?

Several experiments were conducted in the late 1990s to address these questions. In them, participants took turns with another participant (actually a confederate—part of the research team) describing a series of pictures. When the confederate performed certain behaviors, such as face rubbing or foot shaking, participants unintentionally rubbed their faces more or shook their feet more. In some cases, confederates were intentionally unlikable and mimicry still occurred. Participants were not able to report after the interaction what the confederate's mannerisms were, or that they mimicked those mannerisms. In other experiments, the confederate either mimicked the postures, movements, and mannerisms displayed by the participants or not. Mimicked participants liked the confederate more and perceived their interactions as being smoother. Taken together, these studies suggested that mimicry leads to greater rapport, and it occurs at greater than chance levels, in the absence of any overarching goal to affiliate with an interaction partner, and without awareness or intention.

Why Does Mimicry Occur?

One current explanation for why mimicry occurs is the *perception–behavior link.* Essentially, perceiving someone behave in a certain way activates a representation of that behavior in the mind of the perceiver and makes the perceiver more likely to engage in that behavior too. This happens because the mental representation that is activated when a person perceives a behavior overlaps with the mental representation that is activated when the person engages in that behavior himself or herself, so the activation of one leads to the activation of the other.

Although this explanation suggests that mimicry is a by-product of the way concepts in people's minds are structured, this is not to say that social factors do not influence mimicry. Mimicry has evolved in the context of social interactions and serves an important social function. Recent experimental research has shown that people unconsciously mimic more when they have a goal to affiliate with others. Thus, if they want another person to like them, they start to mimic the other person more. Furthermore, a number of social contexts have been identified that seem to heighten people's desire to affiliate with others and therefore heighten their tendency to unwittingly mimic others' behaviors. For example, people are more likely to mimic peers, someone who has power over their outcomes, or someone who has ostracized them. People also engage in mimicry more if they are feeling too distinct from others.

Research has also shown that personality characteristics make certain people more likely to mimic than others. One such personality characteristic is self-monitoring. People who are motivated and able to monitor their public images and adjust to their social contexts are more likely to mimic their interaction partners when there are affiliation cues in the environment than are people who are less concerned with adjusting to their social environment. Another personality characteristic associated with mimicry is interdependent versus independent self-construal. People who perceive themselves to be part of a collective and strive to assimilate to their group—for example, people from Japan—are more likely to mimic their interaction partners than are people who perceive themselves to be distinct from others and possess individualistic ideals—for example, people from the United States. Finally, perspective taking has been related to mimicry, such that people who tend to put themselves in other people's shoes engage in more mimicry than those who do not.

What Are the Consequences?

What are the consequences of behavioral mimicry? For the person who was mimicked, mimicry makes interaction partners seem more likable and makes interactions seem smoother. Mimicry also renders the mimicked person more helpful toward the mimicker

and more open to persuasion attempts by the mimicker. The effects of mimicry appear to generalize beyond the mimicker, making the person who was mimicked feel closer to others in general and engage in more prosocial behaviors, such as donating money to charities. Mimicry can also have consequences for the mimicker. For example, by imitating the postures, gestures, and facial expressions of another, one's own preferences, attitudes, and emotional experiences are affected. The phenomenon whereby feelings are elicited by patterns of one's facial, postural, and behavioral expressions is called *mood contagion* or *emotional contagion*.

Tanya L. Chartrand
Amy N. Dalton

See also Emotional Contagion; Independent Self-Construals; Interdependent Self-Construals; Nonconscious Processes; Self-Monitoring

Further Readings

Chartrand, T. L., Maddux, W. W., & Lakin, J. L. (2003). Beyond the perception-behavior link: The ubiquitous utility and motivational moderators of nonconscious mimicry. In R. Hassin, J. S. Uleman, & J. A. Bargh (Eds.), *Unintended thought 2: The new unconscious.* New York: Oxford University Press.

Dijksterhuis, A., & Bargh, J. A. (2001). The perception-behavior expressway: Automatic effects of social perception on social behavior. *Advances in Experimental Social Psychology, 33,* 1–40.

MINDFULNESS AND MINDLESSNESS

Definitions

What is mindfulness? Phenomenologically, it is the feeling of involvement or engagement. How do people achieve it? Learning to be mindful does not require meditation. It is the simple process of actively noticing new things. It doesn't matter how smart or relevant the new distinctions are; just that they are novel for the person at the time. By actively drawing novel distinctions, people become situated in the present, sensitive to context and perspective, and they come to understand that although they can follow rules and routines, those rules and routines should guide, not govern, their behavior. It is not difficult to understand the advantages to being in the present. When in the present, people can take advantage of new opportunities and avert the danger not yet arisen. Indeed, everyone thinks they are in the present. When they are mindless, however, they're "not there" to know that they are not in the present.

What is mindlessness? It is not the same thing as ignorance. Mindlessness is an inactive state of mind that is characterized by reliance on distinctions drawn in the past. When people are mindless, they are trapped in a rigid perspective, insensitive to the ways in which meaning changes depending on subtle changes in context. The past dominates, and they behave much like automatons without knowing it, where rules and routines govern rather than guide what they do. Essentially, they freeze their understanding and become oblivious to subtle changes that would have led them to act differently, if only they were aware of the changes. As will become clear, mindlessness is pervasive and costly and operates in all aspects of people's lives. Although people can see it and feel it in other people, they are blind to it in themselves.

Mindlessness comes about in two ways: either through repetition or on a single exposure to information. The first case is the more familiar. Most people have had the experience, for example, of driving and then realizing, only because of the distance they have come, that they made part of the trip on automatic pilot, as mindless behavior is sometimes called. Another example of mindlessness through repetition is when people learn something by practicing it so that it becomes like second nature to them. People try to learn the new skill so well that they don't have to think about it. The problem is that if they've been successful, it won't occur to them to think about it even when it would be to their advantage to do so.

People also become mindless when they hear or read something and accept it without questioning it. Most of what people know about the world or themselves they have mindlessly learned in this way. One example of mindlessness is described in the book *The Power of Mindful Learning*. The author was at a friend's house for dinner, and the table was set with the fork on the right side of the plate. The author felt as though some natural law had been violated: The fork "goes" on the left side! She knew this was ridiculous. Who cares where the fork is placed? Yet it felt wrong to her, even though she could generate many reasons it was better for it to be placed on the right. She thought about how she had learned this. The author didn't memorize information about how to set a table. One day as a child, her mother simply said to her that the fork goes on the left. Forever after, that is where she was destined to put it, no matter what circumstances might suggest doing otherwise. The author became trapped without any awareness that the way she learned the information would stay in place in the future. Whether people become mindless over time or on initial exposure to information, they unwittingly lock themselves into a single understanding of information.

Costs of Mindlessness

With this understanding of the difference between mindlessness and mindfulness, the next step is to understand the costs of being mindless. For those who learned to drive many years ago, they were taught that if they needed to stop the car on a slippery surface, the safest way was to slowly, gently, pump the brake. Today, most new cars have antilock brakes. To stop on a slippery surface now, the safest thing to do is to step on the brake firmly and hold it down. When caught on ice, those who learned to drive years ago will still gently pump the brakes. What was once safe is now dangerous. The context has changed, but their behavior remains the same.

Much of the time people are mindless. Of course, they are unaware when they are in that state of mind because they are "not there" to notice. To notice, they must have been mindful. More than 25 years of research reveals that mindlessness may be very costly to people. In these studies, researchers have found that an increase in mindfulness results in an increase in competence, health and longevity, positive affect, creativity, charisma, and reduced burnout, to name a few of the findings.

Absolutes and Mindlessness

Most of what people learn they learn in an absolute way, without regard to how the information might be different in different contexts. For example, textbooks tell us that horses are herbivorous—that is, they don't eat meat. But although typically this is true, if a horse is hungry enough, or the meat is disguised, or the horse was given very small amounts of meat mixed with its feed growing up, a horse may very well eat meat. When people learn mindlessly, they take the information in as true without asking under what conditions it may not be true. This is the way people learn most things. This is why people are frequently in error but rarely in doubt.

When information is given by an authority, appears irrelevant, or is presented in absolute language, it typically does not occur to people to question it. They accept it and become trapped in the mind-set, oblivious to how it could be otherwise. Authorities are sometimes wrong or overstate their case, and what is irrelevant today may be relevant tomorrow. Virtually all the information people are given is given to them in absolute language. A child, for example, may be told, "A family consists of a mommy, a daddy, and a child." All is fine unless, for example, daddy leaves home. Now it won't feel right to the child when told, "We are still a family." Instead of absolute language, if told that one understanding of a family is a mother, father, and a child, the problem would not arise if the circumstances change. That is, mindful learning is more like learning probable "truths" rather than mindlessly accepting absolutes.

Language too often binds people to a single perspective, with mindlessness as a result. As students of general semantics tell us, the map is not the territory. In one 1987 study, Alison Piper and Ellen Langer introduced people to a novel object in either an absolute or conditional way. The subjects were told that the object "is" or "could be" a dog's chew toy. Piper and Langer then created a need for an eraser. The question Piper and Langer considered was who would think to use the object as an eraser? The answer was only those subjects who were told "it could be a dog's chew toy." The name of something is only one way an object can be understood. If people learn about it as if the "map" and the "territory" are the same thing, creative uses of the information will not occur to them.

Meditation and Mindfulness

One way to break out of these mind-sets is to meditate. Meditation, regardless of the particular form, is engaged to lead to post-meditative mindfulness. Meditation grew up in the East. Whether practicing Zen Buddhism or Transcendental Meditation, typically the individual is to sit still and meditate for 20 minutes twice a day. If done successfully over time, the categories the individual mindlessly accepted start

to break down. The path to mindfulness that Langer and her colleagues have studied may be more relevant to those in the West. The two paths to mindfulness are by no means mutually exclusive. In their work, Langer and colleagues provoke mindfulness by active distinction-drawing. Noticing new things about the target, no matter how small or trivial the distinctions may be, reveals that it looks different from different perspectives. When people learn facts in a conditional way, they are more likely to draw novel distinctions and thus stay attentive to context and perspective.

Most aspects of American culture currently lead people to try to reduce uncertainty: They learn so that they will know what things are. Nevertheless, things are always changing. Even the cells in the human body are constantly changing. When people experience stability, they are confusing the stability of their mind-sets with the underlying phenomenon. Instead, they should consider exploiting the power of uncertainty so that they can learn what things can become. Mindfulness that is characterized by novel distinction-drawing and meditation that results in post-meditative mindfulness will lead people in this direction. When people stay uncertain, they stay in the present and they notice; when they notice, they become mindful.

Ellen Langer

See also Automaticity; Conscious Processes; Learning Theory; Meaning Maintenance Model; Meta-Awareness; Metacognition; Need for Closure

Further Readings

Langer, E. (1997). *The power of mindful learning.* Reading, MA: Addison-Wesley.

Langer, E. (2005). *On becoming an artist: Reinventing yourself through mindful creativity.* New York: Ballantine.

MIND-WANDERING

People's experience of their own thoughts is that thoughts rarely stay still; sometimes people's thinking is constrained by the task they are performing; at other moments, people's minds wander easily from topic to topic. The essential property of mind-wandering is that people's attention to the task fluctuates over time; instead of paying attention to the activity in which they are engaged, they often focus privately on their thoughts and feelings. In this entry, what is known about the situations in which mind-wandering is experienced will be described, along with some of the consequences of these experiences when they occur. Finally, what the future may hold for the study of this remarkable yet ill-understood aspect of people's mental lives will be considered. First, the historical context within which to understand the study of mind-wandering will be considered.

Historical Context

People are often told that humans are social animals, so it is a surprise to consider that often what goes on in the *private* mental lives of people is most interesting to psychologists. Mind-wandering is an interesting psychological phenomenon for just this reason: It is a uniquely human act, it is an essential part of a person's internal world, and it is an experience that all readers of this encyclopedia will immediately recognize. Moreover, mind-wandering occurs in almost all circumstances, throughout the life span, and, in all cultures, suggesting that it is a universal part of the human condition. Despite the clear importance of mind-wandering to humans, psychologists are still relatively ignorant about mind-wandering relative to other aspects of social psychology covered in this encyclopedia.

One reason for the relative ignorance about mind-wandering is because the nature of the experience often falls outside the boundaries of phenomena considered important by mainstream psychology. The assumptions of the work of behaviorists in the 20th century provide a clear example. Behaviorists often assumed that, first, the data of psychology should be based on observable facts rather than on the introspective evidence that had formed the focus of research in the previous century, and, second, that applying principles of learning was essential to understanding psychological phenomena. Mind-wandering is a clear candidate for neither—it is *private* experience and so accessible only through introspection. Moreover, because of its privacy, mind-wandering is an experience that is specifically unrelated to the learning that occurs in the environment.

In the 1960s, it became clear that the models of psychological functions based on the behaviorist account were too simple. The cognitive revolution, which occurred in response to these simple models, emphasized the importance of internal cognitive states in determining human behavior. Despite the pioneering work of Jerome Singer and John Antrobus, who developed reliable techniques for measuring private experience, the mainstream of cognitive psychology remained reluctant to embrace mind-wandering research. Many cognitive psychologists felt that these states were best measured by the use of objective measures such as response times, rather than through verbal reports as is the modus operandi for mind-wandering. In addition, many researchers were put off because of researchers' lack of ability to manipulate—switch on and off mind-wandering—preventing the ability to draw causal conclusions.

Thirty years have passed and psychologists have not fully grasped the study of mind-wandering, and yet, interest in these spontaneous aspects of humans' internal lives is growing. One reason for this increase in interest is technological advances in psychophysiological measurement of the brain. The development of tools that allow psychologists to make detailed measurements of the extent to which attention is focused externally, such as event-related potentials, or can pinpoint the network of brain regions that show activation during mind-wandering, such as functional magnetic resonance imaging, suggest that it may be possible to observe changes consequent on mind-wandering in the waking brain. Objective correlates for mind-wandering would reduce researchers' reliance on verbal reports and so improve the status of mind-wandering as an important psychological phenomenon.

The When and Where of Mind-Wandering

Most psychologists would probably agree that mind-wandering occurs most often in simple tasks with few interruptions. It is common, for example, to notice mind-wandering while reading or driving on an empty freeway. Similarly, people who engage in meditation will—all too clearly—recognize the rapidity with which attention can switch away from their breathing to their thoughts. These instincts are borne out by research. In the 1960s, research demonstrated that mind-wandering showed an inverse linear relationship with the time between events in a task. That is, the more targets in a block of a task, the less likely the participants were to report mind-wandering.

Mind-wandering is also frequent when people don't need to hold something in mind. This was demonstrated in a study in which participants either held a number in mind for a short interval, before saying it out loud, or simply repeated the numbers out loud immediately upon hearing them. Mind-wandering was reported less often when people had to remember the numbers for these very short intervals than if they simply repeated them. The act of holding information in mind involves *working memory,* and so it has been suggested that mind-wandering is suppressed by tasks involving working memory load.

These simple information-processing influences, however, do not do justice to the other main influence on the experience of mind-wandering. A quick review of your last enjoyable visit to the cinema or consideration of the last good book you read clearly indicates that often one's mind wanders least when one is interested, intrigued, or absorbed. One study examined the relation between mind-wandering and interest. Participants read a number of texts, selected on the basis of either interest or difficulty. During reading, participants were less likely to be off task when reading interesting, but not difficult, text. When reading dry expository texts (like a social psychology textbook!), the lack of an absorbing narrative meant that participants had to resort to being vigilant regarding their own lapses to ensure they stayed on task.

Oh, No! Mind-Wandering and the Attentional Lapse

All people have at some time made a very simple mistake that occurred, not because the task they were performing was difficult, but instead because they were not giving sufficient attention to what they were doing. Common examples of these sorts of mistakes include pouring coffee, rather than milk, onto your cornflakes or throwing away the vegetables but keeping the peelings. In the literature, these mistakes are referred to as *action slips* and often occur as a consequence of mind-wandering.

Researchers can study an analog of these thoughts under laboratory conditions. In these studies, individuals perform an extremely simple signal detection task. Participants are presented with long sequences of stimuli (e.g., the numbers 0 through 9 in a random order) and are asked to press a key whenever these items appear on the screen. Participants are also told not to respond to a small selection of the items (e.g., the number 3). In these circumstances, because the

task is so straightforward, the failure to correctly inhibit a response is often the result of failure to pay enough attention to the task, and so often results from mind-wandering. After this mistake, normal individuals, but not head-injured participants, usually indicate that they were aware that they made a mistake. This awareness that attention had lapsed is referred to as the *Oops phenomenon* and indicates that the attentional system is tuned to disrupt experiences like mind-wandering if they lead to failures in one's ability to react appropriately to salient external events.

Although the attentional system is very aware of some mistakes, certain sorts of errors seem to fly under people's radar when they are mind-wandering. It is common during reading, for example, to notice that even though the words have been sounding in your head, for some little time your attention was elsewhere. When people notice that their minds have wandered in this fashion, it is often apparent that this has been occurring for some time because they can often reconstruct the narrative of their thoughts or trace back in the book to the last place they were paying attention.

To demonstrate this phenomenon in the laboratory, researchers asked people to detect periods when the text turned to nonsense. People often missed these sentences and read for an average 17 words before they recognized that the text was not making sense. The researchers also demonstrated that periods when participants were missing gibberish were associated with greater frequencies of mind-wandering than would be gained by random sampling alone. These empirical studies provide evidence that when the mind wanders, a person often continues to read for some time without actually registering the meaning of what is being presented. The lengths of time for which these errors occur suggest that during mind-wandering, participants may become so wrapped up in their internal worlds that they lose awareness that they are doing so. This failure to be aware of one's awareness is a failure of *meta-awareness* (i.e., the awareness of one's own experiences).

What's Next?

The questions facing those who study mind-wandering are some of the most intriguing problems in social psychology today. Once research has successfully identified the neural substrates of the system that is responsible for wandering, this will bring exciting questions. One possibility is that the determination of the neural substrates of mind-wandering will allow psychologists to understand the functional purpose of the system that produces these thoughts. Several authors have suggested that mind-wandering is associated with creativity and insight problem solving, and it is possible that functional magnetic resonance imaging could help elucidate this issue.

The most interesting question that arises from consideration of this topic is why the mind wanders. One possibility is that people mind-wander simply because their cognitive system is only able to maintain awareness of their own experiences intermittently. The common experience of catching one's mind wandering provides strong phenomenal support for the notion that people at times are unaware that they have ceased to pay attention to their task. As such, the frequency of mind-wandering could indicate the extent to which people are unaware of their own experiences. A second suggestion is that mind-wandering simply reflects people's inability to control their own cognitive processes. The simple fact that people often experience these thoughts even though they are attempting to concentrate on a task suggests that mind-wandering may occasionally occur without their tacit consent. In fact, a body of research, *ironic processes theory,* demonstrates that attempts at cognitive control often create conditions when the intentional control of experience is undermined. Finally, it is possible that mind-wandering occurs because pertinent personal goals can become automatically activated in people's awareness.

Jonathan Smallwood
Jonathan W. Schooler

See also Attention; Ironic Processes; Memory; Meta-Awareness

Further Readings

Robertson, I. H., Manly, T., Andrade, J., Baddeley, B. T., & Yiend, J. (1997). Oops: Performance correlates of everyday attentional failures in traumatic brain injured and normal subjects. *Neurospsychologia, 35*(6), 747–758.

Singer, J. L. (1966). *Daydreaming.* New York: Random House.

Smallwood, J., & Schooler, J. W. (2006). The restless mind. *Psychological Bulletin, 132*(6), 946–958.

Wegner, D. M. (1997). Why the mind wanders. In J. D. Cohen & J. W. Schooler (Eds.), *Scientific approaches to consciousness* (pp. 295–315). Mahwah, NJ: Erlbaum.

MINIMAL GROUP PARADIGM

Definition

The minimal group paradigm is a procedure that researchers use to create new social groups in the laboratory. The goal is to categorize individuals into groups based on minimal criteria that are relatively trivial or arbitrary. For example, the classic procedure involves asking participants to rate paintings made by two artists with similar abstract styles. Participants are then told that they are members of a group that prefers one of the painters to the other. This is their new ingroup, and the people who prefer the other painter represent a new outgroup. In reality, participants are assigned randomly to one of the two groups. In addition, the members of each group remain anonymous and group members have no interaction or contact with one another. Thus, the minimal group paradigm creates a situation in which individuals are separated into novel ingroups and outgroups, and these individuals have no previous experience with these groups.

Purpose

The minimal group paradigm was first used in the 1960s to examine whether social prejudice and discriminatory behavior result from the mere categorization of people into ingroups and outgroups. Previously, researchers had studied prejudice and discrimination involving preexisting groups with long histories (for example, based on race, ethnicity, or nationality). It largely was believed that these groups perceive real conflict with one another (for example, over resources) and that this conflict leads to beliefs and behavior that favor the ingroup over the outgroup. A European psychologist, Henri Tajfel, wondered whether the experience of conflict was actually necessary to produce ingroup-favoring biases. Perhaps prejudice and discrimination are more fundamental and basic to the human condition. Tajfel and his colleagues demonstrated that participants assigned to groups using the minimal group paradigm behaved in ways that favored their new ingroup and disadvantaged the outgroup. Thus, conflict between groups does not appear to be necessary to produce ingroup favoritism (although conflict is still very important to intergroup relations).

Ingroup Favoritism and Outgroup Derogation

The minimal group paradigm has since been used by researchers hundreds of times. Merely categorizing people into new groups affects a wide variety of perceptions, evaluations, and behaviors that reveal the degree to which people favor new ingroups over new outgroups. For example, group members evaluate new ingroups more positively on personality and other trait ratings (such as "likeable" and "cooperative"), and they evaluate products and decisions made by new ingroups more positively (even when they personally didn't contribute to these products or decisions). Group members also allocate more resources (including money) to members of new ingroups. There is some controversy about the degree to which group members respond in a positive way toward the ingroup (ingroup favoritism) versus a negative way toward the outgroup (outgroup derogation). On the whole, however, it appears that ingroup favoritism is more prevalent than is outgroup derogation in the minimal group paradigm.

The tendency to express ingroup favoritism is very robust and persists even when changes are made to the minimal group paradigm. For example, researchers have changed the basis on which participants believe they are assigned into groups. In the original procedure, participants were led to believe that they shared a preference for a particular artist with their fellow ingroup members. Perhaps this perceived similarity drives ingroup favoritism. However, even when group assignment is completely random (e.g., based on a coin flip), people continue to favor the ingroup over the outgroup in many ways. Researchers also have examined how status differences between the new ingroup and outgroup affect ingroup favoritism. For example, participants have been told that either a majority or a minority of people are classified into their new ingroup. Regardless, participants continue to express ingroup favoritism. Participants also have been told that their new ingroup performed either better or worse on an intelligence test than the outgroup.

Surprisingly, participants who were told that their group performed worse than the outgroup still evaluated the ingroup more positively than the outgroup.

Theoretical Explanations

Social psychologists have suggested several reasons why group members display ingroup favoritism in the minimal group paradigm. Tajfel and his colleagues provided an explanation focusing on social categorization and social identity. Social categorization refers to the way in which people are classified into social groups. Just as people automatically perceive nonsocial objects as belonging to different categories (for example, shoes versus mittens), they also tend to categorize people into different groups. Social categorization is useful because it provides order and meaning to the social environment. For example, it is useful to be able to distinguish police officers from pharmacists. In different situations, different bases for categorizing people become relevant. For example, categorization may be based on gender or sexual orientation when people discuss romantic relationships, whereas it may be based on nationality or religious affiliation when people discuss international terrorism. In addition to classifying others into groups, social categorization also typically results in the classification of the self into a particular group. For example, a man may think of himself primarily as being male in some situations, whereas in other situations, he may think of himself primarily as being an American. Social identity refers to the aspects of the self-image that derive from these group memberships. When a particular group membership is used as the basis for social categorization, the corresponding social identity is based on that group membership. Thus, if a man is thinking about himself as an American (perhaps because he is speaking with a Japanese business associate about differences between the two countries), then his American identity is at the forefront. Importantly, according to Tajfel, social identity can be more or less positive in different contexts, and this has implications for self-esteem. Having positive self-regard (high self-esteem) is a basic human motive. So, people often engage in mental gymnastics (so to speak) to maintain or enhance their self-esteem.

How does all of this help explain ingroup favoritism in the minimal group paradigm? According to Tajfel, the link between social identity and self-esteem creates pressure to evaluate ingroups positively in comparison with outgroups. This is called positive differentiation.

In the minimal group paradigm, the only relevant basis for social categorization is the novel ingroup and outgroup that the participants have just learned about. Thus, participants' social identities and self-esteem are linked to these new groups. Because their self-esteem is on the line, they express favoritism toward the new ingroup (in whatever manner the research context provides) to positively distinguish the new ingroup from the new outgroup. So, participants evaluate the ingroup more positively, rate the ingroup's products and decisions as being superior, and give more resources to the ingroup all as ways to maintain a positive social identity and protect or enhance their sense of self-esteem.

Other researchers have suggested other explanations for ingroup favoritism in the minimal group paradigm. For example, it may be that assigning participants into groups affects their expectancies about the proper way to behave in that context. That is, people may have learned that interactions between groups are typically competitive, and thus they act competitively whenever they are in an intergroup context. Alternatively, people may evaluate the ingroup more positively and give them more resources because they expect their ingroup members to do the same for them. This is known as reciprocity. Another explanation is that learning about new social groups creates uncertainty and ambiguity. Generally speaking, people are uncomfortable in situations in which they are uncertain or unfamiliar. Designating the ingroup as being superior to the outgroup may restore some degree of certainty and order to the social environment that is created by the minimal group paradigm. Finally, several researchers have suggested that when people learn about new social groups to which they belong, they automatically assume that the new ingroup will be similar to themselves. Given that most people perceive themselves positively, the default expectation is that new ingroups are also positive.

Broader Implications

In terms of societal implications, the robust tendency to express ingroup favoritism has two sides. On one hand, the basic tendency appears to be one in which people favor the ingroup rather than derogate the outgroup. This positive orientation toward the ingroup is likely beneficial when interacting with fellow ingroup members. On the other hand, ingroup favoritism sets the stage for negative intergroup relations.

Richard H. Gramzow

See also Ingroup–Outgroup Bias; Self-Categorization Theory; Social Categorization; Social Identity Theory

Further Readings

Aberson, C. L., Healy, M., & Romero, V. (2000). Ingroup bias and self-esteem: A meta-analysis. *Personality and Social Psychology Review, 4,* 157–173.

Brewer, M. B. (1979). In-group bias in the minimal intergroup situation: A cognitive-motivational analysis. *Psychological Bulletin, 86,* 307–324.

Gramzow, R. H., & Gaertner, L. (2005). Self-esteem and favoritism toward novel in-groups: The self as an evaluative base. *Journal of Personality and Social Psychology, 88,* 801–815.

Tajfel, H., & Turner, J. C. (1986). The social identity theory of intergroup behavior. In S. Worchel & W. G. Austin (Eds.), *Psychology of intergroup relations* (2nd ed., pp. 7–24). Chicago: Nelson-Hall.

MINORITY SOCIAL INFLUENCE

Definition

Many tasks and decisions are completed by groups of people instead of by a single person. One challenge of group tasks and decisions is that members of groups are not always in agreement with each other; some members of the group might hold that one view or behavior is preferable, whereas other group members might hold that an opposing view or behavior is preferable. For example, work groups may disagree on business plans, medical teams may disagree on patient diagnoses, and trial juries may disagree on a defendant's guilt or innocence.

In many situations in which group members disagree, opposing views are not equally represented in the group. For example, 4 jurors in a 12-person jury may believe the defendant to be not guilty, whereas the remaining 8 believe the defendant to be guilty. One view is expressed by a numerical minority (e.g., 4 jurors who claim not guilty) and an opposing view is expressed by a numerical majority (e.g., 8 jurors who claim guilty). Although subgroups may differ in aspects such as power, status, or individual characteristics, the terms *majority* and *minority* refer to the number of people who support each view. Both the majority and minority groups may strive to change the opposing views of the other group members.

Minority social influence refers to the minority group's influence on the majority group members' views or behavior. Although minority and majority members may share the goal of influencing group members who hold opposing views, they differ in their underlying motivations, the strategies to achieve influence, and the outcomes of those strategies.

Motivations for Minority Influence

Although a majority is typically thought of as more influential than a minority, minority group members may be particularly motivated to influence the group's views and behaviors in certain situations, such as when minority members are highly invested in the outcome of the group task or decision. This is especially likely if the outcome of the task or decision has direct implications for the minority group members. For example, a work group may decide that an effective way to save money is to eliminate departments. The minority members of the work group who would lose their jobs as a result of this decision have a strong interest in lobbying for an alternative plan that would not eliminate their departments.

Sometimes members of the minority may be motivated to influence majority members because the minority members have more knowledge or expertise than the majority members do. For example, the minority of a medical team might include the most experienced doctors of the group. If the team of doctors is in disagreement about a diagnosis, the experts in the minority may be especially motivated to guide the decision that the group makes. The minority of experts may attempt to convince the majority members to trust the minority's knowledge and expertise.

Personal characteristics of the members of minority groups also might encourage them to influence the outcome of a group task or decision. For example, minority members who are very outgoing or have high self-esteem are more likely to speak up if they disagree with the majority. Some minority members may feel threatened because the majority outnumbers them. This feeling of threat might encourage minority members to increase their number of supporters to be equal to or exceed the majority in size. Also, minority group members may feel a personal responsibility to defend their views if their views are very strong or very important to them. Although it is often easier to side with the majority to bring the group to an agreement, the minority might be motivated to take a stand

and attempt to influence the majority view or behavior for many reasons.

Strategies for Minority Influence

The strategies that minority groups use to influence the majority group are fundamentally different from the strategies majority groups use to influence the minority group. In general, majority group members seek to maintain the status quo, or current majority view and behavior within the group, whereas minority members seek to change the status quo. Stated another way, minority group members work to change the way the group generally believes or acts. In contrast, majority group members tend to play a more defensive role to keep the group view and behavior the way it is. To preserve the status quo, majority members focus on inducing *compliance* in group members to influence them to publicly endorse the majority position, regardless of their private beliefs. Minority members, on the other hand, try to induce *conversion* in group members to change what group members privately believe. Ultimately, minority members hope that the changed private belief will lead to a change in public behavior (e.g., voting) that coincides with the private belief.

To induce conversion, minority members must engage the attention of majority members. Next, minority members should coherently express their alternative view and provide a strong rationale for it. The goal is to cast doubt or uncertainty on the majority view and present the minority's view as the best alternative. After the initial presentation of their position, members of the minority must be consistent in their support for their position over time. In this way, the minority demonstrates that the alternative position is credible and that the minority is committed to the view. Finally, minority members should emphasize that the only way to restore stability and agreement in the group is by majority members changing their views.

Although these general strategies increase the chances that the minority will successfully influence the majority to adopt its position, they might not be effective in all situations. For instance, a particularly powerful majority group might be extremely resistant to the minority view no matter how strong the minority case might be. However, the minority may still influence the majority through indirect routes. For instance, minority members may continuously remind the majority of the importance or implications of the group's task or decision, which may encourage members of the majority to think more critically about their views or delay a final decision until they seek more information. If majority members are willing to collect more information, they may be more willing to consider the details of the minority's viewpoint.

Another important factor in minority social influence is the relationship between the minority and majority in the group at the time that a disagreement occurs. If the members of the minority have established relationships or shared experiences with members of the majority, then attempts at minority influence may be more successful. For example, the minority members might have agreed with majority members in previous tasks or decisions. As a result, majority members might be more welcoming of an opposing view from minority members who have established a positive relationship with the majority in the past.

Outcomes of Minority Influence

In general, minority social influence may differ from majority influence in both the degree and kind of outcomes of their strategies. The social influence that is elicited by a minority group is usually more private and indirect than is influence by a majority group. In addition, the effects of minority influence may not appear immediately. However, minority influence may change majority group members' private beliefs, which can lead to changes in outward behavior later.

Minority social influence also may alter the group's general view on issues that are indirectly related to the task or decision at hand. Minority influence may stimulate divergent thinking among majority members, thus encouraging the majority to consider multiple perspectives on an issue. This increased flexibility in majority members' thinking may lead to changes in some different but related views. For example, a majority group that opposes abortion rights may face a minority that supports abortion rights. Although the majority may refuse to change its view on abortion, it may be willing to consider changing views on related issues such as contraception use. Even if divergent thinking does not change the view that the majority holds on the disagreement at hand (e.g., abortion), flexible thinking may be the first step toward change in the future.

Alecia M. Santuzzi
Jason T. Reed

See also Dual Process Theories; Group Decision Making; Influence; Social Impact Theory

Further Readings

De Drue, C. K. W., & De Vries, N. K. (2001). *Group consensus and minority influence: Implications for innovation.* Oxford, UK: Blackwell.

Nemeth, C. J., & Goncalo, J. A. (2005). Influence and persuasion in small groups. In T. C. Brock & M. C. Green (Eds.), *Persuasion: Psychological insights and perspectives* (2nd ed., pp. 171–194). Thousand Oaks, CA: Sage.

White, E., & Davis, J. H. (Eds.). (1996). *Understanding group behavior: Consensual action by small groups.* Mahwah, NJ: Erlbaum.

MISATTRIBUTION OF AROUSAL

Definition

Misattribution of arousal refers to the idea that physiological arousal can be perceived to stem from a source that is not actually the cause of the arousal, which may have implications for the emotions one experiences. For example, if a professor was unknowingly served a caffeinated latte at her coffee shop one morning instead of the decaf she ordered, and then during her midmorning lecture noticed her heart racing and her hands visibly shaking, she may assess the situation and determine the class full of staring students to be the cause of her arousal (rather than the caffeine buzz actually responsible for the symptoms). Consequently, the professor may feel unusually nervous during her lecture.

Background

The concept of misattribution of arousal is based on Stanley Schachter's two-factor theory of emotion. Although most people probably think they just spontaneously know how they feel, experiencing an emotion is a little more complicated according to the two-factor theory. The theory suggests that two components are necessary to experience an emotion: physiological arousal and a label for it. Schachter suggested that physiological states are ambiguous, so one looks to the situation to figure out how one feels. So if your heart is pounding and you have just swerved out of the way of an oncoming car, you will attribute the pounding heart to the accident you almost had, and therefore will label your emotion "fear." But if your near collision is with a classmate upon whom you have recently developed a crush, you would probably interpret your pounding heart quite differently. You may think, "This must be love that I am feeling." Based on the two-factor theory, emotional experience is malleable because the emotion experienced depends partly on one's interpretation of the events that caused the physiological arousal.

Classic Research

Schachter and his colleague Jerome Singer tested the misattribution of arousal hypothesis in a classic experiment conducted in 1962. They told participants that they were testing the effects of a vitamin on people's vision. In reality, however, some participants were injected with epinephrine (a drug that causes arousal, such as increased heart rate and shakiness). Of these participants, some were warned that the drug causes arousal and others were not. Schachter and Singer predicted that participants who were not informed of the drug's effects would look to the situation to try to figure out what they were feeling. Therefore, participants unknowingly given the arousal-causing drug were expected to display emotions more consistent with situational cues compared with participants not given the drug and participants accurately informed about the drug's effects. The results of the experiment supported this hypothesis. Compared with participants in the other two conditions, participants who had received the drug with no information about its effects were more likely to report feeling angry when they were left waiting in a room with a confederate (a person who appeared to be another participant but was actually part of the experiment) who acted angry about the questionnaire that he and the real participant had been asked to complete. Likewise, when the confederate acted euphoric, participants in this condition were also more likely to feel happy. With no information about the actual source of their arousal, these participants looked to the context (their fellow participants) to acquire information about what they were actually feeling. In contrast, participants told about the drug's effects had an accurate explanation for their arousal and therefore did not misattribute it, and participants

not given the drug did not have any arousal to attribute at all. These findings parallel the example of the professor who did not know that caffeine was responsible for her jitters and therefore felt nervous instead of buzzed. In each case, attributing one's arousal to an erroneous source altered one's emotional experience.

In a classic experiment conducted by Donald Dutton and Arthur Aron in 1974, the misattribution of arousal effect was shown to even affect feelings of attraction. In this experiment, an attractive female experimenter approached men as they crossed either a high, rickety suspension bridge or a low, safe bridge at a popular tourist site in Vancouver, Canada. Whenever an unaccompanied male began to walk across either bridge, he was approached by a female researcher who asked him to complete a questionnaire. Upon completion, the researcher wrote her phone number on a corner of the page and said that he should feel free to call her if he wanted information about the study results. The researchers found that more men called the woman after crossing the rickety bridge compared with the stable bridge. The explanation for this finding is that men in this condition were presumably breathing a bit more rapidly and had their hearts beating a bit faster than usual as a result of crossing the scary bridge, and when these effects occurred in the presence of an attractive woman, they misattributed this arousal to feelings of attraction.

Implications

The misattribution paradigm has been used as a tool by social psychologists to assess whether arousal accompanies psychological phenomena (e.g., cognitive dissonance). For students of social psychology, the message is that, consistent with many findings in social psychology, aspects of the situation can have a profound influence on individuals—in this case, on the emotions an individual experiences. Consequently, you may want to take your date to a scary movie and hope that your date will interpret his or her sweaty palms as attraction to you, but be careful, because in this context, arousal caused by actual feelings of attraction may also be attributed to fear in response to the scary film.

Jamie L. Goldenberg

See also Arousal; Emotion; Excitation-Transfer Theory

Further Readings

Sinclair, R. C., Hoffman, C., Mark, M. M., Martin, L. L., &
Pickering, T. L. (1994). Construct accessibility and the
misattribution of arousal: Schachter and Singer revisited.
Psychological Science, 5, 15–19.

Zanna, M. P., & Cooper, J. (1974). Dissonance and the pill:
An attribution approach to studying the arousal properties
of dissonance. *Journal of Personality and Social
Psychology, 29,* 703–709.

Zillmann, D. (1983). Transfer of excitation in emotional
behavior. In J. T. Cacioppo & R. E. Petty (Eds.), *Social
psychophysiology: A sourcebook.* New York: Guilford Press.

Modeling of Behavior

Definition

Modeling is one way in which behavior is learned.
When a person observes the behavior of another and
then imitates that behavior, he or she is modeling the
behavior. This is sometimes known as observational
learning or social learning. Modeling is a kind of vicarious learning in which direct instruction need not
occur. Indeed, one may not be aware that another is
modeling his or her behavior. Modeling may teach a
new behavior, influence the frequency of a previously
learned behavior, or increase the frequency of a similar behavior.

Components of Modeling

Four steps are involved in the modeling of behavior.
The first is *attention.* Before a behavior can be replicated, one must pay attention to the behavior. The next
step is *retention.* One must be able to remember or
retain the observed behavior. The third stage is *reproduction.* One must be able to translate the images
of another's behavior into his or her own behavior. In
short, one must have the ability to reproduce the
behavior. The final stage is *motivation.* In the end, one
must be motivated to imitate the behavior. Until there
is a reason, one will not model the behavior.

Behaviors Influenced by Modeling

Many categories of behaviors are known to be influenced by modeling. One such category of behavior
is helping. For example, studies have indicated that

children exposed to prosocial models were more helpful than were children who lacked exposure to such
models. Modeling also influences aggression. Children
exposed to a model playing aggressively mimicked the
same aggressive play later, whereas peers unexposed
to the aggressive model did not play as aggressively.
Research has also found that when children observed
an aggressive behavior that produced positive outcomes
for the model, they behaved more aggressively. It seems
that having seen a positive outcome for an aggressive
model increased aggressive behavior in the observer. In
addition, modeling influences gender-role behavior.
Children learn gender-appropriate behaviors and preferences by imitating same sex models.

Effective Models

Many factors contribute to the effectiveness of a
model. Ordinarily, the more attractive or desirable the
model is to the observer, the more likely that model
will be imitated. The desirability or attractiveness of
the model is partially influenced by the prestige the
model has to the observer. This explains why parents
and teachers often serve as models for behavior. The
effectiveness of the model is also to a degree influenced by similarity. The more similar the model is to
the observer, the more effective the model will be.
This explains why peers provide such strong models
for behavior. Furthermore, effective models do not
have to be human or live. Puppets and cartoons, as
well as television and movie characters, often serve as
effective models for behavior.

Natalie Ciarocco

See also Aggression; Bobo Doll Studies; Helping Behavior;
Influence; Social Learning

Further Readings

Bandura, A. (1977). *Social learning theory.* Englewood
Cliffs, NJ: Prentice Hall.

Bandura, A. (1989). Social cognitive theory. In R. Vasta (Ed.),
Annals of child development (Vol. 6, pp. 1–60). Greenwich,
CT: JAI Press.

Bandura, A., Ross, R., & Ross, S. (1961). Transmission of
aggression through imitation of aggressive models.
Journal of Abnormal and Social Psychology, 63, 575–582.

Sprafkin, J. N., Liebert, R. M., & Poulos, R. W. (1975). Effects
of prosocial televised example on children's helping. *Journal
of Experimental Child Psychology, 20,* 119–126.

MODE MODEL

Sometimes people's attitudes predict their behavior and sometimes they don't. Most people have a positive attitude toward donating money to charity, but they don't tend to give their hard-earned cash away whenever a charitable organization requests it. Similarly, many White individuals harbor a negative prejudice toward Blacks, but they often treat many Black individuals they meet with kindness and respect. Why do people's behaviors seem to naturally flow from their attitudes on some occasions but not on others? The MODE model (*motivation* and *opportunity* as *de*terminants of the attitude–behavior relationship) addresses this question.

Key Concepts

Before describing the model, it is important to clarify some concepts. *Attitude* means any positive or negative association that one has with a given object, which can be anything—a person, political issue, food, and so on. According to the MODE model, one's attitude toward an object, say, one's mother, is an association in memory between the attitude object (mother), and one's evaluation of it (positive or negative). Thus, for many objects in one's memory, there is an evaluation directly linked to it. Importantly, the strength of this association can vary. For some attitude objects, there is a very weak link between the object and its evaluation. This would be the case for someone who, for example, has weak attitudes toward various brands of dish detergent. On the other hand, sometimes the link in memory between an object and its evaluation is very strong, as when someone has a strong positive attitude toward his or her mother. Sometimes the link between an object and its evaluation is so strong that merely seeing the object automatically activates the attitude. If seeing a picture of your mother immediately produces warm, positive feelings, then your attitude toward your mother is automatically activated.

Direct Influences of Attitudes on Behavior

The MODE model argues that attitudes, particularly strong attitudes, are functional—they steer people toward positive things and away from negative things. The MODE model argues that strong attitudes—those

that are automatically activated—are more likely to guide behavior. Thus, one way that attitudes and behavior can relate is in a relatively direct fashion. For example, your attitude toward your mother might be automatically activated when you see a picture of her, which then prompts you to pick up the phone and call her. Similarly, if you have a strong attitude toward chocolate, the mere sight of a piece of chocolate might immediately prompt you to pick it up and eat it. In both of these cases, attitude-relevant behavior flows directly from your strong attitude. This direct, attitude-to-behavior route is one of the two ways that the MODE model argues attitudes relate to behavior.

As suggested in the opening paragraph, however, sometimes people's attitudes—even strong ones—don't directly guide their behavior. You might, for example, decide to wait until later to call your mother, and you might remind yourself that you're trying to eat more healthfully and resist devouring that chocolate. The MODE model also describes the conditions under which strong, automatically activated attitudes do not guide behavior. As the MODE acronym implies, two factors—motivation and opportunity—must be present to break the direct attitude-to-behavior link. Each factor will be explained.

Motivation and Opportunity

The term *motivation* is used in a very broad sense within the MODE model, but it refers to any effortful desire one might have to behave in a certain way or reach a certain conclusion. In the example mentioned earlier, you might desire to eat better, which might lead you to overcome your strong positive attitude toward chocolate and avoid eating it. Similarly, you might be motivated to assert your independence from your parents, which might lead you to avoid calling your mother at the mere sight of her picture.

Despite any motivation you might have, however, the opportunity factor must also be present for your behavior not to be determined by your attitude. Opportunity means the time, energy, and ability to overcome the influence of your attitudes. For example, you might be motivated to eat better, but if you don't have the willpower to resist temptation, you might eat the chocolate anyway. Interestingly, there are cases when one lacks the ability to inhibit the influence of one's attitudes on behavior—particularly nonverbal behavior. You might, for example, have a negative attitude toward your boss, yet you are also probably motivated to be nice to him or her. Despite your efforts to be nice to your boss, you might be unable to contain that subtle sneer when you see him or her. In other words, your motivation to be nice is ineffective at curbing the influence of your attitudes because of a lack of ability. Thus, before any motivation can be effective at overcoming the influence of your attitude, the opportunity factor must also be present.

Evidence

A large body of research supports the basic tenets of the MODE model. In one experiment, participants were asked to decide between two department stores in which to buy a camera. One store was excellent overall, except for the camera department. The other store had a good camera department, but was poor overall. Participants' store choice indicated whether they used their attitude toward the stores to guide their decision (if they chose the first) or whether they moved beyond their attitudes and focused on the specific attributes of the stores (if they chose the second). Some participants in this study were also told that they would have to justify their answers to others later, and others were not (a manipulation of motivation). Also, some participants had to reach a decision quickly, and others had unlimited time to decide (a manipulation of opportunity). Consistent with the MODE model, only participants in the high motivation, high opportunity condition chose the department store with the better camera department. People relied on their global attitudes toward the stores to guide their behavior unless both motivation and opportunity were present.

The MODE model has also been applied to the study of racial prejudice. In one experiment, White participants' automatically activated attitudes toward Blacks were assessed using a unique measure that taps people's strong attitudes without having to ask them. In an earlier session, participants also completed a measure of their motivation to control prejudiced reactions toward Blacks, which asked participants to indicate their agreement with items like, "I get angry with myself when I have a thought or feeling that might be considered prejudiced." In a final session, participants were shown pictures of people of various races (e.g., Black, White, Asian) depicted in various occupational roles (e.g., doctor, business person, brick layer), and were asked to make first impressions of them. They had unlimited time to make their ratings, so the opportunity factor was high for all participants. The question this study addressed was whether people's impressions of Black and Whites would be guided directly by their automatically activated racial attitudes, or whether motivation to control prejudice might be used to try to "correct" for their prejudices. The results were consistent with the MODE model: Participants who were not motivated to avoid racial prejudice used their racial attitudes to make their impressions of the people. For those with negative attitudes toward Blacks, their impressions of the Blacks relative to the Whites were negative, and for those with positive attitudes toward Blacks, their impressions of the Blacks relative to the Whites were more positive. However, motivated participants tried to correct for their racial biases. Interestingly, they even appeared to overcorrect. Motivated participants with negative attitudes toward Blacks reported more positive impressions of Blacks relative to Whites. These individuals might have been motivated by a fear of being accused of prejudice. Motivated participants with positive attitudes toward Blacks reported more negative impressions of Blacks relative to Whites. These individuals might have been motivated by a fear of being accused of showing preferential treatment to Blacks.

The MODE model provides a means of conceptualizing situations, such as racial prejudice, where people "can't help" but feel a particular way—that is, when they disagree with their own attitudes. Sometimes people's attitudes influence their behavior directly, through an automatic process. However, as the MODE model states, when both motivation and opportunity are present, people can behave differently than their attitudes would imply.

Michael A. Olson

See also Attitude–Behavior Consistency; Attitudes; Attitude Strength

Further Readings

Fazio, R. H. (1990). Multiple processes by which attitudes guide behavior: The MODE model as an integrative framework. In M. P. Zanna (Ed.), *Advances in experimental social psychology* (Vol. 23, pp. 75–109). New York: Academic Press.

Fazio, R. H., & Olson, M. A. (2003). Attitude structure and function. In M. A. Hogg & J. Cooper (Eds.), *Sage handbook of social psychology* (pp. 139–160). London: Sage.

Olson, M. A., & Fazio, R. H. (2004). Trait inferences as a function of automatically-activated racial attitudes and motivation to control prejudiced reactions. *Basic and Applied Social Psychology, 26,* 1–12.

Sanbonmatsu, D. M., & Fazio, R. H. (1990). The role of attitudes in memory-based decision making. *Journal of Personality and Social Psychology, 59,* 614–622.

MODERN RACISM

See SYMBOLIC RACISM

MORAL COGNITIONS

See MORAL REASONING

MORAL DEVELOPMENT

Definition

Moral development refers to age-related changes in the thoughts and emotions that guide individuals' ideas of right and wrong and how they and others should act. In addressing this broad concept, theorists and researchers have focused on the moral cognitions, feelings, and behaviors that tend to evolve from early childhood to adulthood.

Moral Cognitions

Some researchers have emphasized the cognitive component of morality by studying the development of moral reasoning. Based on his observations of and interviews with 4- to 12-year-old children, Jean Piaget proposed a two-stage model of moral development. In the first stage, young children view rules as rigid, unchangeable, and handed down by authorities. By the second stage, older children have become aware that rules and laws are established and maintained through mutual consent, and as a result, they view rules and laws as flexible and changeable rather than as absolute.

Lawrence Kohlberg revised and extended Piaget's model after extensively interviewing people of different ages about various moral dilemmas (for example, whether a man should steal from a pharmacist an extremely expensive drug that may save his wife's life). The model that Kohlberg proposed describes individuals' moral reasoning as progressing through an age-related sequence of three levels, each composed of two distinct stages. In general, Kohlberg's model describes the basis of individuals' moral judgments as evolving from externally imposed rules and laws to internally determined standards and principles.

There have been numerous criticisms of Kohlberg's conclusions concerning the development of moral judgment. For example, Carol Gilligan argued that Kohlberg's view of moral reasoning emphasizes issues of justice, law, and autonomy, which are associated with a traditionally male perspective of morality, and ignores issues such as a concern for the welfare of others and the preservation of interpersonal relationships, which are associated with a traditionally female perspective of morality. Other critics of Kohlberg's theory and research on moral judgment caution that how a person thinks about morally relevant situations may provide little insight into how that person will act in such situations.

Moral Feelings

Some individuals interested in moral development have focused on various emotions (such as guilt, shame, empathy, and sympathy) that are associated with the enactment of morally acceptable behaviors and the avoidance of morally unacceptable behaviors. For example, Sigmund Freud proposed that, through the process of identifying with the same-sex parent, children take on their parent's moral standards and experience feelings of guilt when engaging in (or anticipate engaging in) behaviors that violate those standards.

A more positive emotion than guilt that has been found to be very important in moral development is empathy. Empathy is said to occur when a person responds to another's feeling, such as sadness, with a similar emotion. Changes in the experience of empathy from infancy onward are believed to be associated with age-related changes in the individual's ability to take others' perspectives, both cognitively and emotionally. Individuals who empathize with the feelings of others have been found to be more likely to engage in positive interpersonal behaviors, and less likely to engage in negative interpersonal behaviors, than are individuals who do not empathize with the feelings of others.

Moral Behaviors

The range of behaviors that have been considered in studies of moral development is extremely broad. Whereas some researchers have focused on the individual's ability and willingness to engage in various prosocial behaviors (such as helping, sharing, and comforting), others have focused on the individual's ability and willingness to resist engaging in various antisocial behaviors (such as aggressing, cheating, and lying). In addition to examining the role of moral cognitions and emotions in moral behaviors, psychologists have devoted considerable attention to identifying the early socialization experiences that promote the expression of prosocial behaviors and the avoidance of antisocial behaviors.

An extensive body of research has demonstrated that moral development is encouraged when parents love and support their children, provide opportunities for their children to learn about other people's views and feelings, model moral thinking and behavior themselves, and provide opportunities for moral thinking and behavior to be expressed and reinforced in their children.

The discipline technique that has been found to be most effective in encouraging moral development is called *induction*. A parent who uses induction explains to the child why his or her behavior is wrong and should be changed by emphasizing the impact of that misbehavior on others. Children whose parents use induction as their primary approach to discipline have been found to display higher levels of empathy and prosocial behaviors, and lower levels of antisocial behaviors, than do children whose parents rely on physical punishment or the withdrawal of love and attention as their primary approach to discipline.

Moral Education

Various educational programs have been designed to enhance the moral development of children and adolescents. As an extension of Kohlberg's view, some schools have set up cognitive moral education programs that encourage groups of adolescents to discuss a broad range of issues in the hope of promoting more advanced moral reasoning. The character education approach tends to be more direct, encouraging students to learn and follow a specific moral code to guide their behaviors in and out of school. Schools with service learning programs attempt to promote social responsibility by encouraging (or, in some cases, requiring) their students to assist needy individuals within their community. Although evidence indicates that providing service to others is beneficial to the young helper as well as to the recipient of the help, the role of service learning and other school-based programs in moral development remains controversial.

Mark A. Barnett

See also Antisocial Behavior; Helping Behavior; Moral Reasoning

Further Readings

Hoffman, M. L. (2000). *Empathy and moral development: Implications for caring and justice.* New York: Cambridge University Press.

Killen, M., & Smetana, J. G. (Eds.). (2006). *Handbook of moral development.* Mahwah, NJ: Erlbaum.

MORAL EMOTIONS

Social psychologists have long known that emotions influence many aspects of decision making, and a growing body of research demonstrates that this is especially true in the domain of morality. Because morality generally consists of rules guiding our treatment of other people, and because emotions are often (though not always) elicited in the context of our interactions with other people, it is possible to conceive of nearly all our emotions as serving morality in some sense. However, most researchers reserve the term *moral emotions* to refer to those emotions whose primary function is the preservation and motivation of moral thoughts and behaviors. In short, they are the emotions that make us care about morality.

Reason Versus Emotion

Morality was traditionally thought to be largely a matter of reasoning. Because the Western philosophical tradition placed such a strong emphasis on the role of reasoning for proper moral judgment, and because emotions were seen as damaging to the reasoning process in general, the study of morality focused heavily on the development of the reasoning ability. If anything, emotions were seen as harmful to the moral process. At first glance, this view is not unreasonable. After all, many emotions further one's own self-interest (such as happiness when one succeeds or anger and sadness when one fails), or bias one toward those individuals who are close to him or her (e.g., you become more angry if someone insults *your* mother than if someone insults a stranger's mother). Because impartiality seems to be critical for proper moral judgment, many thinkers believed that emotions should be eliminated from the process of moral judgment entirely.

Nonetheless, some influential thinkers noted that human morality seemed to depend heavily on the presence of certain emotions. Philosophers such as David Hume and Adam Smith were among the first to implicate emotions (particularly sympathy) as forming the foundations of morality. And recent research seems to support them: Without certain emotions, moral concern would not exist.

Evolutionary Origins

One area of research that elucidates the role of emotion in morality comes from evolutionary theory. However, because morality is inherently other-serving, and evolution was traditionally understood as a selfish mechanism (e.g., survival of the fittest), morality itself was not properly understood by evolutionary theorists for quite some time. Key insights from a few theorists, however, led to an understanding that a trait that encouraged altruistic behavior (helping others at a cost to oneself) could be adaptive, thus increasing the probability that the trait would be passed on to offspring. These traits likely took the form of emotional tendencies to help those in need and punish those who violated rules (e.g., cheaters). The evolutionary etiology of many emotions is still a matter of debate, but most people now believe that the presence of moral emotions is not inconsistent with an evolutionary account.

The Moral Emotions

Broadly speaking, three classes of emotions can be termed *moral emotions:* emotions that encourage people to care about the suffering of others (e.g., sympathy), emotions that motivate people to punish others (e.g., anger), and emotions that are, in essence, punishments upon oneself for violating one's moral code (e.g., guilt). Some researchers also include a class of emotions that are elicited when one sees the positive moral acts of others, such as praise and a form of moral awe termed *elevation.*

Empathy/Sympathy/Compassion

In most discussions of moral emotions, the terms *empathy* and *sympathy* arise. These emotional processes have long been implicated as the very foundation of morality. A clarification about these terms should be made: Empathy is most often defined as feeling what another person is feeling (whether happy, sad, or angry, for instance). It is best described as a sort of emotional contagion and, as such, is not properly an emotion. Sympathy is more generally understood as caring for others. But because these terms often are used interchangeably, some researchers choose to use the term *compassion* to refer to the emotion of caring for the suffering of others. This compassion is often motivated by empathic/sympathetic responses to the suffering of others. These emotions seem to emerge very early on (infants cry at the sound of other infants crying more than to equally loud noncrying sounds), are present to some extent in nonhuman primates, and are disturbingly lacking in psychopathic individuals. This lack of empathy in psychopaths is most likely what allows them to hurt others with little compunction—because they don't feel the pain of others, they are not motivated to compassion for the suffering of others. Having a sympathetic reaction to the suffering of another is also one of the best predictors of altruistic helping behavior.

Anger and Disgust

Much of morality consists of regulating the behavior of others. As moral codes are generated, consequences for the violation of those moral codes become necessary. One way in which individuals mete out immediate consequences to others is by emotional displays of disapproval. Anger is generally a response to a sense of interpersonal violation. Although anger can be elicited across a wide variety of situations, research has demonstrated that many of these situations involve a feeling of betrayal, unfair treatment, or injustice—concerns that fall squarely in the moral domain. The role of disgust in morality is a little less straightforward. Although many individuals report being disgusted by an individual they perceive as morally blameworthy (e.g., being disgusted at a con artist who robs the elderly), it is not clear that they are referring to the same kind of disgust an individual may feel when he or she sees rotting meat or feces (what some researchers term *core* disgust). One possibility is that individuals can recruit this core disgust when presented with a morally shady character.

Guilt and Shame

When people violate what they perceive to be a moral rule, they often respond with a feeling of guilt or shame. These emotions are often referred to as the self-conscious emotions. Shame, and its cousin, embarrassment, regulate people's behavior when others are present. In non-Western cultures in which the hierarchical structure of society is of primary (often moral) importance, these emotions especially keep individuals acting in a manner befitting their lower-status ranking. Guilt, on the other hand, is an inherently interpersonal emotion. It acts as a signal that an individual may have hurt someone with whom he or she has a relationship. As such, guilt often motivates reparatory behavior—it only seems to go away once an individual has righted his or her wrongs.

The Moral-Emotional Life

It is easy to see how these emotions work in concert to uphold morality in everyday life. For instance, consider this simple situation: Someone is suffering and this bothers you (you feel *empathy/sympathy*); you now care for this person (you feel *compassion*). Either you caused his or her suffering (*guilt*) or someone else caused his or her suffering (*anger, disgust*). These emotions then motivate the proper actions to remedy the situation, such as seeking justice or forgiveness.

David A. Pizarro

See also Cheater-Detection Mechanism; Disgust; Emotion; Empathy; Guilt; Moral Reasoning

Further Readings

Frank, R. H. (1988). *Passions within reason: The strategic role of the emotions.* New York: W. W. Norton.

Haidt, J. (2003). The moral emotions. In R. J. Davidson, K. R. Scherer, & H. H. Goldsmith (Eds.), *Handbook of affective sciences* (pp. 852–870). Oxford, UK: Oxford University Press.

Hoffman, M. L. (1990). Empathy and justice motivation. *Motivation and Emotion, 4,* 151–172.

MORAL HYPOCRISY

Definition

Webster's Desk Dictionary of the English Language (1990) defines *moral* as "1. of or concerned with principles of right or wrong conduct. 2. being in accordance with such principles" (p. 586); it defines *hypocrisy* as "a pretense of having desirable or publicly approved attitudes, beliefs, principles, etc., that one does not actually possess" (p. 444). Moral hypocrisy is the motivation to *appear* moral, while, if possible, avoiding the cost of being moral. This is in opposition to moral integrity, which is the motivation to act in accord with moral principles—to actually *be* moral.

Phenomenon

Moral people often fail to act morally. One of the most important lessons to be learned from the atrocities of the past century—mass killings, terrorist bombings, and corporate cover-ups—is that horrendous deeds are not done only by monsters. There are several possible reasons why a typical person might fail to act morally in some situations. One of these may be that people are often motivated by moral hypocrisy rather than by moral integrity.

Moral philosophers often assume a causal link from moral reasoning to moral action, but there is limited evidence for this link. People's ability to see the morally right path does not guarantee that they will follow it. Early in life, most people learn that moral hypocrisy (e.g., appearing to act fairly when not doing so) can be advantageous if one does not get caught. But how best not to get caught? In the moral masquerade, self-deception may be an asset, making it easier to deceive others. Evolutionary biologist Robert Trivers suggested that if one can convince oneself that serving one's own interests does not violate one's principles, one can honestly appear moral and so avoid detection without paying the price of actually upholding the relevant moral principle. Most people are adept at justifying to themselves why a situation that benefits them or those they care about does not violate their moral principles—for example, why storing their nuclear waste in someone else's backyard is fair. Such justification may allow people to apply these principles when judging others, yet avoid following the principles themselves.

Evidence

Research suggests that moral hypocrisy is common. College students given the opportunity to anonymously assign themselves and another person (actually fictitious) to two different tasks—one clearly more desirable than the other—typically assign themselves to the more desirable task 70% to 80% of the time. Students reminded of the moral principle of fairness, and given the chance to flip a coin to fairly determine the task assignment, flip the coin about half the time. Yet, even those who flip the coin assign themselves to the more desirable task 80% to 90% of the time. Clearly, most who lose the coin flip fail to abide by it. Furthermore, those who lose the coin flip but assign themselves the more desirable task rate their action as more moral than do those who assign themselves the more desirable task without going through the charade of flipping the coin. This appearance of fairness (flipping the coin) while avoiding the cost of being fair (assigning oneself the desirable task) has been taken as evidence of moral hypocrisy.

Overcoming Moral Hypocrisy

Procedures that one might think would increase moral integrity often increase moral hypocrisy instead. Both (a) expecting to meet the other person when assigning the tasks and (b) explicitly indicating that fairness is important before assigning the task increased moral hypocrisy. In each case, a larger percentage of participants flipped the coin, but those who did still assigned themselves to the desirable task 80% to 90% of the time.

Two procedures have been found to reduce moral hypocrisy. First, when people are made self-aware (e.g., by looking at themselves in a mirror), they become aware of discrepancies between their behavior and salient personal standards. This awareness creates pressure to act in accord with these personal standards. Among self-aware participants, task assignment following the coin flip has been found to be fair. Supporting the role of self-deception in moral hypocrisy, it seems that participants looking in a mirror could not deceive themselves regarding the fairness of the flip, and so they acted morally.

Second, feeling empathy for the other person seems to reduce moral hypocrisy, but not by increasing moral integrity. Empathy is an other-oriented emotion of sympathy and compassion for someone in distress. When induced to feel empathy for the other participant, many participants assigned the other to the desirable task without flipping the coin, suggesting an altruistic motive. However, those who flipped the coin were no fairer than in other studies, suggesting no increase in moral integrity.

Implications

Moral hypocrisy research highlights the important question of whether widely espoused moral principles such as fairness motivate people to be moral or only to appear moral. If the latter, then psychologists would expect people to act morally only when (a) there is little personal cost, (b) actually being moral is the only way to appear moral, or (c) they care about those that might be harmed by immoral action. Research to date supports this conclusion. Much behavior that has been assumed to be motivated by moral integrity may be motivated by moral hypocrisy instead.

Elizabeth C. Collins
C. Daniel Batson

See also Deception (Lying); Empathy; Moral Reasoning; Self-Awareness; Self-Deception

Further Readings

Batson, C. D., & Thompson, E. R. (2001). Why don't moral people act morally? Motivational considerations. *Current Directions in Psychological Science, 10,* 54–57.

Moral Reasoning

Definition

Moral reasoning refers to the processes involved in how individuals think about right and wrong and in how they acquire and apply moral rules and guidelines. The psychological study of morality in general is often referred to as the study of moral reasoning, although moral psychology is now understood as encompassing more than just the reasoning process.

Many of the topics that social psychologists were originally interested in (such as obedience and conformity) had to do in one way or another with questions of moral judgment and behavior. Despite this early interest in morality, the study of moral reasoning specifically had its beginnings in the work of moral philosophers and developmental psychologists rather than in social psychology.

History

Although morality was originally the domain of religion and theology, interest in the psychology of morality has been around since at least the time of the early Greek philosophers. Plato and Aristotle, for instance, devoted much of their discussion to how people came to acquire moral notions. The tradition continued, as Western philosophers such as Immanuel Kant and David Hume wrote much on the psychological processes involved in moral judgment. These two philosophers famously debated the role of reason versus emotion in moral judgment, with Kant placing a much greater emphasis on rational thought as the proper foundation for moral judgment.

Kant's ideas, particularly his emphasis on reason as the foundation of moral judgment, influenced some of the earliest psychological work on moral reasoning, that of the Swiss psychologist Jean Piaget. Piaget believed that children developed a mature sense of morality as their ability to reason unfolded. Particularly important for Piaget was the idea that mature reasoning caused a shift from children seeing the world from only their perspective (egocentrism) toward being able to take the perspective of others. For Piaget, this developing ability to reason when combined with the natural social interactions children had with one another (which often involved having to share, take turns, and play games together) caused children to move from a morality based on rules, authority, and punishment (heteronomous morality) to a morality based on mutual respect, cooperation, and an understanding of the thoughts and desires of other individuals (autonomous morality).

Lawrence Kohlberg, a developmental psychologist, expanded upon Piaget's stage theory of development to include multiple stages of moral reasoning spanning through adulthood. Kohlberg first outlined his theory of moral development in 1958, in what was to become one of the most influential psychological dissertations of all time. Heavily influenced by the rationalist philosophies of Kant and John Rawls (whose theory of justice was one of the most influential political theories of the 20th century), Kohlberg, like Piaget, believed that as reasoning developed, so did moral judgment. For Kohlberg, individuals progressed from an early, egocentric morality based on the fear of punishment and the desire for reward (stages 1 and 2, preconventional morality), toward a more mature morality based on social norms (stages 3 and 4, conventional morality), and finally (though not always) to an understanding of universal moral principles that existed independently of social convention (stages 5 and 6, post-conventional morality). Like Piaget, Kohlberg believed that being exposed to social interactions involving moral conflicts could cause progression from one stage of moral reasoning to the next.

Although Piaget and Kohlberg set the groundwork for the study of moral reasoning and stimulated a wealth of research in the area (Kohlberg's stage theory continues to stimulate work), their ideas have been challenged. In particular, as the study of moral reasoning expanded from the domain of developmentalists to include other areas of psychology, such as cognitive psychology, evolutionary psychology, social psychology, and cognitive neuroscience, researchers began to question some of the assumptions Piaget and Kohlberg made. For instance, many have argued that stage theories are not the best way to characterize the progression of moral reasoning, and there is mounting evidence that moral emotions may be a greater influence on people's everyday moral thinking than was believed by the developmentalists.

Social Psychology and Moral Reasoning

Because social psychologists have long studied the areas of reasoning and judgment, they have been particularly well suited to investigate the processes involved in everyday moral reasoning. Recently, researchers have taken the wealth of research on topics such as causal reasoning, intentionality, attitudes, heuristics and biases, and emotion, and applied it toward arriving at a better understanding of moral judgment. One of the most interesting findings to emerge about moral reasoning is that it seems to be different from "regular" reasoning (reasoning about nonmoral issues) in important ways.

For instance, there are several differences in the way people think about their moral beliefs and attitudes than about their nonmoral beliefs and attitudes. First, moral attitudes are unlike other attitudes in that they are surprisingly strong and resistant to change. It is very hard, for instance, to convince a pro-life proponent that abortion should be legal, or a pro-choice proponent that abortion should be banned (persuasion in the moral domain is very rare). Second, most people believe that moral truths are universally binding—if a person believes that something is wrong, others should believe this too. Unlike one's attitude toward chocolate ice cream (the person doesn't particularly care whether or not others like it), it is problematic if others don't share a person's attitude toward rape (it is important to the person that others also believe it is wrong). In fact, although Westerners generally appreciate diversity of all sorts, researchers have shown that diversity of moral opinion causes quite a bit of discomfort. Third, individuals often adhere to strong moral rules despite the consequences. For instance, most Westerners believe that it is not permissible to sacrifice one innocent individual to save five. Indeed, the very notion of sacrificing innocent individuals no matter *what* the benefits seems to be seen as impermissible. These rules that are seen as impermissible despite their consequences are often referred to as *deontological* rules. These deontological rules don't always seem rational in the sense that most psychologists use the word, as rationality is often defined as making choices that maximizing good consequences. In short, what research seems to show is that people treat their moral beliefs, attitudes, or opinions as values that should be protected at nearly any cost. Because of this, many researchers have referred to these moral rules as *sacred* or *protected* values.

Although the topic of moral reasoning has a long history, much work remains to be done before psychologists can be satisfied that they have answered the fundamental question of how people think and decide about issues of right and wrong.

David A. Pizarro

See also Guilt; Moral Emotions; Reciprocal Altruism

Further Readings

Greene, J. D., Sommerville, R. B., Nystrom, L. E., Darley, J. M., & Cohen, J. D. (2001, September 14). An fMRI investigation of emotional engagement in moral judgment. *Science, 293,* 2105–2108.

Haidt, J. (2001). The emotional dog and its rational tail: A social intuitionist approach to moral judgment. *Psychological Review, 108,* 814–834.

Sunstein C. R. (2005). Moral heuristics. *Behavioral and Brain Sciences, 28*(4), 531–573.

Mortality Salience

Definition

Mortality salience refers to a psychological state in which a person is consciously thinking about his or her own death.

Background

Jeff Greenberg, Tom Pyszczynski, and Sheldon Solomon coined the term in 1986 to refer to a way to assess terror management theory. The theory posits that the fear of death motivates individuals to sustain faith in a cultural belief system or worldview that makes life seem meaningful and sustain the belief that they are significant and capable of enduring beyond their own death. Greenberg and colleagues proposed that, if the theory is correct, then having people think about their own death—that is, mortality salience—should increase people's support of their own cultural worldview.

Research

The most common method to induce mortality salience is to ask participants to respond to the following two prompts: "Please describe the emotions the thought of your own death arouses in you" and "Jot down, as specifically as you can, what you think will happen to you physically as you die and once you are physically dead." The first finding was that mortality salience led municipal court judges to recommend a much higher bond in a hypothetical prostitution case than they otherwise would. This was interpreted as support for terror management theory because it showed that mortality salience encouraged the judges to uphold their worldview by punishing someone who violated the morals of their worldview.

Studies have shown that mortality salience leads people to react positively to those who support their worldview and negatively to those who violate or criticize their worldview. Additional research has found that mortality salience affects a wide range of judgments and behaviors that preserve faith in either one's worldview or one's self-esteem.

More than 200 studies have made mortality salient in a variety of ways and in comparison with many control conditions. Mortality salience has been induced by exposure to gory accident footage, death anxiety questionnaires, and proximity to funeral homes and cemeteries. Control conditions have reminded participants of neutral topics and aversive topics such as failure, uncertainty, meaninglessness, pain, and social exclusion. These findings have generally supported the specific role of mortality concerns in mortality salience effects.

Studies investigating the cognitive processes involved in mortality salience effects have shown that mortality salience initially leads people toward distracting themselves from thoughts of death. After a delay, thoughts of death return to the fringes of consciousness, at which time the worldview and self-esteem bolstering effects of mortality salience occur. Indeed, similar effects have been shown in response to exposure to brief subliminal flashes of death-related words on a computer screen; these subliminal primes bring death thoughts to the fringes of consciousness without making mortality salient.

Implications

In supporting terror management theory, mortality salience research demonstrates that unconscious concerns about one's own death motivate a wide range of judgments and behaviors to bolster the individual's faith in his or her worldview and self-worth. This work thereby suggests that mortality concerns contribute to nationalism, prejudice, and intergroup aggression, as well as prosocial behavior and cultural achievements.

Jeff Greenberg

See also Consciousness; Meaning Maintenance Model; Priming; Salience; Subliminal Perception; Terror Management Theory

Further Readings

Becker, E. (1974). *The denial of death.* New York: Free Press.

Greenberg, J., Solomon, S., & Pyszczynski, T. (1997). Terror management theory and research: Empirical assessments and conceptual refinements. In M. P. Zanna (Ed.), *Advances in experimental social psychology* (Vol. 29, pp. 61–139). San Diego, CA: Academic Press.

Solomon, S., Greenberg, J., & Pyszczynski, T. (1991). A terror management theory of social behavior: On the psychological functions of self-esteem and cultural worldviews. In M. P. Zanna (Ed.), *Advances in experimental social psychology* (Vol. 24, pp. 93–159). San Diego, CA: Academic Press.

MOTIVATED COGNITION

Definition

When people think and reason, they sometimes have a vested interest in the outcome of their thinking and reasoning. For example, people engage in wishful thinking about whether or not their favorite sports team will win, or whether a relative will survive a risky surgical procedure. In these situations, people may be less open-minded than they might be in other situations in which they do not have a preferred outcome in mind.

Motivated cognition refers to the influence of motives on various types of thought processes such as memory, information processing, reasoning, judgment, and decision making. Many of these processes are relevant to social phenomena such as self-evaluation, person perception, stereotypes, persuasion, and communication. It is important to understand the influence of motivation because such research explains errors and biases in the way people make social judgments and may offer ideas about how to offset the negative effects of such motives.

Examples

One example of a cognitive process influenced by motivation is memory. People tend to remember successes more than failures, and when led to believe that a given attribute is desirable, they are more likely to remember past events where they displayed this attribute than those in which they did not. People overestimate contributions to past events such as group discussions and projects, and revise their memory in accordance with their motives. They might reconstruct their memory of what attributes they considered most important in a spouse after marrying someone who does not have these attributes.

People's motives also influence how they process novel information. They are relatively more likely to trust small samples of information consistent with desired expectations (even when they know that small samples can be unreliable) and are more critical of messages threatening desired beliefs. If they engage in a particular behavior often (e.g., smoking), they are more likely to find fault with information suggesting this behavior is dangerous. Judgments of frequency and probability are also influenced by motives. People overestimate the frequency of events that support their desired beliefs and consider their personal likelihoods of experiencing positive events to be greater than that for negative events.

Another cognitive process is the way in which people make attributions (i.e., search for underlying causes) for events. Motivational factors may cause people to accept responsibility for successes more than failures, and to believe that others who have experienced negative events (e.g., rape, burglarization) were partially responsible and perhaps deserving of those fates. By doing so, they protect themselves from believing that they could also experience these events. Accessing and applying negative stereotypes about others has been shown to help people cope with threats to their own self-concepts. Furthermore, the way in which people define personality traits may be linked to self-serving motives; for example, most people can believe they are better leaders than average if they define leadership according to their own personal strengths.

Types of Motives That Influence Cognition

Many of the previous examples draw on one particular type of motive: to confirm or sustain favorable beliefs (particularly about the self). Many other motives can influence cognition. When people are accountable for their judgments—such as when these judgments can be verified for accuracy—the motive to make accurate, defensible judgments becomes more impactful. The motive to form an accurate impression of another person helps one carefully organize information about that person and remember that information in the future. The motive to belong, exemplified by people's interest in relationships and group memberships, might also influence various types of cognitive processes, such as judgments about romantic partners. The desire to see one's group as different from others may underlie the tendency to view members of outgroups as more similar to each other (relative to ingroups), as well as the tendency to judge members of other groups more harshly.

Another motive that may influence cognition is terror management. According to terror management theory, thinking about one's own mortality can paralyze individuals with terror. One defense against this terror is a bolstering of one's worldview, which offers figurative immortality by being a part of something that will live on even after the individual's demise. In conditions in which the chances of thinking about one's own death are high, individuals are harsher critics of opposing worldviews.

Psychological Processes Linking Motivation and Cognition

People do not simply ignore information inconsistent with their motives. On the contrary, motivation seems to instigate careful scrutiny of the information. In her theory of motivated reasoning, Ziva Kunda argues that motivation formulates directional hypotheses (e.g., "I am a good person") that people then attempt to test using standard cognitive (and dispassionate) strategies. As it turns out, many such strategies are themselves biased. People often exhibit a confirmation bias when testing hypotheses, being more attentive to information confirming their hypothesis than they are to disconfirming information. They remember more vivid and personal information than they do pallid and impersonal information. Individuals also possess crude statistical heuristics (or rules of thumb) they use when making judgments and may be more likely to draw on these heuristics when doing so is consistent with their motives.

When given other opportunities to protect the self-concept (e.g., self-affirmation, or reflection on one's important values), people are less likely to exhibit biases in their judgments. Nonconscious motives may also influence cognition through the automatic activation of concepts relevant to a given judgment. For example, people asked to circle all cases of *I* in a passage (which activates the self-concept below conscious awareness) tend to be faster at identifying whether they possess a given list of traits.

Implications of Motivated Cognition

The effects of motivation on cognition are likely to be a function of several critical psychological needs. For example, people want to protect their limited emotional resources and protect themselves from constant thoughts of their own mortality. Other work suggests that individuals who possess positive illusions—overestimations of one's ability, control over one's environment, and chances of experiencing positive events in the future—are also more healthy (both mentally and physically). Positive illusions may motivate actions designed to achieve positive outcomes. On the other hand, such beliefs could also lead to dangerous behavior. If one is motivated to avoid threatening information about an unhealthy behavior, the outcome is likely to be a continuation of that behavior followed by potential health problems. The extent to which motivated biases in cognition are adaptive is still a matter of debate.

William M. P. Klein
Matthew M. Monin

See also Memory; Positive Illusions

Further Readings

Dunning, D. A. (1999). A newer look: Motivated social cognition and the schematic representation of social concepts. *Psychological Inquiry, 10,* 1–11.

Kunda, Z. (1990). The case for motivated reasoning. *Psychological Bulletin, 108,* 480–498.

Taylor, S. E., & Brown, J. D. (1988). Illusion and well-being: A social psychological perspective on mental health. *Psychological Bulletin, 103,* 193–210.

MOTIVATED REASONING

Definition

Motivated reasoning is a form of reasoning in which people access, construct, and evaluate arguments in a biased fashion to arrive at or endorse a preferred conclusion. The term *motivated* in *motivated reasoning* refers to the fact that people use reasoning strategies that allow them to draw the conclusions they want to draw (i.e., are motivated to draw). Of course, people are not always motivated to confirm their preferred conclusions. Actually, they sometimes are motivated to draw accurate conclusions. However, the term *motivated reasoning* refers to situations in which people want to confirm their preferred conclusion rather than to situations in which people's reasoning is driven by an accuracy motivation.

The Domain of Motivated Reasoning

Motivated reasoning may be observed in virtually any setting. An important trigger of motivated reasoning is the confrontation with a certain threat to the self. In the absence of such a motivating threat, people may have the goal of attaining the most accurate conclusion rather than attaining a preferred conclusion. The following example may illustrate the difference. Someone who wants to buy a used car will try to make the best decision possible and hence be guided by accuracy concerns to avoid buying a lemon. After buying a used car, however, that same person may engage in motivated reasoning to support his belief that the car is not a lemon when the first signs of malfunction appear. For a less involving choice, like the choice of cereals, people will be less motivated to engage in thorough deliberation before the choice but will also be less likely to engage in motivated reasoning if their choice turns out to be bad. People's self-esteem may suffer much less from choosing bad cereals than from being suckered into buying a lemon car.

Threats to the self may come in many different forms, so different types of conclusions may trigger motivated reasoning. A first type is conclusions that bolster people's self-esteem. For instance, people attribute good test results to themselves but construct a motivated reasoning to explain bad test results to uphold the self-serving belief that they are intelligent human beings. A second type is conclusions that make people optimistic about their future. For instance, smokers engage in motivated reasoning when they dispel scientific evidence that suggests that smoking is bad for one's health. People also engage in motivated reasoning to view future competitors as less competent and future cooperators as more competent than they really are. A third type is conclusions that are consistent with strongly held beliefs or strong attitudes. For instance, supporters of a politician might downplay the consequences of an undesirable act committed by the politician they support or might attribute the behavior to situational pressures. In sum, people construct motivated reasonings when their self-worth, their future, or their understanding and valuation of the world are at stake.

The Illusion of Objectivity

That motivated reasoning is not driven by an accuracy motive does not imply that motivated reasoners blatantly disregard the accuracy of their reasoning. Motivated reasoners have to uphold the illusion of objectivity: They cannot ignore the extant evidence regarding the issue at stake. If they are exposed to strong, compelling evidence contrary to their preferred conclusion, they will have to concede that their preferred conclusion is incorrect—the so-called reality constraint. For instance, in the used car example, when the car breaks down very often, the buyer will no longer be able to engage in motivated reasoning to defend his or her belief that the car is not a lemon.

The illusion of objectivity also implies that motivated reasonings must appear logically valid to the motivated reasoners themselves. Still, a motivated reasoning may be compelling only for people who want to endorse its conclusion, but possibly not for neutral observers, and probably not for adversaries, who want to endorse the opposite conclusion.

To uphold the illusion of objectivity, it seems necessary that people are not aware of any bias present in their reasoning; as such, motivated reasoning seems to entail self-deception. The necessity to uphold the illusion of objectivity may seem to entail that people have little latitude in constructing motivated reasonings. Still, to support a preferred conclusion, people may unknowingly display a bias in any number of the cognitive processes that underlie reasoning.

Mechanisms of Motivated Reasoning

First, people may exhibit motivated skepticism: They may examine information consistent with their preferred conclusions less critically than they examine information inconsistent with those conclusions. Although information consistent with a preferred conclusion is accepted at face value, people may spontaneously try to refute information inconsistent with that conclusion. People also view arguments as stronger or as more persuasive if these arguments happen to be consistent with their preferred conclusions than if the arguments are inconsistent with the preferred conclusions. Motivated skepticism implies that people require less information to reach a preferred conclusion than to reach nonpreferred conclusions.

Second, and related to motivated skepticism, people may use statistical information in a motivated way. For instance, people attach more value to evidence based on a small sample size if the evidence supports their position than if it opposes it. Consistent with the

illusion of objectivity that motivated reasoners have to uphold, for large sample sizes, the value attached to favorable and unfavorable evidence is rather similar. Also, although people commonly neglect base rate information, they may use that information if it supports their preferred conclusions.

Third, to justify preferred conclusions, people may need to retrieve information in memory or look for external information. The search for information may be biased toward retrieving or finding information that is consistent with the preferred conclusion. This biased (memory) search may be because people's preferred conclusions function as hypotheses to be tested and that people often exhibit a confirmation bias in hypothesis testing. This confirmation bias implies that people may more readily come up with supporting arguments than with arguments that are not consistent with their preferred conclusions.

Fourth, people not only access information in a biased way, but also apply concepts in a motivated way. For instance, people display motivated stereotyping: They apply stereotypes, sometimes unjustly, if they support their preferred impressions but resist applying these stereotypes if they run counter to their preferred impressions.

The Case for Motivated Reasoning

The idea that motivation may affect information processing, including reasoning, seems intuitively plausible and underlies classic cognitive consistency theories as well as cognitive dissonance theory. However, the problem with many early studies that seemed to evidence the impact of motivation on people's information processing was that they were amenable to a purely cognitive explanation. For instance, the classic finding that people attribute their successes internally but their failures externally may be due to people's motivation to see themselves in the best possible way and therefore points toward motivated reasoning. However, the differential attribution of failures and successes may also be because people's self-schema leads them to expect to succeed and not to fail and that they attribute expected outcomes—successes—internally and unexpected ones—failures—externally. Because the latter explanation does not feature any motivation, it is a purely cognitive explanation of the differential attribution of failure and success.

Recent studies, however, have provided unequivocal support for the hypothesis that motivation affects information processing. For instance, in a study on motivated skepticism, where participants had to choose one of two students they would have to work with on a task, participants required less information to conclude that the more dislikable student was the less intelligent of the two than to decide that he was the more intelligent. The level of knowledge of the two students was equal in both cases, so the obtained results seem to implicate the motivation to see the more likeable student—that is, the one that participants wanted to work with—as the more intelligent one.

Numerous studies have now established that people may reason in a motivated way and have found support for the previously described mechanisms through which motivation may bias reasoning. In addition, studies in motivated social cognition have shown that people may define social concepts, such as traits and abilities, in a self-serving way. Such self-serving social concepts may be used in motivated reasonings to support self-serving beliefs.

Mario Pandelaere

See also Cognitive Consistency; Cognitive Dissonance Theory; Confirmation Bias; Motivated Cognition; Self-Deception

Further Readings

Baumeister, R. F., & Newman, L. S. (1994). Self-regulation of cognitive inference and decision processes. *Personality and Social Psychology Bulletin, 20,* 3–19.

Ditto, P. H., & Lopez, D. L. (1992). Motivated skepticism: Use of differential decision criteria for preferred and nonpreferred conclusions. *Journal of Personality and Social Psychology, 63,* 568–584.

Kunda, Z. (1987). Motivated inference: Self-serving generation and evaluation of causal theories. *Journal of Personality and Social Psychology, 53,* 636–647.

Kunda, Z. (1990). The case for motivated reasoning. *Psychological Bulletin, 108,* 480–498.

Kunda, Z., & Sinclair, L. (1999). Motivated reasoning with stereotypes: Activation, application, and inhibition. *Psychological Inquiry, 10,* 12–22.

Pyszczynski, T, & Greenberg, J. (1987). Toward an integration of cognitive and motivational perspectives on social inference: A biased hypothesis-testing model. In L. Berkowitz (Ed.), *Advances in experimental social psychology* (Vol. 20, pp. 297–340). San Diego, CA: Academic Press.

MUM Effect

Despite the folk wisdom that "no news is good news," almost everyone is reluctant to communicate bad news. For example, your best friend, Tom, has applied for a job that he wants very badly. You learn that he will definitely be offered the job. You can hardly wait to tell him the good news. You will take pleasure in letting Tom know all the details. Now, contrast this with your feelings if you learn that Tom will definitely not get the job he wants so much. In this case, you probably feel awful and do not look forward to communicating the news to Tom. You might even decide to say nothing about what you found out. This reluctance to communicate bad news is very strong under a large variety of types of news, potential recipients, and circumstances. The reluctance to communicate bad news is so general and so robust that it has been given its own name: the MUM effect. When it comes to bad news, it seems that, indeed, "Mum's the word."

Despite its robustness, the reluctance to communicate bad news is not universal. Anyone who has paid attention to the news media can't help forming the impression that bad news is reported with alacrity. Our experience with rumors or gossip or urban myths also suggests that there is no bias against communicating bad news. So, the MUM effect seems to be restricted to situations in which the news affects the well-being of the potential recipient. In one study, for example, participants learned that there was a telephone message telling another participant to call home right away about some good news or about some bad news. When given the opportunity to communicate the message to the person for whom the message was intended, participants were more likely to mention the good news than the bad news. Interestingly, however, this difference disappeared when the participants were given the opportunity to communicate to a bystander. In fact, participants were slightly more likely to mention the bad news than the good news to a bystander. The implication of this is sobering: The person who is affected by the bad news is less likely to learn about it than is a bystander!

Understanding the MUM Effect

Psychologists are rarely content with *just* an empirical regularity like the MUM effect. They want to understand why there is a reluctance to communicate bad news. At least three broad concerns might affect a communicator's propensity to transmit a particular message. Communicators might be concerned with their own well-being, they might be concerned about the potential recipient, or they might be guided by situational norms or what they understand as "the right thing to do."

"Kill the messenger." Folk wisdom suggests that the bearer of bad news may be disliked even if he or she is in no way responsible for the news. And, there is experimental research demonstrating the validity of that suggestion. Perhaps the MUM effect arises because potential communicators fear that they would be disliked if they were to convey the bad news. Another explanation of the MUM effect arising from self-concern implicates guilt. There is a pervasive tendency to believe that the world is (or should be) fair. Perhaps conveying bad news to another tends to make the communicator who is not experiencing the bad fate feel guilty. Because he or she wants to avoid feeling guilty, bad news tends to be withheld. A third self-concern that might account for the MUM effect comes from recognizing that one must adopt a somber if not sad demeanor in conveying bad news. Perhaps potential communicators tend to withhold bad news because they are reluctant to adopt a negative mood. Experimental research has provided evidence for all three of these self-concern factors.

The reluctance to communicate bad news may come from a concern with the recipient. When people are asked to explain why they would or would not communicate good or bad news they seem to focus on the recipient. For example, compared with good news, people are more likely to say that the reason they would communicate bad news is because the recipient might have to use that information in some way. People also say that they withhold bad news because they do not want to put the recipient in a bad mood. Often, communicators assume that potential recipients do not want to hear the bad news. (This assumption is sometimes erroneous. For example, some surveys indicate that medical professionals believe that patients do not want to hear bad news, but patients say they do want to hear such news.) When people are made explicitly aware that a potential recipient wants to hear the news, whether it is good or bad, the MUM effect is reduced.

Finally, the MUM effect may be a result of ambiguous norms. Conveying good news doesn't seem to be an issue. There are few potential costs. On the other hand, if you give a person bad news, there are potential personal costs such as being disliked or feeling guilty. Or, you might upset the recipient or embarrass him or her. Are you the appropriate person to be handling the aftermath? You could be seen as prying or butting in. There simply aren't clear rules telling people what to do with bad news. Indeed, there is a strong positive correlation between how good a message is and people's willingness to relay the message. Although people are reluctant to communicate bad news, there is little correlation between how bad the news is and their (un)willingness to communicate it. More directly touching the norm issue is the agreement among people on their likelihood to communicate news. There is good agreement (clear norms) in the case of good news but lower agreement (unclear norms) regarding the transmission of bad news.

The MUM effect refers to a tendency to withhold bad news compared with good news. This tendency is most likely to show itself when the potential recipient is the person for whom the news is consequential and appears to be the result of communicators' concern with own well-being, recipient well-being, and unclear norms regarding the handling of bad news.

Abraham Tesser

See also Bad Is Stronger Than Good; Empathy; Rumor Transmission

Further Readings

Tesser, A., & Rosen, S. (1975). The reluctance to transmit bad news. In L. Berkowitz (Ed.), *Advances in experimental social psychology* (Vol. 8, pp. 194–232). New York: Academic Press.

MUNDANE REALISM

Definition

Mundane realism describes the degree to which the materials and procedures involved in an experiment are similar to events that occur in the real world. Therefore, mundane realism is a type of external validity, which is the extent to which findings can generalize from experiments to real-life settings.

History and Modern Usage

Elliot Aronson and J. Merrill Carlsmith introduced the concept of mundane realism as a potential threat to external validity in 1968. That is, to the extent that procedures are artificial, it may be more difficult to generalize the findings produced by those procedures to the real world. Mundane realism can be contrasted with experimental realism, which refers to whether an experiment has psychological impact and "feels real" to a participant. Both are important for generalizing findings from the laboratory to the real world, but they are independent and distinct dimensions. That is, any particular experiment might be high or low in either mundane or experimental realism.

For example, Muzafer Sherif's classic Robbers Cave experiment concerning rivalry and hostility between groups at a summer camp is considered to have both high mundane realism and high experimental realism. Sherif randomly divided a group of boys attending a summer camp into two teams. The teams competed against each other in camp activities. This setting closely resembles a typical summer camp experience, so the experiment has a high level of mundane realism. Because of the great psychological impact of the manipulations used in the experiment, the study is also considered to have high experimental realism.

In contrast, Solomon Asch's classic experiment on conformity is considered to be low in mundane realism, but high in experimental realism. Participants were asked to make relatively objective judgments concerning the relative length of three lines after hearing the answers of several of their "peers." Those "peers" were actually confederates of the experimenter, and on critical trials, they were instructed to unanimously provide incorrect answers. Participants had stressful, realistic reactions to the conformity pressure involved in the experiment, demonstrating its experimental realism. However, the experiment was low in mundane realism because it is rare in the real world to have a majority give an incorrect answer to a simple, objective, visual task.

At first glance, it might seem that field studies are always high in mundane realism just because they occur outside of the laboratory. However, because of the potential artificiality of the manipulations that can be used in field studies, they are just as subject to a lack of mundane realism as are experiments conducted in other types of settings.

Janice R. Kelly

See also Conformity; Ecological Validity; Experimental Realism; Robbers Cave Experiment

Further Readings

Aronson, E. R., & Carlsmith, J. M. (1968). Experimentation in social psychology. In G. Lindzey & E. Aronson (Eds.), *Handbook of social psychology* (Vol. 2). Reading, MA: Addison-Wesley.

Asch, S. E. (1956). Studies of independence and conformity: A minority of one against a unanimous majority. *Psychological Monographs, 70* (Whole no. 416).

N

Naive Cynicism

Definition

Naive cynicism is the tendency of laypeople to expect other people's judgments will have a motivational basis and therefore will be biased in the direction of their self-interest. We expect that others will see things in ways that are most flattering to them, while thinking that our own opinions and beliefs are based on objective evidence.

Context and Importance

Naive cynicism is the counterpart to naive realism, the belief on the part of laypeople that they see the world as it really is. Although we often don't believe that the judgments we make are biased, we readily recognize that others' judgments may be. Naive cynicism may even lead people to overestimate the amount of bias in other people's judgments. For example, husbands and wives are known to overestimate their responsibility for household tasks, giving individual estimates that add up to more than 100%; it can't be possible that Mr. Smith washes the dishes 60% of the time while Mrs. Smith washes them 70% of the time. A woman might expect that her husband will overestimate how much he should take credit for positive events and underestimate how much he is to blame for negative events; he might expect the same of her. However, because of the accessibility of their own participation in both positive and negative events, they will each tend to overestimate how much they are responsible for both good *and* bad things, meaning their partners will have cynical views of their beliefs and vice versa. Viewing the other person as part of your ingroup or at least as working in cooperation with you may attenuate this belief; for instance, the happier a married couple was, the less likely they were to show cynical beliefs about each other's judgments. We may be especially likely to be naively cynical when the other person has a vested interest in the judgment at hand, but if that person is a dispassionate observer, we expect that he or she will see things the way we do (the way things "really are"), not biased toward his or her own beliefs. Naive cynicism extends to many of the basic heuristics and biases studied in social psychology; people think that others are prone to commit the fundamental attribution error, the false consensus effect, and self-enhancement bias. Naive cynicism is related to the norm of self-interest. Many intellectual fields, such as classical economics and evolutionary biology, stress how their theories indicate that people should always act in self-interested ways. This emphasis reflects and helps maintain a societal license to act in one's self-interest, and, more importantly, to believe that others will too, even though people are often inclined to behave in a cooperative, empathetic, or altruistic manner.

Elanor F. Williams

See also Lay Epistemics; Naive Realism

Further Readings

Kruger, J., & Gilovich, T. (1999). Naïve cynicism in everyday theories of responsibility assessment: On biased assumptions of bias. *Journal of Personality and Social Psychology, 76*, 743–753.

Pronin, E., Gilovich, T., & Ross, L. (2004). Objectivity in the eye of the beholder: Divergent perceptions of bias in self versus others. *Psychological Review, 111,* 781–799.

NAIVE REALISM

Definition

Naive realism describes people's tendency to believe that they perceive the social world "as it is"—as objective reality—rather than as a subjective construction and interpretation of reality. This belief that one's perceptions are realistic, unbiased interpretations of the social world has two important implications. First, that other, rational people will have similar perceptions as oneself. Second, that other people who have different perceptions from oneself must be uninformed (i.e., not privy to the same information as oneself), irrational, or biased.

Context and Importance

One of psychology's fundamental lessons is that perception is a subjective construction of the world rather than a direct representation of objective reality. That is, people's beliefs and perceptions are a function of both the objective properties of the world and the psychological processes that translate those objective features into psychologically experienced features. Take, for instance, the loving father who happens to be a judge at his daughter's science fair. The father's ranking of his daughter's project in the 90th percentile may result from the fact that his daughter's project truly was above average or from the fact that the father interprets his daughter's science project in a particularly favorable light.

To be sure, people recognize that their initial thoughts, feelings, and behaviors are often subjective and biased. The father may well recognize that his initial inclination to award top honors to his daughter's model volcano is unduly influenced by his desire for his daughter's achievement. After carefully scrutinizing and correcting his initial inclination, then, the father may reign in his judgment, placing his daughter in the 90th percentile rather than the 99th percentile, as he was initially wont to do. In this case, like many others, people's attempts to correct their initially biased judgments are often incomplete.

The important point for naive realism is that people are seldom, if ever, aware of the degree to which their corrective efforts fall short; people consequently infer that their judgments are more accurate, objective, and realistic than they really are. Thus, the loving father truly believes that his daughter's project deserves to be ranked in the 90th percentile, even if a more objective assessment places the project in the 75th percentile.

Lee Ross and his colleagues have discussed several important implications of naive realism for social judgment. One is that because people believe that their perceptions are realistic, it follows that other reasonable people who have access to the same information will share those perceptions. This assumption is one reason why people project their own beliefs, feelings, and opinions on to other people. If one assumes that a preference for 1970s over 1990s music is a consequence of the inherent superiority of Led Zeppelin over M. C. Hammer, it seems only natural that other people would share that preference. By failing to see that one's own preference is partly the result of a particular construal of 1970s and 1990s music, one may fail to recognize that other people may have a different preference arising from a different construal—for example, construing the Village People and Nirvana as typical bands of the 1970s and 1990s. Naive realism tends, therefore, to produce an expectation that others think, feel, and behave similarly as oneself.

Often, however, other people see things differently than the self, and naive realism helps explain people's reactions in these situations. One reaction is that because people's own reactions seem rational and realistic, other people who have different reactions seem uninformed or irrational and biased. When a staunch Democrat learns, for instance, that her cousin is a Republican, she may initially assume that cousin John had not learned about Republican positions on taxation—that John was simply misinformed—and that providing him with the correct information would change his stance. After learning, however, that John knows all about Republican taxation positions, the Democrat might infer that her cousin is simply not a clear thinker or, worse, that he is systematically biased in favor of taxation positions that favor his own income tax bracket at the expense of less financially fortunate individuals.

Because people repeatedly encounter other people who see things differently from themselves, they may become accustomed to thinking that other people are irrational and biased. Over time, people may come to expect others' beliefs and opinions to be based on careless reasoning and systematic bias. The staunch Democrat may come to expect that all Republicans, not just her cousin, are irrational and biased.

Believing the self to be rational and objective whereas others are irrational and biased can pose a substantial barrier to successful dispute resolution. When parties on opposite sides of a conflict both assume that the other side is irrational and biased, achieving a mutually beneficial resolution is that much more difficult. For instance, to the extent that Democrat and Republican members of Congress both assume that lawmakers on the other side of the aisle are self-interested and illogical, they are less likely to craft beneficial and purposeful legislation.

Leaf Van Boven

See also Egocentric Bias; False Consensus Effect; Lay Epistemics; Naive Cynicism

Further Readings

Pronin, E., Gilovich, T., & Ross, L. (2004). Objectivity in the eye of the beholder: Divergent perceptions of bias in self versus others. *Psychological Review, 111,* 781–799.

Ross, L., & Ward, A. (1995). Psychological barriers to dispute resolution. In M. P. Zanna (Ed.), *Advances in experimental social psychology* (Vol. 27, pp. 255–304). San Diego, CA: Academic Press.

NAME LETTER EFFECT

Definition

The name letter effect refers to people's tendency to favor the letters that are included in their names more than letters that are not in their names. In plain terms, people like the letters in their names better than they like the rest of the alphabet. Because the link between name letters and the self is arbitrary, the effect implies that anything that is associated with the self becomes automatically endowed with positive feelings.

History

The name letter effect was discovered in the 1980s by Belgian researcher Jozef Nuttin. Nuttin observed that people prefer their own name letters even when they do not consciously notice the link between name letters and the self. The name letter effect also occurs for infrequent alphabet letters, suggesting that it is not because of more frequent exposure to name letters. The name letter effect is highly robust, particularly for initial letters. Indeed, name letter effects have been observed in at least 15 European countries such as the Netherlands, Poland, and Greece, and at least 3 non-European countries, including Japan, Thailand, and the United States. The name letter effect may thus be universal across different languages and cultures.

Links With Implicit Self-Esteem

The name letter effect seems to be a valid marker of implicit self-esteem, or unconscious positive feelings that people have toward the self. For instance, the name letter effect corresponds more with self-evaluations that are provided very quickly and intuitively than with self-evaluations that are provided more slowly and deliberately. Mothers who report having been more nurturing and less overprotective have children with stronger name letter effects than do mothers who report having been less nurturing and more overprotective. The name letter effect may therefore tap into deeply rooted feelings of self-worth that are formed in early childhood.

Consequences

The name letter effect may influence important decisions. Indeed, Brett Pelham and associates have documented how people gravitate toward other people, places, and things that share their name letters. For instance, people whose surname is Street live disproportionately often at addresses like Lincoln Street. People named Dennis are disproportionately likely to become dentists, whereas people named Laura are disproportionately likely to become lawyers. People also tend to prefer brand names that resemble their own names and are disproportionately likely to marry others whose names resemble their own. Although the influence of the name letter effect on important decisions may seem maladaptive, most researchers believe that the name letter effect is rooted in the adaptive tendency to associate the self with positive qualities.

Sander Koole

See also Implicit Attitudes; Mere Ownership Effect; Self-Esteem

Further Readings

Koole, S. L., & DeHart, T. (in press). Self-affection without self-reflection: Origins, representations, and consequences of implicit self-esteem. In C. Sedikides & S. Spencer (Eds.), *The self.* New York: Psychology Press.

Koole, S. L., & Pelham, B. W. (2003). On the nature of implicit self-esteem: The case of the name letter effect. In S. Spencer, S. Fein, & M. P. Zanna (Eds.), *Motivated social perception: The Ontario symposium* (Vol. 9, pp. 93–116). Mahwah, NJ: Erlbaum.

Pelham, B. W., Carvallo, M., & Jones, J. T. (2005). Implicit egotism. *Current Directions in Psychological Science, 14,* 106–110.

Narcissism

Definition

Narcissism in its extreme forms is considered a personality disorder. It is defined as a syndrome or combination of characteristics that includes the following: (a) a pervasive pattern of grandiosity, self-importance, and perceived uniqueness; (b) a preoccupation with fantasies of unlimited success and power; (c) exhibitionism and attention seeking; (d) emotional reactivity especially to threats to self-esteem; (e) displays of entitlement and the expectation of special treatment from others; and (f) an unwillingness or inability to show empathy.

Researchers have also investigated a less-extreme form of narcissism that is termed the *narcissistic personality type.* These individuals possess most or all of the characteristics of the narcissistic personality disorder but are considered within the normal range of personality. Several self-report measures of narcissistic personality have been used to identify narcissists for research purposes. The most widely used scale is the Narcissistic Personality Inventory (NPI), and it is thought to measure both narcissistic personality disorder as well as narcissism in the normal population. The NPI is understood to contain at least four subscales: leadership/authority, superiority/arrogance, self-absorption/self-admiration, and entitlement/exploitativeness. However, an individual must score fairly highly on each dimension to be considered a narcissistic personality type.

Development

Clinical theories of narcissism posit that adult narcissism has its roots in early childhood experiences. Although Sigmund Freud originally applied the term, Hans Kohut and Otto Kernberg are the two most influential theorists in the area of narcissism. Both Kohut and Kernberg focus on disturbances in early social (parental) relationships as the genesis of adult narcissistic personality disorder. Also, both view narcissism at its core as a defect in the development of a healthy self. According to Kohut, the child's self develops and gains maturity through interactions with others (primarily the mother) that provide the child with opportunities to gain approval and enhancement and to identify with perfect and omnipotent role models. Parents who are empathic contribute to the healthy development of the child's self in two ways. First, they provide mirroring that fosters a more realistic sense of self. Second, parents reveal limitations in themselves that lead the child to internalize or assume an idealized image that is realistic and possible to attain. Problems are introduced when the parent is unempathetic and fails to provide approval and appropriate role models. According to Kohut, narcissism is in effect developmental arrest in which the child's self remains grandiose and unrealistic. At the same time, the child continues to idealize others to maintain self-esteem through association.

Kernberg argues that narcissism results from the child's reaction to a cold and unempathetic mother. His theory is quite the opposite of Kohut's position. According to Kernberg, the emotionally hungry child is enraged by his parents' neglect and comes to view them as even more depriving. Narcissism in this view is a defense reflecting the child's attempt to take refuge in some aspect of the self that his parents valued; a defense that ultimately results in a grandiose and inflated sense of self. Any perceived weaknesses in the self are split off into a separate hidden self. Narcissists, in Kernberg's view, are grandiose on the outside but vulnerable and questioning of their self-worth on the inside. The theories of Kernberg and Kohut are different in many important respects; however, both characterize narcissists as individuals with a childhood history of unsatisfactory social relationships who as adults possess grandiose views of the self that foster a conflicted psychological dependence on others.

Contemporary Views of Narcissism

More recent social and personality psychologists have studied narcissism as a syndrome or collection of traits that characterizes the narcissistic personality type as opposed to narcissistic personality disorder. This perspective views narcissists as people who are preoccupied with maintaining excessively positive self-concepts. These individuals become overly concerned about obtaining positive, self-aggrandizing feedback from others and react with extreme positive or negative emotions when they succeed or fail to receive information that others hold them in high regard. Narcissists want positive feedback about the self, and they actively manipulate others to solicit or coerce admiration from them. In this view, narcissism is thought to reflect a form of chronic interpersonal, self-esteem regulation.

Assessment

The diagnosis of narcissistic personality disorder is usually determined through clinical evaluation of the person. However, the narcissistic personality type is measured through self-report questionnaires such as the NPI. This questionnaire presents respondents with a set of forced-choice items in which they must decide which of two statements is most descriptive of them. For example, a person completing the NPI would be asked whether the statement "people always seem to recognize my authority" or "being an authority doesn't mean that much to me" best describes them. People who score high on the NPI have been shown to display a wide variety of narcissistic behaviors such as arrogance, superiority, and aggressiveness. In addition, people with a clinical diagnosis of narcissistic personality disorder score higher on the NPI than do people with other psychiatric diagnoses or normal controls.

Relevant Research

Research findings employing the NPI describe a portrait of narcissists as possessing inflated and grandiose self-images. It is not surprising then that they report having high self-esteem. However, these positive self-images appear to be based on biased and inflated perceptions of their accomplishments and their distorted views of what others think about them. For example, they overestimate their physical attractiveness relative to judges' ratings of their attractiveness, and they overestimate their intelligence relative to objective assessments of their IQ. In one experiment, narcissistic and nonnarcissistic men were interviewed by a woman whose responses were completely scripted. That is, all men received the same social feedback. Nonetheless, narcissistic men believed that the woman liked them better and was more romantically interested in them than did nonnarcissistic men. Other findings indicate that narcissists take greater credit for good outcomes even when those outcomes occurred by luck or chance.

Although narcissists' self-esteem is high, it is also fragile and insecure. This is evidenced in that their self-esteem is much more variable, fluctuating from moment to moment, day to day, than is the self-esteem of less narcissistic people. Other research indicates that narcissists are more likely to have high explicit self-esteem and low implicit self-esteem. This finding suggests that although narcissists describe themselves in positive terms, their automatically accessible self-feelings are not so positive.

Narcissists' positive but insecure self-views lead them to be more attentive and reactive to feedback from other people. However, not just any response or feedback from others is important to narcissists. They are eager to learn that others admire and look up to them. Narcissists value admiration and superiority more than being liked and accepted. Studies find that narcissists' self-esteem waxes and wanes along with the extent to which they feel admired. Moreover, narcissists are not passive in their desire for admiration from others but, rather, pursue it by attempting to manipulate the impressions they create in others. They make self-promoting and self-aggrandizing statements and attempt to solicit regard and compliments from those around them.

It follows that if narcissists are constantly seeking positive feedback from other people then they should react negatively when people around them fail to provide such support. Accordingly, narcissists respond with anger and resentment when they feel threatened by others. They are more likely to respond aggressively on such occasions. They will derogate those who threaten them even when such hostile responding jeopardizes the relationship.

Narcissists attempt to solicit admiration from those around them, and their hostility when others fail to respond appropriately contributes to the disturbed interpersonal relationships that are a hallmark of the disorder. Research has shown that people describe their narcissistic acquaintances as trying to impress others by bragging and putting down others. These behaviors are initially successful in that interaction partners find narcissists to be competent and attractive. However, over time these partners come to view the narcissist as arrogant and hostile.

Findings from an impressive range of studies suggest a picture of the narcissists as people who use their friends to feel good about themselves. They pander for attention and admiration to support self-images that are positive but easily threatened. They are constantly on alert for even the smallest slight that they perceive as disrespect. Perhaps most important, narcissists' striving to self-enhance at the expense of their friends ultimately costs them the friendships.

Frederick Rhodewalt

See also Narcissistic Entitlement; Self-Enhancement; Self-Esteem; Self-Esteem Stability

Further Readings

Rhodewalt, F. (2005). Social motivation and object relations: Narcissism and interpersonal self-esteem regulation. In J. Forgas, K. Williams, & S. Laham (Eds.), *Social motivation* (pp. 332–350). New York: Cambridge University Press.

Rhodewalt, F., & Morf, C. C. (2005). Reflections in troubled waters: Narcissism and interpersonal self-esteem regulation. In A. Tesser, J. Wood, & D. Stapel (Eds.), *On building, defending, and regulating the self* (pp. 127–151). New York: Psychology Press.

Rhodewalt, F., & Sorrow, D. (2003). Interpersonal self-regulation: Lessons from the study of narcissism. In M. Leary & J. P. Tangney (Eds.), *Handbook of self and identity.* New York: Guilford Press.

NARCISSISTIC ENTITLEMENT

Definition

Narcissistic entitlement refers to a belief that one's importance, superiority, or uniqueness should result in getting special treatment and receiving more resources than others. For example, individuals high in narcissistic entitlement think that they should get more respect, more money, and more credit for doing the same work as everyone else. Narcissistic entitlement also includes a willingness to demand this special treatment or extra resources.

Context and Importance

Narcissistic entitlement contains three components. At the root of narcissistic entitlement, individuals believe that they are uniquely superior. That is, they believe that they are different from others in ways that make them superior. Second, individuals with high levels of narcissistic entitlement feel that they are more deserving of special treatment and limited resources by virtue of their superiority and uniqueness. Finally, they are likely to demand the special treatment and resources to which they believe they are entitled (e.g., receiving a bigger handful of candy than the other children at a holiday party or a paycheck that is larger than what comparable individuals earn). These demands may be in the form of verbal statements, but may also include aggressive and even violent behavior.

Special treatment can include a wide range of things but in general refers to an expectation of treatment that is unique (and usually better) from how others are treated. For example, individuals with high levels of narcissistic entitlement might demand the best seat at a restaurant or not to have to wait in line when everyone else does. They might demand to be called "Sir" or "Doctor" at all times. They might refuse to allow other individuals to be critical of or challenge their thoughts or ideas (a courtesy that they might not reciprocate).

Narcissistic entitlement is traditionally measured with a short subscale of the Narcissistic Personality Inventory as proposed by Robert Raskin and Howard Terry in 1988. This scale has proven to predict narcissistic behavior very well, but also to lack in statistical reliability. As a result, W. Keith Campbell, Angelica M. Bonacci, Jeremy Shelton, Julie J. Exline, and Brad J. Bushman have created other stand-alone measures of entitlement that have greater reliability.

Narcissistic entitlement can have both positive and negative outcomes for the entitled individual. When individuals act in a narcissistically entitled way, they may actually receive better treatment or greater resources than others (and more than they deserve). For example, the person at the airline counter who says he is a very important business person and demands to be seated in first class might actually end up in a first class seat. However, acts of narcissistic entitlement are often perceived by others as rude, selfish, and even pathetic. If upon landing, the businessman appears lost, the other passengers might simply ignore him rather than offering directions. Indeed, narcissistic entitlement by individuals often leads to scorn and replies such as, "Who died and made you king?"

Narcissistic entitlement can be a short-term and context-dependent state of mind. An individual might display narcissistic entitlement in one situation but not in others. For example, a person may display narcissistic entitlement at home around his younger brother, but not around his peers back at school. Narcissistic entitlement can also be a general feature of an individual's personality. Some individuals display more narcissistic entitlement than do others across most situations and at most times. For example, a person might insist upon special treatment from her parents and deference from her younger sister, demand an A from a professor in a class when she really earned a C, and expect everyone to pay for her drinks when she is out.

W. Keith Campbell
Joshua D. Foster

See also Narcissism; Psychological Entitlement

Further Readings

Campbell, W. K., Bonacci, A. M., Shelton, J., Exline, J. J., & Bushman, B. J. (2004). Psychological entitlement: Interpersonal consequences and validation of a new self-report measure. *Journal of Personality Assessment, 83,* 29–45.

Exline, J. J., Baumeister, R. F., Bushman, B. J., Campbell, W. K., & Finkel, E. J. (2004). Too proud to back down: Narcissistic entitlement as a barrier to forgiveness. *Journal of Personality and Social Psychology, 87,* 894–912.

Raskin, R. N., & Terry, H. (1988). A principle components analysis of the Narcissistic Personality Inventory and further evidence of its construct validity. *Journal of Personality and Social Psychology, 54,* 890–902.

NARCISSISTIC REACTANCE THEORY OF SEXUAL COERCION

Definition

The narcissistic reactance theory of sexual coercion and rape explains how the personality of rapists intersects with situational factors to produce reactance. Reactance is a psychological motive to reassert one's sense of freedom when freedom has been denied. In the case of rape, some men will desire sex more after they have experienced a sexual rejection. Rapists will be motivated to reassert their freedom by aggressing against the woman who has denied them sex and by forcing her to have sex. Reactance cannot fully explain rape because most men do not rape when they are refused sex. The narcissistic reactance theory of sexual coercion asserts that men who display narcissistic personality characteristics are more prone to rape in the face of sexual refusal.

Reactance Results From Sexual Refusal

The typical date rape occurs after a man and a woman have engaged in some sexual activity short of intercourse such as kissing or oral sex. The man wants to continue, but the woman refuses. The rapist then uses physical strength or psychological intimidation to force the woman to have sexual intercourse. Theories of psychological reactance help explain why a man might steal sex from a woman who has refused him.

Reactance is a psychological state that results from threats to one's freedom. When a person's freedom has been limited by rejection, reactance theory predicts that the threatened freedom will be viewed as a forbidden fruit. Held out of reach, the forbidden fruit is seen as more important than before. Freedom is reasserted by aggressing against the individual who has refused and engaging in the behavior that has been forbidden.

Reactance theory can apply to the typical date rape scenario. When a woman refuses a sexual advance, a rapist may perceive this refusal as a threat to his freedom. Then he may feel more motivated to have sex with the woman. Some evidence on rape supports this view. Men who are sexually aggressive believe that when a woman "teases" and then denies a man, rape is justified. Ex-lovers and husbands are especially likely to rape women with whom they have had prior sexual relations. It is possible that after the break-up, sex with this woman becomes even more valuable, and the ex-lover feels he must use force to reassert the freedom that he has lost.

The Narcissistic Rapist

Narcissism as a general personality trait may help explain how some men cross the line from sexual rejection to rape. Narcissists are arrogant and feel an exaggerated sense of self-importance. They harbor delusions that they are more successful, important, intelligent, and handsome than the average person. Because of their perceived superiority, narcissists possess strong feelings of entitlement. They tend to be demanding of admiration from others. They are also exploitative and lack empathy for other people. Narcissists also become aggressive when they have been criticized or their egos have been threatened.

Given these characteristics, narcissists would be especially susceptible to reactance following a sexual rejection. The narcissist believes that he is superior to other men in intelligence and attractiveness, and he becomes aggressive when his self-views are challenged. A sexual refusal would likely be the ultimate challenge because the narcissist believes that he is especially deserving and entitled to a woman's admiration and sexual compliance. This increased sense of entitlement intensifies his desire to have sex following a refusal and leads to an increased need to reassert his freedom by forcing a woman to have sex.

Research on rapists supports the idea that rapists have narcissistic qualities. Rapists tend to be arrogant and show cognitive delusions. Rapists also tend to demonstrate a sense of entitlement in that they are likely to feel that they were entitled to sex with a woman whom they had courted with effort and money especially if she had consented to some sexual activity in the past. Rapists often claim that their victims were promiscuous. A narcissist would become especially angry at a woman whom he believed was easy for other men but refusing of him and would likely take this refusal as a personal insult: If she has had sex with an inferior man, she should definitely not refuse the narcissist! Rapists also show the selective empathy that narcissists demonstrate. Rapists are unwilling to see the situation from their victim's perspective. They may report that they never thought about how the woman was experiencing the event or that they believed the woman actually enjoyed the rape.

Evidence for the Theory

Although ethical restraints prohibit direct laboratory tests of this theory, some experimental evidence indicates that narcissism and reactance combine to foster attitudes that are supportive of date rape. Narcissists are more likely to endorse myths about rape and show less empathy for rape victims than are non-narcissists. Although most men are turned off by a rape that occurs after a couple has shown mutual affection, narcissists

find the same scenario enjoyable, entertaining, and sexually arousing. Laboratory tests have also shown that when a female accomplice in an experiment refuses to read a sexually explicit passage to a narcissist, narcissists find this personally insulting and retaliate against her. Men who are not narcissistic do not behave similarly. These results suggest that narcissists support rape that occurs after they believe a man has been led on, and they experience psychological reactance when they undergo a sexual refusal.

Kathleen R. Catanese

See also Date Rape; Narcissism; Rape; Reactance

Further Readings

Baumeister, R. F., Catanese, K. R., & Wallace, H. M. (2002). Conquest by force: A narcissistic reactance theory of rape and sexual coercion. *Review of General Psychology, 6,* 92–135.

Brehm, J. W. (1966). *A theory of psychological reactance.* New York: Academic Press.

Bushman, B. J., Bonacci, A. M., Van Dijk, M., & Baumeister, R. F. (2003). Narcissism, sexual refusal, and aggression: Testing a narcissistic reactance model of sexual coercion. *Journal of Personality and Social Psychology, 84,* 1027–1040.

NEED FOR AFFILIATION

Definition

Human beings differ from each other in how much they like to associate with other people. Some people avoid being alone, put a high priority on their friendships, and try hard to please other people. Others are just the opposite: They are content to be alone, they don't put much effort into their relationships with other people, and they aren't very concerned about making other people happy. Henry Murray coined the term *need for affiliation* to differentiate people who are generally friendly, outgoing, cooperative, and eager to join groups from those who are unfriendly, reserved, and aloof. Most people could probably be described as having a moderate need for affiliation, but some people have an extremely low need and others have an extremely high need.

Murray used the term *need* to describe a kind of force within a person that organizes a person's thoughts, feelings, and behavior. A person with a high need for affiliation is so motivated to build and maintain relationships with other people that many of his or her thoughts, emotions, and actions are directed toward fulfilling this motivation.

Nature of the Need

Having a high need for affiliation probably sounds like an important part of a desirable personality. Many people, after all, would rather think of themselves as being friendly than as cold or standoffish. And there are some advantages to having a high need for affiliation. Murray noted that people with a high need for affiliation try hard to make other people happy, which probably helps them build and maintain strong relationships. But there are also some disadvantages. People with high need for affiliation tend to be conforming and may even go along with unwise choices made by people around them. Under some circumstances, people with a high need for affiliation may also have trouble getting their work done. They may put such a high priority on socializing that they neglect some of their other goals.

Murray believed that the way people express their need for affiliation depends on other aspects of their personality. A person who is high in the need for affiliation and also high in need for nurturance might be extremely kind, but a person who is high in the need for affiliation and high in the need for deference might be extremely compliant. In other words, a group of people who are all high in the need for affiliation might consist of people who are all outgoing, but they would differ in other ways according to their unique need profiles.

Social psychologists have recently shown much interest in the need to belong, and it is important to understand how this related concept is different from the need for affiliation. The need to belong is considered a universal human drive to establish and maintain lasting, positive relationships with other people. Most researchers describe the need to belong as a component of human nature, or something that all normal human beings possess. Much research suggests that if people do not maintain at least a minimum quantity of enduring, healthy relationships, their well-being will suffer. The need for affiliation, on the other hand, is

used to describe people's personalities. People vary in how motivated they are to socialize and establish new contacts, and this is what is meant by the idea that there are individual differences in the need for affiliation. People who are high in the need for affiliation are more motivated to form relationships than other people are, and as a result, they may be more successful at fulfilling their need to belong.

Research Developments

Murray conducted his research on the need for affiliation in the mid-20th century, and researchers have since advanced psychologists' understanding of this motive considerably. Early research on the need for affiliation used the Thematic Apperception Test, which requires respondents to interpret a number of ambiguous pictures, to identify the strength of people's need for affiliation. But since that time, other tests of the need for affiliation have emerged. For example, Douglas Jackson designed a need for affiliation scale as part of his comprehensive measure of personality known as the Personality Research Form. Years later, Craig Hill developed the Interpersonal Orientation Scale, a self-report questionnaire that measures several specific components of affiliation motivation. The development of these and other tests have made it possible for researchers to find out how the need for affiliation shapes people's experiences.

Early research on the need for affiliation yielded results that confirmed Murray's description of the need. Relative to people with a low need for affiliation, people with a high need for affiliation are more concerned about others' acceptance, feel more empathy for others, are more likely to initiate contacts and friendships, and are more likely to conform to the wishes of experts who pressure them into a decision.

Other research has made discoveries that Murray might not have anticipated. For example, Hill's research shows that in some ways women have a higher need for affiliation than men do. Compared with men, women report that they get more pleasure from interacting with other people and are more likely to seek out others' company when they are upset. Hill's research also shows that people with a high need for affiliation can be discriminating when they choose a conversational partner: They prefer people who are warm and friendly to more than reserved people. This result makes sense in light of much social psychological research that shows that people tend to like others who are similar to themselves.

People with a high need for affiliation may also be better leaders than people with a low need for affiliation. In a study conducted by Richard Sorrentino and Nigel Field, students with a high need for affiliation were described by their fellow students as more leader-like than students with a low need for affiliation. But the students who were considered the most leader-like of all were students who were high in both the need for achievement and the need for affiliation. This research suggests that successful leaders are both ambitious and sociable.

Paul Rose

See also Contingency Model of Leadership; Introversion; Need to Belong; Thematic Apperception Test; Traits

Further Readings

Hill, C. A. (1987). Affiliation motivation: People who need people . . . but in different ways. *Journal of Personality and Social Psychology, 52,* 1008–1018.

Murray, H. A. (1938). *Explorations in personality: A clinical and experimental study of fifty men of college age.* New York: Oxford University Press.

Need for Closure

Definition

Need for cognitive closure refers to the desire or motivation to have a definite answer or knowledge instead of uncertainty or doubt. The need for closure is resolved by any answer, and the answer is accepted simply because it is available. Thus, need for closure does not refer to knowledge or decisions regarding a specific question, nor does it refer to the need for accuracy. The need for closure can arise from within the person, as a personality trait—or from the situation, such as when it is urgent to make a decision quickly.

History and Modern Usage

Early psychologists used ideas similar to need for closure, such as openness to experience and intolerance of ambiguity, to refer to broad personality traits and an often dysfunctional style of thinking. Today, need for closure is described as a broader motivation that may affect how a person thinks or reacts in a situation. In addition, need for closure is described as both a stable personality trait and as something that can be provoked by the situation.

Situations that may trigger need for closure include those in which failing to decide has harmful consequences, as well as situations in which the act of thinking about or working on the task is unpleasant. For example, pressure to make quick decisions, boring tasks, and uncomfortable environments (e.g., extreme heat or noise) tend to increase need for closure. In contrast, individuals may avoid closure when the task is enjoyable or the answer is obviously wrong. In addition, individuals vary in their need for closure. Across situations, some individuals prefer to have firm answers quickly, whereas others are more comfortable with uncertainty.

One consequence of need for closure is urgency, or the desire to come to an answer quickly. Urgency leads to a tendency to quickly seize upon the first information that provides an answer. A second consequence of need for closure is permanence, or the tendency to stick to an answer. Permanence leads to a tendency to freeze upon the answer or decision once it is reached. Thus, need for closure may lead individuals to focus only on the initial information provided and to be less likely to change their answers when confronted with new evidence.

The urgency and permanence tendencies of need for closure have been shown to affect how individuals consider information. Need for closure results in focusing on initial information when forming impressions of others, searching for fewer alternative explanations, and using more stereotypes. Need for closure may result in less empathy and perspective taking because these may challenge one's own judgment. Need for closure may also result in being less persuaded by other people's arguments and a preference to interact with people who are more susceptible to persuasion. During group interaction, need for closure may also result in less tolerance of group members who disagree with the majority or who may hinder task completion.

Janice R. Kelly
Jennifer R. Spoor

See also Cognitive Consistency; Mindfulness and Mindlessness; Need for Cognition

Further Readings

Webster, D. M., & Kruglanski, A. W. (1998). Cognitive and social consequences of the need for cognitive closure. In W. Stroebe & M. Hewstone (Eds.), *European review of social psychology* (pp. 133–173). Hoboken, NJ: Wiley.

NEED FOR COGNITION

Definition

Need for cognition refers to an individual's tendency to engage in and enjoy activities that require thinking (e.g., brainstorming puzzles). Some individuals have relatively little motivation for cognitively complex tasks. These individuals are described as being low in need for cognition. Other individuals consistently engage in and enjoy cognitively challenging activities and are referred to as being high in need for cognition. An individual may fall at any point in the distribution, however.

Background and History

The term *need for cognition* was originally introduced by Arthur Cohen and his colleagues in the 1950s and was brought back into popularity by John Cacioppo and Richard Petty in the 1980s. In Cohen's original work, need for cognition was defined as the need to make sense of the world. Therefore, greater need for cognition was associated with preference for structure and clarity in one's surroundings. That approach emphasized intolerance for ambiguity and thus appears closer to contemporary scales that measure need for structure or need for closure than to the current definition of need for cognition. However, Cacioppo and Petty retained the term *need for cognition* in acknowledgment of Cohen and his colleagues' early work.

Cacioppo and Petty conceptualized need for cognition as a stable individual difference (i.e., a personality trait) in the tendency to engage in and enjoy cognitively effortful tasks across a wide variety of domains (e.g., math, verbal, spatial). Need for cognition is assumed to reflect a stable intrinsic motivation that can be developed over time. In the modern way of thinking about need for cognition, the emphasis is on cognitive processing (i.e., the activity of engaging in mentally challenging tasks) rather than on cognitive outcomes (e.g., a structured knowledge of the world). Importantly, need for cognition taps into differences in motivation rather than ability. This is supported by research showing that need for cognition is only moderately related to measures of ability such as verbal intelligence, ACT scores, and high school and college GPA, and continues to predict relevant outcomes after cognitive ability is controlled. It is a matter of whether one likes to think, not whether one is good at thinking.

Measurement

Although the Need for Cognition scale was originally developed as a 34-item inventory, the most commonly used version contains 18 items that people rate on 5-point scales as being characteristic of themselves (or not). Some examples of scale items are "I prefer complex to simple tasks," "The notion of thinking abstractly appeals to me," and "I prefer my life to be filled with puzzles that I must solve." The scale has been established to have high internal consistency, suggesting that the individual scale items tap into the same construct. The scale also demonstrates good validity. That is, the scale correlates with other scales that measure individual differences that should be independent of but related to need for cognition. For instance, the scale correlates positively with other scales that measure the tendency to make complex attributions and the tendency to seek relevant information for decision making and problem solving.

Enjoyment of Cognitive Challenges

Consistent with the definition of need for cognition (NC), research indicates that high NC individuals spontaneously engage in a variety of mentally effortful tasks, whereas low NC individuals will participate in such activities only when there are external incentives to do so. For example, high NC individuals distinguished between strong and weak messages in a persuasive communication. This occurred regardless of whether the message came from a trustworthy or untrustworthy source or took a surprising position or not. Low NC individuals, on the other hand, distinguished between strong and weak arguments only when the arguments came from an untrustworthy source or took a surprising position. This means that low NC individuals scrutinized the message only when there were other motivations to do so (e.g., to check on an untrustworthy source). Other special circumstances that motivate low NC individuals to think include unexpected arguments, an approaching deadline, and a personally relevant topic.

This research suggests that high NC individuals find mentally complex activities inherently enjoyable, but low NC individuals do not. Much evidence indicates that high NC individuals experience cognitively demanding tasks more positively than low NC individuals do. Several studies demonstrated that compared with low NC individuals, high NC individuals reported more positive affective reactions (e.g., ratings of task enjoyment and pleasantness) and less negative ones (e.g., frustration and tension) to mental challenges such as math problems and complex number search tasks. Furthermore, high NC individuals have a greater tendency to seek information about new products and complex issues. For example, they are more likely to tune in to presidential debates. Such active pursuit of information reflects high NC individuals' intrinsic motivation for mental activity and challenges.

Engagement in Cognitively Effortful Tasks

Given their enjoyment of mental challenges, it is expected that high NC individuals have a chronic tendency to participate in cognitively effortful tasks. For example, high NC individuals are more likely to have an abundance of task-relevant thoughts than low NC individuals do. Furthermore, these thoughts are more likely to determine the attitudes of high rather than low NC individuals. For example, in one study, participants saw an advertisement that contained strong arguments for an answering machine. High NC individuals listed more positive thoughts to the strong arguments presented than did low NC individuals. In addition, attitudes toward the answering machine were correlated with thoughts among high NC individuals but not low NC individuals.

High NC individuals have more thoughts regarding persuasive messages and other stimuli, and they are more likely to think about their thoughts, engaging in metacognition. When high NC individuals are confident in their thoughts, they rely on them more than when they lack confidence in them. For low NC individuals, metacognitive processes are less likely. That

is, they are less likely to think about whether the few thoughts they have are valid.

In sum, high NC individuals' thoughts and attitudes are influenced by their effortful assessment of the merits of the information they receive and the perceived validity of their thoughts. Low NC individuals, on the other hand, are more affected by simple cues that are contained in communications. In one study, participants viewed an ad for a typewriter. The ad was endorsed by either two unattractive women or two attractive women. Although high NC individuals gave equally positive ratings to the typewriter regardless of endorser attractiveness, low NC individuals' ratings were more positive when the typewriter was endorsed by attractive than unattractive women. Because the attitudes of high NC individuals are more likely to be based on effortful thought, they tend to be held more strongly. Indeed, research has demonstrated that the attitudes of high NC individuals, compared with low NC individuals, are more persistent, more resistant to attacks, and more predictive of behavior.

Besides attitude-related consequences, another implication of high NC individuals' tendency to process information is that they have better memory for information to which they have been exposed. For instance, when students received arguments about the implementation of senior comprehensive exams, those high in NC recalled a greater proportion of the arguments than did those low in NC. In addition, high NC individuals have more knowledge on a variety of issues. In the domain of politics, high NC individuals listed more information about presidential candidates and more consequences of electing various candidates to office. In other research, high NC individuals listed more types of birds and performed better on a trivia test than low NC individuals did.

Biased Processing

Sometimes, variables can bias one's processing. Because high NC individuals tend to focus on generating their own thoughts to information rather than relying on simple cues, their processing of information is more susceptible to various biases. One source of bias is mood. In one study, positive mood made attitudes more favorable in both high and low NC individuals. The difference is that whereas mood had a direct impact on attitudes in low NC individuals (i.e., mood served as a simple cue), it influenced attitudes in high

NC individuals in a more thoughtful way (i.e., by affecting their perception of the message arguments).

Although high NC individuals may sometimes be biased in their processing, they are also more likely to correct their judgments if biases are detected because they are more likely to engage in the cognitive effort required for such correction. When the biasing factor is subtle and not very salient, it tends to bias the thoughts of high NC individuals (as just described), but when the biasing factor is more blatant, high NC individuals tend to correct for the bias. When they overcorrect for the bias, this can actually lead to a reverse bias.

Need for cognition is an often-researched variable in social psychology because of its implications for people's attitudes, judgments, and decision making. This is because whether an individual is high or low in NC influences how the individual processes information and reacts to variables such as a source's trustworthiness, the individual's own mood, and so on.

Ya Hui Michelle See
Richard E. Petty

See also Elaboration Likelihood Model; Individual Differences; Intrinsic Motivation; Traits

Further Readings

Cacioppo, J. T., Petty, R. E., Feinstein, J. A., & Jarvis, W. B. G. (1996). Dispositional differences in cognitive motivation: The life and times of individuals varying in need for cognition. *Psychological Bulletin, 119,* 197–253.

NEED FOR POWER

Definition

Need for power is defined as the desire to control or influence others. It is not necessarily associated with actually having power, but instead with the *desire* to have power. In 1933, Henry Murray defined a long list of what he considered to be basic human needs. These needs were seen as directing behavior, and people were assumed to vary by how important each need was to them as an individual. One of these needs was the need for power. Some of the early empirical work on need for power was done by David McClelland and David Winter, who refined the definition and developed methods of testing for people's level of need for power. Need for power (also called power motivation) was seen as one of the three fundamental social motives, along with need for achievement and need for affiliation.

Associated Behaviors

Needs for power can be expressed in behavior in many ways. One of these is the use of physical or psychological aggression to force others to comply with what one wants from them. One can also express the need for power through gaining a reputation as an important person. Other behaviors associated with high power motivation include trying to affect the emotions of others. This could be done by telling jokes, or by a musical or dramatic performance. Finally, need for power can be expressed through providing (often unsolicited) advice or help. The association of helping behavior with other expressions of power motivation is not intuitively obvious, but the diverse set of behaviors listed here have been tied together empirically. They are all forms of exerting power over others. This power is sometimes exercised for one's own direct benefit, but can also be done with the apparent goal of doing something good for another person.

Some behaviors that have been found to characterize those high in need for power include having a high level of physical fights or verbal arguments with others. Enjoyment of debating might be a characteristic of someone high in need for power. Those who express their power motivation in this way may be very uncomfortable when others see them as powerless or weak. For this reason, they may be seen as hostile or chronically angry. This type of expression of need for power is often seen in negative terms.

Another type of behavior associated with need for power that is more socially acceptable is taking leadership in group situations. Those high in need for power enjoy running an organization, making decisions, or being in charge of a group. They run for elected office. They define what they are doing as motivated by "service" or "duty," but this labeling of their behavior may be a result of the fact that American society frowns on people openly saying they like to have power.

Gaining a reputation is another expression of power motivation. People may display their need for power by making sure their names are visible on their doors, writing letters that will be published, with their names identified, or doing other things that stand out and lead to other people knowing who they are. One way of building a reputation is to have possessions that are valued by others in the group. These prestige possessions might be particular types of clothing, or music, or any other objects that will impress others. When asked to remember members of a group at a later point, those high in power motivation are more often remembered than are those low in power motivation.

Those high in need for power may also express this by taking a guiding role within their close relationships. They like to give advice to their friends and to propose and plan joint activities. These types of behaviors result in the high-need-for-power individual being more dominant in the relationship. However, when two people who are both high in power motivation do form a relationship, they may alternate in taking the dominant role within the relationship.

Helping behavior resulting from high need for power can be expressed in work roles. One form of this is mentoring, whereby one takes responsibility for guiding a person of lower status within the organization. Mentors motivated by need for power tend to believe that by mentoring others, they will gain a more positive reputation within the organization. By establishing relationships with talented junior members of the organization, they also build a power base that may enable them to gain more power within the organization as those they have mentored rise in the organizational hierarchy.

Knowing levels of need for power provides information that can predict job choice and performance. People who are successful managers within large corporations have been found to be high in need for power. Those working in government positions, where one is providing some type of service, or enforcing regulations, have also been found to be high in power motivation. Being a journalist is another power-related occupation, possibly because of the link with gaining reputation. The set of occupations known as the helping professions are associated with high power motivation. Thus, people who are interested in teaching, being members of the clergy, or being psychologists all tend to be high in need for power. In these types of fields, although the goal is to provide important help to other people, one is also able to exert influence over others and to express desires for power in a way that is socially acceptable, especially for women, who tend to dominate in many of these helping professions.

Although there are many ways of expressing power motivation, those high in the motive may focus on only one type of expression, or they may display many of these. They may express power in one way at one point in their lives, but in another way at a different point. It has been suggested that more aggressive forms of power expression are more common in younger adults, whereas parenting and helping others may be seen more in older adults. Social role expectations affect power motivation expression as well. In general, men are more able to express power through aggression and leadership in large organizations. Women often express power in close relationships or the family.

Testing Methods

Need for power is considered to be an unconscious motivation. People are not necessarily aware of their own level of need for power. In fact, openly admitting a desire to have power or influence is not considered socially acceptable, and many would deny having a high need for power. Because of this, researchers cannot simply ask people if having power is important to them. Instead, a variety of projective techniques are used, where people are given some type of vaguely defined task. One of the best known of these is the Thematic Apperception Test. This involves showing people a series of fuzzy pictures and asking them to write a story about each of them. It is assumed that they will draw details in these stories from their own unconscious as they write these stories. Stories are coded for the existence of specific types of themes and given a score for need for power (or other psychological needs). This coding system is very complex and extensive training is needed to do this well. More recently, power motivation has been measured through asking about some of the behaviors mentioned earlier that are associated with the basic need, as determined by the earlier Thematic Apperception Test story coding. Those who display these power-oriented behaviors are assumed to be high in the need for power.

Irene Hanson Frieze

See also Control; Influence; Leadership; Power; Thematic Apperception Test

Further Readings

Frieze, I. H., & Boneva, B. S. (2001). Power motivation and motivation to help others. In A. Y. Lee-Chai & J. A. Bargh (Eds.), *The use and abuse of power: Multiple perspectives on the causes of corruption* (pp. 75–89). Philadelphia: Psychology Press.

McClelland, D. C. (1975). *Power: The inner experience.* New York: Wiley.

Winter, D. G. (1973). *The power motive.* New York: Macmillan.

NEED TO BELONG

Definition

The need to belong refers to the idea that humans have a fundamental motivation to be accepted into relationships with others and to be a part of social groups. The fact that belongingness is a need means that human beings must establish and maintain a minimum quantity of enduring relationships. These relationships should have more positivity than negativity and be meaningful and significant to the relationship partners.

Background and History

The psychological history of a belongingness motive has a long history, with psychologists including Sigmund Freud recognizing that humans need to be a part of groups and relationships. Freud believed that the desire for relationships comes from people's sex drive or was connected more to bonds between parents and children. Abraham Maslow, whose great psychological legacy was to create a motivational hierarchy, put belongingness needs in between satisfying physical needs (such as being fed and getting enough sleep) and needs for self-esteem. Thus, these early psychologists recognized that humans strive to be a part of relationships, but they did not place supreme significance on this drive.

John Bowlby was probably the first psychologist to develop the idea that belongingness is a special need and was one of the first to perform experimental tests on the idea. Bowlby is best known for his attachment theory, which says that people's early relationships with their caregivers (e.g., parents) are the foundation for how people will respond to others in close, intimate relationships for the rest of their lives. Bowlby saw that people varied in how they behaved toward people they were close to, and that these variations could be observed among children and their mothers.

The most influential version of the need to belong theory was proposed by Roy Baumeister and Mark Leary, whose theory put relationship needs as one of the most important needs that humans must fulfill. They compared satisfying the need to belong to securing necessities, such as food and shelter, which are needed to survive. Baumeister and Leary said that satisfying the belongingness motive requires that two aspects of relationships be met: The first part is that people need to have positive and pleasant, not negative, interactions with others. The second part specifies that these interactions cannot be random but, rather, should take place as part of stable, lasting relationships in which people care about each other's long-term health and well-being.

The reason that the need to belong is essential for humans is that being a part of groups and intimate relationships helped humans to survive in ancestral history. When enemies would attack, when animals would prey, or when it was difficult to find food or shelter, those people who were part of a group were more likely to survive than was the lone man or woman needing to fend for himself or herself. Reproduction too was much easier with another person, as is fairly obvious, and those people who could get into and start a part of a band of others were more likely to have offspring and thus pass their genes onto future generations of humans. Even if loners can create a pregnancy by having sex during a chance encounter with one another, those children would be less likely to survive to adulthood than would children who grow up supported and protected by a group. In these ways, evolution likely favored early humans with a stronger need to belong, and so today's humans are mainly descended from them—and therefore probably inherited that strong need.

Although early theories about the need to belong emphasized one-to-one relationships, more recent work has made clear that larger groups can satisfy the need also. Some people (and perhaps men more than women) can feel connected to a large group, such as a team or company or university, and this bond can take the place of intimate relationships to some extent.

Importance and Consequences

The importance of the need to belong was documented by Baumeister and Leary when they detailed the emotional, cognitive, and physical aspects of the need to belong. One way to look at the importance of the need to belong is to document what happens when the need is unmet. The reason that scientists would examine the consequences of an unsatisfied need to belong is the same reason that scientists would need to study what happens when people fail to get enough food or water; not having enough of something and seeing the negative outcomes that follow gives meaningful scientific information that the missing piece (in this case, relationships with others) is essential for healthy functioning.

Support for need to belong idea was demonstrated by research showing that social bonds are formed easily and without the need for special circumstances or additions. Even when people must part (such as when graduating from college), they are often quite upset about having to part and consequently make promises to keep the relationships going through visits, mail, telephone, and so on. Sometimes people who are not going to see each other again will say "see you soon" as a parting because the idea of not seeing someone again is too unsettling to say aloud.

There are cognitive (mental) components to the need to belong. For instance, people seem to categorize information in terms of relationships, and they readily see relationships between people, even when they do not exist. Have you ever been at a store and had the clerk ask if you and the person next to you in line (a stranger) are on the same bill? This is an example of people's tendency to see relationships between others. When two people are part of a couple, the cognitive representations of the self and the partner get clumped together in mind, making it so that information about the partner is classified in a similar manner as to the self. When relationships break up, people find themselves thinking about the relationship partner over and over again, with thoughts of the other person intruding into other thoughts.

Emotions play a large role in the formation and dissolution of relationships. When people make a new friend or fall in love, they experience happiness and joy. Getting into a desired social group, such as a sorority or academic club, brings people happiness. Despite the stress that comes from having a child, people are excited about becoming a parent before it happens, express positivity with being a parent (usually) during the child's years at home, and look back on the experience as being joyful and rewarding. Having a new relationship, especially one as central to

the person as having one's own child, is likely responsible for those good feelings. In fact, being happy with one's life is largely the result of how many relationships one has and how satisfying those relationships are. Although people may think that money makes them happy, it turns out that being a part of happy, stable relationships is a much bigger influence on happiness.

Conversely, when people are excluded from groups or their relationships fall apart, they feel a variety of negative emotions. Anxiety is one of the primary forms of negative emotions resulting from a loss of a relationship, with children as young as 1 year old showing separation anxiety when they must be without their mothers for some time. Depression and sadness too can result from not being accepted into groups or relationships, and often depression and anxiety go hand in hand when people feel rejected. Jealousy is another negative feeling that is directly related to interpersonal bonds. Jealousy is the feeling that someone is going to (or has) taken away something that one has and does not want to lose (such as a special relationship partner). More than 50% of people say they are jealous people, and the number may be even higher than that because some people try to hide their jealousy. Loneliness is a chronic state of feeling that one does not have enough satisfying relationships. Loneliness is more than not having social contact because a person could have multiple interactions throughout the day but still feel lonely. Feeling lonely is an example of how interactions must take place in the context of long-lasting relationships to satisfy the need to belong.

Researchers have documented physical ills that occur when people are not part of groups or relationships. For instance, married people have better health than single, divorced, or widowed people. Married people live longer, have fewer physical health problems, and have fewer mental health problems. Married people who are diagnosed with cancer survive longer than do single people who have similar forms of cancer. Lonely people are especially known to have ill health. Researchers have studied lonely people for some time and have shown that they get more common illnesses, such as head colds and the flu, as well as have weakened immune systems more generally. Women who have eating disorders are more likely to have had troubled relationships with their mothers when they were young. Veterans who feel they have a lot of social support are less likely to suffer from post-traumatic stress disorder when they return from battle. In short, people have higher quality lives and live longer when they feel a part of supportive, caring relationships.

Individual Differences

People differ in how much they need to be around others and how badly it hurts not to have other people accept them. Mark Leary and his colleagues created a scale, the Need to Belong Scale, to measure people's individual needs for acceptance. People who score high on the Need to Belong Scale want badly to be accepted into social interactions and react strongly to being excluded. People who score low on the scale desire fewer close relationships, although again a minimum number of close ties are important for all human beings.

Kathleen D. Vohs

See also Attachment Theory; Close Relationships; Interdependent Self-Construals; Kin Selection; Rejection

Further Readings

Baumeister, R. F., & Leary, M. R. (1995). The need to belong: Desire for interpersonal attachments as a fundamental human motivation. *Psychological Bulletin, 117*, 497–529.

NEGATIVE-STATE RELIEF MODEL

Definition

The negative-state relief (NSR) model is a theory that attempts to describe how one situational factor—sadness—relates to the willingness to help others. Specifically, this theory predicts that at least under certain circumstances, a temporary feeling of sadness is likely to result in an increased willingness to help others. For example, a person who is sad because a close friend just cancelled a planned visit would be more likely to help a stranger push his or her car out of a snow bank. Why would a sad mood lead to an increased willingness to help others? According to this theory, this is for selfish reasons. Specifically, people have been socialized in such a way that they are rewarded for helping other people. Over time, people internalize this and find helping others rewarding. When a person is sad, he or she is motivated to repair that mood and anticipates that helping another person would do so. More simply, when people are sad, they may be more likely to help others because they believe that doing so will make them feel better.

Significance and History

Human beings would have been unlikely to survive their early history as a species without the existence of helping behavior. Even in modern times, human beings often need assistance from others. Sometimes such assistance is provided; other times, it is not. Knowing why people do or do not help others in particular situations, then, is important both for a complete understanding of human social behavior and for informing attempts to increase helping behavior. The study of helping behavior has a rich history in social psychology, and the NSR model is an early theory of such behavior.

Early studies on the association between positive mood and helping provided unambiguous results. Being in a positive mood is consistently associated with a greater willingness to help others. This might suggest that being in a negative mood ought to make people less likely to help others, but early research on this topic provided less clear results. Some of these studies found that people were more likely to help when in a negative mood whereas others found that people were less likely to help when in a negative mood. The NSR model was an attempt to reconcile these inconsistent findings. This theory suggests that people in a negative mood are more likely to help others only when the helping behavior is not overly aversive and when they have internalized the rewarding nature of helping others. If helping another person is too costly, then doing so is unlikely to improve one's mood. Moreover, if a person does not anticipate that helping another person will improve one's mood, sadness is unlikely to result in increased helping.

Evidence

Considerable evidence indicates that helping other people does indeed improve one's mood. In experimental studies, participants who were able to provide help to another person reported that they were in better moods than did participants who were not given a chance to provide help to another person. This suggests that helping others may be a successful means of repairing a sad mood, and that people may be aware of this. These findings support the NSR model.

Direct evidence also shows that the induction of a sad mood causes people to be more helpful. Pre-teen and teenage research participants who were asked to recall depressing events were more likely to help others when given a chance. However, this pattern was reversed in younger children. These findings provide nice support for the NSR model. Older participants, who presumably have learned that helping other people is rewarding, were more likely to help when they were sad. Younger participants, however, presumably have not yet internalized the lesson that helping others is rewarding, and therefore do not do so as a means of improving their own mood.

Additional evidence is consistent with other aspects of the NSR model. First, research has demonstrated that negative moods only lead to increased helping when the cost of such help is relatively low. This makes sense given that incurring high costs to help someone else is likely to offset any mood improvement resulting from the provision of help. Second, evidence suggests that sad people help even more when they view their own mood as changeable. This, too, makes sense in light of the NSR model. If a person does not believe that his or her mood is changeable, it follows that helping another person will not improve mood. It makes sense, then, that they help less than do people who do think their moods can change.

Whereas the NSR model, as originally written, was intended to apply only to sadness, some evidence suggests that it may apply to at least one other negative emotion. Studies indicate that the experience of guilt is consistently associated with a greater likelihood of helping others. Other studies indicate that negative emotions like anger and anxiety do not increase helping, however.

Controversy

Despite evidence in support of the NSR model, there are critics. Some researchers have found results that seem to contradict the model. For example, evidence indicates that sadness leads to increased helping even when people anticipate that their mood will improve for other reasons. This seems to contradict the NSR model because it shows that sad people are more likely to help even when they do not need to do so to improve their moods. Moreover, an analysis of several

published studies has challenged key assumptions of the NSR model (e.g., that the relationship between sadness and helping increases with age). This analysis has its own critics, however, and there is still disagreement regarding the accuracy of the NSR model.

Regardless, the NSR model has contributed to psychologists' understanding of conditions under which people are more or less likely to help. It has generated a substantial amount of research, continues to do so, and is likely to have an enduring influence, despite differences of opinion regarding its accuracy.

Steven M. Graham

See also Altruism; Empathy–Altruism Hypothesis; Helping Behavior; Prosocial Behavior

Further Readings

Batson, C. D., Batson, J. G., Griffit, C. A., Barrientos, S., Brandt, J. R., Sprengelmeyer, P., et al. (1989). Negative-state relief and the empathy-altruism hypothesis. *Journal of Personality and Social Psychology, 56,* 922–933.

Cialdini, R. B., & Kenrick, D. T. (1976). Altruism as hedonism: A social developmental perspective on the relationship of negative mood state and helping. *Journal of Personality and Social Psychology, 34,* 907–914.

NEUROTICISM

Definition

Neuroticism refers to a broad personality trait dimension representing the degree to which a person experiences the world as distressing, threatening, and unsafe. Each individual can be positioned somewhere on this personality dimension between extreme poles: perfect emotional stability versus complete emotional chaos. Highly neurotic individuals tend to be labile (which means they have plenty of emotional reactions), anxious, tense, and withdrawn. Individuals who are low in neuroticism tend to be content, confident, and stable. The latter report fewer physical and psychological problems and less stress than do highly neurotic individuals.

Neuroticism is associated with distress and dissatisfaction. Neurotic individuals (i.e., those who are high on the neuroticism dimension) tend to feel dissatisfied with themselves and their lives. They are more likely to report minor health problems and to feel general discomfort in a wide range of situations. Neurotic individuals are more prone to negative emotions (e.g., anxiety, depression, anger, guilt). Empirical studies suggest that extremely high levels of neuroticism are associated with prolonged and pervasive misery in both the neurotic individuals and those close to them.

History

The concept of neuroticism can be traced back to ancient Greece and the Hippocratic model of four basic temperaments (choleric, sanguine, phlegmatic, and melancholic, the latter most closely approximating neuroticism). In modern psychometric studies of personality and psychopathology, neuroticism tends to be identified as a first general factor (i.e., the variable with the broadest power in explaining individual differences). For example, as much as 50% of the variability in "internalizing" forms of psychopathology (mental illness) such as depression, anxiety, obsessive-compulsion, phobia, and hysteria can be explained by a general dimension of neuroticism. For this reason, neuroticism almost always appears in modern trait models of personality, though sometimes with slightly different theoretical formulations or names (e.g., trait anxiety, repression-sensitization, ego-resiliency, negative emotionality). Hans Eysenck popularized the term *neuroticism* in the 1950s by including it as a key scale in his popular personality inventory. Neuroticism figures prominently in the influential Big Five model of personality disposition and in tests designed to measure the Big Five, such as the NEO Personality Inventory. Neuroticism is even reflected in inventories designed for clinical psychological use, such as the recently developed "Demoralization" scale on the Minnesota Multiphasic Personality Inventory–2.

Growing but still limited evidence suggests that most major personality traits (including Neuroticism) identified by Western psychology manifest universally. Evidence of the importance of neuroticism in individuals from diverse cultures (and who use different languages) can be found in large-scale cross-cultural studies of personality.

Biological Basis

Accruing research data show persuasively that individual differences in neuroticism are substantially heritable (which means they are passed from parent to child). Heritability estimates based on twin studies generally fall in the 40% to 60% range. The remaining individual differences in neuroticism are attributed primarily to unique (nonfamilial) environmental differences; the shared familial environment appears to exert virtually no reliable influence on individual differences in neuroticism. Researchers speculate that overreactivity of the limbic system in the brain is associated with high levels of neuroticism, but specific neurochemical mechanisms or neuroanatomical loci have not yet been identified.

Costs of Extreme Levels of Neuroticism

Highly neurotic individuals are defensive pessimists. They experience the world as unsafe and use fundamentally different strategies in dealing with distress than non-neurotic people do. They are vigilant against potential harm in their environment and constantly scan the environment for evidence of potential harm. They may withdraw from reality and engage in protective behaviors when they detect danger.

Highly neurotic individuals tend to be poor problem solvers. Because of their tendency to withdraw, they tend to possess an impoverished repertoire of behavioral alternatives for addressing the demands of reality. Consequently, they tend to engage in mental role-play (rumination and fantasy) instead of constructive problem-solving behaviors. In contrast to their impoverished behavioral repertoires, however, they may possess a rich inner world. Introspective and apt to analyze their thoughts and feelings, they are highly invested in seeking the true nature of their intrapsychic experiences. Successful artists (e.g., Woody Allen) are sometimes neurotic individuals who have developed creative channels through which to tap their rich, overpopulated intrapsychic worlds.

Although high neuroticism is related to a deflated sense of well-being, high levels of neuroticism are not always associated with unfavorable characteristics. Neurotic behaviors may be essential for survival by facilitating safety through the inhibition of risky behaviors. Neurotic individuals tend to possess high anticipatory apprehension that may orient them to pay closer attention to contingencies previously associated with punishments. Also, the subjective discomfort (i.e., anxiety) regarding violations of social convention is greater in a neurotic individual than in others; thus, it is less likely that a neurotic individual will become involved in antisocial activity. For instance, adolescents with extremely low neuroticism have been shown to possess a higher risk of adult criminality and to experience low levels of uncomfortable physiological arousal over violations of social conventions.

Keenly attuned to their inner experiences, those high in neuroticism are also attentive to their physical discomforts. Their health maintenance behaviors (e.g., consultations with a physician) are more frequent than those of individuals with less neuroticism. Although their complaints regarding health are more frequent, their objectively assessed health is not poorer than those low in neuroticism. To the contrary, their general health is often found to be better, for example, with less frequent diagnosis of cancer. Researchers hypothesize that this finding is attributable to early detection of potentially harmful symptoms associated with frequent health maintenance behaviors.

Sangil Kwon
Nathan C. Weed

See also Big Five Personality Traits; Defensive Pessimism; Genetic Influences on Social Behavior; Individual Differences; Traits; Twin Studies

Further Readings

Costa, P. T., & McCrae, R. R. (1980). Influence of extroversion and neuroticism on subjective well-being: Happy and unhappy people. *Journal of Personality and Social Psychology, 38,* 668–678.

Goldberg, L. R. (1993). The structure of phenotypic personality traits. *American Psychologist, 48,* 26–34.

Watson, D., & Casillas, A. (2003). Neuroticism: Adaptive and maladaptive features. In E. Chang & L. Sanna (Eds.), *Virtue, vice, and personality: The complexity of behavior* (pp. 145–161). Washington, DC: American Psychiatric Press.

Wiggins, J. S. (Ed.). (1986). *The five-factor model of personality: Theoretical perspectives.* New York: Guilford Press.

NONCONSCIOUS EMOTION

It seems that people can be wrong about or unaware of many things, but at least they can be sure about their own emotions. Yet, psychologists challenge even that certainty and point out that one's emotional life can be a mystery, even to oneself. The idea of nonconscious emotion proposes in its strongest form that people can be in an emotional state (as demonstrated by its impact on behavior, physiology, and cognition) without having any conscious awareness of being in that state.

Evidence

One source of speculation about the relation between emotion and awareness are the works of Sigmund Freud. Freud clearly believed that people can be wrong about the cause of their emotion (as when a person's anger at his or her boss comes from the similarity of the boss to the person's father) or the exact nature of their emotions (as when a person confuses love with hate). There is little empirical support for Freud's most dramatic speculations. However, some evidence indicates that people can be mistaken about some aspects of their emotional states. For example, one study found that in phobic individuals, negative mood can be elicited by presenting them with fear-relevant snakes and spiders. Another study found that positive mood can be elevated by repeated subliminal presentation of simple geometric figures. Many studies demonstrated that arousal resulting from one source (e.g., crossing a bridge) can be mistaken as deriving from another source (e.g., romantic attraction).

Note, however, that in these studies, people were aware of their emotions (though not of the causes). Could an emotion itself be nonconscious? Among psychologists, the issue is somewhat controversial. Some researchers think that the presence of a conscious feeling (the phenomenal component of emotion) is necessary to call a state an emotion. Other researchers think that conscious feeling is only one aspect of emotion, and the presence of emotion can be detected in behavioral and physiological changes. The latter possibility is supported by several lines of evidence.

First, from the standpoint of evolution and neuroscience, at least some forms of emotional reaction should exist independently of subjective correlates. Evolutionarily speaking, the ability to have conscious feelings is a late achievement compared with the ability to have behavioral affective reactions to emotional stimuli. Basic affective reactions are widely shared by animals, including reptiles and fish, and at least in some species may not involve conscious awareness comparable with that in humans. After all, the original function of emotion was to allow the organism to react appropriately to positive or negative events, and conscious feelings might not always have been required.

The neurocircuitry needed for basic affective responses, such as a positive reaction to a pleasant sensation or a disliking reaction to a threatening stimulus, is largely contained in emotional brain structures that lie below the cortex, such as the nucleus accumbens, amygdala, hypothalamus, and even lower brain stem. These subcortical structures evolved early and may carry out limited operations that are essentially preconscious, compared with the elaborate human cortex at the top of the brain, which is more involved in conscious emotional feelings. Yet even limited subcortical structures on their own are capable of some basic affective reactions. A dramatic demonstration of this point comes from affective neuroscience studies with anencephalic human infants. The brain of such infants is congenitally malformed, possessing only a brain stem, and lacking nearly all structures at the top or front of the brain, including the entire cortex. Yet sweet tastes of sugar still elicit positive facial expressions resembling liking from anencephalic infants, whereas bitter tastes elicit negative facial expressions resembling disgust.

Even in normal brains, the most effective "brain tweaks" so far discovered for enhancing basic related affective reactions all involve deep brain structures below the cortex. Thus, animal studies have shown that liking for sweetness increases after a drug that activates opioid receptors is injected into the nucleus accumbens (a reward-related structure at the base of the front of the brain). Liking reactions to sugar can even be enhanced by injecting a drug that activates other receptors into the brain stem, which is perhaps the most basic component of the brain. Such examples reflect the persisting importance of early-evolved neurocircuitry in generating behavioral emotional reactions in modern mammalian brains. In short, evidence from affective neuroscience suggests that basic affective reactions are mediated largely by brain structures deep below the cortex, raising the possibility that these reactions might not be accessible to conscious awareness.

However, neuroscientific evidence from animals and brain-damaged patients by itself is only suggestive about the idea of nonconscious emotion. Fortunately, there are some demonstrations of nonconscious emotion in typical individuals. One study explored nonconscious emotion in a paradigm where participants rated visible Chinese ideographs preceded by subliminal happy or angry faces. Though the subliminal faces influenced the ratings of ideographs, participants interviewed after the experiment denied experiencing any changes in their conscious feelings. Furthermore, participants' judgments were still influenced by subliminal faces even when they were asked not to base their judgments of ideographs on their emotional feelings. Even better evidence for nonconscious emotion comes from a study showing that participants are unable to report a conscious feeling *at the same time* a consequential behavior reveals the presence of an affective reaction. Specifically, in this study participants were subliminally presented with a series of happy, neutral, or angry emotional facial expressions. Immediately after the subliminal affect induction, some participants first rated their conscious feelings (mood and arousal) and then poured themselves and consumed a novel fruit drink. Other participants first poured and consumed a drink and then rated their conscious feelings. The results showed that, regardless of the task order, the ratings of conscious feelings were unaffected by subliminal faces. Yet, participants' consumption behavior and drink ratings were influenced by subliminal affective stimuli, especially when participants were thirsty. Specifically, thirsty participants poured more drink from the pitcher and drank more from their cups after happy, rather than after angry, faces. In short, these results suggest a possibility of nonconscious emotion in the strong sense—a reaction powerful enough to alter behavior, but of which people are simply not aware, even when attending to their feelings.

Implications

Thus, it seems that there are situations when a person can have an emotional reaction without any awareness of that reaction. This phenomenon has several important implications. For example, nonconscious emotions are, almost by definition, hard to control, thus raising the possibility of insidious influence by stimuli strong enough to change behavior without influencing conscious feelings. Clinically, the idea of unconscious emotion is relevant to certain kinds of psychiatric disorder, such as alexithymia, characterized by inability to access or describe one's own feelings. The possibility that emotional behavior may occur without consciousness also raises some troubling questions whether, for example, facial or bodily emotional expressions (including that of pain) of brain-damaged patients reflect an activity of nonconscious emotional programs or some minimal consciousness.

The existence of nonconscious emotional reactions does not mean that conscious feelings are epiphenomenal—which means an interesting but unnecessary "icing on emotional cake" that plays little role in controlling behavior. Clearly, conscious feelings play an important function in what people do and deserve a central place in emotion research and clinical practice. However, the research suggests that many aspects of what is called emotion may be separable from conscious feeling, and that researchers and practitioners of emotion science should not limit themselves to self-reports of subjective experiences when assessing the presence of emotion.

Several critical questions need to be addressed by future research. First, nonconscious states might be primarily differentiated only on a positive-negative valence, rather than on more qualitative aspects associated with specific emotions (fear, anger, disgust, etc.). Some evidence indicates that subcortical circuitry is capable of qualitative differentiation, and studies could test whether different emotional behaviors could be elicited without accompanying conscious feelings. Second, the human studies discussed here relied on simple and highly learned stimuli, such as subliminal facial expressions. Future research should address whether complex, culturally coded stimuli can also elicit valenced behavioral changes without accompanying feelings. Finally, future work should examine what exact psychological and neural mechanisms determine whether an emotional reaction remains nonconscious or is accompanied by conscious feelings. The scientific research on nonconscious emotion has just began, and the near future is certain to bring many exciting findings.

Piotr Winkielman

See also Affect; Emotion; Mere Exposure Effect; Nonconscious Processes

Further Readings

Damasio, A. R. (1999). *The feeling of what happens: Body and emotion in the making of consciousness.* New York: Harcourt Brace.

Ohman, A., Flykt, A., & Lundqvist, D. (2000). Unconscious emotion: Evolutionary perspectives, psychophysiological data and neuropsychological mechanisms. In R. D. Lane, L. Nadel, & G. Ahern (Eds.), *Cognitive neuroscience of emotion* (pp. 296–327). New York: Oxford University Press.

Winkielman, P., & Berridge, K. C. (2004). Unconscious emotion. *Current Directions in Psychological Science, 13,* 120–123.

NONCONSCIOUS PROCESSES

Definition

Nonconscious (or unconscious) processes are all the processes people are not consciously aware of. As opposed to what most people think, nonconscious processes make up most interesting psychological processes. People are only consciously aware of a very limited subset of psychological processes.

Analysis

There is logic behind this division of labor between nonconscious and conscious processes whereby consciousness is only involved in a very limited subset. First, consciousness can generally do only one thing at a time. You cannot simultaneously engage in two activities that both require conscious attention (e.g., watching a good movie and reading a book). Second, the amount of information consciousness can process is very limited. In the 1950s, researchers tried to compare the amount of information consciousness can handle with the amount all our senses (all nonconscious processes combined) can deal with. They measured information in bits—the simple dichotomous unit computers work with. They found, for instance, that when we read, we can process about 50 bits per second (this is a fairly short sentence). Generally, consciousness can process about 70 bits per second. Our senses though, can deal with a stunning amount of information: about 11.2 million bits per second.

It is difficult to quantify the processing capacity of humans, so one should not take these numbers too literally—they are approximations. Still, the difference is enormous. If we translate them to distances, we could say that if the processing capacity of all our senses is the height of the Empire State Building, the processing capacity of consciousness is a tenth of an inch. No wonder most psychological processes are nonconscious!

Structural Versus Learned Nonconscious Processes

Some psychological processes are nonconscious simply because we are the way we are. Other psychological processes are nonconscious because they are well-learned. Initially, such processes are conscious.

It is impossible to provide an exhaustive list of the structural nonconscious processes and the learned nonconscious processes because there are too many. Examples have to suffice.

An example of a structural nonconscious process is search in memory. If I ask you, "What are the three largest cities in the United States?," you will be able to come up with an answer (the correct one is New York, Los Angeles, and Chicago). However, you do not really have conscious insight about how this works. Your nonconscious provides your consciousness with answers, but how you derive the answers is a mystery to consciousness. Memory search is a nonconscious process.

An example of a learned nonconscious process is an increase in achievement motivation when you do an exam. As children, we learn that we when we do an exam or test, we have to do our best. We concentrate hard, we think hard, and we use all our energy to do the test the best we can. Initially, however, we have to learn this. After having taken a few tests, the process becomes nonconscious. The mere fact that we are facing an exam is enough to increase our achievement motivation.

Ap Dijksterhuis

See also Automaticity; Controlled Processes; Dual Process Theories; Memory; Nonconscious Emotions

Further Readings

Wilson, T. D. (2002). *Strangers to ourselves: Discovering the adaptive unconscious.* Cambridge, MA: Harvard University Press.

NONEXPERIMENTAL DESIGNS

Definition

Nonexperimental designs are research methods that lack the hallmark features of experiments, namely manipulation of independent variables and random assignment to conditions. The gold standard for scientific evidence in social psychology is the randomized experiment; however, there are many situations in social psychology in which randomized experiments are not possible or would not be the preferred method for data collection. Many social psychological variables cannot be manipulated, or ethics would keep one from doing so. For example, a researcher cannot randomly assign people to be in a relationship or not or to stay in a relationship for a long versus short period of time. Similarly, research participants cannot be randomly assigned to be male or female, homosexual or heterosexual, or Black or White. Therefore, the impact of important variables such as relationship status, culture, and ethnicity must be studied using nonexperimental designs.

Characteristics of Nonexperimental Research

Many nonexperimental studies address the same types of research questions addressed in experiments. They are aimed at testing whether the variable of interest *causes* people to react in certain ways to social stimuli. When this is the goal, nonexperimental studies often measure the variable of interest, often by asking people to report their beliefs or perceptions (such as measures of amount of self-confidence, of commitment to one's relationship, or of identification with one's ethnic group). Statistical analyses are then used to relate people's ratings to measures of other variables thought to be influenced by the initial variable. Consider a simple example in which a researcher wants to learn whether being committed to remaining in a romantic relationship leads people to be happier than not being committed to a relationship. This researcher might survey research participants who are in relationships, asking them to report their current level of commitment to the relationship and their current level of general happiness. A typical type of statistical analysis in this case might be to correlate relationship commitment with level of happiness. Because correlation is a common type of analysis in these designs, many people use the term *correlational designs* when they are actually referring to nonexperimental designs. The term *nonexperimental* is preferred primarily because the same correlational analyses could be performed on either nonexperimental or experimental data. The status of the study is determined by the research methods, not by the type of statistics used to analyze the data. Yet, the reader should understand that the terms *correlational* and *nonexperimental* are often used interchangeably.

If, in the previous example, the data show that people currently committed to their relationships are happier than are people not committed to their relationships, does this mean that being committed to a relationship *makes* people happier? Maybe, but maybe not. One of the major problems with nonexperimental designs is the result might have occurred in many ways. In this example, it could be that commitment to their current relationships does make people generally happier. However, it could be that people who are generally happier also make more attractive mates. People may flock to those who seem happy (and may want to stay with them), but may shy away from people who seem sullen and unhappy (and may want to leave them). If commitment loves company, being happy may also make people more likely to be committed to a relationship, rather than relationship commitment making people happier. It could also be that a third variable might encourage people to be committed to relationships and might also make people happy. For example, if the research participants are students, it could be that people who are doing well in school are happier than people not doing well in school. It could also be that people who are doing well in school have the time for social activities that draw them closer to their relationship partners. However, if people are doing poorly in school, spending more time outside of class studying to catch up (or the stress of struggling to catch up) may pull them farther away from their relationship partners. Third variables could also be called *confounding* variables, because they confound the original causal link that is hypothesized to exist between the two variables of interest.

In a nonexperimental study, it can be difficult to tell which of a variety of explanations is the best. Because of this, researchers should include additional study features that help determine which explanations are best supported by the data. For instance, if our relationship researcher is concerned that happiness might lead to relationship commitment rather than commitment leading to happiness, he or she might measure people's happiness and relationship commitment over time. If it is true that happiness precedes commitment to a relationship, it should be possible to see that happy uncommitted people are more likely to become highly committed than are unhappy uncommitted people. It would also be possible to look at effects of relationship commitment controlling for one's level of happiness before committing to the relationship. That is, even if happier people want more to stay with their partners, it could be that commitment to the relationship provides an additional boost to happiness beyond the original level of happiness. Measuring the variables over time does not always identify the ordering of the variables in their causal chains, but it can help.

Measuring possible third (confounding) variables can also help in identifying the most likely causal relations among the variables. When these third (confounding)

variables are measured, specific alternative explanations can be tested. For example, if a researcher is concerned that class performance influences both the likelihood of relationship commitment and overall happiness, then a measure of class performance can be used to predict both of these variables. If class performance fails to predict one of the original variables, then it can be rejected as an explanation for the original relation between the two. Even if good class performance was correlated with relationship commitment and with increased happiness, analyses could be conducted using both relationship commitment and class performance to predict happiness. If commitment predicted happiness beyond class performance, this would undermine any concerns about class performance providing the best explanation for a relation between commitment and happiness.

Nonexperimental research can be conducted in laboratories or in naturalistic settings. In general, it might be more likely to see nonexperimental designs when research is conducted in natural (field) settings because the natural settings themselves might make it difficult or impossible to randomly assign people to conditions or to manipulate variables, even though one might still observe or measure the variables in that setting. Yet, it is important to realize that the distinction between experimental and nonexperimental research is not the same as the distinction between lab and field research. Either the laboratory or the field may serve as settings in which to conduct nonexperimental or experimental research.

It is equally important to realize that nonexperimental research includes a wide variety of research methods. Research questions similar to those described earlier (i.e., research aimed at addressing causal relations among variables) can use procedures other than asking research participants to directly report their beliefs or perceptions. For example, researchers might use archival data or direct observation to categorize a research participant's gender, ethnicity, or occupation. If so, the researcher might treat differences between these known groups as reflecting effects of the variables thought to differ between the groups. The problem, of course, is that these known groups might differ in many ways. Therefore, there are many potential third (confounding) variables to consider and possibly to test. Because of this, even if known groups are identified, the study should include direct measurement of the variables thought to differ across the groups to account for the effects of the third (confounding) variables.

Although many nonexperimental studies ask the type of causal questions described earlier, there are also other kinds of research questions. Some research asks whether a set of measures all tap one underlying psychological dimension. Correlational analyses of this type are used to create many of the multi-item scales that are used across areas of psychology. For example, if a researcher wants to create a multi-item measure of political affiliation, research participants might be asked to respond to a large set of measures asking about their liking or disliking of political figures, about political behaviors in which they have engaged, and about social policies they support or oppose. When determining which of these measures best fit together to assess overall political preferences, the research question is not which variables cause the others but instead what the best set of measures is to assess a person's political preferences. Other research questions might simply address which variables are correlated with which other variables or might attempt to identify what a certain group of people does or thinks about a certain issue. These research questions are both nonexperimental and noncausal, though forms of these studies can also be the building blocks for creating hypotheses about the causal relations among the variables of interest.

Duane T. Wegener
Jason T. Reed

See also Experimentation; Research Methods

Further Readings

Pelham, B. W., & Blanton, H. (2003). *Conducting research in psychology: Measuring the weight of smoke* (2nd ed.). Toronto: Thompson/Wadsworth.

Wegener, D. T., & Fabrigar, L. R. (2000). Analysis and design for nonexperimental data: Addressing causal and noncausal hypotheses. In H. T. Reis & C. M. Judd (Eds.), *Handbook of research methods in social and personality psychology* (pp. 412–450). New York: Cambridge University Press.

NONVERBAL CUES AND COMMUNICATION

Definition

Nonverbal cues are all potentially informative behaviors that are not purely linguistic in content. Visible nonverbal cues include facial expressions, head movements, posture, body and hand movements, self- and other-touching, leg positions and movements, interpersonal gaze, directness of interpersonal orientation, interpersonal distance, and synchrony or mimicry between people. Auditory nonverbal cues include discrete nonlinguistic vocal sounds (e.g., sighs) as well as qualities of the voice such as pitch and pitch variation, loudness, speed and speed variation, and tonal qualities (e.g., nasality, breathiness). Several additional behaviors are often included among nonverbal cues even though they are closely related to speech: interruptions, pauses and hesitations, listener responses (such as "uh-huh" uttered while another is speaking), and dysfluencies in speech. Clothing, hairstyle, and adornments, as well as physiognomy (such as height or facial features) are also considered to be nonverbal cues.

Psychologists' interest in nonverbal cues focuses on its relation to encoded meaning, relation to verbal messages, social impact, and development, and on differences between groups and individuals in their nonverbal behavior or skill in using and understanding nonverbal cues. Nonverbal behavior is ubiquitous throughout the animal kingdom, with numerous documented resemblances between the nonverbal behaviors of higher primates and humans. Nonverbal behavior is studied in many disciplines, including ethology, anthropology, sociology, and medicine, as well as all the subdisciplines of psychology. The content of the *Journal of Nonverbal Behavior* reflects the interdisciplinary nature of the field.

The distinction between nonverbal behavior and nonverbal communication is important, but not always easy to maintain in practice. Nonverbal behavior includes behavior that might be emitted without the awareness of the encoder (the one conveying the information), whereas nonverbal communication refers to a more active process whereby encoder and decoder (the one receiving the information) emit and interpret behaviors according to a shared meaning code. Because it is often difficult to distinguish the two, the terms *nonverbal behavior* and *nonverbal communication* are used interchangeably in this entry.

Interpretations

Nonverbal cues emitted by a person are likely to be interpreted by others, whether correctly or not, allowing for misunderstandings to occur. The process of drawing inferences from nonverbal cues is often not in conscious awareness; similarly, encoders may or may not be aware of the cues they are sending. The unintentional conveyance of veridical information through nonverbal cues is called *leakage*.

Nonverbal cues often accompany spoken words, and when they do, the nonverbal cues can augment or contradict the meanings of the words as well as combine with the words to produce unique messages, as in sarcasm, which involves the pairing of contradictory messages through verbal and nonverbal channels. Research has explored the impact of mixed verbal and nonverbal messages.

Some nonverbal behaviors have distinct meanings, most notably the hand gestures called emblems that have direct verbal translations (such as the "A-okay" sign or the "thumbs up" sign in North American usage). However, most nonverbal cues have multiple and often ambiguous meanings that depend on other information for correct interpretation (associated words, situational context, antecedent events, other cues, etc.). Some nonverbal behaviors are discrete (i.e., have distinct on-off properties), examples being nodding, blinking, pausing, and gestural emblems. Others are continuous, such as the fluid movements of the hands while speaking (called speech-dependent gestures), vocal qualities, and movement style.

The face and voice have been extensively studied relative to emotional expression, with at least six emotions having characteristic configurations of facial muscle movements and a variety of acoustic correlates. Nonverbal cues can also contribute to a person's emotional experience and self-regulation via physiological feedback processes; engaging in certain behaviors can produce the associated emotions.

Although it is commonly assumed that the main function of nonverbal behavior is to convey emotions, this is only one of several important purposes served by nonverbal behavior in daily life. Nonverbal cues are used to convey interpersonal attitudes, such as dominance, affiliativeness, or insult. Nonverbal cues of the face, eyes, voice, and hands are used in the regulation of turn-taking in conversation, and also for purposes of providing feedback regarding comprehension and interest to a speaker. Face and hand movements serve dialogic functions, for example, to illustrate, comment, refer, and dramatize. Speech-dependent gestures also contribute to fluent speech by facilitating word retrieval; speakers lose fluency and complexity if they are constrained from gesturing while speaking. Nonverbal cues can also arise from cognitive activity, as when hard thinking produces a furrowed brow or averted gaze.

The coordination of nonverbal behavior between people helps produce and maintain desired levels of arousal and intimacy. People (including infants) often mimic, reciprocate, or synchronize their movements with others. Such behavior matching can contribute to rapport. However, behavioral compensation is also a common occurrence; one person adjusts his or her behavior to compensate for another's behaviors, for example, by gazing less at another, or backing up, if the other is standing too close.

Another important function of nonverbal behavior is self-presentation, that is, to represent oneself in a desired way (as honest, nice, brave, competent, etc.). Related to self-presentation are societal display rules, conventions regarding what kinds of expressions are appropriate at what times and by whom. Examples are norms for how to behave nonverbally in different social situations (when disappointed, at a funeral, etc.) and norms that produce different degrees of outward emotional expressiveness in men and women. At one extreme of self-presentation is deliberate deception.

Nonverbal cues convey information, both intentionally and unintentionally, about emotions, attitudes, personality traits, intelligence, intentions, mental and physical health, physical characteristics, social group membership, deception, and roles, to give a few examples. However, the effects are often small in magnitude, indicating much variation in the predictability of such associations.

The following is a very short list of the many associations that have been found: Lying is associated with blinking, hesitations, and finger movements; a smile of true enjoyment can be distinguished from a polite, social smile by the movement of the muscles at the corner of the eyes; in friendly interaction, more gaze signifies a more positive attitude; persons of higher status or dominance engage in relatively less gazing while listening and relatively more gazing while speaking, and also speak louder and interrupt more; under stress, the pitch of the voice rises; more self-touching is associated with anxiety; women differ from men on a wide variety of nonverbal behaviors (including more smiling and gazing); Mediterranean, Middle Eastern, and Latin American cultures—called contact cultures—display more interpersonal touching and closer interaction distances in public than do non-contact cultures (Asia, Northern Europe); and the personality trait of extraversion is associated with louder and more fluent speech and heightened levels of gaze.

Of course, these are generalizations for which many exceptions can be found.

Nonverbal cues play a role in social influence, for example, persuasion and interpersonal expectancy effects, also called self-fulfilling prophecies. In the latter, one person's beliefs or expectations for another person can be fulfilled via nonverbal cues in a process that can be out of awareness for both parties. Thus, a teacher may be especially warm and nonverbally encouraging to a student believed to be very smart, or a new acquaintance may treat you coolly if he or she has heard you are not a nice person. In both cases, the expected behavior will actually be produced if the student responds with heightened motivation and achievement (confirming the teacher's belief) or if you reciprocate the other's coolness (confirming the acquaintance's belief).

Individuals and groups differ in the accuracy with which they convey information via nonverbal cues (called encoding, or sending accuracy) and interpret others' nonverbal cues (called decoding, or receiving accuracy). Researchers measure encoding accuracy by asking expressors to imagine or pose the intended message, by observing them in specific situations that arouse an intended state, or by observing them displaying their characteristic behavior styles. Accuracy in decoding nonverbal cues is measured by asking perceivers to watch or listen to nonverbal behaviors, either live or recorded, and to make assessments of the meanings of the cues (or to recall what behaviors occurred). The measurement of accuracy requires the establishment of a criterion for deciding what state or trait is actually conveyed in the stimulus.

Nonverbal skills advance over childhood and are often higher in females than in males. There is also evidence for cultural expression "dialects" that allow expressions of emotions to be more accurately judged by other members of that culture, or by people with greater exposure to that culture, than by outsiders. Research shows that nonverbal communication skills are higher in children and adults with healthy mental and social functioning.

Judith A. Hall

See also Babyfaceness; Behavioral Contagion; Crowding; Cultural Differences; Deception (Lying); Emotion; Emotional Intelligence; Expectancy Effects; Facial Expression of Emotion; Facial-Feedback Hypothesis; Mimicry; Nonconscious Processes; Person Perception; Self-Fulfilling Prophecy; Thin Slices of Behavior

Further Readings

Hall, J. A., & Bernieri, F. J. (Eds.). (2001). *Interpersonal sensitivity: Theory and measurement.* Mahwah, NJ: Erlbaum.

Hickson, M., III, Stacks, D. W., & Moore, N. (2004). *Nonverbal communication: Studies and applications* (4th ed.). Los Angeles: Roxbury.

Knapp, M. L., & Hall, J. A. (2005). *Nonverbal communication in human interaction* (6th ed.). Belmont, CA: Wadsworth.

Manusov, V. (Ed.). (2005). *The sourcebook of nonverbal measures.* Mahwah, NJ: Erlbaum.

Russell, J. A., & Fernández-Dols, J. M. (Eds.). (1997). *The psychology of facial expression.* New York: Cambridge University Press.

Normative Influence

Definition

Normative influence refers to the fact that people sometimes change their behavior, thoughts, or values to be liked and accepted by others. This results in conformity, in the form of individuals altering their utterances or demeanor to be more like what they perceive to be the norm. At the individual level, pivotal factors leading to normative influence are the desire to form a good impression and the fear of embarrassment. Normative influence is strongest when someone cares about the group exerting the influence and when behavior is performed in front of members of that group. It is one of social psychology's paradigmatic phenomena because it epitomizes the impact of the social world on an individual's thoughts and actions.

Normative influence has a somewhat negative image in Western industrialized cultures that value independent selves and individualistic values, and where being influenceable is seen as a character flaw. In reality, normative influence regulates people's daily lives much more than they like to recognize. Most people don't pay close attention to the dictum of fashion magazines, yet very few would go out dressed in ways that others might deem inappropriate. Furthermore, social psychological research has shown the surprising power and scope of normative influence: For example, it can lead to conformity to complete strangers, it can cause people to ignore evidence of their senses, it can effect widespread body image issues and eating disorders because of unrealistic ideals of beauty, and it can have disastrous consequences in cases of bystander effect and groupthink.

Normative Versus Informational Influence

Morton Deutsch and Harold Gerard first provided the useful distinction between normative and informational influence: Whereas normative influence results from wanting to fit in regardless of accuracy, informational influence results from believing that the group may know better. If a person enters a room and everyone else is whispering, he or she might start whispering too. If the person does it because he or she assumes others have a good reason that the person doesn't know about (e.g., a baby is sleeping or the roof could collapse at any minute), the person is yielding to informational influence; if the person does it because he or she is afraid of the sideway glances and frowns that the person might get for being loud, then the person is succumbing to normative influence. As this example illustrates, the two forms of influence are often intertwined, but this distinction is useful in analyzing instances of conformity, including some classics in the field. Muzafer Sherif's studies of conformity with the autokinetic effect, for example, are typically interpreted as showing primarily informational influence: Faced with the ambiguous stimulus of an apparently moving dot of light in a dark room, participants converged to a common understanding of their reality when estimating the light's movement. In contrast, Solomon Asch's line-naming paradigm is often seen as demonstrating normative influence: In deciding which stimulus line matched the length of a template, conforming participants chose to suppress the answer they knew to be true to go along with the clearly wrong response endorsed by the majority of their peers. Informational influence is fueled by wanting to know what's right, whereas normative influence is motivated by wanting to get along.

Norms That Influence

The social norms at work in normative influence can be thought as the set of acceptable behaviors, values, and beliefs governing a particular group or situation. They include prescriptions (how one should act) as well as proscriptions (what one shouldn't do). Some are culture-wide (e.g., one wears black at a funeral in the United States), whereas some are more situation-bound (e.g., if everyone else is standing up at a gathering, one might feel uncomfortable sitting down). Some norms are explicit (e.g., announcements about turning off one's cell phone in a movie theater), but some are more implicit and need to be figured out. Humans show remarkable skill at this, enabling them to get along in groups. One way that people discover implicit norms is through behavioral uniformity: If everyone is wearing a suit on a person's first day of work, the person realizes he or she should probably wear one too. Another is by seeing deviants being punished: After hearing several students making fun of a classmate for wearing a tie at a lecture, a professor might realize that the allegedly permissive campus actually has strong implicit norms dictating that one shouldn't dress formally for class. Norms can even be inferred when no one else is around by observing traces of other people's behavior in one's environment: In a littered street, people are more likely to litter than in a perfectly clean one. This last example has sometimes been used as an argument for zero-tolerance approaches to policing, under the assumption that evidence of petty vandalism in a neighborhood communicates a norm of lawlessness that leads to greater crimes.

One interesting feature of normative influence is that people conform to norms as people perceive them, not necessarily as they really are. Because discerning implicit norms is an imperfect inference process, it can lead to misperceptions. And indeed social psychology has documented such breakdowns, leading to conformity to an illusory norm. One such case is pluralistic ignorance, whereby a majority is ignorant of the true attitudes of the rest of the majority. On some college campuses, for example, most incoming students may misperceive that binge drinking is widely accepted, even though most students may in reality have private misgivings about it. Because of this misperception, normative influence leads students to keep their discomfort to themselves, and to boast instead about their drinking exploits. This leads others to believe in turn that drinking is widely accepted, a vicious cycle that ensures that the illusory norm is maintained. This example also illustrates the dynamic nature of normative influence more generally, in that each individual choosing to follow the norm publicly reinforces its grip on other individuals, and this snowballing can be reciprocal.

Deviants and Normative Influence

The weight of normative influence is felt most strongly by individuals who deviate from the group. Stanley Schachter's pioneering research suggested that groups react to deviants by monitoring them, trying to bring them into the fold, and if that doesn't work, rejecting them. Only people who have paid their dues by conforming to the group in the past, thus amassing what has been called idiosyncrasy credit, can express dissenting views with relative impunity. Especially in times of urgency or stress, when a consensus needs to be reached and a decision needs to be made, strong pressures to conform can lead groups to ignore doubts and suppress dissent, sometimes with disastrous consequences. Deviants can disrupt normative influence and instead propagate their own views when they present those consistently and uncompromisingly, a phenomenon called minority influence. They can also loosen the grip of normative influence on others merely by the fact that they exist, regardless of their own message: Studies show that people are less likely to conform when someone else disagrees with the majority, even if their own position differs from the deviant's.

How Deep Is Normative Influence?

How real are the changes brought about by normative influence? Some researchers have argued that whereas normative influence merely leads to compliance, a superficial and temporary behavior change with no accompanying change in values or beliefs, informational influence (as well as minority influence) is more likely to lead to conversion, a deeper reorganization of one's perceptions and attitudes, with longer-lasting consequences. This is suggested because normative influence seems to be strongest when the behavior is performed publicly in front of members of the group exercising the influence, and by the observation that individuals often revert to their initial attitude or belief once they are out of the normative influence situation. This intuition is captured by the use of private voting booths in democratic elections, recognizing that one's true attitude can be adulterated when expressed in the presence of others, but also assuming that it can be rekindled in isolation. By contrast, informational and minority influence has been found to lead to changes even in private responding, and to changes that can still be observed long after the individual left the influence setting.

Benoît Monin

See also Bystander Effect; Conformity; Deviance; Embarrassment; Group Polarization; Groupthink; Informational Influence; Norms, Prescriptive and Descriptive; Pluralistic Ignorance; Risky Shift

Further Readings

Asch, S. E. (1955). Opinions and social pressure. *Scientific American, 193*(5), 31–35.

Deutsch, M., & Gerard, H. G. (1955). A study of normative and informational social influence upon individual judgment. *Journal of Abnormal and Social Psychology, 51,* 629–636.

Moscovici, S. (1985). Social influence and conformity. In G. Lindzey & E. Aronson (Eds.), *Handbook of social psychology* (Vol. 2, pp. 347–412). New York: McGraw-Hill.

Schachter, S. (1951). Deviance, rejection, and communication. *Journal of Abnormal and Social Psychology, 46,* 190–207.

Sherif, M. (1935). A study of some social factors in perception. *Archives of Psychology, 27,* 187.

NORMS, PRESCRIPTIVE AND DESCRIPTIVE

Definition

Social norms are attributes of groups that generate expectations for the behavior of group members. Two types of norms differ in the source of the expectations. Descriptive norms refer to what most people in a group think, feel, or do; prescriptive or injunctive norms refer to what most people in a group approve of. The distinction here is between what is true of group members and what ought to be true of group members. In many cases, these two types of norms overlap. For example, wearing business suits is both a descriptive and a prescriptive norm for executives, just as wearing jeans is both a descriptive and a prescriptive norm for teenagers. Liberal political views are both a descriptive and a prescriptive norm on college campuses, just as traditional values are both a descriptive and a prescriptive norm in wealthy suburbs. However, sometimes descriptive and prescriptive norms diverge. For example, healthy eating and exercising are prescriptive norms for most adult Americans, but less so descriptive norms. Conversely, driving to work (as opposed to taking public transportation) is a descriptive norm in many communities, but certainly not a prescriptive norm.

Analysis

Although both descriptive and prescriptive norms guide behavior, they do so through different psychological processes. Descriptive norms guide behavior because people take them to represent the most sensible course of action, a process known as informational social influence. Prescriptive norms guide behavior because people take them to represent the socially sanctioned course of action, a process known as normative social influence. The two types of norms also differ in how people experience the consequences of violating them. Specifically violating a descriptive norm does not have quite the sting that violating a prescriptive norm has. For example, if knowing Latin is a descriptive norm at College X, a student who does not know Latin may feel relatively Latin-challenged; however, if knowing Latin is a prescriptive norm at College X, this student may very well feel ignorant and uneducated.

One final difference between descriptive and prescriptive norms concerns the scope of their influence on behavior. Descriptive norms influence behavior only within the particular situation and group for which the norm operates. Prescriptive norms have more far-reaching influence; they influence behavior across situations and populations. Thus, a descriptive norm of not smoking at College X will lead students to avoid smoking on campus but not off; a prescriptive norm of not smoking at College X will lead students to avoid smoking all together.

Deborah A. Prentice

See also Conformity; Informational Influence; Normative Influence

Further Readings

Cialdini, R. B., Kallgren, C. A., & Reno, R. R. (1991). A focus theory of normative conduct: A theoretical refinement and reevaluation of the role of norms in human behavior. *Advances in Experimental Social Psychology, 24,* 201–234.

Miller, D. T., & Prentice, D. A. (1991). The construction of social norms and standards. In E. T. Higgins & A. W. Kruglanski (Eds.), *Social psychology: Handbook of basic principles* (pp. 799–829). New York: Guilford Press.

OBJECTIFICATION THEORY

Definition

Objectification theory is a framework for understanding the experience of being female in a culture that sexually objectifies the female body. The theory proposes that girls and women, more so than boys and men, are socialized to internalize an observer's perspective as their primary view of their physical selves. This perspective is referred to as *self-objectification,* which leads many girls and women to habitually monitor their bodies' outward appearance. This, in turn, leads to increased feelings of shame, anxiety, and disgust toward the self, reduces opportunities for peak motivational states, and diminishes awareness of internal bodily states. Accumulations of these experiences help account for a variety of mental health risks that disproportionately affect women: depression, eating disorders, and sexual dysfunction. The theory also helps illuminate why changes in these mental health risks occur alongside life-course changes in the female body, emerging at puberty and diminishing after menopause.

Background and History

At the beginning of the 20th century, American psychologists explored the notion of the looking-glass self, which says that a person's sense of self is a social construction and reflects how others view him or her. This perspective is a precursor to objectification theory, which takes the looking glass, or mirror, component of this metaphor quite literally. The field's earlier notions of self disregarded the physical body as an important component of self-concept and focused almost exclusively on attitudes, values, motivations, and the like. However, studies show that for women, positive self-regard hinges on perceived physical attractiveness, whereas for men, it hinges on physical effectiveness. So objectification theory asks, what would a more embodied view of the self tell us about gender differences in mental health?

Feminist theorists have pointed a finger at Western culture's sexually objectifying treatment of women's bodies for a long time. Psychologist Karen Horney wrote, 75 years ago, about the socially sanctioned right of all males to sexualize all females, regardless of age or status. More recently, Sandra Bartky defined sexual objectification as occurring whenever a woman's body, body parts, or sexual functions are separated from her person, reduced to the status of mere instruments, or regarded as if they were capable of representing her. Furthermore, the notion that within this cultural milieu women can adopt an outside-in perspective on their own bodies has a fairly long history in feminist philosophy. Simone de Beauvoir argued that when a girl becomes a woman, she becomes *doubled;* so instead of existing only within herself, she also exists outside herself. The art historian John Berger showed that women become their own first surveyors as a way of anticipating their treatment in the world.

Objectification theory argues that, with the sexualization of the female body as the cultural milieu in which girls are raised, girls are socialized to treat themselves as objects to be looked at and evaluated for their appearance. The external pressures that encourage girls' own preoccupation with their physical appearances abound. Empirical evidence demonstrates that sexy, eye-catching women receive massive rewards in American culture. For example, compared with average weight or thin girls, heavier girls are less likely to be accepted to college. Physical attractiveness also correlates more highly with popularity, dating experience, and even marriage opportunities for girls and women than for men. It is as if physical beauty translates to power for girls and women. So, what Sigmund Freud called vanity in women, objectification theory explores as a survival strategy in a sexually objectifying culture; a survival strategy that may bring immediate rewards, but carries significant psychological and health consequences.

Importance and Consequences of Self-Objectification

Self-objectification functions as both a trait and a state. That is, some people are simply more likely to define themselves in ways that highlight a third person's, or observer's view, of their bodies. These people are high self-objectifiers. Studies show that, in general, women score higher than men in trait self-objectification. Situations can also call attention to the body as observed by others, and this is when self-objectification is a state. Imagine receiving a catcall or whistle while jogging.

A great deal of research has been conducted on the theorized consequences of self-objectification. The first, and perhaps most insidious, consequence of self-objectification is that it fragments consciousness. The chronic attention to physical appearance that girls and women can engage in leaves fewer cognitive resources available for other mental activities. One study demonstrated this fragmenting quite vividly. In it, college students were asked to try on and evaluate, alone in a dressing room, either a swimsuit or a sweater. While they waited for 10 minutes in the garment, they completed a math test. The results revealed that young women in swimsuits performed significantly worse on the math problems than did those wearing sweaters. No differences were found for the young men. In other words, thinking about the body, comparing it with sexualized cultural ideals, disrupts women's mental capacity.

Other work has demonstrated physical as well as mental capacity can be disrupted by self-objectification. One study showed girls whose bodily self-concepts were more appearance-oriented threw a softball with a less-effective shoulder and humerus swing than did girls with a more competence-based view of their bodily selves. The widely scorned phenomenon of "throwing like a girl," in other words, might better be phrased, "throwing like a self-objectified person."

Studies show that the constant monitoring of appearance that accompanies self-objectification leads to increased feelings of shame and anxiety about one's body. Shame is an emotion that occurs when one perceives one's failure to meet cultural standards of conduct. The chronic comparison of one's own body with the impossible cultural standards of attractive, sexy appearance is a recipe for shame. Most girls and women can never win. Numerous studies have shown stronger body shame, appearance anxiety, and feelings of self-disgust in young women who internalize a sexualized view of self, and also in young women after viewing media portrayals of idealized women's bodies, or even being exposed to sexualizing words that commonly appear on magazine covers such as *sexy* or *shapely*.

These cognitive and emotional consequences can compound to create even more profound mental health risks. Studies have demonstrated a link between the feelings of shame engendered by self-objectification and eating disorders as well as depression in women. Other work has explored the ways in which the mental preoccupation of self-objectification diminishes women's *flow*, or ability to fully absorb themselves in enjoyable activities, and their sexual satisfaction.

Janet Shibley Hyde recently conducted a massive exploration of gender differences in psychological traits and attitudes. She found that there are actually very few such differences, despite the media's emphasis on women and men being from entirely different planets. Men and women are far more alike than different. Self-objectification appears to be one exceptional area. Here researchers do find significant and important differences between men and women. The work of objectification theory helps researchers see the ways that the cultural milieu of sexual objectification diminishes girls' and women's well-being, and limits their potential.

Tomi-Ann Roberts
Barbara L. Fredrickson

See also Gender Differences; Looking-Glass Self

Further Readings

Berger, J. (1973). *Ways of seeing.* London: Penguin.

Fredrickson, B. L., & Roberts, T.-A. (1997). Objectification theory: Toward understanding women's lived experiences and mental health risks. *Psychology of Women Quarterly, 21,* 173–206.

Fredrickson, B. L., Roberts, T.-A., Noll, S. M., Quinn, D. M., & Twenge, J. M. (1998). That swimsuit becomes you: Sex differences in self-objectification, restrained eating, and math performance. *Journal of Personality and Social Psychology, 75,* 269–284.

McKinley, N. M., & Hyde, J. S. (1996). The objectified body consciousness scale. *Psychology of Women Quarterly, 20,* 181–215.

OMISSION NEGLECT

Definition

Omission neglect refers to insensitivity to missing information of all types—including unmentioned or unknown options, alternatives, features, properties, characteristics, possibilities, and events. When people fail to think about what they do not know, they underestimate the importance of missing information, and this leads people to form strong opinions even when the available evidence is weak. This can lead to bad decisions that people later regret.

History and Background

It is often surprisingly difficult to notice that important information is missing. For example, in the story, "The Silver Blaze," Sherlock Holmes asked Inspector Gregory to consider a curious incident involving a dog. Gregory replied that nothing happened, and Holmes proclaimed, "That was the curious incident." This clue enabled Holmes to deduce that the culprit must have been someone familiar to the victim's dog. Most people would miss this important clue because most people, like Gregory, pay little attention to nonevents.

Other types of omissions are also important. It took scientists hundreds of years to discover the importance of using a control group, or a condition involving the omission or the absence of a cause, in their experiments. In fact, scientists failed to recognize the critical importance of a control group until relatively recently in the history of science (following the publication of *A System of Logic* by John Stuart Mill in 1848). Even scientists are surprisingly insensitive to the absence of a property, such as the absence of a cause. Similarly, it took early mathematicians thousands of years to discover the crucial concept of zero, the number that represents nothingness or the absence of quantity.

Omission Neglect in Everyday Life

In everyday life, people typically receive limited information about just about everything—such as political candidates, public policies, job applicants, defendants, potential dating partners, business deals, consumer goods and services, health care products, medical procedures, and other important topics. News reports, advertisements, conversations, and other sources of information typically provide only limited information about a topic. When people overlook important missing information, even a little information can seem like a lot. Ideally, people should form stronger beliefs when a large amount of information is available than when only a small amount is available. However, when people are insensitive to omissions, they form strong beliefs regardless of how much or how little is known about a topic. Furthermore, in rare instances in which a large amount of information is available, forgetting occurs over time and insensitivity to information loss from memory, another type of omission, leads people to form stronger beliefs over time.

For example, consumers should form more favorable evaluations of a new camera when the camera performs well on eight attributes rather than only four attributes. However, research shows that consumers form equally favorable evaluations of the camera regardless of how much attribute information was presented. The amount of information presented matters only when consumers were warned that information might be missing. This warning increased sensitivity to omissions and lead consumers to form more favorable evaluations of the camera described by a greater amount of information.

Similar results are observed in inferences, or judgments that go beyond the information given. Consumers received a brief description of a new 10-speed bicycle and were asked to rate its durability even though no information about durability was provided. When consumers inferred durability immediately after reading the description, they realized that no information about durability was presented and they formed moderately favorable inferences about durability. However, when consumers inferred durability one week after reading the description, extremely favorable and confidently held inferences were formed. This result was observed even though memory tests showed that people forgot most of the information that was presented after the one-week delay. Hence, people's inferences were stronger when they remembered a little than when they remembered a lot. In other words, omission neglect leads people to form less accurate opinions and, at the same time, leads people to hold these opinions with greater confidence.

Why Does Omission Neglect Happen?

Omission neglect occurs for several reasons. First, missing information is not attention drawing: out of sight, out of mind. Second, people often focus on one object at a time rather than comparing many objects. This makes it difficult to determine whether enough information is available. It also makes it difficult to determine how much better or worse one option is relative to another. Third, thinking about presented information can inhibit or prevent people from thinking about nonpresented information.

Fortunately, people are not always insensitive to omissions. People are less likely to overlook missing information when they are highly knowledgeable about a topic or when they are encouraged to compare objects or issues described by different amounts of information. Under these special circumstances, people are less likely to underestimate the importance of missing information, less likely to overestimate the importance of readily available information, and less likely to make bad decisions.

Omission Neglect in Judgments and Decision Making

Although judgments and decisions are often more reasonable when people are sensitive to omissions, people frequently and typically neglect omissions. Research on the feature-positive effect, or the tendency to learn more quickly when a distinguishing feature or symbol (e.g., a letter, number, or geometric figure) is present versus absent, has shown that people find it very difficult to learn that the absence of a feature is informative when people try to categorize a new object.

A fault tree is a list of possible reasons why an object might fail to perform properly, such as why a car will not start. Many people think that a fault tree will help them to determine the cause of a problem more quickly. However, when using fault trees, people typically underestimate the likelihood that an unmentioned alternative could be the cause of a problem. This result is observed regardless of how many or how few alternatives are presented in the fault tree. This result is also similar to previous research results showing that people form strong beliefs regardless of how much or how little is known about a topic.

Missing information is also neglected in the Ellsberg paradox, which is the name given to the fact that people prefer to bet on known probabilities rather than on unknown probabilities. Most people are indifferent between red and black when betting on whether a red or black marble will be drawn from a jar containing 50% red and 50% black marbles. Most people are also indifferent between red and black when betting on whether a red or black marble will be drawn from a jar of red and black marbles with an unknown distribution. When given a choice between the two jars, however, most people prefer to bet on the jar with the 50–50 distribution rather than the jar with the unknown distribution. Hence, making comparisons can help people to notice important omissions and can help people to form better judgments and decisions.

Evolutionary forces may have played a role in the development of omission neglect. The presence of a dangerous predator is a relatively rare event that requires immediate action. However, the absence of a predator is a commonplace event that does not raise a call to action. Because infrequently encountered objects are more informative than frequently encountered objects, it may be more efficient to focus on objects that are encountered rather than not encountered.

People have become accustomed to making judgments and decisions based on whatever information they happen to encounter. Sometimes judgments are based on a relatively large amount of information, and sometimes they are based on a relatively small amount. Regardless of the quality or the quantity of the information that is encountered, omission neglect is common because missing information is not attention drawing, presented information seems more important than it actually is, and presented information interferes with the ability to think about missing information. Frequently, people would be better off if they stopped to think about what they do not know rather than taking whatever information is readily available and running with it.

Frank R. Kardes

See also Attention; Availability Heuristic; Base Rate Fallacy; Decision Making

Further Readings

Kardes, F. R., Posavac, S. S., Silvera, D. H., Cronley, M. L., Sanbonmatsu, D. M., Schertzer, S., et al. (2006). Debiasing omission neglect. *Journal of Business Research, 59,* 786–792.

Kardes, F. R., & Sanbonmatsu, D. M. (2003). Omission neglect: The importance of missing information. *Skeptical Inquirer, 27,* 42–46.

Sanbonmatsu, D. M., Kardes, F. R., Houghton, D. C., Ho, E. A., & Posavac, S. S. (2003). Overestimating the importance of the given information in multiattribute consumer judgment. *Journal of Consumer Psychology, 13,* 289–300.

Sanbonmatsu, D. M., Kardes, F. R., Posavac, S. S., & Houghton, D. C. (1997). Contextual influences on judgment based on limited information. *Organizational Behavior and Human Decision Processes, 69,* 251–264.

Sanbonmatsu, D. M., Kardes, F. R., & Sansone, C. (1991). Remembering less and inferring more: The effects of the timing of judgment on inferences about unknown attributes. *Journal of Personality and Social Psychology, 61,* 546–554.

OPERATIONALIZATION

Definition

Operationalization is the process by which a researcher defines how a concept is measured, observed, or manipulated within a particular study. This process translates the theoretical, conceptual variable of interest into a set of specific operations or procedures that define the variable's meaning in a specific study. In traditional models of science, operationalization provides the bridge between theoretically based hypotheses and the methods used to examine these predictions.

Examples of Operational Definitions

Imagine a researcher who is interested in helping curb aggression in schools by exploring if aggression is a response to frustration. To answer the question, the researcher must first define "aggression" and "frustration," both conceptually and procedurally. In the example of frustration, the *conceptual* definition may be obstruction of goal-oriented behavior, but this definition is rarely specific enough for research. Therefore, an *operational* definition is needed that identifies how frustration and aggression will be measured or manipulated. In this example, frustration can be operationally defined in terms of responses to the question: How frustrated are you at this moment? The response options can be (a) not at all, (b) slightly, (c) moderately, and (d) very. The researcher could then classify people as frustrated if they answered "moderately" or "very" on the scale.

The researcher must also operationalize aggression in this particular study. However, one challenge of developing an operational definition is turning abstract concepts into observable (measurable) parts. For example, most people will agree that punching another person in the face with the goal of causing pain counts as an act of aggression, but people may differ on whether teasing counts as aggression. The ambiguity about the exact meaning of a concept is what makes operationalization essential for precise communication of methodological procedures within a study. In this particular example, aggression could be operationalized as the number of times a student physically hits another person with intention to harm. Thus, having operationally defined the theoretical concepts, the relation between frustration and aggression can be investigated.

The Pros and Cons of Using Operational Definitions

Operationalization is an essential component in a theoretically centered science because it provides the means of specifying exactly how a concept is being measured or produced in a particular study. A precise operational definition helps ensure consistency in interpretation and collection of data, and thereby aids in replication and extension of the study. However, because most concepts can be operationally defined in many ways, researchers often disagree about the correspondence between the methods used in a particular study and the theoretical concept. In addition, when definitions become too specific, they are not always applicable or meaningful.

Jeni L. Burnette

See also Experimentation; Logical Positivism; Research
   Methods

Further Readings

Emilio, R. (2003). What is defined in operational definitions?
   The case of operant psychology. *Behavior and
   Philosophy, 31,* 111–126.
Underwood, B. J. (1957). *Psychological research.* New York:
   Appleton-Century-Crofts.

OPPONENT PROCESS
THEORY OF EMOTIONS

Definition

Richard L. Solomon's opponent process theory of
emotions—also commonly referred to as the opponent process theory of acquired motivation—contends
that the primary or initial reaction to an emotional
event (State A) will be followed by an opposite secondary emotional state (State B). In other words, a
stimulus that initially inspires displeasure will likely
be followed by a pleasurable *after-feeling* and vice
versa. The second important aspect of this theory is
that after repeated exposure to the same emotional
event, the State A reaction will begin to weaken,
whereas the State B reaction will strengthen in intensity and duration. Thus, over time, the after-feeling
can become the prevailing emotional experience associated with a particular stimulus event. One example
of this phenomenon is how, for some people, an initial
unpleasant fear aroused by a good roller-coaster ride
becomes, over time, an enjoyable and much sought-
after experience.

Explanation

According to this theory, a primary *a-process*—
directly activated by an emotional event—is followed
by an opponent process, the secondary *b-process,*
which gives rise to the opposite emotional state. In the
first few exposures to an emotion-eliciting event, such
an opponent process can act to return an organism to a
state of emotional homeostasis or neutrality following
an intensely emotional episode. After repeated exposures, however, the State A response weakens and the

State B response strengthens. Because these states
change over time, the later acquired effects are often
referred to as States A′ and B′ to indicate change over
time. Thus, an initially positive emotional experience
(e.g., love or interpersonal stimulation or drug use) can
eventually give rise to a prevailing negative emotional
experience (e.g., grief or withdrawal), whereas an initially negative emotional experience (e.g., giving blood
or parachuting) can eventually give way to a prevailing
positive experience (e.g., warm-glow effect or exhilaration). As such, this theory has been commonly used
to help explain the somewhat puzzling behavioral tendencies associated with addictive behavior.

Background and Significance

Solomon supported his theory by drawing on numerous examples of opponent process effects in the literature. Four such examples are described in some
detail: (1) love/interpersonal stimulation, (2) drug use,
(3) parachuting, (4) donating blood. The first two of
these represent events that give rise to initially positive emotional states; the others initially create negative emotional states. In each of these examples, two
core aspects of the theory are evident: (1) The emotional value of the primary a-process and opponent
b-process are always contrasting, and (2) repeated
exposures to the same emotion-eliciting event lead the
a-process to weaken and the b-process to strengthen.

In the first example, the initial happiness elicited by
a loving relationship may eventually give rise to a negative emotional state. A common anecdote used to illustrate this point is that of a couple engaged in the height
of sexual passion (highly positive), which is then
abruptly interrupted, giving rise to contrasting irritability, loneliness, perhaps craving in its absence (highly
negative). The opponent process has also been used to
help explain more general separation anxiety in interpersonal relationships as well (e.g., in infant attachment
when a parent leaves the room, and even in ducklings
when the object of their imprinting is removed).

In the second example, the intense euphoria
induced by a drug wears off over time leaving a user
with a prevailing negative withdrawal reaction, making it difficult for him or her to ever return to the original high state first experienced. The acquired nature
of this response may also help explain occurrences of
accidental overdose. If the b-process becomes tied to
environmental cues (e.g., when and where the drug is

generally taken), and the drug is then taken in a different context, the acquired b-process may then not be powerful enough to counteract the initial a-process, resulting in a stronger drug reaction than anticipated.

In the third example, beginning parachuters often report experiencing absolute terror when jumping out of a plane and plummeting to the earth, and are reported to be in a stunned state once they land, gradually returning to neutrality. After many jumps (for those that dare try it again), however, most jumpers cease to be terrified. Instead, they often become expectant, eagerly anticipating the next jump, and feel a strong sense of exhilaration that can last for many hours after the jump is completed. This acquired and intensely positive experience causes some people to continue jumping to recapture the rewarding after-feeling.

The fourth example similarly shows how when people first give blood, they often report feeling anxious during the experience but relief once it is done. Over time, however, most people report experiencing reduced or no anxiety when giving blood but instead report an increasing warm-glow sensation that keeps them returning to donate more.

Implications

Here very different types of effects are explained by a single, simple mechanism, thereby demonstrating the utility of this theory. From this theory, psychologists learn that the initial emotional response elicited by a stimulus event might not necessarily explain the subsequent long-term behavioral tendencies related to that event. In the case of love, for example, which produces intensely euphoric responses initially, the opponent process theory suggests that over time people may become motivated to stay in the love relationship perhaps more in an attempt to avoid feeling lonely or grief stricken than to sustain the loving feeling. Similarly, drug addicts may take drugs in increasingly large doses not to chase the initial high so much as to avoid the increasing feelings of withdrawal. On the other hand, the very events that initially give rise to negative emotional states (e.g., fear or anxiety), such as parachuting or giving blood, over time may be sought after in an attempt to attain the rewarding effects of the after-feelings associated with them. In this way, it becomes apparent how, eventually, initial pleasure can ironically give rise to behavioral tendencies governed by avoidance motivation, and initial negative emotions such as fear by approach motivation.

Reginald B. Adams, Jr.

See also Approach–Avoidance Conflict; Emotion; Learning Theory; Love

Further Readings

Solomon, R. L. (1980). The opponent-process theory of acquired motivation: The costs of pleasure and benefits of pain. *American Psychologist, 35,* 691–712.
Solomon, R. L., & Corbit, J. D. (1974). An opponent-process theory of motivation: I. Temporal dynamics of affect. *Psychological Review, 81,* 119–145.

OPTIMAL DISTINCTIVENESS THEORY

Definition

"Everyone needs to belong." "Everyone needs to be unique." That both of these statements are true is the basis for Marilynn Brewer's theory of optimal distinctiveness, which helps explain why people join social groups and become so attached to the social categories they are part of. Optimal distinctiveness theory is about social identity—how people come to define themselves in terms of their social group memberships.

According to the optimal distinctiveness model, social identities derive from a fundamental tension between two competing social needs—the need for inclusion and a countervailing need for uniqueness and individuation. People seek social inclusion to alleviate or avoid the isolation, vulnerability, or stigmatization that may arise from being highly individuated. Researchers studying the effects of tokenism and solo status have generally found that individuals are both uncomfortable and cognitively disadvantaged in situations in which they feel too dissimilar from others, or too much like outsiders. On the other hand, too much similarity or excessive deindividuation provides no basis for self-definition, and hence, individuals are uncomfortable in situations in which they lack distinctiveness. Being just a number in a large, undifferentiated mass of people is just as unpleasant as being too alone.

Because of these opposing social needs, social identities are selected to achieve a balance between needs for inclusion and for differentiation in a given social context. Optimal identities are those that satisfy the need for inclusion within one's own group and simultaneously serve the need for differentiation through distinctions between one's own group and other groups. In effect, optimal social identities involve shared distinctiveness. (Think of adolescents' trends in clothes and hairstyles; all teenagers are anxious to be as much like others of their age group as possible, while differentiating themselves from the older generation.) To satisfy both needs, individuals will select group identities that are inclusive enough that they have a sense of being part of a larger collective but exclusive enough that they provide some basis for distinctiveness from others.

Importance and Implications

Optimal distinctiveness theory has direct implications for self-concept at the individual level and for intergroup relations at the group level. If individuals are motivated to sustain identification with optimally distinct social groups, then the self-concept should be adapted to fit the normative requirements of such group memberships. Achieving optimal social identities should be associated with a secure and stable self-concept in which one's own characteristics are congruent with being a good and typical group member. Conversely, if optimal identity is challenged or threatened, the individual should react to restore congruence between the self-concept and the group representation. Optimal identity can be restored either by adjusting individual self-concept to be more consistent with the group norms, or by shifting social identification to a group that is more congruent with the self.

Self-stereotyping is one mechanism for matching the self-concept to characteristics that are distinctively representative of particular group memberships. People stereotype themselves and others in terms of salient social categorizations, and this stereotyping leads to an enhanced perceptual similarity between self and one's own group members and an enhanced contrast between one's own group and other groups. Consistent with the assumptions of optimal distinctiveness theory, research has found that members of distinctive minority groups exhibit more self-stereotyping than do members of large majority groups. In addition, people tend to self-stereotype more when the distinctiveness of their group has been challenged.

Optimal identities (belonging to distinctive groups) are also important for achieving and maintaining positive self-worth. Group identity may play a particularly important role in enhancing self-worth and subjective well-being for individuals who have stigmatizing characteristics or belong to disadvantaged social categories. In effect, some of the potential negative effects of belonging to a social minority may be offset by the identity value of secure inclusion in a distinctive social group. Results of survey research have revealed a positive relationship between strength of ethnic identity and self-worth among minority group members, and some experimental studies have demonstrated that self-esteem can be enhanced by being classified in a distinctive, minority social category.

Finally, because distinctive group identities are so important to one's sense of self, people are very motivated to maintain group boundaries—to protect the distinctiveness of their groups by enhancing differences with other groups and limiting membership to "people like us." Being restrictive and excluding others from the group may serve an important function for group members. In effect, exclusion may be one way that individuals are able to enhance their own feelings of group inclusion. Those who are the least secure in their membership status (e.g., new members of a group or marginalized members) are sometimes the most likely to adhere to the group's standards and discriminate against members of other groups. For example, new pledges to a sorority house are often more likely than the more senior sorority members to wear clothing with sorority letters and to attend functions held by the sorority. Ironically, these noncentral group members may be even more likely than those who truly embody the group attributes to notice and punish others for violating the norms and standards of the group. When given the power, marginal group members may also be more discriminating in determining who should belong in the group and who should be excluded—for example, when it comes time to decide on the next group of new pledges.

In experimental studies, it has been demonstrated that when individuals are made to feel that they are marginal (atypical) group members, they become more stringent about requirements for group membership and more likely to exclude strangers from their group. Similarly, when group identity is under threat (e.g., the fear of being absorbed or assimilated into some larger group), members tend to become more exclusionary. Thus, the upside of social identity processes is that secure group identity enhances well-being and motivates positive social behavior. The downside is that insecure group identity motivates exclusion, intolerance, and possibly intergroup hatred.

Marilynn B. Brewer

See also Group Identity; Need to Belong; Rejection; Self-Concept; Self-Stereotyping; Social Identity Theory; Token Effects; Uniqueness

Further Readings

Brewer, M. B. (1991). The social self: On being the same and different at the same time. *Personality and Social Psychology Bulletin, 17*, 475–482.

ORDER EFFECTS

Definition

Order effects refer to differences in research participants' responses that result from the order (e.g., first, second, third) in which the experimental materials are presented to them. Order effects can occur in any kind of research. In survey research, for example, people may answer questions differently depending on the order in which the questions are asked. However, order effects are of special concern in within-subject designs; that is, when the same participants are in all conditions and the researcher wants to compare responses between conditions. The problem is that the order in which the conditions are presented may affect the outcome of the study.

Types of Order Effects

Order effects occur for many reasons. Practice effects occur when participants warm up or improve their performance over time. In reaction time studies, for example, participants usually respond faster as a result of practice with the task.

Participants may also perform differently at the end of an experiment or survey because they are bored or tired. These fatigue effects are more likely when the procedure is lengthy and the task is repetitive or uninteresting.

Carryover effects occur when the effect of an experimental condition carries over, influencing performance in a subsequent condition. These effects are more likely when the experimental conditions follow each other quickly. They also depend on the particular sequence of conditions. For example, people's estimates of height may be lower after they have been exposed to professional basketball players than after they have been exposed to professional jockeys.

Interference effects occur when previous responses disrupt performance on a subsequent task. They are more likely when the second task quickly follows the first and the response required in the second task conflicts with the response required in the first task.

Ways to Control Order Effects

Researchers use a variety of methods to reduce or control order effects so that they do not affect the study outcome. The choice depends on the types of effects that are expected. Practice effects can be reduced by providing a warm-up exercise before the experiment begins. Fatigue effects can be reduced by shortening the procedures and making the task more interesting. Carryover and interference effects can be reduced by increasing the amount of time between conditions.

Researchers also reduce order effects by systematically varying the order of conditions so that each condition is presented equally often in each ordinal position. This procedure is known as counterbalancing. For example, with two conditions, half of the participants would receive condition A first followed by condition B; the other half would receive condition B first followed by condition A.

Sometimes there are so many possible orders that it is not practical to include all of them in a study. Researchers may then present the conditions in a different random order for each participant, or they may include a subset of the possible orders.

Carey S. Ryan
Kelvin L. Van Manen

See also Control Condition; Experimental Condition; Experimentation; Research Methods

Further Readings

Shaughnessy, J. J., Zechmeister, E. B., & Zechmeister, J. S. (2006). *Research methods in psychology.* New York: McGraw-Hill.

ORGANIZATIONAL BEHAVIOR

Organizational behavior (OB) defines a field of applied social science that has two complementary objectives related to the fact that the term *organization* refers both (a) to an entity (e.g., a corporation or business) in which people's behavior is coordinated and regulated, and (b) to the outcome of that coordination and regulation. The first objective is to understand the behavior and experience of people who participate in organizational life. What motivates them to work hard? How can they be influenced and led? What produces effective communication and decision making? How do group affiliations and power affect people's perceptions and interaction? The second objective is to understand how organizations themselves function as a consequence of the social and contextual elements they contain and that impinge on them. How is an organization's performance affected by the knowledge, skills, and abilities of the individuals within it; by group dynamics; and by the economic and political conditions in which it operates? How does the organization respond to change in these elements, and how does it produce it?

To answer such questions, OB draws on insights from a range of disciplines: multiple branches of psychology (e.g., social, personality, cognitive, health, clinical) as well as sociology, anthropology, politics, administration and public policy, management, business, and economics. One consequence of this enormous breadth is that the study of OB is characterized by work that differs greatly in its level of analysis. At a macro-level (broad focus), work focuses on more abstract features of organizations (e.g., their culture, climate, ethics, and design), whereas at a micro-level (narrow, individual focus), attention is paid to more concrete organizational elements (e.g., the personality of employees, the structure of tasks, the nature of rewards). Intermediate levels of analysis focus on the nature of the processes and dynamics that occur within and between different groups and networks (which themselves are defined at more or less inclusive

levels, e.g., the work team, the department, the professional body).

Organizations are a common and important element of social life, and the capacity to analyze them—with a view to understanding both how they work and how they might be improved—is a fundamental human capacity. For this reason, contemplations on the nature of OB are a key component of the earliest human texts on religion and philosophy (a notable early example being Plato's *The Republic*). Nevertheless, formal OB theorizing dates back only about 100 years and is typically traced to Frederick Taylor's writings on scientific management. Taylor sought to identify the one best way to maximize organizational efficiency and placed an emphasis on principles of hierarchical command and control. Critically, these ideas were backed up by experimental research that demonstrated that productivity could be enhanced through the implementation of systems (e.g., of financial reward and task structure) that regularized all aspects of individuals' organizational activity. This work was soon complemented by Hugo Munsterberg's development of personnel selection methods, the purpose of which was to identify the one best worker. These methods emphasized the value of breaking tasks into their constituent parts and then recruiting workers on the basis of their possession of the clearly defined and measurable skills that were associated with superior performance in these discrete areas.

In the 1930s, however, widespread dissatisfaction with individual-level analyses and the philosophy of the one best way led to the growth of the human relations movement. The experimental work on which this was based (notably the Hawthorne studies) pointed to the role played by the informal workgroup (and its norms and values) in determining organizational outcomes. Led by Elton Mayo and later developed by researchers such as Douglas McGregor and Frederick Herzberg, the movement as a whole placed an emphasis on the value of teams, and on processes and practices that recognized, valued, and enriched their experience.

After World War II, there was an explosion of interest in OB as a field, fuelled by the desire to drive and maintain economic performance in a world that was increasingly globalized and appeared to be ever-changing. The massive amount of work that this led to paralleled major developments in OB's various feeder disciplines. Indeed, although the methods of the field have remained avowedly scientific, there is scarcely a significant intellectual development in the last century—from cybernetics and chaos theory to semiotics and post-structuralism—that has not somehow been fed into attempts to understand and improve OB.

Nevertheless, the tension between individual- and group-level approaches continues to be a major defining feature of the field. Moreover, social psychology has played an increasingly important role in the study of OB—largely because its methods and theories are so pertinent to this central debate and to the practices it informs. Typically, this tension is resolved through the development of contingency models that argue that individuals' performance in any domain (e.g., leadership, motivation, decision making, communication, negotiation) is the result of an interaction between their personality (e.g., as measured by personality instruments) and features of the social and organizational context in which they operate. However, although such models remain very popular (not least because they are often translated into lucrative commercial products), they tend to lack predictive ability and fail to account for the capacity (first observed by Mayo) for organizational context to transform individual psychology. Moreover, by breaking down the study of OB into a series of discrete topics, such approaches contribute to a lack of joined up thinking. This means that important connections between topics (e.g., leadership motivation, communication) are not made and that there is a piecemeal quality to both theory and practice. Accordingly, in recent years, social psychologists have led a move toward more integrative approaches (e.g., informed by principles of social cognition and/or social identity) that attempt to address these concerns.

Finally, although OB tends to be concerned primarily with behavior that occurs in the workplace, an organization can be defined more generally as any internally differentiated and purposeful social group that has a psychological impact on its members. In these terms, sporting teams, clubs, societies, churches, and families are all organizations. People do perform work in all these groups, but they are also a locus for leisure and recreation. OB's relation to this breadth of human experience and activity gives it such relevance to people's lives, which in turn makes attempts to understand its social and psychological dimensions so important, so complex and ultimately so interesting.

S. Alexander Haslam

See also Decision Making; Group Dynamics; Group Identity; Group Performance and Group Productivity; Influence; Leadership

Further Readings

Haslam, S. A. (2004). *Psychology in organizations: The social identity approach* (2nd ed.). London: Sage.

Thompson, P., & McHugh, D. (2002). *Work organizations: A critical introduction* (3rd ed.). Houndmills, UK: Macmillan.

OSTRACISM

Definition

Ostracism refers to the act of ignoring and excluding individuals. It is differentiated from social exclusion in that ostracism generally requires ignoring or lack of attention in addition to social exclusion. Ostracism is distinguishable from overt acts of rejection and bullying because rather than combining acts of exclusion with verbal or physical abuse, ostracism involves giving no or little attention to the individual or groups.

Context and Importance

Ostracism is a powerful and universal social phenomenon. Individuals and groups ostracize and are ostracized. A variety of species other than humans have been observed using ostracism, usually to strengthen the group (by eliminating weaker or nonconforming members). Ostracism among humans was first known to be occurring in Athens more than 2,000 years ago, where citizens voted to expel individuals by writing the nominated individual on ostraca—shards of pottery. Nations and tribes, in religious, penal, and educational institutions, and among informal groups, use ostracism. In small groups or dyads, interpersonal ostracism—often referred to as the silent treatment—is common, even in close relationships and among family members.

Humans are social creatures who rely on bonds with others to fulfill fundamental social, psychological, and survival needs. Even when strangers in a minimal interaction context ostracize individuals for a very short time, ostracized individuals show signs of distress and report that their needs have been thwarted. The negative reactions to being ostracized are immediate and robust. The instant unpleasant reaction to even the most minor forms of ostracism indicate that detection of ostracism is a functionally adaptive response. With less than five minutes of exposure to ostracism, individuals report lower satisfaction levels of four fundamental needs—belonging, self-esteem, control, and meaningful existence—and higher levels of sadness and anger. Ostracism appears to be unique in threatening all four of these four basic human needs simultaneously.

Evidence

Reflexive Reactions

The reflexive reaction to ostracism is characterized by immediate and precognitive responses to being ostracized. The same region of the brain that detects physical pain, the dorsal anterior cingulate cortex is similarly activated during a brief episode of minimal ostracism, in which individuals believe others are not including them in a virtual ball-toss game. Researchers propose that social pain and physical pain detection architectures and mechanisms are related to emotional reactions indicative of increased caution and defensiveness such as anxiety, anger, and depression. Essentially, the current thinking is that people have a built-in mechanism that automatically detects social exclusion, registers it as pain, and then triggers coping responses to combat the pain of ostracism.

This effect is argued to be precognitive in the sense that factors that should minimize its distress appear to have no effect as the ostracism occurs. Thus, distress, subjective pain, and thwarted needs are reported whether or not the ostracizers are friends, rivals, or despised others, or even if it is clear to the individuals that they are being ostracized by the computer.

Reflective Responses

The reflective response to ostracism is characterized by deliberate and thoughtful reactions following the social pain reaction to being ostracized. Coping with ostracism is aimed at recovering or fortifying the threatened needs. Because fortifying these needs may result in conflict responses, coping responses are more likely to be variable across situations and people. Thus, one can fortify a loss to belonging or self-esteem by trying to behave in ways that will meet the group's approval, by joining a new group, or even by thinking of strong ties in other realms of one's life. Fortifying control and existence needs, however, might lead to exerting social control over others, provoking recognition

and reactions in others, and even aggression and violence.

The collected findings suggest that with reflection, people can presumably cope with meaningless or inconsequential forms of ostracism, despite the fact that these forms of ostracism are initially detected as painful. Given time to consider the circumstances, individual tendencies for coping and the consideration of relevant situational factors ought to moderate ostracism's negative impact. For example, researchers found that although immediate reactions to ostracism were similarly negative for individuals low and high on social anxiety, only individuals high in social anxiety continued to feel less need satisfaction 45 minutes later. Other research also alludes to the importance of time when it comes to responses to social exclusion.

Methods to Experimentally Induce Ostracism

A variety of interesting and efficient methods have induced ostracism. These include being told that after a group get-acquainted interaction, no one wished to work with the individual, receiving a personality prognosis of living a life alone, and being ignored and excluded in a conversation, ball-toss game, Internet ball-toss game (Cyberball), a chat room, or text messaging on cell phones. Each method has advantages and disadvantages and is likely to contribute to the variety of coping responses that have been observed.

Implications

Ostracism, in all its many forms, permeates almost every aspect of an individual's life. One form of short-term ostracism, time-out, is used routinely in schools and homes, and a majority of individuals report having it used on them by loved ones, and using it on loved ones. Research indicates that on average, individuals report experiencing one act of ostracism a day. Research into the nature and interpersonal and intrapersonal costs of this ubiquitous phenomenon continues. Current research focuses on the conditions under which ostracism leads to generally prosocial responses and when it leads to antisocial, even violent responses.

Kipling D. Williams
Adrienne R. Carter-Sowell

See also Need to Belong; Rejection; Social Exclusion

Further Readings

Eisenberger, N. I., Lieberman, M. D., & Williams, K. D. (2003). Does rejection hurt? An fMRI study of social exclusion. *Science, 302,* 290–292.

Williams, K. D. (2001). *Ostracism: The power of silence.* New York: Guilford Press.

Williams, K. D., Forgas, J. P., & von Hippel, W. (Eds.). (2005). *The social outcast: Ostracism, social exclusion, rejection, and bullying.* New York: Psychology Press.

OTHER–TOTAL RATIO

Part of understanding how groups operate is understanding how the individual within the group looks at the group he or she belongs to. Once dividing the larger group into subgroups, one usually becomes more attached to one subgroup and sees the people in other groups as less distinct from one another. For example, at a party on a college campus with psychology majors and English majors in attendance, the psychology student sees the larger group of students as being made up of two subgroups. That person will feel more attached to the other psychology students and also find the English majors as more similar to each other relative to how varied the group of psychology students.

One way to examine this process comes from self-attention theory. Other–total ratio characterizes what it is like for a person to be part of a group. Specifically, the ratio is the number of Other people divided by the Total number of people in the group. As this number increases, the Others outnumber the people in an individual's own group in relation to the Total number of people. Consequently, the individual focuses more attention on his or her own subgroup and then perceives that subgroup to have salient characteristics. Then, by comparison, the Other group seems to be more similar then the group that the person is in. Using the previous example, if there were 75 English majors out of 100 people at the party, there would be a ratio of .75. Such a high ratio would predict that the psychology major would pay more attention to the subgroup members than if the ratio were a lower number.

This conceptualization of groups has implications for understanding the individual experience of members of minority groups who are part of a larger group. Comprehending how that individual is identifying with certain group members over others can perhaps be applied to how those groups can be brought into greater harmony with each other, perhaps by creating groups with a lower Other–total ratio.

Relatively little empirical work has fully explored this concept, which has been overwhelmed by other theories that address the basic fact that people see other people's groups as homogenous but their own groups as more varied. In a recent overview, the available evidence indicated that the impact of this type of perception is pretty small. It was more important that the other group truly be more variable and that existing groups were studied rather than groups created in the laboratory.

Jennifer R. Daniels

See also Optimal Distinctiveness Theory; Outgroup Homogeneity; Self-Awareness

Further Readings

Mullen, B. (1983). Operationalizing the effect of the group on the individual: A self-attention perspective. *Journal of Experimental Social Psychology, 19,* 295–322.

Mullen, B., & Hu, L. (1989). Perceptions of ingroup and outgroup variability: A meta-analytic integration. *Basic and Applied Social Psychology, 10*(3), 233–252.

OUTGROUP HOMOGENEITY

Definition

Outgroup homogeneity is the tendency for members of a group to see themselves as more diverse and heterogeneous than they are seen by an outgroup. Thus, for example, whereas Italians see themselves as quite diverse and different from one another, Americans view Italians as more similar to each other, or more alike. Democrats see themselves as more diverse than they are viewed by Republicans; Southerners see themselves as more heterogeneous than they are viewed by the rest of U.S. residents, and so on. In examining outgroup homogeneity, it is important to keep the target group constant (e.g., Southerners) and compare the perceptions of two different judge groups (e.g., the judgments of Southerners themselves versus the rest of the country), rather than comparing a single judge group's perceptions of two different targets (e.g., Southerners' judgments of their own group variability relative to their judgments of how variable the rest of the country is). This is because there are differences in how variable groups are, and by holding the target group constant, researchers can control for these.

History and Context

In some of the earliest research on this topic, Bernadette Park and Myron Rothbart explored a number of aspects of outgroup homogeneity. They asked men and women to estimate the percentage of each group that would agree with attitude statements that were chosen to be stereotypic or counterstereotypic of each group, such as, "What percentage of women would agree with the statement, I would rather drink wine than beer." Each group of judges said that a larger percentage of the outgroup would agree with stereotypic statements, and a smaller percentage would agree with counterstereotypic statements, than members of the group themselves said. In another study, young women who belonged to various sororities each said members of their own sorority were more diverse and heterogeneous than they were seen by women who belonged to other sororities. When rating males and females with various college majors, the ingroup ratings were more likely to take into account the college major, whereas ratings made by outgroup members relied simply on the gender category. Thus, a female dance major and a female physics major were seen as relatively more similar to one another by male judges ("they are both women") than by female judges. Finally, when reading about a specific individual, members of the ingroup were more likely to remember specific details about the person (specifically, the person's job category) than were members of the outgroup.

A conceptually similar effect known as *outgroup polarization* has been demonstrated by Patricia Linville and E. Edward Jones. Here, outgroup members are rated in a more extreme or polarized manner than ingroup members. For example, when judging the quality of a law school applicant, White participants rate a strong Black candidate as even better than a comparably strong White candidate, and they rate a weak Black candidate as even worse than a comparably weak White candidate. These researchers suggest

this is because people have a more simplified mental representation of outgroup members; that is, people have many more dimensions along which they think about and evaluate members of their own groups than members of the outgroups. This results in more extreme good-bad judgments of the outgroup. Thus, in outgroup homogeneity, outgroups are viewed in an all-or-none fashion, such that nearly all group members possess an attribute or almost none do. In outgroup polarization, individual outgroup members are similarly judged in an all-or-none fashion.

One possible explanation for this effect is that people are more familiar with members of their own groups than with outgroups, and this causes them to see and appreciate the diversity within their ingroups. Although undoubtedly differences in familiarity do exist, this does not appear to be the whole story. Outgroup homogeneity has been demonstrated even with *minimal groups*. These are artificial groups created in a laboratory setting using some arbitrary means for categorization, such as whether a subject tends to overestimate or underestimate the number of dots in a scatter image of dots. Here, subjects don't know anyone, either ingroup or outgroup members, and yet still they evidence outgroup homogeneity in their judgments. Others have suggested that special knowledge about oneself, who by definition is always a member of the ingroup, leads to perceptions of greater diversity and heterogeneity. Again, although people have more detailed and intricate knowledge of themselves, empirically how one perceives oneself does not account for differences in perceived variability of ingroups and outgroups. A final suggested mechanism is that information about ingroups tends to be organized in a more complex and articulated manner than for outgroups. Specifically, people tend to think about ingroups not as an undifferentiated mass but, rather, as a collection of meaningful subgroups. Thus, women might bring to mind subgroups that are part of the larger group, such as mothers, professional women, college girls, female athletes, and so on. Research has shown that people are able to generate a larger number of such meaningful subgroups for ingroups than for outgroups. Importantly, when one statistically controls for differences in the number of subgroups that are generated, differences in perceived group variability (that is, outgroup homogeneity) go away. When subjects are asked to learn about a group by organizing members into meaningful subgroups, this results in the perception of greater diversity and variability among group members, than when no such study instructions are given.

Bernadette Park

See also Ingroup–Outgroup Bias; Minimal Group Paradigm; Person Perception

Further Readings

Park, B., & Rothbart, M. (1982). Perception of out-group homogeneity and levels of social categorization: Memory for the subordinate attributes of in-group and out-group members. *Journal of Personality and Social Psychology, 42,* 1051–1068.

OVERCONFIDENCE

Definition

Overconfidence refers to the phenomenon that people's confidence in their judgments and knowledge is higher than the accuracy of these judgments. To investigate this effect, the subjective judgment of confidence in the correctness of a set of answers is compared with the objective accuracy of these answers. In a typical study on overconfidence, participants solve a number of two-choice questions, such as "Which of these cities has more inhabitants: (a) Islamabad or (b) Hyderabad?" Participants answer each question and then indicate on a scale from 50% to 100% how confident they are that their answer is correct. The overconfidence effect occurs when the confidence ratings are larger than the percentage of correct responses. For example, typically only 75% of the answers, for which a participant indicates a level of confidence of 90%, are correct. Normatively, however, nine out of ten answers should be correct. Thus, the judge is overly confident because the subjective confidence exceeds the actual accuracy.

Theoretical Explanations

The overconfidence effect has been explained by two classes of explanations: biases in information processing and effects of judgmental error. The first class of explanations considers the overconfidence effect as a result of biases in information processing. According to this line of research, a judgmental process starts with a tentative answer to a given question. Then, when estimating the confidence range, test persons selectively search for evidence that the chosen answer is correct but neglect to search for disconfirming pieces of information. Moreover, because of the associative network structure of the brain, confirming pieces of information come to mind more easily than do disconfirming pieces of information. In addition, people often have reasons why they want a particular answer to be true. For example, if they want to appear knowledgeable, this can also contribute to their biased search for confirming information. All these processes combined often lead to an overrepresentation of confirming information. The judges are not aware that the search for information was biased, so they regard the result of this information search process as support for their initial answer and thus express a high level of confidence.

The second class of explanations purports that judgmental errors can occur even if information processing is unbiased. According to this line of research, overconfidence may, for example, be the result of selected item sampling. When confronted with questions such as "Which city is larger, A or B?" participants in an experiment look for a cue that distinguishes these two cities (e.g., "Only city A has an airport. Normally, only large cities have airports."), and decide accordingly ("City A is larger."). When asked for the level of confidence, they estimate the validity of the cue ("In 90% of the cases, the city with an airport is larger than the city without an airport.") and report this value as confidence judgment. If the questions are harder than normal, the cue leads in the wrong direction more frequently than it normally does (e.g., in an experimental sample of questions, only 60% of the cities with an airport are actually larger). This means that for the sample at hand, the validity of the cue is lower than normal. However, the participants have no reason to assume that the sample is not representative (i.e., that the set of questions is harder than normal), and are therefore entitled to report their initial estimation of cue validity as confidence judgment. They thus appear to be overconfident but the apparent overconfidence is the result of selected item sampling on behalf of the experimenter.

Boundary Conditions

Research has shown that the overconfidence effect does not always occur but is subject to boundary conditions.

First, the size of the overconfidence effect depends on the type of question that has been asked. For two-choice questions, the effect is weaker than for confidence range questions, where participants are asked to estimate a number (e.g., the number of inhabitants of Hyderabad). Instead of estimating the exact number, they have to give a range such that there is a 90% chance that the correct number lies somewhere in the range. Confidence range questions are more prone to effects of biased information processing because there are no explicit alternatives as in the case of two-choice questions. Participants start with guessing a number (e.g., "50,000 inhabitants") that might be far from right and then search for confirming pieces of information.

Second, the degree of overconfidence depends on the domain of questions. For some domains, the effect is stronger than for others. This effect can be attributed to the difficulty of the set of questions. For hard sets of questions, most answers are wrong, whereas for easy sets, most answers are correct. The overconfidence effect is stronger for harder sets of questions, whereas easy sets tend to produce an underconfidence effect.

Third, individual differences contribute to differences in the degree of overconfidence. Some people express more confidence than others do regardless of the domain of questions. Overconfidence is correlated positively with confidence, but negatively with accuracy of judgment. This means that people who are most overconfident are more confident and less accurate in their judgment then are other people.

Fourth, the degree of overconfidence depends on the level of expertise. People who frequently give judgments of the same type display little or no overconfidence effect. They are well calibrated. This effect is restricted to the area of expertise: When confronted with questions from other domains, their calibration is the same as everybody else's.

Implications

The overconfidence effect is not limited to laboratory situations but has been demonstrated in many areas of professional life such as investment banking, clinical psychology, medicine, and others. Unwarranted confidence in one's own knowledge and competence can yield reckless behavior and lack of openness for disconfirming information, and thus lead to poor performance and severe mistakes. On the other hand, displaying high levels of confidence can also be beneficial for two reasons. First, competence cannot always be measured. Therefore, others might not find out that a confident person is actually overconfident. Second, overconfidence in one's competence encourages actions that one wouldn't undertake if one were less confident, but which may nevertheless be successful.

Svenja K. Schattka
Patrick A. Müller

See also Confirmation Bias; Positive Illusions; Self-Serving Bias

Further Readings

Hoffrage, U. (2004). Overconfidence. In R. Pohl (Ed.), *Cognitive illusions: A handbook on fallacies and biases in thinking, judgment, and memory* (pp. 235–254). Hove, UK: Psychology Press.

OVERJUSTIFICATION EFFECT

Definition

Overjustification occurs when play becomes work as a result of payment or other reward. More formally, it is the process by which intrinsic interest in some activity or behavior is supplanted through the presentation of an extrinsic reward. An activity that was once interesting in and of itself becomes less interesting and less attractive after a person is rewarded for completing the activity. This leads to the ironic and surprising result that rewarding a behavior can inhibit future repetitions of that behavior.

The overjustification effect occurs when internalized motives are supplanted by external motives. It occurs because people do not have perfect access to the preferences and motives that guide their decision-making processes. These preferences are often inferred from observation of their own behavior, and sometimes people get it wrong. When two motives exist for a given behavior—both internal and external—people often assume that the more obvious external justification is the cause of their behavior. This observation leads to a permanent change in how people think about the given activity, and it can lead to a loss of the internalized motives for the behavior. Thus, large rewards can extinguish the inherent joy of some positive activity, and large punishments can extinguish the moral inhibitions against some negative activity.

Intrinsic and Extrinsic Reward

Some activities, such as eating, drinking, learning, and socializing, are intrinsically interesting, and people pursue them with little encouragement. Other activities are usually performed only to gain an external reward. For instance, people typically go to work only because they are paid, and children make their beds or take out the trash for praise or an allowance. These behaviors are rewarded by extrinsic sources, and when the rewards stop, so too do the behaviors. Thus, some behaviors are intrinsically rewarding, and some are extrinsically rewarding. In all cases, the rewards lead to an increased likelihood of repeating the given behavior.

However, something strange occurs when extrinsic rewards are given for activities that are already intrinsically interesting. At first, as long as both rewards are present, the person continues the activity. But when the extrinsic rewards are removed, the person stops performing the activity, as if his or her intrinsic interest had been wiped away.

Consider the classic experiment among nursery school students conducted by Mark Lepper and his colleagues. These students were given the opportunity to draw pictures with an attractive set of Magic Markers during their free play time. Hidden observers recorded their behavior and learned, not surprisingly, that children needed little encouragement to play with the markers. Several weeks later, these same students were given another opportunity to play with the markers. But this time some of the students learned that they would receive a very special "good player" award with a ribbon and gold star if they were willing to draw some pictures; others were simply invited to draw for fun. Thus, the experiment had two groups of students involved in an activity with high intrinsic interest: one that received a reward for playing, and one that did not. Several weeks later, the students were again monitored when the markers were brought out during playtime. The results were very clear: Children who had been given an extrinsic reward showed far less interest in playing with the markers than did the children who were not offered the reward. Something about the reward had reduced the children's desire to play with the markers.

These findings are best explained through self-perception theory, which states that people learn about their likes and dislikes by observing their own behavior, and then making inferences from those observations. In this example, the children in the reward condition observed that they had chosen to play with the markers, but they also observed that they were rewarded for that behavior. They concluded, in retrospect, that the reward was the primary reason they had played with the markers. Because no reward was offered for drawing during the subsequent free play period, they chose not to play with the markers. The other students, however, who had not received a reward, saw the scene differently. They observed their previous decision to play with the markers but lacked any obvious explanation for that behavior. In the absence of any other reason, they concluded (correctly) that they must have played with the markers because they enjoyed playing with markers.

This experiment, and the hundreds like it, indicate that human preferences are somewhat more fragile than people expect. When people are given two good explanations for their own behavior (e.g., an external reward and intrinsic interest), they tend to assume that the more obvious and salient explanation is correct. The external reward is generally more obvious and salient than the intrinsic interest is.

Applications

The importance of the overjustification effect lies in its broad application to everyday life. Most people's intuition follows the logic that if one wants to encourage a person to perform an activity, one should offer rewards for doing so. This logic is correct when the activity is inherently unpleasant or unattractive, but not when the activity possesses intrinsic interest. For example, children naturally require little encouragement to learn about their environment and how their world works. This natural curiosity fades in school, and the typical student finds classes and schoolwork downright onerous. There are, no doubt, many reasons for this change, but the fundamental structure of the American educational system and reliance on grading is responsible for a significant part of the decline. Although learning about history or mathematics can be inherently interesting, most students quickly come to believe that their only motivation for learning the material stems from the promise of a reward (an A), or the threat of a punishment (an F). Educational programs that have successfully removed or reduced the importance of grading have shown subsequent increases in intrinsic interest in the topics.

A similar dynamic has been observed when students are rewarded for reading books, completing assignments, or achieving good grades. Parents and teachers with good intentions unwittingly damage the very motivation they are trying to nurture. Beyond school, the effects of overjustification can be equally powerful. Many people choose a career based on their love of the activity, whether as a teacher, a lawyer, a wilderness guide, or a doctor. When the profession pays poorly and there is no overjustification, the original reason for joining the profession (intrinsic interest) remains salient. As a consequence, the person continues to love his or her work. But when the salary increases and provides its own justification, it tends to crowd out the original internal reason, and in so doing, permanently changes the nature of the job for that individual. The person comes to love the paycheck, not the work. Financially, it is always a boon to receive a raise; psychologically, there may be a cost associated with such good fortune.

Punishment

Thus far, the examples have revolved around the effect of external rewards. However, the same conceptual process also applies to punishments and the inhibition of behavior. Imagine, for example, that you are taking an important test and are quite concerned about your performance. You have the opportunity to cheat and thus assure yourself of an excellent score, but choose not to do so. When you later ask yourself "Why didn't I cheat?" your conclusion will likely be "it's wrong to cheat." In fact, the easier it was to cheat, the more strongly you would conclude that you believe cheating

is wrong. Now imagine that there were several proctors closely watching the exam, and that you had been warned of severe consequences for any signs of cheating. When you ask yourself why you refrained from cheating, the salient explanation is "because I would have been caught." As a result, you fail to internalize the belief that cheating is wrong, and you are less likely to conclude that you behaved in line with your moral beliefs. Thus, as the threat of punishment increases, the likelihood that a person will internalize the proscription against the behavior decreases.

This is not to say that punishment doesn't work. It works extremely well, but only when the punishment is certain and swift. If you want to permanently inhibit a person's negative behaviors without providing constant supervision (a goal of all parents and all societies), then it is necessary for that person to internalize the justification for his or her behavior (or, in the present case, the lack of behavior). Thus, the proper amount of punishment should be just sufficient to inhibit the targeted behavior, but not so severe as to provide an overwhelming external justification to the individual.

Kevin M. Carlsmith

See also Attribution Theory; Cognitive Dissonance Theory; Self-Perception Theory

Further Readings

Deci, E. L., & Ryan, R. M. (1985). *Intrinsic motivation and self-determination in human behavior.* New York: Plenum.

Lepper, M. R., Green, D., & Nisbett, R. E. (1973). Undermining children's intrinsic interest with extrinsic rewards: A test of the overjustification hypothesis. *Journal of Personality and Social Psychology, 28,* 129–137.

P

PATH ANALYSIS

Definition

Path analysis is a statistical technique that is used to examine and test purported causal relationships among a set of variables. A causal relationship is directional in character, and occurs when one variable (e.g., amount of exercise) causes changes in another variable (e.g., physical fitness). The researcher specifies these relationships according to a theoretical model that is of interest to the researcher. The resulting path model and the results of the path analysis are usually then presented together in the form of a path diagram.

Although a path analysis makes causal inferences about how variables are related, correlational data are actually used to conduct the path analysis. In many instances, the results of the analysis provide information about the plausibility of the researcher's hypothesized model. But even if this information is not available, the path analysis provides estimates of the relative strengths of the causal effects and other associations among the variables in the model. These estimates are more useful to the extent that the researcher's specified model actually represents how the variables are truly related in the population of interest.

Variables in Path Analysis

Path analysis is a member of a more general type of statistical analysis known as structural equation modeling. The feature of path analysis that separates it from general structural equation modeling is that path analysis is limited to variables that are measured or observed, rather than latent. This means that each variable in a path analysis consists of a single set of numbers in a straightforward way. For example, *extraversion* would be considered a measured or observed variable if each person's level of extraversion was represented by a single number for that person, perhaps that person's score on an extraversion questionnaire. So the variable of *extraversion* as a whole would consist of one number for each person in the sample. Through certain statistical techniques, extraversion could be treated as a latent variable in a structural equation model by using several different measures simultaneously to represent each person's level of extraversion. But by definition, path analysis does not use latent variables.

Model Specification

The researcher must begin a path analysis by specifying the ways in which the variables of interest are thought to relate to one another. This is done based on theory and reasoning, and it is critical that the researcher specify the model thoughtfully. A key aspect of this process is deciding which particular variables causally affect other particular variables. A model in which exercise causes good health has a very different meaning than a model in which good health causes exercise. But in many instances, the numeric results of such alternative path analyses will reveal little or nothing about which model is closer to the truth. Because of this, there is no substitute for the researcher having a sound rationale for the form of the path model.

Path Diagrams

The path diagram is a visual display of the path model and the results of the path analysis. In path diagrams, measured variables are usually represented as squares or rectangles. A single-headed arrow (also known as a *path* or *direct effect*) drawn from one variable to another (say, from *anxiety* to *attention seeking;* see the standardized path diagram shown in Figure 1) means that a change in the value of *anxiety* is thought to tend to cause a change in the value of *attention seeking* (rather than vice versa). It is not necessary for the researcher to specify in advance whether increases in the first variable are thought to cause increases or decreases in the second variable. Mathematical algorithms will estimate both the magnitude of the effect and its positivity or negativity.

A double-headed arrow (sometimes known as a *correlation* in standardized path diagrams, or a *covariance* in unstandardized diagrams) means that the two connected variables are assumed to be associated with one another (again, either positively or negatively), but with no particular cause assumed (as with *income* and *anxiety*). This type of relationship is sometimes referred to as an *unanalyzed association* because the path model does not address why these two variables are associated. They are simply allowed to associate freely.

Data

Once the researcher has specified the path model, it is necessary to have data available to perform the analysis. The variables in the entirely fictional example of Figure 1 are *income* (annual income in dollars), *anxiety* (a score from a psychometric anxiety questionnaire), *attention seeking* (also a questionnaire score), and *impressiveness of jewelry* (say, a rating of each person's jewelry done by a trained coder). What is required is a sample of data in which each of these variables has been measured for each case in the sample. So the researcher would need a sufficiently large group of people for whom values of each of these four variables are available.

The primary inputs to path analysis software are numbers that indicate the strength and the sign (either positive or negative) of the association between each pair of variables. There is one such number for every unique pair of variables. Depending on the form of the analysis, these associations may be referred to as either *correlations* or *covariances*. Regardless, a defining feature of this input information is that no causality among the variables is actually implied in these data themselves. They simply index the strength of the association for each pair of variables in the model, and whether it is positive or negative.

Model Fit

The number of variables used in the path analysis imposes a limit on the complexity of the path model. In most instances, a model is as complex as possible if it has as many paths and correlations as there are unique pairs of variables. Models such as these are known as *just-identified* models. This is not, however, to imply that more complex models are necessarily more desirable; more complex models are less parsimonious.

In Figure 1, there are four variables and thus $4(4-1)/2 = 6$ unique pairs of variables. Because there are fewer paths and correlations in Figure 1 than unique pairs of variables, this model is not just-identified. Models such as this are known as *overidentified* models. A desirable property of overidentified models is that the path analysis can typically provide information about model fit. The most basic piece of this information is known as the *chi-square statistic*. To the extent that the probability value associated with this statistic is relatively low, it is improbable that the researcher has specified a path model that is correct in the population from which the sample data came. In other words, the researcher is confronted with evidence that the specified model is untenable as a representation of what is really happening in the population.

Indices of model appropriateness besides the chi-square statistic are

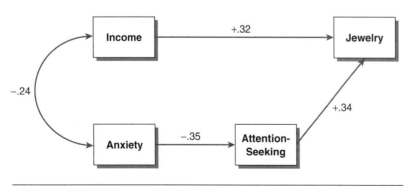

Figure 1   Example Path Analysis Based on Entirely Fictional Data

available and are commonly used. This is partly because many researchers regard the chi-square statistic as too stringent a test for structural equation models in general. Use of these alternative fit indices is associated with a lower likelihood of rejecting a researcher-specified model. The extent to which fit information from the chi-square statistic should counterbalance the generally more lenient criteria of other indices is a controversial issue. Regardless of how a researcher chooses to emphasize each type of fit information, it is important to know that they are only available for overidentified models. Furthermore, it is important to understand that even though poor model fit means that the model specified by the researcher is likely inaccurate, good fit in no way guarantees the correctness of the model. For example, the researcher could have omitted important variables or misspecified the direction of one or more causal arrows, yet still possibly have good fit.

Path Coefficients

All path analyses provide estimates of the values of the paths and correlations that connect the observed variables. Though the researcher specifies the presence or absence of particular paths and correlations, the specific values of these coefficients are entirely calculated by the mathematical algorithms of path analysis acting on the sample data. They are mathematical *best available estimates* of what the coefficients would be if the entire population were available for analysis. These values are typically displayed in the diagram next to the appropriate path (see Figure 1).

Standardized (as opposed to unstandardized) coefficients are typically presented in path diagrams. The use of standardized coefficients attempts to allow comparisons of the relative strengths of the paths and correlations even though the variables involved may have very different scales of measurement. These standardized coefficients can range in value from −1.00 to +1.00. Greater absolute values indicate stronger relationships, and the sign (+ or −) indicates whether an increase in a causal variable results in a predicted increase (+) or decrease (−) in a caused variable or whether a correlation is positive or negative.

Changing the direction of an arrow, eliminating it, replacing it with a correlation, or changing the variables included in the model can result in different values for the strength of that path and can affect other paths in the model in unpredictable ways. Relatedly,

in a path analysis with three or more variables, a path from variable *X* to variable *Y* might have a very different strength or even a different sign (+ versus −) than what might be expected from looking at the simple association between *X* and *Y* alone. For these reasons, path analysis can be a very informative technique. But whether it is informative or misleading depends on the soundness of the researcher's model and the representativeness of the sample data.

In Figure 1, the correlation of *income* and *anxiety* is −.24, meaning that higher incomes are associated with lower levels of anxiety in these sample data. The value of +.32 for the path from *income* to *jewelry* means that increasing income is predicted to directly cause increases in the impressiveness of people's jewelry. Importantly, this model asserts that *income* can be thought to relate to the impressiveness of people's jewelry in two separate ways. Although *income* exerts a direct effect (+.32) on *jewelry*, it is also spuriously associated with *jewelry* via its correlation with *anxiety* because *anxiety* causes changes in *attention seeking*, which in turn causes changes in *jewelry*. The path analysis has decomposed the original, singular sample association between *income* and *jewelry* into these two conceptually distinct parts based on the researcher's theoretical model and the sample data. Theory-based decompositional inferences such as this are the essence of path analysis.

Note also that *anxiety* is not directly linked to *jewelry* in this model. Thus, this model asserts that the association between these variables in the population can be entirely accounted for via *income* and *attention seeking*. To the extent that this theoretical assertion had been wrong, indices of model fit would tend to be worse.

Phillip W. Vaughan

See also LISREL; Nonexperimental Designs; Operationalization; Research Methods; Structural Equation Modeling

Further Readings

Cohen, J., Cohen, P., West, S. G., & Aiken, L. S. (2003). *Applied multiple regression/correlation analysis for the behavioral sciences.* Mahwah, NJ: Erlbaum.

Keith, T. Z. (2006). *Multiple regression and beyond: A conceptual introduction to multiple regression, confirmatory factor analysis, and structural equation modeling.* Boston: Allyn & Bacon.

Kline, R. B. (1998). *Principles and practice of structural equation modeling.* New York: Guilford Press.

Wonnacott, T. H., & Wonnacott, R. J (1981). *Regression: A second course in statistics.* New York: Wiley.

PEACE PSYCHOLOGY

Peace psychology seeks to develop theory and practices that prevent and mitigate both direct violence and structural violence. Direct violence injures or kills people quickly and dramatically, whereas structural violence is much more widespread and kills far more people, by depriving them of basic need satisfaction. When people starve, for example, even though there's enough food for everyone, the distribution system is creating structural violence.

Roots of Peace Psychology

The roots of peace psychology are often traced to William James and a speech he gave at Stanford University in 1906. With World War I on the horizon, James talked about his belief that war satisfied a deeply felt human need for virtues such as loyalty, discipline, conformity, group cohesiveness, and duty. He also observed that individuals who belong to a group, whether military or otherwise, experience a boost in self-pride when they are proud of their group. Most importantly, he argued that war was not likely to be eliminated until humans created a moral equivalent of war, such as public service that allowed people to experience the virtues that were connected with war making.

Many other psychologists and philosophers wrote about the psychology of peace. A partial list includes Alfred Adler, Gordon Allport, Jeremy Bentham, James McKeen Cattell, Mary Whiton Calkins, Sigmund Freud, William McDougall, Charles Osgood, Ivan Pavlov, and Edward Tolman. Even Pythagoras would qualify, because of his writings on nonviolence and appreciation for the more insidious form of violence called structural violence, which kills people slowly by depriving them of basic need satisfaction (e.g., poverty).

Throughout the 20th century, a recurrent theme among peace psychologists has been that war is built, not born, and the related idea that war is biologically possible but not inevitable. These ideas are captured in a number of manifestos issued by psychologists.

One statement was signed by almost 4,000 psychologists after World War II. More recently, the Seville Statement was issued in 1986 by 20 highly respected scientists during the United Nations International Year of Peace.

Because war is built or constructed, a great deal of research in peace psychology has sought to identify environmental conditions that are linked to violence and peaceful behavior. For instance, during the civil rights era in the United States, Floyd Allport's landmark study on the nature of prejudice proposed that contact between conflicted groups (i.e., Blacks and Whites) could improve relations if certain conditions were met, such as cooperative interdependence, equal status, support from authorities. Although integrated schools have not exactly delivered on the promises of the contact hypothesis, numerous studies continue to demonstrate that intergroup contact does improve intergroup attitudes, but only if implemented in accordance with the conditions Allport specified.

Peace Psychology and the Cold War

Peace psychology was given a significant boost during the Cold War when the conflict between the United States and Soviet Union heated up and the threat of nuclear annihilation seemed imminent. At times, the threat of nuclear war was the top fear, even among children in the Soviet Union and United States. These fears were normal responses to the threatening situation.

Why were the superpowers at the brink of nuclear war? Human psychology, and the critical role of emotions and perceptions, provided some insights into the nuclear arms race and the enemy images that dominated U.S.–Soviet relations. Fear was thought to be a key motive: Each side developed and deployed more and more nuclear missiles in an effort to reduce fear and build security, but paradoxically created a security dilemma in which each side responded to the threat of the other side by building more weapons and ultimately becoming even more insecure. Misperception was also a problem. One side would see its actions as defensive (e.g., building more weapons), but the other side would see the same actions as offensive. Mirror images occurred with both sides seeing each other as expansionistic and aggressive. Mutually distorted perceptions, destructive communication patterns, and competition for allies fuelled mistrust. The malignant relationship was reflected in rhetoric, such as President Ronald Reagan's reference to the Soviet Union as "the focus of evil in the modern world."

Some psychologists argued that the policy of deterrence was the main problem. Deterrence is based on the premise that one country, say country A, can deter an attack by country B, if country A has enough retaliatory force. Therefore, decision makers in country B would decide not to attack because the losses for initiating war would outweigh the gains. Psychologists noted that deterrence often breaks down, as it did in 1982, when Argentina launched an offense on Great Britain (over the Falkland Islands) that was quickly put down. Besides, the policy of deterrence culminated in mutually assured destruction whereby both superpowers had so many weapons that both would be destroyed if a nuclear war were started by either side. Some psychologists even wrote about the madness of mutually assured destruction because both sides were behaving irrationally.

Some peace psychologists argued that the only way to improve the relationship was to realize there could be no security for either side unless there was mutual security. Another prescription was for each side to rely less on deterring and more on reassuring each other. A peace-promoting proposal that was widely endorsed was the GRIT Tension Reduction Strategy. To begin GRIT, one of the parties in the conflict unilaterally initiates a cooperative move; the move is announced and reciprocity is invited. If the other side reciprocates, then the cycle would be started and both sides would take turns with tiny steps that deescalate the tension in the relationship.

GRIT was used by President John F. Kennedy in 1963 when he gave a speech at American University and asked all Americans to reexamine their attitudes toward the Soviet Union. He also announced an end to U.S. nuclear tests in the atmosphere as long as the Soviets stopped testing. His speech was followed by a reciprocal initiative by the Soviets—they stopped testing, and soon thereafter, both sides took several more reciprocal steps that led to the Limited Test Ban Treaty, which allowed testing only underground.

Post–Cold War Peace Psychology

The Cold War ended with dramatic events in 1989, most notably the fall of the Berlin Wall that separated the Soviet and U.S. spheres of influence. But the Cold War had given peace psychology a major boost as psychologists created concepts to better understand intergroup conflict and its resolution. Also important was the establishment of the 48th division of the American Psychological Association, called Peace Psychology. Shortly thereafter, a journal was established, *Peace and Conflict: Journal of Peace Psychology,* and even more recently, doctoral-level training programs in peace psychology have begun to spring up around the world.

Peace psychology is now global in scope. It recognizes that violence can be cultural, which occurs when beliefs are used to justify either direct or structural violence. For example, when a person justifies the deaths of starving people by blaming them for their situation (called *blaming the victim*), that person is engaging in cultural violence. Direct violence is supported by the culturally violent notion of just war theory, which argues that under certain conditions, it's acceptable to kill others (e.g., defense of the homeland, using war as a last resort). From the perspective of the United States, one of the main challenges for peace psychology is to deepen understanding of the structural and cultural roots of violence, a problem that is particularly important when security concerns revolve around the prevention of terrorism.

Basically, today, the peace tools of peace psychologists fall into six categories: (1) strengthening relationships that are cooperative already; (2) detecting and responding to early warning signs of cultural violence (e.g., one group beginning to dehumanize another group) before the conflict escalates; (3) using conflict resolution to resolve conflicts and disagreements before they turn violent; (4) organizing antiviolence movements when violence breaks out; (5) mopping up after large-scale violence has occurred, by treating victims and perpetrators of violence and assisting in community development; and (6) building socially just societies and cultures of peace through nonviolent means (e.g., dissent, protest, nonviolent resistance).

Daniel J. Christie
Thomas E. Cooper

See also Contact Hypothesis; GRIT Tension Reduction Strategy; Terrorism, Psychology of

Further Readings

Blumberg, H. H., Hare, A. P., & Costin, A. (2007). *Peace psychology: A comprehensive introduction.* Cambridge, UK: Cambridge University Press.

Christie, D. J. (2006). Post–Cold War peace psychology: More differentiated, contextualized, and systemic. *Journal of Social Issues, 62,* 1.

Peace and Conflict: Journal of Peace Psychology (any articles)

Society for the Study of Peace, Conflict, and Violence: Peace Psychology Division of the American Psychological Association. Retrieved from http://www.webster.edu/peacepsychology

Wessells, M. G. (1996). A history of Division 48 (Peace Psychology). In D. A. Dewsbury (Ed.), *Unification through division: Histories of the divisions of the American Psychological Association, 1* (pp. 265–298). Washington, DC: American Psychological Association.

PERSONALITIES AND BEHAVIOR PATTERNS, TYPE A AND TYPE B

Definition

The type A personality is a collection of behaviors that include impatience and a sense of urgency about accomplishing most tasks; aggressiveness and sometimes hostility toward others, especially those who "get in the way"; and a desire for achievement that leads to exaggerated competitiveness and striving for success. Type A personalities lead fast-paced lives; they speak quickly, walk quickly, eat quickly—all in an attempt to accomplish as much as possible in as little time as possible. By comparison, type B personalities are relaxed and easygoing, less concerned with the pressures of success (but are not lazy), and generally lead less hectic lives.

History and Importance

Interest in type A behavior first arose in the 1950s when two cardiologists, Meyer Friedman and Ray Rosenman, noticed that patients with coronary problems seemed to behave differently from noncoronary patients. Careful observation led Friedman and Rosenman to describe the type A behavior pattern as "an action-emotion complex that can be observed in any person who is aggressively involved in a chronic, incessant struggle to achieve more and more in less and less time, and if required to do so, against the opposing efforts of other things and other persons." Subsequent research sought to validate speculation

that the type A pattern made a person prone to coronary disease. In one of the most famous early studies, the Western Collaborative Group Study (WCGS), more than 3,000 middle-aged men were followed for 8½ years beginning in 1960–1961. All the men were free from coronary disease at the beginning of the study. When data collection was terminated in 1969, nearly twice as many type A personalities as type B personalities had developed coronary heart disease. At the time, type A behavior appeared to be a personality or lifestyle predictor of coronary disease on par with traditional and well-known risk factors such as smoking, high cholesterol, and hypertension.

Other medical research soon followed and with it came mixed results and controversy. Some studies replicated the WCGS, but others (including longer-term follow-ups of the WCGS sample) did not, and the results for women and various ethnic groups were not always consistent. Much of the confusion could be traced to the way type A behavior was measured in research. The original method for identifying type A behavior is called the structured interview (SI). It is time-consuming and requires special training to administer. Alternative questionnaire measures, the most well-known being the Jenkins Activity Survey, were developed to allow faster and more efficient assessment. Unfortunately, the questionnaires mimic the content of the SI but do not include the challenges that are part of the interview nor do they capture the speech style and nonverbal cues that are crucial to identifying type A behavior during the SI. Not surprisingly, research conducted with the two forms of assessment does not always arrive at similar conclusions because different features of type A behavior are being emphasized. In some ways, this problem was a blessing in disguise because it prompted researchers to explore how particular facets of type A behavior are related to coronary risk.

The key problem with questionnaire measures of type A behavior is that they do not provide direct *behavioral* evidence for impatience, anger, and hostility. This proved to be crucial because later research found anger and hostility to be more strongly related to coronary heart disease risk than are the other parts of the type A pattern. Questionnaires such as the Jenkins Activity Survey are perhaps best thought of as measures of self-reported job involvement, competitive achievement striving, and time urgency. These are important parts of the type A pattern and can have health-related consequences, but hostility appears to be especially important in the development of coronary disease.

Underlying Motive

Later research, primarily by psychologists, extended the early work by searching for the motives that give rise to type A behavior. This research showed that type A personalities differ from type B personalities in having a higher need to control their lives and desiring a clear appraisal of their skills. According to this perspective, type A behavior can best be thought of as a tactic for demonstrating control and talent. Situations that are uncontrollable, unpredictable, or create uncertainty about ability are stressful for those with type A personality. Ironically, through their exaggerated attempts to maintain control and achieve success, type A personalities probably create much of the stress that they experience.

Current Status

Other research has shown that type A personalities' fast-paced, stress-filled lives make them susceptible to other health problems. Type A personalities tend to focus their attention on their work to ensure success, but in doing so they ignore other potentially important cues such as physical symptoms that can signal a health problem needing attention. The type A pattern has been of particular interest to organizational psychologists. The behaviors of people with type A personality have obvious and important implications in the work world (e.g., they do not delegate responsibility easily), and their work habits have important implications for their relations with others.

Behavioral Changes

If the type A pattern is related to health problems, it might seem sensible that type A personalities would want to change their ways. Type A personalities are not always aware of their behavioral excesses, however, and even when they are aware, they probably do not see much reason to alter their behaviors. After all, their lifestyle is consistent with American values that emphasize hard work, striving for lofty goals, and competition. Indeed, type A behavior, except for the hostility component, is a recipe for success in Western culture. Yet the health problems do lead some people

with type A personality to seek help, and their behavior can be modified to lessen the problematic features while maintaining the aspects that have made them successful.

Michael J. Strube

See also Personality and Social Behavior; Stress and Coping; Traits

Further Readings

Friedman, M. (1996). *Type A behavior: Its diagnosis and treatment.* New York: Springer.

Friedman, M., & Rosenman, R. (1974). *Type A behavior and your heart.* New York: Knopf.

Glass, D. C. (1977). *Behavior patterns, stress, and coronary disease.* Hillsdale, NJ: Erlbaum.

Strube, M. J., Hanson, J. S., & Newman, L. (2003). The virtues and vices of personal control. In E. Chang & L. Sanna (Eds.), *Virtue, vice, and personality: The complexity of behavior.* Washington, DC: American Psychological Association.

PERSONALITY AND SOCIAL BEHAVIOR

Definitions

Personality is an individual's typical way of feeling, thinking, and acting. Given that personality is typical, it is fairly stable over time. *Social behavior* refers to a person's feelings, thoughts, or actions as he or she relates to other people. These two definitions have a very close relationship. Knowing something about an individual's personality should allow psychologists to predict his or her social behavior. Similarly, knowing about a person's social behavior should give clues to aspects of his or her personality. In other words, an individual's personality and social behavior influence each other, and knowledge of one allows the inference of information about the other.

History and Background

People tend to describe others in terms of personality characteristics. Almost 20,000 English words can be used to describe a person. For example, people can be described as outgoing or shy, dominant or submissive, conscientious or careless, and so forth. People possess different personality characteristics; therefore, it is possible to group people based on these characteristics. The history of psychologists' study of personality has involved several attempts at developing systems that would be helpful in classifying people by their personalities. The ancient Greeks first attempted to broadly describe personality with types. There were four types of personalities (based on which of their body fluids was predominant): cheerful, irritable, depressed, and unemotional. In the past century, personality has also been classified based on three different body types: The endomorph was plump, jolly, and relaxed; the ectomorph was thin, anxious, and unsocial; and the mesomorph was muscular, confident, and active.

More recently, Raymond Cattell's 16 Personality Factors (16 PF) offered a way to classify people based on 16 personality dimensions. The 16 PF includes measures of warmth, reasoning (intelligence), emotional stability, dominance, liveliness, rule-consciousness, social boldness, sensitivity, vigilance (suspiciousness), abstractedness (imaginativeness), privateness, apprehension, openness to change, self-reliance, perfectionism, and tension. To fully describe an individual's personality, the person would be given a rating on how much of each personality factor he or she possesses. However, the most common way of thinking about personality is in terms of the Big Five personality traits. These personality traits are similar to the 16 PF, but they are combined into fewer categories. These traits include Extraversion, Neuroticism (emotional instability), Conscientiousness, Agreeableness, and Openness to Experience (open-mindedness). Describing a person on each of these five dimensions is thought to be enough to give another person a good understanding about what type of person he or she is. Personality traits influence people's behavior. Therefore, if people are described as extraverted, they would be expected to be sociable in groups. If people are conscientious, they would be expected to be hard workers. If people are neurotic, they have the tendency to be anxious.

Identifying Personality Variables

Contemporary personality classification systems (e.g., Big Five, 16 PF) were created by first identifying all the words that people use to describe each other. Next, the researchers created categories by sorting the individual words based on common characteristics. The categories that resulted from this process were called personality traits or factors. For example, the category of Extraversion would have related words like *outgoing, sociable, loud, confident, talkative, friendly,* and so forth. The category of Neuroticism would contain words like *anxious, tense, insecure, paranoid, unstable,* and so on. The Extraversion category would also contain words such as *quiet, shy, unconfident,* and so on because someone can be low on Extraversion. Similarly, the Neuroticism category would also contain descriptive words like *stable, calm,* and *secure* because people can also rate low on Neuroticism.

The categories can further be grouped with the use of a statistical technique called *factor analysis.* Basically, this analysis looks for similarities among categories, and combines multiple categories into a single category if they appear to be describing the same personality dimension. This technique has been used on the 16 PF. For example, the 16 PF categories of liveliness, social boldness, and privateness may be combined to form the Big Five category of Extraversion, and the 16 PF categories of tension, apprehension, and (low) emotional stability may be combined to form the Big Five category of Neuroticism. This process of grouping the personality descriptors is useful because it gives a more simplistic way of describing people. Instead of describing people in terms of 20,000 words, people can be described on the basis of 16, or just 5.

Measuring Personality

To assess personality, people are asked to answer questions about themselves relating to the personality traits of interest. Personality questionnaires or inventories include questions about the person's feelings, preferences, and behaviors. Usually, individuals are asked to respond to questions about themselves and their personality characteristics. However, sometimes people who know the individual, such as work supervisors, friends, or family members, are asked to respond to questions about that individual's personality.

These questionnaires are created by first identifying two groups that are known to differ on the personality trait of interest, administering questions to them regarding their feelings, preferences, and behaviors, and observing which questions the two groups respond differently to. Whichever questions are found to discriminate between those two groups are included in the personality inventory. For example, if the personality inventory is supposed to measure a person's enjoyment of thinking, the researchers may give the questionnaire to university professors and high-school dropouts. It is expected that these two groups would differ on the personality characteristic of interest (enjoyment of thinking), so researchers would identify which questions the two groups respond to differently and include these questions on the personality inventory. Personality inventories can measure any number of personality traits, and they contain a separate scale for each personality trait they are meant to measure. Accurate personality measurement is important, in part, because it is necessary for accurate behavioral prediction. Without quality measures of personality, the influence of personality on social behavior will tend to be underestimated.

Influence of Personality on Important Social Behaviors

Assessing an individual's personality traits is thought to be helpful in predicting his or her future behavior. To assess whether personality influences social behavior, the person's responses on the personality inventory are compared with that person's observed social behavior. If the personality responses on the questionnaire and the social behavior are related, the person's score on the personality inventory should be able to predict the individual's future behavior. Personality variables have been found to influence various social behaviors like helping, conformity, obedience, aggression, and prejudice. In fact, there are personality scales that measure people's tendencies toward aggressiveness, conformity, altruism (an indication of helping behavior), and authoritarianism (an indication of a prejudiced personality), to name a few.

For example, in looking at the 16 PF categories mentioned earlier, the category of apprehension could be used as an indication of a person's tendency toward conformity. People are more likely to conform to others' decisions if they are insecure in their own decision-making abilities. The 16 PF categories of openness to change and dominance may be used as an indication of a tendency toward prejudiced personality. People who want to dominate others and are not open to breaking with traditional ideas are more likely to exhibit prejudice. The 16 PF categories of warmth and sensitivity may be used to indicate tendency toward

helping behavior. Helping others is most likely to come from people who are attentive to others and are sensitive. Many different measures of personality variables can be used to predict social behavior (to some extent).

Importance of the Situation Versus Personality

Although personality is supposed to allow the prediction of a person's behavior, it does not allow perfect prediction in every situation. Unfortunately, research shows that people's behavior is frequently inconsistent. The situation the person is in can also influence behavior. A two-decade-long debate called the *person-situation controversy* involved discussion of when personality or the situation can better predict behavior. Basically, as will be discussed, personality is likely to influence behavior when the situation does not create strong pressures for the person to behave a certain way, when the person is exhibiting dominant personality characteristics, when that person does not care about fitting his or her behavior to situational requirements, and when the person's behavior is observed across a variety of situations over time.

Types of Situations

Not surprisingly, when people are in unfamiliar situations or situations that require more formal behavior (at church or on a job interview), their personalities influence their behavior less than do the situational requirements. On the other hand, when people are in familiar, comfortable situations (with friends or family) their personalities are more likely to influence behavior. For example, if an individual reports having a shy personality, that information may be able to be used to accurately predict behavior in classroom settings or around new, unfamiliar people. However, the information that the person has a shy personality might not be able to be used to accurately predict that his or her behavior will be shy when with close friends. Perhaps the person is a friendly, outgoing person after becoming comfortable with people. Similarly, although some people tend to be helpful, obedient, aggressive, or conformist just because they have that type of personality tendency, the situation can also influence people's behavior, making that personality tendency more or less pronounced. For example, even a very passive person may become aggressive if sufficiently provoked.

The importance of the situation in predicting behavior is determined by carefully controlled experimental research. The researcher creates two or more different situations, exposes each participant to one of the situations, and then measures each participant's reaction or behavior. The difference in participants' behaviors in the two situations is an indication of how much the situation influences behavior. In other words, if the researcher observes the participants (as a group) in one situation behave in a different way from that of participants exposed to a different situation, it is assumed that this difference in behavior is due to the situation rather to than the participants' personalities. In addition, the researcher could both measure personality using an inventory and manipulate the situation to see whether the individual's personality or the situation better predicts behavior.

Types of People and Personality Characteristics

Just as some (strong) situations influence people's behavior more than do others, some people are more influenced by situations in general than are others. Some people consistently monitor and adjust their own behavior to ensure that it fits with the situation (high self-monitors). These people are more likely, for example, to behave differently around different groups of friends. On the other hand, people who do not care about monitoring their behavior to fit in with the social situation (low self-monitors) are more likely to behave consistently with their personalities across situations. They will act the same way, for example, around different groups of friends.

Some personality characteristics are also more dominant for a given person than are other characteristics, and these characteristics are more likely to influence the person's behavior across situations. A person may be extremely neurotic and mildly outgoing. One might expect such a person to be anxious much of the time, regardless of the situation, but only friendly some of the time. Similarly, some personality traits tend to be strong across individuals. For example, expressive traits come out in a person's speech, gestures, and mannerisms. Individuals who have very animated personalities, no matter where they are, will speak loudly with exaggerated hand gestures. Weak personality traits depend on the situation. For example, some people are more concerned about creating a

positive impression than are others. These people might behave differently around people they want to impress (like on a first date) than around people they do not care about impressing.

Types of Behaviors

Furthermore, personality may be a better predictor of how people will usually act (across situations) than in a particular situation. So, instead of looking at a person's behavior in one situation, one should measure the person's behavior averaged across many situations to examine the relationship between personality and behavior. For example, a person who is dishonest may not cheat on a particular exam at school, but that person will tend to engage in more dishonest behaviors across situations (cheating at school, cheating on taxes, lying, etc.) than will someone who is honest. In general, it is important to have good measures of behavior. Such measures of behavior should be obtained through ratings by multiple raters who know the individual well, should be directly observable and related to the personality characteristic of interest, and should be obtained for several situations across time.

Implications

It turns out that the relationship between personality and behavior is very similar in strength to the relationship between the situation and behavior. The relationship between personality and behavior (or between the situation and behavior) allows researchers to predict a person's behavior correctly about 70% of the time. Therefore, personality and situations are both important for predicting behavior.

It is more appropriate to use personality to predict how an individual will *usually* act in most situations, rather than how individuals will act in specific situations. This is because the situation itself often varies and will influence how the individual acts. Sometimes behavior can be predicted mostly from personality. Personality is likely to influence behavior more in situations when the person is exhibiting dominant personality characteristics, when that person does not care about fitting his or her behavior to the situational requirements, or when the situation is weak (no set social rules). On the other hand, the situation will play a bigger role in behavior if the situation is strong (clear social requirements) or if the person cares about keeping his or her behavior consistent with the situational requirements.

Finally, although situations often influence people's behavior, people also choose and influence the situations in which they find themselves. People's personalities influence the types of situations they enter. This increases the likelihood that they will exhibit certain behaviors. For example, people who are outgoing are likely to attend more parties than shy people. This party attendance gives them more opportunities to exhibit outgoing behavior and may actually increase this behavior over time. In turn, the person's behavior may influence the atmosphere of the party itself (the situation).

Laura A. Brannon
Valerie K. Pilling

See also Big Five Personality Traits; Genetic Influences on Social Behavior; Individual Differences; Personality Judgments, Accuracy of; Traits

Further Readings

Kenrick, D. T., & Funder, D. C. (1988). Profiting from controversy: Lessons from the person-situation debate. *American Psychologist, 3,* 23–34.

Mischel, W. (1968). *Personality and assessment.* New York: Wiley.

Snyder, M., & Cantor, N. (1998). Understanding personality and social behavior: A functionalist strategy. In S. Fiske & D. T. Gilbert (Eds.), *The handbook of social psychology* (4th ed., Vol. 1, pp. 635–679). New York: McGraw-Hill.

Snyder, M., & Ickes, W. (1985). Personality and social behavior. In G. Lindzey & E. Aronson (Eds.), *The handbook of social psychology* (3rd ed., Vol. 2, pp. 883–948). New York: Random House.

Personality Judgments, Accuracy of

Definition

The accuracy of personality judgments refers to an area of research in which people evaluate the thoughts, feelings, and behavior of themselves or others and the correctness of their evaluations are determined. The determination of accuracy, or correctness, is a constant challenge for researchers because it is often unclear what to use as the standard for truth. It is straightforward to verify people's estimates of height and weight by using a tape measure and scale, but accuracy researchers must determine, for example, if a person's friendliness rating of a coworker is accurate. The absence of a friendliness "tape measure" requires researchers to use a variety of measurement techniques that together provide a close approximation of the personality characteristic under investigation. Accuracy researchers typically compare a person's friendliness rating to the coworker's observed behavior or to personality ratings of the coworker by close acquaintances. If the person's friendliness ratings predict the coworker's behavior and agree with the close acquaintances' ratings, the friendliness rating is likely to be accurate.

Context and Importance

People make judgments about personality every day and in numerous settings. Clinical psychologists diagnose their clients, human resource managers evaluate prospective employees, and teachers assess the capabilities of their students. In these settings, the judgments that professionals make can either help or harm an individual's life. The judgments that lay people make are equally life affecting, such as the decision to approach or to avoid a stranger. A faulty decision to trust a stranger may lead to physical harm. The misjudgment of a close friend may lead to unpleasant conflict or dissolution of the friendship. The personality judgments that people make of themselves and others can affect their own psychological and physical well-being.

Evidence

Research on the accuracy of personality judgments began by trying to identify the good judge of personality. This research focus represented a mix of theoretical interest and pragmatic concern. Researchers were curious why some people might be better than others at judging personality. From a pragmatic perspective, it was believed that being a good judge of personality was a prerequisite to being a successful clinical psychologist, personnel interviewer, or school counselor. The research evidence is inconsistent regarding the good judge of personality with one exception. Women tend to outperform men when judging the personality characteristics of others.

Despite these inconsistent findings, accuracy researchers continue to search for the good judge of personality and have broadened their research interests to include five additional factors that influence the accuracy and inaccuracy of personality judgments. Each factor will be discussed in turn.

First, *judgability* refers to how accurately people's personalities can be judged by others. Individuals who are high on judgability are like open books, their personalities are easy to read, and they are accurately judged. Those who are low on judgability are closed and enigmatic, and are inaccurately judged by others. Research demonstrates that judgable people tend to score higher on measures of psychological adjustment than do less judgable people.

Second, increased acquaintance produces greater accuracy. Although this might seem fairly intuitive, only recently have researchers provided evidence to support this factor. Considerable evidence now indicates that longer acquaintance leads to greater accuracy because acquainted individuals share more plentiful and intimate information than do people less acquainted.

Third, some personality traits are more accurately judged than other traits. In terms of the Five Factor model of personality (i.e., Neuroticism, Extraversion, Openness to Experience, Agreeableness, Conscientiousness), research consistently points to Extraversion as the most accurately judged trait. Neuroticism is often the most difficult trait to judge. The difference in trait accuracy is due to observability indicating that traits that are easy to see tend to be most accurately judged. Extraverted behaviors such as talking and socializing are easy to see by observers whereas neurotic behaviors such as worrying and feeling anxious are much less observable and more difficult to judge.

Fourth, self-enhancement refers to the tendency for some individuals to hold unrealistically positive self-views. There is currently considerable debate about the topic of self-enhancement. One group of researchers believes that possessing an unrealistically positive self-view is unhealthy. These researchers argue that people should be realistic about their strengths and weaknesses, and only by acknowledging weaknesses can individuals correct them. The other group believes that holding unrealistically positive self-views is mentally healthy. This group argues that these positive beliefs, albeit unrealistic, protect the self-esteem of individuals when negative events occur and motivate individuals to be highly productive. The debate is forcing researchers to carefully consider the nature of mental health and psychopathology.

Fifth, accurate self-knowledge refers to the accuracy of people's beliefs about their own personality and behavior. Despite the belief by many that they possess keen self-insight, Sigmund Freud demonstrated long ago that people do not always know the truth about themselves. Research on accurate self-knowledge indicates that individuals who know themselves well possess positive self-esteem, social skill, and good coping skills. These results are similar to those found for judgability and suggest that to be known by others, a person must also be known to himself or herself.

Implications

Researchers have considerable knowledge about whom and what will be accurately judged, when it will occur, and who will make accurate personality judgments. This information has real-world implications for professionals and lay people alike. A goal of future accuracy research will be to put this knowledge to use. Research-based training may help clinicians better diagnose their patients, teach married couples to communicate more effectively, and help single people to select compatible dating partners.

C. Randall Colvin

See also Big Five Personality Traits; Close Relationships; Individual Differences; Personality and Social Behavior; Person Perception; Self-Enhancement

Further Readings

Funder, D. C. (1999). *Personality judgment: A realistic approach to person perception.* San Diego, CA: Academic Press.

Funder, D. C., & Colvin, C. R. (1997). Congruence of others' and self-judgments of personality. In R. Hogan, J. Johnson, & S. Briggs (Eds.), *Handbook of personality psychology* (pp. 617–647). San Diego, CA: Academic Press.

Kenny, D. A. (1994). *Interpersonal perception: A social relations analysis.* New York: Guilford Press.

PERSONAL SPACE

Definition

Personal space refers to the physical area surrounding an individual that is considered personal or private. Typically, when another person intrudes in this area, the individual experiences discomfort. A related concept, interpersonal distance, refers to the area that people keep between themselves and the interaction partner. As an individual's personal space increases, interpersonal distances will increase as well. The size of personal space largely depends on individual and situational differences. The shape of personal space does not completely follow the lines of a circle or bubble, as the preferred distances at the front of a person are generally found to be larger compared with the rear.

Physical interpersonal spacing behavior serves important functions. Distancing oneself from others promotes control and maintains autonomy. In this case, the influence of others is reduced. Conversely, proximity fosters interpersonal communication and cooperative behavior, smoothes interactions, and increases interpersonal liking.

Determinants of Interpersonal Distance

Personal space should not be considered a static construct because it varies across individuals and situations. Predominantly, interpersonal distance is influenced by the nature of the relationship between the two interacting individuals. Edward Hall distinguished four typical types of interaction distances observed in Western societies: intimate distance (0–18 inches, e.g., two individuals making love); personal distance (18–48 inches, e.g., distance between close friends), social distance (4–12 feet, e.g., personal business); and public distance meetings (12–25 or more feet, e.g., formal interactions like teaching).

Interpersonal distance may also be influenced by a person's mind-set or goals. If an individual adopts the goal to affiliate with another person, he or she may be more likely to sit close to that person. Likewise, a strong need to belong to others also results in a tendency to sit closer to other people. On the other hand, when people focus on personal goals, uniqueness, and autonomy, they are likely to need more distance from others.

Furthermore, individual differences have been linked with proximity behavior. Various studies have provided evidence for personal space to be influenced by sex, showing that two interacting men require more personal space than do two interacting females. Also, personal space seems to increase from childhood to adolescence.

Interpersonal distance also varies across cultures. Members of collectivistic countries prefer stronger interpersonal proximity compared with members of individualistic countries. Interestingly, several studies have shown that members of collectivistic cultures are characterized with a relatively high need to harmonize with others and to have a sense of belonging, whereas members of individualistic cultures have a relatively strong need to distinguish themselves from others and strive for personal achievement. Therefore, these cultural differences in interpersonal distance may be partly explained by cultural differences in goals.

Finally, some aspects of the environment have been shown to influence personal distance. For example, people prefer greater distances when they are in stressful situations, in rooms with low ceilings, or in crowded places.

Compensation for Closeness

Several authors have argued that people strive for balance between several approach/avoidance forces during interaction. Therefore, when the situation forces people to intrude each other's personal space (e.g., standing in a crowded elevator), the decreased interpersonal distance may be compensated for by other psychological mechanisms that are related to intimacy, such as eye contact and topic intimacy. For example, people standing in a crowded elevator avoid making eye contact, look at the elevator doors, and discuss the weather.

Measuring Interpersonal Distance

Interpersonal spacing behavior has been studied using two different kinds of distance measures. Some researchers used projective measures in which individuals are asked to indicate the preferred distance to an imagined other (using miniature figures, dolls, or paper and pencil drawings). These projective measures may be contrasted with real-life measures, including unobtrusive observations of actual spacing and placements or selections of chairs. A popular and efficient measure is to ask a person to take a chair and place it in the vicinity of another person. The distance between the chairs is indicated as the interpersonal distance. As interpersonal spacing behavior is mostly regulated in an automatic fashion, individuals are generally unaware of the distance that they keep from others. As a result, people may find it difficult to explicitly indicate their preferred interpersonal distances. Indeed, projective measures show low correspondence with actual interpersonal behavioral measures and are considered to be less useful in studying personal space.

Benefiting from technical progress, several researchers have recently studied interpersonal spacing behavior using immersive virtual environment technology (virtual reality) in which participants approach virtual other people. People seem to keep distance from these virtual persons quite naturally, as if they approach real individuals. Virtual reality is a potentially useful tool to enlarge researchers' understanding of personal space.

Implications

The implications of personal space can be far-reaching because it can have a strong impact on the quality of the interactions and therefore on the quality of interpersonal relations. The interaction of two persons with different sizes of personal space may result in misunderstanding and become problematic. For example, if a member of an individualistic country (a U.S. citizen) who has large preferred interpersonal distances interacts with a member of a collectivistic country (an India citizen), the latter may stand too close for the American, whereas the Indian person may become irritated because the American stands too far away for conversation. From an applied perspective, the growing body of knowledge in the area of personal space and proximity behavior provides opportunities to adjust spacing behavior and train people to stand closer to or further away from others in specific situations. This may help smooth interactions and reduce psychological discomfort.

Rob W. Holland

See also Close Relationships; Collectivistic Cultures; Cultural Differences; Gender Differences; Need to Belong; Nonconscious Processes; Nonverbal Cues and Communication; Propinquity

Further Readings

Bailenson, J. N., Blascovich, J., Beall, A. C., & Loomis, J. M. (2003). Interpersonal distance in immersive virtual environment. *Personality and Social Psychology Bulletin, 29,* 819–833.

Hayduk, L. (1983). Personal space: Where we now stand. *Psychological Bulletin, 94,* 293–335.

Holland, R. W., Roeder, U., van Baaren, R. B., Brandt, A., & Hannover, B. (2004). Don't stand so close to me: Self-construal and interpersonal closeness. *Psychological Science, 15,* 237–242.

Person Perception

Definition

Person perception refers to a general tendency to form impressions of other people. Some forms of person perception occur indirectly and require inferring information about a person based on observations of behaviors or based on second-hand information. Other forms of person perception occur more directly and require little more than seeing another person. Both of these types of person perception provide a foundation from which subsequent judgments are formed and subsequent interactions are shaped.

History and Background

In social psychology, the phrase *person perception* has historically referred to the perception of others that leads to judgments of traits and dispositions. Given that Bill kicked a dog, what kind of impression is an observer likely to form? Much of the early research investigating such impressions had roots in attribution theory. Fritz Heider proposed that people can attribute the behaviors of others to factors that are internal (personality, dispositions, etc.) or external (situational constraints), but that people are prone to make internal attributions. These basic observations affected decades of research and provided an important foundation for two related theories, in particular. Harold Kelley's covariation model, for example, described how people discern the attitudes of others based on simple factors surrounding observed behaviors. Similarly, Edward E. Jones and Keith Davis's theory of correspondent inferences described why people infer that behaviors reveal personality. Thus, the early research in this area investigated when and how people infer traits from behaviors.

Indirect Person Perception

Many of the personal attributes that observers may want to know about another person (e.g., whether the person is loyal, honest, or contemptible) are not directly observable. Instead, these attributes or traits must be discerned—either from observing the person's actions (actually watching the person behave in a loyal or honest manner) or from interpreting information provided by a third party (e.g., what a roommate conveys about Jill or what the experimenter reveals). In each case, the general perception of a person is the product of inference, and the attribution theories that were proposed a half a century ago remain valid in understanding how such perceptions occur.

Observers watch what people do, and they make judgments about others based on those observations. When a psychology professor is seen responding to an upset student in a dismissive way, for example, one may infer that this occurred because of some aspect of the professor's disposition or because of unfortunate circumstances of the interaction. Classic studies in social psychology attempted to bring similar scenarios into the laboratory. Participants in these studies judged the attitude of a hypothetical person who was described in a vignette as advocating an unpopular political position. Sometimes this action was described to have been voluntary; other times, this action was described to have been compelled (e.g., an experimenter asked the person to advocate a specific position). Across all such studies, participants reported that the target's behavior revealed his or her true attitude, even when that behavior had been coerced by the situation. Thus, observers tend to assume that behaviors convey attitudes and dispositions, and this occurs even when compelling situational grounds for that behavior are present. When perceiving the dismissive professor, therefore, observers are apt to conclude that the professor is callous, and not that the response was compelled by the situation (e.g., the next class that was already streaming into the classroom). These perceptions are called *correspondent inferences,* and the tendency to attribute actions to dispositional factors has been called the *correspondence bias* and the *fundamental attribution error.*

Following the initial insights, many researchers tried to understand precisely what leads to such inferences, and three factors emerged. Harold Kelley, for example, documented that dispositional inferences are especially likely when a particular behavior is (a) distinctive (most professors don't actually respond in a dismissive manner); (b) consistent (this particular professor responds this way in and out of class); and (c) consensual (others have also observed this behavior). Jones and Davis stressed that such inferences are particularly likely when a particular behavior is unexpected (e.g., a known conservative endorsing a liberal position).

More recently, researchers have examined the psychological processes that permit these inferences. Two processes appear to be involved. The initial process is relatively reflexive and leads to dispositional inferences under most circumstances. The second process is considerably more reflective and tends to correct for the constraints imposed by a situation.

Other recent research has explored the extent to which dispositional inferences are ubiquitous. The tendency is so strong that it occurs even when people have no intention to form an impression of others and in the absence of observing actual behaviors. Indeed, much of the research in social psychology has exploited this by presenting research participants with sentences that describe a behavior. Reading about an individual who purportedly solved a mystery novel halfway through a book, for example, might lead an observer to infer that the individual is clever. These rapid judgments that imply enduring traits are typically called *spontaneous trait inferences.*

The attribution approach to the study of person perception revealed much about how impressions of others may emerge from observations. Yet person perception also refers to judgments that occur more directly.

Direct Person Perception

Many of the personal attributes that observers notice about another person need not be inferred because they are directly observable and are therefore noted immediately. Some of these attributes include categorical judgments about other people such as their sex, race, and age. Some researchers have argued that noticing certain personal characteristics is unavoidable, and that observers automatically categorize people according to their group membership. What sex? What race? and How old? are likely to be among the first impressions that observers form of others. Because these particular categorical judgments are made so readily and rapidly, they have been described as obligatory. Two of these obligatory categorical judgments, sex and race, have received considerable attention in social psychology.

Perceiving Sex

In general, observers have little difficulty categorizing others to be men or women. This basic categorization occurs effortlessly, partly because so many individual features differ reliably between men and women. Even apart from primary and secondary sexual characteristics, which are generally not readily visible to observers, men's and women's faces and bodies differ in both absolute and relative measures and in personal grooming, both of which are easily seen. Thus, categorizing individuals by their sex occurs with great facility, and such perceptions are informed by many physical cues.

Perceiving the sex of an individual affects a broad range of other social perceptions and judgments, as well. Many evaluative social judgments, for example, rely heavily on the content of gender stereotypes and role expectations. Exhibiting gender-typical traits and behaviors leads to favorable evaluations; exhibiting gender atypical traits and behaviors, in contrast, leads to unfavorable evaluations. This can pose challenges for certain individuals. Professional women, for example, frequently hold positions that demand characteristics that are stereotypically associated with men. By exhibiting such characteristics, these women are perceived to be competent, but they are not liked.

Perceiving Race

Observers also have little difficulty categorizing the race of others. Much of the research in this area has focused on how race affects observers' recognition or memory of others. Although people are generally quite adept at recognizing the faces of others who they have seen previously, doing so is considerably more difficult for faces of other-race individuals. This tendency has been called the *own-race bias*.

Regardless of whether a particular individual is recognized or not, perceiving a target's race permits racial stereotypes to affect a broad range of social perceptions and judgments, even in the absence of explicit prejudice. In some laboratory studies, for example, participants have been asked to make simple judgments—such as whether a target is holding a gun or a tool—that are objectively unrelated to the target's race. In other studies, participants have been charged with deciding whether or not to "pull the trigger" on a target who is holding either a weapon or another object. In both cases, the race of the target affects the speed and accuracy of judgments.

The facility to perceive others accurately from visual cues alone extends beyond the perception of sex and race. Based on only brief exposures to degraded video images of an individual, observers can accurately judge a range of personal characteristics. These include social categories such as sex, race, and sexual orientation and dispositional characteristics such as teaching

effectiveness. Thus, even from these thin slices, person perception can be remarkably accurate.

Whether person perception occurs by inferring traits from behaviors or by merely perceiving the physical appearance of another, this is the foundation for how people respond to and evaluate others. Given this far-reaching impact, research investigating various aspects of person perception will continue to be an important area in social psychology for years to come.

Kerri L. Johnson

See also Correspondence Bias; Fundamental Attribution Error; Personality Judgments, Accuracy of; Spontaneous Trait Inferences; Thin Slices of Behavior

Further Readings

Ambady, N., & Rosenthal, R. (1992). Thin slices of expressive behavior as predictors of interpersonal consequences: A meta-analysis. *Psychological Bulletin, 111,* 256–274.

Gilbert, D. T. (1998). Ordinary personology. In D. T. Gilbert, S. T. Fiske, & G. Lindzey (Eds.), *The handbook of social psychology* (4th ed., Vol. 2, pp. 89–150). New York: McGraw-Hill.

Jones, E. E. (1990). *Interpersonal perception.* New York: Freeman.

Ross, L., & Nisbett, R. E. (1991). *The person and the situation: Perspectives of social psychology.* New York: McGraw-Hill.

PERSON-POSITIVITY HEURISTIC

Definition

The person-positivity heuristic is a tendency to evaluate individual people more positively than the groups to which they belong. Psychologist David Sears coined the phrase in 1983 because he noticed that results of political polls typically show that although respondents hold political institutions such as the U.S. Congress in low regard, they often have positive impressions of the individuals (senators and representatives) who make up those institutions. The person-positivity heuristic also occurs in evaluations of other types of political figures (governors, mayors), in college students' evaluations of their professors, and even in people's evaluations of small groups of physically attractive and unattractive women.

Application

One explanation of the person-positivity heuristic is that people are predisposed to perceive themselves as similar to other people, and consequently, the closer something is to being a "person," the more positively it will be evaluated. For example, student course evaluations show that courses generally are not liked as well as the professors who teach them. Courses do not exemplify the concept of personhood as well as professors do, and thus students perceive more in common between themselves and professors than between themselves and courses. Groups of individuals or an institution are less like a person than an individual person is. However, because groups and institutions are composed of individual people, they have more personhood than do objects (for example, a car), abstractions (for example, gravity), or an individual person's possessions (for example, a professor's office) or products (for example, the course a professor teaches). Consequently, groups and institutions are liked less than the individuals who compose them, but are liked more than inanimate objects, abstractions, or possessions. For example, Sandra Day O'Connor, who was an individual member of the U.S. Supreme Court, is higher on personhood than her decisions are, and the Court itself falls between Justice O'Connor and her decisions in personhood. The Court as an institution should therefore be liked less than Justice O'Connor, but liked more than her decisions are.

Exceptions and Importance of the Person-Positivity Heuristic

Person-positivity effects are not likely to occur when people evaluate individuals who are members of highly regarded groups. In these cases, the positivity bonus that otherwise accrues to individuals disappears. For example, the U.S. presidency is held in high regard but the U.S. Congress is not. Surveys show that individual presidents of the United States are not evaluated more positively than the office they hold, whereas individual members of Congress are evaluated more positively than Congress itself is. Physically attractive individuals also do not seem to benefit from the person-positivity heuristic as much as their less attractive counterparts do.

The person-positivity heuristic has been important in understanding political attitudes and voting behavior. People hate politicians, but have such high regard for individual politicians that it is usually difficult to unseat an incumbent office-holder. This heuristic also sheds light on how people can have negative stereotypes about a group, but at the same time have positive impressions, and sometimes even close ties with, individual members of the disliked group.

Susan E. Varni
Carol T. Miller

See also Heuristic Processing; Positive–Negative Asymmetry; Similarity-Attraction Effect; Stereotypes and Stereotyping

Further Readings

Granberg, D., & Holmberg, S. (1990). The person positivity and principle actor hypotheses. *Journal of Applied Social Psychology, 20,* 1879–1901.

Miller, C. T., & Felicio, D. M. (1990). Person-positivity bias: Are people liked better than groups? *Journal of Experimental Social Psychology, 26,* 408–420.

Sears, D. O. (1983). The person-positivity bias. *Journal of Personality and Social Psychology, 44,* 233–250.

PERSUASION

Definition

Persuasion is a method of changing a person's cognitions, feelings, behaviors, or general evaluations (attitudes) toward some object, issue, or person. Although any change technique is sometimes referred to as persuasion regardless of the target of influence, the term more commonly refers to a method of change in which a person is deliberately presented with a message containing information intended to alter some general evaluative judgment (e.g., capital punishment is bad). Self-persuasion can occur when people generate their own messages in favor of or against something. Persuasive communication is readily used by advertisers, salespeople, politicians, ministers, attorneys, and people in everyday situations to produce change in others. In democratic societies, persuasion has replaced coercion as the primary means of influence.

History and Background

The power and prevalence of persuasion have led to a great deal of scientific research investigating the factors that make a persuasive appeal effective. In the 1950s, Carl Hovland and his colleagues at Yale University conducted the first systematic analysis of persuasion in what was known as the Yale Communication Project. The Yale group determined that four elements are present in all persuasion settings: (1) a source who delivers the persuasive message, (2) the message itself, (3) a target person or audience who receives the message (recipient), and (4) some context in which the message is received. Adopting an information-processing approach to persuasion, the researchers proposed that for a persuasive appeal to work, the message recipient must pay attention to, comprehend, learn, accept, and retain the message and its conclusion in memory. People's degree of engagement in these steps was thought to be determined by various characteristics of the source, message, recipient, and persuasive context. For example, a highly complex message might be too difficult to comprehend and therefore, unable to be learned, accepted, or retained.

Later research showed, however, that persuasion often does not depend on the specific arguments in a message that people learn and remember but, rather, on what unique cognitive (mental) reactions they have in response to those arguments. That is, what matters most when people are actively processing the message is not learning what is in the message but what people think about the message. According to this cognitive response approach, persuasion is more likely when the recipient has favorable thoughts toward the message and less likely when the recipient's thoughts about the message are unfavorable. For example, two individuals may both learn the same details of a proposal to increase the interstate speed limit and yet have wildly different thoughts (e.g., "I'll be able to get to work faster" versus "It will make driving more dangerous").

Current Theories

The learning and cognitive response approaches to persuasion focused on attitude change through active, effortful thinking. However, research has also shown that sometimes people are persuaded to change their attitudes when they are not thinking much about the information in the message. Instead, they base their attitudes on simple associative or heuristic processes that require less cognitive effort. Incorporating these different ideas, Richard Petty and John Cacioppo's elaboration likelihood model (ELM) and Shelly Chaiken's heuristic-systematic model (HSM) are two similar theories introduced in the 1980s that propose that both effortful and non-effortful processes can produce attitude change in different situations.

According to these models, when people are motivated and able to evaluate all the information relevant to the message's position (high elaboration), they will follow the central or systematic route to persuasion. This corresponds to the cognitive response approach, whereby people's favorable or unfavorable thoughts about the message and their confidence in them determine the degree of attitude change. In contrast, when people are not thinking carefully about the merits of the message (low elaboration), they can still be influenced by processes requiring less cognitive effort. For example, people can rely on mental shortcuts (e.g., "The package is impressive—it must be a good toothpaste.") to decide if they agree with or like something. In these cases, people are said to be taking the peripheral or heuristic route to persuasion. In this case, the models claim that individuals will use the central (systematic) route when they are both motivated and able to consider the contents of the message thoughtfully. If for any reason, they are unwilling or unable to engage in effortful thinking, they will follow the peripheral (heuristic) route to persuasion.

Research using the information-processing and cognitive response approaches identified a number of source, message, recipient, and contextual variables that affect persuasion. Nevertheless, it was not clear from those studies exactly when and how each variable would affect attitude change. For example, in some studies a highly credible source enhanced persuasion, but in others the source inhibited persuasion. However, the two different routes to persuasion outlined in the ELM and HSM provide a valuable framework for determining when and how these variables will lead to attitude change. In particular, the ELM holds that any variable within the persuasion setting may play one of several roles. First, when people are not thinking carefully about the message, the variable is processed as a simple cue that influences attitudes by rudimentary association or heuristic processes. Second, when people are thoroughly considering the merits of the message, the variable will be scrutinized as an argument, bias ongoing processing of the message, or affect confidence in the thoughts generated. Finally, when thinking is not constrained to be high or low by other factors, the variable may affect how much processing occurs by acting as an indicator of whether or not it is worth putting effort into evaluating the message. The multiple roles for variables as explained by the ELM provide the basis for how different source, message, recipient, and context factors affect persuasion.

Source Variables

The source is the person or entity who delivers the persuasive appeal, and a number of source characteristics have been shown to influence attitude change. Two of the most commonly studied source variables are credibility and attractiveness. Credibility refers to the source's (a) expertise and (b) trustworthiness. An expert source is one who has relevant knowledge or experience regarding the topic of the persuasive message. A trustworthy source is one who lacks ulterior motives and expresses honest opinions based on the information as he or she sees it. You may consider a physician (expert) and your best friend (trustworthy) to be credible sources. Attractiveness refers to how physically or socially appealing and likable the source is. For example, television commercials often use fashion models and charismatic celebrities to get people to like their products. In general (but not always), credible and attractive sources are more persuasive than are noncredible and unattractive sources.

Consistent with the ELM's multiple roles hypothesis, source variables have been shown to influence persuasion in several different ways in different situations. Consider, for example, an advertisement for a brand of shampoo that features an attractive person using the product. People often associate attractiveness with positive feelings, and under low elaboration conditions, when there is little effortful thinking about the message, they may decide that they like the shampoo simply because the source makes them feel good. Under high elaboration conditions, when thinking is extensive, people may use the attractiveness of the source as evidence that the product gives them beautiful hair. Or, the source might bias their thinking so that positive thoughts selectively come to mind. Or, they might have more confidence in the thoughts they have if they think that attractive sources know what they are talking about. And if people are not sure how

much to think about the message, the beauty of the source may induce them to pay more attention to the advertisement and its message. This would increase persuasion if what the source says is compelling, but if the message is not very compelling, thinking more about it could lead to less persuasion. Other source variables affect persuasion by the same mechanisms.

Researchers have also documented a delayed persuasion phenomenon that frequently involves source variables. Generally, the effect of an initially compelling persuasive appeal decreases over time as information about the message decays in memory. However, it has been shown that messages associated with a cue that discounts or weakens the initial impact of a message containing strong arguments, such as a noncredible or untrustworthy source, may not change attitudes initially but can lead to persuasion at later. This is called the *sleeper effect*. It happens because the discounting cue decays in memory faster than do thoughts about the message itself, which allows the message to affect attitudes free from the influence of the discounting cue.

Message Variables

The message refers to all aspects of the persuasive appeal itself such as its length, complexity, language, and so forth. One of the central characteristics of the message is the quality of the arguments it contains. The effect of argument quality on persuasion depends on how much the recipient is thinking about the message. When people are unwilling or unable to effortfully process the message, they are influenced by peripheral cues or heuristics rather than by their analysis of the strength or weakness of the evidence presented. Thus, under low processing conditions, a weak message may be persuasive if it is paired with certain factors, such as a credible source. In contrast, when people are motivated and able to think carefully about the message, they will base their attitudes on the analysis of the merits of the evidence. Thus, under high processing conditions, a weak message will be low in persuasiveness even in the presence of a highly credible or likable source. Self-generated arguments (in role-playing, for example) are especially strong because individuals tend to be less resistant to their own thoughts and ideas.

When thinking is high, the message generally becomes more persuasive as argument strength increases. However, if people feel too pressured to change their attitudes, they might respond unfavorably to the message despite the strength of the reasons for change. Also, fear appeals (such as those designed to curb unhealthy behaviors) that are too anxiety arousing can lead people to defensively avoid thinking about the message. In fact, research has shown that fear appeals are most successful when the message is personally relevant, the fear aroused is moderate, and a clear, attainable solution to the problem is presented.

As with source variables, the ELM's multiple roles hypothesis holds that message variables can influence persuasion in several different ways. For example, messages that have been tailored to match the basis of the recipient's attitude are generally more persuasive than messages that mismatch. For example, religious types are more persuaded by messages framed in a religious manner. Also, attitudes based on feelings or affect tend to be more influenced by affectively based messages, whereas attitudes based on thoughts and cognitions tend to be affected more by cognitively based messages. How does matching work? Under low processing conditions, matching may lead to persuasion through a heuristic that messages that match are good. Under high processing conditions, however, matching positively biases processing of the message. That is, strong arguments that match elicit more favorable thoughts than do arguments that mismatch. When the amount of thinking is not constrained to be either high or low, matching increases scrutiny of the message, which leads to persuasion if the arguments in the message are compelling. However, if a matched message is not strong enough to overcome the original attitude, a mismatched message that directs recipients to think about the attitude object in a new way may be more persuasive. Other message variables influence persuasion in a similar manner.

Recipient Variables

The recipient is the target person or audience who receives the persuasive message. As with the source and message, a number of recipient characteristics have been found to influence attitude change. Many of these recipient factors have been shown to follow the multiple roles hypothesis of the ELM and can affect persuasion in several different ways. For example, when effortful thinking is low, a person's mood serves as a simple peripheral cue ("I feel good, so I must agree with the message"). When effortful thinking is

high, however, mood has been shown to serve in other roles. For example, under high thinking conditions, mood has biased the recipient's thoughts. That is, positive mood facilitates the retrieval of other positive thoughts or inhibits the retrieval of negative thoughts. Thinking more positive thoughts will then lead to more favorable attitudes. Under high thinking conditions, a person's mood has also been analyzed as an argument and affected the confidence in people's thoughts. When the amount of thinking was not constrained to be high or low, mood influenced the amount of processing. Specifically, people in positive moods tend not to engage in effortful thinking, presumably because they want to maintain their good moods. However, those in positive moods will think carefully about a message if it is expected to advocate something pleasant. People in negative moods have been shown to engage in effortful processing of the message, regardless of whether it is expected to be pleasant or unpleasant. One explanation for this is that people in bad moods are in a problem-solving frame of mind, and thinking is associated with problem solving.

Some recipient variables influence persuasion by affecting people's motivation to process the message thoughtfully. Need for cognition is an individual difference that refers to how much people engage in and enjoy thinking. Those high in need for cognition tend to like thinking and seek out tasks and activities that are cognitively engaging. In general, these individuals are more likely to carefully consider the merits of the message even when it is not personally relevant. As such, they will base their attitudes on the strength of the evidence. Those low in need for cognition, however, do not enjoy thinking as much and tend to avoid tasks that require extensive thinking. Consequently, they are more likely to form their attitudes based on simple associations and heuristics rather than on effortful assessments of the evidence. Those low in need for cognition can be motivated to process the message carefully, but they require greater incentive to do so.

Context Variables

Contextual factors such as the manner and circumstances in which the message is given can also influence persuasion. That is, *how* the message is presented can be as important as *what* is presented. For example, a persuasive appeal that is introduced in a written format (e.g., in a newspaper) is generally easier to process than is one in an audio format (e.g., on radio) because people can slow the pace of their reading or reread to make sure they understand the arguments. If people are distracted by some variable (e.g., loud noise in the room), they may be unable to think critically about the message and will instead follow the peripheral route to persuasion. In addition, merely associating the message with something positive (e.g., a nice meal) or simply repeating it several times can be used to make the attitude object seem more positive with little or no effortful thinking.

Attitude Strength and Persuasion

As just described, there are a number of ways that source, message, recipient, and context variables can lead to persuasion. Although there are many avenues to attitude change, not all produce equally impactful attitudes. Regardless of the influencing variable, persuasion through effortful (central route) processing generally results in stronger, more durable, and longer-lasting attitudes than does persuasion through less effortful (peripheral route) processing.

Michael McCaslin
Richard E. Petty

See also Attitude Change; Attitudes; Elaboration Likelihood Model; Influence; Metacognition; Need for Cognition; Reactance

Further Readings

Briñol, P., & Petty, R. E. (2005). Individual differences in attitude change. In D. Albarracín, B. T. Johnson, & M. P. Zanna (Eds.). *Handbook of attitudes and attitude change* (pp. 575–615). Mahwah, NJ: Erlbaum.

Petty, R. E. (1995). Attitude change. In A. Tesser (Ed.). *Advanced social psychology* (pp. 195–255). New York: McGraw-Hill.

Petty, R. E., Rucker, D., Bizer, G., & Caciopppo, J. T. (2004). The elaboration likelihood model of persuasion. In J. S. Seiter & G. H. Gass (Eds.), *Perspectives on persuasion, social influence and compliance gaining* (pp. 65–89). Boston: Allyn & Bacon.

Petty, R. E., Wheeler, S. C., & Tormala, Z. L. (2003). Persuasion and attitude change. In T. Millon & M. J. Lerner (Eds.), *Handbook of psychology: Vol. 5. Personality and social psychology* (pp. 353–382). Hoboken, NJ: Wiley.

PHENOMENAL SELF

Definition

The phenomenal self reflects information about oneself that is in a person's awareness at the present time. This salient self-knowledge influences people's thoughts, emotions, and behaviors. The phenomenal self at any given moment is only a portion of all of the self-relevant information an individual has stored in memory. The reason for this is the amount of knowledge that people have about themselves is so vast that it is impossible and impractical for everything that one knows about himself or herself to be in awareness at one time. Thus, the phenomenal self represents that subset of self-knowledge—including beliefs, values, attitudes, self-ascribed traits, feelings of self-worth, autobiographical memories, interpersonal relationship knowledge, and goals and plans—that is currently in consciousness. The concept also recognizes the possibility that on occasion the phenomenal self is not part of one's immediate experience, that is to say, sometimes people are not self-aware. Related constructs in social psychology include terms such as *working self-concept, spontaneous self-concept, relational self,* and *possible selves,* which are similar to the phenomenal self in that they imply that the content of self-awareness is limited and changes across situation and time.

Background

The self is one of the central constructs in personality and social psychology and has generated a great amount of research. The widely accepted view of the self is that it is a set of linked memories that include people's knowledge about who they are, their values, preferences, goals, past experiences, and self-ascribed dispositions and traits. When in awareness, these memories serve as guides for behavior. For example, a person who is made self-aware by being placed before a mirror is more likely to behave in ways that are consistent with his or her traits than if he or she were not self-aware.

A survey of the vast amount of research on the self provides two contradictory pictures. One view is that the self is stable and consistent across time and situations. This view is supported by research that demonstrates that the self is a complex but highly integrated mental representation or set of memories. Moreover, people are motivated to maintain stable, consistent knowledge of who they are through their interactions with others as well as their tendencies to filter and distort information that would challenge their self-conceptions. The second view is that the self is somewhat in flux and changes subtly across time and situations. This view is supported by research that finds even minor changes in context can have pronounced effects on how people think about themselves. For example, asking people to present themselves to another individual as competent or extraverted versus incompetent or introverted, leads to changes in how people think about themselves and behave toward others in terms of competence or introversion–extraversion. This finding has been termed the *carryover* effect in that it reflects the carryover or influence of public, social behavior on people's private views of self.

The phenomenal self implies a view of self that allows the self to be stable in general while fluctuating in response to changes in social context, behavior, motivations, and moods. If available self-knowledge is too vast to fit into consciousness at one time, then the phenomenal self represents a summary statement of self-knowledge that is currently accessible from the potentially vast array of available self-knowledge stored in memory. Social context and current moods and motivations are like a spotlight on the self that illuminates certain pieces of information and makes them more accessible and in awareness than are other pieces of information. As contexts, moods, and motivations change, the spotlight shifts and different information is illuminated and attended to. In technical terms, context, mood, and motivation can lead the individual to a biased scanning of self-knowledge so that relevant information is in awareness while less pertinent information remains outside of awareness. Thus, contexts, moods, and motivations produce moment-to-moment shifts in the phenomenal self, but the underlying available self-knowledge is believed to be relatively stable.

Implications

The demonstration of contextual and motivational influences on shifts in the phenomenal self has relevance to issues such as self-concept change. On the surface, these momentary changes in the phenomenal self seem to be just that, momentary, with no long-term significance for the self. A shift in one direction—for example, spending the day alone at the beach and thinking of oneself as somewhat introverted—will be replaced by new self-views of extraversion after attending a party that evening. Exceptions may lead to more permanent changes in the self. For example, one study reported that actors' self-concepts took the qualities of the characters they portrayed and that these changes persisted 1 month after the close of the play. This finding suggests that repeated exposure to a situation that focuses one on specific aspects of the self will cause those aspects of the self to be more chronically prominent or salient in the phenomenal self. Other findings indicate that momentary shifts in the phenomenal self can influence the impressions that others have of the individual and can lead them to interact with the person based on these impressions. Thus, if because of a momentary shift in the phenomenal self others come to view you as more extraverted than you normally view yourself, they will treat you as if you are an extraverted person and repeated interaction with these people can change the self. Finally, sometimes the context or social pressure induces people to behave in ways that are inconsistent with the self. If people believe that they freely choose to act in this self-contradictory way, they will be motivated to change their self-concept to reduce the inconsistency. In this way, new information about the self becomes available for inclusion in the phenomenal self.

Frederick Rhodewalt

See also Self; Self-Awareness; Self-Concept

Further Readings

Rhodewalt, F. (1998). Self-presentation and the phenomenal self: The "carryover effect" revisited. In J. M. Darley & J. Cooper (Eds.), *Attribution and social interaction: The legacy of Edward E. Jones.* Washington, DC: American Psychological Association.

Placebo Effect

Definition

A *placebo* is a medical term for a drug that has no active ingredient. Biologically, it doesn't do anything, but the patient might mistakenly believe it is a powerful medicine. In fact, in bygone eras, some people who took snake oil and other medically useless substances did get better, partly because they believed that these substances would cure them. The phrase *placebo effect* refers to a person's response to a substance only as the result of the expectation of such a response. The response is called a placebo effect when the substance is known not to induce any response, but a consistent response is found. Because of the placebo effect, people may experience or perceive the effects of medication, such as pain relief or psychotropic effects, even when the "medication" given to them is merely an inert dose that the patient believes to be medicinal (i.e., a pill or serum with no reagent). Placebo effects are one category of expectation effects, though not all expectancy effects are placebo effects because people may expect any outcome for any reason, whether or not they have been given a placebo.

History and Modern Usage

The word *placebo,* in Vulgate Latin, referred to pleasing or satisfying some need or desire. Adopted by the medical community, the term referred to a "drug" given to satisfy a patient's desire for a drug, without giving the patient the actual drug. Because many medications may have negative side effects, doctors began prescribing pills with no medicinal content, informing patients that the pills were indeed the drug they sought. In this manner, patients were satisfied without being exposed to unnecessary, potentially dangerous drugs. These pills were often made out of sugar, and for this reason placebos are often referred to as sugar pills.

Doctors found, however, that some patients who were given these inert pills responded to the treatments, reporting that their symptoms had improved or ceased! Because the "medications" prescribed could not be lauded for the improvements, psychological expectations were used to explain the patients' responses, and still are. People have shown placebo effects for medications expected to relieve pain, prevent heart attacks, heal injuries, and reduce symptoms for depression. Though placebo effects are rarely as effective as actual medication, it is nonetheless impressive that people feel and exhibit responses to nothing more than their expectations.

Today, medical researchers take special care to test for placebo effects by using "double blind" experiments: giving all subjects pills that appear identical, but ensuring that some subjects receive the real drug while others receive a placebo. When neither the subject nor the provider knows whether the subject is getting a real pill or a placebo, all subjects have the same expectations. As such, differences in outcome between subjects who receive real medication and subjects who do not cannot be caused by differences in expectation. Comparing these two groups to subjects in a third "control" condition, in which subjects have been given no treatment (not even a sugar pill) nor told to expect any results, allows researchers to test whether there is a placebo effect present.

Some theorists suggest that placebo effects are physiological responses induced by the placebo. Others hypothesize that motivations (e.g., to please a doctor), or simply expectations alone may cause placebo effects.

Adam D. I. Kramer

See also Demand Characteristics; Expectancy Effects; Expectations

Further Readings

White, L., Tursky, B., & Schwartz, G. (1985). *Placebo: Theory, research, and mechanisms.* New York: Guilford Press.

PLANNED BEHAVIOR THEORY

See THEORY OF PLANNED BEHAVIOR

PLANNING FALLACY

Definition

The planning fallacy refers to a specific form of optimistic bias wherein people underestimate the time that it will take to complete an upcoming task even though they are fully aware that similar tasks have taken longer in the past. An intriguing aspect of this phenomenon is that people simultaneously hold both optimistic beliefs (concerning the specific future task) as well as more realistic beliefs (concerning relevant past experiences). When it comes to planning the future, people can know the past and yet be doomed to repeat it.

The tendency to underestimate task completion times has important practical implications. Governments, businesses, and individuals all spend a considerable amount of time, money, and effort trying to forecast how long projects will take to complete. In daily life, accurate predictions allow individuals to plan effectively and coordinate their schedules with those of friends, family members, and coworkers. Unrealistic completion estimates can have serious economic, personal, and social costs and thus merit research attention.

Evidence and Causes

The most direct evidence for the planning fallacy comes from studies in which people predict how long an upcoming project will take to complete, report completion times for similar projects in the past, and subsequently carry out the project. For example, university students reported that they typically completed their writing assignments about a day before the due date, but predicted that they would complete their current summer essay more than a week before it was due. They tended to finish the essay, as usual, about a day before the deadline. The tendency to underestimate completion times has been observed for a wide variety of activities ranging from daily household chores to large-scale industrial projects.

Why would people repeatedly underestimate how long their tasks will take to complete? According to cognitive explanations, the bias results from the kinds of information that people consider. When generating a task-completion prediction, people's natural inclination is to plan out the specific steps that they will take to successfully complete the project. The problem with this approach is that events don't usually unfold exactly as planned. Given the vast number of potential impediments, there is a great likelihood that people will encounter unexpected problems, delays, and interruptions. When people focus narrowly on a plan for successful task completion, they neglect other sources of information—such as past completion times, competing priorities, and factors that may delay their progress—that could lead to more realistic predictions.

This cognitive explanation has been supported by studies in which individuals describe their thoughts while predicting when they will finish an upcoming project. Most descriptions focus on specific future plans whereas very few descriptions mention relevant past experiences or potential problems. In addition, experimental studies have shown that people who are instructed to develop a detailed future plan for a task make more optimistic predictions than those who are not. These findings imply that people's unrealistic predictions are caused, at least in part, by their tendency to focus narrowly on a plan for successful task completion.

Motivation can also play a role, by guiding the cognitive approach that people take. For example, strong desires to finish tasks early may increase people's focus on future plans and decrease their focus on past experiences, resulting in highly optimistic predictions. The interplay between motivation and cognition was illustrated in a field study. Taxpayers who expected an income tax refund, and were thus strongly motivated to file their tax return early, estimated they would file their return about 10 days earlier on average than did taxpayers who did not expect a refund. In fact, the two groups did not differ in when they filed their returns, which was much later than either group had predicted. Incentives for early task completion appear to increase people's attention to future plans and reduce attention to relevant past experiences—the very pattern of cognitive processes that fuels the planning fallacy.

Moderating Factors and Strategies

Given the potential costs of unrealistic predictions, researchers have attempted to identify factors that may limit their occurrence. The findings suggest that the bias is remarkably robust. It appears for a wide range of tasks and activities, it generalizes across individual differences in personality and culture, and it appears for group predictions as well as individual predictions. One factor that does appear to have a great influence, however, is whether people's predictions involve their own tasks or those of others. When people make predictions about others' tasks, rather than their own, they are less prone to underestimate completion times. This actor–observer difference makes sense given the cognitive and motivational causes of the planning fallacy. Observers typically do not have access to the wealth of information that actors possess about their future plans and circumstances, making it difficult for observers to generate a detailed future plan. Also, neutral observers do not generally share the same motivations as actors (e.g., to complete the task promptly), and thus may be less inclined to focus selectively on information that supports an optimistic forecast. Whenever it is important to avoid unrealistic predictions, then, individuals may be well advised to consult with neutral observers.

Researchers have also examined strategies that individual forecasters can use to avoid underestimating their own completion times. One strategy involves linking past experiences with specific plans for an upcoming task. Specifically, before generating a task-completion prediction, forecasters are asked to recall when they typically finish projects, and then to describe a plausible scenario that would result in the upcoming project being done at the usual time. This procedure should prevent people from either ignoring past experiences or denying the relevance of those experiences, and it has been shown to eliminate the usual optimistic bias. Another strategy that can be effective is to break down a multifaceted task into its smaller subcomponents, and consider how long each of the subcomponents will take.

Roger Buehler

See also Decision Making; Heuristic Processing; Overconfidence

Further Readings

Buehler, R., Griffin, D., & Ross, M. (1994). Exploring the "planning fallacy": Why people underestimate their task completion times. *Journal of Personality and Social Psychology, 67,* 366–381.

Buehler, R., Griffin, D., & Ross, M. (2002). Inside the planning fallacy: The causes and consequences of optimistic time prediction. In T. D. Gilovich, D. W. Griffin, & D. Kahneman (Eds.), *Heuristics and biases: The psychology of intuitive judgment* (pp. 250–270). Cambridge, UK: Cambridge University Press.

Kahneman, D., & Tversky, A. (1979). Intuitive prediction: Biases and corrective procedures. In D. Kahneman, P. Slovic, & A. Tversky (Eds.), *Judgment under uncertainty: Heuristics and biases* (pp. 414–421). Cambridge, UK: Cambridge University Press.

Pluralistic Ignorance

Pluralistic ignorance occurs when people erroneously infer that they feel differently from their peers, even though they are behaving similarly. As one example, imagine the following scenario: You are sitting in a large lecture hall listening to an especially complicated lecture. After many minutes of incomprehensible material, the lecturer pauses and asks if there are any questions. No hands go up. You look around the room. Could these people really understand what the lecturer is talking about? You yourself are completely lost. Your fear of looking stupid keeps you from raising your hand, but as you look around the room at your impassive classmates, you interpret their similar behavior differently: You take their failure to raise their hands as a sign that they understand the lecture, that they genuinely have no questions. These different assumptions you make about the causes of your own behavior and the causes of your classmates' behavior constitute pluralistic ignorance.

Another case of pluralistic ignorance that is familiar to many college students concerns drinking on campus. Alcohol use is prevalent at most colleges and universities. Students drink at weekend parties and sometimes at evening study breaks. Many drink to excess, some on a routine basis. The high visibility of heavy drinking on campus, combined with reluctance by students to show any public signs of concern or disapproval, gives rise to pluralistic ignorance: Students believe that their peers are much more comfortable with this behavior than they themselves feel.

Social Dynamics

Pluralistic ignorance plays a role in many other dysfunctional social dynamics. In addition to the cases already mentioned, researchers have linked pluralistic ignorance to the failure of bystanders to intervene in emergency situations. Bystanders recognize that their own inaction is driven by uncertainty and fear of doing the wrong thing; however, they think other bystanders are not intervening because these others have concluded that the situation is not an emergency and there is no need to intervene. Pluralistic ignorance also acts as an impediment to the formation of new relationships. Consider the case of Jack and Jill, who secretly harbor romantic interest in each other. Jack does not approach Jill because he fears that she will reject him, and Jill does not approach Jack for the same reason. However, Jack assumes that Jill is not approaching him because she is not interested in him, and Jill makes the same assumption about Jack's failure to approach her. In this case, pluralistic ignorance, rather than a lack of interest, is keeping Jack and Jill apart. Finally, pluralistic ignorance keeps nurses from acknowledging the stresses of their jobs, prison guards from showing sympathy for their prisoners, corporate board members from acknowledging their concerns about their firm's corporate strategy, and ordinary citizens from acknowledging concerns about their government's foreign policy. Pluralistic ignorance is a very common dynamic in social life.

Social Norms

Pluralistic ignorance begins with widespread conformity to social norms—norms that govern appropriate behavior in the classroom, at a party, in a boardroom, or in a hospital; norms that regulate behavior with friends, strangers, or colleagues. Indeed, most social contexts and relationships are characterized by normative expectations for behavior, whether people realize it or not. These norms dictate, for example, that one should show unwavering public support for friends and colleagues, should not challenge people's personal choices, and should appear calm, collected, and in control at all times. Of course, often these behaviors do not reflect how people truly feel. Often people have misgivings about their peers' behavior; often they do not agree with their colleagues' proposals; often they feel uncertain, anxious, and fearful. When discrepancies between norm-driven behavior and private feelings arise, pluralistic ignorance is the result. People know that their own behavior does not reflect their true sentiments, but they assume that other people are acting on what they genuinely feel.

Consequences

Pluralistic ignorance has been linked to a wide range of deleterious consequences. For example, victims of pluralistic ignorance see themselves as deviant members of their peer group: less knowledgeable than their classmates, more uptight than their peers, less committed than their fellow board members, less competent than their fellow nurses. This can leave them feeling bad about themselves and alienated from the group or institution of which they are a part. In addition, pluralistic ignorance can lead groups to persist in policies and practices that have lost widespread support: This can lead college students to persist in heavy drinking, corporations to persist in failing strategies, and governments to persist in unpopular foreign policies. At the same time, it can prevent groups from taking actions that would be beneficial in the long run: actions to intervene in an emergency, for example, or to initiate a personal relationship.

Fortunately, pluralistic ignorance can be dispelled, and its negative consequences alleviated, through education. For example, students who learn that support for heavy drinking practices is not as widespread as they thought drink less themselves and feel more comfortable with the decision not to drink. Alcohol intervention programs now routinely employ this strategy to combat problem drinking on campus.

Deborah A. Prentice

See also Bystander Effect; Conformity; Deviance; Norms, Prescriptive and Descriptive

Further Readings

O'Gorman, H. J. (1986). The discovery of pluralistic ignorance: An ironic lesson. *Journal of the History of the Behavioral Sciences, 22,* 333–347.

Prentice, D. A., & Miller, D. T. (1993). Pluralistic ignorance and alcohol use on campus: Some consequences of misperceiving the social norm. *Journal of Personality and Social Psychology, 64,* 243–256.

Todorov, A., & Mandisodza, A. N. (2004). Public opinion on foreign policy: The multilateral public that perceives itself as unilateral. *Public Opinion Quarterly, 68,* 325–348.

Vorauer, J., & Ratner, R. (1996). Who's going to make the first move? Pluralistic ignorance as an impediment to relationship formation. *Journal of Social and Personal Relationships, 13,* 483–503.

Westphal, J. D., & Bednar, M. K. (2005). Pluralistic ignorance in corporate boards and firms' strategic persistence in response to low firm performance. *Administrative Science Quarterly, 50,* 262–298.

POLARIZATION PROCESSES

Definition

Like the North Pole and the South Pole or the opposite ends of a magnet, poles represent extreme endpoints, and polarization indicates movement toward those extremes. In psychological terms, polarization processes describe movement in individuals' views toward opposite extremes. For example, imagine a group of individuals that includes both moderate supporters and moderate opponents of abortion, and imagine they engage in a discussion of the issue. Imagine further that each side then becomes more extreme in its respective support of, or opposition to, abortion. That movement to more extreme positions is said to reflect polarization because each side has moved to a more extreme pole or endpoint on the relevant continuum. In social psychology, polarization processes have been studied in three domains: group decision making, attitudes, and intergroup perception.

Group Decision Making

Beginning in the 1960s, researchers became interested in how individual judgments could be affected by group discussion. A typical study would present individuals with a number of problems, known as *choice dilemmas,* in which the task was to indicate a preference for one of two possible solutions to each problem. For example, participants would be asked to indicate the minimum probability that a new company will survive before a prospective employee should accept a position with the company rather than retain an existing job. In the typical design, participants would indicate their responses individually and then engage in a conversation about the problem with other members of a group. The group would be asked to render its unanimous joint decision, and then each member would be asked to indicate, once again, his or her personal response.

The standard finding from such research was that a group would reach a joint decision favoring more risk than the average response of its constituent members. For example, imagine that a group included three members, and one of those members indicated initially that there had to be a 5 in 10 chance that the hypothetical company would succeed before the employee should accept the new position. Imagine another group member indicated a response of 3 in 10, whereas the final member responded with 1 in 10. The average response of the three members would then be 3 in 10. However, after discussion, the group might come to a joint decision of 2 in 10, and individual members' personal responses might also gravitate toward the riskier end of the probability continuum. This finding was labeled the "risky shift" because group discussion tended to push individuals to adopt, on average, riskier solutions to choice dilemmas than they initially favored.

Later research, however, suggested that the nature of the particular dilemma determined whether groups would end up favoring more risk than their average member or, alternatively, would favor more caution. For some choice dilemma items, for example, after group discussion, individuals who had previously expressed mild endorsement of the safe option would end up endorsing an even safer option. Accordingly, instead of the risky shift, the phenomenon became known as *group polarization,* because groups tended to move individual members to adopt positions that were somewhat more extreme than their initial stances. If those initial positions favored risk, then groups would prompt greater endorsement of risk; if instead, a safe option was preferred, then after group discussion, it would be more preferred.

Two primary factors have been cited as responsible for group polarization effects. The first involves the presence of persuasive arguments. Being a member of a group means that there is an opportunity to be exposed to novel arguments regarding an issue—arguments that can help reinforce and strengthen an individual's initial position, producing movement toward the extremes. In addition, social comparison processes can operate in a group, with each member making an effort to demonstrate that he or she endorses the apparent group norm. Such processes can produce a situation in which individuals move to more extreme positions in an attempt to position themselves squarely on the appropriate side of the safe-risk continuum.

Attitudes

A second domain in which polarization processes have been studied is that of attitudes. Beginning in the 1970s, research on attitude polarization demonstrated that people who were asked to think carefully about a particular attitude that they held ended up endorsing a more extreme version of that attitude.

Related research has suggested that attitudes can become more polarized as a result of a biased search for evidence in support of the initial attitude. For example, in one study, capital punishment opponents and proponents were exposed to written arguments that both supported and refuted some traditional justifications for the death penalty. After being exposed to such mixed evidence, these partisan subjects became more persuaded of the correctness of their initial attitude. This polarization of initial positions appeared to occur because participants engaged in biased interpretation of the relevant evidence, uncritically accepting information that supported their initial positions while subjecting to harsh scrutiny information that contradicted their initial stances, a phenomenon that has been labeled "biased assimilation."

Intergroup Perception

A final domain in which polarization processes have been studied involves intergroup perception, in which, typically, members of opposing groups are asked to make judgments concerning the views of both members of their side and members of the opposite side of some contentious issue. In one study, for example, supporters and opponents of abortion were asked to predict the view that would be espoused by the average pro-choice and the average pro-life member of their respective groups. Members of both groups overestimated the extremity of the average view held by each side, believing that the two groups were farther apart in their views than they actually were, a phenomenon labeled "false polarization." The implication of these inaccurate perceptions is that disputants who overestimate the degree of difference between the views of each side may consequently miss opportunities to resolve intergroup conflict.

Andrew Ward

See also Attitudes; Group Polarization; Outgroup Homogeneity; Risky Shift; Social Comparison

Further Readings

Brown, R. (1986). *Social psychology: The second edition.* New York: Free Press.

Ross, L., & Ward, A. (1995). Psychological barriers to dispute resolution. In M. Zanna (Ed.), *Advances in experimental social psychology* (Vol. 27, pp. 255–304). San Diego, CA: Academic Press.

POLITICAL PSYCHOLOGY

Definition

Political psychology is an interdisciplinary field of study that lies at the crossroads of many fields of research, including psychology, political science, communication, economics, and sociology. Although the field is very broad, much of its research deals with using principles and theories from both psychology and political science to understand and predict people's political opinions, thoughts, feelings, and behaviors.

Political thought and behavior play an important role in determining leaders and how leaders will think and behave. Political psychology attempts to apply scientific principles to better understand these processes. Although this entry presents only the smallest of glimpses into a very limited sample of what political psychology has to offer, it is hoped that the reader will gain an insight into the topics that political psychologists explore and the tools with which they conduct their research.

Areas of Research

As suggested by the definition, political psychology is a vast area of study, encompassing research and theory from a wide variety of other academic disciplines. As such, space limitations make it impossible to discuss all or even most of the areas of study. However, much of the field can be distilled into several important subareas.

Individuals

One area of interest to political psychologists is the prediction and understanding of the political thoughts and behaviors of typical citizens. Much research, for example, has investigated what factors contribute to the choices that people make they vote. Some of the most basic research has investigated the relation between demographics and vote choice, focusing on how, for example, age, race, gender, and household income predict vote choice. Other research has focused on how membership in groups such as political parties, trade unions, and religious organizations can be used to predict vote choice. Still other studies have investigated how a person's stances on political issues such as abortion, taxes, and welfare can predict the candidates for whom he or she will vote.

But voting is only one example of political behavior. Consider the fact that some citizens immerse themselves in the political world, learning a great deal about candidates for political races, donating time and money to their preferred candidates, and never missing an election. Others, however, seem not to care, remaining ignorant of the political world in which they live, unaware of the candidates running for election and rarely if ever taking part in the political process. The study of why people do or do not participate in the political process is another individual-level phenomenon that has garnered much research. For example, some research has investigated how a person's demographics predict political participation, learning that, for example, older people, people of higher income, and people of higher education are more likely to participate. Other research has shown that psychological phenomena such as emotions, feelings of threat, or a perception of a personal stake in an issue can lead a person to participate.

Still other research has explored how political campaigns can influence individuals' political thoughts and behaviors. Stephen Ansolabehere and Shanto Iyengar, for example, have studied the effects of attack advertisements on individuals. They argue that such negative messages can make individuals become more extreme in their political ideologies and, at the same time, make them less likely to vote. Other research has investigated how campaigns are influenced by, for example, media coverage of candidates and issues relevant to the campaign, the amount of money spent on the campaigns, and the state of the economy during the campaign.

Leaders

Whereas some political-psychological research focuses on the typical citizen, other research instead attempts to understand the political leader. Margaret Hermann has argued that to gain insight into what makes a good leader requires understanding several important aspects of the leader and his or her surroundings. The first of these aspects is the context around the leader. For example, one type of leader might be best for a country during years of peace, whereas another type of leader might be best for the same country during wartime. The second aspect is to understand the characteristics and behavioral traits of the leader. For example, Alexander George proposed that some U.S. presidents have shown a formalistic style of leadership in which decisions are made in a highly organized structure, other presidents have shown a competitive style in which power is distributed though conflict and bargaining, and still other presidents have shown a collegial style in which teamwork and interaction are valued. The third of Hermann's aspects is to understand the leaders' constituencies and the relations between

the leader and the constituents. Simply stated, certain groups of people may be best led by certain leaders. Thus, by understanding the context, the leader, and the constituents, one may be able to predict the success or failure of a given leader.

Intragroup Processes

Many political psychologists focus on groups and, in particular, how groups come to make decisions. Although it seems logical that groups of people would come to make more accurate decisions than they might otherwise make individually, this is often not the case. For example, Irving Janis found evidence that, in certain circumstances, groups can be driven more to come to a consensus that keeps members of the group satisfied than to come to an accurate decision that may offend or anger members of the group. Janis termed this phenomenon *groupthink,* suggesting that many of history's worst decisions can be explained in part by its processes, such as the decision to carry out the Bay of Pigs invasion. In a similar vein, David Myers and Helmut Lamm found evidence that members of groups tend to hold more extreme opinions and make more extreme choices when thinking about and discussing options than when formulating such opinions and choices alone. This phenomenon, called *group polarization,* has also garnered much attention by political psychologists.

International Relations

Another area of political psychology deals with understanding nations and countries. One area of study on international relations examines what makes international conflict possible. For example, Jim Sidanius and his colleagues have argued that part of the reason that nations go to war is because of social dominance: that those societies who have disproportionately high resources and power want to maintain this social inequality and will go to great lengths—including waging war—to do so. Others, like Urie Bronfenbrenner, have suggested that enemy nations have negatively distorted images of each other and that these false images can lead to mutual aggression and mistrust. Still other research has investigated other aspects of international relations, such as prejudice, treaties, conflict resolution, alliances, and terrorism.

Methodologies

Because political psychologists attempt to understand myriad political processes at many different levels of analysis, they use a wide range of research techniques to do so.

Surveys

Often, research devoted to understanding individual-level phenomena is conducted using surveys, a technique in which participants provide their opinions, thoughts, and beliefs about various issues, people, and objects. Some surveys are conducted in a respondent's home in a face-to-face format. Others are conducted by telephone, using random-digit-dialing techniques to ensure proper sampling. Other techniques include mail surveys and surveys conducted online. Political psychologists have made especially extensive use of data from the National Election Study surveys, which have been conducted every 2 years since 1948. Participants in these surveys provide a wealth of data about themselves, including their demographics, their political ideologies, and their thoughts and feelings about various candidates, political issues, political parties, public officials, and more.

The Experimental Method

To determine causal relations between variables, political psychologists conduct research using the experimental method. Randomly assigning respondents to conditions and manipulating variables allows such hypotheses of causality to be tested. Although surveys are often conducted using the experimental method, political psychologists often conduct elaborate experimental research that collects data in a way that surveys cannot.

Case Studies

Rather than examining data collected from groups of people like surveys and experiments do, case studies examine one single data point in its naturalistic setting. Thus, instead of learning what a relatively large sample of people think or feel about a particular issue, a case study might examine how decisions made by a person or a group of people during a particular crisis either alleviated or worsened the situation.

Content Analysis

When conducting content analyses, political psychologists examine archived writings and speeches to understand a political phenomenon. Such content analyses can be useful in, for example, distilling a former president's personality from his state of the union addresses, or understanding the main differences between two political parties on an issue by examining transcripts from relevant debates.

George Y. Bizer

See also Group Polarization; Groupthink; Leadership; Social Dominance Orientation

Further Readings

Cottam, M., Dietz-Uhler, B., Mastors, E. M., & Preston, T. (2004). *Introduction to political psychology.* Mahwah, NJ: Erlbaum.

Hermann, M. G. (1986). *Political psychology: Contemporary problems and issues.* San Francisco: Jossey-Bass.

Kuklinski, J. H. (2002). *Thinking about political psychology.* Cambridge, UK: Cambridge University Press.

Monroe, K. R. (2002). *Political psychology.* Mahwah, NJ: Erlbaum.

Sears, D. O., Huddy, L., & Jervis, R. (2003). *Oxford handbook of political psychology.* New York: Oxford University Press.

PORNOGRAPHY

Definition

The term *pornography* refers to sexually explicit media that are primarily intended to sexually arouse the consumer. Such media include magazines, the Internet, and films. They have become very common in many societies and are reported to regularly provide huge profits for the producers and distributors of such media.

Gender Differences

Some of the social scientific research in this area has focused on who are most likely to be the consumers of these media. The findings reveal considerable gender differences in consumption and use of pornography, although within each gender there are also large differences in consumption. Generally, research has found that males are more likely to be consumers of various types of pornography, although some women also do use and enjoy pornography. Men have been found to be much more likely to use pornography on their own, often as a stimulant to masturbation. A considerable number of men and women report using pornography in the context of a relationship where such media are used together by a couple.

Men generally are more likely to be attracted to pornography and to use it more regularly, and they generally have more favorable attitudes, and react with less negative affect, to it. This is particularly true for portrayals featuring nudity of the opposite sex, often in various sexual poses, and portrayals of sexual acts devoid of relationship context. In contrast, men are less likely than women to consume sexually explicit media that emphasize sexual communion and romance.

Effects

The question of what impact exposure to such pornographic materials has on consumers has been debated and researched from many vantage points. Although social psychological research has been designed to be objective, it appears that the types of hypotheses tested have often been guided by ideological/political perspectives on this topic. For example, some researchers, guided by assertions made by conservative thinkers, have tested whether exposure to pornography can affect attitudes about family life and commitment to long-term relationships. Other researchers, guided by concerns of feminists, have tested whether pornography exposure affects attitudes and behaviors toward women, particularly in areas such as violence against women.

Social scientific research on pornography's effects includes primarily three types of studies using differing methodologies. Each type of method has certain advantages and disadvantages. First are studies that seek to find out if there may be causal effects of exposure to different types of pornography. Typically, such studies have randomly assigned participants to different conditions. The researchers then manipulated how much pornography, if any, the participants in the various conditions were exposed to. These studies have usually been conducted in laboratory environments, although some relevant experiments have also been

successfully completed in less artificial environments. The value of such research is that it can determine cause and effect with confidence because participants in the various conditions may be considered equal before their pornography exposure because of random assignment to conditions. Any differences found after different pornography exposure may be attributed to the differences in exposure content and amounts. The second type of research has not involved any manipulation by the researchers of amount of pornography consumption. Instead, people have been surveyed regarding how much and what type of pornography they have been exposed to in their daily lives, and such differences have been correlated with differences in their attitudes and behaviors. Although it is more difficult to identify causal connections in this type of research, there is the advantage of studying what people actually are like in their usual environments. The third type of research has examined in various cultures how much pornography is being consumed in the society at large and changes in such consumption over time. Such changes have then been correlated with other changes in the society, such as changes in sexual crimes. Although such research has provided an interesting window regarding varied cultures, one problem is that it is difficult to relate changes at the larger societal level to individual behavior. Also, there are typically many other changes that have occurred in a society at the same time as changes in pornography consumption have been happening.

Implications

Most of the research using these three types of methodologies has involved male participants, who, as noted earlier, are more frequent consumers of pornography than females are. Although differences have emerged from the various types of studies, some general conclusions seem justified. Overall, it seems that no simple generalizations are justified but that the effects depend largely on the type of person who consumes pornography as well as the content of the material the person uses. In the area of aggression against women, the research suggests that if a man already has relatively strong tendencies to be aggressive toward women, then heavy pornography consumption may increase his aggressive tendencies. This seems to be particularly likely if the type of pornography he is sexually aroused by includes violent content. Conversely, if a man has little risk for being aggressive toward women, then whether or not he consumes pornography does not appear to significantly affect his risk for being aggressive toward women. Moreover, the research suggests that many individuals in some cultures use pornography on a fairly regular basis and, at least in their own self-perceptions, report generally positive and little negative effects. Therefore, the overall findings suggest that there may be considerable variations among individuals within a culture in how pornography affects them. Similarly, differing environments in various cultures, such as the degree of hostility versus trust between males and female and the availability of sex education, may create major individual differences in the role and impact of pornographic stimuli on members of differing societies.

Neil Malamuth

See also Aggression; Gender Differences; Intimate Partner Violence; Media Violence and Aggression; Sex Drive; Sexual Desire

Further Readings

Hald, G. M. (2006). Gender differences in pornography consumption among young heterosexual Danish adults. *Archives of Sexual Behavior, 35,* 577–586.

Kutchinsky, B. (1991). Pornography and rape: Theory and practice? Evidence from crime data in four countries where pornography is easily available. *International Journal of Law and Psychiatry, 14,* 47–64.

Malamuth, N., & Huppin, M. (2005). Pornography and teenagers: The importance of individual differences. *Adolescent Medicine, 16,* 315–326.

Weinstein, J. (1999). *Hate speech, pornography, and the radical attack on free speech doctrine.* Boulder, CO: Westview Press.

POSITIVE AFFECT

Definition

Positive affect is the pleasant state that can be induced by small things that happen in everyday life. It is one of the most exciting topics currently under investigation in the psychological research literature. The findings suggest that there is the potential for a large impact of positive affect on social behavior and interpersonal processes, as well as on thinking, problem solving, and decision making. In addition, the topic has been studied in naturalistic ways and in a diverse range of realistic settings, and results of these studies suggest that positive affect may be important in many contexts of everyday life, from classrooms to boardrooms to physicians' offices. The field itself is still young enough that there remain some controversies about how to understand what the processes are that are fostered by positive affect, which should be inviting to researchers not already in the field.

The noun *affect,* as used in psychology, refers to feelings or emotions, and differs from the noun *effect,* which refers to the result of some action or circumstance. Positive affect, then, refers to pleasant feelings or emotions. From one perspective, *positive affect* is the most general term for pleasant feeling states, encompassing all the different types of positive feelings and all of their effects—neurophysiological, cognitive, motivational, behavioral, and interpersonal (however, in medical and related fields, the term is reserved for only the conscious feeling state). It can include good moods, pleasant emotions (e.g., joy, calmness, love), mild happy feelings, and their consequences.

Further Distinctions

As affect is studied in the psychology research literature, however, some finer distinctions are often made. Thus, *positive affect* usually refers to a mild happy or pleasant general feeling state, induced in some simple way that people may readily experience in daily life. Sometimes specific positive emotions, such as elation, joy, or love, are included under the general heading, "positive affect," but some researchers make a distinction between positive emotions such as love, on the one hand, and positive affect, a more general state, on the other. Some people working on the topic use the term *mood* to refer to this general state. However, some researchers avoid using the term *mood* because that term can carry unwanted connotations such as moodiness, which are not what the researchers in this field study.

Some researchers who study positive affect intend to distinguish between positive affect or mood and positive emotions. A distinction has been proposed between these terms, just for convenience, that suggests that *affect* or *mood* refers to a general state, perhaps a background feeling state, whereas specific emotions refer to more focused feelings. In addition, emotions also seem to be feelings that are targeted at a particular referent person, group, or thing, perhaps the source of the emotion, and they may have specific behaviors associated with them. For example, if someone makes you angry, you become angry *at that person* and you may interrupt what you are doing to say something to that person (or worse). Or if something like a big, barking dog frightens you, you feel afraid *of the dog* and run away from *it,* interrupting your walk down the lane. Notice that these examples are easier to find in the negative domain than in the positive, but perhaps there are focused positive emotions as well, such as love. Affect, in contrast, has been proposed to be less focused and a more generalized feeling state that can occur as a background state even while the person experiencing it can continue to work on some task or play some game or interact with other people. Affect may influence the way the task is done, but the task can be completed.

However, this distinction between affect and emotions is difficult to maintain, and may just come down to degree, or context, because one can think of emotions that are mild and do not interrupt ongoing behavior, or instances where one suppresses the impetus to react to the emotion and goes on with the task one is doing. One can work on a problem while loving someone (positive emotion) or while angry at someone (negative emotion). The usefulness of the distinction is only a practical one, in that it defines not a fundamental difference between affect and emotion, but a situation in which the influence of feeling states on other tasks or processes can be observed.

Positive affect has been defined in this entry as the pleasant state that can be induced by small things that happen in everyday life, so it may be helpful to mention some of the ways in which it can be induced, to understand the state more fully. In research studies, positive affect has been induced by events such as having research participants receive a useful, inexpensive free sample (worth under $1.00), find a dime or quarter in the coin-return of a public telephone that they happened to use in a shopping mall, be offered a cookie while studying in a library, be told that they succeeded (outperformed the average) on a simple, perceptual-motor task, view 5 minutes of a non-aggressive, nonsexual comedy film, or view a few pleasant slides, to mention only a few of the techniques that have been used successfully.

With regard to defining and understanding positive affect, it is important to note that measures of stable personality characteristics thought to reflect people's capacity for happiness or general, underlying tendency to be happy are not mentioned, nor are people's reports of overall well-being, in response to direct questions about it. Positive affect refers to ongoing feelings rather than stable underlying positive dispositions or traits; sometimes, as one might expect, some stable dispositions may also reflect or produce ongoing positive feelings, but in actuality they may not relate to current feelings at any given time. Although it is possible that affective dispositions to be happy or optimistic, for example, may play a role similar to that of induced positive affect, it is important to remember that most of the research on positive affect involves induction of affect among individuals who are randomly assigned to the affect conditions. This means that, without considering the person's underlying affective disposition (or their underlying tendencies to behave in a given way or engage in certain thought processes), the mild interventions such as those described previously have been found to produce the effects described next.

Effects

The focus in the research on positive affect has been on the effects of current feelings on other processes such as brain activity, problem solving, social interaction, and so forth.

A large body of evidence indicates that positive affect fosters mental flexibility, such as the ability to switch among ideas and include a broader range of ideas in mind at any given time. Often, positive affect helps people see how distinct lines of thought can relate to one another or be brought to bear upon one another. This has been found to result in improved creative problem solving, the ability to come up with innovative solutions to difficult problems, and openness to new information, even information that doesn't fit with one's preconceptions or favorite, old ways of thinking about a given situation or problem. This particular finding—improved creative problem solving and innovation—is one that has also been obtained by researchers studying the effects of the relatively stable dispositions of optimism, and of positive affectivity (a tendency to be positive or upbeat). Induced positive affect has also been shown to result in improved judgment and decision making in some circumstances, especially dangerous or genuinely risky situations, and increased social responsibility, helpfulness to others, and concern with the welfare of others as well as oneself. Also observed to result from positive affect have been an increased tendency to see connections between one's behavior, effort, and performance, on the one hand, and one's outcomes, on the other, where those connections actually exist (but not where they do not exist, such as in chance situations). These effects produce increased motivation in achievement or work situations as well as an increased ability to show self-control in situations where self-control would be in the person's long-term best interest. These findings have occurred in several applied contexts, including managerial situations, physicians' diagnostic processes, and consumer decision situations. Many researchers have found these effects exciting, because they open a window to understanding ways of increasing problem-solving effectiveness and creativity and improving thought processes and social interaction, responsibility, and self-control (and a pleasant way, at that!).

However, some researchers believe that positive affect takes cognitive capacity and therefore leads people to be impaired in problem solving and to think sloppily rather than carefully and systematically. Others also see positive affect as interfering with careful thought, but because of an absence of motivation to think carefully, rather than because of capacity deficit. A recent view that is related to these has suggested, likewise, that people who are feeling happy are not careful thinkers, but for the reason that they tend to rely on stored information, schemata, and scripts, rather than taking in new knowledge. There are also a few other variants on these themes, but they are all related in that they result in the idea that positive affect leads to superficial and overly hasty, careless, thought processes, compared with those demonstrated by people in whom affect has not been induced. These researchers argue that the creative problem solving and innovation observed in the studies referred to earlier only results because the problem-solving task can be solved without systematic thought. This latter point, however, has never been demonstrated (and without positive affect or a give-away hint about the solution to the problem, the rate of solution to these problems that require innovative thought is very low—about 15%, for example—whereas it is quite substantial in the positive affect conditions—about 65%, for example).

Finally, this research literature indicates that positive and negative affect are neither the same, nor symmetrical opposites, in their effects on thought processes and behavior. One cannot generalize from what one learns about positive affect to assume that the opposite is true of negative affect, or that the two kinds of feeling states produce the same effects—assuming, for example, that all emotion generally produces the same effect on thinking and behavior. The reasons for this are beyond the scope of this entry, but it is a point worth noting.

Future Research

The research field on the topic of positive affect is currently a very active one, with scientists working to expand understanding of the range of problems and activities and contexts in which positive affect will have effects, and also working to understand exactly what the processes are that have given rise to the opposing views of its overall impact that still exist in the field. The topic is truly an exciting area for continued research, with many avenues for additional research still to be explored.

Alice Isen

See also Affect; Broaden-and-Build Theory of Positive Emotions; Emotion; Happiness

Further Readings

Ashby, F. G., Isen, A. M., & Turken, A. U. (1999). A neuropsychological theory of positive affect and its influence on cognition. *Psychological Review, 106,* 529–550.

Isen, A. M. (1985). Asymmetry of happiness and sadness in effects on memory in normal college students. *Journal of Experimental Psychology: General, 114,* 388–391.

Isen, A. M., Nygren, T. E., & Ashby, F. G. (1988). The influence of positive affect on the perceived utility of gains and losses. *Journal of Personality and Social Psychology, 55,* 710–717.

POSITIVE ILLUSIONS

Definition

Positive illusions refers to a set of three related beliefs that characterize the way people think about (1) themselves, (2) their ability to control environmental events, and (3) their future. Instead of being evenhanded or balanced between the good and the bad, people are unrealistically positive: They believe they have many more positive than negative personal qualities, they exaggerate their abilities to bring about desired outcomes, and they are overly optimistic about their futures.

If not too extreme, these positive illusions promote psychological well-being and psychological functioning.

History and Background

Accurate self-views were once thought to be an essential feature of psychological well-being. It is easy to see why. People who harbor delusions of grandeur or believe they control the moon and stars are not paragons of mental health. Whether accuracy is best, however, is another matter. It is entirely possible that excessively positive self-views are detrimental, but mildly positive ones are beneficial.

One way to address this issue is to ask, "Do most people know what they are really like?" For example, suppose we randomly sample a group of people and ask them, "Compared with most other people, how intelligent are you?" Logically, most of the people in our sample should say they are as intelligent as most other people, with the rest equally split between saying they are less intelligent and more intelligent than most other people. This does not occur. Instead, most people say they are more intelligent than most other people. Furthermore, this effect occurs for a wide variety of personality traits and abilities. People believe they are more competent, flexible, and intelligent than others; drive better than others; are more caring, adaptive, and fairer than others; are happier and have better interpersonal relationships than others; and are more deserving of good fortune and good health. They also believe their judgments are less distorted by greed, self-aggrandizement, or personal gain than are other people's judgments and that their opinions are grounded in facts, but other people's opinions are driven by ideology. The bias even extends to friends, family, loved ones, and fellow group members, and is characteristic of people from a variety of cultures.

People also exaggerate their abilities to bring about desired outcomes. They readily credit themselves when things go well, but deny responsibility when things go awry. Together, these beliefs give rise to unrealistic optimism. Believing they are "good" and "powerful," leads people to believe their futures will be brighter than base rate data justify. For example, even though the current divorce rate in industrialized countries is approximately 50%, roughly three-quarters of newlyweds believe they will never divorce.

The prevalence of illusions does not mean that people are wildly inaccurate. In most cases, the degree of distortion is modest, resulting in a self-portrait that is just a bit too good to be true. Moreover, positive illusions do take reality into account. For example, although smokers think they are less likely to get cancer than are most other smokers, they readily acknowledge they are at greater risk than are nonsmokers.

Benefits

If not too excessive, positive illusions can be beneficial. These benefits fall into four areas. First, positive illusions are linked with subjective well-being. People who hold positive self-views are happier and more content than are those who are more realistic. Second, under some circumstances, positive self-views can also beget success. People who are confident in their abilities often perform better at achievement-related activities (e.g., exams, sporting contests) than do those who are more modest, even when their confidence is not entirely warranted. These effects are most apparent at tasks of moderate difficulty. Third, positive illusions promote interpersonal relationships. People who view their romantic partners through rose-colored glasses are more satisfied with their relationship and more committed to it than are those who have a more realistic view of their partners' actual strengths and weaknesses. Finally, positive illusions help people cope with life's challenges. For example, cancer patients who believe they can prevent the recurrence of cancer enjoy greater health than do those who are realistic, and preoperative patients who are unduly optimistic about their operation's success fare better than those who more accurately perceive the procedure's dangers and risks.

These benefits are achieved through a variety of means, but the most important is that positive illusions promote a problem-focused approach to coping. Rather than assuming that all is lost or blithely adopting a "What, me worry?" attitude, people who exhibit positive illusions roll up their sleeves and actively strive to build brighter lives for themselves. In this sense, positive illusions have motivational consequences. Believing that success is well within one's reach motivates people to work hard to achieve positive outcomes.

Costs

The many benefits of positive illusions should not blind us to their potential costs. First, positive illusions can lead people to undertake activities for which they are ill-suited. For example, an aspiring dancer may invest years pursuing a career in the arts without having the requisite talent. Positive illusions can also lead people to make poor economic decisions or engage in behaviors that are detrimental to their well-being. Gamblers, for example, often exaggerate their ability to control events that are heavily influenced by chance, such as roulette. Finally, positive illusions can have interpersonal costs. Although people generally prefer the company of optimistic people, they are not drawn to people who are boastful or narcissistic.

Importance

Research on positive illusions is important for two reasons. First, it has theoretical implications. Theories of mental health are largely based on what most people do (i.e., what's normative is normal). Evidence that most people possess inaccurate self-knowledge indicates that accuracy is not an essential component of normal psychological functioning. Second, positive illusions have practical implications. The capacity to adapt to life's challenges is one of the most important skills a person can possess. Positive illusions have consistently been shown to play a key role in helping people cope with, and even benefit from, life-threatening illnesses and life-altering tragedies.

Jonathon D. Brown

See also Coping; Illusion of Control; Marital Satisfaction; Narcissism; Self-Concept; Self-Deception; Self-Enhancement; Self-Serving Bias

Further Readings

Taylor, S. E., & Brown, J. D. (1988). Illusion and well-being: A social psychological perspective on mental health. *Psychological Bulletin, 103,* 193–210.

POSITIVE–NEGATIVE ASYMMETRY

Definition

The positive–negative asymmetry refers to two complementary tendencies regarding how people respond to positive and negative events or information. On one hand, there is a tendency for bad events (such as failing a class, being criticized, or experiencing the loss of a close friend) to have more impact on a person than good events (winning a prize, receiving a compliment, or making a new friend). The greater strength of negative information is most obvious in the area of impression formation, where it is called the negativity effect. Accordingly, when people form an impression of another person, they put greater weight on the person's bad behaviors (such as hitting a child for no reason) than on the person's good behavior (such as rescuing a family from a burning house). On the other hand, most of the experiences people have in everyday life are pleasant. As a result, there is a tendency for people to expect positive outcomes and good experiences from other people. In part, this very expectation may lead people to be surprised by and strongly affected by the bad things that occur in life.

Social Domains Where Bad Is Stronger Than Good

Bad events seem to carry more power than do good ones in a variety of domains. To appreciate the negativity effect in impression formation, try this thought experiment. Imagine a person who is very immoral, someone who has done horrendous things. Would you be surprised to learn that this villain did something very positive such as talked a friend out of suicide? Most people would find this mildly surprising. Now imagine a very moral person. Would you be surprised to learn that this person sold narcotics to neighborhood children? Most people would be quite surprised to hear that a very moral person did something so harmful. This thought experiment demonstrates the power of negative information in the impression. A bad act is capable of greatly altering one's impression of a person, whereas a person's good acts seem to count for less in the impression.

The greater weight of negative or immoral behavior also affects the attribution process. Attribution research examines how one's impressions of a person are influenced by both the person's behavior and the situational forces that surround the behavior. For example, if a coworker makes a donation to a charity when asked by the boss, you may discount the possibility that the coworker has a helpful trait. But a person's immoral behavior carries greater weight and may override this discounting tendency. For example, if a coworker is paid handsomely by the boss to swindle poor people, you are likely to see the coworker as immoral. Notice that the presence of the (situational) reward in this situation has little effect on your impression. In summary, when people hear about moral behavior, they take the situation into account when judging the person, but when they hear about a person's immoral behavior, they are likely to judge the person to be immoral, regardless of the situation. People's inferences about a person's underlying motives may help explain this asymmetry. For example, a person who commits a harmful act (such as swindling poor people) for money is probably motivated by selfishness, a motive that is entirely consistent with an immoral trait.

Research on impression formation and attribution focuses on people's reaction to strangers. What about close relationships? Are people more affected by the irritating behaviors of a romantic partner or spouse than by a partner's positive behaviors? Research by John Gottman suggests that negative events count more in this domain as well. The researcher videotaped couples as they discussed conflicts in their relationships. Although couples demonstrated a variety of styles of conflict resolution, negative behaviors by the partners were more strongly related to the couple's relationship satisfaction than were positive behaviors. Positive behaviors such as politeness, compliments, and gifts did help the relationship in minor ways. But negative behaviors such as insults and criticism were more decisive in determining whether the couple stayed together. In fact, Gottman reached the startling conclusion that a healthy relationship requires five times more good interactions than bad interactions.

Why Do Bad Things Have Greater Impact?

The broadest explanation for the negativity effect is that it has survival value. To appreciate this idea, think of the world as if it is a field filled with mushrooms and poisonous toadstools. A mushroom lover must be exceedingly careful when picking fungi for Sunday's dinner. The tastiest mushroom brings only a moment of pleasure. In contrast, eating the wrong toadstool can lead to an untimely and painful death. More generally, people's experiences with positive events (e.g., winning the lottery, sexual orgasm) may have less impact on their survival than their experiences with negative events (particularly those that risk bodily harm). As a result, it is adaptive for people to place greater weight on bad events than on good events.

A variety of specific psychological mechanisms may be involved in producing this negativity effect, including perceptual, cognitive, and affective factors. Bad events tend to receive more attention and more thorough processing than good events do. For example, when people are shown an array of human faces with different expressions, threatening faces are detected more quickly and accurately. This tendency to focus first on the negative may be relatively automatic. In a series of studies based on the Stroop paradigm, participants were shown personality trait adjectives and asked to name the color of ink in which the word was printed. Participants were slower to name the color when the word concerned a negative trait (e.g., sadistic) than a positive trait (e.g., honest). It appears that traits with negative meaning are distracting and slow down the color-naming process. Moreover, the participants in these studies were not deliberately focusing on the trait adjectives and, consequently, were probably unaware of the biasing impact of the negative words.

Perhaps the most elaborate theoretical explanations for the negativity effect involve cognitive mechanisms. For example, in seeking to explain the negativity effect in impressions and attributions, Glenn D. Reeder and Marilyn Brewer described the kinds of behavior that people typically expect from people with different types of traits. These trait-behavior relations often take an asymmetrical form. Specifically, people typically expect a person with a moral trait to emit moral behavior (e.g., helping people in need and giving generously to charity), but not immoral behavior (e.g., hurting other people). In contrast, people expect that a person with an immoral trait will emit both immoral behavior and moral behavior. It follows from these trait-behavior expectations, therefore, that immoral behavior will be more informative (or diagnostic) in the impression process because it must have been performed by an immoral person. Yet moral behavior is less informative because it could have been performed by either a moral person or an immoral person.

Finally, some research suggests that people's evaluation of positive and negative events are governed by separate affective (or feeling) systems. For example, a person may feel ambivalent toward a romantic partner or family member, such that he or she feels both strong positive feelings and strong negative feelings at the same time. In general, however, it appears that the negative system evokes stronger and more rapid responses.

Exceptions to the Rule That Bad Is Stronger Than Good

Although bad seems to outweigh good when the two are juxtaposed, people are generally optimistic about the future, expect the best from other people, and hold pleasant memories of the past. For most people, life is generally a positive experience. Indeed, the preponderance of positive events in everyday life may contribute to the fact that negative events stand out (or are "figural" to the "ground" of positive events). Given the novelty of negative events, it stands to reason that people would pay more attention to them. Thus, people's tendency to expect the best in life is not contradicted by their tendency to react more strongly to the worst in life.

Shelley Taylor described two complementary psychological processes that can account both for people's optimism and their tendency toward the negativity effect. Bad or threatening events create a problem that requires a quick response. In contrast, good or desirable events can be ignored with little penalty. Consequently, negative events cause a quick and intense mobilization to meet the threat. Once the threat is over, a second psychological process of minimization begins to take effect. This second process helps people repair the trauma of the earlier process by directing their attention toward the positive aspects of experience.

Glenn D. Reeder

See also Bad Is Stronger Than Good; Discounting, in Attribution; Person Perception

Further Readings

Baumeister, R. F., Bratslavsky, E., Finkenauer, C., & Vohs, K. D. (2001). Bad is stronger than good. *Review of General Psychology, 5,* 323–370.

Peeters, G., & Czapinski, J. (1990). Positive-negative asymmetry in evaluations: The distinction between affective and informational negativity effects. In W. Stroebe & M. Hewstone (Eds.), *European Review of Social Psychology* (Vol. 1, pp. 33–60). Chichester, UK: Wiley.

Reeder, G. D., & Brewer, M. B. (1979). A schematic model of dispositional attribution in interpersonal perception. *Psychological Review, 86,* 61–79.

Skowronski, J. J., & Carlston, D. E. (1989). Negativity and extremity biases in impression formation: A review of explanations. *Psychological Bulletin, 105,* 131–142.

Taylor, S. E. (1991). Asymmetrical effects of positive and negative events: The mobilization-minimization hypothesis. *Psychological Bulletin, 110,* 67–85.

POSITIVE PSYCHOLOGY

Definition

Positive psychology is the study of the processes and conditions that contribute to optimal functioning and flourishing in human beings. It is the study of positive experiences, positive traits, and positive communities. Examples of topics in positive psychology include the study of positive emotions, such as hope, curiosity, and love; the study of individual strengths, such as wisdom and courage; and the study of positive practices in institutions, such as school policies that foster students' intrinsic motivation to learn. Although interest in such topics has been around since the beginning days of psychology, the term *positive psychology* is quite recent and was coined as part of a concentrated effort by psychologists who saw a need to highlight these relatively neglected areas of research.

History and Background

When *positive psychology* is defined as the study of the ways people flourish and the conditions that contribute to their optimal functioning, it is clear that the concept of positive psychology (if not the term) has existed since the early 1900s and the days of Williams James, who was interested in what he called *healthy mindedness.* Other well-known psychologists interested in topics now classified under the heading of positive psychology included Gordon Allport, who wrote about positive human characteristics, and Abraham Maslow, who asserted that health was not merely the absence of disease. Despite these early seeds of interests in positive topics, in the latter half of the 20th century, psychological research largely focused on disorder, dysfunction, and damage, while the study of the psychological aspects of what makes life worth living receded into the background.

The recent surge in interest in positive psychology was initially a response to clinical psychology's focus on mental illness and the lack of work on healthy mental processes. However, the field of social psychology also showed the same imbalance—focusing the lion's share of effort on human failures, biases, and other ways situations and people can deter or damage themselves and those around them. For example, there is an abundance of studies on emotions such as fear, shame, guilt, anger, disgust, and anxiety, but only few on emotions such as joy, gratitude, and contentment. In the rapidly growing field of close relationships, a disproportionate number of studies have examined how couples weather, or fail to weather, bad relationship behavior such as criticisms and infidelities. But psychologists know little about the how good relationship behaviors such as compliments and displays of affection affect both the individual and the relationship itself. Similarly, there have been hundreds of studies on how couples, families, and friends engage in and manage conflict, but only a few on how they have fun and laugh with one another. In the areas of social cognition and intergroup behavior, social psychologists have focused much of their attention on topics such biases and prejudice, and much less of their attention on accuracy and tolerance. Several notable exceptions to the bias in social psychology have included work on altruism, passionate love, and optimism.

There are likely several reasons that many psychologists, including social psychologists, focus on the more negative or neutral aspects of human existence. First, there is an urgency to try to relieve suffering. Compassion steers psychologists toward helping those who are the worse off before improving the lives of those who are already doing fairly well. The history of research funding in the United States reflects this sentiment. After World War II, most funding agency priorities focused on the description, diagnosis, and treatment of mental illness and disorders. Moreover, some may assume that studying the psychological contributions to flourishing and optimal health cannot and will not help those who are distressed. To the contrary, research suggests just the opposite. For example, Shelley Taylor and her colleagues have demonstrated that optimistic beliefs and a sense of personal control serve as a buffer against both mental and physical disease. That is, people who harbor some degree of positive illusions about their own fate and abilities are less likely to actually become ill or distressed. And, if they do become sick or upset, their prognosis is better than is that of those who do not have these positive beliefs.

A second reason for psychology's overemphasis on human foibles and shortcomings lies in the fact that psychologists are people too. And because they are human, negative stimuli are often more salient, powerful, and memorable than positive stimuli. For example, social psychologists have shown that people often see negative behavior as more diagnostic of a person's character than positive behavior is. People tend to automatically pay more attention to negative cues in their surroundings than to positive cues. And, negative information is often more surprising and memorable than positive information is. In a review of the research bearing on this question, Roy Baumeister and his colleagues concluded that because the evidence so strongly suggests that bad is stronger than good, it should be considered a universal principle in psychology. It is not difficult to imagine how evolutionary pressures would have favored human ancestors who were somewhat more biased toward noticing and reacting to negative and potentially dangerous cues in their surroundings. Likewise, the pressure to document results in researchers' scientific laboratories likely led social psychologists to focus first on the most salient, powerful, and immediate stimuli. However, one explanation for the fact negative stimuli are so strong is because they are far less frequent than positive stimuli. They violate expectations because one's default experience is positive or neutral. The obvious implication is that, over time, positive processes may exert more of an influence on human psychological and physical functioning than negative processes do. Recent evidence suggests that displaying and writing about positive emotions early in life (e.g., young adulthood) has a long-term effect on mental and physical health such that those who seem to experience more positive emotions live longer and more satisfying lives.

The Positive Psychology Movement

The recent movement in positive psychology began in the last few years of the 1990s, during Martin Seligman's tenure as president of the American Psychological Association. The architects of this movement were prominent psychologists who saw a need to highlight the neglected areas of research on optimal human functioning. And the time was right. Many new and established researchers had begun to focus their scientific attention on topics such as positive emotions, morality, optimism, happiness, and well-being. In January 2000, when Martin Seligman and Mihaly Csikszentmihalyi edited a special issue of the journal *American Psychologist* entirely devoted to positive psychology, the positive psychology movement was solidified. In their introductory piece for this issue, they claimed that psychology was not producing enough insights into the conditions and processes that make life worth living. In one metaphor often used by positive psychology's advocates, psychology was said to have already learned how people get from negative eight to zero but learned much less about how people get from zero to positive eight. But was a movement in positive psychology really needed? The answer is straightforward. The science of psychology has made great progress in understanding what goes wrong in individuals, families, groups, and institutions, but these advances have come at the expense of understanding what is right with people.

In the short time since the phrase *positive psychology* came into being, quite a lot has happened. Dozens of conferences, summits, and workshops, both in the United States and abroad, have brought together researchers with diverse backgrounds and skills. Several books, edited volumes, and handbooks have been published. Numerous grants have facilitated the research of young investigators, and courses in positive psychology have appeared in the catalogues of many universities and high schools. Research on positive psychological topics has flourished, and many groundbreaking empirical and theoretical strides have been made. For example, in the field of emotion research, positive emotions had been largely ignored in favor of the study of negative emotions. In 1998, however, Barbara Fredrickson published her broaden-and-build theory of positive emotion in which she hypothesized that the function of positive emotions was to widen the array of thoughts of actions accessible to the individual such that they approach their environment more readily and openly, leading to increased resources. Since then, several empirical studies have provided empirical support for this theory and interest in positive emotions more generally has grown.

Challenges to Positive Psychology

The positive psychology movement has had challenges and criticisms. First, researchers who actually had been studying optimal functioning and flourishing all along may have wondered why a movement was even launched. Second, others have made the assumption that if there is a positive psychology, then the rest of psychology must be negative psychology. Moreover, if a positive psychology movement was needed, then it was because what had been learned in the field thus far was not useful. Actually, most of the work in psychology is neutral, but there is certainly

much more known about negative than positive topics. Moreover, because this previous work has been so extraordinarily successful, the lack of attention to positive topics has become glaring, despite the excellent progress made by the handful of researchers who have been doing positive psychology all along. Another criticism of people involved in positive psychology is that they fail to recognize the indisputable negative sides of life, seeing the world instead through rose-colored glasses. However, the goal of the positive psychology movement was never to erase or supplant work on pathology, suffering, and dysfunction. Rather, the aim is to increase what we know about human resilience, strength, and growth to complement and integrate into the existing knowledge base.

Where does the relatively new field of positive psychology go from here? Interestingly the aim of the positive psychology movement is to make itself obsolete. That is, the goal is to restore the empirical and theoretical effort in psychology to a more balanced profile. To achieve this goal, positive psychology must understand what contributes to individuals' strengths, the factors that lead to resilience, the function of rewarding relationships with others, and the role positive experiences play in human life. Positive psychology needs to understand how all these factors contribute to physical health, psychological well-being, effective groups, and successful institutions. Finally, positive psychology needs to develop effective interventions to increase and sustain these processes.

Shelly L. Gable

See also Bad Is Stronger Than Good; Broaden-and-Build Theory of Positive Emotions; Happiness; Helping Behavior; History of Social Psychology; Positive Affect

Further Readings

Aspinwall, L. G., & Staudinger, U. M. (Eds.). (2003). *A psychology of human strengths: Fundamental questions and future directions for a positive psychology.* Washington, DC: American Psychological Association.

Gable, S. L., & Haidt, J. (2005). What (and why) is positive psychology? *Review of General Psychology, 9,* 103–110.

Kahneman, D., Diener, E., & Schwarz, N. (Eds.). (1999). *Well-being: The foundations of hedonic psychology.* New York: Russell Sage.

Keyes, C. L. M., & Haidt, J. (Eds.). (2003). *Flourishing: Positive psychology and the life well lived.* Washington, DC: American Psychological Association.

Seligman, M. E. P., & Csikszentmihalyi, M. (2000). Positive psychology: An introduction. *American Psychologist, 55,* 5–14.

Snyder, C. R., & Lopez, S. J. (Eds.). (2002). *Handbook of positive psychology.* New York: Oxford University Press.

POWER

Power affects almost all facets of social life, from the food people eat to how long they live. Power concerns are evident in most kinds of relationships, including intimate bonds, parent–child relationships, sibling relations, and relations between group members. This brief entry examines what social psychology has learned with respect to three questions concerning power: What is power? Where does it come from? And how does power influence behavior?

What Is Power?

Power is typically defined according to two attributes: (1) the ability to control one's own outcomes and those of others and (2) the freedom to act. Power is related to but not synonymous with status, authority, and dominance. Status is the outcome of a social evaluation that produces differences in respect and prominence, which contribute to an individual's power within a group. It is possible to have power without status (e.g., the corrupt politician) and status without relative power (e.g., a religious leader in line at the Department of Motor Vehicles). Authority is power that derives from institutionalized roles or arrangements. Nonetheless, power can exist in the absence of formal roles (e.g., within informal groups). Dominance is behavior that has the acquisition or demonstration of power as its goal. Yet, power can be attained without performing acts of dominance, as when leaders attain power through a cooperative and fair-minded style.

Where Does Power Come From?

Starting as early as age 2, people arrange themselves into social hierarchies. Within a day or so, young adults within groups agree with one another about who is powerful and who is not. Where does an individual's power come from? In part, individual differences matter. Thus, extraverted people—that is, those who are gregarious, energetic, and likely to express

enthusiasm—often attain elevated power within natural social groups. People with superb social skills are more likely to rise in social hierarchies. And even appearance matters. People who are physically attractive, males who are taller and have large muscle mass, and even males with large, square jaws, often attain higher positions in social hierarchies.

Power also derives from facets of the interpersonal context. Authority-based roles within groups endow some individuals with power. This is true in formal hierarchies, such as the workplace, as well as in informal hierarchies, such as family structures in cultures that have historically given older siblings elevated power vis-à-vis younger siblings. Power can derive from knowledge-based expertise. Medical doctors wield power over their patients because of their specialized knowledge. Power can derive from coercion based on the ability to use force and aggression. Power can stem from the ability to provide rewards to others. This helps explain why members of elevated socioeconomic status and majority group status tend to experience greater levels of power than do people of lower socioeconomic status and minority group status. Finally, power derives from the ability to serve as a role model, which is known as *reference power.*

How Does Power Influence Behavior?

The English language is rich with aphorisms that concern the effects of power: "Power corrupts." "Money [a source of power] is the root of all evil." A recent theoretical formulation known as the approach-inhibition theory of power has offered two broad hypotheses concerning the effects of power.

Elevated power is defined by control, freedom, and the lack of social constraint. As a consequence, elevated power tends to make people less concerned with the evaluations of others, more automatic in social thought, and more disinhibited in action. In general, power predisposes individuals to approach-related behavior, moving toward satisfying goals. In contrast, reduced power is associated with increased threat, punishment, and social constraint. As a result, being in low-power positions tends to make people more vigilant and careful in social judgment and more inhibited in social behavior.

A first hypothesis that derives from this approach/inhibition theory of power is that high-power individuals should be less systematic and careful in how they judge the social world. One result is that high-power individuals should be more likely to thoughtlessly stereotype others, rather than carefully relying on individuating information. Several experimental studies support this hypothesis: Participants given power in experiments are indeed less likely to attend to individuating information and more likely to rely on stereotypes in judging others. Individuals who desire to see their own group dominate other groups, known as the *social dominance orientation,* are also more likely to stereotype.

Predisposed to stereotype, high-power individuals should tend to judge others' attitudes, interests, and needs in a less accurate fashion—a hypothesis that has received support from numerous studies. A survey study found that high-power professors were less accurate in their judgments of the attitudes of low-power professors than were low-power professors in judging the attitudes of their high-power colleagues. In a similar vein, power differences may account for the tendency of males to be slightly less accurate than females in judging expressive behavior. Power may even be at work in the striking finding that younger siblings, who experience reduced power vis-à-vis older siblings, outperform their older siblings on theory-of-mind tasks, which assess the ability to construe correctly the intentions and beliefs of others.

Power even seems to prompt less careful thought in individuals who experience a tremendous incentive to demonstrate sophisticated reasoning—Supreme Court justices. A study compared the decisions of U.S. Supreme Court justices when they wrote opinions endorsing the positions of coalitions of different sizes. In some cases, justices wrote on behalf of a minority, typically equated with low power; in other cases, justices wrote on behalf of the victorious majority. Justices writing from positions of power crafted less complex arguments in their opinions than did those writing from low-power positions.

The theory's second hypothesis is that power should make disinhibited (less constrained) social behavior more likely. Support for this hypothesis is found in numerous studies. Individuals given power experimentally are more likely to touch others and to approach them closely physically, to feel attraction to a random stranger, to turn off an annoying fan in the room where the experiment is being conducted, and to flirt in overly direct ways. In contrast, low-power individuals show inhibition of a wide variety of behaviors.

Individuals with little power often constrict their posture, inhibit their speech and facial expressions, and clam up and withdraw in group interactions.

Perhaps more unsettling is the wealth of evidence showing that elevated power makes antisocial communication more likely. For example, high-power individuals are more likely to violate politeness-related communication norms: They are more likely to talk more, to interrupt more, and to speak out of turn more. They are also more likely to behave rudely at work. They are more likely to tease friends and colleagues in hostile, humiliating fashion. Low-power individuals, in contrast, generally speak politely, making requests indirectly or by asking vague questions, whereas high-power individuals speak forcefully and directly, asking pointed questions and making commands. Power even influences patterns of gaze. A clear indicator of power is the following pattern of gaze: High-power individuals look at listeners when speaking and are looked at when speaking, whereas low-power individuals look away when speaking but look at others when listening.

Power disinhibits more harmful forms of aggression as well, leading to violent behavior against low-power individuals. For example, power asymmetries predict the increased likelihood of sexual harassment. Across cultures and historical periods, the prevalence of rape rises with the cultural acceptance of male dominance and the subordination of females. Furthermore, the incidence of hate crimes against disliked minority groups (that is, non-Whites) was highest when the proportion of demographic majority members (that is, Whites) in a particular neighborhood was largest relative to the proportion of minority members.

Research suggests that we should be careful about who gains power, for power seems to allow individuals to express their true inclinations, both good and bad. If the person is inclined toward malevolent or competitive behavior, power will only make him or her more so. If, on the other hand, the person is more benevolent or good natured, power will amplify the expression of those tendencies. In a study that nicely illustrates this claim, Serena Chen and colleagues identified and selected participants who were either more self-interested and exchange-oriented, or more compassionate and communal-oriented. Each participant was then randomly assigned to a high-power or low-power position in a clever, subtle manner: High-power individuals were seated in a snazzy leather professorial chair during the experiment; low-power individuals were seated in a plain chair typical of psychology experiments. Participants were then asked to volunteer to complete a packet of questionnaires with the help of another participant, who was late. Consistent with the idea that power amplifies the expression of preexisting tendencies, the communal-oriented participants with high power took on the lion's share of filling out the questionnaires. In contrast, the exchange-oriented participants with high power acted in more self-serving fashion, leaving more of the task for the other participant. The effects of power, then, depend quite dramatically on who is in power.

Dacher Keltner
Carrie Langner

See also Approach–Avoidance Conflict; Authoritarian Personality; Extraversion; Group Dynamics; Leadership; Nonverbal Cues and Communication; Power Motive; Roles and Role Theory; Self-Regulation; Social Dominance Orientation; Social Relations Model

Further Readings

Keltner, D., Gruenfeld, D. H., & Anderson, C. (2003). Power, approach, and inhibition. *Psychological Review, 110,* 265–284.

POWER MOTIVE

The key defining element of the power motive is one person having an impact on the behavior or emotions of another, or being concerned about prestige and reputation. This basic imagery is often elaborated with anticipations, actions designed to have impact, prestige, pleasure at reaching the goal, and so forth. The measure is implicit, tapping a motivation system based on emotional experience rather than conscious verbal processing, which is affected by language, defenses, and rationalizations. Thus, the content analysis measure of the power motive is usually uncorrelated with direct questionnaire measures—that is, what people believe or consciously report about their need for power.

A power motive should be distinguished from other power-related psychological concepts. For example, power motive is not related to power styles or traits (such as dominance or surgency), beliefs about power (such as authoritarianism or Machiavellianism), the sense of having power (internal control of reinforcements), occupying power positions, or having the skills to get or use power.

History

Power is a concept fundamental to human social life. Hence, the idea that people have a power drive or power motive has a long history in philosophy and psychology. The ancient Greek philosopher Empedocles wrote of "strife" as a master motive opposed to "love." The 19th-century German philosopher Friedrich Nietzsche introduced the term *will to power,* which psychologist Alfred Adler later adapted as the *striving for superiority.* In his later work, Sigmund Freud postulated an aggressive or destructive instinct, whereas Henry Murray included a need for dominance in his catalog of human motives.

Measurement

In modern psychology, the power motive (also labeled "*n* Power") is measured through content analysis of imaginative verbal material—typically, stories that people tell or write in response to vague or ambiguous pictures on the Thematic Apperception Test. The power motive scoring system was developed experimentally, by comparing the stories of people whose power concerns had been aroused with the stories of a control group that had no arousal experience. It was later adapted to score any kind of imaginative verbal or written material, such as fiction, political speeches, and interviews.

Characteristics

People express their need for power in a variety of different ways, often depending on other moderating variables such as social class, responsibility, or extraversion. They are drawn to careers involving direct and legitimate interpersonal power, where they can direct other people's behavior through positive and negative sanctions, within a legitimate institutional structure: for example, business executive, teacher, psychologist or mental health worker, journalist, and the clergy. They also are active members and officers in organizations.

Power-motivated people try to become visible and well-known. They take extreme risks and use prestige (or self-display). They are good at building alliances, especially with lower-status people who aren't well-known, who have nothing to lose and so become a loyal base of support. In small groups, people high in power motivation tend to define the situation, encourage others to participate, and influence others; however, they are not especially well-liked, and they do not work particularly hard or offer the best ideas. As leaders, they are able to create high morale among subordinates. Political and organizational leaders high in *n* Power are often viewed by their associates as charismatic and judged by historians as great. In times of social stress, therefore, voters turn to them.

Research

Several studies suggest a negative side to the power motive, supporting Lord Acton's famous comment, "Power tends to corrupt and absolute power corrupts absolutely." In experimental studies, small-group leader-managers high in power motivation are vulnerable to flattery and ingratiation. Although more cohesive and higher in morale, their groups are less effective in gathering and using information, and pay less attention to moral concerns. In negotiation or bargaining, power-motivated people tend to break agreements to demand better terms. If they lack a sense of responsibility, they engage in a variety of "profligate impulsive" behaviors: verbal and physical aggression, excessive drinking and multiple drug use, gambling, and exploitative sex. Finally, they are vulnerable to boredom, sometimes finding it difficult to take pleasure in their lives.

Most of these actions associated with power motivation are true for women as well as for men. However, power-motivated men may be more likely to be abusive and oppressive to their partners.

Recent research suggests that the need for power is related to certain physiological processes, mechanisms, and hormones. Power-motivated people show greater sympathetic nervous system arousal in response to stress and threat. This leads, in turn, to lower immune system efficiency and more infectious diseases. Power motivation is also related to higher blood pressure and cardiovascular problems.

High levels of power motivation are associated with aggression, both among individuals and among political leaders, governing elites, and societies, especially in times of crisis. International crises in which both sides express high levels of power motivation are likely to escalate to war, whereas crises with lower levels are more likely to be resolved peacefully.

Not much research has been done on the developmental origins of the power motive. Many theorists (for example, Adler and political scientists Harold Lasswell and Alexander George) believe that power strivings originate from an early sense of weakness or lacking power. Some longitudinal research suggests, however, that *n* Power is fostered by early parental permissiveness rather than restriction, especially permissiveness about the expression of sex and aggression.

Are there good and bad kinds of the need for power? Can power motivation be tamed or tempered by some other psychological variables into prosocial rather than antisocial behavior? Different research studies have suggested that affiliation motivation, maturity, sense of responsibility, self-control, and inhibition can—sometimes but not always—play such a role.

David G. Winter

See also Aggression; Power; Thematic Apperception Test

Further Readings

De Hoogh, A. H. B., Den Hartog, D. N., Koopman, P. L., Thierry, H., Van den Berg, P. T., Van der Weide, J. G., et al. (2005). Leader motives, charismatic leadership, and subordinates' work attitude in the profit and voluntary sector. *Leadership Quarterly, 16,* 17–38.

McClelland, D. C. (1975). *Power: The inner experience.* New York: Irvington.

Winter, D. G. (1973). *The power motive.* New York: Free Press.

Winter, D. G. (1993). Power, affiliation and war: Three tests of a motivational model. *Journal of Personality and Social Psychology, 65,* 532–545.

Zurbriggen, E. L. (2000). Social motives and cognitive power-sex associations: Predictors of aggressive sexual behavior. *Journal of Personality and Social Psychology, 78,* 559–581.

PREFERENCE REVERSALS

Definition

Preference reversals refer to the observation that there are systematic changes in people's preference order between options. Preference order refers to an abstract relation between two options. It is assumed that when an individual is presented with options A and B, he or she either prefers A to B or prefers B to A (or is indifferent between A and B). Systematic changes refer to the observation that people exhibit different or even *reverse* preferences for the same options in normatively equivalent evaluation conditions (i.e., conditions that differ at first sight but in which the options that people are presented with have essentially remained the same).

History and Background

The preference reversal phenomenon was first observed in the late 1960s and the early 1970s by Sarah Lichtenstein and Paul Slovic in a gambling context. They observed that if people are asked to choose between a relatively safe bet with a low payoff and a relatively risky bet with a high payoff, and if they are asked to indicate their selling prices if they were to sell these very lotteries, people's choice ordering is systematically different from their price ordering. More specifically, people tend to state a preference for the safer bet but tend to state a higher selling price for the riskier one. Very soon, this finding was replicated several times.

Although the theoretical concept of preferences as an abstract relation between two options seems very clear and natural, this abstract relation is a psychological construct that must be operationalized or measured by some observable behavior. Researchers have introduced multiple elicitation methods or methods that enabled them to observe decision makers' preferences. Besides asking individuals to choose among different options or to indicate how much they are willing to accept to forego or sell an option (i.e., willingness to accept), people have been asked to indicate how much they are willing to pay to obtain an option (i.e., willingness to pay), to state a price that is considered to be equivalent to an option (i.e., a certainty equivalent), or to give the probability of winning an option that is considered equivalent to another option (i.e., a probability equivalent). Researchers then use this information to rank order people's preferences. Consistently, the rank order of preferences produced by one measurement method did not correspond with the rank order produced by a second measurement method. In other words, systematic preference reversals were found repeatedly.

In addition, the preference reversal phenomenon has not stopped at lotteries. Rather than being a peculiar characteristic of a choice between bets, it has been found to be an example of a general pattern. Research has also shown preference reversals when options offering a certain but delayed outcome are used. When faced with a choice between delayed payments, decision makers often select the short-term option but assign a higher certainty equivalent to the long-term option. Different descriptions of the same problem also cause individuals to exhibit different preferences.

Nowadays, preference reversals are firmly established as robust phenomena. Contrary to what researchers assumed originally, preferences do depend on the method of elicitation (i.e., there is no procedure invariance) and they do depend on how the options are described (i.e., there is no description invariance). Rather than trying to eliminate the preference reversal phenomenon as they tend to have done in the past, researchers are now trying to explain it.

Context and Importance

The study of preference reversals has led to a conception of preferences that differs from the classical assumption that decision makers have a stable preference order for all options under consideration and consistently select the option highest in that order. An ever-growing body of evidence suggests that the so-called assumption of context-free preferences is not tenable. Instead, preferences appear to be context-specific. The preference reversal phenomenon has contributed to knowledge that decision making is a constructive process. Preferences are often constructed in the elicitation process, rather than only being revealed. This new conception of preferences particularly applies to judgments and choices among options that are important, complex, and perhaps unfamiliar or novel, such as careers and cars for instance. It has been shown empirically that people display more preference reversals for options that they are unfamiliar with. Especially in these circumstances, preferences are not simply read off some master list but are constructed on the spot by an adaptive decision maker.

Different construction can easily lead to different choices. One important construction strategy that has received a lot of empirical attention is so-called anchoring and adjustment, meaning that when decision makers state a price for a given option, they "anchor" on the highest possible outcome. Subsequently, decision makers adjust downward from this anchor toward the true value. If these adjustments are insufficient, then preference reversals can occur. Another important construction strategy is to focus on the most important attribute in the decision process and to select the alternative that is superior on it. This prominent attribute weighs more heavily in choice than in other elicitation procedures.

Implications

One area of research in which the preference reversal phenomenon might be of particular importance is the study of consumer behavior, and, more specifically, consumer choice making. Consumers, like other decision makers, will have to construct product preferences right on the spot. This means that product preferences might reverse depending on numerous contextual factors such as product descriptions and time pressure.

Sabrina Bruyneel

See also Behavioral Economics; Consumer Behavior; Decision Making; Prospect Theory

Further Readings

Bettman, J. R., Luce, M. F., & Payne, J. W. (1998). Constructive consumer choice processes. *Journal of Consumer Research, 25,* 187–217.

Lichtenstein, S., & Slovic, P. (1973). Response-induced reversals of preference in gambling—Extended replication in Las Vegas. *Journal of Experimental Psychology, 101,* 16–20.

PREJUDICE

Definition

Prejudice is defined as an attitude toward people based on their membership in a group (e.g., their racial group, gender, nationality, even the college they attend). Critical to prejudice is an inflexibility in the reaction to the target person whereby the responses to the target are not based on the target's behaviors or characteristics (good or bad) but instead are based on the target's membership in a group. Prejudice is most often negative, although it is also possible to be positively prejudiced. Prejudice involves three key components: an emotional response to members of the group; beliefs about the abilities, behaviors, and characteristics of group members; and behaviors directed at group members. For example, imagine that a person was negatively prejudiced against people from country X. That person may feel angry, anxious, or disgusted when he or she interacts with people from X. In addition, the person may believe that people from country X are stupid, lazy, or untrustworthy. The person may also try to keep people from country X from visiting his or her own country. A person who is prejudiced toward a group may not engage in all three types of responses. For example, it is possible to have prejudiced thoughts and feelings but never engage in prejudiced behavior.

Research Into Prejudice

Understanding prejudice and unraveling its causes, consequences, and potential cures has been of great interest to social psychologists for more than 50 years. There continues to be great debate among psychologists about the origin or cause of prejudice. Some believe that prejudice is the result of people's desire to feel better about the groups to which they belong (e.g., "We are better than they are!") and, thereby, better about themselves. Others believe prejudice comes from competition between groups for scarce resources (e.g., food, jobs). Still others argue that prejudice is an innate human response that developed to protect humans from dangerous strangers. The list of potential causes goes on, but like most social psychological phenomena, there is likely to be more than one correct answer and many factors likely contribute to prejudice.

Prejudiced responses toward others can range from making unfair judgments and harboring unkind feelings to brutal attacks and, at its most extreme, genocide. Prejudice can be overt and unmistakable, but it can also be subtle and difficult to detect. Prejudice takes many forms, and the nature of prejudice can change over time. For example, many social psychologists argue that in response to social and legal pressure, most White Americans have learned to conceal overt expressions of prejudice toward Black people and instead express prejudice in indirect and subtle ways. Thus, social psychologists argue that prejudice has gone underground and, therefore, may be particularly pernicious and difficult to eradicate.

The ultimate goal of those who study prejudice is to find ways to promote intergroup harmony and encourage people to treat others based on individual characteristics and not group membership. Social psychologists have uncovered some potential routes to prejudice reduction. For example, forming friendships with people from another social group is strongly related to positive attitudes toward that group. Also, getting people to reframe their views of "us" and "them" into "we" can decrease prejudice. Although progress has been made, much remains to be understood about the elimination of prejudice.

E. Ashby Plant

See also Intergroup Emotions; Intergroup Relations; Racism; Sexism; Stereotypes and Stereotyping

Further Readings

Allport, G. W. (1954). *The nature of prejudice.* Reading, MA: Addison-Wesley.

PREJUDICE REDUCTION

Definition

Prejudice reduction refers to a decrease in (most often) negative attitudes or evaluations that individuals hold in relation to other people. These negative attitudes are based on the groups to which people belong, such as a White person disliking someone because he or she is a Black person. Although social psychologists have linked the idea of prejudice reduction most directly with changing negative attitudes, this term is also used to refer to decreasing stereotypic beliefs (such as the belief that all gay men are promiscuous), outward expressions of bias, or negative behaviors.

Background and History

Prejudice reduction was first studied only when prejudice was seen as a social problem in the United States. Until the 1920s, there was widespread belief among nonscientists and scientists alike in the racial superiority of Whites. Indeed, prejudice was considered perfectly defensible and rationale. Between the 1920s and 1940s, scientists increasingly viewed prejudice as problematic and certain aspects of World War II (e.g., anti-Semitism and genocide) underscored this.

Prejudice clearly was a social problem and strategies for curbing it needed to be understood.

In 1954, Gordon Allport published his book *The Nature of Prejudice,* which provided the first comprehensive analysis of prejudice and laid the foundation for decades of subsequent research. Allport's writing provides many roots of modern work, three of which are especially important. First, Allport discussed the natural human tendency to categorize to simplify the world, noting that this includes categorizing people into groups. Many mental tricks allow people to place others into categories and, once categorization occurs, many other processes naturally occur to make categories resistant to change. For example, a boy who tugs on a girl's pigtails may be viewed as an aggressive Black boy, whereas the same behavior by a White boy may be interpreted as playful. Therefore, reducing prejudice often involves getting people to alter the nature of the categories in their minds so they can perceive people differently.

A second root of modern work on prejudice reduction is Allport's discussion of the inner conflict that people can experience in relation to their prejudices and the motivation that this conflict provides for prejudice reduction. Here Allport referred to Gunnar Myrdal, who in 1944 discussed the "American dilemma." According to Myrdal, many Americans are prone to a moral conflict between the ideas of equality on which the nation was founded and the racist traditions of prejudice and discrimination. The idea that conflict between values and prejudiced tendencies can spur people to reduce their prejudice later became a cornerstone of various strategies for reducing prejudice.

A third root found in Allport's work is his intergroup-contact hypothesis. The idea that contact between people of different backgrounds and races can help people realize that some of their beliefs are incorrect or that they do like people who are different from themselves is straightforward. However, making contact between groups work to reduce prejudice is more complicated. Allport correctly noted this and described some of the conditions that must be met for contact to reduce prejudice successfully.

At different points in time, different prejudice reduction strategies have become more or less important in the field of social psychology. These changes often can be traced to the combination of historical or societal changes and with popular methods within the field. For example, starting in the 1980s, blatant prejudice became less accepted and prevalent in the

United States while subtle biases and prejudices remained quite common. Also, social psychologists interested in prejudice were adopting many techniques from cognitive psychology to study the mind's use of social stereotypes. The result was the discovery that prejudiced responses sometimes occur not because people consciously hold prejudiced beliefs and attitudes but, rather, because learned prejudices and stereotypes can be activated and used without people even being aware that this is happening. Patricia Devine formally advanced and tested this argument. A new view of prejudice reduction emerged from this line of thinking that involved learning to control and change biases resulting from nonconscious processes.

Norms

Society's norms or expectations of what is acceptable behavior greatly influence when people will try to reduce their prejudice and why they do so. Not all bias is looked upon in the same way. For instance, blatant racial prejudice is not considered politically correct nowadays; however, other prejudices are considered acceptable (such as not wanting a convicted sex offender to babysit a child). As such, the social norms of a particular time or geographic location in part dictate what people deem as important prejudices to curb. If a prejudice is recognized as problematic and labeled as inappropriate in society, people are likely to act accordingly and not express bias to avoid violating important social norms. For example, if an individual is surrounded by people who value equality among men and women, this person is likely to reduce his or her prejudice by also endorsing those values and acting in ways that are not biased.

Values

Early research by Milton Rokeach highlighted that people can be motivated to reduce their prejudice when they are made aware of the conflict between the values they hold and their actions. In his classic research, he suggested that people were potentially more concerned about their own personal freedom than equality for others. Awareness of this conflict between people's values and actions prompted them to change their behavior and participate in activities promoting equality. For example, someone may embrace cultural values like racial equality but still have a preference for hiring a White applicant over a Black applicant. When people become aware of this hypocrisy, it can make them feel dissatisfied with themselves and motivate them to act in line with their values and reduce their prejudice. Months after these types of experiences, people can continue to show positive changes consistent with equality.

Contact

The idea that intergroup contact may reduce prejudice was a driving force behind the introduction of laws that required desegregation of, for example, schools. However, contact between members of different groups can increase tension and reinforce prejudice if certain conditions are not met. Decades of research have revealed that for contact to reduce prejudice, people in contact should have equal status (e.g., one is not designated as the person in charge), they should be working together on common goals (e.g., a school project) rather than competing, institutional support should be present (such as when school officials encourage the contact), and the contact should be intimate rather than casual so that friendships can develop. Although all of these conditions are not always necessary, the more that are met the greater the potential is for prejudice reduction. An excellent example of a strategy that meets these conditions is Elliot Aronson's jigsaw classroom technique, where each student working in a group is provided with a segment of important information from a lesson to teach the others.

Researchers have also studied how contact can lead people to view others who are different from themselves in new ways, such as leading people to view themselves as members of one large, superordinate group rather than as members of smaller separate groups. For example, people of different races in the United States could focus on their common American identity.

Individual Efforts

Even if people do not hold prejudices of which they are consciously aware, they may be in the habit of responding in biased ways toward members of certain groups. These more automatic prejudices can be combated with individual efforts to change what feelings and thoughts immediately come to mind. One approach involves spending time thinking about people who are very different than a stereotype of a group (such as imagining a strong and independent woman). Another approach involves intensive training to think "no" whenever members of stereotypes groups are paired with stereotypes, such as when a picture of a Black person is presented along with the word *lazy*. Finally, research shows that people who are aware of their automatic prejudices and who feel bad about them can learn to associate certain stimuli with prejudiced responses they have had in the past and their negative feelings about having had such responses. When these stimuli are present in a subsequent situation, they can trigger people to slow down and respond more carefully so that they can reduce their prejudiced responses. As these examples of individual effort strategies illustrate, people must be highly motivated and vigilant in their attempts to control and change engrained prejudices.

Margo J. Monteith
Aimee Y. Mark

See also Ingroup–Outgroup Bias; Intergroup Relations; Jigsaw Classroom; Prejudice; Racism; Sexism; Stereotypes and Stereotyping

Further Readings

Devine, P. G., & Monteith, M. J. (1999). Automaticity and control in stereotyping. In S. Chaiken & Y. Trope (Eds.), *Dual process theories in social psychology* (pp. 339–360). New York: Guilford Press.

Dovidio, J. F., Glick, P., & Rudman, L. A. (Eds.). (2005). *On the nature of prejudice: Fifty years after Allport.* Oxford, UK: Blackwell.

Gaertner S. L., & Dovidio, J. F. (2000). *Reducing intergroup bias: The common ingroup identity model.* Philadelphia: Psychology Press.

PRIMACY EFFECT, ATTRIBUTION

Definition

The primacy effect concerns how one's impressions of others are formed. Thus, it relates to the field of psychology known as person perception, which studies how people form impressions of others. The word *primacy* itself is generally defined in the dictionary as the state of being first in order or importance. In a similar manner, according to the primacy principle, when generating impressions of others, what we think and feel about a person is strongly influenced by our very first impressions of that person. Therefore, when one is making judgments of others, first impressions are more important than later impressions. It seems that first impressions tend to color or bias later judgments of a person. They do this in a way that is consistent with those initial assessments. Thus what someone first sees, hears, or reads about a person tends to serve as a primary reference point or anchor for later judgments, so that later judgments are overly influenced by a person's initial judgment. In essence, first impressions count.

Background and History

Since the early 20th century, psychologists have been concerned with how the impressions we make of others are formed. Early on, psychologists tried to see if there were any stable patterns regarding how people formed these impressions. However, the primacy principal was not established by scientific study until the 1940s. Solomon Asch is credited with discovering the primacy principal. His early experiments were quite simple: People were read a list of words that one might use to describe a person. Sometimes these lists were long, sometimes they were short, and most importantly, where each word appeared the list appeared was varied. Sometimes a certain word appeared in the beginning, sometimes in the middle, and sometimes at the end. After they heard a particular list, participants in the study were then asked to give their impressions of what a person who fit the description that they had just heard might be like. What Asch's early studies found was that the order in which people heard the words mattered greatly. It seemed that people used these lists to form an overall unified impression of a person, and the words that people heard first set the tone for everything else a person heard. So, a list of words like intelligent, industrious, impulsive, and critical tended to result in positive ratings when compared with the same list in reverse order, that is, critical, impulsive, industrious, and intelligent. In effect, the early words dominated the impression that people formed.

Summary of Types, Amount, and Quality of Evidence

Asch's early work inspired a large number of studies that supported the primacy effect in person perception. In addition to overall impressions, it was also discovered that the primacy effect also affects specific judgments about others. These judgments include how generally intelligent and successful we perceive others to be and how well we expect them to perform in the future. Assuming that the number of successes and failures are equal, one might think that whether a person experiences success early or late shouldn't matter when we judge them, but it does. Perceptions of intelligence along with future expectations of success depend on the pattern of a person's successes and failures. When comparing people who have early success and then get worse to those who start poorly and then get better, or have a mixed pattern of success and failure, people rate those with the early success higher. Thus, it is better to start strong and finish weak, than to start weak and finish strong or have a random pattern of successes and failures. Everything else being equal, those who have early successes and then descend in performance are judged to be both smarter and more likely to perform better than others.

Physical attractiveness can be part of the primacy effect. When rating others, it has been shown that physically attractive people tend to receive generally high ratings regardless of how they perform on a series of tasks. Those who were physically unattractive, however, tended to be rated lower even when their performance was the same as that of the attractive people. Consistent with the primacy effect, this only occurred if people knew what the person looked like before they judged his or her performance. However, if a person's performance was judged without knowing how he or she looked, finding out how the person looked later didn't change the ratings. Being good looking is a generally positive attribute, but it only seems to affect judgments if people know about it before initial judgments are made. Like the word studies discussed earlier, if a judgment of attractiveness is the first thing in a chain of judgments, it tends to color subsequent judgments in a manner consistent with the general goodness that people associate with physical attractiveness.

Importance of Topic

Besides beginning a whole new field of inquiry in psychology, the primacy effect has broader implications.

The effect is important because the first thing that we do when we are making a judgment of another person is to categorize him or her, and because of the primacy effect, the category that we first put people into tends to influence our subsequent judgments about that person. When we encounter people, the process of categorization starts with the most noticeable categories of that person such as sex, race, social class, or age. We then use this category to make initial assumptions about the person, and because these initial assumptions affect our later judgments, they are the most important assumptions one makes.

Implications

Because of the primacy effect, the judgments others make about a person may not be accurate, and this inaccuracy is likely to persist over time. People may be judged by who they first appear to be, rather than by who they actually are. If first judgments are positive, this could give someone an undeserved advantage; if negative, it could put someone at an unfair disadvantage.

Gregg Gold

See also Attributions; Person Perception; Primacy Effect, Memory; Recency Effect

Further Readings

Asch, S. E. (1946). Forming impressions of personality. *Journal of Abnormal and Social Psychology, 1,* 1956–1972.

Jones, E. E. (1968). Pattern of performance and ability attribution: An unexpected primacy effect. *Journal of Personality and Social Psychology, 10,* 317–340.

PRIMACY EFFECT, MEMORY

Definition

The primacy effect denotes the phenomenon that after encountering a long list of items, one will more likely be able to recall the first few items from that list than items than from later parts of the list. In a typical study investigating the primacy effect, participants are sequentially presented with a list of words, each being presented for a fixed amount of time. After the words have been presented, participants are asked to write down all the words from the list that they recall. A primacy effect is found when participants correctly recall words from the first few positions in a list more often than they recall words from later list positions.

History and Importance

The primacy effect and its counterpart, the recency effect, which describes a recall advantage for the last few items of a list compared with items in the middle, combine to form the U-shaped serial position curve of list recall. This phenomenon was interpreted as evidence for two different memory systems—a long-term store that is the basis for the primacy effect, and a short-term store that is responsible for the recency effect. This distinction has influenced many theories of human memory.

Evidence

The primacy effect has been explained by a rehearsal advantage for words presented early in the list: They are rehearsed more often than subsequent words. This was found in an early study, in which participants were asked to overtly rehearse the words they were to memorize. Results showed that the first few words were rehearsed more often than were words presented later in the list. The more frequent rehearsal of an item leads to a stronger long-term memory for that item, and thus a better chance to recall that item, compared with less frequently rehearsed items.

Further evidence for the rehearsal-based explanation of the primacy effect comes from studies that modify participants' rehearsal. For example, one study presented words at a faster rate, thus reducing participants' opportunity to rehearse. Under those conditions, the magnitude of the primacy effect is reduced. Additional evidence showing that rehearsal is the basis for the primacy effect comes from studies that modified participants' rehearsal strategies. When participants were asked to rehearse only the item that is currently presented, no primacy effect was found.

The primacy effect is a general phenomenon that occurs beyond laboratory settings where participants are explicitly asked to memorize a list of items. A primacy effect has also been found in studies in which participants were unaware of a subsequent memory test. A primacy effect has also been shown in the domain of television commercials: Participants viewing a television program that was interrupted by blocks of commercials showed better memory for the first three commercials than for commercials broadcast later in the block.

Christoph Stahl

See also Memory; Primacy Effect, Attribution; Recency Effect

Further Readings

Glanzer, M., & Cunitz, A. R. (1966). Two storage mechanisms in free recall. *Journal of Verbal Learning & Verbal Behavior, 5,* 351–360.

PRIMING

Definition

Priming is the process by which perception (or experience) of an item (or person or event) leads to an increase in its accessibility and the accessibility of related material and behaviors. Priming is a phenomenon that is enormously influential in people's everyday lives, yet people are typically unaware of its operation and impact. For example, if you pass a telephone and it reminds you to call your mother, priming is at work. If middle-aged women make you feel nervous after watching *Desperate Housewives,* once again priming can be blamed. Priming is particularly important in social psychology because of the inherent complexity of social information processing—when many interpretations and behavioral options are available, the accessibility determined by priming can constrain perception, cognition, and action.

How Does Priming Work?

Psychologists' understanding of priming is based on the idea that information is stored in units (schemas) in long-term memory, whose activation levels can be increased or decreased. When the activation of a schema is increased, it becomes more accessible— that is, more likely to enter consciousness or direct behavior. Priming research has capitalized on the connectionist idea that when schemas are frequently activated together, connections form between them, thereby creating networks in the mind. Activation can spread through these networks such that following activation of one schema, the activation of associated schemas in the network is also increased. This is a very useful tool because it helps prepare the mind for what it is likely to encounter next, or may have to think about very soon. When a cat is perceived, for instance, the "cat" schema will be activated, and activation will spread to cat-related concepts such as "cat's meow" and "cat's scratch." This activation means that potentially important information is then more accessible, enabling people to behave toward the cat in an appropriate manner.

Empirically, this priming process would not be investigated by watching a perceiver's behavior toward the cat, but by testing the accessibility of the relevant schema using techniques such as word recognition or lexical decision tasks. For example, research has shown that reading the word *bread* will prime associated items such as butter, but not unrelated items such as bikini. Experiments of this kind confirm that priming does indeed increase the activation of associated schemas.

Types of Priming

Repetition Priming

At its simplest level, priming can apply to a single word: Reading a word once will increase the speed at which that same word will subsequently be recognized. This effect is known as repetition priming and occurs because once a schema has been activated, it takes less energy to reactivate the construct on a subsequent occasion. Furthermore, if a schema is frequently activated, it can become hyperaccessible, and the rate at which it decreases its activation is reduced. This pattern is optimal because it keeps schemas that are encountered frequently activated for longer, so that they are more easily accessible if required again.

Associative Priming

Priming is known as associative when it increases the activation of associated knowledge, such as "bacon" priming "eggs." This effect can be subcategorized according to the type of association through which the activation has spread, such as through shared perceptual components, phonological features, or semantic relations. An example of perceptual priming would be a facilitated response to the word *lost* following presentation of the word *most*. These two words are orthographically similar, although they do not sound the same or have similar meanings. Phonological

priming might occur between the words *foul* and *trowel* because they rhyme even though they do not share perceptual or semantic qualities. Priming between words that belong to the same semantic category is semantic priming, such as between *baby* and *diaper* or *leaf* and *flower*.

Semantic priming is the type most often studied in social psychology because it allows researchers to investigate semantic links between schemas. For example, stereotyping research has shown that people respond more quickly to words such as *warm* and *caring* after being shown stereotypic pictures of women than men. This suggests that people have developed associations between women and these traits, associations that are stored in semantic memory.

An important subtype of semantic priming is affective priming—the increase in activation of words of the same valence (i.e., positive or negative) as the prime. This phenomenon is elicited primarily when priming stimuli are presented for very short periods, so for example, if a smiling man is presented for a short duration, positive traits will be primed more than with masculine traits. The existence of affective priming suggests that valence is elicited from stimuli before priming spreads through more complex semantic associations, indicating the fundamental importance of this quality.

Negative Priming

The effects described earlier all concern facilitation effects: increased activation of concepts related to a prime. However, in some cases priming can actually *decrease* the activation of particular schema, spreading inhibition rather than activation. This effect may arise from the way the brain deals with schema that are competing for attention. For example, making coffee might prime the milk and sugar schemas, but it is not physically practical for both to appear simultaneously in behavior. The solution is for whichever concept is primary (most highly activated) to decrease or laterally inhibit the activation of the competing schema. Stereotyping research has provided examples of this effect, demonstrating negative priming when a target person belongs to two stereotypic categories containing competing information. For example, a person might belong to the category "mother," priming traits such as caring and unselfish, but also be a member of the "lawyer" category, perhaps priming opposite traits. To interact effectively with this person, the perceiver has to make a judgment about which traits to expect. If the "mother" stereotype is more highly activated (by contextual cues), then the lawyer stereotype will be inhibited. As with facilitation effects, therefore, negative priming can achieve useful and preparative ends.

Consequences of Priming

As the stereotyping examples suggest, priming is not just a cognitive phenomenon; its importance stems from the consequences that it has for people's thoughts, behaviors, and interactions with others.

Priming can influence the way in which people perceive others and interpret their behavior, even without awareness of the prime. For example, after subliminal priming with aggressive words like *hostile,* participants are more likely to rate ambiguous behaviors (such as a playful shove) as being aggressive. In this case, participants' social perception has been altered by the increased accessibility of aggressive traits, without them being aware of the priming experience. Priming social categories has a similar effect as priming individual traits because it increases the activation of all the traits contained within the category network. For example, presenting either the stereotype label "vegetarian" or "murderer" before asking participants to form an impression of a target person is likely to produce different impressions—the former presumably less brutal than the latter.

The phenomenon of increased accessibility altering perception is well-established. However, more contentious research suggests that even complex social behaviors can be primed and produced in behavior without perceivers' awareness, a phenomenon referred to as the *perception-behavior* link. For example, participants who sit near a gun while giving electric shocks in an experiment show more aggression than those who are not near a weapon—the so-called weapons effect. Participants who have been primed with behavioral characteristics like "polite" or "rude" are more likely to behave in line with these traits in subsequent tasks. Again, this priming can be category based, so for example, priming with the "accountant" stereotype can increase conformity because this trait is contained within the occupational stereotype. Importantly, behavioral consequences of priming are elicited in situations that offer a relevant context for the behavior to be produced. If participants have been primed with aggression, they are unlikely to randomly produce aggressive acts. Rather, if they are put in a situation in which they perceive a potentially aggressive incident or are forced to choose to behave with high or low aggression, then the priming is likely to be influential. This may be why people are so often unaware of the influence of priming: It does not change the availability of thoughts or actions but, rather, alters the accessibility of the available options.

Sheila Cunningham
C. Neil Macrae

See also Accessibility; Automatic Processes; Schemas; Social Cognition; Stereotypes and Stereotyping

Further Readings

Bargh, J. A., Chen, M., & Burrows, L. (1996). Automaticity of social behaviour: Direct effects of trait construct and stereotype activation on action. *Journal of Personality and Social Psychology, 71,* 230–244.

Bodenhausen, G. V., & Macrae, C. N. (1998). Stereotype activation and inhibition. In R. S. Wyer (Ed.), *Advances in social cognition XI: Stereotype activation and inhibition* (pp. 1–51). Mahwah, NJ: Erlbaum.

Meyer, D. E., & Schvanevedt, R. (1971). Facilitation in recognising pairs of words: Evidence of a dependence between retrieval operations. *Journal of Experimental Psychology, 90,* 227–234.

Srull, T. K., & Wyer, R. S. (1979). The role of category accessibility in the interpretation of information about persons: Some determinants and implications. *Journal of Personality and Social Psychology, 37,* 1660–1672.

Zajonc, R. B. (1980). Feeling and thinking: Preferences need no inferences. *American Psychologist, 35,* 151–175.

PRISONER'S DILEMMA

Definition

Beyond any doubt, Prisoner's Dilemma is the best-known situation in which self-interest and collective interest are at odds. The situation derives its name from the classic anecdote about two prisoners who were accused of robbing a bank. In this anecdote, the district attorney, unable to prove that the prisoners were guilty, created a dilemma in an attempt to motivate the prisoners to confess to the crime. The prisoners were put in separate rooms, where each prisoner was to make a choice: to confess or not to confess.

The attorney sought to make confessing tempting to the prisoners by creating a situation in which the sentence was determined not only by their own confessing or not but also by the fellow prisoner's confessing or not. Yet irrespective of the fellow prisoner's choice, the choice to confess yielded a better outcome (or less worse outcome) than did the choice not to confess. Specifically, when the other confessed, confessing yielded *only* an 8-year sentence, whereas not confessing yielded a 10-year sentence. And when the other did not confess, confessing yielded only a 3-month sentence, whereas not confessing yielded a 1-year sentence. So, from this perspective, it seems rational for each prisoner to confess to the crime. However, the crux of the dilemma is that the outcome following from both confessing (an 8-year sentence) is worse than the outcome following from both not confessing (a 1-year sentence). Thus, if both prisoners were completely trusting of each other, and strongly committed to supporting or helping each other, neither would confess, despite the attorney's attempt to make confessing attractive. (The four possible sentences following from both prisoners' choices are derived from R. Duncan Luce and Howard Raiffa; some other sources report slightly different sentences.)

The Single-Trial Prisoner's Dilemma

This classic Prisoner's Dilemma describes a situation in which the prisoners were to make their choices simultaneously, irrevocably (i.e., they could not undo or take back their choices), and therefore independently of one another. The independence of their choices was also ensured by putting the prisoners in separate cells, thereby excluding any possibility for communication relevant to the choices that they were going to make. In doing so, the attorney created a rather uncommon situation because people are usually able to interact in ways that permit them to respond to each other's behavior or communicate about their choices.

Nevertheless, some situations that people encounter in real life resemble aspects of the classic Prisoner's Dilemma. For example, it occasionally may be tempting to prepare less than fully for a working meeting with a partner to save time and energy for another activity that is more pressing or interesting. Yet, the meeting would be more fruitful if both partners invest time and effort and prepare well for the meeting. More generally, the Prisoner's Dilemma represents exchange situations, which in the real world often occur under more flexible conditions, where both partners make choices in turn and every now and then can undo their choices. An example is the exchange of baseball cards, or cards of well-known soccer players, where two children can, at a little cost, provide each other with the card the other desires very much (e.g., to own the last card that completes one's set of cards). In that sense, the Prisoner's Dilemma represents a situation in which people "do business," exchanging money, products, or services, that is more desirable to the other than to the self.

Researchers often use the single-trial Prisoner's Dilemma when they want to study how people approach one another in the absence of a history of interaction and in the absence of a future of interaction. Hence, these choices are not influenced by considerations regarding the past (e.g., retaliation) or the future (e.g., adopting a strategy so as to obtain mutual cooperation). In these situations, impressions of the other play a very important role. In particular, any information that is relevant to one's expectations regarding the other's probable choice is useful, at least when one's own choice depends on what the other is going to choose. For example, people expect much more cooperation from another perceived as honest than from another perceived as dishonest. Also, people may also derive expectations from stereotypical information. People expect more cooperation from a theology student than from student in economics or public administration.

More recently, it has been shown that choices can also be influenced in very subtle ways. In this research, participants typically first engage in a different task in which they unscramble sentences (putting scrambled sentences together in the correct order) that contain words having to do either with morality (e.g., *honest, dishonest*) or might (e.g., *strong, weak*). This task, or related task, seeks to activate morality-related concepts or might-related concepts—rather unconsciously. As it turns out, people are more likely to make a cooperative choice when morality was activated in such a task than when might was activated.

The Iterated Prisoner's Dilemma

The Prisoner's Dilemma has often been used to study repeated choices by which people respond to one another's choices, a situation that captures interaction. Actually, most of the examples discussed so far illustrate the Prisoner's Dilemma but do not perfectly match the features of a single-trial Prisoner's Dilemma because there usually is a history or future of interaction that accompanies working meetings or exchanges of products (e.g., baseball cards). As such, single-trial interactions are more common in dealings with relative strangers rather than with partners, friends, or acquaintances. In contrast, the iterated Prisoner's Dilemmas, characterized by repeated interaction, is more relevant to processes that shape people's interactions with partners, friends, or acquaintances.

This research has focused on a variety of processes. One such process is the role of verbal communication. Often, cooperation can be enhanced if people are able to communicate before their choices in a Prisoner's Dilemma. The more important question is, of course, how one can persuade the other to cooperate. Some research has compared the effectiveness of four messages: (1) "I will cooperate." (2) "I would like you to cooperate." (3) "If you don't cooperate, then I will choose so that you can't win." (4) "If you now decide to cooperate and make a cooperative choice, I will cooperate." This research has shown that a message that communicates conditional cooperation involving threats and promises tend to be somewhat more effective than those that do not incorporate such messages. These principles were subsequently used in designing strategies for building trust and resolving conflict, as well as further theorizing on these topics.

The iterated Prisoner's Dilemma has also been used to examine the effectiveness of behavioral strategies. How should one behave if one seeks to obtain stable patterns of mutual cooperation? Or how can a person motivate, through his or her own behavior, the other person to make cooperative choices? Consider, for example, the tit-for-tat strategy that begins with a cooperative choice and subsequently imitates the partner's previous choice. This strategy has been shown to yield greater outcomes than a 100% cooperative or 100% noncooperative strategy. Following early experiments examining this strategy, Robert Axelrod in 1984 organized a computer tournament in which several social and behavioral experts submitted programmed strategies that they believed would, when pitted against other possible programs, produce the highest outcomes. Each strategy then played against (or with) each other strategy. The interesting result was that tit for tat yielded far better outcomes for itself than did any of the other strategies.

An important feature accounting for tit for tat's effectiveness is its niceness, in that the self is never first to make a noncooperative choice, and therefore cannot be perceived as exploitative or aggressive. Tit for tat is also effective because it is retaliatory: Noncooperative behavior is responded to with a reciprocal noncooperative action. Furthermore, tit for tat is forgiving, in that noncooperative choices by the other in one situation are easily remedied in subsequent situations. Finally, tit for tat is also a clear strategy, readily understood by others, and indeed it tends to be experienced as directed toward establishing cooperation.

At the same time, tit for tat fails to initiate cooperation after there has been a lapse in it. Hence, a limitation of tit for tat is that it may give rise to the so-called echo effect (or negative reciprocity), that is, interaction patterns whereby the two persons are "trapped" in cycles of noncooperative responses. This limitation is especially important in situations characterized by *noise*—when there are discrepancies between intended and actual outcomes for an interaction partner because of unintended errors (e.g., not being able to respond to an e-mail because of a local network breakdown). In such situations, an unintended error may lead to misunderstanding ("why hasn't he responded to my e-mail") and eventually a noncooperative response ("I will make him wait as well"), which may instigate the echo effect. Indeed, some recent research indicates that some level of generosity might be important in overcoming the detrimental effects of such unintended errors. That is, when unintended errors are likely to occur with some regularity, strict forms of reciprocity will give rise to the echo effect, which can be prevented or overcome by adding a little generosity to reciprocity: that is, by consistently behaving a little more cooperatively than the other did in the previous interaction.

Moreover, the Prisoner's Dilemma also often operates in situations involving more than two individuals (the so-called N-person Prisoner's Dilemma; also referred to as social dilemma). For example, everyone enjoys clean public places, such as clean parks or sports stadiums. Yet people often find litter in such places, indicating that it is somewhat tempting to litter. As another example, whether or not to exercise restraint in the use of energy represents such a dilemma because overuse eventually leads to depletion of natural resources. In N-person Prisoner's Dilemmas, threats or promises, or tit for tat, are generally less effective because there are so many people involved so that they are harder or even impossible to implement (to whom should I give tit for tat?). Typically, the level of cooperation is much lower in N-person Prisoner's Dilemmas than in two-person Prisoner's Dilemmas. Also different mechanisms tend to underlie behavior in N-person situations. For example, feelings of perceived efficacy, the feeling that one can make a difference and affect collective outcomes in a positive manner, feelings of personal responsibility (feeling responsible for a positive collective outcome), and feelings of identifiability (whether to feel anonymous or identifiable such that others can tell who cooperated and who did not) are all important ingredients of cooperation. These and other findings may be effectively used in public campaigns, which emphasize that people can make a difference ("all pieces help" to enhance perceived efficacy), or that people need to do so out of moral obligation or concern with the group (to enhance feelings of responsibility).

And finally, there are Prisoner's Dilemmas between groups, or between representatives of two groups. Two companies may compete for the same clients, even though they both enjoy the public attention for their new products. Nations also often face such conflicts between their own group's interest and both groups' interests. Frequently, interactions between groups (or their representatives) are often less cooperative than are interactions between individuals. One reason is that groups do not tend to trust each other as much as individuals do, in that groups often rely on a scheme of distrust—which is not too surprising because groups often do compete in everyday life. A second reason is that group members tend to support their representative, and one another, for actions that serve the interest of their group (and themselves), but not that of the two groups together. The Prisoner's Dilemmas of this sort have received relatively little attention, but may well be one of the most challenging to manage.

Paul A. M. Van Lange
Anthon Klapwijk

See also Cooperation; Social Dilemmas; Trust

Further Readings

Dawes, R. M. (1980). Social dilemmas. *Annual Review of Psychology, 31,* 169–193.

Hamburger, H. (1979). *Games as models of social phenomena.* San Francisco: Freeman.

Kelley, H. H., Holmes, J. W., Kerr, N. L., Reis, H. T., Rusbult, C. E., & Van Lange, P. A. M. (2003). *An atlas of interpersonal situations.* New York: Cambridge University Press.

Pruitt, D. G., & Kimmel, M. J. (1977). Twenty years of experimental gaming: Critique, synthesis, and suggestions for the future. *Annual Review of Psychology, 28,* 363–392.

Van Lange, P. A. M., Ouwerkerk, J., & Tazelaar, M. (2002). How to overcome the detrimental effects of noise in social interaction: The benefits of generosity. *Journal of Personality and Social Psychology, 82,* 768–780.

PROCEDURAL JUSTICE

Procedural justice is the study of people's subjective evaluations of the justice of decision making of conflict resolution procedures—whether they are fair or unfair, ethical or unethical, and otherwise accord with people's standards of fair processes for interaction and decision making. Procedural justice is usually distinguished from subjective assessments of the fairness of outcomes (distributive justice) and the degree to which people feel that they are gaining or losing resources in the group (outcome favorability). Subjective procedural justice judgments have been the focus of a great deal of research attention by psychologists because people are widely found to be more willing to defer to others when they act through just procedures.

John W. Thibaut and Laurens Walker presented the first system set of experiments designed to show the impact of procedural justice. Their studies demonstrate that people's assessments of the fairness of third-party decision-making procedures shape their satisfaction with their outcomes. This finding has been widely confirmed in subsequent laboratory and field studies of procedural justice.

What do people mean by a fair procedure? Four elements of procedures are the primary factors that contribute to judgments about their fairness: opportunities for participation, having a neutral forum, trustworthy authorities, and treatment with dignity and respect.

People feel more fairly treated if they are allowed to participate in the resolution of their problems or conflicts. The positive effects of participation have been widely found. People are primarily interested in presenting their perspective and sharing in the discussion over the case, not in controlling decisions about how to handle it.

People are also influenced by judgments about neutrality—the honest, impartiality, and objectivity of the authorities with whom they deal. They believe that authorities should not allow their personal values and biases to enter into their decisions, which should be made based on consistent rule application and the use of objective facts. Basically, people seek a level playing field in which no one is unfairly disadvantaged.

Another factor shaping people's views about the fairness of a procedure is their assessment of the motives of the third-party authority responsible for resolving the case. People recognize that third parties typically have considerable discretion to implement formal procedures in varying ways, and they are concerned about the motivation underlying the decisions made by the authority with which they are dealing. They judge whether that person is benevolent and caring, is concerned about their situation and their concerns and needs, considers their arguments, tries to do what is right for them, and tries to be fair. In other words, people assess the degree to which they trust the authority.

Studies suggest that people also value having respect shown for their rights and for their status within society. They want their dignity as people and as members of the society to be recognized and acknowledged. Because it is essentially unrelated to the outcomes they receive, the importance that people place on this affirmation of their status is especially relevant to conflict resolution.

Tom R. Tyler

See also Conflict Resolution; Distributive Justice

Further Readings

Lind, E. A. & Tyler, T. R. (1988). *The social psychology of procedural justice.* New York: Plenum.

Thibaut, J., & Walker, L. (1975). *Procedural justice.* Hillsdale, NJ: Erlbaum.

Tyler, T. R. (2000). Social justice: Outcome and procedure. *International journal of psychology, 35,* 117–125.

Tyler, T. R., & Smith, H. J. (1998). Social justice and social movements. In D. Gilbert, S. Fiske, & G. Lindzey (Eds.), *The handbook of social psychology* (4th ed., Vol. 2, pp. 595–629). New York: Oxford University Press.

PROCRASTINATION

Definition

Procrastination refers to wasting time before a deadline. The tendency to procrastinate involves putting off work that must be completed to attain a certain goal, such as watching television instead of working on a term paper. Procrastination has a negative impact on the quality of one's work and is linked to a variety of negative physical and psychological outcomes.

History and Background

Procrastination lies at the heart of the psychological study of goal attainment. To attain a goal, people must have adequate motivation and ability to perform the necessary actions involved in satisfying the goal. Procrastination is particularly relevant in cultures that are industrialized and place a high priority on adherence to schedules. Philip DeSimone has shown that procrastination becomes a more salient concept as a society becomes more industrialized. Although some researchers have argued that procrastination is a completely modern phenomenon, similar words and concepts related to procrastination have existed throughout history. Ancient Egyptians used words related to procrastination to describe both useful habits of avoiding unnecessary work and harmful habits indicative of laziness that preclude the possibility of completing an important activity. The *Oxford English Dictionary* states that the word *procrastination* was frequently used by the early 17th century to describe situations in which people intelligently chose to restrain their behavior to arrive at a better conclusion. Procrastination began to be used as a means of the negative consequences of squandering time before a deadline during the mid-18th century, which coincides with the emergence of the Industrial Revolution. Thus, the tendency to procrastinate has existed for many years but became problematic when societies placed a high priority on faithfulness to schedules.

Consequences

Procrastination is a difficulty that is pervasively reported in everyday settings among people who are otherwise psychologically healthy. As many as 20% of nonclinical adult men and women report that they chronically procrastinate. And although procrastination may offer people a temporary break from an upcoming deadline, the consequences of procrastination are almost uniformly negative. Chronic procrastination has been linked to low self-esteem, self-control, and self-confidence. Other research has shown that chronic procrastinators are more likely than are nonprocrastinators to have increased levels of depression, anxiety, perfectionism, self-deception, and noncompetitiveness. Compared with nonprocrastinators, chronic procrastinators also show signs of dysfunctional impulsivity, suffer more ill health effects, and tend to score low on measures of the Big Five factor of Conscientiousness. People who procrastinate on a regular basis make inaccurate predictions of the amount of time needed to complete activities and tend to focus on past events rather than anticipating future events. Thus, chronic procrastination is related to a wide variety of negative physical and psychological outcomes.

Causes

In addition to documenting the consequences of procrastination, psychologists have investigated the possible reasons why people procrastinate. One explanation is that people procrastinate to protect their self-images from the negative consequences that accompany poor performance. From this perspective, placing a barrier in the way of completing a task (by procrastinating) can allow the person to explain the causes of their behavior in a positive or negative manner. If the person procrastinates and performs well on a task, then the person can explain the causes of the successful performance as having the ability to overcome an obstacle. If the person procrastinates and performs poorly, in contrast, then the person can explain his or her performance by the procrastinating behavior that caused the person to perform at a suboptimal level. Some research has shown that behavioral procrastination is related to the extent to which people place barriers in the way of completing activities to manipulate whether their performance can be explained positively or negatively. Joseph Ferrari and Dianne Tice showed that chronic procrastinators engaged in procrastination when an upcoming task was evaluative and potentially threatening. Thus, one possible cause of procrastination is that people place barriers in the way of their goal to minimize the negative impact of possible poor performance.

Another possible cause of procrastination is a sense of self-uncertainty early in life. According to this perspective, the bonds that people form with their primary caregiver from an early age can influence the degree to which people procrastinate later in life. People who grow up knowing that their caregiver is loving and responsive are less likely to procrastinate later in life, whereas people with a less secure attachment to their primary caregiver are more likely to

procrastinate later in life. Other research has demonstrated that children raised by overcontrolling parents are more likely to procrastinate later in life than are children who were raised by noncontrolling parents. These findings suggest that insecure attachment to primary caregivers at an early age is associated with a tendency to procrastinate later in life.

Prevention

Researchers have recently begun to explore prevention strategies that may reduce the negative consequences of procrastination. One strategy is to teach chronic procrastinators to restructure their mistaken thoughts regarding goal completion. Chronic procrastinators rely on thoughts that either increase task anxiety (e.g., "It's hopeless to complete this task") or decrease task anxiety (e.g., "I'll do it tonight, so I don't have to worry"). Teaching chronic procrastinators to identify and challenge these anxiety-producing thoughts may reduce the likelihood of continued procrastination. Another treatment strategy has been to boost concern and forethought for behaviors. As noted earlier, chronic procrastination is associated with low scores on the Big Five factor of Conscientiousness. Ferrari and colleagues have demonstrated that putting emphasis on the existent pattern of self-deceptive thinking aids in the reduction of procrastination among people low in Conscientiousness. The findings from these prevention strategies, though still preliminary, offer evidence that procrastination and its negative effects can be reduced.

Dianne M. Tice
C. Nathan DeWall

See also Anxiety; Attachment Styles; Big Five Personality Traits; Goals; Planning Fallacy; Self-Defeating Behavior; Self-Handicapping

Further Readings

Ferrari, J. R., Johnson, J. L., & McCown, W. G. (1995). *Procrastination and task avoidance: Theory, research, and treatment.* New York: Plenum.

Tice, D. M., & Baumeister, R. F. (1997). Longitudinal study of procrastination, performance, stress, and health: The costs and benefits of dawdling. *Psychological Science, 8,* 454–458.

PROJECTION

Definition and History

Many biases affect the impressions people form of each other, and a great deal of work by social psychologists explores those biases. For example, people often do not take into account how others' behaviors are constrained by the situations they are in (the fundamental attribution error). Impressions can also be biased and distorted because of the influence of stereotypes. Yet another bias—and a more subtle one—is the tendency for people to see in others characteristics that they are motivated to deny in themselves. For example, a woman tempted to cheat on a test might accuse others of dishonesty, a man with unwanted sexual fantasies and desires might become obsessed with the immorality of his neighbors, and another with an urge to commit violence against someone might come to believe that the other person is the potential aggressor. All these hypothetical cases are examples of *projection*—specifically, defensive projection (also sometimes referred to as direct or classical projection).

Sigmund Freud provided some of the earliest descriptions of projection, and his daughter Anna Freud further elaborated on his ideas. As a result, defensive projection is strongly associated with psychoanalytic theory. For psychoanalysts, projection was one of many defense mechanisms (along with repression, denial, reaction formation, and others)—psychological processes used to help people avoid becoming aware of anxiety-provoking thoughts or feelings.

Outside of psychoanalytic circles, though, the phenomenon was long viewed with a great deal of skepticism. Experimental social psychologists in particular doubted the very existence of defensive projection. The difficulty of figuring out how to study projection in a careful and systematic way was only part of the problem. Further complicating matters was confusion about how to define the phenomenon. For example, some argued that projection of a trait required actually possessing that trait. Unfortunately, it is not clear how to establish that a person can unambiguously be characterized by traits such as dishonesty, lustfulness, or aggressiveness. Still other researchers insisted that lack of awareness was a necessary characteristic of projection. It was never clear, though, what the awareness criterion referred to: Not being aware that one has a characteristic? Not being aware that one despises the characteristic? Not being aware that one is attributing the characteristic to another person? Not being aware that one's attribution of the trait to another person is a function of one's own motivation to deny the trait?

Contemporary Research

In the 1990s, however, projection was revived as a topic of study, and several studies support a general account of how it comes about. Although many unfavorable traits are almost universally disliked, individual people might be motivated to avoid and deny some of them more than others would. One person might desperately want not to be seen as incompetent; another might be most motivated to steer clear of dishonesty; still another might most despise cowardliness. Unfortunately, human behavior being as complex, ambiguous, and multidetermined as it is, it is hard to avoid ever doing, saying, thinking, or feeling anything that might be seen as evidence that one has a hated trait. One way of dealing with the distress that results is to simply try not to think about that evidence—that is, to suppress thoughts about the trait and about the possibility that it might at least to some extent characterize one's behavior. For example, one might try to forget about a nasty comment one just made and try to avoid thinking about how making such a comment suggests at least a certain amount of nastiness. Unfortunately, a great deal of research suggests that thought suppression can backfire. In other words, directly trying not to think about something can lead those thoughts to be harder to avoid than if one had never tried to suppress them. As a result, thoughts about the trait will have a tendency to pop into mind when interacting with other people, and therefore, it will dominate the impressions one forms of others. It should be noted that this account does not require a person to objectively possess a trait before he or she can project it; it is enough that people just be strongly motivated to deny it and be vigilant for any traces of it in their behavior.

Research supports the claim that efforts to deny a trait increase the likelihood that people will come to believe that others can be labeled with that very trait. In addition, people with a general and long-standing tendency to suppress thoughts (people known as repressors) project more than others. Finally, recent research has begun to address the possibility (long suggested by students of intergroup relations) that stereotypes and prejudices can develop as a result of defensive projection.

Projection is seen as a defense mechanism. That can mean at least two different things. Projection is related to defense in that it results from people's efforts to defend themselves against the possibility of perceiving themselves in certain ways. In other words, it comes about as a result of the suppression of threatening thoughts. But does projection itself work as a defense—that is, do people feel better about themselves and experience less anxiety as a result of projecting unwanted traits onto others? Recent research suggests that projection can be considered to be a defense in that sense as well. People have been found to report more positive self-concepts and less distress after they are led to project.

Many people seem to have pet peeves about the deficiencies of their fellow human beings. Some people gripe about others' stupidity and laziness, some are struck by others' cruelty, and others are flabbergasted at the selfishness they see around them. Research on defensive projection suggests that these tendencies often are more revealing of the observers' anxieties and fears about themselves than they are about the nature of the people that arouse their disgust.

Leonard S. Newman

See also Defensive Attributions; Fundamental Attribution Error; Ironic Processes; Meta-Awareness; Social Projection; Stereotypes and Stereotyping

Further Readings

Newman, L. S., & Caldwell, T. L. (2005). Allport's "Living Inkblots": The role of defensive projection in stereotyping and prejudice. In J. F. Dovidio, P. Glick, & L. A. Rudman (Eds.), *On the nature of prejudice: 50 years after Allport* (pp. 377–392). Malden, MA: Blackwell.

Newman, L. S., Duff, K. J., & Baumeister, R. F. (1997). A new look at defensive projection: Thought suppression, accessibility, and biased person perception. *Journal of Personality and Social Psychology, 72*, 980–1001.

Schimel, J., Greenberg, J., & Martens, A. (2003). Evidence that projection of a feared trait can serve a defensive function. *Personality and Social Psychology Bulletin, 29*, 969–979.

PROPINQUITY

Definition

Propinquity refers to the proximity or physical closeness of one person to another. The greater the degree of propinquity, the more likely that two people will be attracted to each other and become friends. Propinquity is usually thought of in terms of functional distance—that is, the likelihood of coming into contact with another person—rather than sheer physical distance.

Background and Modern Usage

Research on the effects of propinquity rests on the common-sense premise that one is unlikely to become friends with someone whom one has never met. Beyond this simple principle, however, is a set of observations and implications with considerable relevance for understanding how people move from initial encounters to the development of friendship. The power of propinquity is illustrated by a well-known finding from the Maryland State Police Training Academy. When aspiring police officers were asked to name their best friend in their training class, most named someone whose name, when placed in alphabetical order, was very close to their own. This result is readily attributed to the use of alphabetical name position for dormitory assignments and training activities.

Among the various explanations for propinquity effects, two have received the most support. One is termed the *mere exposure effect*. All other things being equal, the more often a person is exposed to a particular stimulus, the more favorably that stimulus tends to be evaluated. This has been shown with abstract paintings, letters of the alphabet, names, faces, and people. Thus, according to the mere exposure explanation, propinquity influences attraction because physical closeness increases familiarity and hence liking for other persons.

A second explanation is more interactive in nature. Physical proximity increases the frequency of encounters, and thereby creates opportunities for interaction. Because most of our interactions tend to be on the positive side of neutral, propinquity breeds positive experiences, which in turn foster attraction and friendship. In other words, propinquity creates opportunities to interact with others; more often than not, these interactions are rewarding and enjoyable in a way that promotes friendship formation. This explanation suggests an important exception to the propinquity-attraction rule: In circumstances in which people are predisposed in a more negative way—for example, because of substantial value differences, bias, or competing interests—propinquity should increase the likelihood of disliking. Research has shown that this is indeed the case.

The idea that functional distance may matter more than simple physical proximity reflects both of these explanations. Many factors other than sheer distance affect the frequency with which people encounter one another—for example, the physical and temporal layout of everyday routines such as going to work, health clubs, and recreation. Moreover, in the modern world, propinquity may also be cultivated electronically, such as by e-mail, instant messaging, and cell phones. Although the principle of propinquity may be timeless, the ways in which propinquity is established are ever-changing.

Harry T. Reis

See also Attraction; Contact Hypothesis; Mere Exposure Effect; Personal Space; Positive–Negative Asymmetry

Further Readings

Bornstein, R. F. (1989). Exposure and affect: Overview and meta-analysis of research, 1968–1987. *Psychological Bulletin, 106,* 265–289.

Segal, M. W. (1974). Alphabet and attraction: An unobtrusive measure of the effect of propinquity in a field setting. *Journal of Personality and Social Psychology, 30,* 654–657.

PROSOCIAL BEHAVIOR

Definition

Prosocial behavior is voluntary behavior intended to benefit another. Thus, it includes behaviors such as helping, sharing, or providing comfort to another. Prosocial behavior is evident in young children but changes in frequency and in its expression with age. Individual differences in prosocial behavior are caused by a combination of heredity, socialization, and situational factors. Prosocial behaviors can be preformed for a variety of reasons, ranging from selfish and manipulative reasons (e.g., helping get something in return) to moral and other-oriented reasons (e.g., helping because of moral principles or sympathy for another's plight). Prosocial behavior that is not performed for material or social rewards (e.g., rewards, approval), but is based on concern for another or moral values, is usually labeled "altruism."

A topic of attention in the social psychological literature is whether there is true altruism—that is, if people ever help others for reasons that are not really selfish. Although people sometimes assist others even when they receive no social or material benefits, some psychologists argue that there is always a selfish reason underlying altruistic motives. For example, they argue that people actually help because of the psychological merging of the self with another, the desire to elevate one's own mood or to avoid negative feelings or a negative self-evaluation (for not helping). People sometimes help others to alleviate their own feelings of distress when dealing with someone else in distress or need, or primarily because of personal ties to needy others. Nonetheless, C. D. Batson has provided evidence that people often assist for other-oriented sympathy, and there is likely at least some selfless motivation for some types of prosocial actions.

Importance

Prosocial behavior is relevant to both the quality of close interpersonal relationships and to interactions among individuals and groups without close ties. People, as individuals or as members of a group, often assist others in need or distress, as well as others whose needs are relatively trivial. Charities and societies depend on people helping one another. In addition, prosocial behavior has benefits for the benefactor. For example, children who are more prosocial tend to be better liked by peers, and adults who engage in helping activities tend to have better psychological health.

Personal Characteristics Associated With Prosocial Behavior

As is evident in everyday life, some people are more prosocial than others. Prosocial children and adults tend to be prone to sympathize with others. They also are more likely to understand others' thoughts and feelings and to try to take others' perspectives. In addition, people who tend to assist others often hold other-oriented values (e.g., value others' well-being) and tend to assign the responsibility for actions such as helping to themselves. Prosocial children tend to be positive in their emotional expression, socially competent, well adjusted, well regulated, and have a positive self-concept. In both childhood and adulthood, people who reason about moral conflicts in more mature ways (e.g., use more abstract moral reasoning, with more sophisticated perspective taking and a greater emphasis on values) are also more likely than their peers are to help others. Of particular note, preschool children who engage in spontaneous, somewhat costly prosocial behaviors (e.g., sharing a toy they like) engage in more prosocial behavior as adolescents and tend to be sympathetic and prosocial as adults. Thus, there appears to be some continuity in prosocial responding from a fairly early age.

Situational Factors

Even though some people are more prone to help than are others, situational factors also can have a powerful effect on people's willingness to help. For example, people are less likely to help when the cost of helping is high. They also are more likely to help attractive people and to help if they are the only ones available to help (e.g., there are no other people around who see an individual who needs assistance). People in good moods are likely to assist others more than are people in neutral moods, although sometimes people in bad moods seem to help others to raise their moods. People also are more likely to help if they are exposed to models of prosocial behavior. Moreover, the interaction of situational factors with personality characteristics of potential helpers is important; for example, sociable people seem more likely to provide types of helping that involve social interaction whereas shy individuals often may tend to help in situations in which they do not need to be outgoing or socially assertive.

Origins

Prosocial behavior is a complex behavior affected by numerous factors, both biological and environmental. Findings in twin studies support the view that heredity plays a role: Identical twins (who share 100% of their genes) are more similar to each other in prosocial behavior, as well as sympathetic concern, than are fraternal twins (who share only 50% of their genes). Heredity likely affects aspects of temperament or personality such as self-regulation, emotionality, and agreeableness, which contribute to people engaging in higher levels of prosocial behavior.

Considerable evidence also indicates that individual differences in prosocial behavior also are linked to socialization. For example, adults are more likely to help others if, as children, their parents were models of prosocial behavior. Warm, supportive parenting, especially if combined with the use of positive discipline (e.g., the use of reasoning with children about wrongdoing), has also been linked to prosocial tendencies in children, whereas punitive parenting (e.g., parenting involving physical punishment, the deprivation of privileges, or threats thereof) has been inversely related. Parents who help their children to attend to and understand others' feelings tend to foster prosocial tendencies in their offspring. Appropriate levels of parental control, when combined with parental support, prosocial values, and behaviors that help children to attend to and care about others' needs, seem to foster prosocial responding.

Age and Sex Differences

Even very young children, for example, 1-year-olds, sometimes help or comfort others. However, the frequencies of most types of prosocial behavior increase during childhood until adolescence. It currently is unclear if prosocial tendencies increase or not in adulthood. This increase in prosocial behavior with age in childhood is likely caused by a number of factors, including increased perspective-taking skills and sympathy, internalization of other-oriented, prosocial values, greater awareness of the social desirability of helping, and greater competence to help others.

There also are sex differences in sympathy and prosocial behavior. In childhood, girls tend to be somewhat, but not greatly, more likely to engage in prosocial behavior. Girls also are more empathic or sympathetic, albeit this sex difference is small and depends on the method of assessing empathy or sympathy. Women are perceived as more nurturant and prosocial, although they likely help more only in certain kinds of circumstances. Indeed, men are more likely to help when there is some risk involved (e.g., interactions with a stranger on the street) or if chivalry might be involved.

Nancy Eisenberg

See also Altruism; Empathy; Empathy–Altruism Hypothesis; Gender Differences; Helping Behavior; Kin Selection; Moral Reasoning; Twin Studies

Further Readings

Eisenberg, N. (1992). *The caring child.* Cambridge, MA: Harvard University Press. (Also in published in Japanese)

Eisenberg, N., & Mussen, P. (1989). *The roots of prosocial behavior in children.* Cambridge, UK: Cambridge University Press. (Also published in Japanese by Kaneko Shobo, 1991)

Penner, L. A., Dovidio, J. F., Piliavin, J. A., & Schroeder, D. A. (2005). Prosocial behavior: Multilevel perspectives. *Annual Review of Psychology, 56,* 365–392.

Schroeder, D. A., Penner, L. A., Dovidio, J. F., & Piliavin, J. A. (1995). *The psychology of helping and altruism: Problems and puzzles.* New York: McGraw-Hill.

PROSPECT THEORY

Definition

Prospect theory is a psychological account that describes how people make decisions under conditions of uncertainty. These may involve decisions about nearly anything where the outcome of the decision is somewhat risky or uncertain, from deciding whether to buy a lottery ticket, to marry one's current romantic partner, to undergo chemotherapy treatment, or to invest in life insurance.

Prospect theory predicts that people go through two distinct stages when deciding between risky options like these. In the first phase, decision makers are predicted to edit a complicated decision into a simpler decision, usually specified as gains versus losses. Purchasing a car is simplified into losing $20,000 and gaining a car, whereas buying a lottery ticket is simplified into losing $1 and gaining a small chance to win $100,000. A key feature of this editing phase is that the way in which people edit or simplify a decision may vary from one moment to the next, depending on situational circumstances. A person may think of a lottery as a .001% chance to gain $1 million, for instance, or as a 99.999% chance to lose $1. People make decisions based on these edited prospects, and the way that prospects are edited is therefore a critical determinant of the decisions they will make.

In the second phase, decision makers choose between the edited options available to them. This choice is based on two dimensions: the apparent value of each attribute or option and the weight (similar, although not identical to, the objective likelihood) assigned to those values or options. These two features—overall value and its weight—are then combined by the decision maker, and the option with the highest combined value is chosen by the decision maker.

The most interesting feature of prospect theory for most psychologists is that it predicts when (and why) people will make decisions that differ from perfectly rational or normative decisions, and has therefore figured prominently in explanations of why people make a variety of transparently bad decisions in daily life.

Background and History

Decision-making research before the 1970s was dominated by normative theories that prescribe how people "ought" to make decisions in a perfectly rational way, and many implicitly assumed that most people, in daily lives, followed these normative rules. Prospect theory was a notable departure from these existing theories because it offered a descriptive theory of how people actually make decisions, rather than providing a perfectly rational account of how they ought to do so.

The simplest way to choose between risky options is to choose the option with the highest expected value—the likelihood that an option will occur, multiplied by the value of that option. Imagine, for instance, that you are deciding whether to pay $1 for a lottery ticket that offers a 10% chance of winning $10. The expected value of this lottery ticket is $1 (0.1 × $10), the same as the cost of the ticket. Rationally speaking, you should therefore be perfectly indifferent about buying this ticket or not. The problem, noted by both economists and psychologists, is that rational theories did not always describe people's actual behavior very well. Few people, for instance, would actually purchase the lottery ticket in the last example. The certain loss of $1 simply does not compensate for the 10% chance of winning $10 and a 90% chance of winning nothing. In general, research found that people were more averse to taking risks than the expected value of outcomes would predict.

The inability of expected value calculations to explain people's decisions then led to the development of *expected utility theory,* which essentially incorporated people's attitude toward risk into their expected value calculations. Expected utility theory assumed that attitudes toward risk were stable within individuals, were not influenced by the way a particular decision was described (or framed), and was not influenced by the mood or situational context of the decision maker. However, experiments again revealed that decision makers often violate the predictions made by expected utility theory. For instance, a terminal cancer treatment with a 1 in 10 chance of saving the patient's life is identical to a cancer treatment with a 9 in 10 chance of death (assuming people can only live or die), and yet terminally ill cancer patients themselves would likely be more interested in pursuing this treatment when described as the likelihood of living than when described as the likelihood of dying.

Prospect theory was motivated by these failures of rational models to describe actual decision making in everyday life. Daniel Kahneman, one of the founders of prospect theory along with the late Amos Tversky, won the 2002 Nobel Prize in economics, at least in part, for this work.

Value and Weighting Functions

Prospect theory's central prediction is that choices between uncertain outcomes are determined by the combination of an outcome's apparent value (predicted by the *value function*) and the importance or weight assigned to a particular outcome (called the *weighting function*).

Value Function

There are three critical aspects of the value function (see Figure 1). First, value is assigned to changes in value rather than to absolute value. Almost no attribute can be judged in isolation, but can be judged only in relation to something else. A person is tall, for instance, only in comparison with others who are shorter. Or a person is happy only in relation to those who are sadder. So too, prospect theory predicts that the value assigned to an option is determined only by comparison with other options, and the option used in this comparison is therefore of critical importance. Winning an all-expenses-paid trip to Florida might sound wonderful compared with an all-expenses-paid trip across the street. But that trip to Florida might not sound nearly as wonderful when compared with an all-expenses-paid trip to Fiji. This comparison in prospect theory is called a *reference point,* and the value of an object is determined by the change in

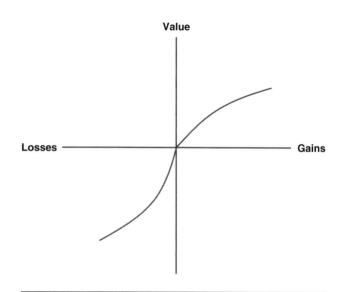

Figure 1   A Hypothetical Value Function

value between an object under consideration and that reference point, rather than by the absolute value of an object. This means that people might accept an option in one situation that they reject in another.

Second, the value function is S-shaped (see Figure 1), and predicted to be concave for gains above the reference point and convex for losses below the reference point. This means that differences between small gains or losses close to the reference point are assigned a high value, whereas differences farther away from the reference point are assigned smaller values. The difference between winning $5 versus $10 seems rather large, for instance, but winning $1,000 and winning $1,005 seems relatively small, even though the objective difference ($5) is identical.

Third, the value function is steeper for losses than for gains (see Figure 1). This means that a loss is assigned greater value than is a gain of an objectively identical amount. The prospect of losing $10 in a gamble, for instance, seems worse than the prospect of gaining $10 seems good. This difference helps explain why few people are interested in betting money on the outcome of a fair coin, even though the probability of winning money on this gamble is identical to the probability of losing money.

These two features of the value function have at least three profound effects on decision making. First, the S-shape of the value function means that minor changes near a reference point are likely to have a much more dramatic influence on decisions than are equivalent changes further from the reference point.

A person might drive across town, for instance, to buy a $10 book on sale for $5, but would not do so to buy a $1,005 TV on sale for $1,000. Or a person might be very enthusiastic about taking a new drug that reduces his or her risk of contracting a disease from 5% to 1%, but much less enthusiastic about a new drug that reduces the risk from 50% to 46%. Second, the asymmetry between gains and losses means that people will generally be loss-averse, which explains why people are not indifferent to gambles that have an equal probability of losing versus winning the same amount of money. What is more, this asymmetry explains why framing a decision in terms of gains or losses can have such a profound influence on behavior. People are unlikely to choose an option framed as a loss from a reference point compared with the same option framed as a gain from a reference point. Third, the asymmetry between gains and losses means that people are likely to be risk seeking in the domain of losses, but risk averse in the domain of gains. Because the prospect of losses hurts more than the prospect of gains feels good, people are likely to take greater risks to avoid a foreseeable loss than to ensure a foreseeable gain. People who fear falling short of a goal, for instance, may choose to adopt a riskier course of action to eventually achieve that goal (that may leave them even further from their goal), compared with people who believe they will exceed their goal.

Weighting Function

Rational models of decision making assume that people multiply the perceived value of an outcome by the objective likelihood that the outcome will occur. Prospect theory modifies this slightly and predicts that instead, people multiply the perceived value of an outcome by a decision weight. The major difference between the decision weights and objective probabilities is observed with extreme probabilities (either very low, e.g., 1%, or very high, e.g., 99%). For instance, moving from having no chance of contracting a terminal illness to having a 1% chance has a much larger effect on one's decision making than moving from a 50% chance to a 51% chance. Although the increase in the likelihood of contracting a terminal illness is the same (1%), the influence this increase has on one's decision—considered its weight in the decision—is not. In general, people tend to overweight low-probability events in judgment, which helps explain the irrational appeal of gambling and insurance for very low-probability events. At the other extreme, people tend to underweight highly certain outcomes. People will pay much less, for instance, for a lottery in which they have a 99% chance of winning $1,000 than they will for a lottery in which they have a 100% chance of winning $1,000, but there is little difference between the amount people would pay for a 50% versus 51% chance of winning $1,000. Again, the objective difference in probabilities (1%) is identical, but its impact on one's decision is not.

Evidence

Support for prospect theory can be found in a wide variety of disciplines, including sociology, psychology, and many areas within economics. Much of the empirical support comes from studies in which people make hypothetical or real choices between gambles. These gamble studies are ideal because they allow researchers to clearly specify the value and probabilities associated with each gamble, and provide an analogy to many, if not all, risky decisions made in daily life. Substantial empirical support exists for the major tenets of prospect theory: the importance of reference points in decision making, the asymmetry between gains and losses of equivalent magnitudes, and the weighting function that overweights low-probability events and underweights high-probability events. Recent advances in prospect theory involved demonstrations in field settings (such as with New York taxi drivers), and the more complicated treatment of decisions with a very large number of possible outcomes (called *cumulative prospect theory*). None of these recent advances challenged the major tenets of the original formulation.

Importance for Social Psychology

At its heart, social psychology investigates how situations—typically social situations—influence judgment and behavior. Prospect theory explains how situational variability in the way a decision is framed can have a dramatic impact on the decisions people make. These decisions are not restricted to any particular domain. They can be decisions to accept a financial gamble as much as they can be decisions about whether to marry one's high-school sweetheart, whether to fund social welfare policies, or whether to help a person in need.

In particular, the overall prediction from prospect theory that judgments and decision are determined by comparisons to an existing reference point has figured prominently in many areas of social psychology. For instance, White Americans in public opinion surveys typically report that racial conditions have improved significantly more than Black Americans do. One of the reasons for this difference appears to be that minority groups frame their progress as falling short of a goal compared with majority groups and, therefore, are more likely to consider what still needs to be accomplished rather than what has already been gained. Research on social comparisons similarly highlights the importance of reference points for determining one's self-concept, and research on social judgment shows that people often use their judgments as a reference point for others' judgments.

The asymmetry between gains and losses has similarly influenced several areas of social psychology. For instance, people tend to react much more strongly to threatening social cues in the environment than to helpful or supportive social cues. This pattern has been termed the *negativity bias* and is both informed by, and an extension of, the gain–loss asymmetry documented by prospect theory. The gain–loss asymmetry has also figured prominently in theories of motivation and goal pursuit. Focusing on preventing a loss versus achieving a gain activates very different kinds of psychological states and behaviors, a line of research clearly inspired by the insights of prospect theory. Finally, people's tendency to be risk seeking in the domains of losses but risk averse in the domain of gains has been applied to political attitudes for change versus stability and has therefore shed light on the origins of conservative versus liberal social attitudes.

One very specific phenomenon that has been of particular interest to social psychologists is the endowment effect. Empirical evidence demonstrates that people are more reluctant to give up or sell an item once they own it than they are interested in acquiring it if they do not. In the most common experimental demonstration, participants were randomly assigned to either receive a mug to take home or to receive no mug. Those who received a mug later state the amount of money they would ask to sell the item, and those who do not have a mug indicate the amount they would spend to buy the object. Despite being randomly assigned to own the mug, results show repeatedly that selling prices are higher than buying prices. The reason is that buyers are gaining an object and therefore value it less than do sellers who are losing an object. The power of this situational influence, unfortunately, is generally lost on buyers and sellers themselves who instead explain the other role's behavior as an instance of greed—not wanting to pay or sell an object for what it is "really" worth.

Ayelet Gneezy
Nicholas Epley

See also Behavioral Economics; Consumer Behavior; Decision Making; Mere Ownership Effect

Further Readings

Eibach, R. P., & Ehrlinger, J. (2006). Keep your eyes on the prize: Reference points and racial differences in assessing progress toward equality. *Personality and Social Psychology Bulletin, 32,* 66–77.

Kahneman, D., & Tversky, A. (1979). Prospect theory: An analysis of decision under risk. *Econometrica, 47,* 263–291.

Rottenstreich, Y., & Hsee, C. K. (2001). Money, kisses, and electric shocks: On the affective psychology of risk. *Psychological Science, 12,* 185–190.

Thaler, R. H. (1980). Towards a positive theory of consumer choice. *Journal of Economic Behavior and Organization, 1,* 39–60.

Tversky, A., & Kahneman, D. (2000). Advances in prospect theory: Cumulative representation of uncertainty. In D. Kahneman & A. Tversky (Eds.), *Choices, values, and frames* (pp. 44–65). New York: Cambridge University Press.

Van Boven, L., Dunning D., & Loewenstein G. (2000). Egocentric empathy gaps between owners and buyers: Misperceptions of the endowment effect. *Journal of Personality and Social Psychology, 79,* 66–76.

PROTOTYPES

Definition

A prototype is the best or most central member of a category. An object can be described in terms of prototypicality, which refers to the degree to which it is a good example of a category. For example, baseball is a more prototypical sport than is billiards or bullfighting, and an automobile is a more prototypical vehicle than is a sled or skateboard.

Background

The idea that category members differ in how well they fit their category is an important component of what is known as the natural view of categories, which emerged in the 1950s with the publication of Ludwig Wittgenstein's *Philosophical Investigations.* Radically transforming how categories were understood, the natural view replaced the classical view, a perspective originating from Aristotle's thinking about categories that had been the accepted belief for two millennia.

According to the classical view, a category, like a formal set, has specific defining characteristics that make the determination of category membership unambiguously clear. Objects that possess all the defining characteristics are category members and objects that do not are nonmembers. Having an absolute criterion for category membership implies that there is no gradation among category members. All objects that meet the standard for inclusion are equivalently good category members. The classical view also assumes that categories are arbitrary, as expressed in Benjamin Lee Whorf's writing on language and thought, which portrays categorization as a linguistic community's agreement about how to organize its otherwise chaotic reality. In this view, a category is merely sociolinguistic convention, without any inherent order or constraint in which attributes cluster together to define it.

The Natural View and Categorization

Despite its longevity, the classical view ultimately gave way because the natural view better describes how people actually categorize objects. The natural view recognizes that most categories are not defined by a set of specific properties that are true of all category members. Instead, category members are linked by family resemblance, a group of related characteristics that category members will likely, but not necessarily, possess. For example, a number of things are typically found on vehicles, such as wheels and a motor. However, none of these typical attributes are found on all vehicles, and there is no essential characteristic that an object must possess to be categorized as a vehicle.

Family resemblance implies that category members may not be equivalent. When individual category members possess some but not all of the category's common features, an object with more of these common features will be considered a better example of the category than one that has fewer. Natural categories have an internal structure, with the prototype, or best example of the category, at the center and less prototypical objects radiating away from it. Although the category's center is clear, its boundaries are fuzzy. There is no definite point at which one can say the category ends. People will agree about the status of most objects. Things like cars and bicycles are clearly vehicles, but coffeepots and neckties are obviously not. However, at the margins of a category, there will be objects whose status is unclear. People will disagree about whether things like a wheelbarrow, an elevator, or a pair of skates can be considered a vehicle. According to the natural view, no absolute boundary divides the things that are vehicles from those that are not.

The natural view rejects the idea that categories are arbitrary. It contends that a category's common attributes are things that naturally belong together. For example, it is not merely chance that attributes like feathers, beaks, laying eggs, and the capacity to fly are characteristic of the category "bird." They form a meaningful category because these things naturally occur together. Creatures that possess any one of these attributes are also very likely to have the others.

Substantial empirical evidence indicates that the natural view provides a more accurate account of categorization than does the classical view, much of which was obtained by Eleanor Rosch and her collaborators in the 1970s. For example, research participants uniformly find it to be an easy and reasonable task to rate whether an object is a better or worse example of a category. There is remarkable consensus in their ratings, and their level of agreement is usually greatest for the most typical category members. Consistent with the idea of family resemblance, objects that possess more of a category's common attributes are judged to be more prototypical. When listing members of a category, people generate the highly prototypical examples first, and less prototypical examples come later, if they are produced at all. People recognize category membership more quickly for highly prototypical objects than for less prototypical objects. Similarity ratings between high and low prototypicality objects are asymmetrical, with less prototypical objects being seen as more similar to highly prototypical objects than vice versa; for example, people more strongly endorse the statement "a sled is similar to a car" than "a car is similar to a sled." Interestingly, prototypicality effects also extend to categories with specific defining characteristics, such as geometric shapes or even numbers. People reliably judge 4 to be a "better" example of an even number than 104, though they equally satisfy the formal definition of an even number.

Categorization involves making generalizations that are essential for people to organize and make sense of the information they encounter. However, that people readily generate highly prototypical examples when thinking about categories can be problematic for social judgments. Many members of a social group will not share all the characteristics of the most prototypical member. Failure to recognize this may contribute to pervasive errors in social judgment, such as overestimating the degree to which group members possess certain characteristics, underestimating the variability among group members, and focusing on category membership at the exclusion of relevant information such as base rates.

Mark Hallahan

See also Need for Closure; Representativeness Heuristic; Schemas; Subtyping

Further Readings

Brown, R. (1976). Reference: In memorial tribute to Eric Lenneberg. *Cognition, 4,* 125–153.

Brown, R. (1986). Language and thought. In *Social psychology: The second edition* (Chap. 13, pp. 467–494). New York: Free Press.

Khorsroshahi, F. (1989). Penguins don't care, but women do: A social identity analysis of a Whorfian problem. *Language in Society, 18,* 505–525.

Lakoff, G. (1987). *Women, fire, and dangerous things: What categories reveal about the mind.* Chicago: University of Chicago Press.

Mervis, C. B., & Rosch, E. (1981). Categorization of natural objects. *Annual Review of Psychology, 32,* 89–115.

Whorf, B. L. (1956). *Language, thought and reality: Selected writings of Benjamin Lee Whorf* (J. B. Carroll, Ed.). Cambridge: MIT Press.

PSYCHOLOGICAL ENTITLEMENT

Definition

Psychological entitlement refers to a general belief that one deserves more or is entitled to more than others are. Psychological entitlement is defined as a general belief because it is consistent over time and across different situations.

Context and Importance

The concepts of entitlement and deservingness play an important role in much of social life. They both reflect the commonly held idea that when individuals contribute to a situation, they should get something back in return. When individuals do not get what they feel they are entitled to or deserve, they consider the situation unjust or unfair, and may get upset or angry and seek redress.

Entitlement and deservingness are similar but have slightly different meanings. Entitlement usually refers to a reward that a person should receive as the result of a social contract. For example, a person would say that she is entitled to receive a pension because she worked at a job for a set number of years. In the United States, government programs like Social Security are actually called entitlement programs. Deservingness, in contrast, usually refers to a reward that a person should receive as a result of his or her efforts or character. For example, a person may say that he deserves a larger salary because he is such a hardworking employee and keeps such a positive attitude in the workplace.

Psychological entitlement encompasses the experience of both entitlement and deservingness across time and across situations. In this sense, psychological entitlement can be considered an individual difference variable. That is, it reflects a very general difference between persons in beliefs and behaviors: Some individuals have chronically high levels of psychological entitlement, others have moderate levels of psychological entitlement, and still others have low levels of psychological entitlement. Individuals who have high levels of psychological entitlement think that they deserve more than do others in most situations. For example, a student with a high level of psychological entitlement will think that she deserves an A in a class, even if it is clear to the professor and the other students that she does not. Furthermore, this same student will likely feel that she deserves A's in all of her classes because psychological entitlement is a general trait and not limited to one specific situation. In contrast, another student with a low sense of psychological entitlement would not think that he deserved an A if he did not clearly earn it.

An individual's level of psychological entitlement is typically measured with a self-report scale, the Psychological Entitlement Scale. This scale asks individuals to rate the extent that they agree with certain statements. These include "I deserve more things in my life," "People like me deserve an extra break now and then," and "I feel entitled to more of everything." Individuals who have high levels of psychological entitlement are more likely to agree with these and similar statements.

Psychological entitlement has a wide range of important and often negative consequences for human thoughts, feelings, and behavior. In the workplace, for example, individuals who have high levels of psychological entitlement often believe that they should be paid more than are others in similar positions. This can potentially lead to conflict or divisiveness at work and leave the psychologically entitled person constantly dissatisfied. In romantic relationships, psychological entitlement is also related to many negative consequences. Individuals who have high levels of psychological entitlement report responding more negatively to conflict in the relationships, being less empathic, less respectful, and less willing to take their partners' perspective. They also report being more selfish and more game-playing. Finally, individuals who have high levels of psychological entitlement are more prone to aggression. These individuals believe that they deserve special treatment, so they are particularly likely to be aggressive toward those who criticize them. In short, individuals who have high levels of psychological entitlement often feel shortchanged by others. This is linked to feelings of resentment or anger, selfish and self-centered behaviors, and even hostility and aggression.

Although psychological entitlement is usually linked with negative outcomes, it may also benefit individuals in some situations. For example, employees who have high levels of psychological entitlement may actually end up making more money at work simply because they ask for it. Likewise, students who think they deserve higher grades and demand them might in some cases actually receive higher grades. Of course, these benefits of psychological entitlement may be short-lived. Individuals who constantly demand more resources or better treatment than they truly deserve might well gain bad reputations and eventually be avoided by others.

Finally, psychological entitlement might also operate at the level of social groups. When there is conflict between groups, excessive levels of psychological entitlement by one group may be blamed. In the United States (and this certainly occurs in other countries), many social groups have been referred to as "entitled." These include CEOs, celebrities, professional athletes, the young, the old, the poor, and the rich. In each of these cases, the label "entitled" applied to a social group implies that members of that group believe that society owes them special treatment. Furthermore, the implication is often that this special treatment is not deserved. For example, if a professional athlete is caught committing a crime, the comment is often made that it is typical of these entitled athletes to think that the rules that apply to everyone else do not apply to them.

W. Keith Campbell
Laura E. Buffardi

See also Narcissism; Narcissistic Entitlement

Further Readings

Campbell, W. K., Bonacci, A. M., Shelton, J., Exline, J. J., & Bushman, B. J. (2004). Psychological entitlement: Interpersonal consequences and validation of a new self-report measure. *Journal of Personality Assessment, 83*, 29–45.

PSYCHOLOGY OF TERRORISM

See TERRORISM, PSYCHOLOGY OF

PUBLIC GOODS DILEMMA

Definition

Public goods dilemma refers to a real-world decision whereby the outcome for any individual depends on the decisions of all involved parties. More specifically, these dilemmas are decisions in which individuals must weigh personal interests against the collective interest, which is typically a communal resource, a public good.

Examples of Public Goods Dilemmas

Real-world public goods dilemmas are quite common. For example, the existence of public radio stations is based on listener donations, but any one individual can save money by listening without contributing. Voting, actions by the United Nations, and many environmental problems are all examples of public goods dilemmas.

One of the original public goods dilemmas is Garrett Hardin's "Tragedy of the Commons." In his example, a community uses a common pasture to graze sheep. As long as each rancher uses the pasture for a small number of sheep, the pasture provides plenty of grazing. However, because each rancher sees the logic in adding a few more sheep (a large benefit for each rancher, only minor impact on the pasture), soon the pasture is well beyond its capacity and unusable by all.

Empirical Study

Public goods games are used to study these dilemmas in the laboratory. In one version, players are given some amount of money either to keep for themselves, or contribute to a shared pool. Typically, any contributions to the shared pool are multiplied to reflect the shared benefit of such contributions. The total amount that a player receives is the sum of (a) the amount that the player kept for himself or herself, and (b) that player's share of the shared pool.

By varying the specifics of these games, much has been learned about how people make public goods decisions. For example, punishments for noncontributors tend to increase contributions. Anonymous players tend not to contribute, whereas players who know each other are more likely to contribute. Similarly, a sense of belonging to a team tends to increase contributions, especially when one's team is competing against another team in a different game.

Strategies

It may be easiest to illustrate the strategies and payoffs in a public goods game with an example. Imagine a simple four-player game in which players are given $10 to keep or contribute (with no partial contributions), and contributions get multiplied by 2. Each player's profit is the $10 he or she kept or an equal share of the total contributions. Assume that Players 2, 3 and 4 will all make the same choice. Table 1 shows Player 1's total profit. Regardless of whether the other players keep or contribute the money, Player 1 profits most by keeping the money, and profits least by contributing it. Thus, although it is illogical for any one player to contribute, if all players contribute, the total benefit for the group is greatest. Hence, the dilemma: Contributing is risky, but it can lead to a larger benefit for the group as a whole.

Table 1 Player 1's Total Profit

		All Other Players	
		Keep	*Contribute*
Player 1	*Keep*	$10	$25
	Contribute	$0	$20

Travis Carter

See also Altruism; Cooperation; Intergroup Relations; Social Dilemmas; Social Loafing

Further Readings

Baron, J. (2000). *Thinking and deciding* (3rd ed.). New York: Cambridge University Press.

Rapoport, A. (1987). Research paradigms and expected utility models for the provision of step-level public goods. *Psychological Review, 94,* 74–83.

QUASI-EXPERIMENTAL DESIGNS

Definition

A quasi-experimental design is a research methodology that possesses some, but not all, of the defining characteristics of a true experiment. In most cases, such designs examine the impact of one or more independent variables on dependent variables, but without assigning participants to conditions randomly or maintaining strict control over features of the experimental situation that could influence participants' responses.

Example of a Quasi-Experimental Design

Quasi-experimental designs are most often used in natural (nonlaboratory) settings over longer periods and usually include an intervention or treatment. Consider, for example, a study of the effect of a motivation intervention on class attendance and enjoyment in students. When an intact group such as a classroom is singled out for an intervention, randomly assigning each person to experimental conditions is not possible. Rather, the researcher gives one classroom the motivational intervention (intervention group) and the other classroom receives no intervention (comparison group). The researcher uses two classrooms that are as similar as possible in background (e.g., same age, racial composition) and that have comparable experiences within the class (e.g., type of class, meeting time) except for the intervention. In addition, the researcher gives participants in both conditions (comparison and motivation

intervention) pretest questionnaires to assess attendance, enjoyment, and other related variables before the intervention. After the intervention is administered, the researcher measures attendance and enjoyment of the class. The researcher can then determine if students in the motivation intervention group enjoyed and attended class more than the students in the comparison group did.

Interpreting Results From a Quasi-Experimental Design

How should results from this hypothetical study be interpreted? Investigators, when interpreting the results of quasi-experimental designs that lacked random assignment of participants to conditions, must be cautious drawing conclusions about causality because of potential confounds in the setting. For example, the previous hypothetical example course material in the intervention group might have become more engaging whereas the comparison group started to cover a more mundane topic that led to changes in class enjoyment and attendance. However, if the intervention group and comparison group had similar pretest scores and comparable classroom experiences, then changes on posttest scores suggest that the motivation intervention influenced class attendance and enjoyment.

The Pros and Cons of Using Quasi-Experimental Designs

Quasi-experiments are most useful when conducting research in settings where random assignment is not possible because of ethical considerations or constraining situational factors. In consequence, such designs are more prevalent in studies conducted in natural settings, thereby increasing the real-world applicability of the findings. Such studies are not, however, true experiments, and thus the lack of control over assignment of participants to conditions renders causal conclusions suspect.

Jeni L. Burnette

See also Ecological Validity; Experimentation; Nonexperimental Designs; Research Methods

Further Readings

Cook, T. D., & Campbell, D. T. (1979). *Quasi-experimental: Design and analysis issues for field settings.* Boston: Houghton Mifflin.

Shadish, W. R., Cook, T. D., & Campbell, D. T. (2002). *Experimental and quasi-experimental designs for generalized causal inference.* Boston: Houghton Mifflin.

R

RACIAL RESENTMENT

See SYMBOLIC RACISM

RACISM

Definition

Racism is the systematic implementation of a doctrine of racial supremacy that maintains the superiority of one race over another.

Background, Components, and Modern Usage

Racial supremacy is the hallmark of racism, but it is also often characterized by a belief that racial groups are genetically isolated, biologically based entities that exist in nature. Racists believe that the biology of their group has afforded them greater intellect and moral fiber than the biology of other groups, and, therefore, they must control the behaviors of members of lesser groups to maintain the purity (and supremacy) of their own group.

Racism builds upon prejudice and discrimination, phenomena that have been studied in social psychology for more than 100 years. Prejudice is the affect or emotion, usually negative, an individual feels toward members of a particular racial group. For instance, the negative attitudes regarding Arab Americans that surfaced in response to the September 11, 2001, terrorist attacks can be thought of as prejudice. Discrimination is treating people differently from one another based on their racial group membership, often resulting in the relative advantage of one group. For example, if an individual owns a store and decides that he or she will only sell goods to members of one racial group, then he or she is discriminating against all the other racial groups. Violent hate crimes, such as lynching, are the most extreme form of discrimination. Racism, prejudice, and discrimination can each take three forms: interpersonal, institutional, and cultural. Consider, for instance, discrimination. Individual discrimination is the unfair treatment of one individual by another, such as attempting to keep a member of a different race from joining your fraternity. Institutional discrimination is the unfair treatment of members of an entire race that is sanctioned by societal institutions, norms, or governing bodies. The Jim Crow laws of the U.S. South that mandated separate public facilities for Whites and Blacks, such as drinking fountains and bathrooms, constituted institutional discrimination. Cultural discrimination entails the promotion and normalization of the practices, values, and products of one race, coupled with the marginalization of those of other races. The use of a White norm for "skin colored" pantyhose and bandages is a form of cultural discrimination.

Many scholars argue that prejudice and discrimination transform into racism when the members of the discriminating group have societal power over the members of the discriminated group. Such societal power allows the dominant group to define racial category boundaries; promote and communicate stereotypes about the other racial groups in schools, churches, and the media; and control the minority groups' access to educational, economic, and other societal resources. In other words, racism presupposes the power to affect individuals' lives on a large scale.

J. Nicole Shelton
Jennifer A. Richeson

See also Contact Hypothesis; Prejudice; Sexism; Stereotypes and Stereotyping; Subtyping; Symbolic Racism

Further Readings

Allport, G. (1979). *The nature of prejudice.* Reading, MA: Perseus Books. (Original work published in 1954)

Dovidio, J. F., & Gaertner, S. L. (Eds.). (1986). *Prejudice, discrimination, and racism.* San Diego, CA: Academic Press.

RAPE

Rape occurs when one individual forces another into sexual intercourse against his or her will. Other instances in which one of the individuals participates in sexual acts without fully consenting to them (e.g., unwanted kissing) are encompassed within the more general term *sexual coercion.* Males are much more frequently than females the perpetrators of rape and sexual coercion, not only in humans but also in nonhuman animals. In a recent review of research literature, the researchers could not find one animal species (other than human beings) where females actually force sex on males.

Although there are differences among studies, partly depending on how questions are asked and who the participants are, survey data on average indicate that almost half of all college women have experienced at least one sexual coercion incident since age 14, and 6% to 15% of college women have experienced rape. About 15% to 30% of male college students report having engaged at least once in some level of actual sexual aggression, and about a third of college men avow some likelihood of raping if they could be assured that no one would know. Acquaintance rape (e.g., by dates and boyfriends) is reported to be as common as stranger rape and usually does not lead to similar adjustment difficulties in the aftermath. Compared with other types of physical assaults, victims of rape suffer relatively higher trauma from sexual assaults, even when the degree of actual physical severity of the act remains constant. Young women are raped more frequently than are other women and experience the greatest psychological distress following the rape.

Compared with criminologists, who primarily study characteristics of incarcerated rapist populations, social psychologists have focused their research on college students and participants from the general community. The distinctive types of populations they have focused on may help explain some differences between criminologists and social psychologists regarding the proposed characteristics of sexual aggressors. Criminologists have generally concluded rape is typically the result of the same types of characteristics and factors that cause other antisocial acts such as stealing, killing, and cheating. In other words, incarcerated rapists appear to be criminal generalists who commit many different types of antisocial acts. Accordingly, criminologists have found convicted rapists to be comparable with other types of violent criminals on most measures of antisocial traits and behaviors, and the criminal records of rapists often resemble those of other offenders. In contrast, social psychologists have discovered that men in the general population who self-identify as having committed sexual coercion are more specialized in their coercive tendencies. For these men, sexually aggressive behaviors are much less likely to correlate significantly with measures of general antisocial behavior (e.g., drug use, lying, hitting, kicking, fraud, or killing).

An important objective of social psychological research has been to identify risk factors associated with an increased probability of committing sexual coercion among noncriminal populations. Several researchers have found a relation between men's hostile masculinity characteristics and the likelihood of committing sexually coercive acts. Such hostile masculinity includes callous attitudes toward women (e.g., rape myth acceptance and acceptance of interpersonal violence against women), feelings of hostility toward women, and sexual gratification from dominating and controlling women. Related research indicates that being sexually aroused by forced sex, even in fantasy, correlates with self-reported likelihood of raping and actual sexual coercion, and that for such males, but not other participants, the addition of power cues in a simulated relationship with a woman makes females over whom they have power more sexually attractive to them.

Notably, if a man has a hostile masculinity profile, and he also has a generally promiscuous or impersonal sexual lifestyle, then the combination makes him considerably more likely to be sexually coercive. Men who possess a promiscuous sexuality are identified by certain prior experiences. These men generally have had sexual intercourse at a relatively early age as well as quite a few short-term sexual relationships, without much personal attachment or intimacy. Individuals who come from homes where there was much conflict, including aggression by the parents against each other or sexual abuse of the child, have also been found to be more likely to adopt an impersonal sexual lifestyle. It has also been found that engaging in delinquent acts in adolescence or having close friends who participate in such delinquent acts during adolescence also increases the likelihood of developing an impersonal sexual lifestyle.

Although no single risk factor is strongly predictive of actual sexual aggression, if a man possesses several of these risk factors, these, in combination, can become quite predictive of his propensity to sexually aggress. The risk for sexual coercion is further exacerbated if significant alcohol consumption occurs by either individual on a date or during other social interactions, because inhibitions are likely to be reduced by drinking.

Importantly, risk factors for sexual aggression can be counteracted by certain cultural and individual variables. To illustrate, it has been found that among Asian American men but not European Americans, early risk factors for rape (e.g., abuse and violence in the family of origin) are tempered by the importance one assigns to the preservation of his own social integrity. For example, those males who are more concerned about being shamed by their actions are less likely to commit acts of sexual aggression. This result probably reflects differing norms between Asian and European cultures. Because concerns about losing face and upsetting interpersonal harmony are more characteristic of Asian culture, those Asian men who highly identify with norms of societal interdependency are expected to have this identification as an added cultural incentive not to sexually aggress. Likewise, certain personality traits can serve as possible inhibitory factors against the commission of sexual aggression. For instance, some research has found that males who were otherwise at high risk for sexual coercion were less likely to aggress if they also possessed high levels of empathy and compassion for the feelings of others.

Neil Malamuth
Mark Huppin

See also Date Rape; Hostile Masculinity Syndrome; Narcissistic Reactance Theory of Sexual Coercion

Further Readings

Abbey, A., Parkhill, M. R., BeShears, R., Clinton-Sherrod, A. M., & Zawacki, T. (2006). Cross-sectional predictors of sexual assault perpetration in a community sample of single African American and Caucasian men. *Aggressive Behavior, 32,* 54–67.

Lalumière, M. L., Harris, G. T., Quinsey, V. L., & Rice, M. E. (2005). *The causes of rape: Understanding individual differences in the male propensity for sexual aggression.* Washington, DC: American Psychological Association.

Malamuth, N., Huppin, M., & Bryant, P. (2005). Sexual coercion. In D. Buss (Ed.), *Evolutionary psychology handbook* (pp. 394–418). New York: Wiley.

REACTANCE

Definition

Broadly, reactance refers to the idea that people become upset when their freedom is threatened or eliminated, so much so that they attempt to reassert their lost freedom. The theory is relevant to the idea that humans are motivated to possess and preserve as many options and choices as possible. When people's options are restricted, they experience aversive emotional consequences. Reactance is very similar to a layperson's idea of reverse psychology: Humans will tend to do the opposite of what they are told to. Being ordered to do something by an external person or source implies that someone is trying to reduce one's freedom. Reactance also refers to the idea that people will want something more if they are told they cannot have it. As a result, humans may act in a manner that will oppose a resistance presented to their freedom.

Background and History

Psychological reactance theory was first proposed by the social psychologist Jack Brehm in 1966. Reactance theory is still considered to be one of the basic psychological theories; it has withstood decades of testing and can be applied to many aspects of human behavior.

Reactance theory is important because it highlights people's need for control, freedom of action and choice, as well as people's desire to preserve as many options as possible. Indeed, the theory was devised during a decade when people were constantly advocating and rallying about freedom of choice and action. Brehm observed that humans react strongly to having options taking away by external forces; they become quite upset and will take action to preserve or regain their lost options.

Many psychologists have noted that humans have a very strong aversion to loss, both in options and choices. Essentially, humans value freedom greatly. They like having options so much that they will incur costs to their own self just to maintain options, even if the options they keep open aren't that important or profitable. Think about what would happen if you woke up one day and heard on the news that you no longer have the right to vote; most likely you would become very upset—people value the ability to vote in a democratic society. Though this may seem like an extreme example, even people who do not exercise the right to vote would be upset. Indeed, many people would immediately revolt because someone else is trying to infringe on one of their basic freedoms.

Reactance theory highlights the simple, but important, fact that people value their freedom: When this freedom of behavior and choice is threatened, people will engage in motivated behavior, designed to take steps that will reassert and regain that freedom. In the former example, citizens will rally, petition, they may even become aggressive, if necessary, to try and regain freedom or options they feel are jeopardized.

A subtler example can be demonstrated by one of the original studies on reactance. Participants were asked to rate a series of records and then list the three they desired the most. Importantly, participants were promised that they could keep one of the records. After ranking their top three choices, participants were told that their third choice was unavailable. The researchers found that when participants were asked to rate the records again, the choice that was no longer available (their third choice) would then be rated as more attractive than it originally was. Simply because the option was no longer available, people actually valued it more.

Consequences

When people react, they become aroused. That is, they become upset, distressed, angry, or emotionally charged. Over the decades, researchers have been able to identify three main ways that people direct this arousal. These are known as the main consequences of psychological reactance.

First, an object, action, or freedom becomes more attractive after it has been eliminated or threatened. That is, the desire for that behavior or object will increase, as seen in the previous example. This consequence also applies to things such as people and behaviors, not just objects. For example, teenagers who are told by their parents that they cannot attend a party on the weekend want to go to that party more than before their parents restricted the teenagers' behavior. Even if the teenagers originally had no intention of attending the party, once they are told they cannot, they will desire going to the party more than before.

Second, people will engage in behavioral attempts to reassert the threatened or eliminated freedom. That is, a person will try to regain his or her freedom or options. According to reactance theory, when parents forbid teenagers to attend the party, the teenagers will engage in behaviors that they think will increase their chances of regaining their options. For example, they may begin arguing with their parents about the benefits (e.g., social acceptance) and costs (e.g., exclusion, being the only one in the class not attending) of attending the party. Hence, the teenagers will try to regain the ability to attend the party.

Often people will even engage exactly in the same behavior that was threatened or eliminated. Thus, if the teenagers cannot convince their parents to let them go, they may go anyway, either by sneaking out of the house or pretending to do something else, such as going to a respected friend's house.

Finally, reactance may lead people to feel or act aggressively toward the person who is attempting to restrict their freedom. For example, in times of war, citizens whose country is being occupied may feel intense hatred toward the enemy (occupiers) such that they have aggressive thoughts, and sometimes even aggressive actions, toward the enemy.

Influences on Degree of Reactance

The magnitude of reactance is not exactly the same for each person, nor for each situation. Rather, it depends on several key factors. First, the importance of the action or choice determines the degree of reactance to the loss. That is, when something that is very important to a person is in jeopardy, that person will probably experience stronger reactance (i.e., more arousal, increased attempt to regain). For example, students wishing to enroll in a course would probably value enrolling in it more if it is required to graduate than if it is only an elective. Consequently, if it is required to graduate and they are unable to enroll in it because the course is full, they will react more strongly than if they had wanted to take it simply as an elective. Moreover, the students who value it more will probably try and reassert their ability to take that course by pleading their case to the professor or department, whereas those students who wanted to take it as an elective might just attempt to enroll in the course next semester (though, to be sure, they will probably want to take the course more than before).

If an option or behavior has not been taken away, but has only been threatened to be taken away, the perceived magnitude of the threat (that is, if only a threat exists) will determine the strength of the reactance experienced by the person. If the threat is blatantly strong, then the person will experience stronger psychological reactance in response to the threat.

Importance

Having control over their actions and behavior is one of human beings' most important and valued needs. Indeed, people become distressed, angry, and even aggressive to actual loss of freedom, even perceived infringement on freedom. For example, after a couple breaks up, the person who initiated the end of the relationship is better able to cope and often feels a maintained sense of control. The person who did not have control over the termination of the relationship, however, will typically want his or her ex-partner back even more. That person also tends to feel a lack of control over the situation, which can be accompanied by wanting the ex-partner back more, being unable to think about anything else, and taking extreme steps to try and win that person back.

Men who are refused by women they believe they should have the opportunity to sleep with may become angry and coercive, even to the point of raping her. Moreover, sometimes reactance will produce behavior that is opposite of what was intended. This could be one reason why restrictions on violent video games and movies, pornographic material, or unhealthy behaviors such as smoking or drinking underage leads to the opposite of the intended effect. Humans will even use this basic knowledge to their advantage. For example, some parents may try to have their children cooperate by using reverse psychology on them.

Nicole L. Mead

See also Free Will, Study of; Narcissistic Reactance Theory of Sexual Coercion

Further Readings

Brehm, J. W., & Brehm, S. S. (1981). *Psychological reactance.* New York: Wiley.

REALISTIC GROUP CONFLICT THEORY

Definition

Between the borders of Pakistan and India lies a fertile valley known as Kashmir. Since 1947, India and Pakistan have fought three wars over this valuable territory. Unfortunately, the wars have contributed to hostilities and prejudice experienced by people on both sides. These tensions can be described by the realistic group conflict theory (RGCT). RGCT is a well-established theory with robust research support from both laboratory and field studies. It is used to understand many of the local and global intergroup conflicts that besiege the world. That a solution to end conflict is incorporated within this theory makes it one of the most applicable and compelling social psychological theories existing today.

This theory emerged in the 1960s to describe how perceived competition for limited resources can lead to hostility between groups. Unlike theories that use psychological factors such as personality or value differences to explain conflict and prejudice, RGCT focuses on situational forces outside the self. When valuable resources are perceived to be abundant, then groups cooperate and exist in harmony. However, if valuable resources are perceived as scarce (regardless of whether they truly are), then these groups enter into competition and antagonism ensues between them. The resources in question can be physical (such as land, food, or water) or psychological (such as status, prestige, or power).

One group need only believe that competition exists for hostile feelings and discriminatory behavior to follow. For example, if ethnic group A believes that members of ethnic group B pose a threat to them by "stealing jobs," then regardless of whether this is true, ethnic group A will feel resentment and hostility. The extent to which ethnic group A holds any power to follow through on its hostile feelings determines if unfair or discriminatory behavior toward ethnic group B will occur. At the very least, negative stereotypes about the other group will be created and mistrust and avoidance will result. How long and how severe the conflict becomes is determined by the perceived value and scarcity of the resource in question.

RGCT is unique because it does not discuss any personal features of the individuals engaged in the conflict. Other psychological theories use personality factors (such as authoritarianism) or ideologies (such as social dominance orientation) to explain why these hostilities exist. In RGCT, if individuals in a group believe that the two groups share a zero-sums fate, meaning that the other group's success feels like a failure or loss for one's own group, then no matter what outside group members say or do, feelings of resentment and discriminatory behavior will result. As the conflict unfolds, the members of each group will close ranks with their fellow members and will come to believe that their fate is connected with each other.

Classic Study

Muzafer Sherif's Robbers Cave experiment is a demonstration of this theory. Sherif is credited as one of the most important social psychologists of his time. With his colleagues, he set up a 2-week experiment involving White, middle-class, 12-year-old boys at a summer camp. At first, the boys interacted only with their own group members because Sherif wanted them to develop a sense of group identity. The boys did develop a group identity and called themselves the Eagles or the Rattlers. In the second phase of the study, the boys were introduced to the other group and were required to engage in a series of competitive activities. Rewards and prizes were handed out to the winning team. Sherif and his colleagues purposely set up these games and rewards so that the boys would have reason to compete intensely. During these fierce competitions, both groups became suspicious of and hostile toward one another. As tensions increased, the boys demonstrated allegiance to their group by discouraging one another from establishing friendships across group lines. No one wanted to be seen as a traitor, so the boys stuck to their own groups. Hostility increased to the point that physical fights and acts of

vandalism broke out. Despite direct interventions by adults, the two groups could not seem to reconcile.

Unity was restored only when Sherif and colleagues created situations requiring both groups of boys to depend on each other to achieve important goals equally valued by both groups. In other words, harmony was restored when both groups were equally invested in achieving a goal that required everyone's help and cooperation. For example, Sherif set up a situation in which a truck carrying their food supply broke down and the help of all the boys was needed to bring the food to camp. After completing a series of such tasks requiring interaction and everyone's involvement, positive behavior toward the other group members increased. The boys began to behave more like individuals rather than group members and formed friendships across group lines. Psychologically, they began as two distinct groups, but when the perception of threat was replaced by cooperation and interdependence, the groups reestablished themselves as one large group. Therefore, the group distinctions made between Eagles and Rattlers disappeared and everyone felt as if they belonged to the same group.

Research Support

RGCT has received support from both psychological and sociological studies. For example, RGCT has been used to explain Whites' opposition to civil rights policies for Blacks. This research indicates that for some Whites, losing certain privileges is at the root of their resistance to racial policies rather than a dislike for Blacks. There has also been cross-cultural research using RGCT to analyze conflict between different ethnic and religious groups of people. These studies show that violence between different groups will escalate in societies experiencing shortages in vital resources. Research has shown that competition can lead to hostile behaviors in children, adolescents, and adults alike.

Saera R. Khan
Viktoriya Samarina

See also Intergroup Relations; Prejudice; Robbers Cave Experiment; Stereotypes and Stereotyping

Further Readings

Jackson, J. (1993). Realistic group conflict theory: A review and evaluation of the theoretical and empirical literature. *Psychological Record, 43,* 395–413.

REASONED ACTION THEORY

Definition

The theory of reasoned action (TRA) is a model for predicting people's behavior, which states that the best predictor of people's behavior in any given situation is their intention to perform the behavior. Not surprisingly, the best predictor of whether people will actually do something is whether they intend to do it. The intention to perform the behavior is influenced by a person's own attitude toward (feelings or evaluations of) the behavior as well as the attitudes of people who are important to the person and the associated perceived social pressures (subjective norms).

Background and Importance

Social psychologists have demonstrated that knowledge of people's attitudes and feelings frequently allows one to predict their behavior. However, research also indicates that sometimes people's behavior is not consistent with their attitudes. For example, students might believe that studying for exams is good because it leads to better grades; however, they still might not study. Therefore, more variables must be influencing the behavior than just attitudes. The TRA was an attempt to identify other factors, such as social pressures, that could be useful in predicting behavior. The result was the better prediction of behavior.

Components of the Theory and Evidence

According to the TRA, individuals' intention to perform a behavior (their behavioral intention) determines what they do, and it is based on two things: their own attitudes about the behavior and perceived social pressures from people whom they want to please (technically referred to in the theory as subjective norms). Usually, people intend to perform behaviors that they feel positively about or that are popular with other people, and they do not intend to perform behaviors that they feel negatively about or that are unpopular with other people. Once the intention to behave a certain way is determined, people tend to follow through with the intention and engage in the behavior.

Research demonstrates that people tend to perform behaviors about which they have positive attitudes and avoid behaviors toward which they have negative attitudes. The TRA states that attitudes toward specific behaviors are based upon expectations or beliefs about what the likely consequences of the behavior will be. If people believe that primarily positive consequences will result from the behavior (and negative consequences seem unlikely), they will have positive attitudes toward the behavior. If they believe that primarily negative consequences will result from the behavior (and positive consequences seem unlikely), they will have negative attitudes toward the behavior. For example, a student might believe that studying will lead to better grades but also to missed opportunities to socialize with friends. If socializing is more important to the student than are good grades, or if the student is not confident that he or she would get good grades even with more studying, the student would probably have a negative attitude toward studying. On the other hand, if getting better grades is more important to the student than socializing, and if the student is confident that studying will lead to better grades, he or she will probably have a positive attitude toward studying.

Although research demonstrates that people's own attitudes concerning a behavior significantly influence whether they intend to do it, research has also shown that attitudes are not always sufficient for predicting behavior. According to the TRA, behavioral intentions are also influenced by perceived social pressures. For example, even if a student has a positive attitude toward studying, if the student's friends have negative attitudes toward studying, it is likely that the student will not study much either because of conformity pressures. Whether the student conforms to perceived social pressures will depend largely on the extent to which the student is concerned about what those individuals think. In other words, the perceived social pressure is the result of the beliefs of other people (friends, family, etc.) concerning how the individual should behave as well as how motivated the individual is to comply with those people. For example, even if there is perceived pressure from parents to study, the student may be more motivated to comply with friends' wishes. Studies have demonstrated that the consideration of perceived social pressures in addition to attitudes enhances the prediction of behavioral intention, and thus behavior. However, research shows that some people, as well as some behaviors, are more influenced by social pressure than others.

Typically, TRA researchers ask participants to report their attitudes concerning a specific behavior, including its likely consequences, the perceived social pressures from important others concerning the behavior, and their intention toward performing the behavior. Researchers then contact participants later to ask them whether they have actually engaged in the behavior. Such research generally supports the theory. Behavioral intentions are better predictors of behavior than are attitudes alone, and considering perceived social pressures in addition to attitudes usually increases prediction of a person's behavioral intention. Therefore, all the components of the TRA are important.

Implications

The TRA has been used to predict a wide range of behaviors relating to health, voting, consumer purchases, and religious involvement. Although the TRA predicts behavior more successfully than do models that only consider attitudes, the TRA is only applicable to behavior that is deliberate and under the person's control. In instances when there are barriers to engaging in a behavior (for example, students who just do not have enough time to study even though they and their friends have positive attitudes toward studying), a recent extension of the TRA, the theory of planned behavior, must be applied.

Laura A. Brannon
Valerie K. Pilling

See also Attitude–Behavior Consistency; Attitudes; Normative Influence; Theory of Planned Behavior

Further Readings

Ajzen, I., & Fishbein, M. (1975). *Belief, attitude, intention and behavior: An introduction to theory and research.* Reading, MA: Addison-Wesley.

Ajzen, I., & Fishbein, M. (1980). *Understanding attitudes and predicting social behavior.* Englewood Cliffs, NJ: Prentice Hall.

Sheppard, B. H., Hartwick, J., & Warshaw, P. R. (1988). The theory of reasoned action: A meta-analysis of past research with recommendations for modifications and future research. *Journal of Consumer Research, 15,* 325–343.

RECENCY EFFECT

Definition

The recency effect is an order of presentation effect that occurs when more recent information is better remembered and receives greater weight in forming a judgment than does earlier-presented information. Recency effects in social psychology have been most thoroughly studied in impression formation research. Typically, researchers investigate how impressions are formed on the basis of sequentially presented information. For example, a recency effect occurs if a person who is described in terms of three positive traits followed by three negative traits is subsequently evaluated more negatively than is a person described by exactly the same traits but presented in a reverse order (negative traits followed by positive traits). The opposite of a recency effect is a primacy effect, when early information has a disproportionate influence on subsequent impressions compared to more recent information. Both recency and primacy effects have important consequences in many everyday impression formation judgments. One might wonder, for example, whether the most effective strategy in a job interview is to present your best points first (expecting a primacy effect), or present your best points last (expecting a recency effect)? To answer such questions, we need to understand the mechanisms that produce recency effects.

Mechanism

The most plausible explanation of recency effects emphasizes memory processes: More recent information is simply better remembered and so more available to be used when forming a judgment. Numerous studies have found that immediate past events are usually better remembered than are more distant past events. There are, however, a number of specific conditions that influence the likelihood of recency effects.

Facilitating Conditions

Two kinds of factors seem to influence the presence and strength of recency effects in impression formation: (1) how the task is structured and presented (*task factors*) and (2) how judges process the available information (*processing factors*). Task factors include the length and distribution of the information array over time. When the information array is long, or there is a long delay or other activity interposed between early and late items of information, or judgments are formed immediately after the presentation of the last information, recency effects are more likely, simply because judges will disproportionately rely on recent and better remembered details. In contrast, when the information sequence is short and is presented without interruption, primacy effects are the more likely result.

The way judges *process* the available information is also important in explaining recency effects. When judges are instructed to use step-by-step processing and update their impressions after each piece of information is received, primacy effects are reduced and recency effects become more likely. Recency effects are also more likely when judges do not know that they need to form an impression until after all the information is received. In the absence of an a priori impression formation goal, judges must rely on their memories for input into the impression formation judgment. Under such circumstances recent, better remembered information receives more weight and a recency effect results. In contrast, when judges know from the beginning that impression formation is the goal, a primacy effect is more likely.

Simon Laham
Joseph P. Forgas

See also Heuristic Processing; Memory; Person Perception; Primacy Effect, Memory

Further Readings

Jones, E. E., & Goethals, G. R. (1972). Order effects in impression formation: Attribution context and the nature of the entity. In E. E. Jones, D. E. Kanouse, H. H. Kelly, R. E. Nisbett, S. Valins, & B. Weiner (Eds.), *Attribution: Perceiving the causes of behavior* (pp. 27–46). Morristown, NJ: General Learning Press.

RECIPROCAL ALTRUISM

Altruism refers to behaviors that are performed for the sake of benefiting others at a cost to oneself. Reciprocal altruism is when altruistic behaviors are performed because they increase the likelihood of repayment in the future. For quite some time the presence of altruistic behaviors in animals and humans was a genuine puzzle for the Darwinian account of evolution through natural selection. It seemed impossible for an organism that acts unselfishly for the sake of another (nonrelated) organism to benefit in any way that would encourage that organism's reproductive success. This is simply because selfish (non-altruistic) individuals

would on average have more resources than altruistic individuals. After many generations, natural selection seemed to dictate that any genetic basis for altruistic behavior should be eliminated from a population. The theory of reciprocal altruism was first described by the evolutionary biologist, Robert Trivers, as a solution to the problem of how altruistic behaviors directed toward nonkin could have emerged through natural selection.

Trivers's insight was that often an individual could act in such a manner (e.g., by sharing food) as to increase its chance of survival if it could depend on similar altruistic behavior from another individual at some point in the future. For the strategy of reciprocal altruism to work, however, a few conditions must be met: Individuals must interact more than once (so that the opportunity to be repaid can arise), individuals must be able to recognize other individuals reliably, and individuals must be able to remember the past behavior of those with whom it interacts. Because of these constraints, reciprocal altruism is less common than is kin-directed altruism, where individuals act for the good of individuals who share their genes.

Reciprocal altruism is often discussed in the context of *game theory,* particularly the Prisoner's Dilemma Game. This Prisoner's Dilemma provides an elegant way to test cooperative behavior in the simplified context of a game. An influential analysis by the political scientist Robert Axelrod and the evolutionary biologist William Hamilton demonstrated that in this game, in which two isolated "prisoners" must decide whether to "cooperate" and refuse to confess, or to "defect" and confess for a lesser sentence, the most effective strategy (submitted by the mathematical psychologist Anatol Rapoport)—that is, the strategy with the best payoff across repeated interactions—was a tit-for-tat strategy—a strategy that repays in kind. If your partner cooperates, you return the favor. If he or she cheats, you do the same. Because this strategy is essentially reciprocal altruism, Axelrod and Hamilton's analysis was able to demonstrate that evolution could easily have selected for genes that might encourage such altruistic behavior.

It is often remarked that reciprocal altruism is not genuine altruism because it has the seemingly selfish goals of repayment, whereas true altruism is usually defined as self-sacrifice for the sole sake of benefiting others. The fact that altruistic behaviors could emerge through natural selection via the mechanism of reciprocal altruism, however, says nothing about the motives of the organism engaged in the altruistic act. It is important to recognize that reciprocal altruism is a theory of how cooperation could have evolved, not a theory of the psychological states of the altruist.

David A. Pizarro

See also Altruism; Evolutionary Psychology; Helping Behavior; Moral Reasoning; Prisoner's Dilemma; Prosocial Behavior

Further Readings

Pizarro, D. (2000). Nothing more than feelings? The role of emotions in moral judgment. *Journal for the Theory of Social Behaviour, 30,* 355–375.

Trivers, R. (1971). The evolution of reciprocal altruism. *Quarterly Review of Biology, 46,* 35–37.

RECIPROCITY NORM

Definition

Reciprocity norm is the rule of human interaction that says people need to reciprocate the action of another person. Simply, this means that when a person is given a gift (which can take any number of forms) by another, the person must repay the gift. Every investigated society has a version of the reciprocity norm. The reciprocity norm has also been termed *a web of indebtedness* by cultural anthropologists.

The reciprocity norm's presence in every investigated society points to its importance and function. The reciprocity norm has many benefits for society, such as reciprocal altruism. There are also important sanctions for those who do not follow the norm in its prescribed mannerisms (which can vary from society to society). It is important that one is aware of how the norm can be abused.

Aspects of the Norm

The fact that the norm is present in every investigated society suggests that it is a vital component of human interaction. Evolutionary psychologists have suggested that reciprocity was clearly present in human beings' ancestral past and has contributed to human survival. They point to various experiments where reciprocity helps explain the mystery of altruism. "If you scratch my back, I will scratch yours" is common colloquialism that is based on reciprocity.

Reciprocity will occur regardless of whether the reciprocation is done publicly or privately. Studies have investigated the extent to which people will reciprocate even if the original gift-giver is completely unable to tell if the gift was reciprocated. It has been found that people reciprocate the gift, although gift recipients donated slightly less than they might have in a more public situation.

People are very good at detecting cheating in social situations, such as receiving a favor without repaying it. Humans excel in tasks in which the problem is set up as a social cheating scenario, whereas the same task set up as a purely numerical task results in much worse performance.

Other limits on the potential for cheating are enforced by society. Societies have various sanctions for people who break the reciprocity norm, ranging from calling someone a "mooch," to social isolation, to serious legal consequences, which includes death in some cultures. Third parties will often intervene on behalf of someone who has just been shorted by a violation of the reciprocity norm, even if it means incurring some penalty of their own.

Abuses of the Norm

Importantly, the reciprocity norm itself does not have rules of interaction in most cultures (but see the cross-cultural section later for an important caveat); instead, the norm simply says that the gift must be reciprocated in some fashion. This leaves open the potential for very uneven exchanges.

Dennis Regan clearly demonstrated this effect by setting up an experiment that was purportedly on art appreciation. In this experiment, a participant would come in and rate a painting. Another "participant" (who actually was working for the experiment—also known as a confederate) was also there to rate art. During the course of the experiment, the confederate gave the participant an unsolicited gift of a can of Coca-Cola. The confederate later asked the participant to purchase raffle tickets. Regan found that the gift of the Coke doubled the number of tickets purchased over a control condition. This is important because the cost of the Coke was significantly less than the cost of a single ticket. In fact, the confederate was able to get a 500% return on the cost of the gift in terms of raffle tickets purchased.

Also, it does not matter if the original gift was not wanted, or even forced onto the receiver; they are still obligated to reciprocate. This has been demonstrated in a number of experimental studies; however, perhaps the best example is the Hare Krishnas.

The Hare Krishnas are a religious organization that used reciprocity very effectively in the 1970s and 1980s. The Krishnas would give a small gift to a traveler, often a flower, and then solicit the traveler to make a donation to their religion. The travelers would begrudgingly give the donation, and then could often be seen throwing the flowers away in disgust. As evidenced by their facial expressions and the frequency they threw the flowers away, the travelers had been forced into giving a donation to a religion that most did not support through the reciprocity norm.

To date, it appears that there is only one limit on reciprocity: when the gift-giver asks the receiver to participate in an antisocial activity. In these cases, the norm of reciprocity does not increase compliance with the request. However, this occurs only in a strictly antisocial activity, such as abetting cheating on a test. More ambiguous circumstances show the increase in compliance to a reciprocity-based request.

Cross-Cultural Aspects

Another important topic when discussing reciprocity norm is its cross-cultural relevance. It appears that reciprocity occurs in every known society; however, not all societies have the same rules regarding reciprocity. Some have formal, ritualized rules that parse out the debts. For instance, Vartan Bhanji is a ritual form of gift exchange in Pakistan and India. This system ensures that there are no outstanding debts left unpaid. The gifts that are exchanged are often weighed out to ensure the equality of the exchange. Other societies, such as the one in the United States, do not have formalized rules. Despite the lack of formalized rules, there is a clear norm of reciprocation, and when one breaks the norm, there are consequences.

John Edlund

See also Cheater-Detection Mechanism; Conformity; Norms, Prescriptive and Descriptive; Persuasion

Further Readings

Cialdini, R. B. (2001). *Influence: Science and practice.* Boston: Allyn & Bacon.

Fehr, E., & Fischbacher, U. (2004). Third-party punishment and social norms. *Evolution and Human Behavior, 25,* 63–87.

Regan, D. (1971). Effects of a favor and liking on compliance. *Journal of Experimental Social Psychology, 7,* 627–639.

REDUCTIONISM

Definition

Reductionism means that complex principles can be reduced to simpler or more fundamental principles. Social psychologists often oppose reductionism and emphasize instead the social context that surrounds the individual. There are two basic types of reductionism: psychological and methodological.

Psychological Reductionism

One can often identify reductionism with the mind-body problem, which is the question about the relationship between mental and physiological processes. Psychological reductionism is the idea that one can completely explain the human psyche by breaking it down into several general principles. Social reductionism explains social events in terms of the qualities of the individuals who are involved. For example, a social reductionist would explain the aggression of a football crowd by saying that it is made up of aggressive individuals, whereas another explanation might be that when you take ordinary, non-aggressive people and place in them in a certain social context, they act as an aggressive group.

Proponents of the neuronal reductionism argue that thoughts and feelings consist simply of electrical or chemical changes in the brain, whereas proponents of genetic reductionism argue that genes alone determine human behavior. Reductionism in social psychology also tries to explain social psychological group processes by looking at individual differences (e.g., type A personality) rather than at contextual factors (e.g., frustrations).

Sociobiology embraces several reductionistic approaches to explain human behavior. Some social psychologists, however, argue that breaking psychological processes to individual, neuronal, or genetic levels disregards meaningful information about the social context and history of an individual. The constant tension between those who emphasize basic principles and those who emphasize social context has led to divergent streams of investigation throughout history.

Methodological Reductionism

Methodological reductionism deals with the selection of one theory among other competing theories. All other things being equal, the best theory is the most parsimonious one. Methodological reductionism is often identified with Ockham's razor (named after William of Ockham), which proposes that if competing theories have equal predictive powers, you should choose the one that makes the fewest assumptions, shaving off those theories that make no difference in the observable predictions of the explanatory hypothesis.

Modern Developments

In the recent past, there has been a movement within social psychology toward an interactionist approach, which acknowledges the interaction of individual factors (e.g., brain activity, genetics) with the social factors. For instance, social neuroscience proposes the multilevel analysis of psychological factors, trying to combine psychobiological knowledge with social psychological knowledge. This idea is different from the traditional reductionism, in which lower-level processes replace upper-level social processes.

In general, one can also see the current tendency toward using multiple methods in social psychology as an effort to bring together sociobiological knowledge with the knowledge gained through the traditional experiments or surveys.

Igor Grossmann
Brad J. Bushman

See also Social Cognitive Neuroscience, Social Neuroscience; Sociobiology

Further Readings

Ariew, R. (1976). *Ockham's razor: A historical and philosophical analysis of Ockham's principle of parsimony.* Urbana: University of Illinois.

Berntson, G. G., & Cacioppo, J. T. (2004). Multilevel analyses and reductionism: Why social psychologists should care about neuroscience and vice versa. In J. T. Cacioppo & G. G. Berntson (Eds.), *Essays in social neuroscience* (pp. 107–120). Cambridge: MIT Press.

REFERENCE GROUP

A reference group is any group that people use as a point of comparison to form their own attitudes, values, beliefs, and behaviors. For example, new college students may use older (and presumably wiser) college students as a reference group to form their attitudes about politics, what clothes to wear, how much alcohol to drink, what music to listen to, what restaurants to frequent, and so on. In one classic study, college women attending Bennington College in Vermont between 1935 and 1939 reported their political attitudes. These women came from politically conservative, wealthy families who could afford to send their daughters to a private college during the Great Depression. At Bennington, these women encountered faculty members and older students who were much more politically liberal than their parents were. The new students used these faculty and older students (rather than their parents) as a reference group for their own political attitudes. The students in the study consistently voted against their families' political ideology, even 50 years later.

People also use reference groups to evaluate other people. For example, a student might find a professor to be unintelligent. That judgment is not made in comparison with the entire population (relative to which that professor may be quite smart) but, rather, in comparison with other professors (relative to whom that professor may not be very smart). In evaluating members of stereotyped groups people tend to use members of that group, rather than the population as a whole, as the reference group.

Finally, people use reference groups to evaluate themselves. When people are trying to self-enhance, they tend to compare themselves with others who are less skilled than they are. When people are trying to gain an accurate understanding of their abilities, they tend to compare themselves with others who are more skilled than they are.

Although people use different reference groups for different purposes, they are probably not aware they are doing this. Comparisons with different reference groups occur largely at an unconscious level.

The reference group effect can pose significant problems when researchers design psychological questionnaires. For example, questionnaires designed to measure people's independence by asking them how independently they feel or behave do not work well across different cultures. This is because behavior that would be considered independent in collectivist societies (e.g., Japan, China), would be considered much less independent in individualist societies (e.g., United States, Western Europe). However, a person filling out a survey asking how much the person agrees with the statement "I tend to act independently" is not thinking about how independent he or she is relative to other people in general, but rather in comparison with other people in their society.

Michael E. W. Varnum
Brad J. Bushman

See also Bennington College Study; Cultural Differences; Person Perception; Social Comparison

Further Readings

Heine, S. J., Lehman, D. R., Peng, K., & Greenholtz, J. (2002). What's wrong with cross-cultural comparisons of subjective Likert scales?: The reference-group effect. *Journal of Personality and Social Psychology, 82*(6), 903–918.

Sherif, M., & Sherif, C. W. (1964), *Reference groups: Exploration into conformity and deviation of adolescent.* New York: Harper & Row.

REGRET

Definition

Regret is the negative emotion that people experience when realizing or imagining that their present situation would have been better had they decided or acted differently. Regret thus originates in a comparison between outcomes of a chosen option and the nonchosen alternatives in which the latter outperforms the former. This painful emotion reflects on one's own causal role in the current, suboptimal situation. The emotion regret is accompanied by feelings that one should have known better, by having a sinking feeling, by thoughts about the mistake one has made and the opportunities lost, by tendencies to kick oneself and to correct one's mistake, by desires to undo the event and get a second chance, and by actually doing this if given the opportunity. Put differently, regret is experienced as an aversive state that focuses one's attention on one's own causal role in the occurrence of a negative outcome. It is thus a cognitively based emotion that motivates one to think about how the negative event came about and how one could change it, or how one could prevent its future occurrence.

Relation to Decision Making

As such, regret is unique in its relation to decision making and hence to feelings of responsibility for the negative outcome. One only experiences regret over a bad outcome when at some point in time one could have prevented the outcome from happening. Of course, other emotions can also be the result of decisions; for example, one may be disappointed with a decision outcome, or happy about the process by which one made a choice. But, all other emotions can also be experienced in situations in which no decisions are made, whereas regret is exclusively tied to decisions. For example, one can be disappointed with the weather and happy with a birthday present, but one cannot regret these instances (unless the disappointing present was suggested by oneself). Thus, in regret, personal agency and responsibility are central, whereas in other aversive emotions such as anger, fear, and disappointment, agency for the negative outcomes is either undetermined, in the environment, or in another agent. Hence, regret is the prototypical decision-related emotion in the sense that it is felt in response to a decision and that it can influence decision making.

The relation between regret and decision making is also apparent in regret's connection to counterfactual thinking. Counterfactual thoughts are thoughts about what might have been. It is important to note that not all counterfactual thoughts produce regret, just specifically those that change a bad outcome into a good one by changing a decision or a choice. Thus, when it rains on the way home from work and a person gets wet, the person feels regret when he or she generates a counterfactual thought in which the person brought an umbrella, but not when he or she generates a counterfactual in which it would be a beautiful day. In the latter case, counterfactual thoughts about better weather that could have been would result in disappointment but not in regret (there was nothing the person could have done about the weather, so there is nothing to regret).

Intensity of Reaction

Experiences of regret can be the result of a negative outcome that was produced by a decision to act or a decision not to act. In other words, one may regret sins of omission and sins of commission. Early regret research focused on whether people regret their actions (commissions) more than their inactions (omissions). This research indicated that people tend to regret their actions more than their inactions. Later research showed that which type of regret is most intense (action regret or inaction regret) depends on the time that has elapsed since the regretted decision. In the short run, people tend to feel more regret about their actions (the stupid things they did or bought), but in the long run, they tend to feel more regret over their inactions (the school they never finished, the career or romance never pursued). This temporal pattern to regret is mainly of the result of several factors that decrease the regret for action over time (e.g., people take more reparative action and engage in more psychological repair work for action regrets than for inaction regrets), and factors that increase the regret for inaction over time (e.g., over time people may forget why they did not act on opportunities, making the inaction inexplicable). An additional factor producing this temporal pattern is that people forget regrettable actions easier than regrettable failures to act, resulting in a greater cognitive availability for failures to act.

Another factor determining the intensity of regret is the justifiability of the decision. People feel most regret over decisions that are difficult to justify. Decisions that are based on solid reasons produce less regret than do decisions that are not well thought through. This justifiability may also explain when actions are more regretted than inactions and when the reverse is true. Consider the following example. There are two coaches of soccer teams. One of them decides to field the same players as last week; the other decides to change the team. Now both teams play and lose. Which coach would feel most regret? Research showed that participants point at the active coach, the one who changed his or her team, as the one who will feel most regret. This clearly shows more regret for action than for inaction (replicating the traditional action-inaction difference). But now consider the same situation, but with the additional information that the current decision to change the team or not follows a prior defeat. Who would now feel most regret, the coach who actively tries to better the situation by changing the

team, or the coach who simply fields the same players that lost the previous game? In this case, participants point to the passive coach as the one feeling most regret. This decision was clearly ill justified and therefore produces more regret. A losing record calls for action, and inexplicable inaction produces more regret in situations that call for action. Thus, both decisions to act and decisions to forgo action may result in regret. The intensity of regret depends on the time since the decision and the justifiability of this decision.

Influence

Psychologists became interested in studying regret partly because it is a passive emotional reaction to bad decisions, but also because it is a major influence on day-to-day decision making. This influence can take two forms. First, the experience of regret may produce a behavioral inclination to reverse one's decision or undo the consequences. Second, decision makers may anticipate possible future regret when making decisions, and choose in such a way that this future regret will be minimal.

The influence of experienced retrospective regret on ensuing behavior can be functional. The aversive experience prompts people to undo the cause of the regret. For example, after buying a product that proves to be suboptimal, regret can motivate a person to ask for his or her money back, or it may result in apologies in the case of interpersonal regrets. In both instances regret can help people satisfy their needs. It protects people from wasting money and helps them maintain good social relationships. In addition, regret can be functional in the sense that the painful self-reflective nature of the experience is one of various ways by which people learn. The feeling of regret over bad decisions and wrong choices makes them stand out in people's memory and helps people make better decisions in the future. This is also shown by the finding that people tend to feel most regret about things that they can still improve in the future, sometimes referred to as the opportunity principle in regret. Another functional aspect of regret is that it stems from its influence on cognitions. Instead of going back to the shop to undo the regretted purchase or apologizing to the person central in the regret, the person can imagine various ways in which the current situation could have been more favorable to him or her. So regret motivates people to engage in reparative action and helps them remember their mistakes and missed opportunities; by making cognitively available counterfactual worlds in which one would have arrived at a better outcome, it also prepares people to behave more appropriately when they are confronted with similar choices in the future.

The idea that people, when making decisions, might consider future emotional reactions to possible decision outcomes has some history in research on decision making, starting with economists studying rational choice in the early 1980s. We now know that the influence of anticipated future regret on current decision making can take several forms. First, people may avoid deciding so they can avoid making the wrong decision. However, this inactive attitude may result in regret as well because in the long run inactions produce most regret. People may also avoid or delay their decisions because they want to gather more information so they can make better decisions.

Another way in which anticipated regret can influence decision making is related to post-decisional feedback. Regret stems from comparisons between outcomes of the chosen and nonchosen options, so decision makers can try to avoid regret by avoiding feedback about nonchosen options. In real-life decisions, people may occasionally receive information about foregone outcomes. For example, people choosing to invest in particular stocks will learn about future stock prices for the chosen stocks, but also for the nonchosen stocks. Likewise, gamblers who decide not to bet on the long shot in a horse race will learn after the race is over the position at which this horse finished and, thus, whether this option would have been better. In these cases, one can expect to feel regret if the decision goes awry. For some quite important life decisions, however, such feedback is often not present. If a person decides to go into business with someone or to marry someone, the person will never find out how successful each enterprise would have been had he or she chosen another partner or spouse, or none at all. In these cases, there is only feedback on the chosen option.

The knowledge that this future feedback will or will not be present influences current decision making, as revealed in the following example. Imagine that you have the choice between a sure $100 or a 50% chance of $200 (depending on the toss of a coin). If you opt for the sure thing (the $100), you normally do not learn whether the gamble (the 50% of winning $200) would have been better. If you opt for the gamble, you will always learn the outcome of the gamble and the outcome of the sure thing. Hence, you will always know whether the sure thing would have been

better. Thus, the sure thing protects you from regret, whereas the gamble carries some risk of regret. In this case, the anticipation of regret promotes a preference for the sure thing, revealing risk aversion. However, when the outcome of the gamble will become known irrespective of one's choice (e.g., the coin will always be tossed), one may also end up regretting the choice for the sure $100. This may lead to an increased preference for the gamble, revealing risk seeking. Thus, the anticipation of regret may produce risk-seeking and risk-avoiding choices, depending on which alternative minimizes the future regret. Research has shown that these anticipations of regret can influence many real-life decisions, such as stock market investments, salary negotiations, lottery play, prenatal screening decisions, and condom use.

Implications

Regret is an aversive emotional state that is related to counterfactual thoughts about how one's present situation would have been better had one chosen or acted differently. Therefore, people are motivated to avoid or minimize post-decisional regret. This has several implications for decision making because people may employ different strategies to prevent regret from happening or to cope with regret when it is experienced. In principle, the effects of regret can be considered rational because they protect the decision maker from the aversive consequences of the experience of regret. There might be cases, however, in which an aversion to regret leads one to avoid counterfactual feedback and, hence, results in reduced learning from experience. This might be considered irrational. But, irrespective of this rationality question, regret has shown to be a fundamental emotion in the behavior decisions of most, if not all, people.

Marcel Zeelenberg

See also Counterfactual Thinking; Decision Making; Emotion; Moral Emotions

Further Readings

Gilovich, T., & Medvec, V. H. (1995). The experience of regret: What, when, and why. *Psychological Review, 102,* 379–395.

Landman, J. (1993). *Regret: The persistence of the possible.* New York: Oxford University Press.

Loomes, G., & Sugden, R. (1982). Regret theory: An alternative theory of rational choice under uncertainty. *Economic Journal, 92,* 805–824.

Roese, N. J. (2005). *If only.* New York: Broadway Books.

Zeelenberg, M., & Pieters, R. (2007). A theory of regret regulation 1.0. *Journal of Consumer Psychology, 17*(1), 3–18.

REGULATORY FOCUS THEORY

For centuries, the hedonic principle that people approach pleasure and avoid pain has been the dominant motivational principle for many disciplines and across all areas of psychology. Even when Sigmund Freud discussed the need to go beyond the pleasure principle because people were controlled by the reality principle—environmental demands—he was simply modifying the pleasure principle such that avoiding pain became almost equal in importance to approaching pleasure. But is that the end of the story of motivation? How does the hedonic principle itself work? Might not there be different ways to approach pleasure and avoid pain that tell us something about motivation beyond the hedonic principle per se? Regulatory focus theory was developed in response to these questions.

Evolutionary Perspective

Regulatory focus theory starts with an evolutionary perspective on motivation. What are the survival motives? To survive, people (and other animals) need both nurturance and security, support or nourishment from the environment (often provided by others), and protection from dangers in the environment (social and nonsocial dangers). Regulatory focus theory proposes that two distinct regulatory systems have developed to deal with each of these distinct survival concerns. When people succeed in satisfying a concern they experience pleasure, and when they fail they experience pain. Thus, both of these regulatory systems involve approaching pleasure and avoiding pain. But this does not mean that the motivational principles underlying these systems are the same. Regulatory focus theory emphasizes the motivational significance of the differences in how actors approach pleasure and avoid pain when they regulate within these distinct systems.

Regulatory focus theory associates the nurturance motive with the development of promotion focus concerns with accomplishment, with fulfilling hopes and aspirations (ideals). It associates the security motive with the development of prevention focus concerns with safety, with meeting duties and obligations (oughts). Once again, people can succeed or fail to fulfill their promotion or prevention focus concerns. But the emotional and motivational consequences of success or failure in these two regulatory focus systems are not the same. When people are in the promotion focus system (either from a chronic predisposition to be in that system or from a current situation activating that system), they experience cheerfulness-related emotions following success (e.g., happy, joyful) and dejection-related emotions following failure (e.g., sad, discouraged). The pleasure of success and the pain of failure are not the same in the prevention focus system. People experience quiescence-related emotions following success (e.g., calm, relaxed) and agitation-related emotions following failure (e.g., nervous, tense). Individuals in a promotion focus also appraise objects and events in general along a cheerfulness-dejection dimension more readily than along a quiescence-agitation dimension, whereas the opposite is true for individuals in a prevention focus.

Strategic Preferences

Success and failure in promotion versus prevention is also not the same motivationally. To understand why this is, a critical difference between promotion and prevention proposed by regulatory focus theory needs to be introduced. Regulatory focus theory proposes that when people pursue goals, their strategic preferences are different in a promotion versus a prevention focus. The theory proposes that individuals in a promotion focus prefer to use *eager* strategies to pursue goals—strategies of advancement (a gain), which move the actor from neutral (the status quo) to a positive state. In contrast, individuals in a prevention focus prefer to use *vigilant* strategies to pursue goals (a nonloss)—strategies of carefulness, which stop the actor from moving from neutral to a negative state. Why this difference in strategic preferences? Research has found that individuals in a promotion focus experience a world of gains and nongains because their concerns are about accomplishments and aspirations. Strategic eagerness is also about ensuring gains and not wanting to miss gains, so eagerness should fit a promotion focus. Individuals in a prevention focus, however, experience a world of nonlosses and losses because their concerns are about safety and meeting obligations. Strategic vigilance is also about trying to be careful and not wanting to commit mistakes that produce a loss, so vigilance should fit a prevention focus. Indeed, many studies have found that individuals in a promotion focus prefer to use eager strategies to pursue goals whereas individuals in a prevention focus prefer to use vigilant strategies.

This difference in strategic preferences when people are in a promotion versus a prevention focus is why success and failure in promotion versus prevention is not the same motivationally (or emotionally). When individuals succeed in a promotion focus, it increases their eagerness (experienced as high-intensity joy). In contrast, when individuals succeed in a prevention focus, it reduces their vigilance (experienced as low-intensity calmness). When individuals fail in a promotion focus, it reduces their eagerness (experienced as low-intensity sadness). In contrast, when individuals fail in a prevention focus, it increases their vigilance (experienced as high-intensity nervousness). Evidence indicates that this regulatory focus difference in the motivational impact of success and failure influences postperformance expectations as well. Consistent with people attempting to maintain the strategic state that sustains their focus, individuals in a promotion state raise their expectations for the next trial after success on the initial trial of a task much more than do those in a prevention state (because optimism increases eagerness but reduces vigilance), whereas individuals in a prevention state lower their expectations for the next trial after failure on the initial trial much more than do those in a promotion state (because pessimism increases vigilance but reduces eagerness).

Regulatory focus differences in strategic preferences have other effects as well. Often the differences are revealed when there is a conflict between different choices or different ways to proceed on a task. One conflict is between being risky or conservative when making a judgment. When people are uncertain, they can take a chance and accept something as true, thereby risking an error of commission. Alternatively, they can be cautious and reject something as true. Studies on memory and judgment have found that individuals in a promotion focus take more risks than do those in a prevention focus. Consistent with individuals in a promotion focus being more willing to

consider new alternatives under conditions of uncertainty rather than simply sticking with the known (albeit satisfactory) current state of affairs, evidence shows that they are more creative than are those in a prevention focus and are more willing to change and try something new when given the opportunity. The trade-off, however, is that prevention focus individuals are more committed to their choices and thus stick to them even when obstacles arise.

Other Conflicts and Implications

Another conflict on many tasks is between speed (or quantity) and accuracy (or quality). Individuals in a promotion focus emphasize speed more than accuracy whereas individuals in a prevention focus emphasize accuracy more than speed. A third conflict concerns whether to represent objects or events in a more global and abstract manner or in a more local and concrete manner. Evidence indicates that individuals in a promotion focus are more likely to represent objects and events in a global and abstract manner (as well as more temporally distant) than in a local and concrete manner, whereas the opposite is true for those in a prevention focus.

There are additional implications of the difference between a promotion focus on gains versus a prevention focus on nonlosses. Studies have found, for example, that promotion focus individuals perform better when success on a task is represented as adding points toward a desired score or as attaining some desired prize rather than when it is represented as not subtracting points or as maintaining some desired prize. Other studies have found that the nature of ingroup versus outgroup bias varies by regulatory focus. For individuals in a promotion focus, ingroup members are treated with a positive bias ("promoting us"), but there is little bias regarding outgroup members. For individuals in a prevention focus, however, outgroup members are treated with a negative bias ("preventing them"), but there is little bias regarding ingroup members.

Motivational theories in psychology have mostly emphasized people's needs and desires for particular outcomes, from physiological needs to belongingness needs to achievement needs to autonomy needs. Most generally, the emphasis has been on the hedonic needs for pleasure and against pain. Regulatory focus theory differs from this traditional emphasis in highlighting people's desires to use certain strategies in goal pursuit—an emphasis on the *how* of goal pursuit rather than on the consequences of goal pursuit. Studies that have tested regulatory focus theory have shown that promotion and prevention strategic preferences are a major determinant of the motivational and emotional lives of people.

E. Tory Higgins

See also Emotion; Goals; Ingroup–Outgroup Bias; Self-Discrepancy Theory

Further Readings

Crowe, E., & Higgins, E. T. (1997). Regulatory focus and strategic inclinations: Promotion and prevention in decision-making. *Organizational Behavior and Human Decision Processes, 69,* 117–132.

Forster, J., Higgins, E. T., & Idson, L. C. (1998). Approach and avoidance strength during goal attainment: Regulatory focus and the "goal looms larger" effect. *Journal of Personality and Social Psychology, 75,* 1115–1131.

Higgins, E. T. (1997). Beyond pleasure and pain. *American Psychologist, 52,* 1280–1300.

Higgins, E. T., Friedman, R. S., Harlow, R. E., Idson, L. C., Ayduk, O. N., & Taylor, A. (2000). Achievement orientations from subjective histories of success: Promotion pride versus prevention pride. *European Journal of Social Psychology, 30,* 1–23.

Liberman, N., Idson, L. C., Camacho, S. J., & Higgins, E. T. (1999). Promotion and prevention choices between stability and change. *Journal of Personality and Social Psychology, 77,* 1135–1145.

REJECTION

Definition

Defined broadly, social rejection refers to one's perceived reduction of social acceptance, group inclusion, or sense of belonging. Social psychologists study real, imagined, and implied rejection in a variety of forms and contexts. Explicit rejection, exclusion, and ostracism are different kinds of rejection than can occur within groups or dyadic relationships of a romantic or platonic nature. Rejection typically produces negative immediate effects and leads to either antisocial or prosocial behavior, depending on the context of subsequent interactions.

History

Even though philosophers, writers, and laypeople have contemplated the nature of social rejection for centuries, social scientists had not formulated cohesive theories about social rejection and acceptance until relatively recently. In the 1950s, psychologists such as Stanley Schachter began examining the motivations that underlie social contact, and Abraham Maslow, in particular, argued that individuals seek relationships to fulfill a need to belong—belonging being a fundamental need secondary only to nourishment and safety needs. By the 1960s, psychologists began fleshing out attachment theories, which argued that parental rejection powerfully influences children's thoughts, feelings, and behaviors. Notwithstanding this early work on belonging needs and attachment, social psychological research examining the characteristics, antecedents, and consequences of rejection has only come of age in the last decade.

Complexities of Rejection

Contemporary social psychologists study rejection in an array of forms and contexts. Rejection may be active or passive and involve physical or psychological distancing or exclusion. For example, individuals may be actively rejected when others voice negative views of them or tell them that their presence is not wanted. In comparison, individuals may be passively rejected when others pay little attention to them or ignore them altogether (e.g., the silent treatment). Physical exclusion from a group elicits feelings of rejection in most circumstances (e.g., when an individual is purposefully left out), and psychological exclusion (e.g., when one's opinions are discounted or ignored) is also experienced as a rejection.

Rejection may be derived from individuals or groups, and the nature of these relationships influences the severity of the rejection. Romantic partners, friends, acquaintances, strangers, and group members can all serve as a source of rejection. Although the causes and characteristics of these rejections are arguably different on average (e.g., a stranger's insult has different connotations than that of a friend), the most powerful rejections are dispatched by individuals or groups that are important to a person. In other words, the more important a relationship is to a person, the more painful its weakening or dissolution will be.

Similarly, the further one falls in liking after a rejection, the more robust the consequences. In other words, the change in a person's opinion of another has more impact than the absolute level of that opinion. When an individual's positive initial opinion of another person dwindles to a negative opinion over time, this person will feel worse than had the individual always thought poorly of him or her. Likewise, even a drop in positive regard can feel like a rejection. A close friend who is suddenly treated like a casual acquaintance may feel rejected even though general liking remains. Consequently, initial liking needs to be taken into account when considering the impact of a rejection.

As discussed previously, *social rejection* (as well as *social acceptance*) is a multifaceted term that encompasses a number of behaviors and experiences that occur in a variety of contexts. To predict rejection outcomes with the most accuracy, a researcher would require knowledge of the source, the individual's relationship with the source, the nature of the rejection, and so forth. Most researchers find this narrow vision too restrictive and instead choose to blend or mix these variants of rejection together in an effort to generate broad theories that speak to the nature of social rejection more generally. Most of this research has addressed the responses to and consequences of social rejection.

Responses to Rejection

Immediate reactions to rejection are typically negative. Rejected individuals report feeling worse about themselves in general. In addition to lowered self-esteem, people usually describe their feelings as hurt. Furthermore, people seem to experience social pain and distress after a rejection much like physical pain, according to recent neuroscientific evidence. Rejection also hinders individuals' ability to rein in impulses and make difficult decisions. Given their impoverished decision-making abilities, rejected individuals tend to perform more self-defeating behaviors such as procrastinating and making risky, irrational choices than do accepted individuals. Moreover, rejection impairs individuals' logic and reasoning abilities, and this results in poor performance on tasks that require complex intelligent thought.

The negative consequences of rejection are not confined to the individual who experienced the rejection.

In addition to hurting themselves, rejected individuals also perform antisocial behaviors that hurt others. After being rejected, individuals are especially likely to lash out against the rejecter and to aggress against innocent bystanders as well. Roy Baumeister, Jean Twenge, and colleagues have shown, for instance, that study participants who were told that no one wanted to work with them in a group were more willing to blast innocent others with loud, uncomfortable bursts of noise than were participants who were told that they were accepted into the group. These researchers also demonstrated that rejected individuals feel less empathy for others and are, consequently, less willing to cooperate with and help them. When given an opportunity to cooperate with an unknown partner, rejected individuals choose to cheat the partner instead.

Despite these negative initial reactions, rejection also elicits prosocial behaviors under some circumstances. Rejected individuals try to strengthen social bonds with others by working harder on group tasks, publicly agreeing with others' opinions, and displaying positive, affiliative nonverbal behavior (e.g., smiling, making eye contact, mimicking others' actions). To make subsequent social interactions smoother, rejected individuals pay more attention to subtle social cues like facial expressions and vocal tones than accepted individuals do. When rejected individuals are unable to form new social attachments or mend broken social bonds (e.g., when interaction partners are not available), they attempt to regain a sense of belonging by other means. In comparison with accepted individuals, those who are rejected reflect upon and affirm their own relationships to a greater extent and prefer tasks of a social nature (e.g., looking at photographs of loved ones) rather than those of a nonsocial nature (e.g., looking at a magazine). Among individuals with a strong need to belong, rejected individuals can find companionship with their pets and even atypical targets such as favorite television characters.

On the whole, research on rejection indicates that the consequences of rejection are mixed. Some studies find evidence of antisocial behavior following rejection whereas others find evidence of prosocial behavior. The literature currently suggests that rejected individuals will act in prosocial ways (e.g., being agreeable) when they foresee future interactions with a partner and in antisocial ways (e.g., being aggressive) if they expect little or no contact with a partner. An aim of ongoing and future research is to uncover the circumstances under which social rejection elicits more prosocial than antisocial effects and vice versa.

Long-Term Consequences

Even though individuals can recover from a single rejection, the experience itself is unpleasant and detrimental in many ways. Individuals who experience rejections repeatedly, however, suffer even more serious consequences. Such individuals may internalize these rejections and behave in self-fulfilling ways that actually elicit subsequent rejection. In other words, perpetually rejected individuals will come to expect rejection and will push away potential friends and partners and choose to isolate themselves. Stuck in this vicious circle, these individuals' feelings of loneliness, helplessness, and worthlessness will bring about poor mental and physical health outcomes.

Megan L. Knowles
Wendi L. Gardner

See also Need to Belong; Ostracism; Rejection Sensitivity; Self-Esteem; Social Exclusion

Further Readings

Baumeister, R. F., & Leary, M. R. (1995). The need to belong: Desire for interpersonal attachments as a fundamental human motivation. *Psychological Bulletin, 117,* 497–529.

Leary, M. R (2001). *Interpersonal rejection.* New York: Oxford University Press.

Williams, K. D., Forgas, J. P., & von Hippel, W. (2005). *The social outcast: Ostracism, social exclusion, rejection, and bullying.* New York: Psychology Press.

REJECTION SENSITIVITY

Definition

Everyone desires acceptance and dislikes rejection from people who are important to them. Some people, however, are more concerned with rejection, a quality known as rejection sensitivity. Thus, rejection sensitivity refers to a trait that makes some people different from others. Rejection-sensitive people (unlike, or more than, other people) come into new situations feeling anxious and expecting rejection. For example, when Kate attends a party where she knows only the host, she gets sweaty palms (i.e., indicating high anxiety) and doesn't think anyone will want to talk with her (i.e., rejection expectancy). Rejection-sensitive individuals also perceive rejection in situations more often than others do, tending to read rejection into others' actions and words. Luke is a reserve player on the school's basketball team. Sometimes when his teammates only pass him the ball a few times in a game, he believes they don't like him. Rejection sensitivity also shows itself in how a person reacts to a rejection. Rejection-sensitive people often react to rejection with strong hostility and aggression or severe anxiety and withdrawal. Anna gave her professor low ratings on the teacher evaluation form after she found out she didn't do well on the final. Jake didn't leave the house all summer after his girlfriend broke up with him. The rejection sensitivity model was developed to explain all of these elements—expectation of rejection, perception of rejection, reaction to rejection.

Context and Background

Psychology has long emphasized the importance of a relationship of trust between children and their primary caregivers. One of the most influential models of the link between early relationship experiences and later interpersonal functioning is John Bowlby's attachment theory. This theory suggests that early experiences cause children to create mental representations (i.e., ideas or images of what close relationships are like) that influence subsequent social interactions. If they can trust their caregiver to meet their needs, they form secure representations. If their needs are met with rejection through the form of unavailability or nonloving responses, then they will become insecure and unsure in their relationships. Other researchers have proposed that these early relationship representations carry over into adulthood, particularly in intimate relationships. Early experiences of rejection can lead to rejection sensitivity as an adult.

Research on rejection sensitivity illuminates how insecure attachment may play out in everyday life. Anticipating and fearing rejection influence people's thoughts and feelings, which in turn influence their behavior in social situations.

In general, rejection sensitivity is correlated with low self-esteem. However, rejection sensitivity involves insecurity about relationships with others more than about the doubt about one's worth as an individual.

Evidence and Implications

Research has documented support for the various links of the rejection sensitivity model. Studies of childhood experiences have established that anxious expectations of rejection are associated with exposure to family violence, emotional neglect, harsh discipline, and conditional love by parents. Experiments have shown that anxious expectations of rejection predict a readiness to perceive rejection in others' behavior. Perceiving rejection predicts cognitive, emotional, and behavioral reactions that damage significant relationships and can trigger withdrawal or aggression.

These reactions of hostility and depression may lead to a self-fulfilling prophecy (a prediction that becomes true through its influence on people's thoughts and behavior). This is because rejection-sensitive people perceive rejection in ambiguous situations and overreact to it, making it more likely that their partners will actually reject them. Rejection sensitivity can also hinder people from forming close, meaningful relationships. When combined with other factors, rejection sensitivity may put people at risk for clinical syndromes such as depression, social anxiety, and borderline personality disorder.

Status-Based Rejection

Rejection sensitivity was originally conceptualized as a tendency to believe potential rejection was caused by personal characteristics. Further work has expanded rejection sensitivity research to address rejection based on group membership such as race or gender. If you believe you may be or are rejected because you are a member of a stigmatized minority group, this can affect how you interact with members of the majority group or social institutions such as schools or workplaces. One study showed that for African American students entering a predominantly White college, higher levels of race-based rejection sensitivity were associated with less racially diverse friendships, less trust that the school had their best interests in mind, more anxiety about seeking help from teachers, and lower grades by the end of the year. Similarly, recent evidence suggests that women who are sensitive to being rejected because of their sex may have more trouble coping well in environments that have traditionally been dominated by men, such as math or engineering.

Rejection Sensitivity Measure

The original Rejection Sensitivity Questionnaire (RSQ) assesses anxious interpersonal rejection expectations using 18 scenarios relevant to a college student population. The measure asks participants to imagine themselves in various situations in which they need to ask something of a valued other, such as, "You ask someone you don't know well out on a date." They are then asked to answer the following questions:

How *concerned or anxious* would you be about how the other person would respond?

| Very unconcerned | 1 | 2 | 3 | 4 | 5 | 6 | Very concerned |

How do you think the other person would be likely to respond?

I would expect that the person would want to go out with me.

| Very unlikely | 1 | 2 | 3 | 4 | 5 | 6 | Very likely |

The expectation answer is reverse scored (subtracted from 7) so that higher numbers mean more expectation for rejection. Then for each scenario, the anxiety number and the expectation number are multiplied, and an average is taken across the 18 scenarios. This total RSQ score has a possible range of 1 to 36, with higher numbers indicating greater rejection sensitivity.

The original RSQ has been adapted for an adult population and for group-based rejection sensitivity in the form of the RS-Race questionnaire and the RS-Gender questionnaire. The RS measures can be found at http://www.columbia.edu/cu/psychology/socialrelations/.

Jan Kang
Geraldine Downey

See also Attachment Theory; Individual Differences; Rejection; Social Exclusion

Further Readings

Downey, G., & Feldman, S. (1996). Implications of rejection sensitivity for intimate relationships. *Journal of Personality and Social Psychology, 70,* 1327–1343.

Social Relations Laboratory. Columbia University Department of Psychology. Retrieved April 5, 2007, from http://www.columbia.edu/cu/psychology/socialrelations/

RELATIONAL MODELS THEORY

Definition

The relational models theory describes the four fundamental forms of social relationships: communal sharing, authority ranking, equality matching, and market pricing. People in communal sharing relationships feel that they have something essential in common, whereas outsiders are different. Participants in an authority ranking relationship see themselves as ordered in a legitimate linear hierarchy. In an equality matching relationship, people keep track of whether each separate individual is treated equally. In market pricing, people use ratios or rates, according to some standard of due proportions, such as price. People in all cultures use combinations of these four models to organize nearly all interactions, from close relationships to casual and distant ones. The relational models are innate and intrinsically motivated. But children rely on cultural prototypes and precedents to discover how to implement them in culture-specific ways.

Relational models theory integrates classical theories of social relations and society, and it connects natural selection, neurobiology, child development, cognition, emotion, communication, psychological disorders, norms and ideology, religion, social and political structures, and culture. The theory is supported by ethnographic and comparative cultural studies, and by psychological experiments using a variety of methods. Alan Page Fiske formulated the theory; Nick Haslam did much of the early experimental work on it and developed the theory in relation to clinical psychology and social cognition. Research using relational models theory has provided insights into political psychology, cross-cultural interaction, attitudes toward immigration, behavioral and anthropological economics, the social systems of classical Greece, sociolinguistics, business management, group and family processes, moral judgment, social motives and emotions, gifts and other exchanges, time perspectives, tobacco use, personality disorders, autism, schizophrenia, and vulnerability to other psychological disorders.

Four Relational Models

Communal Sharing

In communal sharing, everyone in a group or dyad is all the same with respect to whatever they are doing: They all share some food, or living space, or responsibility for some work. If one has a problem, it concerns them all. Outsiders treat them as collectively responsible for what they do, punishing any or all of them indiscriminately. Communal relationships involve a sense of oneness and identity, which can be as strong as the connection between mother and child or romantic lovers, or as weak as national or ethic identity. The most intense communal sharing relationships are based on participants' feeling that their bodies are essentially the same or connected because they are linked by birth, blood, appearance, and body marking or modification such as a form of circumcision or excision. Synchronous rhythmic movement can also connect people in this way, for example, in military drill or ritual dance. Sharing food, drink, or substances such as tobacco also underlies communal relationships. So does physical contact, such as caressing, cuddling, kissing, or sleeping close. By making their bodies alike or connected, people create communal relationships, and at the same time communicate the existence and intensity of their relationship. People also think of themselves as the same; their cognitive and emotional representation of the relationship corresponds to the ways they express it. Infants intuitively respond to these expressions of communal sharing, which is how they connect and identify with their families and caretakers.

Authority Ranking

In authority ranking, people are linearly ordered in a proper hierarchy of privileges and responsibilities. Superiors are entitled to deferential respect, but have pastoral responsibility to represent, stand up for, and protect subordinates. In an authority ranking relationship, people think of their superiors as above, greater than, in front of, having more power or force than, and preceding them. Subordinates are perceived as below, lesser than, following behind, weaker than, and coming after. This cognitive representation of social ranking corresponds to the social displays of rank that people use to communicate their relative positions, for example, when a person bows to superiors or waits for them to start eating first. In many languages, people respectfully address or refer to superiors using plural forms and use singular forms when speaking to subordinates (for example, French *vous* vs. *tu*). Children intuitively recognize the meaning of being bigger or higher, being in front, or going first.

Equality Matching

Equality matching is the basis of turn-taking, equal rights, even sharing, voting, decision by coin flip or lottery, and balanced reciprocity whereby people return the same kind of thing they received. This is the universal structure of games and sports, where opponents have equal numbers of players or pieces, employ a fair way to decide who chooses first, play on a symmetrical field or board, take turns, have equal time to play, and often use dice or other devices that add uncertain but equal chances. In an equality matching relationship, the participants may be even or uneven at any given point, but when they are uneven, they know how to even things up again—for example, by taking the next turn. In equality matching, people use concrete matching operations to demonstrate equality, such as starting a race side by side, flipping a coin, or lining up the opposing teams one-to-one. These concrete operations are procedural demonstrations of equality: The actions show that the sides are manifestly equal. Casting ballots is an operational definition of equality in political choice; setting up the two corresponding sets of chess pieces and punching the clock at the end of each move are operational definitions of a fair game. Adhering to these rules makes the game a demonstrably fair and proper game. For children and adults, equality matching is intrinsically important; people get very upset when they have less than their peers.

Market Pricing

Market pricing is a relationship governed by ratios, rates, or proportions. The most obvious examples are prices, wages, rents, taxes, tithes, and interest. But market pricing is also the basis for formal and informal cost–benefit analyses in which people make decisions on the basis of what they are investing in proportion to the returns they can expect to get out. Market pricing

always involves some universal standard by which the values of everything in the relationship can be compared. This need not be money; utilitarianism is the moral philosophy based on giving the greatest good to the greatest number, where all good and evil is compared in a metric of utility. Similarly, grades and grade point averages are the product of ratio-based calculations that combine all aspects of academic performance in a single score. People also measure social ratios in terms of time or effort. Market pricing transactions rely on abstract conventional symbols, such as numbers or linguistic descriptions of the features of an item or the terms of a contract. The arbitrary symbols in a used car ad, for example, are totally unintelligible to anyone unfamiliar with the arbitrary conventions of the specific market system: "2000 Ford Mustang GT 39M, conv, auto, lthr, alrm, Alpine snd syst, BBK air intake, Flowmasters, 18 X 10 Saleen whls, new pnt, body kit & more, slvg, pp, $9,500." The most abstract conventional symbols are prices, which represent the ratios of exchange of all valued features of all commodities in a market system.

Four Ways of Organizing Any Interaction

These four relational models are the components for all kinds of coordinated interactions and social institutions. For example, moral evaluations and sentiments can be based on the communal sense that everyone in the group feels the suffering of everyone else: one for all and all for one. Another form of morality is obedience to superiors such as elders, religious leaders, or gods; conversely, superiors have pastoral responsibilities to protect their flocks. Another moral framework is equality: equal rights, equal opportunities, equal shares, or equal outcomes. Finally, there is justice as proportionality: giving each person what he or she deserves, either punishment in proportion to the crime or reward in proportion to merit. However, the four relational models also structure aggressive, hostile, and violent interactions. When people try to "purify" a group or nation to rid it of others whom they view as inherently different, communal sharing may result in ethnic cleansing and genocide. Acting in an authority ranking system, rulers punish dissidents, kill rebels and traitors, and make war to extend their dominions. Feuding and retaliation typically take the equality matching form of "life for life, eye for eye, tooth for tooth, hand for hand, foot for foot, burning for burning, wound for wound" vengeance. And the planning of modern warfare is often based on kill ratios and other *ratio*nal cost–benefit calculations. The relational models also organize the social meanings of material things. Studies show that the economic value that people place on objects depends on the social relationships that the objects signify. Indeed, objects such as a wedding ring may have virtually infinite economic value—people refuse to sell them. Cultural and historical research shows that land can be held communally, shared by all: a village commons or a park. Land can be a feudal dominion, such that all who reside on it are subjects of the king and the lord of the manor. People may be entitled to equal plots of land, as represented by homesteading laws, or land can also be what makes people equal, as when owning land is a requirement for voting. Or land can be a commodity that people invest in for the rent or appreciation in market value. In virtually every domain of social life in every culture, people use the four relational models to generate their own actions, to understand others' actions, to evaluate or sanction their own and others' actions, and to coordinate joint activities.

Complex, long-term social relationships and institutions are composed of combinations of discrete relational models. For example, a dean has an authority ranking relationship with a professor, who in turn has an authority ranking relationship with students. But the dean should treat professors equitably, and professors should give each student the same opportunities and apply the same standards to all, according to equality matching. Similarly, within each department, faculty may have equal teaching loads. At the same time, students pay tuition and buy textbooks, and professors receive a salary. Yet professors and students have communal access to the library and the Internet services that the university provides; deans, professors, and students also have a shared identification with the university and its teams.

Research on Relational Models

Ample and diverse evidence supports relational models theory, including ethnographic participant observation, ethnologic comparison across cultures, research on naturally occurring social cognition in everyday life, and experimental studies using rating scales and artificial stimuli. One set of studies analyzed social errors when people called someone by the wrong name, directed an action at the wrong person, or misremembered with whom they had interacted. In five cultures, when people make these types of errors, they typically substitute another person with whom they have the same type of relationship. So, for example, I may call Susan, Gwen, because I have communal sharing relationships with each of them. Other studies have shown that people intuitively categorize their own relationships into groups roughly corresponding to the four relational models, and judge any two of their relationships to be most similar when the relationships are organized by the same relational model.

People interacting with each other may use different models without realizing it. When this happens, they are likely to get frustrated or disappointed, and to feel that the others are doing something wrong. For example, if Tom assumes that he and Alesha are doing the dishes in a communal framework, he expects them both to wash dishes whenever they can. But suppose Alesha implicitly assumes that dish washing should be based on equality matching. When Tom is busy and Alesha is not, he will be angry if Alesha fails to do the dishes, but if she sees it as his turn, she'll be angry that he fails to do them. Studies of families, research groups, corporations, and inter-ethnic relations show that mismatching of relational models produces distress and recriminations: Everyone perceives themselves to be acting properly in accord with the relational model *they* are applying, whereas others are transgressing that model. Research also indicates that some people persistently try to apply relational models in ways that are inconsistent with prevalent cultural expectations; this leads to chronic problems associated with personality disorders and vulnerability to other psychological disorders.

Alan Page Fiske

See also Authoritarian Personality; Awe; Communal Relationships; Culture; Deindividuation; Dominance, Evolutionary; Envy; Equity Theory; Ethnocentrism; Exchange Relationships; Group Cohesiveness; Group Identity; Groupthink; Ingroup–Outgroup Bias; Mere Ownership Effect; Milgram's Obedience to Authority Studies; Minimal Group Paradigm; Moral Emotions; Moral Reasoning; Need for Affiliation; Need for Power; Need to Belong; Outgroup Homogeneity; Power; Power Motive; Public Goods Dilemma; Reference Group; Social Dominance Orientation

Further Readings

Fiske, A. P. (1991). *Structures of social life: The four elementary forms of human relations.* New York: Free Press.

Fiske, A. P., & Haslam, N. (2005). The four basic social bonds: Structures for coordinating interaction. In M. Baldwin (Ed.), *Interpersonal cognition* (pp. 267–298). New York: Guilford Press.

Fiske, A. P., Haslam, N., & Fiske, S. (1991). Confusing one person with another: What errors reveal about the elementary forms of social relations. *Journal of Personality and Social Psychology, 60,* 656–674.

Haslam, N. (Ed.). (2004). *Relational models theory: A contemporary overview.* Mahwah, NJ: Erlbaum.

Relational Models Theory. Retrieved April 5, 2007, from http://www.rmt.ucla.edu

RELATIONSHIP VIOLENCE

See INTIMATE PARTNER VIOLENCE

RELIGION AND SPIRITUALITY

Definition

Religion and spirituality refer to a search for the sacred dimension of life. The sacred refers to a transcendent realm of experience, one often seen as including a God or a Higher Power, that addresses existential questions about life's meaning and purpose. Religion refers to socially organized forms of the sacred search. Spirituality refers to a personal side of the sacred search, one that may or may not involve organized religion.

History and Background

Historically, spiritual topics have been neglected within psychology. As a group, psychologists are less religious than is the general population, and many social scientists see religious topics as inappropriate for empirical study. Indeed, with the exception of Gordon Allport's research on religion and prejudice and Daniel Batson's work on religion and helping, most religious topics are just beginning to receive attention within mainstream social psychology.

Socialization and Religious Faith

Social factors are a major predictor of religious belief and practice. Although cultural factors, peer groups, and religious education all predict religious commitment, parental religiosity (by both mothers and fathers) is a particularly strong predictor. Several studies suggest that people's images of God mirror their images of their fathers.

Religious doubts and questions are common, particularly in the adolescent and early adult years. Religious doubts have many sources, including unanswered prayers, hypocrisy by religious leaders, and unresolved questions about the reasons for suffering and evil. Religious doubts often lead to fluctuations in faith. Although there are exceptions, most people who permanently abandon religious faith come from homes where religion was not strongly emphasized.

Religion and Well-Being

During the past decade, many studies from medicine and social science have demonstrated positive associations between religious involvement and health, including both physical and mental health. The association appears to be the result of at least three factors. First, religious involvement often provides a sense of community and ongoing social support. Social support, in turn, predicts better health. Second, most religious belief systems include codes of moral behavior that, if followed, reduce risky health behaviors. For example, most major world religions include prohibitions against sexual promiscuity, poorly controlled anger, and the abuse of alcohol and other drugs. Third, religion and spirituality can provide a sense of meaning or purpose to life while offering answers for deep existential questions. This overarching sense of meaning can help people make decisions, set goals, and find comfort in difficult times. Many people turn to religion as a means of coping with stressful life events, ranging from everyday hassles to bereavement or trauma. The constructive use of religious coping can, in turn, lead to better adjustment.

Followers of virtually all world religions have some means of trying to connect with a sacred or transcendent realm of experience. However, some traditions (typically Western ones) also contend that people can connect with God on a deeply personal level. Studies suggest that when people see themselves as having a loving, close relationship with God, this perception can help to meet attachment needs. Yet, it cannot be assumed that this relationship will always be positive. Many people have negative images of God, viewing God as cruel, uncaring, punitive, or untrustworthy. In the wake of negative life events, people often become angry toward God. They may also have difficulty trusting God, believing that God is punishing, rejecting, or abandoning them. These negative feelings toward God can lead to crises of faith. Studies are now beginning to use frameworks from social psychological research to explore the dynamics of people's perceived relationships with God, including the potential for both intimacy and conflict.

Religion and Social Behavior

In social terms, several sources of evidence demonstrate that religious involvement leads to higher levels of altruistic giving and volunteerism. In addition, most religions include a code of moral behavior that focuses on helping and serving others. Religious institutions can be a powerful source of socialization, meaning that people who are strongly committed to a particular religious system are likely to internalize its moral principles. For example, research has demonstrated a consistent connection between religiosity and the value assigned to humility and forgiveness. Yet, as demonstrated across many areas of psychology, the translation from values and principles to actual behavior tends to be imperfect. Therefore, although highly religious people may be especially likely to believe that they should be kind, helpful, or forgiving, they often behave similarly to nonreligious people in controlled laboratory situations. Other personality factors, such as agreeableness or dispositional guilt, may be better predictors of social behavior than religiosity.

As described earlier, religious systems provide meaning systems for answering existential questions. These meaning systems can be helpful in psychological terms. However, believing that one's beliefs are rooted in divine revelation can also promote conflict with groups who hold different beliefs. As such, strongly held religious identities can foster ingroup–outgroup thinking and negative attitudes toward other groups, particularly when people are convinced that their group possesses the only correct view. For example, some studies suggest a positive link between religious fundamentalism and prejudice. The evidence is mixed, however, and depends partly on how prejudice is framed. Fundamentalists and highly religious persons sometimes appear prejudiced because they express disapproval of behaviors that violate their religious beliefs (e.g., drug abuse; certain sexual behaviors). However, this behavioral disapproval does not necessarily translate to prejudice on nonbehavioral domains such as race. A much clearer association has emerged between prejudice and right-wing authoritarianism—a tendency toward rigidity, conventionality, and unquestioning obedience toward authority. Although right-wing authoritarians tend to score high on fundamentalism measures, it seems to be authoritarianism— rather than religiosity or fundamentalism per se—that predicts prejudice.

Julie Exline

See also Beliefs; Prejudice; Search for Meaning in Life; Values

Further Readings

Hill, P. C., & Pargament, K. I. (2003). Advances in the conceptualization and measurement of religion and spirituality. *American Psychologist, 58,* 64–74.

Spilka, B., Hood, R. W., Jr., Hunsberger, B., & Gorsuch, R. (2003). *The psychology of religion: An empirical approach* (3rd ed.). New York: Guilford Press.

REPRESENTATIVENESS HEURISTIC

Definition

According to some social psychologists, human beings have the tendency to be cognitive misers—that is, to limit their use of mental resources when they need to make a quick decision or when the issue about which they must make a decision is unimportant to them. People have several strategies they can use to limit their use of mental resources; one such group of strategies is heuristics. Heuristics are cognitive shortcuts or rules of thumb that are used when one must make a decision but lacks either ample time or the accurate information necessary to make the decision. Heuristics are advantageous in that they aid in quick decision making, but the use of heuristics can lead to inaccurate predictions. In general, heuristics are automatic cognitive processes; that is, people use them in decision-making situations without necessarily being aware that they are doing so.

One common heuristic is the representativeness heuristic, a rule of thumb used to determine whether a person or an event should be put into a certain category by judging how similar the person or event is to the prototypical person or event of that category. The prototypical person or event of a given category is the one that possesses the highest number of representative characteristics of that category; for example, the prototypical chair might have four legs, a seat, and some sort of back. If the person or event one is judging is similar to the prototype, then the person or event is likely to be placed in that category. If there is no similarity to the prototype, then the person or event may be judged as unlikely to be a member of the category. For example, in a freshman psychology course, Andrew meets Anne. Andrew notices that Anne is petite, blonde, and very outgoing. Andrew tells his friend Jeff that he met Anne in class, and Jeff asks if Andrew met Anne the cheerleader or Anne the biology major. Andrew matches the petite, blonde, outgoing Anne he met to prototypes from the categories "cheerleader" and "biology major" and matches Anne to the "cheerleader" category because the prototypical cheerleader is petite, blonde, and outgoing. Because she fits the prototype of one category, Andrew may quickly categorize her and subsequently ignore information that would lead him to place Anne more accurately. Conversely, Andrew meets Heidi, who is tall, has short dark hair, and wears glasses. Because Heidi does not match the prototype of "cheerleader," Andrew will likely assume that Heidi is not a cheerleader and may ignore evidence that indicates that she is a cheerleader.

Representativeness Heuristic and Decision Making

The representativeness heuristic can hinder accurate judgments of probability by emphasizing aspects of the event in question that are similar to the prototype or by masking other diagnostic information that demonstrates the event's dissimilarity to the prototype. For example, in the previous Andrew and Anne scenario, Andrew assumes Anne is a cheerleader because she closely matches his prototype of that category. However, Andrew has ignored important information that might cause him to make a different judgment of Anne; in particular, he has ignored base rates, or the rate at which any one type of person or event occurs in the population at large. At any given university, the number of cheerleaders is typically quite small. On the other hand, the number of biology majors at any given university is much larger than the number of cheerleaders. If Andrew had used base rates instead of the representativeness heuristic as a basis for determining category membership, it is far more likely that he would determine that Anne is a biology major

rather than a cheerleader. This example demonstrates the danger of relying on the representativeness heuristic when making decisions about category membership because the desire to use cognitive shortcuts may supersede the desire to seek accurate and complete information. Andrew's dismissal of Heidi as a cheerleader is equally erroneous; it is just as likely that Heidi is a cheerleader as it is that Anne is a cheerleader, but because she does not appear to represent the cheerleader category, Andrew is unlikely to judge that she belongs to that category.

Representativeness Heuristic and Social Psychology

The representativeness heuristic is typically mentioned in the contexts of social cognition (the way people think about the people and situations with which they interact) and categorization (the process of classifying people and events based on their prominent attributes).

Jennifer A. Clarke

See also Base Rate Fallacy; Decision Making; Fast and Frugal Heuristics; Heuristic Processing; Illusory Correlation; Prototypes; Social Cognition

Further Readings

Kahneman, D., & Tversky, A. (1972). Subjective probability: A judgment of representativeness. *Cognitive Psychology, 3,* 430–454.

Kahneman, D., & Tversky, A. (1982). On the psychology of prediction. In D. Kahneman, P. Slovic, & A. Tversky (Eds.), *Judgment under uncertainty: Heuristics and biases.* New York: Cambridge University Press.

Tversky, A., & Kahneman, D. (1993). Probabilistic reasoning. In A. I. Goldman (Ed.), *Readings in philosophy and cognitive science.* Cambridge: MIT Press.

RESEARCH METHODS

Definition

Research methods are the ways in which researchers measure variables and design studies to test hypotheses. For example, if a researcher wants to study whether people in a happy mood are more likely to offer help to a stranger than are people who are not happy, the researcher might measure or manipulate how research participants feel and then measure how likely people are to offer help.

Overview

Researchers can choose among many different ways to measure variables. They can directly observe people's behaviors, directly ask people for their perceptions, or infer people's perceptions on the basis of behaviors or responses that only indirectly relate to the variables of interest. In most areas of social psychology, researchers want to learn what causes the phenomenon of interest (in the example, whether differences in mood causes differences in helping). Thus, whenever possible, researchers seek to manipulate variables of interest (e.g., mood) in an effort to make confident claims about causes (e.g., happy mood causing larger amounts of helping). Of course, for some variables or in some settings, the researcher cannot or chooses not to manipulate variables but instead looks at the relations between presumed cause and effect variables (such as mood and helping, respectively, in the example).

Measurement techniques will be discussed first and then research designs. Social psychologists commonly use a variety of measurement techniques including self-report, behavioral observation, response latency (time to answer), and physiological measures. Each type of measure has its strengths and limitations, but the extent to which one can draw conclusions from measured data is also a function of the type of research design employed. Social psychological research designs can be broadly classified into experimental and non-experimental research methods. Nonexperimental approaches are well-suited for identifying associations among variables; however, these approaches are less well-suited to determining cause-and-effect relations. However, experimental designs can demonstrate causal relations because of random assignment to conditions and greater control over variables that may covary (go along) with the cause variables under study.

Measurement Techniques

Whenever possible, researchers try to collect supporting evidence using more than one type of measure. By doing this, the strengths of some measures can offset the weaknesses of other measures. Researchers often have greater confidence in the research conclusions when a particular theory can be supported by more than one type of measure.

Self-Reports

Self-reports are perhaps the most widely used measurement technique in social psychology. Self-report measures ask people to directly report their feelings, behaviors, or thoughts. In some cases, self-report questions may require open-ended responses (e.g., "What is your current mood state?"). Other types of self-reports may require people to respond according to a provided scale (e.g., "Please rate your current mood state." 1 = negative mood to 7 = positive mood). Using a set of items that all tap into the variable of interest (e.g., asking people to rate mood on measures of how negative/positive, bad/good, and unpleasant/pleasant their mood is) generally provides a better measure than using only a single item (e.g., only the negative/positive question). The primary advantage of self-report measures is that variables of interest can be directly measured from the source of those experiences.

However, at times, people may not be able or willing to provide accurate reports. When this is true, data collected from self-reports may be inaccurate or misleading. In some cases, for example, the validity of self-reports may depend on respondents' verbal abilities. Self-report data from children or those who have cognitive deficits may be inaccurate because of an inability to understand the questions or express responses. Even when ability to accurately report is not in question, people may not be willing to express their true feelings, thoughts, and behaviors. For example, when asked about socially undesirable opinions or behaviors, people may be inclined to respond in ways that make them look good to themselves and others (i.e., social desirability bias). Thus, when there are concerns that research participants might lie on self-reports (e.g., when addressing socially sensitive issues such as stereotyping, prejudice, or aggression), other forms of measurement may provide especially useful information.

Behavioral Measures

Behavioral measurement consists of observing and recording people's actions. Social psychologists typically measure a particular behavior(s) (e.g., smiling) because the behavior directly relates to a variable of interest (e.g., mood). Unlike self-reports, one advantage of behavioral measures is that assessment can occur without participants realizing that the measurement is taking place. Thus, researchers might be able to assess reactions that research participants would not willingly share.

However, one limitation of behavioral measurement is that researchers must infer the reasons for the behavior. For example, imagine a study of opinions toward consumer products where participants are asked to choose one product (from several) that they can take from the study. If a participant selects one product rather than another, this could indicate that he or she has a more positive opinion of the chosen product, but this choice could have also been made for other reasons unrelated to his or her opinion (e.g., taking it to give to a friend). Another possible limitation of behavioral measures (and of some self-reports) is that behaviors are often situation-specific. That is, the behavior may occur in one situation, but not in another similar situation. In most social psychological studies, people's behaviors are assessed in only a single situation. Therefore, the behavior-based assessment of the variable might not reflect a general perception that would work across circumstances; it may reflect a more limited tendency to act a certain way in a certain circumstance.

Response Latency

Researchers may often be able to make inferences about psychological variables based on how quickly or slowly people make responses. More often than not, computers are used to present words or pictures on screen, and the computer records how quickly people respond to the word or picture (e.g., pronouncing the word, naming the pictured object, or evaluating the object). When speed of response is important, responses often take the form of hitting one of two computer keys as quickly but accurately as possible. One common use of response time is to index whether people have recently been thinking about a concept related to the word or picture on the computer screen. For example, imagine that a researcher believes people are likely to spontaneously think about the concept of race in a certain circumstance. If so, reaction time to label a pictured person as belonging to one racial category or another might be faster in that condition than would the same reactions to the same picture in a condition where previous consideration of race is unlikely.

Like behavioral measures, reaction times may be less susceptible than self-reports are to participant control over socially undesirable responding. Because response times often differ across conditions in very small amounts (fractions of seconds), participants may not even realize that they are responding more quickly to some stimuli than to others, and they may be even less likely to identify any such differences as reflecting the conceptual relations between certain conditions of the study and the critical responses to the specific words or pictures. Like behavioral measures, however, the researcher must infer the meaning of relatively fast or slow responses. Research participants can take time to engage in many different psychological processes. If a number of different processes would make people take longer to respond, then long response times alone may not help the researcher to distinguish among those potential thought processes. This may be especially true when time measures are taken for engaging in an activity such as reading information, rather than responding to a question. People can take a long rather than short time to read a passage for many different reasons. Thus, measures of time taken to read (or, in some cases, respond) may require additional measures or manipulations to help characterize why the additional time was taken.

Physiological Measures

Social psychologists (and perhaps especially social neuroscientists) may use a variety of measures that assess physiological responses to social stimuli. These measures include those that assess brain or muscle activity, activation of the autonomic nervous system, and others. For example, even if observers cannot see that a participant is smiling, electrical activity may be greater in the smiling muscles when the person is listening to information with which they agree rather than disagree.

Physiological responses are often involuntary or not under people's conscious control. Therefore, concerns about people's inability or unwillingness to respond in a certain way are minimal. Thus, like behavioral and response latency measures, physiological measures can be useful when measuring reactions to socially sensitive material. Disadvantages include the time and expense involved in taking physiological measures. Even relatively minimal physiological recording equipment is expensive, and more advanced physiological measures (especially scanning techniques) involve very expensive equipment. Most physiological measures are also especially sensitive to participant movements during the study and to the environment in which the measurements are taken. Thus, relatively long periods are taken to acquaint participants with the recording equipment and to get baseline measures (to control for individual differences in baseline activation of the systems under study). In addition, limitations in movement for many physiological measures restrict the kinds of interactions in which research participants can engage while physiological recording occurs. Finally, much remains to be learned about how various patterns of physiological reaction relate to particular psychological processes and variables. Many physiological systems become active during more than one type of psychological process. Therefore, in many circumstances, there may not be a one-to-one mapping of activation of a particular brain area or a particular system with one particular psychological process or outcome. This can make inferences based on physiological measures quite complex when compared with other types of measurement.

Research Designs

Experimental Design

Experiments are perhaps the most prominent research approach used in social psychology. Experiments offer many advantages over nonexperimental approaches. In particular, because experiments control extraneous variables through random assignment to conditions, they allow researchers to confidently determine cause-and-effect relations. Random assignment is the procedure of assigning research participants to different experimental groups such that each participant has an equal chance of being assigned to any experimental condition. This is important because researchers can be assured that the background characteristics of the participants in each group are equivalent before a manipulation is applied. For example, let's return to our example of a study of mood and helping. Some people may simply be more likely to offer help to a stranger. Yet, if each person has an equal chance of being assigned to a happy mood group or a neutral mood group, then personal tendencies to offer help should be equal across the groups before any mood manipulation takes place. Later, if

there are differences in helping across mood groups, this difference cannot be attributed to differences across groups in the background tendencies of the people in each group; the differences must have been created by the manipulation.

Even though experimental designs offer many advantages, they do have limitations. For instance, experimentation cannot be performed when variables such as gender, personality traits, or ethnicity are under study because these variables cannot be manipulated. Also, many possible manipulations of variables such as ethnic prejudice, marital status, and physical aggression would not be undertaken because of ethical concerns. Therefore, research addressing influences of variables such as these must be conducted nonexperimentally.

Another potential issue with experimental designs concerns to the extent to which findings can generalize to real life. Increases in experimental control can result in increased artificiality of the experimental setting. This is less of an issue when the goal of the study is to test psychological theory rather than to produce results that are relevant to a particular applied setting. For instance, a researcher may believe that ethnic categories are activated when people encounter group members as they walk down a hallway. Yet, it may be much more straightforward to show such activation in a laboratory showing pictures or video on a computer screen. However, all else being equal, researchers would often prefer that their research findings (or at least the psychological processes that produced the findings) would translate to real world settings. Researchers can increase the likelihood of their results translating to real world contexts by using experimental activities that closely reflect similar activities in everyday life, by showing that the research findings are the same across different kinds of manipulations and measures, or by conducting field research that shows parallel effects without the same level of experimental control over extraneous variables.

Nonexperimental Design

Although experimentation is the primary way to determine causal relations among variables, a nonexperimental design may be more appropriate for some research questions. Some research questions do not involve cause and effect. For example, when a researcher is developing a multi-item measure of a particular concept or idea, the researcher may only be interested in identifying the presence of relations among those items, not causal relations. Even when researchers are interested in cause and effect, some variables cannot be experimentally manipulated (e.g., gender, personality traits) or manipulation would not be ethical (e.g., marital status, physical aggression). When this is the case, nonexperimental research is the best that researchers can do. In addressing cause and effect relations, however, nonexperimental approaches face a number of challenges.

Consider nonexperimental investigation of the question of whether people are more likely to offer help while in happy moods. For example, participants could be asked to complete diaries in which they report their moods and their major activities each day for a month or more. It could be, in such a study, that people who report being generally happy also more often report helping others. One of the problems with non-experimental designs is that causes might often occur in either direction (i.e., happy mood could increase helping, or increased helping could create happy mood). Even when this is not as likely (e.g., if mood were measured before a specific opportunity to help, so the helping opportunity itself cannot be the source of the mood), a measurement of the independent variable (mood) might identify people who are also disposed to help for reasons other than their mood per se. For example, the people who report being happy at a particular point in time may be happy because of positive events in their lives (e.g., getting a raise at work), and those positive events themselves may make helping more likely separate from mood (e.g., by making people feel like they have an excess of resources, so they can afford to share). At times, the researcher can measure potential alternative reasons for the effects or can include measurements over time that make a stronger case for the preferred explanation. However, these solutions are often less compelling than running an experiment in which random assignment to conditions equate the conditions on variables not influenced by the manipulation of interest.

Duane T. Wegener
Jason K. Clark

See also Control Condition; Ecological Validity; Experimental Condition; Experimentation; Nonexperimental Designs; Quasi-Experimental Designs; Self-Reports; Social Desirability Bias; Social Neuroscience

Further Readings

Pelham, B. W., & Blanton, H. (2003). *Conducting research in psychology: Measuring the weight of smoke* (2nd ed.). Toronto: Thompson/Wadsworth.

Reis, H. T., & Judd, C. M. (Eds.). (2000). *Handbook of research methods in social and personality psychology.* New York: Cambridge University Press.

Sansone, C., Morf, C. C., & Painter, A. T. (Eds.). (2004). *The Sage handbook of methods in social psychology.* Thousand Oaks, CA: Sage.

RESISTING PERSUASION

Resistance is central to persuasion. Without resistance, persuasion is not necessary. Resistance to persuasion can be desirable, for example, when non-smokers repeatedly resist advertisements and peer pressure encouraging them to smoke. But resistance can also be an undesirable characteristic, as when smokers resist the many strong messages encouraging them to stop smoking and prolong their lives.

Effective resistance can be used to ward off unwanted persuasion, but inappropriate resistance can close a person off to meaningful changes. Skepticism, reactance, and inertia are three kinds of resistance that work in different way to limit persuasion. People can do many things to increase or to decrease their own or other people's resistance to persuasion.

Three Kinds of Resistance

Resistance to persuasion is not just one single thing. One encounters three kinds of resistance: skepticism, reactance, and inertia.

Skepticism is resistance to the content of the message. Skepticism focuses on the logic and evidence of the arguments in the message, and produces a desire to critically evaluate and refute those arguments.

Reactance refers to the negative reaction people have to someone else telling them what to think or do. Reactance is resistance to the influence attempt itself. The contrariness produced by reactance leads people to counter the persuasion, no matter what it advocates, and to reestablish their freedom to think by choosing the opposite.

Inertia is an objection to change itself, no matter which change is advocated. With inertia, people don't pay attention to the message. They aren't interested in the change. They just want to keep things the way they are.

Increasing Resistance to Persuasion

Sometimes it is advisable to increase one's own resistance or someone else's resistance to unwanted persuasion. Skepticism can be strengthened by (a) increasing a person's motivation to examine the message and (b) assembling information and tools to effectively evaluate a message. Realizing that persuasion is coming will energize both aspects of skepticism. Also, considering the ways this topic is personally important will increase the energy available to critically and carefully think through a message or proposal.

Reactance can be increased by focusing on how the persuasion is manipulative and aimed at limiting freedom. Reactance is stronger when the unwanted influence is directed toward more important values and actions, and when the unwanted influence is more intrusive and offensive. Thoughts that emphasize these aspects of the influence increase the reactance form of resistance.

Inertial resistance can be strengthened by focusing on the current situation, particularly on what is liked about the present situation, and how difficult it would be to change. The nonsmoker who makes a mental list of the top five things to like about being a nonsmoker is bolstering inertia.

Decreasing Resistance to Persuasion

There are times when a person meets resistance, even his or her own resistance to a proposal, and feels that it is baseless and that it prevents a recommendation or change from being realistically considered. In these cases, it may be useful for the person to think of ways to minimize or reduce resistance. Most people think first to overwhelm resistance with debate, explaining why resistance is unreasonable or unnecessary. This tactic rarely works, and most often creates reactance. But some more subtle and effective ways do allow resistance to be minimized.

Skepticism is usually a good quality, but it can be overused and get in the way of making good decisions. A subtle way to diminish skepticism is to provide a guarantee, which eliminates the need for skepticism and scrutiny by assuring that a bad outcome will be repaired. When a guarantee is not feasible, asking the person (or yourself) to consider the proposal for the future—for example, "What if next year at this time you were a nonsmoker?"—can reduce skepticism. Assessing a proposal for the future (next week, next month, next year) diminishes the influence of the costs and allows the benefits to be considered more clearly.

Framing proposals differently can also greatly affect how the request is considered. Listen to these two ways of framing a request and their respective result: Pat asked her father if she could watch TV while she did homework, and he said "Certainly not!" Pat's sister asked her father if she could do homework while she watched TV, and he said, "That would be great!" Framing this case as a request about changing TV watching was much more effective than framing it as a request about how one does homework.

Reactance can be lessened by minimizing the pushiness or offensiveness of the request. This can be done by making a smaller request, which might be followed later by a larger one. Reactance can also be diminished by making the request politely. Saying, "I know that you might not want to, but would you . . ." rather than simply saying "Would you . . ." increases persuasion dramatically. Another way to minimize reactance is to put the message into a story about someone who acted in a certain way and achieved a certain result. A story sidesteps reactance because the message is not, "you should . . . ," but "Jesse did and it worked for her." With stories, people are interested in what happened next, without analyzing or contesting what happened they way they would with a direct message.

The interesting problem with inertia is that this form of resistance is unresponsive to persuasion. It is the tuning out of persuasive messages. So, to reduce inertia, one has to do something to make the person tune in to the message. Many television ads are designed on the principle that they first have to capture the audience members' attention before they can hear the message. Bright lights, loud sounds, humor, confusing beginnings, and unexpected events are all ways that advertisements use to overcome inertia.

Eric S. Knowles
Jessica M. Nolan
Dan D Riner

See also Compliance; Influence; Persuasion; Reactance

Further Readings

Ahluwalia, R. (2000). Examination of psychological processes underlying resistance to persuasion. *Journal of Consumer Research, 27*(2), 217–232.

Hogan, K. (2004). *The science of influence.* New York: Wiley.

Knowles, E. S., & Linn, J. A. (2004). The future and promise of resistance to persuasion. In E. S. Knowles & J. A. Linn (Eds.), *Resistance and persuasion* (Chap. 15). Mahwah, NJ: Erlbaum.

Knowles, E. S., & Riner, D. (2007). Omega approaches to persuasion: Overcoming resistance. In A. R. Pratkanis (Ed.), *The science of social influence* (Chap. 2). New York: Psychology Press.

RESPONSIBILITY ATTRIBUTION

A responsibility attribution relates to beliefs about the cause of an event, or outcome, or state. The event in question may be positive (success) or negative, but responsibility is used more in association with aversive outcomes. Hence, a responsibility attribution is linked with terms such as *fault* and *blame,* with the individual held accountable for an unwanted experience. In addition, a responsibility attribution may apply to the self or to others. This entry focuses on social perception and judgments about others, rather than on self-perception.

Responsibility attributions are of central importance in studies of thinking, feeling, and behavior (motivation). Social psychologists therefore have devoted much attention to this topic, and that interest remains central.

How Does One Know If Another Is Responsible?

If an earthquake leveled a house, then it is unlikely that a particular individual will be held responsible. A responsibility attribution presumes that a person brought about the outcome. But responsibility implies more than an attribution to a person. It also embraces a guilty mind and the belief that it could have been otherwise. Hence, although effort and ability are person characteristics, lack of effort resulting in failure elicits judgments of responsibility, whereas this is not the case given lack of aptitude as the cause, which is presumed not to be subject to volitional control and

change. In a similar manner, obesity caused by love of eating or HIV/AIDS caused by promiscuous sexual behavior gives rise to responsibility ascriptions, whereas obesity because of a thyroid disorder or HIV/AIDS traced to a transfusion with contaminated blood results in beliefs of nonresponsibility. The former are "sinners," the latter are "sick."

These can be difficult judgments, prone to influence by biases and affected by a variety of information. For example, situational causes of behavior tend to be underestimated in comparison with personal causes, so that an individual may be blamed for a car accident on a rainy day because the severity of the road conditions is underestimated (what is called *discounting*).

Judgments of responsibility embrace complex issues at the intersection of law, philosophy, and psychology, and scholars with these interests often pose odd dilemmas to tease apart the essence of responsibility. Consider the following: Robber #1 is about to rob a bank when Robber #2 enters that bank, holds a gun to the head of Robber #1, and demands that he help rob the bank or else he will be shot. Is Robber #1 responsible for the robbery? Similarly, when a severely abused woman intentionally kills her abusive spouse when he is asleep, is she fully responsible for this action? Judgments of responsibility are lessened given mitigating circumstances, such as mental state at the time of the behavior. Hence, the abused spouse is likely to receive a more lenient sentence than is one who has not been victimized.

Consequences of Responsibility Beliefs

Responsibility attributions affect emotions. Some psychologists contend that feeling is directly determined by thinking, that is, what is thought determines what is felt. The task for this group of emotion theorists is to specify the key thoughts linked with emotions and identify the feelings they generate. Perceived responsibility for an aversive event gives rise to anger and related emotions such as annoyance. For example, you are mad when a roommate fails to clean up the kitchen or when a friend misses an appointment. Furthermore, the greater the perceived responsibility is, the more intense the anger is. Hence, an intentionally missed appointment gives rise to greater anger than does one forgotten (an unintentional cause revealing a less guilty mind). On the other hand, nonresponsibility for a negative event or state gives rise to sympathy and pity. People feel sorry for the mentally handicapped person who cannot complete an academic task and for the physically handicapped individual who cannot compete in an athletic event. Thus, responsibility judgments provide one key to thinking–feeling linkages.

In addition, responsibility judgments and their linked feelings give rise to important behavioral reactions. For example, charity is more likely to be endorsed for those considered not responsible for their plights. Hence, it is easier to solicit financial assistance for the blind than for drug abusers. This is one reason why so many have contributed charity to those suffering from hurricane damage in New Orleans and other southern cities. Similarly, welfare payments are denounced by individuals who see these recipients as lazy rather than unemployed because of harsh economic conditions. Political ideology affects these judgments and how the political parties perceive one another and themselves. Democrats (liberals) accuse Republicans (conservatives) of holding others responsible when this is not the case—for example, blaming those in need of welfare for being lazy, when their poverty is caused by the minimum wage being too low or by some other uncontrollable factor. Conversely, Republicans accuse Democrats of being bleeding hearts, giving out public funds to those who are truly responsible for their plights, and not differentiating between the deserving and the undeserving needy. There are kernels of truth in both positions, but of greater importance here is that this debate illustrates the central role responsibility beliefs play in political life.

Responsibility attributions and their consequences are pervasive in other aspects of everyday life as well. For example, teachers and parents are likely to punish failure because of lack of studying but not if this failure is attributed to lack of aptitude; spouses in distressed marriages are more likely to fault their partners for aversive events than are partners in successful marriages; caregivers blame the mentally ill more for passive symptoms (e.g., apathy) than for active symptoms (e.g., hallucinations); and on and on. Thus, responsibility judgments and their linked affects loom large in people's lives.

Altering Responsibility Beliefs

Inasmuch as being held responsible for a negative event has great personal costs, individuals strive to reduce such judgments. Impression management techniques are available to meet this goal, including denial of the

event; providing an excuse (ex = from, cuse = cause) that is external to the person or uncontrollable ("I am late because the subway broke down"), giving a justification so that the punishable behavior is regarded as serving a higher goal ("I missed the appointment to take my mother to the hospital"), or confessing, which has the paradoxical effect of maintaining responsibility yet reducing punishment. This is likely because the act and the actor are separated—the confessor is perceived as a good person who happened to perform a bad act.

Bernard Weiner

See also Attributions; Excuse; Fundamental Attribution Error; Person Perception; Self-Serving Bias

Further Readings

Malle, B. (2004). *How the mind explains behavior.* Cambridge: MIT Press.
Weiner, B. (1995). *Judgments of responsibility.* New York: Guilford Press.
Weiner, B. (2006). *Social motivation, justice, and the moral emotions.* Mahwah, NJ: Erlbaum.

RINGELMANN EFFECT

Definition

The Ringelmann effect refers to individuals expending less individual effort on a task when working as part of a group than when working alone.

Background and History

Max Ringelmann was a French agricultural engineer who was interested in examining various aspects related to agricultural efficiency. He was primarily interested in conditions under which draft animals such as horses and oxen—and men—are more or less efficient in their work performance. Ringelmann's research represents some of the earliest systematic social psychological research. Because he was also interested in the process by which animals and men could be more efficient, his research also represents some of the earliest known human factors research. Actually, the human factors aspect of his research represented the primary focus of his research, whereas comparisons of individual and group performance were only a secondary interest at the time of his original research.

In some of his preliminary research, Ringelmann had male participants pull horizontally on a rope for approximately 5 seconds. Participants pulled on a rope individually, in groups of 7, or in groups of 14. During this time, their maximum pulling effort was recorded via a dynamometer (a device that measures maximum force exerted). Those participants who pulled alone exerted a mean force of 85.3 kg per person. When participants pulled in 7- and 14-person groups, the mean force exerted per person was 65.0 kg and 61.4 kg, respectively. Thus, as group size increased, the average force exerted per individual decreased. Ringelmann found similar results when participants were asked to push a crossbar connected to a two-wheeled cart. When participants pushed alone they exerted more force (170.8 kg), on average, than when they pushed together with another person (154.1 kg).

Some of Ringelmann's most cited findings involve examining relative group performance as a function of group size in groups ranging in size from one to eight participants. Similar to his research mentioned previously, individual effort decreased as a function of group size. For example, assuming that the total force exerted for one worker was 1.00, the force exerted for two through eight workers was 1.86, 2.55, 3.08, 3.50, 3.78, 3.92, and 3.92, respectively, indicating a curvilinear relation among group size and group performance. That is, as group size increased, the total force exerted for the group decreased but the difference between two- and three-person groups was greater than the difference between four- and five-person groups and the difference between seven- and eight-person groups was still smaller. Interestingly, Ringelmann did not clearly specify what types of tasks these data were based on. They may or may not come from research specific to rope pulling as is often assumed.

Ringelmann acknowledged two potential reasons underlying this decrement of individual performance when working in groups. The first was that the effect was caused by coordination losses. For example, two people pulling on a rope would be more coordinated in their pulling (more likely to be in sync in their pulling) than would a group of seven or eight people putting together. For Ringelmann, this was the most likely explanation. Nonetheless, he also acknowledged the fact that such an effect might be the result of decreased motivation. For example, with more people pulling on a rope, individuals may feel that the work of their coworkers will be enough to successfully accomplish the task at hand, thus individual effort decreases as the result. Others did not attempt to disentangle the mystery of the Ringelmann effect until nearly a century after Ringelmann's original work.

Contemporary Research

Until the mid-1970s, researchers cited Ringelmann's work, but no one had attempted to replicate his findings. Then in 1974, researchers sought to better understand the Ringelmann effect. Is this effect real? Would similar findings emerge if Ringelmann's research had been conducted in a controlled laboratory environment? Are the effects Ringelmann obtained primarily because of coordination losses involved with working together on a task? Alternatively, can Ringelmann's data be explained primarily through other mechanisms such as decreased individual motivation?

Similar to Ringelmann's original research, more contemporary findings indicate that individual effort does decrease as a function of group size. These findings have been replicated using a number of different group sizes and a number of different tasks (clapping, shouting, brainstorming, job evaluation, etc.), including one of Ringelmann's original tasks, rope pulling. Moreover, both reduced motivation and coordination losses contribute to decreased group performance on a task, with coordination playing a bigger role as group size increases. At least two possible causes have been suggested to account for decreased motivation. The first is that as group size increases so does an individual's belief that other group members will be able to successfully accomplish the task at hand, thus leading to decreased effort (i.e., motivation). This is referred to as the free-rider effect. A second explanation for motivation decrements concerns the perception that other group members are not putting forth their best effort. As a result, an individual will reduce his or her effort, compared with when the individual is working alone, so as not to appear as a sucker (i.e., the sucker effect). This research also led to a change in terminology used to describe this effect; the original Ringelmann effect was replaced with a term that more aptly describes this phenomenon, *social loafing*. When working on a task as part of a group, many times people are apt to loaf or work less hard than they would if working alone.

Since the reemergence of research in this area, several variables have been found to moderate or mediate the extent to which individuals will tend to loaf while performing a group task. A few of these variables are identifiability, personal relevance, group cohesiveness, and task interdependence. For example, individuals are less likely to decrease their individual effort within a group if they believe their individual effort is identifiable, the group task has some personal relevance for the individual (i.e., is important), the group is more cohesive or tight-knit, and successful completion of a task depends on the effort of all group members.

Robert Thomas Hitlan

See also Group Dynamics; Group Performance and Productivity; Social Loafing

Further Readings

Ingham, A. G., Levinger, G., Graves, J., & Peckham, V. (1974). Ringelmann effect: Studies of group size and group performance. *Journal of Experimental Social Psychology, 10,* 371–384.

Karau, S. J., & Williams, K. D. (1993). Social loafing: A meta-analytic review and theoretical integration. *Journal of Personality and Social Psychology, 65,* 681–706.

Kravitz, D. A., Martin, B. (1986). Ringelmann rediscovered: The original article. *Journal of Personality and Social Psychology, 50,* 936–941.

RISK APPRAISAL

Definition

The term *risk appraisal* refers to an evaluation of the chances that a future event may occur. Similar terms include *risk assessment, risk perception, perceived likelihood,* and *perception of vulnerability.* One might appraise the risk of globally significant events (e.g., terrorism, natural disasters) as well as those that are personally relevant (e.g., losing a child, developing a disease). People's beliefs about risk influence a wide variety of decisions and behaviors in many life domains including careers, relationships, and health. As examples, college students are relatively less likely to choose careers in which the chances of getting a job are low, and women are unlikely to get mammographies if they do not feel at risk for breast cancer. If risk appraisals are incorrect, they may lead to faulty decision making and counterproductive behavior, necessitating the development of strategies to correct these appraisals. Laypeople evaluate risk very differently than experts do, and such differences can have public policy implications.

Measurement

A common method of assessing perceptions of risk is to ask individuals whether an event will or will not happen, or have them estimate the chances it will happen on a percentage (0%–100%) scale. One problem with the latter approach is that people often have difficulty thinking about risk in numerical terms and think about probabilities differently than experts do. For example, when people estimate that an event has a 50% chance of happening, what they really mean is that it might or might not happen and they are not sure. Several other numerical measures attempt to minimize this problem, such as a magnifier scale in which the lower end of a percentage scale (between 0% and 1%) is divided into smaller units to encourage respondents to use this part of the scale for rare events. Another approach is to have individuals make relative judgments, such as how the risk of one event compares with that of another (e.g., having cancer vs. having heart disease) or how one person's risk compares with that of another person or persons. Still another is to use a verbal scale (ranging, for example, from "very unlikely" to "very likely"). Any of these measures can be designed to be conditional on some behavior (e.g., "If you continue to smoke, what are your chances of getting lung cancer?"). Affective risk appraisals such as worry or the feeling that something will happen can also be assessed.

The choice of measures can greatly influence the findings of a given study. For example, people's verbal risk appraisals are more sensitive to new information than are their numerical risk appraisals, and people may be pessimistically biased regarding their absolute risk of an event yet optimistically biased about their risk relative to that of their peers. Affective perceptions of vulnerability (e.g., "feeling at risk") are sometimes more predictive of behaviors such as vaccination than are cognitive perceptions of vulnerability.

Errors in Risk Appraisal

People often make errors when appraising their risk. They tend to overestimate small risks and underestimate large risks, and perceive positive events as more likely to occur than negative events. A disproportionate number of individuals consider their level of personal risk to be lower than that of their peers, a bias called *unrealistic optimism*. People also tend to overestimate the risk of outcomes that have a low probability of occurring and yet result in major consequences (e.g., nuclear reactor explosions, airplane accidents). These events are often marked by a feeling of dread, lack of control, and the potential for extremely negative outcomes. Indeed, people often believe that high risk initiatives have low benefit, whereas experts believe exactly the reverse (as in the case of nuclear energy).

People may be able to estimate the likelihood of a single event occurring (e.g., getting a job), but they often have trouble estimating the probability of a compound event (e.g., getting a job and being promoted). They also have trouble understanding how quickly risk accumulates; for example, smokers do not realize that their risk of lung cancer relative to that of nonsmokers gets substantially higher the more years they continue to smoke. People have trouble making decisions where the risk of one outcome increases and the risk of another decreases (as is the case for many health therapies), and they have trouble considering all possible outcomes when assessing likelihood. For example, when a sample of smokers was asked how many smokers out of 100 would die of lung cancer, the average response was 42, but when asked the same question with a longer list of possible diseases, the average response for lung cancer was much lower. People's risk perceptions are often constructed on the spot based on the way these risk perceptions are measured and the information available to the respondent at that moment. This may explain why risk appraisals are often not as predictive of behavior as one might expect.

Influences on Risk Appraisal

Many of the errors contaminating people's risk appraisals can be explained by a set of basic psychological phenomena. Amos Tversky and Daniel Kahneman found that people rely on a variety of heuristics, or rules of thumb, when assessing the likelihood of events. An example of such a heuristic is the availability heuristic, whereby people estimate the probability of an event occurring based on how easy it is to think of an instance of that event. People tend to remember (and thus overestimate) events that happened relative to events that did not happen and are likely to remember vivid events more than mundane

events. For instance, people may overestimate the number of times that disclosing personal information on a date backfired, yet suppress memory of many times that it did not. Highly publicized events such as airplane crashes raise risk appraisals for air travel, despite the fact that thousands more die in less publicized car accidents. People also engage in egocentrism, which means that thoughts about the self are more prominent than are thoughts about other people. As a result, when comparing their risk with that of others, people rely on the abundance of information they have about themselves, leading to errors like unrealistic optimism.

People think differently about frequencies than they do about proportions. For example, upon hearing that 10 individuals (of 100) were infected with a communicable disease, people worry more than if they hear that 10% of this group was infected, despite the statistics being equivalent. People seem to focus exclusively on the 10 people who might have been infected. People also fail to acknowledge the actual chances of an event when assessing their own (or another person's) risk. For example, when determining whether a young woman is anorexic, people might compare her build and symptoms with that of other anorexic women and pay little attention to the actual prevalence of anorexia (which is lower than that of other health problems with similar symptoms). Such a bias results from a heuristic called the *representativeness heuristic,* which is used to make judgments of similarity.

People tend to judge risks higher when sad, and lower when angry or happy. Their motivation to believe that good things will happen to them and bad things will not often color their risk perceptions in a self-enhancing direction. As a result, they may be resistant to information designed to increase their risk perceptions, which explains why many health promotion campaigns are unsuccessful. People high in self-esteem, extraversion, dispositional optimism, or sensation-seeking tend to estimate their personal risks as relatively lower, whereas those who are depressed tend to be more pessimistic (though some evidence suggests that depressed people are more realistic about their risk than are nondepressed people). Contrary to popular belief, adults and adolescents do not vary greatly in their appraisals of the risk of various activities, and even older adults have been found to be unrealistically optimistic about their chances of experiencing negative events relative to peers.

Improving Risk Appraisal

Given the many errors in the way people appraise risk, and given the association of risk appraisals with important decisions and behaviors, it is important to devise ways to improve the accuracy of risk appraisals. The increasing use of computer aids and the Internet will be helpful in this regard. Several Web sites provide personalized risk information to individuals about their chances of getting a disease, and decision aids are now available to patients who need to appraise the risk of competing options (e.g., watchful waiting vs. surgery) when making important medical decisions. These decision aids collect information about patients' values (such as whether years of life matter more than quality of life) to help them understand their risk and to make informed decisions. Evidence also indicates that training in the social sciences, and psychology in particular, improves the ability to reason and make probabilistic judgments, which is necessary to appraise risk accurately. If made available to a wider audience, similar training may reduce errors in risk appraisal on a wider scale.

William M. P. Klein
Jennifer L. Cerully

See also Availability Heuristic; Decision Making; Egocentric Bias; Heuristic Processing; Representativeness Heuristic; Risk Taking

Further Readings

Slovic, P. (1987). Perception of risk. *Science, 236,* 280–285.
Tversky, A., & Kahneman, D. (1974). Judgment under uncertainty: Heuristics and biases. *Science, 185,* 1124–1131.
Weinstein, N. D. (2003). Exploring the links between risk perceptions and preventive health behavior. In J. Suls & K. A. Wallston (Eds.), *Social psychological foundations of health and illness* (pp. 22–53). Malden, MA: Blackwell.

RISK TAKING

Definition

When people take risks, they engage in behaviors that could lead to negative consequences such as physical injury, social rejection, legal troubles, or financial losses. Behaviors that are more likely to lead to such outcomes are considered riskier than behaviors that are less likely to lead to such outcomes. Regardless of the degree of risk involved, however, behaviors of any type can lead to both positive and negative consequences. People who take risks think about consequences in one of two ways. The first way involves an awareness that a behavior such as gambling could lead to both positive and negative consequences (e.g., their winnings could increase further or they could lose all of their money), but people engage in the behavior anyway because they assume that the positive consequences are more likely than the negative consequences. In contrast, people who think about consequences in the second way do not seem to consider both positive and negative consequences at the time when they are thinking about engaging in the behavior. Instead, they only seem to consider the possible positive consequences. If they had considered the negative consequences as well, they might not have taken the risk.

Major Issues in Risk-Taking Research

Researchers from a wide range of disciplines have been interested in risk taking for a variety of reasons. Economists and other financial experts, for example, have considered the implications of philosophical, mathematical, and psychological analyses of risk taking for making wise investment decisions. Given that nearly all financial decisions carry some degree of risk, the focus is not on how one can avoid taking risks. Rather, the focus is on how one can maximize financial gains while minimizing financial losses.

Cognitive psychologists, in contrast, have been less interested in financial decisions and more interested in the ways in which the human mind copes with all the information and possibilities that may be present in a risk-taking situation. People cannot consider all the possible positive and negative consequences of their choices because doing so would require much more memory ability and processing capacity than the human mind possesses. Instead, they simplify the task for themselves by only considering certain kinds of information, narrowing down their options to one or two, and relying on rules of thumb that are usually (but not always) useful guides to selection. Whereas many scholars (especially evolutionary psychologists) now argue that such strategies are highly adaptive and usually inconsequential, others have shown in experiments how simplifying tendencies can lead to systematic decision errors and inconsistent choices across similar situations.

For example, when presented with hypothetical health policy choices, people make different choices depending on how the information is "framed." In one study, one group of participants was willing to implement a risky health policy involving a vaccination plan when they were told only that the vaccination would likely "save the lives of 600 people" in a particular town (population = 1,000). A second group, in contrast, was unwilling to implement the policy when they were only told that "400 people might die" if the plan were implemented. Thus, people made different choices even though the choices were formally identical. People presented with the first frame failed to realize that although 600 would be saved, 400 would not be. People presented with the second frame failed to draw the opposite inference.

Although studies of framing and other effects have been of interest to social psychologists as well, other issues currently predominate in the social psychological literature on risk taking. The goal of most studies is to identify the psychological factors that seem to predict who is likely to engage in unhealthy behaviors such as unprotected sex, reckless driving, or cigarette smoking. Some researchers argue that people engage in these unhealthy behaviors because the long-term, negative consequences of these behaviors are outweighed in their minds by the short-term, positive consequences that they produce.

Risk taking is particularly likely when the short-term positive consequences include reductions in both negative emotion and high self-awareness, combined with increases in physical pleasure or arousal. That is, people are drawn to risks that promise a quick positive outcome that will feel good, be exciting, help them forget themselves, and get rid of unpleasant emotions. Experimental procedures that increase negative emotion or self-awareness (e.g., leading people to believe they will never form close relationships; reminding them that they will die someday) increase tendencies toward risk taking. Further work has shown that risk-taking is more likely when (a) factors such as stress or alcohol decrease the number of consequences considered, (b) the risky behaviors serve a variety of goals and needs (e.g., need for intimacy; self-esteem), and (c) people have favorable stereotypes about the kind of person who engages in the behavior, believe that most people engage in the behavior, and their friends would approve of their engaging in the behavior.

Developmental (child) psychology often builds on scholarship in the fields of cognitive and social psychology. Developmental psychologists have given many of the same tasks and measures used by cognitive and social psychologists to children in an effort to document developmental increases or decreases in risk-taking tendencies. Although adolescents are more likely to engage in certain kinds of risky behaviors than are preadolescents and children (e.g., smoking, binge drinking, unprotected sex), age differences have not been found on a variety of other risk-taking measures. Hence, there does not appear to be a global increase in risk taking with age because age differences vary by topic. Similarly, there does not appear to be a general tendency for males to take more risks than females do. Although some studies have found that males engage in certain risky behaviors more than females (e.g., reckless driving), other studies have either found no gender differences or found that females engaged in certain risky behaviors more than males (e.g., females in their 20s smoke more than males in their 20s).

Hence, financial scholars and scholars in various subfields of psychology have had somewhat divergent interests. Nevertheless, several findings and issues have been of interest to scholars in all these disciplines. One issue pertains to the question of whether a person who engages in one kind of risky behavior (e.g., smoking) is also likely to engage in other kinds as well (e.g., binge drinking, reckless driving). Again, the findings seem to show that the degree of consistency depends on which behaviors are presented to participants in studies. Certain kinds of risky behaviors do tend to cluster together (e.g., smoking and binge drinking in teens), but other kinds do not (e.g., trying out for a sport and smoking). Whenever larger lists of risky behaviors are presented to participants, less consistency in the tendency to take risks emerges.

The second issue of interest to scholars in multiple disciplines pertains to the relation between risk taking and rationality. In classical terms, rational people are people who behave in ways that are consistent with their beliefs and values. To illustrate, people who drive recklessly with their children in their cars can be said to behave irrationally if they (a) believe that driving recklessly could lead to the injury or death of any passengers in their cars and (b) consider it very important to protect their children. Similarly, the act of smoking cigarettes is irrational for any person who believes that smoking causes premature death and considers it important to live a long and healthy life.

Several studies of risk taking have shown that adolescents and adults can deviate from the classical norms of rationality. Scholars have reacted to such deviations in one of two ways. Some have argued that the classical criteria for rational behavior need to be discarded in favor of other criteria. In other words, there is nothing wrong with the human mind; there is something wrong with the definition of rationality. These scholars suggest that millions of years of evolution could not have produced a mind that is designed for self-destruction. Other scholars, in contrast, have accepted the classical criteria and sought to determine the psychological and contextual factors that cause people to sometimes behave irrationally. As noted previously, for example, social psychologists have appealed to constructs such as negative emotion, self-awareness, social exclusion, lack of self-regulation, and positive views of risk-takers to explain irrational risky behavior. Developmental psychologists have also appealed to lack of self-regulation, but have added an emphasis on other factors such as impulsivity and sensation-seeking as well. In contrast, cognitive psychologists have focused on various cognitive processes that keep people from attending to, or recalling, the right kinds of information.

The issue of rationality also arises in legal settings. When adults or adolescents engage in criminal behaviors, the question arises whether they should be held accountable for their behavior. Are their beliefs in accord with reality? Do they value their own lives or the lives of others? Did psychological factors such as extreme emotion or uncontrollable impulsivity cause them to behave irrationally? If so, should they be held accountable for not controlling their emotions or impulses?

James P. Byrnes

See also Decision Making; Emotion; Self-Defeating Behavior; Self-Regulation

Further Readings

Baumeister, R. F. (1997). Esteem threat, self-regulatory breakdown, and emotional distress as factors in self-defeating behavior. *Review of General Psychology, 1,* 145–174.

Byrnes, J. P., Miller, D. C., & Schafer, W. D. (1999). Gender differences in risk-taking: A meta-analysis. *Psychological Bulletin, 125,* 367–383.

Jacobs, J. E., & Klaczynski, P. A. (2005). *The development of judgment and decision-making in children and adolescents.* Mahwah, NJ: Erlbaum.

Romer, D. (2004). *Reducing adolescent risk.* Thousand Oaks, CA: Sage.

Risky Shift

Risky shift occurs when people change their decisions or opinions to become more extreme and risky when acting as part of a group, compared with acting individually; this is one form of the phenomenon known as group polarization. The result is that group decisions are bolder and more adventurous than those made by individuals alone and even riskier than the average of the individuals' opinions and decisions before group discussion. However, sometimes people in groups shift such that the group decision is actually more conservative, which is known as cautious (or conservative) shift. The group's initial tendency toward risk is important in predicting if risky shift will occur. The direction of the shift (to be more risky or more conservative) tends to be in line with the general direction of group initial viewpoints.

The term *risky shift* was coined by James Stoner in 1961. To examine group decision making, he asked participants to make decisions about real-life scenarios that involved some amount of risk. Participants first gave their own individual ratings. Then they got together in groups and arrived at a decision together. Following this, participants made their own individual ratings again. Contrary to what was expected, he found that group decisions were more risky. In addition, the postdiscussion individual decisions also showed a shift toward increased risk. Subsequent research has shown that people in groups may make more risky decisions in a variety of situations including, but not limited to, gambling and consumer behavior, and people in groups can become more prejudiced in their opinions of minorities or more liberal on issues such as feminism.

This risky shift in group decision making may occur for a variety of reasons. First, the individuals with more extreme views may be more confident, committed, and persuasive, compared with the more conservative members of the group. In addition, as people present their arguments to the group members, they may come to hold a stronger belief in their own opinions and, in turn, be willing to make more extreme decisions. These stronger opinions may carry more weight in determining the final decision.

Another reason for the occurrence of risky shift is that the group may fail to consider all available opinions and possibilities. There may be biased filtering and communicating of views, facts, and findings because of motivation by an individual to promote his or her own opinion. This insufficient exploration by the group of costs and benefits of each choice may lead to assumptions in which negative outcomes are overlooked.

Although the goal and desire of committee and group decision making is ultimately to result in more educated, well-rounded, and better decisions, risky shift may be a deterrent to this. In groups such as juries or panels of judges, committees of generals, or boards of directors, as a result of group discussion, the group may choose a more risky option than a single juror or judge, general, or CEO alone would. Unfortunately, in some cases, this may result in poor, even disastrous, decisions and outcomes.

Carrie L. Wyland

See also Group Polarization; Groups, Characteristics of

Further Readings

Isenberg, D. J. (1986). Group polarization: A critical review and meta-analysis. *Journal of Personality and Social Psychology, 50,* 1141–1151.

Johnson, N. R., Stemler, J. G., & Hunter, D. (1977). Crowd behavior as risky shift: A laboratory experiment. *Social Psychology Quarterly, 40,* 183–187.

Stoner, J. A. F. (1961). *A comparison of individual and group decisions involving risk.* Unpublished master's thesis, Massachusetts Institute of Technology, Cambridge.

Stoner, J. A. F. (1968). Risky and cautious shifts in group decisions: The influence of widely held values. *Journal of Experimental Social Psychology, 4,* 442, 459.

Wallach, M. A., Kogan, N., & Burt, R. B. (1962). Group influence on individual risk taking. *Journal of Abnormal Social Psychology, 65,* 75–86.

ROBBERS CAVE EXPERIMENT

Definition

The Robbers Cave experiment demonstrated that an attempt to simply bring hostile groups together is not enough to reduce intergroup prejudice. Rather, this experiment confirmed that groups must cooperate and have common goals to truly build peace. Thus, although contact is vital to reducing tensions between groups, interdependence is essential for establishing lasting intergroup harmony. This experiment is a classic in social psychology and is important because it has implications for reducing conflict between real social groups. In addition, this study has implications for a number of prominent social psychological theories, including realistic conflict theory and social identity theory.

Background

The purpose of this study was to create conflict and hostility between groups, and then employ interventions designed to reduce it. Researchers accomplished this goal by sending two groups of adolescent boys to a remote location where both the creation and resolution of intergroup conflict could be manipulated. Twenty-two 11-year-old boys were transported to a summer camp located in Oklahoma's Robbers Cave State Park (hence the name by which this experiment has come to be known). All the boys were similar on important demographic features, with each exhibiting satisfactory academic performance and coming from stable, middle-class families. In addition, the boys did not know one another and had no idea that they were about to participate in a psychology experiment. Researchers divided the boys into two equal-sized groups that were taken to opposite sides of the camp. These groups were initially unaware of each other's existence, but this soon changed.

The study took place in three separate stages that were approximately 1 week apart: (1) group formation, (2) intergroup competition, and (3) intergroup cooperation. The purpose of the first stage was to encourage the development of unique ingroup identities among the groups. This occurred as a result of the boys engaging in shared activities (e.g., swimming, hiking) with their own groups, which indeed led to the spontaneous emergence of norms, leaders, and identities. In fact, the groups even chose distinct names for themselves, with one referring to itself as the Rattlers and the other as the Eagles.

In the second stage, the groups were introduced and placed in direct competition with one another. Thus, the boys competed in a series of contests involving activities such as baseball and tug-of-war. The group that won overall was to be awarded a trophy and other prizes, and the losing group was to receive nothing. The result was a vicious rivalry between the groups, with both verbal and physical attacks being commonplace. For instance, the boys engaged in name-calling and taunting, as well as more physical acts of aggression such as stealing the winning group's prizes and burning each other's team flags. Clearly, the researchers' goal of creating intergroup conflict was easily achieved. However, resolving this conflict turned out to be a more difficult task.

In the final stage of the experiment, researchers arranged specific situations designed to reduce the severe hostility between groups. First, the groups were provided with noncompetitive opportunities for increased contact, such as watching movies and sharing meals together. However, these getting-to-know-you opportunities did little to defuse intergroup hostility. In fact, many of these situations resulted in an exchange of verbal insults and, occasionally, food fights.

As an alternative strategy, the groups were placed in situations that required them to cooperate with one another (i.e., the situations involved superordinate goals). For instance, one situation involved a broken-down truck carrying supplies to the camp. Another involved a problem with the camp's water supply. In both cases, the groups needed to work together because the resources at stake were important to everyone involved. This cooperation resulted in more harmonious relations between groups, as friendships began to develop across group lines. As a telling sign of their newfound harmony, both groups expressed a desire to return home on the same bus.

Implications and Importance

The Robbers Cave experiment has had an enormous impact on the field of social psychology. First, this study has implications for the contact hypothesis of prejudice reduction, which, in its simplest form, posits that contact between members of different groups improves how well groups get along. This experiment illustrates how contact alone is not enough to restore intergroup harmony. Even after the competition between the boys ended, the hostility did not disappear during future contact. Competition seemingly became incorporated into the groups' identities. The hostility did not finally calm down until the context changed and cooperation between groups was required. Thus,

beyond mere contact, groups also need to be interdependent and have common goals.

Second, this study validated the claims of realistic conflict theory, which specifies that prejudice and discrimination result when groups are placed in competition for valuable resources. The boys in this experiment clearly demonstrated that competition breeds intergroup hostility. More importantly, however, this study highlights the significance of the social context in the development of prejudice and discrimination. The boys selected to participate in this study were well-adjusted and came from stable, middle-class families. Thus, it is unlikely that individual characteristics such as socioeconomic status and family life were responsible for the observed effects because these factors were held constant. Rather, the context of intergroup relations (i.e., competition) led to the observed conflict and hostility. This suggests that prejudice is largely a product of social situations and that individual pathology is not necessary to produce outgroup hatred. Therefore, the results of this experiment speak to a number of social psychological theories that emphasize the importance of the social context in understanding group prejudice, such as social identity theory and self-categorization theory.

Justin J. Lehmiller

See also Contact Hypothesis; Prejudice; Racism; Realistic Group Conflict Theory; Self-Categorization Theory; Social Identity Theory

Further Readings

LeVine, R. A., & Campbell, D. T. (1972). *Ethnocentrism: Theories of conflict, ethnic attitudes and group behavior.* New York: Wiley.

Sherif, M., Harvey, O. J., White, B. J., Hood, W. R., & Sherif, C. W. (1988). *The Robbers Cave experiment.* Middletown, CT: Wesleyan University Press.

ROLES AND ROLE THEORY

"All the world's a stage, and all the men and women merely players": With these lines from *As You Like It,* William Shakespeare succinctly captured the essence of role theory. In short, people's behavior stems from the parts they play in life. In social psychology, a *role* is defined as the collection of expectations that accompany a particular social position. Indeed, the word originates from the French *rôle,* which denoted the parchment from which an actor read his lines. Each individual typically plays multiple roles in his or her life; in different contexts or with different people, a particular person might be a student, a friend, or an employee. Each of these roles carries its own expectations about appropriate behavior, speech, attire, and so on. What might be rewarded for a person in one role would be unacceptable for a person occupying a different role (e.g., competitive behavior is rewarded for an athlete but not a preschool teacher). Roles range from specific, in that they only apply to a certain setting, to diffuse, in that they apply across a range of situations. For example, gender roles influence behavior across many different contexts; although someone may be a cashier when she is on the clock, she is a woman across all settings. Role theory examines how these roles influence a wide array of psychological outcomes, including behavior, attitudes, cognitions, and social interaction.

Background

Within social psychology, role theory has generally focused on roles as causes of (a) behaviors enacted by individuals or groups and (b) inferences about individuals or groups. One of the fundamental precepts of social psychology is that the social and physical environment exerts a profound influence on individuals' thoughts and behavior. Role theory posits that the roles that people occupy provide contexts that shape behavior. For example, the Stanford Prison Experiment demonstrated that normal college students displayed strikingly different behaviors depending on whether they were assigned to be guards or prisoners in a simulated prison environment. Within a short time, prisoners began to show meek, submissive behaviors, whereas prison guards began to show dominant, abusive behaviors. In general, people are motivated to behave in ways that fit valued social roles. Rewards stem from alignment to valued social roles, and punishments stem from misalignment to such roles.

Role theory also examines how observers form inferences about others' personality and abilities based on their roles. Indeed, one of the first questions asked to get to know someone is, "What do you do?" A classic illustration of the power of roles to influence beliefs about others is a study in which individuals participated in a quiz show with a partner. Their roles as questioner or contestant were randomly assigned by a flip of a coin, in plain sight of both participants. The questioner was instructed to write a series of general knowledge questions based on anything that he or she knew, and then the questioner posed these questions to the contestant. After this trivia game, participants rated the general knowledge ability of themselves and their partners. Both the contestants and observers rated the questioners as more knowledgeable than the contestant. In fact, according to objective tests, the questioners and the contestants did not differ in knowledge. This study clearly showed that observing someone in a particular role leads to the inference of related traits, even when his or her behaviors are required by a particular role, that role is arbitrarily assigned, and role assignment is obvious to all involved.

These trait judgments form partly because observers infer that individuals possess the personality traits that equip them to perform their roles. For example, seeing someone care for a puppy would likely lead to the inference that this individual is sensitive and kind. In contrast, seeing someone play a game of basketball would lead to the inference that the individual is aggressive and competitive. Observers typically assume that people have the personal qualities or motivation to behave a certain way, and thus observers underestimate how much roles elicit behaviors.

Mechanisms: How Do Roles Lead to Behavior?

External Mechanisms

One basic way in which roles influence behavior is via role affordances, or opportunities for different actions. For example, competitive roles typically promote self-assertion but inhibit kindness. In the quiz-show study described earlier, the role of questioner afforded the display of knowledge. This display led to the inference that the questioner was extremely knowledgeable, even though both partners tested similarly in general knowledge and the questioner was allowed to pick questions that he or she knew.

The expectations of others based on one's role also powerfully influence behavior. Many experiments have documented the effects of the self-fulfilling prophecy, in which an individual's beliefs about a target are confirmed because the individual elicits such behavior from the target. For example, Robert Rosenthal and colleagues demonstrated the power of expectancies on others by providing teachers with lists of students who had been identified as likely to develop special abilities throughout the school year. In truth, these students did not initially differ from other students. However, the teachers assessed these children as more curious, interesting, and likely to succeed, and by the end of the school year, the "late bloomer" students actually performed better than other students. Studies of the self-fulfilling prophecy have effectively demonstrated how expectancies about different role occupants (e.g., that CEOs will be aggressive or women are emotional) can become reality.

Internal Mechanisms

With repeated experience in a role, aspects of that role can become internalized in the self-concept—for example, repeated experience of competing against others might lead one to identify as "competitive." These internalized constructs become an important part of identity and are carried across the boundaries of different roles. Indeed, identity transformations frequently happen when individuals enter or leave roles. Major life transitions, such as going to college, starting a new job, or getting married, represent some of these role-identity shifts.

When someone occupies a certain role, he or she is socialized to perform certain behaviors. In addition, more experience in role-related tasks fosters comfort and expertise in specific domains. Individuals may thus begin to feel greater self-efficacy in roles they have previously occupied. Moreover, socialization into diffuse roles (e.g., gender roles) can lead to greater comfort in activities that are compatible with those roles, with the result that individuals choose specific roles that fit with their diffuse role socialization. For example, the tendency to socialize girls more than boys to attend to others' needs can contribute to women's greater selection of communal or caring-oriented careers.

Implications

Role theory has provided an important framework for understanding perceived and actual group differences. Just as perceivers fail to correct for the influence of roles on individuals' behavior, they fail to correct for the influence of roles on group members' behaviors. The role perspective on stereotype content has been applied to understand stereotypes based on gender, age, ethnicity, and culture. According to the social role theory of sex differences and similarities, the traditional division of labor (in which women are concentrated in caretaking roles and men in breadwinner roles) leads to the inference that men and women possess the traits that equip them to perform their roles. Moreover, group members may differ in their behaviors because of current or historical distributions into certain social roles. As detailed previously, role occupancy can lead to constraints on the performance of behaviors, as well as to the development of skills and abilities associated with those roles.

Role theory also provides an explanation of the sources of prejudice against certain groups. Role congruity theory posits that negativity stems from the lack of fit between the requirements of valued social roles and the perceived characteristics of an individual or group. For example, negativity occurs when a group's stereotype (e.g., women are kind) does not align with the characteristics required by the role (e.g., leaders are aggressive). As a way of understanding how behavior derives from the surrounding context, role theory thus provides a useful framework to understand the behaviors, thoughts, and attitudes of oneself and others.

Amanda B. Diekman

See also Fundamental Attribution Error; Looking-Glass Self; Self-Categorization Theory; Self-Fulfilling Prophecy; Sex Roles; Stanford Prison Experiment

Further Readings

Eagly, A. H., & Karau, S. J. (2002). Role congruity theory of prejudice toward female leaders. *Psychological Review, 109,* 573–598.

Eagly, A. H., Wood, W., & Diekman, A. B. (2000). Social role theory of sex differences and similarities: A current appraisal. In T. Eckes & H. M. Trautner (Eds.), *The developmental social psychology of gender* (pp. 123–174). Mahwah, NJ: Erlbaum.

Moskowitz, D. S., Suh, E. J., & Desaulniers, J. (1994). Situational influences on gender differences in agency and communion. *Journal of Personality and Social Psychology, 66,* 753–761.

Rosenthal, R., & Jacobson, L. (1968). *Pygmalion in the classroom.* New York: Holt, Rinehart & Winston.

Ross, L. D., Amabile, T. M., & Steinmetz, J. L. (1977). Social roles, social control, and biases in social-perception processes. *Journal of Personality and Social Psychology, 35,* 485–494.

ROMANTIC LOVE

Romantic love has been found in every historical era and in every culture for which data are available. To those familiar with the research literature, romantic love today is no longer the mystery it has been considered to be throughout the ages. Nevertheless, there is much more to learn, and romantic love remains a thriving topic of research for social psychologists.

Aspects of romantic love are found in many animal species, and love may have played a central role in shaping human evolution. In humans, romantic love is a source of some of the deepest joys and greatest problems, including depression, abandonment rage, stalking, suicide, and homicide. Therefore, social psychologists and other scientists have devoted a great deal of research to understanding romantic love.

Definition

People generally understand love by its resemblance to a prototype, which means a standard model or idea (as one would recognize a bird by its resemblance to a robin). The protoypical features of love encompass, in order of centrality, intimacy, commitment, and passion. Scientists, by contrast, define love in a more formal way—for example, as the constellation of behaviors, cognitions, and emotions associated with a desire to enter or maintain a close relationship with a specific other person.

Much research on love has focused on types of love, including distinguishing romantic love from more general kinds of love, such as familial love or compassionate love for strangers. Romantic love, which is associated with dependence, caring, and exclusiveness, is also distinguished from liking, which emphasizes similarity, respect, and positive evaluation. Moreover, passionate love (the fervent desire for connection with a particular other person) is also distinguished from companionate love (the warm feelings one has for people with whom one's life is interconnected). Items on the standard research measure of passionate love focus on such things as wanting to be with this person more than with anyone else, and melting when looking into this person's eyes. A similar distinction is between those whom one "loves" and the subset of these with whom one is "in love."

Another well-researched approach identifies six love styles: *eros* (romantic, passionate love), *ludus* (game playing love), *storge* (friendship love), *pragma* (logical, "shopping-list" love), *mania* (possessive, dependent love), and *agape* (selfless love). Yet another influential approach, the triangular theory, conceptualizes love in terms of intimacy, commitment/decision, and passion, the various combinations of which define diverse types of romantic love.

Biological Basis

Biological research suggests that birds and mammals evolved several distinct brain systems for courtship, mating, and parenting, including (a) the sex drive, characterized by a craving for sexual gratification; (b) attraction, characterized by focused attention on a preferred mating partner; and (c) attachment, characterized by the maintenance of proximity, affiliative gestures and expressions of calm when in social contact with a mating partner, and separation anxiety when apart. Each neural system is associated with a different constellation of brain circuits, different behavior patterns, and different emotional and motivational states. With regard to human love, one can equate "attraction" with passionate love and "attachment" with companionate love. Recent studies using functional magnetic resonance imaging of the brain indicate that these three neural systems are distinct yet interrelated.

Predicting Falling in Love

Numerous experiments have identified factors that lead to liking, in general, and to many forms of loving. These factors include discovering that the other person likes one's self; attraction to the other's characteristics, including kindness, intelligence, humor, good looks, social status; similarities with one's self, especially in attitudes and background characteristics; proximity and exposure to the other; and confirmation and encouragement from one's peers and family that this is suitable partner. In the context of falling in love, discovering that the other likes one's self and that he or she has desirable and appropriate characteristics is especially important. In addition, a well-researched predictor specific to falling in love is the arousal-attraction effect—being physiologically stirred up at the time of meeting a potential partner (e.g., one study found that men who met an attractive woman when on a scary suspension bridge were more romantically attracted to her than were men who met the same woman on a safe bridge; another study found that individuals felt greater romantic attraction to an individual whom they met just after running in place for a few minutes!).

Effects of Falling in Love

Those experiencing intense passionate love report a constellation of feelings including focused attention on the beloved, heightened energy, sleeplessness, loss of appetite, euphoria and mood swings, bodily reactions such as a pounding heart, emotional dependence on and obsessive thinking about the beloved, emotional and physical possessiveness, craving for emotional union with the beloved, and intense motivation to win this particular partner. Studies have also found that when someone is intensely in love, and that person's romantic passion is reciprocated, the lovers experience an increase in self-esteem and an expanded, more diverse sense of one's self.

Unreciprocated Love

Autobiographical accounts of being rejected and of being the undesired object of someone's attraction have reported that rejection can lead to strong organization as well as strong disorganization of thoughts, behaviors, and emotions. Both the rejector and rejectee largely express passive behaviors, both are unhappy with the situation, and both usually end up disappointed. A large survey study found that the intensity of a person's feelings of unrequited love can be predicted by how much the individual wants the relationship, how much he or she likes the state of being in love (whether reciprocated or not), and whether the rejectee initially believed his or her love would be reciprocated.

Maintaining Love Over Time

Longitudinal studies report that passionate love regularly declines after an initial relationship period of 1 to 3 years. Evolutionary anthropologists suggest that this decline is because the basic function of love (to promote the breeding process with a specific individual) was designed to dissipate and change into feelings of attachment so partners could rear their child together in a calmer state. One psychological explanation for this emphasizes habituation. Another psychological explanation argues that passionate love arises from the rapid increase in intimacy or interpersonal connection, which inevitably slows down as one gets to know the partner. Whatever the reason for the typical decline, love does not *inevitably* weaken. In one study following newlyweds for 4 years, about 10% maintained or increased their relationship satisfaction.

Furthermore, some studies have found a small percentage of long-term married people have very high levels of passionate love. How might this happen? One clue is from experiments and surveys showing an increase in passionate love in long-term relationships in which partners do challenging and novel activities together.

How Does Love Work?

Love as Emotion and Motivation

Love, especially "moments of love," are very emotional (indeed, "love" is the first example most people give when asked to name an emotion). However, love, especially passionate love, may not be a specific emotion in its own right. Rather, passionate love may be better described as a goal-oriented state (the desire for a relationship with a particular partner) that can lead to a variety of emotions depending on the partner's response. Also, unlike basic emotions, passionate love is not associated with any specific facial expression, it is more focused on a highly specific goal, and it is particularly hard to control (it is almost impossible to make yourself feel passionate love for someone). Similarly, brain scan studies show that passionate love engages a common reward-area brain system across individuals, a system similar to that which becomes active when one takes cocaine, but the emotional parts of the brain show different patterns for different individuals.

Love and Sex

People typically feel sexual desire for a person they passionately love, but they may not feel passionate love for all of the people whom they sexually desire. This distinction between these systems is also seen in studies of neural systems active in brain functioning and in varying behavioral responses in laboratory experiments.

Love and Attachment

Attachment theory posits that a key factor in adult love is whether during infancy one's primary caregiver (usually one's mother) provided a secure base for exploration. Research shows that those who had inconsistent caregiving are much more likely to experience intense passionate love as adults; those who had consistent lack of attention in infancy are especially unlikely to experience passionate love. Some evidence also indicates that the brain systems engaged by passionate love may differ according to one's attachment history.

Self-Expansion

The self-expansion model posits, with research support, that the exhilaration and intense focused attention of passionate love arise from the rapid rate of coming to feel as if the other is part of oneself that is often associated with forming a new romantic relationship, but that companionate love arises from the ongoing greater opportunities offered by the partner and the potential for loss to the self of losing the partner.

Love as a Story

An influential (though little researched) idea is that loving relationships can be described accurately by the people involved through narrative autobiographies, often suggesting culturally prototypical "stories." For example, the story of a couple locked in constant struggle is common, as is the story of couples growing to love each other over time.

Evolutionary Approaches

One evolutionary view (noted earlier), based on animal studies and some recent brain scanning studies, proposes that passionate romantic love evolved to motivate individuals to select among potential mating partners and focus their courtship attention on these favored individuals, thereby conserving precious courtship and mating time and energy. Another influential line of evolutionary thinking is based on the idea that when choosing a mate, a woman is making a bigger investment than is a man. This approach has emphasized gender differences, for example, in what features are desirable in a mate (across cultures, women give more weight to a man's social status; men, to a woman's good looks). Finally, some recent theorists interpret various studies as suggesting that romantic love is an elaboration of the basic bonding system between infants and parents.

Arthur Aron
Helen E. Fisher
Greg Strong

See also Attachment Theory; Close Relationships; Love; Self-Expansion Theory; Sexual Desire; Triangular Theory of Love; Unrequited Love

Further Readings

Aron, A., Fisher, H., & Strong, G. (2006). Romantic love. In D. Perlman & A. Vangelisti (Eds.), *Cambridge handbook of personal relationships* (pp. 595–614). Cambridge, UK: Cambridge University Press.

Baumeister, R. F., & Wotman, S. R. (1992). *Breaking hearts: The two sides of unrequited love.* New York: Guilford Press.

Fisher, H. (2004). *Why we love: The nature and chemistry of romantic love.* New York: Henry Holt.

Pines, A. M. (1999). *Falling in love: Why we choose the lovers we choose.* London: Routledge.

Tennov, D. (1999). *Love and limerence: The experience of being in love.* Lanham, MD: Scarborough House.

ROMANTIC SECRECY

Definition

Romantic secrecy is the process by which an individual deliberately conceals his or her ongoing romantic relationship from a person or persons outside of the relationship. Romantic secrecy is typically associated with deception about the nature of a romantic relationship. Romantic secrecy occurs most clearly when an individual conceals all aspects of his or her romantic relationship from others. An individual can maintain such pretenses by meeting privately with only his or her romantic partner or by concealing the romantic nature of the relationship when in public. Romantic secrecy occurs similarly when an individual acknowledges an ongoing romantic relationship, but conceals the romantic partner. Finally, romantic secrecy occurs to a lesser degree when an individual acknowledges a romantic relationship, but goes to lengths to hide the emotional depth of the relationship.

Romantic secrecy occurs for two general reasons. First, individuals commonly engage in romantic secrecy during early relationship development. That is, individuals frequently maintain the privacy of a new relationship until they consider it the right time to reveal the relationship to others. For example, an individual might wait until a new relationship becomes more serious before disclosing the relationship to friends. This form of romantic secrecy is probably benign insofar as it involves low levels of deliberate deception and any relationship concealment can be regulated easily by romantic relationship partners. Second, and more important, individuals might maintain romantic secrecy because of identifiable external constraints that make relationship disclosure appear harmful. The notion of romantic secrecy generally refers to these kinds of relationships. In these cases, romantic secrecy goes beyond the relatively brief romantic relationship concealment that partners might invoke in developing relationships. Instead, relationship partners experience heightened anxiety about possible romantic relationship disclosure and maintain romantic secrecy for extended periods. For example, romantic partners in an interreligious relationship might keep their relationship secret because they anticipate strong disapproval from friends and family.

Relationships that contain high levels of romantic secrecy are often thought of as "secret relationships." However, even relationships that appear to be nonsecret can contain milder levels of romantic secrecy. To illustrate, partners who conceal their romantic relationship from one person might not identify their own relationship as secret but still engage in some elements of romantic secrecy.

Prevalence of Romantic Secrecy

Individuals usually maintain romantic secrecy to avoid negative outcomes that they believe would result from relationship disclosure. Individuals might engage in romantic secrecy to avoid personal harm (e.g., an individual might hide a homosexual relationship to avoid social disapproval). Similarly, individuals might engage in romantic secrecy to protect their romantic partners from harm (e.g., an individual might conceal a romantic relationship to avoid creating a rift between the partner and the partner's parents). Lastly, individuals might maintain romantic secrecy to protect others outside of the relationship (e.g., single parents might keep newer, unstable romances secret from children to avoid causing them distress).

Individuals might underestimate the prevalence of romantic secrecy because it does not seem a part of the prototypical adult romantic relationship. However, some common forms of romantic secrecy demonstrate the ubiquitous nature of this phenomenon. To begin, workplace romances are common, and romantically involved coworkers frequently conceal their relationships to avoid gossip and potential administrative repercussions. Members of homosexual, interracial, and interreligious relationships might maintain romantic secrecy because others are more likely to disapprove of these relationships. Members of these so-called stigmatized relationships, particularly members of homosexual relationships, might also worry about more serious issues such as employment termination and even violence.

Romantic affairs are another common source of romantic secrecy. Romantic affairs are noteworthy because they can create two simultaneous forms of romantic secrecy. Romantic affairs might be kept secret from long-term relationship partners, and long-term relationships (e.g., marriages) might be kept secret from extra-relationship partners. For obvious reasons, romantic affairs often require inordinately high levels of romantic secrecy. On a related note, individuals who do not have full-scale affairs might still employ romantic secrecy to leave open the option to "trade up." Put differently, individuals might avoid revealing their existing romances when in the presence of romantically intriguing and newly met others, particularly when their current relationships are less satisfactory than they used to be.

Romantic Secrecy and Relationship Quality

Many individuals believe that romantic secrecy increases romantic attraction. According to one theory, romantic secrecy causes individuals to think more frequently about their romantic partners, which, in turn, heightens romantic attraction. Although some evidence supports this theory, research indicates generally that romantic secrecy decreases relationship quality. Individuals in ongoing romantic relationships who report greater levels of romantic secrecy also tend to report reduced relationship quality (e.g., love). Similarly, members of interracial and homosexual relationships appear to find the requirements of romantic secrecy aversive rather than alluring. Romantic secrecy might inhibit relationship quality because relationships with greater levels of romantic secrecy are more difficult to manage and receive less social support. Individuals should be aware of these potential challenges when entering or maintaining relationships that require romantic secrecy.

Craig Foster

See also Close Relationships; Deception (Lying); Self-Presentation; Social Support

Further Readings

Baxter, L. A., & Widenmann, S. (1993). Revealing and not revealing the status of romantic relationships to social networks. *Journal of Social and Personal Relationships, 10*, 321–337.

Foster, C. A., & Campbell, W. K. (2005). The adversity of secret relationships. *Personal Relationships, 12*, 125–143.

Wegner, D. M., Lane, J. D., & Dimitri, S. (1994). The allure of secret relationships. *Journal of Personality and Social Psychology, 66*, 287–300.

ROSENTHAL EFFECT

See EXPERIMENTER EFFECTS

RUBICON MODEL OF ACTION PHASES

To differentiate and integrate both the selection and realization of goals, the Rubicon model of action phases was developed. The model describes successful goal pursuit as solving four consecutive tasks: choosing between potential goals, planning the implementation of a chosen goal, acting on the chosen goal, and assessing what has been achieved by acting on the goal and what still needs to be achieved by further acting on the goal. Thus, the Rubicon model of action phases posits four distinct phases of goal pursuit: (1) the predecisional phase, in which the pros and cons of one's wishes and desires are deliberated by assessing the desirability of expected outcomes and the question of feasibility (i.e., Can I obtain the desired outcomes if I wanted to?); (2) the postdecisional phase, in which the implementation of the chosen goal is planned by deciding on when, where, and how one wants to act toward the goal; (3) the actional phase, in which one progresses toward the goal by initiating goal-directed behaviors and bringing them to a successful ending; (4) finally, the postactional phase in which the achieved outcomes of the goal-directed behavior are evaluated by looking backward (i.e., How successfully did I perform the goal-directed behavior?)

and forward (i.e., What needs to be done still to achieve the desired outcomes implied by my goal?).

These four phases are separated by three clear transition points: (1) deciding to strive for the realization of certain wishes and desires, thus transforming them into goals (at the end of the predecisional phase); (2) the initiation of actions suited to attain these goals (at the end of the preactional phase); and (3) the evaluation of the achieved outcomes of these goal-directed actions (at the end of the actional phase). The transition point at the end of the first phase is called *the transition of the Rubicon*. This metaphor comes from Julius Caesar's crossing of the northern Italian Rubicon River with his army after some hesitations in 49 B.C.E., thereby initiating a civil war. By crossing the Rubicon, Caesar committed himself to conquer or to perish. Thus, the metaphor "crossing the Rubicon" symbolizes that as soon as one has decided to pursue a select wish or desire, the pro versus con deliberation is terminated, and one is strongly committed to act. Thus, at the end of the predecisional phase, the deliberation is replaced by a sense of determination to actually realize the former wish or desire that is now experienced as a firm goal.

Different modes of thought are associated with each of the four action phases—the so-called action mind-sets. By getting involved with the distinct tasks posed in each of the four phases, certain ways of thinking become more prominent (i.e., unique cognitive procedures are activated). The deliberative mind-set is associated with the predecisional phase. It emerges when people start to think about an unresolved personal problem that is still a wish or desire, thinking of the short-term and long-term pros and cons of both making and not making the decision to realize it. The implemental mind-set is associated with the postdecisional phase. It originates when people start to plan the steps they want to take to actually realize a chosen goal. These plans specify when, where, and how one intends to execute each of these steps.

To investigate the cognitive, self-evaluative, and behavioral consequences of the deliberative and implemental mind-sets, the following experimental paradigm was invented. Research participants are made to believe that they have to perform two different, subsequent experiments (usually performed by two different experimenters). The first experimenter then induces the deliberative and the implemental mind-sets. The deliberative mind-set is induced by having participants deliberate a still unresolved personal problem (e.g.,

Should I move to a different apartment?). The implemental mind-set is induced by having participants plan the implementation of a chosen project to be resolved in the near future (e.g., moving into a different apartment). The second experimenter, being blind to this manipulation of mind-sets, then asks participants to perform certain tasks or answer questionnaires that tap into the hypothesized cognitive features of the two mind-sets. Numerous studies in social and motivation psychology have used this paradigm showing that the deliberative and the implemental mind-sets thus created have distinct consequences.

People in a deliberative mind-set usually show the following attributes: (a) They evaluate their selves accurately (i.e., rate themselves realistically with regard to intelligence, attractiveness, etc.), (b) they show reduced positive illusions of control over frequent outcomes that are uncontrollable, (c) they make less positive illusionary judgments of their invulnerability to controllable (e.g., divorce, having a drinking problem) and uncontrollable risks (e.g., death of a loved one), (d) they are impartial in the sense that they appraise desirability-related information even-handedly, (e) they are particularly effective in processing desirability-related information, and (f) they are open-minded as their processing of incidental information is generally very effective.

In contrast, people in an implemental mind-set show quite different attributes: (a) They evaluate themselves in a very positive illusionary manner (e.g., they rate themselves as much more intelligent and attractive than the average person in their peer group), (b) they show strong illusions of control over frequent, but uncontrollable outcomes, (c) they make very positive illusionary judgments of their vulnerability to controllable and uncontrollable outcomes, (d) they are partial in the sense that they focus on positive desirability-related information more than on negative desirability-related information, (e) they are particularly effective in processing information related to the realization of goals, and (f) they are closed-minded in the sense that they are rather sluggish in processing incidental information.

Recently, these effects of implemental mind-sets (enhanced self-efficacy, optimistic outcome expectations, perceptions of the task at hand as easy, etc.) were shown help people to succeed in their ongoing goal pursuits. Furthermore, people in an implemental mind-set are more optimistic in their forecasts of the survival of their romantic relationships than deliberative mind-set

individuals. When choosing test materials of different difficulty, people in implemental mind-sets preferred more difficult tasks than did people in deliberative mind-sets. Moreover, those in implemental mind-sets overestimated their probability of success as compared with people in deliberative mind-sets.

Finally, there are individual differences in the ability of activating deliberative and implemental mind-sets and their effects on cognition and behavior. Deliberative and implemental mind-set effects are moderated by a person's level of achievement motivation, social anxiety, and goal commitment. For instance, people whose achievement motive is strongly determined by hope for success (in contrast to fear of failure) show a strong illusionary optimism when they are in an implemental mind-set compared with a deliberative mind-set. Conversely, fear of failure people when in a deliberative mind-set boost their self-perception of competence (i.e., show illusionary optimism), but not when they are in an implemental mind-set.

The Rubicon model of action phases with its associated mind-set theory has stimulated a re-conceptualization of the classic concept of motivation. In the past, the term *motivation* referred to both the readiness to choose a certain course of action and the intensity and effectiveness with which the chosen course of action was implemented. Nowadays, one discusses only issues of choosing a course of action in motivational terms by pointing to the motivational variables of desirability and feasibility. However, the issue of successful implementation of a chosen course of action is considered to be volitional in nature. That is, it depends on people's willpower and their possession of relevant self-regulation skills whether a chosen course of action is ultimately implemented. The mind-set theory associated with the Rubicon model turned out to be conceptually very influential too. Theories of action control that distinguish between types of goals (e.g., abstract vs. concrete, promotion vs. prevention, learning vs. performance) have tried to test their hypotheses by creating respective mind-sets—for instance, creating why versus how mind-sets to assess differences between the pursuit of goals construed at a high versus low level of abstraction.

Anja Achtziger
Peter M. Gollwitzer

See also Goals; Implementation Intentions; Positive Illusions; Reasoned Action Theory

Further Readings

Achtziger, A., & Gollwitzer, P. M. (2006). Motivation and volition in the course of action. In J. Heckhausen & H. Heckhausen (Eds.), *Motivation and action.* Oxford, UK: Oxford University Press.

Bayer, U. C., & Gollwitzer, P. M. (2005). Mindset effects on information search in self-evaluation. *European Journal of Social Psychology, 35,* 313–327.

Gollwitzer, P. M. (1990). Action phases and mindsets. In E. T. Higgins & R. M. Sorrentino (Eds.), *Handbook of motivation and cognition: Foundation of social behavior* (Vol. 2, pp. 53–92). New York: Guilford Press.

RUMOR TRANSMISSION

Definition

Rumors are unverified information statements that people circulate to make sense of an unclear situation or to deal with a possible threat. Rumors are about issues or situations of topical interest. Rumors are like news except that news is accompanied by solid evidence; rumor is not. A classic example: "I heard that our department is being downsized; what have you heard?" Rumor discussions are thus collective sense-making and threat-management efforts. The threat could be physical or psychological. In either case, the rumor helps people actively or emotionally prepare for negative events, or to defend against threats to their self-esteem.

Although most people use *gossip* and *rumor* interchangeably, they are different. Gossip is evaluative social talk about individuals outside of their hearing. Gossip may or may not be verified. It is entertaining tittle-tattle of the sort: "Did you hear what Kyle did at the Christmas party?!" Urban legends—sometimes called contemporary or modern legends—also differ from rumor. Urban legends are funny, horrible, or tall tales that amuse us or teach us a moral lesson. They are longer narratives than rumor, with a setting, plot, climax, and denouement. Many people have heard the story of the man who lost his kidney. Away from home on a business trip, he is enticed by a woman at a bar and they return to his room; after a drink, his next memory is waking up the next morning in a bathtub packed with ice, his kidney removed—sold on the black market. Moral of the story: *Indiscretions can be costly!*

Types, Frequency, and Effects

Social psychologists have been interested in rumors since the 1930s. They often categorize them as one of three types: *Dread* rumors convey fear about a potential negative event: "The 'good-times' virus will erase your hard drive!" *Wish* rumors relate a desired outcome: "Have you heard? We're getting a big bonus this year!" *Wedge-driving* rumors divide people groups, such as this false one from World War II: "The Catholics are evading the draft." Unfortunately, wedge-driving rumors may be the most numerous of the three. Rumors have been categorized in other ways that indicate what people are collectively concerned about: Stock market rumors suggest ever-present stockholder worries over portfolio value, job-security rumors convey anxiety over possible job losses, personnel-change rumors evidence concern about how one's job duties might change with a new boss.

Rumors appear to be a regular feature of social and organizational landscapes. For example, in corporations, rumors reach the ears of management about once per week on average. Rumor activity waxes and wanes, but seems especially prevalent when important changes occur that are not well understood and may be potentially threatening. Rumors cause or contribute to a variety of attitudes and behaviors. Negative rumors can lower morale, reduce trust, and sully reputations. Wedge-driving rumors help form or strengthen prejudicial attitudes. Rumors have long been implicated in sparking riots during times of ethnic/racial tension, altering stock market trading, and changing behaviors that affect health or disease detection. Interestingly, rumors may not have to be believed to have such effects: Burger sales at McDonald's once dropped because of a false rumor that McDonald's used worm-meat—this even though people disbelieved the rumor!

Transmission and Belief

People spread rumors for three broad reasons. First, to find the facts so they can act effectively in a given situation: "I heard that I might get laid off—is this true? I'll put out my resume." Second, to enhance their relationship with the rumor recipient: Being in the know with the latest information, for example, increases one's social standing. Third, to boost one's self-esteem, often by derogating rival groups: By putting other groups down, people sometimes build up their own group—and by extension themselves—by comparison.

People are more likely to spread rumors when they are anxious (worried about a dreaded event or simply anxiety-prone), uncertain (filled with questions about what events mean or what will happen), or feel that they have lost control in a situation that is important to them. These conditions are more likely to occur when people distrust either formal news sources ("That TV news channel is biased!") or the group the rumor targets ("Management are aliens!"). Finally, rumors that are believed are more likely to be spread than are those in which we have less confidence.

People believe rumors—even fantastic ones—when the rumor accords with their previously held attitudes, it comes from a credible source, is heard repeatedly, and is not rebutted. Rumors that the leader of political party *x* tried to cover up illegal activity, for example, are believed more strongly by members of rival party *y,* who hear these rumors repeatedly from trusted party *y* officials and do not hear a rebuttal of any sort. For these reasons, the plausible rumors circulated in one community are considered fantastic in another. For example, false rumors that the AIDS virus was concocted in a Western laboratory, tested on 100,000 Africans, and led to the current African pandemic are believed by some in the U.S. African American community.

Content Change and Accuracy

In the course of rumor transmission and discussion, rumors change. Four types of change have been identified: *leveling* is the reduction of the number of details in the rumor message, *adding* is when the rumor becomes more elaborate, *sharpening* is when certain details are accentuated, and *assimilation* is the overall shaping of the rumor to fit preconceived ideas. Sharpening and assimilation occur in all forms of rumor transmission. For example, rumors about an intoxicated football player's auto accident tend to retain those elements of the story that match athlete stereotypes. Leveling tends to happen especially when rumor are transmitted serially—as in the "telephone game" or "whisper-down-the-lane." For example, 20 details may be leveled to 5 after several transmissions. In contrast, adding tends to occur in very active high-involvement rumor discussions: A rumor about a sensational murder in one's local high school is likely to be extensively elaborated.

Rumors have a reputation as being inaccurate and false, but this reputation may not be deserved.

Some situations—such as established organizational grapevines—tend to produce highly accurate rumors, whereas others—such as natural disasters—give rise to grossly inaccurate ones. Several factors affect accuracy. Accuracy is generally reduced by limits to attention and memory, relationship- and self-enhancement motives, high anxiety, the inability to check rumor veracity, and transmitting the rumor without discussion. Accuracy is enhanced when transmitted by persons who are motivated by fact-finding and situated in an established communication channel. Organizational rumors—often transmitted in communication channels that have existed for some time, checked against one another, transmitted with lots of discussion to ensure precision, and discussed by people who want to ferret out the facts—are often extremely accurate. In one organization that underwent radical downsizing, a rumor listing the names of all the people to be cut was circulated one week before the official layoff announcement—the rumor was 100% accurate.

Managing Rumors

People often desire to prevent or neutralize harmful rumors. Prevention is best accomplished by reducing the uncertainty that gives rise to rumor and by developing trust in formal sources of information. Uncertainty can be reduced even when the rumor cannot be confirmed or disconfirmed by setting a timeline for when more information will be forthcoming, stating the values and procedures by which changes and policies will be made, and stating precisely what *is* known. Rumors cannot always be prevented however. In such cases, rebuttals—of false rumors—offered by a source perceived to be appropriate and honest, conveying anxiety-reducing information, and relating the context for why the rebuttal is being offered, are most effective in reducing harmful rumor effects. Credible third parties are often effective in refuting rumors. False tales that the Procter & Gamble Corporation contributed to the Church of Satan, for example, were quickly squelched when transmitters were given "truth kits" containing letters from religious leaders stating that these malicious rumors were false.

Nicholas DiFonzo
Prashant Bordia

See also Attitude Change; Gossip; Prejudice; Self-Esteem Stability

Further Readings

Allport, G. W., & Postman, L. J. (1947). *The psychology of rumor.* New York: Holt, Rinehart & Winston.

Bordia, P., & DiFonzo, N. (2002). When social psychology became less social: Prasad and the history of rumor research. *Asian Journal of Social Psychology, 5,* 49–61.

DiFonzo, N., & Bordia, P. (2007). *Rumor psychology: Social & organizational approaches.* Washington, DC: American Psychological Association.

Rosnow, R. L. (1991). Inside rumor: A personal journey. *American Psychologist, 46,* 484–496.

Shibutani, T. (1966). *Improvised news: A sociological study of rumor.* Indianapolis, IN: Bobbs-Merrill.

S

SALIENCE

Definition

The term *salient* refers to anything (person, behavior, trait, etc.) that is prominent, conspicuous, or otherwise noticeable compared with its surroundings. Salience is usually produced by novelty or unexpectedness, but can also be brought about by shifting one's attention to that feature. Salience usually depends on context. A child would not be particularly salient at his or her school, but would be at a nursing home. The act of crying would not be salient at a funeral, but would be at a job interview. A salient feature can be thought of as the "figure" that stands out against the "ground" of all other nonsalient features.

Importance

Humans have a limited ability to process information; they cannot attend to every aspect of a situation. Salience determines which information will most likely grab one's attention and have the greatest influence on one's perception of the world. Unfortunately, the most salient information is not always the most accurate or important. Salient media coverage might cause people to overestimate the frequency of relatively unusual dangers (e.g., airplane crashes) and underestimate much more common threats (e.g., colon cancer) that do not receive salient coverage. People are not usually consciously aware of the extent to which salience affects them.

Effects

Salience has been shown to influence people's perception of the causes of events, particularly other people's behaviors. Behaviors have two possible causes: the traits of the person who performs the behavior, or aspects of the situation in which the behavior took place. Researchers have repeatedly shown that the situation in which behaviors takes place is usually not very salient to observers. Instead observers almost always focus on the behavior itself, which leads them to infer the traits of the person. If someone snaps at you, you are more likely to think that this is a mean person than that he or she is simply having a bad day. Although behaviors are quite salient for observers, the situational context is often more salient to the actors themselves, for example, "I'm smiling because one *has* to smile at job interviews." Interesting, some studies have increased the salience of actors' behavior to themselves, for example, by having them perform a task in front of a mirror, or watch a videotape of themselves performing the behavior. In this case, actors attributed their behavior to their own disposition rather than to the situation, just as an observer would, for example, "I'm smiling because I'm a happy person."

How Do Researchers Manipulate Salience?

Researchers can increase the salience of a person in a number of ways. First, they can simply direct observers' attention to that person. Second, they can change the visual characteristics of the person relative to others in the situation. For example, one person may wear a brightly colored shirt instead of a dull one, or rock in a rocking chair instead of sitting motionless. Third, researchers can arrange a situation so that the feature is more noticeable to observers. In a classic experiment by Shelley Taylor and Susan Fiske, for example, two actors were seated facing each other having a get-acquainted conversation, while other observers sat in a circle around them. If an observer could see the face of one actor better than the other, that salient actor was believed to have set the tone of the conversation, and have greater influence over the behavior of the other nonsalient actor. Similar results have been shown by having observers watch a video-taped conversation shown from different camera angles. Whichever actor is most visually salient (e.g., has their face shown by the camera) will be judged by most people to control the conversation. In an interesting twist on this experiment, the conversation being observed is between a police officer and someone confessing to a crime. People who viewed the police officer's face were more likely to perceive the confession as coerced, that is, caused by the police officer. Other research has shown that simply sitting at the head of a table will increase one's salience and cause observers to judge that person as having more leadership qualities.

Salience, Sex, and Race

Salience can affect perceptions of people who are members of minority or stereotyped groups. Researchers have manipulated the uniqueness of an actor's sex or race by changing the composition of a group the actor is in. In one study, participants listened to a tape-recorded conversation between six men. A photograph of each man appeared on a screen as he spoke, allowing researchers to manipulate the proportion of Black to White men in the group. Compared with a situation with equal representation of both races, a person who occupied solo status (the only Black person in the room) was perceived to have spoken more, and to have been more influential in the conversation. Similar studies have shown that the only woman in a room full of men is more likely to be stereotyped than is a woman in a more balanced environment. In general, salient persons and objects are evaluated more extremely than are other targets.

Salience also affects perceptions of entire groups. Smaller minority groups tend to be more salient than larger, majority groups. Observers often perceive members of smaller groups to be more similar to each other than are members of larger groups. Interesting, members of salient groups are also more likely to overestimate how much they agree with each other, and to show a stronger bias in favor of their own group.

In addition, research has shown that because salient pairings (e.g., violent crime and minority race) are more available in memory, they are likely to be overestimated when people later recall their frequency. This may contribute to the perpetuation of certain stereotypes.

Mark V. Pezzo

See also Availability Heuristic; Mortality Salience; Priming

Further Readings

Taylor, S. E., & Fiske, S. T. (1978). Salience, attention, and attribution: Top of the head phenomena. In L. Berkowitz (Ed.), *Advances in experimental social psychology* (Vol. 11, pp. 249–288). New York: Academic Press.

SATISFICING

Definition

Satisficing refers to making a decision with the goal of satisfying or fulfilling some acceptable minimum requirement (instead of choosing the best option). Decision makers who adopt a satisficing strategy do not evaluate all the available alternatives. Instead, they accept the first "good enough" option that they encounter. Satisficing is thought to be a useful decision-making strategy given that people live with limited information-processing capacity in a world of complicated and difficult choices. The cost of expending the resources required to evaluate every available option is thought to be greater than the additional value that will be gained by selecting the best option instead of the good enough option. Satisficing is typically discussed as an alternative to maximizing (maximizing the value of a decision by comparing the value of all options and selecting the best one).

Background and History

Historically, rational choice theory has strongly influenced how people study and think about decision making. When John von Neumann and Oskar

Morgenstern published *Theory of Games and Economic Behavior* in 1944, they introduced several different elements of rational decision making to the field of economics. Expected utility theory specifies that decision makers can assign an expected value to every alternative course of action. After an expected utility is assigned to every option, the alternative with the highest expected value will be selected.

However, although von Neumann and Morgenstern's work played a key role in the field of economics, psychologists began to demonstrate key ways in which actual decision makers systematically deviate from rational choice models. In the 1950s, Nobel Prize winner Herbert Simon (economist and psychologist) published a series of papers in which he suggested that it is more useful to approach the study of decision making by acknowledging that actual decision makers have to approach complicated choices with limited information and limited cognitive resources available to them. Rational choice theory requires that all options can be thoroughly evaluated, which is not the case in the real world. Simon was the first to coin the term *satisficing* when he suggested that decision makers conserve resources by choosing to fulfill some minimum requirement instead of maximizing expected value. In more recent years, psychologist Barry Schwartz borrowed Simon's term and discovered that individual people differ in the degree to which they tend to approach decisions with the goal of satisficing.

Individual Differences

Schwartz divided the world into "satisficers" versus "maximizers" when he identified existing individual differences in people's tendencies to approach decisions with the goal of satisficing versus maximizing. He measured these differences through a maximization scale that he developed and administered to several thousand participants. Following are some examples of items found on the maximization scale:

"Renting videos is really difficult. I'm always struggling to pick the best one."

"When I am in the car listening to the radio, I often check other stations to see if something better is playing, even if I am relatively satisfied with what I'm listening to."

"Whenever I'm faced with a choice, I try to imagine what all the other possibilities are, even ones that aren't present at the moment."

Participants rated each statement on a 1 to 7 scale (ranging from *completely disagree* to *completely agree*). Schwartz did not define a strict cutoff that identifies maximizers versus satisficers, but he generally calls people maximizers if their average score is higher than 4 for all the items. Satisficers generally have an average score of less than 4. The distribution of scores for his participants was relatively symmetrical about the midpoint of the scale. About one third received an average score of more than 4.75 and one third scored under 3.25. The final third scored closer to the middle, somewhere between 3.25 and 4.75. In addition, approximately 1 of every 10 participants had an average score of more than 5.5 (extreme maximizers), and similarly, about 1 of every 10 had an average score of less than 2.5 (extreme satisficers).

Importance and Implications

Schwartz also investigated implications of satisficing versus maximizing for decision makers' experiences both during and after making a choice. People who are more apt to satisfice complete a less thorough search of all available options, make decisions faster, and are less likely to engage in social comparison while choosing. After the decision, satisficers are also more likely to evaluate decision outcomes more positively, despite apparently expending less effort in the process of making the choice. For example, after making a consumer choice, satisficers are less likely to reflect on the products that they didn't choose and engage in "what if" thinking. Satisficers are happier with their choices and don't feel as regretful as maximizers. They are less likely to ruminate and think counterfactually. In addition, satisficers are less aversely affected by an increase in the number of available alternatives. For the maximizer, more options can create anxiety because they make the goal of identifying the best one more difficult to achieve.

Satisficing has also been linked to many positive psychological outcomes. Schwartz administered general well-being scales to subjects and found that satisficers are less likely to be perfectionists and less likely to suffer from depression. They are happier, more optimistic, more satisfied with life, and have higher self-esteem. People who are least likely to employ satisficing strategies (extreme maximizers) tend to demonstrate depressive symptoms that are in the borderline clinical range.

Ironically, striving for the best and adopting an approach that most closely mirrors rational choice strategies can have negative consequences. People seem to need some choice to maintain happiness, and an initial increase in choice can increase happiness. However, evidence suggests that having too much choice can decrease happiness, particularly if a person does not adopt a satisficing approach. In a complicated world with limitless options, satisficing might be the most rational approach to making decisions.

Erin Sparks

See also Decision Making; Individual Differences

Further Readings

Schwartz, B. (2004). *The paradox of choice: Why more is less.* New York: HarperCollins.

Schwartz, B., Ward, A., Monterosso, J., Lyubomirsky, S., White, K., & Lehman, D. R. (2002). Maximizing versus satisficing: Happiness is a matter of choice. *Journal of personality and social psychology, 83*(5), 1178–1197.

von Neumann, J., & Morgenstern, O. (1944). *Theory of games and economic behavior.* Princeton, NJ: Princeton University Press.

SCAPEGOAT THEORY

Definition

Scapegoat theory refers to the tendency to blame someone else for one's own problems, a process that often results in feelings of prejudice toward the person or group that one is blaming. Scapegoating serves as an opportunity to explain failure or misdeeds, while maintaining one's positive self-image. If a person who is poor or doesn't get a job that he or she applies for can blame an unfair system or the people who did get the job that he or she wanted, the person may be using the others as a scapegoat and may end up hating them as a result. However, if the system really is unfair and keeps the person from succeeding financially, or the other people got the job because of nepotism or illegitimate preferential treatment, then blaming those factors would not be scapegoating. Essentially, scapegoating generally employs a stand-in for one's own failures so that one doesn't have to face one's own weaknesses.

Origins

The term itself comes from the Bible's reference to a goat upon which Aaron cast all the sins of Israel and then banished to the wilderness. Hence, the goat, though presumably blameless, was essentially punished for the sins of the people of Israel. Psychologists have expanded the concept to include not only someone else to pay the price for one's own immorality but also a target of blame and explanation when outcomes are not what one hoped for.

Historical and Research Applications

History contains a number of examples of political leaders using scapegoats to rally their people at the expense of a despised group. In perhaps the most blatant and tragic example, Adolf Hitler notoriously scapegoated Jews for the fact that other Germans were suffering after World War I. By depicting Jews as more commercially successful than the average German citizen—and unfairly so, by favoring other Jews—he rallied his citizens to extreme levels of nationalism at the expense of Jews and other groups. He thus conjured resentment and hatred toward the group, simultaneously unifying other Germans to a singular cause: the perceived improvement of Germany.

The concept of scapegoating is also somewhat consistent with Sigmund Freud's notions of displacement or projection as defense mechanisms. According to Freud, people displace hostility that they hold toward unacceptable targets (e.g., parents, the boss) onto less powerful ones. Similarly, projection refers to one's tendency to attribute one's own unacceptable feelings or anxieties onto others, thus denying them within oneself. Both mechanisms protect people from their illicit desires or fears by helping them reject the notion that they are the holders of such feelings. As such, the target of their displacement or projection may serve as a scapegoat.

More recently, social psychologists have explained the tendency to scapegoat in similar terms, but with some qualifications and clarifications. For example, the notion of displaced aggression has received a good deal of attention in the field. If a woman has a fight with her boyfriend, she may come home and kick her dog for a minor misbehavior. The dog, then, is her scapegoat and is paying the price for the fight with the boyfriend. The aggression that the fight produced is not being directed toward its true cause, but instead is directed at the dog, which is a more acceptable target because it cannot retaliate or argue back, as the boyfriend is likely to do. In addition, the theory of relative deprivation is relevant as an explanation for people's tendency to scapegoat. This theory suggests that people experience negative emotions when they feel as though they are treated relatively poorly for illegitimate reasons. For example, a person may be satisfied with his or her salary until the person learns that a colleague whose work is not great but who is friends with the boss gets a raise. Now the person is relatively deprived and may resent the colleague for the person's lower salary.

Other researchers have specified some conditions in which scapegoating against a particular group is most likely to occur. For example, the scapegoated group tends to be one of relatively low power. Otherwise, the group would be able to stamp out the opposition brought from the masses. The scapegoated group also tends to be a group that is somehow recognizable as distinct from the ingroup (the group to which one belongs), so that group members can be easily identified and associated with the undesired situation. Finally, the scapegoat tends to pose a real threat to the ingroup, intentionally or unintentionally. For example, lynchings against Blacks rose dramatically when the economic prospects for Whites began to drop off. African Americans were perceived as a greater threat to the increasingly scarce jobs and opportunities and so were punished in brutally tragic ways. In a land of plenty or when a group is kept completely under wraps, that group poses no threat and therefore does not present the opportunity to serve as a scapegoat.

Elliott D. Hammer

See also Displaced Aggression; Intergroup Relations; Projection; Self-Serving Bias

Further Readings

Glick, P. (2002). Sacrificial lambs dressed in wolves' clothing: Envious prejudice, ideology, and the scapegoating of Jews. In L. S. Newman & R. Erber (Eds.), *Understanding genocide: The social psychology of the Holocaust* (pp. 113–142). New York: Oxford University Press.

SCARCITY PRINCIPLE

Definition

According to the scarcity principle, objects become more attractive when there are not very many of them. This scarcity may be either real or imagined. People assume that because others appear to want something, and it is in short supply, it must be valuable. In a classic demonstration of the scarcity principle, students were divided into two groups. One group was asked to choose a cookie from a jar with two cookies. The other group was asked to choose a cookie from a jar that contained ten cookies. Consistent with the scarcity principle, students who chose from the jar with two cookies (scarce condition) rated the cookies as more desirable than students who chose from the jar with ten cookies (plentiful condition).

Importance of Topic

Imagine the following scenario, which illustrates several strategic compliance techniques, most notably the scarcity principle. A family's dinner is interrupted by a knock on the door. The father, Fred, answered the door to find an older gentleman, Al, who was holding a bundle of sketches. Al greeted Fred and told him of a great opportunity. For the low, low price of $249, Al would sketch a portrait of Fred's house. By this time, Fred's wife, Mary, had come outside with their two young sons. The man quickly commented on how cute the boys were and proceeded with his pitch. "This type of sketch normally costs $700," he informed the couple. Knowing the perils of making quick, emotional decisions, Fred asked Al for his phone number to call him back after discussing his offer. Al quickly replied, "I can't really come back because of time constraints. I do all the sketches and all the door-to-door contacting, so it's simply not efficient for me to return. I really need to know tonight." Mary remarked that she really wanted to have a portrait of their house in the living room and Fred reluctantly agreed. They discussed it briefly and told Al they'd give him $200. Al countered with $225 and no sales tax, and they agreed on a deal. Fred and Mary thought, "Wow, did we ever get a bargain: from $700 to $249 to $225 without sales tax! We had saved nearly $500!"

It was only after Fred and Mary sat down later that evening that they realized Al was indeed an artist: both a sketch artist and a master in the art of persuasion! Maybe, instead of saving money, they unexpectedly spent $225 more than they planned to at the outset of the evening. Al had skillfully employed a number of compliance techniques, particularly in his use of the scarcity principle. By telling the couple they had to decide immediately, Al created the illusion that this opportunity would not be available again. Notice how Al did not even respond to their question of whether they could call him. If he had, the sketch would no longer be scarce. By creating the false impression that they had to decide now, Al invoked the scarcity principle, a powerful weapon of social influence.

Of course, Al is not alone in his recognition of the power of a scarce resource. Walk through any mall to find any number of messages alerting people to unbelievable opportunities to purchase items they have always (or never) wanted. But, to take advantage of these fabulous offers, one must act now. Consider the following signs:

"Hurry, while supplies last!" (Presumably supplies will be around as long as people keep buying.)

"Don't miss out!" (Who wants to miss out, on anything?)

"Don't be left out in the cold!" (People in cold climates are particularly sensitive to this one.)

"Buy today—save thousands!" (Who in their right mind doesn't want to save thousands?)

Employed effectively, the scarcity principle is a subtle way to take advantage of the fact that most people assume that if something is in short supply, others must like it, it must be good, and a purchase ought to be made quickly. The scarcity principle has the potential to make something good seem great, and something undesirable seem desirable. The belief that one may miss out on a fabulous opportunity creates a sense of urgency, leading individuals to make emotional, rather than rational, decisions. Thus, one may end up purchasing unwanted items, simply because of what psychologist Robert Cialdini has termed a *feeding frenzy*, not unlike that witnessed among fish when food is sprinkled in a lake. This explains why every holiday season, parents and children line up and fight for the hottest new toys. By creating the perception of scarcity, corporations recognize their products will be more appealing. Hence, the race to purchase Cabbage Patch Kids in the 1980s, Beanie Babies in the 1990s, and sadly, gasoline in the 21st century.

Implications

Fortunately, there are ways to avoid falling prey to the scarcity principle. First, when people start feeling emotional during a decision, they can stop, and promise to return to the decision when they feel more rational. Although a salesperson may claim that one must act now, odds are the same offer will still be around tomorrow. Actually, many stores seem to have a once-a-year sale on a nearly weekly basis! Second, individuals can limit their purchases to items they had already planned to buy. Anytime people are caught off guard by an offer, they should consciously choose to wait some time before deciding whether or not to purchase the item. Legendary economist John Galbraith theorized that business manufactures the needs it seeks to satisfy. Consumers will be far better off if they decide what they need and make their purchases accordingly, rather than letting others create and decide these needs for them.

John M. Tauer

See also Consumer Behavior; Decision Making

Further Readings

Cialdini, R. B. (2001). *Influence: Science and practice.* Needham Heights, MA: Allyn & Bacon.
Levine, R. (2003). *The power of persuasion.* Hoboken, NJ: Wiley.

SCHEMAS

Definition

A schema is a cognitive representation of a concept, its associated characteristics, and how those characteristics are interrelated. Social schemas are representations of social concepts and may include notions of physical appearance, traits, behavioral information, and functions. Social schemas may be relatively concrete (e.g., one's fifth-grade teacher) or abstract (e.g., likable person). When a schema is activated, the characteristics of the concept are evoked spontaneously. For example, the concept "librarian" may bring to mind a drably attired unmarried woman, who is quiet, reads books, and helps one conduct a literature search. Those characterizations may be entirely false in general, and certainly many specific librarians will differ from that stereotype, but they are the characteristics that the observer associates with the concept. Although social schemas for the same concept vary somewhat from person to person, observers who share a common culture or upbringing often hold strikingly similar schemas. In short, social schemas comprise the expectations that observers have for the characteristics and behavior of themselves, other people, and social situations.

Types of Social Schemas

Observers develop schemas for individual social roles (e.g., librarians) and social groups (e.g., ethnic and cultural outgroups). Schemas for social groups fall under the rubric of stereotypes, and the basic principles discussed later apply to them as well as to other types of schemas.

An event schema, sometimes termed a script, prescribes a chronological order to the relation among the characteristics. Going out to dinner at a four-star restaurant, one expects first to be greeted, then guided to a table, then order drinks, and so forth. Violation of the event schema (e.g., a pronounced delay in ordering drinks) may elicit surprise and possible substitution of another script. Scripts that additionally require causal coherence among the characteristics are termed *narratives*. In a murder trial, for instance, a prosecuting attorney may outline a plausible sequence of events that explains the body of evidence. In a related vein, people form excuses by purporting a narrative of unforeseeable and unavoidable events, thereby reducing their apparent responsibility for negative outcomes. Schemas thus can play an important role in how people understand the causes of behavior and events.

A self-schema is an integrated collection of knowledge, beliefs, attitudes, and memories about the self. Self-schemas may develop around personality traits, roles in relationships, occupations, activities, opinions, and other characteristics that are part of an individual's definition of self. Typically, individuals form self-schemas for characteristics that they believe to be important or central to who they are. In other words, individuals are schematic on central characteristics, but may be aschematic on less central characteristics. For example, individuals who believe that their friendliness is a particularly defining characteristic of their self-concepts probably have a self-schema for friendliness. If such individuals do not consider politics interesting or important, they likely are aschematic on a dimension such as political activism.

Self-schemas, and schemas in general, may vary in their degree of complexity. For example, some people might off-handedly acknowledge their own intelligence, but may view friendliness as more self-defining and important. Their mental representation of friendliness would be more complex, including detailed memories of their own friendly behaviors, stable beliefs about the causes and consequences of friendliness, and certainty about their own friendliness. They also might categorize other people's behaviors in terms of friendliness, thereby using the self-schema as a filter for interpreting their social world.

Uses of Social Schemas

Schemas can affect whether observers notice information as well as the inferences that they draw about that information. Specifically, schemas can affect how observers categorize a situation or group, process information about it, and then remember that information. Schemas encourage information processing through the schematic lens, often overlooking the unique qualities of the social situation or person. For example, a library patron hurrying to find assistance may notice and approach a drably attired person perusing a heavy reference volume, only to suffer embarrassment when the person denies being the librarian. Relying primarily on the librarian schema led to a categorization error. Later, when the actual librarian is identified, the hurried patron notices sensible shoes and eyeglasses, but misses schema-irrelevant qualities such as the tarnished school ring and brown eyes. Generally speaking, schema-consistent information is noticed and remembered better than schema-irrelevant information, sometimes yielding judgment errors.

The previous example also illustrates that schema use is influenced by observer goals. The patron has a pressing goal to find immediate assistance. Thus, the patron relies on the librarian schema and schema-consistent information to accelerate the process. If the patron had a different goal or fewer time constraints, the impression formation process likely would change. For instance, if the patron hopes to contest a large library fee, a more careful search process might be desired. An accuracy goal generally discourages reliance on schemas and encourages attention to unique behaviors and qualities in forming impressions. When seeking accuracy, even schema-inconsistent information may be remembered better than it typically would be because observers feel compelled to expend extra effort to reconcile such information in light of the schema.

Implications

In general, schemas help to organize social information and facilitate navigation through social environments. This organization allows people to use fewer cognitive resources in the detection and interpretation of schema-relevant information, thus increasing efficiency and sparing important resources that could be used for interacting with novel and complex stimuli. However, overreliance upon schemas may lead observers to miss important information. For instance, mistaking a patron for the librarian both interferes with the search for the real librarian and yields an embarrassing interaction with the nonlibrarian. When relying on schemas to guide social experiences, the cost of missing important information must be weighed against the benefit of efficiency.

Janet B. Ruscher
Alecia M. Santuzzi

See also Impression Management; Roles and Role Theory; Scripts; Stereotypes and Stereotyping

Further Readings

Fiske, S. T., & Taylor, S. E. (1991). *Social cognition* (2nd ed.). New York: McGraw-Hill.

Kunda, Z. (2001). *Social cognition: Making sense of people.* Cambridge: MIT Press.

SCRIPTS

Let me tell you a simple story: John went to a restaurant. He ordered lobster. He paid the check and left.

Now let me ask you some questions about your understanding of this story: What did John eat? Did he sit down? Whom did he give money to? Why?

These questions are easy to answer. Unfortunately, your answers to them have no basis in actual fact. John may have put the lobster in his pocket. He might have been standing on one foot while eating (if he was eating). Who really knows whom he paid?

You feel we know the answer to these questions because you are relying on knowledge you have about common situations that you have encountered in your own life. What kind of knowledge is this? Where does it reside? How is it that your understanding depends on guessing?

People have scripts. A *script* can be best understood as a package of knowledge that a person has about particular kinds of situations that he or she has encountered frequently. Some scripts are culturally common, everyone you know shares them, and some scripts are idiosyncratic, which means that only you know about them. When you refer to something that takes place in a restaurant you can leave out most of the details because you know that your listener can fill them in. You know what your listener knows. But, if you were telling a story about a situation that only you were familiar with, you would have to explain what was happening in great detail. Knowing that your listener has the baseball script, you can describe a game to him or her quite quickly. But, if you were speaking to someone who had never seen a baseball game you would either have to make reference to a script the listener already had (cricket perhaps) or else you would be in for a long explanation.

Scripts help people understand what others are telling them and also help people comprehend what they are seeing and experiencing. When a person wants to order in a restaurant and starts to talk to the waiter and he hands the person a piece of paper and a pencil, the person is surprised. He or she may not know what to do. But, the person may have had experience with private clubs that want orders written down. If not, the person will ask. When expectations are violated, when a script fails and things don't happen the way a person expected, he or she must adjust.

Adjustments in daily life to script violations are the basis of learning. Next time the person will know to expect the waiter to hand him or her a paper and pencil. Or the person might generalize and decide that next time doesn't only mean in this restaurant but in any restaurant of this type. Making generalizations about type is a major aspect of learning. Every time a script is violated in some way, every time a person's expectations fail, he or she must rewrite the script, so as not to be fooled next time.

Scripts are really just packages of expectations about what people will do in given situations, so one is constantly surprised since other people don't always do what one expects. This means in effect, that although scripts serve the obvious role of telling people what will happen next, they also have a less obvious role as organizers of the memories of experiences people have had.

Remember that time in the airplane when the flight attendant threw the food packages at the passengers? You would remember such an experience, and might tell people a story about it: "You know what happened on my flight?" Stories are descriptions of script violations of an interesting sort. But, suppose that this happened twice, or five times; suppose it happened every time you flew a particular airline. Then, you would match one script violation with another, to realize that it wasn't a script violation at all, just a different script you hadn't known about. Learning depends on being able to remember when and how a script failed, marking that failure with a memory or story about the failure event, and then being able to recognize a similar incident and make a new script.

Scripts fail all the time. This is why people have trouble understanding each other. Their scripts are not identical. What one person assumes about a situation—the script he or she has built because of the experiences he or she has had—may not match another's because that person has had different experiences. Children get upset when their scripts fail. They cry because what they assumed would happen didn't happen. Their world model is naive and faulty. But they recover day by day, growing scripts that are just like the ones that adults have. They do this by expecting, failing, explaining their failure (maybe they ask someone for help), and making a new expectation, which will probably fail too someday. This cycle of understanding is a means by which people can learn every day from every experience.

Some people stop learning. They expect all scripts to be followed the way they always were. They get angry when a fork is on the wrong side of a plate because that's the way it has always been and has to be. All people have such rigidity in their scripts. They have scripts that others wouldn't consider violating because they want to live in an orderly world. People confuse other people when they fail to follow culturally agreed upon scripts. People depend on other people to follow the rules. And, their understanding of the behavior of others depends on everyone agreeing to behave in restaurants the way people behave in restaurants. It is so much easier to communicate that way.

Scripts dominate people's thinking lives. They organize people's memories, they drive people's comprehension, and they cause learning to happen when they fail.

Roger C. Schank

See also Expectations; Memory; Schemas

Further Readings

Schank, R. C. (with Abelson, R.). (1977). *Scripts, plans, goals and understanding: An inquiry into human knowledge structures.* Hillsdale, NJ: Erlbaum.

Schank, R. C. (1982). *Dynamic memory: A theory of learning in computers and people.* Cambridge, UK: Cambridge University Press.

Schank, R. C. (1986). *Explanation patterns: Understanding mechanically and creatively.* Hillsdale, NJ: Erlbaum.

Schank, R. C. (1995). *Tell me a story: Narrative and intelligence.* Evanston, IL: Northwestern University Press.

SEARCH FOR MEANING IN LIFE

Definition

The search for meaning in life refers to the idea that individuals are strongly motivated to find meaning in their lives, that is, to be able to understand the nature of their personal existence, and feel it is significant and purposeful. Life feels meaningful to people when they can satisfactorily answer the big questions about their lives, such as who am I, why am I here, what is truly important to me, what am I supposed to do with my life. That finding meaning in life is considered a fundamental motivation by some means that human beings must perceive a sufficient amount of meaning in their lives. In other words, feeling that one's life is significant, comprehensible, or purposeful may be necessary for human psychological functioning.

Background and History

For millennia, attempting to understand what makes life meaningful had been the task of artists, theologians, and philosophers. Following World War I, some influential philosophers asserted that life is inherently meaningless. They believed that there was no higher purpose to the universe, and therefore people were all alone in trying to figure out what their individual lives were all about. However, people will go to great lengths to defend their ideas of what life is really all about. In other words, they firmly hold onto their life meanings. For example, many people strive to defend specific religious, moral, or scientific beliefs in the face of contradictory opinions or beliefs. From this observation, several psychologists proposed that people must be motivated to find meaning in their lives.

Alfred Adler said that people innately strive to accomplish the purpose of their lives, particularly through participation in social activities. Erik Erikson proposed the need for self-integration in later life. In this approach, searching for meaning focuses on struggling to understand one's life experiences and what it all has meant in the Big Picture. Eric Fromm stressed the importance of meaning in human life and suggested that feeling alienated from others and mindlessly feeling, thinking, and acting during daily and work activities reduces our ability to find life meaningful. Abraham Maslow thought meaning would arise from self-actualization, or achieving one's full potential.

Fromm's ideas about alienation and automatization in modern life echo work by Viktor Frankl, the person who is most closely associated with psychological work on meaning in life. Frankl's experiences as a survivor of Germany's World War II concentration camps convinced him of the importance of finding a purpose for living. He felt that the biggest difference between those who did and did not survive the horrific camps was not how much they were forced to work, how little they had to eat, or how exposed to the elements they were (everyone had to work to exhaustion, no one had enough to eat, and all were greatly exposed to adverse weather). Instead, Frankl believed that Friedrich Nietzsche's maxim— by having "our own *why* of life we shall get along with almost any *how*"—made the critical difference. Frankl believed that all people must find their own, unique why—in other words, their purpose in life. He wrote that those who found some meaning or purpose were more likely to survive the concentration camps, and those who had lost their purpose were almost certainly doomed. Following Frankl's writings, and his founding of logotherapy (literally, meaning-healing), psychological work on the importance of searching for meaning accelerated dramatically. Roy Baumeister's argument that meaning in life is rooted largely in people's strivings for feelings of purpose, value in what they do, control and capability, and self-worth ushered in the modern era of social psychological research into the search for meaning.

Two important distinctions must be made between the search for meaning in life and related psychological processes. First, although Frankl wrote that the will to meaning drove each person to find the unique meaning of his or her own life, others distinguished between searching for meaning and having meaning. A common assumption is that only people without

meaning in life would search for it. Essentially, the assumption was that searching for and feeling the presence of meaning in life were opposite ends of the same continuum.

Several lines of research, however, demonstrate that searching for meaning is different from having meaning. Psychological measures of how much people are searching for meaning and how much meaning people feel in their lives have very little overlap. Also, the assumption that searching for and having meaning are opposite versions of the same thing may be culturally bound. That is to say, among European Americans (who often think in terms of individuality and dichotomies), there is a small, inverse relation between the two (the less you have, the more you search, and vice versa), whereas some evidence suggests that among people from cultures that are more traditionally collectivistic or holistic (who often think in terms of relationships or harmony, e.g., Japan), the two variables may be positively related (the more you search, the more you feel you have, and vice versa). Those whose cultural influences are somewhere in between (e.g., Spaniards) appear to report no relation between them. Finally, some evidence also indicates that searching for meaning and having meaning fluctuate in their relation to each other depending on age and stages in life. For example, the relation may be less strong in youth and stronger in older adulthood. A younger person might be searching for more meaning and also feel life is meaningful, whereas an older adult is more likely to search for meaning in life if he or she feels that life is somewhat meaningless.

The second important distinction to make is between searching for meaning in life and searching for some sort of meaning in a traumatic or aversive event. Those who have experienced traumatic events, such as being assaulted, losing a loved one, or having a miscarriage, often struggle with the question, why did this happen. Frequently, attempts to answer such questions are referred to as a search for meaning. It is probably more accurate to refer to them as efforts to find situational meaning or attributions. The search for meaning in life refers to attempts to understand what one's life as a whole means, rather than more circumscribed efforts to understand a particular event.

Importance

If the search for meaning in life is an important psychological motivation, it should be important to human welfare. We know with certainty that the presence of meaning in life is related to more well-being in relationships, work, and life in general, as well as to less psychological distress. However, we cannot assume that people who are searching for meaning in life are simply less happy and more distressed. The search for meaning in life might motivate people to immerse themselves in religion, volunteering, wilderness adventures, or philosophy just as much as it might drive them to despair. Even people who already feel that their lives are full of meaning might be searching for a deeper understanding of that meaning, or be trying to adjust to a big life change such as having children, or they might be looking for new sources of meaning. For example, a successful athlete might derive meaning from athletic competition. A career-ending injury might take away that source of meaning, and the athlete might look to family, friends, religion, or social service as potential new sources of meaning.

Those highest in the search for meaning appear somewhat less happy, more anxious, and more depressed, but they also appear more open-minded and thoughtful in some ways, reflecting on their past experiences and asking questions about the nature of their religious beliefs. How much people are searching for meaning also varies from day to day. On days when people are searching for meaning in life, they are actually happier. So, even though people who are usually searching for meaning are less happy, people who momentarily search for meaning enjoy the process in the short term. In some ways this supports the theory that the search for meaning is an important psychological motivation: Those who are able to meet temporarily strong needs for meaning over a day or two are happy with their success, whereas those who must search for longer periods, or who are almost always trying to meet this need, are unhappy.

Individual Differences

People differ in the strength and intensity of their search for meaning in life. Psychologists have developed questionnaires in recent years to measure these differences. Recent efforts to develop psychometrically sound measures of the search for meaning in life appear promising, although more research and theory development are needed. People who score high on search for meaning measures are usually looking for more meaning and purpose in their lives. People who score low are rarely looking for meaning and purpose. Scores on this scale are stable, even over 1 year,

meaning that people who are usually searching for meaning in life now will probably still be searching next year.

Michael F. Steger
Todd B. Kashdan

See also Happiness; Phenomenal Self; Self-Awareness

Further Readings

Baumeister, R. F. (1991). *Meanings of life.* New York: Guilford Press.

Frankl, V. E. (1963). *Man's search for meaning: An introduction to logotherapy.* New York: Washington Square Press.

Steger, M. F., Frazier, P., Oishi, S., & Kaler, M (2006). The Meaning in Life Questionnaire: Assessing the presence of and search for meaning in life. *Journal of Counseling Psychology, 53,* 80–93.

SELF

Definition

In psychology, the notion of the self refers to a person's experience as a single, unitary, autonomous being that is separate from others, experienced with continuity through time and place. The experience of the self includes consciousness of one's physicality as well as one's inner character and emotional life.

People experience their selves in two senses. The first is as an active agent who acts on the world as well as being influenced by that world. This type of self is usually referred to as the *I*, and focuses on how people experience themselves as doers. The second is as an object of reflection and evaluation. In this type of self, people turn their attention to their physical and psychological attributes to contemplate the constellation of skills, traits, attitudes, opinions, and feelings that they may have. This type of self is referred to as the *me,* and focuses on how people observe themselves from the outside looking in, much like people monitor and contemplate the competence and character of other people.

History and Development

Everyone has an experience of self. That self, however, can be quite different from the one experienced by another person. For example, historians suggest that people in medieval times experienced themselves quite differently from the way people do today. Literature from that time suggests that people did not possess the rich interior lives that people experience today but, rather, equated a person's self with his or her public actions. Not until the 16th century, according to the literature of the time, did people conceive of an inner self whose thoughts and feelings might differ from the way he or she acted. Over time, that inner self would become to be considered as the individual's *real self,* which reflected who the person really is. Today, people feel their selves are more accurately revealed by their interior thoughts and feelings rather than by the actions they take (although people often reverse this stance in their opinions of others, thinking others are revealed more by their actions than by their feelings and beliefs they express about those actions).

People also differ in their experience of self as they age and develop. Indeed, evidence indicates that people are not born with a sense of self, but that the notion that one is a separate and autonomous being is one that the child must develop. For example, suppose you placed a large orange mark on the forehead of a toddler, and then put the toddler in front of a mirror, a procedure known as a *mark test.* Children don't begin to show any recognition that it is *their self* that they are seeing in the mirror, reaching for their own foreheads to touch the mark, until they are between 18 and 24 months old.

The senses of self that children develop may also differ from the mature one they will attain when they are older. In 1967, Morris Rosenberg asked 10-year-olds to describe themselves in 10 sentences. The children tended to describe themselves in physical terms. Not until a few years later did children, at the edge of adolescence, began to describe themselves in terms of their personality and character. However, some psychologists believe that a psychological rather than a physical sense of self develops much earlier than 10 years old. For example, ask young children if someone would be a different person if that person's body were replaced by someone else's, and children generally say no. However, if that person's personality were replaced by another individual's personality, children argue that that person's self has now been changed.

People in different cultures may also differ in the elements that make up their sense of self. North Americans and Western Europeans tend to view themselves as independent beings. Ask them to describe themselves, and they tend to dwell on their individual skills and personality traits (e.g., as an intelligent, moral, and hardworking individual). Individuals from the Far East (e.g., Japan), however, tend to ascribe to a more interdependent view of self, defining who they are in terms of their social relations and place in the world. Ask them to describe themselves, and they tend to focus more than do Americans on social roles that they fill in their everyday life (e.g., as mother, or daughter, or as a manager in a local firm).

Some mental illnesses, such as Alzheimer's or bipolar affective disorder, alter or disrupt people's experience of the self. For example, people suffering from autism appear to possess rather concrete, physical experiences of self. They do not experience the self at a more abstract level. If they answer a questionnaire about their personality traits, they later do not remember the traits that they said they possessed. This is in sharp contrast to people not suffering from autism, who show a strong memory bias toward recalling the traits they said were self-descriptive. This difference can be explained if one assumes that nonsufferers have a *self-schema* about themselves, that is, a cognitive representation of their inner personality that aids their later memory. Those with autism, it appears, do not have a self-schema that is as richly developed.

In addition, schizophrenia can damage a person's experience of self. The disordered thought associated with schizophrenia can lead people to lose the experience of themselves as an individual with an unbroken history from the past to the present. Schizophrenia can also lead a person to confuse where his or her self ends and the outside world begins. This can be an important aspect of hallucinations and delusions. People suffering from schizophrenia may lose track of how much they themselves author their hallucinations, instead thinking that the hallucinations come from the outside world.

Implications

The self that people possess has profound implications for their thoughts, emotional reactions, and behavior. For example, the thoughts people have often are crafted to maintain the sense of self that they possess. This is especially true for thoughts about other people. The impressions that people tend to have about themselves (their "me's"), at least in North America and Western Europe, tend to be rather positive ones with many strengths and proficiencies. People tend to see other people who share some similarity as also imbued with these same strengths and weaknesses, whereas people who are different are more likely to be seen as having shortcomings and weaknesses. In this way, people can bolster their self-impressions as lovable and capable people.

A sense of self also influences the emotions people feel. People do not feel merely bad or good, but experience an entire panoply of emotions. Some emotions arise because people view that they authored the actions that produced them. When students study hard and do well on tests, they feel happy and proud. If they wrong a friend, they do not feel unhappy; they feel guilty. If they are worried about how their action looks to others, they feel shame, or perhaps embarrassment. Many emotions involve self-consciousness, and the experience of all these emotions requires a sense of self.

Finally, people's views of themselves can significantly affect their behavior. People often act in ways to maintain the view of self they possess. For example, if you ask people whether they would give to charity, they will likely say yes. If someone else approaches them a few days later and asks them to donate, people are then more likely to donate (relative to a group not asked), even though they do not connect the second request to the original question. In a similar way, if you ask a person whether people should save water during a drought, he or she typically responds that they should and do. If you then point out what a long shower the person just had (such as is done in studies of hypocrisy), the person is much more likely to take shorter showers in the future. In short, the actions people take are constrained by the views they have of themselves, especially if those views are made salient to them.

David Dunning

See also Independent Self-Construals; Interdependent Self-Construals; Looking-Glass Self; Phenomenal Self; Schemas; Self-Enhancement

Further Readings

Baumeister, R. F. (1997). How the self became a problem: A psychological review of historical research. *Journal of Personality and Social Psychology, 52,* 163–176.

Baumeister, R. F. (1998). The self. In D. T. Gilbert, S. T. Fiske, & G. Lindzey (Eds.), *The handbook of social psychology* (4th ed., Vol. 1, pp. 680–740). Boston: McGraw-Hill, 1998.

Brown, J. D. (1998). *The self.* New York: McGraw-Hill.

Leary, M., & Tangney, J. (Eds.). (2002). *Handbook of self and identity.* New York: Guilford Press.

SELF-AFFIRMATION THEORY

Definition

The self-affirmation theory posits that people have a fundamental motivation to maintain self-integrity, a perception of themselves as good, virtuous, and able to predict and control important outcomes. In virtually all cultures and historical periods, there are socially shared conceptions of what it means to be a person of self-integrity. Having self-integrity means that one perceives oneself as living up to a culturally specified conception of goodness, virtue, and agency. Self-affirmation theory examines how people maintain self-integrity when this perception of the self is threatened.

Background and History

From humanist psychologists like Abraham Maslow and Carl Rogers to contemporary investigators examining the psychology of self-esteem, there has been a historical emphasis in psychology on the importance of people's sense of personal regard. Some have suggested that a sense of personal regard emerges early in the life of an infant and remains relatively stable through the lifetime.

Contemporary researchers have documented the various adaptations people deploy to maintain self-regard. The social psychologist Daniel Gilbert and his colleagues have suggested that people have a psychological immune system that initiates psychological adaptations to threats to self-regard. Indeed, these protective adaptations may lead to rationalizations and even distortions of reality. The social psychologist Tony Greenwald described the self as totalitarian in its ambition to interpret the world in a way congenial to its desires and needs. People view themselves as able to control outcomes that they objectively cannot. They take excessive credit for success while denying responsibility for failure. They are overoptimistic in their predictions of future success and are blind to their own incompetence. People resist updating their beliefs and behavior in light of new experience and information, preferring to maintain the illusion that they were right all along. Although people are certainly capable of realism and self-criticism, ego-defensiveness nevertheless seems to be a pervasive human penchant.

The social psychologist Claude Steele first proposed the theory of self-affirmation. A major insight of this theory involves the notion that although people try to maintain specific self-images (such as "being a good student" or "being a good family member"), that is not their primary motivation. Rather, individuals are motivated to maintain *global* self-integrity, a general perception of their goodness, virtue, and efficacy. There is thus some fungibility in the sources of self-integrity. If individuals feel relatively positive about themselves in one domain, they are willing and able to tolerate a threat to their self-integrity in another domain.

Self-affirmation theory led to a reinterpretation of classic research findings in cognitive dissonance. In a classic cognitive dissonance study, people are shown to change their attitudes to bring them in line with their past behavior. People led to commit an action espousing a position with which they disagree (for example, students who write in favor of tuition increases) subsequently come to agree with the position when they believe that their actions were freely chosen. Doing so is a form of rationalization and self-justification; it convinces the individual that his or her action was the right one. Previously, such effects had been viewed as evidence of a basic motivation for psychological consistency; people want to see their attitudes as consistent with their actions. However, Steele and colleagues demonstrated that these effects arise, in part, from the motivation to maintain self-integrity. Thus, when people are given an opportunity to affirm their self-integrity in an alternative domain, the rationalization effect disappears. For example, when people were given the opportunity to express the importance of a cherished personal value (for example, when science students were allowed to don a white lab coat, or when people who valued aesthetics were allowed to assert their love of art), these individuals did not defensively change their attitudes to make them concordant with their behavior.

Contributions of Self-Affirmation Theory

When self-integrity is threatened, according to self-affirmation theory, people need not defensively rationalize or distort reality. Instead, they can reestablish self-integrity through affirmations of alternative domains of self-worth unrelated to the provoking threat. Such self-affirmations, by fulfilling the need to protect self-integrity in the face of threat, can enable people to deal with threatening events and information without resorting to defensive bias. Self-affirmations can take the form of reflections on important, overarching values (such as relationships with friends and family) or on a prized skill.

Numerous studies demonstrate that individuals are less likely to rationalize, deny, or resist threatening information in one domain if their sense of self-integrity is affirmed in another domain. People have been shown to be more open to persuasive information, and less biased in their evaluations of political information and health risk warnings if they are first permitted to self-affirm in an unrelated domain, for instance, by reflecting on an important personal value. Self-affirmed individuals are also more likely to acknowledge their own personal responsibility (and their group's collective responsibility) for defeat. In addition, people are more open to threatening courses of action—for example, compromising with an adversary in a divisive social-political dispute—when self-affirmed. Self-affirmation theory also illuminates the way in which prejudice and stereotyping are forms of self-integrity maintenance. The social psychologists Steven Fein and Steven Spencer showed that respondents were less likely to discriminate against a Jewish job candidate if they had previously been provided with a self-affirmation. People, it seems, can use a negative stereotype as a cognitively justifiable way of putting other people down, to make themselves feel good. However, if their needs for self-integrity are met in another domain, they have less need to resort to negative stereotypes.

Self-affirmations can also help to reduce physiological and psychological stress responses. David Creswell and colleagues had participants complete a self-affirmation procedure before engaging in the stressful experience of public speaking and mental arithmetic in front of a hostile audience. Unlike those in a control condition, those in the self-affirmation condition did not show any changes from baseline in their levels of the stress hormone cortisol. Because chronic stress is linked to physical illness, this finding also suggests that affirming the self could have positive effects on health outcomes.

One of the most important implications of contemporary research on self-affirmation theory involves its demonstration that seemingly small interventions can have large effects, if they are attuned to psychological processes of self-integrity maintenance. Self-affirmation was used successfully to mitigate the psychological threat associated with being the target of a negative stereotype in school. Previous research had demonstrated that African Americans experience threat and its concomitant stress, in situations in which they know that they or fellow group members could be judged in light of a negative racial stereotype. This stress, in turn, can undermine performance. A series of field experiments demonstrated that a self-affirmation, administered for 15 minutes in the context of students' classroom activities, improved African American students' end-of-term course grades and thus reduced the racial achievement gap by 40%. Although the affirmed state stemming from a self-affirmation may appear relatively brief, the changes in attributions and information processing it prompts can become self-reinforcing or self-sustaining over time.

Research and theorizing inspired by self-affirmation theory has led to theoretical advances in social psychology, with wide-ranging implications for many instances of human functioning and frailty. Self-affirmation theory research suggests that defensive resistance, self-serving illusions, intransigence in social dispute, prejudice and stereotyping, stress, illness, and intellectual underperformance can be understood as arising, in part, from threats to self-integrity and the motivation to protect it. Self-affirmation theory provides a framework for understanding the origins of these problems and an optimistic perspective for their resolution.

Geoffrey L. Cohen
David K. Sherman

See also Cognitive Dissonance Theory; Ego Shock; Goals; Stress and Coping; Values

Further Readings

Cohen, G. L., Garcia, J., Apfel, N., & Master, A. (2006). Reducing the racial achievement gap: A social-psychological intervention. *Science, 313,* 1251–1252.

Creswell, J. D., Welch, W., Taylor, S. E., Sherman, D. K., Gruenewald, T., & Mann, T. (2005). Affirmation of personal values buffers neuroendocrine and psychological stress responses. *Psychological Science, 16,* 846–851.

Sherman, D. K., & Cohen, G. L. (2006). The psychology of self-defense: Self-affirmation theory. In M. P. Zanna (Ed.), *Advances in experimental social psychology* (Vol. 38, pp. 183–242). San Diego, CA: Academic Press.

Steele, C. M. (1988). The psychology of self-affirmation: Sustaining the integrity of the self. In L. Berkowitz (Ed.), *Advances in experimental social psychology* (Vol. 21, pp. 261–302). New York: Academic Press.

SELF-ATTRIBUTION PROCESS

Definition

Self-attribution refers to the process through which people determine the antecedents and consequences of their behaviors. Because people do not have access to their internal states—attitudes, beliefs, emotions, motives, traits—they must infer these from observations of their own behaviors and the situational contexts in which they occurred.

Historical Background

Theoretical and empirical accounts of the self-attribution process developed from attribution theory, which addressed how individuals infer the internal states of others from observable behaviors. The theory was derived from the work of Fritz Heider, who suggested that behavioral perceptions are a function of how observers make attributions for the causes of behavior. According to Heider, behavioral causes can be attributed either to the person who performed the behavior (i.e., internal cause) or to the environment in which the behavior occurred (i.e., external cause). If an attribution is made to an internal cause, intentionality can be assigned to the person, and thus both stable and temporary characteristics of the actor can be inferred. More recently, Daryl Bem developed self-perception theory as an account of how people determine their own internal states. Bem suggested that people determine their own internal states by inferring them from observations of their own behavior and the situational context in which the behavior occurred.

The Process of Self-Attribution

Theoretically, self-attribution occurs in a manner that is similar to the process of person perception. Specifically, individuals observe their overt behavior, assign intentionality through an attribution to either internal or external causes, and infer their own internal states from their behavioral observations. For example, some students often read about social psychology, enjoy the topic, and even read when not studying for an exam; from this, they can make internal attributions of causality. Thus, they can infer that they hold favorable attitudes toward social psychology.

Errors in Self-Attribution

The process of self-attribution is far from perfect. One exemplary error is known as the self-serving bias, which suggests that people tend to attribute positive outcomes to internal causes but negative outcomes to external causes. For example, if students receive an A, they are likely to attribute the good grade to their own abilities; in contrast, if they receive a D, they are likely to attribute the poor grade to the difficulty of the assignment or to the harshness of the professor.

Implications

Errors in self-attribution may be responsible for poor psychological health. For example, depression is widely viewed as a function of a maladaptive style of self-attribution that is opposite to the self-serving bias. Specifically, depressed people often attribute positive outcomes to external causes but negative outcomes to internal causes. As a result, depressed people view positive outcomes as the result of chance or fate and view themselves as personally responsible for negative outcomes.

Christopher P. Niemiec

See also Attribution Theory, Self-Perception Theory; Self-Serving Bias

Further Readings

Heider, F. (1958). *The psychology of interpersonal relations.* New York: Wiley.

Miller, D. T., & Ross, M. (1975). Self-serving biases in the attribution of causality: Fact or fiction? *Psychological Bulletin, 82*, 213–225.

SELF-AWARENESS

Self-awareness is often defined in terms of an ability to engage in reflective awareness. According to most theorists, this requires certain types of cognitive abilities. Even in its most primitive form (visual self-recognition and the ability to recognize oneself in a mirror), self-awareness appears to be restricted to a small subset of animals including humans, chimpanzees, orangutans, and dolphins. In humans, this ability is not present at birth and only begins to appear around 12 to 18 months of age. Furthermore, there appears to be some support for George Herbert Mead's claim that development of this ability requires a social rearing history in which the individual comes to recognize that he or she is distinct from others.

Beyond an ability to be reflectively aware of oneself, self-awareness is often associated with executive processes essential to self-regulation. Thus, the self-aware individual is often viewed as more controlled and intentional in his or her actions. Within social psychology, self-awareness is often associated with a theory of objective self-awareness by Shelley Duval and Robert Wicklund. According to this theory, situational cues that remind individuals of themselves (e.g., mirrors and video cameras) lead to attention focused on the self and away from the environment. The result is a self-aware state in which individuals are proposed to compare their current selves with ideal self-standards. Because the current or actual self is usually found to be lacking when compared with these standards, Duval and Wicklund proposed that self-awareness creates a negative emotional reaction. This negative affect then motivates the individual either (a) to regulate his or her behavior with respect to the standard in an effort to reduce the discrepancy, or (b) to avoid the self-aware state.

Although this theory has yielded a great deal of research in support of its basic tenets, several researchers noted that self-awareness inducing stimuli often motivate self-regulation without inducing self-criticism and negative affect. Charles Carver and Michael Scheier proposed an alternative theory of self-awareness that retained some features of the Duval and Wicklund model (e.g., self-focused attention), but argued that the comparison of the current self with an ideal standard is itself sufficient to motivate behavior without creating negative affect. Their model of self-awareness was inspired by other cybernetic models of behavior. Jay G. Hull and Alan Levy proposed a more drastic departure from the original Duval and Wicklund model. According to Hull and Levy, self-awareness inducing stimuli essentially act as self-symbolic primes that activate self-knowledge and cause the individual to process situations as personally relevant. Behavior follows as a consequence of focusing on the self-relevant aspects of the environment (as opposed to focusing inward and evaluating self).

Although social psychologists are typically interested in situationally manipulated self-awareness, personality researchers are interested in individual differences in tendency to become self-aware. To measure such differences, Alan Fenigstein, Michael Scheier, and Arnold Buss created the Self- Consciousness Scale. This personality inventory has three subscales: private self-consciousness, public self-consciousness, and social anxiety. Private self-consciousness focuses on the internal experience of self-awareness. It is measured with items such as "I'm always trying to figure myself out," "I reflect about myself a lot," and "I'm alert to changes in my mood." Public self-consciousness focuses on the self-presentational motives sometimes associated with self-awareness and is measured with items such as "I'm concerned about the way I present myself," "I'm concerned about what other people think of me," and "I'm usually aware of my appearance." Social anxiety focuses on negative emotions sometimes associated with being the focus of attention of others and is measured with items such as "I get embarrassed very easily," "I feel anxious when I speak in front of a group," and "Large groups make me nervous." Although the social anxiety subscale captures the colloquial understanding of what it means to be self-conscious, the private and public self-consciousness scales assess individual differences in the psychological processes most often theorized to be associated with the self-aware state.

Given that both public and private self-consciousness measures focus on self, it is not surprising that they tend to be modestly correlated. Similarly, both public self-consciousness and social anxiety tend to be modestly correlated. Private self-consciousness tends not to be correlated with social anxiety. Recently, some researchers have argued that private self-consciousness is itself associated with two subcomponents: internal state awareness characterized by items such as "I am alert to changes in my mood," and reflectiveness characterized by items such as "I reflect about myself a lot." This issue has yet to be resolved.

With respect to individual differences in self-regulation, the components of the Self-Consciousness Scale are often compared with those of the Self-Monitoring Scale introduced by Mark Snyder.

Individuals high in self-monitoring are motivated by self-presentational concerns, whereas individuals low in self-monitoring are motivated by personal concerns. Perhaps the best way to think about the relation of these individual differences is that high self-monitors are both high in public self-consciousness and low in private self-consciousness. Conversely, low self-monitors are both low in public self-consciousness and high in private self-consciousness.

The effects of individual differences in private self-consciousness have often been found to parallel the effects of situational manipulations of self-awareness (e.g., the presence or absence of a mirror). Similarly, the effects of individual differences in public self-consciousness have often been found to parallel the effects of situational manipulations that remind the individual of their appearance to others (e.g., video cameras). As a consequence, researchers often distinguish between situational manipulations of private and public self-awareness along the same lines that they distinguish individual differences of private and public self-consciousness.

Research has regularly demonstrated that both situational manipulations of self-awareness and individual differences in self-consciousness are associated with increased self-regulation. Manipulations of private self-awareness and individual differences in private self-consciousness have been associated with increased attitude–behavior consistency, increased emotional reactivity to success and failure feedback, and increased self-regulation with respect to standards of appropriate conduct (e.g., increased helping when helping is defined as situationally appropriate, and decreased aggression when aggression is defined as situationally inappropriate). Private self-awareness has also been associated with an increased motivation to avoid self-awareness when it is personally painful (e.g., following failure). Indeed, evidence shows that the latter motivation to avoid self-awareness can lead individuals to consume drugs such as alcohol that can lower self-awareness.

Manipulations of public self-awareness and individual differences in public self-consciousness have been associated with increased self-presentation and impression management. For example, individuals high in public self-consciousness demonstrate a greater emphasis on social rather than personal identities, a concern over body image (body weight, clothing, makeup use), and an increased concern with the perspective of others. Although this focus on self-presentational concerns can be useful in gaining the approval of others, it can also lead to somewhat self-destructive impression management strategies (e.g., increased self-handicapping) and even paranoia regarding others' intentions.

Whereas most research on this topic has investigated the effects of manipulations that heighten self-awareness, some research has examined manipulations that lower self-awareness. In addition to alcohol use mentioned previously, these include deindividuation manipulations that render the individual indistinguishable from others (e.g., through anonymity, being in a crowd, darkness, or wearing masks). Such manipulations typically increase disinhibited behavior that does not conform to social and personal norms. One popular account of how this occurs is that deindividuation manipulations lower self-awareness. Paralleling the previous arguments, researchers have distinguished both public and private components of the deindividuated experience. Situations that foster anonymity are thought to reduce aspects of public self-awareness whereas situations that reduce the individual's ability to distinguish themselves from others are thought to reduce aspects of private self-awareness.

In summary, at its most basic, self-awareness is associated with a reflective awareness of self. Within social psychology, self-awareness is typically viewed as involving cognitive and affective processes essential to self-regulation. A variety of theories have been offered that describe these processes. Both social psychologists and personality psychologists have actively pursued research on this topic. As a consequence, research has investigated the effects of both situational manipulations (of self-awareness) and individual differences (in self-consciousness). Within each of these approaches, researchers usually distinguish between more personal, private aspects of self-awareness and more public, self-presentational aspects of self-awareness. This has been true both for variables associated with increased self-awareness as well as variables related to deindividuation and decreased self-awareness. Because of its relevance to self-regulation of a variety of different types of behavior, research and theory on self-awareness has integrated topics as disparate as helping, aggression, and self-presentation and bridged traditional divisions between social and personality psychology.

Jay Hull

See also Deindividuation; Impression Management; Self-Monitoring; Self-Presentation

Further Readings

Carver, C. S., & Scheier, M. F. (1981). *Attention and self-regulation: A control theory approach to human behavior.* New York: Springer.

Duval, S., & Wicklund, R. A. (1972). *A theory of objective self-awareness.* New York: Academic Press.

Fenigstein, A., Scheier, M. F., & Buss, A. H. (1975). Public and private self-consciousness: Assessment and theory. *Journal of Consulting and Clinical Psychology, 43,* 522–527.

Hull, J. G., & Levy, A. S. (1979). The organizational functions of the self: An alternative to the Duval and Wicklund model of self-awareness. *Journal of Personality and Social Psychology, 37,* 756–768.

SELF-CATEGORIZATION THEORY

Self-categorization theory addresses the problem of the psychological group. Are there such things as psychological groups? How do they form? How is a collection of individuals able to act, think, and feel as a group, collectively, as if, in the extreme, the group members shared a common mind? It is taken for granted that human beings are individual persons, that they have unique personalities and differ from other individuals, but it is also known that they belong to social groups and that these social groups can have a psychological reality for their members. People do not just describe others as belonging to groups, they describe themselves as groups (not as if they were groups, but as groups). They talk about "we" and "us" as well as "I" and "me"; they act under the right circumstances in a highly uniform, consensual, unified way as a crowd, a nation, an army, a mob, an audience, and so on; they experience collective emotions and feelings and share similar attitudes, beliefs, and values. Can people be or become a group, psychologically, subjectively, in terms of their identities, perceptions, feelings, beliefs, motives, and so on? Or is it just an illusion because people are really, fundamentally, nothing but individuals?

Self-categorization theory, in contrast to a popular point of view in North American social psychology, asserts that human beings are and are able to act as both individual persons and social groups. The theory assumes that a person might act as a unique personality in one context, but display collective similarities as a group member in another. Human beings are very good at varying the degree to which they act in terms of either individual differences or collective similarities, and the theory tries to explain how such flexibility is possible.

Self-categorization theory explains individuality and group behavior (and the relationship between them) in terms of the way that people define and perceive themselves. Like many other theories, it focuses on what is called the *self-concept,* the collection of identities, definitions, descriptions, categories, concepts, and so on, that people use to define and experience themselves, the self-categories that people use to answer the question, who am I? or who are we? Like other theories, the theory assumes that people define themselves differently in different situations and that the way they categorize themselves will influence how they will react to that situation. For example, you may react very differently to a news story about the criminal behavior of a young child if you think of yourself as a police officer rather than as a parent. Self-categorizing is simply the process whereby a person defines the self in terms of varying kinds of "I," "me," "we," or "us" categories such as "the real me," or "me as opposed to you," or "we Australians compared with you Americans" or "us Earth people as opposed to you alien Martians." Nearly all theories before self-categorization theory tended to assume that the self-concept was basically, primarily, or predominantly about defining the person as a unique individual being, that it revolved around ways of defining *I* or *me.* Self-categorization theory holds that people see themselves at different levels, of which the individual level is only one. In particular, it makes a distinction between personal and social identity.

Think of a "chair." This is a category we might use to describe four-legged objects we sit on in contrast to a "table." The same object could also be considered "furniture," a category we might use to refer to both chairs and tables in contrast to, say, "objects not designed for human use." It could also be called an "old chair" to distinguish it from a "new chair." In these three cases the object is put into categories at a lower (more specific), intermediate or higher (more inclusive) level as we move from old chair to chair to furniture. With each step, it becomes similar to more objects, which were different from it at more specific levels. The process is just the same with the self the

theory states. People can define themselves as "the me as I was in my youth" in contrast to "the me as I am today," or "I the writer" in contrast to "you the reader," or "we English people" as opposed to "you continental Europeans," or "we Europeans" in contrast to "you Americans," right up to "we human beings" as opposed to other animals, and beyond. In principle, an endless number of levels of self-categorizing are possible, limited only by reality and one's imagination, and higher levels include more people (are more collective) than lower levels.

The theory describes the individual level (e.g., "I John Smith" as opposed to "you Jane Brown") as one's personal identity and the various possible group levels (e.g., "we Europeans" versus "you Americans") as social identity. Every person has many different actual and possible personal and social identities. The theory holds that the way that people define and see themselves in any particular situation moves up and down between these levels and between the different identities at each level and that this is completely normal. It also holds that as self-definition shifts from personal to social identity and people see themselves differently, then psychologically and behaviorally people change from being individuals to being group members, from making responses based on individual personality to making responses based on shared social identity and collective similarities.

In sum, people define themselves in terms of social identities as well as personal identities; under certain circumstances, social identities become more important or influential than personal identities in the perception of oneself, and behavior changes from individual to group as people act more in terms of social than personal identity. Much research has looked at how and when people define themselves in terms of personal or social identity, how and why this makes people's behavior and psychology more collective and less personal, and how these basic ideas can be used to explain the whole variety of phenomena related to group psychology.

Particular social identities become salient as a result of both psychological factors having to do with the perceiver such as his or her experience, habits, motives, beliefs and knowledge, and the nature of the social relationships perceived in a given social situation. One important finding is that people are much more likely to see themselves as individuals in settings where only people from their own group are present than where members of other groups are present.

Social identity comes to the fore more in the presence of outgroup than ingroup members. For example, research shows that a woman who is asked to judge herself against other women will define herself in terms of her personal identity, how she differs from other women as an individual, but one asked to judge herself against other men is likely to emphasize her social identity and see herself as much more like other women and different from men. In the former situation, she may see herself and be faster to rate herself as more masculine (different from the typical woman), but in the latter she may see herself and be faster to rate herself as more feminine (similar to the typical woman and different from men). She can see herself as having completely opposite traits depending on whether her personal or social identity is salient. Another strongly supported finding consistent with this idea is that social identity tends to be especially strong and powerful in situations of social conflict between groups. Americans may see themselves as very individualistic, but if attacked as a group by an enemy, they may pull together behind their leaders and conform strongly to group attitudes in their reactions.

Why do people become more group-oriented when social identity is salient? One reason is that social identities tend to have the same meaning for people because they arise in the same culture and are used in the same situation. Australians asked to say what Australians are like, for example, will agree about a lot of things. Because social categories have similar meanings for the people who use them, people will see themselves as more similar and actually become more similar when they define themselves in terms of the same group. If one asks a group of Australians to discuss their individual views about what Americans are like, one will find that they happily disagree on many points, but if one asks them to think about their views "as Australians," one will now find a very high degree of uniformity in their views of Americans, just as one will in their views of Australians. Thus, a social identity that is shared by people makes people more similar in their self-described traits, goals, attitudes, beliefs, definition of the situation and behavior when it is made salient in a specific situation. This leads their behavior to become more consensual and unitary; they act alike. It also leads them to expect to be similar and encourages them to influence each other to produce agreement even when it was not originally present.

Also, people who define each other in terms of the same social category share an inclusive self that shapes their self-interest and emotions. If the self becomes a "we" instead of an "I," then people can cooperate and be altruistic because helping an ingroup member is helping oneself. Similarly, people can feel the experiences of others because what happens to others is also happening to themselves if they see themselves as members of the same inclusive self-category. If a police officer beats Rodney King, then any African American or any American who identifies with King can react as if he or she were the victim. He or she can feel empathy and sympathy. A person can have collective emotions that go beyond the experience of the individual person.

Research backs up the idea that people's self-perception, behavior, and psychology change qualitatively as psychological or situational factors make social identity more salient and personal identity less salient. Under these conditions, people see themselves as more similar to ingroup members (and different from outgroup members); they feel closer and more attracted to ingroup members; they are more influenced by ingroup members and agree with them more; they are more likely to cooperate and pursue joint interests, to obey and comply with ingroup members' authority; they feel ingroup members' emotions and are motivated by their needs and goals. Self-categorization theory explains how and why people are much more than merely unique persons, and why they are capable of a collective as well as an individual psychology, without any unscientific assumptions about a group mind.

John C. Turner

See also Collective Self; Intergroup Relations; Self; Self-Concept

Further Readings

Onorato, R. S., & Turner, J. C. (2004). Fluidity in the self-concept: The shift from personal to social identity. *European Journal of Social Psychology, 34,* 257–278.

Turner, J. C. (1985). Social categorization and the self-concept: A social cognitive theory of group behaviour. In E. J. Lawler (Ed.), *Advances in Group Processes* (Vol. 2, pp. 77–122) Greenwich, CT: JAI Press.

Turner, J. C. (2005). Explaining the nature of power: A three-process theory. *European Journal of Social Psychology, 35,* 1–22.

Turner, J. C., Oakes, P. J., Haslam, S. A., & McGarty, C. A. (1994). Self and collective: Cognition and social context. *Personality & Social Psychology Bulletin, 20,* 454–463.

SELF-COMPLEXITY

Definition

People differ substantially in how extremely they react to good and bad events in their lives. Some people experience dramatic swings in mood and self-appraisal in response to the ups and downs of life, whereas others do not. Some experience adverse mental and physical health consequences of stressful events, but others do not. The self-complexity concept helps us understand these differences.

According to Patricia Linville's original formulation of the self-complexity model, people differ in the degree to which they maintain a complex, differentiated view of the self. This model assumes that the representation of the self in memory consists of multiple self-aspects, which may be organized in terms of contexts (home, school, with friends), roles (student, athlete), traits (creative, nurturing), behaviors (studying, playing tennis), and time frames (past, present, and future selves). Intuitively, greater self-complexity involves having a more differentiated view of the self. The greater the extent to which a person makes distinctions among the attributes or features associated with various self-aspects, the greater the person's self-complexity is. Furthermore, a person who is higher in self-complexity is likely to associate different emotions and self-appraisals with different self-aspects. For example, a person may feel good about himself or herself as an athlete but not as a student.

History and Background

The concept of self-complexity provides a perspective on several enduring issues and paradoxes in the psychology of the self. First, it is directly related to a classic debate about whether people have a unified, single self (a view espoused by many early self theorists) or multiple selves (espoused by William James and most contemporary researchers). The current self-complexity concept assumes that self-knowledge is represented and processed in terms of multiple self-aspects related to various contexts of experience. Second, the self-complexity concept helps people understand the classic paradox—How can a person maintain seemingly discrepant beliefs about the self? A person may associate different self-attributes or behaviors with different aspects of the self, allowing

inconsistent self-knowledge to coexist. For example, a woman may perceive herself as outgoing in small social gatherings yet shy at large parties. Third, the self-complexity concept helps explain the enduring paradox—How can the self be both stable yet malleable? Different self-aspects may be cognitively activated or accessible at different points in time or in different contexts, thus creating a flexible working self. Furthermore, certain core self-aspects (e.g., self as a moral person) may be stable over long periods, whereas others may adapt rapidly in the face of changing experience (e.g., self as a competitive athlete). Also, one may develop entirely new self-aspects as one enters new realms of experience (e.g., self as a parent).

Importance and Consequences

People differ substantially in their degree of self-complexity. Do these differences have any important consequences for their lives? People also differ substantially in how they react to good and bad events in their lives. The self-complexity concept is important largely because it helps to explain these differences in reactions to life events.

Self-Complexity and Affective Extremity

According to the self-complexity model, those lower in self-complexity will experience greater swings in affect and self-appraisal in response to life events such as success or failure. They will evaluate themselves more positively (and experience more positive emotion) when good things happen, but they will also evaluate themselves more negatively (and experience more negative emotion) when bad things happen. Why? People who are lower in self-complexity tend to maintain stronger ties among the traits or behaviors describing various self-aspects. Thus, a positive or negative event that has a direct impact on one self-aspect is likely to have a relatively broad overall impact on the self because strong ties among the traits and behaviors describing various self-aspects will lead to greater spillover (generalization) from one trait to another or one self-aspect to another. In contrast, with greater self-complexity, there will be less generalization across traits or self-aspects, so a smaller proportion of the self will be affected by any given positive or negative event.

Several types of evidence support this general hypothesis. First, studies of reactions to performance feedback show that those lower in self-complexity experience both a greater increase in affect and self-appraisal following success feedback and a greater decrease in affect and self-appraisal following failure feedback. Second, assuming that people experience both positive and negative events over time, the self-complexity model predicts that those lower in self-complexity will experience greater mood variability over time. This prediction was supported in a mood diary study in which participants filled out a set of mood scales each day over a 2-week period. In short, higher self-complexity buffers a person against the bad times but also keeps his or her feet on the ground in good times.

Self-Complexity as a Stress Buffer

Stressful events can lead to mental and physical health problems. Furthermore, people higher in self-complexity experience less negative emotional reactions following negative events. If these negative emotional reactions contribute to stress-related depression and illness, then greater self-complexity may also reduce the adverse health and mental health effects of negative stressful events. As this line of reasoning suggests, several studies have found that greater self-complexity moderates the adverse mental and physical health effects of stressful life events; that is, those higher in self-complexity are less adversely affected by stressful events. They seem less prone to both physical illnesses (e.g., upper respiratory infections) and depressive symptoms 2 weeks after experiencing high levels of stressful life events.

Related Findings and Research

In an interesting extension of self-complexity to present and future goals, Paula Niedenthal and her colleagues showed that the complexity of the present self moderates reactions to feedback about current goals, whereas complexity of possible selves moderates reactions to feedback about future goals. Roy Baumeister and others have extended self-complexity to the realm of self-regulation. One interesting finding is that those lower in self-complexity are more threatened by failure and consequently are more motivated to escape from self-awareness following failure. Consistent with this prediction, those lowest in self-complexity were the quickest to finish an essay on self goals in front of a mirror following failure. Another

interesting finding is that those who are higher in self-complexity regarding activities have higher optimal activity levels. Greater activity complexity appears to reduce the rate at which performing additional tasks leads to ego depletion and fatigue.

Another important issue concerns the source of differences in self-complexity. Peter Salovey has shown that both positive and negative mood lead to greater self-complexity because both lead to greater self-focused attention than a neutral mood state. Similarly, individuals with greater attentional resources (e.g., working memory capacity) also display higher levels of self-complexity.

Yet another set of interesting issues concerns the mechanisms underlying the link between self-complexity and emotional extremity. Recent research supports the assumption that the emotional consequences of positive and negative experiences spill over from the most directly affected self-aspects to others. As predicted, the degree of spillover is greater for those lower in self-complexity.

Measuring Self-Complexity

The self-complexity concept is quite intuitive, but applications of self-complexity require a precise measure. Linville's original formulation of self-complexity theory relies on a card-sorting procedure in which people sort a set of features (e.g., smart, shy) into piles describing different self-aspects. Using the results of this sorting task, one can compute a complexity measure known as the H-statistic, which reflects the number of independent dimensions implicitly present in the self-aspects created. The self-complexity model and findings rely heavily on the properties of this measure of differentiation. Recently, there have been several attempts to reformulate the self-complexity concept in terms of separate measures of number of self-aspects and degree of feature overlap between self-aspects. At present, it appears that a reformulation of self-complexity in terms of feature overlap often fails to confirm the theoretical predictions of the self-complexity model. Consequently, almost all of the findings reported here were obtained in studies in which the H-statistic was computed from feature sorting tasks. The self-complexity hypotheses described here are closely tied to the properties of the H-statistic. These hypotheses may not hold for other conceptual definitions or measures of self-complexity. In this context, the specific measure used matters.

Related Concepts and Research

The term *self-complexity* has close links to other concepts such as *self-schemas* and *self-differentiation.* Self-complexity also has links to other cognitive complexity concepts. In general, experts about a domain perceive objects in the domain in a more differentiated or complex way. For example, ingroup members tend to have a more differentiated view of their group than do outgroup members and political experts have a more complex view of political candidates than do nonexperts. Finally, the self-complexity model has close ties to the complexity-extremity model of social judgment, developed by Linville and Edward Jones.

Patricia Linville

See also Phenomenal Self; Self; Self-Esteem; Stress and Coping

Further Readings

Dixon, T. M., & Baumeister, R. F. (1991). Escaping the self: The moderating effect of self-complexity. *Personality and Social Psychology Bulletin, 17,* 363–368.

Linville, P. W. (1985). Self-complexity and affective extremity: Don't put all of your eggs in one cognitive basket. *Social Cognition, 3,* 94–120.

Linville, P. W. (1987). Self-complexity as a cognitive buffer against stress-related depression and illness. *Journal of Personality and Social Psychology, 52,* 663–676.

Linville, P. W., & Carlston, D. E. (1994). Social cognition of the self. In P. G. Devine, D. L. Hamilton, & T. M. Ostrom (Eds.), *Social cognition: Its impact on social psychology* (pp. 143–193). New York: Academic Press.

Niedenthal, P. M., Setterlund, M. B., & Wherry, M. B. (1992). Possible self-complexity and affective reactions to goal-relevant evaluation. *Journal of Personality and Social Psychology, 48,* 575–584.

SELF-CONCEPT

Definition

Self-concept refers to people's characteristic ideas about who they are and what they are like. Although psychologists often talk about *the* self-concept, a person's self-concept typically consists of a loose collection of ideas rather than a single unified conception of the self. The self-concept is grounded in subjective experience. This means that a person's self-concept may be different from what he or she is actually like.

History

One of the first psychologists who wrote about the self-concept was William James, a psychologist in the late 19th century. James distinguished between the *I* and the *ME.* The I is the part of the self that is actively perceiving and thinking. The ME is the part of the self that becomes an object of the person's thoughts and perceptions. The self-concept relates primarily to the ME.

Adaptive Functions of the Self-Concept

Having a self-concept is a uniquely human trait. The capacity to form a self-concept presumably evolved because it promoted survival and reproduction among early humans. Because people have a self-concept, they can consider themselves in alternative times and circumstances. Thus, one adaptive function of the self-concept lies in helping people plan for the future. Goals, particularly ideals and obligations, are indeed central to people's self-concepts. When a person's current self differs from his or her desired self, this motivates the person to take action to move closer to the desired self. Another adaptive function of the self-concept is to facilitate social behavior. When people view themselves similarly as their interaction partners, this helps people predict how others will behave toward them. A shared cultural background may lead people to construe their self-concepts in a similar manner. For instance, people living in Western cultures like the United States or France tend to regard themselves as more independent from others. By contrast, people living in Eastern cultures such as Japan or India tend to think of themselves as more mutually dependent. When people have similar self-concepts, they may understand each other better.

Structure of the Self-Concept

Self-concepts have a certain structure. One important aspect of the structure of the self-concept is self-complexity. Individuals with a complex self-concept distinguish between many distinct aspects or dimensions of themselves. Individuals with a simple self-concept view themselves in terms of only a few broad aspects or dimensions. Individuals with a simple self-concept are more vulnerable to stress than are individuals with a complex self-concept. This is because individuals with a complex self-concept can overcome negative feedback in one self-domain (e.g., getting fired from one's job) by turning their attention to other self-domains (e.g., one's family life, religion). Individuals with a simple self-concept cannot follow this strategy.

Another important aspect of the structure of the self-concept is whether self-views are implicit or explicit. Explicit self-views are ideas about the self of which people are consciously aware. Implicit self-views are ideas about the self that are unconsciously held. Self-views may become unconscious when people use them over and over again, so that these ideas become like automatic mental habits. Explicit self-views are easier to observe than implicit self-views are. This is mainly because people themselves do not know about their implicit self-views. Nevertheless, implicit self-views can be observed indirectly because they influence how people respond to self-relevant objects or situations. Implicit self-views are especially likely to guide people's behavior when people rely on their immediate intuitions, for instance, when people are responding very quickly or when they are distracted.

Self-Concept Motives

When people learn about themselves, certain kinds of information are especially valuable to them. It seems intuitively plausible that people should be interested in obtaining accurate information about themselves. The desire for accurate information about the self has been called the self-assessment motive. As it turns out, self-assessment is not the only motive surrounding the self-concept. Three additional motives have been found to influence how people construct their self-concepts. First, people want to receive positive, self-enhancing feedback, which is known as the self-enhancement motive. Second, people want to confirm what they already believe about themselves, which has been called the self-verification motive. Third, people want to learn things that help them to improve themselves, which is known as the self-improvement motive.

Self-assessment, self-enhancement, self-verification, and self-improvement jointly determine which information people use to construct their self-concepts.

However, the motives sometimes conflict. For instance, self-enhancement leads people to prefer positive feedback, even when their self-concepts are negative. However, self-verification leads people with negative self-concepts to prefer negative feedback. The conflict between self-enhancement and self-verification motives has been extensively studied by psychologist Bill Swann and associates. These researchers found that self-enhancement drives people's immediate emotional reactions to self-relevant information. However, self-verification may still prevail in people's cognitive beliefs about themselves. People with a negative self-concept may thus internalize negative feedback, even when this feedback is emotionally painful to them. People with a positive self-concept don't experience this conflict because for them, both self-enhancement and self-verification foster a preference for positive feedback.

The different self-concept motives become dominant under different circumstances. Self-enhancement is the most automatic motive, at least among people living in the West. Self-enhancement therefore becomes stronger when people are distracted or emotionally aroused. Self-assessment becomes stronger when people are deliberating about the pros and cons of a course of action. Self-verification becomes stronger when people possess great confidence in their beliefs about themselves. Finally, self-improvement becomes stronger when people believe that they can change their self-attributes. Moreover, self-improvement is particularly strong among people in Eastern cultures.

Sander Koole

See also Independent Self-Construals; Interdependent Self-Construals; Self; Self-Complexity; Self-Enhancement; Self-Verification Theory

Further Readings

Baumeister, R. F. (1998). The self. In D. Gilbert, S. T. Fiske, & G. Lindzey (Eds.), *Handbook of social psychology* (4th ed., Vol. 1, pp. 680–740). New York: McGraw-Hill.

Kihlstrom, J. F., & Klein, S. B. (1994). The self as a knowledge structure. In R. S. Wyer, Jr., & T. K. Srull (Eds.), *Handbook of social cognition* (Vol. 1, pp. 153–208). Hillsdale, NJ: Erlbaum.

Sedikides, C., & Skowronski, J. J. (1997). The symbolic self in evolutionary context. *Personality and Social Psychology Review, 1,* 80–102.

SELF-CONCEPT CLARITY

Definition

Some individuals possess a clear sense of who they are and where they are going in life. They are aware of their strengths and weaknesses, the nature of their personalities, and where they stand on important attitudes and values. Other individuals have less clear self-concepts. These individuals may not be confident in who they are, may not really know where they stand on important issues, and may not be certain about their abilities. Self-concept clarity refers to the extent to which people with a clear self-concept know who they are, do not have beliefs that conflict with each other, and have viewpoints that are consistent over time. Whereas self-esteem is seen as an overall evaluation of the self as good or bad, self-concept clarity is seen as the way in which people's knowledge about themselves is cognitively organized. One would hypothesize that self-concept clarity is a good thing, providing individuals with a greater sense of understanding and meaning and allowing them to make life decisions that result in greater well-being.

Measurement

The initial measurement of self-concept clarity was somewhat indirect. For example, the variable was first measured by such factors as the confidence with which individuals reported holding various self-beliefs (e.g., "I am confident," "I am extraverted"), the stability of self-ratings over time (e.g., the consistency between the same self-reports taken 9 weeks apart), and how fast individuals were able to respond to questions about themselves (with a faster reaction time seen as indicating higher self-concept clarity). However, researchers later developed a self-report measure to assess self-concept clarity, whereby individuals are asked to rate the extent to which they have clear self-beliefs that do not conflict with each other. A 12-item scale was ultimately created that asks individuals the extent to which they agree with such items as "In general I know who I am and where I'm headed in life," and "I spend a lot of time wondering what kind of person I really am" (reverse-scored). This scale has been used in many different studies to assess the relationships between self-concept clarity and a

number of additional variables (e.g., self-esteem, psychological adjustment, self-focus).

Outcomes

One of the earliest and consistent correlates of self-concept clarity was self-esteem. Individuals with high levels of self-esteem are more likely to have positive, well-articulated views of the self, whereas individuals with low self-esteem report inconsistent, uncertain, and unstable views of themselves. Research has also shown that individuals with high levels of self-concept clarity also report lower levels of depression, anxiety, neuroticism, and perceived stress and report higher levels of perceived social support and psychological adjustment than do individuals with low levels of self-concept clarity.

In addition to examining the relationships between self-concept clarity and psychological health, researchers have also assessed whether people high versus low in clarity use different types of coping strategies when dealing with life's challenges. Individuals with clearer self-concepts are more likely to take action, plan, and use positive reinterpretation (trying to view the situation in a more positive, less stressful way) to deal with stressful situations. However, those with a less clear self-concept are more likely to use denial, mental disengagement (e.g., try not to think about the stressful situation), behavioral disengagement (e.g., physically leave the stressful situation), and drugs or alcohol. These relationships are seen even when controlling for the effects of gender, perceived social support, anxiety, depression, and self-esteem.

Relationships of self-concept clarity with motivational factors have also been found. For example, self-concept clarity has been found to be related to the degree of personal engagement an individual feels for his or her occupation. Individuals higher in self-concept clarity are more likely to report a high level of connection with their jobs than are individuals low in self-concept clarity. This could be a result of individuals high in self-concept clarity choosing occupations that are more consistent with their self-views.

Finally, self-concept clarity has also been found to influence how people respond to others. The concept was first linked to a phenomenon known as the foot-in-the-door-technique, whereby individuals who agree to a small favor (e.g., to donate $1 to a charity) are more likely to agree to a larger favor when asked later (e.g., to donate $50 to a charity) than if the smaller favor had not been asked. Interestingly, individuals higher in self-concept clarity were more likely than those low in clarity to comply with a second, larger request. This effect likely stems from those high in clarity wanting to ensure consistency between their behaviors so that agreeing to the small request creates a greater need to agree to the second, larger request. Although individuals high in self-concept clarity are more likely to fall victim to the foot-in-the-door technique, individuals low in self-concept clarity are more likely to have difficulties in conflict resolution because of a need to take ownership over arguments in a dispute. This effect is most likely due to the need that low-clarity individuals have for connecting reality to their self-concept.

Future Research

Self-concept clarity is a useful variable in understanding psychological health, coping, and reactions to one's interpersonal world. One of the biggest areas in need of future research is how self-concept clarity develops, and what contributes to low versus high clarity. Can someone have high self-concept clarity and then experience life events that lead to lower clarity? Do certain parental behaviors contribute to high versus low self-concept clarity? The answers to these questions await future research.

Thomas W. Britt
Heather N. Odle-Dusseau

See also Foot-in-the-Door Technique; Self-Concept; Self-Esteem; Stress and Coping

Further Readings

Burger, J. M., & Guadagno, R. E. (2003). Self-concept clarity and the foot-in-the-door procedure. *Basic and Applied Social Psychology, 25,* 79–86.

Campbell, J. D. (1990). Self-esteem and clarity of the self-concept. *Journal of Personality and Social Psychology, 59,* 538–549.

Campbell, J. D., Assanand, S., & Di Paula, A. (2003). The structure of the self-concept and its relation to psychological adjustment. *Journal of Personality,71,* 115–140.

Campbell, J. D., Trapnell, P. D., Heine, S. J., Katz, I. M., Lavellee, L. F., & Lehman, D. R. (1996). Self-concept clarity: Measurement, personality correlates, and cultural boundaries. *Journal of Personality and Social Psychology, 70,* 141–156.

SELF-CONTROL MEASURES

Self-control (also commonly referred to as self-regulation) is the ability to control one's thoughts, emotions, urges, and behaviors. A person might exert self-control, for example, by trying to stop thinking about something unpleasant, escape a bad mood and feel better, or refrain from cursing in front of his or her parents. Self-control is conceptually similar to what many people refer to as self-discipline, willpower, or self-change. Although self-control can be regarded as an act, the capability for it is a personality trait. Some people are better at self-control than are others, not in every single occasion, but overall. Self-control measures are designed to identify which people are generally good at self-control and which ones are not.

The ability to exert self-control is vital to maintaining a successful and healthy lifestyle. People must frequently exert self-control in many areas of their lives, such as when trying to diet, quit smoking or drinking, control their spending, or refrain from engaging in undesirable sexual acts. Life requires constant self-change and adaptation, such as a new college student who must motivate himself or herself to study in the absence of parental supervision. Self-control is essential in this regard.

Likewise, people who are more capable than others at self-control experience numerous benefits as a result. For instance, they receive better grades, are more popular with peers, have better social relationships and mental health, and cope better with stress. They are also less likely to suffer from eating disorders or have substance problems. High self-control even helps people to follow the law and stay out of jail.

Researchers have developed several different ways to measure self-control. One method is to directly assess people's self-control behaviors. For instance, a researcher might give a person some delicious cookies or ice cream and measure how much the person eats. People typically try to limit how much of these foods they eat, and so eating a larger amount indicates a lack of self-control. One method commonly used with children is to assess the ability to delay gratification.

For instance, a researcher might give a child a marshmallow and tell the child that he or she can eat it immediately or wait to eat it until the researcher retrieves a second marshmallow. The researcher then measures how long the child is willing to resist eating the marshmallow and wait (up to about 20 or 30 minutes) for the second marshmallow. Experiments using this and other similar procedures have shown that children more capable of delaying gratification are more successful (e.g., more popular and healthier mentally) than others many years later, even during adulthood.

Questionnaires are also used frequently to assess self-control. For instance, a research participant might indicate how much he or she agrees with statements such as, "I have a hard time breaking bad habits," "I never allow myself to lose control," or "I am able to work effectively toward long-term goals." Alternatively, participants might be asked to report their recent self-control behaviors, such as how often they have eaten too much or lost control of their temper. Some self-control questionnaires measure the ability to exert self-control more generally, whereas other questionnaires focus on more specific self-control behaviors, such eating, illegal activities, or drug and alcohol use. One measure of personality assesses the related construct of conscientiousness. Questionnaire measures, like direct assessments of behavior, have also linked self-control with several positive outcomes.

Studies on self-control have demonstrated how self-control operates. When exerting self-control, individuals first monitor themselves or pay attention to the target behavior. For instance, a dieter will first keep track of how much food he or she eats. Progress toward a goal is then compared with some standard, such as an ideal diet. People are far more successful at self-control if they monitor their behavior and set realistic standards than if they do not monitor their behavior or do not set standards.

If a person's behavior or current state matches the desired goal, then the person no longer exerts self-control. A dieter who reaches his or her ideal weight, for instance, will probably stop dieting. If a person's behavior or current state falls short of the goal, however, then the person will exert self-control by changing his or her behavior until the desired goal is reached.

Although the process of self-control may seem straightforward, actually exerting self-control is difficult and demanding. Many people fail at self-control. For example, many people fail to follow their New Year's resolutions, even during the first week of the year.

Why is exerting self-control so difficult? One reason seems to be that the ability to exert self-control is limited. Consistent with the idea of willpower, people seem to use up their self-control energy, and so they are less likely to succeed at self-control later on. In one study, for instance, participants were given a plateful of delicious cookies and a bowl full of radishes. Some participants were told they could eat whatever they wanted, whereas other participants were told to resist eating the cookies and to eat the radishes instead. It takes self-control to avoid eating cookies and instead eat radishes, and so participants who had to eat the radishes should have used up their self-control energy. To test this idea, the researchers then had participants watch a funny film and asked them to hide or suppress any signs of enjoyment or laughter. Participants who had resisted eating the cookies were less able to hide their enjoyment than were participants who had eaten freely, consistent with the idea that exerting self-control had depleted their self-control or willpower. Thus, people probably fail at self-control because they have limited self-control energy. Indeed, after completing an initial task requiring self-control, people show poorer self-control in numerous areas. They fail to control their spending, inappropriate sexual behavior, and drinking, and they seem less able to avoid thinking about unpleasant topics, such as death!

Matthew T. Gailliot

See also Delay of Gratification; Ego Depletion; Individual Differences; Research Methods; Self-Regulation; Traits

Further Readings

Baumeister, R. F., Heatherton, T. F., & Tice, D. M. (1994). *Losing control: How and why people fail at self-regulation.* San Diego, CA: Academic Press.

Mischel, W., Shoda, Y., & Peake, P. K. (1988). The nature of adolescent competencies predicted by preschool delay of gratification. *Journal of Personality and Social Psychology, 54,* 687–696.

Tangney, J. P., Baumeister, R. F., & Boone, A. L. (2004). High self-control predicts good adjustment, less pathology, better grades, and interpersonal success. *Journal of Personality, 72,* 271–322.

SELF-DECEPTION

Definition

Self-deception is the act of lying to yourself. You have likely noticed this puzzling behavior in others, that is, cases in which people apparently believe something that they must know is false. This behavior does not include exaggeration, faking, or simple lying—those are cases in which the individual is well aware of uttering a falsehood. Instead, self-deception is something deeper and more complicated, even paradoxical.

Consider some typical examples. An otherwise pleasant young man drinks too much alcohol but gets angry if anyone suggests he has a drinking problem. He refuses to believe he is an alcoholic even though the evidence is obvious: Empty bottles are hidden throughout his apartment, and his boss has often sent him home for drinking on the job. Again, it does not count as self-deception if he knows he is an alcoholic but is simply lying about it.

Consider another case in which a young woman has a deep-seated hatred of her mother but cannot admit it to herself. The signs of this hatred are abundant; she angers quickly at any mention of her mother and makes a face when mentioning her. But the young woman cannot admit it because much guilt and shame would ensue.

The mother of a criminal cannot believe the things the police say about him. Her reason for living, her pride and joy, would be destroyed, so she won't let herself believe it. Still she startles at every ring of the phone, fearing that it is the police calling about her son again.

The more one analyzes such cases, the more complex the notion of self-deception appears. Explaining them requires an acknowledgment of the unconscious part of the mind. Only in the unconscious can an emotional conflict actually influence an individual's behavior and yet be inaccessible. At a conscious level, the truth about an individual's particular problem area is unavailable or, at least, obscure. The unconscious, however, knows the truth.

Therefore, self-deception is not simply being mistaken about oneself. You may well be in error about many aspects of your life. But most of them are not the result of any self-deceptive process. For example, you may not have been told that you are adopted: In that case, others may have purposely deceived you. Or you may believe that you have a genius-level IQ because you accidentally mis-scored a take-home IQ test. Your recall of the fact that you hated your parents at age 10 may have faded along with other memories. None of these cases qualifies as self-deception.

History and Background

Because the unconscious appears to be involved, self-deception is often discussed in the context of Sigmund Freud's famous psychoanalytic theory. Rather than being one of the traditional defense mechanisms, self-deception is thought to be a necessary component of all defense mechanisms. Each one has the paradoxical element noted earlier: There must be at least one moment of self-deception for a defense mechanism to work. Those readers familiar with such defenses as projection, intellectualization, and repression will understand that, in each case, a person has to be both unaware and hyperaware of the disturbing information.

Psychoanalytic theory is pessimistic about your ability to ever recognize self-deception in yourself. That conclusion is probably too severe: A person should be able to recognize his or her own self-deception at some point after it occurs—when the person has cooled down and has a more objective perspective on the issue.

The Paradox of Self-Deception

When Freud first wrote about self-deception, he was attacked by a famous philosopher, Jean-Paul Sartre. Like many nonphilosophers, Sartre dismissed the idea of self-deception as impossible. How can you know something and not know it at the same time?

This criticism is a powerful one. How can you avoid a thought without knowing it is there? An analogy would be the goal of avoiding someone you hate: You cannot effectively avoid the fellow unless you are continuously vigilant for his possible appearance. Similarly, the task of avoiding potentially upsetting self-knowledge requires that you continuously turn your mind away from it. Success at this task would seem impossible if you don't know the threatening thought is even there.

Freud flatly rejected Sartre's critique. A true understanding of the unconscious, Freud argued, would reveal that self-deception can occur. Its feasibility has indeed been supported by recent developments in cognitive psychology.

For example, we now know that many processes are unconscious. Moreover, we know humans' cognitive apparatus allows for multiple versions of the same information: Contradictory information can be stored in two different parts of the brain. Finally, we also know that the emotional part of a stimulus is processed more quickly than is the content. For example, with a polygraph, the emotional impact of a word can be detected before the word is understood.

Given the solid evidence for these mental processes, the possibility of self-deception becomes quite feasible. Incoming information is processed by two different brain systems. One is the cognitive system that deals with the informational value of the stimulus; the other is the emotional system. Furthermore, the emotional system operates first, thereby allowing the mind to set up preemptive roadblocks for the informational system.

Evolutionary Basis

Given that self-deception has been mentioned from the earliest writings of human beings, many psychologists suspect that it has an evolutionary basis. That is, human beings engage in self-deception because it is built in to the genes of our species. According to evolutionary theory, such psychological tendencies are part of our genetic makeup because they proved to give a survival advantage to those who engaged in it. Individuals without this tendency did not survive as well as those who did.

But how could such irrationality be adaptive? An anthropologist, Robert Trivers, pointed out that complete awareness of our motives would interfere with their effectiveness. Your ability to remain brave in the face of extreme danger is enhanced if you really believe you can deal with the threat. Your overconfidence that you can make the Olympic team will actually aid in making it come true. In both cases, there are negative consequences if you are wrong: In one case, you may exhaust yourself in 4 years of futile workouts; in the other case, you may unnecessarily risk your life.

The Evidence for Self-Deception

Thus, it appears that self-deception is possible. But the bulk of the direct evidence for its existence comes from the clinical experiences of psychologists and psychiatrists. Most clinicians can report instances where their patients have clearly deceived themselves, usually with unhealthy consequences.

The experimental evidence for self-deception is much less abundant. In fact, only the two studies described later claim to have demonstrated

self-deception. Of course, it just takes one valid demonstration to prove that human beings can self-deceive. But such demonstrations have proved to be extremely difficult to carry out even in controlled laboratory studies. The reader can decide whether the two studies are convincing or not.

Psychologists Harold Sackeim and Ruben Gur started with the idea that people typically don't like the sound of their own voices. On the main experimental task, participants were asked to pick out their own voices from a series of voices that did, in fact, include their own. They said "Me" or "not Me" to indicate that a voice was theirs or not. At the same time, they are hooked up to a polygraph, which measures emotional response. So we have two pieces of information, an oral response and an emotional response measured by polygraph.

The polygraph invariably shows a blip when the subject's own voice comes on, but many false denials can occur. The oral response is not accurate; it is your voice and you deny it, but the polygraph recognizes it as you. The false denials, coupled with the polygraph, suggest the person knows something and does not know it at the same time; the person is unaware of his or her own beliefs.

When Sackeim and Gur lowered the self-esteem of subjects beforehand, there were more false denials. False denials substantially increased when the person was motivated to avoid self-confrontation.

According to Sackeim and Gur, the false denials show that subjects believe X and do not believe X at the same time. Their lack of awareness is motivated by lowering their self-esteem. They argue that this single demonstration of self-deception is all that is needed to show self-deception occurs.

The second study claiming to demonstrate self-deception was conducted by psychologists George Quattrone and Amos Tversky. They used a cold pressor test, in which participants are asked to immerse one hand in very cold water and keep it there as long as they can stand it.

Some of the participants in the study were told something scary before taking the test: "People who feel a lot of pain from the cold water have a weakness in their cardiovascular system. This defect leads to early heart attacks and a short lifespan."

Results showed that participants receiving this information rated the task as less painful. They even held their hand in the cold water longer. They seemed to be trying to convince themselves that they didn't have the life-threatening cardiovascular problem.

They were engaging in self-deception, according to Quattrone and Tversky, because they wouldn't acknowledge, even to themselves, the pain that they surely were experiencing.

You may or may not be convinced that these studies demonstrate self-deception. What you should be convinced of is that proving self-deception is incredibly difficult. Remember that a convincing experiment has to show that a person believes something and disbelieves it at the same moment. It is not surprising then that only two empirical studies have claimed to demonstrate the phenomenon. Instead, the bulk of writing on self-deception is published by philosophers who, unlike psychologists, do not have to collect data to support their claims. Instead, philosophers' method consists of developing logical, persuasive arguments for their position on an issue.

The Importance of Self-Deception

The examples discussed earlier suggest a deep-seated powerful psychological process. In each case, the person has the information to draw the correct conclusion but, for strong emotional reasons, will not do so.

A number of everyday positive illusions seem to have the flavor of self-deception but are less dramatic. You might set your watch 10 minutes ahead to ensure that you get to an appointment on time. How can that possibly work? You know very well your watch is 10 minutes fast; you aren't fooling anyone. Yet people say it helps them to be on time. Or take procrastination: People know the strategy hasn't paid off in the past, yet they promise themselves that they'll make that unpleasant phone call later. They come up with amazing rationalizations for staying in bed or waiting until the last minute to write a paper.

Labeling such cases as self-deception is a stretch. They are better placed into the category of strategic coping mechanisms. The term *self-deception* should be reserved for cases in which strong psychological forces prevent a person from acknowledging a threatening truth about himself or herself.

In short, the importance of self-deception to social psychology cannot be overestimated. The concept is central to the human necessity to trade off or, at least, balance two fundamental motivations. People want accurate information about their world and its complexity; at the same time, they need to defend against information that would destroy the ideas that their lives are built on.

Delroy L. Paulhus

See also Deception (Lying); Dual Process Theories; Nonconscious Processes; Positive Illusions; Procrastination; Projection; Self-Enhancement; Self-Esteem

Further Readings

Baumeister, R. F. (1993). Lying to yourself: The enigma of self-deception. In M. Lewis & C. Saarni (Eds.), *Lying and deception in everyday life* (pp. 166–183). New York: Guilford Press.

Goleman, D. (1985). *Vital lies, simple truths: The psychology of self-deception.* New York: Simon & Schuster.

Gur, R. C., & Sackeim, H. A. (1979). Self-deception: A concept in search of a phenomenon. *Journal of Personality and Social Psychology, 37,* 147–169.

Krebs, D. L., & Denton, K. (1997). In J. A. Simpson & D. T. Kenrick (Eds.), *Evolutionary social psychology* (pp. 21–48). Hillsdale, NJ: Erlbaum.

Lockard, J. S., & Paulhus, D. L. (1988). *Self-deception: An adaptive mechanism?* New York: Prentice Hall.

SELF-DEFEATING BEHAVIOR

For social psychologists, a self-defeating behavior is any behavior that normally ends up with a result that is something the person doing the behavior doesn't want to happen. If you are trying to accomplish some goal, and something you do makes it less likely that you will reach that goal, then that is a self-defeating behavior. If the goal is reached, but the ways you used to reach the goal cause more bad things to happen than the positive things you get from achieving the goal, that is also self-defeating behavior. Social psychologists have been studying self-defeating behaviors for at least 30 years. And although they have identified several things that seem to lead to self-defeating behaviors, much more can be learned about what self-defeating behaviors have in common, and how to get people to reduce the impact of these behaviors in their lives.

Background and History

Social psychologists began thinking about self-defeating behaviors as a class of behaviors in the late 1980s. Interest in this topic spread following the controversy that took place in the 1980s about whether or not a psychological disorder called the *self-defeating personality disorder* should be included in the official handbook of mental disorders, the *Diagnostic and Statistical Manual of Mental Disorders* (*DSM*).

The group revising the *DSM* in the 1980s wanted to include a disorder where people showed "a pervasive pattern of self-defeating behaviors." Some people didn't want this to be included because they said that there wasn't enough research to show that a disorder like this really existed; some people didn't want it to be included because they said that the behaviors that supposedly made up the self-defeating personality disorder were really parts of other personality disorders; and finally, some people didn't want it to be included because they were afraid that the disorder would be biased against women and would excuse spouse abusers, blaming their victims by claiming that the victims had self-defeating personality disorder.

In the edition of the *DSM* published in 1987 (called the *DSM-III-R*), self-defeating personality disorder was included in an appendix and was not considered an official diagnosis. More recent editions of the *DSM* do not mention the self-defeating personality disorder at all.

Even though social psychologists were inspired by this controversy, they are interested in studying behaviors of normal people, not those of people who are mentally ill. Although some psychiatrists believe that all humans are driven to harm themselves, most people are not motivated in this way. Most humans are interested in accomplishing their goals, not in harming themselves.

Types

Social psychologists have divided self-defeating behaviors into two types. One type is called *counterproductive behaviors*. A counterproductive behavior happens when people try to get something they want, but the way they try to get it ends up not being a good one. One type of counterproductive behavior occurs when people persevere at something beyond the time that it is realistic for them to achieve the desired outcome. For example, students taking a class, and doing very poorly, sometimes refuse to drop the class. They think that if they stick it out, they will be able to pull their grades up and pass the class. But, it may just be too late for some, or they may not have the ability to really pass the class. Most students' goals are to get a degree with as high a grade point average as possible, so refusing to drop the class is a self-defeating behavior. Counterproductive behaviors usually happen because the person has a wrong idea either about himself or herself or about the situation the person is in. The students have an incorrect idea about their own abilities; they think they can succeed, but they can't.

The second type of self-defeating behavior is called *trade-offs*. We make trade-offs in our behavior all the time. For example, you may decide not to go to a party so you can study for an exam. This is a trade-off: You are trading the fun you will have at the party for the benefit you will get from studying (a better grade).

This example of a trade-off is not self-defeating. You are probably going to come out a winner: The benefit of studying will, in the end, outweigh the benefit of going to the party. But, some kinds of trade-offs are self-defeating: The cost that you have to accept is greater than the benefit that you end up getting. One example is neglecting to take care of yourself physically. When people don't exercise, go to the dentist, or follow the doctor's orders, they are risking their health to either avoid some short-term pain or discomfort (such as the discomfort of exercise or the anxiety that the dentist causes).

Another example of a self-defeating trade-off is called self-handicapping. Self-handicapping is when people do something to make their success on a task less likely to happen. People do this so that they will have a built-in excuse if they fail. For example, students may get drunk the night before a big exam. If they do poorly on the exam, they have a built in excuse: They didn't study and they were hungover. This way they avoid thinking that they don't have the ability to do well in the class.

Some common self-defeating behaviors represent a combination of counterproductive behaviors and trade-offs. Procrastination is a familiar example. When you think about why people procrastinate, you probably think about it as a trade-off. People want to do something more fun, or something that is less difficult, or something that allows them to grow or develop more, instead of the thing they are putting off. But, sometimes people explain why they procrastinate in another way: That they do better work if they wait until the last minute. If this is really the reason people procrastinate (instead of something people just say to justify their procrastination), then it is a counterproductive strategy; they believe that they will do better work if they wait until the last minute, but that is not usually the case. (Research shows that college students who procrastinate get worse grades, have more stress, and are more likely to get sick.)

Alcohol or drug abuse is another self-defeating behavior. Many people use alcohol and drugs responsibly, and do it to gain pleasure or pain relief. But for addicts, and in some situations for anyone, substance use is surely self-defeating. Substance use may be a trade-off: A person trades the costs of using drugs or alcohol (health risks, addiction, embarrassing or dangerous behavior, legal problems) for benefits (feeling good, not having to think about one's inadequacies). Usually over the long run, however, the costs are much greater than the benefits.

Even suicide can be looked at as either a self-defeating trade-off or counterproductive behavior. People who commit suicide are trying to escape from negative things in their life. They are trading off the fear of death, and the good things in life, because they think the benefit of no longer feeling the way they do will be greater than what they are giving up. But, suicide can also be thought of as a counterproductive behavior. People may think that taking their life will allow them to reach a certain goal (not having problems).

Causes and Consequences

Causes of different self-defeating behaviors vary; however, most self-defeating behaviors have some things in common. People who engage in self-defeating behaviors often feel a threat to their egos or self-esteem; there is usually some element of bad mood involved in self-defeating behaviors. And, people who engage in self-defeating behaviors often focus on the short-term consequences of their behavior, and ignore or underestimate the long-term consequences.

Procrastination is an example that combines all three of these factors. One reason people procrastinate is that they are afraid that when they do the thing they are putting off, it will show that they are not as good or competent as they want to be or believe they are (threat to self). Also, people procrastinate because the thing they put off causes anxiety (a negative emotion). Finally, people who procrastinate are focusing on the short-term effects of their behavior (it will feel good right now to watch TV instead of do my homework), but they are ignoring the long-term consequences (if I put off my homework, either I'll get an F or I will have to pull an all-nighter to get it done).

These three common causes are all related to each other. If you have a goal for yourself, or if other people expect certain things from you, and you fail or think you will fail to meet the goal, this is a threat to your self-esteem or ego. That will usually make you feel bad (negative mood). So, ego-threats make you have negative moods.

But, negative moods also can lead to ego threats. When people are in negative moods, they set higher

standards or goals for themselves. So, this will make them more likely to fail. Here is a vicious cycle: Failing to meet your goals is a threat to your ego, which leads to negative emotion, which leads you to set higher standards, which makes you fail more. Negative moods also can lead you to think more about the immediate consequences of your actions, instead of the long-term consequences. This, too, can make people do something self-defeating.

Steve Scher

See also Procrastination; Risk Taking; Self-Handicapping; Suicide; Sunk Cost; Threatened Egotism Theory of Aggression

Further Readings

Baumeister, R. F. (1997). Esteem threat, self-regulatory breakdown, and emotional distress as factors in self-defeating behavior. *Review of General Psychology, 1,* 145–174.

Baumeister, R. F., & Scher, S. J. (1988). Self-defeating behavior patterns among normal individuals: Review and analysis of common self-destructive tendencies. *Psychological Bulletin, 104,* 3–22.

Curtis, R. C. (Ed.). (1989). *Self-defeating behaviors: Experimental research, clinical impressions, and practical implications.* New York: Plenum.

Fiester, S. J. (1995). Self-defeating personality disorder. In W. J. Livesley (Ed.), *The DSM–IV personality disorders* (pp. 341–358). New York: Guilford Press.

Widiger, T. A. (1995). Deletion of self-defeating and sadistic personality disorders. In W. J. Livesley (Ed.), *The DSM–IV personality disorders* (pp. 359–373). New York: Guilford Press.

SELF-DETERMINATION THEORY

The self-determination theory (SDT), formulated by Edward L. Deci and Richard M. Ryan, is a broad theory of human motivation for which the concept of basic or universal psychological needs for competence, relatedness, and self-determination and the differentiation of types of motivation (autonomous, controlled) are central and defining features. SDT posits that the type, rather than amount, of motivation is the more important predictor of outcomes, and that the type of motivation is determined by the degree of satisfaction of the basic needs. The theory predicts, and empirical evidence has confirmed, that satisfaction of the basic needs, and being motivated autonomously, are associated with important positive outcomes, such as enhanced well-being, improved learning, and greater persistence. Studies also show that when authority figures are autonomy supportive, taking the other person's perspective and providing choice, the other person tends to become more autonomously motivated.

Basic Psychological Needs

SDT proposes that, in addition to requiring various physical forms of sustenance (e.g., food and water), humans have evolved to require certain psychological experiences for optimal functioning and psychological health. SDT has identified three psychological experiences that are universally required for optimal growth, integrity, and well-being: the needs for competence, relatedness, and self-determination. The postulate that these needs are universal means that they are essential for all people, regardless of sex, ethnicity, socioeconomic status, or cultural values. Consider each need in turn.

The first psychological experience that has been identified as a need is the feeling of competence, that is, the feeling that one is effective in dealing with one's inner and outer worlds. This concept originated in the writings of Robert White, who spoke of being motivated by *effectance*. White suggested that when children play, they do it because it is fun, but children are also learning and becoming more effective or competent while they are playing. The feeling of competence or effectance applies to learning to manage oneself, for example, learning to regulate one's emotions effectively, just as it applied to learning to function in the larger social milieu. The realization that one is improving in any important activity or meaningful aspect of one's life is very gratifying and can be understood as representing satisfaction of the basic need for competence.

The second type of psychological experience that is a need within SDT is relatedness. The experience of relatedness is broadly defined as feeling connected to other human beings: of loving and being loved, of caring for and being cared for, of belonging to groups or collectives, and of having enduring relationships characterized by mutual trust. When someone shares a meaningful conversation, writes or receives a letter from a friend or family member, or hugs someone he or she cares for, the person is likely to experience satisfaction of the need for relatedness.

The third basic need within self-determination theory is the need for autonomy or self-determination. The concept of self-determination evolved from the writings of Richard deCharms, who distinguished between internal and external perceived loci of causality. DeCharms suggested that when people have an internal perceived locus of causality, they will feel as though they are the origin of their own actions, rather than being a pawn, which involves feeling pushed around by external forces. Being self-determined involves feeling a sense of volition or full willingness, having a feeling of choice about what one is doing, of endorsing one's actions fully, and experiencing freedom in one's thoughts, feelings, and actions. Having these experiences provides satisfaction of the basic need for autonomy or self-determination. Although other psychologists may use one or another of these terms to mean something other than what it means in self-determination theory, the use of these multiple descriptors is intended to give one a real sense of what the terms mean within SDT. In short, SDT maintains that human beings have a fundamental need to fully endorse their actions and to feel free with respect to constraints and pressures.

To summarize, SDT posits that each of these three types of experiences—the experiences of competence, relatedness, and autonomy—contribute importantly to people's psychological and physical well-being. To the extent that any one of these needs is thwarted or denied to people, they will suffer some type of psychological or physical decrement as a result. Furthermore, these psychological needs are identified as the sources of energy for one type of motivation referred to as *intrinsic motivation.*

Intrinsic Motivation and Extrinsic Motivation

Intrinsic motivation is the type of motivation characterized by the experience of interest and enjoyment. The reward for intrinsic motivation is said to be in the doing of the activity rather than in what it leads to. In other words, intrinsically motivated behaviors are maintained by the spontaneous feelings that accompany the activity. Activities that you truly enjoy— perhaps playing lacrosse or golf, perhaps reading or drawing, perhaps climbing a mountain or taking a dip in the ocean—are intrinsically motivated. The concept of intrinsic motivation is used to describe the full range of behaviors that are willingly enacted in the absence of contingencies of reward or punishment. The prototypic example of intrinsic motivation is a child at play, running madly around the playground, building a snowman, digging in a sandbox, or turning a large cardboard box into a clubhouse. All these activities require the exertion of energy, yet the rewards are entirely intrinsic to the activities themselves. From an SDT perspective, the energy for such activities originates from the basic psychological needs (e.g., competence, relatedness, and autonomy).

The complement to intrinsic motivation, that is, the type of motivation that energizes and directs other human activities, is referred to as *extrinsic motivation*. This type of motivation is characterized by an instrumentality between the behavior and some separable consequence. The classic example of extrinsic motivation is doing an activity for a reward. In that case, the person is not doing the activity because the activity itself is interesting and enjoyable but rather because doing the activity allows the person to earn the reward. Doing things to avoid a punishment, to please a parent or spouse, to be accepted by a group, to look better than someone else are all examples of being extrinsically motivated.

Undermining Intrinsic Motivation

One of the phenomena for which SDT is well known is the undermining of intrinsic motivation by extrinsic rewards. In the early 1970s, some surprising research suggested that there might be a dark side to using task-contingent tangible rewards, such as money or prizes, to help motivate people to do interesting activities, such as learning or playing. The initial experiment by Deci found that when college students worked on interesting puzzles to earn money, they ended up finding the puzzles less interesting and enjoyable than did other students who had worked on the same puzzles without being offered money. The students who had been paid for solving the puzzles were less likely to return to the puzzle activity during a subsequent free-play period. In other words, when people were given a reward for doing an interesting activity, they lost interest in the activity and were less likely to engage the activity later.

From the perspective of SDT, the reason for this drop in intrinsic motivation was that the rewards tended to make individuals feel controlled. They became dependent on the rewards and lost their sense of doing the activity autonomously. Because satisfaction of the need for autonomy is essential for maintaining people's interest and vitality for the activity—that is, their intrinsic motivation—they lost intrinsic motivation when their behavior was controlled.

Interestingly, another early experiment by Deci showed that when people received positive feedback for doing an interesting activity, their intrinsic motivation tended to increase rather than decrease. The SDT explanation was that the information contained in the positive feedback about people's effectiveness at the activity provided satisfaction of the need for competence and enhanced their intrinsic motivation. Because positive feedback is sometimes referred to as verbal rewards, this experiment helped make the important point that rewards do not always undermine intrinsic motivation. Instead, they tend to undermine intrinsic motivation when people *feel* controlled by the rewards.

More than 100 published experiments have explored the effects of rewards on intrinsic motivation. In general, across all these studies, the results indicate that tangible rewards tend to decrease intrinsic motivation whereas verbal rewards tend to enhance it. Still other studies have examined the effects of other motivators such as surveillance, deadlines, evaluations, and pressure to win a competition. These studies suggest that each of these motivators tends to undermine intrinsic motivation because they diminish people's experience of autonomy.

Autonomous Motivation and Controlled Motivation

The diminishment of intrinsic motivation by extrinsic motivators via the thwarting of people's need for autonomy raised an interesting question: Do all extrinsic motivations tend to *control* people? Put differently, is it possible to be self-determined while doing an extrinsically motivated activity? SDT proposes that people can internalize external prompts or contingencies and accept them as their own. For example, a request from a parent that a child participate in the chores around the house to help the family would be an extrinsic motivator. The child might initially do the chores to please the parent. Gradually, however, the child could internalize the value of helping and the regulation of the behavior and, thus, would be more autonomous in doing the chores. However,

SDT also suggests that values and regulations can be internalized to varying degrees. If the child were simply to take in the regulation and use it to force himself or herself to help, the child would still be relatively controlled. The child might be doing it to avoid feeling guilty or worthless, which, although internalized, does not represent autonomous self-regulation. To become autonomous, the child would need to identify with the importance of the activity and integrate its value and regulation into his or her own sense of who he or she is. Considerable research has shown that it is possible to internalize and integrate values and regulations, and that doing so is associated with higher levels of psychological well-being. Accordingly, over time, SDT changed the most important differentiation in the theory from intrinsic and extrinsic motivation to autonomous and controlled motivation. *Autonomous motivation* consists of intrinsic motivation plus fully internalized extrinsic motivation. *Controlled motivation,* in contrast, consists of regulation by external contingencies and by partially internalized values or contingencies—what in SDT are called *introjects.*

Being autonomously motivated involves feeling a sense of choice as one fully endorses one's actions or decisions. People do intrinsically motivated behaviors because they find the activities interesting and enjoyable; they do well-internalized extrinsically motivated behaviors because they find them personally important. So, interest and importance are the two bases of autonomous motivation, and doing activities for either reason allows people to feel satisfaction of the three basic psychological needs. Controlled motivation, in contrast, involves acting because one feels pressured to do so, either through coercion or seduction. When controlled, people may behave because they feel lured into it by seductive rewards, feel forced into it by authority figures, or have introjected a demand and do it to bolster a fragile sense of self-esteem. When controlled, people might feel a sense of competence or relatedness, but they will not be satisfying their need for autonomy. From the prospective of SDT, satisfaction of all three of the basic psychological needs is necessary for autonomous motivation and for optimal well-being.

Positive Outcomes Associated With Autonomous Motivation

By virtue of the definition of basic needs within SDT, satisfaction of these needs promotes positive psychological health. More than three decades of research has confirmed that being autonomously motivated and satisfying the psychological needs are vital to both mental and physical well-being. Greater autonomous motivation relative to controlled motivation has been linked to more positive emotions and less stress. This pattern emerges in samples of both children and adults, in countries as varied as Germany, Bulgaria, Russia, South Korea, Turkey, and the United States, among others.

Autonomous motivation also leads to greater maintained lifestyle change, better conceptual understanding and deep learning, greater job satisfaction and performance, and higher creativity. For example, research has demonstrated that when people are autonomously motivated to eat a healthier diet and exercise more, they tend to maintain those behaviors more effectively over the long run. When students in school are more autonomously motivated, they tend to get better grades and are less likely to drop out. Employees at large companies are more likely to receive positive work evaluations when they are autonomously motivated. And the paintings and collages created by individuals whose motivation is autonomous are likely to be rated as more creative by expert judges. The merits of autonomous motivation are numerous and varied.

Promoting Autonomous Motivation

Many studies have shown that it is possible to enhance autonomous motivation. Research has indicated that when authority figures, such as parents, managers, teachers, coaches, or physicians are more autonomy supportive, their children, subordinates, students, athletes, or patients become more autonomously motivated. Being autonomy supportive means that authority figures consider and understand the other person's perspective and relate to that person with consideration of this perspective. For example, autonomy-supportive teachers relate to their students in terms of the students' skill levels and encourage them to move on from there. Furthermore, the autonomy-supportive authority figure offers choice, provides meaningful explanations for why requested behaviors are important, and encourages exploration and experimentation. In these ways, authority figures can facilitate autonomous motivation, basic psychological need satisfaction, and greater health and well-being.

Arlen C. Moller
Edward L. Deci
Richard M. Ryan

See also Autonomy; Control; Intrinsic Motivation; Self-Regulation

Further Readings

Deci, E. L., Koestner, R., & Ryan, R. M. (1999). A meta-analytic review of experiments examining the effects of extrinsic rewards on intrinsic motivation. *Psychological Bulletin, 125,* 627–668.

Deci, E. L., & Ryan, R. M. (1985). *Intrinsic motivation and self-determination in human behavior.* New York: Plenum.

Ryan, R. M., & Deci, E. L. (2000). Self-determination theory and the facilitation of intrinsic motivation, social development and well-being. *American Psychologist, 55,* 68–78.

White, R. W. (1959). Motivation reconsidered: The concept of competence. *Psychological Review, 66,* 297–333.

SELF-DISCLOSURE

Definition

Self-disclosure refers to the process of revealing personal, intimate information about oneself to others. Through self-disclosure, two individuals get to know one another. Self-disclosure is considered a key aspect of developing closeness and intimacy with others, including friends, romantic partners, and family members. However, self-disclosure also functions as a way for people to express their feelings about a situation, to give others their thoughts and opinions about a topic, to elicit reassurance about their feelings, or to get advice.

Context and Importance

Self-disclosure varies by the level of intimacy. For example, information can range from being relatively superficial, such as disclosing where you are from and what your favorite flavor of ice cream is, to being more private, such as revealing that your parents are going through a divorce or that you once cheated on your boyfriend or girlfriend. Self-disclosure also varies in how many different topics that are disclosed. When individuals disclose private information, their disclosure is high in *depth*. When individuals disclose a wide range of topics about themselves, their disclosure is high in *breadth*. Most relationships begin with the exchange of superficial information, which gradually turn into more meaningful disclosures when the superficial conversation is rewarding. That is, people are likely to move the conversation to a deeper level by increasing both the breadth and the depth of the conversation when they are enjoying a conversation they are having.

When a relationship is new, early conversations tend to involve self-disclosure reciprocity. Put another way, new acquaintances tend to match one another's disclosures; when one partner opens up and discloses, the other ends up disclosing as well. As one partner's disclosure increases in intimacy, so too does the other partner's disclosure. Because self-disclosure is reciprocal, it both influences and is influenced by the intimacy level between two people. Thus, if you want to get to know someone, one strategy is to disclose personal information about yourself to the person you want to get to know. Most likely, this person will open up to you in turn. Over time and over the course of a number of conversations, a relationship becomes increasingly more intimate.

Three important factors determine whether an interaction will be intimate. First is the content of the individual's disclosure. For example, the disclosure of personal desires, fantasies, anxieties, and emotions is more important for the development of intimacy than is the disclosure of facts. This is because the disclosure of emotions provides an opportunity for the partner to validate and demonstrate that he or she cares for, supports, and accepts the individual. The second is the partner's response to the disclosure. When the partner is responsive, feelings of closeness are increased and further communication is facilitated. When a partner is not responsive, he or she is indicating a lack of interest in further conversation and intimacy is decreased. Third is the individual's interpretation of and reaction to the partner's behavior. If the individual perceives the partner as supportive and understanding, the conversation is likely to become more intimate because the individual is likely to disclose again or prompt the partner to disclose. If the individual perceives the partner as unsupportive or intrusive, the conversation is not likely to become intimate. Thus, when disclosure is high, the partner is responsive and the individual perceives the partner as caring, the conversation will most likely become more intimate over time.

Pioneering research by Sidney Jourard revealed that self-disclosure and liking for another person are linked. Later research has demonstrated that people (a) like those who disclose, (b) disclose to those they like, and (c) after disclosing, like the person to whom they disclosed even more. It feels good to disclose your inner feelings to another, and it is gratifying to be singled out for somebody else's disclosure because it is a signal that they like and trust you. Furthermore, it is rewarding to find out that someone has the same beliefs and values you do.

However, social norms govern appropriate self-disclosure. When people are just getting to know each other, a person who discloses at a medium level of intimacy is better liked than is a person who discloses at a too low or too high level. People like those who disclose at the same level as they do and are deterred by those who are too reserved or too revealing. In addition, a person who reciprocates an intimate self-disclosure is liked more than is a person who reciprocates an intimate disclosure with a superficial one. When a person reciprocates an intimate disclosure with a superficial disclosure, it is a signal that they do not want to get to know the other person and the conversation is not as rewarding. Typically, however, superficial information is disclosed to strangers and more intimate information is disclosed to close others. Revealing highly personal information to a stranger is perceived as inappropriate. For example, it is improper for somebody you barely know to come up to you and reveal the intimate details of his or her sex life. Yet in a close relationship, such a revelation could strengthen the relationship and make two people even closer. A person who reveals too much information early on is perceived by others as unbalanced.

Self-disclosure fosters love as well as liking. Couples who engage in more extensive and intimate self-disclosure to one another tend to have longer, more satisfying relationships. This is because disclosing personal information about yourself is one way to get your needs met, and having your needs met increases feelings of love and affection, companionship, and a sense of belonging. Partners believe that their relationship contains a high level of intimacy when they can express their thoughts, opinions, and feelings to their partners, and feel their partners are able to express themselves as well. This is why many researchers believe that experiencing intimacy through self-disclosure may be the most important factor that determines the health of a relationship.

Gender and Individual Differences

We expect women to be more expressive than men. When a woman is not expressive, others perceive her as maladjusted. Likewise, men are expected to be inexpressive, and when a man is expressive, he is perceived as unstable. And, in fact, women tend to disclose more than men do in general. However, although women disclose more to their female friends and to their romantic partners than men do, they do not disclose more to their male friends any more than men do. Furthermore, women tend to elicit self-disclosure from others, even from those who do not usually disclose very much about themselves. One reason for this is that women tend to be responsive listeners, which in turn promotes further disclosure by the speaker.

Traditional gender roles are changing, however, and men are becoming more expressive in the context of their close romantic relationships and view disclosure as an important part of the relationship. Therefore, couples nowadays are exhibiting patterns of full and equal self-disclosure, which has produced relationships that foster mutual respect and trust. Relationships that contain a high level of self-disclosure have been found to be both more intimate and more satisfying for both partners.

Some people are better able to self-disclose than others are. This is because self-disclosure can be threatening. Self-disclosure can leave you vulnerable to rejection, manipulation, and betrayal. Some individuals are so concerned about these dangers of self-disclosure that they have trouble opening up and revealing intimate details about themselves, even in the appropriate contexts. They worry about the impression they are making on others and readily perceive rejection in others' intentions. Consequently, these individuals frequently feel lonely and isolated from others and tend to have fewer close, satisfying relationships with others.

Amy B. Brunell

See also Intimacy; Need to Belong; Social Support

Further Readings

Altman, I., & Taylor, D. A. (1973). *Social penetration: The development of interpersonal relationships.* New York: Holt, Rinehart & Winston.

Collins, N. L., & Miller, L. C. (1994). Self-disclosure and liking: A meta-analytic review. *Psychological Bulletin, 116,* 457–475.

Laurencau, J., Barrett, L. F., & Pietromonaco, P. R. (1998). Intimacy as an interpersonal process: The importance of self-disclosure, partner disclosure, and perceived partner responsiveness in interpersonal exchanges. *Journal of Personality and Social Psychology, 74,* 1238–1251.

Reis, H. T., & Shaver, P. (1988). Intimacy as an interpersonal process. In S. Duck (Ed.), *Handbook of personal relationships: Theory, research, and interventions* (pp. 239–256). New York: Wiley.

SELF-DISCREPANCY THEORY

Self-discrepancy theory was developed in an attempt to answer the following question: Why is it that when people are emotionally overwhelmed by tragedies or serious setbacks in their lives—such as the death of their child, the loss of their jobs, or the break-up of their marriages—some suffer from depression whereas others suffer from anxiety? Even when the tragic event is the same, people's emotional reactions can be very different. The answer proposed by self-discrepancy theory is that even when people have the same specific goals, such as seniors in high school wanting to go to a good college or older adults wanting a good marriage, they often vary in how they represent these goals. Some individuals represent their goals (or standards), called self-guides in self-discrepancy theory, as hopes or aspirations: ideal self-guides. Other individuals represent their self-guides as duties or obligations: ought self-guides. According to self-discrepancy theory, this difference between ideals and oughts holds the answer to the mystery of people having different emotional reactions to the same negative life events.

Self-Guides

Self-discrepancy theory proposes that people represent a negative life event as saying something about their current state, their *actual self* now. This actual self is compared with their self-guides, the kind of person they want or desire to be (e.g., going to a good college, having a good marriage). When there is a discrepancy between individuals' actual self and their self-guides, a *self-discrepancy,* people suffer emotionally. When the actual self is discrepant from an ideal, people feel sad, disappointed, discouraged—dejection-related emotions that relate to depression. When the actual self is discrepant from an ought, people feel nervous, tense, and worried—agitation-related emotions that relate to anxiety. Thus, self-discrepancy theory proposes that people's emotional vulnerabilities depend on the type of self-guide that motivates their lives: dejection/depression when ideals dominate and agitation/anxiety when oughts dominate.

The rationale behind these predictions is that different emotions are associated with different psychological situations that people experience: Success or failure to meet your ideals produce different psychological situations than success or failure to meet your oughts. Specifically, with an ideal (i.e., one of your hopes and aspirations), you experience success as the presence of a positive outcome (a gain), which is a happy experience, and you experience failure as the absence of positive outcomes (a nongain), which is a sad experience. In contrast, with an ought (i.e., one of your duties and obligations), you experience success as the absence of a negative outcome (a nonloss), which is a relaxing experience, and you experience failure as the presence of a negative outcome (a loss), which is a worrying experience.

Self-discrepancy theory also makes predictions about the kind of parenting that is likely to result in children having strong ideal self-guides and the kind that is likely to result in children having strong ought self-guides. Again, these predictions are based on the underlying idea that self-regulation in relation to ideals involves experiencing successes in the world as the presence of positive outcomes (gains) and failures as the absence of positive outcomes (nongains), whereas self-regulation in relation to oughts involves experiencing successes as the absence of negative outcomes (nonlosses) and failures as the presence of negative outcomes (losses). When children interact with their parents (or other caretakers), the parents respond to the children in ways that make the children experience one of these different kinds of psychological situations. Over time, the children respond to themselves as their parents respond to them, producing the same specific kinds of psychological situations, and this develops into the kind of self-guide (ideal or ought) that is associated with those psychological situations. The pattern of parenting that is predicted to create strong ideals in children is when parents combine bolstering (when managing success) and love withdrawal (when disciplining failure). Bolstering occurs, for instance, when parents encourage the child to overcome difficulties, hug and kiss the child when he or she succeeds, or set up opportunities for the child to engage in success activities; it creates an experience of the presence of positive outcomes in the child. Love withdrawal occurs, for instance, when parents end a meal when the child throws some food, take away a toy when the child refuses to share it, or stop a story when the child is not paying attention; this creates an experience of the absence of positive outcomes in the child.

The pattern of parenting that is predicted to create strong oughts in children is when parents combine prudence (when managing success) and punitive/critical (when disciplining failure). Prudence occurs, for instance, when parents childproof the house, train children to be alert to potential dangers, or teach children to mind their manners; this creates an experience of the absence of negative outcomes in the child. Punitive/critical occurs, for instance, when parents play roughly with children to get their attention, yell at children when they don't listen, or criticize children when they make mistakes; this creates an experience of the presence of negative outcomes.

Self-discrepancy theory makes another distinction: between when individuals' self-guides are from their own independent viewpoint or standpoint ("What are my own goals and standards for myself?") and when individuals' self-guides are from the standpoint of a significant person in their lives, such as their father or mother ("What are my mother's goals and standards for me?"). The theory proposes that there are individual differences in whether it is discrepancies from independent self-guides or discrepancies from significant other self-guides that most determine individuals' emotional vulnerabilities.

Research

Research testing these predictions of self-discrepancy theory has been conducted with both clinical and nonclinical populations. A questionnaire has been developed that measures individuals' actual self-discrepancies from their ideals and from their oughts (for both their own independent self-guides and their significant others' guides for them). Research with clinically depressed and clinically anxious patients has found that discrepancies between patients' actual selves and their ideal self-guides predict their suffering from depression more than such discrepancies predict their suffering from anxiety disorders, whereas discrepancies between patients' actual selves and their ought self-guides predict their suffering from anxiety disorders more than such discrepancies predict their suffering from depression. Because some individuals have actual-self discrepancies from both their ideal and their ought self-guides, one or the other kind of discrepancy can be made temporarily more active by exposing them either to words related to an ideal they possess or to an ought they possess. When such priming of either an ideal or an ought occurs in an experiment, participants whose actual-ideal discrepancy is activated suddenly feel sad and disappointed and fall into a depression-like state of low activity (e.g., talk slower). In contrast, participants whose actual-ought discrepancy is activated suddenly feel nervous and worried and fall into an anxiety-like state of high activity (e.g., talk quicker).

The results of many such studies support the predictions of self-discrepancy theory regarding the distinct emotional vulnerabilities from actual-self discrepancies to ideals versus oughts. Moreover, consistent with the underlying logic of the theory, several studies have found that individuals with strong ideals are especially sensitive to events reflecting the absence or the presence of positive outcomes (gains and nongains), whereas individuals with strong oughts are especially sensitive to events reflecting the presence or absence of negative outcomes (nonlosses and losses). Evidence also supports the predicted parenting relations between bolstering plus love withdrawal parenting and developing strong ideals, and between prudence plus critical/punitive parenting and developing strong oughts. Finally, as predicted, individual differences have been found in whether discrepancies from independent self-guides or discrepancies from significant other self-guides that most determine emotional vulnerabilities. In particular, in North America at least, discrepancies from independent self-guides are a more important determinant of emotional vulnerabilities for males than for females, whereas discrepancies from significant other self-guides are more important for females than for males.

Impact

Self-discrepancy theory has had both a practical and a theoretical impact. Practically, a new method of clinical treatment for depression and for anxiety, called *self-system therapy,* is based on the conceptual and empirical contributions of self-discrepancy theory. This new therapy has been shown to help some patients more than does standard drug treatment or cognitive-behavioral therapy. Studies have also found that actual-self discrepancies from ideals is a vulnerability factor for bulimic eating disorders, whereas discrepancies from oughts is a vulnerability factor for anorexic eating disorders. Theoretically, the psychological mechanisms identified by self-discrepancy theory were the foundation for another psychological theory, regulatory focus theory, which itself has increased understanding of the motivational underpinnings of decision making and performance. What self-discrepancy theory highlights is that it is not the specific goals of people that are critical. Rather, the more general concerns, the viewpoints on how the world works—a world of gain and nongains or a world of nonlosses and losses—determine the quality of people's emotional and motivational lives.

E. Tory Higgins

See also Anxiety; Bulimia; Depression; Goals; Emotion; Self-Awareness; Self-Concept

Further Readings

Higgins, E. T. (1987). Self-discrepancy: A theory relating self and affect. *Psychological Review, 94,* 319–340.

Higgins, E. T., & Tykocinski, O. (1992). Self-discrepancies and biographical memory: Personality and cognition at the level of psychological situation. *Personality and Social Psychology Bulletin, 18,* 527–535.

Moretti, M. M., & Higgins, E. T. (1999). Internal representations of others in self-regulation: A new look at a classic issue. *Social Cognition, 17,* 186–208.

Strauman, T. J. (1989). Self-discrepancies in clinical depression and social phobia: Cognitive structures that underlie emotional disorders? *Journal of Abnormal Psychology, 98,* 14–22.

Strauman, T. J., & Higgins, E. T. (1987). Automatic activation of self-discrepancies and emotional syndromes: When cognitive structures influence affect. *Journal of Personality and Social Psychology, 53,* 1004–1014.

SELF-EFFICACY

Definition

Self-efficacy is defined as people's beliefs in their capabilities to produce desired effects by their own actions. Self-efficacy theory maintains that self-efficacy beliefs are the most important determinants of the behaviors people choose to engage in and how much they persevere in their efforts in the face of obstacles and challenges. Self-efficacy theory also maintains that these self-efficacy beliefs play a crucial role in psychological adjustment, psychological problems, and physical health, as well as in professionally guided and self-guided behavioral change strategies.

Since the publication of Albert Bandura's 1977 *Psychological Review* article titled "Self-Efficacy: Toward a Unifying Theory of Behavior Change," the term *self-efficacy* has become ubiquitous in psychology and related fields. Hundreds of articles on every imaginable aspect of self-efficacy have appeared in journals devoted to psychology, sociology, kinesiology, public health, medicine, nursing, and other fields. This article addresses three basic questions: What are self-efficacy beliefs? Where do they come from? Why are they important?

History and Background

Although the term *self-efficacy* is recent, interest in beliefs about personal control has a long history in philosophy and psychology. Benedict Spinoza, David Hume, John Locke, William James, and (more recently) Gilbert Ryle have all struggled with understanding the role of volition and the will in human behavior. In the 20th century, the theories of effectance motivation, achievement motivation, social learning, and learned helplessness are just a few of the many theories that sought to explore relationships between perceptions of personal competence and human behavior and psychological well-being. Bandura's 1977 article, however, both formalized the notion of perceived competence as self-efficacy and offered a theory of how it develops and how it influences human behavior and defined it in a way that made scientific research on it possible. The essential idea was not new; what was new and important was the empirical rigor with which this idea could now be examined. Bandura also has placed self-efficacy theory in the context of his broader social cognitive theory.

What Are Self-Efficacy Beliefs?

One of the best ways to get a clear sense of how self-efficacy is defined and measured is to distinguish it from related concepts. Self-efficacy is not *perceived skill;* it is what one believes one can do with one's skills under certain conditions. Self-efficacy beliefs are not simply *predictions* about behavior. Self-efficacy is concerned not with that one believes one *will* do but with what one believes one *can* do. Self-efficacy is not an *intention* to behave or an intention to attain a particular goal. An intention is what one says one will probably do, and research has shown that intentions are influenced by several factors, including, but not limited to, self-efficacy beliefs. A self-efficacy belief is not the same as a *goal* but is a belief about one's ability to do what it takes to achieve one's own goals. Self-efficacy is not *self-esteem*. Self-esteem is what one generally believes about oneself, and how one generally feels about what one believes about oneself. Self-efficacy beliefs are specific beliefs about exercising specific abilities in specific domains. Self-efficacy is not a *motive, drive,* or *need for control*. One can have a strong need for control in a particular domain but still hold weak beliefs about one's self-efficacy for that domain. Self-efficacy beliefs are not *outcome expectancies* (or *behavior-outcome expectancies*). An outcome expectancy is one's belief that a specific behavior may lead to a specific outcome in a specific situation. A self-efficacy belief, simply put, is one's belief that one can perform the behavior that produces the outcome. Self-efficacy is not a *personality trait* but, rather, beliefs about one's own ability to coordinate skills and abilities to attain desired goals in particular domains and circumstances. Self-efficacy beliefs can generalize from one situation to another, but specific self-efficacy beliefs are not caused by a personality trait called *general self-efficacy.*

Where Do Self-Efficacy Beliefs Come From?

Self-efficacy beliefs develop over time and through experience. The development of such beliefs begins in infancy and continues throughout life. The early development of self-efficacy is influenced primarily by two interacting factors: the development of the capacity for symbolic thought, particularly the capacity for understanding cause–effect relationships, and the capacity for self-observation and self-reflection. The development of a sense of personal agency begins in infancy and moves from the perception of the causal relationship between events to an understanding that actions produce results, to the recognition that one can produce actions that cause results. Children must learn that one event can cause another event, that they are separate from other things and people, and that they can be the origin of actions that effect their environments. As children's understanding of language increases, so does their capacity for symbolic thought and, therefore, their capacity for self-awareness and a sense of personal agency.

Second, the development of self-efficacy beliefs is influenced by the responsiveness of environments, especially social environments, to the infant or child's attempt at manipulation and control. Environments that are responsive to the child's actions facilitate the development of self-efficacy beliefs, whereas nonresponsive environments retard this development. Parents can facilitate or hinder the development of this sense of agency by their responses to the infant or child's actions and by encouraging and enabling the child to explore and master his or her environment.

Self-efficacy beliefs and a sense of agency continue to develop throughout the life span as people continually integrate information from five primary sources, presented here in roughly their descending order of importance in shaping self-efficacy beliefs. People's own performance experiences—their own attempts to control their environments—are the most powerful source of self-efficacy information. Successful attempts at control that one attributes to one's own efforts will strengthen self-efficacy for that behavior or domain. Perceptions of failure at control attempts usually diminish self-efficacy. Self-efficacy beliefs are influenced also by observations of the behavior of others and the consequences of those behaviors—referred to as *vicarious experiences*. People use this information to form expectancies about their own behavior and its consequences. People also can influence self-efficacy beliefs by imagining themselves or others behaving effectively or ineffectively in hypothetical situations. Self-efficacy beliefs can be influenced by verbal persuasion—what others say to a person about what they believe the person can or cannot do. The potency of verbal persuasion as a source of self-efficacy expectancies will be influenced by such factors as the expertness, trustworthiness, and attractiveness of the source. Physiological and emotional states influence self-efficacy when a person learns to associate poor performance or perceived failure with aversive physiological arousal and success with pleasant feeling states. In activities involving strength and stamina, such as exercise and athletic performances, perceived self-efficacy is influenced by such experiences as fatigue and pain.

Why Are Self-Efficacy Beliefs Important?

Self-efficacy beliefs influence everyday behavior in multiple and powerful ways. Most philosophers and psychological theorists agree that a sense of control over one's behavior, one's environment, and one's own thoughts and feelings is essential for happiness and a sense of well-being. Feelings of loss of control are common among people who seek the help of psychotherapists and counselors. Self-efficacy beliefs play a major role in several common psychological problems, as well as in successful interventions for these problems. Low self-efficacy expectancies are an important feature of depression. Depressed people usually believe they are less capable than are other people of behaving effectively in many important areas of life. Dysfunctional anxiety and avoidant behavior are often the direct result of low self-efficacy expectancies for managing threatening situations. Self-efficacy beliefs play a powerful role in attempts to overcome substance abuse problems and eating disorders. For each of these problems, enhancing self-efficacy for overcoming the problem and for implementing self-control strategies in specific challenging situations is essential to the success of therapeutic interventions.

Self-efficacy beliefs influence physical health in two ways. First, they influence the adoption of healthy behaviors, the cessation of unhealthy behaviors, and the maintenance of behavioral changes in the face of challenge and difficulty. All the major psychological theories of health behavior, such as protection motivation theory, the health belief model, and the theory of reasoned action/planned behavior include self-efficacy as a key component. In addition, enhancing self-efficacy beliefs is crucial to successful change and maintenance of virtually every behavior crucial to health, including exercise, diet, stress management, safe sex, smoking cessation, overcoming alcohol abuse, compliance with treatment and prevention regimens, and disease detection behaviors such as breast self-examinations.

Second, self-efficacy beliefs influence a number of biological processes that, in turn, influence health and disease. Self-efficacy beliefs affect the body's physiological responses to stress, including the immune system. Lack of perceived control over environmental demands can increase susceptibility to infections and hasten the progression of disease. Self-efficacy beliefs also influence the activation of catecholamines, a family of neurotransmitters important to the management of stress and perceived threat, along with the endogenous painkillers referred to as endorphins.

Self-efficacy beliefs are also crucial to successful self-regulation. Self-regulation depends on three interacting components: goals or standards of performance, self-evaluative reactions to performance, and self-efficacy beliefs. Goals are essential to self-regulation because people attempt to regulate their actions, thoughts, and emotions to achieve desired outcomes. Self-evaluative reactions are important in self-regulation because people's beliefs about the progress they are making (or not making) toward their goals are major determinants of their emotional reactions during goal-directed activity. These emotional reactions, in turn, can enhance or disrupt self-regulation. Self-efficacy beliefs influence self-regulation in several ways. First, self-efficacy influences the goals people set. The higher people's self-efficacy in a specific achievement domain, the loftier will be the goals that they set for themselves in that domain. Second, self-efficacy beliefs influence people's choice of goal-directed activities, expenditure of effort, persistence in the face of challenge and obstacles, and reactions to perceived discrepancies between goals and current performance. Strong self-efficacy beliefs make people more resistant to the disruptions in self-regulation that can result from difficulties and setbacks. As a result, strong self-efficacy beliefs lead people to persevere under difficult and challenging circumstances. Perseverance usually produces desired results, and this success then strengthens self-efficacy beliefs. Third, self-efficacy for solving problems and making decisions influences the efficiency and effectiveness of problem solving and decision making. When faced with complex decisions, people who have confidence in their abilities to solve problems use their cognitive resources more effectively than do those people who doubt their cognitive skills. Such self-efficacy usually leads to better solutions and greater achievement.

Self-efficacy beliefs are crucial to the success of psychotherapy and other interventions for psychological problems. Different interventions, or different components of an intervention, may be equally effective because they equally enhance self-efficacy beliefs for crucial behavioral and cognitive skills. Self-efficacy theory emphasizes the importance of arranging experiences designed to increase the person's sense of self-efficacy for specific behaviors in specific problematic and challenging situations. Self-efficacy theory suggests that formal interventions should not simply resolve specific problems, but should provide people with the skills and sense of self-efficacy for solving problems themselves.

The notion of self-efficacy can also be extended from the individual to the group through the concept of collective efficacy—the extent to which members of a group or organization believe that they can work together effectively to accomplish shared goals. Collective efficacy has been found to be important in several domains. The more efficacious that spouses feel about their shared ability to accomplish important shared goals, the more satisfied they are with their marriages. The collective efficacy of an athletic team can be raised or lowered by false feedback about ability and can subsequently influence its success in competitions. The individual and collective efficacy of teachers for effective instruction seems to affect the academic achievement of school children. The effectiveness of work teams and group brainstorming also seems to be related to a collective sense of efficacy. Researchers also are beginning to understand the origins of collective efficacy for social and political change.

James E. Maddux

See also Achievement Motivation; Control; Depression; Learned Helplessness; Reasoned Action Theory; Self-Regulation; Social Learning; Stress and Coping

Further Readings

Bandura, A. (1977). Self-efficacy: Toward a unifying theory of behavioral change. *Psychological Review, 84,* 191–215.

Bandura, A. (1997). *Self-efficacy: The exercise of control.* New York: Freeman.

Maddux, J. E. (Ed.). (1995). *Self-efficacy, adaptation, and adjustment: Theory, research and application* (pp. 143–169). New York: Plenum.

Maddux, J. E. (1999). Expectancies and the social-cognitive perspective: Basic principles, processes, and variables. In I. Kirsch (Ed.), *How expectancies shape behavior* (pp. 17–40). Washington, DC: American Psychological Association.

SELF-ENHANCEMENT

Definition

People engage in self-enhancement whenever they seek, interpret, or distort evidence about themselves in a way designed to maintain, create, or amplify a positive self-image. Self-enhancement is cognitive or interpersonal activity aimed at boosting beliefs that one is a lovable and capable human being. A related concept is *motivated reasoning,* which is thought that is expressly aimed at reaching congenial conclusions about one's self and place in the world.

Self-enhancement needs to be distinguished from other similar activities that people may engage in.

Self-improvement refers to the motive to become a better individual in reality; self-enhancement instead refers to the motive to create the perception that one is a competent and capable individual, regardless of reality. *Self-assessment* refers to the motive to obtain an accurate view of the self, whether that view be positive or negative; people engage in self-enhancement when they shade their treatment of the evidence toward creating positive perceptions of self. *Self-verification* refers to activity people engage in to confirm previously held notions about themselves, whether those perceptions be desirable or undesirable; people engaging in self-enhancement only want to confirm the desirable and deny the undesirable in themselves.

Self-enhancement is also related to a *self-protection* motive. People engage in self-protection when they strive to deny undesirable aspects of themselves. Self-enhancement refers to claiming as much good as one can about one's strengths and achievements. Self-enhancement is also related to, but different from, a *self-presentation* motive, which is creating a positive self-image to convince other people that one is competent and capable, regardless of what one believes about one's self.

History and Evidence

The idea that people manage information about themselves to convince themselves that they are capable beings has a long history, at least in Western thought. Indeed, in ancient Greece, the Epicureans raised self-enhancement to a moral principle, asserting that people should entertain only those thoughts about themselves that gave them pleasure.

Scholars in Western thought and in psychology have long assumed that people gather and distort evidence about themselves to maintain positive self-images, and modern psychology has spent a good deal of effort cataloging many of the tactics that people use in the service of self-enhancement. A few of the major ones, all somewhat interrelated, are discussed here.

Biased Hypothesis Testing

People frame the questions they ask themselves to bolster a perception of competence and success. For example, if students contemplate whether they will obtain a good job after they graduate, they usually frame the question as, "Will I get a good job?" Framing the question in this way tends to make people think about positive evidence of success (e.g., "Gee,

I've gotten good grades so far"). People do not adopt a frame that would pull for negative evidence, such as using a negative frame like "Will I fail to get a good job?" Asking the question this way tends to pull for negative and unpleasant evidence (e.g., "Gee, a lot of other people have good grades, too").

Breadth of Categorization

People adopt broad categorizations to describe their successes and narrow ones to characterize their failures. Suppose two people take a test of South American geography. The first does well and is likely to categorize the behavior broadly as indicating intelligence and worldliness. The second person does poorly and is likely to conclude narrowly that this performance only indicates that he or she does not know much about that particular continent.

Self-Serving Attributions

People reach self-serving conclusions about the causes of their successes and failures. People who succeed make internal attributions and give credit to themselves, thus enhancing their self-images as capable human beings. People who fail make external attributions and blame the failure on luck, difficulty of the task, or some outside agent, thus avoiding the conclusion that their failures indicate personal weakness.

Differential Scrutinization of Good and Bad News

People tend to accept good news at face value. They hold bad news to a higher standard and scrutinize it more closely. For example, if people take a medical test that shows that they are healthy, they accept the verdict and move on. However, if the test indicates they have a health problem, they are likely to search more carefully for reasons to accept or reject the test's verdict—or even ask to retake the test.

Differential Discounting of Good and Bad News

Whereas people take self-enhancing news at face value, and thus rarely question it, they try to find reasons to discount, dismiss, or belittle bad news. That is, the scrutiny that people give to bad news is often not even-handed but instead an attempt to find ways to discredit the evidence. If a student fails a course exam,

he or she might expressly look for reasons to suggest that his or her failure was an aberration. The student might conclude that he or she was ill the night before the test, or that the questions on the test were picky, or the professor unfair. The key for this student is that he or she is discounting the relevance of the test performance for predicting future outcomes.

Re-Analyzation of Importance

If people fail in their attempts to discount or dismiss bad news, they may then downplay the importance of the outcome. For example, if a pre-medical student unambiguously fails a math test, he or she might decide that knowing math is not all that important for being a good doctor. On the other hand, students excelling at a task may decide that it is an important one. A student who aces the same math test may decide that mathematical ability is an essential attribute for being a successful doctor.

Definition of Success

People may also define success in ways to ensure a positive image of self. People often want to claim positive traits, such as intelligent, for themselves. One easy route to do so is to define those traits in ways that ensure a positive self-concept. A person who is good at math, knows a foreign language, and can play the violin can guarantee a positive self-image by merely concluding that those skills are central to intelligence. Students who lack those skills can de-emphasize those skills in their definition of intelligence and instead emphasize those idiosyncratic skills that they possess.

Implications

A lifetime of self-enhancement activity can leave one with significantly distorted and unrealistic views of self. And, indeed, a good deal of recent research suggests that people tend to hold positive views of themselves that simply cannot be true. These unrealistic self-views are exhibited in a number of ways. Here are some of the ones that have received the most attention in recent research.

Above-Average Effects

People on average think they are anything but average. The typical person, for example, thinks he or she is more disciplined, socially skilled, idealistic, and moral than the average person, but this is impossible. It is impossible for the average person to be above average, given the logic of mathematics. People also think they are more likely to achieve positive outcomes (have a happy marriage, get a high-paying job) and less likely to face aversive ones (get fired, contract cancer) than are their peers, although, again, it is mathematically impossible for the average person to be more likely to achieve good outcomes and avoid bad ones than the mathematical average.

Overpredictions of Desirable Actions and Outcomes

When forecasting the future, people overpredict the chance that they will take desirable actions and achieve favored outcomes. Business school students overpredict the likelihood that they will receive a high-paying offer. College students overpredict, for example, how likely they are to give to charity, vote, and maintain their romantic relationships. These types of overpredictions can have economic consequences: People often predict they will work out frequently when they buy gym memberships—and then fail to go to the gym on more than a sporadic basis. Indeed, often, they would have been better off financially if they had just paid for the few individual visits they actually did manage to make rather than buying the more expensive membership.

One caveat, however, must be made about the motive to self-enhance and the unrealistic self-images that the motive creates. Researchers have found ample evidence that people consistently engage in self-enhancement in North America and Western Europe, but there is increasing (albeit controversial) evidence that people in some other parts of the world do not engage in such activity. Namely, people in Far East Asia appear not to extol the positive in themselves and to deny the negative. Indeed, they show signs of attuning to failures and weaknesses so that they may improve upon them. They also show less evidence of the above-average effect described earlier. As such, the motive to self-enhance may be pervasive, but only within certain cultures.

David Dunning

See also Motivated Reasoning; Self-Affirmation Theory; Self-Evaluation Maintenance; Self-Presentation; Self-Serving Bias

Further Readings

Baumeister, R. F., & Newman, L. S. (1994). Self-regulation of cognitive inference and decision processes. *Personality and Social Psychology Bulletin, 20,* 3–19.

Dunning, D. (2005). *Self-insight: Roadblocks and detours on the path to knowing thyself.* New York: Psychology Press.

Kunda, Z. (1990). The case for motivated reasoning. *Psychological Bulletin, 108,* 480–498.

SELF-ESTEEM

Definition

Self-esteem is such a commonly used term you probably already know what it is: thinking highly of yourself. You have probably heard self-esteem mentioned on talk shows, in magazine articles, and even in popular songs (the song "The Greatest Love of All" is about loving yourself, and there's a song by the band The Offspring called "Self-Esteem.") But social psychology research has discovered a lot of things about self-esteem that have not yet made it to popular culture, and this research might surprise you.

Academic psychologists recognize two types of self-esteem. The first is general self-esteem, often measured using the Rosenberg Self-Esteem Scale (which includes items such as "I take a positive attitude toward myself"). The second type of self-esteem is specific, often measuring self-esteem in a particular domain such as school, work, athletics, or appearance. These subdomains are then combined to form a complete self-esteem score (for example, in scales such as the Tennessee Self-Concept Scale or the Coopersmith Self-Esteem Inventory). Although nonpsychologists sometimes use the term *self-esteem* to refer to body and appearance concerns, a psychologist is more specific and instead calls these *body image* or *appearance self-esteem.*

People high in self-esteem seem to know more about themselves and their preferences. They can furnish longer lists of their likes and dislikes, and they are more confident about their self-ratings. They are also more self-serving; they are more likely to take credit for their successes and blame outside sources for their failure. Self-esteem is also correlated with emotional stability: People with low self-esteem experience negative moods more often and report more fluctuation in their moods.

Differences and Predictors

Which groups of people are high in self-esteem, and which are low? You might have heard that teenage girls have very low self-esteem, but this is not true. Men and boys do score higher on self-esteem than women and girls, but the difference is small; gender explains only about 1% of the differences in self-esteem (this number tells you how much of the variation in self-esteem is caused by a specific variable—here, gender—rather than by other factors). The gap does widen a bit during adolescence, with gender explaining about 2.6% of the differences and boys scoring higher. But this doesn't happen because girls' self-esteem drops at adolescence; girls' self-esteem rises between middle school and high school, but just not as much as boys' does. Between high school and college, women's self-esteem increases sharply, and the gender difference shrinks back to 1% of the variance.

Are rich and well-educated people higher in self-esteem? Yes, but not by much—socioeconomic status explains less than 1% of the variance in self-esteem. The correlation between socioeconomic status and self-esteem peaks during middle age, but even then, it accounts for only 1.5% of the differences. So social status and money are only very weak predictors of self-esteem.

What about racial and ethnic differences—are racial minorities, many of whom experience prejudice, more likely to be low in self-esteem? The answers here are complex: Overall, racial differences in self-esteem seem to be caused more by cultural differences than by racial discrimination. Black Americans, who probably experience the most prejudice and discrimination in the United States, actually score higher in self-esteem than are White Americans (though this is yet another of those 1% of the variance small findings). This might occur because they protect their self-esteem by attributing criticism to prejudice (a theory called *stigma as self-protection*). However, Hispanic Americans score lower than Whites do in self-esteem (though this is a very small difference accounting for only about .2% of the variance), and they experience prejudice as well. So prejudice alone cannot explain why Blacks score higher on self-esteem measures. Cultural differences provide a more consistent explanation. Black American culture champions self-respect, whereas Asian cultures emphasize humility and self-criticism. Sure enough, Asian Americans score lower on self-esteem than do Whites, a somewhat larger difference that explains 2.2% of the variance. Asians living in Asia score even lower compared with White Americans, a difference that explains about 4.5% of the variance. These differences are all consistent with the idea that cultural ideas about the self influence levels of self-esteem.

Cultural differences can happen over time and generations as well. The culture of 1950s America was very different from the culture of 1990s America, and one of the main differences is the increased emphasis on the self during recent decades. And indeed, 1990s college students scored higher on self-esteem measures than did 1960s college students, a difference that explains 9% of the variance in self-esteem scores. Overall, culture (of time and regions) is a stronger influence on self-esteem than is being a certain race, gender, or income level.

Outcomes

So what does self-esteem cause? In psychological language, what are the outcomes of self-esteem? You might have heard that high self-esteem leads to better academic achievement and less bad behavior like aggression and teen pregnancy. However, a large body of research suggests that this is not the case. Self-esteem does explain about 5% of the variance in school achievement, a small but statistically significant effect. However, as in any correlational study, there are three possibilities: High self-esteem could cause school achievement, school achievement could cause high self-esteem, or a third variable (such as income level) could cause both. To use a common analogy, the horse could be pulling the cart, or things could be reversed and the cart has been put before the horse. A third variable resembles the horse and the cart being towed on a flatbed truck: Neither the cart nor the horse is causing the motion in the other even though they are moving together.

Most studies have found that achievement leads to self-esteem, not vice versa. Another set of studies finds that controlling for third variables (such as family income) eliminates the correlation. This occurs because rich kids are both higher in self-esteem and do better in school. Self-esteem is also not consistently correlated with alcohol and drug abuse or teen pregnancy. Some studies have found that high self-esteem actually predicts earlier intercourse among teens. Overall, self-esteem does not seem to cause good outcomes for kids; the two are unrelated.

Despite this research, numerous school programs aim to increase children's self-esteem. A 2006 Google search showed that more than 300,000 elementary schools mention self-esteem in their mission statements. Most of these say that they seek to encourage or develop children's self-esteem. Some of these programs promote self-esteem without rooting it in achievement, in the belief that children should feel good about themselves no matter what they do. Although the results of these programs are continuing to be debated, it seems likely that they will not have much impact if self-esteem does not cause achievement and good behavior (which appears to be the case).

There has recently been some debate about whether low self-esteem leads to antisocial behavior. Experimental lab studies consistently find no correlation between self-esteem and aggression. Two recent correlational studies, however, found that low self-esteem was correlated with delinquent behavior in a sample of adolescents, even after controlling for academic achievement, income, and parental support. Other variables, such as associating with delinquent friends, might explain the effect, which accounts for about 4% of the variance in delinquent behavior. Overall, the evidence suggests that self-esteem is not correlated with aggression, but that low self-esteem is linked to a slightly higher incidence of delinquent behavior.

Some evidence also indicates that low self-esteem is linked to eating disorders such as anorexia and bulimia. However, low self-esteem only predicts eating disorders when women are perfectionistic and feel overweight. Low self-esteem might also follow, rather than precede, eating disorders: People might start to feel badly about themselves after they develop an eating disorder.

One thing self-esteem does strongly predict is happiness. People who are high in self-esteem report being happy, and they are also less likely to be depressed. However, these studies have not proven causation and ruled out other third variable explanations, so further research needs to be done: It is not yet known if self-esteem causes happiness, happiness causes self-esteem, or if some other variable causes both. Self-esteem also leads to greater persistence on tasks, though the causation is not known here, either, and self-control is a better predictor of persistence. Self-esteem is also correlated with greater relationship confidence. High self-esteem people who experience a threat to their self-worth are subsequently more certain of their partners' regard for them; in contrast, low self-esteem people began to doubt their partners' feelings, which can cause problems in the relationship.

The stability of self-esteem also plays a role. People whose self-esteem fluctuates wildly, or whose self-esteem heavily depends on a particular outcome, are more likely to be depressed and anxious. Stable self-esteem, and self-esteem that does not depend on certain things happening, is correlated with better mental health.

Origins

Where does self-esteem come from, and how does it develop in a child? One theory proposes that self-esteem is a sociometer, or a gauge of how accepted people feel by other people. Thus, self-esteem arises from feeling loved by others and belonging to groups. This theory also helps explain the main difference between self-esteem and narcissism. Narcissism is an inflated sense of self, but it goes beyond simply having very high self-esteem. Narcissists believe that they are better than others in achievement realms such as intellectual ability and sports. However, they acknowledge that they are not particularly friendly or moral. Perhaps as a result, narcissism is correlated with poor relationship outcomes: Narcissists lack empathy, are more likely to derogate their partners, and are more likely to cheat. They are also more aggressive in response to threat.

Implications

People are very motivated to preserve their self-esteem and good feelings about themselves, and this motive explains a surprising amount of human behavior. Many people tend to credit themselves when things go well, and blame others or luck when things go badly. This is called *self-serving bias,* and you can easily see how it preserves good self-feelings. Self-esteem boosting also explains ingroup bias, in which people believe that their own group is better than other groups. In other words, prejudice against people unlike ourselves may be rooted in our desire to feel good about ourselves. One set of researchers believes that the ultimate self-preservation—pushing away thoughts about death—explains patriotism and ingroup bias. They find that when people are reminded of death, they strongly defend their own worldviews. Another study found that when high self-esteem people are threatened, they respond by acting more boastful and rude.

Overall, self-esteem does not explain as many things as most people believe it does. Self-esteem is good for relationships, but only if it does not cross over into narcissism. People with high self-esteem are happier, but their self-esteem does not cause good things to happen in their lives. Instead, the pursuit of self-esteem can sometimes lead people to behave in ways that they might later regret.

Jean M. Twenge

See also Contingencies of Self-Worth; Happiness; Narcissism; Self-Esteem Stability; Sociometric Status; Threatened Egotism Theory of Aggression

Further Readings

Baumeister, R. F., Campbell, J. D., Krueger, J. E., & Vohs, K. D. (2003). Does high self-esteem cause better performance, interpersonal success, happiness, or healthier lifestyles? *Psychological Science in the Public Interest, 4,* 1–44.

Twenge, J. M., & Campbell, W. K. (2001). Age and birth cohort differences in self-esteem: A cross-temporal meta-analysis. *Personality and Social Psychology Review, 5,* 321–344.

SELF-ESTEEM STABILITY

Definition

Some people possess immediate feelings of self-worth that fluctuate considerably from day to day or even within a given day. These people are said to have unstable self-esteem. Other people possess immediate feelings of self-worth that rarely, if ever, change. These people are said to have stable self-esteem. Consider Ashley who, when asked to consider the question "How worthy a person do you feel at this moment?" each morning and evening for 5 days, gives answers that vary considerably from "I feel very worthy" to "I feel useless." Ashley possesses unstable self-esteem. In contrast, Heather's responses to that same question remain essentially the same over the same period ("I feel very worthy"), as do Mark's responses ("I feel pretty useless"). Both Heather and Mark possess stable self-esteem. Importantly, considerable research indicates that the degree to which one's self-esteem is stable or unstable has important implications for one's psychological health and well-being.

Unstable Self-Esteem

Unstable self-esteem reflects fragile and vulnerable feelings of self-worth that are affected by positive and negative experiences that either are internally generated (i.e., a person's own negative self-evaluations) or externally provided (e.g., getting an A+ on an exam). Moreover, people with unstable self-esteem are said to be highly ego-involved in their everyday activities, which means that they experience their self-esteem as continually *being on the line* as they go about their lives. For example, whereas someone with unstable self-esteem feels stupid and worthless (reactions that imply negative feelings of self-worth) after receiving a poor grade, someone with stable self-esteem feels badly (e.g., feels disappointed or frustrated) about his or her performance without implicating his or her overall feelings of self-worth. Researchers have examined a number of implications of the heightened self-esteem investment of individuals with unstable self-esteem.

First, daily negative events have a greater adverse impact on individuals with unstable as opposed to stable self-esteem. Researchers found that daily hassles (those irritating events that people experience at times, such as having too much work to do or not enough money to buy what they want), or doing poorly on an important exam, triggers greater increases in depressive symptoms among people with unstable as opposed to stable self-esteem.

Second, people with unstable self-esteem are especially concerned about, and responsive to, potential self-esteem threats. Among sixth-grade children, those with unstable self-esteem report that they are more likely to get angry because of the self-esteem threat (e.g., feeling weak) rather than the goal-thwarting aspect (e.g., having to be thirsty longer) of negative interpersonal events (e.g., someone butting ahead of you in line at the water fountain).

Third, everyday positive and negative events have a greater immediate impact on the self-feelings of people with unstable as opposed to stable self-esteem. When asked to rate the extent to which their most positive and negative daily events made them feel better or worse about themselves over a 2-week period, college students with unstable as opposed to stable self-esteem reported that positive events made them feel better about themselves and negative events made them feel worse about themselves to a greater extent.

Fourth, people with unstable self-esteem have a weaker sense of self (i.e., are less self-determining, have relatively confused self-concepts) than do people with stable self-esteem. Possessing a strong sense of self is a marker of positive mental health. Research has shown that individuals who feel autonomous and self-determining (i.e., make choices about how to behave based on their own values and interests) have more positive mental health than do individuals who feel controlled and pressured about how to behave by outside people and events. The same is true for individuals who have a clear rather than confused sense of their identity. Researchers have shown that, compared with individuals with stable self-esteem, individuals with unstable self-esteem report feeling less autonomous and self-determining and have less clear self-concepts than do individuals with stable self-esteem.

Childhood Factors

Of considerable importance is the role that family environments play in the development of children's self-esteem. Researchers asked 12- and 13-year-old children to report individually on how their mothers and fathers communicated with them. Importantly, children's perceptions of many aspects of parent–child communication patterns (especially with respect to fathers) related to the extent to which they possessed unstable self-esteem. For example, children who perceived their fathers to be highly critical, to engage in insulting name calling, and to use guilt arousal and love withdrawal as control techniques, had more unstable (as well as lower) self-esteem than did children who did not perceive their fathers in this manner. Moreover, compared with children with stable self-esteem, children with unstable self-esteem indicated that their fathers less frequently talked about the good things that they (the children) had done and were less likely to use value-affirming methods (e.g., hug or spend time with them) when they did show their approval. Still other findings indicated that, compared with fathers of children with low self-esteem, fathers of children with stable high self-esteem, but not unstable high self-esteem, were perceived as using better problem-solving methods to solve disagreements with their children. Perceptions of mothers' communication styles more consistently related to children's self-esteem level than to their self-esteem stability. The findings for self-esteem stability that did emerge, however, were largely consistent with those that emerged for fathers.

Levels of Self-Esteem

Level of self-esteem refers to people's general or typical feelings of self-worth, whereas stability of self-esteem refers to whether people's immediate feelings of self-worth exhibit considerable short-term fluctuations. These two self-esteem components (level, stability) are relatively independent of each other. Thus, people can have high self-esteem that is stable or unstable, or low self-esteem that is stable or unstable. Considerable research indicates that whereas unstable high self-esteem is fragile, stable high self-esteem is secure. For example, people with unstable high self-esteem are more defensive and self-promoting than are their stable high self-esteem counterparts, yet they are lower in psychological health and well-being. Feelings of self-worth are more brittle among unstable as compared with stable high self-esteem individuals. Compared with individuals with stable high self-esteem, individuals with unstable high self-esteem are more (a) prone to anger and hostility, (b) likely to show increased depression in the face of daily hassles, (c) verbally defensive when interviewed about potentially threatening events in their past, (d) likely to report increased tendencies to get even in response to hypothetical romantic partner transgressions, and (e) likely to report lower quality romantic relationships. These and other findings indicate that stable high self-esteem is a healthy form of self-esteem whereas unstable high self-esteem is an unhealthy form of self- esteem. Thus, a more complete understanding of self-esteem requires taking into consideration both level and stability of self-esteem.

Michael H. Kernis

See also Contingencies of Self-Worth; Narcissism; Self-Esteem

Further Readings

Kernis, M. H. (2003). Toward a conceptualization of optimal self-esteem. *Psychological Inquiry, 14,* 1–26.

Kernis, M. H. (2005). Measuring self-esteem in context: The importance of stability of self-esteem in psychological functioning. *Journal of Personality, 73,* 1569–1605.

Kernis, M. H., & Goldman, B. M. (2006). Assessing stability of self-esteem and contingent self-esteem. In M. H. Kernis (Ed.), *Self-esteem issues and answers: A sourcebook of current perspectives* (pp. 77–85). New York: Psychology Press.

Kernis, M. H., Grannemann, B. D., & Barclay, L. C. (1989). Stability and level of self-esteem as predictors of anger arousal and hostility. *Journal of Personality and Social Psychology, 56,* 1013–1022.

Self-Evaluation Maintenance

Sometimes the success of others is a source of good feelings. People take pride in their friends' or their spouse's accomplishments, and this brings people closer to their friends or spouse. Sometimes the accomplishments of friends are threatening and may even disrupt the relationships. These kinds of complex interpersonal dynamics are the focus of the self-evaluation maintenance (SEM) model.

The SEM model is based on two broad assumptions: (1) People want to maintain a positive evaluation of the self. (2) The way people evaluate themselves is at least partially determined by the accomplishments of the people around them, particularly the people to whom they are close. These assumptions appear to be useful in understanding a variety of social and personal behaviors. The SEM model specifies two antagonistic processes: A comparison process in which a close other's achievements are threatening and could lead to changes in self-identity and negative consequences for the interpersonal relationship, and a reflection process in which a close other's good performance has positive personal and relational consequences.

Reflection and Comparison Processes

Everyone has seen the reflection process in action. Imagine a conversation at a cocktail party. Inevitably someone casually lets it be known that he or she has some connection with someone who is notably rich, smart, creative, well connected, and so on. That person has not been instrumental in the accomplishments of those others, so it appears as if he or she points out these associations simply to bask in reflected glory. Such associations appear to raise the individual's self-evaluation and are associated with feelings such as pride in the other.

The reflection process has two distinct components: closeness and performance. The reflection process is not enabled by any successful other person. To bask in reflected glory, one must have some connection to the other. Thus, closeness counts. Closeness is defined in very broad terms. Anything that psychologically connects one individual to another increases closeness. Closeness may be based on similarity, family relationships, geographic proximity, and so on.

The second component of the reflection process is the other's performance. If the other's performance is not particularly good, then regardless of how psychologically close he or she is, self will not gain in reflected glory. For example, it is difficult to imagine anyone basking in the reflected glory of a neighbor who tried out for the local orchestra but was not selected or a cousin who was the 25th out of 100 to be eliminated in a spelling bee.

According to the SEM model, the closeness and performance components combine multiplicatively. If there is no association between self and another, then even if that other's performance is superb, there is little potential for gains to the self via reflection. When closeness goes to zero, the level of performance ceases to matter—anything multiplied by zero is zero. In short, the reflection process will produce gains in self-evaluation to the extent that another is psychologically close and that his or her performance is good.

A close other's good performance can raise self-evaluation through the reflection process, but it can also lower self-evaluation through the comparison process. Self's own performance pales in comparison with that of someone who performs better, resulting in a lower self-evaluation and emotions such as envy and jealousy, and decreases in pride. Closeness and performance also play a leading role in the comparison process. If a person has nothing in common with another person, if a person is different with respect to age, gender, race, ethnicity, and so forth, he or she is unlikely to draw comparisons with the other person. However, if the other is psychologically close, comparison processes are more likely to be engaged. A performance that is better than one's own can be a blow to self-evaluation, whereas a mediocre performance is not threatening. Again, closeness and performance combine multiplicatively. If there is no connection to the other person, that is, closeness, then even if the other's performance is superb, there is little threat from comparison. If the others' performance is mediocre, not as good as one's own, then regardless of how close the other is, there is little threat from comparison.

Weighting by Relevance

The reflection and comparison processes have identical components but opposite effects on self-evaluation. However, these processes are generally not equally important. Sometimes self-evaluation will be more affected by the reflection process; other times self-evaluation will be more affected by the comparison process. Which process will be more or less important is determined by the relevance of the other's performance to one's self-definition.

People recognize and value good performance on any number of dimensions: marathon running, violin playing, and so on. One's own aspirations, however, exist only with respect to a small subset of these. A person wants to be a good cabinetmaker, or a good tennis player, or a physician. But almost no one aspires to all these things. Another's performance, then, is relevant to the extent that it is on one of those few dimensions that are self-defining for a person. (A performance dimension is any dimension that has a "good" pole and along which it is possible to rank order people. For example, even though beauty does not require the kind of skill we usually think of when we think of performance, it is better to be beautiful than ugly and it is possible to rank order people with respect to their looks.) Thus, if one aspires to be a good surfer, but does not play the piano, then another's surfing performance is high in relevance but his or her piano performance is not.

The relevance of another's performance increases the importance of the comparison process relative to the reflection process. When relevance is high, a good performance by another is threatening to self-evaluation (via comparison) and the closeness of that other increases the threat. When relevance is low, another's good performance will bolster one's self-evaluation (via reflection), especially when that other is close.

Understanding and Predicting Behavior

The reflection and comparison processes are crucial to understanding and predicting behavior. However, only performance, closeness, and relevance actually manifest themselves in behavior, and the theory aspires to predict and understand performance, closeness, and relevance. The predictions derived from the SEM model regarding performance, closeness, and relevance have been confirmed in several studies.

Predicting Performance

When will a person help another do well? Who is most likely to receive such help? According to the SEM model, when relevance is high, the comparison process is important and another's good performance is threatening to self-evaluation, particularly the performance of a close other. Thus, to avoid the threat of being outperformed, when relevance is high, the model predicts interference rather than helping, particularly when the other person is close. When relevance is low, the reflection process is important. The good performance of another provides a potential gain to self-evaluation. To realize this gain, the model predicts helping, particularly when the other person is close. Contrary to common sense, these predictions suggest that people are sometimes kinder to strangers than to friends.

Predicting Closeness

When will a person try to spend more time with another? When less? When will a person initiate a relationship? When will a person terminate it? The predictions for closeness follow the SEM logic: When relevance is high, comparison is important and self will suffer by the better performance of another. Thus, when relevance is high, the better another's performance is, the more the self should distance himself or herself from the other. When relevance is low, however, the better another's performance is, the greater is the potential boost to self-evaluation via reflection. Closeness should intensify those positive self-feelings, so when relevance is low, the better the other's performance, the more the self should increase closeness. The SEM model suggests that the aphorism, "Everyone loves a winner," is only half true, that is, only when the performance dimension is low in personal relevance.

Predicting Relevance

Relevance refers to the importance of a performance domain to one's own self-definition. Related to relevance are questions such as, What should I major in? How will I spend my free time? What kind of work should I choose? Although common sense might suggest that people want to be like those closest to them, the SEM model reminds us that performance differentials will play an important role in this. Again, relevance determines the relative importance of the comparison process over the reflection process. If another person outperforms the self, then comparisons would be threatening, particularly if the other person were close. Reducing relevance avoids the threat of comparison and increases the potential for reflection, particularly if the other is psychologically close. When self performs better than the other, however, there is little to be gained by reflection and the comparison may be flattering. Thus, self will be motivated to increase relevance, particularly with a close other.

Abraham Tesser

See also Basking in Reflected Glory; Close Relationships; Self

Further Readings

Tesser, A. (1988). Toward a self-evaluation maintenance model of social behavior. In L. Berkowitz (Ed.), *Advances in experimental social psychology* (Vol. 21, pp. 181–227). New York: Academic Press.

SELF-EXPANSION THEORY

Definition

Close relationships open up new worlds to people. As you interact with roommates, close friends, and relationship partners in college, you will probably start to notice small parts of yourself changing to become a little more like them and vice versa. For example, you might notice that you start taking more interest in sports if you have a partner who always watches basketball and football games on television. Before you know it, you might think of yourself as a sports buff!

Relationships can help shape our identities, and they can provide us with shared resources. If your partner owns a car and you do not, you will likely occasionally get a ride to get groceries or go out to dinner. Or if you have a nicer apartment than your partner's, he or she will likely benefit by spending more time at your place. Besides developing a sense of ourselves and receiving extra resources, we can also develop different perspectives from close relationships. For example, if your partner is from a small town in the Midwest and you are from a large East Coast city, you will likely learn a lot about each other's worldviews just by interacting and talking.

These changes to people's identities, resources, and perspectives that occur in relationships are described in and explained by *self-expansion theory*. This theory says that it is very important for people's sense of self to expand and grow throughout their lives for them to feel satisfied with their lives. Although close relationships can provide us with a rich source of potential expansion, people can experience this type of growth in other ways: through spirituality, creativity, and their interactions with valued objects.

People really enjoy the feeling of self-expansion, and as a result, they try very hard to look for self-expansive opportunities. People can do this in various ways. For example, some people might look for new relationships to keep the positive feeling of growth alive, whereas others might instead try new activities with current relationship partners as a way to increase their self-expansion.

What happens if your best friend bombs a chemistry midterm? Will you react to his or her failure as if it was your own, or will you suddenly want to shrink away from your friend? It makes sense that people include others' positive elements in their self-concepts when they grow. After all, it usually feels good to have successful friends. However, self-expansion is not necessarily selfish: People don't only include the good elements of others in themselves when they grow. The fact that some people might even include others' negative elements in themselves shows how strong the need to self-expand is; it might even be stronger than our need to make ourselves feel good! Finally, like other human motivations, self-expansion is not necessarily a conscious one; a person may not always be aware of why he or she wants to meet new people and try new things.

Background and History

The motivation to self-expand is tied to people's ability to accomplish their goals, thus self-expansion is related to psychological models of self-efficacy, intrinsic motivation, self-actualization, and the self-improvement motivation. The idea that the self is created through relationships with close others goes back to Martin Buber's conception of the "Thou" and "I" uniting and is also related to George Herbert Mead's work on social interactions. Carl Jung believed that relationship partners could draw out otherwise hidden aspects of the self to create greater wholeness, and

Abraham Maslow thought that loved ones could be included in people's self-concepts. Within social psychology, Fritz Heider's concept of the unit relation that can form between close others comes closest to Art and Elaine Aron's recent idea of inclusion of others in the self.

Research Evidence

One of the most common ways that humans self-expand is through their relationships with others. In relationships, people can feel distant and completely different from the other person, or they can feel a close sense of oneness called *psychological overlap.* Psychological overlap with close others is measured with the Inclusion of Other in the Self Scale, which is a set of seven pairs of circles with gradually increasing levels of overlap. Participants are asked to select the pair of circles that most represents their relationship.

This scale measures both feelings of closeness and behaviors related to closeness. Psychological overlap as measured by this scale is strongly related to relationship satisfaction, commitment, relationship investment and importance, and the percentage that dating partners use the pronouns *we* and *us* when discussing their relationship. This scale also predicts whether people stay in a relationship in a 3-month posttest.

According to research, the idea that the self expands through relationships can be taken literally. For example, people in close relationships describe their self-concepts with more complexity do than those who are not in close relationships. As well, people who report falling in love describe themselves with more different domains of self-content compared with their baseline "not in love" state and compared with those who are not in love.

Relationships high in self–other overlap are characterized by expanded identities, resources, and perspectives from the relationship partner. When the self expands to include another, people may even confuse their own personality traits and memories with close others' traits and memories. Identity and self-knowledge literally overlap with a highly overlapped other.

In a sense, there is also a literal overlap of resources and possessions with highly overlapped others, perhaps reflecting an awareness of shared outcomes. People treat close others as if they are indistinguishable from themselves: They allocate more resources to close others, giving approximately equal amounts to themselves and their partner when the partner in a money allocation game is a close other but giving more to themselves when the partner is an acquaintance or stranger.

Self-expansion theory also suggests that people may make more situational and less dispositional attributions to explain the behavior of close others, an evaluation more consistent with how information is processed about the self. For example, when your best friend fails on a chemistry test, you will likely consider situational variables that affected your friend's performance (e.g., having a cold that day) in the same way that you would for yourself, rather than making trait-based attributions as you would for strangers or acquaintances (e.g., they are unmotivated or unintelligent).

Implications

Self-expansion theory can help provide explanations for both people's initial attraction to others and the eventual decline in relationship satisfaction that occurs over time. It suggests that one of the main reasons people initially enter romantic relationships is because of the opportunity to self-expand and that attraction is the result of a nonconscious calculation of how much the potential partner can contribute to one's self-expansion. Extremely high levels of relationship satisfaction that typically occur at the beginning of a relationship are explained by positive feelings resulting from self-expansion, which quickly fade as the two people get to know each other better and opportunities for self-expansion decline. Importantly, the model specifies why relationship satisfaction declines over time and how to increase relationship satisfaction. This has been successfully done in the laboratory through inducing couples to participate in self-expanding activities together (e.g., completing a difficult maze) and in real life by asking couples to spend time doing exciting things together (e.g., learning to dance).

Sara Konrath

See also Close Relationships; Interdependent
    Self-Construals; Romantic Love; Transactive Memory

Further Readings

Aron, A., & Aron, E. (1997). Self-expansion motivation and including other in the self. In S. Duck (Ed.), *Handbook of personal relationships* (2nd ed., pp. 251–270). Chichester, UK: Wiley.

Aron, A., McLaughlin-Volpe, T., Mashek, D., Lewandowski, G., Wright, S., & Aron, E. (2004). Including others in the self. *European Review of Social Psychology, 15,* 101–132.

Aron, A., Norman, C., & Aron, E. (1998). The self-expansion model and motivation. *Representative Research in Social Psychology, 22,* 1–13.

SELF-FULFILLING PROPHECY

Definition

A self-fulfilling prophecy is a process through which someone's expectations about a situation or another person leads to the fulfillment of those expectations. Thus, the expectancy becomes a cause, so that what is expected comes true because it was expected. The process includes three steps: (1) A perceiver forms an expectation of a situation or target person, (2) the perceiver's expectations affects how he or she behaves in the situation or treats the target person, and (3) the situation or the target person is affected by the perceiver's behavior in a way that confirms the perceiver's initial expectation.

Background and History

The concept of the self-fulfilling prophecy was initially introduced by a sociologist, Robert K. Merton. In Merton's conception, a self-fulfilling prophecy applied to social as well as nonsocial phenomena. For example, Merton discusses how a self-fulfilling prophecy could lead a stable bank to experience failure. Imagine that a group of individuals comes to believe that a bank is on the verge of bankruptcy. As a result, those individuals withdraw their savings from the bank. In turn, other depositors start to worry that their funds are not safe and consequently withdraw their funds. In the end, many depositors withdrawing their funds actually leads to the bank becoming bankrupt. Therefore, the individuals' expectations influenced their own behavior and ultimately the very situation about which they were concerned. The type of self-fulfilling prophecy that leads to a bank failure is one that depends on the beliefs and actions of many individuals. However, most of the social psychological research on self-fulfilling prophecies has focused on how one person's belief about another person leads to confirmation of that belief.

One of the best-known studies that demonstrates the effect of self-fulfilling prophecies at the interpersonal level was conducted by Robert Rosenthal and Lenore Jacobson in the late 1960s. In this study, the researchers led classroom teachers to believe that some of their students were "potential bloomers," who would show substantial IQ gains during the school year. In actuality, the students labeled as "bloomers" were randomly chosen by the researchers and were not really different from their classmates. So the teachers' beliefs about the potential bloomers were initially false. Nonetheless, at the end of the school year, these bloomers had higher gains in their IQ compared with the other students. The teachers' expectations that bloomers would experience IQ gains caused them to treat these students differently. For example, teachers were more likely to give feedback to the bloomers and challenge them more than they did their other students. These differences in the teachers' behavior led these students to perform better. This study was important in demonstrating that individuals may unwittingly cause outcomes that they expect by changing their own behavior and thereby influencing the behavior of others.

The early research on the self-fulfilling nature of teacher expectations on student achievement faced criticism about the ethics of the research and the very existence of the self-fulfilling prophecy. Experimental laboratory research, however, convincingly demonstrated that people can subtly affect the behavior of others because of their own expectations and that these self-fulfilling prophecies do occur in many situations. The experimental studies on self-fulfilling prophecies typically led perceivers to expect something of a target and then measured the target's behavior. Because the expectations perceivers held for the targets were initially false, if the behavior of the target confirmed the expectation, this was taken as evidence of a self-fulfilling prophecy. For example, perceivers might be led to believe that a target person with whom they would interact was physically attractive by showing the perceiver a picture of an attractive person. Because people tend to believe that physically attractive individuals are friendly and outgoing, perceivers would expect an attractive interaction partner to be sociable. Perceivers would then interact with someone who was objectively physically attractive or not. In general, perceivers acted in ways that elicited the type of behavior they expected from their interaction partners. So, for example, perceivers were themselves more friendly and outgoing if they believed that they were interacting with an attractive person rather than if they thought they were interacting with an unattractive person. In turn, targets who experienced friendliness from the perceiver responded by being warm and friendly, regardless of their objective levels of physical attractiveness. These types of laboratory studies were important in demonstrating that self-fulfilling prophecies do occur, even in situations in which people do not know each other very well or have repeated contact, as a teacher might have with students. Recent research has even demonstrated that perceivers' expectations may lead to self-fulfilling prophecies even when perceivers are unaware or not consciously thinking of their beliefs. Something in the environment may bring to mind a perceiver's expectation, and even if the perceiver is not actively thinking about the belief, it might influence his or her behavior, and the behavior of individuals with whom they interact, leading to self-fulfilling prophecies.

Although false expectations can lead to self-fulfilling prophecies, some researchers questioned whether these effects occur in the real world and how powerful they are. For example, do teacher expectations that have not been created by researchers influence student performance in real classrooms? Although self-fulfilling prophecies are not as powerful in the real world as they are in the laboratory, perceivers' expectations do have a small effect on targets' behaviors. But, in some situations perceivers' expectations are unlikely to lead to the target confirming those expectations. If a person knows that others have negative expectations about him or her, he or she may work hard to disconfirm, rather than confirm, the expectations. The result might thus be a self-defeating prophecy, the opposite of a self-fulfilling prophecy.

Importance

Self-fulfilling prophecies demonstrate that people often play an active role in shaping, and even creating, their own social realities. Self-fulfilling prophecies can influence many interactions and situations, but the impact of these prophecies is particularly evident in two major areas: (1) stereotyping and perceptions of members of groups that are negatively viewed in society and (2) the effects of teacher expectations on student achievement.

Stereotypes are beliefs about the traits, personalities, and abilities that characterize the typical individual of a group, and these beliefs are often difficult to change. Self-fulfilling prophecies may be one reason that this is the case. As an example, consider the case of women. One component of the stereotype of women is that the typical group member is dependent. A perceiver who expects women to be dependent may

be especially likely to treat women in ways that elicit dependence. For example, a perceiver may offer help to a woman with a flat tire (even if help is not requested, or is unnecessary), and the woman may respond by accepting the offer. In such an interaction, the woman depended on another person for help, and therefore the perceiver's stereotype of the group is confirmed. Because stereotypes are usually widely shared within a society, these types of stereotype confirming interactions are likely to occur repeatedly in the society and thus have a much stronger impact than the idiosyncratic expectations that one individual has about another individual. But the influence of self-fulfilling prophecy on stereotypes is even more pernicious when one considers that individuals do not need to be actively or consciously thinking about a stereotype for it to affect their behavior. Just being aware of a stereotype may lead the belief to automatically come to mind and influence the behavior of the perceiver when he or she interacts with members of the stereotyped group.

The second application of research on self-fulfilling prophecies harkens back to the original research of Rosenthal and Jacobson on the effect of teachers' expectation on student achievement. Rosenthal and Jacobson showed that high expectations from teachers can improve student performance, but the converse is also true; teachers' negative expectations may impair student performance. Students from some ethnic minority groups and those with low socioeconomic status tend to achieve less academically than do their White and more economically advantaged students. These outcome differences may be partly due to teachers' expectations. Teachers' expectations do affect performance in real classrooms. Research has shown that self-fulfilling prophecies have stronger effects on poor and ethnic minority students, about whom teachers are likely to have the most negative expectations. So, it is important for teachers to think about their expectations for their students because these expectations have real consequences for important outcomes.

Collette Eccleston

See also Expectations; Experimenter Effects; Stereotypes and Stereotyping

Further Readings

Jussim, L., Eccles, J., & Madon, S. (1996). Social perception, social stereotypes, and teacher expectations: Accuracy and the quest for the powerful self-fulfilling prophecy.

In M. P. Zanna (Ed.), *Advances in experimental social psychology* (Vol. 28, pp. 281–388). San Diego, CA: Academic Press.

Rosenthal, R., & Jacobson, L. (1968). *Pygmalion in the classroom: Teacher expectations and student intellectual development.* New York: Holt, Rinehart & Winston.

Snyder, M., Tanke, E. D., & Berscheid, E. (1977). Social perception and interpersonal behavior: On the self-fulfilling nature of social stereotypes. *Journal of Personality and Social Psychology, 35,* 656–666.

SELF-HANDICAPPING

Definition

Self-handicapping was first defined in 1978 by Steven Berglas and Edward Jones as "any action or choice of performance setting that enhances the opportunity to externalize (or excuse) failure and to internalize (reasonably accept credit for) success." Self-handicapping involves putting a barrier or handicap in the way of one's own success. If one fails, then the failure can be blamed on the handicap rather than on (the lack of) one's innate ability. If one succeeds despite the handicap, then one can claim extra credit for success because one succeeded despite the impediment to success. Thus, self-handicapping both protects the person from the implications of failure and enhances the success if one should succeed despite the handicap. Self-handicapping may be used to protect or enhance a person's own self-image and public reputation. Although self-handicapping may protect one from implications of failure, self-handicapping is a trade-off, and there are both short and long-term consequences of self-handicapping. Self-handicapping limits success and increases the probability for failure, both immediately and in the future. Chronic self-handicappers also exhibit poorer achievement and poorer adjustment over time.

Examples

One example of self-handicapping is staying out and partying the night before a big exam. If the person does poorly on the exam, he or she can blame it on partying all night. If the person does well on the exam, he or she can take credit for doing well on the exam despite partying the night before. Researchers have cited many other examples of self-handicapping, which include procrastination, underachievement (or low effort), alcohol or drug use or abuse, test anxiety, getting too little sleep, underpreparing or inadequate practice before evaluation, exaggerating the effects of an injury or illness, complaints of physical symptoms or hypochondriacal complaints, traumatic life events, shyness, and choosing extremely difficult or unattainable goals.

Causes and Purpose

Researchers believe that self-handicapping is caused by feelings of uncertainty about future performance, especially when others have high expectations of success. Self-handicapping appears to be a self-protective mechanism, protecting one's self-esteem from the potentially damaging effects of failure while enhancing attributions for success. If one fails, a self-handicapper can blame failure on external causes and can thus maintain and protect self-esteem. If one succeeds, a self-handicapper can take credit for succeeding despite external obstacles, increasing self-esteem.

There has been debate about whether one engages in self-handicapping to protect and enhance one's own self-image or to protect and enhance one's public reputation. Berglas and Jones's original self-handicapping construct defined self-handicapping as a strategy to protect both a person's self and public images and presented evidence consistent with both the public and private functions of the attributions. Other research has suggested, however, that self-handicapping only protects a person's public reputation. For instance, one study found that self-handicapping was reduced when others were not present to evaluate the person's performance on a task. Current consensus is that self-handicapping sometimes may occur for the protection of private self-image, but it is even more common in public circumstances.

If a person self-handicaps to protect his or her public image, however, the strategy may backfire and may not improve a person's reputation. Research has found that people do not like those who self-handicap. Self-handicappers are disliked more and rated more negatively on several variables by others evaluating them than are those who do not self-handicap.

Costs and Benefits

Self-handicapping has both immediate costs and benefits, thus representing a trade-off. Self-handicapping involves constructing a barrier to one's own success. The self-handicapper reduces his or her chances for success, but also protects himself or herself from the implications of failure. Self-handicapping, however, also appears to have long-term costs. For instance, research has shown that chronic self-handicappers do more poorly academically and have poorer adjustment over time. In addition, as mentioned previously, there may be several interpersonal consequences for a person who engages in self-handicapping. Furthermore, some researchers believe that frequent self-handicapping may lead to the development of chronic self-destructive patterns, such as alcoholism or drug abuse.

A person's self-esteem affects the motivation for self-handicapping. People with high self-esteem self-handicap for self-enhancement motives (or to enhance their success). People with low self-esteem, however, self-handicap for self-protective motives (or to protect themselves from the esteem-threatening implications of failure). Research has also suggested that high self-handicappers actually enjoy an activity more when they engage in self-handicapping strategies, supposedly decreasing worries about failure and increasing the intrinsic motivation for engaging in or completing the activity.

Gender Differences

Gender differences in self-handicapping have been studied extensively. Some research has shown that men are more likely to self-handicap than women are. Other research has shown that men and women self-handicap differently, with men being more likely to engage in behavioral self-handicapping, such as using alcohol or underpreparing, and women being more likely to engage in self-reported handicapping, such as complaining of illness or traumatic life events. Other research, however, has found no sex differences in the incidence of self-handicapping. Research has found, however, that women are more critical of those who self-handicap, evaluating self-handicappers more negatively than men do. Women were also less likely to excuse self-handicapping than were men.

Dianne M. Tice

See also Anxiety; Procrastination; Self-Defeating Behavior; Self-Enhancement; Self-Esteem; Self-Fulfilling Prophecy; Self-Serving Bias

Further Readings

Baumeister, R. F., & Scher, S. J. (1988). Self-defeating behavior patterns among normal individuals: Review and analysis of common self-destructive tendencies. *Psychological Bulletin, 104,* 3–22.

Berglas, S., & Jones, E. E. (1978). Drug choice as a self-handicapping strategy in response to noncontingent success. *Journal of Personality and Social Psychology, 36,* 405–417.

Hirt, E. R., McCrea, S. M., & Boris, S. I. (2003). "I know you self-handicapped last exam": Gender differences in reactions to self-handicapping. *Journal of Personality and Social Psychology, 84,* 177–193.

Tice, D. M. (1991). Esteem protection or enhancement? Self-handicapping motives and attributions differ by trait self-esteem. *Journal of Personality and Social Psychology, 60,* 711–725.

Zuckerman, M., Kieffer, S. C., & Knee, C. R. (1998). Consequences of self-handicapping: Effects on coping, academic performance, and adjustment. *Journal of Personality and Social Psychology, 74,* 1619–1628.

SELF-MONITORING

Definition

Self-monitoring is a personality trait that captures differences in the extent to which people control the image they present to others in social situations. High self-monitors are motivated and skilled at altering their behavior to influence the impressions others have of them. In contrast, low self-monitors tend to focus on remaining true to their inner attitudes by presenting a relatively consistent image of themselves to others regardless of the situation.

Background and History

The theory of self-monitoring was introduced by Mark Snyder in 1974 at a time when personality and social psychologists were grappling with two fundamental debates. First, the impact of personality traits versus the situation on behavior was a source of contention between personality and social psychologists. Second, the disconnect between inner attitudes and external behavior was also perplexing researchers at that time. Self-monitoring offered a partial resolution to these debates by introducing an individual difference variable that addressed both sides of the debate;

self-monitoring emphasized the power of the situation on high self-monitors' behavior and the power of personality traits on low self-monitors' behavior. Moreover, self-monitoring partly addressed the attitude–behavior consistency debate because such consistency could be expected among low but not high self-monitors.

Measurement Issues

Perhaps because it dealt with such contentious issues, the theory and measurement of self-monitoring have been subject to much scrutiny and debate. Individual differences in self-monitoring are typically measured using a version of Snyder's paper-and-pencil Self-Monitoring Scale that was revised and shortened by Snyder and Steve Gangestad in 1986. There has been some debate about whether three or four components make up the self-monitoring scale. This debate prompted researchers to clearly distinguish the concept of self-monitoring from other similar concepts, most notably the Big Five trait Extraversion. Currently, the three most commonly accepted components measured by the self-monitoring scale are acting, extraversion, and other-directedness. The role of each component is generally recognized as vital for identifying and measuring self-monitoring.

Another long-standing debate in the measurement of self-monitoring concerns whether there are two distinct categories of people, high and low self-monitors, or whether there is a self-monitoring continuum. This debate reaches beyond the trait of self-monitoring to the theoretical foundations of personality psychology, and so is mentioned only briefly here. Researchers investigating self-monitoring tend to follow Snyder's original method of creating and comparing dichotomous categories of high and low self-monitoring.

Much of the work on self-monitoring was conducted in the 1980s when researchers were first identifying the implications and limitations of this trait. Research continues, further refining and applying our understanding of self-monitoring in light of modern developments in both social and personality psychology.

Importance and Implications

Self-monitoring is important for understanding how people behave in social situations. Research has examined the influence of self-monitoring in many ways, including but not limited to how people behave over time, express their attitudes, perceive social cues and others' behavior, approach interpersonal relationships, behave nonverbally, and make consumer judgments.

Because of their sensitivity to the situation, high self-monitors behave less consistently across different situations than do low self-monitors and, hence, have relatively weaker correspondence between their attitudes and behavior. In addition, high self-monitors tend to tailor the attitudes they express to correspond with those of their audience and to appreciate the effect of the social context on others' behavior. Self-monitoring also influences the types of situations people select for themselves. High self-monitors prefer to engage in situations that are clearly defined to facilitate their behavior adaptation, whereas low self-monitors select situations that converge with their personal dispositions.

Interpersonal Relationships

The social worlds of high and low self-monitors are characterized distinctly. The social groups of high self-monitors tend to differ depending on the context; they have different friends in different situations. Conversely, low self-monitors tend to have a stable group of friends who are similar to them in a global way.

Commitment and relationship longevity differ between high and low self-monitors in a way that corresponds to the contextually driven versus constant approaches to their social networks. Both friendships and romantic relationships tend to be approached with greater sense of commitment and intimacy among low self-monitors relative to high self-monitors. High self-monitors tend to report having more casual friendships and sexual partners, having greater quantities of shorter romantic liaisons, and relying on outward appearances when judging others to a greater degree than do low self-monitors.

Nonverbal Cues

The tendency to use nonverbal displays of behavior strategically is also influenced by self-monitoring, at both conscious and nonconscious levels, stemming from differences in attempts to control images presented to others. High self-monitors are better able to expressively convey internal states and to actively conceal socially inappropriate emotional displays than are low self-monitors.

In general, people will nonconsciously mimic the nonverbal behavior (e.g., foot shaking) of others. Mimicry is a strategy used nonconsciously to achieve social connection. The mimicry of high self-monitors is context dependent. They mimic especially when the other person is affiliated with them in some way (e.g., has power over them in an upcoming task, or is a member of a peer group instead of a more senior or junior group). Thus, the process of regulating behavior to accord with social cues may operate outside of conscious awareness among high self-monitors. Low self-monitors do not show this sensitivity to affiliation with others when nonconsciously mimicking behavior.

Application to Consumer Behavior

The study of consumer behavior is one area to which researchers have applied knowledge of self-monitoring. In line with their propensity toward managing outward appearances, high self-monitors tend to prefer advertisements that appeal to a particular image and will select products that will help them convey an image in a certain situation. Low self-monitors prefer advertisements that focus on a product's quality and are less swayed by attractive packaging than are high self-monitors.

Catherine D. Rawn

See also Impression Management; Mimicry; Self-Presentation; Traits

Further Readings

Gangestad, S. W., & Snyder, M. (2000). Self-monitoring: Appraisal and reappraisal. *Psychological Bulletin, 126,* 530–555.

Snyder, M. (1987). *Public appearances/public realities: The psychology of self-monitoring.* New York: Freeman.

SELF-PERCEPTION THEORY

In everyday life, people observe other people's actions and behaviors and make inferences about others' attitudes based on what they observe. When people see how another person acts in a particular situation, they often attribute the behavior to the person's traits and attitudes. For example, if you view someone in a park recycling a plastic water bottle rather than throwing it in the garbage, you might infer that the individual is concerned about the environment. Similarly, if you witness a school child scowling at her teacher, you might infer that she is upset or angry with the teacher. Interestingly, sometimes people also observe their own behavior, much as an outsider might do, and make similar inferences about their own attitudes based on their behavior. According to self-perception theory, when people are unsure of their own attitudes, one way to infer them is by looking at their behaviors. Daryl Bem proposed self-perception theory in 1967 when he argued that people sometimes analyze their own behavior in the same fashion as they would analyze someone else's behavior.

At the time, Bem was proposing something that was counter to how people's attitudes and behaviors were thought of. Most people would agree, for example, that a person who perceives himself or herself as interested in road biking may, as a result of that interest, buy bicycling equipment and go on long cycling rides. That is, the person's attitudes and self-perception influence his or her behavior. Bem, however, reversed this relation by suggesting that it is also possible that people understand their attitudes and interests because they have made inferences based on their behavior. Thus, this person could infer that he or she is interested in road biking on the basis of frequent cycling trips and lavish spending on a nice road bike.

Self-perception theory provides a similar explanation for emotion by suggesting that people infer their emotions by observing their bodies and their behaviors. In other words, people's emotions and other feelings come from such actions as facial expressions, postures, level of arousal and behaviors. In this way, feelings are consequences of behavior rather than the other way around. People are angry because they scowl and are happy because they smile—this is the self-perception effect.

Everyone has experienced the self-perception effect. Imagine for a moment that you have had a terrible day—several things have gone wrong and you feel very irritable and grouchy. However, you have made previous plans to meet up with some friends for a small social gathering that evening. When you arrive, you smile and elicit warm, polite behavior. When others at the gathering greet you with "Hi, how's it going?" you respond with "Fine, how are you?" It is challenging to scowl and maintain your irritability at a party with friends. So, you smile instead and—in effect—pretend to be happy. For most of us, our original feelings of irritability decrease after smiling and exhibiting "happy" behavior. Our behavior changes our attitude.

Even the way people walk can affect the way they feel. Test this with yourself. When you get up, walk back and forth across the room, shuffling with your shoulders hunched and your eyes looking down at the floor. What do you feel? Similarly, imagine sitting slouched over all day, sighing when people speak to you and talking in a really low voice. You probably feel a bit down or depressed. Now try walking across the room taking long strides, swinging your arms high, and smiling. These different behaviors can elicit a different emotional experience.

Research Support

Several studies have been done since the proposal of self-perception theory that support Bem's hypothesis. As self-perception theory predicts, research has demonstrated that people who are induced to act as if they feel something, such as happiness, report actually feeling it, even when they are unaware of how their feelings arose. This effect has been demonstrated for a wide variety of feelings and with an even wider variety of behaviors.

For example, in a simple study designed to demonstrate whether facial expression influenced affective responses—a phenomenon closely related to self-perception—psychologists examined whether facial expressions influenced individuals' emotion responses to cartoons. To manipulate facial expressions or facial activity, subjects were asked to hold a pen in their mouth in one of two ways: (1) between their teeth with their lips open to facilitate the muscles typically associated with smiling or (2) pursed between their lips because it inhibited the muscles used during smiling. (Try this to see if you can get a sense of what your facial expressions would have been if you were in the experiment.) The task for the participants was to read a series of cartoons, with the pen in their mouth, and rate them for their degree of funniness. As self-perception theory would predict, the psychologists found that those who were holding the pen in between their teeth (facilitating a smile) reported higher levels of humor based on the cartoons than did the participants who were holding the pen between their lips. The researchers concluded that the perceived funniness of the cartoons depended on producing the muscle action involved in smiling.

The self-perception effect might also carry over to later behavior. For example, imagine that ordinarily you are shy at parties but have recently decided that you want to make new friends. You have decided that at the next party, you will make an effort to be especially talkative to meet new people and it goes well. This behavior influences your attitude about social behavior and leads you to perceive a greater outgoingness in yourself. The next time you are at a party, you exhibit outgoing social behavior without nearly as much effort. Act as if you are outgoing and you might become more so.

In a study demonstrating this carryover effect, researchers looked at the impact of a community service experience on adolescent volunteers' levels of empathy, social responsibility, and concern for others. The findings from this study suggest that community service positively influences sympathy and compassion for others, sense of concern for society at large, and a willingness to take action to help others and the community. This demonstrates that the behavior—engaging in volunteer helping experience—can create a shift toward more caring and helping attitudes *and* sustained action in service.

In another interesting investigation of how behaviors affect attitudes, Mark Lepper and colleagues found giving people external reasons (e.g., monetary rewards) for performing a behavior they already enjoy decreases their intrinsic motivation to do it—a phenomenon called *overjustification effect*. For example, in a study testing this effect, children who were initially interested in a drawing activity reported significantly lower intrinsic interest in drawing after two weeks of receiving extrinsic reward, whereas children who did not receive external reward for engaging in the activity did not report a reduction in interest after the two weeks. According to self-perception theory, people undergo overjustification effect when their actions can no longer be attributed to their intrinsic motivation but, rather, to the anticipation of an extrinsic reward. In the previous example, the principles of self-perception theory would argue that the children's initial interest in the activity was undermined by creating a situation in which activity was an explicit means to an extrinsic goal—in other words, the extrinsic rewards turned "play" (i.e., an activity engaged in for it's own sake) into "work" (i.e., an activity engaged in only when extrinsic incentives are present).

In the decades following Bem's original article, a great deal of research was aimed at trying to distinguish self-perception theory from the widely accepted cognitive dissonance theory, which argues that the inconsistency presented by believing one thing and doing another generates emotional discomfort that directs behavior toward the goal of reducing the inconsistency or dissonance. However, dissonance arises when there is inconsistency or hypocrisy between attitudes, beliefs, or behaviors. Thus, attitudes or beliefs in these situations are known. Years of research in this area have led to the conclusion that cognitive dissonance and self-perception theories have different applications: Self-perception theory is more applicable in situations in which people's attitudes are initially vague, ambiguous, or weak.

Importance and Implications

Because self-perception theory suggests that when people's internal awareness of their attitudes or emotions is weak or ambiguous they can view themselves in much the same way as an outside observer, it is possible to rely upon external cues or behaviors to infer people's inner states. You may be able to relate to the following experiences: "This is my second sandwich; I guess I was hungrier than I thought," or, "I've been biting my nails all day; something must be bugging me." In both cases, attitudes or emotions are inferred from the behavior. Thus, even if people are generally self-aware, they cannot always be accurate about why they feel the way they do. The self-perception effect allows people to gather important cues from their external environment and apply them to understand what attitudes or emotions they are experiencing internally.

The self-perception effect also may have an important application when attitudes and behaviors are incongruent or when behavior change is desired. For example, therapists working with individuals with alcohol addiction have reported that the principles of self-perception theory assist in creating change. Individuals who begin to consciously observe the amount they are drinking might infer from their behavior that they are tense or anxious and then do something about it other than drinking. Similarly, behavior change might inform individuals of their internal attitudes about drinking. For example, individuals who communicate their intentions about drinking out loud may infer their attitudes about drinking from hearing themselves speak. In other words, the behavior of telling others, "I am going to cut down on my drinking" may allow individuals to infer the attitude or internal awareness that their

drinking has created problems for themselves or others. In sum, researchers in psychology have applied the self-perception theory to a wide variety of attitudes and behaviors with very interesting and important implications.

Shelly Grabe
Janet Shibley Hyde

See also Attitude Change; Attitudes; Cognitive Dissonance Theory; Emotion; Facial Expression of Emotion; Facial-Feedback Hypothesis; Introspection; Looking-Glass Self; Overjustification Effect

Further Readings

Bem, D. J. (1967). Self-perception: An alternative interpretation of cognitive dissonance phenomena. *Psychology Review, 74,* 183–200.

Bem, D. J. (1972). Self-perception theory. In L. Berkowitz (Ed.), *Advances in experimental psychology* (Vol. 6, pp. 1–62). San Diego, CA: Academic Press.

Lepper, M. R., Greene, D., & Nisbett, R. E. (1973). Undermining children's intrinsic interest with extrinsic reward: A test of the "overjustification" hypothesis. *Journal of Personality and Social Psychology, 28,* 129–137.

SELF-PRESENTATION

Definition

Self-presentation refers to how people attempt to present themselves to control or shape how others (called the audience) view them. It involves expressing oneself and behaving in ways that create a desired impression. Self-presentation is part of a broader set of behaviors called *impression management.* Impression management refers to the controlled presentation of information about all sorts of things, including information about other people or events. Self-presentation refers specifically to information about the self.

History and Modern Usage

Early work on impression management focused on its manipulative, inauthentic uses that might typify a used car salesperson who lies to sell a car, or someone at a job interview who embellishes accomplishments to get a job. However, researchers now think of self-presentation more broadly as a pervasive aspect of life. Although some aspects of self-presentation are deliberate and effortful (and at times deceitful), other aspects are automatic and done with little or no conscious thought. For example, a woman may interact with many people during the day and may make different impressions on each person. When she starts her day at her apartment, she chats with her roommates and cleans up after breakfast, thereby presenting the image of being a good friend and responsible roommate. During classes, she responds to her professor's questions and carefully takes notes, presenting the image of being a good student. Later that day, she calls her parents and tells them about her classes and other activities (although likely leaving out information about some activities), presenting the image of being a loving and responsible daughter. That night, she might go to a party or dancing with friends, presenting the image of being fun and easygoing. Although some aspects of these self-presentations may be deliberate and conscious, other aspects are not. For example, chatting with her roommates and cleaning up after breakfast may be habitual behaviors that are done with little conscious thought. Likewise, she may automatically hold the door open for an acquaintance or buy a cup of coffee for a friend. These behaviors, although perhaps not done consciously or with self-presentation in mind, nevertheless convey an image of the self to others.

Although people have the ability to present images that are false, self-presentations are often genuine; they reflect an attempt by the person to have others perceive him or her accurately, or at least consistent with how the person perceives himself or herself. Self-presentations can vary as a function of the audience; people present different aspects of themselves to different audiences or under different conditions. A man likely presents different aspects of himself to his close friends than he does to his elderly grandmother, and a woman may present a different image to her spouse than she does to her employer. This is not to say that these different images are false. Rather, they represent different aspects of the self. The self is much like a gem with multiple facets. The gem likely appears differently depending on the angle at which it is viewed. However, the various appearances are all genuine. Even if people present a self-image that they know to be false, they may begin to internalize the self-image and thereby eventually come to believe the self-presentation. For example, a man may initially present an image of being a good student without believing it to be genuine, but after attending all his classes for several weeks, visiting the professor during office hours, and asking questions during class, he may come to see himself as truly being a good student. This internalization process is most likely to occur when people make a public commitment to the self-image, when the behavior is at least somewhat consistent with their self-image, and when they receive positive feedback or other rewards for presenting the self-image.

Self-presentation is often directed to external audiences such as friends, lovers, employers, teachers, children, and even strangers. Self-presentation is more likely to be conscious when the presenter depends on the audience for some reward, expects to interact with the audience in the future, wants something from the audience, or values the audience's approval. Yet self-presentation extends beyond audiences that are physically present to imagined audiences, and these imagined audiences can have distinct effects on behavior. A young man at a party might suddenly think about his parents and change his behavior from rambunctious to reserved. People sometimes even make self-presentations only for themselves. For instance, people want to claim certain identities, such as being fun, intelligent, kind, moral, and they may behave in line with these identities even in private.

Goals

Self-presentation is inherently goal-directed; people present certain images because they benefit from the images in some way. The most obvious benefits are interpersonal, arising from getting others to do what one wants. A job candidate may convey an image of being hardworking and dependable to get a job; a salesperson may convey an image of being trustworthy and honest to achieve a sale. People may also benefit from their self-presentations by gaining respect, power, liking, or other desirable social rewards. Finally, people make certain impressions on others to maintain a sense of who they are, or their self-concept. For example, a man who wants to think of himself as a voracious reader might join a book club or volunteer at a library, or a woman who wishes to perceive herself as generous may contribute lavishly to a charitable cause. Even when there are few or no obvious benefits of a particular self-presentation, people may simply present an image that is consistent with the way they like to think about themselves, or at least the way they are accustomed to thinking about themselves.

Much of self-presentation is directed toward achieving one of two desirable images. First, people want to appear likeable. People like others who are attractive, interesting, and fun to be with. Thus, a sizable proportion of self-presentation revolves around developing, maintaining, and enhancing appearance and conveying and emphasizing characteristics that others desire, admire, and enjoy. Second, people want to appear competent. People like others who are skilled and able, and thus another sizable proportion of self-presentation revolves around conveying an image of competence. Yet, self-presentation is not so much about presenting desirable images as it is about presenting desired images, and some desired images are not necessarily desirable. For example, schoolyard bullies may present an image of being dangerous or intimidating to gain or maintain power over others. Some people present themselves as weak or infirmed (or exaggerate their weaknesses) to gain help from others. For instance, a member of a group project may display incompetence in the hope that other members will do more of the work, or a child may exaggerate illness to avoid going to school.

Avenues

People self-present in a variety of ways. Perhaps most obviously, people self-present in what they say. These verbalizations can be direct claims of a particular image, such as when a person claims to be altruistic. They also can be indirect, such as when a person discloses personal behaviors or standards (e.g., "I volunteer at a hospital"). Other verbal presentations emerge when people express attitudes or beliefs. Divulging that one enjoys backpacking through Europe conveys the image that one is a world-traveler. Second, people self-present nonverbally in their physical appearance, body language, and other behavior. Smiling, eye contact, and nods of agreement can convey a wealth of information. Third, people self-present through the props they surround themselves with and through their associations. Driving an expensive car or flying first class conveys an image of having wealth, whereas an array of diplomas and certificates on one's office walls conveys an image of education and expertise. Likewise, people judge others based on their associations. For example, being in the company of politicians or movie stars conveys an image of importance, and not surprisingly, many people display photographs of themselves with famous people. In a similar vein, high school students concerned with their status are often careful about which classmates they are seen and not seen with publicly. Being seen by others in the company of someone from a member of a disreputable group can raise questions about one's own social standing.

Pitfalls

Self-presentation is most successful when the image presented is consistent with what the audience thinks or knows to be true. The more the image presented differs from the image believed or anticipated by the audience, the less willing the audience will be to accept the image. For example, the lower a student's grade is on the first exam, the more difficulty he or she will have in convincing a professor that he or she will earn an A on the next exam. Self-presentations are constrained by audience knowledge. The more the audience knows about a person, the less freedom the person has in claiming a particular identity. An audience that knows very little about a person will be more accepting of whatever identity the person conveys, whereas an audience that knows a great deal about a person will be less accepting.

People engaging in self-presentation sometimes encounter difficulties that undermine their ability to convey a desired image. First, people occasionally encounter the *multiple audience problem,* in which they must simultaneously present two conflicting images. For example, a student while walking with friends who know only her rebellious, impetuous side may run into her professor who knows only her serious, conscientious side. The student faces the dilemma of conveying the conflicting images of rebellious friend and serious student. When both audiences are present, the student must try to behave in a way that is consistent with how her friends view her, but also in a way that is consistent with how her professor views her. Second, people occasionally encounter challenges to their self-presentations. The audience may not believe the image the person presents. Challenges are most likely to arise when people are managing impressions through self-descriptions and the self-descriptions are inconsistent with other evidence. For example, a man who claims to be good driver faces a self-presentational dilemma if he is ticketed or gets in an automobile accident. Third, self-presentations can fail when people lack the cognitive resources to present effectively because, for example, they are tired, anxious, or distracted. For instance, a woman may yawn uncontrollably or reflexively check her watch while talking to a boring classmate, unintentionally conveying an image of disinterest.

Some of the most important images for people to convey are also the hardest. As noted earlier, among the most important images people want to communicate are likeability and competence. Perhaps because these images are so important and are often rewarded, audiences may be skeptical of accepting direct claims of likeability and competence from presenters, thinking that the person is seeking personal gain. Thus, people must resort to indirect routes to create these images, and the indirect routes can be misinterpreted. For example, the student who sits in the front row of the class and asks a lot of questions may be trying to project an image of being a competent student but may be perceived negatively as a teacher's pet by fellow students.

Finally, there is a dark side to self-presentation. In some instances, the priority people place on their appearances or images can threaten their health. People who excessively tan are putting a higher priority on their appearance (e.g., being tan) than on their health (e.g., taking precautions to avoid skin cancer). Similarly, although condoms help protect against sexually transmitted diseases and unwanted pregnancy, self-presentational concerns may dissuade partners or potential partners from discussing, carrying, or using condoms. Women may fear that carrying condoms makes them seem promiscuous or easy, whereas men may fear that carrying condoms makes them seem presumptuous, as if they are expecting to have sex. Self-presentational concerns may also influence interactions with health care providers and may lead people to delay or avoid embarrassing medical tests and procedures or treatments for conditions that are embarrassing. For example, people may be reluctant to seek tests or treatment for sexually transmitted diseases, loss of bladder control, mental disorders, mental decline, or other conditions associated with weakness or incompetence. Finally, concerns with social acceptance may prompt young people to engage in risky behaviors such as excessive alcohol consumption, sexual promiscuity, or juvenile delinquency.

Meredith Terry
Kate Sweeny
James A. Shepperd

See also Deception (Lying); Ego Depletion; Goals; Impression Management; Phenomenal Self; Self-Defeating Behaviors; Self-Perception Theory; Social Desirability Bias

Further Readings

Jones, E. E., Pittman, T. S. (1982). Toward a general theory of strategic self-presentation. In J. Suls (Ed.), *Psychological perspectives on the self* (Vol. 1, pp. 231–260). Hillsdale, NJ: Erlbaum.

Leary, M. R. (1996). *Self-presentation: Impression management and interpersonal behavior.* Boulder, CO: Westview Press.

Leary, M. R., Tchividjian, L. R., & Kraxberger, B. E. (1994). Self-presentation can be hazardous to your health: Impression management and health risk. *Health Psychology, 13,* 461–470.

Schlenker, B. R. (1980). Imp*ression management: The self-concept, social identity, and interpersonal relations.* Monterey, CA: Brooks/Cole.

SELF-PROMOTION

Definition

Self-promotion refers to the practice of purposefully trying to present oneself as highly competent to other people. When people self-promote, their primary motivation is to be perceived by others as capable, intelligent, or talented (even at the expense of being liked). Self-promotion becomes especially useful and prominent when a person competes against others for desirable—often scarce—resources, such as a good job or an attractive partner. People can self-promote their abilities in general or in a specific domain.

Context

Self-promotion exists as part of a general yet extremely pervasive human motivation: to be perceived favorably by others. In the case of self-promotion, people want to be perceived by others as being competent. Not surprisingly, then, people generally only self-promote in public, and around people they want to impress, such as superiors at work. For example, someone completing a self-evaluation at work would be much less likely to self-promote if a supervisor would never read the self-evaluation, or if the self-evaluation was anonymous.

How Do People Self-Promote?

Researchers have identified several tactics people use to self-promote. First, people may self-promote by speaking of themselves in flattering terms: They may highlight their leadership skills, prowess at school or work, or adeptness at overcoming obstacles. Second, if they are personally involved in a positive event, they may claim more responsibility for the event than they objectively deserve, or they may exaggerate the importance of the event in the hopes it will sound more impressive. People can self-promote more tactfully by (1) guiding the course of a conversation to a point where it is fitting to mention prior achievements and honors, (2) trying to avoid conversation topics in which others may be experts, or (3) providing opportunities for other people to promote them, such as by covertly making a substantial salary raise known to gossipy coworkers.

The Problem of Integrating Self-Promotion and Likeability

When self-promoting, people face an important problem: Their behavior might come across as conceited, if not fraudulent. Although the key motivation underlying self-promotion is to be perceived as competent, situations arise where self-promotion must be successfully integrated with likeability, even though these two motivations may conflict. Probably the most prominent example of this concern is the classic job interview. Applicants interviewing for a job need to appear both competent and likeable to impress their potential supervisor, but expressing both of these qualities during the interview may be tricky! For example, to convey confidence and competence, applicants know they must highlight their relevant experience and accomplishments. At the same time, applicants do not want to appear conceited or arrogant to the interviewer.

Evidence: Does Self-Promotion Work?

Researchers have examined quite extensively whether self-promotion actually helps people appear more competent. By far the biggest research arena for self-promotion has been in business settings, especially in the interview process, for reasons mentioned previously. Specifically, researchers have studied whether self-promotion helps people secure jobs and promotions.

In a typical study, researchers will ask both the applicant and the interviewer to complete post-interview surveys that ask about instances of self-promotion used by the applicant throughout the interview; researchers might also ask permission to film the interview. The researchers then either contact the participants later to see if they secured the job for which they interviewed or subsequently ask the interviewers which applicants they might consider hiring. With this information, the researchers can then examine whether self-promotion during the interview influenced hiring decisions.

Results from these studies are mixed. Overall, researchers often conclude self-promotion has little effect on hiring decisions (though studies certainly exist that find either positive or negative effects). Unfortunately, researchers have not offered conclusive reasons to account for these null findings, but they probably reflect the interviewers' expectation that most people will self-promote in some way during the interview, thus negating the self-promotion attempt.

The effect of self-promotion on job promotions is largely inconclusive as well. Self-promoting at work can sometimes result in promotion, but plenty of studies demonstrate self-promotion really has no effect on being promoted. These conflicting results probably reflect the intricacies of the individual job environments, as well as personal characteristics and preferences of the people involved.

The Added Problem of Gender

Self-promotion poses a unique problem for women because women have been traditionally perceived as less competent and competitive than men. To counteract such stereotypes, women probably need to highlight their skills and talents more than men do, especially when competing for the same job. Unfortunately, self-promotion by women is generally received more poorly than is self-promotion by men. In fact, studies have shown women themselves rate other women who self-promote less favorably than men who self-promote! This discrepancy may stem from culturally ingrained stereotypes, wherein women have been traditionally socialized to adopt more passive, subservient, and modest roles compared with men. Therefore, self-promotion may enhance how others perceive a woman's qualifications, but at the expense of social appeal. Indeed, women who self-promote are often perceived as competent, yet socially unattractive.

Implications

Self-promotion is an extremely common strategy people employ to create and maintain an impression of competence. Sometimes self-promotion works, but other times it fails. The factors underlying successful self-promotion have not been conclusively determined, but it seems likely that tactful self-promotion would work best. Unfortunately, women shoulder the additional burden of battling ingrained social stereotypes that prescribe female modesty. Historically, these stereotypes may have contributed both to the disproportionate rates of hiring men over women for certain positions, as well as fewer opportunities for women to be promoted. However, the ever-changing role of women in present-day society may eventually help lessen these disparities.

Scott J. Moeller
Brad J. Bushman

See also Impression Management; Self-Enhancement; Self-Presentation

Further Readings

Higgins, C. A., & Judge, T. A. (2004). The effect of applicant influence tactics on recruiter perceptions of fit and hiring recommendations: A field study. *Journal of Applied Psychology, 89,* 622–632.

Rudman, L. A. (1998). Self-promotion as a risk factor for women: The costs and benefits of counterstereotypical impression management. *Journal of Personality and Social Psychology, 74,* 629–645.

SELF-REFERENCE EFFECT

Definition

The self-reference effect refers to people's tendency to better remember information when that information has been linked to the self than when it has not been linked to the self. In research on the self-reference effect, people are presented with a list of adjectives (e.g., intelligent, shy) and are asked to judge each word given a particular instruction. Some people are told to decide whether each word describes them. In this case, people make a decision about each word in relation to their knowledge of themselves—a self-referent comparison. Other people are instructed to decide whether each word is long—a nonself-referent comparison that requires making a decision about each word that does not use information about the self. According to the self-reference effect, if people are later asked to remember the words they rated in a memory task that they do not expect, they will be more likely to remember the words if they thought about them in relation to the self (Does the word describe them?) than if they thought about them without reference to the self (Is the word long?). Although some studies have failed to support the self-reference effect, a recent meta-analysis supports that, overall, the self-reference effect is robust.

The different instructions are thought to lead to differences in the likelihood of self-referent encoding. Encoding is the process putting information into memory, of taking a stimulus from the environment and processing it in a way that leads to storage of that stimulus in a person's mind. In the case of the self-reference effect, the stimulus is encoded or processed with information about the self. Information about the self is highly organized in memory because people frequently use and add to their information about themselves. Therefore, information encoded with respect to self becomes part of a highly organized knowledge structure. The benefit of encoding something with respect to an organized knowledge structure is that new information is encoded more efficiently and effectively, which can lead to easier retrieval and recall. People also tend to think deeply about concepts that relate to the self. Therefore, when people are asked to think about words in relation to the self, those words benefit from deeper encoding and are better elaborated, connected, and integrated in memory. Because people habitually use the self to process information in their daily lives, they are particularly practiced at encoding information in a self-referent way. More elaborated encoding provides additional cues for words to be later retrieved from memory.

One extension of the self-reference effect examined whether memory after self-referent judgments differed from other-referent judgments (Does this word describe someone else?). Self-referent memory is superior to other-referent memory when people are asked to rate whether words describe a person who is not well known (Does this word describe the study experimenter?). The memory advantage of self-referent encoding decreases, but is not eliminated, if people rate whether the words describe an intimate other (Does this word describe your mother?) whose characteristics may also be well-organized and elaborated in memory.

Background and History

The first research on the self-reference effect was published by T. B. Rogers and colleagues in 1977. Research at that time was particularly interested in how personality information was organized in people's minds, and Rogers and his colleagues set out to extend Fergus I. M. Craik's and Endel Tulving's research on depth of processing. The depth of processing perspective suggests that certain types of information are processed more deeply, or in a more elaborated way, than are other types of information. For example, words are better remembered when people are asked to think about them in a semantic way (Does the word mean the same thing as another word?) than when people are asked to think about them phonemically (Does the word rhyme with another word?), and are remembered least if people are asked to think about them in a structural way (Is the word written in capital letters?). These three instructions differ in the depth of processing required to make the judgment (it requires more processing to make judgments of meaning of the word compared with the sound or the structure of the word). Memory for words is weaker when depth of processing is lower. Rogers and colleagues hypothesized that self-referent encoding would involve even deeper processing than semantic encoding and would result in better memory for the words. Research supported this hypothesis, thereby supporting the idea that self-knowledge was uniquely represented in memory.

Individual Differences

Among people given the self-referent instructions, research consistently shows a memory bias for words that they rate as like themselves (This word describes me) compared with words that people rate as unlike themselves (This word doesn't describe me). This suggests that the self-reference effect is strongest for traits that people actually endorse about themselves. Follow-up studies confirm this bias in various groups and situations in which the self-reference effect is observed. For example, depressed individuals show increased memory for depressed traits, and non-depressed individuals showed increased memory for nondepressed traits. People given failure feedback show a greater self-reference effect for negative traits, whereas those who are given success feedback show a greater self-reference effect for positive traits. People also differ in the degree to which they chronically think about the world in self-referent ways. People who are high in private self-consciousness are more likely than are those low in private self-consciousness to think about the world in terms of self, and low private self-conscious people are less likely to show the self-reference effect compared with high private self-conscious people. Similarly, situations in which people experience low self-awareness (e.g., people who are intoxicated) reduce the likelihood of self-referent encoding and thus the self-reference effect.

Jennifer J. Tickle

See also Encoding; Memory; Salience; Self; Self-Awareness

Further Readings

Rogers, T. B., Kuiper, N. A., & Kirker, W. S. (1977). Self-reference and the encoding of personal information. *Journal of Personality and Social Psychology, 35,* 677–688.

Symons, C. S., & Johnson, B. T. (1997). The self-reference effect in memory: A meta-analysis. *Psychological Bulletin, 121,* 371–394.

SELF-REGULATION

Definition

Self-regulation refers to the self exerting control over itself. In particular, self-regulation consists of deliberate efforts by the self to alter its own states and responses, including behavior, thoughts, impulses or appetites, emotions, and task performance. The concept of self-regulation is close to the colloquial terms *self-control* and *self-discipline,* and many social psychologists use the terms interchangeably.

History and Background

Early social psychologists did not use the term *self-regulation* and, if they thought about it at all, regarded it as a minor, obscure, technical problem. However, as the study of the self expanded and researchers became more interested in inner processes, interest in self-regulation expanded. By the 1990s, self-regulation had become widely recognized as a central function of the self, with both practical and theoretical importance, and a broad range of research sought to contribute to the rapidly expanding research literature on self-regulation.

Modern self-regulation theory has several roots. One is in the study of animal learning. Skinnerian behaviorists taught that animals learn behaviors based on past rewards and punishments. In that way, behavior patterns are molded by the external environment. Recognizing that human behavior was more complex and internally guided than much animal behavior, thoughtful behaviorists such as Albert Bandura proposed that people self-regulate by administering rewards and punishments to themselves. For example, a person might say, "If I can get this task done by 7 o'clock, I will treat myself to ice cream," or "If I don't get this paper written today, I won't go to the movies."

A second root is in research on delay of gratification. In the 1960s, researchers such as Walter Mischel began to study how people would choose between a small immediate reward and a larger, delayed one. For example, a child might be told, "You can have one cookie now, but if you can wait for 20 minutes without eating it, you can have three cookies." In adult life, most work and study activities depend on the capacity to delay gratification, insofar as work and studying bring delayed rewards but are often not immediately satisfying (as compared with relaxing or engaging in hobbies). This line of research found that successful delaying of gratification depended on overriding immediate impulses and focusing attention away from the immediate gratification. The immediate response to a tempting stimulus is to enjoy it now, so it requires self-regulation to override that response to wait for the delayed but better reward.

A third root is in the study of self-awareness. During the 1970s, researchers began studying how behavior changes when people focus attention on themselves. In 1981, the book *Attention and Self-Regulation* by Charles Carver and Michael Scheier proposed that one main function of self-awareness is to aid in self-regulation. That is, you reflect on yourself as a way of deciding how and whether improvement would be desirable.

The fourth root of self-regulation theory is in research on human personal problems, many of which revolve around failures at self-control. Across recent decades, research has steadily accumulated to reveal the importance of self-regulation in many spheres of behavior. Eating disorders and obesity partly reflect failures to regulate one's food intake. Alcohol and drug addiction likewise indicate poor regulation of use of these substances. Research on these and related issues has provided much information that self-regulation theorists could use.

Importance

Self-regulation has implications for both psychological theory and for practical, applied issues. In terms of theory, self-regulation has come to be seen as one of the most important operations of the human self. Indeed, the human capacity for self-regulation appears to be far more advanced and powerful than is self-regulation in most other animals, and it helps set the human self apart from selfhood in other species. Some theorists believe that the capacity for self-regulation was one decisive key to human evolution.

Self-regulation depicts the self as an active controller. Social psychology's early theories and research on the self focused mainly on issues such as self-concept and self-knowledge, and in that sense, the self was treated as an accumulated set of ideas. In contrast, self-regulation theory recognizes the self as an active agent that measures, decides, and intervenes in its own processes to change them. Some psychologists link self-regulation to the philosophical notion of free will, understood as the ability to determine one's actions from inside oneself rather than being driven by external forces.

The practical importance of self-regulation can scarcely be understated. Most personal and social problems that plague modern society have some degree of self-regulation failure at their core. These include addiction and alcoholism, obesity and binge eating, anger management, and other emotional control problems. Crime and violence are often linked to poor self-regulation (especially of aggressive and antisocial impulses). Sexual problems, including unwanted pregnancy and sexually transmitted diseases, can be avoided with effective self-regulation. underachievement in school and work often reflects inadequate self-regulation. Money problems, whether in the form of gambling losses, failure to save for the future, or impulsive shopping and credit card debt, can also indicate inadequate self-regulation. Many health problems could be prevented by self-regulation, such as to ensure that one exercises regularly, brushes and flosses teeth, takes vitamins, and eats a proper diet.

More broadly, self-regulation appears to be an important predictor of success in life. People with good self-regulation have been shown to be more popular and have better, more stable relationships, to get better grades in school and college, to have fewer personal pathologies, and to have better adjustment.

Self-regulation is also a key to moral behavior, and some theorists have argued that it is the master virtue that underlies most or all virtuous behavior because such behavior typically requires overcoming an anti-social or immoral impulse (e.g., to cheat, harm, or betray someone) to do what is morally valued.

Standards and Goals

Effective self-regulation requires standards, which are concepts of how something ideally should be. Researchers on self-awareness noted very early that when people reflect on themselves, they do not simply notice how they are. Rather, they compare how they are with some standard, such as their personal ideals, other people's expectations, how they were previously, or the average person. Self-regulation begins by noting discrepancies between how you are and how you want to be. For example, a diet often begins by noting that the person weighs more than his or her ideal weight, and the diet is intended to bring the weight down to the desired weight (the standard).

Self-regulation can be impaired if standards conflict, such as if two parents make inconsistent demands on the child. A lack of clear standards also makes self-regulation difficult.

Self-regulation goals can be sorted into prevention and promotion. Preventive self-regulation focuses on some undesirable outcome and seeks to avoid it. In contrast, promotional self-regulation focuses on some desirable outcome and seeks to approach it. A related distinction is between *ideal* and *ought* standards. Ideals are positive concepts of how one would like to be. Ought standards, such as moral rules, typically emphasize some bad or undesired possibility and center on the importance of not performing such actions.

Standards do not automatically activate self-regulation. People must be motivated to change. How people choose their goals and standards, and why they sometimes abandon these, is an important topic for further study.

Monitoring and Feedback Loops

Monitoring refers to keeping track of particular behaviors. It is almost impossible to regulate a behavior effectively without monitoring it. (Imagine trying to have a successful diet without ever weighing yourself or keeping track of what you eat.) As stated earlier, many experts believe that a main functional purpose of self-awareness is to serve self-regulation by enabling people to monitor their behavior. Monitoring is more than noticing the behavior itself, though, because it also compares the behavior to standards.

Poor monitoring is an important cause of self-regulation failure. People lose control when they stop keeping track of their behavior. Alcohol intoxication leads to many kinds of self-regulation failure (including overeating, violent activity, overspending, and further drinking), partly because intoxicated people cease to monitor their actions. In contrast, the simplest way to improve self-regulation is to improve monitoring, such as by using external records. For example, people who want to control their spending can often benefit by keeping a written record of each time they spend money.

Self-regulation theory has incorporated the concept of feedback loops from cybernetic theory (that is, a theory originally designed for guided missiles and other mechanical control devices). The feedback loop is represented by the acronym TOTE, which stands for test, operate, test, exit. One commonly invoked example is the thermostat that controls indoor room temperature. The test phase compares the present status with the standard (thus, is the room as warm as the temperature setting?). If there is a discrepancy, then the operate phase begins, which initiates some effort to resolve the problem and bring the reality in line with the standard, just as a thermostat will turn on the furnace to heat the room when it is too cold. As the operate phase continues, additional tests are performed. These will indicate whether progress is being made and, if so, whether the goal or standard has been reached. As long as the reality is still short of the standard, the operations are continued. At some point, the reality reaches the standard, and the test will reveal this. There is then no need for further operations, and the loop is exited (the exit phase).

Unlike machines, humans often feel emotions during self-regulation. Noticing a discrepancy between self and standard can produce negative emotions, such as guilt or sadness or disappointment. Reaching a goal or standard after a successful operate phase can produce positive emotions such as joy, satisfaction, and relief. However, it is not necessary to reach the goal entirely to feel good. Many people experience positive emotions simply because they note that they are making progress toward the standard. In these ways, emotions can sustain and promote effective self-regulation.

Strength and Depletion

Successful self-regulation depends on the capacity to bring about the desired changes. It is not enough to have goals or standards and to keep track of behavior, if one lacks the willpower or other capacity to make the necessary changes. Some people knowingly do things that are bad for them or that violate their values.

As the colloquial term *willpower* implies, the capacity to regulate oneself seems to depend on a psychological resource that operates like strength or energy. Exerting self-regulation uses up some of this resource, leaving the person in a weakened state called *ego depletion*. In that state, people tend to be less effective at further acts of self-control. Moreover, the same resource is used for many different kinds of self-regulation and even for making difficult decisions. For example, when a person is using self-regulation to try to cope with stress or meet deadlines, there will be less available for regulating other habits, and the person may resume smoking or have atypical emotional outbursts. Some evidence indicates that strength can be increased with regular exercise (just like with a normal muscle). That is, if people regularly perform acts of self-regulation, such as trying to maintain good posture or speaking carefully, their capacity for successful self-regulation in other spheres may improve.

Trait Differences

Different people are successful at self-regulation to different degrees, though each person's ability to self-regulate may fluctuate across time and circumstances. Some research has shown that children who were more successful at a delay of gratification task at age 4 years grew up to be more successful academically and socially, and this suggests that there is an important element of stability in people's self-regulation. (That is, if someone is good at self-regulation early in life, he or she is likely to remain good at it for many years.)

June Tangney and colleagues have reviewed some of the scales designed to measure the capacity for self-regulation. It does appear to be quite possible to rely on a self-report measure to distinguish people by how good at self-regulation they are, although some responses may be tainted by boastfulness, self-report bias, and social desirability bias.

Other Issues

Although self-regulation offers human beings a powerful psychological tool for controlling and altering their responses, its effectiveness has important limits. As already noted, consecutive efforts at self-regulation can deplete the capability for further regulation. Another important limit is that not all behaviors can be regulated. Many responses are automatic or otherwise strongly activated. The popular term *impulse control* (referring to self-regulation of impulsive behaviors such as alcohol and substance abuse, or violence, or sex, or eating) may be a misnomer because usually the impulse itself is not controlled but only the behavior stemming from it. That is, a reformed smoker usually cannot refrain from wanting a cigarette and has to be content with refusing to act on that impulse and to smoke.

Controlling emotions, or affect regulation, is an important category of self-regulation that confronts limited power. Most people cannot alter their emotional states simply by deciding to do so. Put another way, emotions tend to be beyond conscious control. Affect regulation typically proceeds by indirect means, such as by distracting oneself, inducing a different emotion, or calming oneself down.

An ongoing debate concerns the extent to which self-regulation failure stems from irresistible impulses, rather than simply acquiescing. Many people say that they couldn't resist, such as when they spent too much money shopping or ate something fattening (or indeed engaged in proscribed acts of sex or violence). However, some research suggests that people could resist most of the time if they were sufficiently motivated. Self-deception may be involved in the process by which people allow themselves to fail at self-regulation. Undoubtedly, however, there are some irresistible impulses, such as to breathe, or go to sleep, or urinate.

Once self-regulation begins to break down, additional psychological processes may accelerate the failure. These have been called *lapse-activated patterns* or, in the case of alcohol and drug abuse, *abstinence violation effects.* A recovering alcoholic may be very careful and scrupulous about avoiding all alcohol, but after taking a drink or two on one occasion may cease to keep track and hence drink more, or may even decide that because the zero-tolerance pattern has been broken, he or she might as well enjoy more. Dieters seem particularly vulnerable to the fallacy that if a caloric indulgence has spoiled one's diet for the day, one might as well eat more forbidden foods and then resume the diet tomorrow. Such spiraling processes can turn a minor failure at self-regulation into a destructive binge.

Roy F. Baumeister

See also Ego Depletion; Goals; Self-Control Measures

Further Readings

Baumeister, R. F., & Vohs, K. D. (Eds.). (2004). *Handbook of self-regulation: Research, theory, and applications.* New York: Guilford Press.

Carver, C. S., & Scheier, M. E. (1981). *Attention and self-regulation: A control theory approach to human behavior.* New York: Springer.

Higgins, E. T. (1996). The "self digest": Self-knowledge serving self-regulatory functions. *Journal of Personality and Social Psychology, 71,* 1062–1083.

Tangney, J. P., Baumeister, R. F., & Boone, A. L. (2004). High self-control predicts good adjustment, less pathology, better grades, and interpersonal success. *Journal of Personality, 72,* 271–322.

SELF-REPORTS

Definition

The term *self-reports* refers to information that is collected from an individual's own description of the events, sensations, or beliefs under scrutiny. Self-reports may be collected with any of several different methods: for example, surveys and questionnaires, electronic diaries, and clinical interviews. Self-reports are distinguished from other methods of data collection because their only source is the respondent's personal account.

Issues Surrounding the Use of Self-Reports

Most researchers agree that it is naive to believe that all self-reports are fully accurate. However, it is also simplistic to assume that because self-reports can be erroneous, they are not valuable or informative. A better approach is to attend closely to the various cognitive and motivational factors that influence people's ability and willingness to report on their beliefs, feelings, and activities. Numerous such factors have been identified. Although some of these factors concern outright deception (e.g., when accurate self-reports would be embarrassing or harmful), more commonly self-reports are distorted by the limits of people's ability to store, save, recall, and summarize information. For example, research has shown that when asked to describe events from their past, people are prone to report whatever information is most accessible at that moment, regardless of whether that information is correct or was made accessible by an experimental manipulation.

Self-reports are also known to be biased by an individual's motives, goals, and personality. For example, people high in the personality trait of neuroticism tend to experience and describe events in their lives (for example, everyday stressors, pain symptoms) as more distressing than do people low in neuroticism.

Whenever possible, it is useful to corroborate self-reports through other sources, such as historical records, reports by informed friends and family members, psychophysiological recording, or behavioral observation. Systematic comparison of self-reports with these other sources of data can provide valuable insights into the processes that contribute to accuracy and inaccuracy in self-reports. Nevertheless, many important concepts are either intrinsically subjective and internal, and therefore measurable only through self-reports (for instance, pain, momentary mood, attitudes, feelings about of another person), or are for pragmatic reasons impossible to appraise otherwise (for instance, behavior over a month's time, events in the distant past). For this reason, substantial effort has gone into developing instruments and procedures that maximize the validity of self-reports.

Harry T. Reis

See also Motivated Cognition; Neuroticism; Self-Deception; Self-Presentation; Social Cognition

Further Readings

Stone, A. A., Turkhan, J. S., Bachrach, C. A., Jobe, J. B., Kurtzman, H. S., & Cain, V. S. (Eds.). (2000). *The science of self-report.* Mahwah, NJ: Erlbaum.

SELF-SCHEMAS

See SCHEMAS

SELF-SERVING BIAS

Definition

The self-serving bias refers to the tendency to take credit for successful outcomes in life, but to blame the situation or other people for failing outcomes. For example, when an individual gets a promotion at work, he or she will explain this by citing an internal cause, such as his or her ability or diligence. In contrast, when the same individual is fired from a job, he or she will explain this by pointing to an external cause, such as an unfair boss or bad luck. In general, the self-serving bias allows individuals to feel positively about themselves and to protect themselves from the negative psychological consequences of failure.

Background and History

The self-serving bias is part of a larger area in social psychology known as causal attributions, or the way individuals explain events in the social world. Fritz Heider, a social psychologist, argued in his classic work on attribution theory that four basic types of attributions can be made regarding an individual's behavior. These include two internal attributions, ability and effort, and two external attributions, difficulty and luck. Internal attributions apply to something about the person and external attributions apply to something about the situation. For example, if a person successfully rows a boat across a lake, his or her success could be attributed to internal factors: the person's ability (e.g., strength or rowing skill) or effort (e.g., the person was motivated because he or she had a good friend on the other side or was being chased). The person's success could also be attributed to external factors: the difficulty of the task (e.g., it was a small lake) or luck (e.g., an unexpected breeze blew him or her across). Bernard Weiner, who played a central role in creating modern attribution theory, later expanded on these ideas.

The self-serving bias occurs when individuals make attributions for their own (rather than others') behavior. When the outcome is positive, individuals make more internal attributions; when the outcome is negative, individuals make more external attributions. This difference in attributions for positive and for negative outcomes is why the self-serving bias is considered a bias. This bias is readily apparent when you think about a group situation. Imagine a classroom of students who have just gotten grades back on a test. The students who get A's are likely to explain their success by ascribing it to their intelligence and work ethic; the students who failed are likely to explain their failure by ascribing it to the fact that the test was too hard or unfair, or only asked questions about the one area they didn't study. Both groups of students

cannot be correct in their attributions. Either the test was fair and the students who failed were not smart enough or did not study sufficiently, or the test was truly unfair and the students who received A's really just got lucky. Importantly, although the self-serving bias in this example leads to a distortion of reality by many students, it also leads to all students feeling as good about themselves as possible. The students with A's think they are smart, and the students with F's think it was not a reflection of their ability or effort.

Situations and Measurement

The self-serving bias can be observed in a wide range of situations. Individual situations are the most commonly studied. These simply involve a person engaging in a task by himself or herself, and then receiving positive or negative feedback about the performance. Taking an exam would be an example of an individual task. Dyadic tasks and group tasks involve more than one person. In a dyadic task, a person and a partner work together on a task, and feedback is directed toward their combined efforts. For example, if two students worked together on a class project, they would only receive a single grade for their combined effort. A group task is similar, but involves more than two people. For example, a team playing a soccer game would be an example of a group task. Finally, there are situations that involve two or more people, but in which the performance feedback is given to a single person whom the other directs. For example, in a teacher–student task, a teacher who has a failing student might be asked how personally responsible the student is, relative to the teacher, for the failure. Likewise, a therapist might be asked how personally responsible the client is, relative to the therapist, for the failure to get well.

There are two basic strategies for assessing the self-serving bias. The first is to ask someone to complete a task, give that person success or failure feedback, and then ask him or her to attribute responsibility for the performance to internal or external factors. When this strategy is completed in a psychology lab, the participant usually completes a task, such as a novel creativity test, and then is given randomly determined success or failure feedback. In other words, the experimenter will tell the participants at random that half of them succeeded and half of them failed. When this strategy is used in a classroom setting and the participants are students, the students simply take a test and are given accurate results. They are then asked to attribute the results to internal or external causes.

The second basic strategy for assessing the self-serving bias is to use paper and pencil questionnaires. Participants are presented with a series of hypothetical situations that have positive or negative outcomes and then are asked to what they would attribute each outcome. The most used questionnaire of this type is the Attributional Style Questionnaire.

Causes, Consequences, and Contexts

The primary cause underlying the self-serving bias is the desire to protect or enhance the positivity of the self. The self-serving bias allows individuals to maintain positive feelings about themselves in the face of failure ("it wasn't my fault") or to feel particularly good about themselves following success ("I am a genius!"). This means that the self-serving bias will be most evident in those individuals or in those situations in which the desire to protect or enhance the self is the strongest.

Certain individuals or groups are more likely to show the self-serving bias than are others. Individuals who feel particularly good about themselves, such as those who are narcissistic or in happy moods are more likely to show the self-serving bias. In contrast, depressed individuals are less likely to show the self-serving bias. Individuals who care more about achievement and success also report a greater self-serving bias.

At a group level, men show a greater self-serving bias than do women. This is because men, on average, are more narcissistic and have higher self-esteem than do women. Similarly, U.S. citizens and Westerners more generally show a greater self-serving bias than do East Asians. Again, this parallels the great narcissism and higher self-esteem found in the West.

Certain situations also can increase or reduce the self-serving bias. If the task is important, such as a major exam, individuals are more likely to show the self-serving bias than they are on unimportant tasks. Likewise, moderately challenging tasks are more likely to elicit the self-serving bias than very easy tasks. Individuals also show the self-serving bias more when they choose the task they are participating in rather than being told what task to complete. For example, if an individual wants to play tennis in school, he or she is more likely to show the self-serving bias than if his or her parents force the individual to play. Furthermore, the self-serving bias will be greater when the individual expects to do well on a task than when he or she expects to perform poorly.

Finally, any situation that makes an individual more self-aware is likely to increase the self-serving bias. This is because self-awareness makes people think about their own internal goals and standards. For example, if someone completes a musical performance while being filmed (a simple way to increase self-awareness), the self-serving bias will increase.

One particularly interesting situation is when the self-serving bias is reported publicly. In public, individuals are less likely to show the self-serving bias. The reason for this is that it often looks better to take responsibility for failure and share credit for success. For example, imagine if a quarterback after a winning football game said at an interview: "I won this game single-handedly!" The fans would think he was an arrogant jerk and his teammates would stop supporting him. This is why most athletes on a winning team will readily share the credit with other players and even the fans.

W. Keith Campbell
Elizabeth A. Krusemark

See also Attribution Theory; Narcissism; Self-Enhancement; Self-Presentation

Further Readings

Campbell, W. K., & Sedikides, C. (1999). Self-threat magnifies the self-serving bias: A meta-analytic integration. *Review of General Psychology, 3,* 23–43.

Mezulis, A., Abramson, L. Y., Hyde, J. S., & Hankin, B. L. (2004). Is there a universal positivity bias in attributions? A meta-analytic review of individual, developmental, and cultural differences in the self-serving attributional bias. *Psychological Bulletin, 130,* 711–747.

Miller, D. T., & Ross, M. (1975). Self-serving biases in the attribution of causality: Fact or fiction? *Psychological Bulletin, 82,* 213–225.

Peterson, C., Semmel, A., Von Baeyer, C., Abramson, L. Y., Metalsky, G. I., & Seligman, M. E. P. (1982). The Attributional Style Questionnaire. *Cognitive Therapy and Research, 6,* 287–300.

Weary Bradley, G. (1978). Self-serving biases in the attribution process: A re-examination of the fact or fiction question. *Journal of Personality and Social Psychology, 36,* 56–71.

Weiner, B. (1974). *Achievement motivation and attribution theory.* Morristown, NJ: General Learning Press.

Zuckerman, M. (1979). Attribution of success and failure revisited, or: The motivational bias is alive and well in attribution theory. *Journal of Personality, 47,* 245–287.

SELF-STEREOTYPING

Definition

Self-stereotyping occurs when individuals' beliefs about their own characteristics correspond to common beliefs about the characteristics of a group they belong to. This is generally measured in one of two ways. The first involves measuring the degree to which individuals describe themselves using characteristics that are commonly thought to describe members of their group in general. For example, it is a common belief that women in general are poor at math. Assessing whether individual women feel as if they are poor at math would be consistent with this way of measuring self-stereotyping. The second way researchers measure self-stereotyping is by determining the amount of similarity between how individual group members see their group (or a typical group member) and how they see themselves. For example, researchers may ask individual members of a fraternity how similar they are to a typical member of their fraternity. Some researchers use the term *self-stereotyping* to describe when being a member of a group that is viewed negatively decreases self-esteem, when members of a group endorse stereotypic beliefs about their group, or when the behaviors of individual group members are consistent with stereotypes about their group. However, these uses of the term do not fit the prevailing definition.

Importance

Historically, self-stereotyping has been important in social psychology because prominent theorists thought that it was an unavoidable consequence of group membership. Conceptualizing self-stereotyping more broadly than is done today, they argued that being viewed a certain way because of one's group membership undoubtedly should affect how individual group members see themselves. The modern importance of self-stereotyping stems from the functions it is thought to serve. Some researchers argue that self-stereotyping can translate into beliefs and behaviors that help support existing inequalities between groups in society. Other researchers argue that self-stereotyping fulfills the need to feel close to other group members. From this perspective, self-stereotyping is beneficial in that it creates a sense of

group unity and solidarity. Research documenting other functions of self-stereotyping needs to be done.

When and Why

Although early theorists thought self-stereotyping was virtually unavoidable, modern researchers show that the occurrence of self-stereotyping depends on several things. One is how easily one's group membership comes to mind. The more easily this occurs, the more likely an individual is to self-stereotype in line with beliefs about that group. How easily a group membership comes to mind increases as a function of how unusual it is within a given social environment. For example, being the only woman or African American at a board meeting will bring these group memberships to mind and, therefore, enhance the likelihood of self-stereotyping. A group membership will also come to mind more easily if divisions between different groups are made noticeable. For example, if two men and two women engage in a discussion and tend to find agreement, then their respective gender identities will remain largely in the background. However, if a disagreement along gender lines emerges, then their gender identities will become more noticeable and self-stereotyping will be more likely to occur.

Self-stereotyping is also determined by efforts to maintain an optimal level of closeness to the group. The closer individuals feel to the group, the more likely they are to see themselves as possessing characteristics associated with the group. Conversely, when group members perceive themselves as distinctly different from other members of their group, they engage in self-stereotyping to lessen this feeling.

Feelings as if one's group is threatened also increase self-stereotyping. Threat can come in the form of being a low-status or minority group, as well as feeling that the group is not sufficiently different from other groups. Response to threat, however, depends on how close a person feels to the group. People who feel very close to their groups are more likely to respond to temporary and chronic threats to status with increased self-stereotyping than are people who feel less close to their group. People who feel very close to the group are motivated to maintain ties to the group and thus cope with the threat in ways that protect the group and their place within it.

Finally, interpersonal relationships act as pathways through which individuals come to self-stereotype.

People who think close others, or a new person with whom they want to affiliate, hold stereotypic beliefs about their group, are more likely to see themselves in a stereotypic manner.

Future Directions

The understanding of self-stereotyping has evolved over time. Researchers are now in a better position to describe how and when it will emerge. However, several important unanswered questions remain. One question is whether self-stereotyping occurs for both positive and negative group characteristics. Some research has found that self-stereotyping only occurs for positive traits, whereas other research has found self-stereotyping on positive and negative traits. Another question concerns the consequences of self-stereotyping. For example, it would be useful to know when self-stereotyping does and does not lead to corresponding behavior.

Stacey Sinclair
Jeffrey R. Huntsinger

See also Self; Self-Categorization Theory; Self-Concept; Stereotypes and Stereotyping

Further Readings

Hogg, M. A., & Turner, J. C. (1987). Intergroup behavior, self-stereotyping, and the salience of social categories. *British Journal of Social Psychology, 26,* 325–340.

Pickett, C. L., Bonner, B. L., & Coleman, J. M. (2002). Motivated self-stereotyping: Heightened assimilation and differentiation needs result in increased levels of positive and negative self-stereotyping. *Journal of Personality and Social Psychology, 82,* 543–562.

Sinclair, S., Huntsinger, J., Skorinko, J., & Hardin, C. D. (2005). Social tuning of the self: Consequences for the self-evaluations of stereotype targets. *Journal of Personality and Social Psychology, 89,* 160–175.

SELF-VERIFICATION THEORY

The self-verification theory proposes that people want others to see them as they see themselves. For example, just as those who see themselves as relatively extraverted want others to see them as extraverted, so too do those who see themselves as relatively introverted want others to recognize them as introverts. The theory grew out of the writings of the symbolic interactionists, who held that people form self-views so that they can predict the responses of others and know how to act toward them. For example, a person's belief that he or she is intelligent allows the person to predict that others will notice his or her insightfulness. This prediction, in turn, may motivate the person to pursue higher education at a premier university. Because people's self-views play such a critical role in their lives, they become invested in maintaining them by obtaining self-verifying information.

Among people with positive self-views, the desire for self-verification works hand-in-hand with another important motive, the desire for self-enhancing or positive evaluations. For example, those who view themselves as organized will find that their desires for both self-verification and self-enhancement compel them to seek feedback that others perceive them as organized. In contrast, people with negative self-views will find that the two motives push them in opposite directions. Those who see themselves as disorganized, for example, will find that whereas their desire for self-verification compels them to seek evidence that others perceive them as disorganized, their desire for self-enhancement compels them to seek evidence that others perceive them as organized. Self-verification theory suggests that under some conditions people with negative self-views will resolve this conflict by seeking self-enhancement, but that under other conditions they will resolve it by seeking self-verification.

Seeking Self-Verifying Settings and Partners

Considerable evidence supports self-verification theory. In one study, researchers asked participants with positive and negative self-views whether they would prefer to interact with evaluators who had favorable or unfavorable impressions of them. Not surprisingly, those with positive self-views preferred favorable partners, but contrary to self-enhancement theory, those with negative self-views preferred unfavorable partners.

Many replications of this effect using diverse methods have confirmed that people prefer self-verifying evaluations and interaction partners. Both men and women display this propensity, even if their self-views happen to be negative. Moreover, it does not matter whether the self-views refer to characteristics that are relatively immutable (e.g., intelligence) or changeable (e.g., diligence), whether the self-views happen to be highly specific (e.g., athletic) or global (e.g., low self-esteem, worthless), or whether the self-views refer to the individual's personal qualities (e.g., assertive) or group memberships (e.g., Democrat). Furthermore, when people choose negative partners over positive ones, they do not do so merely to avoid positive evaluators (out of a concern that they might disappoint them). To the contrary, people choose negative partners even when the alternative is participating in a different experiment.

Just as self-verification strivings influence the contexts people enter initially, so too do they influence whether or not people remain in particular contexts. Research on married couples, college roommates, and dating partners show that people gravitate toward partners who provide verification and drift away from those who do not. For instance, just as people with positive self-views withdraw (either psychologically or through divorce or separation) from spouses who perceive them unfavorably, people with negative self-views withdraw from spouses who perceive them favorably. Similarly, the more positively college students with firmly held negative self-views are perceived by their roommates, the more inclined they are to plan to find a new roommate (students with positive self-views displayed the opposite pattern). Finally, self-views determine how people react to the implicit evaluations conveyed by the salaries they receive. In one study examining self-esteem and job turnover, among people with high self-esteem, turnover was greatest among those who failed to receive raises; for people with low self-esteem, turnover was greatest among people who did receive raises. Apparently, people gravitate toward relationships and settings that provide them with evaluations that confirm their self-views.

Bringing Others to See Them as They See Themselves

Even if people wind up with partners who do not see them in a self-verifying manner, they may correct the situation by changing their partners' minds. One way they may do this is by judiciously displaying identity cues. The most effective identity cues are readily controlled and reliably evoke self-verifying responses from others. Physical appearances represent a particularly salient class of identity cues. The

clothes one wears, for instance, can advertise numerous self-views, including those associated with everything from political leanings to income level and religious convictions. Similarly, people routinely display company or school logos, buttons, and bumper stickers, and wear uniforms to evoke reactions that verify their self-views. Consistent with this, one set of researchers discovered that dress, style, and fabric revealed a great deal about individuals' jobs, roles, and self-concepts. Even body posture and demeanor communicate identities to others. Take, for example, the CEO who projects importance in his bearing or the new employee who exudes naïveté. Such identity cues announce their bearer's self-views to all who are paying attention. Moreover, self-verification theory predicts that people should display identity cues to communicate socially valued and devalued identities. Some highly visible examples include skinheads and members of the Ku Klux Klan.

Even if people fail to gain self-verifying reactions through their choice of environments or through the display of identity cues, they may still acquire such evaluations by the way they act toward other people. One group of researchers, for example, found that college students who were mildly depressed as compared with nondepressed were more likely to solicit negative evaluations from their roommates. Moreover, students' efforts to acquire negative feedback appear to have borne fruit in the form of interpersonal rejection: The more unfavorable feedback they solicited in the middle of the semester, the more apt their roommates were to derogate them and plan to find another roommate at the semester's end.

If people are motivated to bring others to verify their self-conceptions, they should intensify their efforts to elicit self-confirmatory reactions when they suspect that others might be misconstruing them. Researchers tested this idea by informing participants who perceived themselves as either likable or dislikable that they would be interacting with people who probably found them likable or dislikable. Participants tended to elicit reactions that confirmed their self-views, especially if they suspected that evaluators' appraisals might disconfirm their self-conceptions. Therefore, participants intensified their efforts to obtain self-verification when they suspected that evaluators' appraisals challenged their self-views.

People will even go so far as to cease working on tasks that they have been assigned if they sense that continuing to do so will bring them nonverifying feedback. One researcher recruited participants with positive or negative self-views to work on a proof-reading task. He then informed some participants that they would be receiving more money than they deserved (i.e., positive expectancies) or exactly what they deserved (i.e., neutral expectancies). Self-verification theory predicts that people's self-views will influence how they respond to positive compared with neutral feedback. This is precisely what happened. Whereas participants with positive self-views worked the most when they had positive expectancies, participants with negative self-views worked the least when they had positive expectancies. Apparently, people with negative self-views withdrew effort when expecting positive outcomes because, unlike those with positive self-views, they felt undeserving.

Seeing More Self-Confirming Evidence Than Actually Exists

The research literature provides abundant evidence that expectancies (including self-conceptions) channel information processing. This suggests that self-conceptions may systematically channel people's perceptions of their experiences to make their experiences seem more self-verifying than they actually are.

Self-views may guide at least three distinct aspects of information processing. One research team focused on selective attention. Their results showed that participants with positive self-views spent longer scrutinizing evaluations when they anticipated that the evaluations would be positive, and people with negative self-views spent longer scrutinizing evaluations when they anticipated that the evaluations would be negative.

In a second study, the researchers examined biases in what people remembered about an evaluation that they had received. They found that participants who perceived themselves positively remembered more positive than negative statements. In contrast, those who perceived themselves negatively remembered more negative than positive statements.

Finally, numerous investigators have shown that people tend to interpret information in ways that reinforce their self-views. For example, one investigator found that people endorsed the perceptiveness of an evaluator who confirmed their self-conceptions but derogated the perceptiveness of an evaluator who disconfirmed their self-views. Similarly, another researcher reported that just as people with high self-esteem remembered feedback as being more favorable

than it actually was, people with low self-esteem remembered the feedback as being more negative than it actually was.

In summary, evidence suggests that people may strive to verify their self-views by gravitating toward self-confirming partners, by systematically eliciting self-confirming reactions from others, and by processing information in ways that exaggerate the extent to which it appears that others perceive them in a self-confirming manner. Although these forms of self-verification may be implemented more or less simultaneously, people may often deploy them sequentially (although probably not consciously). For example, people may first strive to locate partners who verify one or more self-views. If this fails, they may redouble their efforts to elicit verification for the self-views in question or strive to elicit verification for a different self-view. Failing this, they may strive to see more self-verification than actually exists. And, failing this, they may withdraw from the relationship, either psychologically or in actuality. Through the creative use of such strategies, people may dramatically increase their chances of attaining self-verification.

Self-Verification and Related Processes
Self-Verification and Desire for Novelty

Too much predictability can be oppressive. No matter how much we like something at first—a scrumptious meal, a beautiful ballad, or a lovely sunset—eventually it may become too familiar. In fact, researchers have shown that people dislike highly predictable phenomena almost as much as they dislike highly unpredictable ones. People seem to prefer modest levels of novelty; they want phenomena that are new enough to be interesting, but not so new as to be frightening.

This does not mean that people like their relationship partners to treat them in a novel (i.e., nonverifying) manner, however. Evidence that people desire novelty comes primarily from studies of people's reactions to art objects and the like. If novel art objects become overly stimulating, people can simply shift their attention elsewhere. This is not a viable option should their spouse suddenly begin treating them as if they were someone else, for such treatment would pose serious questions about the integrity of their belief systems. In the final analysis, people probably finesse their competing desires for predictability and novelty by indulging their desire for novelty within contexts in which surprises are not threatening (e.g., leisure activities), while seeking coherence and predictability where it really counts—within their enduring relationships.

Self-Verification and Self-Enhancement

People's self-verification strivings are apt to be most influential when the relevant identities and behaviors matter to them. Thus, for example, the self-view should be firmly held, the relationship should be enduring, and the behavior itself should be consequential. When these conditions are not met, identity issues will be of little concern and people will self-enhance, that is, prefer and seek positive evaluations.

That self-verification strivings trump self-enhancement strivings when people have firmly held negative self-views does not mean that people with negative self-views are masochistic or have no desire to be loved. Even people with very low self-esteem want to be loved. What sets people with negative self-views apart is their ambivalence about praise and acceptance; although positive evaluations initially foster joy and warmth, these feelings are later chilled by incredulity. Tragically, people with negative self-views are also ambivalent about negative evaluations; although such evaluations may reassure them that they know themselves, their feelings of reassurance are tempered by sadness that the truth is not kinder.

Happily, people with negative self-views are the exception rather than the rule. That is, on the balance, most people tend to view themselves positively. Although this is beneficial for people themselves, it presents a challenge to the researchers who study them. That is, for theorists interested in determining whether behavior is driven by self-verification or self-enhancement, participants with positive self-views will reveal nothing because both motives encourage them to seek positive evaluations.

Self-Verification and Self-Concept Change

Although self-verification strivings tend to stabilize people's self-views, change may still occur. Perhaps the most common source of change is set in motion when the community recognizes a significant change in a person's age (e.g., when adolescents become adults), status (e.g., when students become teachers), or social role (e.g., when singles get married). The community may abruptly change the way that it treats the person. Eventually, the target of such differential treatment will bring the person's self-view into accord with the treatment he or she receives.

Alternatively, people may themselves initiate a change in a self-view when they conclude that the self-view is blocking an important goal. Consider, for example, a person who decides that his or her negative self-views have led the person to tolerate neglectful and irresponsible relationship partners. When he or she realizes that such partners are unlikely to facilitate the goal of raising a family, the person seeks therapy. In the hands of a skilled therapist, the person may develop more favorable self-views, which, in turn, steer him or her toward relationship partners who support those goals.

Implications

Self-verification strivings bring stability to people's lives, making their experiences more coherent, orderly, and comprehensible than they would be otherwise. These processes are adaptive for most people because most people have positive self-views and self-verification processes enable them to preserve these positive self-views. Because self-verification processes facilitate social interaction, it is not surprising that they seem to be particularly beneficial to members of groups. Research indicates that when members of small groups receive self-verification from other group members, their commitment to the group increases and their performance improves. Self-verification processes seem to be especially useful in small groups composed of people from diverse backgrounds because it tends to make people feel understood, which encourages them to open up to their coworkers. Opening up, in turn, fosters superior performance.

Yet, for people with negative self-views, self-verification strivings may have undesirable consequences. Such strivings may, for example, cause them to gravitate toward partners who undermine their feelings of self-worth, break their hearts, or even abuse them. And if people with negative self-views seek therapy, returning home to a self-verifying partner may undo the progress that was made there. Finally, in the workplace, the feelings of worthlessness that plague people with low self-esteem may foster feelings of ambivalence about receiving raises or even being treated fairly, feelings that may undercut their propensity to insist that they get what they deserve from their employers.

William B. Swann, Jr.

See also Expectations; Self; Self-Concept; Self-Enhancement; Self-Esteem; Symbolic Interactionism

Further Readings

Swann, W. B., Jr. (1983). Self-verification: Bringing social reality into harmony with the self. In J. Suls & A. G. Greenwald (Eds.), *Social psychological perspectives on the self* (Vol. 2, pp. 33–66). Hillsdale, NJ: Erlbaum.

Swann, W. B., Jr. (1987). Identity negotiation: Where two roads meet. *Journal of Personality and Social Psychology, 53,* 1038–1051.

Swann, W. B., Jr. (1996). *Self-traps: The elusive quest for higher self-esteem.* Freeman: New York.

Swann, W. B., Jr., De La Ronde, C., & Hixon, J. G. (1994). Authenticity and positivity strivings in marriage and courtship. *Journal of Personality and Social Psychology, 66,* 857–869.

Swann, W. B., Jr., Rentfrow, P. J., & Guinn, J. (2002). Self-verification: The search for coherence. In M. Leary & J. Tagney, *Handbook of self and identity* (pp. 367–383). New York: Guilford Press.

SEMANTIC DIFFERENTIAL

Definition

The semantic differential is a method of measurement that uses subjective ratings of a concept or an object by means of scaling opposite adjectives to study connotative meaning of the concept or object. For example, the first level meaning of a car is that of a transportation device; the second level meaning of a car can also be its value as a status symbol. The semantic differential is designed to measure these second levels—in other words, connotative meanings of an object. The semantic differential is mostly used for measuring attitudes toward social and nonsocial objects, but also to assess quality and type of interactions between people. The method was developed by Charles Osgood in the 1950s and has been broadly used in and outside of psychology.

The semantic differential usually consists of 20 to 30 bipolar rating scales (i.e., the scale is anchored by an adjective on each side, for example *warm–cold*) on which the target object or concept is judged. Basis for the judgment is not so much the denotative or objective relation of the object and the adjective anchors of the bipolar scales (because it may not be given at first glance given our car example earlier and the rugged *warm–cold* adjective pair) but, rather, the metaphoric or connotative closeness of the object and the anchors of the bipolar scales. For example, on a metaphorical or connotative level, a family car might be judged as warm, whereas a delivery truck might be judged as more cold. The denotative meaning, that is, firsthand meaning, might be quite similar, in terms of being an adequate transportation device in both cases.

Background

Social psychologists, but also market researchers or public pollsters, are often interested in the subjective (i.e., somewhat hidden and varying between individuals) definition of meaning that an object or concept has beyond its mere brute facts, as well as in the attitude of a certain group of people concerning a certain object or concept.

Meaning can be divided into four different dimensions: structural (a possible higher-level similarity to other objects, e.g., a sports car and a truck are different, but structurally similar because they are both means of transportation), contextual (depending on the current context, e.g., a truck serves as a transportation device, but can also be an vintage car later on), denotative (objective, brute facts of the car, such as horsepower), and connotative (more metaphoric, second-level associations). Osgood was particularly interested in this fourth dimension of meaning. His scaling method was meant to measure individual differences in the connotation of a word describing an object or a concept.

Construction and Use of Semantic Differentials

The actual questionnaire consists of a set of bipolar scales with contrasting adjectives at each end. The positions on the scale in between can be numbered or labeled. Note that the neutral middle position is usually marked by zero and the other positions by numbers increasing equally in both directions. Thus, each scale measures the directionality of a reaction (e.g., good vs. bad) and its intensity (from neutral via slight to extreme). In most cases, the universal adjective pairs are used because translations in many languages are available. Besides universal semantic differentials, object- or concept-specific sets of adjective pairs can be used. For the latter, great care while constructing the respective semantic differentials is necessary to avoid problems (outlined in the next section). For the universal semantic differential, cross-cultural comparisons revealed that three basic dimensions of response account for most of the covariation. These three dimensions have been labeled "evaluation, potency, and activity" (EPA) and constitute the semantic space (i.e., the set of descriptive attributes) of the target to be judged. Some of the adjective pairs are direct measures of the dimensions (e.g., *good–bad* for evaluation, *powerful–powerless* for potency, and *fast–slow* for activity); others rather indirectly relate to the single dimensions of the EPA structure. Given the research conducted, for each new case meaning of the scales should not just be inferred from previous results. Dimensionality should be checked so that scales that do not represent a unidimensional factor are not summed up.

Analysis of Data

At first glance, analysis of semantic differential data seems easy, but actually, it is a rather complex procedure. It is not sufficient to simply average scale ratings for each individual and to use mean differences on a judged object or concept. In fact, the underlying factor structure must be determined and correlations of similarity between the profiles must be computed. Data from semantic differentials contain three levels or modes: the target objects or concepts, the scales themselves, and the responding individuals. Thus, before factor analysis, these three-mode data need to be collapsed into a two-mode structure. This can be done either by summing over targets for each individual and scale or by averaging over individuals for each scale-concept combination. Also, one can deal with target objects separately, likewise with individuals. Finally, each individual target object–concept response can be transferred in a new matrix and inter-scale correlations can be computed. Note that different methods of collapsing modes can produce rather different correlation patterns.

The original semantic differential is currently rarely used in social psychology (but widely outside this field). Yet, a lot of related measurement methods in social psychology have been influenced by it. Almost every stereotype rating using, for example, competence or warmth as its basic dimensions follows

the idea of the original concept. The use of the original concept is not without pitfalls and problems. This is especially crucial because many researchers outside of social psychology are not aware of these issues. First, the method is partly self-contradictory: For some words (in this case, the concepts to be measured), people's connotations are assumed to differ, but for other words (in this case the adjectives used as endpoints of the single scales), this assumption should not hold. Second, scales may be relevant to the target objects or concepts to a different degree. These concept-scale interactions are to be treated carefully by determining the structure of the dimensions by using a factor analysis instead of the blind adoption of the EPA structure. Third, a number of problems arise during the administration itself. For some individuals, judging objects on the given scales is hard because the adjective pairs seem unrelated to the target object. In addition, respondents may give socially desirable answers, or can develop a so-called response set, meaning that they would consistently give moderate or very extreme answers. Some of these problems can be overcome by anonymity of the respondents, inclusion of irrelevant target words to disguise the true purpose of the semantic differential, or by checking for response sets. Finally, some problems with the semantic differential arise from a thoughtless use, administration of the method, and analysis of its data. Not every set of bipolar scales and given adjective pairs constitute a semantic differential. The underlying dimensions and possible overlap of the adjective pairs are not assessed in many cases and consequences resulting from it are ignored.

The semantic differential can be an informative and economic measure for the connotation of objects or concepts. However, the user should be fully aware of the complexity of the method and reflect its value carefully.

Kai J. Jonas

See also Attitudes; Research Methods; Social Desirability Bias

Further Readings

Heise, D. R. (1970). The semantic differential and attitude research. In G. F. Summers (Ed.), *Attitude measurement* (pp. 235–253). Chicago: Rand McNally.

Osgood, C. E., Suci, G. J., & Tannenbaum, P. H. (1957). *The measurement of meaning.* Urbana: University of Illinois Press.

SENSATION SEEKING

Definition

Sensation seeking is a personality trait defined by the degree to which an individual seeks novel and highly stimulating activities and experiences. People who are high in sensation seeking are attracted to the unknown and as a result consistently seek the new, varied, and unpredictable. Examples of such behaviors are varied, but sensation seekers may be attracted to extreme sports, frequent travel, diverse foods and music, new sexual partners and experiences, and challenging existing viewpoints. Often, sensation seekers are likely to be impulsive and engage in behaviors that others would find too risky. The risks may be physical (e.g., skydiving), social (e.g., risking embarrassment by dressing unusually), financial (e.g., gambling), or legal (e.g., vandalism). Because sensation seekers are easily bored, they actively avoid situations and activities likely to be overly repetitive and predictable.

Theory

Marvin Zuckerman originally developed the concept of sensation seeking and has contributed the most important research and relevant theory. Zuckerman's work is especially noteworthy because of his firm and long-standing emphasis on the biological and evolutionary bases of sensation seeking (and personality more generally). Specifically, Zuckerman's basic proposition is that sensation seeking is based on individual differences in the optimal level of sensation caused by biological nervous-system differences. People who are high in sensation seeking are individuals who have relatively low-level nervous system activation and therefore seek arousal from their external environment by looking for novel stimuli and engaging in varied experiences. In contrast, individuals who are low in sensation seeking have a naturally higher level of internal activation and thus do not tend to seek sensation from external sources. Zuckerman posits that sensation seeking is genetically influenced because it is evolutionary adaptive. Across the animal kingdom, engaging in a certain degree of risky behaviors will increase the likelihood of survival and reproductive success (e.g., seeking new territories for food and new potential mates).

Measurement

Zuckerman first created the Sensation Seeking Scale in 1964 to measure an individual's overall level of susceptibility to excitement or boredom in the context of sensory deprivation experiments. Current versions of the self-report measure include four subscales: (1) Thrill and Adventure Seeking—the extent to which individuals engage in or are interested in participating in risky activities such as parachuting or skiing; (2) Experience Seeking—the degree to which one seeks excitement through the mind, such as from music, art, and travel; (3) Disinhibition—seeking sensations through social stimulation and disinhibitory behaviors such as drinking and sex; and (4) Boredom Susceptibility—avoiding monotonous, repetitive, and boring situations, people, and activities.

Research Findings

Zuckerman has generated an impressive amount of research on sensation seeking, and his biologically based approach to understanding personality and social behavior likely influences the current emphasis on behavioral genetics and neuroscience in social psychology. Research supports Zuckerman's biologically based theory and has revealed that sensation seeking plays an important role in many social behaviors.

High sensation seekers have a stronger orienting response to new stimuli, and their physiological response is indicative of sensation seeking rather than avoidance (e.g., decreasing heart rate and increasing brain activity in the visual cortex). In addition, sensation seeking has been found to be related to levels of important brain neurotransmitters (e.g., monoamine oxidase, norepinephrine, and dopamine), which in turn have been found to be genetically influenced. Furthermore, studies of identical and fraternal twins have found sensation seeking to be one of the personality traits most likely to be genetically influenced, with a high degree of heritability (nearly 60%) for the trait. Evidence also indicates that men tend to score higher than women in sensation seeking, which is likely related to the finding that sensation seeking is positively correlated with testosterone levels. In addition, sensation seeking appears to peak during late adolescence and then decrease with age.

Sensation seeking has been found to be related to a wide range of overt social behaviors, some of which are likely caused by the tendency for sensation seekers to perceive less risk in a given situation than do low sensation seekers. For example, sensation seekers more frequently engage in adventure sports (e.g., scuba diving); are more likely to work in dangerous occupations (e.g., firefighter); and have a preference for rock music, entertainment that portrays humor, and "warm" paintings with red, orange, and yellow colors over "cold" paintings with green and blue colors. Sensation seeking has been suggested as a disease-prone personality because many of the behaviors associated with sensation seeking are potentially harmful to health whereas others concern social problems. For example, sensation seeking has been found predictive of reckless driving, sexual activity, adolescent delinquency, aggression, hostility, anger, personality disorders, criminal behavior, alcohol abuse, and illicit drug use. Not all studies, however, have found sensation seeking to be a strong predictor of such behaviors, likely because research also indicates that the environment and experiences play important roles in the expression of behaviors such as aggression.

Michael J. Tagler

See also Evolutionary Psychology; Genetic Influences on Social Behavior; Individual Differences; Personality and Social Behavior; Risk Taking; Social Neuroscience; Traits; Twin Studies

Further Readings

Stelmack, R. M. (Ed.). (2004). *On the psychobiology of personality: Essays in honor of Marvin Zuckerman.* San Diego, CA: Elsevier.

Zuckerman, M. (1994). *Behavioral expressions and biosocial bases of sensation seeking.* New York: Cambridge University Press.

SEQUENTIAL CHOICE

Definition

The term *sequential choice* is mostly used in contrast to *simultaneous choice*. Both terms refer to the selection of a series of items for subsequent consumption, for example, when selecting a set of snacks to be consumed one per day during the next week. Sequential choice refers to choosing a single product at a time and consuming this product before selecting the next one (e.g., selecting one of the snacks on the day of its consumption). In contrast, simultaneous choice is the selection of several items all at once for consumption one after another over time (e.g., selecting all snacks simultaneously before or on the first day of its consumption).

Explanation and Details

The concepts of sequential and simultaneous choice are used primarily in consumer psychology. Research shows that the two strategies lead to different decision outcomes. A person who is choosing products sequentially makes less diverse decisions than does a person who is choosing products simultaneously. For example, a person making a sequential choice often chooses identical products (e.g., the same chocolate bar) rather than different ones, whereas a person making choices simultaneously often chooses a greater variety of products (e.g., chocolate bars of different tastes). Explanations for this difference have been studied experimentally: When making a simultaneous choice, a person has to think simultaneously about various consumption situations in the future; that is, in one situation a person has to select several products that will be consumed later in several different occasions. This process requires a lot of time and effort. People also overestimate the possibility that their preference for a product will change in the future. Consequently, people choose a greater variety of products to simplify their decision. These aspects have no or only little influence when making choices sequentially. Compared with a simultaneous choice, sequential choice is the easier task: A person only has to select the most preferred product out of several products. Consequently, experiments show that people making decisions sequentially feel more confident about their decisions than making decisions simultaneously.

Which strategy yields a better outcome depends on the situation: Studies show that especially in situations when independent products have to be selected (e.g., music CDs, snacks), the chosen product is liked more when choices are made sequentially instead of simultaneously. The reason is that people who make sequential choices focus on their needs in a given situation disregarding any irrelevant information (e.g., product preferences in the future). Instead, in situations when interdependent items have to be selected (e.g., furniture for an apartment), the outcomes of simultaneous choices are favored over those of sequential choices because the products will be used together.

Examples of products that have been used to investigate sequential and simultaneous choices are food (e.g., snacks, yogurt, meals), drinks (e.g., soft drinks, juices), music songs, and gambles.

Ursula Szillis
Anke Görzig

See also Consumer Behavior; Decision Making; Satisficing; Simultaneous Choice

Further Readings

Simonson, I. (1990). The effect of purchase quantity and timing on variety-seeking behavior. *Journal of Marketing Research, 27,* 150–162.

SEX DRIVE

Definition

Sex drive represents a basic motivation to pursue and initiate sexual activity and gratification and is tightly regulated by sex hormones—testosterone in men and both testosterone and estrogen in women. In other words, sex drive can be thought of as a person's general urge to have sex.

History and Modern Usage

Sex drive is thought to have evolved to ensure the survival of the species by motivating sexual behavior and hence reproduction. This is consistent with the fact that children who have not yet reached puberty, who have low levels of sex hormones and are incapable of reproduction, do not typically report strong urges for sex (although they are capable of sexual arousal). The importance of sex hormones (such as testosterone) to sex drive has been demonstrated by studies showing that individuals with abnormally low levels of these hormones report very weak sexual urges and that these urges can be increased by administering corrective doses of such hormones.

Much research has focused on gender differences in sex drive, specifically the fact that women typically report weaker motivations for sexual activity than do

men and fewer spontaneous sexual urges and fantasies. Considerable debate exists about whether such gender differences reflect cultural repression of female sexuality or biological differences between men and women. Both factors likely play a role, but it is not clear whether one factor is uniformly more important than the other. Some researchers have argued that instead of viewing women as having *weaker* sex drives, it is more appropriate to view the female sex drive as more *periodic* than men's—that is, showing notable peaks and valleys over time—because of fluctuations in women's hormone levels across the menstrual cycle. Whereas men have fairly high and constant levels of testosterone, women's estrogen levels peak around the time of ovulation (when pregnancy is most likely to occur), and this surge corresponds to an increase in sexual motivation. When estrogen levels subsequently fall, so does sexual motivation. This may be an evolved mechanism ensuring that women are most likely to pursue sexual activity when such activity is most likely to produce offspring.

Although sex drive is regulated by sex hormones, it can also be influenced by social, psychological, and cultural factors. Psychological stress, for example, is commonly associated with decreased sex drive. Finally, it is important to distinguish between sex drive and sexual orientation. Although there have long been stereotypes that individuals with lesbian, gay, or bisexual orientations are more sexual in general than are heterosexuals, and thus have stronger sex drives, there is no evidence that this is the case. Rather, the strength of one's overall sexual motivation appears to be independent of the object of one's sexual motivation.

Lisa M. Diamond

See also Erotic Plasticity; Sexual Desire; Testosterone

Further Readings

Baumeister, R. F., Catanese, K. R., & Vohs, K. D. (2001). Is there a gender difference in strength of sex drive? Theoretical views, conceptual distinctions, and a review of relevant evidence. *Personality and Social Psychology Review, 5,* 242–273.

Baumeister, R. F., & Twenge, J. M. (2002). Cultural suppression of female sexuality. *Review of General Psychology, 6,* 166–203.

Fisher, H. E. (1998). Lust, attraction, and attachment in mammalian reproduction. *Human Nature, 9,* 23–52.

Tolman, D. L., & Diamond, L. M. (2001). Desegregating sexuality research: Combining cultural and biological perspectives on gender and desire. *Annual Review of Sex Research, 12,* 33–74.

Wallen, K. (2001). Risky business: Social context and hormonal modulation of primate sexual desire. In W. Everaerd & E. Laan (Eds.), *Sexual appetite, desire and motivation: Energetics of the sexual system* (pp. 33–62). Amsterdam: Koninklijke Nederlandse Akademie van Wetenschappen.

Sexism

Definition

Sexism refers to prejudice or bias toward people based on their gender; it encompasses beliefs (e.g., in different roles for men and women), emotions (e.g., disliking powerful women), and behavior (e.g., sexual harassment) that support gender inequality. Although originally conceived as antipathy toward women, sexism includes subjectively positive but patronizing beliefs (e.g., that men ought to provide for women). There can also be sexism against men, insofar as people believe women are superior to men.

History and Current Usage

Research on sexism developed rapidly in the 1970s. Initially, researchers assumed that sexism, like other prejudices, represents an antipathy (dislike or hatred) toward an oppressed group (specifically women, who have historically had less power than men). The Attitudes toward Women Scale, which measured whether respondents thought that women ought to remain in traditional gender roles (e.g., raising children rather than working outside the home), became the most prominent measure of sexist attitudes.

Sexist attitudes, however, inherently involve comparisons between the sexes. In the late 1980s, Alice H. Eagly and Antonio Mladinic contrasted attitudes toward each sex, finding the *women are wonderful effect:* As a group, women are rated more favorably than men (by both women and men). This effect challenged the idea of sexism as antipathy toward women because subjectively positive views of women can nevertheless support gender inequality.

Specifically, women are viewed favorably because they are perceived as more *communal* (nice, nurturing,

empathetic), whereas men are viewed as more *agentic* (competent, competitive, ambitious). Although women are likeable, their assigned traits suit them to domestic, lower status roles (which require nurturing others), whereas men's stereotypical traits suit them for high status, leadership roles. In short, women are better liked but less well respected than men. Recent research measuring implicit attitudes (what people automatically and nonconsciously think) supports this conclusion.

In the 1990s, Peter Glick and Susan T. Fiske coined the term *benevolent sexism* to refer to subjectively favorable but patronizing attitudes toward women (e.g., that women, though wonderful, are weak and need men's help). Sexists tend to endorse both benevolent sexism and hostile sexism (negative attitudes toward women who seek equality or powerful roles in society). Benevolent sexism rewards women for staying in traditional (e.g., domestic) roles, whereas hostile sexism punishes women who attempt to break out of those roles. The two forms of sexism work together to maintain gender inequality. Cross-cultural comparisons reveal that nations in which people most strongly endorse benevolent sexism also exhibit the most hostile sexism and the least gender equality (e.g., lower living standards for women relative to men).

Peter Glick

See also Benevolent Sexism; Prejudice, Racism; Stereotypes and Stereotyping

Further Readings

Eagly, A. H., & Mladinic, A. (1989). Gender stereotypes and attitudes toward women and men. *Personality and Social Psychology Bulletin, 15,* 543–558.

Glick, P., & Fiske, S. T. (2001). An ambivalent alliance: Hostile and sexism as complementary justifications of gender inequality. *American Psychologist, 56,* 109–118.

Rudman, L. A. (2005). Rejection of women? Beyond prejudice as antipathy. In J. F. Dovidio, P. Glick, & L. A. Rudman (Eds.), *On the nature of prejudice: Fifty years after Allport.* Malden, MA: Blackwell.

Sex Roles

Definition

Sex roles, or gender roles, consist of the social expectations about the typical and appropriate behavior of men and women. Generally, the female gender role includes the expectation that women and girls exhibit communal traits and behaviors, which focus on interpersonal skill, expressivity, and emotional sensitivity. In contrast, the male gender role includes the expectation that men and boys exhibit agentic traits and behaviors, which focus on self-orientation, independence, and assertiveness. In addition, gender roles include expectations about other elements, such as cognitive skills, hobbies and interests, and occupational choice. Because gender roles transcend many different situations, they can exert considerable influence, and thus studying them is critical to understanding the psychology of men and women.

Gender roles include both descriptive norms, which describe the behavior that is typically observed in men and women, and injunctive or prescriptive norms, which mandate the behavior that is socially approved for men and women. These beliefs are often consensually held: Studies of gender stereotypes, or beliefs about men and women, across a wide range of cultures have found that although some variability exists, people of different cultures generally agree about what men and women are like. In general, people believe that women tend to be more communal than men, and men tend to be more agentic than women. Regardless of the accuracy of such beliefs, this widespread consensus lends them considerable power. Moreover, gender roles tend to be socially approved; not only do people agree that men and women differ, but they also agree that such differences are good.

Writers and philosophers have long considered the impact of different expectations for men and women (for example, Mary Wollstonecraft's *Vindication of the Rights of Woman,* published in 1792). The scientific study of sex roles began in earnest during the second wave of feminism in the 1970s, when psychologists began to document and explain sex differences in behavior and cognitive skills. Explanations of sex-related differences include a wide range of social and biological causes. Although the general convention is to use the term *gender* to describe the social and cultural systems (e.g., socialization) and *sex* to describe the biological groupings of men and women, growing consensus suggests that these causes may not be easily separated. For instance, biological differences (e.g., pregnancy) can assume greater or lesser meaning in cultures with different social or economic demands.

Roots of Gender Roles

Gender roles are closely intertwined with the social roles of men and women. In the traditional division of labor, men occupy high status or leadership roles more than women do, and women occupy caretaking and domestic roles more than men do. When a group of people occupies a particular type of social role, observers infer that the group possesses the internal qualities suited to such roles, thereby failing to account for the power of the role to affect behavior. In the case of the gender groups, the observation that men occupy leadership roles and women occupy caretaking roles leads to the assumption that each group possesses role-congruent personality traits. Initial evidence supporting this inferential process came from a series of experiments in which respondents read brief scenarios about individuals who were described as (a) male, female, or sex-unspecified, and (b) an employee, homemaker, or occupation-unspecified. When no occupation was specified, inferences followed traditional gender stereotypes (i.e., that women were more communal and that men were more agentic). However, when the target individual was described as a homemaker, the respondents inferred that the individual was highly communal and not very agentic—whether the target individual was male or female. Conversely, when the target individual was described as an employee, the respondents inferred that the individual was highly agentic and not very communal—again, regardless of the sex of the target individual. Thus, gender stereotypes stem from the assumption that men and women occupy different types of social roles. The expectation that men and women possess gender-stereotypic traits is then elaborated into broader gender roles, including beliefs that men and women are especially suited for their social roles and approval for gender-stereotypic traits.

Effects of Gender Roles

Because of the consensual and widely approved nature of gender roles, they have considerable impact on behavior. Expectations related to gender may begin to exert an influence extremely early in life. Indeed, within 24 hours of birth, parents have been found to describe male and female infants in gender-stereotypic terms, although the infants did not differ on any objective measures. Such expectations elicit confirming behavior, as demonstrated in several experiments studying the self-fulfilling prophecy. In a classic experiment, each participant was asked to complete a set of male- and female-stereotypic tasks along with a partner, whom they did not meet. The experimenters varied whether participants *believed* they were interacting with a male or female partner. Task assignments followed gender-stereotypic lines: When participants believed they were interacting with a partner of the other sex, they negotiated a more traditional division of labor. Importantly, this gender-stereotypic division of labor occurred regardless of the actual sex of the partner. The simple belief that someone is a man or a woman—even if incorrect—can elicit behavior that conforms to gender role expectations.

The power of expectations to elicit confirming behavior within one specific situation is compelling, but even more so is the consideration of the power of expectations culminated over a lifetime. A wide variety of sources, including parents, teachers, peers, and the media, convey these expectations, which can have considerable impact on life choices. For example, the Eccles model of achievement choices has explicated how parent and teacher expectations about gender differences in ability lead to boys' greater tendency to excel in achievement-related domains. Moreover, repeated experience in certain activities may lead to the development of congruent personality characteristics, which then may guide behaviors across different situations.

An important element of the power of gender roles is that people are rewarded for compliance and punished for transgressions. Those who violate gender-stereotypic expectations, whether because of sexual preference, occupational choice, or personality characteristics, often meet with derogation in their social environment. Such negativity has been documented in experimental findings that women who adopt dominant or self-promoting speech and behavior are penalized compared with similar men. This derogation can include sexism, heterosexism, and discrimination.

Sex-role expectations also contribute to differences in men and women's behavior. For example, the tendency for men to aggress more than women is exacerbated for male-stereotypic behaviors, such as physical aggression, compared with psychological or verbal aggression. In contrast, the sex difference decreases or reverses for relational aggression, in which elements of relationships are used to harm others. Similarly, men's greater tendency to help others especially appears in unfamiliar or potentially dangerous situations. Analyses of heroic behavior suggest that women tend to help in contexts that require long-term commitment (e.g., kidney donation), whereas men tend to help in physically demanding or immediate-response contexts. These patterns of behavior cohere with gender role expectations that emphasize women's close relationships and men's physicality.

Implications

Despite widespread persistence, gender roles have also shown malleability. Since the mid-20th century, these expectations have changed a great deal in the United States and many other cultures. Women's entry into the paid labor force, and especially into formerly male-dominated professions, has resulted in the relaxation of many restrictions placed on women's behavior. People generally believe that women have adopted many male-stereotypic qualities from the past to present, and they expect women to continue to adopt these qualities in the future. Men's roles also reveal some signs of change, although less so than women's roles. Time-use data suggest that men have increased their time spent caring for children since the 1960s, and expectations of more involved fatherhood continue to grow. Even so, men or women who transcend the boundaries of their gender roles still meet with resistance in many domains. Nonetheless, the belief that gender roles are changing may ultimately provide more men and women with the opportunity to follow their individual preferences and desires, rather than be bound by societal expectations.

Amanda B. Diekman

See also Gender Differences; Norms, Prescriptive and Descriptive; Roles and Role Theory; Sexism

Further Readings

Diekman, A. B., & Eagly, A. H. (2000). Stereotypes as dynamic constructs: Women and men of the past, present, and future. *Personality and Social Psychology Bulletin, 26,* 1171–1188.

Eagly, A. H., Beall, A. E., & Sternberg, R. J. (Eds.). (2004). *The psychology of gender* (2nd ed.). New York: Guilford Press.

Eagly, A. H., Wood, W., & Diekman, A. B. (2000). Social role theory of sex differences and similarities: A current appraisal. In T. Eckes & H. M. Trautner (Eds.), *The developmental social psychology of gender* (pp. 123–174). Mahwah, NJ: Erlbaum.

Eccles, J. S. (1994). Understanding women's educational and occupational choices: Applying the Eccles et al. model of achievement-related choices. *Psychology of Women Quarterly, 18,* 585–609.

Prentice, D. A., & Carranza, E. (2002). What women should be, shouldn't be, are allowed to be, and don't have to be: The contents of prescriptive gender stereotypes. *Psychology of Women Quarterly, 26,* 269–281.

Skrypnek, B. J., & Snyder, M. (1982). On the self-perpetuating nature of stereotypes about women and men. *Journal of Experimental Social Psychology, 18,* 277–291.

SEXUAL DESIRE

Definition

Sexual desire is typically viewed as an interest in sexual objects or activities. More precisely, it is the subjective feeling of wanting to engage in sex. Sexual desire is sometimes, but not always, accompanied by genital arousal (such as penile erection in men and vaginal lubrication in women). Sexual desire can be triggered by a large variety of cues and situations, including private thoughts, feelings, and fantasies; erotic materials (such as books, movies, photographs); and a variety of erotic environments, situations, or social interactions.

Background and History

Sexual desire is often confused with sex drive, but these are fundamentally different constructs. Sex drive represents a basic, biologically mediated motivation to seek sexual activity or sexual gratification. In contrast, sexual desire represents a more complex psychological experience that is not dependent on hormonal factors. One useful way to think about the distinction between sex drive and sexual desire comes from research on nonhuman primates. This research distinguishes between *proceptivity* and *receptivity.* Proceptivity refers to a basic urge to seek and initiate sexual activity and is regulated by hormones (for example, testosterone in men and estrogen in women). Receptivity, sometimes called *arousability,* represents the capacity to become sexually interested or aroused upon exposure to certain stimuli. Unlike proceptivity, arousability is not hormone-dependent; in fact, even individuals with no circulating gonadal hormones show arousability to erotic stimuli, although they are not typically motivated to seek sexual gratification.

Proceptive desire and arousability are probably experienced differently (for example, proceptive desire feeling more like a strong, motivating craving or hunger for sex), although no research has directly addressed this question.

Evidence Regarding Hormonal and Physiological Aspects

Although the capacity to experience sexual desire is not hormone-dependent, developmental research suggests that it might be facilitated or intensified by hormones. For example, children typically report their first awareness of sexual desires and attractions as early as 9 years of age, and some researchers have linked this transition to the development of the adrenal gland and the corresponding secretion of adrenal hormones (which are considered weaker than gonadal hormones). Notably, however, these experiences do not typically involve a motivation to seek sexual gratification or activity. Such a motivation does not typically develop until after age 12, when the maturational changes of puberty produce notable surges in levels of gonadal hormones.

Sexual desire is often accompanied by physiological sexual arousal, most notably increased blood flow to the genitals. Yet, this is not always the case. Some individuals report feeling sexual desire even when their genitals show no signs of arousal, whereas others show genital arousal in the absence of psychological feelings of desire. Thus, physiological arousal is not a necessary element of sexual desire and should not be considered a more valid marker of sexual desire than individuals' own self-reported feelings. Researchers do not yet understand why some individuals, in some situations, show differences between their psychological and physiological experiences of sexual desire. These differences are likely influenced by the large variety of psychological, emotional, cultural, social, and political factors that can affect individuals' experiences of sexual desire. In particular, an individual's immediate social and interpersonal context can have a profound affect on how he or she experiences and interprets moments of desire.

Evidence Regarding Gender Differences

Cultural, social, and political factors are also thought to influence the notable gender differences that have been documented regarding sexual desire. One of the most consistent gender differences is that women tend to place greater emphasis on interpersonal relationships as a context for the experience of sexual desire. This may be because women have been historically socialized to restrict their sexual feelings and behaviors to intimate emotional relationships, ideally marital relationships, whereas males have enjoyed more social freedom regarding casual sexual behavior. Another consistent gender difference is that women typically report less frequent and less intense sexual desires than do men. In fact, among adult women, the most common form of sexual disorder is low or absent sexual desire, which is reported by nearly one third of American women. Some adolescent and adult women have difficulty even identifying their own experiences of desire or find that sexual desires are always accompanied by feelings of anxiety, shame, fear, or guilt. This may reflect the fact that women's sexuality has historically faced stricter social regulation and repression than has been the case for men, and that women have always faced greater danger of sexual violence and violation than have men. In addition, however, some researchers have attributed gender differences in sexual desire to the different evolutionary pressures that have faced women and men over the course of human evolution. Specifically, these researchers have argued that the different strategies associated with maximum male versus female reproductive success—respectively, multiple matings with different females versus selective mating with a few, carefully chosen males—may have favored the evolution of stronger sexual desires in men than in women.

Broader Implications and Importance

There has been much interest in sexual desire as an index of sexual orientation, typically defined as an individual's general sexual disposition toward partners of the same sex, the opposite sex, or both sexes. Historically, researchers have considered same-sex sexual desires to be the most important indicator of a same-sex (i.e., gay, lesbian, or bisexual) orientation. In recent years, however, scientific understanding of same-sex desire and sexual orientation has become more complicated. It used to be thought that gay, lesbian, and bisexual individuals were the only people who ever experienced same-sex sexual desires. We now know that many individuals who are otherwise completely heterosexual periodically experience same-sex sexual desires, even if they have little motivation to act on those desires. These periodic same-sex desires might occur at any stage of the life course and can be triggered by a variety of different stimuli, situations, or relationships. Having such an experience does not appear to indicate that an individual will eventually want to pursue same-sex sexual behavior or will eventually consider himself or herself lesbian, gay, or bisexual. Thus, researchers now generally believe that lesbian, gay, and bisexual orientations are characterized by persistent and intense experiences of same-sex desire that are stable over time.

Some individuals' desires appear to be more plastic, meaning flexible, changeable, and sensitive to external influence than are other individuals' desires. In particular, research increasingly suggests that women's desires are more plastic than men's. This is reflected in the fact that women are more likely than men to report patterns of bisexual desire (i.e., desires for partners of both sexes) and more likely to report desires that run contrary to their general sexual orientation (i.e., periodic same-sex attractions among heterosexuals and periodic opposite-sex attractions among lesbians). For example, recent research has found that gay men report strong feelings of sexual desire, accompanied by genital arousal, when shown sexual depictions of men, but not of women. Correspondingly, heterosexual men report strong feelings of sexual desire, accompanied by genital arousal, when shown sexual depictions of women but not of men. Very different patterns, however, were found among women. Specifically, both lesbian and heterosexual women reported some degree of sexual desire and genital sexual arousal to both men and women. Women's sexual desires also appear to be more sensitive than do men's to experiences of emotional bonding. Some heterosexual women, for example, report having experienced periodic same-sex desires for close female friends with whom they share an intense emotional attachment.

Researchers do not fully understand why this occurs, nor do they understand how feelings of romantic affection are linked to, although distinct from, sexual desire. This is one of the most interesting directions for future research on sexual desire. Other promising areas for future research include how the experiential quality of sexual desire develops and changes over the entire life course, from childhood to late life, and how various biological and cultural factors interact to shape individuals' experiences of desire.

Lisa M. Diamond

See also Erotic Plasticity; Hormones and Behavior; Pornography; Sex Drive

Further Readings

Baumeister, R. F. (2000). Gender differences in erotic plasticity: The female sex drive as socially flexible and responsive. *Psychological Bulletin, 126,* 347–374.

Diamond, L. M. (2003). What does sexual orientation orient? A biobehavioral model distinguishing romantic love and sexual desire. *Psychological Review, 110,* 173–192.

Heiman, J. (2001). Sexual desire in human relationships. In W. Everaerd, E. Laan, & S. Both (Eds.), *Sexual appetite, desire and motivation: Energetics of the sexual system* (pp. 117–134). Amsterdam: Royal Netherlands Academy of Arts and Sciences.

Regan, P. C., & Berscheid, E. (1996). Beliefs about the state, goals, and objects of sexual desire. *Journal of Sex & Marital Therapy, 22,* 110–120.

Wallen, K. (1995). The evolution of female sexual desire. In P. R. Abramson & S. D. Pinkerton (Eds.), *Sexual nature/sexual culture* (pp. 57–79). Chicago: University of Chicago Press.

SEXUAL ECONOMICS THEORY

Definition

Sexual economics theory is an idea about how men and women think, feel, respond, and behave in a sexual context. More specifically, this theory says that men's and women's sexual thoughts, feelings, preferences, and behavior follow fundamental economic principles.

The basic premise is that sex is something that women have and men want. Sex is therefore a female resource that is precious, and hence, women hold on to it until they are given enough incentive to give it up. Men's role is to offer resources that will entice women into sex. The resources that men give women include commitment, affection, attention, time, respect, and money. Note that in this theory, the term *sex* is used rather broadly, to refer to not only intercourse but also touching, kissing, fondling, talking about sex, and other aspects of sexual behavior.

Sex as a Female Resource

Sexual economics theory uses as a starting point social exchange theory, which is an idea about how each person in a dyad gives up something that he or she holds to get something of greater benefit in return. For instance, if a person owns a puppy and a family wants to buy it, then the family has to want the puppy more than the money it will give to the person and the person has to want the money more than the puppy he or she will give up. If both parties want what the other has more than what they themselves hold, then the exchange takes place.

Sometimes one party wants the exchange to take place more than does the other. This situation gives rise to an imbalance in power: The party who wants the exchange less has more control over the relationship because he or she can hold out until a highly tantalizing offer is made. In the context of sexual exchange, men are eager to get sex whereas women are less interested. Women have more power when men want sex, and therefore women should be able to get something valuable in return for giving up sex.

Do men really want sex more than women? The answer is a definite yes. When researchers have reviewed all the findings on men's and women's sexual responses, they have observed a strong and consistent difference, with men (as a group) uniformly liking and wanting sex more than women do. This gap means that men have a stronger motivation to obtain sex than do women, and therefore, they must attempt to persuade potential sexual partners. According to sexual economics theory, men give women resources so that women will allow sex to take place.

This trade of resources in the context of sex has happened consistently enough through eras and cultures that societies recognize that female sexuality has value, whereas male sexuality has no value. Ample evidence supports the idea that female sexuality is perceived as having value. For instance, men's and women's feelings about their own virginity are vastly different, and in line with sexual economic theory. Far more women than men think of their virginity as a precious gift to be given only at the most ideal time. Men, in contrast, far more than women see their virginity as a shameful condition from which they want to escape. Society places positive value on female virginity but not on male virginity.

Another piece of evidence comes from violent relationships. A woman with a violent partner apparently would offer sex to distract or soothe her partner if he seemed to be heading for abuse. In this way, women traded sex with their partners to lower their risk for being beaten. Men with violent partners cannot usually escape victimization by offering sex.

In one international study of the reasons why marriages are allowed to dissolve, wives' adultery was punished far more severely than was husbands' adultery. In fact, in many places wives' adultery was a viable reason for husbands to be granted a divorce, whereas husbands' adultery did not justify divorce. These findings fit the idea that sex is a female resource that, in this case, is traded in exchange for being married. When a woman has sex outside her marriage, she is in effect giving away something that the husband considers his.

In one graphic illustration, women prisoners in Australia who had to endure public floggings could have the amount of punishment cut in half if they agreed to be whipped naked to please the male onlookers. Male prisoners were not given any sex-related options as trade for a reduced punishment.

Last, and more germane to the current analysis, recent research reveals that being around sexual cues prompts men to give up monetary resources. When men saw photos of scantily clad women (versus land-scape scenes) or they felt bras (versus T-shirts), they were willing to part with monetary resources.

Hence, psychological experiments and historical records show that men trade resources to convince women to be sexual. These patterns spring from men's stronger motivation to obtain sex than women's, which leads men to offer women resources in the hope that they will respond favorably and offer sex.

At What Price?

Women, in general, want to obtain many, high-quality resources in exchange for providing sex. Men, on the other hand, want to get sex without having to give up much. So, in other language, women want to set a high price, but men only want to pay a low price. The actual price, the going rate, is influenced by what others in a given community are doing. For instance, if women in a given community wait until they receive an engagement ring before they have any sexual inter-actions with their partners, then a specific woman has a good chance of getting her partner to give her a ring before she agrees to sex. However, if the women in the area collectively give sex away cheaply, then any one woman who wants to receive a marriage proposal and ring before having sex will likely be unable to ask such a high price. Seen this way, women are sellers, and according to basic economic principles, sellers compete with each other. The more competition among women, the lower the prices for the men. However, to curb this downward trend in prices, women exert pressure on each other to keep the price of sex high. Women do this mainly through social punishment (via rumors, interpersonal exclusion, etc.) of women who offer cheap sex.

Men want the opposite of what women want: They want low-cost sex. Men would prefer to get sex with-out giving up money, commitment, affection, or time—or at least, to give up these resources when they want to, not only when they want sex. Just like bidders in an online auction, men as buyers at times compete with other men to get sex from a specific woman. In an opposite fashion to what happens with female com-petition, male competition results in the woman being able to command a higher price.

How do people know what others in the local mar-ket are doing and for what price? Often, they do not know, although gossip about the sex acts of one's neighbors and friends are key determinants of what people think is going on. Because people often do not have direct knowledge of the going rate for sex in their community, perceptions of norms become important. Men attempt to convince women that sex occurs quite frequently and at a low price, and women claim that sex happens much less frequently and only after appropriate resources have been exchanged. This amounts to each partner portraying sexual norms in line with a price level they prefer.

In sum, sexual economics theory is a way of explaining heterosexual sexual interactions. Women sell sex (so to speak) and men buy sex, and in doing so they are exchanging valuable resources. Women give sexual access to men after men have given them money, commitment, affection, respect, or time. It seems crude to think about sexual relations in this way, but sexual economics theory demonstrates that basic economic tenets can explain men's and women's negotiations about whether to have sex.

Kathleen D. Vohs

See also Sex Drive; Sexual Desire; Social Exchange Theory

Further Readings

Baumeister, R. F., & Vohs, K. D. (2004). Sexual economics: Sex as female resource for social exchange in heterosexual interactions. *Personality and Social Psychology Review, 8,* 339–363.

SEXUAL HARASSMENT

Definition

The term *sexual harassment* came into use in the U.S. federal courts in the 1970s to describe a form of gender-based discrimination in the workplace. There are two legally recognized forms of workplace sexual harassment: quid pro quo and hostile environment sexual harassment. In quid pro quo, unwanted sex or gender-related behavior constitutes a term or condition of employment or advancement at work. For example, an employer might require employees to tolerate the employer's sexual advances to maintain employment or gain promotions. In hostile environment, unwelcome sex or gender-related behavior creates an intimidating, hostile, or offensive work environment. For example, employees might be offended by their coworkers' displays of pornography in the workplace. U.S. law also recognizes sexual harassment as a form of discrimination in academic settings and in obtaining fair housing. Although U.S. law does not stipulate the gender of either perpetrator or target of sexual harassment, most perpetrators historically have been male and most targets have been female. Central to the legal definition of sexual harassment is the notion that sexual harassment is unwelcome or unwanted behavior. Whether a behavior is deemed unwelcome ultimately depends on the interpretations made by the target of the behavior. In discerning whether something constitutes sexual harassment, U.S. courts consider whether a reasonable person similar to the target would judge such a behavior to be unwelcome under similar circumstances. Internationally, there are variations in both the legal and lay understanding of sexual harassment across countries. However, since the term was first coined in the United States, the meaning of sexual harassment in other countries has generally been influenced by its roots in the U.S. legal system.

Research

Most of the early studies of sexual harassment within social science were primarily aimed at capturing the sexually harassing experiences of women in the workplace. Although different survey researchers have devised different ways of operationally defining sexual harassment, the most common experience of sexually harassing behavior reported by women in the workplace is generally called *gender harassment.*

Gender harassment is essentially the overt sexist treatment of women at work. It may include such things as being told that women are incapable of performing a job because they are women, having to endure a litany of offensive and sexist epithets from coworkers or supervisors, or being inundated with offensive pornographic images at work. The aim of gender harassment is not to gain sexual access to the target; rather, it is to express hostile attitudes based on a target's gender. The next most common experience reported by working women in surveys is called *unwanted sexual attention.* This type of sexual harassment may include verbal behavior such as persistent requests for dates despite rejection and nonverbal behavior such as unwelcome sexual touching, conspicuous leering, and sexually suggestive gestures. The third and rarest type of sexually harassing behavior documented from surveys of female workers is called *sexual coercion.* Sexual coercion is essentially synonymous with the legal term *quid pro quo* sexual harassment. It is attempting to use threats or bribes to gain sexual access to a target. As research began to explore men as well as women as the potential targets of sexually harassing behavior, it became clear that even though men were less often targeted, a significant portion of men also experienced such behavior. In addition, a form of gender harassment sometimes called *gender role enforcement* or *challenges to sexual identity* was identified as an experience for men. This form of sexually harassing behavior includes ridiculing men who do not conform to masculine stereotypes. More recent studies have found that women may also experience similar harassment and find it just as emotionally upsetting as men do.

Social scientists have devoted a great deal of attention to the study of factors that influence interpretations of behaviors as sexual harassment. Although women and men more often agree than disagree on what should be considered sexual harassment, women have been found to interpret a broader range of behaviors as potentially sexual harassment. Women and men are less likely to disagree when it comes to more severe behaviors like sexual coercion and more likely to show some disagreement when it comes to less severe behaviors like unwanted sexual attention and gender harassment. Labeling one's experiences as sexual harassment is related in part to their frequency and the severity of the consequences of these experiences. Many people who do not label their experiences as sexual harassment nevertheless suffer from negative psychological effects as the result of having been subjected to sexually harassing behavior. Experiencing sexually harassing behavior at work may be considered a form of work-related stress and has negative consequences on the personal and professional lives of men and women.

Research has found that sexually harassing behavior is more likely to occur in organizational settings where such behavior is tolerated or condoned. Traditionally masculine jobs where men dominate in numbers are settings in which sexually harassing behavior is also more likely to occur. As mentioned earlier, most perpetrators are men, but researchers have found that men vary widely in their proclivities for sexually harassing behavior. Individual differences in basic social cognition processes, such as associating ideas about sexuality with ideas about social power, seem to be correlated with male proclivities for some forms of sexually harassing behavior.

Interventions

Research on interventions designed to reduce sexually harassing behavior has produced mixed results. Although participants in training and educational programs conducted in organizational contexts generally report that such experiences are useful, there is little evidence that the mere experience or even the thoroughness of training actually reduces sexual harassment rates in organizations. In fact, some studies have found increased reporting of sexual harassment following training, perhaps attributable to enhancements of awareness. One possible way that training in an organization can have a positive effect is simply by communicating to employees that management takes the topic seriously and providing awareness of mechanisms for targets to report complaints.

John B. Pryor
Amy Mast

See also Bullying; Discrimination; Sexism

Further Readings

Gutek, B. A., & Done, R. S. (2001). Sexual harassment. In R. K. Unger (Ed), *Handbook of the psychology of women and gender* (pp. 367–387). Hoboken, NJ: Wiley.

Pryor, J. B., & Fitzgerald, L. F. (2003). Sexual harassment research in the United States. In S. Einarsen, H. Hoel, D. Zapf & C. L. Cooper (Eds.), *Bullying and emotional abuse in the workplace: International perspectives in research and practice* (pp. 79–100). London: Taylor & Francis.

SEXUAL SELECTION

Definition

Evolution is driven not just by the survival of the fittest (natural selection) but also by the reproduction of the sexiest (sexual selection). If an animal finds food and avoids predators but can't find a mate, the animal is an evolutionary dead end. Its genes will die out when it dies. This is why sexual selection is so important: It is the evolutionary gateway to genetic immortality. Every one of your ancestors managed not just to survive to adulthood but also to attract a willing sexual partner. Every one of your 30,000 genes has passed through thousands of generations of successful courtship, mating, and parenting. *Sexual selection* is another term for *reproductive competition,* competition to attract more high-quality mates than one's sexual rivals, to have more high-quality offspring.

History and Background

Charles Darwin discovered sexual selection and published a massive book about it in 1871, but sexual selection was usually ignored in biology until the 1970s and in psychology until the 1990s. Since then, biologists have realized that many traits in animals have been shaped by sexual selection, either as sexual ornaments to attract mates (e.g., the peacock's tail, the nightingale's song, the female baboon's bright red bottom) or as weapons for sexual competition against rivals (e.g., deer antlers, gorilla muscles, big male baboon teeth). Since about 1990, evolutionary psychologists have also realized that many human traits have been shaped by sexual selection. These sexually selected traits include (a) socially salient physical traits such as female breasts and buttocks, and male beards, upper-body muscles, and penises; (b) person-perception abilities to judge the attractiveness of potential mates, including their beauty, kindness, intelligence, and status; (c) self-presentation abilities (ways of showing off in courtship) such as language, art, music, and humor; and (d) social emotions such as lust, love, jealousy, anger, and ambition.

Importance

Sex differences in bodies and brains are usually the result of sexual selection. Male mammals can produce offspring just by having sex for a few minutes if they find a willing female, whereas female mammals can only produce offspring if they get pregnant for a long time and produce milk for their offspring. Thus, males can potentially have a lot more offspring than females can. This makes fertile females a much more precious, limited resource than fertile males are. For these reasons, male mammals typically compete much more intensely to attract mates than females do, and females are typically much more choosy about their mates than males are. This leads to many human sex differences that appear across all known cultures, including stronger male motivations to seek status, kill rivals, seduce multiple partners, and take conspicuously heroic risks for the public good.

Yet, sexual selection is not restricted to explaining sex differences. Sexual selection can also explain mating-related traits that are shared by both sexes, including many uniquely human physical traits (e.g., long head hair, everted lips, smooth hairless skin) and mental traits (e.g., creativity, language, social intelligence, moral virtues). Humans can feel lust for other people's bodies, but humans typically fall in love with other people for their impressive minds, great personalities, and social virtues. Or, humans fall out of love with other people because they realize the other people are stupid, boring, selfish, or violent. Thus, human mate choice (choice of sexual partners) depends a lot on the social psychology shared by both sexes, the way people perceive what others are thinking and feeling.

Sexual selection can also explain sexual maturation, the changes from puberty through adolescence and young adulthood, as male and female bodies and brains get ready to enter the mating market. Sexual selection may also be important in explaining individual differences in personality (such as the Big Five personality traits: Openness to Experience, Conscientiousness, Extraversion, Agreeableness, and Neuroticism), which can be understood as different mating strategies that have different strengths and weaknesses. Finally, sexual selection is important in understanding many social psychology topics related to sexual competition, such as aggression, status, self-presentation, prejudice, and prosocial behavior.

Sexual selection is especially good at explaining weird social behavior. If someone is doing something that seems irrational, foolish, bizarre, or risky, it's probably because that person is producing some sort of courtship display to attract a mate, by trying to attain higher sexual status in some subculture that you don't understand. Just as different animal species have very different sexual ornaments, different human cultures develop different ways to compete for sexual status, to attract mates, and to derogate rivals. But underneath this cultural variability, a few key traits are always displayed and considered attractive: physical health and fertility, mental health, intelligence, kindness, charisma, social popularity, and social status.

Geoffrey Miller

See also Big Five Personality Traits; Evolutionary Psychology; Sexual Economics Theory

Further Readings

Buss, D. M. (2003). *The evolution of desire: Strategies of human mating* (2nd ed.). New York: Basic Books.

Cronin, H. (1993). *The ant and the peacock: Altruism and sexual selection from Darwin to today.* New York: Cambridge University Press.

Judson, O. (2003). *Dr. Tatiana's sex advice to all creation.* New York: Owl Books.

Miller, G. F. (2000). *The mating mind: How sexual choice shaped the evolution of human nature.* New York: Doubleday.

Ridley, M. (2003). *The red queen: Sex and the evolution of human nature.* New York: HarperPerennial.

SEXUAL STRATEGIES THEORY

Definition

Strategies are the means people use to achieve goals. If the goal is to obtain food, for example, one strategy might be to hunt, another strategy to gather, and a third strategy to scavenge. Sexual strategies are the means people use to achieve sexual or mating goals. Humans have evolved a menu of sexual strategies that includes, at a minimum, short-term and long-term mating. The sexes differ sharply in the adaptive problems they must solve to carry out each strategy successfully and so have evolved profoundly different sexual psychologies. Nonetheless, they share a universal emotion of love, which unites their reproductive interests in mutually produced children and reveals a feature of human sexual strategies that they profoundly share.

Critical Variables

The sexual strategies theory begins with two critical variables that heavily influence sexual or mating behavior. The first is the temporal variable (time span), which ranges from short-term at one end to long-term mating at the other. Short-term mating has been given many names: one-night stands, hooking up, brief affairs, temporary liaisons. Long-term mating typically involves a prolonged commitment to one mate during a period of years, decades, or a lifetime. The ends of this temporal dimension are anchored using the descriptively neutral terms *short-term mating* and *long-term mating*. Matings of intermediate duration, such as dating, going steady, brief marriages, and intermediate-length affairs, fall between these points. Before the advent of sexual strategies theory in 1993, theories designed to explain human mating focused nearly exclusively on long-term mating and neglected the fact that short-term mating is a common sexual strategy across most cultures.

The second critical variable that forms the foundation of sexual strategies theory is biological sex—whether one is male or female. Biological sex becomes critical to human mating because men and women have recurrently faced profoundly different adaptive mating problems. These recurrently different problems stem from sexual asymmetries in human reproductive biology. Fertilization occurs internally within women, not within men; this has created an adaptive problem for men that no woman has ever faced—the problem of paternity uncertainty. Men never know if they are the biological fathers of their children. Women always know that they are the biological mothers.

Internal female fertilization also creates a critical adaptive problem for women: the selection of which male will fertilize her eggs. Women, not men, bear the metabolic costs of pregnancy and breast-feeding. This has rendered women, the high-investing sex, an extraordinarily valuable reproductive resource for men, the lower investing sex.

As a rule, across thousands of species, the higher investing sex (often, but not always, the female) tends to be choosy or discriminating about its choice of a mate. The reasons center on the costs of making a poor mate choice and the benefits of making a wise mate choice. The higher investing sex suffers greater costs of making a poor mate choice. A woman who makes a poor mate choice, for example, risks becoming pregnant with a man who will not stay around to help her and invest in her child. She also risks passing on genes to her children that are inferior (e.g., genes for poor health) to those that would occur if she were to make a wiser choice (e.g., genes for good health). The lower-investing sex, in contrast, suffers fewer costs of making a poor mate choice—he can go on to reproduce with other partners, an option the higher investing sex is less free to do.

Another general rule of mating is that the lower investing sex tends to be more competitive with members of its own sex for sexual access to members of the valuable members of the high-investing sex. In summary, considering only the obligatory investment, one could predict that women would be generally more choosy and discriminating than men in their mate choices, whereas men more than women would be more competitive with their own sex for sexual access.

Adaptive Problems and Evidence

According to sexual strategies theory, however, both men and women have evolved to pursue both short-term (sometimes purely sexual) and long-term mating strategies. Sexual strategies theory provides a theory of the different adaptive problems men and women confront when pursuing short-term and long-term mating strategies. This entry describes a few of these adaptive problems and a few pieces of evidence supporting hypotheses about how they evolved to solve those problems.

Short-Term Mating

Consider first the adaptive problems men must solve when pursuing a short-term mating strategy. One is identifying women who are potentially sexually accessible. A second is identifying women who are fertile. A third adaptive problem is providing the motivational impetus for pursuing a variety of different sexual partners. A fourth is deploying successful strategies of seduction. A fifth is minimizing the time that elapses before seeking sexual intercourse. A sixth is avoiding becoming encumbered in high-investment, high-commitment relationships that would interfere with the successful pursuit of short-term mating.

Empirical studies support several hypothesized evolved solutions to these problems. Men pursuing a short-term mating strategy, for example, avoid women who are prudish and are not deterred by women who show signs of promiscuity (sexual accessibility problem). Men typically express a desire for a variety of different sex partners, have frequent sexual fantasies involving different women, and let less time elapse before seeking sexual intercourse (compared with women). Men are more likely than women to lie about the depth of their emotional commitment to seduce a woman. Men who pursue short-term mating experience a psychological shift, such that they find their sex partners less attractive immediately after intercourse—a possible adaptation to motivate these men to seek a hasty postcopulatory departure. The success of short-term mating requires not becoming entangled in a relationship with heavy commitment. In short, men show many psychological, emotional, and behavioral characteristics that suggest that short-term mating has evolved as one strategy within their mating menu.

Women confront a somewhat different suite of adaptive problems when pursuing a short-term mating strategy. For men, the adaptive function of short-term mating is straightforward, a direct increase in reproductive success as a consequence of successfully inseminating a variety of women. Women, in contrast, cannot increase their offspring production directly through short-term mating. Adding an additional sex partner does not directly translate into additional offspring, given their heavy metabolic investment to produce a single child (a 9-month pregnancy). Instead, women can potentially benefit, in the currency of reproductive success, by obtaining at least three potential benefits from short-term mating: (1) obtaining superior genes from a man who is high in desirability; (2) obtaining additional resources for herself or her children, which could be critical in lean times, food shortages, or other evolutionary bottlenecks; and (3) using short-term mating as a mate-switching strategy, either to provide a means for exiting one relationship or as a means of trading up to a better mating relationship.

Empirical studies support the hypothesis that women pursue short-term matings to obtain each of these benefits. For example, women pursuing short-term mating place a greater premium on physically symmetrical, masculine-looking, and physically attractive men, markers of good genes. They also state that obtaining economic and material resources are one of the reliable benefits they obtain from short-term mating. And women dissatisfied with their existing long-term relationship are more likely than are satisfied women to have short-term sexual affairs, using them as a means of exiting an existing relationship or exploring whether they can locate better mates.

Long-Term Mating

Short-term mating, of course, is not the only strategy in the menu of human mating strategies. Both sexes also pursue long-term mating: forming an emotional bond with one partner and committing sexual, psychological, and economic resources to that partner over the long term. When pursuing a long-term mating strategy, however, women and men still differ in several important respects. The sexes differ in their mate selection criteria, what they want in a long-term mate.

Men seeking a long-term mate historically have had to solve the problem of identifying a fertile woman. Men mating with infertile women failed to become ancestors. All modern humans are descendants of men who mated with fertile women. As their descendants, modern men carry with them the psychological desires that led to the success of their ancestors.

How did men solve the problem of selecting a fertile woman? They focused on two important classes of cues known to be linked to fertility: cues to youth and cues to health. Physical appearance provides a wealth of information about youth and health status, and hence fertility status. A study of 10,047 individuals from six continents and five islands discovered that men in all cultures on average place a greater premium on physical attractiveness when seeking a long-term mate, compared with women. Men universally also desire women who are young, and typically younger than they are; in contrast, women desire men who are a bit older than they are. In summary, men's desires in long-term mating center heavily on cues to youth and health, and hence fertility.

Ancestral women faced a different adaptive problem: securing resources for herself and her offspring to increase the odds that she would survive through pregnancy and breast-feeding, and that her children would survive and thrive. Ancestral women who were indifferent to a man's ability and willingness to commit resources to her and her children suffered in survival and reproductive success. Modern women have inherited the mate preferences of their successful ancestral mothers. In the 37-culture study, women indeed placed a greater value on a man's financial status, social status, and cues known to lead to resources: ambition, hard work, and intelligence.

Love

Although there are universal sex differences in what women and men want in a long-term mate, both sexes universally want love. Love is a powerful evolved emotion that helped men and women remain committed to each other through thick and thin. Love helped bond ancestral men and women together, unite their reproductive interests in mutually produced offspring, and is powerfully linked to long-term mating.

David M. Buss

See also Evolutionary Psychology; Love; Romantic Love; Sexual Selection

Further Readings

Bleske-Rechek, A., & Buss, D. M. (2006). Sexual strategies pursued and mate attraction tactics deployed. *Personality and Individual Differences, 40,* 1299–1311.

Buss, D. M. (2000). *The dangerous passion: Why jealousy is as necessary as love and sex.* New York: Free Press.

Buss, D. M. (2003). *The evolution of desire: Strategies of human mating* (Rev. ed.). New York: Basic Books.

Buss, D. M. (2003). Sexual strategies: A journey into controversy. *Psychological Inquiry, 14,* 217–224.

Buss, D. M. (2005). True love. In J. Brockman (Ed.), *What we believe but cannot prove: Today's leading thinkers on science in the age of uncertainty* (pp. 55–56). New York: Free Press.

Haselton, M., Buss, D. M., Oubaid, V., & Angleitner, A. (2005). Sex, lies, and strategic interference: The psychology of deception between the sexes. *Personality and Social Psychology Bulletin, 31,* 3–23.

SHAME

Definition

Shame is one of the most overlooked emotions, at least among individuals residing in Western cultures. Feelings of shame can have a profound effect on one's level of psychological adjustment and one's relationships with others, but these feelings nonetheless often go undetected. People rarely speak of their shame experiences. Denial and a desire for concealment are part of the phenomenology of shame itself. People shrink from their own feelings of shame, just as they recoil from others in the midst of a shame experience. To further complicate matters, shame can masquerade as other emotions, hiding behind guilt, lurking behind anger, fueling despair and depression.

People's tendency to confuse shame with guilt has helped relegate shame to a footnote in psychology's first century. In professional writings and in everyday conversation, *shame* and *guilt* are mentioned in the same breath as emotion synonyms, or (perhaps more often) *guilt* is used as a catchall term for elements of both emotions. Even the father of psychoanalysis, Sigmund Freud, rarely distinguished between shame and guilt.

Difference Between Shame and Guilt

Numerous psychologists and anthropologists have attempted to differentiate between these moral emotions. Accounts of the difference between shame and guilt fall into three categories: (1) a distinction based on the types of events that give rise to the emotions, (2) a distinction based on the public versus private nature of the transgression, and (3) a distinction based on the degree to which the person views the emotion-eliciting event as a failure of self or behavior.

Theorists who focus on types of events assume that certain kinds of situations lead to shame, whereas other kinds of situations lead to guilt. For example, behaviors that cause harm to others elicit guilt, whereas behaviors that violate social conventions (e.g., burping in public, poor table manners, unusual sexual behavior) elicit shame. Social psychological research, however, indicates that the type of event has surprisingly little to do with the distinction between shame and guilt. When people are asked to describe personal shame and personal guilt experiences, most types of events (e.g., lying, cheating, stealing, sex, failing to help another, disobeying parents) are cited by some people in connection with feelings of shame and by other people in connection with guilt. Some evidence indicates that shame is evoked by a broader range of situations including both moral and nonmoral failures and transgressions (e.g., harming others and violating social conventions) whereas guilt is more specifically linked to transgressions in the moral realm, as traditionally defined. But on balance, the types of situations that cause shame and guilt are remarkably similar.

Another frequently cited distinction between shame and guilt is the long-standing notion that shame is a more public emotion than guilt is, arising from public exposure and disapproval, whereas guilt is a more private experience arising from self-generated pangs of conscience. As it turns out, research has not supported this public–private distinction in terms of the actual characteristics of the emotion-eliciting situation. For example, when researchers analyze people's descriptions of personal shame and guilt experiences, others are no more likely to be aware of shame-inducing behaviors than of guilt-inducing behaviors.

Where does this notion that shame is a more public emotion come from? Although shame- and guilt-inducing situations are equally public (in the likelihood that others are present and aware of the failure or transgression), people pay attention to different things when they feel shame compared with when they feel guilt. Specifically, when feeling guilt, people are apt to be aware of their effects on others (e.g., how much a careless remark hurt a friend or how much they disappointed their parents). In contrast, when feeling shame, people are more inclined to worry about how others might evaluate them (e.g., whether a friend might think he or she is a jerk, or whether the parents might regard him or her as a failure). In short, when feeling shame people often focus on others' evaluations, but actual public exposure isn't any more likely than in the case of guilt.

A third basis for distinguishing between shame and guilt centers on the object of one's negative evaluation, and this is the distinction most strongly supported by social psychological research. When people feel guilt, they feel badly about a specific behavior. When people feel shame, they feel badly about themselves. Although this differential emphasis on self ("*I* did that horrible thing") versus behavior ("I *did* that horrible *thing*") may seem minor, it sets the stage for very different emotional experiences and very different patterns of motivation and subsequent behavior.

Shame is an especially painful emotion because one's core self, not simply one's behavior, is the issue. Shame involves a painful scrutiny of the entire self, a feeling that "*I* am an unworthy, incompetent, or bad person." People in the midst of a shame experience often report a sense of shrinking, of being small. They feel worthless and powerless. And they feel exposed. Although shame does not necessarily involve an actual observing audience present to witness one's shortcomings, there is often the imagery of how one's defective self would appear to others—as unworthy and reprehensible.

Motivations and Behaviors Associated With Shame

Phenomenological studies indicate that shame often motivates avoidance, defensiveness, and denial. People feeling shame often report a desire to flee from the shame-inducing situation, to "sink into the floor and disappear." Denial of responsibility (or of the behavior itself) is not uncommon. Shamed individuals are motivated to hide their misdeeds and their very selves from others, in an effort to escape the pain of shame. In addition to motivating avoidant behavior, research indicates that shame often prompts externalization blame and anger. During a shame experience, hostility is initially directed inward, toward the self ("*I*'m such a loser"). But because this entails such a global negative self-assessment, the person in the midst of a shame episode is apt to feel trapped and overwhelmed. As a consequence, shamed people are inclined to become defensive. One way to protect the self, and to regain a sense of control, is to redirect that hostility and blame outward. Rather than accepting responsibility for having hurt a friend's feelings, for example, a shamed individual is apt to come up with excuses, deny that he or she said anything offensive, and even blame the friend for overreacting or misinterpreting. Not all anger is based in shame, especially irrational rage and anger, seemingly erupting out of the blue, has its roots in underlying feelings of shame.

In the extreme, shame can lead to aggression and violence, with tragic consequences. Clinicians and researchers identify shame as a common element in situations involving domestic violence. During the months leading up to the Columbine killings and other school shootings, the shooters appear to have experienced deep feelings of shame. Collective shame and humiliation has even been cited by historians and political observers in analyses of the causes of ethnic strife, genocide, and international conflict.

Shame and Psychological Symptoms

Researchers consistently report a relationship between shame and whole host of psychological symptoms, including depression, anxiety, post-traumatic stress disorder, substance abuse, eating disorders, sexual dysfunction, and suicidal ideation. People who frequently experience shame are at greater risk to develop psychological symptoms, compared with their nonshame-prone peers.

Is Shame Really a Moral Emotion?

Shame is often cited as a moral emotion, caused by violations of important moral or social standards. A widely held assumption is that painful feelings of shame help people avoid doing wrong, decreasing the likelihood of transgression and impropriety. As it turns out, there is surprisingly little evidence of this inhibitory function of shame. Shame is not as effective as guilt in guiding one down a moral path. For example, adults' self-reported moral behaviors are substantially positively correlated with proneness to guilt but unrelated to proneness to shame. Similarly, children with a well-developed capacity to feel guilt are less likely to be arrested and incarcerated in their teens. Shame-prone children are not so advantaged. Among incarcerated offenders, guilt but not shame is associated with lowers levels of "criminal thinking." Together with research linking shame to impaired empathy, denial of responsibility, and destructive expressions of anger, there is good reason to question the moral self-regulatory function of shame.

Adaptive Functions of Shame

The theory and research reviewed thus far has emphasized the dark side of shame, underscoring its negative consequences for psychological adjustment and for interpersonal behavior. Why, then, do people have the capacity to experience this emotion? What adaptive purpose might it serve?"

Psychologists taking a sociobiological approach have focused on the appeasement functions of shame. In the social hierarchy of apes, shame serves as an important signal to dominant apes that lower ranked animals recognize their place. Submissive, shame-like reactions (hunched posture, downcast eyes) reaffirm the social hierarchy and seem to diffuse aggressive interactions. Dominant apes are much less likely to attack subordinate apes when subordinates signal submission in this way. At earlier stages of human evolution, shame likely served similar functions. It has also been suggested that the motivation to withdraw, so often a component of the shame experience, may be useful in interrupting potentially threatening social interactions until the shamed individual has a chance to regroup. Overall, the weight of scientific evidence indicates that guilt is the more moral, adaptive response to sins and transgressions in a contemporary human society that is more egalitarian than hierarchical in structure.

June Price Tangney

See also Approach–Avoidance Conflict; Guilt; Moral Emotions; Self; Sociobiology

Further Readings

Tangney, J. P. (1990). Assessing individual differences in proneness to shame and guilt: Development of the Self-Conscious Affect and Attribution Inventory. *Journal of Personality and Social Psychology, 59,* 102–111.

Tangney, J. P., Miller, R. S., Flicker, L., & Barlow, D. H. (1996). Are shame, guilt, and embarrassment distinct emotions? *Journal of Personality and Social Psychology, 70,* 1256–1269.

SHIFTING STANDARDS

Definition

Much of people's conversation about others includes descriptions such as "he's very tall" or "she's smart" or "he's really aggressive!" The concept of shifting standards refers to the idea that these descriptions are made with reference to some standard of judgment, and that this standard may shift depending on the person or object being described. How tall is tall? Presumably, standards of tallness—what qualifies as tall versus short—differ depending on whether a man or a woman (or a child) is being described. Similarly, standards for judging intelligence, aggressiveness, or any other attribute may shift or vary for different categories of people. Research on shifting standards has suggested that stereotypes about groups, such as beliefs that men are more aggressive than women or that African Americans are better athletes than White Americans, may lead to the use of different (shifting) standards to judge individual members of these groups. The result is that the same description or adjective label may mean something substantially different depending on whom it describes. For example, because standards for height and aggression are lower for women than men, a woman might be labeled "tall" if she were 5'9" whereas a 5'9" man would not; "interrupting a conversation" might warrant a label of "assertive" in a woman more so than in a man.

Background

Many psychologists have been interested in how judgments are made—whether they involve objects (such as estimating the brightness of lights or the heaviness of weights), other people, or the self. Every type of judgment must be made with reference to some standard, and usually that standard is based on the immediately preceding context, or on what a person has come to expect. As psychologist Harry Helson noted in his theory of adaptation level, a normally lighted room will seem bright if you've been adapted to the dark, but will seem dark if you've previously been exposed to bright sunlight. With regard to judgments of people, a 1986 experiment by Paul Herr demonstrated that an individual may seem hostile if you've recently been thinking about nonhostile people such as Santa Claus or the Pope, but rather nonhostile if you've previously been thinking about hostile people such as Adolf Hitler and Charles Manson. The previous exposure provides the context in which the new target stimulus or person is judged.

Monica Biernat and her colleagues first argued in a 1991 paper that stereotypes about groups function in the same way as other context effects. Stereotypes provide people with expectations about what other people will be like, and therefore serve as standards against which we judge them. If one expects that men have lesser verbal skills than women do, or that African Americans are more athletic than Whites are, the standards will shift depending on whether one is judging men or women, African Americans or Whites. The result could be, paradoxically, that a man is judged even more verbally skilled than a comparably performing woman, or that a White actor is judged more athletic than a Black actor (because standards are lower in each case). But this doesn't mean that no stereotyping has occurred, or even that reverse stereotyping has occurred. Instead, the stereotype gives rise to different standards, which leads people to judge individual members of groups in comparison with expectations for their groups as a whole.

Evidence

To demonstrate that stereotypes lead to the use of shifting standards, a line of research has compared the kinds of subjective judgments people make of others with more objective judgments. For example, when asked to judge the heights of individual men and women (depicted in photographs), estimates in inches provide an objective indicator, but estimates in short versus tall descriptors are subjective (i.e., their meaning is not fixed). A typical finding in research comparing these judgments is that objective judgments reveal that people perceive the pictured men as taller than the pictured women. But when asked to estimate how short versus tall these same individuals are, perceivers generally judge the men and women as equally tall. Presumably this occurs because the standard has shifted: Even though the men are seen as objectively taller, they are not so subjectively tall because standards for tallness are higher.

In another demonstration of shifting standards, judges were asked to view photographs of men and women and estimate either how much money they made (in dollars earned per year) or to estimate how financially successful they were (a subjective judgment). The men were judged to earn more money than the women, but the women were judged more financially successful than the men. Again, because standards for financial success are higher for men than women, a woman could earn $9,000 less than a man and still be considered more financially successful.

Across a wide variety of domains—including estimates of athletic ability and verbal skill in the case of racial groups; estimates of writing quality and leadership competence in the case of gender groups—similar patterns have emerged. Indeed, the signature evidence that standards have shifted is that objective judgments reveal straightforward stereotyping effects (e.g., men are judged objectively better leaders than women), but subjective judgments show reductions or reversals of this pattern.

Evidence also indicates that this pattern extends to how individuals actually behave toward members of stereotyped groups. For example, in one study focusing on gender and athleticism, role-playing managers of a coed softball team favored male over female players in many decisions: Managers were more likely to choose men for the team and assign them to valued positions. At the same time, however, female players were praised more than were male players when they successfully hit a single while at bat. Because expectations for women were low, judges were more impressed by a hit from a woman than from a man.

Implications

Judging others is a big part of social life, and in some settings, such as school or the workplace, the judgments people form may have real implications for their life outcomes. That stereotypes may tarnish these judgments has always been a cause for concern, but research on shifting standards has highlighted that the effects of stereotypes on judgments may be quite complex. Imagine the female softball player who finds herself benched, but patted on the back when she does get the chance to occasionally catch a ball. Or think of the African American employee who finds that he is lavishly praised for completing the simplest of tasks, but is nonetheless passed over for a promotion. This pattern of conflicting feedback must be disconcerting at best. It may also allow judges (the team manager, the employer) to deny the fact that bias is operating. More generally, the fact that standards shift means that the language we use to describe others is often slippery and imprecise. How tall is tall? How smart is smart? That depends on the standard at hand.

Monica Biernat

See also Reference Group; Self-Reports; Stereotypes and Stereotyping

Further Readings

Biernat, M. (2003). Toward a broader view of social stereotyping. *American Psychologist, 58,* 1019–1027.

Biernat, M., Manis, M., & Nelson, T. E. (1991). Stereotypes and standards of judgment. *Journal of Personality and Social Psychology, 60,* 485–499.

Shyness

Definition

Shyness is the ordinary language term most often used to label the emotional state of feeling anxious and inhibited in social situations. As would be expected from a social psychological perspective, situations differ in their power to elicit reactions of social anxiety. Ratings of shyness-eliciting events reveal that interactions with strangers, especially those of the opposite sex or in positions of authority; encounters requiring assertive behavior; and explicitly evaluative settings such as job interviews provoke the strongest feelings of social anxiety. Quietness, gaze aversion, and awkward body language are the most common behavioral signs of shyness.

Emotional State and Personality Trait

Viewed as an emotional state, shyness is an almost universal experience, with less than 10% of respondents to cross-cultural surveys reporting that they had never felt shy. The ubiquity of shyness raises the question of its possible adaptive value. Contemporary psychologists who take an evolutionary perspective on emotional development point out that a moderate amount of wariness regarding strangers and unfamiliar or unpredictable situations may have considerable adaptive value. Social anxiety is functional when it motivates preparation and rehearsal for important interpersonal events, and shyness helps facilitate cooperative group living by inhibiting individual behavior that is socially unacceptable. Moreover, the complete absence of susceptibility to feeling shy has been recognized as an antisocial characteristic since at least the time of the ancient Greeks. Situational shyness as a transitory emotional state thus appears to be a normal and functional aspect of human development and everyday adult life.

For some people, however, shyness is more than a temporary situational response; it occurs with sufficient frequency and intensity to be considered a personality trait. About 30% to 40% of adults in the United States label themselves as dispositionally shy persons. Three quarters of the shy respondents said that they did not like being so shy, and two thirds of them considered their shyness to be a personal problem. Although shyness does have some positive connotations, such as modesty or gentleness, it is generally rated as an undesirable characteristic, especially for men. Recent research supports this negative image of the trait by documenting how shyness can be a barrier to personal well-being, social adjustment, and occupational fulfillment.

Some people prefer to spend time alone rather than with others but also feel comfortable when they are in social settings. Such people are nonanxious introverts, who may be unsociable but are not shy. The opposite of shyness is social self-confidence, not extraversion. The problem for truly shy people is that their anxiety prevents them from participating in social life when they want to or need to.

Individual Differences

One way to approach the distinction between shy people and those who are not shy is simply quantitative: Dispositionally shy people experience physical tension, worry, and behavioral inhibition more frequently, more intensely, and in a wider range of situations than do people who do not label themselves as being shy. There are also qualitative differences in psychological processes. For example, shy people perceive various situations as being inherently less intimate and more evaluative, and they perceive the same interpersonal feedback as being more evaluatively negative, compared with those who are not shy. When they encounter social difficulties, shy people also tend to make more self-blaming causal attributions and to remember more negative details than do people who are not shy.

Research studies of identical and fraternal twins indicate that the temperamental predisposition for shyness has a substantial genetic component. Infants with this highly reactive temperament in the first year of life are more likely to be wary or fearful of strangers at the end of the second year, and they are also more likely to be described as shy by their kindergarten teachers than are children with an opposite, behaviorally uninhibited temperament. Temperamental inhibition in infancy does not lead invariably to childhood shyness. Parents who are sensitive to the nature of their inhibited child's temperament, who take an active role in helping the child to develop relationships with playmates, and who facilitate involvement in school activities appear to ameliorate the impact of shyness on the child's subsequent social adjustment. Childhood shyness is a joint product of temperament and socialization experiences within and outside the family. Retrospective reports indicate that 75% of young adults who say they were shy in early childhood continue to identify themselves as shy persons. Equally significant, however, is that about half of shy adults report that they did not become troubled by shyness until they were between the ages of 8 and 14.

Most of the children who first become shy in later childhood and early adolescence do not have the temperamental predisposition for shyness. Instead, late-developing shyness is usually caused by adjustment problems in adolescent social development. The bodily changes of puberty, the newly acquired cognitive ability to think abstractly about the self and the environment, and the new demands and opportunities resulting from changing social roles combine to make adolescents feel intensely self-conscious and socially awkward. Adolescent self-consciousness gradually declines after age 14, and less than 50% of individuals who first became shy during later childhood and early adolescence still consider themselves to be shy by age 21.

Cultural Differences

Sex role socialization puts different pressures on adolescent girls and boys. In the United States, teenage girls experience more symptoms of self-conscious shyness, such as doubts about their attractiveness and worries about what others think of them, whereas teenage boys tend to be more troubled by behavioral symptoms of shyness because the traditional male role requires initiative and assertiveness in social life. Cultural differences in the prevalence of shyness also may reflect the impact of socialization practices. In Israel, children tend to be praised for being self-confident and often are included in adult conversations, two factors that may account for the low level of shyness reported by Israelis. In Japan, on the other hand, the incidence of shyness is much higher than in the United States. Japanese culture values harmony and tends to encourage dependency and quiet loyalty to one's superiors. Talkative or assertive individuals risk being considered immature or insincere, and there is a high level of concern about avoiding the shame of failure. All these values may promote shyness yet also make it a somewhat less socially undesirable personality trait. In contrast, American cultural values that emphasize competition, individual achievement, and material success appear to create an environment in which it is particularly difficult for the shy person to feel secure and worthwhile.

Jonathan M. Cheek

See also Anxiety; Cultural Differences; Embarrassment; Gender Differences; Genetic Influences on Social Relationships; Individual Differences; Introversion; Social Anxiety; Traits

Further Readings

Cheek, J. M., & Krasnoperova, E. N. (1999). Varieties of shyness in adolescence and adulthood. In L. A. Schmidt & J. Schulkin (Eds.), *Extreme fear, shyness, and social phobia: Origins, biological mechanisms, and clinical outcomes* (pp. 224–250). New York: Oxford University Press.

Crozier, W. R. (Ed.). (2001). *Shyness: Development, consolidation, and change.* London: Routledge.

Leary, M. R., & Kowalski, R. M. (1995). *Social anxiety.* New York: Guilford Press.

SIMILARITY-ATTRACTION EFFECT

Definition

The similarity-attraction effect refers to the widespread tendency of people to be attracted to others who are similar to themselves in important respects. Attraction means not strictly physical attraction but, rather, liking for or wanting to be around the person. Many different dimensions of similarity have been studied, in both friendship and romantic contexts. Similarity effects tend to be strongest and most consistent for attitudes, values, activity preferences, and attractiveness. Personality similarity has shown weaker, but still important, effects on attraction.

Background and Modern Usage

Similarity-attraction research embodies the popular adage, "birds of a feather flock together." This effect has been studied extensively, usually in one of two ways. First, in laboratory experiments, participants are given descriptions of a person they are about to meet. These descriptions are manipulated to vary in their degree of similarity, from very similar to very dissimilar, to the participant's own standing on whatever dimensions the investigator wishes to study. The second method entails correlational studies, which assess the properties of interest in relationship partners, often by questionnaire. The degree of correspondence between partners is then compared with that of random pairs of people, people with a tepid attraction to each other or, more commonly, chance. Years of research have produced such robust evidence that one researcher referred to the effects of similarity on attraction as a "law." In striking contrast, many attempts to find support for a sister principle, known as the *complementarity principle* ("opposites attract") have failed to find more than a highly selective effect in limited contexts.

Why does similarity attract? At least four explanations have received consistent empirical support. First, because similar others are more likely than are dissimilar others to possess opinions and worldviews that validate one's own, interaction with similar others is a likely source of social reinforcement. Second, all other things being equal, people more readily expect rejection by dissimilar others than by similar others. As other research has shown, anticipated rejection usually diminishes attraction. Third, interaction with similar others may be more enjoyable than interaction with dissimilar others, inasmuch as similar others tend to share one's own interests, values, and activity preferences. Finally, fortune or chance also seems to play a part. Because attitudes and values direct much of a person's behavior (for example, people who love

baseball attend more baseball games than people who don't), he or she is simply more likely to encounter others who have similar attitudes and values than others with dissimilar preferences. Obviously, attraction cannot develop between persons who have not encountered each other. Overall, all four of these explanations likely contribute to the effect of similarity on attraction.

People sometimes question evidence about the similarity-attraction link for subjective reasons. After all, when a person reflects on his or her own friendships, he or she often notices the differences more than the similarities. This is probably a healthy part of the process of expressing and accepting one's individuality. However, similarity is relative. When asked to consider the degree of similarity between the self and a close friend, compared with the self and a random inhabitant of planet Earth, or, for that matter, a random person living elsewhere in the same country, state, or neighborhood, the relevance of similarity for friendship usually becomes quickly apparent.

Harry T. Reis

See also Attraction; Complementarity, of Relationship Partners; Rejection

Further Readings

Berscheid, E., & Reis, H. T. (1998). Interpersonal attraction and close relationships. In S. Fiske, D. Gilbert, G. Lindzey, & E. Aronson (Eds.), *Handbook of social psychology* (Vol. 2, pp. 193–281). New York: Random House.

Newcomb, T. M. (1961). *The acquaintance process.* New York: Holt, Rinehart & Winston.

SIMULATION HEURISTIC

Definition

The simulation heuristic focuses on what occurs after a person has experienced an event in his or her life. According to the simulation heuristic, a person imagines possible simulations or alternative outcomes to events that he or she encounters. The imagined alternatives, in turn, affect how a person feels about the event in question.

Implications

When faced with questions about events that occur in life, a person may react in many ways. Sometimes a person may choose to put off dealing with the event until later or perhaps even ignore it altogether. However, usually a person eventually comes to confront life events. How a person deals with these situations has great importance for how he or she comes to think about, perceive, and eventually react to the event.

According to the simulation heuristic, one way that a person confronts a life event is to construct alternatives or simulations to the event in question. This means that when a person encounters some events he or she mentally creates other possible scenarios for how the event could have turned out differently. The simulation heuristic also addresses the emotional impact that imagining the possible outcomes can have for a person. Specifically, imagining better alternative outcomes can make a person feel worse about the event that he or she has experienced. Originally, these mental simulations were compared with computer-based programming models.

In the computer analogy, the simulation model can be constrained so that only predetermined contingencies can occur, or it may be limited to a particular outcome. The output of the simulation is the ease with which the person can generate the simulations. The computer analogy is helpful as an example, but it is lacking in many respects. Consequently, it has been replaced by a more elaborate cognitive processing model of event construction that includes an emotional presence.

Although the simulation heuristic may have influence in many situations such as prediction and probability assessment, its influence is most evident in the study of counterfactual influences. Counterfactuals deal with other possible outcomes to an event. For example, imagine a situation in which two people had missed the school shuttle that only runs on the hour. And because they missed the shuttle, they did not make it to a test in a class in which the professor does not allow makeup exams. One person learns that the shuttle had run on time. The other person learns that the shuttle was running late and left just before they got there. Who would be more upset? Most people would agree that the person who missed the shuttle by only moments would be more upset. The reason for this, according to the simulation heuristic, is that it is easier to generate simulations to the event when the shuttle was missed by only moments. And this construction of mental simulations of the event or *counterfactual production* is what leads people to feel more regret about events that they encounter.

Research investigating the simulation heuristic has found that people can create simulations to an event in many different ways, and these simulations can have distinct differences in how people perceive the event. For example, a person could create a simulation that is better or a simulation that is worse than the actual event, which, in turn, may have profoundly different effects on how the person perceives the event. Differences such as these have proven important for understanding many areas of research including planning, decision making, and emotional response.

Todd McElroy

See also Counterfactual Thinking; Decision Making; Emotion

Further Readings

Kahneman, D., & Miller, D. T. (1986). Norm theory: Comparing reality to its alternatives. *Psychological Review, 93,* 136–153.

Kahneman, D., & Tversky, A. (1982). The simulation heuristic. In D. Kahneman, P. Slovic, & A. Tversky (Eds.), *Judgment under uncertainty: Heuristics and biases* (pp. 201–208). New York: Cambridge University Press.

Simultaneous Choice

Definition

The term *simultaneous choice* is mostly used in contrast to sequential choice. Both terms refer to the selection of a series of items for subsequent consumption, for example, when selecting a set of three soft drinks to be consumed one per day during the next three days. Simultaneous choice is the choice of several items ahead of time (e.g., selecting all three soft drinks before or on the first day of consumption) whereas sequential choice refers to single decisions, where each item is chosen at the time of its employment (e.g., selecting each of the three soft drinks on the day of its consumption).

Explanation and Details

Simultaneous and *sequential choice* derive from the area of consumer research. Decision outcomes from simultaneous choice and sequential choice tend to differ because of different decision strategies. People choose a greater variety of things when making simultaneous choices rather than sequential choices. For example, a person who is consuming one yogurt daily is more likely to select a greater variety of flavors when buying yogurts for the next week within one shopping trip than when going shopping daily and buying only one yogurt for immediate consumption each day.

Several reasons for this seeking of greater variety in simultaneous choice have been discussed and experimentally tested. When making a simultaneous choice a person tends to overpredict satiation with one item (e.g., a particular yogurt flavor) because of an underestimation of the time interval from one consumption period to the other. The result is the selection of a greater variety of items. In addition, simultaneous choice requires the prediction of future preferences, which are prone to be uncertain. For example, a person's taste might change over time. It seems less likely that a person's taste will change for each variation, so selecting a variety of items is less risky than choosing the same item for all consumption periods. Selecting a series of items during simultaneous choice also requires more time and effort than selecting one item at a time. Determining the best item for each of the consumption occasions within a simultaneous choice is a time consuming and cognitively demanding task. Consequently, selecting a greater variety of items can be a means of simplifying the decision task.

Research examining whether simultaneous or sequential choice is better for the consumer in liking and objective value of items yields no definite results. A simultaneous choice is possibly a better strategy for a simultaneous experience (e.g., choosing a set of interdependent items such as furniture for an apartment) whereas a sequential choice seems to be best for sequential experience (e.g., choosing a set of independent items such as different music compact discs).

Some items that have been used in simultaneous choice experiments include compact disk tracks, gambles, groceries, movies, and snacks.

Anke Görzig
Ursula Szillis

See also Consumer Behavior; Decision Making; Satisficing; Sequential Choice

Further Readings

Simonson, I. (1990). The effect of purchase quantity and timing on variety-seeking behavior. *Journal of Marketing Research, 27,* 150–162.

SLEEPER EFFECT

Definition

A sleeper effect in persuasion is a delayed increase in the impact of a persuasive message. In other words, a sleeper effect occurs when a communication shows no immediate persuasive effects, but, after some time, the recipient of the communication becomes more favorable toward the position advocated by the message. As a pattern of data, the sleeper effect is opposite to the typical finding that induced opinion change dissipates over time.

Discovery and Original Interpretation

The term *sleeper effect* was first used by Carl Hovland and his research associates to describe opinion change produced by the U.S. Army's *Why We Fight* films used to improve the morale of the troops during World War II. Specifically, Hovland found that the film *The Battle of Britain* increased U.S. Army recruits' confidence in their British allies when the effect of this film was assessed 9 weeks after it was shown (compared with an earlier assessment).

After the war, Hovland returned to his professorship at Yale University and conducted experiments on the sleeper effect to determine its underlying causes. According to Hovland, a sleeper effect occurs as a result of what he called the *dissociation discounting cue hypothesis*—in other words, a sleeper effect occurs when a persuasive message is presented with a discounting cue (such as a low-credible source or a counterargument). Just after receiving the message, the recipient recalls both message and discounting cue, resulting in little or no opinion change. After a delay, as the association between message and discounting cue weakens, the recipient may remember what was said without thinking about who said it.

History of Research

The Hovland research gave the sleeper effect scientific status as a replicable phenomenon and the dissociation discounting cue hypothesis credibility as the explanation for this phenomenon. As a result, the sleeper effect was discussed in almost every social psychology textbook of the 1950s and 1960s, appeared in related literatures (such as marketing, communications, public opinion, and sociology), and even obtained some popular notoriety as a lay idiom.

However, as the sleeper effect gained in notoriety, researchers found that it was difficult if not impossible to obtain and replicate the original Hovland findings. For example, Paulette Gillig and Tony Greenwald published a series of seven experiments that paired a persuasive message with a discounting cue. They were unable to find a sleeper effect. They were not the only ones unable to find a sleeper effect, prompting the question "Is it time to lay the sleeper effect to rest?"

The Differential Decay Hypothesis

Two sets of researchers working independently of each other were able to find reliable empirical conditions for producing a sleeper effect. In two sets of experiments conducted by Charles Gruder, Thomas Cook, and their colleagues and by Anthony Pratkanis, Greenwald, and their colleagues, reliable sleeper effects were obtained when (a) message recipients were induced to pay attention to message content by noting the important arguments in the message, (b) the discounting cue came *after* the message, and (c) message recipients rated the credibility of the message source immediately after receiving the message and cue. For example, in one experiment, participants underlined the important arguments as they read a persuasive message. After reading the message, subjects received a discounting cue stating that the message was false and then rated the trustworthiness of the message source. This set of procedures resulted in a sleeper effect.

The procedures developed by these researchers are sufficiently different from those of earlier studies to warrant a new interpretation of the sleeper effect. As a replacement for the dissociation hypothesis, a differential decay interpretation was proposed that hypothesized a sleeper effect occurs when (a) the impact of the message decays more slowly than the impact of the discounting cue and (b) the information from the message and from the discounting cue is not immediately integrated to form an attitude (and thus the discounting cue is already dissociated from message content).

The procedures associated with a reliable sleeper effect and the differential decay hypothesis do not often occur in the real world. However, one case in which these conditions are met is when an advertisement makes a claim that is subsequently qualified or modified in a disclaimer (often given in small print and after the original message). In such cases, the disclaimer may not be well integrated with the original claim and thus its impact will decay quickly, resulting in the potential for a sleeper effect.

Other Sleeper Effects

Although much of the research on the sleeper effect has focused on the discounting cue manipulation, researchers have developed other procedures for producing sleeper effects including (a) delayed reaction to a fear-arousing message, (b) delayed insight into the implications of a message, (c) leveling and sharpening of a persuasive message over time, (d) dissipation of the effects of forewarning of persuasive intent, (e) group discussion of a message after a delay, (f) the dissipation of reactance induced by a message, (g) delayed internalization of the values of a message, (h) wearing-off of initial annoyance with a negative or tedious message, (i) delayed acceptance of an ego-attacking message, and (j) delayed impact of minority influence. Although these other procedures for obtaining a sleeper effect have been less well researched, they may indeed be more common in everyday life than are sleeper effects based on the differential decay hypothesis.

Anthony R. Pratkanis

See also Persuasion; Resisting Persuasion

Further Readings

Gillig, P. M., & Greenwald, A. G. (1974). Is it time to lay the sleeper effect to rest? *Journal of Personality and Social Psychology, 29,* 132–139.

Gruder, C. L., Cook, T. D., Hennigan, K. M., Flay, B. R., Alessis, C., & Halamaj, J. (1978). Empirical tests of the absolute sleeper effect predicted from the discounting cue hypothesis. *Journal of Personality and Social Psychology, 36,* 1061–1074.

Hovland, C. I., Janis, I. L., & Kelley, H. H. (1953). *Communication and persuasion.* New Haven, CT: Yale University Press.

Pratkanis, A. R., Greenwald, A. G., Leippe, M. R., & Baumgardner, M. H. (1988). In search of reliable persuasion effects: III. The sleeper effect is dead. Long live the sleeper effect. *Journal of Personality and Social Psychology, 54,* 203–218.

Social Anxiety

Definition

Social anxiety, as the term implies, refers to anxiety (a feeling of emotional distress akin to fear or panic) experienced in interpersonal situations, such as job interviews, dates, public presentations, or casual social gatherings. Because of the variety of situations in which people experience social anxiety, several specific types of social anxiety have been investigated in the literature, including public speaking anxiety, audience anxiety, stage fright, sport performance anxiety, and physique anxiety, to name a few. Regardless of the specific situation in which social anxiety occurs, the physical and psychological feelings that accompany social anxiety are common to all: butterflies in the stomach, increased heart rate, light-headedness, sweaty palms, and fear.

Background and History

Although everyone experiences social anxiety from time to time, some people experience debilitating levels of social anxiety, so much so that they avoid social situations altogether. The pervasiveness of social anxiety might lead one to believe that extensive theoretical and empirical attention has been devoted to the topic. On the contrary, however, empirical research on social anxiety is relatively recent, with an explosion of research on the topic within the past decade.

Charles Darwin addressed the topic of social anxiety in his book *The Expression of the Emotions in Man and Animals.* In a comparison of shyness and fear, Darwin noted that shyness, although similar to fear is still distinct from it. A person who is shy may not enjoy being around other people, but does not fear those others. Shortly after the turn of the century, the Japanese philosopher Yoritomo-Tashi, in his book entitled *Timidity: How to Overcome It,* examined the topic of social anxiety, as well as ways to combat it.

Darwin's and Yoritomo-Tashi's contributions to our knowledge of social anxiety were largely conceptual. Empirical attention to the topic of social anxiety began when feelings of distress in social situations emerged during the 1940s and 1950s as one of the core dimensions of personality. Still, another 15 to 20 years passed before focused research attention was devoted to social anxiety, fueled largely by the creation of two trait measures of social anxiety: The Social Avoidance and Distress Scale and the Personal Report of Communication Apprehension. With scales to measure subjective and behavioral indices of social anxiety, a flurry of research on the topic began.

Not surprisingly, these initial studies focused primarily on individual differences in social anxiety. With time, however, three other directions for research on social anxiety took root. Some researchers turned their attention to situational determinants of social anxiety. Others focused more on developmental issues related to social anxiety, examining specifically the reasons why some people are more socially anxious than others. A third area of research examined the treatment of social anxiety.

From these studies, several theories developed to account for why people experience social anxiety. The most recent and compelling of these models is the self-presentational theory of social anxiety developed by Barry Schlenker and Mark Leary. According to this model, people experience social anxiety when two conditions are met: They are motivated to make an impression on other people, and they doubt their ability to do so. Imagine, for example, a person applying for a very desirable job. This individual is motivated to make a favorable impression on the interviewer. If he or she is certain that the desired impression will be made, then social anxiety is not experienced. If, on the other hand, he or she doubts that the desired impression will be made, then social anxiety creeps in. Should the person fail to make the desired impression and actually make an undesired impression, a self-presentational predicament is created and he or she experiences embarrassment.

Importance and Consequences of Social Anxiety

The universality of the experience of social anxiety and the array of situations that precipitate it suggest that it plays an important role in interpersonal behavior. Indeed, social anxiety may help keep people from behaving in ways that damage their social images and undermine their acceptance by other people. A person who never felt socially anxious would not care about the impressions he or she makes or would be overconfident regarding his or her success at making desired impressions. The experience of social anxiety may interrupt social behavior and alert people that their behavior may not be making the desired impression. Viewed in this way, the experience of social anxiety provides people with a warning to change the course that their behavior is taking.

Even so, when social anxiety is experienced too frequently, too intensely, or in situations in which concerns with others' impressions are misplaced, it can become maladaptive. Excessive social anxiety can disrupt people's life goals, such as being a competitive athlete or effective salesperson, and impair the development or maintenance of social relationships. For some people, the experience of social anxiety is so debilitating that they simply avoid the social situations that precipitate the anxiety. For example, people may avoid medical examinations, such as pelvic exams, because of the potential for anxiety and embarrassment. Similarly, they may fail to reveal embarrassing medical conditions because of the anxiety surrounding such disclosures.

Individual Differences

Whereas some people experience social anxiety only rarely, others experience chronic social anxiety. Furthermore, for some people social anxiety is only mildly uncomfortable, whereas for others (at least 2% of the population), it is debilitating enough to be labeled "social phobia" according to psychiatric diagnostic criteria. Several scales have been developed to measure individual differences in social anxiety. Some of these scales, such as the Social Avoidance and Distress Scale, measure both the subjective and behavioral manifestations of social anxiety. However, many people feel very anxious in social situations yet come across to others as if they were not nervous at all. Therefore, some other scales were created, such as the Interaction Anxiousness Scale, that focus exclusively on the subjective feeling of social anxiety, independently of how a socially anxious person might behave.

Robin M. Kowalski

See also Anxiety; Embarrassment; Individual Differences; Shyness; Spotlight Effect; Traits

Further Readings

Leary, M. R., & Kowalski, R. M. (1995). *Social anxiety.* New York: Guilford Press.

Schlenker, B. R., & Leary, M. R. (1982). Social anxiety and self-presentation: A conceptualization and model. *Psychological Bulletin, 92,* 641–669.

SOCIAL CATEGORIZATION

Definition

Social categorization refers to the way a person's mind clusters together individuals who share important characteristics. A person mentally groups people on the basis of their demographic features (e.g., sex, age, ethnicity, or religion), personality and interests (e.g., extraverts, nerds), and occupation, to name some of the most common types of social categories. This process has several important functions. It provides a person with a way to organize and structure his or her understanding of the social world. For each meaningful social category, a person is likely to have some preconceptions about what members of the category are like. Rather than having to start from scratch in figuring other people out, a person often identifies the groups they belong to and then makes some starting assumptions about their characteristics, given these group memberships. If you learn that your new next-door neighbor is a lawyer, for example, you can start to form an impression just on the basis of this category membership.

Sometimes a person is provided with categories (as when someone tells a person his or her occupation), and sometimes a person must infer another person's category membership based on observable evidence (e.g., one can often—but not always—easily infer someone's sex or approximate age on the basis of physical appearance). Membership in some categories is based on very clear criteria (e.g., the category "college students" is defined by attending a college), but some categories are much fuzzier. There is no strict criterion for being a nerd, for example. However, a set of characteristics seems typical of nerds, resulting in a mental image, or prototype, of the category. In such a case, putting someone into the category is based more on how much the person resembles one's mental image of that category, rather than on meeting a clear set of rules about category membership. Even in the case in which there are clear criteria, resemblance to a mental image of the category may still be important. A divorced homemaker in her 50s who returns to school to get her bachelor's degree may technically be a member of the category "college students," but perceivers may not think of her as a member of the category because she does not match the common prototype of the category.

Context and Importance

Whether discussing people, objects, or events, categories are essential for mental functioning. Without them, people would not be able to make sense of the complex, multifaceted environment around them. By grouping similar items into categories, the world acquires structure and meaningfulness. This process of organizing and structuring the world into categories involves two related processes. First, when thinking about people who belong in a particular category, one mentally emphasizes their shared characteristics while minimizing their differences or unique individual characteristics. When one thinks of the category "nerds," one thinks about the characteristics that are common to members of the category. Second, one also accentuates, or emphasizes, differences between different categories. When a person thinks of nerds, he or she thinks of the ways nerds are different from other comparable kinds of people (such as jocks or artsy types).

By identifying category memberships, people can make inferences about individual members when they have incomplete information about them. For example, a person might feel confident that the nerd would be interested in going to the *Star Wars* film festival. "Likes science fiction" may be a facet of his or her image of what nerds are like, so once the person categorizes the other person as a member of the "nerd" category, he or she feels confident in making this assumption. Applying typical features of the social category to individual category members facilitates the social judgments people make, but the benefit of this increased facility comes at the cost of potential inaccuracy. Some nerds actually don't like science fiction, some men don't like sports, and some women don't love taking care of children. A major by-product of social categorization is the process of stereotyping. Generalizations will rarely if ever apply to all category members, and in some cases, people might even hold generalizations about social groups that do not even apply to most category members. Social psychologists have identified several ways that people

come to hold erroneous or greatly exaggerated stereotypes about social groups.

Social categorization differs from other kinds of categorization in that the person doing the categorization is also potentially included into the relevant category. Social categorization results in carving the world into ingroups (the groups to which one belongs) and outgroups (the groups to which one does not belong). Because people have a strong tendency to think favorably about themselves, they also tend to evaluate their ingroups favorably. This tendency, paired with the previously mentioned tendency to accentuate the differences between groups, results in another potentially toxic result of social categorization: prejudice. If a person feels that his or her group is superior to other groups, ingroup favoritism and discrimination against outgroups may be common by-products. Given the widespread existence of prejudice and intergroup conflict, from Northern Ireland to South Africa and right around the globe, the potential dangers of social categorization are evident. Social psychologists have been keenly interested in understanding whether social categorization, per se, is sufficient to explain prejudice and ingroup favoritism or whether other conditions must also be present.

Implications

Social categorization is inevitable, as people could not function without some way of organizing and simplifying the complex social world around them. However, social categorization carries with it the risk of stereotyping and prejudice and the injustices sometimes associated with them. Fortunately, there is flexibility in the way people categorize other people. People need not always focus on race or sex or other common bases for prejudice and conflict but can look to shared categories that unite them with others (e.g., "members of our community" rather than ethnic subgroups). And they can emphasize multiple category memberships of others, rather than reducing them to a single dimension (e.g., "intelligent Mexican female actress" rather than just "Mexican"). When people think in terms of multiple categories, they begin to recapture the constellations of characteristics that make each of them unique.

Galen V. Bodenhausen
Monika Bauer

See also Intergroup Relations; Minimal Group Paradigm; Prejudice; Stereotypes and Stereotyping

Further Readings

Bodenhausen, G. V., Macrae, C. N., & Hugenberg, K. (2003). Social cognition. In I. Weiner (Ed.), *Handbook of psychology* (Vol. 5, pp. 257–282). Hoboken, NJ: Wiley.

SOCIAL COGNITION

For thousands of years there has been philosophical debate about what it is that makes humans different from other species of animals on Earth. Whether one believes that humans are just another step in the evolutionary process or descended from aliens, there is no denying that humans are different from other animals. Although many aspects of psychology, such as perception, learning, and memory, can be generalized across species, the field of social cognition deals exclusively with thoughts and behaviors that are (arguably) uniquely human. This is because social cognition is concerned with the mental processes that subserve people's understanding of both self and other individuals. By default, it takes a social agent to know one. For this reason, a great deal of social cognition research has focused on determining whether or not the thoughts people have about other people are driven by the same basic mental operations that regulate humans' understanding of tables, automobiles, and seafood gumbo. For example, are there dedicated systems that deal with information about the social world and its diverse inhabitants?

Social cognition draws heavily on material within cognitive psychology and social psychology to examine the relationship between basic cognitive operations and fundamental social problems. In this respect, work in this domain has attempted to show that, during his or her lifetime, an individual's thoughts and behaviors are influenced by his or her preceding social experiences, but at the same time, these experiences are modified by the individual's current behaviors. This dynamic relationship between cognition and social experience means that social cognition affects almost every area of human existence. To help explain the importance of social cognition in everyday life, this entry will explore what it would perhaps be like to try to live without the capacity to understand self and others. The examples that follow will therefore speculate on what it would be like if you encountered an alien (called Todf) who was human-like in every respect, apart from the fact that Todf has no social-cognitive abilities. Would such a person be able to cope with everyday social situations?

One of the central topics in social cognition is person perception, the way in which people collect and use information about other people to guide their interactions with them. From infancy, humans have an in-built preference for human beings (i.e., social agents) over other objects, and the face is a stimulus of particular interest. Even before humans can walk or talk, they begin to learn the skills of nonverbal communication that provide them with their first interactive social experiences. Within only a few months of birth, human infants can decode facial expressions and begin to make sense of their social world and the people around them. Imagine the problems that Todf would experience if he were unable to produce and decipher the meaning inherent in facial expressions; successful social interaction would be beyond his grasp. Humans constantly rely on very subtle facial cues to determine what other people are intending (e.g., I'm going to kiss you), thinking (e.g., You look just like Pamela Anderson), and feeling (e.g., I love you). People can usually determine from a face whether someone is behaving threateningly toward them, when a friend is entertained by an anecdote, or when a partner is annoyed by one's behavior. Although it is possible to use language to convey the contents of their inner mental lives, frequently people rely on faces to do the talking. Without such a capacity, Todf would be mind blind.

Social cognition allows people to read the faces of other people and enables them to decode the contents of their minds. Imagine the alien Todf in a classroom with children ages 5 or 6 years old. If the teacher pointed out of the window to an oak tree in the school yard and asked the class, "What is that?" they would probably all reply, "A tree." Although answering this question correctly may not seem like a tricky task, without social cognition Todf would probably furnish an incorrect response. He may even be confused as to why tree was the appropriate response. Why not window, bird, leaf, or trunk? The reason that children performed the task with aplomb is because they were all able to read the teacher's mind, they knew exactly what it was she was asking when she pointed her index finger toward the window. This ability to work out what other people are thinking is known as *theory of mind* and is a core component of human social cognition Arguably, the capacity sets humans apart from other species and makes them different. Indeed, without a theory of mind, people would find it impossible to empathize or sympathize with other people. They would never be able to climb into the shoes of another person and experience the world through their eyes. Without such a capacity, successful social interaction would be impossible.

The previous example highlights another important core aspect of social cognition, the observation that social agents continually strive to simplify and structure their knowledge of the world. Children probably possess extensive knowledge of trees and could provide this material when requested. This is because information about the world is stored in extensive networks in memory, networks, or schemas that can be accessed with rapidity and ease. The simplest way of thinking about schemas is to imagine that the brain contains many locked filing cabinets, with numerous files stored within each cabinet. These files contain information, varying in specificity, with respect to the content of the file. For example, when the category "tree" is probed, the relevant cabinet (or schema) is unlocked and all the information is made available. Storing related information in this way enables us to access material just when it is needed most. It also prevents irrelevant knowledge from entering consciousness at the wrong time. Although storing information in this way is useful, it can have some interesting consequences when the files contain information about other people and the cabinets are organized in a group-based manner (e.g., men, women, plumbers, bodybuilders).

One consequence of schema-based organization of information about people is that the tendency to neatly arrange information in this way can lead to stereotyping and prejudice. Stereotyping involves the generalization of specific features, beliefs, or properties to entire groups of people (e.g., if he's a man, he must be aggressive, ambitious, and unemotional). Prejudice occurs when people act on these beliefs. This is one area whereby the alien Todf may, on the surface, appear to have a slight advantage over people. If he did not have the ability to create stereotypes based on his previous knowledge and experience of people, then he would be free from any possible prejudices. People would be treated as unique entities and social interaction would be free from discrimination. However, to form individual, accurate, well-informed impressions of every person he encounters, Todf would require enormous amounts of time and energy. Suppose the alien and a human were both given the task of selling 100 tickets for a nightclub. Armed with

their stereotypic knowledge (or not, as the case would be) of the kinds of people most likely to enjoy dancing, drinking, and falling over, the human may attempt to sell the tickets to students on a university campus. The alien on the other hand, completely clueless about the vagaries of human social behavior, may consider retirement homes as an ideal place to sell the tickets, as there is a captive audience of potential buyers with disposable income. Who do you think would sell their tickets fastest? Although potentially troublesome, generalized beliefs about groups of people can be handy at times.

All of the previous examples have shown the problems an alien without social cognition would encounter when dealing with other people. Several difficulties may arise from another core component of social cognition, an understanding and appreciation of self. The self is generally considered the conscious insight a person has into his or her own existence. As such, this construct gives human life meaning, order, and purpose. People's memories are based on their own unique experience of events, their current activity is construed in a personalized way, and their view of the future is theirs and theirs alone. As the self and consciousness are so intertwined, and because they are at the very center of what is consider to be human, it does not seem possible to imagine an alien that is humanlike but that does not possess a self. Without a self, the alien would merely be an automaton, a robot capable of mimicking human actions but incapable of understanding them. When it comes to being a person, social cognition matters.

Douglas Martin
C. Neil Macrae

See also Attributions; Cultural Animal; Theory of Mind

Further Readings

Baron-Cohen, S. (1995). *Mindblindness: An essay on autism and theory of mind*. Boston: MIT Press/Bradford Books.

Bless, H., Fiedler, K., & Strack, F. (Eds.). (2003). *Social cognition: How individuals construct social reality*. Hove, UK: Psychology Press.

Cacioppo, J. T., & Berntson, G. G. (2005). *Social neuroscience*. New York: Psychology Press.

Moskowitz, G. B. (2005). *Social cognition: Understanding self and others*. New York: Guilford Press.

Srull, T. K., & Wyer, R. S. (Eds.). (1994). *Handbook of social cognition*. Hillsdale, NJ: Erlbaum.

SOCIAL COGNITIVE NEUROSCIENCE

Definition

Social cognitive neuroscience is the study of the processes in the human brain that allow people to understand others, understand themselves, and navigate the social world effectively. Social cognitive neuroscience draws on theories and psychological phenomena from across the social sciences, including social cognition, political cognition, behavioral economics, and anthropology. The tools used to study these topics are also wide-ranging, including functional magnetic resonance imaging (fMRI), positron emission tomography, transcranial magnetic stimulation, event-related potentials, single-cell recording, and neuropsychological lesion techniques.

Background and History

The notion that social behavior and social cognition have biological roots extends back thousands of years to at least Galen in ancient Greece who suggested that our social nature was influenced by the admixture of four substances in our bodies called *humors*. These four substances (blood, black bile, yellow bile, and phlegm) were linked to personality and interpersonal styles (sanguine, melancholic, choleric, phlegmatic). Although the humors have long since fallen out of favor in scientific attempts to understand the mind, the notion that the material body, including the brain, contributes directly to psychological processes has become increasingly important in psychological research during the past two centuries.

Of particular interest to social psychology is the case of Phineas Gage in the 1860s. Gage was considered a socially agreeable and savvy individual until an explosion sent a tamping iron in one side of his brain and out the other. Miraculously, Gage retained his motor skills and cognitive abilities; however, socially and emotionally, he was a changed man. During the years after the accident, Gage made a series of ill-advised social decisions that left him unemployed, penniless, and divorced. By all accounts, his social and emotional makeup was quite different, largely because of damage to the ventromedial prefrontal cortex, a region of the brain located behind the eye sockets. Other cases of neurological damage have also shown neural contributions to social function. Prosopagnosic patients cannot recognize faces as faces even though they can recognize other objects. Damage to a region of the parietal cortex can lead individuals to feel as though other people are controlling their bodily movements. Individuals who have had their corpus callosum severed, cutting off communication between the hemispheres of the brain, will respond appropriately to cues shown exclusively to the right hemisphere of the brain but then provide strange rationalizations for this behavior using the left hemisphere, which was unaware of the original cue. In each of these cases, some social function that humans take for granted is profoundly altered because of localized brain damage.

These case studies have been extremely provocative; however, such cases are rare and thus are not sufficient to sustain a new area of research. Two developments took place in the 1990s that laid the groundwork for the explosion of research that is now taking place in social cognitive neuroscience. First, social psychologists such as John Cacioppo, Stanley Klein, and John Kihlstrom began to apply much more sophisticated experimental methods to brain-damaged patients and healthy individuals using event-related potentials, to test social psychological hypotheses. These researchers used the brain to test questions about what kinds of processes are involved in normal social cognition, rather than focusing on describing what is impaired in brain-damaged patients. Just as other social psychologists use self-report measures and reaction time measures to test their hypotheses, these scientists used neural measures.

The second major development was the use of fMRI to study social cognition. Although neuroscientists used fMRI throughout the 1990s, social psychologists only began to use this technique in the new millennium (although several British scientists, including Chris Frith, Uta Frith, and Raymond Dolan, did use positron emission tomography in the 1990s to conduct social cognitive neuroscience studies). Starting in the year 2000, social cognitive neuroscience research began to grow exponentially in the number of studies, number of topics studied, and number of researchers. Currently, active research programs are examining the automatic and controlled aspects of attitudes and prejudice, theory of mind, dispositional attribution, empathy, social rejection, social connection, interpersonal attraction, self-awareness, self-recognition, self-knowledge, cognitive dissonance reduction, placebo effects, social factors in economic decision making, moral reasoning, and emotion regulation. Many of these topics are in their infancy with no more than a handful of studies attempting to identify the brain regions that are involved in the process of interest. One might remark, "What good is it to know that social psychological processes take place in the brain? Of course they do, so what?" Indeed, if social cognitive neuroscience began and ended with showing which parts of the brain "light up" when engaging in different social psychological processes, it would be of little significance. Fortunately, most social cognitive neuroscience does not begin and end as an expensive game of Lite-Brite.

The Importance of Social Cognitive Neuroscience

In the best social cognitive neuroscience research, the *where* (in the brain) question is merely a prelude to the *when, why,* and *how* questions. Social cognitive neuroscience has many of the same goals as social psychology in general, but brings a different set of tools to bear on those scientific goals. These new tools have several advantages and disadvantages, and although a debate about whether reaction time measurement or functional neuroimaging is a better tool for hypothesis testing may be a useful pedagogical exercise, it ultimately makes about as much sense as asking whether hammers or screwdrivers are better. They are both useful tools for some jobs and less useful for others.

Before turning to what fMRI is useful for, it is worth noting some of the limitations of this technique. First, there can be no face-to-face interactions during fMRI. When subjects have their brains scanned, they lay on a narrow bed, which slides into a long narrow tube, and there is no room for multiple people to be scanned in the same scanner while interacting. Second, because of the nature of the imaging procedure, it is critical that subjects keep their heads absolutely still. As a result, subjects cannot speak while the images are being taken. Subjects typically reply to computer tasks that are watched with video goggles by pressing buttons on a small keypad. Finally, because the signals detected in the brain are noisy signals, many pictures must be taken and then averaged together. This means that subjects must perform the same task repeatedly before useful information can be extracted from the scans. The problem with this is that most social psychological research depends on having a large number of subjects each perform a task once. Many of these tasks will quickly lose their psychological meaning if they are repeated

again and again. For all these reasons and more, many social psychological questions cannot easily be addressed with fMRI.

An fMRI can make important contributions to social psychology in at least three ways: First, sometimes two psychological processes experientially feel similar and produce similar behavioral results but actually rely on different underlying mechanisms. For instance, the ability to remember social information and nonsocial information does not feel all that different, and for decades social psychologists debated whether social and nonsocial information is encoded and retrieved using the same mechanisms. Although no strong conclusions were reached (and if anything the standard tools of social cognition suggested that there were no special mechanisms for social information processing), recent fMRI research has definitively changed the debate. Jason Mitchell and his colleagues have shown in a series of fMRI studies that the brain regions involved in encoding social and nonsocial information are quite distinct. Encoding nonsocial information in a way that could be later remembered is related to activity in the hippocampus, whereas encoding social information in a way that could be later remembered is related to activity in dorsomedial prefrontal cortex. Thus, two processes that superficially seem quite similar and are difficult to disentangle with behavioral methods were clearly distinguished when examined with fMRI.

Conversely, sometimes one would not think that processes rely on the same mechanisms, when in fact they do. For instance, Naomi Eisenberger and her colleagues have demonstrated that social pain, resulting from being socially excluded, produces activity in a similar network of brain regions as the experience of physical pain. Although physical pain words are typically used to describe feelings of social pain ("He *hurt* my feelings"; "She *broke* my heart"), the relation between physical and social pain was primarily thought to be metaphorical. Physical pain seems real because one can see physical injuries, whereas social pain seems as though it's all in one's head. Nevertheless, both seem to rely on similar mechanisms in the brain. Perhaps this overlap evolved because infants need to stay connected to a caregiver to survive and thus feeling hurt in responses to social separation is an effective mechanism for maintaining this connection.

Finally, as more and more is learned about the precise functions of different regions of the brain, it may be possible to infer some of the mental processes that an individual is engaged in just from looking at the activity of his or her brain. The advantage of this would be that researchers would not need to interrupt subjects to find out an individual's mental state. For instance, if a region of the brain was primarily invoked during the experience of sadness, one could know whether a subject was experiencing sadness based on the activity of this region rather than having to ask the subject. This would be useful because subjects may not always want to report the state that they are in, subjects may not always accurately remember what state they were in before the experimenter asked, and because reporting on one's current state may change that state or contaminate how the subject will perform in the rest of the experiment. This is one of the loftier goals of social cognitive neuroscience and is not something that can be done currently with precision; however, this kind of analysis may be possible in the future.

Matthew D. Lieberman

See also Biopsychosocial Model; Social Neuroscience; Social Psychophysiology

Further Readings

Lieberman, M. D. (2007). Social cognitive neuroscience. A review of core processes. *Annual Review of Psychology, 58,* 18.1–18.31.

Social Comparison

Definition

Social comparison involves thinking about information about one or more other people in relation to the self. People may compare themselves with other people for a variety of reasons: to evaluate themselves (e.g., How good at math am I?), to learn from others (e.g., How much did that person study to ace that exam?), and to feel better about their own situation (e.g., I may not be great at algebra, but I'm better than 70% of my classmates), to name a few.

History and Background

Early research in social psychology on level of aspiration and on reference groups contributed to Leon Festinger's social comparison theory, which he proposed in 1954. Festinger argued that humans have a drive to evaluate their opinions and abilities. When objective standards for self-evaluation are unavailable, he said, they compare themselves with other people. According to Festinger's similarity hypothesis, people prefer to compare themselves with others who are similar to themselves. He also noted that people have a drive to improve themselves, which often results in upward comparisons, comparisons with others who are superior to themselves or more advantaged in some way.

Social comparison theory has inspired a great deal of research, but the history of the literature is uneven, with spikes of activity in 1966 and 1977, and then a more steady output since the early 1980s. The theory has been applied beyond opinions and abilities to emotions and to all kinds of personal attributes (e.g., personality traits). Although Festinger devoted much of his theory to interpersonal processes—for example, he proposed that the need for similar comparison with others leads to pressures toward uniformity in groups—social comparison researchers have focused mostly on individuals and their selections of individual comparison targets. During the 1990s, studies of the individual's reactions to social comparisons grew more numerous as well.

Who Is a Relevant Comparison Target?

The most frequently asked question in the social comparison literature has been, "With whom do people choose to compare themselves?" Festinger's similarity hypothesis was ambiguous as to whether similarity concerns the specific dimension under evaluation or other dimensions. For example, guitarists may compare their playing ability with those of others who are similar in their guitar-playing ability, or with others who are similar in more general ways, such as the kind of guitar and music they play (acoustic or electric, classical or folk) or gender. The most informative, meaningful comparisons may occur with others who are similar in attributes related to the dimension under evaluation. For example, guitarists can best evaluate their playing ability if they compare themselves with other guitarists who play similar instruments and who have been playing about the same amount of time.

Considerable evidence has attested to the importance of such related attributes. It is perplexing, however, that the dimensions of similarity need not always be related to the dimension under evaluation to be relevant. For example, people often compare themselves with same-sex others, even if the dimension of comparison has little to do with gender. Similarly, the effects of comparisons are especially strong when they are with others who are similar, even if the dimension of similarity seems to bear no relation to the dimension of comparison (e.g., comparisons with friends are more potent than comparisons with strangers).

Recent efforts to resolve such puzzles have focused on the question that the individual is seeking an answer to, such as, "What kind of person am I?" or "Can I accomplish this task?"

Goals and the Selection of Comparison Targets

A great deal of research has focused on how goals guide the selection of comparison targets. In the 1980s, researchers increasingly viewed the individual not as an unbiased self-evaluator but as a person with needs to feel good about himself or herself. Thomas Wills's downward comparison theory argued that people who are unhappy seek to feel better by comparing themselves with others who are less fortunate or who are inferior to themselves.

This theory inspired a resurgence of interest in social comparison that has not abated. The 1980s also saw a shift toward field research, and considerable evidence of downward comparisons has emerged from diverse samples of people under psychological threat. Women with breast cancer and people with eating disorders, for example, have been shown to compare themselves with others who are less fortunate than themselves.

More generally, the traditional view that self-evaluative motives lead to comparisons with similar others, self-improvement motives lead to upward comparisons, and self-enhancement motives lead to downward comparisons, is giving way to the view that multiple targets can serve one's goal, depending on the comparison context. Individuals also may use comparison strategies that do not involve target selection, such as avoiding comparisons altogether or carefully selecting one's comparison dimensions. For example, breast cancer patients who are disadvantaged on one dimension (e.g., prognosis) may focus on a dimension on which they are relatively advantaged (e.g., "At least I'm married; it must be difficult for single women").

Some researchers have even argued that people may create imaginary comparison targets to serve their goals. This view turns the original theory on its head; whereas Festinger viewed the individual as seeking comparisons to establish reality, this view holds that the individual fabricates reality to serve his or her goals. However, this view is by no means universally accepted.

Another relatively new view that is more widely shared is that people frequently make comparisons without deliberately *selecting* comparison targets. This view holds that people make comparisons by relatively automatically comparing themselves with the others they come across in their daily lives.

Effects of Social Comparisons

The traditional assumption has been that upward comparisons make people feel worse about themselves and that downward comparisons make them feel better, but research has revealed that both types of comparisons can be either inspiring or dispiriting. What determines the impact of comparisons? One important variable is whether the comparison involves a dimension that is central to one's self-definition. For example, a musician may take pride in her brother's superior cooking ability but be demoralized by his superior musical ability.

Additional factors that may determine the impact of comparisons include one's beliefs about one's control over the dimension of comparison and whether one will improve or worsen on that dimension. An upward comparison with a superior other may be inspiring, rather than demoralizing, if one thinks that one will improve and can attain the level of the upward target. In contrast, a downward comparison with an inferior other may be frightening rather than self-enhancing if one fears one will worsen, for example, that one's illness prognosis is unfavorable.

Measurement Issues

Social comparison has been operationalized in many ways, including the choice of another person's score to see, the desire to affiliate, self-reports of past comparisons, the effects of comparisons on mood and self-evaluation, and ratings of self versus others. These operationalizations have yielded results that do not always converge, perhaps partly because they capture different meanings or facets of social comparison. The possibility that comparisons may be made automatically, perhaps even outside of awareness, also threaten the validity of such measures as self-reported comparisons. Social desirability concerns also may inhibit respondents' self-reports; people do not want to appear to be competitive, dependent on others, or, in the case of downward comparisons, as taking pleasure in others' misfortune. Increasingly, researchers have used methods that are more naturalistic (e.g., diaries of social comparisons in daily life) or that offer richer information to research participants than did earlier methods.

Importance of Social Comparison

Comparisons with other people are widely believed to be a ubiquitous (ever-present) aspect of social life. Social comparison is also believed to have powerful effects on such outcomes as people's well-being, their motivation to succeed, their satisfaction with their economic circumstances, and their very identities. Yet, when people are asked how they evaluate themselves and their lives, they mention social comparison infrequently. Although social comparisons might occur less frequently than social psychologists initially thought, it seems equally possible that respondents' self-reports are inhibited by a lack of awareness that they make comparisons and by social desirability concerns.

Indeed, social comparisons may sometimes be more important than objective information. Contrary to Festinger's belief that people rely on social comparisons only when objective standards are unavailable, research has indicated that individuals often want to know their rank relative to others in addition to, or even in preference to, objective standards. For example, a runner who already knows that he or she ran 100 meters in 15 seconds may still want to know that his or her time was the second fastest. And people do not usually regard themselves as smart, attractive, or wealthy unless they see themselves as ranking higher on these dimensions than the other people in their nearby surroundings.

Joanne V. Wood
Karen Choi
Danielle Gaucher

See also Downward Social Comparison; Self-Evaluation Maintenance

Further Readings

Suls, J., & Wheeler, L. (Eds.). (2000). *Handbook of social comparison: Theory and research.* New York: Plenum.

Suls, J., & Wills, T. A. (Eds.). (1991). *Social comparison: Contemporary theory and research.* Hillsdale, NJ: Erlbaum.

Wood, J. V. (1989). Theory and research concerning social comparisons of personal attributes. *Psychological Bulletin, 106,* 231–248.

SOCIAL COMPENSATION

Definition

Social compensation refers to the phenomenon that individuals increase their effort on a collective task (compared with how hard they try when working individually) to compensate for the anticipated poor performance of other group members. People are more likely to compensate when they think their coworkers are not going to perform well and when the outcomes of the group performance are perceived to be important.

Background and History

Many of life's most important tasks can be accomplished only in groups, and many group tasks require the pooling of individual members' inputs. Government task forces, sports teams, organizational committees, juries, and quality control teams are good examples of groups that combine individual efforts to form a single product. Social psychologists have always been interested in whether individual motivation, effort, and productivity are influenced by working in groups. Indeed, the first experiments in social psychology dealt with these very issues, including Norman Triplett's work showing motivation gains when performing alongside other performing individuals, and Max Ringelmann's demonstration of motivation losses when men collectively pulled on a rope. Research in the late 1960s and early 1970s consistently found that individuals tried harder on tasks when they were in the presence of others (who could be either coworkers or audience members), and this effect was referred to as *social facilitation.* Trying harder meant doing better on easy, well-learned tasks, but doing worse on novel or difficult tasks. Research in the 1970s and 1980s tended to find robust motivation losses, a phenomenon known as *social loafing.* The major difference between social facilitation and social loafing was that with social facilitation, individuals were working in the evaluative presence of others, but in social loafing, they were working on tasks in which they shared contributions with the others. As a result, the presence of others implied less evaluation. Still to be demonstrated, however, were conditions in which individuals would work harder when working collectively than when they worked individually. Lay theories focus on *esprit de corps,* in which individuals working in collective groups are infused with team spirit and work harder than they do individually; however, there is little evidence that this occurs. At best, highly cohesive teams were simply less likely to loaf.

But consider a classroom situation in which a teacher divides a class into small groups in which each group works on a project for which they share a grade. Social loafing occurs in this type of situation, but under what conditions would a student feel especially obligated to compensate for others?

When People Compensate

For social compensation to occur, two criteria must be satisfied. The first is that individuals must, for some reason, distrust their fellow coworkers to put forth an acceptable contribution to the group task. This can happen several ways. Some individuals are chronically distrustful of others, feeling they cannot rely on others to do their part. Research has shown that those low in interpersonal trust are more likely to compensate on a collective task. Ironically, high-trusting individuals seem most likely to take advantage of a collective task and let others do most of the work. Distrust can also develop when individuals suspect that their coworkers do not intend to exert much effort on the collective task. Social compensation is likely to occur when coworkers indicate their lack of intended effort. Finally, individuals are more likely to socially compensate when they are led to believe their coworkers lack the ability to do well on the collective task.

The second criterion is that the task must be sufficiently important to the individual before he or she will feel compelled to exert greater amounts of effort. If the task is relatively meaningless or unimportant, then regardless of one's trust level or perceptions of coworker effort or ability, individuals will be most likely to socially loaf. Only if the task is perceived to be important to the individual, and expectations of coworker contributions are low, will social compensation occur.

Limitations and Boundary Conditions

Several factors could affect the likelihood of social compensation as well. The existing research has only examined collective effort in a short-term task (usually less than an hour), in which there is no possibility for exiting the group. Whether individuals will socially compensate for their coworkers if the individual has other options, such as working alone or with a new group, is unknown. Also, even when someone does compensate for coworkers, he or she probably will not do this forever. At the beginning, individuals may be more likely to compensate for others' poor performance, but if their coworkers keep performing poorly for a long period, resentment is likely to build, and individuals may be no longer inclined to compensate. Finally, social compensation is less likely as group size increases. If the group is large, and the outcome of the group depends on each individual's contribution, then it becomes impossible in some cases to compensate for the poor performance of coworkers, and individuals are likely to be unwilling to carry the burden of many poorly performing coworkers.

Implications

The factors that lead to social compensation could conceivably aid in understanding and managing group performance, although not without caution. One possible way to reduce social loafing and promote social compensation is to encourage individuals to value the outcomes of the group performance and to simultaneously suggest that their coworkers may engage in social loafing. This strategy, of course, may work initially but, over time, may backfire and lead to resentment or early exit. As yet, little research has addressed the persistence of social compensation over time. More important, perhaps, is the unfortunate conclusion that esprit de corps is still not readily observed, and that to achieve high individual contributions to collective tasks, the opposite must occur: a general lack of regard for one's fellow coworkers' willingness or ability to contribute adequately.

Kipling D. Williams
Zhansheng Chen
Eric D. Wesselmann

See also Group Dynamics; Ringelmann Effect; Social Facilitation; Social Loafing

Further Readings

Kerr, N. L. (2001). Motivational gains in performance groups: Aspects and prospects. In J. Forgas, K. Williams, & L. Wheeler (Eds.), *The social mind: Cognitive and motivational aspects of interpersonal behavior* (pp. 350–370). New York: Cambridge University Press.

Williams, K. D., Harkins, S. G., & Karau, S. J. (2003). Social performance. In M. A. Hogg & J. Cooper (Eds.), *Handbook of social psychology* (pp. 328–346). London: Sage.

Williams, K. D., & Karau, S. J. (1991). Social loafing and social compensation: The effects of expectations of coworker performance. *Journal of Personality and Social Psychology, 61*, 570–581.

Social Desirability Bias

In the context of participating in a psychology study, social desirability bias refers to the tendency to present one's self in a favorable way rather than to give accurate answers. In other words, participants have a tendency to answer in ways that make them look good in the eyes of others, regardless of the accuracy of their answers. For example, most people would deny that they drive after drinking alcohol because it reflects poorly on them and others would most likely disapprove.

Psychologists have long been interested in people's thoughts, feelings, and behaviors, and have often relied on self-reports to gather information. For example, a person may be asked to indicate which items in a list of characteristics describe him or her. The underlying assumption in the use of self-reports to collect information is that people are experts in knowing themselves. However, researchers recognize that individuals can distort their responses to self-reports in ways that are inaccurate and misleading. Distortion of responses may be to the result of an individual's disposition (i.e., their personality) or caused by aspects of the situation (e.g., the way a statement is phrased). Social desirability bias is one way of distorting responses that has received a large amount of empirical investigation.

In general, social desirability bias can take one of two forms. One involves self-deception, whereby a person provides inaccurate information but believes that it is accurate. For example, reporting that one is better than average on any given attribute could suggest a distorted response that is a subjectively honest response. A second form of social desirability is impression management whereby people intentionally distort responses to appear better than what they are. A good example of impression management occurs in the context of job interviews where applicants present themselves in ways to make themselves appear best suited for the job.

The literature shows that self reports are especially vulnerable to inaccurate responses caused by social desirability. As a result, some researchers suggest alternative ways to collect information such as through direct observation or having others report information about the respondents. However, because self-reports remain an economical way to gather information, one focus in the research on social desirability concerns how best to deal with this bias. For example, evidence suggests that this bias may be reduced through careful wording of questions and the assurance of anonymity. Some researchers take the approach of measuring for social desirability bias and statistically controlling for its influence.

Louise Wasylkiw

See also Impression Management; Self-Deception; Self-Enhancement; Self-Presentation; Self-Reports

Further Readings

Paulhus, D. L. (1991). Measurement and control of response bias. In J. P. Robinson, P. R. Shaver, & L. S. Wrightsman (Eds.), *Measures of personality and social psychological attitudes* (pp. 17–59). San Diego, CA: Academic Press.

Paulhus, D. L., & Reid, D. B. (1991). Enhancement and denial in socially desirable responding. *Journal of Personality and Social Psychology, 60*, 307–317.

Social Dilemmas

Definition

A social dilemma is a situation in which a group of people must work together to achieve some goal that no one person could easily meet alone. However, if the goal is met, all group members, even those who did not help toward the goal, can enjoy its benefits.

This feature introduces a temptation to let others do the work and then enjoy the fruits of their labors after the goal is met. However, this same temptation exists for all other group members, and if everyone succumbs to it, then no one will be working toward the goal: The goal will not be met, and everyone will be worse off than if everyone had contributed effort. Thus the dilemma: Should you do what's best for yourself and hope that others work hard, or do what's best for the group and hope that others don't take advantage of your efforts? Social dilemmas are generally separated into two types: *commons dilemmas* (also called *resource dilemmas* or *social traps*), under which a short-term gain may lead to a long-term loss, and *public goods* (or *social fences*), under which a short-term loss may lead to a long-term gain.

Commons Dilemmas

The commons dilemma has its roots in a famous 1968 article in *Science,* "The Tragedy of the Commons" by Garrett Hardin. Imagine that all houses in a neighborhood have access to a water table. Economically, the ideal strategy for each household is to use as much water as the family desires; all of their needs will be met. However, if all households do this, the water will deplete more quickly than rain and snowmelt can replenish it, and eventually the table will go dry. At that point, the neighbors will have to begin purchasing all their water, which will be a considerable expense. Thus, the people realized an immediate benefit but suffered a long-term loss. If all households had instead forgone some luxuries and curbed their water use, the table could have replenished at an adequate rate and would have lasted much longer, perhaps indefinitely. However, if everyone else is indeed conserving, the temptation will be strong to not do one's part and revert to maximum-use behavior—how much damage can one abuser cause? Unfortunately, this temptation usually proves to be so strong that most people eventually succumb to it, and the resource eventually dies; hence, the tragedy.

Research on Commons Dilemmas

Research clearly shows that people are not good at maintaining a resource over a long period. Psychologists have tried to identify factors that encourage people to be better resource managers. Some of these factors are internal to the person, and some are external. Much work on internal characteristics has centered on social value orientation, and this remains a popular topic. There is also quite a bit of research on situational perceptions. Many have been studied, and a good number seem to be important in the odd situation, but far fewer have broad impact. The best evidence shows that people are generally likely to be conserving if they feel the need to offset overuse by others, perceive conformity pressure to conserve, believe that the resource is inadequately sized, have previously caused (rather than merely experienced) resource failure, and socially identify with the group.

Regarding external factors, research has concentrated on the effectiveness of leader-based (rather than free-choice) systems of resource sampling, under which a single person determines how much of the resource each person receives. Though the leader system is typically more effective at resource maintenance than free choice, group members generally dislike it, so much so that they will abandon it at first opportunity, all the while acknowledging its effectiveness. Emerging evidence indicates that the leader can develop a sense of entitlement and start to claim a disproportionate amount of the resource for himself or herself.

An emerging issue is the amount of information group members have, and how specific that information is, regarding the commons. In real commons dilemmas, group members almost always lack some information about the commons, their fellow group members, or both, and researchers are trying to understand the impact of this uncertainty. A general finding is that people become more consuming as the specificity of commons information gets less, and this is magnified if some people get to sample the commons before others. Early samplers will be especially abusive (and interestingly, people seem to expect this will happen).

Public Goods

A public good is an entity that exists only after a sufficient number of group members contribute toward its provision; hence, the social fence: You must give up something now to experience the benefit later. However, once the good is provided to all members, contributors and noncontributors alike can share in it. Thus, the dominant motive is to let others work to provide the good, and then take advantage once they succeed. This is termed *free riding*. But if everyone responds to this motive, then no effort will be put forth, and everyone will be denied the good. Public television is a well-known example. Stations solicit funds during pledge drives, but everyone can access its shows, so there is no obvious incentive to give money. However, low donation levels will force the station to forgo expensive programs, and as expensive shows are usually the most popular, it follows that everyone will be denied the opportunity to watch their favorite programs. Researchers distinguish between a *discrete* good, which is provided only after a minimum total contribution has been reached, and a *continuous* good, which is provided in proportion to the total amount given. Small amounts of the good are available when contributions are few, and large amounts are available when contributions are plentiful.

Research on Public Good Dilemmas

Public goods have been studied by economists since at least the 1930s, and their work has largely focused on external influences. Psychologists began systematically investigating internal factors in the 1970s. Of these, strong support exists for self-efficacy, and especially criticality, as a key factor. People who believe that their efforts will make a difference in determining whether the good is provided are much more likely to help than are people who do not. The best-case scenario is when people believe provision will fail without their involvement. All else being equal, efficacy goes down as group size increases, so this is a very real problem in large groups. Evidence shows that discussion of the dilemma among group members enhances contributions, though it is not clear why; group identity, promise making, coordination of actions, and normative influence have all been suggested as explanations. Research also supports the value of a sanctioning system for increasing contribution. Under such a system, group members socially punish noncontributing others, usually by criticizing or stigmatizing them. People are also influenced by the knowledge of how many others have already declined to contribute. As that number increases, people become more likely to give, possibly because they feel they do not have a choice, possibly because their sense of efficacy increases.

Other factors have also been shown to influence public goods behavior, but the nature of the influence is not yet understood. For example, a person's wealth is predictive of whether he or she will contribute, but some studies show wealthy people to be more likely to give than poor people (because the wealthy can more easily afford a contribution), whereas others show the reverse (the public good may be the poor person's only means of realizing the benefit associated with the good, whereas the wealthy person may have many alternatives; hence, the poor person has greater incentive to see the good provided). Also, greed is definitely a motivator of noncontribution, though whether it is the dominant motive or secondary to a fear of being exploited by free riders is not clear.

An interesting relationship exists between willingness to accept a leader-based solution and dilemma type. At the start, people in a public goods problem are even less supportive of a leader than are those in a commons problem because the leader will be taking some of their personal property. In the commons problem, the leader simply restricts access to the commons. However, in the wake of a failed public goods problem, people are *more* supportive of a leader system than are those experiencing failed commons management. This is because a failed public good produces a net loss for contributors: Something was given up, but nothing was received in return. By contrast, a failed commons still produces a net gain; the dilemma is simply that the gain is not as large as it could have been. The specific experience of loss seems to be crucial for gaining support for a leader-based system.

Craig D. Parks

See also Cooperation; Interdependence Theory; Prisoner's Dilemma; Social Value Orientation; Trust

Further Readings

Kelley, H. H., Holmes, J. G., Kerr, N. L., Reis, H. T., Rusbult, C. E., & Van Lange, P. A. M. (2003). *An atlas of interpersonal situations.* Cambridge, UK: Cambridge University Press.

Komorita, S. S., & Parks, C. D. (1996). *Social dilemmas.* Boulder, CO: Westview Press.

Van Vugt, M., Snyder, M., Tyler, T. R., & Biel, A. (2000). *Cooperation in modern society.* New York: Routledge.

SOCIAL DOMINANCE ORIENTATION

Definition

Social dominance orientation (SDO) is a measure of an individual's support for group-based hierarchies. It reflects a person's attitudes toward hierarchies in general, as well as beliefs about whether one's own group should dominate other groups. People with high SDO believe that society should be structured in terms of inequality, with some groups at the top (i.e., possessing more power and resources) and others at the bottom. People with low SDO, in contrast, believe that society should be structured in terms of equality, with no single group dominating others.

Background and Importance

Social dominance orientation is based on social dominance theory, which was developed by Jim Sidanius and Felicia Pratto. According to social dominance theory, all societies are composed of group-based hierarchies. Group-based hierarchy refers to the notion that some people dominate others by virtue of their membership in powerful groups, independent of their individual-level characteristics such as charisma and intelligence. These groups can be organized by gender, race, ethnicity, social class, religion, sports teams, or any other social category relevant to the context at hand.

Social dominance theory postulates that group-based hierarchies are reinforced by *legitimizing myths,* or belief systems that indicate how power and status should be distributed among groups of people. Legitimizing myths can take one of two forms. First, they can be hierarchy-enhancing, meaning that they promote social inequality. Examples include racism, sexism, nationalism, and social Darwinism. Second, they can be hierarchy-attenuating, meaning that they promote social equality. Examples include multiculturalism, beliefs in the universal rights of humankind, and socialism.

Hierarchy-enhancing myths justify group-based domination. For instance, a central idea of social Darwinism is that certain groups are at the top of the hierarchy because they are more fit and capable than are those at the bottom. Hierarchy-attenuating myths, in contrast, counteract these belief systems to regulate the degree of inequality in society. Individuals with high SDO tend to support hierarchy-enhancing myths, whereas individuals with low SDO tend to support hierarchy-attenuating myths.

Social dominance orientation is an important measure because it shows that people's general feelings toward social inequality can predict their beliefs about whether their own group should dominate other groups (e.g., nationalism), their endorsement of specific social policies (e.g., capital punishment), and even their choice of occupation or college major. In turn, these beliefs, attitudes, and choices can influence individuals' levels of SDO because they perpetuate

the idea that certain groups should be at the top of the hierarchy, whereas other groups should stay at the bottom. Thus, SDO is both a cause and a consequence of hierarchy-enhancing myths and practices.

Antecedents

SDO stems from at least three sources, one of which is group status or power. Members of high-status groups generally have higher SDO than do members of low-status groups. For example, men have higher SDO than women, White Americans have higher SDO than non-Whites, and heterosexuals have higher SDO than gays. A possible reason for such patterns of SDO endorsement is that groups at the top of the hierarchy would like to maintain their dominant position, whereas groups at the bottom of the hierarchy would like to change their subordinate position. As a result, the former support social inequality and the latter oppose it.

Another source of SDO involves socialization and background. In general, individuals who were raised in unaffectionate families have higher SDO than do those who were raised in affectionate families, most likely because unaffectionate families promote fewer ideas of equality. Furthermore, people who consider themselves religious typically have lower SDO than do their nonreligious counterparts because religious faith predicts endorsement of many hierarchy-attenuating legitimizing myths.

A third source of SDO is personality or temperament. People who are tough-minded tend to have high SDO because they are concerned with group-based competition and domination. In contrast, people who are empathetic and concerned about others tend to have low SDO because they care about cooperation and the reduction of group-based inequality.

Consequences

As noted previously, high SDO is associated with the promotion of hierarchy-enhancing myths, and low SDO is associated with the promotion of hierarchy-attenuating myths. Endorsing these myths in turn leads people to support social policies that either heighten or attenuate social inequality. For instance, hierarchy-enhancing myths trigger favorable attitudes toward war, the military, and capital punishment. Hierarchy-attenuating myths, on the other hand, induce favorable attitudes toward affirmative action, women's rights, and gay rights.

In addition to predicting endorsement of legitimizing myths and social policies, SDO predicts selection into particular organizational roles. To illustrate, police recruits and law students have higher SDO than do public defenders and psychology students. Presumably, the reason for this is that the former two roles are hierarchy-enhancing and attract people with high SDO, whereas the latter two roles are hierarchy-attenuating and attract people with low SDO.

Importantly, hierarchy-enhancing roles can heighten the SDO of individuals who enact them. In one study, the magnitude of the difference between law and psychology students' levels of SDO increased with the amount of time that these students spent in college. This finding suggests that hierarchy-enhancing roles, such as being a law student, can breed positive feelings toward social inequality. In contrast, hierarchy-attenuating roles, such as being a psychology student, can trigger negative feelings toward social inequality.

Kimberly Rios Morrison
Oscar Ybarra

See also Attitudes; Beliefs; Equity Theory; Ideology; Intergroup Relations

Further Readings

Pratto, F., Sidanius, J., Stallworth, L. M., & Malle, B. F. (1994). Social dominance orientation: A personality variable predicting social and political attitudes. *Journal of Personality and Social Psychology, 67,* 741–763.
Sidanius, J., & Pratto, F. (1999). *Social dominance: An intergroup theory of social hierarchy and oppression.* New York: Cambridge University Press.

SOCIAL EXCHANGE THEORY

Definition

Social exchange theory is a broad social psychological perspective that attempts to explain how human social relationships are formed, maintained, and terminated. The basic premise of this theory is that how people feel about a given interaction or relationship depends fundamentally on the outcomes that they perceive to be associated with it. More specifically, the perceived costs and benefits that accompany a person's interactions determine how he or she evaluates them. To the extent that rewards are seen as high and costs are seen as low, a person tends to feel good about a relationship and will stay in it. If perceived costs increase or perceived benefits decrease, however, satisfaction with the relationship will decline and the person is more likely to end it.

Because social exchange theory is very general in nature, it can be readily applied to understanding a variety of different social relationships and situations. For instance, social exchange principles can provide insight into people's business relationships, friendships, and romantic partnerships, among other types of social involvements. In addition, these principles can be applied to understanding relationships involving individual people or social groups.

Theoretical Background and Principles

Social exchange theory is based on the idea that people seek to maximize rewards and minimize costs in any given social relationship. Rewards can consist of anything tangible or intangible that an individual considers valuable. For instance, business relationships may provide several concrete benefits, such as income or material goods, in addition to several more abstract benefits, such as prestige and a sense of security. Costs include anything that an individual considers to be unrewarding or sees as requiring a significant amount of time or effort. For example, romantic relationships may involve costs such as shared housework and spending vacations with one's in-laws (which, for some people, can be extremely unpleasant). Of course, the evaluation of rewards and costs is highly subjective because that which is rewarding for one individual might not be quite as rewarding for another person. Similarly, that which is considered rewarding in one relationship might not be perceived as rewarding in a different social involvement.

People's evaluations of perceived rewards and costs influence how satisfied they are with their relationships and the relative stability of those relationships. Satisfaction with a relationship is determined by considering one's outcome *comparison level* (i.e., the standard by which one judges his or her current relationship's outcomes). For instance, a person may compare his or her current outcomes with those he or she has received in a past relationship of a similar type. So, you might compare how things are going now with your current boyfriend or girlfriend with how things went with past romantic partners. To the extent that a person's current outcomes exceed his or her previous outcomes, the person is satisfied with a relationship and desires it to continue. However, if a person's current outcomes don't compare favorably to his or her previous outcomes, the person becomes dissatisfied and is less likely to work at furthering the relationship. People compare their current outcomes not only to past outcomes but also to those that they could be receiving now in other potential relationships (referred to as the *comparison level for alternatives*). To the extent that the outcomes people perceive as possible within an alternative relationship are better than those that they are receiving in their current relationship, they are less likely to continue in the current relationship.

Reward-to-cost ratios and comparison levels are subject to change over time, as individuals continually take stock of what they have gained and lost in their relationships. This implies that relationships that a person found satisfying at one point in time may become dissatisfying later because of changes in perceived rewards and costs. This may occur because certain factors may become less rewarding or more costly over time. For instance, sex may be extremely rewarding for members of a newly married couple but may become less so as passion and spontaneity decrease over the years.

Finally, people's perceptions of their relationships also depend on whether the exchanges that occur are viewed as equitable. Equitable or fair exchanges are necessary to avoid conflict between relationship partners. For instance, assume that there is favorable exchange for all parties involved in an ongoing relationship, but one party is receiving substantially greater benefits than the other. Such a scenario may be perceived as unfair because *distributive justice* is not present (i.e., outcomes are being distributed unequally). In this case, individuals with worse outcomes may feel exploited and have negative feelings about their exchange partner, which may ultimately affect how committed they are to continuing the relationship.

Example

A recent college graduate accepts his or her first job with a large corporation because it has an excellent reputation and pays well. At first, the graduate loves the new job. Eventually, however, he or she comes to realize that his or her supervisor does not treat the graduate with respect, and he or she is so overworked that there is little time to enjoy the large salary. The graduate considers leaving the current job and starting

his or her own company. This is seen as desirable because it would allow the graduate to be his or her own boss and set his or her own hours. Then the graduate receives a promotion at work. No longer having to work as many hours and free from the previous supervisor, the graduate decides to renew the contract with the corporation.

Limitations

Social exchange theory is limited in some ways. For example, the theory does not address the role of altruism in determining relationship outcomes. That is, people do not always act in self-interested ways (i.e., maximizing rewards and minimizing costs). For instance, in intimate relationships, people act communally, working for the benefit of their partner or relationship, sometimes even at great cost to oneself. Although evidence for this has been found for romantic relationships, this may not hold for other types of involvements, such as business relationships. Therefore, although social exchange principles have implications for a variety of different types of social relationships, they may explain some types of relationships better than others.

Christopher R. Agnew
Justin J. Lehmiller

See also Distributive Justice; Equity Theory; Interdependence Theory; Reciprocity Norm

Further Readings

Blau, P. M. (1964). *Exchange and power in social life.* New York: Wiley.

Cook, K. S., & Rice, E. (2003). Social exchange theory. In J. Delamater (Ed.), *Handbook of social psychology* (pp. 53–76). New York: Kluwer.

Homans, G. C. (1961). *Social behavior and its elementary forms.* New York: Harcourt, Brace, and World.

Thibaut, J. W., & Kelley, H. H. (1959). *The social psychology of groups.* New York: Wiley.

SOCIAL EXCLUSION

Definition

Social exclusion refers to keeping an individual or group out of social situations. It typically occurs in the context that the individual or group is believed to possess undesirable characteristics or characteristics deemed unworthy of attention. Acts of social exclusion are observed in humans and other social animals. Researchers agree that social exclusion serves a specific function for those who employ it, and that it is unpleasant and painful for those who are denied inclusion.

Context, Importance, and Evidence

Researchers suggest four main functions for social exclusion. The first function is as a way of enforcing social rules. Societies operate on rules that apply to various situations, and if members violate these rules, they are often excluded from social activities. Individuals who break criminal laws are often excluded from society. Children who perpetually ignore the rules of a game are subsequently excluded from future games.

The second function is for the distribution of resources to group members. Most resources are in limited supply; thus, the group must decide which members receive these resources. If members are judged by the majority to be unfit for social exchange, then the majority may decide to exclude those members from social interactions and deny them resources. This often occurs in children, for example, when smaller or less coordinated children are excluded from athletic games. It also occurs on a societal level when laws are enacted that hinder fringe groups from benefiting from governmental programs.

The third function involves group identity, often resulting in justification for discrimination. The need for belonging is an important basic human need; group identity is often a way of fulfilling this need. Group identity categories are formed on biological factors (e.g., race, sex), socially constructed factors (e.g., social class), or personal beliefs and opinions (e.g., religion, politics). These divisions often lead to an "Us versus Them" mentality, serving as a way of solidifying group identity, and keeping dissimilar groups on society's fringes. Young children tend to socially avoid members of the opposite sex, but play with same-sex members. Exclusion can be the first step toward discrimination, which can lead to large-scale segregation and aggression.

The fourth function is to increase the strength or cohesiveness of the excluding group. Social exclusion is used to reduce vulnerability or weakness in the group. In social animals, the member who is weak or puts the group at risk is excluded, thus strengthening the group. The act of excluding can strengthen the perceived cohesiveness and power of the group. Acts of exclusion provide an immediate sense of power, control, and cohesiveness.

Implications

Social exclusion (and related phenomena such as rejection and ostracism) is a powerful and universal social tool. Those who employ it receive some immediate benefits. For those on which it is used, it can sometimes lead them to correct their behaviors so that they can be re-included, but often, it is painful and can lead to depression and, in some cases, aggression. Researchers are actively investigating under what conditions each of these paths are taken, and when social exclusion becomes harmful to the larger group, as well.

Kipling D. Williams
Eric D. Wesselmann
Zhansheng Chen

See also Need to Belong; Ostracism; Rejection

Further Readings

Williams, K. D., Forgas, J. P., & von Hippel, W. (Eds.). (2005). *The social outcast: Ostracism, social exclusion, rejection, and bullying.* New York: Psychology Press.

SOCIAL FACILITATION

Definition

Social facilitation refers to the general phenomenon that physical and cognitive performance is improved when other people are present (and possibly watching the performer). Psychologists use the term *social facilitation/inhibition* to indicate that performance is sometimes facilitated while being observed, and other times inhibited in the presence of others. The critical factor for determining whether performance is facilitated or inhibited is whether the task that the individual is performing is well learned (simple) or novel (difficult). Research has shown that well-learned tasks are facilitated under observation, whereas novel tasks are inhibited under observation.

History and Background

One of the first documented studies in social psychology appeared in Norman Triplett's 1898 article "The Dynamogenic Factors in Pacemaking and Competition," which described observational data from competitive cyclists and an experimental study on the speed at which children could spin a fishing reel. Triplett demonstrated that competitive cyclists paired with other cyclists yielded faster racing times than did cyclists racing against the clock. In the experimental section of the article, children were instructed to spin a fishing reel as quickly as possible to move a figure along a racecourse, either with other children (coaction) or alone. Children in the coaction setting were more likely to spin the reel faster than were those performing the task alone. These findings led to the conclusion that the presence of others, particularly coacting others, improved performance.

By the mid-20th century, social facilitation research had waned. A cursory examination of the literature revealed inconsistent findings regarding how the presence of others affected performance. Though it appeared that performance improved when in the presence of others, not all the data supported this conclusion. Even in Triplett's research, only 50% of the children performed faster when coacting, and among the remaining children 25% performed the same and 25% performed worse when paired with others.

In the mid-1960s, Robert Zajonc published an influential article on social facilitation that brought order to these inconsistent findings. Zajonc argued that the presence of others could bring about facilitated or impaired performance depending on the type of task being performed. When the task at hand was well learned, observers or coactors could facilitate performance, but when the task was novel, the presence of others could inhibit performance. Zajonc argued that the underlying reason for these differences was an arousal or drive component. According to the drive theory, the presence of others evoked an undifferentiated arousal or drive that increased the likelihood of a dominant response. (The dominant response is whatever response is most likely in that exact situation.) In well-learned or easy tasks, the dominant response would be the correct answer. In novel or complex tasks, however, the dominant response is likely to be the incorrect answer. Zajonc's distinction explained the inconsistencies in social facilitation studies and why tasks that involved well-established and fluid responses were improved by the presence of

an audience or coactors, but tasks that required problem-solving skills were impaired.

Zajonc demonstrated support for this theory in one of the classic social psychology studies. Instead of studying task performances of college sophomores, Zajonc enlisted 72 female cockroaches (*Blattis orientalis*, to be exact) to run an easy or a difficult maze. In addition to the difficulty of the maze, Zajonc manipulated whether the cockroach ran the maze with an audience of other cockroaches (the cockroaches were in clear boxes adjacent to the maze) or without a cockroach audience. The final critical factor was whether cockroaches ran the maze alone or paired with another cockroach. Zajonc found that the presence of conspecifics (i.e., members of the same species) as either coactors or as observers (the audience) increased running time in the easy maze, but decreased running time in the difficult maze relative to running times in the alone condition. These findings were interpreted as support for the drive hypothesis of social facilitation, specifically that the presence of conspecifics increased general arousal states and that arousal facilitated dominant responses and impaired nondominant responses.

Zajonc's provocative theory and empirical data renewed interest in social facilitation research and a flurry of empirical investigations followed. As a way to make sense of the many studies, researchers in the 1980s examined all the studies simultaneously (a process called meta-analysis) to extract generalizable constructs and gauge the reliability of the phenomenon. After reviewing 241 studies comprising more than 24,000 subjects, the authors concluded that the presence of others did indeed inhibit complex performance accuracy and decreased speed of responding. Also consistent with the theory, the meta-analysis showed that the presence of others facilitated simple performance speed, but there was less evidence that accuracy of performance increased in the presence of others. This finding could be caused by ceiling effects; performance is already so close to perfect in simple tasks that the additive benefit derived from the presence of others may be difficult to detect.

Why Is Performance Improved or Impaired?

The meta-analysis strongly supported social psychologists' claims that these effects were robust. However, the demonstration of social facilitation/inhibition, though important, does not address the question of *why* the effects occur. What is the process by which performance is facilitated or inhibited? In social facilitation research, social psychologists have focused on three reasons to explain social facilitation/impairment effects. These reasons can be broadly construed as physiological, cognitive, and affective mechanisms. The physiological explanation was discussed briefly earlier—the generalized drive and arousal hypothesis; the cognitive explanation focuses on distraction and attention; and the affective component focuses on the anxiety and self-presentational aspects related to performing in front of others.

Physiological Mechanisms

The drive-arousal hypothesis received some support, using a variety of methodological techniques. In a naturalistic setting, social psychologists examined running speeds of joggers who were filmed unobtrusively as they rounded a footpath. The experimenters manipulated the presence of others using three conditions: mere presence, evaluative, and alone conditions. The experimenters operationalized these conditions using a female confederate placed strategically along the footpath. As runners rounded a bend in the footpath, the female confederate sat with her back to the runners (mere presence), the female confederate sat facing the runners (evaluative), or the female confederate was not present (alone). Only runners in the evaluative condition (confronted with a person watching them run) significantly accelerated their running pace, demonstrating support for the drive aspect of facilitation effects.

Though the studies examining running time were consistent with the arousal explanation, they did not directly measure physiological arousal. Not until advances in the field of psychophysiology (the science of linking psychological states with physiological responses) occurred were social psychologists able to properly test the arousal hypothesis of social facilitation effects. A century after the publication of Triplett's seminal article, social psychophysiologist Jim Blascovich tested the arousal mechanisms that were believed to underlie social facilitation effects. This research found that as Zajonc had originally hypothesized, present others did significantly increase sympathetic activation during performance tasks relative to alone conditions (e.g., heart rate and other cardiac measures increased). However, even though general autonomic reactivity increased for everyone in the audience condition, very different physiological profiles were produced, depending on whether the cognitive task was novel or well learned. Specifically, people completing the well-learned task in the presence of an audience had changes in cardiovascular responses consistent with a benign (healthier) profile. These changes included stronger contractility force of the heart ventricles, more blood ejected from the heart, and overall dilation of the arterioles, which allows faster blood flow to the periphery. In stark contrast, when people completed a novel task in the presence of an audience, their cardiovascular responses were consistent with a malignant (unhealthier) profile that included greater contractile force and co-occurring decreases in blood volume (indicating less heart efficiency), and constriction of the arterioles. This research demonstrated that although Zajonc was correct in identifying arousal as a critical explanation in social facilitation/inhibition effects, arousal is not unidirectional. Instead, while in the presence of others, different cardiovascular profiles co-occur when completing novel versus well-learned tasks.

Cognitive Mechanisms

Evidence for the cognitive mechanisms underlying social facilitation effects are best articulated by the distraction-conflict theory. This theory suggests that the presence of others is distracting and that distraction creates cognitive overload, which restricts attentional focus. This results in different effects in simple versus complex tasks. In simple tasks performance is improved because attentional focus on present others results in screening out nonessential stimuli, leading to better performance. In complex tasks, attentional focus impairs performance because the complex tasks require attention to wider ranges of stimulus cues. Some persuasive evidence for this explanation of social facilitation/inhibition effects comes from studies examining attentional focus as a result of present others using the Stroop task. In the Stroop task, participants are instructed to say aloud the ink color of a word. This task is difficult because the word is a color word printed in an incongruent color (e.g., the word *red* would be printed in blue ink); participants have to say the word *blue*—the ink color—and simultaneously suppress the desire to say the word *red*. The Stroop task thus requires the inhibition of the dominant response (reading) and requires the person to focus on the details of the printed word. In support of the distraction-conflict theory, researchers found that, compared with the alone condition, participants in the audience condition had less Stroop interference, meaning that attention shifted away from the central or dominant response tendency (reading) and toward processing the stimulus details (the ink color).

Affective Mechanisms

A final related explanation for social facilitation effects is one that focuses on the affective responses associated with being evaluated in the presence of others. This explanation emphasizes the importance of self-presentational concerns related to performing in front of others. Some psychologists have argued that the most significant consequence of an audience (or coactors) is that their presence shapes the behaviors of the performer and emphasizes the importance of making a good impression or avoiding a bad impression. To the extent that individuals feel that they can self-present positively while being observed, which they would be more likely to believe if the tasks were simple or well learned, then present others would facilitate performance. If, on the other hand, the task is difficult or novel, the individual may expect to perform poorly. This anxiety or evaluation apprehension associated with performing well may ironically worsen their performance. Persuasive evidence for this idea comes from studies that found no differences in task performance when participants performed a task alone or in the presence of a blindfolded audience. These findings suggest that the ability of the present others to evaluate the performance is critical to social facilitation/inhibition effects.

Related Constructs

Several related constructs appear in the social psychological literature, but the construct most commonly confused with social facilitation is *social loafing.* Social loafing is the tendency for individuals to perform worse in a group setting. For example, when a group of participants was asked to pull on a rope, they pulled with less strength than when pulling the rope alone as an individual. This might seem to be a direct contradiction to social facilitation. However, the constructs can be clearly differentiated. Social loafing is more likely to occur when the task performance is evaluated at a group level. Therefore, any one individual's performance cannot be evaluated. In contrast,

social facilitation occurs when an individual's performance can be directly evaluated and the performance is unambiguously related back to the individual.

Implications

Unlike other contemporary psychological theories, social facilitation/inhibition theory predicts changes in performance in both physical and cognitive domains. The utility and application of these findings are relevant to educational settings, sports psychology, and organizational behavior, to name a few. Implications from this theory are particularly relevant to educational settings where the goal is both effective learning and testing of knowledge. Social facilitation/inhibition theory suggests that to increase learning comprehension, one should try to learn new material while alone (in this case, the material being learned is presumed to be novel, difficult, and non-dominant), but one should be tested on well-learned material in the presence of others.

In addition, sports psychologists use the knowledge gleaned from social facilitation/inhibition theory on how to best improve physical performance in observed domains. They can predict that when athletes are competing against a clock or their own time, performance will be worse compared with environments in which athletes are competing against a present other. Similarly, games or events that have spectators may produce better performance than do games with no spectators. An interesting application of the theory is the *championship choke,* which suggests that the home field advantage may actually be a disadvantage. Related to the affective mechanisms of social facilitation, Roy Baumeister has argued that competing in the most important games in the presence of a home crowd increases one's level of self-awareness, which would not be the case for the visiting team. This increased self-consciousness, like social inhibition effects, can produce worse performance.

On some occasions, dominant responses are unhealthy, and presence of others may encourage these responses. Social facilitation has been applied to the study of activities such as teenage drinking, drug use, overeating, and even acting with more prejudice. In a recent study, psychologists showed that people most concerned about appearing prejudiced acted more prejudiced with others present than when alone. The authors argued that observers decreased cognitive control, resulting in more (unintended) prejudice. In other words, observers facilitated biases and prejudice.

The presence of evaluative others affects one's performance, for better or worse. Whether the effect is positive (better test scores, more touchdowns) or negative (forgetting lines during a presentation, dropping a pass on a football field) depends on whether the task is familiar or novel, the nature of the audience (friendly or hostile, friends or strangers), and one's physiological responses (benign or maladaptive).

Wendy Berry Mendes

See also Choking Under Pressure; Self-Presentation; Social Compensation; Social Loafing

Further Readings

Blascovich, J., Mendes, W. B., Hunter, S., & Salomon, K. (1999). Social facilitation as challenge and threat. *Journal of Personality and Social Psychology, 77,* 68–77.

Bond, C. F., & Titus, L. J. (1983). Social facilitation: A meta-analysis of 241 studies. *Psychological Bulletin, 94,* 265–292.

Geen, R. G. (1991). Social motivation. *Annual Review of Psychology, 42,* 377–399.

Harkins, S. G. (1987). Social loafing and social facilitation. *Journal of Experimental Social Psychology, 23,* 1–18.

Huguet, P., Galvaing, M. P., Monteil, J. M., & Dumas, F. (1999). Social presence effects in the Stroop task: Further evidence for an attentional view of social facilitation. *Journal of Personality and Social Psychology, 77,* 1011–1025.

Triplett, N. (1898). The dynamogenic factors in pacemaking and competition. *American Journal of Psychology, 9,* 507–533.

Zajonc, R. B., Heingartner, A., & Herman, E. M. (1969). Social enhancement and impairment of performance in the cockroach. *Journal of Personality and Social Psychology, 13,* 83–92.

SOCIAL IDENTITY THEORY

Definition and History

Social identity theory explains how the self-concept is associated with group membership and group and intergroup behavior. It defines group membership in terms of people's identification, definition, and evaluation of themselves as members of a group (social identity) and specifies cognitive, social interactive and societal processes that interact to produce typical group phenomena.

Originating in the work of Henri Tajfel in the late 1960s and collaboration with John Turner in the 1970s, social identity theory has a number of different conceptual foci. The two most significant are the social identity theory of intergroup relations and the social identity theory of the group, the latter called *self-categorization theory.* Social identity theory has developed to become one of social psychology's most significant and extensively cited analyses of intergroup and group phenomena, for example, prejudice, discrimination, stereotyping, cooperation and competition, conformity, norms, group decision making, leadership, and deviance.

How People Represent Themselves

People have a repertoire of different ways to conceive of themselves; they have many different identities that can be classified as personal identities or social identities. Personal identities are definitions and evaluations of oneself in terms of idiosyncratic personal attributes (e.g., generous, shy), and one's personal relationships (e.g., X's friend, Y's spouse). Social identities are definitions and evaluations of oneself in terms of the attributes of specific groups to which one belongs (e.g., male, nurse, Hindu). Personal identity is tied to the personal self and associated with interpersonal or idiosyncratic individual behaviors; social identity is tied to the collective self and associated with group and intergroup behaviors. Recently, theorists have argued that in some cultures, social identity rests more on networks of relations within a group and is thus associated with the relational self.

How People Represent Groups

Human groups are social categories that people mentally represent as *prototypes,* complex (fuzzy) sets of interrelated attributes that capture similarities within groups and differences between groups. Prototypes maximize *entitativity* (the extent to which a group is a distinct entity) and optimize *metacontrast* (the extent to which there is similarity within and difference between groups). If someone says to you, "Norwegian," what comes immediately to mind is your prototype of that national group. Overwhelmingly, people make binary categorizations in which one of the categories is the group that they are in, the ingroup. Thus, prototypes not only capture similarities within the ingroup but also accentuate differences between a person's group and a specific outgroup. Ingroup prototypes can therefore change as a function of which outgroup you are comparing your group to. In this way, prototypes are context dependent.

Categorization and Depersonalization

The process of categorizing someone has predictable consequences. Rather than seeing that person as an idiosyncratic individual, you see him or her through the lens of the prototype; the person becomes depersonalized. Prototype-based perception of outgroup members is more commonly called *stereotyping;* you view them as being similar to one another and all having outgroup attributes. You can also depersonalize ingroup members and yourself in exactly the same way. When you categorize yourself, you view yourself in terms of the defining attributes of the ingroup (self-stereotyping), and, because prototypes describe and prescribe group-appropriate ways to think, feel, and behave, you think, feel, and behave group prototypically. In this way, self-categorization produces normative behavior among members of a group.

Feelings for Group Members

Social categorization affects how you feel toward other people. Feelings are governed by how prototypical of the group you think other people are, rather than by personal preferences, friendships, and enmities; liking becomes depersonalized *social attraction.* Furthermore, because within one's group there is usually agreement over prototypicality, prototypical members are liked by all; they are popular. Likewise, less prototypical members are unpopular and can be marginalized as undesirable deviants. Another aspect of social attraction is that outgroup members are liked less than ingroup members; outgroupers are very unprototypical of the ingroup. Social attraction also occurs because one's ingroup prototypes are generally more favorable than one's outgroup prototypes; thus, liking reflects prototypicality and the valence of the prototype.

Intergroup Behavior

The tendency for ingroup prototypes to be more favorable than outgroup prototypes represents *ethnocentrism,* the belief that all things ingroup are superior to all things outgroup. Ethnocentrism exists because of the correspondence, through social identity, between

how the group is evaluated and how a person is evaluated. Thus, intergroup behavior is a struggle over the relative status or prestige of one's ingroup, a struggle for positive ingroup distinctiveness and social identity. Higher status groups fight to protect their evaluative superiority; lower status groups struggle to shrug off their social stigma and promote their positivity.

The strategies that groups adopt to manage their identity depend on *subjective belief structures,* members' beliefs about the nature of the relationship between their group and a specific outgroup. Beliefs focus on status (What is my group's social standing relative to the outgroup?), stability (How stable is this status relationship?), legitimacy (How legitimate is this status relationship?), permeability (How easy is it for people to change their social identity by passing into the outgroup?), and cognitive alternatives (Is a different intergroup relationship conceivable?).

A *social mobility* belief structure hinges on a belief in permeability. It causes members of lower status groups as isolated individuals to disidentify from their group to try to join the higher status outgroup; they try to "pass." A *social change* belief structure hinges on acceptance that permeability is low. It causes low status groups to engage in *social creativity,* behaviors aimed at redefining the social value of their group and its attributes, coupled with attempts to avoid (upward) comparison with higher status groups and instead engage in (lateral or downward) comparisons with other groups lower in the social pecking order. Where a social change belief structure is coupled with recognition that the social order is illegitimate, group members engage in *social competition,* direct competition with the outgroup over status, which can range from debate through protest, to revolution and war.

Social Identity Motivations

The group pursuit of positive distinctiveness is reflected in people's desire to have a relatively favorable self-concept, in this case through positive social identity. The *self-esteem hypothesis* draws out this logic: Social identity processes are motivated by the individual pursuit of a relatively favorable self-concept and possibly by the global human pursuit of self-esteem. Research suggests that group membership generally does make people feel good about themselves, even if the group is relatively stigmatized, but feeling good or bad about oneself does not easily predict whether one will actually identify with a group.

According to *uncertainty reduction theory,* there is another basic motivation for social identity processes. People strive to reduce feelings of uncertainty about their social world and their place within it; they like to know who they are and how to behave, and who others are and how they might behave. Social identity ties self-definition and behavior to prescriptive and descriptive prototypes. Social identity reduces uncertainty about who you are and about how you and others will behave, and is particularly effective if the social identity is clearly defined by membership in a distinctive high entitativity group. Research confirms that uncertainty, especially about or related to self, does motivate identification particularly with high entitativity groups.

When Does Social Identity Come into Play?

A social identity comes into play psychologically to govern perceptions, attitudes, feelings, and behavior when it is psychologically salient. People draw on readily accessible social identities or categorizations (e.g., gender, profession), ones that are valued, important, and frequently employed aspects of the self-concept (*chronically accessible* in memory), or because they are self-evident and perceptually obvious in the immediate situation (*situationally accessible*). People use accessible identities to make sense of their social context, checking how well the categorization accounts for similarities and differences among people (*structural/comparative fit*) and how well the stereotypical properties of the categorization account for people's behavior (*normative fit*). People try different categorizations, and the categorization with optimal fit becomes psychologically salient. Although largely an automatic process, salience is influenced by motivations to employ categorizations that favor the ingroup and do not raise self-uncertainty.

Social Influence in Groups

People in groups adhere to similar standards, have similar attitudes, and behave in similar ways. They conform to group norms and behave group prototypically. Self-categorization is the cognitive process responsible for an individual group member behaving prototypically, transforming his or her self-concept and behavior to be identity-consistent. In gauging what the

appropriate group norm is, people pay attention to the behavior of people who are most informative about the norm, typically highly prototypical members and leaders, but also, as contrast anchors, marginal members and deviants, and even outgroup members (*referent informational influence theory*).

Michael A. Hogg

See also Group Identity; Ethnocentrism; Self-Categorization Theory; Self-Concept

Further Readings

Hogg, M. A. (2006). Social identity theory. In P. J. Burke (Ed.), *Contemporary social psychological theories* (pp. 111–136). Stanford, CA: Stanford University Press.

Hogg, M. A., & Abrams, D. (1988). *Social identifications: A social psychology of intergroup relations and group processes.* London: Routledge.

Tajfel, H., & Turner, J. C. (1986). The social identity theory of intergroup behavior. In S. Worchel & W. Austin (Eds.), *Psychology of intergroup relations* (pp. 7–24). Chicago: Nelson-Hall.

Turner, J. C., Hogg, M. A., Oakes, P. J., Reicher, S. D., & Wetherell, M. S. (1987). *Rediscovering the social group: A self-categorization theory.* Oxford, UK: Blackwell.

SOCIAL IMPACT THEORY

Definition

Social impact theory proposes that the amount of influence a person experiences in group settings depends on (a) strength (power or social status) of the group, (b) immediacy (physical or psychological distance) of the group, and (c) the number of people in the group exerting the social influence (i.e., number of sources). Thus, a group that has many members (rather than few members), high power (rather than low power), and close proximity (rather than distant proximity) should exert the most influence on an individual. Conversely, if the strength of the person exposed to the social influence (i.e., target) increases, the immediacy of the group decreases, or if the number of targets increases, the amount of influence exerted by the group on the individual decreases. The theory therefore has direct applications to persuasion and obedience.

Social impact theory differs from other models of social influence by incorporating strength and immediacy, instead of relying exclusively on the number of sources. Although criticisms have been raised, the theory was (and continues to be) important for the study of group influence. Reformulating social impact theory to accommodate the influence of targets on sources (i.e., dynamic social impact theory) has further increased its validity and range of explainable phenomena. Furthermore, pushing social impact theory into applied areas in social psychology continues to offer fresh perspectives and predictions about group influence.

Tests of Social Impact Theory

Number of Sources

Social impact theory predicts multiple sources will have more influence on a target than will a single source. Research has generally supported this prediction: Many studies have shown a message presented by multiple people exerts more influence than does the same message presented by a single person. However, the effect of multiple sources only holds true under three conditions. First, the influencing message must contain strong (rather than weak) arguments. Weakly reasoned arguments, whether given by multiple sources or not, result in little attitude change. Second, the target must perceive the multiple sources to be independent of one another. The effect of multiple sources disappears if the target believes the sources "share a single brain." The colluding party will in such cases be no more effective than will a single source. Third, as the number of sources grows large, adding additional sources will have no additional effect. For example, the effect of 4 independent sources substantially differs from the effect of 1 source, but the effect of 12 independent sources does not substantially differ from the effect of 15 independent sources.

Strength and Immediacy

The inclusion of strength and immediacy as variables is unique to social impact theory; no other social influence theory includes these variables. Defining strength and immediacy in research studies is less straightforward than is defining the number of sources, but the operational definitions have been relatively consistent across studies. Researchers usually vary the source's strength with differences in either age or occupation (adults with prestigious jobs presumably have more strength than do young adult college students). Researchers usually vary the source's immediacy either with differences in the physical distance between the source and the target (less distance means more immediacy) or, in cases of media presentation, with differences in the size of the visual image of the source (a larger image focused more on the face relative to the body means more immediacy).

Surprisingly, however, these two components of the model have received considerably less empirical investigation than has the number of sources; therefore, the effects of strength and immediacy on influence are less clear. A statistical technique called meta-analysis, which allows researchers to combine the results of many different studies together, has helped researchers draw at least some conclusions. Across studies, meta-analyses on these two variables indicate statistically significant effects of low magnitude (i.e., the effects, though definitely present, are not very strong). Furthermore, strength and immediacy appear to only exert influence in studies using self-report measures; the effects of strength and immediacy wane when more objective measures of behavior are examined.

Dynamic Social Impact Theory

In its traditional form, social impact theory predicts how sources will influence a target, but neglects how the target may influence the sources. Dynamic social impact theory considers this reciprocal relationship. The theory predicts people's personal attitudes, behaviors, and perceptions will tend to cluster together at the group level; this group-level clustering depends on the strength, immediacy, and number of social influence sources. Day-to-day interaction with others leads to attitude change in the individual, which then helps contribute to the pattern of beliefs at the group level. In support of the immediacy component of dynamic social impact theory, for example, studies have shown randomly assigned participants were much more likely to share opinions and behaviors with those situated close to them than with those situated away from them, an effect which occurred after only five rounds of discussion.

New Directions for Social Impact Theory

Recently, researchers have pushed social impact theory outside the areas of persuasion and obedience into more applied areas of social psychology. For example, recent studies have examined social impact theory in the context of consumer behavior. In one study, researchers varied the size and proximity of a social presence in retail stores, and examined how this presence influenced shopping behavior. Furthermore, several tenets of social impact theory seem to predict political participation. One study found as the number of people eligible to vote increases, the proportion of people who actually vote asymptotically decreases. This finding accords with social impact theory, which predicts an increasingly marginal impact of sources as their number grows very large.

Social impact theory has enjoyed great theoretical and empirical attention, and it continues to inspire interesting scientific investigation.

Scott J. Moeller
Brad J. Bushman

See also Attitude Change; Influence; Persuasion

Further Readings

Harkins, S. G., & Latané, B. (1998). Population and political participation: A social impact analysis of voter responsibility. *Group Dynamics: Theory, Research, and Practice, 2,* 192–207.

Latané, B., & Wolf, S. (1981). The social impact of majorities and minorities. *Psychological Review, 88,* 438–453.

SOCIAL INFLUENCE

See INFLUENCE

SOCIAL JUSTICE ORIENTATION

Definition

When, why, and how do people decide that something is fair or unfair? For the past half-century, social justice has been an active area of study for social psychologists. Social justice researchers study both individuals and groups, trying to understand how people make justice decisions and what they perceive and feel about the fairness of others' decisions.

Social Justice Theories

Just-World Theory

Do most people care about justice? Cynics say no and point out people's inhumanity to each other as proof. But Melvin Lerner proposed a theory called *belief in a just world,* stating that all people want to imagine that they live in a just world. Experiments show people's desire to maintain the illusion of fairness often leads them to do cruel acts. If someone receives bad outcomes, others look at the person and believe that he or she did something to deserve the bad outcomes. This belief shields observers from feeling vulnerable to unjust outcomes because they know that they themselves are not bad people, but the process also results in victim blaming.

Distributive Justice

How do people decide that something is just or not? In social psychology, early research approached this question by focusing on distributions, arguing that it is how things of value are distributed that guides people's feelings and perceptions regarding justice. Of particular importance to researchers was equity theory. The central point of equity theory states that every justice decision is determined by comparisons between people. According to equity theory, one person will compare his or her inputs and outcomes to the inputs and outcomes of another. An input is what you put into the situation (e.g., studying for an exam, being smart in a subject) and the output is what you get out of the situation (e.g., the grade on the test).

An example illustrates the process. Imagine that two coworkers in a firm are working equally hard and well on an important project that will determine the amount of their bonus checks. If the supervisor decides to give a big bonus check to one and a little check to the other, the latter employee would likely find the situation unjust and would find the situation more unjust than if no bonus were given.

Equity theory applies well to most economic transactions, but the input-outcome calculations are not the only method for deciding whether a distribution of rewards is fair. According to Morton Deutsch, when people make justice decisions regarding social relationships, equality is preferred over equity. In a social situation, an equal division of costs and benefits seems the most fair. Thus, for example, when you go out to dinner with friends, it usually seems as fair just to split the bill as it does to calculate precisely the cost of each person's meal. A third consideration is need. Deutsch argued that when making justice decisions regarding personal development and welfare, people will be most likely to consider the needs of those affected by the justice decision. It seems fair to buy shoes for the baby even though the baby has brought no income into the house, and it seems fair to put the baby's needs in front of the mother's or father's needs.

Procedural Justice

Researchers have noticed that sometimes people feel upset with an interaction even though they obtain the desired outcome. People also often accept decisions that are not to their advantage if they view the decision-making process as fair. The researchers began to look beyond simple questions about distributions of outcomes and instead turned their attention toward the *ways* in which outcomes are distributed; thus, the field of procedural justice was born.

A good example of the power of procedural justice is an effect researchers call *voice.* If a person has an opportunity to express his or her views to decision makers, that person will be more likely to find the outcome fair. Imagine, for example, that your town wants to knock down several houses to make way for a new interstate highway. If the town holds hearings where citizens can voice their concerns, homeowners will find the situations less unjust than if the town has no meetings—even if the meetings occur after the decision to demolish!

Why do procedures have such an effect on the perception of justice? Tom Tyler has noticed that procedures matter to people because fair treatment signals that one is regarded as a good person. When a person is treated fairly by other members of his or her group, the person feels respected, and when the person is treated fairly as a member of the group, he or she feels pride.

Retributive Justice

For a long time, researchers concentrated on how people make decisions about justice but did not emphasize how people react in situations in which a wrong has already been committed. Several factors influence how people react to wrongs. If the harmful outcome seems accidental, there is less outrage; if the harm seems intentional, there is more outrage. Low outrage results in low punishment. Moderate outrage results in punishments that emphasize righting the wrong done to the victim. High outrage results in punishment that takes away the privileges, rights, and even the life of the offender.

Implications

Social justice continues to remain an important topic to study because of its far-reaching implications for both oppressed and powerful individuals and groups, particularly in the realm of affirmative action, legal, welfare, and environmental policy.

Kristina R. Schmukler
Elisabeth M. Thompson
Faye J. Crosby

See also Attitudes; Blaming the Victim; Distributive Justice; Equity Theory; Just-World Hypothesis; Procedural Justice

Further Readings

Deutsch, M. (1985). *Distributive justice: A social-psychological perspective.* New Haven, CT: Yale University Press.

Lerner, M. J. (1980). *The belief in a just world: A fundamental delusion.* New York: Plenum.

Skitka, L. J., & Crosby, F. J. (Eds.). (2003). New and current directions in justice theorizing and research [Special issue]. *Personality and Social Psychology Review, 7*(4).

Tyler, T., & Blader, S. L. (2000). *Cooperation in groups: Procedural justice, social identity and behavioral engagement.* Philadelphia: Psychology Press.

SOCIAL LEARNING

Definition

Social learning refers to the learning that occurs in social contexts. More precisely, it refers to adaptive behavior change (learning) stemming from observing other people (or other animals), rather than learning from one's own direct experience. People acquire and change social behaviors, attitudes, and emotional reactions from observing and imitating the actions demonstrated by models such as parents or peers. This learning occurs from merely observing the actions of others and from observing the consequences of their actions. For example, if you see someone else touch a hot plate and then pull his or her hand away in pain, you do not have to imitate or repeat the action yourself:

You will avoid touching the hot plate as if you yourself had been burned by it.

Background and History

In the first half of the 20th century, psychological theories of learning were primarily behavioral in nature, focusing on direct consequences of one's own actions. For example, in B. F. Skinner's operant conditioning theory, learning occurs through the experience of rewards or reinforcements, such as studying behaviors being reinforced with good grades. The rigid adherence to environmental rewards and punishments in the behaviorist models was addressed by John Miller and Neal Dollard's work in the 1940s on social learning that highlighted the importance of the social setting on learning. Although this research had limitations (e.g., they maintained that learning could not occur without imitation and reinforcement), it did underscore the role of internal, cognitive processes in learning and it spurred considerable theoretical work and empirical research into social learning.

Probably the most influential and comprehensive researcher and theorist in social learning is Albert Bandura. He introduced his social learning theory in the 1970s, which suggests that although humans do learn from the responses they receive when they engage in behaviors (such as a painful burn reinforcing the need to use a potholder to remove items from a hot oven), most human behavior is learned through the observation and modeling of others' behaviors. According to social learning theory, children may learn how to behave in a restaurant setting by mimicking the behavior of their parents, and adolescents may learn their political attitudes by listening to conversations of adults. Social learning theory is a synthesis of cognitive and behavioral approaches to understanding learning: It is behavioral in its emphasis on the observation and mimicking of models, but it is cognitive in that it highlights the human ability to think, anticipate outcomes, and symbolize.

In the 1970s, Bandura expanded his theory to include an important element missing from theories on social learning: self-beliefs. He renamed his theory social cognitive theory to highlight the importance of cognition in learning, motivation, and behavior. From this theoretical perspective, human functioning is a product of the dynamic interaction between environmental, personal, and behavioral influences; this dynamic interplay is referred to as *reciprocal determinism*. For example, if an individual receives a poor grade on an exam (environmental factor) that may affect his or her belief (personal factor) about his or her ability in that domain, which in turn would influence his or her behavior (changed approaches to studying), and his or her behavior influences his or her environment (the individual now convenes a study group to prepare for exams).

Vicarious Learning, Modeling, Self-Regulation, and Self-Efficacy

Social learning theory contends that people do not need to imitate behavior for learning to occur. An important element of social learning is observing the consequences others receive when they engage in behaviors, which is termed *vicarious learning*. These consequences inform the learner about the appropriateness of the behavior and the likely outcomes of the behavior. People are more likely to model behavior that has been rewarded and is deemed appropriate than behavior that has been punished. Thus, a boy seeing his sister get punished for lying to their father is likely to learn that he shouldn't lie, and he does not need to engage in that behavior himself for learning to occur.

Modeling, or observing others' actions and their resultant consequences, can influence behavior in a number of ways. First, modeling can teach people new behaviors, such as how to swing a golf club properly. Next, modeling can facilitate existing behaviors, such as deciding it is time to leave a party. Modeling also changes people's inhibitions (self-imposed restrictions on behaviors); for example, the inhibition against passing notes in the classroom can be strengthened by seeing the teacher reprimand a note-passing peer. Finally, emotional reactions can be changed by observing a model's emotions, for example, watching an uneasy speaker will likely increase one's own fear of public speaking.

Research into social learning has revealed that not all models are equally effective. Individuals are most likely to model behavior of those who are perceived to be similar to them (for example, same-sex models are generally more influential than opposite-sex models), to be competent, and to have high status (such as admired athletes or influential leaders). In addition, models can either be real people, such as parents or best friends, or they can be symbolic, such as a book or a film character.

Bandura's social cognitive theory also highlights the important concepts of self-regulation and self-reflection. Self-regulation involves goal setting, self-observation, self-assessment, and self-reinforcement.

Once goals have been set, people monitor their behavior, judge it against their own standards, and reinforce or punish themselves. Importantly, standards for behavior are quite variable, and although one person may pat himself or herself on the back for a job well done after receiving a B on an exam, another may kick himself or herself for such poor performance. Self-reflection is expressed in the concept of self-efficacy, which refers to individuals' perceptions of their competence to perform a specific task or a range of tasks within a certain domain. Self-efficacy is context dependent, and although a person may have high self-efficacy in one domain (such as math), he or she may have low self-efficacy in another domain (such as leadership). Ample empirical evidence suggests that self-efficacy is an important motivational construct that influences the choices people make, the goals they set for themselves, the effort and persistence put forth toward their goal, and their performance within a given domain.

Processes

According to social learning theory, four subprocesses underlie the social learning process: attention, retention, production, and motivation. First, to learn from others, individuals must pay attention to the relevant aspects of the behavior being modeled. For example, a child learning to tie his or her shoelaces must pay close attention to the finger movements of the model. Next, the learner must also remember what the model did by committing the lace-tying movements into memory; often this information is committed to memory in either symbolic or verbal form. The next, likely difficult, step is for the learner to translate his or her understanding of how to tie his or her laces into overt lace-tying behaviors. Finally, people are more likely to attend to, remember, and engage in the modeled behavior if they are motivated to do so, and doing so will result in rewarding outcomes. Thus, the child is most likely to effectively engage in these social learning processes if he or she is adequately motivated to, for example, stop tripping on his or her laces or gain the approval of his or her parents.

Importance and Consequences of Social Learning

Although social learning has been thought to be particularly important for children, it has been broadly applied to learning that occurs over a person's life span. The social learning perspective has been very important for developing techniques for promoting behavior change (such as health promotion) and reducing unwanted behaviors such as aggressive behavior. Social learning has also contributed to our understanding of a wide range of phenomena including classroom learning, the influence of groups and leaders on individual behavior, health-related issues such as medical therapy compliance and alcohol abuse, and the moral and value internalization of children.

Perhaps the area of research most influenced by the social learning perspective is the study of antisocial, aggressive behavior. Significant research in this area indicates that an array of aggressive models can elicit a wide variety of aggressive behaviors. In a set of well-known BoBo doll experiments, Bandura and colleagues successfully demonstrated that children learned behaviors by simply watching others. They examined the behavior of mildly frustrated children who were previously exposed to an adult who either kicked, threw around, and punched an inflatable BoBo doll or was quiet and reserved around the doll. Children who were exposed to the aggressive adult were themselves more aggressive with the doll than were those exposed to the docile adult. However, children were less likely to imitate the aggressive behavior when they saw the adult get punished for the behavior.

Importantly, the models do not need to be physically present to influence the learner, aggressive models on television (including cartoon characters) can serve as effective models of aggressive behavior. Children are particularly vulnerable to this influence, and they learn that violence is acceptable because they see "good" people aggress, and they learn how to aggress from models. In addition to learning specific aggressive behaviors, they also learn attitudes regarding aggression as well as "scripts" to guide social behavior in different situations that may lead people to engage in aggressive behaviors by following the scripts that have been learned. On a more optimistic note, changing the model can influence behavior such that nonaggressive models decrease aggressive behavior. In addition, social learning has also been shown to play a large role in the learning of prosocial, helping behavior.

Crystal L. Hoyt

See also Bobo Doll Studies; Modeling of Behavior; Self-Efficacy; Self-Regulation

Further Readings

Bandura, A. (1977). *Social learning theory.* New York: General Learning Press.

Bandura, A. (1986). *Social foundations of thought and action: A social cognitive theory.* Englewood Cliffs, NJ: Prentice Hall.

SOCIAL LOAFING

Definition

Social loafing refers to a decline in motivation and effort found when people combine their efforts to form a group product. People tend to generate less output or to contribute less effort when working on a task collectively where contributions are combined than when working individually. The consequence is that people are less productive when working as part of a group than when working individually. Social loafing is similar to the *free rider effect,* whereby people contribute less to a collective effort when they perceive their contributions are dispensable. This is also similar to the *sucker effect,* whereby people withhold their contributions to a group to avoid being the victim of the social loafing or free riding efforts of other group members. However, the *free rider effect* and the *sucker effect* are narrower terms that refer to specific causes of social loafing. *Social loafing* is a broader construct that refers to any reduction in motivation and effort that occurs when contributions are pooled compared with when they are not pooled.

History and Modern Usage

Social loafing was first documented in the latter half of the 19th century by a French engineer named Max Ringelmann who observed men pulling or pushing a two-wheeled cart. Ringelmann noted that doubling or tripling the number of men performing the task did not produce a doubling or tripling of output, that is, two-man groups did not perform twice as well as individual men. More recently, researchers have observed social loafing on other physical tasks such as pulling a rope in a tug-of-war game, generating noise by clapping and cheering, swimming in a relay race, pumping air, and wrapping pieces of candy, and on cognitive tasks such as solving mazes, evaluating an editorial or poem, and generating uses for objects. For example, participants wearing blindfolds were instructed to pull a tug-of-war rope as hard as they could. Although participants believed they were pulling alone in some trials and as part of a group in other trials, in all conditions participants pulled the rope alone. Participants pulled harder on the rope when they believed they pulled alone than when they believed they pulled as part of a group.

Research reveals a variety of circumstances that influence whether people work hard versus loaf. For example, people work hard when offered strong external rewards for a good group performance, when they find the task intrinsically interesting or personally involving, and when they believe low effort will be punished. Conversely, people loaf when they perceive their efforts or contributions as redundant with the efforts or contributions of fellow group members. They loaf when they perceive the task as unimportant. They are more likely to loaf when the task is easy than when it is difficult. Perhaps most important, people loaf when they believe that their contributions cannot be identified, allowing them to hide in the crowd.

Understanding when people loaf requires distinguishing between effort (the contribution individuals make), performance (the product of those contributions), and outcome (the reward or consequences attached to the performance). With this distinction in mind, the various circumstances that influence social loafing can be organized under three broad conditions, and people will loaf when any of the conditions occur. First, people loaf when they perceive their individual efforts as unrelated or inconsequential to a good performance. For example, if a student working on a group project believes that the group will produce a good performance regardless of whether he or she individually works hard, then he or she is likely to loaf. Likewise, if the student believes that a good group product is unachievable regardless of whether he or she works hard, then he or she is likely to loaf.

Second, people loaf when they perceive that the outcome is unrelated to the quality of the performance. For example, if group members perceive that the group's performance will be rewarded regardless of the quality of the group performance, they will loaf. Likewise, if people perceive that the group's performance will go unrewarded regardless of the quality of the group performance, they will loaf.

Third, people will loaf when they do not value the outcome. More specifically, people will loaf when they perceive the costs of achieving the outcome exceed any benefits of achieving the outcome. For example, students may understand that a good group project in a class will receive an A, but also recognize that the time required to produce a good group project will impinge on the time they need to study for other classes. Thus, they may loaf because they are unwilling to sacrifice study time for their other classes to achieve a good group project. Notably, the finding that people loaf when contributions cannot be identified also illustrates the third condition. When contributions cannot be identified, individual contributors cannot be appropriately rewarded for their high efforts but also cannot be appropriately punished should they loaf.

Social loafing is often described as a group problem that only occurs when individual members combine their efforts toward a common goal. Indeed, group settings seem particularly vulnerable to social loafing. However, the conditions that prompt social loafing in group settings can also prompt a reduction in motivation and effort among people undertaking individual tasks. Specifically, people will withhold efforts on individual tasks to the extent that they perceive no relationship between their efforts and their performance, no relationship between their performance and the outcome, do not value the outcome, or believe that the costs of achieving a good outcome outweigh the benefits of receiving a good outcome.

Social loafing has often been characterized as a social disease. However, it is a disease with a cure. Managers, teachers, and other people who depend on groups, as well as people working in groups, can reduce or eliminate social loafing by making sure that each of the following conditions is in place. First, people must believe that their efforts make a difference and that their contributions are essential to achieve a good performance. Second, people must perceive a strong link between performance and the outcome. They must believe that a good performance (both individual and group) will be rewarded and that a poor performance will not. Often, this condition requires making individual contributions identifiable. Finally, the outcome must be important to the contributors. Moreover, the benefits of achieving a good performance must exceed the costs of achieving a good performance.

Jodi Grace
James A. Shepperd

See also Effort Justification; Group Performance and Productivity; Social Facilitation; Social Compensation

Further Readings

Karau, S. J., & Williams, K. D. (1993). Social loafing: A meta-analytic review and theoretical integration. *Journal of Personality and Social Psychology, 65,* 681–706.

Latané, B., Williams, K., & Harkins, S. (1979). Many hands make light the work: The causes and consequences of social loafing. *Journal of Personality and Social Psychology, 37,* 822–832.

Shepperd, J. A. (1993). Productivity loss in performance groups: A motivation analysis. *Psychological Bulletin, 113,* 67–81.

Shepperd, J. A., & Taylor, K. M. (1999). Social loafing and expectancy-value theory. *Personality and Social Psychology Bulletin, 21,* 1147–1158.

Social Neuroscience

Definition

Social neuroscience is an interdisciplinary field of science that deals with the biological mechanisms underlying social processes and behavior, considered by many to be one of the major problems for the neurosciences to address in the 21st century. Social neuroscience also involves using biological concepts and methods to develop and refine theories of complex human behavior in the social and behavioral sciences.

Background and History

During the 20th century in the biological sciences, the architects of development and behavior were conceived as anatomical entities (e.g., genes) sculpted by the forces of evolution and located within living cells far from the reaches of the social world. The brain was treated as a rational information-processing machine. Social factors, such as early family environment or social isolation later in life, were thought to have minimal implications for basic development, structure, or processes of the brain, which meant that social factors need not be considered to understand the human mind and behavior. And even if relevant, the notion was that considering social factors made the study of the human mind and behavior too complicated to sustain scientific progress.

The embrace of the neurosciences by cognitive and social scientists throughout most of the 20th century was no less antagonistic. World wars, a great depression, and civil injustices made it clear that social and cultural forces were too important to address to await the full explanation of cellular and molecular mechanisms. Given the antagonism between biological and social sciences that characterized psychology throughout most of the 20th century, research crossing social and biological levels of analysis was relatively rare.

By the dawn of the 21st century, neuroscientists, cognitive scientists, and social scientists began to collaborate more systematically, joined by the common view that complex human behavior must consider both biological and social factors and mechanisms. The research in social neuroscience has quickly grown to be broad and diverse. Investigations in the field include genetic studies of social recognition and affiliation in mice, research on social perception in stroke patients, animal studies of nurturance and affiliation, autonomic (e.g., neural pathways to and from internal organs) and neuroendocrine (e.g., hormones) research of social stressors and morbidity, and brain imaging studies of racial prejudice, social cognition, decision making, and interpersonal processes—to name but a few. The meteoric growth in research crossing social and biological levels of analysis during the past decade is testimony that the gap between the neurosciences and social sciences can be bridged, that the mechanisms underlying complex human behavior will not be fully explicable by a biological or a social approach alone, and that a common scientific language grounded in the structure and function of the brain and biology can contribute to this end point.

Reductionism Versus Substitutionism

Reductionism means that the nature of complex things can be explained by (i.e., reduced to) simpler or more fundamental things. The term *reductionism* comes from reducing something complex, such as the human mind, to something simpler, such as areas of brain activity. The sensitive issue that has worried social scientists about brain studies is that scientists might want to reduce all behavior to brain processes, as if self, attitudes, and other social processes are nothing else but brain activity. Extreme reductionists may even say there is no need for social psychology

research because studies of brain processes can replace everything that social psychologists do.

All human social behavior, at some level, is biological, but this is not to say that biological description or reductionism yields a simple or satisfactory explanation for complex behaviors, or that molecular forms of representation provide the only or best level of analysis for understanding human behavior. Scientific constructs such as those developed by social psychologists provide a means of understanding highly complex activity without needing to specify each individual action of the simplest components, thereby providing an efficient means of describing the behavior of a complex system. Social psychologists are not alone in their preference for the simplest form of representation to perform certain tasks. Chemists who work with the periodic table on a daily basis nevertheless use recipes rather than the periodic table to cook, not because food preparation cannot be reduced to chemical expressions but because it is not cognitively efficient to do so. In other words, even though cooking can be reduced to chemical processes, it is still useful and more efficient to think about it and do it at a higher level.

Reductionism, a systematic approach to investigating the parts to understand better the whole, is sometimes confused with substitutionism, which is the denial of the value or usefulness of a higher level of representation once one has a lower level description. The chemist who sees no value in recipes when cooking because these recipes can be described in chemical equations illustrates substitutionism. Reductionism, in fact, is one of various approaches to better science based on the value of data derived from distinct levels of analysis to constrain and inspire the interpretation of data derived from other levels of analysis. In scientific reductionism, however, the whole is as important to study as are the parts, for only in examining the interplay across levels of analysis can the beauty of the design be appreciated. Social neuroscience is a reductionistic rather than a substitutionistic approach to the study of complex human behavior, and as such, it also seeks to contribute to theory and research in social psychology and related sciences.

Organizing Principles

Contemporary work has demonstrated that theory and methods in the neurosciences can constrain and inspire social psychological hypotheses, foster experimental tests of otherwise indistinguishable theoretical explanations, and increase the comprehensiveness and relevance of social psychological theories. That is, social neuroscience improves scientific understanding of complex human behavior. Several principles from social neuroscience indicate why this might be the case.

The principle of *multiple determinism* specifies that human behavior can have multiple antecedents within or across levels of organization. For instance, one might consume a considerable quantity of pizza in an effort to remedy a low blood-sugar condition (biological determinant) or win a food-eating contest (social determinant). If either the biological or social level of analysis is regarded as inappropriate for its science, then that science will be ignoring an entire class of determinants and, therefore, will not be able to provide a comprehensive explanation for such behaviors.

The principle of *nonadditive determinism* specifies that properties of the whole are not always readily predictable from the properties of the parts. Nonadditive determinism is also sometimes called *emergent properties* because the higher-level entity has properties that are not predictable by the properties of the lower-level pieces. In an illustrative study, the behavior of nonhuman primates was examined following the administration of amphetamine or placebo. No clear pattern emerged until each primate's position in the social hierarchy was considered. When this social factor was taken into account, amphetamine was found to increase dominant behavior in primates high in the social hierarchy and to increase submissive behavior in primates low in the social hierarchy. A strictly physiological (or social) analysis, regardless of the sophistication of the measurement technology, may not have unraveled the orderly relationship that existed.

Finally, the principle of *reciprocal determinism* specifies that there can be mutual influences between microscopic (e.g., biological) and macroscopic (e.g., social) factors in determining behavior. For example, the level of testosterone in nonhuman male primates promotes sexual behavior; however, the availability of receptive females increases the level of testosterone in nonhuman primates. That is, the effects of social and biological processes can be reciprocal.

Social neuroscience, which is built on these principles, makes it more likely that comprehensive accounts of complex human behavior can be achieved because the biological, cognitive, and social levels of organization are considered as relevant.

Throughout most of the 20th century, social and biological explanations were cast as incompatible. Advances in recent years have led to the development of a new view synthesized from the social and biological sciences. The new field of social neuroscience emphasizes the complementary nature of the different levels of organization spanning the social and biological sciences (e.g., molecular, cellular, system, person, relational, collective, societal) and how multilevel analyses can foster understanding of the mechanisms underlying the human mind and behavior.

John T. Cacioppo

See also Biopsychosocial Model; Reductionism; Social Cognitive Neuroscience; Social Psychophysiology

Further Readings

Cacioppo, J. T. (2002). Social neuroscience: Understanding the pieces fosters understanding the whole and vice versa. *American Psychologist, 57,* 819–830.

Cacioppo, J. T., & Berntson, G. G. (2005). *Social neuroscience.* New York: Psychology Press.

Frith, C. D., & Wolpert, D. M. (2004). *Neuroscience of social interaction: Decoding, imitating, and influencing the actions of others.* New York: Oxford University Press.

Gazzaniga, M. (2004). T*he cognitive neurosciences* (3rd ed.). Cambridge: MIT Press.

Harmon-Jones, E., & Winkielman, P. (2007). *Social neuroscience.* New York: Guilford Press.

Social Power

Definition

Social power is the potential for social influence. The available tools one has to exert influence over another can lead to a change in that person. Social power and social influence are separate and distinct concepts. Although social power is potential (which may or may not be used), social influence is an effect, an actual change (or deliberate maintenance) in the beliefs, attitudes, behavior, emotions, and so on, of someone because of the actions or presence of another. The person or group that is the source of influence is commonly known as the influencing agent, whereas the object of the attempted or successful influence attempt is commonly known as the target (of the influence). Thus, influencing agents have social power, which are the means they may use to influence targets.

Background and History

The ability of one person (or group) to get others to do his or her will, also known as social power, has long been of interest to social psychologists. Perhaps this is because so much of human interaction involves the change or the attempt to change the beliefs, attitudes, or behaviors of another. Because of the long-standing interest in the topic, several different investigations have used different definitions of social power and different ways of measuring power. However, an extensive survey has found that the approach most commonly used originally identified five distinct potential tactics one could use in an influence attempt. This approach was updated some years ago and now includes six distinct tactics that can be subdivided into 11 varieties. Of course, in an influence attempt multiple types of influence are often used at the same time. The types of social power are as follows:

Informational. This type is the ability to rationally persuade someone.

Expert. This social power is similar to informational power except that arguments are not necessary because the target trusts the influencing agent.

Referent. The referent type is based on the target's identifying and liking the influencing agent and, because of this, wanting to comply with his or her requests.

Coercive power. This type involves threat of punishment. These can be things such as monetary fines (impersonal) or simply personal disapproval (personal).

Reward power. This social power type stems from the ability of the influencing agent to grant some kind of reward, either impersonal or personal.

Legitimate power. Based on what general society typically expects of us, this includes (a) the formal legitimate (or position) norm, which is the right to ask for something based simply on position or job title; (b) the reciprocity norm, whereby if someone does something for you, you owe him or her the favor in return; (c) the equity norm, the idea that one is expected to help others receive what they deserve, for example, if you work hard, you should get rewarded; and (d) social responsibility (or dependence), whereby people are obligated to help those who depend on them.

The type of social power used in an influence attempt often depends on a person's motivations. Sometimes people are consciously aware of their motivations, and sometimes they are not. Clever influencing agents often choose the kind of influence they use based on considerations of potential effectiveness and other factors. These factors can be quite varied. For example, some people are motivated by the desire to appear powerful. To feel powerful, an influencing agent may choose a type of influence strategy that makes him or her feel as though he or she is in control of the target of influence. If so, the influencing agent may choose to use coercion or reward in the influence attempt. Similarly, a desire to enhance one's sense of power in the eyes of others, status, security, role requirements, the desire to harm a target of influence, and self-esteem considerations might lead one to choose the more controlling, stronger, or harsher types of influence tactics (such as coercion). Others may wish to maintain a friendship or appear humble. In that case, they would rely more on information.

When these stronger or harsher types of power are used effectively, they enhance the influencing agent's view of himself or herself because the influencing agent can attribute subsequent change in the target to himself or herself. When this occurs, the powerholder then tends to think less of the target of influence. It has been argued that simply through the continual exercise of successful influence, the powerholder's view of others and himself or herself changes in a harmful way. The powerholder begins to view himself or herself as superior to the person that over which he or she is exercising power, and because of this feeling of superiority, may treat the target of influence in a demeaning manner. This effect would be consistent with the common belief that power is a corrupting influence.

Evidence

Hundreds of studies published in respected scientific journals involving social power as described earlier have been conducted in several diverse fields, including health and medicine, family relations, gender relations, education, marketing and consumer psychology, social and organizational psychology, and examinations of confrontation between political figures. Studies have been conducted in the context simulations and questionnaires, strictly controlled laboratory settings using traditional experimental methods, real-world settings such as hospitals and other large organizations, and through historical case study analysis.

Importance

Much of what humans do as individuals and society involves influencing others. People want and need things from others, things such as affection, money, opportunity, work, and justice. How they get those things often depends on their abilities to influence others to grant their desires. In addition, people are also the constant targets of the influence attempts of others. Thus, it is important to understand what causes people to comply with others' wishes, and how the exercise of power affects both targets and influencing agents. The study of social power provides that knowledge.

Gregg Gold

See also Compliance; Influence; Power; Power Motive

Further Readings

Gold, G. J., & Raven, B. H. (1992). Interpersonal influence strategies in the Churchill-Roosevelt bases for destroyers exchange. *Journal of Social Behavior and Personality, 7*, 245–272.

Kipnis, D. (1972). Does power corrupt? *Journal of Personality and Social Psychology, 24*, 33–41.

Raven, B. H. (2001). Power/interaction and interpersonal influence: Experimental investigations and case studies. In A. Y. Lee-Chai & J. A. Bargh (Eds.), *The use and abuse of power* (pp. 217–240). Ann Arbor, MI: Sheridan Books.

SOCIAL PROJECTION

Definition

Social projection refers to the tendency to assume that others are similar to oneself. Students who cheat on their statistics exams, for example, probably believe that many others cheat as well, whereas honest students think that cheating is rare. Projection is not limited to value-laden behaviors such as cheating versus being honest, and therefore, projection is not necessarily a defense mechanism. Statistically, projection is simply a positive correlation between what people say about themselves and what they believe is common in the group.

Though not considered a defense mechanism, it was believed for a long time that projection is a judgmental bias that people should rather get rid of. Surely, the argument was, people have enough information about others to make accurate estimates about the group. An individual's own attitude, preference, or personality trait is but a single bit of data that should not make a difference. It is now recognized, however, that projection can improve the accuracy of the perception of the group when knowledge of the self is all a person has.

Useful Projection

Suppose a person is brought to the laboratory and told that there are different types of people, and that each individual's type can be measured by a new test. After testing, the person is informed of being type T. Not knowing anything about how many different types there are and how common each one of them is, the person can speculate that his or her type is the most common one. Now, the person's single data point is useful. This is a good guessing strategy because most people are by definition in the majority rather than the minority.

Consider another example. A new gene is discovered, but it is unknown whether many (e.g., 90%) or few people (10%) have it. Both possibilities seem equally likely at first. Now a randomly chosen person tests positive for the gene. Because this person is more likely to represent a group in which the gene is common than a group in which it is rare, it can be inferred that the gene is common. This kind of inductive reasoning supports the idea that social projection is rational when a person has little knowledge other than self-knowledge. The more that is known about individual others, the more projection should diminish—and generally does.

A good example of a situation in which a person knows little about others is the one-shot Prisoner's Dilemma. To illustrate, suppose each of two players has a coin that must be placed heads up or tails up. If both choose heads, both get $15; if both choose tails, both get $5; if they make different choices, the one choosing heads gets nothing, whereas the one choosing tails gets $20. Heads is the *cooperative* choice because it leads to the best result for the group; tails is the *defecting* choice that yields the best outcome for the individual regardless of what the other person does. Most people project after making a choice, irrespective of what that choice was. Cooperators expect cooperation, and defectors expect defection. More important, social projection can increase the probability that a person chooses to cooperate. People who strongly believe that others will make the same choices as they themselves do will expect to receive the payoff for mutual cooperation ($15) rather than the sucker's payoff ($0) if they don't cooperate.

Harmful Projection

Sometimes people project when they should not. Public speakers, for example, know certain things about themselves that are hidden from the audience. They know how well they prepared, how anxious they feel, or which critical piece of information they forgot to mention. Many people cannot help but assume that the audience knows what they themselves know, especially when their own experiences are as emotional and vivid as their awareness of their own stage fright. Here, the projective assumption that one's own feelings and thoughts are transparent to others leads to overprojection. Unfortunately, efforts to suppress awareness of these unpleasant states or self-consciousness do not diminish projection. Instead, the unwanted thoughts become hyperaccessible, that is, they push themselves back into consciousness and are then projected even more strongly onto others.

Even seasoned public speakers must be wary of projection. The more knowledgeable they are about their topic, the more they are inclined to assume the audience already knows what they are about to say. To appreciate the actual differences between themselves and the audience, these speakers must deliberately adjust their expectations. Students can experience how difficult it is to overcome this projection of knowledge when taking an exam. They can predict the performance of others from their own experience with the test's difficulty. In this regard, students are similar to one another and projection is useful. When, however, students have been informed of the actual test results, they also project this knowledge to others who do not have it, and their predictions get worse.

Variations in Social Projection

Social projection tends to be strong regardless of whether people predict attitudes, behaviors, or personality traits. This is so, partly because people have some latitude to define the meaning of these attributes in self-serving terms. A person who cheats on exams may downplay the severity of the offense and thereby conclude that cheating is common. A lover of Pinot may think that the superiority of this grape is a fact of nature, to be recognized by all except the most boorish of people. Estimates regarding abilities are different because abilities are defined as relative. To believe that one has a high ability to play chess is to believe that one can beat most competitors. It is not possible to predict that most others will also beat most others. By contrast, it is easy to project one's love for the game to others.

For any type of personal attribute, projection is weak when people make predictions for groups to which they themselves do not belong. Men, for example, project their own attributes only to other men (the ingroup) but not to women (the outgroup), whereas women project to other women but not to men. Because most people's self-concepts comprise mostly desirable attributes, the lack of projection to outgroups has serious consequences for social stereotyping and intergroup relations. Inasmuch as they limit their projections to ingroups, people come to see these groups as extensions of themselves, and thus, as mostly desirable. Their perceptions of outgroups, which do not benefit from projection, are comparatively neutral. In the context of intergroup relations, an increase of projection to the outgroup would be a good thing.

Joachim I. Krueger

See also Attribution Theory; False Consensus Effect; Projection

Further Readings

Krueger, J. I., Acevedo, M., & Robbins, J. M. (2005). Self as sample. In K. Fiedler & P. Juslin (Eds.), *Information sampling and adaptive cognition* (pp. 353–377). New York: Cambridge University Press.

Robbins, J. M., & Krueger, J. I. (2005). Social projection to ingroups and outgroups: A review and meta-analysis. *Personality and Social Psychology Review, 9,* 32–47.

Savitsky, K., & Gilovich, T. (2003). The illusion of transparency and the alleviation of speech anxiety. *Journal of Experimental Social Psychology, 39,* 618–625.

Social Psychophysiology

Definition

Broadly defined, social psychophysiology is the study of human social behavior as it relates to and is revealed by physiological or bodily responses. Hence, social psychophysiologists investigate the interplay between social psychological and physiological processes. Generally, and in distinction to what has come to be known as social neuroscience, social psychophysiology focuses largely on the relationship between skeletal-muscular and visceral physiological processes controlled via the peripheral nervous system rather than on central nervous system or brain physiology.

History

Although social psychophysiology's history can be traced to the ancient Greeks and Romans, its modern roots stem from theory and empirical work at the end of the 19th and beginning of the 20th centuries by William James, James Cannon, Hans Selye, and others. By the late 1960s, an important chapter, "Physiological Approaches to Social Psychology," that appeared in the second edition of the prestigious *Handbook of Social Psychology,* marked the recognition of the value of interdisciplinary work combining social psychology and physiology for the field of social psychology. Similar recognition by the field of physiology occurred only indirectly a decade or two later when the relevance of social psychophysiological research for health and illness became established.

Social psychologists provided the main impetus and the lion's share of the work in this relatively new field. But they generally lacked training in physiology. As a consequence, their investigation and use of physiological measures were overly simplistic. Specifically, early social psychophysiologists focused on general arousal theory rather loosely defined, which basically assumed that physiological measures such as heart rate, blood pressure, skin conductance, respiration rate, muscle tension, and so forth were interchangeable measures, an assumption that today we know is wrong (see later discussion).

By the 1980s, however, this overly simplistic view of physiological processes began to come undone as social psychophysiologists such as John Cacioppo and Louis Tassinary became as well versed in physiology as they were in social psychology. Furthermore, they piqued the interest of physiological experts and others in social psychophysiology. Equally important, they became the primary disseminators of physiological knowledge, methodologies, and technical expertise to social psychologists. Their efforts included an edited volume of social psychophysiological research in 1983, a series of month-long intensive advanced physiological training institutes for social psychological researchers during the summers of 1986 through 1990, and two comprehensive handbooks of social pstychophysiology, one published in 1990 and the other in 2000. This group pioneered and revolutionized the field of social psychophysiology, paving the way for much more sophisticated and important research linking social psychology and physiology, and laying the groundwork for the field of social neuroscience as well.

Background

Social psychophysiology fits within the broader category of mind-body interactions, thereby rejecting centuries-old notions of mind-body dualism or separation. Social psychophysiology is based on the assumption that is termed the *identity thesis*. This thesis states that all mental, and hence psychological, states and processes are embodied rather than unembodied (e.g., spiritual). It suggests that understanding bodily responses helps the understanding of mental states and processes, and vice versa. The identity thesis implies that psychological (including social psychological) and biological (including physiological) disciplines must be combined if the mind-body relationship is to be understood.

The aspects of human physiology most pertinent to social psychophysiology can be divided into control and operational systems. Control systems include the central nervous system (brain and spinal cord) and the endocrine system, which includes all the glands (e.g., pituitary, adrenal) that excrete hormones (e.g., adrenalin) into the bloodstream. Operational systems control various bodily responses and include, for example, the cardiovascular (heart, vasculature, and blood), the somatic (skeletal muscle) system, and the visceral (stomach, small and large intestines) systems. The central nervous system operates by transmitting operating instructions via one type (efferent) of neurons and monitoring operational systems via another type (afferent) of neurons. Similarly, the endocrine system transmits operating instructions and monitors operational systems via circulating hormones.

Physiological Measures of Social Psychological Constructs

Social psychophysiologists pursue research questions that involve the interaction of intra-individual and interindividual psychological processes and physiological control and operating systems. Most social psychophysiologists seek to understand the effects of social psychological variables on physiological responses, and to be able to use that understanding to create physiological measures of those social psychological variables.

To create physiological measures of variables of interest, social psychophysiologists, as social psychologists, define the nature of their social psychological variables or constructs as precisely as possible. Further, social psychophysiologists as physiologists identify candidate physiological measures that should be related to the variable of interest and specify a plausible physiological rationale for linking physiological measures to the variables.

As mentioned previously, the specification of a physiological rationale was quite limited (e.g., general arousal) and overly simplistic (e.g., increases in psychological states are accompanied by across the board increases in sympathetically (neurally) controlled autonomic) responses, resulting in the use of simple unitary physiological measures such as heart rate and skin conductance to index literally dozens of constructs. However, therein is the problem. The psychological-sympathetic nervous system rationale failed to provide social psychophysiologists with distinctive physiological indexes of their constructs. For example, heart rate increases occurred during both approach and avoidance states. Today, social psychophysiologists strive to identify more specific (and complex) physiological theories and rationales to support their choice of sets of physiological responses to measure their constructs of interest. The pattern of increases and decreases from rest among these multiple measures provides distinctive physiological indexes of the constructs.

A good case in point is affect, a central construct for many research questions in social psychology. *Affect* is defined as the general emotional state that results in either an overall positive or negative feeling state. In the case of affect, Charles Darwin's ethological observations of the expressions of emotions provides a theoretical physiological formulation pointing toward specific physiological measures of it. Briefly, Darwin pointed to the face as the location of emotional expression in primates. Later, others identified specific facial muscles involved in the experience of positive and negative affect. More specifically, an increase in zygomaticus majori (smile muscles) activity and a decrease in corrugator supercilii (frown muscles) activity occur during the experience of positive affect; and, the reverse during the experience of negative affect. Muscle activity is typically measured using electromyographic (EMG) techniques. Cacioppo and his colleagues validated these patterns of EMG activity as measures of positive and negative affect. An interesting aspect of EMG activity is that it can measure positive or negative affect even if one could not detect it from just looking at the person.

Examples

Social psychophysiologists are not merely interested in identifying and validating physiological indexes of constructs. Rather, they use these indexes to test theories involving the constructs.

Racial Prejudice

For example, facial EMG has been used to study racial prejudice. Theoretically, prejudice involves negative affect toward members of a group. A long-standing problem for prejudice researchers is that people are reluctant to self-report their own prejudices. An advantage of physiological measures is that they are not subject to self-presentation problems.

Eric Vanman found that White research participants self-reported more positive affect for imagined Black than for imagined White partners but exhibited more facial EMG activity indicative of negative affect for Blacks than for Whites. In addition, he found that during presentations of photos of Blacks and Whites, high-prejudice participants exhibited lower zygomaticus and higher corrugator activity during presentation of Black than of White target photos, indicating higher negative affect; in contrast, low-prejudice participants did not differ in EMG activity between photo groups.

Psychological Threat

Social psychophysiologists are also interested in social factors that influence whether individuals experience psychological threat in potentially stressful performance situations (e.g., taking exams, giving speeches, negotiations). Threat occurs when an individual's perceived resources fail to meet the demands of the situation. Richard Dienstbier's theory of physiological toughness and weakness based on animal work suggests a pattern of cardiovascular responses that should occur during threat in humans. Specifically, both heart rate and heart muscle contractility should increase during threat, but cardiac output (the amount of blood pumped by the heart) should remain stable or decrease because of relative increases in total peripheral resistance (constriction of the arteries).

Jim Blascovich and his colleagues validated this pattern in humans. They also used the cardiovascular threat index to test many theoretical notions including the long-held assumption by stigma theorists that individuals interacting with members of stigmatized groups (e.g., people with physical deformities, people with low socioeconomic status). In several studies, Blascovich and colleagues demonstrated that individuals engaged in a cooperative task evidenced the threat pattern when playing with a stigmatized than with a nonstigmatized individual.

Implications

Physiological measures are now well established in the methodological toolbox of social psychologists. As more researchers become interested in mind-body interactions, its value will increase.

Jim Blascovich

See also Biopsychosocial Model; Health Psychology; Research Methods; Social Neuroscience

Further Readings

Blascovich, J. (2000). Psychophysiological methods. In H. T. Reis & C. M. Judd (Eds.), *Handbook of research methods in social and personality psychology* (pp. 117–137). Cambridge, UK: Cambridge University Press.

Blascovich, J., Mendes, W. B., Hunter, S.B., Lickel, B., & Kowai-Bell, N. (2001). Perceiver threat in social interactions with stigmatized others. *Journal of Personality and Social Psychology, 80,* 253–267.

Blascovich, J., Mendes, W., Hunter, S., & Salomon, K. (1999). Social facilitation, challenge, and threat. *Journal of Personality and Social Psychology, 77,* 68–77.

Cacioppo, J. T., Petty, R. E., Losch, M. E., & Kim, H. S. (1986). Electromyographic activity over facial muscle regions can differentiate the valence and intensity of affective reactions. *Journal of Personality and Social Psychology, 50,* 260–268.

Shapiro, D., & Crider, A. (1969). Psychophysiological approaches in social psychology. In G. Lindzey & E. Aronson (Eds.). *The handbook of social psychology* (2nd ed., Vol. 3, pp. 19–49). Reading, MA: Addison-Wesley.

SOCIAL RELATIONS MODEL

Definition

The social relations model is a theoretical and statistical approach to studying how people perceive others. Although investigations of person perception have a long history in social psychology, early methodological approaches relied on research participants reporting their perceptions of fictitious others who were described in brief stories. The social relations model allows researchers to move beyond such vignette studies and address a variety of questions related to interpersonal perception while studying real people engaged in real social interactions.

Background and History

Perceptions of other people are fundamental components of social interactions and, therefore, have a prominent place in social psychology. A person must perceive other people's traits accurately so that he or she can predict how they will behave. If you correctly perceive that someone is friendly, then you can probably expect that person to help you. What is more, people should also value knowing what other people think of them. For example, knowing that someone doesn't like you might be useful so that you can avoid interactions with that person. Such beliefs about how others perceive one's self are termed *metaperceptions*. Because person perception is so basic to social interaction, researchers have conducted many studies to learn how people form perceptions (Is John seen as friendly?), the attributions people make following perceptions (Why is John seen as friendly?), and the relative accuracy or inaccuracy of perceptions (Is John really friendly?).

Many of the early person perception studies, however, relied on vignettes, or stories, about imaginary other people. So, for example, a research participant might be given a paragraph that purportedly describes another student. After reading the paragraph, the participant would be asked to report his or her perceptions of the student in the story. Using such an approach makes person perception akin to object perception. That is, the target person becomes static and noninteractive, no different than perceptions about a chair or book. The vignette method has a clear advantage in that the researcher can control and manipulate the information that participants receive about the target person. Yet relying on written descriptions of another person removes much of the richness of real social interactions. Some researchers have improved the vignette approach by using videotapes of a person's behavior, which allows for a more vivid portrayal of the target person. Regardless of whether the vignette is presented as written or videotaped, participants in these studies know that the perceptual process is a one-way street. That is, although participants can make perceptions of the person in the vignette, the fictitious character cannot make a perception of the participant. Therefore, it would be unrealistic to ask participants to report on metaperceptions in such circumstances.

To further enhance the vignette method, some researchers have used assistants (called *confederates*) to pretend as if they are participants and engage the real participant in a seemingly authentic social interaction. Thus, participants believe that they are having an active, spontaneous interaction with another person. Under these conditions, participants should be able to report both perceptions and metaperceptions. Yet even a confederate approach to person perception is limited because the research assistant is generally required to play a prespecified role and use scripted responses. Thus, regardless of the specific approach described earlier, the researcher is not able to study the real give-and-take of an unscripted social interaction.

Given the problems associated with vignette and confederate approaches to studying person perception, one might conclude that an easy solution is to study real interactions between real people. Unfortunately, the major strength of such an approach (the give-and-take of real interactions) leads to challenges when interpreting data. Specifically, the perceptions in a real interaction depend on a variety of factors, including the particular person making the perception, the particular person being perceived, and the unique relationship between those two people. For example, John's perception of Mary's friendliness could be due to the way John perceives most people, the way Mary is perceived by most people, or something about the specific relationship between John and Mary. This situation is often referred to as a problem of *nonindependence* between the perceiver and the target (e.g., John's perception of Mary might be dependent on John, Mary, or both people). Thus, until the development of the social relations model, it would have been difficult for most researchers to account for these different components of perceptions that are generated by real social interactions.

Details of the Model

David Kenny developed the social relations model to give researchers a means to account for the nonindependence of perceivers and targets that emerges from real social interactions. The social relations model provides a theoretical way to conceptualize interpersonal perceptions, a methodological guide for designing studies that use real interactions, and a statistical approach to analyze the data from these studies. According to the model, interpersonal perceptions are a function of five components: a constant, a perceiver effect, a target effect, a relationship effect, and error. These components, described further later, can be summed to yield the overall perception or metaperception. So John's perception of Mary's friendliness (P) could be described with the following equation:

$$P = \text{constant} + \text{John's perceiver effect} + \text{Mary's target effect} + \text{relationship effect} + \text{error}$$

The constant is the average score on the perception across all perceivers and all targets. Perhaps, on average, people are seen as somewhat friendly. The perceiver effect is how a participant views others in general. For example, John might view everyone as very friendly, including Mary. The target effect is the degree to which a person elicits a certain perception. So Mary might be somewhat reserved and, in turn, be rated as less friendly by most of her interaction partners. The relationship effect represents the variance caused by the unique combination of a specific perceiver and a specific target. John may view Mary as especially friendly beyond his perceiver effect and beyond her target effect. Although social relations model analyses often lump together the relationship effect and error, it is possible to separate these two components. If a researcher has John rate Mary on friendliness using multiple measures or on multiple occasions, one can determine how much of the rating is due to the John-Mary relationship and how much is random across measure or time.

Conducting a study to use the social relations model requires a particular methodological approach. Specifically, multiple perceivers must rate multiple targets. So John would need to report not only Mary's friendliness but Bill's and Sally's too. Having multiple raters and targets can be accomplished in several ways, but is most easily done using a round-robin design in which each person rates, and is rated by, each other person in the group. A block design, in which people rate some members of the group but not others, is a common alternative to the round-robin study. Block designs are often used when a researcher is specifically interested in intergroup perceptions. For example, do men perceive women in the same way that women perceive men? Specialized software programs (SOREMO and BLOCKO) are used to analyze data from the different social relations model designs.

Using the social relations model, a researcher can investigate a variety of topics, including what Kenny calls the nine basic questions of interpersonal perception. Three of these questions can be answered by evaluating variability in the perceiver, target, and relationship effects. If perceptions are largely a function of the perceiver effect, then one has evidence for *assimilation.* That is, perceivers tend to see all of their targets in a similar way. For example, John might see Mary, Bill, and Sally as friendly, regardless of actual differences among them. Conversely, when perceptions are driven by the target effect, a researcher has evidence for *consensus.* In this case, perceivers tend to agree on which targets are high or low on a trait. John, Bill, and Sally might concur that Mary is somewhat unfriendly. Finally, strong relationship effects make the case for *uniqueness:* A given person's perception of another person is idiosyncratic.

The remaining basic questions are addressed by evaluating the degree to which the social relations model effects are related to each other, self-perceptions, or metaperceptions. For example, one might wonder whether people see others as others see them, called *reciprocity.* Evidence for reciprocity would be documented by an overlap between perceiver effects (how people see others) and target effects (how people are seen by others). Another intriguing possibility is assessing *meta-accuracy,* which is the degree to which people know how others see them. This would be evaluated by related perceiver effects in metaperceptions (how people think they are seen by others) with target effects in perceptions (how people are actually seen by others). The last four questions include assessing whether people can accurately perceive another person's traits (*target accuracy*), whether people assume others see them as they see others (*assumed reciprocity*), whether people see others as they see themselves (*assumed similarity*), and whether people see themselves as others see them (*self-other agreement*).

P. Niels Christensen

See also Empathic Accuracy; Personality Judgments, Accuracy of; Person Perception

Further Readings

DePaulo, B. M., Kenny, D. A., Hoover, C. W., Webb, W., & Oliver, P. V. (1987). Accuracy of person perception: Do people know what kinds of impressions they convey? *Journal of Personality and Social Psychology, 52,* 303–315.

Kenny, D. A. (1994). *Interpersonal perception: A social relations analysis.* New York: Guilford Press.

Kenny, D. A., Albright, L., Malloy, T. E., & Kashy, D. A. (1994). Consensus in interpersonal perception: acquaintance and the Big Five. *Psychological Bulletin, 116,* 245–258.

SOCIAL SUPPORT

Definition

In general, social support refers to the various ways in which individuals aid others. Social support has been documented as playing an important and positive role in the health and well-being of individuals. To receive support from another, one must participate in at least one important relationship. However, social support has often been summarized as a network of individuals on whom one can rely for psychological or material support to cope effectively with stress. Social support is theorized to be offered in the form of instrumental support (i.e., material aid), appraisal/informational support (i.e., advice, guidance, feedback), or emotional support (i.e., reassurance of worth, empathy, affection).

Perceived and Conditional Social Support

Perceived social support is support that an individual believes to be available, regardless of whether the support is actually available. Perception of support may be a function of the degree of intimacy and affection within one's relationships. Compared with actual support, perceived support may be just as important (and perhaps more so) in improved health and well-being. Actually, perceived support appears to correlate more closely with health status than does actual social support. Similar to actual support, perceived support may heighten the belief that one is able to cope with current situations, may decrease emotional and physiological responses to events, and may positively alter one's behavior.

Conditional support is defined as one's expectation of receiving support only after fulfilling certain expectations or requirements. Conditionality of support is correlated with actual support. For example, those who offer little support will only be supportive given the fulfillment of certain expectations.

Buffering and Direct Effects Hypotheses

Social support is theorized to affect health through one of two routes: (1) an indirect, buffering, or mediational route and (2) a direct, main-effects route. The stress-buffering hypothesis has been more frequently studied than the main-effects hypothesis. The stress-buffering hypothesis asserts that an individual's social network supplies the individual with the resources needed to cope with stressful events and situations. Accordingly, the beneficiary aspects of support are only seen during stressful periods. That is, the stress-buffering hypothesis posits that social support tends to attenuate (weaken) the relationships between stressful life events and negative physical or psychological difficulties, such as cardiovascular disorders and depression. In addition, proponents of the stress-buffering model believe that support will only be effective when there is good support-environment fit (i.e., type of support provided matches the situational demands). For example, having someone offer empathy and reassurance will be helpful when a person has lost a loved one, but receiving empathy may be useless when one is facing stresses associated with financial difficulties.

Conversely, the main-effects hypothesis postulates that social support is beneficial whether one is going through a stressful event or not. The main-effects hypothesis asserts that the extent of an individual's participation in the social network plays a vital role in the degree of social support benefits. In other words, there is a direct monotonic link between social support in one's social network and well-being (i.e., the more support, the greater one's well-being).

A related concept to social support is social integration. Social integration is defined as an individual's involvement in a wide variety of social relationships. Social integration can also refer to the quality of the social relationship. For example, negative social

relationships could have negative effects on health, whereas positive social relationships and interactions usually have a beneficial effect on health and well-being. Previous research has demonstrated that social integration tends to be a main effect. That is, one's relationships with others may provide multiple avenues of information to influence health-related behaviors.

Social Support and Stress

The presence of a support network has been found to reduce the negative effects of stress. The support of one's social network can act as a buffer to stress in many ways. For example, individuals in one's support network can offer less threatening explanations for stressful events (e.g., instead of being called into the boss's office to be fired, perhaps it is to be asked to head a special committee instead). A positive social support network can also increase an individual's self-esteem and self-efficacy. For example, effective coping strategies may be suggested (e.g., a list of pros and cons or a priority list). In addition, the support network may suggest solutions to current problems or stressors being faced. Having a support group can also alter perceptions of the stressor by decreasing the perceived importance of the stress. Furthermore, having a supportive group of people surrounding a person can result in increased positive behaviors such as more exercise, proper rest, and better eating habits. Likewise, interactions with others may help distract attention from the problem.

Strong social networks can buffer against social pain (e.g., loss of a loved one, betrayal, exclusion) as well as buffer against negative aspects of other relationships. For example, widows with a confidant (someone to talk to about personal things) were less depressed than were widows without a confidant. One caveat to this buffering effect is that for support to buffer the effects of stress, the supporter cannot also be a source of conflict or additional stress. As such, having a strong and stable support network may lessen the negative effects of stress. In addition, support is associated with adaptive coping to stressful events and greater protection from the negative effects of stress.

Social Support and Health

Social support also has important effects on one's health and well-being. Overall, support has been linked with good health and well-being as well as improved adjustment to specific illnesses, such as cardiovascular disorders and cancer. For example, having a strong support network has been correlated with lower mortality rates, less depression, better adherence to medical treatment, greater health-related behaviors (e.g., lower rates of smoking), maintenance of health behaviors, lower incidences of cardiovascular disorders, and improved adjustment to breast cancer. Furthermore, social support has been linked to adaptation to surgery. That is, patients who had a social support network received lower doses of narcotics, displayed less anxiety, and were released from the hospital sooner than were individuals who had no type of social support.

Conversely, lack of social support has been associated with increased anxiety and depression, an increase in cardiovascular problems, feelings of helplessness, and unhealthy behaviors (e.g., sedentary lifestyle, habitual alcohol use). For example, a lack in parental support predicted potential increases in depressive symptoms and onset of depression in adolescent girls. That is, girls who had very little to no support from their parents were more likely to develop depression than were girls who had parental support. In addition, females reporting low levels of perceived support also have more eating problems than do females reporting high levels of support.

Social Support and Self-Esteem

Researchers have suggested that social support is one of the key elements that influence self-esteem, especially the support of one's parents early in development. Perceived support, rather than actual support, has been most frequently examined in relation to self-esteem. Researchers have found that the best predictor of self-esteem in adolescents is the amount of perceived social support from their classmates and the degree of parental approval they receive. In other words, an individual's perceptions of support tend to influence his or her reports of self-esteem. Therefore, the more support one believes he or she is receiving, the higher his or her self-reported self-esteem. Furthermore, social support moderates the level of self-esteem depending on the degree of competence in an area. In other words, people who are highly competent in an area but receive little support report lower levels of self-esteem than do people who are highly competent but receive a lot of social support. In addition, the higher the degree of conditional support, the lower one's self-esteem will be.

Negative Aspects of Social Support

Although the benefits of social support are well known, there may also be negative aspects. For example, a difference in the desired support and actual support received can result in poorer psychosocial adjustment in breast cancer survivors. Among older adults, too much social support can heighten the negative impact of stress, perhaps by eliciting feelings of incompetency, lower self-esteem, and less self-control. In addition, being the provider of social support may take a toll on the providers' physical health, psychological well-being, and emotional resources. The act of providing support, especially over a long duration, may be taxing because of the amount of emotional, financial, and mental resources that must be made available to provide such support.

Attachment Style and Social Support

Adult attachment style has been consistently linked to individual differences in actual and perceived social support. The relative quality of support caregivers provide young children is believed to influence how they perceive themselves and others in the future. In other words, internal working models that involve expectations about whether others will provide support develop. Research has found that adults with secure working models are more likely to believe they will receive support when needed and are more satisfied with the support they receive compared with adults with insecure working models. In addition, secure attachment has been positively associated with seeking social support and providing support to others.

Personality and Social Support

Evidence supports a link between Big Five personality traits (i.e., Extraversion, Agreeableness, Conscientiousness, Neuroticism, Openness to Experience) and social support. Specifically, there appears to be a reciprocal relationship between personality characteristics and support. Personality traits likely influence relationships (and thus support and perceptions of support). In turn, support will affect relationships. As such, changes in personality characteristics have been positively related to changes in perceptions of support.

Agreeableness and Extraversion are two dimensions that have been previously related to interpersonal behavior. For example, Agreeableness has been linked to interpersonal behaviors reflecting a need to maintain positive relations with others. Consequently, Agreeableness has been found to be most strongly associated with support and perceived support. Research has shown that Agreeableness positively predicts the amount of support received. Furthermore, providing job-related support mediates the relationship between Agreeableness and received job-related support. Similarly, Extraversion has been linked to support in non–job-related and positive job-related events. Extraversion and received job-related support are mediated by job-related support provided. In addition, Extraversion plays a role in the perceived support received by children from parents, but not vice versa.

Gender Differences in Social Support

Much of the early research in gender differences of social support used self-report measures and found that women are more skillful providers of support than are men. For example, wives affirm their husbands at a greater rate than husbands affirm their wives and more frequently offer support in post-stress situations than husbands offer. In addition, wives will complete more household chores (and thus relieve some stress and pressure) when the husband has had a stressful workday. Studies observing support behavior (i.e., observing supportive behavior rather than self-report measures) among marital couples have not found these gender differences and instead find that husbands and wives offer comparable support to one another.

Recent research indicates that the skill of providing social support is similar among husbands and wives. It has been suggested that the key distinction in previously found gender differences lies in *when* spouses offer support. For example, wives offer greater amounts of support when their husbands are experiencing greater stress whereas when wives experience increased stress, husbands do not necessarily offer greater support. In other words, women are more likely to provide greater support during severely stressful times than are men.

Evidence indicates that social support may differentially affect men and women. For example, widows with support experienced improved quality of life, greater well-being, and increased self-esteem, whereas these elements were negatively correlated with received social support among widowers. Support received by men can be moderated by their desire to be independent. Men who have a strong desire to be independent

are more likely to react negatively to social support than are men who do not have a strong desire to be independent or who desire to be dependent. In women, the influence of social support does not appear to be contingent on the desire to be independent.

Culture and Social Support

A possible determinant in the decision to seek or solicit social support may be one's culture or the norms that govern that culture. For example, individuals in Eastern cultures are less likely to solicit social support from their social network than individuals in Western cultures are. This cultural pattern seems counterintuitive since Eastern cultures tend to be collectivistic and emphasize interdependence, whereas Western cultures tend to be individualistic and emphasize independence. It would seem as though individuals in collectivistic cultures would be the ones to seek and solicit help from their social support network. However, research has shown that the opposite is true. That is, individuals in individualistic cultures are those who are soliciting help from their social support network. The underlying reason for this counterintuitive pattern may be the result of cultural norms, such as cultural norms that discourage the use of a social support network when solving problems and coping with stress.

Workplace Social Support

The amount of social support one receives from others in the workplace depends on numerous factors such as social competence, reciprocity relationships, and job commitment. For example, individuals who are socially competent tend to receive a greater amount of emotional and instrumental support from coworkers than do individuals who are not as socially competent. However, many studies show that an individual's support network is usually a network of people outside of his or her job such as family members, spouses, and so forth. In any case, support given in the workplace positively predicts support received.

Social support has also been shown to moderate the relationship between long work hours and physical health symptoms. In other words, physical health tends to decrease when an individual has long work hours and lacks social support. Conversely, individuals who have a social support network tend to be buffered against the adverse effects of longer working hours.

Influences

Perceived social support and actual social support are both influential in a multitude of facets in one's life. Social support can have either a direct (or main) effect or a buffering (or mediation) effect on one's health. The influence of social support can be seen widely from an effect in the workplace to intimate relationships. In addition, social support has effects on one's health, ability to handle stress, and self-esteem level. Furthermore, one's personality, cultural background, and gender may influence or moderate the effects of stress.

Jennifer M. Knack
Amy M. Waldrip
Lauri A. Jensen-Campbell

See also Buffering Effect; Cultural Differences; Gender Differences; Helping Behavior; Need to Belong; Self-Efficacy; Self-Esteem; Stress and Coping

Further Readings

Cohen, S. (2004). Social relationships and health. *American Psychologist, 59*(8), 676–684.

Collins, N. L., & Feeney, B. C. (2004). Working models of attachment shape perceptions of social support: Evidence from experimental and observational studies. *Journal of Personality and Social Psychology, 87,* 363–383.

Krohne, H. W., & Slangen, K. E. (2005). Influence of social support on adaptation to surgery. *Health Psychology, 24*(1), 101–105.

Taylor, S. E., Sherman, D. K., Kim, H. S., Jarcho, J., Takagi, K., & Dunagan, M. S. (2004). Culture and social support: Who seeks it and why? *Journal of Personality and Social Psychology, 87*(3), 354–362.

SOCIAL TRAP

See SOCIAL DILEMMAS

SOCIAL VALUE ORIENTATION

People differ in how they approach others. Some people tend to approach others in a cooperative manner, whereas other people tend to approach others in a more self-centered manner. Such social dispositions have been demonstrated to be quite important in various contexts and are often examined under the heading of social value orientation. This concept refers to preferences for particular distributions of outcomes for self and others. One could discriminate among various social value orientations, such as altruism, equality, cooperation, individualism, competition, aggression, and the like. However, research has supported a three-category typology that discriminates among three orientations—prosocial orientation, individualistic orientations, and competitive orientation.

Prosocial orientation is defined in terms of enhancing one's own and another's outcomes ("doing well together") as well as equality in outcomes ("each receiving an equal share"), individualistic orientation is defined in terms of enhancing outcomes for self and being largely indifferent to outcomes for another person ("doing well for oneself"), and competitive orientation is defined in terms of enhancing the difference between outcomes for self and another in favor of oneself ("doing better—or less worse—than another person").

Measurement

The concept of social value orientation is rooted in classic research on cooperation and competition, which revealed (largely unexpected, at that time) a good deal of individual stability in behavior over a series of interactions and across situations. These considerations, as well as the aim of disentangling (or decomposing) interpersonal goals underlying behavior in experimental games, have inspired researchers to design a measure that is closely linked to game behavior. Rather than focusing on a 2-by-2 matrix game, such as the Prisoner's Dilemma Game, the instrument represents decompositions of game situations, capturing consequences of one's behavior for oneself and another person. A frequently used instrument is the Triple-Dominance Measure of Social Values. In this instrument, outcomes are presented in terms of points said to be valuable to self and the other, and the other person is described as someone the person does not know and that he or she will never knowingly meet in the future (in an effort to exclude the role of considerations relevant to the future interactions).

An example of a decomposed game is the choice among three options:

Option A: 480 points for self and 80 points for the other person

Option B: 540 points for self and 280 points for the other person

Option C: 480 points for self and 480 points for the other person

In this example, option A represents the competitive choice because it yields the greatest outcomes for self relative to the other (480 − 80 = 400 points); option B represents the individualistic choice because it yields the greatest absolute outcomes for self (540 points); and option C represents the prosocial choice because it yields the greatest joint outcomes (480 + 480 = 960 points) as well as the smallest absolute difference between outcomes for self and other (480 − 480 = 0 points). In research using this instrument, most individuals are classified as prosocial (about 60%–65%), followed by individualists (about 25%), and only a small minority is classified as competitive (about 10%–15%). Of course, these percentages might differ as a function of the sample, depending on variables such as (sub)cultural differences, gender, number of siblings, and age. For example, prosocial orientation is more likely to be observed in collectivistic cultures (as opposed to individualistic cultures), in women (as opposed to men), and among people with a large number of siblings, especially sisters. And prosocial orientations are more commons among older people (at least up to 65 years) than among younger people.

Research

Research revealed that social value orientation exhibited considerable ability to predict actual behavior in a variety of different experiment games, with prosocial exhibiting greater cooperation than individualists and competitors. Moreover, social value orientations often exert their influence not only in terms of independent effects but also in combination with several variables, such as personality impressions of the partner, or the strategy pursued by the interaction partner. Also, social value orientation is associated with several cognitive processes, including the use of morality (good versus bad) versus competence (intelligent versus stupid, weak versus strong) in person judgment and impression formation. For example, whereas prosocials tend to judge cooperative and noncooperative others in terms of good and bad (e.g., fair or unfair), individualists and competitors tend to judge these people in terms of strong versus weak or smart versus dumb.

Recent research has also examined how individual differences in social value orientation could have an impact on cognition, affect, and behavior in contexts outside of the laboratory, that is, in everyday life. Evidence increasingly reveals that prosocials and individualists report a greater willingness to sacrifice for their partners than do competitors. Prosocials also report working harder for their housemates (to maintain a clean apartment), which is an interesting finding because prosocials were judged by their roommates and friends as more philosophical than individualists and competitors. Also, prosocials are more likely than individualists and competitors to volunteer in participating in psychological experiments. Last but not least, social value orientation is also very important at the large societal level, showing that prosocials are more likely to make donations to noble causes than are individualists and competitors, and prosocials are more likely to hold a left-wing political orientation (valuing equality and solidarity), whereas individualists and competitors are more likely to hold a right-wing political orientation.

Implications

In short, what is fascinating about social value orientation is that only a small number of games (which can be assessed in only a couple of minutes) appear to be useful tools for understanding prosocial behavior as diverse as sacrifice in ongoing relationships, citizenship in groups, participation in experiments, and donations to help the poor and the ill. This is remarkable from a measurement perspective and from the theoretical perspective. Recall that many theories tend to portray individuals as self-interested individuals, calculated or not. This view on human nature appears to be incomplete, and therefore partially inaccurate, so it is good to realize that some people may be quite prone to value good (and equal) outcomes for all, whereas others want to make sure that they do not get less than others. Outcomes are inherently social.

Paul A. M. Van Lange
Chris P. Reinders Folmer

See also Cooperation; Prosocial Behavior; Social Dilemmas; Values

Further Readings

Kuhlman, D. M., & Marshello, A. (1975). Individual differences in game motivation as moderators of preprogrammed strategic effects in prisoner's dilemma. *Journal of Personality and Social Psychology, 32,* 922–931.

Liebrand, W. B. G., Jansen, R. W. T. L., Rijken, V. M., & Suhre, C. J. M. (1986). Might over morality: Social values and the perception of other players in experimental games. *Journal of Experimental Social Psychology, 22,* 203–215.

Messick, D. M., & McClintock, C. G. (1968). Motivational bases of choice in experimental games. *Journal of Experimental Social Psychology, 4,* 1–25.

Van Lange, P. A. M. (1999). The pursuit of joint outcomes and equality in outcomes: An integrative model of social value orientation. *Journal of Personality and Social Psychology, 77,* 337–349.

Van Lange, P. A. M., Otten, W., De Bruin, E. N. M., & Joireman, J. A. (1997). Development of prosocial, individualistic, and competitive orientations: Theory and preliminary evidence. *Journal of Personality and Social Psychology, 73,* 733–746.

SOCIOBIOLOGICAL THEORY

In 1975, Harvard biologist Edward O. Wilson published *Sociobiology: The New Synthesis*, wherein he outlined a framework for investigating the biological basis of social behavior. As a branch of evolutionary biology, sociobiology aims to use demographic parameters (e.g., growth and mortality rates, gender and age distributions) and the genetic structure of populations to predict patterns of social organization across species. One of the conceptual tools sociobiology contributes to investigations of social behavior is an analysis of ultimate causation. Whereas proximate causal analyses focus on, for example, the behavioral, developmental, physiological, or neural mechanisms operating within an individual's lifetime to produce a particular phenotype, an ultimate causal analysis focuses on the selective forces that operated over generations and led to the evolution of the specific phenotype manifest in the individual. In this way, proximate explanations answer the question of how mechanisms operate (e.g., the catalog of hormones, neurotransmitters, and brain regions governing behavior); ultimate explanations answer the question of why they were selected for (i.e., how a particular trait affected the probability of survival and reproduction).

Sociobiologists have made progress in understanding a wide range of behaviors, both their proximate mechanisms and ultimate functions, including altruism, patterns of communication, aggression, mating systems, and parental care of offspring. Such behaviors have been investigated in a wide range of species including ants, birds, frogs, and chimps. Wilson's volume sparked heated controversy regarding his last chapter, which extended the principles of evolutionary ultimate causation and population genetics to explain the social behavior of humans. Among the many reasons for this controversy were (a) misunderstandings about sociobiology and genetic determinism and, (b) the long-held view in the social sciences that social behavior in humans is the product of cultural forces, rather than biological ones. Many opponents mistook sociobiology for arguing that social behaviors are genetically fixed and immutable when, in fact, much of sociobiology focuses on how evolved social behavior is capable of adapting to different environmental situations (e.g., morphological and behavioral change given particular environmental cues). Controversy also occurred because sociobiology ran counter to the prevailing view in the social sciences. Indeed, one goal of sociobiology is the reshaping of the humanities and social sciences to make them consistent with the principles of modern evolutionary biology.

Though based on many of the same principles, sociobiology is distinct from *evolutionary psychology*. Although both disciplines consider ultimate causal explanations, evolutionary psychology uses this level of analysis to construct models of the information processing circuitry (i.e., the cognitive programs) required to produce an adaptive response. In contrast, sociobiology steps from selective forces (e.g., limited resources) to social behavior (e.g., aggression) without making explicit the kinds of cognitive programs required to produce a particular behavior. So, though related, there exists a set of non-overlapping goals distinct to each field. Nevertheless, sociobiology and its related disciplines take seriously the claim that principles derived from the *modern synthesis*, which united Darwin's theory of evolution and Mendelian genetics, can be used to explain the constellation of behaviors in humans and nonhumans alike.

Debra Lieberman

See also Evolutionary Psychology; Genetic Influences on Social Behavior; Sociobiology

Further Readings

Wilson, E. O. (1975). *Sociobiology: The new synthesis.* Cambridge, MA: Belknap.

SOCIOBIOLOGY

Definition

Sociobiology is an approach to studying the biological bases of social behavior that focuses on applying evolutionary theory and the principles of genetics to explain specific instances of social behavior in a wide variety of species.

Background

John P. Scott coined the term *sociobiology* in 1948, but it was not until 1964 that William Hamilton laid the theoretical foundations of the field. Hamilton introduced the idea that, in the evolution of species, the transmission of genes from one generation to the next matters much more than any individual organism's success in survival and reproduction. He and others went on to conclude that, because social behaviors may aid in the passing on of genes, such behaviors may have evolutionary, and ultimately biological, bases.

The modern era of sociobiology effectively began in 1975, however, with the publication of entomologist E. O. Wilson's *Sociobiology: The New Synthesis.* Wilson's prominent yet controversial work advocated the integrative and systematic application of many disciplines, including evolutionary theory and genetics, to the study of social behavior. With the release of Wilson's book, the amount of work in this area increased dramatically. Many of the core principles of sociobiology persist today in the field of evolutionary psychology.

What Sociobiologists Study

Sociobiologists try to identify the evolutionary origins of social behaviors in all species. To do this, they examine specific social behaviors and the environments in which they occur, and then infer how such behaviors may have been adaptive in enabling species to pass on their genes. Although most sociobiological research has focused on behavior in nonhuman animals, sociobiologists have also examined the evolutionary bases of human social behavior. Research on helping, for instance, has shown that the likelihood that people will aid those in distress depends partly on how genetically related the helper is to the person in need. This supports the idea that altruism has an evolutionary basis in aiding the survival of those who share one's genes.

Constraints on Human Sociobiology

Although many interpret sociobiological research on humans to suggest that people's behavior can be explained using evolutionary theory, others have argued that this approach is limited because the precise influence of genes in most human behavior is difficult to pinpoint. This is because most of the social behaviors sociobiologists attribute to genetic influence also can be explained by the influence of cultural norms and learning. For example, cultural norms promote helping one's close relatives over helping strangers. In addition, sociobiologists have difficulty specifying the adaptive value of complex cultural phenomena such as art and religion. Nonetheless, study of the evolutionary bases of human behavior has proved a novel, and increasingly influential, approach to understanding human social behavior.

Spee Kosloff

See also Evolutionary Psychology; Genetic Influences on Social Relationships; Sociobiological Theory

Further Readings

Dawkins, R. (1976). *The selfish gene.* Oxford, UK: Oxford University Press.

Hamilton, W. D. (1964). The genetical theory of social behavior: I and II. *Journal of Theoretical Biology, 7,* 1–52.

Wilson, E. O. (1975). *Sociobiology: The new synthesis.* Cambridge, MA: Belknap.

SOCIOECONOMIC STATUS

Definition

Socioeconomic status (SES) is an indicator of an individual's social and economic standing in society and often is determined by a combination of ratings on occupational status, income level, and education. Individuals with low SES ratings tend to have low-status occupations, such as service industry jobs; income at or below the poverty level; and low levels of formal education. These individuals have limited access to the kinds of financial, educational, and social resources that could promote their own health and well-being and that of their families. Individuals with high SES ratings are likely to work in prestigious positions, such as in medicine or law; have higher salaries; and have more advanced education. These individuals have greater access to resources that can contribute to their success and to the perpetuation of similar benefits for their families.

Importance

Low SES has been associated with a variety of negative developmental and social outcomes, especially for children. For example, low SES is associated with health problems, such as premature birth, low birth weight, respiratory illnesses, and iron deficiencies in children. Children in low-SES households are more likely to be exposed to tobacco, less likely to have adequate nutrition, less likely to be immunized, and less likely to receive high-quality health care than their higher SES peers. These conditions also affect the health of adults, with women living in poverty being more likely than their higher SES counterparts to suffer from disease, chronic health conditions, and disabilities.

Low SES also is associated with lower academic performance and IQ scores for children. Low-SES parents likely have limited access to high-quality books, libraries, and schools for their children, and they may provide fewer enriching educational opportunities for their children to develop their intellectual skills. Teachers also may unknowingly contribute to the lower academic performance of these children, by subtly conveying their low expectations in a way that actually undermines performance. Ultimately, a low-SES child's poor performance may confirm the teacher's original negative expectation, creating a self-fulfilling prophecy. Some experts think the causation goes in the opposite direction, that low IQ (which they regard as genetically determined) causes people to end up with low SES.

Low SES also has been linked with maladaptive social functioning. Children and adolescents growing up in low-SES households exhibit more aggressive and delinquent behavior, and both low SES children and adults have a higher likelihood of suffering from psychological disorders, such as depression. Moreover, individuals with limited financial resources likely have more difficulty finding and receiving appropriate, affordable, and effective mental health treatment, further limiting their functioning.

Low SES often co-occurs with minority, recent immigrant, and disability status; single-parent households; and exposure to violence, making low-SES individuals frequent targets of prejudice. People may assume that low SES reflects personal failings, without considering possible societal constraints. This assumption may undermine their willingness to help low-SES individuals improve their social standing, further perpetuating a cycle of social inequality.

Elizabeth L. Cralley

See also Prejudice; Self-Fulfilling Prophecy

Further Readings

Bradley, R. H., & Corwyn, R. F. (2002). Socioeconomic status and child development. *Annual Review of Psychology, 53,* 371–399.

SOCIOLOGICAL SOCIAL PSYCHOLOGY

Definition

Although most social psychologists are psychologists working in psychology departments, an important minority are sociologists working in sociology departments. The two groups share an interest in many of the same research problems, but their approaches are distinct. Psychological social psychologists tend to focus on the single person, on how an individual's perceptions of a social situation affect how she or he thinks, feels, and behaves in that situation. Sociological social psychologists, however, tend to focus on the relationship between the individual and larger social systems (e.g., society). Beyond this general orientation, however, sociological social psychology consists of a diverse set of perspectives and theories. Most often, sociologists distinguish between two major variants of sociological social psychology—symbolic interactionism and social structure and personality—though an emerging third variant has come to be called structural social psychology.

History and Background

Symbolic Interactionism

Symbolic interactionism is itself a diverse variant of sociological social psychology, the rise of which is connected with the emergence of American sociology in the early part of the 20th century, largely because of George Herbert Mead's ideas concerning the self-society relationship. At the core of Mead's theorizing is the idea that society gives rise to the self, the self in turn influences behavior, and behavior acts back to maintain society, though emergent behavioral patterns may also promote societal change.

Toward the mid-20th century, symbolic interactionism split into two different strands, often referred to as the Chicago School and the Iowa School. Although both claimed inspiration from Mead's ideas on self and society, the two schools make different assumptions about the nature of the individual, the nature of interaction, and the nature of society. Consequently, the two schools offer contrasting views regarding the kinds of empirical and theoretical methods that are appropriate for sociological analysis.

The Chicago School. After Mead's death in 1931, a version of his work was carried on at the University of Chicago by his student Herbert Blumer, who posthumously published Mead's lecture notes and is credited with coining the phrase *symbolic interactionism.* Blumer's interactionism emphasizes the ever-changing, chameleon-like nature of the self and its tentative role in social interaction (i.e., the self is only one object among many objects that can influence a person's behavior in a situation). Accordingly, Blumer viewed social interaction as largely unpredictable, and society as carefully balanced, infinitely alterable, and thus full of potential for change. As such, Blumer advocated explorative methodologies and inductive theory-building as a means of achieving an interpretive understanding of social life.

The Iowa School. An alternative view of Mead's interactionism was developed by Manford Kuhn, who taught at the State University of Iowa from 1946 until his death in 1963. Compared with Blumer, Kuhn saw far more constancy in the self, arguing that people have a core self (i.e., a set of stable meanings toward themselves) arising from the social roles they occupy. According to Kuhn, the core self constrains a person: Each person experiences social reality and chooses behaviors in line with his or her core self across situations. Thus, Kuhn viewed social interaction as highly patterned and predictable, and society as a relatively stable place relating people in role networks. Accordingly, Kuhn argued on behalf of developing deductive theories from which predictions about human behavior could be formed and subsequently tested. Toward this effort, Kuhn developed the now-famous Twenty Statements Test in 1950, which within a few years became a popular research tool used for assessment of the core self. In this test, respondents are asked to provide 20 responses to the statement, "Who am I?"

Recent Advances. Major developments in modern symbolic interactionism represent ongoing efforts to translate Mead's ground-breaking yet vague ideas about self and society into testable claims. Central to some of these noteworthy efforts is the concept of identity, which refers to the components of the self containing the specific meanings that individuals assign to themselves because of the roles they occupy in society. Modern theories of identity fall under two distinct (though not competing) approaches. The *structural approach,* represented by the pioneering work of Sheldon Stryker and his colleagues, focuses on how social structures shape identities that, in turn, influence social behavior. *Cognitive approaches,* represented by Peter Burke's identity control theory and David Heise's affect control theory, focus on the psychological mechanisms that affect how individuals express identities in social interaction. One important similarity between Burke's theory and Heise's theory is that both offer a "control systems" view of the relationship between identities and behavior. In other words, identity meanings work like a temperature setting in a thermostat. When a room gets too cool, the thermostat tells the furnace to turn on and heat the room to the desired temperature. Similarly, if a person receives feedback from the environment (i.e., from others) that is not consistent with meanings associated with an identity, then the person will change her or his behavior to try to bring feedback into line with the identity.

An important difference between Burke's identity control theory and Heise's affect control theory, however, concerns the assumptions each makes about what people strive to control. Burke's view is more individualistic: People behave in ways that confirm their own self meanings. For example, a person who thinks of herself or himself as a bright student will behave in ways (e.g., working hard, striving to achieve excellent grades, participating frequently) to produce social feedback from others (parents, teachers, classmates) that confirms this self-view. By contrast, Heise argues that people behave in ways to create situations that confirm not only their own self meanings but also the meanings of other objects in the situation, including other people. Thus when a bright student interacts with a hardworking teacher in a classroom, each is motivated to behave toward the other in a manner that creates a socially appropriate situation for these identities in this particular context (i.e., the classroom). In this respect, Heise's theory is consistent with Blumer's view that the self is only one object that influences social behavior. Yet Heise's theorizing, unlike Blumer's, shows how behavior can nonetheless be predicted amid such incredible social complexity.

Social Structure and Personality

Social structure and personality shares many of symbolic interactionism's general ideas and concerns, yet it has traditionally emphasized how societal features influence many different aspects of people's individual lives. In this perspective, individuals are viewed as occupying different positions in a society. The relationships among the positions characterize the system's social structure. Social-structural positions place individuals in different social networks (including family, friendship, and coworker networks), involve specific expectations for behavior, and convey different levels of power and prestige. In turn, these features of social-structural positions affect their occupants in numerous ways. Social structure and personality studies have shown how the positions that people occupy in society (e.g., in terms of factors such as their occupational roles, gender, race, and relationship status) determine a variety of outcomes, including physical and mental health, involvement in criminal behavior, personal values, and status attainment. Mark Hayward at the University of Texas Population Center has conducted fascinating research showing that social conditions in childhood (such as socioeconomic status, whether the child grew up with both biological parents or in another type of family structure, whether the child's mother worked outside the home, etc.) affect age of death in adulthood. In recent years, however, analyses of social structure and personality have begun to place more emphasis on how individuals can influence societal patterns and trends. The actions of members of disadvantaged groups can sometimes lead to societal-level changes in the distribution of power, prestige, and privileges. A classic example is that of Rosa Louise McCauley Parks, an African American woman whose refusal to give up her bus seat to a White passenger in 1955 eventually led to the overturning of racial segregation laws across the United States. Indeed, Congress awarded Parks the prestigious Congressional Gold Medal in 1999, recognizing that she is widely hailed as the first lady of civil rights and the mother of the freedom movement.

Structural Social Psychology

Structural social psychology is an emerging variant of sociological social psychology that is similar to symbolic interactionism and social structure and personality in its recognition that social structures influence social interaction, and that social interaction perpetuates and sometimes leads to changes in social structure. However, the most distinctive and controversial feature of structural social psychology is its minimalist view of individuals. Although, for example, some social structure and personality researchers have called for richer, more detailed descriptions of individuals (incorporating a wide range of personality attributes, personal interests, goals, desires, etc.), structural social psychological theories stress just the opposite: Only those qualities of individual actors thought to be relevant to a specific theoretical question ought to be included. The guiding principle of this approach is what is referred to as scientific parsimony. That is, structural social psychologists aim to develop general theories that explain as much as possible while employing as few concepts and assumptions as possible. In contrast to a "more is better" ambition, structural social psychologists advocate a "less is more" approach. Major theories in this tradition include (but are not limited to) Joseph Berger and colleagues' expectation states theory, Noah Friedkin's social influence network theory, Barry Markovsky's multilevel theory of distributive justice, and Barry Markovsky and colleagues' network exchange theory.

An especially promising aspect of structural social psychological theorizing is its compatibility with agent-based modeling (ABM), the most recent approach to designing computer simulations of complex phenomena. Using what is called a bottom-up strategy, ABMs illustrate how complex system-level patterns emerge from the coordinated behaviors of actors assumed to follow very simple interaction rules (i.e., minimalist actors). For example, Craig Reynolds from Sony Corporation developed a now-famous ABM called *boids* that shows how complex and elegant flocking formations exhibited by birds in the real world are produced by computer-simulated birds that follow just three simple collision-avoidance rules. ABMs are now being used to model emergent complex patterns of human social behavior, including crowd behavior, cooperation, learning, and social influence. ABMs and structural social psychology have much to gain from one another. ABMs currently stress how complex social patterns and structures emerge from individual behavior, whereas structural social psychological theories have tended to emphasize (though not by necessity) the opposite (i.e., how social structures influence individual behavior). In the future, the two will realize their full potential by drawing from one another's strengths.

Implications

What do we make of the diversity of approaches to social psychology within the field of sociology? On one hand, the diverse character of sociological social psychology (and of sociology more generally) may in part indicate a lack of shared standards for developing and testing theories, which, as Barry Markovsky has argued in various places, lends itself to the creation of nebulous theories that lack true explanatory power. On the opposing hand, one might argue that the wide variety of approaches in sociological social psychology may reflect the diverse and multifaceted nature of the social phenomena under investigation, so theoretical and methodological differences ought to be tolerated, if not appreciated and cultivated. Resolution of this ongoing debate is perhaps one of the most important tasks facing sociology today.

Will Kalkhoff

See also History of Social Psychology; Self; Symbolic Interactionism

Further Readings

Axelrod, R., & Tesfatsion, L. (2006). *On-line guide for newcomers to agent-based modeling in the social sciences.* Retrieved September 29, 2006, from http://www.econ.iastate.edu/tesfatsi/abmdemo.htm

Cook, K. S., Fine, G. A., & House, J. S. (Eds.). (1995). *Sociological perspectives on social psychology.* Boston: Allyn & Bacon.

Heise, D. (n.d.). *Affect control theory.* Retrieved from http://www.indiana.edu/~socpsy/ACT/

House, J. S. (1977). The three faces of social psychology. *Sociometry, 40*(2), 161–177.

Lawler, E. J., Ridgeway, C., & Markovsky, B. (1993). Structural social psychology and the micro-macro problem. *Sociological Theory, 11*(3), 268–290.

Macy, M. W., & Willer, R. (2002). From factors to actors: Computational sociology and agent-based modeling. *Annual Review of Sociology, 28,* 143–166.

SOCIOMETRIC STATUS

Definition

Sociometric status refers to how much a child is liked and noticed by peers. It reflects a broader categorization of peer acceptance than simple friendships. Sociometric categories include popular, rejected, neglected, controversial, and average children. Sociometric status is important because peer relations play a significant role in the social and emotional development of children.

Evaluation

Sociometric status is evaluated by asking children to nominate the peers whom they most like and dislike, rate each peer on a scale ranging from *like very much* to *dislike very much,* or indicate their preferred playmates from among different pairs of children. Teachers, parents, and researchers also can provide their observations. Researchers use these positive and negative nominations to categorize each child's sociometric status.

Sociometric Categories

Popular

Popular children receive many positive and few negative nominations. They are well liked by others. Popular children are cooperative, sociable, friendly, and sensitive to others. Although they are assertive and capable of using aggression, they exhibit few disruptive and negative behaviors. Instead, they appear to use their social skills to get what they want without resorting to aggression. Popular children also tend to show high levels of academic and intellectual abilities. Children, teachers, and parents generally agree which children are popular. Overall, popular children are skilled in initiating and maintaining positive social interactions and relationships.

Rejected

Rejected children receive many negative and few positive nominations. They are actively disliked. Rejected children exhibit fewer positive social skills and traits than do children in the other groups, and they show weaker academic and intellectual abilities. Recent research indicates two types of children who are rejected: Children who display disruptive and aggressive behavior, and children who are socially anxious and withdrawn.

Children in the rejected-aggressive group display high levels of hostile and threatening behavior, physical aggression such as pushing and fighting, and disruptive behavior such as breaking rules. They also may display a hostile attribution bias or a tendency to assume that other children have hostile intentions in ambiguous situations. For example, if one child drops an art project and a second child steps on it before it can be retrieved, the scenario is ambiguous; it is unclear whether the second child stepped on it on purpose or by accident. Although nonrejected children recognize the ambiguity, rejected-aggressive children may assume that the negative act was purposeful, subsequently responding with aggressive retaliation. This aggressive retaliation is perceived as unwarranted by those who recognized the situational ambiguity, which feeds into the cycle of peer rejection.

Other children may be rejected because they display socially anxious behavior. These children are not overly aggressive. Rather, they are timid and wary in social situations, leading to uncomfortable, awkward interactions. Peers may find it difficult to predict how these children will act and may be less willing to approach them. Socially anxious children may then withdraw from future social situations. Rejected-withdrawn children appear to lack the social skills that make smooth interactions with peers possible.

Neglected

Neglected children receive few positive and few negative nominations. They engage in few disruptive and aggressive behaviors, and they show less sociability than their peers. However, research indicates that neglected children are not at great risk for negative outcomes. Indeed, in more structured activities, these children show more sociability. Otherwise, they may prefer solitary activities, ultimately contributing to their neglected status. Neglected children are not disliked. They simply are not noticed.

Controversial

Controversial children receive both positive and negative nominations. They are well liked by some children but actively disliked by others. These children engage in as much aggressive behavior as rejected-aggressive children. However, they compensate for their aggression with positive social behaviors. Similar to popular children, they tend to have high levels of academic and intellectual abilities. Their positive behaviors and attributes offset their higher levels of aggression. Ratings by children, teachers, and parents are less consistent regarding controversial children, perhaps because controversial children curb their aggressive displays when adults are present. Although controversial children engage in aggressive behavior, they are also cooperative and sociable.

Average

Average children receive an average number of positive and negative nominations. They do not fit into one of the more extreme categories. Most children fit into this category. They are more sociable than rejected and neglected children but not as sociable as popular and controversial children.

Stability and Implications

Over short periods, such as a few weeks or months, ratings for popular and rejected children remain fairly stable. Children in the neglected and controversial categories may fluctuate as school activities change and social skills develop. Over longer periods, stability ratings for rejected children are higher than for the other groups. In other words, children who are popular, neglected, or controversial when they are young may or may not hold that status several years later. However, children who are actively rejected at a young age still tend to be rejected several years later. Without intervention, they do not acquire the social skills they need to experience peer acceptance.

Rejected children, especially rejected-aggressive children, are at high risk for negative outcomes such as delinquency, hyperactivity, attention deficit hyperactivity disorder, conduct problems, and substance abuse. In addition, they are at higher risk than are the other groups for feelings of loneliness, depression, and for obsessive-compulsive disorder. However, these children can benefit from interventions. Parents and teachers who coach children on how to deal with conflict and difficult social situations, how to meet and interact with unfamiliar peers, and who also model and reinforce socially competent behavior can assist children in developing their social skills. Ultimately, children who learn about appropriate social behaviors, how to implement them, and how to interpret social feedback from others should become more socially competent and experience better peer relations.

Elizabeth L. Cralley

See also Aggression; Hostile Attribution Bias; Ostracism; Rejection; Research Methods

Further Readings

Newcomb, A. F., Bukowski, W. M., & Pattee, L. (1993). Children's peer relations: A meta-analytic review of popular, rejected, neglected, controversial, and average sociometric status. *Psychological Bulletin, 113,* 99–128.

SPONTANEOUS TRAIT INFERENCES

Definition

The notion of spontaneous trait inferences (STIs) refers to a frequently demonstrated empirical finding. Observing behaviors or reading behavior descriptions gives rise to immediate trait inferences, beyond the actually given information. Thus, somebody who steps on a partner's feet on the dance floor elicits the inference *clumsy*. Witnessing a student succeeding on a difficult task gives rise to the spontaneous inference *clever*. Such inferences take place even though the trait is not strictly implicated. Stepping on someone's feet can happen to nonclumsy people, just as even a dull student can solve a task under auspicious conditions. Logically, singular behaviors do not imply general traits. STIs are called spontaneous because they can be assumed to occur in the absence of explicit task instructions and deliberate intentions to think about

the traits that correspond to a given behavior. In STI experiments, researchers make serious attempts to conceal their interest in trait inferences, ruling out demand characteristics that might account for controlled trait inferences.

Measurements

Several paradigms have been developed to investigate STI effects experimentally. In the original cued-recall paradigm, participants are exposed to a list of behavior descriptions (e.g., "Steven stepped on his partner's feet on the dance floor"). Then, on a so-called cued-recall test, their task is to recall the previously presented behavior descriptions based on variable cue words or phrases. The specific types of cues given in the recall test are manipulated. As it turns out, trait words that represent reasonable inferences but that never appeared in the original sentences (such as *clumsy*) provide more effective retrieval cues than such words or phrases that actually occurred in the list, suggesting that traits must have been inferred spontaneously. In another word-fragment completion paradigm, being exposed to behavior descriptions facilitates the subsequent generation of a corresponding trait concept from an incomplete letter string. For instance, a person who has been primed with the earlier sentence takes less time to generate the word concept *clumsy* from the word fragment c–m–y than does somebody who was not exposed to that behavior. The faster response latency provides evidence that the trait concept has already been inferred implicitly. Unlike the cued-recall method, this method warrants trait inferences that occur immediately after the behavior has been presented, ruling out inferences during a later recall stage.

In a picture-priming paradigm, behaviors are presented in pictures or moving pictures (film clips), and participants have to identify a trait word that is first hidden behind a mask and that appears only gradually (over 3 seconds or so) as small pieces of the mask are removed in random order. Again, an STI effect is evident in response speed. When the trait to be identified constitutes a reasonable inference from the behavior presented in the preceding picture or film, the identification time is slower than on nonmatching trials. This method has been extended to control for the mental activity during behavior presentation, by inserting a verification task. Thus, participants have to verify an aspect of the picture or film (e.g., whether the presented behavior is an instance of *hitting* or *attacking* or an instance of *hostile*), before the trait identification task (e.g., involving the trait *aggressive*) starts. In this fashion, the trait inference process can be guided or tuned experimentally.

In still another method based on response latencies, the probe-recognition paradigm, the reaction time required to correctly falsify a trait word as having not appeared in a text passage is prolonged if that trait constitutes a plausible inference from a behavior read in a preceding sentence. Last but not least, the savings-in-relearning paradigm measures STI effects in terms of the reduced time required to relearn trait words when the list to be learned involves traits inferred from previously presented behaviors.

Practical and Theoretical Relevance

STIs have important practical and theoretical implications. Practically, drawing quick and unreflected inferences about people's traits can lead to premature action, uncritical decisions, and serious conflicts in diverse areas, such as personnel assessment or legal decisions. STIs can contribute to social stereotypes and cultural knowledge.

Theoretically, STI research is expected to further the understanding of quick and seemingly automatic social judgments based on unintended thought and unplanned, effortless cognitive operations. However, although trait inferences can occur spontaneously, in the absence of deliberate instructions or intentions, and demand little mental resources, other evidence suggests that the process is not fully automatic in some respects. First, STIs are stronger when inferred traits are consistent with an existing stereotype of the target. Accordingly, the trait *submissive* is more likely to be inferred from a corresponding behavior when the target person is female than male because submissive is part of the female gender stereotype. Second, trait inferences depend on the linguistic implications of the verbs used to describe a behavior. The same aggressive behavior will more likely elicit the trait inference *aggressive* when an action verb (such as *attack*) is used to describe this behavior than when a state verb (*hate*) is used because action verbs imply internal causes within the actor, whereas state verbs imply external causes outside the actor. Third, trait inferences can be influenced through attentional manipulations; they are bound to persons or faces that are the focus of attention when behaviors are observed.

The STI effect provides a theoretical model for the interpretation of several intriguing phenomena. These include the correspondence bias (default tendency to attribute behavior internally to person dispositions,

while neglecting situational constraints), spontaneous trait transference (blaming or praising communicators of unpleasant or pleasant messages), and perseverance effects (adhering to premature inferences that full debriefing has revealed to be wrong). Importantly, STI must not be equated with internal attributions of behaviors to person dispositions. Behaviors can also give rise to spontaneous situation inferences, implying external causes of the observed behavior in the environment.

Current Issues

Current research and theoretical discussions revolve around such issues as the cognitive states or mind-sets that facilitate STI tendencies, the binding of trait inferences to particular persons of faces associated with the observed behavior, and the intriguing issue of differences between cultures. Members of (Eastern) collectivist cultures have been shown to be less prone to trait inferences than are members of (Western) individualist cultures, in accordance with the assumption that collectivist cultures put less weight on personal factors in explaining the world than individualist cultures do.

Klaus Fiedler

See also Attributions; Collectivistic Cultures; Personality Judgments, Accuracy of; Priming

Further Readings

Newman, L. S., & Uleman, J. S. (1989). Spontaneous trait inference. In J. S. Uleman & J. A. Bargh (Eds.), *Unintended thought* (pp. 155–188). New York: Guilford Press.

Skowronski, J. J., Carlston, D. E., Mae, L., & Crawford, M. T. (1998). Spontaneous trait transference: Communicators take on the qualities they describe in others. *Journal of Personality and Social Psychology, 74*, 837–848.

Uleman, J. S., Hon, A., Roman, R., & Moskowitz, G. (1996). On-line evidence for spontaneous trait inferences at encoding. *Personality and Social Psychology Bulletin, 22*, 377–394.

SPOTLIGHT EFFECT

Definition

The spotlight effect is a very common psychological phenomenon that psychologists define as a person's tendency to overestimate the extent to which others notice, judge, and remember his or her appearance and behavior. In other words, it represents a person's conviction that the social spotlight shines more brightly on him or her than is actually the case. Would you be reluctant to go to the movies alone because of a fear that others might see you there and conclude that you don't have many friends? Do you spend long periods in front of the mirror each day making sure that your hair is groomed just right or that your clothes create just the right impression? Does it feel like all eyes are on you when you walk into a classroom a few minutes late? If you answered yes to any of these questions, you are prone to the spotlight effect.

Evidence

It's easy to find evidence of the spotlight effect. In one study, students arrived individually at a laboratory and were asked to don a T-shirt with a large picture of the pop singer Barry Manilow on the front. (This student population generally regarded Manilow as corny and uncool.) Students were then instructed to report to another laboratory down the hall. When they did so, they encountered another experimenter and several students seated around a table filling out questionnaires. After a brief time in this room, the student was told to wait outside because everyone else was too far ahead with the day's tasks. After waiting outside for a few minutes, the second experimenter emerged from the laboratory and asked the student a simple question: "How many of the students who were filling out questionnaires in the laboratory would be able to state who was pictured on your T-shirt?" Consistent with the idea that people tend to overestimate the extent to which others attend to them, the students wildly overestimated the number of students who noticed that it was Barry Manilow depicted on their T-shirts. The students thought that roughly half of those in attendance noticed, when in reality only about a quarter of them did so.

Other research has demonstrated that people overestimate the extent to which their own contributions to a group discussion are noticed and affect the other group members, that people think their absence from a group will stand out to others more than it actually does, and that people are convinced that the ups and downs of their performances—their good days and bad days—will register with others more than it truly does. Research has also shown that people tend to overestimate the extremity of others' judgments of them: They think they will be judged more harshly for potentially embarrassing mishaps and judged more favorably for their momentary triumphs than is actually the case.

People of all ages are prone to the spotlight effect, but it appears to be particularly pronounced among adolescents and young adults. This can be attributed to the fact that people are intensely social creatures, and so a heightened concern with how one stands in the eyes of others is an essential component of successful group life. But having a heightened concern with one's social standing means, by its very nature, that one is vulnerable to having an *excessive* concern with one's standing—and hence, is likely to overestimate the extent to which one is the target of others' thoughts and attention.

Implications

Should knowing about the spotlight effect encourage people to act differently than they would otherwise? Perhaps. One must often decide whether to act or not—to dive in the waves or stay on the beach, to go to the dance or stay home, to audition for a theater production or join a softball league—and sometimes social considerations play a prominent role in these calculations. What would others think? How would I look if I tried (and possibly failed)? What the existence of the spotlight effect suggests is that if these sorts of social considerations are largely making one lean against pursuing such actions, perhaps one should be more venturesome and take the plunge. After all, fewer people are likely to notice, and the social consequences are likely to be less pronounced, than one imagines.

Not that one should be cavalier about taking such actions. These calculations are rarely simple and, given that humans are fundamentally social creatures, their excessive sensitivity to what others think of them exists for a reason. What knowledge of the spotlight effect can contribute to these internal debates is a focus on the opinions that really matter—who the audience is that individuals are most concerned about—and a recognition that they are less salient to most audiences than they tend to think.

Thomas Gilovich

See also Self-Awareness; Social Anxiety; Social Comparison

Further Readings

Gilovich, T., Medvec, V. H., & Savitsky, K. (2000). The spotlight effect in social judgment: An egocentric bias in estimates of the salience of one's own actions and

appearance. *Journal of Personality and Social Psychology,
78,* 211–222.

Gilovich, T., & Savitsky, K. (1999). The spotlight effect and
the illusion of transparency: Egocentric assessments of
how we're seen by others. *Current Directions in
Psychological Science, 8,* 165–168.

Savitsky, K., Epley, N., & Gilovich, T. (2001). Is it as bad as
we fear? Overestimating the extremity of others'
judgments. *Journal of Personality and Social Psychology,
81,* 44–56.

SPREADING OF ALTERNATIVES

Inspired by cognitive dissonance theory, hundreds of
experiments have demonstrated that following a difficult decision, compared with an easy one, individuals
change their attitudes to be more consistent with their
decisions. That is, following a decision, individuals
evaluate the chosen alternative more positively and
the rejected alternative more negatively than they did
before the decision. This effect has been referred to as
spreading of alternatives because the attitudes toward
the chosen and rejected alternatives spread apart.
Attributes of decision alternatives also become more
coherent or more related with each other following
decisions. Memories are also affected by choice, such
that individuals incorrectly remember more positive
features of chosen options and more negative features
of rejected options.

In experiments on spreading of alternatives, people
are induced to make an easy or difficult decision.
An easy decision is created by having people chose
between two things that are very different in value,
with one being liked much and the other not being
liked as much. A difficult decision is created by having people chose between two things that are close in
value but with different attributes. According to the
theory of cognitive dissonance, after one makes a difficult decision, one will evaluate the chosen alternative as more positive and the rejected as more
negative. The decision does not need to be between
two initially positively valued items; negatively valued items cause spreading of alternatives too.

After the person makes a decision, each of the negative aspects of the chosen alternative and positive
aspects of the rejected alternative is dissonant (that is,
inconsistent) with the decision, whereas each of the
positive aspects of the chosen alternative and negative
aspects of the rejected alternative is consonant or (that

is, consistent) with the decision. Difficult decisions
arouse more dissonance than do easy decisions
because there are a greater proportion of dissonant
cognitions after a difficult decision than after an easy
one. Because of this, there will be greater motivation
to reduce the dissonance after a difficult decision.
Dissonance following a decision can be reduced by
removing negative aspects of the chosen alternative or
positive aspects of the rejected alternative, or adding
positive aspects to the chosen alternative or negative
aspects to the rejected alternative.

Research in both lab and field settings has provided
support for the prediction that difficult decisions cause
more spreading of alternatives than easy decisions do.
Most evidence has been in the form of self-reported
attitudes, though some research used behavioral and
physiological measures. Research has revealed that
individuals high in action orientation (who efficiently
implement actions) show greater spreading of alternatives than do individuals low in action orientation.
Spreading of alternatives research has implications for
life satisfaction, interpersonal relationships, gambling, smoking, and many other issues. For example,
when persons make a decision to commit to a relationship, they would be expected to increase their positive
evaluations of the relationship partner and decrease
their negative evaluations. This would lead to greater
relationship satisfaction.

Eddie Harmon-Jones
Cindy Harmon-Jones

See also Attitude Change; Cognitive Dissonance Theory;
Decision Making

Further Readings

Beauvois, J. L., & Joule, R. V. (1996). *A radical dissonance
theory.* London: Taylor & Francis.

Harmon-Jones, E., & Mills, J. (1999). *Cognitive dissonance:
Progress on a pivotal theory in social psychology.*
Washington, DC: American Psychological Association.

Wicklund, R. A., & Brehm, J. W. (1976). *Perspectives on
cognitive dissonance.* Hillsdale, NJ: Erlbaum.

STANFORD PRISON EXPERIMENT

The Stanford Prison Experiment (SPE) is a highly
influential and controversial study run by Philip

Zimbardo and his colleagues at Stanford University in 1971. The researchers originally set out to support the notion that situational forces are just as powerful and perhaps more powerful than dispositional forces in influencing prison behavior. In addition to providing support for their hypothesis, the study was heavily covered in the mainstream media and had far-reaching ethical implications. Regardless, and perhaps because of its controversial nature, the SPE remains one of the most well-known experiments in social psychology.

Purpose

The SPE was conceived as a reaction to the popular belief that the violent and oppressive nature of U.S. prisons and subsequent reports of humanitarian violations were due to the unique personality characteristics of the prisoners and guards. Because of self-selection, prison guards were believed to possess characteristics such as sadism and a lack of sensitivity. Prisoners, of course, are usually incarcerated because at some point in time they exhibited illegal behavior. Zimbardo and colleagues argued that this view discounts the powerful influence of the social situation in which guards are pitted against prisoners under a variety of social and political influences.

Methodology

To test their hypothesis, Zimbardo and colleagues created a realistic mock prison in the basement of Stanford University. The participants included 21 male college students, specifically chosen for their normal responses on a battery of background questionnaires. The participants were randomly assigned to be either a guard or a prisoner, with an undergraduate research assistant acting as warden and Zimbardo himself taking on the role of superintendent. The prisoners stayed in the prison 24 hours per day, while the guards worked 8-hour shifts. Aside from a restriction on physical violence, guards were given great latitude in how they could deal with prisoners, including the rules they could establish and punishments they could dole out.

The experimenters went to great lengths to establish realism. Prisoners were unexpectedly "arrested" at their houses by the local police department, were taken to the police station to be charged their "crime" and brought to the prison at Stanford. Prisoners were assigned a number and wore only a smock, which was designed to deindividuate the prisoners. Guards were fitted with a uniform, nightstick, and reflective sunglasses to establish power. The prison cells consisted of a 6- by 9-foot space furnished with only a cot. To further increase realism, a catholic priest and attorney were brought in and a parole board was established.

Once the participants had arrived at the prison, the situation escalated at a surprising rate. On the second day, a prisoner rebellion was quickly quelled by the guards, who punished the prisoners through means conceived without guidance from the experimenters. For example, prisoners were stripped naked, forced to do menial tasks, and in many cases were deprived of their cots, meals, and bathroom privileges. After the attempted revolt and subsequent punishment, five prisoners began to experience extreme emotional reactions and were eventually released. As the obedience tactics became more brutal and humiliating and prisoners displayed increasingly negative affectivity, Zimbardo eventually decided to end the study on the sixth day of what had been planned as a 2-week study.

Findings

Zimbardo and colleagues construed the increasingly hostile behavior of the guards and increasingly passive behavior of the prisoners, each of which had started out as groups of normal young men, as evidence that the extreme nature of the prison situation breeds such volatile and desperate behavior. Indeed, the SPE is often cited as evidence for the strong role of the situation over individuals in ways in which they often do not predict. The researchers also compared their work to Stanley Milgram's research on obedience in that both provide support for the notion that given an extreme situation, good people can be coerced into doing evil things. Despite these exciting findings, the SPE has been criticized from both a methodological and ethical standpoint.

Methodological Criticisms

Methodologically, critics have argued that participants of the SPE never fully accepted the situation as real and were merely playing the stereotypic roles of prisoners and guards. In essence, it was argued that the results were driven by demand characteristics of the experimental situation. It did not help the original authors' argument that Zimbardo himself played a prominent role in the experiment, sometimes guiding the way in which the study played out. Regardless, evidence suggests that participants did internalize the situation, as well as their roles in the situation. For instance, only one-tenth of the conversations between prisoners contained speech about life outside of the experiment.

Ethical Criticisms

The SPE was likely more controversial from an ethical point of view. The ethical implications of the study, as well as Zimbardo's dual role as investigator and superintendent of the Stanford prison were highly criticized at the time. Zimbardo himself admitted that his own acceptance of the prison situation and his desire to run a good prison clouded his judgment, suggesting that even he had internalized his role in the situation. Although the experiment did conform to the guidelines set forth by the ethics review board at the time, few would argue that the sadistic and humiliating acts performed during the study were ethical by today's standards. Even Zimbardo admits that it was unethical for the study to continue after the first prisoner showed an extreme negative reaction.

Replications

Stephen Reicher and S. Alexander Haslam attempted to replicate the SPE, skirting ethical guidelines through allowing the experiment to take place in the context of a British reality television show. The results of the SPE were not replicated; in Reicher and Haslam's version, the guards never organized themselves and were eventually overthrown.

Jason Chin

See also Aggression; Fundamental Attribution Error; Milgram's Obedience to Authority Studies; Robbers Cave Experiment

Further Readings

Adam, D. (2002). Reality TV show recreates famed social study. *Nature, 417,* 213.

Haney, C., Banks, C., & Zimbardo, P. (1973). Interpersonal dynamics in a simulated prison. *International Journal of Criminology and Penology, 1,* 69–97.

Zimbardo, P. G., Maslach, C., & Haney, C. (1999). Reflections on the Stanford Prison Experiment: Genesis, transformations, consequences. In T. Blass (Ed.), *Obedience to authority: Current perspectives on the Milgram paradigm* (pp. 193–237). Mahwah, NJ: Erlbaum.

STEALING THUNDER

Definition

Stealing thunder is a social influence tactic in which in anticipation of negative information being revealed about a person, that person chooses to reveal it first. By doing so, the negative impact is reduced or, in some cases, eliminated. An individual's representative can also steal thunder with similar consequences, as in the case of an attorney who steals thunder by revealing the worst bit of evidence before the opposing counsel brings it out.

Courtrooms provide the best example of the use of stealing thunder. Defense attorneys may reveal incriminating evidence about their clients, for instance that they had a prior conviction, before prosecuting attorneys can reveal it. The defense attorney might use the stealing thunder technique to minimize the damage caused by incriminating evidence against his or her client.

Evidence

Based on naive theories and research, beginning an interaction by revealing damaging information about one's self would seem to backfire by creating a negative first impression that would negatively bias future information and impressions. In many circumstances, the fact that the negative information is revealed again (as in the case of a courtroom trial) by someone else would also increase the salience of the information. Nevertheless, research has demonstrated that stealing thunder can be quite effective. In mock trial studies, researchers have found that both the defense (in a criminal trial) and plaintiffs (in a civil trial) can benefit by stealing thunder. Legal experts suggest that the reason that stealing thunder is potentially effective is that the attorney who reveals it first can put a positive spin on the negative information.

In addition to showing the effectiveness of stealing thunder in courtroom settings, research has also found positive benefits in a political domain. Voters (or mock voters) are more likely to indicate a willingness to vote for a candidate who reveals a transgression himself or herself, than they are if an adversary (or the media) reveals the same information. News editors also indicate less interest in pursuing the story when candidates reveal the information.

Reasons for Effectiveness

Recent research suggests several reasons stealing thunder might work. One is that the revealer appears to be credible, and thus, likeable. Another is that because the negative self-revelation is so unexpected, message recipients force the meaning of the information to be less damaging. Another reason is that stealing thunder allows the revealer to cast the information in a favorable light, but the available research suggests that putting a positive spin on the information is not necessary for the effect to emerge. Still another reason that stealing thunder may work is that by making the information more public and common, less attention and value are placed on it. When people perceive information to be scarce or secret, they think it is more valuable. Stealing thunder diminishes the perception that the information is scarce.

Limitations

The question still remains, when will stealing thunder work and not work? Do factors such as the timing of stealing thunder, the seriousness of the thunder information, and the use of compelling spin moderate the effects? In a courtroom context, the existing research suggests that the timing of stealing thunder does not seem to affect how well thunder stealing works. Damaging information presented by the defendant's lawyer earlier or later in the case did not reduce the benefits of stealing thunder. Nor did it matter if the opposing counsel chose not to reveal the negative information after all. However, acknowledging incriminating evidence after it has been disclosed does not reduce the impact of negative information.

Regardless of how serious the damaging information is (bouncing a series of check compared with smuggling drugs), stealing thunder appears to reduce the information's negative impact. Stealing thunder continues to work even if the information is very damaging. In a mock court case involving homicide resulting from reckless driving, stealing thunder remained effective at reducing negative information even when the defendant admitted veering into the oncoming traffic lane. One boundary condition discovered so far

is that if the message recipients (in this case, mock jurors) are told during closing arguments that the other attorney manipulated their opinions by using the stealing thunder tactic, then they are no longer positively influenced by stealing thunder.

Whether stealing thunder works best under heuristic (i.e., low effort) or systematic (i.e., high effort) processing remains to be determined. Whereas source credibility is often used as a short-cut to message processing, changing the meaning of the message to be consistent with the message source would require considerable cognitive effort and elaboration.

Implications

Stealing thunder has been demonstrated to be an effective way to minimize (or eliminate) the impact of incriminating information in a variety of different contexts. Most legal experts already are aware of its benefits (even if they are not aware of the reasons why it works) and use it regularly in court. Ironically, politicians (many of whom are lawyers) are generally not willing to take the chance of stealing thunder and are more likely to deny wrongdoings to the bitter end.

Kipling D. Williams
James Wirth

See also Embarrassment; MUM Effect; Self-Presentation

Further Readings

Williams, K. D., & Dolnik, L. (2001). Revealing the worst first: Stealing thunder as a social influence strategy. In J. P. Forgas, & K. D. Williams (Eds.), *Social influence: Direct and indirect processes* (pp. 213–231). Philadelphia: Psychology Press.

STEREOTYPES AND STEREOTYPING

Definition

A stereotype is a generalized belief about the characteristics that are associated with the members of a social group. In 1922, the journalist Walter Lippmann first popularized the term *stereotype,* which he described as the image people have in their heads of what a social group is like. Early researchers examined the content of social stereotypes by asking people to indicate which psychological traits they associate with various ethnic and national groups (e.g., Germans, Blacks, Jews). This research indicated that there was a good deal of consensus in the public's image of these social groups, with generally strong agreement about which characteristics are typical of each group. There was also a tendency for these "pictures in our heads" to contain more negative than positive characteristics.

Origins

Having cataloged the content of stereotypes, subsequent generations of researchers sought to explain how and why stereotypes develop. One approach examined how socialization processes perpetuate stereotypes, emphasizing the ways whereby parents, peers, and the media communicate and reinforce stereotypic images of social groups. The consensus of stereotypes can be explained, from this perspective, by the transmission of broader cultural biases to new generations of children as they develop within a society. However, this approach does not explain where the stereotypes came from in the first place. To answer that question, some researchers turned to motivational approaches. From this perspective, stereotypes arise to satisfy important psychological needs. For example, a person's stereotypes about other groups may make the person feel superior. In support of that possibility, researchers have shown that after experiencing a threat to one's self-esteem, stereotypic thoughts about a minority group are more likely to come to mind. Stereotypes also function to support and rationalize intergroup conflict over valuable resources, making one social group feel justified in hostile actions taken toward other groups. In addition, as noted in system justification theory, stereotypes work to justify the status quo, making a person feel comfortable with the disparities that are present in society. That is, stereotypes provide people with a way of convincing themselves that there are good (and fair) explanations for social inequality. For example, a person might reason that if some social groups have achieved less economic success, it must be because of their inherently deficient characteristics (e.g., laziness, lack of ability). In this way, social inequality can be blamed on the disadvantaged groups themselves (rather than on unfair discrimination or the legacy of historical disadvantages). Interestingly, the need to justify the social system appears to be so strong that even disadvantaged minorities themselves sometimes accept these negative stereotypes of their own groups. These kinds of motivational explanations can readily account for the predominantly negative quality of many social stereotypes.

Recent research shows that stereotypes tend to cluster around two broad themes. One theme concerns competence: Are members of the group smart and successful? The second theme concerns warmth: Are members of the group likeable, friendly, and unthreatening? Perhaps unsurprisingly, members of the dominant (majority) social group tend to regard their own group as both competent and warm. Many other groups are regarded with a mixture of ambivalent stereotypes. Some groups, such as women and the elderly, are commonly seen as being quite warm but lacking competence, whereas other groups, such as Asians and Jews, tend to be seen by the majority group as being quite competent but lacking in warmth. Only relatively few groups (e.g., the homeless, drug addicts) are seen as lacking on both dimensions. In general, however, this research confirms that the stereotypes of many social groups are marked by at least one negative theme.

Much research in recent decades has examined the cognitive processes underlying stereotyping. From this perspective, stereotypes serve a knowledge function, organizing and structuring one's understanding of the social environment. The social cognition perspective emphasizes that stereotypes arise from the normal, everyday operation of basic mental processes such as attention, memory, and inference. In everyday life, a person is potentially exposed to information about the members of various social groups in diverse ways. One may see them on TV, hear friends talk about them, or actually encounter them in person. The social cognition perspective asserts that the stereotypes a person forms will be determined by which aspects of this parade of information he or she pays attention to and remembers. Essentially, there is a basic process of learning involved in the formation of stereotypes, but this process may not necessarily be objective and unbiased. Indeed, an important question that has not yet been fully addressed is the extent to which everyday learning processes result in stereotypes that are reasonably accurate.

Certainly, it seems intuitively unlikely that one would form wildly inaccurate stereotypes, and even if one did, it is still unclear how he or she could maintain them in the face of continual disconfirmation. Yet social cognition research suggests that it is indeed possible for people to be systematically biased in what they "know" about social groups. People often possess an extensive mental database containing evidence supporting the apparent accuracy of their stereotypes, but this seemingly compelling evidence may be substantially illusory. First, for people to form accurate images of a social group, they would need to be exposed to representative samples of group members; however, representative samples may be hard to come by (especially for groups that are personally encountered less frequently) if the media, gossip, and other forms of public discourse focus selectively on the more negative aspects of a social group's behavior. Even if a representative sample of behavior is available, people would still have to be equally sensitive to all types of presented information for their mental image of a group to be objectively accurate. Research suggests that again, there is a tendency to pay greater attention to negative information, especially when it is associated with a distinctive social group (such as a minority group). And when people start out with a clear expectation about what a group is like, they may be biased in what they perceive and remember in subsequently encountered information about the group. Although it is an open question just how accurate most social stereotypes are, available research shows that exaggerated and inaccurate stereotypes can form and be maintained under at least some circumstances.

Consequences

When a person encounters a member of a stereotyped group, the stereotypes associated with that group may be automatically *activated;* that is, the specific characteristics that are seen as typical of the group may become more accessible in the person's mind. This process of stereotype activation can happen even in cases in which a person does not personally endorse or accept the stereotype as accurate. As long as there is an association between the group and the stereotypic characteristic stored in memory (e.g., from frequent exposure to common cultural images of a group), the stereotype can become activated upon encountering a member of the stereotyped social group. If this happens, the stereotype can exert a host of effects on the way this person is perceived and treated. Most of these effects occur rapidly, involuntarily, and often without any awareness that they are taking place.

Social psychologists have developed several ways of detecting that stereotypes become activated in people's minds rapidly and automatically. For example, research indicates that many people are influenced by gender stereotypes in this manner. Participants are exposed to a series of photographs of men and women, and after each photograph, they have to respond to a target word as quickly as possible. After seeing a picture of a man, people tend to be reliably

faster to respond to stereotypically masculine concepts (e.g., "strong") but reliably slower to respond to stereotypically feminine concepts (e.g., "soft"). The converse pattern happens after exposure to a picture of a woman. Thus, merely encountering a picture of a person is all it takes for gender-related stereotypic concepts to become more accessible in the minds of perceivers. The automatic activation of stereotypes is common but by no means universal. Substantial individual differences exist, and the immediate context is important too. For example, in a situational context in which ethnicity is more salient than sex, the same set of target photos might evoke automatic racial stereotypes but not gender stereotypes. In most cases, however, a person does form some kind of rapid impression of another person, and often this impression is based partly on the application of activated stereotypes regarding some (but probably not all) of the target person's social groups.

Once activated, stereotypes can exert a host of important effects on the way a person sees the world. For example, once a stereotype is activated, it can bias the way the person interprets ambiguous behavior. If one holds the stereotype that Arabs are dangerous, then even fairly mundane behavior by an Arab (or someone who looks vaguely like an Arab) can take on seemingly sinister overtones in one's mind. In this kind of situation, ambiguous behavior is *assimilated* to the stereotypic ideas that are activated in the perceiver's mind. Stereotypes can also bias the way a person explains social events. For example, leadership skill is stereotypically associated more with men than with women. A successful male executive is often credited with business savvy and leadership skill, whereas a successful female executive's performance might be explained by favorable economic conditions or even blind luck. Because the causes of most events are often at least somewhat ambiguous, stereotypes can influence which elements of the situation stand out as causally important. Stereotypic outcomes readily suggest stereotypic personal causes (e.g., a male's leadership skill), whereas counterstereotypic outcomes call for situational or temporary causes (e.g., favorable market conditions). Notice that these biasing effects of stereotypes tend to reinforce the stereotype's apparent accuracy by adding to one's mental database of confirmatory instances (simultaneously overlooking or discounting disconfirming instances).

Stereotypes may also be self-perpetuating in the sense that people who hold strong stereotypes may act in ways that bring about the confirmation of their beliefs. For example, if a person believes that African Americans are hostile, then he or she may interact with African Americans in a relatively unfriendly way; such treatment often tends to elicit a response that is also unfriendly, thereby seeming to confirm the expected hostility. This kind of self-fulfilling prophecy adds to the appearance of stereotype accuracy.

People form stereotypes about all kinds of social groups, but much of the focus of social psychological research has been on stereotypes about groups defined by basic demographic features (such as ethnicity, sex, or age). Because of the historical injustices associated with racism, sexism, and ageism, researchers have sought to understand the connections between stereotypes and discrimination in these particular domains. In most cases, it does not seem that people engage in generalized discrimination toward minority groups; that is, they do not tend to respond negatively or unfairly to group members generally, irrespective of context or circumstances. Instead, the forms of discrimination often align with the content of stereotypes. Sexist discrimination provides a clear example. Women face employment discrimination primarily in situations in which they seek to take on traditionally masculine roles (e.g., business executive), but not in cases in which they seek traditionally feminine roles (e.g., school teacher). Stereotypes create the expectation that women, despite their many positive qualities, "don't have what it takes" to be forceful, effective business leaders. Research on racial stereotypes similarly shows that race-based discrimination against ethnic minorities is much more likely in stereotypic cases. In some studies, for example, African Americans and Latinos have been judged more likely to be guilty of blue-collar crimes (such as theft or assault) than a White defendant, but the pattern reverses for white-collar crimes (such as embezzlement or computer hacking). Thus, people do not discriminate against any particular group across the board; rather, the content of social stereotypes directs the focus and form of discrimination faced by the members of stereotyped groups.

Social psychologists are not the only ones to notice these connections between stereotyping and discrimination. During the 20th century, the general public also came to associate stereotyping of these groups with social injustice, leading to the common view that stereotyping is inappropriate and unacceptable. As a result, people often disavow stereotypic ideas, yet as previously noted, this personal rejection of stereotypes provides no guarantee that their activation and

influence will be avoided. One strategy for avoiding unwanted stereotypic reactions is to try to suppress stereotypes, or prevent them from coming into one's mind. Numerous studies have examined the effects of trying not to have stereotypic thoughts come to mind. This research emphasizes that, although the process of activating and using stereotypes is often quite efficient and largely automatic, the process of trying to squelch these stereotypes is typically much more effortful. It takes mental energy and focused effort to do it successfully. If perceivers have consistent motivation and ample free attention, they can succeed in suppressing stereotypic responses, but if their motivation lapses, or they become distracted, trying to suppress stereotypes can actually result in a rebound effect, in which the stereotypes become even more accessible than they would have been if suppression had never been attempted. Fortunately, there is growing evidence that it is possible for perceivers to unlearn unwanted cultural stereotypes and to become quite efficient in inhibiting these stereotypes. Research examining the most rapid responses that happen in the first seconds of encountering a member of a stereotyped group confirm that individuals can succeed in overcoming stereotypic biases and that this process of inhibiting stereotypic responses does not have to remain effortful and taxing (although it may start out that way).

Implications

Stereotypes play an important role in how people perceive and form impressions of others. Once an individual is categorized as a member of a particular group, he or she can come to be judged in terms of group-based expectations. In the absence of clear disconfirmation, the person can easily be seen as a "typical" member of that group, interchangeable with other group members. In contrast to such category-based impressions, perceivers can instead judge individuals on the basis of personal attributes, some of which may be typical of their group, but many of which are not. This process of *individuation*, though escaping the risks of inaccurate or exaggerated stereotyping, requires a much larger investment of time and energy. To come to know an individual's personal attributes, rather than simply assuming that he or she possesses group-typical attributes, requires fairly extensive contact and unbiased appraisals of the individual who is encountered. Given these demands, stereotyping may often be the default process guiding social perception when the need or desire for accurate impressions is not especially pressing.

Galen V. Bodenhausen
Andrew R. Todd
Andrew P. Becker

See also Automatic Processes; Expectancy Effects; Mental Control; Outgroup Homogeneity; Prejudice; Racism; Self-Stereotyping; Sexism; Social Categorization; Subtyping; System Justification

Further Readings

Jost, J. T., & Hamilton, D. L. (2005). Stereotypes in our culture. In J. F. Dovidio, P. Glick, & L. A. Rudman (Eds.), *On the nature of prejudice: Fifty years after Allport* (pp. 208–224). Malden, MA: Blackwell.

Lippmann, W. (1961). *Public opinion.* New York: Macmillan.

Operario, D., & Fiske, S. T. (2004). Stereotypes: Content, structures, processes, and context. In M. B. Brewer & M. Hewstone (Eds.), *Social cognition* (pp. 120–141). Malden, MA: Blackwell.

Quinn, K. A., Macrae, C. N., & Bodenhausen, G. V. (2003). Stereotyping and impression formation: How categorical thinking shapes person perception. In M. A. Hogg & J. Cooper (Eds.), *The Sage handbook of social psychology* (pp. 87–109). London: Sage.

Schneider, D. J. (2003). *The psychology of stereotyping.* New York: Guilford Press.

STEREOTYPE THREAT

Definition

Stereotype threat arises from the recognition that one could be judged or treated in terms of a negative stereotype about one's group. This sense of threat usually happens when one is doing something to which such a stereotype applies. Then one knows that one is subject to be judged or treated in terms of that stereotypes—as when, for example, an older person is trying to remember where he or she placed the house keys. The negative stereotype alleging poorer memory among older people applies. As the person searches, he or she is aware of confirming this stereotype or being seen as confirming it. If the person is invested in having a good memory, the prospect of being judged or treated this way could be upsetting, distracting. It could even have the ironic effect of interfering with the person's ability to find the lost keys. Most research on stereotype threat has examined how this threat affects the intellectual performance of groups whose intellectual abilities are negatively stereotyped in the larger society—for example, women performing advanced math, as well as minority groups performing difficult cognitive tasks in general.

Most often stereotypes are seen to affect their targets through the discriminatory behavior and judgment of people who hold the stereotype. An implication of stereotype threat, however, is that stereotypes can affect their targets even before they are translated into behavior or judgments. The mere threat of such judgment and treatment—like the threat of a snake loose in the house—can have effects of its own.

Stereotype threat has several features and parameters.

General Features

Stereotype threat is situational in nature. It arises from situational cues signaling the relevance of a stereotype to one's behavior. Experiencing it doesn't depend on a particular state or trait of the target such as believing in the stereotype, or holding low expectations that might result from chronic exposure to the stereotype. Such internal states or traits are neither necessary nor sufficient to the experience of stereotype threat.

Stereotype threat is a general threat that is experienced in some setting or another by virtually everyone. All people have some social identity for which negative stereotypes exist—the elderly, the young, Methodists, Blacks, Whites, athletes, artists, and so forth. And when they are doing things for which those stereotypes apply, they can experience this threat.

The nature of the threat depends on the content of the negative stereotype. The specific meaning of the stereotype determines the situations, the people, and the activities to which it applies, and thus becomes capable of causing a sense of stereotype threat. For example, the type of stereotype threat experienced by men, women, and teenagers would vary considerably, focusing on sensitivity in the first group, math skills in the second, and maturity and self-control in the third. And for each group, the threat would be felt in situations to which their group stereotype applies, but not in other situations. For example, a woman could feel stereotype threat in a math class where a negative group stereotype applies but not in an English class where it doesn't apply.

The Strength of a Stereotype Threat

The strength of a stereotype threat also depends, in part, on the meaning of the stereotype involved. Some stereotypes have more negative meaning than others do. A stereotype that demeans a group's integrity should pose a stronger threat than a stereotype that demeans a group's sense of humor, for example.

How much a person identifies with the domain of activity to which a stereotype applies should also affect the strength of the stereotype threat he or she experiences. The more one cares about a domain, the more upset one is likely to be over the prospect of being stereotyped in it.

The more one cares about the group identity that is being stereotyped, the more upset one should be by the prospect of being group stereotyped

Generally, the more capable one feels about coping with the threat, the less intense the experience of stereotype threat should be.

Claude Steele
Joshua Aronson
Steve Spencer

See also Identity Status; Self-Stereotyping; Stigma

Further Readings

Spencer, S. J., Steele, C. M., & Quinn, D. M. (1999). Stereotype threat and women's math performance. *Journal of Experimental Social Psychology, 35,* 4–28.

Steele, C. M. (1997). A threat in the air: How stereotypes shape the intellectual identities and performance of women and African-Americans. *American Psychologist, 52,* 613–629.

Steele, C. M., & Aronson, J. (1995). Stereotype threat and the intellectual test performance of African-Americans. *Journal of Personality and Social Psychology, 69,* 797–811.

STERNBERG'S TRIANGULAR THEORY OF LOVE

See TRIANGULAR THEORY OF LOVE

STIGMA

Definition

Stigma is an attribute or characteristic that marks a person as different from others and that extensively discredits his or her identity. Ancient Greeks coined the term *stigma* to describe a mark cut or burned into the body that designated the bearer as someone who was morally defective, such as a slave, criminal, or traitor. Sociologist Erving Goffman resurrected the term, defining *stigma* as an attribute that spoils a person's identity, reducing him or her in others' minds "from a whole and usual person to a tainted, discounted one." Stigmatizing marks are associated with negative evaluations and devaluing stereotypes. These negative evaluations and stereotypes are generally well known among members of a culture and become a basis for excluding, avoiding, and discriminating against those who possess (or are believed to possess) the stigmatizing mark. People who are closely associated with bearers of stigma may also experience some of the negative effects of stigma, a phenomenon known as *stigma by association.*

Stigma does not reside in a person but in a social context. For example, within the United States, gays and lesbians are stigmatized across a range of situations, but not in a gay bar. African Americans are stigmatized in school but not on the basketball court. This contextual aspect of stigma means that even attributes that are not typically thought of as being stigmatizing may nonetheless lead to social devaluation in some social contexts (e.g., being heterosexual at a gay pride rally). Some marks, however, are so pervasively devalued in society that they cause bearers of those marks to experience stigmatization across a wide range of situations and relationships. The consequences of stigmatization are far more severe for these individuals than for those who experience stigmatization only in very limited contexts.

Types and Dimensions

Goffman categorized stigmatizing marks into three major types: tribal stigma, abominations of the body, and blemishes of character. Tribal stigmas are passed from generation to generation and include membership in devalued racial, ethnic, or religious groups. Abominations of the body are uninherited physical characteristics that are devalued, such as obesity or physical deformity. Blemishes of character are individual personality or behavioral characteristics that are devalued, such as being a child abuser or rapist.

Stigmas also differ on important dimensions, such as the extent to which they are concealable, controllable, and believed to be dangerous. These differences have important implications for how the stigmatized are treated by others, and how stigma is experienced by those who have a stigmatizing condition.

Some marks (e.g., obesity) are visible or cannot be easily concealed from others, whereas others (e.g., being a convicted felon) are not visible or can more easily be concealed. Individuals whose stigma is visible must contend with different issues than do those whose stigma is invisible. The visibly stigmatized are more likely to encounter avoidance and rejection from others than those whose stigmas are concealed. Consequently, the former may be more likely to interpret others' behavior in terms of their stigma and be more concerned with managing others' treatment of them. People whose stigmas are concealable, in contrast, have a different set of concerns. Although they may be able to "pass" or hide their stigma from others, they may be preoccupied with figuring out the attitudes of others toward their (hidden) stigma and with managing how and when to disclose their stigma to others. They must live with the fear of others finding out about their stigma, and of being discredited. They may also have a harder time finding others like themselves to interact with, which may lead to social isolation and lowered self-esteem.

The perceived controllability of a stigma is also important. Stigmas are perceived as controllable when the bearer is thought to be responsible for acquiring the stigmatizing mark or when it is thought that the condition could be eliminated by the behavior of the bearer. Obesity, drug addiction, and child abuse are examples of marks generally perceived to be controllable; whereas skin color and physical disability are examples of marks generally thought to be uncontrollable. People with stigmas that are believed to be controllable are more disliked, rejected, and less likely to receive help than are people whose stigmas are perceived as uncontrollable. Perceived controllability can also affect the bearer's behavior. Those who view their stigma as controllable, for example, may focus more on escaping or eliminating it than might those who perceive their stigma as uncontrollable.

Functions

Most scholars regard stigma as socially constructed, meaning that the particular attributes or characteristics that are stigmatized are determined by society. This view is supported by evidence of variability across cultures in the attributes that are stigmatized. For example, obesity is severely stigmatized in the United States, far less so in Mexico, and is prized in some cultures. Even within the same culture, the degree to which a particular attribute is stigmatizing can change over time. For example, in the United States, being divorced was much more stigmatizing in earlier than it is today. Some commonalities exist across cultures, however, in what attributes are stigmatized.

Social stigma occurs in every society. This universality suggests that stigmatization may serve some functional value for individuals, groups, or societies. At the individual level, putting someone else down may make one feel better about oneself as an individual. At the group level, devaluing other groups may help people feel better about their own groups by comparison. At the societal level, negatively stereotyping and devaluing people who are low in social status may make their lower status seem fair and deserved, thereby legitimizing social inequalities in society. Stigmatization may also serve a fourth function. Evolutionary psychologists propose that it may have evolved among humans to avoid the dangers that accompany living with other people. Specifically, they posit that humans have developed cognitive adaptations that cause them to exclude (stigmatize) people who possess (or who are believed to possess) attributes that (a) signal they might carry parasites or other infectious diseases (such as a having a physical deformity or AIDS), (b) signal that they are a poor partner for social exchange (such as a having a criminal record), or (c) signal they are a member of an outgroup that can be exploited for one's own group's gain.

Consequences

Stigmatization has profound and wide-ranging negative effects on those who bear (or who are thought to bear) stigmatizing marks. Stigmatization has been linked to lower social status, poverty, impaired cognitive and social functioning, poorer physical health, and poorer mental health. These negative effects can occur through several pathways.

Direct Effects

Stigma has direct negative effects on bearers by increasing their likelihood of experiencing social rejection, exclusion, prejudice, and discrimination. Research has established that the stigmatized are vulnerable to a variety of types of social rejection, such as slurs, slights, derision, avoidance, and violence. People who are stigmatized also receive poorer treatment in the workplace, educational settings, healthcare system, housing market, and criminal justice system. Stigma even has negative effects on family relationships. For example, parents are less likely to pay for the college education of their daughters who are heavy than of daughters who are thin. Discrimination can be interpersonal (e.g., when a woman is rejected by a man because of her weight) or institutional (e.g., when a woman is denied a job as a flight attendant because of institutionalized height and weight requirements).

Stigma also can have direct, negative effects on the stigmatized through the operation of expectancy confirmation processes. When people hold negative beliefs about a person because of the person's stigma (e.g., believe that someone who has been hospitalized for mental illness is dangerous), their beliefs (incorrect or correct) can lead them to behave in certain ways toward the stigmatized that are consistent with their beliefs (e.g., avoid the stigmatized, watch them suspiciously, refuse to hire them). These behaviors can cause the stigmatized to respond in ways that confirm the initial evaluation or stereotype (e.g., they get angry, hostile). This can happen without the stigmatized person even being aware that the other person (perceiver) holds negative stereotypes, and even when the perceiver is not conscious of holding negative stereotypes.

People who are stigmatized are not always treated negatively by those who are not stigmatized. People often feel ambivalence toward the stigmatized; they may feel sympathy for the plight of the stigmatized while feeling that the stigmatized are dependent, lazy, or weak. People may also experience aversion and negative affect toward the stigmatized yet also desire to respond positively toward them to avoid appearing prejudiced, either to others or to themselves. As a result of these conflicting motives and feelings, bearers of stigma sometimes are treated extremely positively, and at other times extremely negatively. People behave more positively toward the stigmatized in public settings than in private settings, and report being less prejudiced on explicit measures of liking (such as attitude questionnaires) than implicit measures of liking (such as reaction time, or other measures of attitudes

that are not under conscious control). These conflicting responses can make it difficult for the stigmatized to gauge how others really feel about them.

Indirect Effects

Stigma also has indirect effects on the stigmatized by influencing how they perceive and interpret their social worlds. Virtually all members of a culture, including bearers of stigma, are aware of cultural stereotypes associated with stigma, even if they do not personally endorse them. People who are stigmatized are aware that they are devalued in the eyes of others, know the dominant cultural stereotypes associated with their stigma, and recognize that they could be victims of discrimination. These beliefs are *collective representations,* in that they are typically shared by others who bear the same stigma. These collective representations influence how bearers of stigma approach and interpret situations in which they are at risk of being devalued, negatively stereotyped, or targets of discrimination. For some, their stigma may become a lens through which they interpret their social world. They may become vigilant for signs of devaluation and anticipate rejection in their social interactions.

Collective representations can have negative effects on the stigmatized by increasing their concerns that they will be negatively evaluated because of their stigma, a psychological state termed *identity threat.* Identity threat is not chronic, but situational; it occurs only in situations in which people are at risk of devaluation because of their stigma. When experienced, identity threat can interfere with working memory, performance, and social relationships and can increase anxiety and physiological stress responses. One form of identity threat is *stereotype threat,* concern that one's behavior will be interpreted in light of or confirm negative stereotypes associated with one's stigma. Stereotype threat occurs in situations in which negative group stereotypes are relevant and may be applied to the self and can impair performance in those domains.

Collective representations can also lead bearers to experience *attributional ambiguity* in situations in which their stigma is relevant. Attributional ambiguity stems from bearers' awareness that they may be targets of prejudice and discrimination. As a consequence of this awareness, bearers of stigma (particularly those whose stigma is visible) who are treated negatively may be unsure whether it was caused by something about themselves (such as their performance or lack of qualifications) or was caused by prejudice and discrimination based on their stigma. Positive outcomes can also be attributionally ambiguous. As noted earlier, bearers of stigma are often exposed to inconsistent treatment and are aware of discrepancies between how the nonstigmatized feel and how they behave toward the stigmatized. As a consequence, bearers of stigma may mistrust the validity, sincerity, and diagnosticity of positive as well as negative feedback. This, in turn, can negatively affect their social relationships as well as interfere with their abilities to make accurate self-assessments.

Collective representations associated with stigma influence how bearers of stigma perceive, interpret, and interact with their social world. Through this process, stigma can have negative effects on bearers in the absence of any obvious forms of discriminatory behavior on the part of others, even if a stigmatizing mark is unknown to others, and even when no other person is present in the immediate situation.

Coping Strategies

Some psychological theories describe bearers of stigma as passive victims who cannot help but devalue themselves because they are devalued by society. In fact, research shows that not all bearers of stigma are depressed, have low self-esteem, or perform poorly. Indeed, members of some stigmatized groups have higher self-esteem on average than do members of nonstigmatized groups. How bearers of stigma respond to their predicament varies tremendously. An important determinant of their response is how they *cope* with the threats to their identity that their stigma poses.

Bearers cope with stigmatization in a variety of ways. Some coping efforts are problem focused. For example, the stigmatized may attempt to eliminate the mark that is the source of stigmatization, such as when an obese person goes on a diet or a stutterer enrolls in speech therapy. This strategy, of course, is not available to bearers whose stigma cannot be eliminated. Bearers may also cope by trying to avoid stigmatization, such as when a person with a concealable stigma "passes" as a member of more valued group, or an overweight person avoids going to the gym or the beach. This coping strategy may severely constrain the everyday lives of the stigmatized. The stigmatized may also cope by attempting to overcome stigma by compensating, or striving even harder in domains where they are negatively stereotyped or devalued. For example, one study showed that overweight women who believed that an interaction partner could see them (and hence believed their weight might negatively affect the interaction)

compensated by behaving even more sociably compared with overweight women who thought their interaction partner could not see them. Although this strategy can be effective, it can also be exhausting, especially in the face of enormous obstacles.

Other coping strategies focus on managing the negative emotions or threats to self-esteem that stigmatization may cause. For example, the stigmatized may cope with threats to their identity by disengaging their self-esteem from domains in which they are negatively stereotyped or fear being a target of discrimination and investing themselves more in domains in which they are less at risk. When they encounter negative treatment, another coping strategy they may use is to (often correctly) shift the blame from stable aspects of themselves ("I am stupid," "I am unlikable") to the prejudice of others. This strategy may protect their self-esteem from negative outcomes, especially when prejudice is blatant. Bearers of stigma may also cope by identifying or bonding with others who share their stigma. Similarly stigmatized others can provide social support, a sense of belonging, and protect against feelings of rejection and isolation. Furthermore, bonding with others who are similarly stigmatized may also enable bearers to enact social changes that benefit their stigmatized group, as demonstrated by the success of the civil rights movement and the gay pride movement. In sum, through various coping strategies, bearers of stigma may demonstrate resilience even in the face of social devaluation.

Brenda Major

See also Attributional Ambiguity; Coping; Expectancy Effects; Ostracism; Rejection; Social Exclusion; Social Support; Stereotype Threat

Further Readings

Allport, G. W. (1954). *The nature of prejudice.* Boston: Addison-Wesley. (See, especially, chapter on "Traits due to victimization.")

Crocker, J., & Major, B. (1989). Social stigma and self-esteem: The self-protective properties of stigma. *Psychological Review, 96,* 608–630.

Crocker, J., Major, B., & Steele, C. (1998). Social stigma. In D. Gilbert, S. T. Fiske, & G. Lindzey (Eds.), *Handbook of social psychology* (4th ed., pp. 504–553). Boston: McGraw-Hill.

Goffman, E. (1963). *Stigma: Notes on the management of spoiled identity.* Englewood Cliffs, NJ: Prentice Hall.

Heatherton, T. F., Kleck, R. E., Hebl, M. R., & Hull, J. G. (Eds.). (2000). *The social psychology of stigma.* New York: Guilford Press.

Jones, E. E., Farina, A., Hastorf, A. H., Markus, H., Miller, D. T., & Scott, R. A. (1984). *Social stigma: The psychology of marked relationships.* New York: Freeman.

Link, B. G., & Phelan, J. C. (2001). Conceptualizing stigma. *Annual Review of Sociology, 27,* 363–385.

Major, B., & O'Brien, L. T. (2005). The social psychology of stigma. *Annual Review of Psychology, 56,* 393–421.

Steele, C. M. (1992). A threat in the air: How stereotypes shape intellectual identity and test performance. *American Psychologist, 52,* 613–629.

Steele, C. M., Spencer, S. J., & Aronson, J. (2002). Contending with group image: The psychology of stereotype and social identity threat. In M. P. Zanna, (Ed). (2002). *Advances in experimental social psychology* (Vol. 34, pp. 379–440). San Diego, CA: Academic Press.

STRESS AND COPING

Definition

Stress occurs when an individual perceives that the demands of a personally important situation tax or exceed his or her capabilities and resources. The situation can be a major event such as the death of a loved one, an interaction with another person such as a disagreement with a coworker, or even an internal event such as a realization that one is aging but has not accomplished important life goals. Stress, especially if experienced chronically, can have serious negative physical and psychological consequences. Coping consists of the individual's thoughts and behaviors aimed at eliminating the source of the stress, reducing the negative emotions associated with the stress, or increasing positive emotion in the context of stress. The study of coping is important because adaptive coping can be taught, which can help short-circuit the potentially harmful effects of stress on mental and physical health.

History and Background

Stress is a ubiquitous term that is commonly used to describe a wide range of situations, experiences, and states of being. Practically everyone has had personal, often daily, experience with stress, and the idea that stress is harmful to mental and physical well being is well ensconced in popular culture. Empirical studies of stress began early in the 20th century with research focused on the biological aspects of the stress response. In 1932, Walter Cannon outlined the fight-or-flight response in which the organism reacts to a threat by releasing catecholamines that ready the organism physically to respond to the stressor. Increased heart rate, blood pressure, blood sugar, and respiration are among the physiological results of catecholamine release. The fight-or-flight response is adaptive in the sense that it provides the necessary physical resources for the organism to react to acute stress. When the fight-or-flight response is repeatedly or chronically triggered, there are likely to be harmful physical consequences. Hans Selye discovered that a variety of stressors such as extreme cold or fatigue caused enlarged adrenal glands, shrinking of the thymus, and bleeding ulcers in rats. Selye outlined a three-stage process called the General Adaptation Syndrome in which prolonged stress leads to a breakdown of bodily resistance leaving the organism vulnerable to what he called diseasesof adaptation such as cardiovascular disease, kidney disease, or arthritis.

Early biological theories of stress led researchers to investigate the types of occurrences or events that resulted in biological changes. A natural outgrowth of the research of Cannon and Selye was stressful life events research. Researchers in this tradition were interested in quantifying the impact of various life events by their effects on psychological and physical well-being. Initially, the idea was that those individuals who experienced life events that required some sort of adjustment (such as marriage, death of a close family member, pregnancy, or changing to a different line of work) would be more likely to experience distress, depression, and physical illness than would those who experienced fewer life events. Results of these studies indicated that although there is a significant association between life events and well-being, the link is not particularly strong. Even among those individuals who are categorized as high risk for deleterious effects based on the number of stressful life events they experience, a substantial number do not show increased illness. Thus, the research focus in stressful life events turned from an emphasis on the stressful events per se to the study of other factors that play a role in the association between stressful events and physical or psychological well-being. Coping is one such factor. Two people who experience the same objectively stressful event can have very different psychological and physical outcomes depending on how they cope with the event.

The concept of coping was born out of the psychodynamic work on defenses. The theory developed by

Sigmund Freud in the late 1800s and early 1900s was that each form of psychopathology stemmed from unconscious reliance on a particular defense mechanism in response to uncomfortable thoughts or feelings. For example, paranoia was thought to stem from the defense mechanism of projection—attributing one's own unacceptable thoughts and feelings to someone else. Subsequent theorists classified defense mechanisms into adaptive (mature) and maladaptive (immature) with responses such as humor, suppression, and sublimation considered mature and responses such as projection and passive aggression considered immature.

One of the hallmarks of defense mechanisms is that they are relatively unconscious and traitlike. Although research on defenses continues, in the 1960s, researchers set a new course for the study of stress and coping by conceptualizing coping as a context-dependent, conscious process of thoughts and behaviors that ordinary people use in response to the events in their lives that they perceive as stressful.

Stress and Coping Theory

The stress and coping theory developed by Richard Lazarus and Susan Folkman has served as the foundation for decades of coping research in several different samples experiencing a vast variety of types of stress. The key components of the theory are appraisal and coping, along with emotion, which is central to both components.

Appraisal

Appraisal is the evaluation of an event in terms of its significance for well-being. Whether the individual appraises the event as stressful depends on characteristics of the individual (such as personality, goals, and beliefs) as well as characteristics of the event. Appraisal is an assessment that focuses on the meaning of an event or situation for the individual and occurs on a continuous basis. Humans naturally appraise or evaluate their surroundings and experiences constantly in relation to their own well-being. *Primary appraisal* addresses the question of whether anything is at stake for the individual in the context of the event. *Secondary appraisal* indicates what, if anything, can be done in response to the event and involves the assessment of available coping resources (e.g., money, time, social support, self-esteem) and options for coping and whether these are likely to be

effective in the particular situation. For example, imagine you have an exam coming up in your most difficult class and you must do well on it to pass the class and graduate. If graduation is something you value, your primary appraisal is likely to be one of threat—there is a lot at stake in the situation for you. As part of the secondary appraisal process you inventory the resources at your disposal for addressing the stressor/upcoming exam. Your coping resources may include textbooks and other reading materials on the test topic, notes taken by other students in the class, the willingness of the teaching assistant to spend time helping you prepare for the exam, and perhaps your own confidence in your test-taking ability. Upon reflection on your coping resources, you may reappraise the upcoming test as more of a challenge than a threat. Together, primary and secondary appraisal determine the extent to which the event is perceived as stressful.

Appraisals are associated with emotional responses. Those stressful events appraised as threatening are usually associated with negative emotions such as anxiety. Events appraised as harmful are associated with negative emotions such as sadness or anger. A challenge appraisal—the evaluation of a situation as having the potential for gain—is usually associated with both positive and negative emotions. Whereas an appraisal of challenge is likely to prompt feelings such as excitement and enthusiasm, there is also the potential for anxiety and fear because the outcome is uncertain.

Early stress and coping research focused almost exclusively on negative emotions. However, several studies have now documented that positive emotion can occur with relative high frequency, even in the most dire stressful context, even during periods when depression and distress are significantly elevated. Positive emotion in the stress process is thought to sustain coping, restore depleted resources, and provide a respite from negative emotions, particularly under conditions of chronic stress. Furthermore, positive and negative emotions are associated with different types of coping. Therefore, it is important to consider the role of positive as well as negative emotion in the coping process.

Coping

The appraisal of the event as a harm, threat, or challenge prompts a coping response. This coping response may influence the event itself, the individual's appraisal of the event, or the emotions associated with the event. In the context of a given stressful event, appraisal produces emotion and prompts coping, which, in turn, influences emotion and subsequent reappraisal of the situation. This appraisal-emotion-coping-emotion-reappraisal process continues until the situation is resolved or the appraisals are such that the event is no longer viewed as stressful.

Although there are potentially an infinite number of ways of coping (e.g., making a plan of action, fantasizing about an ideal outcome, reminding oneself of the good that will come out of the situation, pretending the stressful event didn't happen), on a theoretical level, there are two major functions of coping. *Problem-focused coping* involves taking steps to deal with the problem directly, whereas *emotion-focused coping* is aimed at reducing the negative emotions associated with the problem. Some examples of problem-focused coping are making a plan of action or concentrating on the next step. Some examples of emotion-focused forms of coping are engaging in distracting activities or using alcohol or drugs. Getting drunk doesn't really solve the problem, but people often think it will help them feel better.

The theoretical distinction between problem- and emotion-focused types of coping is useful for classifying and discussing the many types of coping, and it is used extensively in the coping literature. In practice, however, the distinction between coping aimed at addressing the problem and coping aimed at addressing the emotion isn't always clear. Problem-focused coping can also serve an emotion-focused function because by addressing the problem itself, the individual is also addressing the source of his or her negative emotions. Thus, if the problem-focused efforts are successful, the negative emotions associated with the problem will also be reduced. For example, a problem-focused response to having a car that repeatedly breaks down would be to buy a new car. Buying a new car effectively eliminates the negative emotions associated with the repeated breakdowns of the old car. Thus, the problem-focused coping response has also served an emotion-focused function. Sometimes, emotion-focused types of coping can ultimately serve a problem-focused function. Studying in response to an upcoming exam is a form of problem-focused coping. However, high levels of anxiety may prohibit effective studying. Therefore, doing something to reduce the anxiety such as going to the gym or getting a massage may facilitate subsequent problem-focused coping. People rarely rely on just problem-focused or just emotion-focused types of coping. Usually, in response to a given stressful event, they employ a mix of problem- and emotion-focused responses.

Although many stressful events are short-lived and require only an abbreviated coping response, many types of life stress are ongoing. These chronically stressful situations call for repeated and continued coping efforts over a long period. Examples of such ongoing stressors include one's own or a loved one's chronic illness, a dysfunctional work environment, or living in the aftermath of traumatic life events such as a major natural disaster. Because it calls for sustained coping efforts over a long period, chronic stress can deplete an individual's coping resources. In this context, *meaning-focused* coping becomes important. Meaning-focused coping responses draw on deeply held values, goals, and beliefs and help motivate and sustain coping efforts and bolster coping resources over the long term. These responses are linked to positive emotion, which reinforces their motivational and sustaining qualities. Meaning-focused coping, for example, includes identifying realistic coping outcomes that are valued by the person. For example, a husband providing care to his wife in the terminal stages of cancer who ensures that his wife is cleaned up and dressed every day because that helps her retain a sense of normalcy even though she is unable to leave the house is engaging in meaning-based coping. The pursuit of these outcomes creates a sense of control, which produces positive emotion, which, in turn, helps reinforce coping effort. Meaning-focused coping is used when a person reorders priorities so that they are in alignment with his or her underlying values, goals, and beliefs. The reordering helps the person allocate attention, resources, and efforts according to what matters. Benefit-reminding, a form of positive reappraisal in which the individual appraises benefit in a stressful situation (e.g., improved personal relationships, appreciation of the little things in life, greater sense of self-worth), is also considered a form of meaning-focused coping.

What Is Effective Coping? A central tenet of stress and coping theory is that coping is not inherently adaptive or maladaptive. Instead, coping effectiveness must be judged in the context of the stressful situation. A given form of coping may be effective in one situation but not in another. For example, in a situation in which the individual has some control, problem-focused forms of coping are likely to be beneficial. But in situations that are completely out of the individual's control, problem-focused coping is less likely to be effective. Furthermore, the effectiveness of a given coping strategy will depend on the outcome of interest. A given coping response can be beneficial in terms of one outcome but detrimental in terms of another. For example, increasing the amount of time you spend on a project at work may be effective for your career success but damaging to your relationship with your spouse. Another consideration in judging coping effectiveness is proximity of the outcome. A particular coping strategy may be beneficial in the short run (e.g., confronting the person responsible for the problem may make you feel better) but detrimental in the long run (damage the potential for working with the person you confronted in the future). Thus, in judging coping effectiveness, it is important to identify the outcome, the time point (proximal vs. distal), and the context.

Can Coping Be Changed? Part of the appeal of studying coping is that because it is a conscious response, it is potentially amenable to change. A growing body of evidence indicates that coping can be changed and people can be taught to cope more effectively with a variety of stressors. One approach to improving coping effectiveness is to help individuals identify whether a situation is changeable or not and then to match the form of coping to the situation (problem-focused types of coping for changeable situations, emotion-focused types of coping for unchangeable situations, meaning-focused coping in chronic situations). Another type of coping intervention targets the individual's appraisals of the stress and works to enhance confidence in his or her coping skills. Traditional stress management interventions can be viewed as training in emotion-focused coping, and problem-solving interventions can be thought of as training in problem-focused coping. In addition, coping training can take the form of enhancing coping resources such as social support.

Judith Tedlie Moskowitz

See also Anxiety; Coping; Emotion; Health Psychology; Projection; Search for Meaning in Life; Stress Appraisal Theory (Primary and Secondary Appraisal)

Further Readings

Cannon, W. B. (1939). *The wisdom of the body* (Rev. ed.). New York: W. W. Norton.

Folkman, S., & Moskowitz, J. T. (2004). Coping: Pitfalls and promise. *Annual Review of Psychology, 55,* 745–774.

Lazarus, R. S., & Folkman, S. (1984). *Stress, appraisal, and coping.* New York: Springer.

Park, C. L., & Folkman, S. (1997). Meaning in the context of stress and coping. *Review of General Psychology, 1,* 115–144.

Selye, H. (1956). *The stress of life.* New York: McGraw-Hill.

Zeidner, M., & Endler, N. S. (1996). *Handbook of coping.* New York: Wiley.

STRESS APPRAISAL THEORY (PRIMARY AND SECONDARY APPRAISAL)

Definition

Stress appraisal refers to the process by which individuals evaluate and cope with a stressful event. It is concerned with individuals' evaluation of the event, rather than with the event per se. People differ in how they construe what is happening to them and their options for coping. Stress appraisal comes in two forms, primary and secondary appraisal, which should be considered as two stages of appraisal or evaluation. These two types of appraisal are not mutually exclusive; they work in concert with one another to complete the appraisal process.

Primary Appraisal

Primary appraisal is the cognitive process that occurs when one is appraising whether an event is stressful and relevant to him or her. During this phase, a decision is made about whether the event poses a threat, will cause harm or loss, or presents a challenge. Harm or loss is associated with damage that has already occurred, such as a death or a job loss. Threat is the possibility of a harm or loss in the future, such as sickness or poor job performance. Conversely, challenge consists of events that provide a person an opportunity to gain a sense of mastery and competence by confronting and overcoming a dilemma. Such a struggle would be considered a positive type of stress and allows a person to expand one's knowledge and experience, and to develop extra tools to embrace future challenges or stresses. Finishing a marathon or writing a book might be an example of a challenge.

Secondary Appraisal

Secondary appraisal is the cognitive process that occurs when one is figuring out how to cope with a stressful event. During this process, a person decides what coping options are available. A harmful event requires immediate evaluation of coping options because it has already occurred, whereas threatening or challenging events allow one time to gather more information about events. Prior experience or being exposed to similar situations previously provides a frame of reference to determine the options available for dealing with the situation.

Background

Richard Lazarus, the originator of stress appraisal theory, became interested in the early 1950s in studying differences between individuals with relation to stress and the coping mechanisms. He was deeply impressed by a monograph written by two psychiatrists, Roy Grinker and John Spiegel, about how flight crews dealt with the constant stress of air war. He came to realize that stress was associated with the subjective meaning of what was happening to the personnel, who, in combat, were in imminent danger of being killed. A person constantly weighs coping options to deal with stress in the context of his or her personal goals or resources or environmental constraints. Lazarus argued that individuals differ in how they perceive circumstance as relevant and in how they react to and cope with situations.

Environmental and Person Variables

Stress appraisal theory takes into consideration precursory conditions that affect the process of appraisal. These antecedent conditions are divided into two classes, environmental variables and personal variables. Environmental variables are those that are beyond the person and lend rules of behavior that are governed by societal norms. Environmental variables include demands, constraints, opportunity, and culture. Person variables are those that lie within the person, including goals and goal hierarchies, beliefs about self and world, and personal resources.

Demands

Demands are pressures from the social environment to behave in certain ways and to conform to social conventions. Examples of demands include helping others in need, taking care of children, and performing well at one's job. Although demands originate from external pressure, they are later internalized.

Constraints

Constraints are composed of the behaviors in which one should not engage. They are defined by social norms or laws and are usually backed by punishment if violated. The punishment can come in social form, such as in banishment, or in legal form such as a fine or incarceration.

Opportunity

Opportunity refers to taking the right action at the right moment. Being able to take advantage of an opportunity involves recognizing the opportunity and knowing when to take action. An example of an opportunity would be making a decision right away to take a job that has been offered.

Culture

Culture generally refers to cultural norms and how those norms shape emotional perception. An example of a cultural norm would be understanding that (in most Western cultures) you should strive for individuality and distinction. This is inherent knowledge because of where you grew up, who your peers are, how people behave around you, and so on.

The four environmental variables—demands, constraints, opportunities, and culture—do not operate alone on the appraisal of an event. They interact with person variables on the appraisal of harm or loss, threat, and challenge, and the coping process. The person variables—goals and goal hierarchies, beliefs about self and world, and personal resources—give meaning to the events encountered and order them into an implicit understanding of how things work and how to cope with stresses elicited by environmental variables.

Goals and Goal Hierarchies

Goals and goal hierarchies refer to motivations to achieve one's objectives and to order them into a meaningful succession of importance. When a person attempts to fulfill goals or has multiple goals in conflict, stress will arise. It is important to determine which goals he or she values most and least. An example of goal and goal hierarchies would be that a person contemplates current goals in term of importance, such as striving to achieve a good grade in one's classes, getting more involved in community services, and cleaning one's apartment every Sunday.

Beliefs About Self and World

Beliefs about self and world refer to what one thinks of oneself and the world. These beliefs form perceptions and emotions, lending information as to what one expects to happen in a given situation. A person operates in a certain way because he or she *knows* what the outcome will be. For instance, a person knows that one's parents would withdraw their financial support if one fails one's classes. Even though studying is not fun, this person studies hard to conceive of oneself as a good student for his or her parents.

Personal Resources

Personal resources are those things that a person has at his or her disposal that influence what he or she can and cannot do to satisfy his or her needs. Some of these resources a person is born with; others are acquired by effortful measures. Some examples of personal resources include intelligence, physical attractiveness, social standing, and money.

During the process of primary appraisal, environmental and person variables interact to determine whether an event is considered a threat, harm or loss, or challenge. If an event is considered a harm, threat, or challenge, the relationship between environmental and person variables is considered again during the secondary appraisal process to determine appropriate coping options. Take two persons, A and B, who have recently lost their jobs. Person A feels threat because A has a large family to support (demands) with little savings (personal resources). Person A decides to look for a job right away because supporting family is one's most important role (beliefs about self and culture). Meanwhile, person B feels challenge because losing the job provides an opportunity to do something B has always wanted to try (opportunity and goal). Person B decides to send out applications to graduate schools because obtaining an advanced degree has long been one of B's goals, and B's partner can provide financial support (opportunity, goal, and personal resources).

Importance and Implications of Stress Appraisal

Stress appraisal theory considers how individual differences play a critical role in assessing stressors and

determining appropriate coping responses. By understanding how stress is appraised, one obtains information about the best methods for coping with stress. Understanding how stress occurs and the way in which one deals with it is important so that one can become more effective at reducing the adverse effect of negative stress and the ability to maximize positive stress.

Tamara Stone
Kyunghee Han

See also Coping; Culture; Goals; Health Psychology; Personality and Social Behavior; Stress and Coping

Further Readings

Lazarus, R. S. (1963). A laboratory approach to the dynamics of psychological stress. *Administrative Science Quarterly, 8*(1).

Lazarus, R. S. (1999). *Stress and emotion: A new synthesis.* New York: Springer.

Lazarus, R. S. (2000). Relational meaning and discrete emotions. In K. R. Scherer, A. Schorr, & T. Johnstone (Eds.), *Appraisal processes in emotion: Theory, methods, research,* New York: Oxford University Press

Tomaka, J., Blascovich, J., Kibler, J., & Ernst, J. M, (1997). Cognitive and physiological antecedents of threat and challenge appraisal. *Journal of Personality and Social Psychology, 73*(1), 63–72.

STRUCTURAL EQUATION MODELING

Structural equation modeling (SEM) is a particular form of data analysis. According to this approach, a researcher begins with a model that specifies how multiple variables are related to each other. These theorized relationships are formalized into a set of equations that include the variables in question. These variables are then measured and their relations to each other are quantified. The test of the model involves an assessment of how well the equations can reproduce or "fit" the observed relations.

As a simple example, consider a model in which the researcher theorizes that variable A influences C because of its influence on B. Schematically, A → B → C. This model has two equations, one that predicts B using A and one that predicts C using B. To test this model, the researcher measures the observed relations between A, B, and C. Application of SEM provides tests of (1) whether A is actually a useful predictor of B, (2) whether B is actually a useful predictor of C, and (3) whether the model as a whole fits the observed data. The latter test is not simply redundant with the previous two tests. The reason for this is that the model specifies that A is *only* a predictor of C because of its relation to B. A might be a useful predictor of B, and B of C, but the model might provide a poor fit because the researcher has incorrectly specified that A has no direct relation with C.

As can be seen, the proper use of SEM requires that the researcher has carefully thought about the ways variables are related to each other before collecting the data. In this sense, application of SEM is typically considered to be confirmatory in nature rather than exploratory. Although researchers often conceptualize the associations among variables in terms of causal influences, causality cannot be inferred simply from observed relations (the term *causal modeling* is therefore a misnomer). Once a relation has been identified and placed in the context of a larger set of variables using SEM, researchers are best advised to test for causality using experimental designs.

As might be imagined, SEM can be an extremely powerful and flexible data analytic technique. Indeed, many other data analytic strategies can be thought of as specific forms of SEM, including linear and nonlinear regression, path analysis, factor analysis, and hierarchical modeling. SEM actually allows the researcher to combine several of these simpler data analytic techniques in a single analysis rather than conducting separate analyses using multiple steps. For example, one of the more popular applications of SEM involves a combination of factor analysis and path analysis. Because factor analysis deals with latent, or unobserved, variables, this form of analysis is often referred to as latent variable modeling.

As might be expected, most application of SEM are computationally complex and require sophisticated statistical computer packages. Among the most popular of these is LISREL.

Jay Hull

See also LISREL; Nonexperimental Designs; Research Methods

Further Readings

Bollen, K. A. (1989). *Structural equations with latent variables.* New York: Wiley.

Kline, R. B. (2004). *Principles and practice of structural equation modeling* (2nd ed.). New York: Guilford Press.

McDonald, R., & Ho, M. R. (2002). Principles and practice in reporting structural equation analyses. *Psychological Methods, 7,* 64–82.

Raykov, T., & Marcoulides, G. A. (2006). *A first course in structural equation modeling.* Mahwah, NJ: Erlbaum.

SUBLIMINAL PERCEPTION

The term *subliminal* is derived from the terms *sub* (below) and *limen* (threshold), and it refers to perception so subtle it cannot reach conscious awareness. Most of the research on subliminal perception is done on visual subliminal perception. For instance, one can flash words or pictures so quickly on a computer screen (generally faster than 10–15 milliseconds) that perceivers have the feeling they do not see anything at all. In other words, they are not consciously aware of the presented words or pictures. However, such visual stimuli are processed unconsciously, and they can have brief and subtle effects on our feeling and thinking. In addition, some research has been done on auditory subliminal perception. No reliable scientific evidence exists, however, for psychological effects of auditory subliminal perception.

The idea of an objective "threshold" is misleading. No objective threshold exists for conscious perception. Whether a briefly presented stimulus reaches conscious awareness depends on many different factors, including individual differences. The threshold is merely subjective.

Effects of subliminal perception are generally small and not easy to establish in controlled laboratory research. However, a few findings are reasonably well established, the most prominent being subliminal mere exposure; Repeated subliminal exposure to a stimulus (for example a picture) leads perceivers to like this picture a little more. Effects of mere exposure have even been obtained for stimuli that were perceived for only one millisecond. Perceivers can to some extent infer the valence (is something good or bad?) from subliminal stimuli. This is shown in research on the subliminal perception of short positive (e.g., sun) and negative (e.g., death) words.

Subliminal perception is controversial mainly because of the notion of subliminal persuasion: The strategy that may be used by marketers or politicians to deliberately influence customers or voters subliminally. In 1957, James Vicary claimed that he increased the sale of cola and popcorn in a New Jersey cinema by subliminally flashing "Drink Coke" and "Eat popcorn" during movies. This however, turned out to be a myth. Perhaps because of the media attention subliminal perception and persuasion sometimes receives, most of the American population does believe subliminal persuasion to have far reaching consequences. However, although subliminal perception exists, research shows the effects to be minor and usually short-lived. There is no scientific reason to believe it can substantially change consumer behavior.

Ap Dijksterhuis

See also Automatic Processes; Mere Exposure Effect; Nonconscious Processes; Persuasion; Priming

Further Readings

Dijksterhuis, A., Aarts, H., & Smith, P. K. (2005). The power of the subliminal: Subliminal perception and possible applications. In R. R. Hassin, J. S. Uleman, & J. A. Bargh (Eds.), *The new unconscious*. New York: Oxford University Press.

Dijksterhuis, A., & van Knippenberg, A. (1998). The relation between perception and behavior or how to win a game of Trivial Pursuit. *Journal of Personality and Social Psychology, 74*, 865–877.

SUBTYPING

Definition

Subtyping refers to a process whereby people come to view individuals who don't fit a stereotype as exceptions or as poor members of a group. The concept is important because it explains why people often do not change their stereotypes in the face of disconfirming information. Subtyping involves psychologically fencing off deviant group members so that perceivers need not consider information about those individuals when thinking about the group as a whole.

Background and Research

Early research on stereotype change showed that the same amount of stereotype disconfirming information was more likely to weaken a stereotype when it was dispersed across many group members rather than concentrated in only a few. In these studies, participants read about multiple group members who each exhibited various behaviors. Participants who read about many group members who committed one disconfirming behavior each later reported weaker stereotypes than those who read that the disconfirming behaviors were all committed by a small subset of the group. This finding suggests that it may be easy to subtype, and therefore ignore, small numbers of extreme deviants.

Researchers have gone on to study specific conditions that promote subtyping. Strong evidence indicates that people are especially likely to subtype individuals who seem atypical rather than typical of their group. For example, in one study, people were more likely to change their stereotype that lawyers are extraverted if they learned about an introverted lawyer who seemed otherwise typical of the group (e.g., was White), rather than one who seemed deviant on multiple dimensions (e.g., was Black). Other research suggests that people are more likely to subtype individuals who deviate a lot on a particular stereotypic trait rather than just a little, presumably because extreme deviants seem more atypical of the group. At least one study points to the disturbing finding that getting to know someone in a stereotyped group personally can promote subtyping, suggesting that making friends across group boundaries is not enough to change stereotypes. Research also suggests that people may perceive neutral information about a disconfirming group member in ways that promote subtyping and stereotype preservation.

Subtyping is not an inevitable process. When people encounter large numbers of disconfirming individuals, subtyping may become more difficult. In addition, if perceivers view disconfirming individuals as legitimate group members, a process referred to as subgrouping rather than subtyping, then perceivers may come to see the group as more diverse, and the stereotype may eventually weaken. As predicted by this theoretical distinction, people encouraged to pay attention to similarities and differences among all group members, a manipulation intended to induce subgrouping, later report weaker stereotypes than those in a subtyping condition instructed to think about distinctions between typical and atypical group members.

Carolyn Weisz

See also Contact Hypothesis; Person Perception; Prejudice; Stereotypes and Stereotyping

Further Readings

Kunda, Z., & Oleson, K. C. (1995). Maintaining stereotypes in the face of disconfirmation: Constructing grounds for subtyping deviants. *Journal of Personality and Social Psychology, 68,* 565–579.

Park, B., Wolsko, C., & Judd, C. M. (2001). Measurement of subtyping in stereotype change. *Journal of Experimental Social Psychology, 37,* 325–332.

SUICIDE

Definition

Suicide is the act of intentionally taking one's life. This definition, however, has been expanded to describe the range of thoughts and behaviors that are exhibited by individuals who are in some manner considering suicide. *Suicidal ideation* involves having thoughts of killing oneself or of being dead. *Suicidal intent* involves having a plan for how to kill oneself and intending to carry that plan out. *Suicidal behavior* is a broad term that includes all actions related to suicide (i.e., all the terms in this paragraph), but also includes some behaviors not captured by the other terms listed here, including actions related to suicide that did not result in an attempt, such as gathering bottles of pills (without taking them), or tying a noose (without using it). A *suicide attempt* occurs when an individual intends to take his or her own life, acts on that intent, but does not die. A *suicide completion* occurs when an individual intends to take his or her own life and dies as a result. One way to understand *suicidal behavior* is to think of it as a continuum with ideation at the far left and completion to the far right: In this way, behaviors toward the left of the continuum are relatively less severe and behaviors to the right are relatively more severe because of their differing proximities to suicide completions. This continuum view has not been empirically validated (e.g., it is possible that suicidal ideation differs from suicide attempt in kind rather than just in degree), and in any event, all suicidal behaviors are serious and warrant assessment by a mental health professional.

Importance and Context

Suicide is a serious health problem worldwide, including in the United States. In 2002, it is estimated that 31,655 individuals died by suicide, making suicide the 11th leading cause of death (homicide ranks 14th). Although rates vary somewhat year to year, approximately 30,000 people in the United States, and almost a million people die by suicide each year worldwide. On one hand, 30,000 U.S. deaths per year—one every 18 minutes or so—is a lot. On the other hand, suicide is a rare cause of death compared with other causes of death in the United States. For example, given that a person has died, the chance that the cause was heart disease or cancer is 52%. Given that someone has died, the chance that the cause of death was suicide is a little over 1%. However, the number of deaths by suicide (i.e., the number of suicide completions), though an accurate representation of the fact that death by suicide is rare, also greatly underestimates the magnitude of the problem: For every death by suicide, there are as many as 25 nonfatal attempts. Suicidal ideation is even more common than attempts: Estimates suggest that approximately 13% of individuals in the United States will experience substantial suicidal ideation at some point in their lifetime. Thus, suicide completions are relatively rare in the United States, but attempts are more common, and ideation is even more common.

The prevalence of suicidal behavior (i.e., how common it is) differs for men and women. Males complete suicide more often than females do, but females attempt suicide more often than males do. More specifically, men are approximately 4 times more likely than are women to die by suicide; women are approximately 3 times as likely as men to attempt suicide. This pattern can be explained in part by research showing that, in general, men engage in more violent behavior than women. Suicide attempts by women, on average, use methods that are less violent, and therefore are less likely to be lethal. For example, 2 of 3 male suicide victims in the United States die by firearm, whereas 1 of 3 female suicide victims in the United States die by firearm. The most common method for female victims is overdosing or poisoning.

Measurement

Although attempts and completions can be investigated with medical records, the other aspects of suicidality (i.e., ideation and intent) cannot be measured in such a straightforward manner. One commonly used measure is the Beck Suicide Scale, a self-report measure with 21 questions. For each of the questions, respondents pick one of three statements that best describes how he or she has been feeling; each statement is scored as 0, 1, 2 with increasing level of severity. For example, one of the items that indicates suicidal ideation is as follows: "I have no desire to kill myself" (0 point response), "I have a weak desire to kill myself" (1 point response), and "I have a moderate to strong desire to kill myself" (2 point response). Higher scores on the Beck Suicide Scale indicate more severe suicidal ideation or intent.

Theories of Suicide

One of the most prominent theorists of suicide is Edwin Shneidman. His theory states that suicide results from the perception of unendurable psychological pain, which he calls *psychache*. Another researcher of suicide, Aaron Beck, theorizes that our thoughts (i.e., cognitions) play a causal role in the development of suicidal behavior. This theory proposes that suicide results from cognitions that involve hopelessness—beliefs that things will not get better in the future. Roy Baumeister proposed that suicide results from a desire to escape from painful self-awareness resulting from discrepancies between expectations and actual events. A more recent theory was proposed by Thomas Joiner. This theory states that suicide results from the combination of three factors: thwarted belongingness, perceived burdensomeness (i.e., the belief that one is a burden on others), and an acquired ability to enact lethal self-injury. The last component of the theory, acquired ability, involves the idea that it is difficult to overcome the most basic instinct of all—self-preservation—and that individuals acquire this capability through experience with painful and provocative events. Through these experiences, individuals get used to the pain of self-injury, become less afraid of self-injury, and build knowledge that facilitates self-injury.

Risk Assessment

Suicide risk assessment is a process conducted by a mental health professional to determine if an individual is at risk for engaging in suicidal behavior. Two main questions guide suicide risk assessment: Is the individual being assessed a danger to himself or herself and is the danger both immediate and severe? The answer to these questions can come from the use of standardized assessment measures (such as the Beck Suicide Scale) as well as clinical interviews. A thorough risk assessment for suicide gathers information from the individual on both present suicidal symptoms as well as past suicidal behavior, current stressors, and other psychological symptoms (e.g., hopelessness). For example, individuals who suffer psychiatric disorders are at higher risk for suicide. A disorder with one of the highest rates is major depressive disorder. One of the strongest predictors of completed suicide is a prior attempt; thus, considering presenting symptoms is not sufficient for thorough risk assessment.

If risk is deemed to be immediate or severe, emergency mental health services are used, most often involving hospitalization until the individual is no longer at imminent risk for suicide. If risk is not deemed immediate or severe, alternatives to emergency mental health can be used. For example, with the help of a trained mental health professional, individuals may be helped to create a coping card that lists concrete steps to take in the event that suicidal symptoms intensify.

Warning Signs

Members of the American Association of Suicidology are researchers and clinicians who research and treat suicidal behavior. This group devised a list of warning signs for suicide that indicate severe and immediate risk for suicide. These warning signs are designed for the friends, family members, and any other people who may come into contact with a suicidal individual. The warning signs instruct that a person should get help immediately if he or she witnesses, hears, or sees any one or more of the following:

- Someone threatening to hurt or kill himself or herself
- Someone looking for ways to kill himself or herself by seeking access to pills, weapons, or other means
- Someone talking or writing about death, dying, or suicide

The warning signs also instruct that should seek immediate help if one witnesses, hears, or sees someone exhibiting any one or more of the following:

- Hopelessness
- Rage, anger, seeking revenge
- Acting reckless or engaging in risky activities, seemingly without thinking
- Feeling trapped—like there's no way out
- Increasing alcohol or drug use
- Withdrawing from friends, family, or society

- Anxiety, agitation, unable to sleep or sleeping all the time
- Dramatic changes in mood
- No reason for living
- No sense of purpose in life

Kimberly A. Van Orden
Theodore W. Bender
Thomas E. Joiner, Jr.

See also Depression; Need to Belong; Rejection; Social Exclusion

Further Readings

American Association of Suicidology. (n.d.). *Understanding and helping the suicidal person.* Retrieved September 29, 2006, from http://www.suicidology.org/displaycommon.cfm?an=2

Joiner, T. E. (2005). *Why people die by suicide.* Cambridge, MA: Harvard University Press.

Sunk Cost

Definition

Sunk cost refers to money, time, or effort that has already been spent on a particular endeavor and that cannot be recovered. Economic principles dictate that sunk costs should not be considered when making decisions about whether to continue one's present course of action or to divert resources elsewhere. Such decisions rationally should be based only on consideration of the anticipated costs and benefits of current options.

For example, after 6 months of exclusively dating one man, a woman ponders whether it makes sense to maintain the relationship. Upon weighing the positives and negatives, she comes to the realization that continuing to date this same man will not allow her to achieve the quality of relationship she desires. That being the case, the clearly rational thing for the woman to do is to immediately terminate the relationship.

Unfortunately, people do not always make decisions in accord with rational principles. In this instance, the woman may factor into her deliberations what she has already invested in the relationship. Perhaps she has put considerable time, effort, and money into helping the man update his wardrobe, tolerated many insufferable visits to his parents, and passed up opportunities to date more promising long-term partners. Although these prior investments cannot be undone or canceled out by staying in the relationship (or leaving for that matter), they often lead decision makers to choose to hang on to a current relationship despite knowing that it will never fully meet their expectations. This kind of irrational behavior has been described as throwing good money after bad. More formally, psychologists identify such behaviors as instances of the sunk-cost fallacy.

Sunk-Cost Fallacy: Scientific Evidence

Scientific demonstrations of the sunk-cost fallacy are numerous. For example, in one study some people were asked to imagine that they enjoy playing tennis, but that on one occasion they develop a bad case of tennis elbow, thereafter making it extremely painful for them to play. Their doctor tells them to expect to experience pain while playing for approximately a year. People were then asked to estimate the number of times they would play tennis over the next 6 months. Another group of people was presented with a similar scenario, but were additionally told to imagine that they had recently paid a $400 nonrefundable fee for a tennis-club membership, which expires in 6 months. If people were making a decision rationally, the two versions of the scenario should produce comparable estimates. Their decision to play tennis in both instances should be determined by an evaluation of the costs and benefits of engaging in this activity. If people believe that their enjoyment will exceed the physical discomfort, then they should decide to play. If they instead anticipate that the pain will sap any pleasure from the experience, they should logically choose not to play. Whether or not they paid the $400 fee should not influence their decision. Play or not play, that money is irretrievably lost and thus should be irrelevant to any decision to play tennis in the near future. However, people estimated that they would play tennis 2.5 times more in the situation in which they had paid the membership fee, thereby honoring sunk cost.

Although the sunk-cost fallacy has been shown to be a fairly common judgment error, whether it occurs may depend on aspects of the situation and characteristics of the decision makers themselves. For example, people are more likely to fall prey to the sunk-cost fallacy in circumstances in which they feel personally responsible for making the initial investment in an endeavor. Also, some evidence demonstrates, interestingly, that adults are more susceptible to the sunk-cost fallacy than are 5- and 6-year-olds. This seems at odds with common sense because young children have more modest cognitive abilities to apply to any decision-making task and, therefore, should have even more difficulty than adults sidestepping maladaptive decisions. This finding, however, becomes more understandable once possible explanations for the sunk-cost fallacy are examined.

Why Sunk-Cost Fallacy Occurs

One explanation for the sunk-cost fallacy is that people tend to justify their behavior. According to this self-justification account, people continue to invest in endeavors that are unlikely to produce desired outcomes because failing to do so could be interpreted as an admission that their initial decision to invest was a mistake. Abandoning the initial course of action could also make decision makers appear inconsistent. Neither of these possibilities is tolerated well, so people choose instead to escalate their commitment to the initial decision in a misguided attempt to reaffirm its "correctness" to themselves and others. This self-justification explanation receives support from the previously mentioned study showing that greater personal responsibility for the initial decision heightens the likelihood of the sunk-cost fallacy occurring.

Another possible explanation for the sunk-cost fallacy is people's desire not to be wasteful. "Waste not, want not" is a maxim that most Americans have been exposed to since childhood, and it may be that this generally beneficial rule is inappropriately applied in sunk-cost situations. That is, abandoning a failing course of action could be construed as wasting the resources that have already been expended. As noted earlier, children have been found to be less likely to manifest the sunk-cost fallacy. This may be because children tend to stay focused on the immediate consequences of their actions, whereas adults are sidetracked by abstract rules such as "Don't waste," which most of the time help simplify decision-making tasks. But in situations in which sunk costs are involved, the misapplication of well-ingrained rules on waste may only make it more difficult to ignore prior investments when deciding whether anticipated benefits outweigh anticipated costs for any given course of action.

G. Daniel Lassiter
Jennifer J. Ratcliff
Matthew J. Lindberg

See also Cognitive Consistency; Consumer Behavior; Decision Making

Further Readings

Arkes, H. R., & Ayton, P. (1999). The sunk cost and Concorde effects: Are humans less rational than lower animals? *Psychological Bulletin, 125,* 591–600.

SUPPLICATION

We often want to influence the way other people perceive us. For instance, a professor might want her class to see her as intellectual and competent, whereas a boxer might want his competitors to see him as physically powerful and mean. Both the professor and the boxer are likely to act in ways that influence how others see them. The professor might take extra time preparing her notes for class or use impressive words in her lectures, whereas the boxer might affect a scowl or show off his muscles before a match. These are examples of strategic self-presentation—the term for acting in a manner that shapes how people view us.

Supplication is one kind of strategic self-presentation. Although most strategic self-presentations strategies are designed to make positive impressions on others, sometimes we lack the ability or impress others with our capabilities. Supplication is a strategy for this kind of situation. Rather than trying to look able, strong, or smart, people using supplication as a self-presentation strategy purposely emphasize their incompetence or weakness. They want to appear helpless. The purpose of appearing helpless is to advertise their dependence on others to get help or sympathy. For example, a schoolchild might feign a complete inability to do homework to a parent. This seeming dependence on the parent is designed to provoke the parent's sense of nurturance toward the child, resulting in the parent doing the homework for the child. However, supplication does not necessarily entail pretending to be dependent; it can refer to emphasizing actual inadequacies. Panhandlers frequently emphasize their destitute condition to increase their chances of getting money. The need for money may or may not be real, but the advertising of need constitutes supplication. Another example familiar to most people is crying. The student who cries to a professor over a grade or the driver who cries to the police officer over a ticket may be supplicating—trying to get help or mercy via pity.

Whether the supplicant is a family member, a coworker, or a stranger, the purpose is to arouse a sense of obligation toward the supplicant. Supplicants exploit their weakness by throwing themselves on the mercy of others, which places both supplicant and target in an uncomfortable position. This may explain why, of the many different methods of strategic self-presentation, supplication is used infrequently. The extreme difference in power inherent is a supplication disrupts the day-to-day stability of close relationships. Most people to whom supplication is directed will quickly tire of repeated demands on their pity. Supplication is also distasteful to the supplicant because it is personally demeaning, which limits how much an individual would want to resort to using it.

Tyler F. Stillman

See also Helplessness, Learned; Self-Handicapping; Self-Presentation

Further Readings

Jones, E. E., & Pittman, T. S. (1982). Toward a general theory of strategic self-presentation. In J. Suls (Ed.), *Psychological perspectives of the self* (pp. 231–261). Hillsdale, NJ: Erlbaum.

SURPRISE

Definition

Surprise is the sense of astonishment, wonder, or amazement that is caused by something sudden or unexpected. The experience of surprise varies with the importance of the outcome, as well as beliefs about the outcome. Some formalists have offered mathematical definitions of surprise (i.e., a comparison of Bayesian priors and posteriors), but there is little consensus about a psychological definition. Some researchers treat surprise as a cognitive assessment based on the probability of an event, whereas others treat it as an emotion, on par with happiness, sadness, anger, disgust, and fear because of its unique pattern of facial expressions. If surprise is an emotion, it is an unusual one; it can be positive or negative, and it dramatically shapes the experience of other emotions.

Importance

The concept of surprise is relevant to many aspects of human behavior. Humans notice and focus on surprising events and are more likely to attend to surprising events. Surprise facilitates curiosity and learning. It also affects beliefs about other events. When a person takes an unexpected stance that violates his or her self-interest, the person's arguments are surprising and quite often more persuasive.

Surprise is a key factor in emotional life. Neurological studies show that when monkeys expect a reward, dopamine neurons fire. When monkeys get the reward, neuronal firing depends on prior expectations. Unexpected rewards lead to greater firing than expected rewards. Apparently, unexpected pleasures are more rewarding than expected ones.

What Makes Something Unexpected?

If surprise depends on sudden or unexpected events, what makes something unexpected? An unexpected event is a low-probability event. Surprise usually follows the event, but it can also be anticipated. However, the intensity and duration of surprise may be harder to forecast than the valence of a future event.

An unexpected event may be an unfamiliar event. A tourist who travels to Hawaii may be surprised to see 30-foot waves, despite the fact that such waves are common during the winter months and familiar to local inhabitants. An unexpected event may also be a novel event. Most people expect swans to be white, so a black swan is unique and rare.

Unexpectedness depends on the ease with which a person can imagine an event. Some people are more surprised to draw a red ball at random from an urn containing 20 balls, 1 of which is red, than to draw a red ball from an urn with 200 balls, 10 of which are red. Although the two events are equally likely, the first event can happen in only *one* way, whereas the second event can happen in 10 different ways.

Unexpectedness also varies with the ability to imagine other events unfolding. Some people are more surprised to select a red ball at random from a jar with 1 red ball and 19 blue balls than to pick a red ball from a jar with 20 balls, each a different color. In the first case, the blue ball is the only referent, but in the second, there are many referents. In a similar fashion, a negative event is often more surprising, and more tragic, if there were many ways it could have been avoided than if there was only one way.

Finally, unexpectedness depends on social and cultural norms. A person learns how to react to events from his or her social environment. Research shows that East Asians tend to take contradictions and inconsistencies for granted and are less surprised by most events than are Americans.

Magnifier of Emotions

Psychologists have developed a theory that connects surprise to the pleasure or pain of an outcome. Decision affect theory predicts that surprising outcomes have greater emotional intensity than expected outcomes; a surprising positive event is more pleasurable than an expected positive event, and a surprising negative event is more painful than an expected negative event.

In gambling studies, a surprising outcome had a small probability of occurrence. Surprising wins or losses are more intense than expected wins or losses. In studies of skill, a surprising outcome is one that deviates from expectations. A person may expect to succeed or fail at a task. In this case, surprising success is more pleasurable than expected success, and surprising failure is more painful than expected failure.

When assessing the ability to be successful, a person often sees himself or herself through rose-colored glasses. Inaccurate self-assessments are sometimes called *positive illusions.* One such illusion is overconfidence, the tendency of a person to believe he or she will do better at a task of skill than reality suggests. Overconfidence has two detrimental effects on affective experiences. It makes successes less surprising and therefore less pleasurable, and it makes failures more surprising and therefore more painful.

Another positive illusion is called hindsight. After learning what happened, a person thinks he or she knew it all along. The person recollects past beliefs as too accurate. Hindsight makes events seem less surprising, and it has one detrimental effect on emotional experiences. An expected negative event will be less painful than a surprising negative event, but an expected positive event will be less pleasurable than a surprising positive event.

Strategic Shifts

Can beliefs be systematically altered before an event occurs to make a person feel better? People are aware that bad news feels worse when unexpected, and some lower their expectations to avoid a surprising disappointment. In one experiment, researchers asked college sophomores, juniors, and seniors to estimate their starting salary for their first job at the beginning and end of the spring term. Sophomores and juniors showed no change, but seniors lowered their estimates. They were the only group that would soon face reality.

People also shift their beliefs after the event, especially if it was bad. They convince themselves that the event was inevitable. For example, sports fans might convince themselves that their team lost because the umpire was biased. Such thoughts diminish the pain by making the loss seem expected. To feel better about negative events, people should remember that much of life is unpredictable, and surprises should be expected.

Barbara Mellers

See also Affect; Beliefs; Emotion; Expectations; Hindsight Bias

Further Readings

Mellers, B. A. (2000). Choice and the relative pleasure of consequences. *Psychological Bulletin, 126,* 910–924.

Mellers, B. A., & McGraw, A. P. (2004). Self-serving beliefs and the pleasure of outcomes. In J. Carrillo & I. Brocas (Eds.), *The psychology of economic decisions. Vol. 2: Reasons and choices* (pp. 31–48). New York: Oxford University Press.

Symbolic Interactionism

Definition

Symbolic interactionism is a major theoretical perspective in North American sociological social psychology that studies how individuals actively define their social reality and understand themselves by interacting with others. Symbolic interactionism has its origins in pragmatism, the American philosophy of how living things make practical adjustments to their surroundings. American sociologist and pragmatist philosopher George Herbert Mead (1863–1931) is generally identified as the founder of this theory, although the term *symbolic interactionism* was actually coined by Mead's student, Herbert Blumer, who formally articulated Mead's ideas following his death.

Assumptions and Implications

According to symbolic interactionism, social reality is not fixed and unchanging. Instead, people are continually constructing (and reconstructing) the meaning of their social lives through interacting with others. An essential component of this creative interaction is the use of symbols. Spoken or printed words are symbols, as are many nonverbal gestures. Symbols in their various forms are the basis of social life because they create a shared meaning in both the expresser and the recipient. When socializing, people interpret others' expressions and respond on the basis of this interpreted meaning. However, the meaning of these words and gestures may differ depending on the social context. For example, the question "Do you want to spend the night at my place?" may have a very different meaning when spoken by a romantic partner rather than by a platonic friend.

To understand others' intentions during social interactions, Mead argued that people engage in role taking, which is imaginatively assuming the point of view of others and observing their own behavior from this other perspective. Mead believed that through such symbolic interaction, humans cease being puppets controlled by environmental strings and, instead, become coactors who have control in creating their social reality. Thus, unlike many social scientists who believe that society dictates meanings to people, interactionists believe that meaning emerges and is transformed as people interact. Although society does shape the conduct of its individual members, those same individuals have the capacity to shape society by redefining their social reality.

Reflected Appraisal and Self-Development

Through symbolic interaction, individuals also develop a sense of themselves as they learn to use symbols, but this self-development occurs in stages. Mead asserted that children become selves as they begin taking the role of other people in their play activities. The roles they adopt in the first stage of self development, the play stage, are those of specific others, such as parents and siblings, and they can only adopt one role at a time. For example, after disobeying a family rule, a young child may spontaneously adopt the perspective of "Daddy" and reprimand himself or herself. Through such role taking, children develop an understanding of societal norms, and they develop beliefs about themselves, which are largely a reflection of how they believe others evaluate them. This reflected appraisal is an important determinant of the beliefs and attitudes that form people's self-concepts. In other words, individuals develop a sense of themselves as they learn to see themselves the way they believe others see them.

As children mature, Mead stated that they learn to take the role of many others simultaneously and, as a result, the self becomes more cognitively complex. In this second stage of self-development, the game stage,

they can engage in complex activities (often in the form of games) involving the interaction of many roles. An example of such role taking would be people playing soccer. To play effectively, players must understand how everyone on the field is related to one another, and each player must cognitively adopt these multiple roles simultaneously. Mead stated that as the self becomes increasingly complex, older children begin responding to themselves from the point of view of not just several distinct others, but from the perspective of society as a whole. By internalizing the attitudes and expectations held by the larger society— what Mead called the *generalized other*—the person becomes a mature self.

Presentation of Self and Social Roles

The emphasis that symbolic interactionists place on symbols, negotiated reality, and the ever-changing social construction of society explains their interest in the social roles people play. Erving Goffman, a prominent theorist in this tradition, suggests that social life is like a theatrical performance, with people behaving like actors on stage playing prescribed roles. Goffman's approach is called *dramaturgy,* and it focuses on the techniques people use to manage the impression they make on others by carefully constructing and monitoring their presented selves. According to Goffman, while "on stage," people act out "lines" and attempt to maintain competent and appropriate presented selves. In observing this performance, the audience generally accepts the presented selves at face value and treats them accordingly because to do otherwise would disrupt the smooth flow of social interaction. Figuratively "booing" performers off stage by rejecting their presented selves typically occurs only when performers are so incompetent that they cannot adequately play their roles.

Research Focus

Because symbolic interactionists view human societies as consisting of actively created realities among individuals, their research focuses on observable face-to-face interactions. Furthermore, because symbolic interactionists believe that social reality is continually being modified, they tend to shift their focus away from stable norms and values in society toward more fluctuating and continually adjusting social processes. Regarding the scientific methods employed by symbolic interactionists, they tend to rely on participant observation, although some interactionists employ surveys, interviews, and experiments. This emphasis on participant observation is based on the belief that close contact and immersion in the everyday lives of participants is necessary for understanding the meaning of actions, the definition of the situation itself, and the process by which actors construct the situation through their interaction. Symbolic interactionists have been criticized for being overly subjective and impressionable in their reliance on qualitative methods, as well as being somewhat unsystematic in their theoretical formulations. However, although more quantitatively oriented social psychologists find fault in this methodology, symbolic interactionists contend that their approach allows them to watch behavior in its "wholeness," providing the full context in which to understand it.

Stephen L. Franzoi

See also Interpersonal Cognition; Self; Self-Presentation; Social Cognition; Sociological Social Psychology

Further Readings

Goffman, E. (1958). *The presentation of self in everyday life.* Edinburgh, UK: University of Edinburgh, Social Sciences Research Centre.

Hewitt, J. P. (2003). *Self and society: A symbolic interactionist social psychology* (9th ed.). Boston: Allyn & Bacon.

Mead, G. H. (1934). *Mind, self, and society.* Chicago: University of Chicago Press.

Stryker, S. (1980). *Symbolic interactionism: A structural version.* Caldwell, NJ: Blackburn Press.

SYMBOLIC RACISM

Definition

Symbolic racism is a form of prejudice that Whites in particular hold against Blacks, although it is likely to be held in some measure by other American ethnic groups, and in principle some version of it may target groups other than Blacks. Symbolic racism is usually described as a coherent belief system that can be expressed in several beliefs: that Blacks no longer face much prejudice or discrimination, that Blacks' failure to progress results from their unwillingness to work hard enough, that they make excessive demands, and that they have gotten more than they deserve. The theory of symbolic racism centers on four essential propositions: (1) Symbolic racism has largely replaced old-fashioned racism, in that only a tiny minority of Whites still accept the latter, whereas they are about evenly divided about the beliefs contained in symbolic racism; (2) symbolic racism now influences Whites' political attitudes much more strongly than does old-fashioned racism; (3) Whites' opposition to racial policies and Black candidates is more influenced by symbolic racism than by realistic self-interest, defined as threats posed by Blacks to Whites' own lives; and (4) the origins of symbolic racism lie in a blend of negative feelings about Blacks, acquired early in life, with traditional moral values. The label "symbolic" therefore highlights its roots in abstract moral values rather than in concrete self-interest or personal experience, and its targeting Blacks as a group rather than as specific Black individuals. The label "racism" reflects its origins partly in racial antagonism.

Background

Symbolic racism has been the most influential form of racial prejudice in American political life since the civil rights era of the 1960s. Racial conflicts have plagued the United States from its very beginnings, driven in particular by prejudice against Blacks. At the end of World War II, African Americans were second-class citizens, denied the pursuit of the American dream socially, economically, and politically. Since then, the Southern system of institutionalized Jim Crow segregation has been eliminated, as has most formal racial discrimination elsewhere. Old-fashioned racism, embodying beliefs in the biological inferiority of Blacks and support for formal discrimination and segregation, has greatly diminished. However, African Americans continue to experience substantial disadvantages in most domains of life. A variety of government race-targeted policies have addressed those disadvantages, such as busing for racial integration, affirmative action in university admissions, protection of equal opportunity in hiring and promotion, and special assistance in housing. These racial policies have been greeted with much White opposition. One explanation for that opposition is that some new form of racism, such as symbolic racism (also known as modern racism or racial resentment), has become influential in contemporary politics.

Contemporary Politics

Research on symbolic racism finds it to be the most powerful influence over Whites' attitudes toward racial issues and that it strongly influences Whites' voting behavior in election campaigns that involve Black candidates or racial issues. Its explanatory power typically outweighs that of other important political attitudes, such as conservative ideology, preference for smaller government, or of more traditional racial attitudes such as old-fashioned racism, negative stereotypes, or pure anti-Black feelings. This has even affected the politically crucial change of the once solidly Democratic White vote in the South to conservative Republican dominance. The especially high levels of symbolic racism among White Southerners and its especially strong influence over their voting preferences seem to be leading factors in that change.

The symbolic racism claim is an important one that the politics of race are not merely politics as usual, but that they are significantly distorted by the underlying racial prejudice held by many racial conservatives, with ostensibly race-neutral rhetoric often disguising underlying racial animosity. Not surprisingly, then, the theory has stimulated some heated criticism.

Criticism

Some conservatives say that racial prejudice has become only a minor political force, and that the theory of symbolic racism mistakenly treats ordinary political conservatism as reflecting racial prejudice. Its political effects might not be the result of racial prejudice, but of unprejudiced conservatives' aversion to large, active government programs. However, symbolic racism invariably has far greater power than does ostensibly race-neutral conservatism in explaining White opposition to racial policies, such as affirmative action, when both are considered.

Critics on the political left say that symbolic racism theory ignores the vested interest that Whites have in maintaining their privileged position as the dominant group in a racially hierarchical society. In their view, symbolic racism is not the product of early acquired prejudices, but is a way of rationalizing Whites' defense of their own and their group's privileges. But considerable research shows that neither White opposition to greater racial equality nor symbolic racism stems to an important degree from Whites' feelings of personal racial threat, their degree of identification with other Whites, or their perceptions that Blacks threaten Whites' interests.

Relevance

These controversies are of more than mere academic relevance. They go to the substantive core of America's longest-running and most difficult social problem. If the symbolic racism claim is right, much remedial work of a variety of kinds needs to be done on the White side of the racial divide. If it is wrong, and racial conservatives' views about the optimal relative balance of governments and markets in modern societies are largely free of underlying racial prejudice, much obligation would be placed upon Blacks to adapt to a society in which they no longer are being treated much less fairly than other Americans.

David O. Sears
P. J. Henry

See also Discrimination; Political Psychology; Prejudice; Racism; Stereotypes and Stereotyping

Further Readings

Sears, D. O., & Henry, P. J. (2005). Over thirty years later: A contemporary look at symbolic racism. In M. P. Zanna (Ed.), *Advances in experimental social psychology* (Vol. 37, pp. 95–150). San Diego, CA: Academic Press.

Sears, D. O., Sidanius, J., & Bobo, L. (Eds.). (2000). *Racialized politics: The debate about racism in America.* Chicago: University of Chicago Press.

Valentino, N. A., & Sears, D. O. (2005). Old times there are not forgotten: Race and partisan realignment in the contemporary South. *American Journal of Political Science, 49,* 672–688.

SYMBOLIC SELF-COMPLETION

Definition

Symbolic self-completion refers to having or seeking social symbols of achievement regarding a goal important to one's self-identity. R. A. Wicklund and P. M. Gollwitzer's symbolic self-completion theory was based on the pioneering work of Kurt Lewin and his collaborators. Wicklund and Gollwitzer posited that once an individual commits to a goal, psychological tension exists until the goal is achieved. If the individual engages in a task to accomplish the goal but is interrupted, the tension will motivate a return to the task or to a substitute task that could also lead to goal accomplishment. Personality psychologists, beginning with Alfred Adler, proposed a similar notion of substitutability in their concept of compensation, in which the individual compensates for perceived deficiencies through renewed efforts in either the domain in which one feels inferior or in other domains that could also broadly compensate for the deficiency.

Theory and Research

The theory proposes that when an individual is committed to a self-defining goal, such as a role like physician or an attribute like intelligence, that individual will seek symbols of completeness, socially acknowledged indicators that one has achieved that goal. For example, a medical degree is one symbol of being a physician and high scores on the Scholastic Aptitude Test are symbols of intelligence. When an individual has an ample supply of symbols regarding a particular self-defining goal, he or she will not need to seek additional symbols of completeness. However, if the individual perceives a deficit in symbols, efforts will be made to display symbols that restore completeness.

Two strategies have been used to test these ideas. The first is to compare people with and without a strong background of symbols of completeness. For example, one study asked people with extensive and limited educational backgrounds in their self-defining domains to admit to mistakes in that domain. As symbolic self-completion theory predicts, individuals with limited educational backgrounds, being more incomplete, were far more reluctant to admit mistakes.

The second strategy is to bring participants into the lab and induce half of them to believe they are incomplete with regard to a self-defining goal. In one study, participants were asked to write about mistakes they had made in a self-defining domain or in an unimportant domain. The participants were then asked to write a self-descriptive essay regarding the self-defining domain. As the theory predicted, those led to feel incomplete in the self-defining domain spent more time writing the essay, presumably to restore completeness.

Theoretical implications

Symbolic self-completion theory provides insight into goal striving and has been used to help explain the desire for cosmetic surgery, impulsive shopping, and subscription to particular magazines. The theory and research also indicate that those who feel the least adequate in an important domain may be most boastful, least willing to admit mistakes, and most likely to display degrees and awards. This suggests that people should not judge the competence of a person based solely on that person's outward presentation of their own qualifications and attributes. If one does so, one's judgments may be quite contrary to the truth.

Jeff Greenberg

See also Goals; Self-Affirmation Theory; Self-Presentation; Self-Promotion

Further Readings

Wicklund, R. A., & Gollwitzer, P. M. (1982). *Symbolic self-completion theory*. Hillsdale, NJ: Erlbaum.

SYSTEM JUSTIFICATION

Definition

System justification refers to a social psychological propensity to defend and bolster the status quo, that is, to see it as good, fair, legitimate, and desirable. A consequence of this tendency is that existing social, economic, and political arrangements tend to be preferred, and alternatives to the status quo are disparaged. System justification refers, therefore, to an inherently conservative tendency to defend and justify the status quo simply because it exists, sometimes even at the expense of individual and collective self-interest.

System Justification Theory

To understand how and why people accept and maintain the social systems that affect them, social psychologists have developed system justification theory. According to system justification theory, people want to hold favorable attitudes about themselves (ego-justification) and their own groups (group-justification), and they want to hold favorable attitudes about the overarching social order (system-justification). Importantly, system justification theory holds that this motive is not unique to members of dominant groups, who benefit the most from the current regime; it also affects the thoughts and behaviors of members of groups who are harmed by it (e.g., poor people, oppressed minorities, gays, and lesbians). System justification theory therefore accounts for counter-intuitive evidence that members of disadvantaged groups often support the societal status quo (at least to some degree), even at considerable cost to themselves and to fellow group members.

Evidence for the System Justification Motive

Several lines of research have documented the means by which individuals engage in system justification. First, sociologists and psychologists have identified several distinct but related system-justifying ideologies adopted by members of both advantaged and disadvantaged groups in the service of rationalizing the status quo, including the belief in a just world, Protestant work ethic, meritocratic ideology, fair market ideology, power distance, opposition to equality, and political conservatism.

Second, evidence indicates that most people want to perceive existing authorities and institutions as largely benevolent and legitimate. The dominant tendency, at least in the Western world, is for people to trust and approve of their government, to restrict criticism of it, and to believe in the fairness of their own system. Similarly, most people disapprove of protest and radical social change. Paradoxically, these tendencies are (at least sometimes) most pronounced for members of disadvantaged groups, who would have the most to gain from the implementation of a new system.

Third, members of advantaged and disadvantaged groups tend to internalize intergroup preferences that reinforce and legitimate the existing social hierarchy. Hundreds of studies have shown that members of advantaged groups tend to exhibit ingroup favoritism (preferences for their own kind), whereas members of disadvantaged groups exhibit this tendency to a much lesser extent and in many cases show outgroup favoritism (preferences for others who are more advantaged), especially but not exclusively on implicit (nonconscious) measures of preference. Outgroup favoritism among the disadvantaged maintains the status quo by accepting rather than supplanting existing forms of inequality.

Fourth, studies have also shown that consensual stereotypes (as well as evaluations) are used to differentiate between advantaged and disadvantaged groups

in such a way that the existing social order, with its attendant degree of inequality, is seen as legitimate and even natural. For example, members of low-status groups are routinely stereotyped by themselves and by others as less intelligent, competent, and hardworking than members of high-status groups. At the same time, complementary, off-setting stereotypes also lead people to show increased support for the status quo, insofar as such stereotypes maintain the belief that every group in society benefits from the existing social system. For example, individuals who are exposed to "poor but happy," "poor but honest," "rich but miserable," and "rich but dishonest" stereotype exemplars score higher on a measure of system justification than do individuals who are exposed to non-complementary stereotype exemplars.

If there is indeed a psychological motive to defend and justify the status quo, as system justification theory suggests, then people should be especially likely to exhibit the patterns of behavior described previous when the legitimacy or stability of the social system is threatened, as in the terrorist attacks of September 11, 2001. Numerous studies have indeed shown that there are increases in the endorsement of system-justifying beliefs and ideologies and the use of evaluations and stereotypes to differentiate between groups of unequal status in response to threats directed at the status quo.

Consequences of System Justification

In accordance with the motivational perspective of system justification theory, the successful rationalization of the status quo is associated with reduced negative affect and satisfaction of basic epistemic and existential needs (e.g., uncertainty reduction, threat management) for everyone in the system. However, the long-term consequences of system justification can differ for members of advantaged and disadvantaged groups. Whereas members of advantaged groups experience increased self-esteem and subjective well-being to the extent that they engage in system justification, members of disadvantaged groups who buy into the legitimacy of the system suffer in self-esteem and subjective well-being and hold more ambivalent attitudes about their own group membership.

System justification may also have detrimental consequences for society as a whole. Although there are hedonic benefits associated with minimizing the unjust and oppressive aspects of everyday life, processes of rationalization inhibit the motivation to change and improve the status quo, thereby undermining efforts to reform society's institutions and to redistribute social and economic resources in a more just manner. By highlighting the ways in which people consciously and unconsciously defend and bolster the status quo, system justification theory helps explain why acquiescence in the face of injustice is so prevalent and why social change is so rare and difficult to accomplish.

John T. Jost
Ido Liviatan

See also False Consciousness; Ideology; Political Psychology; Prejudice

Further Readings

Jost, J. T., & Banaji, M. R. (1994). The role of stereotyping in system-justification and the production of false consciousness. *British Journal of Social Psychology, 33,* 1–27.

Jost, J. T., Banaji, M. R., & Nosek, B. A. (2004). A decade of system justification theory: Accumulated evidence of conscious and unconscious bolstering of the status quo. *Political Psychology, 25,* 881–919.

Jost, J. T., & Hunyady, O. (2005). Antecedents and consequences of system-justifying ideologies. *Current Directions in Psychological Science, 14,* 260–265.

Kay, A. C., & Jost, J. T. (2003). Complementary justice: Effects of "poor but happy" and "poor but honest" stereotype exemplars on system justification and implicit activation of the justice motive. *Journal of Personality and Social Psychology, 85,* 823–837.

SYSTEMS THEORY

See DYNAMICAL SYSTEMS THEORY

T

TEASING

Teasing is central to human social life. In fact, in one study of grade-school children, more than 96% of respondents said they had been teased, and more than 50% admitted to teasing others. Teasing is as varied as the people doing the teasing and being teased. Teasing can be purely physical or verbal, and ranges widely in its affiliative or hostile intent. People tease to socialize, negotiate conflicts, flirt, and play. Empirical studies of this pervasive social practice have yielded answers to several intriguing questions.

Definition

A first question may be the most basic and most elusive to answer: What is teasing? Empirical studies of teasing lead to the following definition: *Teasing* is a behavior designed to provoke a target through the use of playful commentary on something relevant to the target. This provocation can be verbal (a cutting remark) or physical (an embarrassing gesture) and, by definition, threatens the teaser's and the target's desired social identity, or what some call "face." If the tease is too harsh, the target risks embarrassment or hurt feelings, and the teaser risks looking overly aggressive. To minimize these risks, teases are often accompanied by playful behaviors designed to signal that the tease is not meant to be taken too literally and that it is delivered, in part, in the spirit of play. Some examples of these behaviors, called off-record markers, include using a singsong voice, exaggerated facial expressions, metaphors, and unusual speed of delivery. Lastly, the tease is directed at something relevant to the target: either a commentary on the target himself or herself, the relationship between the target and the teaser, or some object of interest to the target. This definition helps clarify the differences between teasing and other related behaviors. The most common of these is bullying, which is a direct act of hostility that lacks the playful markers that signal playful, even affectionate, intent.

Occurrence

Equipped with a working definition of teasing, a second question can be asked: When do people tease? Observational studies in which researchers have documented the occurrence of teasing in naturalistic contexts, for example, in family dinner conversations or at work, reveal that teasing usually occurs in response to two kinds of social disturbances: norm deviations and interpersonal conflicts. First, individuals often tease others who have violated social norms. Elementary school children have been observed teasing each other for playing with classmates of the opposite sex or following violations of gender norms. Parents sometimes tease their children when they sulk or act selfishly. Coworkers tease one another in response to violations of the ethics and standards of the workplace.

Teasing often arises in a second context of social tension: conflict. Studies have indicated that siblings tease each other more during conflict situations, friends are more likely to tease each other during discussions of their conflicting goals and beliefs, and coworkers are more likely to tease when addressing hot-button issues, such as allocation of office space. Provocative and at times unpleasant, teasing in fact serves important prosocial functions, enabling individuals to signal and negotiate norm violations and interpersonal conflict.

Variations in Contexts

Given that teasing socializes and figures in conflict resolution, how then does it vary across different contexts? The same tease, it seems on the surface, acquires radically different meaning when delivered by superiors rather than peers or in formal as opposed to informal settings. Several studies have documented how the nature of the social context influences the content and meaning of a tease. Qualities of the relationship between the teaser and the target, such as social power and familiarity, have been found to influence teasing. High-power individuals are less dependent on others and are thus less concerned with the risks associated with teasing. High-power individuals, it should come as little surprise, are more likely to tease than low-power individuals, and they tease in a more hostile, less playful manner. The degree of closeness between teaser and target also affects teasing behavior, as individuals are less concerned about saving face in front of close others. As a result, people are more likely to tease close others than strangers, and to do so in a more direct manner. This may account in part for the ironic tendency for teasing, although aggressive, to be a signal of affection.

There also exist developmental differences in the content and meaning of teasing. Teasing, by its very nature, involves several capacities that develop with age. Among these are the ability to understand non-literal communication and many of the playful tactics used in teasing such as irony and sarcasm. As a result, older children are more likely to tease than are younger children, and to do so in a more subtle and sophisticated manner. The content of teasing also changes with age, as certain social norms become more or less relevant. For example, possessiveness and aggression are important topics for teasing in preschool, whereas experimental behaviors related to sex and drug use are focused on in adolescence and young adulthood.

Teasers

Who, then, is more likely to tease? Gender is one important determinant of the frequency and content of teasing. In general, men have been found to tease more than women when interacting with same- and opposite-sex friends as well as with children. Some studies suggest that while men have been observed to tease in more hostile and direct ways, women use more indirect methods, such as social exclusion. Gender has also been related to differences in teasing content, with men teasing more about physical appearance and women teasing more about the target's relationships.

The personalities of the individuals involved also shapes teasing in important ways. Highly agreeable individuals, who report great warmth and cooperativeness, tease less often in general, and when they do tease, they do so in more affectionate, less hostile fashion. In addition, Agreeableness has also been associated with stronger feelings of remorse after teasing someone. Highly extraverted individuals tease more often and feel less empathy toward the target than do those low in Extraversion. In addition, the target's personality and past history of teasing have been related to reactions to being teased. Among individuals who have been teasers themselves, individuals high on Agreeableness and Extraversion respond more positively to being teased than those low in Agreeableness and Extraversion.

Research

The empirical study of teasing is relatively new, and numerous questions await empirical answers. Current research is systematically examining how culture shapes the content and meaning of teasing. Studies within development are exploring how teasing is involved in language acquisition. Other studies are exploring how individuals with deficits in the cognitive capacities required of teasing understand teasing and tease themselves. It looks as though high-functioning autistic children have particular difficulties in seeing the playful intent of teasing and generating playful teasing. Still other lines of research are exploring how the teasing of bullies goes woefully awry and how to intervene. Continued research of these and other important issues pertaining to teasing will continue to enhance understanding and appreciation of this complex social phenomenon.

Dacher Keltner
Maria Logli Allison

See also Bullying; Conflict Resolution

Further Readings

Keltner, D., Capps, L., Kring, A. M., Young, R. C., & Heerey, E. A. (2001). Just teasing: A conceptual analysis and empirical review. *Psychological Bulletin, 127,* 229–248.

Keltner, D., Young, R. C., Heerey, E. A., Oemig, C., & Monarch, N. D. (1998). Teasing in hierarchical and intimate relations. *Journal of Personality and Social Psychology, 75,* 1231–1247.

Kowalski, R. M. (2000). "I was only kidding!": Victims' and perpetrators' perceptions of teasing. *Personality and Social Psychology Bulletin, 26,* 231–241.

Kowalski, R. M. (2004). Proneness to, perceptions of, and responses to teasing: The influence of both intrapersonal and interpersonal factors. *European Journal of Personality, 18,* 331–349.

Temporal Construal Theory

Definition

Temporal construal theory is a general theoretical framework that describes the effects of psychological distance on thinking, decision making, and behavior. Psychologically distant objects and events are those beyond one's direct experience of the here and now and can be distant on a number of dimensions: time, space, social distance (self vs. other, ingroup vs. outgroup), and hypotheticality. A central proposition of temporal construal theory is that psychologically distant objects or events evoke mental representations, or construals, that capture the general and essential features of the objects or events (i.e., high-level construals), whereas psychologically near objects or events bring to mind unique, concrete, and incidental features (i.e., low-level construals). The activation of high-versus low-level construals produces systematic differences in individuals' understanding of objects and events, leading to changes in evaluation, judgment, and action.

Background

Temporal construal theory (also referred to as construal level theory) was originally proposed by Nira Liberman and Yaacov Trope as an integrative framework for understanding the effects of time on decision making and behavior. Objects and events, however, can be distant not only in time but also in space, social distance, and hypotheticality. As such, the theory has since been expanded beyond time to incorporate these other dimensions of psychological distance. The term *construal* refers to the construction of knowledge structures that represent objects or events in an individual's mind (i.e., how information is processed so that an individual can think about and understand an object or event).

When objects and events are psychologically distant, less information is known about them. An individual can learn about a dog, but without direct experience, there is little to distinguish this particular dog from other dogs. Without such information, individuals can only think of objects and events in broad, general terms (i.e., high-level construals). Thus, the individual might know that the dog has four furry legs and barks. As the objects and events become more psychologically near, direct experience of these objects and events becomes increasingly available. This allows individuals to think about objects and events in more concrete details, highlighting their specific, unique, incidental features (low-level construals). Through more direct experience, for example, an individual might learn about the unique properties or characteristics of a dog: the breed, specific coloration, or temperament. This association between the psychological distance of an object and its corresponding level of construal is thought to be so ingrained that respective construals are activated even when all necessary information is available. That is, even if an individual knows that a dog is called Fluffy and is a white poodle, when the dog is psychologically distant (e.g., far away in time or space), the individual is more likely to think of the dog as a furry animal with four legs rather than as Fluffy.

As high- and low-level construals bring to mind different features of objects and events, they can systematically change individuals' decisions and behavior. They can focus individuals on contrasting aspects of a situation and lead to very different evaluations and judgments of the same thing. Going on a vacation in the abstract (high-level construal) may evoke images of the beach and pleasant company. When psychologically distant, going on a vacation should therefore engender positive feelings. Going on a vacation, however, more concretely (low-level construal) entails making plans, dealing with travel agencies, and having to bear the inconveniences of traveling. Thus, when psychologically near, going on a vacation may evoke more negative evaluations. Hence, psychological distance, through the activation of different levels of construal, plays an important role in human decision making and behavior.

Evidence

Empirical data have supported the proposition that increasing psychological distance leads individuals to construe objects and events more broadly and generally (i.e., activate high-level construals). Research has shown, for example, that individuals organize objects associated with temporally distant events in fewer, broader, and more abstract categories than objects associated with temporally near events. Similarly, when feeling socially distanced from others, individuals are more accurate in recalling the gist rather than the specifics of material that they have seen before. Individuals are also more likely to access global, abstract concepts, such as stereotypes and traits, when making judgments about psychologically distant others, whether they be distant by physical space, time, or social distance.

There is also accumulating evidence that by changing how individuals construe situations, psychological distance can influence the kinds of judgments and decisions individuals make. High-level construals, when activated by increasing psychological distance, lead individuals to be more concerned with high- rather than low-level features of objects and events. That is, individuals are more likely to make choices on the basis of global, primary concerns over local, secondary considerations when events are psychologically distant rather than near. For example, increasing the temporal distance of an event leads individuals to make decisions more on the basis of ends (why they might engage in an action) rather than means (how they would perform an action). They also prefer activities that accord with their goals and values to a greater extent when those activities are associated with distant future rather than near future events.

All of the research described here has suggested that increasing any dimension of psychological distance—time, space, social distance, or hypotheticality—leads to similar effects on mental representation (i.e., activates high-level rather than low-level construals) and decision making (i.e., preferences and choices based on high-level rather than low-level features). Providing additional support for the notion that these various dimensions of psychological distance are interrelated is research that suggests that thinking about one type of distance facilitates thinking about others. That is, thinking about "here" leads one also to think about "now" and "us," whereas thinking about "there" leads to thoughts of "then" and "them."

Beyond Psychological Distance

The psychological distance of objects and events are not the only factor that leads individuals to evoke high- versus low-level construals. It has been found, for example, that positive moods tend to activate higher-level construals as compared to negative moods. Moreover, engaging in any mental process that leads one to extract generalized properties of objects and events, such as causal reasoning or superordinate categorization, can activate high-level rather than low-level construals. Construals can also carry over from unrelated prior contexts. For example, imagining one's life at a distant location or distant time can lead individuals to use high-level construals in subsequent contexts, even those that had nothing to do with what one imagined.

In addition, there may be individual differences in the use of high- versus low-level construals. That is, in addition to situational factors, there may be personality factors in the tendency to represent objects and events at different levels of construal. Some individuals may habitually use high-level construals, whereas others tend to use low-level construals.

Importance

Individuals make decisions about objects and events that are psychologically distant in almost every domain of life. Indeed, the ability to make choices about objects and events beyond one's direct experience is one of the hallmarks of the human mind. Despite this remarkable ability, individuals are fallible decision makers, often making decisions that seem good at the time but that they later regret. Temporal construal theory provides a general framework for understanding why and how this occurs and has important implications for interventions aimed at improving decision making. As such, the theory has been applied to a wide array of research topics in psychology that range from attribution, attitudes, and self-control to interpersonal perception, social power, and negotiation.

Kentaro Fujita
Yaacov Trope
Nira Liberman

See also Action Identification Theory; Actor–Observer
Asymmetries; Delay of Gratification; Ingroup–Outgroup
Bias; Outgroup Homogeneity; Self-Regulation

Further Readings

Trope, Y., & Liberman, N. (2003). Temporal construal.
Psychological Review, 110, 403–421.

TEND-AND-BEFRIEND RESPONSE

In times of stress, humans and many animal species
tend and befriend. Tending involves quieting and caring for offspring during stressful times, and befriending involves engaging the social network for help in
responding to stress.

Background

Threatening circumstances trigger a cascade of neuroendocrine responses to stress, including engagement of the sympathetic nervous system and
corticosteroids that mobilize a person or animal to
cope with stress. Consequently, stress responses are
heavily marked by physiological arousal. Historically,
the prototypical response to stress has been regarded
as fight or flight. That is, in response to a threat,
arousal mobilizes the person to behave aggressively or
assertively (fight), or flee or withdraw instead (flight).
Contemporary manifestations of fight responses in
humans assume the form of aggressive reactions to
stressful circumstances, and flight responses are often
manifested as social withdrawal or substance abuse,
as through alcohol or drugs.

Although fight or flight is somewhat descriptive
of human responses to stress, scientists have noted
that social affiliation distinguishes human responses
to stress as well, and it has long been known to protect against the adverse changes in mental and physical health that stress can produce. Social support
from a partner, relative, friend, or coworkers and
from social and community ties reliably reduces cardiovascular and neuroendocrine stress responses and
psychological distress. Correspondingly, social isolation has been consistently tied to poor health and a
higher risk of mortality in both animal and human
studies. Taken together, these findings may account
for the robust relations between social support and a

lower likelihood of illness, faster recovery from illness, and greater longevity.

Further refining of these social responses to stress
has led to the characterization "tend and befriend."
That is, the fight-or-flight response seems incomplete
when one realizes that humans have few of the physical resources necessary to do either (e.g., sharp claws,
speed). Instead, human survival has depended on
group living. From an evolutionary standpoint,
humans would not have survived had they not evolved
ways of coping with stress that involved the protection
of offspring from harm and group living to fend off
threats and predators.

Gender Differences

The tend-and-befriend response to stress appears
to be especially characteristic of females. Historically,
females have had primary responsibility for the care
of offspring, and consequently, the tend-and-befriend
responses may have evolved in females especially
in light of these selection pressures. That is, a female
stands a better chance of protecting both herself and
her immature offspring if she tends to those offspring
and enlists the help of the social group for protection
as well.

What is the evidence that tend-and-befriend characterizes females' responses to stress? Across the
entire life cycle, girls and women are more likely to
mobilize social support, especially from other
females in times of stress. Compared to men,
women seek out social contact more, they receive
more social support, they provide more social support to others, and they are more satisfied by the
support they receive. Whereas men also draw on
social support, especially from their partners,
women seek more social support from a broader
array of sources, including friends and relatives, and
these findings are consistent across many different
cultures. The sex difference in women's seeking of
social support in times of stress is modest in size but
very robust.

Research suggests that there may be biological
underpinnings of these tending and befriending
responses. In particular, oxytocin has been identified
as an affiliative hormone that is known to increase
maternal behavior and affiliative activity. Because the
effects of oxytocin are strongly enhanced by the
presence of estrogen, oxytocin has been thought to
have more important effects on the social behavior of

females than males. Although there is modest evidence to date that oxytocin is implicated in these affiliative processes under stress, studies do suggest that oxytocin levels rise when women experience gaps in their social network, potentially providing a neuroendocrine basis for an increased desire to affiliate with others in difficult times. Studies also show that oxytocin reduces sympathetic nervous system arousal and corticosteroid activity and that it is associated with reduced anxiety and a sense of calm. Consistent with this point, tending activities represent adaptive responses to stress, not only because of the protection they provide for offspring but also because tending quells biological stress responses in both offspring and mother. Endogenous opioid peptides, that is, opioids naturally produced by the body, also appear to play a role in these tending and befriending processes.

The exploration of the tend-and-befriend response is a relatively new theoretical and empirical undertaking for social psychologists. This is in large part because, until recently, stress studies were based heavily on animal studies and on males. As females have been included in stress studies, the fact that their responses to stress are more social than men's has come into focus. This gender difference must not be overstated, however. Both men and women demonstrate affiliative responses to stress, and men profit from social support just as women do. Although oxytocin may not play a role in men's affiliative behavior (because of its regulation by estrogen), possibly vasopressin, a hormone similar to oxytocin that is regulated in part by androgen, may be implicated. Vasopressin appears to underpin male monogamous behavior, protection of mate and offspring, and guarding of territory, for example, in some rodent studies; however, whether vasopressin plays a role in human behavior is not yet known.

Shelley E. Taylor

See also Fight-or-Flight Response; Social Support; Stress and Coping

Further Readings

Carter, C. S. (1998). Neuroendocrine perspectives on social attachment and love. *Psychoneuroendocrinology, 23,* 779–818.

Hrdy, S. B. (1999). *Mother nature: A history of mothers, infants, and natural selection.* New York: Pantheon Books.

Repetti, R. L., Taylor, S. E., & Seeman, T. E. (2002). Risky families: Family social environments and the mental and physical health of offspring. *Psychological Bulletin, 128,* 330–366.

Tamres, L., Janicki, D., & Helgeson, V. S. (2002). Sex differences in coping behavior: A meta-analytic review. *Personality and Social Psychology Review, 6,* 2–30.

Taylor, S. E. (2002). *The tending instinct: How nurturing is essential to who we are and how we live.* New York: Henry Holt.

Territoriality

Definition

Territoriality is a pattern of attitudes and behavior held by a person or group that is based on perceived, attempted, or actual control of a physical space, object, or idea, which may involve habitual occupation, defense, personalization, and marking of the territory. Marking means placing an object or substance in a space to indicate one's territorial intentions. Cafeteria diners leave coats or books on a chair or table. Prospectors stake claims. Personalization means marking in a manner that indicates one's identity. Many employees decorate their workspaces with pictures and mementoes. Some car owners purchase vanity license plates. Territoriality usually is associated with the possession of some physical space, but it can also involve such processes as dominance, control, conflict, security, claim staking, vigilance, and identity. If a territory is important to a person, his or her sense of identity may be closely tied to it. Although it is sometimes associated with aggression, territoriality actually is much more responsible for the smooth operation of society because most people, most of the time, respect the territories of others.

Types of Territories

Territoriality is extremely widespread. Once you recognize them, the signs of human territoriality are everywhere: books spread out on a cafeteria table to save a place, nameplates, fences, locks, no-trespassing signs, even copyright notices. There are billions of territories in the world; some are large, others small, some are nested within others (such as a person's "own" chair within a home), and some are shared.

Primary territories are spaces owned by individuals or primary groups, controlled on a relatively permanent basis by them and central to their daily lives. Examples include your bedroom or a family's dwelling. The psychological importance of primary territories to their owners is always high.

Secondary territories are less important to their occupiers than primary territories, but they do possess moderate significance to their occupants. A person's desk at work, favorite restaurant, locker in the gym, and home playing field are examples. Control of these territories is less essential to the occupant and is more likely to change, rotate, or be shared with strangers.

Public territories are areas open to anyone in good standing with the community. Beaches, sidewalks, and hotel lobbies are public territories. Occasionally, because of discrimination or unacceptable behavior, public territories are closed to some individuals. Retail stores, for example, are public territories open to anyone. However, someone who causes trouble may be banned from a particular store.

The physical self may be considered as a body territory. The boundary is at one's skin. Bodies may be entered with permission (as in surgery) or without permission (as in a knife attack). Some people mark and personalize their own bodies with makeup, jewelry, tattoos, piercings, and clothing, but they certainly defend and try to control access to their bodies by other people.

Two other types of territories exist, although they are not universally considered territories. Objects meet some of the criteria for territories—we mark, personalize, defend, and control our possessions. Ideas are also, in some ways, territories. We defend them through patents and copyrights. There are rules against plagiarism. Software authors and songwriters try to protect ownership of their programs and songs.

Infringements

Even though territories usually work to keep society hassle-free, sometimes they are infringed upon. The most obvious form of infringement is invasion, in which an outsider physically enters someone else's territory, usually with the intention of taking it from its current owner. One obvious example is one country trying to take the territory of another.

The second form of infringement is violation, a temporary infringement of someone's territory. Usually, the goal is not ownership but annoyance or harm. Vandalism, hit-and-run attacks, and burglary fall into this category.

Sometimes a violation occurs out of ignorance, as when a boy who cannot yet read walks into a women's washroom. Other times the violation is deliberate, such as computer pranksters worming their way into others' machines. Violation may occur without the infringer personally entering the territory. Jamming radio waves and playing loud music are some examples.

The third form of infringement is contamination, in which the infringer fouls someone else's territory by putting something awful in the territory. Examples would be a chemical company leaving poisonous waste in the ground for later residents to deal with, a houseguest leaving the kitchen filthy, or pesticide spray drifting into your yard.

Defenses

Just as there are a three general ways to infringe on territories, there are three different types of defense. When someone uses a coat, sign, or fence to defend a territory, it is called a *prevention defense*. One anticipates infringement and acts to stop it before it occurs.

Reaction defenses, on the other hand, are responses to an infringement after it happens. Examples range from slamming a door in someone's face or physically striking the infringer to court actions for copyright violations.

The third type is the social boundary defense. Used at the edge of interactional territories, the social boundary defense consists of a ritual engaged in by hosts and visitors. For example, you need a password to enter many Web sites. Another example is the customs office at the national border. Social boundary defenses serve to separate wanted visitors from unwanted ones.

Territoriality in Everyday Life

One way territoriality has been used in everyday life involves defensible space theory, sometimes called crime prevention through environmental design. The theory proposes that certain design features, such as real or symbolic barriers to separate public territory from private territory and opportunities for territory owners to observe suspicious activity in their spaces, will increase residents' sense of security and make criminals feel uneasy. It has been used widely to reduce crime in residences, neighborhoods, and retail stores.

Robert Gifford

See also Control; Identity Status; Personal Space

Further Readings

Edney, J. (1974). Human territoriality. *Psychological Bulletin,* *81,* 959–975.

Taylor, R. B. (1988). *Human territorial functioning: An empirical, evolutionary perspective on individual and small group territorial cognitions, behaviors, and consequences.* New York: Cambridge University Press.

TERRORISM, PSYCHOLOGY OF

Terrorism is certainly the scourge of our times. Considerable economic, military, political, and scientific resources are devoted these days to the "war on terrorism." Psychological research is not only relevant but also essential to understanding this issue. Indeed, the psychology of terrorism has become one of psychology's major growth markets. Books and journals on the topic have been published in unprecedented quantities. Terrorists' acts of self-destruction and their indiscriminate killings of innocent civilians cry out for a psychological explanation. But what explanations has psychology provided? How do psychologists analyze the phenomenon of terrorism? And how can psychology help eradicate it?

What Is Terrorism?

Before answering these questions, it is important to first describe what terrorism is. This is not an easy task. Terrorism researchers have proposed over a hundred different definitions of the phenomenon. Why is it so hard to agree on a definition?

A major problem is that this term carries a negative connotation. It is for that reason that one person's terrorist is another's person freedom fighter. Thus, applying the "terrorism" label to an act depends not only on the act but also on who is applying the label.

The U.S. Department of State formally defines *terrorism* as "premeditated, politically motivated violence conducted in times of peace, perpetrated against noncombatant targets by sub-national groups or clandestine state agents, usually intended to influence an audience to advance political ends." This definition contains a number of ingredients: For it to be called terrorism, an act needs to be planned ("premeditated"), to be politically motivated, to involve violence, to be carried out in peacetime, to be directed against civilians (i.e., "noncombatants"), and to involve no government directly. Such a multidimensional definition allows one to set terrorism apart from (1) state-originated violence at times of war (e.g., the bombings of German or Japanese cities during World War II), (2) incidental killings of noncombatants (so-called collateral damage), and (3) underground resistance to occupation.

Terrorism as Syndrome Versus Terrorism as Tool

Over the years, two psychological approaches to terrorism have appeared. One approach treats terrorism as a syndrome; the other treats it as a tool. The syndrome view treats terrorism as a unique phenomenon with its own psychology. From this perspective, terrorists are considered different from nonterrorists. They are assumed to differ not only in *what* they do, but also in *who* they are, and *why* they do what they do. In this respect, terrorism is considered akin to a mental disorder, like depression or schizophrenia. The syndrome view of terrorism also suggests that there could exist external root causes of terrorism, such as poverty or political oppression, which inevitably breed terrorism.

In contrast, the tool view of terrorism does not assume anything psychologically abnormal or unique about terrorists. This view depicts terrorism as a means to an end, a tactic of warfare that anyone could use. It suggests that like the rocket launcher, the tank, or the AK-47 assault rifle, terrorism may be used by nonstate militias, state-sponsored military, and even lone perpetrators. If one assumes that terrorism is a means to an end, its psychology can be well understood by general theory and research on goals and motivations. Basically, this body of knowledge has taught psychologists that a specific means is used when a person considers it of a high expected utility. That is, if a person wants to achieve something, he or she is more likely to use a tool or means, if it is seen as helpful to such attainment. If it is so seen, the tool or means is considered to have high expected utility. Moreover, a tool is particularly high in expected utility if the thing the person wants to achieve is important to him or her. Thus, to the extent that a tool is highly helpful to the achievement of important goals, it is said to have high psychological utility.

What does this mean for the psychology of terrorism? As the name implies, the tool view of terrorism suggests that the tool of terrorism may, for some individuals and under some circumstances, be particularly high in expected utility. In such cases, terrorism may be seen as helpful to the achievement of highly important goals, and the actors involved may feel they have no other means that are equally helpful. The goals of the terrorists and their available means are of great relevance for understanding the psychology of terrorism.

In light of these ideas, it may be possible to think of various ways in which terrorism is used by different organizations. Utopian Islamist groups, for example, have doctrines and convictions that leave little room for negotiation, dialogue, or peacemaking. For them terrorism and violence represent the only available means. Given such depth of commitment to violence, it is unlikely that anything short of a total defeat will convince the Utopian Islamists to give up their use of terrorism. The situation is different for terrorism-users for whom terrorism represents merely one among several available instruments. Though not shy of using terrorism, Hamas, Hezbollah, and Sinn Féin, for example, have other means at their disposal (diplomacy, media campaigns) as well as other goals (of a political or social variety). All three have mitigated their use of terrorism or withheld it for a time when alternative means to their purpose appeared feasible or when other goals existed to which terrorism appeared inimical.

In short, different organizations may differ in their potential for relinquishing the use of terrorism. Whereas negotiating with terrorists is unlikely to work with terrorists whose commitment to terrorism is total, it might work with terrorist groups who may entertain alternative means and value alternative goals. On the level of terrorist organizations, then, the terrorism-as-a-tool view helps to explain how terrorism could be of use.

Root Causes Versus Contributing Factors

What are the factors that lead individuals to embrace the goal of terrorism? This question has been answered in two ways. Some have tried to identify the root causes assumed to underlie terrorist engagement, whereas others have argued that there is no single root cause but rather several contributing factors that may help motivate an individual to embrace terrorism. The root cause concept implies a factor that constitutes both a necessary and a sufficient condition for some effect. The concept of a contributing factor raises doubts about whether any given personality trait, need, or situational circumstance could constitute such a condition, inevitably giving rise to terrorism. But if an individual were presented with the idea of terrorism, traits, motivations, and situational conditions might well affect the likelihood of his or her embracing it.

Although it may be appealing to identify a single cause for terrorist activity, research thus far has failed to provide supportive evidence that such cause exists. Early psychological investigations asked whether terrorists are driven by some kind of psychological disturbance. However, painstaking empirical research conducted on various terrorist organizations didn't reveal anything particularly striking about the psychological makeup of terrorists.

That does not mean that psychological factors do not matter. Decades of psychological research have demonstrated that motivation significantly affects the tendency to embrace beliefs on various topics, and beliefs in the efficacy and justifiability of terrorism are no exception. Thus, individuals with appropriate motivations (deriving from their stable personality traits or situational pressures) might be more prone to endorse terrorism under the appropriate circumstances than might individuals with different motivations. In this context, it has been found that whereas in Iran, mortality salience enhanced support for suicide terrorism, in the United States, it enhanced the support for tough antiterrorist measures. In Lebanon, right-wing conservatism predicted the support for terrorism, whereas in the United States, it predicted the support for counterterrorism. In other words, mortality salience and conservative attitudes do not in and of themselves produce terrorism. They are not the root causes of terrorism, but in a social and cultural environment where terrorism is viewed as an acceptable tool, they may contribute to individuals' endorsement of terrorism.

Research has also failed to find evidence for a relation between poverty or education and terrorism, although some investigators have found that many terrorists come from countries that suffer from political repression. However, from the standpoint of psychological theory, there are reasons to doubt a general causal link between either poverty or political repression and terrorism. Presumably, the underlying logic of such a hypothesized link is that poverty and oppression foster frustration, fomenting aggression against others, ergo terrorism. But in scientific psychology, the simple frustration–aggression hypothesis has long been questioned. Just because one is frustrated does not necessarily mean that one would become a terrorist. Instead, one could escape, withdraw, or aggress against self rather than against others. Thus, again, poverty, lack of education, and political repression may not be considered root causes of terrorism. However, being deprived of opportunities, and hence suffering and frustrated, may be considered a contributing factor in the emergence of terrorism.

Discouraging Terrorism

The tool view of terrorism suggests that terrorism may particularly thrive in circumstances under which no alternative tools are available to achieve one's goals and in which the individual has a strong conviction that these goals are important to attain. According to this view, discouraging terrorism amounts to convincing the perpetrator that (a) this means is not of use to achieve the goal, (b) there are alternative and better means to achieve the goal, and (c) once terrorism is chosen to achieve particular goals, it will be carried out at the expense of other goals that may also be worthwhile to attain.

Perceived Use of Terrorism

Though schematically simple, implementation of these strategies is anything but that. A major difficulty is that events are perceived differently by different parties. Such perceptions are often biased by interests and motivations. For example, throughout much of the second intifada, about 80% of the Palestinian population supported the use of terror tactics against the Israelis, believing this to be an effective tool of struggle. By contrast, the majority of the Israelis (85%) viewed Palestinian terror as counterproductive. It seems plausible to assume that the divergent motivations of Israelis and Palestinians importantly colored their beliefs in this matter.

Terrorism may be difficult to give up also because, apart from presumably helping to achieve the ideological (political, religious, ethnonationalistic) objectives of the terrorist, it brings about the emotional satisfaction of watching the enemy suffer. In that sense, terrorism is multipurpose, adding up to its appeal or the total value of objectives to which it appears of use. Such counterterrorist policies as ethnic profiling, targeted hits, or inadvertent collateral damage might further enhance the terrorists' rage, amplifying the emotional goal of vengeance against the enemy. A recent empirical analysis suggests that targeted hits by the Israeli forces boosted the estimated recruitment to the terrorist stock, presumably due to Palestinians' revenge motivation. Thus, whereas targeted hits do hurt the terrorist organizations and may decrease the perceived efficacy of terrorism, they may also increase the appeal of terrorism by increasing the intensity of the emotional goal it may serve.

Feasibility of Alternatives to Terrorism

Whereas alternative goals (such as revenge) may increase terrorism's appeal by increasing the total expected utility of terrorism, perceived availability of alternative means to the terrorism's ends may decrease it. Such availability brings about the possibility of shifting to a different means and abandoning terrorism, at least for a time. For instance, following the election in 2005 of Mahmud Abbas to the presidency of the Palestinian Authority and a renewed chance for a peace process (i.e., an alternative means potentially helpful to end the Israeli occupation), support for suicide attacks among the Palestinians dipped to its lowest in 7 years: a mere 27%.

Alternative Objectives

Discouraging people from using terrorism may also be attained by making potential users of terrorism aware of alternative objectives that do not fit well with terrorism. In the Palestinian context, the opposition to suicide attacks is particularly pronounced among Palestinians likely to possess the means to alternative, individualistic goals, for example, professional, family, or material goals. Such opposition reached 71% among holders of B.A. degrees compared to 61% among illiterates, 75% among employees compared to 62% among students, and, curiously enough, 74% among individuals willing to buy lottery tickets (i.e., individuals presumably interested in material goals) compared to 64% among those unwilling to buy them.

Arie W. Kruglanski
Mark Dechesne

See also Aggression; Frustration–Aggression Hypothesis; Goals; Ideology; Mortality Salience; Peace Psychology; Political Psychology

Further Readings

Crenshaw, M. (2000). The psychology of terrorism: An agenda for the 21st century. *Political Psychology, 21,* 405–420.

Kruglanski, A. W., & Fishman, S. (2006). The psychology of terrorism: Syndrome versus tool perspectives. *Terrorism and Political Violence, 18,* 193–215.

McCauley, C. (2002). Psychological issues in understanding terrorism and the response to terrorism. In C. Stout (Ed.), *The psychology of terrorism: Vol 3. Theoretical underpinnings and perspectives* (pp. 3–30). Westport, CT: Greenwood Press.

TERROR MANAGEMENT THEORY

Definition

Terror management theory is an empirically supported theory developed to explain the psychological functions of self-esteem and culture. The theory proposes that people strive to sustain the belief they are significant contributors to a meaningful universe to minimize the potential for terror engendered by their awareness of their own mortality. Cultures provide their members with meaning-imbuing worldviews and bases of self-esteem to serve this terror management function.

Background

Former University of Kansas graduate student colleagues Sheldon Solomon, Jeff Greenberg, and Tom Pyszczynski developed terror management theory in 1984. These social psychologists were searching for answers to two basic questions about human behavior: Why do people need self-esteem? Why do different cultures have such a difficult time coexisting peacefully? The trio found potential answers to these questions in the writings of anthropologist Ernest Becker. Becker integrated insights from psychoanalysis, psychology, anthropology, sociology, and philosophy into a framework for understanding the motives that drive human behavior. Solomon, Greenberg, and Pyszczynski designed terror management theory to summarize, simplify, and elaborate Becker's scholarly synthesis into a unified theory from which they could generate new testable hypotheses regarding the psychological functions of self-esteem and culture, and thereby address the two basic questions they originally posed.

The Theory

Terror management theory begins with two simple assumptions. The first is that, being evolved animals with a wide range of biological systems serving survival, humans have a strong desire to stay alive. The second is that, unlike other animals, humans have evolved cognitive abilities to think abstractly; to think in terms of past, present, and future; and to be aware of their own existence. Although these cognitive abilities provide many adaptive advantages, they have led to the realization that humans are mortal, vulnerable to all sorts of threats to continued existence and that death, which thwarts the desire to stay alive, is inevitable. According to the theory, the juxtaposition of the desire to stay alive with the knowledge of one's mortality creates an ever-present potential to experience existential terror, the fear of no longer existing. To keep the potential terror concerning mortality at bay, people need to sustain faith in a meaning-providing cultural worldview and the belief they are significant contributors to that meaningful reality (self-esteem). By psychologically living in a world of absolute meaning and enduring significance, people can obscure the possibility that they are really just transient animals in a purposeless universe destined only to absolute annihilation upon death.

The terror management functions of worldviews and self-esteem emerge over the course of childhood. Parents are the initial basis of security for the small vulnerable child and convey the core concepts and values of the prevailing cultural worldview. Throughout socialization, religious, social, and educational institutions reinforce and further elaborate this worldview. As part of this process, parents impose conditions of worth on the child that reflect the culture's customs and standards of value. These conditions must be met to sustain the parental love and protection and, later, the approval of one's peers, teachers, and cultural ideals and authority figures. In this way, believing in and living up to the values of the culture confer self-esteem and become the individual's basis of psychological security. As the child matures, the limits of the parents become apparent and the basis of security gradually shifts to the culture's broader spiritual and secular ideals and figures. Each cultural worldview offers its own bases of self-esteem, such that what bolsters self-esteem in one culture might not in another.

The most obvious examples of how worldviews provide the basis for terror management are religious worldviews such as Christianity and Islam, in which one's earthly purpose is to serve one's deity, after which those who have been true to the teachings of the deity will be rewarded with eternal life. Indeed, a spiritual dimension and concept of eternal soul had been central to all known cultures until the rise of science-based secular worldviews in the 19th and 20th centuries. These forms of literal immortality (or death transcendence) are supplemented by symbolic modes of immortality offered by secular components of culture. Symbolic immortality can be achieved in modern society through identification with collectives and causes that transcend individual death, such as one's nation; it can also be achieved through offspring, inheritances, memorials, and many forms of cultural achievement in the arts and sciences (novels, paintings, sculptures, discoveries, etc.). Thus, as a result of the socialization process, people everywhere live out their lives ensconced within a culturally derived orderly and meaningful construal of reality in which they strive to be significant beings qualified for transcendence of death through an eternal soul and/or permanent contributions to the world.

Terror Management Theory and Social Behavior

Terror management theory can help explain much of what has been learned about humans from history and the social sciences. People by and large conform to their culture's ways, following its norms and obeying authorities. People vehemently defend their cherished beliefs and rituals. Religious, governmental, and educational institutions reinforce cultural beliefs and values in myriad ways. Cultural belief systems provide explanations of where the world and humans come from, what humans should strive for, and how humans will persist in some form after individual death.

The theory answers basic questions about self-esteem and intercultural disharmony. Self-esteem, the belief that one is a valuable member of a meaningful universe, serves to minimize anxiety concerning one's vulnerability and mortality. This view of self-esteem can help explain why those with high self-esteem fare much better in life than those with low self-esteem and why threats to self-esteem engender anxiety, anger, and defensive reactions, ranging from self-serving attributions to murder.

The theory also offers an explanation for what is perhaps humankind's most tragic flaw: people's inability to get along peacefully with those different from themselves. People who subscribe to a different cultural worldview call into question the validity of one's own, thus threatening faith in one's own basis of security. To minimize this threat, people derogate those with different beliefs, perhaps labeling them "ignorant savages"; try to convert them, as in missionary activity; or, in extreme historical cases such as Hitler's Germany and Stalin's Soviet Union, try to annihilate them.

Research

Since its initial development, a body of more than 250 studies conducted in 14 different countries has supported terror management theory. Prominent contributors to this research in addition to the codevelopers of the theory include Linda Simon, Jamie Arndt, Jamie Goldenberg, Victor Florian, Mario Mikulincer, Mark Dechesne, Eva Jonas, and Mark Landau.

The first research based on the theory tested the idea that self-esteem protects people from anxiety. A series of studies showed that when people feel really good about themselves, they can deal with potentially threatening situations in an especially calm manner. One such study showed that when people are given a very favorable report regarding their personality, they perspire less while anticipating exposure to painful electric shocks. Follow-up research found that high self-esteem is particularly protective regarding death-related concerns.

Subsequent studies examined the idea that if self-esteem protects people from their concerns about death, making people think about their own mortality (known as mortality salience [MS]) should lead them to defend their self-esteem more fervently and strive harder to exhibit their worthiness. For example, research has shown that MS leads people who base their self-esteem partly on their driving ability to drive more boldly, those who base it partly on physical strength to display a stronger hand grip, and those who base it on their appearance to become more interested in tanning. In addition, MS leads people to give more generously to valued charities, to strengthen their identification with successful groups, and to reduce their identification with unsuccessful groups.

The other general terror management idea tested early on was that MS would lead people to strongly defend and uphold the beliefs and values of their own worldview. Using a variety of approaches, more than 100 studies have supported this idea. The first such study found that MS led municipal court judges to set higher bonds for an alleged prostitute in a hypothetical but realistic case. Many subsequent studies have supported the idea that MS increases harsh judgments of others who transgress the morals of one's worldview. But MS also increases favorable treatment of those who uphold the worldview, such as heroes. Furthermore, MS increases favorable reactions to others who praise or otherwise validate one's worldview and intensifies negative reactions to others who criticize or otherwise dispute the validity of one's worldview. For example, a study using American participants found that MS increased positive reactions to a pro-U.S. essayist and negative reactions to an anti-U.S. essayist. Similarly, a study using Christian participants found that MS engendered positive reactions to a fellow Christian and negative reactions to a Jewish person.

These studies have reminded people of their mortality in a variety of ways and in comparison with many control conditions. Reminders of mortality have included two questions about one's own death, gory accident footage, death anxiety scales, proximity to funeral homes and cemeteries, and exposure to extremely brief subliminal flashes of death-related words on a computer screen. Control conditions have reminded participants of neutral topics such as television, and aversive topics such as failure, worries after college, uncertainty, meaninglessness, pain, and social exclusion. These findings support the specific role of mortality concerns in MS effects.

Once support for these basic terror management hypotheses had accumulated, a variety of additional directions were pursued. One body of research explored the processes through which thoughts of death produce their effects. This research has shown these effects do not occur while people are consciously aware of death-related thoughts and are not triggered by consciously experienced emotion. Rather, thoughts of death that are outside of but close to consciousness signal heightened potential for anxiety, which triggers intensified

efforts to bolster the worldview and one's self-esteem. This work shows that cultural investments and self-esteem striving often serve existential needs outside of conscious awareness.

Another set of studies has examined the effects of MS on basic ways in which people preserve their sense that life is orderly and meaningful. This work shows that MS leads people to increase their preference for believing that the world is a just place, for art that seems meaningful, and for people who behave consistently and who conform to prevailing stereotypes of their group. Thus, concerns about mortality help shape people's basic beliefs about their world.

Recent work in the political realm has shown that MS leads people to prefer charismatic leaders who emphasize the greatness of one's own group and the need to heroically triumph over evil. Because of this latter tendency, MS increases support for violent actions against those designated by one's culture as evil. One study found that although Iranian college students generally were more favorable to a fellow student who advocated peaceful strategies over one who advocated suicide bombings of American targets, after being reminded of their mortality, this preference reversed, with the students generally siding more with the advocate of suicide bombing. Similarly, although American college students were generally not supportive of extreme military actions against terrorists (including use of nuclear weapons) that would kill many innocent people, MS led politically conservative students to shift toward advocacy of such measures.

Research has also addressed the implications of the theory for people's attitudes toward their own body and its activities. The physical body is what dooms humans to death and is therefore a continual reminder of mortal fate. MS should therefore lead people to distance from reminders of their animal nature. Consistent with this idea, studies have shown that MS reduces the appeal of physical aspects of sex and increases disgust reactions to reminders of the body. MS also leads men to deny attraction to women who arouse lustful feelings in them. This body of work helps explain why all cultures try to control and disguise bodily activities, imbuing them with ritualistic and spiritual elements.

Although MS increases wariness about physical aspects of sex, the theory also posits that romantic relationships serve a valuable terror management function. Love relations serve terror management by helping people feel that their lives are meaningful and that they are valued. Love relationships may also provide a fundamental source of comfort because, as attachment theory proposes, they hark back to the earliest security-providing relationships with one's parents. In support of these ideas, a substantial body of research has shown that MS increases the desire for close relationships and appreciation of one's romantic partner. In addition, threat to a relationship brings death-related thought close to consciousness.

Implications

Terror management research indicates that concern about mortality play a significant role in prejudice and investment in cultural stereotypes of women and minority groups. This work suggests a variety of measures that could help reduce intergroup violence, prejudice, and discrimination. Reducing the salience of mortality could be helpful. This would be difficult in places where violence is already prevalent but could be accomplished by minimizing actions likely to increase focus on death, whether by terrorists or military forces. The mass media could also play a role given the prevalence of reminders of death in news reports, films, and television shows.

A second possibility is to alter the cultural worldviews in which we embed our children. Studies show that worldviews that are more global and that more strongly advocate tolerance of diverse beliefs and customs should reduce the propensity for feeling threatened and needing to defend against those with different customs and beliefs. Worldviews and cultural practices that reduce the fear of death, such as death awareness courses in schools, could also be helpful. Addressing the matter of our mortality in a thoughtful, conscious manner may encourage more constructive approaches to coping. Indeed, preliminary research suggests that extensive contemplation of death, long practiced in some forms of Buddhism, may actually promote tolerance rather than punitiveness toward others who do not conform to the dictates of one's own worldview.

The theory has implications for individual mental health as well as intergroup harmony. People should function securely in their daily lives as long as they have strong faith in a meaning-providing worldview and believe they are significant contributors to that meaningful world. This suggests that buttressing these psychological resources should be an important goal for psychotherapists. This goal should also

be embraced by educators and policy makers, for the culture at large provides the critical bases for viewing life as meaningful and oneself as significant. If the standards for significance offered by a culture are too narrow, too stringent, or too unavailable for many individuals or for certain minority groups within a culture, mental health problems, alternative subcultures, and drug abuse are likely to be prevalent.

The knowledge of mortality is a difficult problem that has haunted humanity since its emergence. Terror management theory offers insights into the productive and destructive ways people cope with this problem and thereby offers a psychological basis for considering potential avenues for optimizing modes of death transcendence.

Jeff Greenberg

See also Attachment Theory; Culture; Intergroup Relations; Mortality Salience; Prejudice; Self-Esteem

Further Readings

Becker, E. (1974). *The denial of death.* New York: Free Press.

Greenberg, J., Koole, S., & Pyszczynski, T. (Eds.). (2004). *Handbook of experimental existential psychology.* New York: Guilford Press.

Greenberg, J., Solomon, S., & Pyszczynski, T. (1997). Terror management theory and research: Empirical assessments and conceptual refinements. In M. P. Zanna (Ed.), *Advances in experimental social psychology* (Vol. 29, pp. 61–139). San Diego, CA: Academic Press.

Pyszczynski, T., Solomon, S., & Greenberg, J. (2003). *In the wake of September 11: The psychology of terror.* Washington, DC: American Psychological Association.

Solomon, S., Greenberg, J., & Pyszczynski, T. (1991). A terror management theory of social behavior: On the psychological functions of self-esteem and cultural worldviews. In M. P. Zanna (Ed.), *Advances in experimental social psychology* (Vol. 24, pp. 93–159). San Diego, CA: Academic Press.

TESTOSTERONE

Definition

Testosterone is a hormone that is responsible for the development and maintenance of masculine characteristics. Testosterone is released into the bloodstream by the testes (testicles) in males and to a lesser extent, by the adrenal cortex and ovaries in females. Not only does testosterone influence the growth and development of masculine physical characteristics, such as the penis and the beard, but testosterone is also related to masculine psychological characteristics and social behaviors, including aggression, power, sexual behavior, and social dominance. In addition, social experiences such as competition can cause testosterone levels to rise or fall.

Background and History

The history of testosterone research dates back to ancient times, when farmers observed that castrated animals (animals whose testes had been removed) were not very aggressive and had low sex drives. Castrated humans showed similar changes in behavior.

In 1849, German scientist Arnold Berthold conducted the first formal experiment involving testosterone. It was already known that when chickens were castrated during development, they became more docile than normal roosters. These castrated chickens, called *capons*, did not fight with others and did not show normal mating behavior. But when Berthold implanted testes from other birds into the abdomen of these capons, they developed into normal roosters. Berthold concluded that the testes must influence aggression and sexual behavior by releasing a substance into the bloodstream.

In 1935, Dutch researchers identified this substance, a hormone that they named *testosterone*. Later that same year, another group of researchers developed a method for producing testosterone from cholesterol. Through the development, in the 1960s, of a method called *radioimmunoassay*, researchers were able to measure the amount of testosterone circulating in the bloodstream, and shortly after that, a technique was developed to measure testosterone levels in saliva. The ability to measure testosterone levels through saliva rather than blood has made it easier and more practical to conduct research in humans.

Effects

Testosterone exerts its effects during three different life stages: the perinatal period (which includes pregnancy and the period shortly after birth), puberty, and adulthood.

Perinatal Period

During the perinatal period, testosterone influences the development of the sexual organs (e.g., the penis). Animal studies show that high testosterone levels during the perinatal period also cause the nervous system to develop in a more malelike way and cause more masculine adult behaviors. The evidence in humans for the effects of testosterone during the perinatal period is less clear. Some human studies have actually found an effect of perinatal testosterone in females but not in males. For example, high perinatal testosterone levels in females are associated with more masculine behaviors in early childhood and with more masculine personality traits, such as sensation seeking and emotional stability, in adulthood.

Puberty

Testosterone levels rise during puberty, and this rise is related to the deepening of the voice, muscle growth, facial and body hair growth, and increased sex drive. There is also evidence in animals that a rise in testosterone level at the beginning of puberty influence competitive behaviors, including aggression and dominance, although scientists are not sure whether this relationship exists in humans.

Adulthood

Across a number of animal species, high testosterone concentrations in adult males are associated with high sex drive, and seasonal rises in testosterone (e.g., during the breeding season) are related to an increase in sexual behaviors. In humans, testosterone increases sex drive and sexual behaviors among men with abnormally low levels of testosterone but not among men who already have testosterone levels within the normal range.

Adult levels of testosterone are also associated with aggression and competition over food and mates. In animals, seasonal rises in testosterone (e.g., during the breeding season) are associated with increases in aggression and mate competition. There is also a small relationship between testosterone and aggression in humans. For example, several studies of male and female prisoners have found that prisoners with higher testosterone commit more violent crimes and break more rules in prison.

Testosterone is also related to power and social dominance. Animals with high testosterone levels tend to have high social rank within status hierarchies. In humans, high testosterone levels are associated with more masculine, dominant facial characteristics and with personality styles that are related to power and dominance. In addition, individuals with high testosterone levels are more reactive to and pay more attention to threats to their status, such as losing in a competition. For example, one study found that individuals with high testosterone levels felt badly (e.g., irritable, hostile) and could not concentrate after they lost in a competition but felt fine and could concentrate quite well after they won in a competition.

Changes in Levels

Testosterone levels can change in both the short term and the long term. In humans, testosterone levels peak in the late teens to early 20s and decline slowly but steadily after that. Testosterone levels also change throughout the day: They are highest in the morning, drop over the course of the day, and rise again in the evening. In a number of animal species, there are seasonal changes in testosterone, and testosterone levels are typically highest during the breeding season. Social experiences can also cause testosterone levels to change. In animals and in humans, winners of competitions tend to increase in testosterone, whereas losers tend to drop in testosterone. In addition, testosterone can increase in response to sexual stimuli, such as the presence of a female.

Gender Differences

Most of the research on testosterone has focused on men, but more studies have begun examining women. Although women have only about one-seventh the testosterone levels as men, testosterone still seems to play a role in women. For example, research has found that women with higher testosterone levels tend to smile less often, score higher on tests of social dominance, and are more vulnerable to stereotype threat.

Pranjal Mehta
Robert Josephs

See also Aggression; Dominance, Evolutionary; Hormones and Behavior; Sex Drive

Further Readings

Archer, J. (2006). Testosterone and human aggression: An evaluation of the challenge hypothesis. *Neuroscience and Biobehavioral Reviews, 30,* 319–345.

Dabbs, J. M., & Dabbs, M. G. (2000). *Heroes, rogues, and lovers: Testosterone and behavior.* New York: McGraw-Hill.

Mazur, A., & Booth, A. (1998). Testosterone and dominance in men. *Behavioral and Brain Sciences, 21,* 353–397.

THEMATIC APPERCEPTION TEST

Definition

The Thematic Apperception Test (TAT) is a psychological assessment device used to measure an individual's personality, values, or attitudes. The TAT is a projective test that is made up of 30 pictures that show persons in black and white, engaged in ambiguous activities. The test may be adapted for adults and children, males or females by using particular cards within the set. The test taker is asked to make up a story, telling what led up to the scene in the picture, what is happening at the current moment, how the characters are thinking and feeling, and what the outcome will be.

The original purpose of the TAT was to assess Henry Murray's need theory of personality. Currently, clinicians or researchers use it more generally to assess personality, attitudes, and values.

Background and History

The TAT is based on the projective hypothesis. Projective tests assume that the way that a test taker perceives and responds to an ambiguous scene reveals inner needs, feelings, conflicts, and desires. The responses are a "projection" of the self and are thought to be indicative of an individual's psychological functioning. This type of testing was influenced by Freudian thought and theories and became popular in the 1940s.

Projective tests have been used in psychological testing since the 1940s and remain popular in clinical settings. They have been criticized, however, for having poor reliability and validity. While the tests seem to generally reflect a participant's feelings or personality, they are also potentially influenced by other variables. In particular, there is a lot of random error introduced into these tests. The participant can be influenced by temporary states, such as hunger, sleep deprivation, drugs, anxiety, frustration, or all of these things. The results could be influenced by instructional set, examiner characteristics, the respondent's perception of the testing situation, or all three elements. Finally, ability factors influence all projective tests, particularly verbal ability. A meaningful interpretation of projective tests must consider all of these factors.

The TAT is the most popular projective test after the Rorschach Inkblot Test, and when scored using the standardized procedure developed by Bellak or used for well-defined constructs such as achievement motivation or affiliation, it is fairly reliable and valid.

The TAT was developed as measure of Henry Murray's need theory. Murray proposed a set of psychological needs that determined personality. He also defined common environmental forces—presses—which acted on personality and behavior. Murray believed that the projective responses to the ambiguous TAT cards would reveal an individual's needs and presses. Currently, the TAT is used in clinical as well as research settings to measure personality constructs. In social psychology the TAT might be used to assess individual differences in relating to others within social settings or groups.

Elizabeth K. Gray

See also Need for Affiliation; Projection; Research Methods

Further Readings

Bellak, L., & Abrams, D. M. (1996). *The T.A.T., C.A.T., and S.A.T. in clinical use* (6th ed.). Boston: Allyn & Bacon.

THEORY OF MIND

Definition

Theory of mind (ToM) refers to humans' everyday mind reading. It is the commonsense ability to attribute mental states (such as beliefs, desires, and intentions) to one's self and to other people as a way of making sense of and predicting behavior. For example, your thought that "John thinks I ate his sandwich" reflects a basic understanding that John has internal mental states much like your own, though the specific content of those mental states may differ from your own (in this case, perhaps you believe that Mary ate John's sandwich). ToM is fundamental to everyday social life: Normally it is taken for granted that others have beliefs and desires and that they act in accordance with those mental states; furthermore, it is assumed that other people use *their* ToM to think about *another's* mental states (e.g., "John believes that I intend to make him believe that I didn't crave his sandwich"). Although potatoes and houseflies are considered incapable of these complex forms of thought, it is less obvious whether or not other mammals and birds have a ToM. The emerging consensus on this issue is that other species have either highly limited or, more often the case, no ToM abilities resembling those of humans. Therefore, ToM may be one of the crucial attributes that make humans human and distinguish humans' social lives from the experience and behavior of all other social animals. Also, among humans, it is possible that newborn babies do not have a ToM, and so child psychologists are very interested in understanding when and how children acquire this ability.

Background

The term *ToM* was coined by primatologists David Premack and Guy Woodruff, who were interested in whether chimpanzees could use abstract concepts such as desire and memory to interpret others' behavior. Although the matter remains controversial, ToM capabilities appear to be uniquely human. Other species may communicate with elaborate signaling and vocalizations, but they are probably not drawing on a rich understanding of mental states and how they influence behavior. Their social interactions might be characterized in the same way as your interaction with a vending machine: You do such-and-such, this thing responds in a useful and predictable way, but you don't necessarily believe that it thinks, feels, or has any intentions of its own.

Basic Research

In addition to primatologists, scholars in diverse disciplines have taken an interest in ToM. Evolutionary psychologists have noted that the evolution of human language and social cooperation may have built on ToM. That is, without ToM, human language probably would not have developed into its present state. Some philosophers contend that ToM figures centrally in human consciousness, since the appreciation that one's perception of the world may differ from others' requires *knowing* that one *knows* (i.e., metacognition). The most extensive ToM research comes from developmental psychologists. ToM may seem like a perfectly obvious and basic capacity, but humans are not born with it. As the psychologist Jean Piaget noted, young children have difficulty appreciating that their construal of reality may not be shared by everyone. Gradually they begin to understand that their mental states are unique to their perspective and begin to represent others' perspectives based on knowledge of their mental states. ToM is often assessed in children using a false belief task: Show a child that a container labeled "lollipops" actually contains pencils rather than the expected candy. Ask the child what someone else who has not seen the contents of the container will think it contains. Most 3-year-olds incorrectly predict "pencils," whereas most 4-year-olds predict "lollipops." Passing this test requires thinking through what another person would think given knowledge that differs from one's own.

Implications for Everyday Life

Everyday social activities—communicating, navigating public spaces, or outsmarting a basketball opponent—depend crucially on everyday mind reading. How fundamental ToM is to everyday social life isn't realized until seeing cases where it is impaired. This seems to be the case with autistic individuals, who lack normal social insight and communication skills in part because of selective deficits in the capacity to reason about others' mental states. The following are some everyday social phenomena involving ToM.

Communication

In normal, reciprocal communication, a person uses ToM to monitor whether the person and his or her communication partner are still attending to the same topic, to shift topics, and to discuss imaginary or hypothetical situations. ToM is also instrumental in understanding subtle or indirect meanings, such as those conveyed through sarcasm, humor, and nonverbal communication (e.g., facial expressions). Conversely, everyday types of miscommunication occur when people fail to take into account each other's perspective. For example, you might be confused if a friend called and abruptly announced, "I refuse to do that!" because she has failed to think through what knowledge is only in her head and what knowledge is mutually shared, or common ground.

Persuasion

The ability to reason about what others think, and how certain messages are likely to affect attitudes, is critical for influencing beliefs and actions. For example, if you attempted to use persuasion to influence your boss's attitude about the importance of conserving water, you would need to adopt his or her point of view and to anticipate his or her reactions to your persuasive appeal. On a similar note, effectively deceiving someone, from telling a white lie to staging an elaborate ruse, demands that the deceiver see the world through another's eyes. It would be quite impossible to tailor a persuasive or deceptive message without first appreciating what others already know, want, or feel.

Empathy and Helping

Imagine seeing someone struggling to open a door while negotiating six bags of groceries and three children. Would you offer help even if there was nothing in it for you? According to Daniel Batson, if you empathize with the person—that is, vicariously experience the person's suffering—you will be likely to help regardless of what you stand to gain by doing so. Whether a person lends a hand to those in need can thus depend crucially on his or her ability to put him- or herself in their shoes, to experience events and emotions the way they experience them.

Explaining Behavior

People often act as amateur psychologists, trying to interpret others using what Fritz Heider called a naive or commonsense psychology about how minds and actions interrelate. People use information about traits and situations, but they also interpret others' actions from the perspective of their predisposing desires and beliefs ("He's upset because he thinks I ate his sandwich"). Interestingly, people are also prone to attribute human-like mental states to nonhuman entities that presumably don't have minds ("This butterfly came by to cheer me up!" or "I think my computer hates me!"). Cultural practices (e.g., rain dances) and beliefs (e.g., karma, fate) suggest that the young child's animism, the belief that the physical world is endowed with mental life, retains its appeal well into adulthood.

Conflict

To have a mind is what it really means to be human. Historically, one way that people have justified their incessant brutalization and annihilation of each other is to deny that their victims are possessed of mind—they are "rats," "bugs," or even "filth"—and are thus (the reasoning goes) appropriate to enslave, belittle, or extinguish without compunction. Consistent with this notion is recent evidence that humans are more likely to attribute mind to those they like. Future research should explore not only the capacity for ToM but also the social ramifications of people's motivations for admitting or denying certain others into the charmed circle of mental beings.

Mark J. Landau

See also Attributions; Empathy

Further Readings

Carruthers, P., & Smith, P. (1996). *Theories of theories of mind.* Cambridge, UK: Cambridge University Press.

Heider, F. (1958). *The psychology of interpersonal relations.* New York: Wiley.

Mitchell, P. (1997). *Introduction to theory of mind: Children, autism, and apes.* London: Arnold.

Premack, D., & Woodruff, G. (1978). Does the chimpanzee have a theory of mind? *Behavioral and Brain Sciences, 4,* 515–526.

THEORY OF PLANNED BEHAVIOR

Developed by Icek Ajzen in 1985, the theory of planned behavior (TPB) is today perhaps the most popular social-psychological model for the prediction of behavior. It has its roots in Martin Fishbein and Ajzen's theory of reasoned action, which was developed in response to observed lack of correspondence between general dispositions, such as racial or religious attitudes, and actual behavior. Instead of dealing with general attitudes of this kind, the TPB focuses on the behavior itself and goes beyond attitudes to consider such other influences on behavior as perceived social norms and self-efficacy beliefs.

Conceptual Framework

According to the theory, human social behavior is guided by three kinds of considerations: beliefs about the behavior's likely positive and negative outcomes, known as *behavioral beliefs;* beliefs about the normative expectations of others, called *normative beliefs;* and beliefs about the presence of factors that may facilitate or impede performance of the behavior, termed *control beliefs.* For example, people may believe that the behavior of exercising, among other things, improves physical fitness and is tiring (behavioral beliefs), that their family and friends think they should exercise (normative beliefs), and that time constraints make it difficult to exercise (control belief). Taken together, the total set of behavioral beliefs produces a favorable or unfavorable attitude toward the behavior; the total set of normative beliefs results in perceived social pressure to perform or not to perform the behavior, or subjective norm; and, in their totality, control beliefs give rise to a sense of self-efficacy or perceived control over the behavior.

Attitude toward the behavior, subjective norm, and perceived behavioral control jointly lead to the formation of a behavioral intention. The relative weight or importance of each of these determinants of intention can vary from behavior to behavior and from population to population. However, as a general rule, the more favorable the attitude and subjective norm are, and the greater the perceived behavioral control is, the stronger is the person's intention to perform the behavior in question. Finally, people are expected to carry out their intentions when the appropriate opportunity arises. However, successful performance of a behavior depends not only on a favorable intention but also on a sufficient level of volitional control, that is, on possession of requisite skills, resources, opportunities, and the presence of other supportive conditions. Because many behaviors pose difficulties of execution, the TPB adds perceived behavioral control to the prediction of behavior. To the extent that perceived behavioral control is accurate, it can serve as a proxy of actual control and can, together with intention, be used to predict behavior.

Beliefs play a central role in the TPB, especially those salient behavioral beliefs that are most readily accessible in memory. In applications of the theory, these salient beliefs are elicited in a free-response format by asking a representative sample of respondents to list the advantages and disadvantages of performing a behavior of interest (behavioral beliefs), to list the individuals or groups who approve or disapprove of performing the behavior (normative beliefs), and to list the factors that facilitate or inhibit performance of the behavior (control beliefs). The most frequently emitted behavioral, normative, and control beliefs are assumed to be the salient beliefs in the population and to determine prevailing attitudes, subjective norms, and perceptions of behavioral control. These salient beliefs are focused on the particular behavior of interest, and they serve as the fundamental explanatory constructs in the theory. More general factors, such as personality traits, gender, education, intelligence, motivation, or broad values are assumed to influence behavior only indirectly by their effects on salient beliefs. Assume, for example, that women are found to drink less alcohol than men. The TPB would explain this gender effect by predicting that men hold more favorable behavioral, normative, or control beliefs about drinking than women do.

The TPB assumes that human social behavior is reasoned or planned in the sense that people are assumed to take into account a behavior's likely consequences, the normative expectations of important referents, and factors that may impede performance of the behavior. Although the beliefs people hold may sometimes be inaccurate, unfounded, or biased, their attitudes, subjective norms, and perceptions of behavioral control are thought to follow spontaneously and reasonably from these beliefs, to produce a corresponding behavioral intention, and ultimately to result in behavior that is consistent with the overall tenor of the beliefs. This does not necessarily presuppose a deliberate, effortful retrieval of information and construction of attitudes prior to every enactment of a behavior. After at least minimal experience with the behavior, attitude, subjective norm, and perceived behavioral control are assumed to be available automatically as performance of the behavior is contemplated.

Successful application of the TPB is predicated on two conditions. First, the measures of attitude, subjective norm, perceived behavioral control, and intention must be compatible with one another and with the measure of behavior relative to the action involved, the target at which the action is directed, and the context and time of its enactment. Second, attitude, subjective norm, perceived behavioral control, and intention must remain relatively stable over time. Any changes in these variables prior to observation of the behavior will tend to impair their predictive validity.

Empirical Support

The TPB has been applied in research on a great variety of behaviors, including investment decisions, high-school dropout, mountain climbing, driving violations, recycling, class attendance, voting in elections, extramarital affairs, antinuclear activism, playing basketball, choice of travel mode, tax evasion, and a host of other activities related to protection of the environment, crime, recreation, education, politics, and religion. It has found its most intense application, however, in the health domain, where it has been used to predict and explain such varied behaviors as drinking, smoking, drug use, exercising, blood donation, dental care, fat consumption, breast self-examination, condoms use, weight loss, infant sugar intake, getting medical checkups, physician referrals, protection of the skin from the sun, living kidney donation, and compliance with medical regimens. The results of these investigations have, by and large, confirmed the theory's structure and predictive validity, especially when its constructs were properly assessed. Even without this caveat, the TPB has fared very well. Meta-analytic reviews of close to 200 data sets in a variety of behavioral domains have found that the theory accounts, on average, for about 40% of the variance in intentions, with all three predictors—attitude toward the behavior, subjective norm, and perceived behavioral control—making independent contributions to the prediction; the reviews also found that intentions and perceptions of behavioral control explain about 30% of the behavioral variance.

Given its predictive validity, the TPB can serve as a conceptual framework for persuasive messages and other interventions designed to influence intentions and behavior. Influence attempts directed at one or more of the theory's predictors have been found to increase use of public transportation among college students, to raise the effectiveness of job search behavior of unemployed individuals, to promote testicular self-examination among high-school and college students, and to induce alcoholics to join a treatment program.

Intention–Behavior Relation

For the TPB to afford accurate prediction, intentions must remain relatively stable prior to observation of the behavior. Empirical evidence supports this expectation, showing that the intention–behavior relation declines with instability in intentions over time. More important, the theory also assumes that people will act in accordance with their intentions under appropriate circumstances. This expectation has frequently been challenged, beginning with R. T. LaPiere's classic study in which ready acceptance of a Chinese couple in hotels, motels, and restaurants contrasted sharply with stated intentions not to accept "members of the Chinese race" in these same establishments. Similar discrepancies have been revealed in investigations of health behavior where it is found that large proportions of participants fail to carry out their intentions to use condoms, to undergo cancer screening, to exercise, to perform breast self-examination, to take vitamin pills, to maintain a weight-loss program, and so forth.

A variety of factors may be responsible for observed failures of effective self-regulation, yet a simple procedure can often do much to reduce the gap between intended and actual behavior. When individuals are asked to formulate a specific plan—an implementation intention—indicating when, where, and how they will carry out the intended action, the correspondence between intended and actual behavior often increases dramatically. Behavioral interventions of this kind that focus on implementation intentions have been shown to produce high rates of compliance with such recommended practices as cervical cancer screening and breast self-examination.

Critiques

Although popular and successful, the TPB has not escaped criticism. One type of critique has to do with the theory's sufficiency—the proposition that attitudes, subjective norms, and perceptions of behavioral control are sufficient to predict intentions and behavior. Investigators have suggested a number of variables that might be added to the theory to improve its predictive validity. Among the proposed additions are desire and need, affect and anticipated regret, personal and moral norms, past behavior, and self-identity (i.e., the extent to which people view themselves as the kind of person who would perform the behavior in question).

In another major critique, investigators have challenged the theory's reasoned action assumption, or more precisely, they have argued that reasoned action may represent only one mode of operation, the controlled or deliberate mode. According to Russell Fazio's MODE model, reasoned action occurs when people are motivated and capable of retrieving their beliefs, attitudes, and intentions in an effortful manner. When they lack motivation or cognitive capacity to do so,

they are said to operate in the spontaneous mode where attitudes must be strong enough to be activated automatically if they are to guide behavior.

A related critique of the TPB's reasoned action assumption relies on the well-known phenomenon that, with repeated performance, behavior becomes routine and no longer requires much conscious control for its execution. Some have suggested that as a result of this process of habituation, initiation of the behavior becomes automatic, and control over the behavior is transferred from conscious intentions to critical stimulus cues. The finding that frequency of past behavior is often a good predictor of later behavior and, indeed, that it has a residual impact on later behavior over and above the influence of intention and perceived behavior control, has been taken as evidence for automaticity in social behavior.

Icek Ajzen

See also Attitude–Behavior Consistency; Implementation Intentions; Reasoned Action Theory

Further Readings

Ajzen, I., & Fishbein, M. (2005). The influence of attitudes on behavior. In D. Albarracín, B. T. Johnson, & M. P. Zanna (Eds.), *The handbook of attitudes* (pp. 173–221). Mahwah, NJ: Erlbaum.

THIN SLICES OF BEHAVIOR

Definition

Thin slices of behavior is a term coined by Nalini Ambady and Robert Rosenthal in their study examining the accurate judgments of teacher effectiveness. They discovered that very brief (10-second and even 2-second) clips of dynamic silent video clips provided sufficient information for naive raters to evaluate a teacher's effectiveness in high correlation with students' final course ratings of their instructors. Distinctively, *thin slices* are thus defined as brief excerpts of expressive behavior, sampled from the behavioral stream, that contain dynamic information and are less than 5 minutes long. Thin slices can be sampled from any available channel of communication, including the face, the body, speech, the voice, transcripts, or combinations of all of these. Hence, static images (e.g., photographs) and larger chunks of dynamic behaviors would not qualify as thin slices. Thin slices retain much, if not most, of the information encoded via dynamic, fluid behavior while reducing or sometimes eliminating the information encoded within the ongoing verbal stream, the past history of targets, and the global, comprehensive context within which the behavior is taking place.

Impact

Since its introduction to the field of psychology, research on thin-slice judgments has had a distributed impact across social, applied, and cognitive psychology, and it has recently penetrated the popular literature as well. For instance, judgments based on thin slices have been shown to accurately predict the effectiveness of doctors treating patients, the relationship status of opposite-sex dyads (pairs) interacting, judgments of rapport between two persons, courtroom judges' expectations as to a defendant's guilt, and even testosterone levels in males.

Evidence

Recent research on thin-slice judgments has revealed that the accuracy of such judgments is bounded by several factors. Overall, the thin-slice methodology is useful only so long as relevant and valid information can be extracted from a behavioral stream. Factors that influence the accuracy of thin-slice judgments include culture and exposure, individual differences in the ability to decode information accurately, differences in accuracy based on expertise and group membership, and the type of judgment being made. Although, overall, both children and adults who enjoy greater interpersonal success are generally better decoders of nonverbal behavior, individual differences are tempered by cultural and subcultural exposure. Specifically, people are better at accurately judging targets from their own culture and cultures similar to their own than they are those more foreign. Similarly, ingroup benefits exist for groups such as homosexuals, who show an advantage at accurately determining the sexual orientation of others based on thin slices of behavior. More individually, thin-slice judgments can be affected by people's expertise and competency with the particular social context being assessed. Together, these caveats regarding thin slices illustrate

how the validity and utility of a thin slice ultimately depends both on the construct being evaluated and on the context within which accuracy is being judged.

For example, although a thin slice may provide valid information regarding an individual's affective state, it may provide entirely invalid information regarding other aspects of that individual, such as future intentions. Much of this variance due to culture and exposure is cogently explained by recent work suggesting the existence of nonverbal dialects and accents that are culturally determined. Exposure to particular dialects and familiarity with cultural norms and constructs contribute to the increased accuracy. Thus, exposure to information about persons based on their group membership and familiarity with the context of evaluation bolsters expertise and accuracy.

The type of judgment being made has an effect on accuracy as well. Thin-slice judgments are predictive and accurate only to the extent that relevant variables are observable from the thin slice sampled. Thus, thin-slice judgments of observable variables revealed through demeanor and behavior, such as how warm or likeable someone appears to be, tend to be more predictive in contrast to thin-slice judgments of less observable variables that cannot be observed rapidly through behavior, such as how persevering someone appears to be. This is because information regarding how perseverance is more likely revealed through actions and behaviors that unfold over a relatively long period of time. Such information is less likely to be gleaned from thin slices of behavior. Consequently, variables that are easily observable, such as extraversion, show the highest reliability across judges.

Mental Processes

What mental processes underlie this ability to make accurate judgments based on thin slices? Because of the brevity of the stimuli being perceived, as well as the nature of the information being conveyed, judgments based on thin slices of behavior likely rely on a nonconscious, relatively automatic form of cognitive processing. In this way, important social information can be gleaned without the perceiver having to rely on elaborate information-processing strategies, which strain precious cognitive resources. Thus, thin-slice judgments seem to be made rapidly and efficiently. Depletion of cognitive resources does not seem to disrupt accuracy based on thin slices. In other words, even when people are distracted or preoccupied, they can still form accurate impressions based on thin slices. Conversely, practice does no better to facilitate accurate judgments, nor does providing incentives such as monetary reward for higher accuracy. In sum, the accurate impressions and judgments formed from thin slices occur automatically, are intuitive in nature, and seem to proceed outside of conscious awareness or control.

Implications

Thin slices of behavior are diagnostic of many affective, personality, and interpersonal conditions. Examining judgments based on thin slices can inform us about the sensitivity people have to this information as well as the process by which immediate impressions are formed. This scrutiny will then lead to a better understanding of how subsequent expectations of, and behavior toward, others come about.

Nalini Ambady
Nicholas O. Rule

See also Nonconscious Processes; Nonverbal Cues and Communication

Further Readings

Ambady, N., Bernieri, F. J., & Richeson, J. A. (2000). Toward a histology of social behavior: Judgmental accuracy from thin slices of the behavioral stream. In M. P. Zanna (Ed.), *Advances in experimental social psychology* (Vol. 32, pp. 201–271). San Diego, CA: Academic Press.

Ambady, N., & Rosenthal, R. (1992). Thin slices of expressive behavior as predictors of interpersonal consequences: A meta-analysis. *Psychological Bulletin, 111,* 256–274.

THREATENED EGOTISM THEORY OF AGGRESSION

Definition

The threatened egotism theory of aggression states that violence is related to a highly favorable view of the self, combined with an ego threat. This theory does not suggest that high self-esteem necessarily causes violence or that there is any direct relationship between self-esteem and violence. Furthermore,

although there is evidence that most violent criminals, bullies, and terrorists tend to think highly of themselves, most people who think highly of themselves are not violent. An accurate characterization of the theory is that violence is perpetrated by a subset of people who exhibit an unstable and overly inflated high self-esteem. They respond with hostile aggression to what they perceive as challenges to these self-views to express the self's rejection of ego-threatening feedback.

Context and Importance

This theory runs counter to the widely held belief that low self-esteem is the cause of violent behavior. High self-esteem has traditionally been viewed as an unqualified asset and something that everyone should strive to achieve. Much of the self-help literature stems from this notion that high self-esteem is essential for success in one's relationships and careers and that one can develop high self-esteem by adhering to prescribed formulas. Many school systems have adopted policies that operate on this premise and offer praise and rewards to children for effort as much as for achievement. The threatened egotism theory of aggression casts serious doubt on this school of thought and instead suggests that artificially inflating self-esteem without accompanying boosts in achievement or other bases for feeling good about one's self can do more harm than good. The theory suggests that it is these people—those with grandiose, unstable self-esteem—who are most likely to respond violently in response to unfavorable feedback or other types of threats to their self-conceptions. It is these people who find criticism particularly threatening and lash out against its source.

Evidence

Evidence supporting this theory comes from diverse sources, such as studies of violence in laboratory settings, criminological surveys, and historical accounts, and includes a wide range of violence, such as murder, assault, rape, domestic violence, bullies, youth gangs, terrorism, repressive governments, tyranny, warfare, prejudice, oppression, and genocide. The common theme throughout these studies is that those who perceive a threat to their high self-esteem are most likely to perpetrate violence. Threatened egotism has been measured in a variety of ways as well, such as perceived disrespect, wounded pride, insults, verbal abuse, or unfavorable feedback. In addition, the same pattern was found for nations, medium and small groups, and lone individuals. It is important to note that the theory does not claim that threatened egotism is the only cause of aggression since there are likely numerous other factors, such as biochemical or genetic causes, family environment, and other factors that have yet to be identified. Studies indicate that threatened egotism is a cause of violence in a substantial number of contexts, but there are other possible variables that might play important roles in predicting violence.

Evidence from research examining how violent groups and individuals view themselves provides support for this theory, as does an examination of how egotism predicts violent behavior. Research studies with narcissistic people (those who are likely to have high self-esteem that is not well founded) have shown that they respond to negative interpersonal feedback with aggression toward the source of the feedback. In one laboratory study, participants were instructed to write an essay expressing a particular attitude toward abortion and were then led to believe that another participant was going to evaluate the essay and give feedback. The feedback was construed so that it was positive for half the participants and negative for the rest of the participants. The researchers found that when the essay was evaluated negatively, participants were more likely to blast the other participant with loud noise on a subsequent competitive task that involved punishments for incorrect answers. These aggressive responses were the strongest among the participants who scored high on a narcissism scale, indicating that an inflated view of the self that is challenged is most associated with aggressive behavior.

Some research compares rates of aggression between groups that are known to differ on egotism. Psychopaths, for example, commit a disproportionately high level of violent crimes and exhibit a highly inflated view of their abilities and importance in the world. In addition, the well-documented relationship between alcohol consumption and aggression can be understood in the context of this theory. Evidence indicates that when people drink, they tend to rate themselves more favorably than they would otherwise, creating a temporary state of high self-esteem. An examination of violent offenders also suggests strong tendencies toward egotism. Men who are imprisoned for murder or assaults tend to commit these crimes in response to when they perceive they were insulted, belittled, or simply had their pride wounded.

Implications

This theory has had a strong influence on how violent behavior has been understood and on the development of appropriate interventions. Although it may, in some ways, seem counterintuitive that high self-esteem would not be protective against ego threats, an important component of this theory is that an unstable, inflated sense of self is the type that is most harmful. This form of self-esteem is particularly vulnerable to threats and proneness to violence. This theory provides compelling evidence that attempting to boost self-esteem to cure underachievement, social exclusion, and aggressive tendencies is counterproductive and potentially harmful.

Laura Smart Richman

See also Aggression; Ego Shock; Narcissism; Self-Esteem

Further Readings

Baumeister, R. F., Smart, L., & Boden, J. M. (1996). Relation of threatened egotism to violence and aggression: The dark side of self-esteem. *Psychological Review, 103*, 5–33.

Bushman, B. J., & Baumeister, R. F. (1998). Threatened egotism, narcissism, self-esteem, and direct and displaced aggression: Does self-love or self-hate lead to violence? *Journal of Personality and Social Psychology, 75*, 219–229.

Kernis, M. H., Grannemann, B. D., & Barclay, L. C. (1989). Stability and level of self-esteem as predictors of anger arousal and hostility. *Journal of Personality and Social Psychology, 56*, 1013–1022.

THREE-DIMENSIONAL MODEL OF ATTRIBUTION

Definition

The three-dimensional model of attribution posits that the explanations people give for the things that happen to them can vary on three distinct factors, and these variations have consequences for people's mood, self-perception, and well-being. Attributions can be stable (true across time) or unstable (temporary); they can be internal (stemming from the person) or external (stemming from the environment); and they can be global (applying to many domains) or specific (limited to one area).

Background

According to initial work on learned helplessness, exposure to uncontrollable negative events can lead to depression. Upon further research, however, Martin Seligman and colleagues, who originally developed the theory of learned helplessness, found that this was true for some people but not for others. Their research showed that what separated the depressed from the nondepressed was a tendency to attribute those negative events to factors that were stable, internal, and global, despite their inherent uncontrollability. While the type of attribution people make can vary on all three dimensions, depending on the event being considered as well as many other factors, people often show a general tendency across attributions toward one pattern of explanation or another. Seligman developed a test to measure this individual difference, called the Attributional Style Questionnaire. This questionnaire has people give explanations for a series of hypothetical positive and negative events; the general patterns of responses that they give can be used to make diagnoses or predictions. For example, a person who fails a test and explains his or her poor grade by saying, "I never do anything right," which is a stable, internal, global explanation, is more likely to become depressed than a person who explains away their failure by saying, "That test was especially difficult," an unstable, external, specific explanation.

This latter type of attribution for negative events may in fact be more common. Nondepressed people also make stable, internal, global attributions, but they tend to make them for *positive* events instead. Most people feel that the positive things that happen to them are due to their person and therefore they were the direct cause, and negative events are due to the situation and therefore those events shouldn't reflect poorly on them. They may believe, for example, that when they pass a test, it is because they are smart (which is stable, internal, and global), and when they fail, it is because of the test or some other situational factor (which is unstable, external, and specific). This tendency to take credit for successes and shirk blame for failures is part of what underlies people's tendencies toward positive self-esteem and even self-enhancement.

Elanor F. Williams

See also Attribution Theory; Learned Helplessness

Further Readings

Abramson, L. Y., Seligman, M. E. P., & Teasdale, J. D. (1978). Learned helplessness in humans: Critique and reformulation. *Journal of Abnormal Psychology, 87,* 49–74.

Peterson, C., & Seligman, M. E. P. (1984). Causal explanations as a risk factor for depression: Theory and evidence. *Psychological Review, 91,* 347–374.

TOKEN EFFECTS

Definition

A token is the only person of his or her category, or one of very few persons, in an otherwise homogeneous group. A sole female in a group of males is an example of a token individual, as is the only Latino in a group of Caucasians. Being numerically distinctive produces effects on one's thoughts and capabilities. When an individual is a token (or solo) in a group, he or she generally becomes preoccupied with evaluative or self-presentational concerns, such as "What do they think of me? How am I coming across?" Frequently, the attention diverted to these concerns interferes with the token's ability to concentrate on the central group activity, yielding diminished performance. This phenomenon is called the *token deficit effect.* There are instances, however, when the priming of self-presentation concern is concordant with the group task. In these instances, numerical distinctiveness facilitates performance, resulting in the *token surfeit effect.*

Research Findings

Past research has shown that individuals' memory for group interaction and their problem-solving skills are impaired when they are the numerical token in the group. In parallel, tokens' memory for their own performance, and for that of others, during a group session is actually enhanced. In short, they are so worried about how they are being evaluated and about how well they are performing relative to others that they fail to perform; instead, they focus on tracking how well they are doing and how well everyone else is doing and are consequently able to report very accurately on this dimension.

Token deficit effects have been demonstrated with different types of tasks (memory, problem solving) and with different types of tokens. Early work showed that gender tokens evinced deficits; later work demonstrated the same pattern with ethnic/racial tokens. Note that the token deficit effect is not limited to one sex or ethnic/racial minority group—both males and females, and Whites and minorities show similar deficits when they are numerically distinctive. Moreover, members of categories that are not visibly distinctive but socially meaningful show similar results. For example, being the only one from a particular school in a group of persons from a rival school also produces deficits, even when the token looks no different from the other group members.

The latest work in this area indicates that tokens might not always be at a disadvantage. In fact, there is evidence for a *token surfeit effect,* wherein tokens outperform their nontoken counterparts. How can this be the case? In fact, because tokens are compelled to focus on evaluation in the group, they are especially attentive to information that relates to interpersonal evaluation, requires taking the perspective of others, or both. When they are assigned tasks that draw on these inclinations, they show superior performance to nontokens. Group tasks that rely on memory for evaluative words (trait ratings of self and others) and those that depend on being able to take different perspectives (coming up with solutions when two or more parties are at odds) are compatible with the token mindset. Accordingly, when faced with these tasks, tokens do very well.

Numerical distinctiveness as manifested in tokens can yield deficits and surfeits. Being one-of-a-kind can produce benefits as well as disadvantages.

Delia S. Saenz

See also Decision Making; Group Dynamics; Intergroup Relations; Interpersonal Cognition; Self-Presentation

Further Readings

Lord, C. G., & Saenz, D. S. (1985). Memory deficits and memory surfeits: The differential cognitive consequences of tokenism for tokens and observers. *Journal of Personality and Social Psychology, 49,* 918–926.

Saenz, D. S. (1994). Token status and problem-solving deficits: Detrimental effects of distinctiveness and performance monitoring. *Social Cognition, 12,* 60–74.

Saenz, D. S., & Lord, C. G. (1989). Reversing roles: A cognitive strategy for undoing memory deficits associated with tokenism. *Journal of Personality and Social Psychology, 56,* 698–708.

TRAITS

Definition

When people describe themselves and others, they tend to use trait descriptors. A trait is marked by the tendency to act, think, and feel in a certain way—over time and across situations. Terms such as *disposition, construct, dimension,* and *personality variable* have very similar meanings and psychologists often use them interchangeably.

Traits indicate that the probability of certain behavior is high, but they are not to be understood in a deterministic sense. Even the cruelest person will have moments of tenderness. Strictly speaking, traits describe behavior but do not explain it. Socialization or genetic factors can be used to explain how traits develop in a person. Some authors have regarded traits as fictions that do not exist outside the mind of observers; others have searched for their neurophysiological basis.

Historical and Contemporary Approaches to Traits

Hippocrates (460 B.C.E.) stated that an imbalance of body fluids leads to physical and mental illness. Galen (130–200 C.E.) asserted that four temperaments are based on the dominance of one of those fluids: blood (sanguine, optimistic), yellow bile (choleric, irritable), black bile (melancholic, sad), and phlegm (phlegmatic, calm). These historical assumptions influenced the development of other trait theories. Gordon Allport (1897–1967) supported an idiographic approach and emphasized that there are unique personal dispositions in addition to general dispositions. Raymond B. Cattell (1905–1998) used factor analysis, a statistical tool, to identify the traits that are most relevant in distinguishing people. He proposed 16 Personality Factors (16 PF). Hans Eysenck (1916–1997) identified three supertraits (the Gigantic Three): extraversion (outside or inward orientation), neuroticism (emotional stability or lability), and psychoticism (antisocial behavior or friendliness). In the 1970s, Paul Costa and Robert McCrae suggested that five trait dimensions are optimal for describing personality. Even though there are authors who favor six, four, or three factors, the Big Five (Openness to Experience, Neuroticism, Extraversion, Agreeableness, and Conscientiousness) are currently the most popular approach in studying traits.

Traits or Situations?

In the late 1960s, Walter Mischel dealt a heavy blow to the trait approach. He pointed out that traits lack cross-situational consistency and predictive validity. In other words, what we do depends a lot on the situation, and what we will do in the future cannot be easily predicted with the help of personality questionnaires. The fact that someone who is outgoing in one situation might be shy in another situation led to the situationist approach: People's behavior was understood as a consequence of situational forces. Later on, Walter Mischel left that radical position and proposed an interactionist approach that considers behavior to be guided by situational cues as well as traits. Recently Yushi Shoda and Walter Mischel have used situation profiles to describe the stable patterns with which individuals react to different situations. Today one will not find a reasonable theorist who will deny the relevance of traits or the relevance of situations.

Astrid Schütz
Aline Vater

See also Big Five Personality Traits; Individual Differences

Further Readings

Matthews, G., Deary, I. J., & Whiteman, M. C. (2003). *Personality traits* (2nd ed.). New York: Cambridge University Press.

TRANSACTIVE MEMORY

Definition

An important function of relationships is information sharing. People often look to their interpersonal and work relationships for needed information: the forgotten name of a common acquaintance, an opinion on possible investment strategies, or help with an unfamiliar task such as setting up a wireless network. People in relationships often share the burden for learning and remembering information by dividing responsibility for different knowledge areas; for example, in a work team, one member may be responsible for all information related to Client X while another member may be responsible for all information related to Client Y. When one person needs information in another's area, they can simply ask the person responsible rather than taking the time and energy to learn the information themselves. The knowledge sharing system that often develops in relationships and in groups where people assume responsibility for different knowledge areas and rely on one another for information is called *transactive memory*.

Transactive memory refers to the idea that people in continuing relationships often develop a specialized *division of labor*; that is, specific roles with respect to the encoding, storage, and retrieval of information from different knowledge domains. Each member of the relationship becomes a "specialist" in some areas but not others, and members rely on one another for information. For example, among life partners, one partner might be responsible for knowing the couples' social calendar and car maintenance schedule, while the other might be responsible for knowing when the bills need to be paid and what is in the refrigerator. Such specialization reduces the memory load for each individual, yet each individual has access to a larger pool of information collectively. For transactive memory to function effectively, individuals must also have a shared conceptualization of "who knows what" in the group.

Transactive memory is more than knowing who to ask for information in different knowledge areas. It also involves retrieval and communication processes: knowing how to ask for information from others in the system, knowing how to communicate information effectively to those who need it, and knowing how to use retrieved information in collective decisions. What makes transactive memory "transactive" are the "transactions" (i.e., communications) among individuals to encode, store, and retrieve information from their individual memory systems. Transactive memory theory and research borrows heavily from what is known about the memory processes of individuals and applies it to groups.

Evidence of transactive memory systems has been demonstrated in a variety of relationships and groups, including married couples, dating couples, families, friends, coworkers, and project teams in both organizational and laboratory settings.

Transactive Memory Development

One necessary condition for transactive memory development is cognitive interdependence: Individuals must perceive that their outcomes are dependent on the knowledge of others and that those others' outcomes are dependent on their knowledge. Cognitive interdependence often develops in close interpersonal relationships, in which people share responsibilities, engage in conversations about many different topics, and make joint decisions. It can also arise as a result of a reward system or the structure of a group task.

Transactive memory develops as individuals learn about one another's expertise and begin to delegate and assume responsibility for different knowledge areas. The delegation process by which members are associated with knowledge areas is often implicit and informal, emerging through interaction. Individuals can become linked to knowledge-based relative expertise (the best cook is likely to become the person in charge of knowing what is in the refrigerator), negotiated agreements (one person agrees to keep track of car maintenance if the other will keep track of when bills are due), or through circumstance (the person who answered the phone when Client X called the first time becomes the "Client X" expert). In newly formed groups, individuals are likely to rely on stereotypes based on personal characteristics (such as age, gender, ethnicity, social class, and organizational role) to infer what others know. In some cases, these initial assumptions can become self-fulfilling prophecies: Individuals are assigned knowledge areas that are consistent with social stereotypes, even though they may not fit with their actual expertise, and eventually become experts as a result of those assignments. For example, a male group member might be assigned to set up a wireless network because the group assumes that he knows more about technology than his female group members when in fact he does not. Through the slow and cumbersome learning process of setting it up, he ultimately becomes an expert on wireless networks.

Informal interactions and shared experiences provide opportunities for members to learn about the relative expertise of other members, to indicate their interests and preferences, to coordinate who does what, to observe members' skills in action, and to evaluate the willingness of others to participate in the transactive memory system. Those systems set up by formal design (such as a listing of job responsibilities of staff in an office procedures handbook) are either validated or modified over time as individuals discover whether individuals assigned to specific knowledge roles are able and willing to perform them.

Processes in Transactive Memory

A directory-sharing computer network has been used as a metaphor for illustrating key processes of transactive memory systems. The first process is *directory updating,* whereby individuals develop a working directory or map of "who knows what" and update it as they obtain relevant new information. The second process is *information allocation,* whereby new information that comes into the group is communicated to the person whose expertise will facilitate its storage. The third process is *retrieval coordination,* which involves devising an efficient and effective strategy for retrieving needed information based on the person expected to have it.

Unlike the literal and straightforward ways that computer networks update directories, and locate, store, and retrieve information, transactive memory systems among human agents are often flawed. Transactive memory systems can vary in accuracy (the degree to which group members' perceptions about other members' expertise are accurate), sharedness (the degree to which members have a shared representation of who knows what in the group), and validation (the degree to which members accept responsibility for different knowledge areas and participate in the system). Transactive memory systems will be most effective when knowledge assignments are based on group members' actual abilities, when all group members have similar representations of the system, and when members fulfill expectations.

Context and Importance

In recent years, a renewed interest in the collective aspects of cognition has emerged. Proponents argue that contrary to current social psychological conceptions of social cognition as individual thought about social objects, social cognition should be thought of as a product of social interchange and is constructed, shared, and distributed among groups of people during the course of interaction. Theory of and research on transactive memory examine the collective aspects of cognition. Transactive memory helps explain how people in collectives learn, store, use, and coordinate their knowledge to accomplish individual, group, and organizational goals.

Implications

People in close interpersonal and work relationships often perform their tasks and make decisions more effectively than strangers, because they are better able to identify experts and make better use of knowledge through their transactive memory system. Transactive memory systems can lead to improved group performance on tasks for which groups must process a large amount of information in a short period of time and on tasks that require expertise from many different knowledge domains. However, there may be situations in which too much specialization may impede group performance, for example, when assigned experts are unavailable, unable, or unwilling to contribute their knowledge. Even when specialization leads to better outcomes, some redundancy may be useful. It helps members to communicate more effectively, it can encourage group members to be more accountable to one another, and it can provide a cushion for transitions in relationships when, for example, the designated expert leaves the group. New technologies facilitating the development of transactive memory are emerging to help people locate and retrieve information from experts in their organizations and in their social networks.

Andrea B. Hollingshead

See also Group Decision Making; Interpersonal Cognition; Memory

Further Readings

Hollingshead, A. B. (1998). Retrieval processes in transactive memory systems. *Journal of Personality and Social Psychology, 74,* 659–671.

Liang, D. W., Moreland, R. L., & Argote, L. (1995). Group versus individual training and group performance: The mediating role of transactive memory. *Personality and Social Psychology Bulletin, 21,* 384–393.

Wegner, D. M. (1987). Transactive memory: A contemporary analysis of the group mind. In B. Mullen & G. R. Goethals (Eds.), *Theories of group behavior* (pp. 185–208). New York: Springer.

TRIANGULAR THEORY OF LOVE

Definition

The triangular theory of love characterizes love in terms of three underlying components: intimacy, passion, and commitment. People love each other to the extent they show these three components, and different combinations of the components yield different kinds of love.

The Three Components

The three components of love are each different in nature. Intimacy is characterized by feelings of caring, concern, understanding, trust, and closeness between two partners. Intimate partners are good friends and support each other in times of need. Intimacy is primarily emotional in nature. Passion is characterized by intense desire, feelings of longing, need of the partner, and joy at the thought of seeing the partner (and anxiety or worry at the thought of separation). Passionate partners crave each other's presence, much as do people who experience an addiction. Passion is primarily motivational in nature. Commitment is characterized by cognitions of the long-lasting nature or even permanence of a relationship, the stand that one will stay with the partner, despite any hardships that may evolve, and the confidence that the relationship is the right one to be in. Committed partners view themselves as in the relationship over the long term. Commitment is primarily cognitive in nature.

Time Courses of the Three Components

The three components show somewhat different time courses. Intimacy usually develops somewhat slowly, over the course of time. In relationships that succeed, intimacy continues to develop; in those that fail, intimacy may go up and then start to go down. However, in many long-term relationships, high levels of intimacy may be difficult to sustain over periods of many years. A good test of intimacy is whether, when there is some disruption in a relationship, the disruption brings the partners closer together or further apart. Passion usually develops quickly but also may fade quickly. It shows a course similar to that of addictions. After a while, the "high" of the relationship is less rewarding than the "low" of the thought of termination of the relationship seems punishing. Commitment typically develops slowly and may continue to increase in successful relationships and fade in unsuccessful ones. Fading of commitment can be caused by problems in the relationship or by the entrance of competition to the relationship.

Kinds of Love

According to the theory, different combinations of intimacy, passion, and commitment yield different kinds of love.

None of the components = nonlove.

Intimacy alone = friendship. This is the type of love experienced by good friends. It is a limiting case of love.

Passion alone = infatuated love. This is the kind of love one experiences in love at first sight. It is a limiting case of love.

Commitment alone = empty love. This is the kind of love one experiences when all that holds a couple together is the cognition that one should stay in the relationship. It is characterized by the beginning of arranged relationships and marriages and the (emotional) end of relationships that have failed over time.

Intimacy + passion = romantic love. This is the type of love experienced by those who fall in love with each other but who are not ready to commit for the long term, such as students whose future lives are yet uncertain.

Intimacy + commitment = companionate love. This is the kind of love that often develops over the course of many years, when the passion begins to flicker. Many long-term, stable relationships are based on companionate love.

Passion + commitment = fatuous (foolish) love. This is the kind of love, sometimes seen in movies, in which partners commit to each other on the basis of passion without even truly getting to know each other. These kinds of relationships do not have a good prognosis.

Intimacy + passion + commitment = consummate (complete) love. This is the kind of love to which many people aspire: It is difficult to attain and even more difficult to maintain. People generally have to work at relationships and mutual growth to maintain consummate love.

Origins of the Components

The origins of the components are in stories one develops about what love should be like. In the United States, there are about two dozen common stories. Examples are a *fairy-tale story,* in which partners view each other as a prince and a princess; a *travel story,* in which partners see themselves traveling through life together over a sometimes rocky road; a *business story,* in which partners view the relationship as a business, much like any other business; the *pornography story,* in which love is viewed as exciting to the extent it is "dirty"; and a *horror story,* in which one partner terrorizes the other.

Data Regarding the Theory

Empirical tests of the theory have yielded several interesting findings. For example, it has been found that higher levels of intimacy, passion, and commitment all tend to be associated with greater happiness and satisfaction in relationships. The patterns of the three components also play a role in happiness and satisfaction. Partners whose patterns of intimacy, passion, and commitment are more similar (e.g., both needing high levels of intimacy, or neither caring much about commitment) tend to be more satisfied that partners whose patterns differ (e.g., one needing a high level of intimacy and the other caring much more about the level of passion). In addition, different loving relationships, such as with father, mother, lover, sibling, show quite different patterns of intimacy, passion, and commitment. Stories also have been shown to have effects on relationships. For example, partners with more similar stories about relationships tend to be happier than partners with less similar stories (e.g., two partners with a fairy-tale story will be happier, on average, than one with a fairy-tale story and the other with a business story). However, stories do not in and of themselves predict happiness, independent of match to the partner's story, but certain stories are associated with unhappiness, such as the horror story and the pornography story.

Robert J. Sternberg

See also Companionate Love; Decision and Commitment in Love; Love; Romantic Love

Further Readings

Sternberg, R. J. (1998). *Cupid's arrow.* New York: Cambridge University Press.
Sternberg, R. J. (1998). *Love is a story.* New York: Oxford University Press.

TRUST

Definition

Trust refers to a person's confident belief that another's motivations are benevolent toward him or her and that the other person will therefore be responsive to his or her needs. Trust is typically viewed as a belief about a specific person, though it has also been viewed as a personality trait characterizing people's tendency to trust or distrust others in general.

Evolutionary Foundations

Evolutionary thinkers have argued that issues of trust were critical to the survival of early humans. Because one's welfare depended on cooperation and exchange with others, for instance in trading berries or other fruit for meat, people needed to anticipate who they could count on to engage in fair exchanges and who, instead, deserved their suspicions as possible cheaters. They also needed to understand who among their significant others could be truly relied on to take care of them in times of serious need and who, instead, were fair-weather friends. Given that issues of trust were so important for early humans' welfare, evolutionary theorists contend that specific mechanisms likely exist in the modern brain that allow people to monitor behaviors relevant to others' motivations and calibrate the level of trust that a person warrants—a suspicion meter, if you will.

Trust in Close Relationships

Trust, of course, remains very critical in modern life, especially in one's significant relationships with family, friends, and romantic partners. Close attachments such as these oblige people to depend and rely on others' good intentions, that is, to become more heavily interdependent with others to satisfy their own central needs. As the extent of risk and possible costs of rejection and betrayal increase in such relationships, the stakes become much higher and trust becomes all the more critical. It is therefore unsurprising that research on trust has been most prevalent within the contexts of these close relationships.

The development of trust in a relationship is usually a gradual process that requires social interactions and experiences with a person that suggest he or she is predictable and dependable, especially in situations in which costly sacrifices by another may be necessary to be responsive to one's own needs. Such situations are seen as diagnostic because clearer conclusions about others' motives can be drawn when helping is costly to another and not in their short-term interests. However, to achieve a true sense of confidence in

another person, one must eventually go beyond the available evidence and make a leap of faith. Past evidence can never fully predict future behavior, so to genuinely trust and achieve some peace of mind about a significant other, people must set aside their uncertainties and simply act in a trusting way.

The amount of trust that develops in a relationship is crucial because it regulates the extent to which people allow themselves to be committed to and invested in that relationship. That is, people will only take the risk of caring and becoming attached to someone they believe reciprocates their affections. Uncertainty or insecurity about whether a partner has a strong positive regard for them can result in people pulling back or increasing their psychological distance from the partner, a self-protective behavior that reduces the risk of being hurt and let down.

Researchers who study romantic relationships from the perspective of attachment theory, a theory of personality based on early experiences with caregivers, have demonstrated that trust has two components. People who are most able to trust a close partner have a *secure personality style.* They view themselves as worthy of love (they have a positive model of self or low anxiety about being loved), and view their attachment figures as generally capable of being loving and responsive (they possess a positive model of others or low avoidance of closeness). Insecurity about either belief or about whether a partner is both willing and able to be available and responsive to one's self diminishes trust in another and results in a less satisfying relationship.

Trust in another person is determined by one's personality and the qualities of one's relationship and greatly affects how secure one feels in a relationship. However, pressures from social networks, such as social norms within extended families and communities, may also influence feelings of security. This type of assurance is most typical in more traditional societies and also in Asian societies. Asian people who believe that their parents like and accept their partner feel more secure about their relationship, which in turn allows them to risk depending more on their partner even though their trust in that partner may not have increased.

Finally, some scientists have studied people's general beliefs about the motivations of strangers. Interestingly, trusting individuals do not naively believe that everyone is good but instead are selective about whom they trust and cooperate only when they believe that another has positive motivations. In contrast, competitive people tend to distrust the motives of others, believing that it is a dog-eat-dog world and that they must consider their own interests first.

John G. Holmes
Justin V. Cavallo

See also Dependence Regulation; Love

Further Readings

Holmes, J. G., & Rempel, J. K. (1989). Trust in close relationships. In C. Hendrick (Ed.), *Review of personality and social psychology: Close relationships* (Vol. 10, pp. 187–219). Newbury Park, CA: Sage.

Murray, S. L., Holmes, J. G., & Griffin, D. (2000). Self-esteem and the quest for felt security: How perceived regard regulates attachment processes. *Journal of Personality and Social Psychology, 78,* 478–498.

Shaver, P. R., & Hazan, C. (1993). Adult romantic attachment: Theory and evidence. In W. H. Jones & D. Perlman (Eds.), *Advances in personal relationships* (Vol. 4, pp. 29–70). London: Jessica Kingsley.

Simpson, J. A. (2007). Foundations of interpersonal trust. In A. W. Kruglanski & E. T. Higgins (Eds.), *Social psychology: A handbook of basic principles* (2nd ed., pp. 597–621). New York: Guilford Press.

Tooby, J., & Cosmides, L. (1996). Friendship and the banker's paradox: Other pathways to the evolution of adaptations for altruism. *Proceedings of the British Academy, 88,* 119–143.

Twin Studies

Twin studies can tell us about how genes and environments affect behavioral and physical development. There are two kinds of twins: identical and fraternal. Identical twins result when one fertilized egg splits during the first two weeks of pregnancy. These twins share all their genes and are always of the same sex. They occur in about one third of natural twin conceptions. Fraternal or nonidentical twins result when two eggs released by the mother are fertilized by two sperm from the father. These twins share half their genes, on average, just like ordinary siblings. Fraternal twins can be same-sex or opposite-sex.

The classic twin design involves comparing the similarity of identical and fraternal twins. If identical twins are more alike in intelligence, personality, or physical skills this demonstrates that the trait is probably influenced by genetic factors. Some people have objected that identical twins are alike because people treat them alike, not because of their shared genes. However, careful studies have ruled out this criticism after finding that identical twins who are treated alike are not more similar than identical twins who are treated differently.

There are many ways to study twins. A powerful method is studying identical twins reared apart from birth. Reared-apart identical twins resemble one another only because of their shared genes. Interestingly, research shows that identical twins reared apart and together are about equally similar in personality traits such as aggression and traditionalism. The twin-family method includes identical twins, their spouses, and their children. The children of identical twins are cousins, but they are also "half-siblings" because they have a genetically identical parent. These children's aunts and uncles are like their "mothers" and "fathers" because they are genetically identical to the children's own parents. It is possible to compare the behavioral similarity of a twin mother and her daughter (who share genes and environments) and a twin aunt and her niece (who share genes but not environments). Research has shown that parent–child and aunt/uncle–niece/nephew similarity is the same on a spatial visualization test. A more recent research design uses a unique twin-like pair called virtual twins. Virtual twins are same-age individuals who are raised together, but are not genetically related. Virtual twins show modest similarity in intelligence, despite their shared environment, a finding that supports genetic influence.

The multiple birth rate (especially the fraternal twinning rate) has increased from 19.3 to 30.7 multiple births per 1,000 births in recent years. This is primarily due to new reproductive technologies but also to the fact that women are having children at older ages. The increased twinning rate is good news for researchers. However, the downside is that twins are more likely than non-twins to suffer from birth difficulties.

It is likely that twins will continue to play significant roles in psychological and medical research.

Identical twins differing in traits, such as novelty-seeking, schizophrenia, or breast cancer may help identify which genes are expressed and which genes are not expressed. Thus, twin studies can help clarify the origins of behavior in everyone else.

Nancy L. Segal
Kevin A. Charvarria

See also Genetic Influences on Social Behavior; Research Methods

Further Readings

Machin, G. A., & Keith, L. G. (1999). *An atlas of multiple pregnancy: Biology and pathology.* New York: Parthenon.

Segal, N. L. (2000). *Entwined lives: Twins and what they tell us about human behavior.* New York: Plume.

Segal, N. L. (2005). *Indivisible by two: Lives of extraordinary twins.* Cambridge, MA: Harvard University Press.

TYPE A PERSONALITY

See PERSONALITIES AND BEHAVIOR PATTERNS, TYPE A AND TYPE B

TYPE B PERSONALITY

See PERSONALITIES AND BEHAVIOR PATTERNS, TYPE A AND TYPE B

U

UNIQUENESS

Definition

Uniqueness involves a person's distinctiveness in relation to other people. Such uniqueness can reflect actual behaviors or a person's perceptions regarding his or her differences. People can vary in the degree to which they want such distinctiveness, with some being highly desirous of specialness (high need for uniqueness) and others who do not want to stand out from other people (low need for uniqueness).

History

Uniqueness seeking probably is a modern phenomenon because people centuries ago were concerned about fundamental survival issues and did not have the time to attend to their uniqueness. Toward the 19th, 20th, and 21st centuries, however, people were more assured of meeting their basic survival needs, and accordingly, they turned to issues involving the maintenance of their self-concepts. Thus, in increasingly technological and highly populated societies, people became more focused on matters pertaining to their uniqueness.

Although there were 17th- and 18th-century books and stories about people who were worried about preserving their distinctiveness (known under the German term *doppelgänger*), prior to the mid-1970s, the shared view among social psychologists was that people did not want to be special. This latter anti-uniqueness view stemmed from both conformity research, showing that people often wanted to go along with the crowd, and

interpersonal attraction research, which showed that people wanted to be as similar as possible to others. Likewise, during this pre-1970s period, clinical psychologists and sociologists viewed any differences that people displayed as being abnormal, deviant, or pathological.

Moving into the 1970s and the early 1980s, however, social psychological researchers began to perform robust experimental manipulations that were aimed at studying how people would react when they were given feedback indicating that they were extremely similar to other people. Contrary to the pre-1970s findings, these new research findings showed that people did not like such extremely high similarity and, indeed, wanted to feel some sense of specialness in relation to other people. The terms *individuation, need for uniqueness,* and *uniqueness theory* were applied to this latter research. Later, it was called *optimal distinctiveness theory.*

Evidence

Studies on need for uniqueness basically involved giving self-report tests that asked research participants to describe themselves on a variety of dimensions and thereafter delivering feedback to these people about how similar they were to other people who supposedly had taken the same tests. (In actuality, this similarity feedback was bogus, but the research participants believed it.) Before their purported meetings with these other people, various measures were taken of the research participants' emotional and behavioral reactions. Results showed that when people were given feedback that they were very highly similar, as compared to moderately similar, to others who had taken the same tests, these former people reported feeling more negative emotions and engaging in behaviors to reestablish their specialness. For example, the behaviors aimed at showing their uniqueness included the endorsing of unusual self-descriptive words, conforming less, expressing less popular ideas, producing more creative uses for objects, and valuing scarce objects. On this last point, need for uniqueness has been used to explain why people are attracted to products that are only available to a few persons (e.g., "Hurry on down while the supply lasts!"), as well as why changing product styles each year makes those products very appealing to people.

Self-report scales also were developed and validated to measure the degree to which a person has a low, moderate, or high need for uniqueness. In other words, some people are especially desirous of displaying distinctive attitudes, beliefs, behaviors, and so forth, whereas other people do not want such distinctiveness. These need-for-uniqueness scales have been used successfully to predict the propensity of people to seek unusual activities and scarce commodities.

The societally acceptable dimensions on which people can manifest their distinctiveness have been called uniqueness attributes, and research shows that people use the following attributes to display their specialness: (a) attitudes, (b) beliefs, (c) personal appearance (including clothing), (d) friends and mates, (e) personality characteristics, (f) group membership, (g) signatures, (h) performances, and (i) consumer products. Furthermore, people display their uniqueness on those dimensions that are important to their self-concepts. For example, a person for whom personal appearance is crucial will dress in a manner that shows him or her to be different from other people.

The research shows that people generally want to establish a sense of specialness when they are given feedback that they are highly similar to others. Moreover, most people use societally acceptable uniqueness attributes to show some sense of specialness relative to other people. Finally, self-report scales also reveal that some individuals are extremely desirous of displaying their uniqueness.

Importance and Implications

Uniqueness seeking allows people to attain satisfaction about their specialness. Also, uniqueness seeking may increase the diversity in society. This happens because the people with high needs for uniqueness

seek different goals and interests, and in so doing, they open up new arenas in which other people can succeed. In pursuing their uniqueness, people also are likely to produce new skills, knowledge, beliefs, and attitudes that may be helpful in solving problems. The acknowledgment and pursuit of uniqueness foster greater societal toleration and appreciation of differences among people.

C. R. Snyder

See also Conformity; Independent Self-Construals; Optimal Distinctiveness Theory; Self-Concept; Self-Presentation

Further Readings

Brewer, M. B. (1991). The social self: On being the same or different at the same time. *Personality and Social Psychology Bulletin, 17,* 475–482.

Lynn, M., & Snyder, C. R. (2002). Uniqueness. In C. R. Snyder & S. J. Lopez (Ed.), *Handbook of positive psychology* (pp. 395–410). New York: Oxford University Press.

Maslach, C. (1974). Social and personal bases of individuation. *Journal of Personality and Social Psychology, 29,* 411–425.

Snyder, C. R., & Fromkin, H. L. (1977). Abnormality as a positive characteristic: The development and validation of a scale measuring need for uniqueness. *Journal of Abnormal Psychology, 86,* 518–527.

Snyder, C. R., & Fromkin, H. L. (1980). *Uniqueness: The human pursuit of difference.* New York: Plenum.

Unrequited Love

Definition

Unrequited love refers to instances when one person (the would-be lover) feels romantic, passionate feelings for an individual who does not return the same feelings (the rejector). Research indicates that unrequited love is quite common. Almost everyone in the United States has either loved someone who did not love them in return or been loved by someone they did not love in return by the time they reach college.

Background and History

For centuries, unrequited love has been a prevalent theme in the cultural arts (e.g., poetry, music, literature), as well as the popular media. If you turn on your radio, there is a good chance you will hear a melancholy singer lamenting over having his or her love refused by the object of his or her affection. Despite societies' fascination with the topic, psychologists devoted little attention to the topic until more recently. In the early 1990s Roy Baumeister and colleagues collected autobiographical narratives written by college students from the perspective of the rejector and from the perspective of the would-be lover. Comparisons made between the roles of would-be lover and rejector provided insight into the process of unrequited love, forming the basis of what social psychologists know about unrequited love to this day.

Common Pathways

Unrequited love occurs for multiple reasons; there is no one specific reason why romantic attraction goes unreciprocated. Several common reasons emerged in the collected narratives, however. For instance, people will reject offers of love if they come from people who do not live up to standards they hold for a romantic partner. For example, one important standard people set is physical attractiveness. Research in social psychology indicates that people tend to prefer a romantic partner who is as physically attractive as, if not more physically attractive than, they are. So if Lauren develops a romantic attraction for Joe, she runs the risk of having her love rejected if Joe thinks that he is more physically attractive than Lauren.

Physical attractiveness is not the only mismatch that can lead to a rejection of love. People tend to marry those who are similar on a whole host of domains, such as level of intelligence and socioeconomics. Thus, when people fall in love with targets perceiving themselves to be superior on mate-valued traits, the admirer is liable to having their love rejected. Luckily, as people grow older they learn to better estimate their mate value and level of physical attractiveness. Consequently, they experience fewer instances of unrequited love and more instances of reciprocated love.

Platonic friendships can also lead to unrequited love. Friendships can exist between two people who differ in mate standards. Even though love will often go unreciprocated because of mismatches in mate value, would-be lovers could misread or misinterpret positive gestures and intimacies from a platonic friend as romantic feelings. This can lead would-be lovers to overinterpret the likelihood of gaining the love of their friend and want more from the platonic friendship than is desired by the target of their affection.

Developing relationships can also lead to unrequited love. Sometimes the rejector is initially interested but, after several dates, loses interest in the would-be lover for a variety of reasons. Perhaps the rejector is put off by certain values the would-be lover holds, the would-be lover could resemble the rejector's mom or dad, or maybe the rejector comes to realize that he or she is not sexually attracted to the would-be lover despite finding the would-be lover to be physically attractive. Long-term relationships can even end in unrequited love, with one person wanting to continue the relationship while the other is losing interest. Although one may think all these different pathways will lead to very different experiences of unrequited love, research indicates that they are surprisingly similar.

Experience of Unrequited Love

Unrequited love is characterized by mutual incomprehension. Would-be lovers characterize the rejector as sending mixed signals and acting in inconsistent ways, whereas rejectors typically do not understand why the would-be lover continues to pursue them past the point of rejection.

Rejectors commonly grapple with feelings of guilt. Despite the portrayal of rejectors in the mass media as uncaring and cold, rejectors typically are quite concerned about whether they are leading the would-be lover on. Rejectors typically do not want to hurt the would-be lover, who is often a friend or colleague, and struggle with guilt that can accompany rejecting a person's offer of love. Guilt, combined with the difficulty in delivering bad news to others, can often cause the rejector to send the message of rejection in a more indirect way to spare the person's feelings and salvage the relationship. This, in turn, can confuse the would-be lover as to the rejector's intentions. Or it can cause the would-be lover to maintain hope, prolonging the experience of unrequited love for both parties.

Would-be lovers, who do not want to hear the bad news of rejection, will often misconstrue, reinterpret, or completely ignore such ambiguous messages of rejection. If the rejector says no to Friday because he or she is busy, what would stop the would-be lover from trying for Saturday? No one wants to be rejected; it is very painful to know that someone does not feel the same way about you that you do for him or her. To ward off the negative experience of realizing the offer of love will not be returned by the object of affection is potentially one reason would-be lovers typically pursue the rejector long after the rejector feels it is appropriate to do so. Research indicates that once the would-be lover picks up on the message of rejection, he or she experiences a decline in self-esteem, signaling the end of the pursuit and the beginning of recovery.

Who Is Worse Off?

Despite the pain that often accompanies having love rejected, would-be lovers look back at the experience with a mixture of positive and negative emotions. Would-be lovers describe the experience as a roller coaster of emotions, filled with many euphoric highs but also devastating lows. For example, the state of being in love with someone alone can keep the would-be lover in pursuit of his or her target. Rejectors, however, typically describe the experience as mainly a negative one consisting of few, if any, positives. Targets of affection may gain slight boosts in self-esteem from the flattery of being loved by someone, but this is offset by the moral guilt of rejecting someone and by the annoyance and frustration experienced if the would-be lover does not desist pursuit.

Unrequited love has allowed researchers to examine reasons why people reject love despite humans' fundamental need for mutually caring relationships. That people should endure personal costs, such as emotional discomfort and personal humiliation, to find such a person highlights just how important the search is for humans.

Nicole L. Mead
Roy F. Baumeister

See also Autobiographical Narratives; Interdependence Theory; Love; Need to Belong; Rejection

Further Readings

Baumeister, R. F., & Wotman, S. R. (1992). *Breaking hearts: The two sides of unrequited love.* New York: Guilford Press.

Baumeister, R. F., Wotman, S. R., & Stillwell, A. M. (1993). Unrequited love: On heartbreak, anger, guilt, scriptlessness and humiliation. *Journal of Personality and Social Psychology, 64,* 377–394.

URBAN MYTH

See RUMOR TRANSMISSION

Validity of Personality Judgments

See Personality Judgments, Accuracy of

Value Pluralism Model

Definition

What happens when two or more values come into conflict? What will determine the level of conflict a person experiences, and how will the person go about resolving it? The value pluralism model (VPM) addresses these questions. The VPM, in its original form, consists of three interrelated sets of propositions:

1. Underlying all belief systems are core or terminal values that specify what the ultimate goals of life should be (e.g., economic efficiency, social equality, individual freedom). Different values may point to different and often contradictory goals.

2. People find value conflicts challenging for at least three reasons. First, people confronted with conflicting values find it cognitively difficult to make apples-and-oranges comparisons between them (e.g., How much of my economic prosperity am I willing to give up to help promote social equality?). Second, value conflict is emotionally painful. Most people faced with a situation in which they must sacrifice one important value for another experience dissonance. The more important the value, the more painful the

dissonance will be. Third, trade-offs between core values can be politically embarrassing: If one chooses one value over the other, one may feel he or she is letting down those who feel they have received the short end of the trade-off stick.

3. Given these formidable obstacles, explicit reasoning about trade-offs between core values is stressful. In the short term, the motivation to reduce cognitive discrepancy stems from the need to reduce negative emotion, but in the long term, the motivation stems from the requirement for effective action. Whenever feasible, people should prefer modes of resolving conflict that are simple and require minimal effort. However, how much mental effort is required to resolve the dissonance will depend on the magnitude of the dissonance. Specifically, when a person is confronted with a situation that requires choosing between two values held with unequal strength, he or she will experience low dissonance. This occurs when a person believes more strongly in the importance of value A over value B. Under these circumstances, the model hypothesizes that people will rely on the simple cognitive solution of denying or downplaying the weaker value and exaggerating or bolstering the stronger value. This process will suffice to resolve the dissonant reaction. In contrast, when dissonance is high, the simple solutions of bolstering and denial no longer offer plausible solutions. This occurs when the person not only perceives the conflicting values as important but also perceives them to be equally important. Under such circumstances, the person must turn to more effort-demanding strategies, such as differentiation (weighing the merits of each value) and integration (developing rules for

trading off values). These are the two components of integrative complexity.

Extending the Model

It often proves difficult, however, to motivate integratively complex processing even when important values clearly come into conflict. According to the revised VPM, two classes of variables must also be taken into account to determine whether people will indeed respond in integratively complex ways to high-value conflict situations. First, the social content of the colliding values has important implications for which conflicts people are likely to view as legitimate. Specifically, people are likely to accept trade-offs between secular values, such as money, time, and convenience, much more readily than they are willing to accept what are considered taboo trade-offs, such as those between secular values and sacred values (e.g., life, liberty, and justice). For example, although attaching monetary value to the services provided by an employee may be cognitively demanding, it is not normatively unacceptable. In contrast, attaching monetary value to human life is. Confronted with the need to conduct such forbidden trade-offs, decision makers are likely to rely on massive impression-management efforts to conceal, obfuscate, or redefine what they are doing to protect themselves from the harsh judgment of observers.

Second, the social context of decision making is also important. Specifically, the types of accountability pressures people experience can dramatically lower or raise thresholds for complex trade-off reasoning. For example, if individuals, unconstrained by prior commitments, are confronted with a single audience whose views are known, they will tend to adjust their opinions in the direction of the audience and show no awareness of counterarguments or trade-offs. Alternatively, if decision makers believe that they will be blamed for whatever position they take on a trade-off problem, they are likely to resort to the avoidance tactics of buck-passing (shifting responsibility to others) or procrastination (delaying decision making). In contrast, when people are accountable for the long-term consequences of their decisions or when they are confronted with an audience with unknown views or with conflicting views, there is no simple solution available and no opportunity to delay. People have no choice but to respond complexly. Thus, complex reasoning will only be activated when decision makers are accountable to an audience that cannot be easily appeased.

Evidence and Implications

The model was initially developed to explain individual differences in political reasoning. For example, it was able to resolve a long-standing puzzle in political psychology of why advocates of centrist and moderate left-wing causes tend to discuss issues in more complex trade-off terms than do advocates of conservative or right-wing causes. Indeed, in support of the VPM, evidence suggests that the former are more likely to attach high importance to potentially contradictory values. Numerous archival and laboratory studies have since confirmed the basic predictions of the model and have extended its implications to other social domains, such as tolerance of outgroup members, resource distribution decisions, religious orthodoxy, and media and rhetoric effects on attitude change. Recently it has been used to explain the cognitive changes that occur when individuals are exposed to a second culture. Specifically, it has been suggested that individuals who cope with the social and cultural conflict situations associated with the acculturation process by internalizing the values of both old and new cultural groups (i.e., become bicultural) will become more integratively complex than those who choose to adhere to the values of only one cultural group. This will be due to the greater dissonance bicultural individuals experience during the acculturation process.

Importantly, although integrative complexity was originally viewed as a relatively stable personality trait, recent research inspired by the VPM has highlighted the fact that no stable individual differences should be expected. Rather, the complexity of one's reasoning on an issue is a function of the intensity of value conflict activated by that issue and the accountability pressures the individual faces. Indeed, similar levels of integrative complexity should be expected only to the degree that the issues sampled activate similar levels of value conflict and when the accountability pressures are conducive to complex thought. Moreover, evidence suggests that, contrary to popular belief, complex solutions should not be viewed as either cognitively or morally superior to simple reasoning. Rather, whether integrative complexity should be viewed as beneficial is context dependent.

Significance

The VPM explains how people deal with value conflicts of varying intensity and types. It suggests that although individuals may prefer to be cognitive misers and favor simple strategies to minimize cognitive dissonance, under conditions of high value conflict, they can be motivated to evoke more effort-intensive strategies.

Carmit T. Tadmor
Philip E. Tetlock

See also Accountability; Integrative Complexity; Value Priorities; Values

Further Readings

Tadmor, C. T., & Tetlock, P. E. (2006). Biculturalism: A model of the effects of second-culture exposure on acculturation and integrative complexity. *Journal of Cross Cultural Psychology, 37*(2), 173–190.

Tetlock, P. E. (1986). A value pluralism model of ideological reasoning. *Journal of Personality and Social Psychology, 50*(4), 819–827.

Tetlock, P. E., Peterson, R. S., Lerner, J. S. (1996). Revising the value pluralism model: Incorporating social content and context postulates. In C. Seligman, J. M. Olson, & M. P. Zanna (Eds.), *The Ontario symposium: The psychology of values* (Vol. 9, pp. 25–49). Mahwah, NJ: Erlbaum.

VALUE PRIORITIES

Definition

Value priorities are principles that provide people with a way of knowing what they must do and what type of person they must be so that they can live the best way possible, taking into account their environment and personal attributes. Value priorities therefore provide people with a way of knowing what is important and less important to being happy and getting along in their worlds. Because what these principles mean in people's lives develops as a result of experience, they operate like analogies (in an analogy, one thing is compared to another). When people encounter new situations, new people, or new objects, they can use their value principles to see similarity and therefore respond according to those principles. People often are not aware that these principles are operating, but even when they are unaware, these principles provide the basis for judging and responding in everyday life. For example, if people have equality as a very important value priority and they live in an environment in which

equality means treating people fairly, then if they believe another person is being treated unfairly they will feel a real need to repair this situation; they may or may not know why they are responding this way.

Value priorities are central to a person's sense of self. People use their value priorities not only as standards for self-evaluation but also as standards for evaluating other people, things, actions, and activities. Because value priorities provide a structure for knowing what is important and less important to living the best way possible, they assist people in making choices. Perhaps the most important feature of value theory—past and present—is the assumption (which is supported by research) that all people, everywhere, have the same values but differ in terms of the relative importance they place on each value. This means that to be accurate, discussion should be about people's value priorities (and not just, e.g., "values") or should emphasize the existence of relations among value priorities, their value systems.

Important Distinctions

When value priorities are discussed, focus is generally on people's personal value priorities. However, not only do people have a *personal value system*, but they also have perceptions of others' value systems (these are sometimes referred to as *social value systems*). Others can be other people, groups, organizations, or institutions, and their value priorities are transmitted implicitly through both overt and covert behavior. It is assumed that perceptions of others' value priorities have the same organization as the personal value system, although there is very little research in this area.

Not only can personal value priorities be distinguished from perceptions of others' value priorities, but they also can be distinguished from what can be referred to as *ideological value systems*. Because such promotions are often explicitly created to provide a particular image (e.g., for an organization's mission statement), they may not have the same implicit structure as personal value systems in which there are predictable relations among value types. Again, there is very little theory-directed research into ideological value systems.

The concept of value priorities can be distinguished from the concepts of attitude (an evaluation of a specific entity), worldview (a collection of conscious beliefs about how the world is or should be), and ideology (a rhetorical—i.e., language-based—association or set of associations between things, people, actions or activities and value priorities). Nevertheless, in past research these distinctions are not always clear, and the term *value* has been used in referring to each of these concepts.

Value Theory

Discussion of the huge amount of theory concerning human values typically includes Milton Rokeach's influential work. Shalom Schwartz built on and extended Rokeach's work and developed a values inventory to measure value priorities. A version of this inventory has also been developed for use with younger people. Currently, Schwartz's theory is the most influential and respected in the field.

Schwartz provided evidence in support of the assumption (made by all previous theorists) that important human values can be understood in terms of a relatively small set of value types that would be important to all people throughout the world. Schwartz's theory includes 10 value types: Universalism (understanding, appreciating, tolerating, and protecting people and nature); Benevolence (preserving and enhancing the welfare of those with whom we have frequent contact); Tradition (respecting, being committed to, and accepting traditional customs and ideas); Conformity (also known as Dutifulness; having the self-control required to ensure behavior does not upset or harm others or violate social expectations or norms); Security (maintaining stability to ensure safety and harmony within the self, relationships, and society); Power (having control and dominance over people and resources that results in social status and prestige); Achievement (gaining personal success that results from demonstrating competence according to social standards); Hedonism (indulging one's own pleasure and having sensuous gratification); Stimulation (having excitement, experiencing novelty, and feeling challenged); and Self-Direction (being able to think and behave independently and creatively). For each value type, Schwartz described representative values. For example, creativity and independence are two of the values that represent the Self-Direction value; politeness and self-discipline are two that represent the Conformity value type.

Analysis of the value priorities reported by many, many people from different countries around the world showed that the 10 value types can be arranged in a circular structure. This makes it possible to see how priorities on one value type have implications for

priorities on other value types. Value types that are adjacent to the highest priority value type also will be held with high priority, whereas the value type positioned directly opposite to the highest priority value type will be held with the lowest priority. Underlying the relations among priorities are two motivational dimensions.

One dimension concerns whether focus is on individual outcomes or on social context outcomes (Schwartz referred to this as the Self-Enhancement–Self-Transcendence dimension). A focus on individual outcomes is thinking about the self and others in terms of achievements and successes. People may develop this focus because of a belief that others' assistance is not dependable, and therefore they must develop expertise or dominance to enhance their survival; this type of focus will mean high priorities on Achievement and Power value types. A focus on social context outcomes refers to the acceptance of others and being concerned for others' welfare. People may develop this focus as a result of a belief in a shared fate, and therefore they have the incentive to ensure others' welfare and comfort ("to the extent others are doing well, so will I"); this type of focus will mean high priorities on Universalism and Benevolence value types.

The second dimension (Schwartz referred to this as the Openness to Change–Conservation dimension) concerns whether focus is on opportunity (that highlights independent thought and action as well as change) or on organization (that highlights stability and maintaining the status quo). A focus on opportunity will mean high priorities on Self-Direction and Stimulation value types, whereas a focus on organization will mean high priorities on Tradition, Conformity, and Security value types. High priorities on the Hedonism value type reflect both a focus on opportunity and a focus on individual outcomes.

Important Issues

People's value priorities are stable and relatively resistant to change, even though researchers have found that reports of value importance can be influenced temporarily. The success of such manipulations arises because human values have been shown to be universal—all humans, everywhere, believe that particular values are important, even though people differ in the relative importance placed on each of those values. For example, a person with highest value priorities on Benevolence values (e.g., honesty, loyalty, responsibility) will also say that Achievement values (e.g., success, ambition, influence) are important if attention is focused on these, even though in the value system, Benevolence and Achievement values are maximally different in terms of value priorities. Stability of reported value priorities also might not be observed in people who do not have explicit awareness of their value priorities or who confuse personal value priorities with their perceptions of important value priorities of others (so reliable measurement is difficult).

Value priorities transcend situations, and therefore it is difficult to interpret research in which distinctions are made between, for example, personal values, work values, and family values. The confusion that sometimes arises in this and related research may concern the distinction between personal value priorities, perceptions of others' value priorities, and ideological values, as well as the focus on single values rather than on value systems in which priorities on one value has implications for priorities on other values. Confusion may also concern the recognition that different environments provide differing opportunities for satisfaction. In addition, people who differ in their value priorities may choose the same behavior to enable value satisfaction. For example, excellence in a university course for one person satisfies high Power value priorities because he or she gains status and recognition, whereas for another it satisfies high Self-Direction value priorities because he or she gains greater choice in future options for study or career.

The connection between people's personal value priorities and their self-esteem has yet to be investigated fully, but there is growing recognition that people's feelings of self-esteem implicitly signal how well they are getting along in their world. Because value priorities serve to indicate what living the best way possible means, then to the extent a person is satisfying his or her personal value priorities or working toward doing so, he or she is more likely to have optimal self-esteem. Complications arise because people have perceptions of others' value priorities (and exposure to ideological value priorities), and others' value priorities may be more salient to people than their own value priorities. As a result, attitudinal or behavioral decisions may be influenced by these salient perceptions rather than by personal value priorities. Because value systems often operate outside awareness, people also may misperceive their own value priorities and behave according to their misperceptions.

Failing to behave in line with one's own value priorities will induce dissatisfaction—and chronic behavior of this type may lead to dissatisfaction that is reflected in self-esteem.

Meg J. Rohan

See also Self; Social Value Orientation; Values

Further Readings

Rohan, M. J. (2000). A rose by any name? The values construct. *Personality and Social Psychology Review, 4,* 255–277.

Schwartz, S. (1996). Value priorities and behavior: Applying a theory of integrated value systems. In C. Seligman, J. M. Olson, & M. P. Zanna (Eds.), *The Ontario symposium: The psychology of values* (Vol. 8, pp. 1–24). Mahwah, NJ: Erlbaum.

VALUES

Definition

The term *value* has two related yet distinct meanings. The value of an object or activity is what the object or activity is worth to a person or community; this is the economic or decision-making meaning of value. In its social-psychological meaning, by contrast, a value is an abstract, desirable end state that people strive for or aim to uphold, such as freedom, loyalty, or tradition. Only this second meaning is used in the plural form *values,* and public and political discussions refer to such values in many ways, speaking of the decline of values, a clash of values, or an election being about values. This entry describes the ways in which human values in the second sense select for certain attitudes, goals, and preferences that in turn guide concrete actions. Although there is not yet a consensus on a taxonomy of human values, research is converging on a set of basic dimensions.

Nature of Values

Many theorists have pointed out that values are distinct from attitudes, norms, beliefs, goals, and needs. Values, such as equality, friendship, or courage, are more abstract and general, and they not only are directed at specific objects (as attitudes are), behaviors (as norms are), or states of reality (as beliefs are) but also represent very general, and at times vague, end states. The end states described by many values also benefit the community, unlike goals or needs, which typically benefit the individual. Compare such values as honesty, forgiveness, and democracy to the goals of wealth, fame, and healthiness. Finally, most values are never quite reached, such as equality, national security, or world peace. In sum, prototypical values refer to abstract states that typically benefit the community, not just the individual, and that people strive for without ever quite reaching them.

Talking about values can be hard because the idea of value is so abstract. As long as people believe they share the same values, there is no need to define those values. But when people try to ascertain a definition of something like freedom or true friendship, heated debates can ensue. Likewise, the vagueness of many value concepts (consider the term *family values*) subtly removes these concepts from open, shared discourse and can make them subject to arbitrary and rhetorical use in propaganda. For example, politicians can try to win votes by saying they stand for family values, even though they don't have a very clear idea what family values are.

Even though all values are somehow represented in the individual, the more abstract among them are less likely to guide directly an individual's concrete behaviors. How many decisions and actions can you recall from yesterday that were directly guided by your values of freedom, democracy, or salvation? Goals are more apt to influence behavior directly, as people are more aware of their goals, and goals are more imminent and context-specific than are values. Values that resemble goals, however, such as excitement, independence, or respect for tradition, can directly influence behaviors. These considerations are largely supported by empirical research, which shows lower correlations between concrete behavior and abstract values than between behavior and specific or goal-like values. Furthermore, values appear to relate to preferences and attitudes, which themselves predict behavior. So even highly abstract values can have an impact on concrete behavior when that impact is mediated by less abstract psychological forces. For example, the value of freedom might make someone study hard for a driver education test, because getting a driver's license increases one's freedom of movement. The broad, abstract value of freedom leads to the specific, concrete goal of getting a license, which guides behavior.

Values can strongly influence behavior when they are perceived to be threatened and are therefore defended. A threat can "activate" a value, and defending and fighting for it entails a number of concrete behaviors (though rarely of the prosocial variety). For example, many Americans considered the attacks on New York's World Trade Center on September 11, 2001, as a threat to the value of freedom, and numerous actions following those attacks were directly motivated, and claimed to be justified, by the defense of that freedom.

Taxonomies

A taxonomy is an organized list, especially a thorough list. A taxonomy of values would be a list of all the values that people hold, sorted into several sublists according to different types of values. Considerable effort has gone into trying to put together a taxonomy of values, and in this endeavor, researchers have drawn from varying sources: reviews of value-related constructs in the scholarly literature, interviews and questionnaires that assess ordinary people's conception of values, and systematic analyses of value-related terms in lexicons. These sources show that individuals and groups can hold a wide range of values. However, researchers have tried to identify an underlying structure for this multitude of values. (The structure of the taxonomy would be what determines the different types of values.) They use statistical tools (e.g., factor analysis) to reduce the large number of specific values down to a small set of fundamental value dimensions, not unlike the effort that has led personality psychologists to the Five-Factor Theory of personality.

Different proposals exist regarding the number, specificity, importance, and content of human values. Milton Rokeach distinguished between 18 terminal values, which are desirable end states (e.g., self-respect, freedom), and 18 instrumental values, which refer to modes of conduct (e.g., helpful or forgiving). Contemporary researchers, such as Shalom Schwartz or Walter Renner, have proposed that both instrumental and terminal values fall into a smaller and more fundamental set of value orientations, such as power, achievement, tradition, and profit. Individuals differ reliably in these value orientations, but there is uncertainty over the particular orientations that make up the fundamental set. The inclusion of specific value words (test items) in value measures can change the discovered structures across data sets, and even though the value orientations from different data sets overlap, their numbers and content also vary. Thus, currently there is no consensus on the fundamental dimensions of values, but research is converging on these dimensions.

One complication is that when people get a chance to judge whether such concepts as power, achievement, or profit are values or goals, most people agree that they are goals. So the question arises whether the fundamental dimensions onto which research is converging depicts only values or actually mixes values with goals. It is currently not established whether goals and values are the same, both operating as motivational forces in the individual, or whether values have unique social functions and consequences that goals do not.

Function

What are values for? In people's own understanding, values regulate society and interpersonal relations, and they guide moral behavior, the distinction between right and wrong. In this sense, values are not just motives but socially shared concepts that serve a communal function. Evolutionary theorist David Sloan Wilson argues that values bind communities together, and those communities that agree on a value system (and on a system of sanctions in case the values are threatened) may be more successful over the course of human cultural history. Wilson shows through historic analysis that, for example, those religious groups that formed an agreed-upon value system became stronger than their competitors and outlived them. Values create a group bond at an abstract level that unifies individual actions into a group-level mind-set and organization. In this sense, values may be a uniquely human adaptation to the demands of a social reality in which not only individuals but also groups compete with each other. However, while values increase organization and cohesion within a group, they also sharpen boundaries to other groups (those who don't share the same value system), and indeed, intergroup conflict is often motivated, or at least rationalized, by a clash of values.

If there is only a small set of human values, these values should be relatively constant across cultures and history. The reason for this limited and stable set may be the invariable demands on human survival to serve biological needs, succeed in social interaction, and negotiate conflicts between biological needs and social interaction. But the evidence on historic and cultural variations is only beginning to be available.

Historic and Cultural Differences

Some values that communities uphold may have changed relatively little over documented history. In contrast to norms and laws, which have changed substantially, standards such as freedom, courage, fairness, and even honesty have remained the same at least since ancient Greece. Some values have been applied selectively to certain groups, such as equality and forgiveness, which are often extended only to members of the dominant group; other values have increased in importance in recent times, such as democracy and diversity.

Recent research by Schwartz, using questionnaires presented to people from different cultures, offers evidence for the universality of fundamental standards. Cultures differ, of course, in the extent to which they regard particular values as more or less important, but the set of fundamental dimensions within which cultures express their values may be universal. This evidence, however, is not without its critics. For one thing, translating words across languages such that their meaning stays truly constant is challenging. Moreover, the presentation of questionnaires, which fix the relevant value dimensions at the outset, does not establish which dimensions people would have picked as fundamental values if given no researcher-devised measure. To illustrate, gender equality is seen as an important value in many cultures. But highly patriarchic cultures not only may consider gender equality as less important but also may not even conceptualize it as a value. Future research will help clarify whether some of these dimensions operate more like goals and others constitute values "proper," with their own unique social functions and consequences.

Bertram F. Malle
Stephan Dickert

See also Attitudes; Big Five Personality Traits; Goals; Group Cohesiveness; Value Priorities

Further Readings

Rohan, M. J. (2000). A rose by any name? The values construct. *Personality and Social Psychology Review, 4*, 255–277.

Rokeach, M. (1973). *The nature of human values.* New York: Free Press.

Schwartz, S. H. (1994). Are there universal aspects in the content and structure of values? *Journal of Social Issues, 50,* 19–45.

VISCERAL INFLUENCES

Definition

Visceral factors are states such as hunger, thirst, sexual desire, drug cravings, physical pain, and fervent emotion that influence how much goods and actions are valued. When experiencing a visceral state, people focus primarily on goals associated with their current state and downplay the importance of other goals. For example, when a person is thirsty, finding water becomes the most important goal and other goals tend to be overlooked. Although visceral factors can have a powerful influence on behavior, people fail to recognize this influence. That is, they don't anticipate the influence that visceral factors will have on their future behavior, remember the influence that visceral factors have had on past behavior, or recognize the influence that visceral factors have on other people. People may think that they (or others) are acting irrationally because it is difficult for people in a "cold state" (not under the influence of a visceral factor) to predict or remember what it is like to be in a "hot state" (under the influence of a visceral factor). This difficulty in prediction is referred to as the *hot-cold empathy gap.*

Importance

Researchers who study decision making struggle to understand why people knowingly behave at odds with their long-term goals. Why do dieters who claim that losing weight is important to them and can avoid ordering dessert from a restaurant menu, succumb to temptation when a fresh batch of cookies is pulled from the oven? Why do people who claim that they will never have sexual intercourse without a condom find themselves doing just that when they are in a sexually arousing situation? Many decision-making models have difficulty describing such "irrational" behavior. George Loewenstein, a behavioral economist, proposed that one reason people seem to behave against their long-term interests is that long-term interests are often generated while in a cold state, and behavior often occurs while in a hot state. Loewenstein has offered several mathematical propositions to specify how visceral factors will influence behavior, the prediction of behavior, and the recollection of behavior.

Implications for Behavior

Because the experience of a visceral state leads people to focus on the goals associated with the current state at the exclusion of other goals, the more intensely people experience a visceral factor, the more they tend to act against their stated long-term goals. In other words, the more intense the visceral state, the more likely desire is to win over reason. For example, the hungrier dieters are, the more likely they are to cheat on their diets (especially if the cues to cheating are vivid, such as when the cookies can be seen or smelled). And, the more sexually aroused people are, the more likely they are to indulge their sexual desire at the expense of other goals. In a recent study, men who were sexually aroused indicated that they would be willing to go to further lengths to have sex compared to men who answered the questions when they were not aroused. Specifically, the aroused men stated that they would be more willing to tell a woman that they loved her (if they did not), to encourage their date to drink, and to slip a woman a drug in order to have sex with her. It seems that the visceral state of sexual desire crowded out their long-term goals.

Implications for Predicting and Recollecting Behavior

Despite the powerful influence that visceral states have on behavior, people underestimate this influence when predicting their future behavior. Thus, people say that they will never have sex without a condom because they fail to recognize how their sexual desire will change their feelings about various goals and actions. While predicting behavior from a cold state, the goal of being safe may be paramount. But, in the heat of the moment, the goal of having sex may crowd out the goal of being safe.

Research on pregnant women's decisions regarding anesthesia for delivery illustrates the difficulty of predicting future visceral states. When predicting from a cold state whether or not they would want anesthesia during childbirth, a majority of women said that they would not want it, but once in the hot state of pain, most women changed their preference and chose the painkillers.

Just as people fail to anticipate the influence of visceral factors on future behavior, as time passes people forget the influence visceral factors had on their past behavior. Although people can remember the circumstances that evoked a visceral state and can remember being in a certain state, they cannot reproduce the sensation the same way they can recall words or visual images. Even pregnant women who had experienced the pain of childbirth before mispredicted their interest in painkillers for an upcoming delivery. This is because they misremembered how much the actual sensation of pain influenced their desire for painkillers.

The tendency for people to underweight the influence of visceral factors when they are not currently experiencing the visceral state also leads to a hot-cold empathy gap between people. Those in a cold state often fail to appreciate how someone in a hot state feels. When someone is in pain, hungry, or depressed, it is difficult to empathize with that person without experiencing the pain, hunger, or depression oneself. Furthermore, when people are in a hot state, research suggests that it is difficult for them to make predictions for others without being influenced by the goals associated with their own current visceral state. For example, compared to nonthirsty participants, thirsty participants were more likely to claim that lost hikers would be more bothered by a lack of water than a lack of food.

It seems, then, that recognizing the power of visceral influences may help people predict and understand their own behavior. By recognizing people's tendency to underweight visceral factors, decision-making researchers may be better able to predict and understand when and why people will act against their stated long-term interests.

Jane L. Risen

See also Arousal; Behavioral Economics; Decision Making; Delay of Gratification

Further Readings

Loewenstein, G. (1996). Out of control: Visceral influences on behavior. *Organizational Behavior and Human Decision Processes, 65,* 272–292.

Metcalfe, J., & Mischel W. (1999). A hot/cool-system analysis of delay of gratification: Dynamics of willpower. *Psychological Review, 106,* 3–19.

VOLUNTEERISM

Definition

Volunteerism is voluntary, deliberate service to others over time and without compensation. A key element of volunteer behavior is that the person freely chooses to help and has no expectation of pay or other compensation. Mandatory public service required by courts or schools would not meet the definition of volunteerism. The volunteer behavior must include service work, not simply a donation of money or goods. This service is long-term, repeated service, such as giving time weekly to help at a local hospital. The volunteer service is only a service if it benefits others who want help. For example, the Boy Scout who helps the blind person across the street when the blind person wants to move independently (and perhaps in another direction) would not be a volunteer.

Who Are Volunteers?

People from youth to older adulthood engage in volunteering. The organization Independent Sector estimates that about 44% of adults and 59% of teenagers volunteer, with the largest group of volunteers being from 35 to 55 years old. Wealthier people volunteer more because they have more spare time and more flexibility in their jobs. The wealthy may also have a social obligation, called *noblesse oblige,* to engage in philanthropy and good works. Those who volunteer are likely also to be the most generous givers. Women volunteer slightly more often than men do, but men give more money to charities. Better-educated people also volunteer more than less-educated people, because of the skills and resources they have to offer. Finally, those people with more connections to the community, such as people living in smaller, rural communities and people who have connections to religious and cultural group memberships, volunteer more often.

What Motivates People to Volunteer?

E. Gil Clary, Leslie Orenstein, Mark Snyder, and others have examined motivations for volunteering. A person is driven by *value expressive* motivation if his or her reasons for volunteering derive from the values he or she holds dear, such as a concern for the poor. When a person's primary goal is to learn about a particular problem or group of people or to have new experiences, his or her primary motivation is *understanding* or *knowledge*. Those with a *social adjustive* motive volunteer because friends, family, or social demands encourage them to do so. Others are motivated by career aspirations. For example, college students may volunteer to enhance their job skills or increase their probability of educational or career goals. Some people volunteer to relieve their personal problems, such as the guilt of having too much time on their own hands or needing a positive outlet for their insecurities. This is called *ego-defensive* or a *protective* function. On the other hand, those with an *ego-enhancing* motivation volunteer to increase their own self-esteem. In a volunteer job, a person can be valued by the staff and feel competent at a minor job. Finally, some people volunteer out of *community concern*. They demonstrate concern for a particular community as defined by geography (a neighborhood) or by a particular condition or need (concern for those with cancer).

Allen M. Omoto and Mark Snyder have discovered that when motivation type matches recruiting strategy, people are more likely to volunteer. For example, when a student is motivated to seek a job, he or she would be more likely to volunteer in response to advertisements highlighting job skills. When motivation is met in volunteering experience, people are likely to continue to volunteer. For example, a person who wishes to build confidence will be more likely to continue volunteering when a coordinator praises him or her for a job well done. Contrary to expectations, researchers found that "mandatory volunteerism" as a college requirement made some students *less* likely to freely volunteer in the future. This is one reason why volunteerism requires helping to be freely chosen.

Benefits and Costs of Volunteering

Benefits to an organization that uses volunteers include the money saved from having to hire staff to do the same job. A research report from Independent Sector puts the 2005 value of volunteer time at $18.04 per hour, including wages and benefits, saved by an organization for each hour a volunteer serves. The organization also benefits indirectly because volunteers become representatives and advocates for the organization, sharing information and positive views with the community. Costs to the organization include the

costs of training the volunteers, the staff time to coordinate volunteers, and the chance that volunteers may offer lower-quality service than paid staff.

Benefits to the recipients of help from well-trained volunteers can be obvious: The homeless mother gets served a meal, the immigrant learns to read and write, and so forth. Costs include not getting expert help or receiving inconsistent help when volunteers are not available. Benefits to the volunteers themselves include increases in their sense of self-esteem and self-confidence, decreased loneliness, the making of friends, and more favorable attitudes toward clients served. In older adults, the increased activity and social stimulation of volunteering has positive health effects and increases life satisfaction. In youth, those who volunteer have a lower likelihood of being arrested. Costs to the volunteer include any costs associated with volunteering itself, such as transportation, and emotional costs of working with those in need, such as sadness when a client dies. Conflicts between volunteer time and time spent with family and friends and the potential stigma of associating with those who have less desirable traits in society are social costs that volunteers incur. Benefits to society include the promotion of the common welfare of the community, the ability to expand services, the defrayal of dollar costs, the increase of the skills base in the community, and the instillation of norms of prosocial behavior.

Shelley Dean Kilpatrick

See also Altruism; Compassion; Cooperation; Empathy; Empathy–Altruism Hypothesis; Moral Development; Prosocial Behavior; Reciprocal Altruism; Reciprocity Norm; Social Support

Further Readings

Clary, E. G., Snyder, M., Ridge, R. D., Copeland, J., Stukas, A. A., Haugen, J., et al. (1998). Understanding and assessing the motivations of volunteers: A functional approach. *Journal of Personality and Social Psychology, 74,* 1516–1530.

Independent Sector. (2001). *Giving and volunteering in the United States: Key findings.* Washington, DC: Author.

Snyder, M., Omoto, A. M., & Lindsay, J. J. (2004). Sacrificing time and effort for the good of others: The benefits and costs of volunteerism. In A. G. Miller (Ed.), *The social psychology of good and evil* (pp. 444–468). New York: Guilford Press.

Z

ZEAL

Definition

The term *zeal* came into common usage in reference to a sect of 1st-century-C.E. religious fanatics who were uncompromising in their opposition to Roman rule. Some of them carried daggers under their cloaks and killed anyone who did not fully support their views. Such extremism brought reprisals that ultimately crushed their sect. Accordingly, *zeal* refers to extreme ideological conviction that belligerently insists on consensus, without regard for practical consequences.

Zeal is puzzling because it can be unreasonable and self-defeating. Just as the original Zealots' aggressive fervor led to the annihilation of their sect, thousands of naively unprepared crusaders were killed from 1086 C.E. to 1270 C.E. in seemingly foolhardy campaigns to seize Jerusalem for their ideological cause. Their consensual zeal inflated them with a righteous euphoria that was insensitive not only to obstacles and dangers but also to their own atrocities.

Zeal is an important social phenomenon to understand because although it sometimes animates devoted philanthropy, it often fuels militant religious and political conflicts that can have devastating social consequences. The first systematic investigation of zeal was reported a hundred years ago in William James's classic, *The Varieties of Religious Experience.* James concluded, from dozens of interviews with religious converts, that moral and religious zeal helps people forget about their personal problems. At around the same time, Freud observed that his neurotic patients repressed taboo thoughts by rigidly focusing on other, extremely intense trains of thought. Thus, both classic theorists viewed zeal as a tool for coping with self-threatening thoughts and problems.

Research on Zeal

The horror of World War II spurred systematic research aimed at understanding zealous bigotry, nationalism, and fascism. Thousands of in-home interviews about respondents' life experiences and zealous tendencies informed the conclusion that zeal arises from feelings of personal vulnerability. Cross-sectional research supports the general conclusion. For example, during wars, political leaders tend toward black and white certainty in their speeches, dogmatic religious denominations flourish, and children's books become more moralistic than usual. These findings are consistent with historians' observations that religious movements tend to sprout during times of social insecurity and that religious fundamentalism and extremism are especially likely to foment under conditions of social turmoil and threat. (Accordingly, enthusiasm for the crusades spiked under conditions of unprecedented social and political insecurity.)

Laboratory research supports the conclusions from interview and cross-sectional research. Hundreds of studies, conducted by dozens of researchers in North America and Europe in the past 20 years, have found that people react with exaggerated zeal to experimental manipulations of experiential self-threats such as mortality salience, personal uncertainty, social rejection, loneliness, isolation, failure, inferiority, confusion, and exposure to people who violate their cherished ideals.

Such threats cause people to exaggerate pride and conviction in favor of their worldviews, countries, groups, causes, values, opinions, romantic relationships, and personal goals. Such threats also increase people's willingness to fight for their more certain causes and to exaggerate social consensus for them.

Importantly, zeal reactions occur even in domains that are not related to the eliciting threats. Thus, zeal can be regarded as a generalized, compensatory response to poignant self-threats. Why do people turn to compensatory zeal when threatened? Just as James and Freud proposed, zeal insulates people from threatening thoughts. Laboratory experiments show that zealous expressions of worldviews, value ideals, personal convictions, or pride cause previously bothersome thoughts to recede from awareness. Moreover, even if repeatedly reminded of distressing thoughts after zeal expression, the distressing thoughts still feel less important, less urgent, and less pressing than they normally do. This means that zeal is not simply a form of distraction. It somehow makes distressing thoughts loom less large even when they are in focal awareness. These experimental findings are consistent with James's early observation that religious zealots seem exceptionally able to cope with challenging circumstances and to joyfully tolerate severe hardship. (One mystic saint reputedly demonstrated piety by cheerfully licking the suppurating wounds of hospital patients.)

How Does Zeal Work?

Recent research is beginning to reveal how compensatory zeal alleviates distress. Whereas poignant self-threats activate a system in the brain that specializes in avoidance motivation and prevention of unwanted outcomes, zealous and angry thoughts activate a system in the brain that specializes in approach motivation and promotion of desired outcomes. When one system is active, stimuli and experiences relevant to the other system loom less large and seem less vital. Preliminary research indicates this may occur because of reciprocal inhibition of activity between brain areas that are centrally involved in approach processes (left frontal lobe) and those that are centrally involved in avoidance processes (right frontal lobe). Zeal may thus be an appealing response to threat because it effectively turns down activity in brain areas that process threatening stimuli.

Zealous Personalities and Cultures

Defensive zeal is most pronounced among individuals who (a) explicitly claim high self-esteem but who show evidence of low implicit self-esteem on assessments that bypass conscious awareness, (b) defensively avoid close personal relationships, or (c) have narcissistically inflated claims of superiority. These three personality tendencies are empirically related and share felt insecurity at the core. Thus, zeal can be seen as a defensive maneuver in which outwardly proud people engage when situational threats resonate with inner insecurities. Defensive zeal is also most prominent in cultures (e.g., Judaic, Christian, and Muslim) influenced by ancient Greek ideas that champion independent pursuit of ideal truth. Zeal is less evident in cultures influenced by Taoist and Confucian norms that promote yielding of confrontational opinions to dialectical perspective taking.

Ian McGregor

See also Attitude Strength; Authoritarian Personality; Beliefs; Ideology; Mortality Salience; Motivated Cognition; Regulatory Focus Theory; Religion and Spirituality; Self; Self-Esteem; Social Neuroscience; Terror Management Theory; Values

Further Readings

Adorno, T. W., Frenkel-Brunswik, E., Levinson, D. J., & Sanford, R. N. (1950). *The authoritarian personality.* New York: Harper.

Armstrong, K. (2000). *The battle for God: A history of fundamentalism.* New York: Ballantine Books.

James, W. (1958). *The varieties of religious experience.* New York: Mentor. (Original work published 1902)

McGregor, I., & Marigold, D. C. (2003). Defensive zeal and the uncertain self: What makes you so sure? *Journal of Personality and Social Psychology, 85,* 838–852.

McGregor, I., Nail, P. R., Marigold, D. C., & Kang, S.-J. (2005). Defensive pride and consensus: Strength in imaginary numbers. *Journal of Personality and Social Psychology, 89,* 978–996.

Index

need to belong and, **2:**616
neuroticism, **2:**619
Neuroticism and, **1:**117
prevalence, consequences of, **1:**240
procrastination and, **2:**705
rejection perception and, **2:**741
self-discrepancy and, **2:**812, **2:**813
self-efficacy and, **2:**815
self-serving bias and, **2:**790
serotonin and, **1:**240, **1:**444
shame and, **1:**404
stress generation and contagious depression, **1:**241
See also **Depressive realism**
Depressive realism, 1:242–243
cognitive theory, cognitive therapy and, **1:**242
control over outcomes and, **1:**242–243
definition of, **1:**242
implications of, **1:**243
Descartes, René, **1:**171
Descriptive invariance principle, **1:**371
Desegregation of schools. *See* Integration of schools
DeSimone, Philip, **2:**705
Determinism
free will *vs.,* **1:**3, **1:**363, **1:**364
de Tocqueville, Alexis, **1:**208
Deutsch, Morton, **1:**480, **2:**628, **2:**906
Developmental psychology
achievement motivation research in, **1:**5
cultural differences studied in, **1:**5, **1:**209
emotion studied in, **1:**286
environmental psychology and, **1:**302
executive function of self in, **1:**324
memory research in, **2:**553
moral development and, **2:**586–587
moral reasoning and, **2:**591
theory of mind research in, **2:**986
Deviance, 1:243–245
anomie concept and, **1:**244–245
definition of, **1:**243
group dynamic theory on, **1:**244
implications of, **1:**244–245
looking-glass self concept and, **1:**244, **1:**245, **2:**631
pluralistic ignorance and, **2:**674
social norms focus and, **1:**244–245
structural functionalism theory on, **1:**243–244, **1:**245
symbolic interactionism theory on, **1:**244
Devine, Patricia, **2:**696
Dewey, John, **1:**437
Diagnostic hypothesis testing, **1:**245
Diagnosticity, 1:245–247
definition of, **1:**245
diagnostic *vs.* pseudodiagnostic hypothesis testing and, **1:**245–246
dispositional bias implications of, **1:**246
self-evaluation and, **1:**246–247
Diener, Ed., **1:**468
Diensbier, Richard, **2:**916
Different-consequences framing, **1:**371
Differential psychology, **1:**472

Diffusion of responsibility, 1:247–248
in bystander effect, **1:**133
in helping behavior, **1:**423
Dilution effect, 1:248–249
definition of, **1:**248
intuitive knowledge *vs.,* **1:**249
real world contexts of, **1:**249
stereotyping and, **1:**249
Direct access processing strategy, **1:**17
Direct aggression, **1:**20
Discontinuity effect, 1:250–251
definition of, **1:**250
generality of, **1:**251
intergroup competitiveness reduction and, **1:**251
laboratory evidence of, **1:**250–251
mechanisms producing the effect and, **1:**251
nonlaboratory evidence of, **1:**250
Prisoner's Dilemma Game and, **1:**165, **1:**189, **1:**250, **2:**701–704, **2:**729
Discounting. *See* **Discounting, in attribution; Hyperbolic discounting**
Discounting, in attribution, 1:252
hyperbolic discounting and, **1:**451–462
responsibility attribution and, **2:**753
Discourse analysis. *See* **Discursive psychology**
Discrimination, 1:253
just-world hypothesis and, **2:**514
sexual harassment as, **2:**865–866
See also **Prejudice; Racism**
Discursive psychology, 1:254
critical social psychology and, **1:**202–204
Disgust, 1:255–257
animal nature reminder and, **1:**256
bad taste reaction and, **1:**255
contamination response and, **1:**255
core disgust concept and, **1:**255, **2:**589
cultural differences in, **1:**256
elicitors of, **1:**255–256
facial expression of, **1:**339
humor in, **1:**256–257
immorality and, **1:**256
moral emotion of, **2:**588–589
other people and, **1:**256
responses to, **1:**255
variations of, **1:**256–257
Displaced aggression, 1:20, 1:257–258
definition of, **1:**257
excitation transfer concept and, **1:**257–258, **1:**320–322
scapegoating and, **1:**257–258, **2:**778–779
tit-for-tat rule of, **1:**189, **1:**257, **2:**703
triggered displaced aggression and, **1:**257–258
Dispositional bias, **1:**246, **1:**475
Dissociation discounting cue sleeper effect hypothesis, **2:**878
Dissonance processes
attitude change through, **1:**64
See also **Cognitive dissonance theory**
Distinctiveness, in attribution, 1:76–77, 1:258–259
distinctiveness-based illusory correlation and, **1:**460–461
Kelley's covariation model and, **2:**518